SOCIOLOGICAL THEORY
in the CONTEMPORARY ERA

SOCIOLOGICAL THEORY
in the CONTEMPORARY ERA
Text and Readings

Scott Appelrouth ▪ Laura Desfor Edles

California State University, Northridge

PINE FORGE PRESS
An Imprint of Sage Publications, Inc.
Thousand Oaks • London • New Delhi

For information:

Pine Forge Press
An imprint of Sage Publications, Inc.
2455 Teller Road
Thousand Oaks, California 91320
E-mail: order@sagepub.com

Sage Publications Ltd.
1 Oliver's Yard
55 City Road
London EC1Y 1SP
United Kingdom

Sage Publications India Pvt. Ltd.
B-42, Panchsheel Enclave
Post Box 4109
New Delhi 110 017 India

Printed in the United States of America

Library of Congress Cataloging-in-Publication Data

Appelrouth, Scott, 1965-
Sociological theory in the contemporary era: Text and readings/
Scott Appelrouth, Laura Desfor Edles.
        p. cm.
Includes bibliographical references and index.
ISBN 0–7619–2801–4 or 978-0-7619-2801-0 (pbk.)
    1. Sociology. 2. Sociology—Philosophy. I. Edles, Laura Desfor. II. Title.
HM586.A67 2007
301.01—dc22   2006004952

This book is printed on acid-free paper.

06   07   08   09   10   10   9   8   7   6   5   4   3   2   1

Acquiring Editor:	Benjamin Penner
Associate Editor:	Margo Beth Crouppen
Editorial Assistant:	Camille Herrera
Production Editor:	Beth A. Bernstein
Copy Editor:	Barbara Ray
Typesetter:	C&M Digitals (P) Ltd.
Cover Designer:	Glenn Vogel

CONTENTS

List of Illustrations and Photos

LIST OF FIGURES AND TABLES

Figures

Tables

ABOUT THE AUTHORS

Scott Appelrouth (Ph.D., New York University, 2000) is an associate professor of sociology at California State University, Northridge. His interests include social theory, cultural sociology, and social movements. He teaches classical and contemporary theory at both the graduate and undergraduate levels and has published several articles in research and teaching journals.

Laura Desfor Edles (Ph.D., UCLA, 1990) is the author of *Symbol and Ritual in the New Spain* (Cambridge University Press, 1998), *Cultural Sociology in Practice* (Blackwell Publishers, 2002), and various articles on social theory, culture, and social movements. Currently an associate professor of sociology at California State University, Northridge, she has taught at a number of universities including the University of Hawaii, Manoa; Boise State University; and Vanguard University in Costa Mesa, California.

PREFACE

Every semester we begin our sociological theory courses by telling students that we love sociological theory, and that one of our goals is to get each and every one of them to love theory, too. This challenge we set for ourselves makes teaching the course exciting. If you teach "sexy" topics like the sociology of drugs, crime, or sex, students come into class expecting to be titillated. By contrast, when you teach theory, students tend to come into class expecting the course to be abstract, dry, and absolutely irrelevant to their lives. The fun in teaching sociological theory is in proving students wrong, in getting them to see that the subject matter is absolutely central to their everyday lives—and fascinating as well. What a reward it is to have students who adamantly insisted that they "hated" theory at the beginning of the semester "converted" into theorists by the end!

In teaching sociological theory, we use original texts. We rely on original texts in part because every time we read these works, we derive new meaning. Core sociological works tend to become "core" precisely for this reason. However, using original readings requires that the professor spend lots of time and energy explaining issues and material that is unexplained or taken for granted by the theorist. This book was born of this process—teaching from original works and explaining them to our students. Hence, this book includes the original readings we use in our courses, as well as our interpretation and explanation of them.

Thus, this book is distinct in that it is both a reader *and* a text. It is unlike existing readers in several ways, however. First and foremost, this book is not just a collection of seemingly disconnected readings. Rather, in this book we provide an overarching theoretical framework with which to understand, compare, and contrast these selections. In our experience, this overarching theoretical framework is essential in explaining the relevance and excitement of sociological theory. In addition, we discuss the social and intellectual milieu in which the selections were written, as well as their contemporary relevance. Thus, we connect these seemingly disparate works not only theoretically but also via concrete applications to today's world.

Finally, this book is unique in that we provide a variety of visuals and pedagogical devices—historical and contemporary photographs and diagrams and charts illuminating core theoretical concepts and comparing specific ideas—to enhance student understanding. Our thinking is, why should only introductory-level textbooks have visual images and pedagogical aids? Most everyone, not just the youngest audiences, enjoys—and learns from—visuals.

As is often the case in book projects, this turned out to be a much bigger and thornier project than either of us first imagined. And, in the process of writing this book we have accrued many intellectual and social debts. First, we especially thank Jerry Westby of Sage/Pine Forge Press for helping us get this project started. Jerry walked into our offices at California State University, Northridge, and turned what had been a nebulous, long-standing idea into a concrete plan. Several months later, Ben Penner joined Sage/Pine Forge and began to attend to the myriad of details this project entailed. We greatly appreciate "Ben and Jerry's" continuous support and enthusiasm for our work, and also for inspiring us and keeping us on task. Associate editor Margo Beth Crouppen, production editor Beth Bernstein, permissions editor Karen Wiley, and editorial assistants Annie Louden, Camille Herrera, and copyeditor Barbara Ray saw this book through its final stages, and we thank them for their conscientiousness.

At California State University, Northridge, we thank our department chair, Nathan Weinberg, and our Dean of the College of Social and Behavioral Sciences, Stella Theodoulou, for supporting this undertaking. We are particularly grateful for having received college grants that allowed us to complete this volume. We are also especially indebted to our friend and colleague David Boyns, who helped us out when things got tight. This book is much better because of David's pivotal contributions to Chapter 8 on poststructural and postmodern theories and to the section on Jürgen Habermas in Chapter 9. We are also indebted to Laura's colleagues at Vanguard University in Costa Mesa, California, for their support. Professors Ed Clarke, Elizabeth Leonard, and Phil Robinette all graciously excused her from administrative and teaching tasks so that she could find time to complete this book.

We thank the following reviewers for their comments: Harry Dahms, University of Tennessee, Knoxville; Melanie Hildebrandt, Indiana University; Amanda Kennedy, Ohio State University; John Murray, Manhattanville College; Anne Szopa, Indiana University East; John Bartkowski, Mississippi State University; Chris Hunter, Grinnell College; Paul-Brian McInerney, Indiana University—South Bend; David Schweingruber, Iowa State University; Matthew Bond, Oxford University; Brian Rich, Transylvania University; Joy Crissey Honea, Montana State University–Billings; Elizabeth Mitchell, Rutgers, the State University of New Jersey; Stephen B. Groce, Western Kentucky University; Neil Gross, Harvard University; Mathieu Deflem, University of Southern California; Laurel Holland, University of West Georgia; William Outhwaite, University of Sussex; William Nye, Hollins University; Leslie Cintron, Washington and Lee University; Robert Bausch, Cameron University; Darek Niklas, Rhode Island College; Scott Schaffer, Millersville University of Pennsylvania. Finally, we both want to thank our families—Amie, Alex, and Julia; and Mike, Benny, and Ellie—for supporting us while we spent so much time and energy on this project.

1

INTRODUCTION

Key Concepts

❖ Theory
❖ Order
    Collective/Individual
❖ Action
    Rational/Nonrational
❖ Enlightenment
❖ Counter-Enlightenment

SOURCE: *Alice's Adventures in Wonderland and Through the Looking-Glass,* by Lewis Carroll; illustration by John Tenniel. (1960) New York: Penguin.

"But I'm not *a serpent, I tell you!" said Alice. "I'm a—I'm a—"*

"Well! What *are you?" said the Pigeon. "I can see you're trying to invent something!"*

"I–I'm a little girl," said Alice, rather doubtfully, as she remembered the number of changes she had gone through that day.

"A likely story indeed!" said the Pigeon, in a tone of the deepest contempt. "I've seen a good many little girls in my time, but never one with such a neck as that! No, no! You're a serpent; and there's no use denying it. I suppose you'll be telling me next that you never tasted an egg!"

"I have *tasted eggs, certainly," said Alice, who was a very truthful child; "but little girls eat eggs quite as much as serpents do, you know."*

"I don't believe it," said the Pigeon; "but if they do, why, then they're a kind of serpent: that's all I can say."

~Lewis Carroll,
Alice's Adventures in Wonderland (1865) [1960:54]

In the passage above, the Pigeon had a theory—Alice is a serpent because she has a long neck and eats eggs. Alice, however, had a different theory—that she was a little girl. Yet, it was not the "facts" that were disputed in the above passage. Alice freely admitted that she had a long neck and ate eggs. So why did Alice and the Pigeon come to such different conclusions? Why didn't the facts "speak for themselves"?

Alice and the Pigeon both *interpreted* the question (what *is* Alice?) using the categories, concepts, and assumptions with which each was familiar. It was these unarticulated concepts, assumptions, and categories that led the Pigeon and Alice to have such different conclusions.

Likewise, social life can be perplexing and complex. It is hard enough to know "the facts"—let alone to know *why* things are as they seem. In this regard, theory is vital to making sense of social life because it holds assorted observations and facts together (as it did for Alice and the Pigeon). Facts make sense only because we interpret them using preexisting categories and assumptions, that is, "theories." The point is that even so-called facts are based on implicit assumptions and unacknowledged presuppositions. Whether we are consciously aware of them or not, our everyday life is filled with theories as we seek to understand the world around us. The importance of formal sociological theorizing is that it makes assumptions and categories explicit, hence open to examination, scrutiny, and reformulation.

To be sure, some students find sociological theory as befuddling as the conversation between Alice and the Pigeon in *Alice's Adventures in Wonderland*. Some students find it difficult to understand and interpret what sociological theorists are saying. Thus, the purpose of this book is to provide students not only with core sociological readings but also with a framework for comprehending them. In this introductory chapter we discuss (1) *what* sociological theory is, (2) *why* it is important for students to read the original works of the "core" figures in contemporary sociological theory, (3) *who* these "core theorists" are, and (4) *how* students can develop a more critical and gratifying understanding of some of the most important ideas advanced by these theorists.

WHAT IS SOCIOLOGICAL THEORY?

Theory is a system of generalized statements or propositions about phenomena. However, there are two additional features that, together, distinguish scientific theories from other idea systems such as those found in religion or philosophy. "Scientific" theories:

1. explain and predict the phenomena in question.

2. produce testable and thus falsifiable hypotheses.

Universal laws are intended to explain and predict events occurring in the natural or physical world. For instance, Isaac Newton established three laws of motion. The first law, the law of inertia, states that objects in motion will remain in motion, while objects at rest will remain at rest unless either is acted on by another force. In its explanation and predictions regarding the movement of objects, this law extends beyond the boundaries of time and space. For their part, sociologists seek to develop or refine general statements about some aspect of *social* life. For example, a long-standing (although not uncontested) sociological theory predicts that as a society becomes more modern, the salience of religion will decline. Similar to Newton's law of inertia, the secularization theory, as it is called, is not restricted in its scope to any one time period or population. Instead, it is an abstract proposition that can be tested in any society once the key concepts making up the theory, "modern" and "religion," are defined and observable measures are specified.

Thus, sociological theories share certain characteristics with theories developed in other branches of science. However, there are significant differences between social and other scientific theories (i.e., theories in the social sciences as opposed to the natural sciences) as well. First, sociological theories tend to be more evaluative and critical than theories in the natural sciences. Sociological theories are often rooted in implicit moral assumptions, which contrast with traditional notions of scientific objectivity. In other words, it is often supposed that the pursuit of scientific knowledge should be free from value judgments or moral assessments; that is, that the first and foremost concern of science is to uncover what *is*, not what *ought* to be. Indeed, such objectivity is often cast as a defining feature of science, one that separates it from other forms of knowledge based on tradition, religion, or philosophy. While some sociologists adopt this model of scientific inquiry, others tend to be interested not only in an objective understanding of the workings of society but also in realizing a more just or equitable social order. As you will see, the work of many theorists is shaped in important respects by their own moral sensibilities regarding the condition of modern societies and what the future may bring. Thus, sociological theorizing at times falls short of the "ideal" science practiced more closely (although still imperfectly) by "hard" sciences like physics, biology, or chemistry. The failure to consistently conform to the ideals of either science or philosophy is, for some observers, a primary reason for the discipline's low status within the world of academics. For others, it represents the opportunity to develop a unique understanding of social life.

A second difference between sociological theories and those found in other scientific disciplines stems from the nature of their respective subjects. Societies are always in the process of change, while the changes themselves can be spurred by any number of causes including internal conflicts, wars with other countries (whether ideological or through direct invasion), scientific or technological advances, or through the expansion of economic markets that in turn spread foreign cultures and goods. As a result, it is more difficult to fashion universal laws to explain societal dynamics. Moreover, we must also bear in mind that humans, unlike most other animals or naturally occurring elements in the physical world, are motivated to act by a complex array of social and psychological forces. Our behaviors are not the product of any one principle; instead they can be driven by self-interest, altruism, loyalty, passion, tradition, or habit, to name but a few factors. From these remarks you can see the difficulties inherent in developing universal laws of societal development and individual behavior, this despite our earlier example of the secularization theory as well as other efforts to forge such laws.

These two aspects of sociological theory (the significance of moral assumptions and the nature of the subject matter) are responsible, in part, for the form in which much sociological theory is written. While some theorists construct formal propositions or laws to explain and predict social events and individual actions, more often theories are developed through storylike narratives. Thus, few of the original readings included in this volume will contain explicitly stated propositions. One of the intellectual challenges you will face in studying the selections is to uncover the general propositions that are embedded in the texts. Regardless of the style in which they are presented, however, the theories (or narratives, if you prefer) that you will explore in this text answer the most central social questions, while uncovering taken-for-granted truths and encouraging you to examine who you are and where we, as a society, are headed.

WHY STUDY SOCIOLOGICAL THEORY?

Some professors agree with students that original works are just too hard to decipher. These professors use secondary textbooks that interpret and simplify the ideas of core theorists. Their argument is that you simply can't capture students' attention using original works; and because students must be engaged in order to understand, secondary texts ultimately lead to a better grasp of the covered theories.

However, there is an important problem with only reading secondary interpretations of original works: the secondary and the original text are not the same thing. Secondary texts do not simply translate what the theorist wrote into simpler terms; rather, in order to simplify, they must revise what an author has said.

The problems that can arise from even the most faithfully produced interpretations can be illustrated by the "telephone game." Recall that childhood game in which you sit in a circle, and one person thinks of a message; then he or she whispers the message to the next person, and then that person passes the message on to the next person, until the last person in the circle announces the message aloud. Usually, everyone roars with laughter because the message at the end typically is not the same as the one circulated at the beginning. This is because the message inadvertently gets misinterpreted and changed as it goes around.

In the telephone game the goal is to repeat exactly what has been said to you. Nevertheless, misinterpretations and modifications are commonplace. Consider now a secondary text in which the goal is not to restate exactly what was originally written, but to take the original source—that is by nature open to multiple interpretations—and make it "easier" to understand. While this process of simplification perhaps allows students to understand the secondary text, they are at least one step removed from what the original author actually wrote.[1] At the same time, you have no way of knowing what was written in the original works. Moreover, when you start thinking and writing about the material presented in the secondary reading, you are not one—but *two*—steps removed from the original text. If the object of a course in sociological theory is to grapple with the ideas that preoccupied the core figures of the field—the ideas and analyses that currently shape the direction of sociology—then studying original works must be a cornerstone.

To this end, we provide excerpts from the original writings of those we consider to be sociology's core contemporary theorists. We believe that if students are to understand Habermas, they must read Habermas and not a simplified interpretation of his ideas. They must learn to study for themselves what the leading theorists have said about some of the most fundamental social issues, the relevance of which are timeless.

Nevertheless, in this book we also provide a secondary interpretation of the theorists' overall frameworks and the selected readings. Our intent is to provide a guide (albeit simplified) for understanding the original works. The secondary interpretation will help you navigate the different writing styles often resulting from the particular historical, contextual, and geographical locations in which the theorists were and are rooted. Bear in mind, however, that our secondary explanations are just that—*secondary*. You should not take our secondary explanations at face value or, even worse, read only the secondary explanations and not the original texts. Instead, our secondary interpretations, examples, and visual aids are intended to serve as a tool for enabling you to better understand the original texts. The secondary explanations can be used as a launching pad for discussion as well.

WHO ARE SOCIOLOGY'S CORE CONTEMPORARY THEORISTS?

Our conviction that students should read the core contemporary sociological theorists raises an important question: who are the core theorists? After all, the discipline of sociology has been influenced by dozens of philosophers and social thinkers. Given this fact, is it right to hold up a handful of scholars as *the* most important theorists while necessarily excluding others?

In our view, the answer is yes, it is right (or at least not wrong) to cast a select group of intellectuals as the core writers in the discipline. To better understand our rationale for including some theorists while excluding others, it is important to briefly consider (1) the historical context that set the stage for the development of sociology as a discipline in the late nineteenth century, (2) the central ideas of the core figures of the classical period, and (3) how these ideas and thinkers continue to impact contemporary sociological theorists today.

The Enlightenment

Many of the seeds of what would become sociology were first planted with the **Enlightenment**, a period of remarkable intellectual development that occurred in Europe during the late seventeenth and early eighteenth centuries. During the

---

[1] Further complicating the matter is that many of the original works that make up the core of sociological theory were written in a language other than English. Language translation is itself an imperfect exercise.

Enlightenment, a number of long-standing ideas and beliefs on social life were turned upside down. The development of **civil society** (open spaces of debate relatively free from government control) and the rapid pace of the modern world enabled a critical mass of literate citizens to think about the economic, political, and cultural conditions that shaped society. Before that, explanations of the conditions of existence were so taken for granted that there was no institutionalized discipline examining them (Seidman 1994). Enlightenment intellectuals advocated rule by rational, impersonal laws and the end of arbitrary, despotic governments. They sought to define the rights and responsibilities of free citizens. In so doing, Enlighteners called into question the authority of kings whose rule was justified by divine right.

However, the Enlightenment was not so much a fixed set of ideas but a new attitude, a new method of thought. One of the most important aspects of this new attitude was an emphasis on *reason*. Central to this new attitude was questioning and reexamining received ideas and values.

The Enlightenment emphasis on reason was part and parcel of the rise of science. Scientific thought had begun to emerge in the fifteenth century through the efforts of astronomers and physicists such as Copernicus, Galileo, and Newton. Enlightenment intellectuals developed an approach to the world based on methodical observations. Rather than seeing the universe as divinely created and hierarchically ordered, Enlighteners insisted that the universe was a mechanical system composed of matter in motion that obeyed natural laws. Moreover, they argued that these laws could be uncovered by means of science and empirical research. In advocating the triumph of reasoned investigation and systematic observation of phenomena over religious faith and common-sense ways of understanding, Enlightenment intellectuals rebuked existing knowledge as fraught with prejudice and mindless tradition (Seidman 1994:20–1). Not surprisingly, such views were dangerous, for they challenged the authority of religious beliefs and those charged with advancing them. Indeed, some Enlighteners were tortured and imprisoned, or their work was burned for being heretical.

The rise of science and empiricism would give birth to sociology in the midnineteenth century. The central idea behind the emerging discipline was that society could be the subject of scientific examination in the same manner as biological organisms or the physical properties of material objects. Indeed, the French intellectual **Auguste Comte** (1798–1857), who coined the term "sociology" in 1839, also used the term "social physics" to refer to this new discipline and his organic conceptualization of society. The term "social physics" reflects the Enlightenment view that the discipline of sociology parallels other natural sciences. Comte argued that like natural scientists, sociologists should rationally and scientifically uncover the laws of the social world.[2] For Enlighteners, the main difference between scientific knowledge and either theological explanation or mere conjecture is that scientific knowledge can be tested. Thus, for Comte, the new science of society—sociology—involved (1) the analysis of the central elements and functions of social systems, using (2) concrete historical and comparative methods in order to (3) establish testable generalizations about them (Fletcher 1966:14).[3]

---

[2]Physics is often considered the most scientific and rational of all the natural sciences because it focuses on the basic elements of matter and energy and their interactions.

[3]Of course, the scientists of the Enlightenment were not uninfluenced by subjectivity or morality. Rather, as Seidman (1994:30–1) points out, paradoxically, the Enlighteners sacralized science, progress, and reason; they deified the creators of science such as Galileo and Newton and fervently believed that "science" could resolve all social problems and restore social order, which is itself a type of "faith."

However, it was the French theorist **Émile Durkheim** (1858–1917) who arguably was most instrumental in laying the groundwork for the emerging discipline of sociology. Durkheim emphasized that while the primary domain of psychology is to understand processes internal to the individual (for example, personality or instincts), the primary domain of sociology is "social facts," that is, conditions and circumstances external to the individual that, nevertheless, determine one's course of action. As a scientist, Durkheim advocated a systematic and methodical examination of social facts and their impact on individuals.

Yet interestingly, sociology reflects a complex mix of Enlightenment and **counter-Enlightenment** ideas (Seidman 1994). In the late eighteenth century, a conservative reaction to the Enlightenment took place. Under the influence of Jean-Jacques Rousseau (1712–1778), the unabashed embrace of rationality, technology, and progress was challenged. Against the emphasis on reason, counter-Enlighteners highlighted the significance of nonrational factors, such as tradition, emotions, ritual, and ceremony. Most important, counter-Enlighteners were concerned that the accelerating pace of industrialization and urbanization and growing pervasiveness of bureaucratization were producing profoundly disorganizing effects. In one of his most important works, *The Social Contract* (1762), Rousseau argued that in order to have a free and equal society, there must be a genuine social contract in which everyone participates in creating laws for the good of society. Thus, rather than being oppressed by impersonal bureaucracy and laws imposed from above, people would willingly obey the laws because they helped make them. Rousseau's challenge of the Age of Reason echoed Pascal's view that the heart has reasons that reason does not know. When left to themselves, our rational faculties leave us lifeless and cold, uncertain and unsure (see McMahon 2001:35).

In a parallel way, Durkheim was interested in both objective or external social facts and the more subjective elements of society, such as feelings of solidarity or commitment to a moral code. Akin to Rousseau, Durkheim felt that it was these subjective elements that ultimately held societies together. Similarly, **Karl Marx** (1818–1883), who is another of sociology's core classical figures (although he saw himself as an economist and social critic), fashioned an economic philosophy that was at once rooted in science and humanist prophecy. Marx analyzed not only the economic dynamics of capitalism but also the social and moral problems inherent to the capitalist system. So too, the third of sociology's core classical theorists, **Max Weber** (1864–1920), combined a methodical, scientific approach with a concern about both the material conditions and the idea systems of modern societies.

Economic and Political Revolutions

Thus far we have discussed how the discipline of sociology emerged within a specific intellectual environment. But of course, the Enlightenment and counter-Enlightenment were both the cause and effect of a whole host of political and social developments that also affected the newly emerging discipline of sociology. Tremendous economic, political, and religious transformations had been taking place in western Europe since the sixteenth century. The new discipline of sociology sought to scientifically explain both the causes and effects of such extraordinary social change.

One of the most important of these changes was the **Industrial Revolution,** which began in England in the eighteenth century. The Industrial Revolution refers to the application of power-driven machinery to manufacturing. Although industrialization began in remote times and continues today, this process completely transformed Europe in the eighteenth century. It turned Europe from a predominantly agricultural to a predominantly industrial society. It not only radically altered how goods were produced and distributed but galvanized the system of capitalism as well.

Specifically, with the Industrial Revolution large numbers of people began to leave farms and agricultural work to become wage earners in factories located in the rapidly growing cities. Indeed, although most of the world's population was rural before the Industrial Revolution, by the mid-nineteenth century half of the population of England lived in the cities, and by the end of the nineteenth century so did half of the population of Europe. Moreover, while there were scarcely twenty-five cities in Europe with a population of one hundred thousand in 1800, there were more than 150 cities this size a century later. At the same time, factories were transformed by a long series of technological changes. Ever more efficient machines were adopted, and tasks were routinized. Thus, for instance, with the introduction of the power loom in the textile industry, an unskilled worker could produce three and a half times as much as the best handloom weaver.

However, this rise in efficiency came at a tremendous human cost. Mechanized production reduced both the number of jobs available and the technical skills needed for work in the factory. A few profited enormously, but most worked long hours for low wages. Accidents were frequent and often quite serious. Workers were harshly punished and/or their wages were docked for even the slightest mistakes. Women and children worked alongside men in noisy, unsafe conditions. Most factories were dirty, poorly ventilated and lit, and dangerous.

Karl Marx was particularly concerned about the economic changes and disorganizing social effects that followed in the wake of the Industrial Revolution. Marx not only wrote articles and books on the harsh conditions faced by workers under capitalism, but was also a political activist who helped organize revolutionary labor movements to provoke broad social change.

Max Weber also explored the profound social transformations taking place in European society in the eighteenth and nineteenth centuries. Akin to Marx, Weber was concerned about the social consequences wrought by such profound structural change. However, in contrast to Marx, Weber argued that it was not only modern economic structures (e.g., capitalism) but also organizational structures—most important, bureaucracies—that profoundly affected social relations. Indeed, in one of the most famous metaphors in all of sociology, Weber compares modern society to an "iron cage." Even more important, in contrast to Marx, Weber also examined the particular systems of meaning, or ideas, that both induced and resulted from such profound structural change.

The eighteenth century was a time of not only tremendous economic but also political transformation. One of the most significant political events of that time was the French Revolution, which shook France between 1787 and 1799 and toppled the ancien régime. Inspired in large part by Rousseau's *Social Contract*, the basic principle of the French Revolution as contained in its primary manifesto, *The Declaration of Rights of Man and of the Citizen*, was that "all men are born free and equal in rights." The French revolutionaries called for "liberty, fraternity, and equality." They sought to substitute reason for tradition and equal rights for privilege. Because the revolutionaries sought to rebuild government from the bottom up, the French Revolution stimulated profound political rethinking about the nature of government from its inception and set the stage for democratic uprisings throughout Europe.

However, the French Revolution sparked a bloody aftermath, making it clear that even democratic revolutions involve tremendous social disruption and that heinous deeds can be done in the name of freedom. During the Reign of Terror led by Maximilien Robespierre, radical democrats rounded up and executed anyone—whether on the left or right—suspected of being opposed to the revolution. In the months between September 1793 (when Robespierre took power) and July 1794 (when Robespierre was overthrown), revolutionary zealots arrested about three hundred thousand people, executed some seventeen thousand, and imprisoned thousands more. It was during this radical period of the Republic that the guillotine, adopted as an efficient and merciful method of execution, became the symbol of the Terror.[4]

The Ins and Outs of Classical and Contemporary "Canons"

Thus far we have argued that the central figures at the heart of classical sociological theory all sought to explain the extraordinary economic, political, and social transformations taking place in Europe in the late nineteenth century. Yet, concerns about the nature of social bonds and how these bonds can be maintained in the face of extant social change existed long before the eighteenth century and in many places, not only western Europe. Indeed, in the late fourteenth century, Abdel Rahman Ibn-Khaldun (1332–1406), born in Tunis, North Africa, wrote extensively on subjects that have much in common with contemporary sociology (Martindale 1981:134–36; Ritzer 2004:5). And long before the fourteenth century, Plato (circa 428–circa 347 B.C.), Aristotle (384–322 B.C.), and Thucydides (circa 460–circa 400 B.C.) wrote about the nature of war, the origins of the family and the state, and the relationship between religion and the government—topics that have since become central to sociology (Seidman 1994:19). Aristotle, for example, emphasized that human beings were naturally political animals (*zoon politikon*; Martin 1999:157), and he sought to identify the "essence" that made a stone a stone or a society a society (Ashe 1999:89). For that matter, well before Aristotle's time, Confucius (551–479 B.C.) developed a theory for understanding Chinese society. Akin to Aristotle, Confucius maintained that government is the center of people's lives and that all other considerations derive from it. According to Confucius, a good government must be concerned with three things: sufficient food, a sufficient army, and the confidence of the people (Jaspers 1957:47).

Yet, these premodern thinkers are better understood as philosophers, not sociologists. Both Aristotle and Confucius were less concerned with explaining social dynamics than with prescribing a perfected, moral social world. As a result, their ideas are guided less by a scientific pursuit of knowledge than by an ideological commitment to a specific set of values. Moreover, in contrast to modern sociologists, premodern thinkers tended to see the universe as a static, hierarchical order in which all beings, human and otherwise, have a more or less fixed and proper place and purpose, and they sought to identify the "natural" moral structure of the universe (Seidman 1994:19).

Our key point here is that while the ideas of Marx, Durkheim, and Weber are today at the heart of the classical sociological theoretical canon, this does not mean that they are inherently "better" or more original than those of other intellectuals who wrote before or after them. Rather, it is to say that, for specific historical, social, and cultural as well as intellectual reasons, their works have helped define the discipline

---

[4]R. W. Connell (1997) notes that sociology was born during a decisive period of European colonial expansion. In turn, much of the discipline was devoted to collecting information about the colonizers' encounters with "primitive Others." Early sociologists' views on progress, human evolution, and racial hierarchies, however, were largely marginalized as the process of canon formation began during the 1930s. This had the effect of purging the discourse of imperialism from the history of the discipline.

of sociology, and that sociologists refine, rework, and challenge their ideas in different ways to this day.[5]

This brings us to contemporary sociological theory, which can be periodized roughly from 1935 to the present. (Classical theory generally refers to the era during which sociology first emerged as a discipline and was then institutionalized in universities—the mid-nineteenth to early twentieth centuries.) Of course, these dates are not set in stone, and a few classical thinkers, such as W. E. B. Du Bois (1868–1963), wrote from the late 1800s right up until the 1960s! The question as to who are our core contemporary sociological theorists today is not easy to answer. There are a myriad of possibilities, and contemporary sociologists disagree not only as to who is a core theorist and who is not, but even as to the major genres or categories of contemporary theory. For that matter, as you will see in Chapter 8, even defining what theory "is" or should be is a far from settled issue. Tied to this state of affairs is the increasing fragmentation of sociological theory during the past twenty-five years. During this period, sociology has become both increasingly specialized (breaking into such subspecialties as sociology of emotions and world-systems theory) and increasingly broad, as sociologists have built new bridges between sociology and other academic fields (for instance, anthropology, psychology, biology, political science, and literary studies), further contributing to the diversity of the discipline.

That said, in identifying the core contemporary theorists, we consider the extent to which a writer extends and expands on the theoretical issues at the heart of sociology. In our view, core contemporary theorists are those who write on the central questions of social order and social change and whose ideas are widely disseminated. In addition, to a person, core contemporary theorists all talk back to, revise, and reformulate the ideas of the "founding" theorists of sociology while taking up important issues raised by the social context in which they were/are writing and by the human condition itself. In sum, here we take a broad, historical perspective, prioritizing individuals who have significantly influenced others—and the discipline—from the mid-twentieth century until today.

In the end, however, determining the "ins and outs" of contemporary theory is a controversial and subjective matter, and, as such, the writers whose work we feature in this volume are by no means unanimously "core." To address this issue within the space constraints of this book, we expand our coverage by providing a brief look at a number of important theorists in the "Significant Others" section of the chapters that follow.

We begin this volume with the tradition of **structural functionalism** and the work of Talcott Parsons and one of his most prolific students, Robert Merton. From the 1930s through the 1970s, functionalism was the dominant theoretical approach in American sociology. A major emphasis of this approach lies in analyzing the societal forces that sustain or disrupt the stability of existing conditions. Functionalists introduced central concepts, such as "role," "norm," and "social system," into the discipline of sociology.

---

[5]For that matter, Marx, Weber, and Durkheim have not always been considered the core theorists in sociology. On the contrary, until 1940, Marx, Weber, and Durkheim were not especially adulated by American sociologists; up to this time, discussions of their work were largely absent from sociological theory textbooks (Bierstedt 1981). Meanwhile, even a cursory look at midcentury textbooks reveals an array of important "core figures" including Sumner, Sorokin, Sorel, Pareto, Le Play, Ammon, Veblen, De Tocqueville, Cooley, Spencer, Tönnies, and Martineau. Moreover, many important writers—for instance, W. E. B. Du Bois, Georg Simmel, George Herbert Mead, and Charlotte Perkins Gilman (see Edles and Appelrouth, *Sociological Theory in the Classical Era,* 2005)—whose works were ignored or underappreciated while they were alive, have become central to contemporary sociological theorizing.

They also coined several concepts (such as "role model" and "self-fulfilling prophecy") that are in widespread colloquial as well as academic use today.

Chapter 3 examines the work of the Frankfurt School of **critical theory**. Due in large measure to the dominance of the functionalist paradigm, the ideas expressed within this perspective would not find wide dissemination in the United States until the 1960s, when the sweeping social and cultural changes occurring in the broader society demanded a radically different theoretical approach for their explanation. Rather than emphasizing societal cohesion or consensus (as functionalists typically did), critical theorists underscore the divisive aspects of the social order. Drawing particularly from the works of Karl Marx and Max Weber, the theorists presented in this section seek to expose the oppressive and alienating conditions that are said to characterize modern societies.

As you will see, one of the most important characteristics of both functionalism and critical theory is their collectivist or "macro" approach to social order. (This point is further explained below.) However, a variety of more individualistic perspectives focusing more on the "micro" dimension of the social order was developing alongside these two theoretical camps. In Chapter 4 we examine one of the most important of these perspectives: **exchange theory**. Instead of looking to social systems or institutions for explanations of social life, exchange theorists emphasize individual behavior. Moreover, they consider individuals to be strategic actors whose behavior is guided by exchanges of benefits and costs. Based on rational calculations, individuals use the resources they have at their disposal in an effort to optimize their rewards. We focus especially on the work of two renowned exchange theorists: George Homans, who draws principally from behavioral psychology and neoclassical economics; and Peter Blau, who, while sympathetic to economics, evinces a greater indebtedness to the German sociologist Georg Simmel.

In Chapter 5, **symbolic interactionism** and **dramaturgical theory**, we continue our discussion of analyses of everyday life by examining the work of three theorists: Herbert Blumer, Erving Goffman, and Arlie Russell Hochschild. Blumer's contribution to symbolic interactionism cannot be overstated. Not only did he coin the term, but in advancing George Herbert Mead's analyses of the self and its relationship to language, Blumer outlined the central concepts and premises that would form the foundation of the tradition. As the leading proponent of dramaturgy, Erving Goffman occupies a unique place in the pantheon of contemporary theorists. While rooted in part in a symbolic interactionist approach, Goffman also drew from the work of Émile Durkheim and Georg Simmel. In doing so, he developed a fascinating account of the commonplace rituals that pervade daily interaction and their significance for constructing and presenting an individual's self. Arlie Hochschild's work bears the imprint of Goffman but incorporates a focus on a crucial, although often neglected, aspect of social life: emotions. In addition, she brings within her purview an examination of gender and family dynamics in contemporary capitalist society.

In Chapter 6 we discuss **phenomenology** and **ethnomethodology**, perspectives that, akin to exchange theory and symbolic interactionism, focus not on political, economic, and social institutions at the collectivist level but on the everyday world of the individual. Focusing especially on the work of the phenomenologists Alfred Schutz and Peter Berger and Thomas Luckmann, you will see that phenomenologists explore the subjective categories behind and within which everyday life revolves. They are interested in how people actively produce and sustain *meaning*. In this chapter you will also see that ethnomethodology, which was developed in the 1950s and 1960s primarily by Harold Garfinkel, focuses not on how actors internalize specific norms, ideas, and values but rather on the actual *methods* people use to accomplish their everyday lives.

Arlie Hochschild's integration of questions of gender into symbolic interactionism and dramaturgical theory brings us to an obvious but all too often overlooked point: sociological theory has been traditionally written by men from the perspective of men. In Chapter 7, we focus on perspectives that take seriously both the dearth of female voices in sociological theorizing and the distinct social situation of women in society: **feminist theory**. As you will see, feminist theory is very diverse. Feminist theorists all address a specific topic—gender equality (or the lack thereof)—but they examine this issue from a number of theoretical perspectives. Indeed, in this chapter you will read selections from the works of psychoanalytic feminist Nancy Chodorow, who turns Freud on his head; institutional ethnographer Dorothy Smith, who extends and integrates the seemingly disparate traditions of phenomenology and Marxism; neo-Marxist feminist Patricia Hill Collins, whose black feminist thought speaks to the particular situation of African American women; and postmodernist Judith Butler, who rejects the very idea that "woman" can be understood as a concrete category at all and, instead, construes gender identity as unstable "fictions" (1990:145–7).

Judith Butler's postmodern approach brings us to the topic of Chapter 8: **poststructuralism** and **postmodernism.** The theorists whose work you will read in this chapter, Michel Foucault, Jean Baudrillard, and Jean-François Lyotard, all critically engage the meaning of modernity by emphasizing how all knowledge, including science, is a representation of reality—not reality itself. Baudrillard goes the furthest here, by contending that in contemporary society "reality" has completely given way to a simulation of reality, or *hyperreality*, as simulated experience has replaced the "real."[6]

In Chapter 9, we present the work of three leading contemporary theorists: Pierre Bourdieu, Jürgen Habermas, and Anthony Giddens. Each of these theorists has been involved in a similar project, namely, developing a multidimensional approach to social life that integrates elements from distinct theoretical orientations. In articulating their perspectives, each has emphasized a different theme. Bourdieu develops his project through an emphasis on the reproduction of class relations; Habermas's approach addresses the prospects for democracy in the modern world. For his part, Giddens explores the effects of modernity on trust, risk, and the self.

We conclude this book with an examination of various theories pertaining to **contemporary global society**. As you will see, while the work of Immanuel Wallerstein, Leslie Sklair, and Edward Said is quite distinct, these theorists all focus not on the dynamics of interpersonal interaction (à la symbolic interactionism; see Chapter 5) or the forces that give form to a single society per se (à la functionalism; see Chapter 2), but rather on how such aspects of social life are themselves embedded in a global context, and how what happens in any given country (or geographical zone) is a function of its interconnections with other geographical regions. Indeed, these theorists all underscore that, given the increasingly unrestricted flow of economic capital and cultural images across countries, the nation-state—a self-governing territory demarcated by recognized spatial boundaries—can no longer serve as the dominant unit of analysis today.

HOW CAN SOCIOLOGICAL THEORY BE UNDERSTOOD?

Thus far we have (1) explained the importance of sociological theory, (2) argued that students should read original theoretical works, and (3) discussed the social theorists

---

[6]Thus, for instance, by the time they are school-aged, many American children will have watched more hours of television than the total number of hours they will spend in classroom instruction (Lemert 1997:27).

Figure 1.1   Basic Theoretical Continuum as to the Nature of Social Order

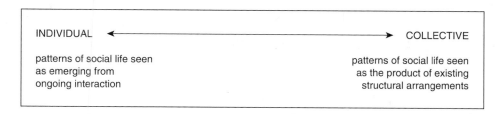

who we consider to be at the heart of classical and contemporary sociological theory. Now we come to the fourth question: how can we best navigate the wide range of ideas that these theorists bring to the fore? To this end, in this section we explain the analytical frame or "map" that we use in this book to explore, compare, and contrast the work of each theorist.

The Questions of "Order" and "Action"

Our analytical frame or map revolves around two central questions that social theorists and philosophers have grappled with since well before the establishment of sociology as an institutionalized discipline: the questions of *order* and *action* (Alexander 1987). Indeed, these two questions have been a cornerstone in social thought at least since the time of the ancient Greek philosophers. The first question, that of order, asks what accounts for the patterns and/or predictability of behavior that leads us to experience social life as routine. Or, expressed somewhat differently, how do we explain the fact that social life is not random, chaotic, or disconnected but instead demonstrates the existence of an ordered social universe? The second question, that of action, considers the factors that motivate individuals or groups to act. The question of action, then, turns our attention to the forces that are held to be responsible for steering individual or group behavior in a particular direction.

Similar to how the north-south, east-west coordinates allow you to orient yourself to the details on a street map, our analytical map is anchored by four "coordinates" that assist in navigating the details of the theories presented in this volume. In this case, the coordinates situate the answers to the two questions. Thus, to the question of order, one answer is that the patterns of social life are the product of structural arrangements or historical conditions that confront individuals or groups. As such, preexisting social arrangements produce the apparent orderliness of social life as individuals and groups are pursuing trajectories that, in a sense, are not of their own making. Society is thus pictured as an overarching system that works *down* on individuals and groups to determine the shape of the social order. Society is understood as a reality "sui generis" that operates according to its own logic distinct from the will of individuals. This orientation has assumed many different names—macro, holistic, objectivist, structuralist, and the label we use here, **collectivist**.

By contrast, the other answer to the question of order is that social order is a product of ongoing interactions between individuals and groups. Here, it is individuals and groups creating, recreating, or altering the social order that works *up* to produce society. This position grants more autonomy to actors, as they are seen as relatively free to reproduce the patterns and routines of social life (i.e., the social order) or transform them. Over time, this orientation has earned several names as well—micro, elementarism, subjectivist, and the term we adopt, **individualist**.

Figure 1.2   Basic Theoretical Continuum as to the Nature of Social Action

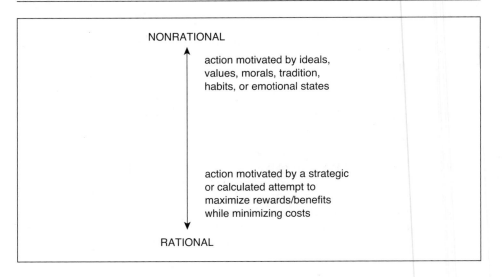

Figure 1.3   Core Classical Theorists' Basic Orientation*

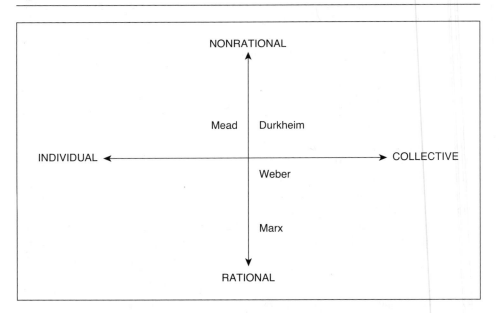

NOTE: *This diagram reflects the basic theoretical orientation of a few core classical sociological theorists: George Herbert Mead, Émile Durkheim, Max Weber, and Karl Marx. However, each of these theorists—as well as every theorist in this volume—is far more nuanced and multidimensional than this simple figure lets on. The point is not to "fix" each theorist in a particular box, but, rather, to provide a means for illuminating and discussing each theorist's orientation relative to one another and within their various works.

Turning to the question of action, we again find two answers, labeled here **nonrational** and **rational**. A "nonrational" basis for action refers to the extent to which the motivation for action is guided by values, morals, norms, traditions, the quest for meaning, unconscious desires, and/or emotional states. A "rational" basis for action means that individual and group actions are motivated primarily by the attempt to maximize rewards while minimizing costs.[7] In contrast to the nonrationalist orientation, which is relatively broad in capturing a number of motivating forces, the rationalist orientation is far less encompassing. Here, individuals and groups are viewed as essentially calculating and strategic as they seek to achieve the "selfish" goal of improving their position. In short, interests, not values, motivate action.

Intersecting the two questions and their answers, we can create a four-celled map on which we are able to plot the basic theoretical orientation of some of the core classical theorists (see Figure 1.3) and some of the major contemporary perspectives (see Figure 1.4) discussed in this book. The four cells are identified as individual-nonrational, individual-rational, collective-nonrational, and collective-rational. Yet, we

Figure 1.4   Basic Orientation of Core Perspectives in Contemporary Sociological Theory*

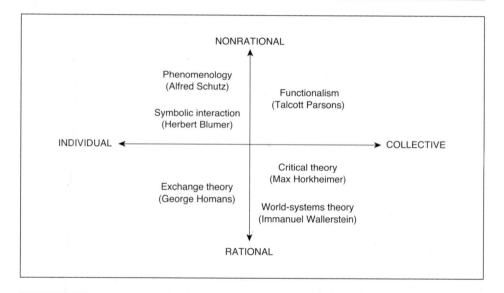

*This simplified diagram is intended to serve as a guide to comparing and contrasting the theoretical orientations underlying several contemporary theoretical perspectives and the work of authors who are aligned with them. For the sake of visual clarity, we include only the names of those theorists who arguably are most commonly associated with a given perspective, although, as the contents alone of this book suggest, any number of theorists are aligned with a given approach. The point is not to "fix" each theorist in a particular box; nor do all of the works associated with a given perspective fit neatly in a given quadrant. Indeed, each of the theorists and perspectives in this diagram is far more nuanced and multidimensional than this simple figure suggests. Moreover, several perspectives discussed in this book—for instance, postmodernism and feminist theory—are not included in this diagram. Postmodern theory deliberately challenges the very idea of fixed categories such as those that form the basis of this figure, while feminist theories draw from, extend, and fuse a wide variety of perspectives and traditions.

[7]The terms "rational" and "nonrational" are problematic in that they have a common-sensical usage that is at odds with how theorists use these terms. By "rational" we do not mean "good and smart," and by "nonrational" we do not mean irrational, nonsensical, or stupid (Alexander 1987:11). Despite these problems, however, we continue to use the terms "rational" and "nonrational" because the semantic alternatives (subjectivist, idealist, internal, etc.) are problematic as well.

cannot overemphasize that these four coordinates are "ideal types"; theorists and theories are never "pure." Implicitly and/or explicitly, theorists inevitably incorporate more than one orientation in their work. This is even more true today than in the past, as today's theorists explicitly attempt to bridge the theoretical gaps and dilemmas left by earlier thinkers. Thus, these coordinates (or cells in the table) are best understood as endpoints to continua on which theories typically occupy a position somewhere between the extremes. This multidimensionality and ambiguity is reflected in our maps by the lack of fixed points.

In addition, it is important to note that this map is something *you* apply to the theories under consideration. Although each theorist addresses the questions of order and action, they generally do not use these terms in their writing. For that matter, their approaches to order and action tend to be implicit, rather than explicit, in their work. Thus, at times, you will have to read between the lines to determine a theorist's position on these fundamental questions. While this may pose some challenges, it also expands the opportunities for learning.

Consequently, not everyone views each theorist in exactly the same light. Moreover, even within one major work, a theorist may draw from both ends of the continua. Nevertheless, these maps enable you to (1) recognize the general tendencies that exist within each theorist's body of work and (2) compare and contrast (and argue about) thinkers' general theoretical orientations.

Put another way, when navigating the forest of theory, individual theorists are like trees. Our analytic map is a tool or device for locating the trees within the forest so that you can enter and leave having developed a better sense of direction, or in this case, having learned far more than might have otherwise been the case. By enabling you to compare theorists' positions on two crucial issues, their work is less likely to be seen as a collection of separate, unrelated ideas. Bear in mind, however, that the map is only a tool. Its simplicity does not capture the complexities of the theories or of social life itself.

In sum, it is essential to remember that this four-cell table is an analytical device that helps us understand and compare and contrast theorists better, but it does not mirror or reflect reality. The social world is never a function of either "individuals" or "social structures" but a complex combination of both; so too, motivation is never completely rational or completely nonrational. To demonstrate this point as well as how our analytical map on "action" and "order" works in general, we turn to a very simple example.

Consider the question: why do people stop at red traffic lights? First, in terms of *action*, the answer to this question resides on a continuum with rational and nonrational orientations serving as the endpoints. On one hand, you might say that people stop at red traffic lights because it's in their best interest to avoid getting a ticket or into an accident. This answer reflects a rationalist response. A nonrationalist answer to this question is that people stop at red traffic lights because they believe that it is good and right to follow the law. Here the individual takes her bearings from unquestioned morals or values. Interestingly, if this moral or normative imperative is the only motivation for action, the individual will stop at the traffic light even if there is no police car or oncoming cars in sight. External circumstances, such as whether or not she will get hit or caught if she goes through the red light, are irrelevant. By contrast, if one's only motivation for action is rationalist, and there are absolutely no visible dangers (i.e., no other cars in sight and hence no possibility of getting a ticket or getting into an accident), the driver will *not* stop at the red light. Rather, on the basis of a calculated appraisal of the relevant conditions, she will go.

Another nonrationalist answer to the question "Why do people stop at red traffic lights?" involves "habits" (see Table 1.1). By definition, habits are relatively unconscious; that is, we don't think about them. They come "automatically," not from strategic calculations of interests or a concern for consequences; that is why they are typically considered

Table 1.1   Why Do People Stop at Red Traffic Lights? Basic Approaches to Order and Action

<table>
<tr><td rowspan="6">ACTION</td><td colspan="3" align="center">ORDER</td></tr>
<tr><td></td><td>Individual</td><td>Collective</td></tr>
<tr><td>Nonrational</td><td>Individual believes it is good and right to follow the law.

Habit: Individual stops without thinking.</td><td>Hegemonic moral order: Society teaches that it is "wrong" to disobey the law.

"Red" means "stop" and "green" means "go" in hegemonic symbolic system.</td></tr>
<tr><td>Rational</td><td>Individual does not want to get a ticket.

Individual does not want to get into an accident.</td><td>Hegemonic legal structure: Society punishes those who break the law.</td></tr>
</table>

nonrationalist. Interestingly, habits may or may not have their roots in morality. Some habits are "folkways," or routinized ways that people do things in a particular society (paying your bills by mail rather than in person; driving on the right side of the road), while other habits are attached to sacred values (putting your hand over your heart when you salute the flag). Getting back to our example, let's say you are driving your car on a deserted road at two o'clock in the morning, and you automatically stop at a red traffic light out of habit. Your friend riding with you might say, "Why are you stopping? There's not a car in sight." If your action were motivated simply from habit and not a moral imperative to follow the law, you might say, "Hey, you're right!" and run through the red light.

Of course, actions often have—indeed, they usually have—both rational and nonrational dimensions. For instance, in this last example, you may have interpreted your friend's question "Why are you stopping? There's not a car in sight" to mean "Don't be a goody-goody—let's go!" In other words, you may have succumbed to peer pressure even though you knew it was wrong. If such was the case, you may have wittingly or unwittingly felt that your ego, or "sense of self," was on the line. Thus, it was not so much that rational trumped nonrational motivation; rather, you acted out of a complex combination of your assessment of the traffic conditions, pressure from your friend to do the "cool" thing, and your desire to be the particular type of person you want to be.

Indeed, a basic premise of this book is that because social life is extremely complex, a complete social theory must account for multiple sources of action and levels of social order. Theorists must be able to account for the wide variety of components (individual predispositions, personality and emotions, social and symbolic structures) constitutive of this world. Thus, for instance, our rationalist response to the question as to why people stop at red traffic lights—that people stop simply because they don't want to get a ticket or get into an accident—is, in fact, incomplete. It is undercut by a series of unacknowledged nonrational motivations. There is a whole host of information that undergirds the very ability of an individual to make this choice. For example, before one can even begin to make the decision as to whether to stop for the red light or not, one must know that normally (and legally) "red" *means* "stop" and "green" *means* "go." That we know and take for granted that "red" means "stop" and "green" means "go," and then consciously think about and decide to override that cultural knowledge (and norm), indicates that even at our most rationalist moments we are still using the tools of a largely taken-for-granted, symbolic or nonrational realm (see Table 1.1 above).

Now let's turn to the issue of *order*.

If we say that people stop at red lights because they don't want to get a ticket, this can reflect a collectivist approach to order if we are emphasizing that there is a coercive state apparatus (e.g., the law, police) that hems in behavior. If such is the case, we are emphasizing that external social structures precede and shape individual choice. This collectivist approach to order (and rationalist approach to action) is illustrated in Table 1.1.

If we say that people stop because they believe it is good and right to follow the law, we might be taking a collectivist approach to order as well. Here we assume that individuals are socialized to obey the law. We emphasize that socially imposed collective morals and norms are internalized by individuals and reproduced in their everyday behavior. Similarly, if we emphasize that it is only because of the preexisting symbolic code in which "red" means "stop" and "green" means "go" that individuals can then decide what to do, we would be taking a collectivist approach. These versions of order and action are illustrated in Table 1.1.

On the other hand, that people stop at red traffic lights because they don't want to get into an accident or get a ticket also might reflect an individualist approach to order, if the assumption is that the individual determines his action using his own free will, and from this the traffic system is born. At the same time, another important individualist, albeit nonrationalist, answer to this question emphasizes the role of emotions. For instance, one might fear getting a ticket or into an accident, and to the extent that the fear comes from within the individual, rather than from a set of laws or socialization into a preexisting symbolic code, we can say that this represents an individualist explanation for the patterning of social life.

Sociological theorists hold a variety of views on the action/order continua even within their own work. Overall, however, each theorist can be said to have a basic or general theoretical orientation. For instance, in terms of the classical theorists discussed above, Marx was most interested in the collectivist and rationalist conditions behind and within order and action, while Durkheim, especially in his later work, was most interested in the collectivist and nonrationalist realms. Thus, juxtaposing Figure 1.3 and Table 1.1, you can see that if we were to resurrect Marx and Durkheim from their graves and ask them the hypothetical question "Why do people stop at red traffic lights?" it would be more likely that Marx would emphasize the rationalist motivation behind this act (they seek to avoid getting a ticket), while Durkheim would emphasize the nonrational motivation (they consider it the "right" thing to do)—although both would emphasize that these seemingly individualist acts are actually rooted in collectivist social and cultural structures (that it is the law with its coercive and moral force that undergirds individual behavior). Meanwhile, at the more individualist end of the continuum, Mead (whose pivotal contributions to symbolic interactionism are discussed in Chapter 4) would probably emphasize the immediate ideational process in which individuals interpret the meanings for and consequences of each possible action (although obviously each of these theorists is more complex and multidimensional than this simple example lets on).

Of course, the purpose of this book is not to examine the work of sociological theorists in order to figure out how they might answer a hypothetical question about traffic lights. Rather, the purpose of this book is to examine the central issues that contemporary theorists themselves raise and analyze the particular theoretical stance they take as they explore these concerns. These tasks are particularly challenging because the contemporary theorists and perspectives you will encounter in this book tend to be even more theoretically complex than sociology's classical founding figures. This is because contemporary theorists are not only drawing from and extending the classical

Figure 1.5   Basic Orientation of Core Classical Theorists and Contemporary Perspectives
in Sociological Theory

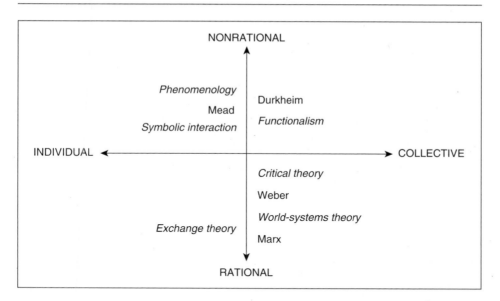

theorists' ideas; they are also seeking to better them. For instance, Jürgen Habermas, Pierre Bourdieu, and Anthony Giddens, whose works are discussed in Chapter 9, have each set out to develop a theoretical model that explicitly synthesizes and bridges nonrationalist and rationalist, and individualist and collectivist, concerns and ideas.

However, *all* of the theorists whose works you will read in this book are well aware of, and seek to correct in some way, the theoretical dilemmas posed by sociology's founding figures. Some thinkers, for instance those aligned with exchange theory, symbolic interactionism, and phenomenology and ethnomethodology (see Chapters 4, 5, and 6), look to address more fully the individualist realm that Marx, Weber, and Durkheim underemphasized (see Figures 1.4 & 1.5). Some of these analysts (e.g., phenomenologists) focus, above all, on how individuals apprehend social life on the basis of taken-for-granted assumptions, thereby emphasizing the individual/nonrational realm (see Figures 1.4 and 1.5). Others (e.g., exchange theorists) emphasize that individuals make relatively conscious attempts to satisfy their interests, which reflects a more individualist/rationalist theoretical orientation.

Unlike the individualist perspectives just outlined, collectivist approaches argue that individual and group conduct is largely shaped by external forces. For instance, as you will see in the following chapter, functionalism posits that societies are self-contained systems that possess needs necessary to their survival. Following Durkheim, functionalists tend to emphasize that a system of shared values and morals must be developed in order to establish the basis for consensual relations. As depicted in Figures 1.4 & 1.5, these assumptions reflect an emphasis on the collective/nonrational realm.

By contrast, the critical theorists whose works you will read in Chapter 3 followed Marx in emphasizing the oppressive nature of modern capitalistic societies, thereby exhibiting a predominantly collectivist/rationalist approach. To be sure, as you will see, critical theorists expounded on issues of ideology and consciousness more so than Marx (thereby reflecting a nonrationalist bent); however, above all, they emphasized the driving force of technological and instrumental conditions. For its part, world-systems theory, discussed in Chapter 10, explores the historical dynamics that have created the modern capitalist economy, an economy whose reach spans the globe. Far from studying the routines of everyday interaction or the consciousness of individuals, world-systems theory explores how distinct regions of the world are tied to one another by relations of domination and subordination that in turn affect economic and social dynamics within a given country. This argument reflects a collectivist/rationalist orientation.

Yet, it cannot be overemphasized that the point is not to "fix" each theorist or tradition in a particular box. All of the theorists and traditions presented in this book are far more complex than these simple figures let on. Moreover, as you will see, poststructural and postmodern thinkers, such as Judith Butler (see Chapter 7), Michel Foucault, Jean-François Lyotard, and Jean Baudrillard (see Chapter 8), seek to correct sociology's so-called theoretical dilemmas by throwing out metatheorizing altogether. Postmodernists, generally speaking, dismiss—rather than advance—overarching theoretical frameworks as "essentializing" and misguided. Throughout this book (but particularly in Chapters 7–10), we will explore the ideas of these provocative thinkers who challenge some of sociology's central tenets.

Discussion Questions

1. Explain the difference between "primary" and "secondary" theoretical sources. What are the advantages and disadvantages of reading each type of work?

2. Using Table 1.1 as a reference, devise your own question and give hypothetical answers that reflect the four basic theoretical orientations: individual/rational, individual/nonrational, collective/rational, and collective/nonrational. For instance, why do sixteen-year-olds stay in (or drop out of) school? Why might a man or woman stay in a situation of domestic violence? What are possible explanations for gender inequality? Why are you reading this book?

3. Numerous works of fiction speak to the social conditions that early sociologists were examining. For instance, Charles Dickens's *Hard Times* portrays the hardships of the Industrial Revolution, while Victor Hugo's *Les Miserables* addresses the political and social dynamics of the French Revolution. Read either of these works (or watch the play) and discuss the tremendous social changes they highlight.

4. One's answers to the questions of order and action have methodological as well as theoretical implications. Theories, after all, should be testable through the use of empirical data. Particularly with regard to the question of order, the perspective one adopts will have an important bearing on what counts as evidence and how to collect it. Consider both an individualist and collectivist perspective: How might you design a research project studying the causes and effects of job outsourcing, or the causes and effects of affirmative action? How about a study of the causes and effects of the rising costs of college tuition, or the causes and effects of drug and alcohol abuse? What types of questions or data would be most relevant for each approach? How would you collect the answers to these questions? What are some of the strengths and weaknesses associated with each approach?

2

STRUCTURAL FUNCTIONALISM

Key Concepts

Talcott Parsons	*Robert K. Merton*
❖ Role/Role-Set	❖ Manifest Function
❖ Values	❖ Latent Function
❖ Unit Act	❖ Deviance
❖ Social System	❖ Dysfunction
❖ Cultural System	
❖ Personality System	
❖ Pattern Variables	

A particularly important feature of all systems is the inherent limitation on the compatibility of certain parts or events within the same system. This is indeed simply another way of saying that the relations within the system are determinate and not just anything can happen.

~Parsons and Shils,
Toward a General Theory of Action (2001/1951:107)

From the 1930s through the 1970s, structural functionalism was the dominant theoretical approach in American sociology. Functionalists coined pivotal concepts, such as "role," "norm," and "social system," that came to form the basic building blocks of sociology. Moreover, a few functionalist concepts, such as "role model" and "self-fulfilling prophecy," have entered our colloquial vocabulary as well. Yet, structural functionalism is most well known not for the specific concepts that it introduced but rather for the metatheoretical framework on which it is based. Structural functionalists envision society as a system of interrelated parts, and they emphasize how the different parts work together for the good of the system. The classic structural functionalist image of society is as an organism, such as the body, with different parts (e.g., limbs, brain, liver, etc.) working together in an interdependent way.

In addition, structural functionalists emphasize "systems within systems." For instance, while each family can be considered its own self-contained "system" or unit, it is also a *component* of society as a whole. Other major components of society include the economy—the *system* for providing goods and services to members of that society; the government (or political realm)—the *system* for determining the rules for that society and the distribution of power; and the religious system—the *system* that provides individuals with core values and a sense of meaning. In short, for structural functionalists, just as the body is a system with specific parts (e.g., arms, legs, liver, etc.) that ensure its overall functioning, so, too, society is a system with specific parts (family, government, economy, religion, etc.) necessary for its very survival. While each of these components can and must be studied separately in order to thoroughly understand them, structural functionalists typically emphasize how the various systems and subsystems work together.

During the 1970s, the image of society as a system of interrelated parts was harshly rejected by those sociologists who emphasized that society was based on conflict, not consensus, among social groups. These sociologists, called "conflict theorists" (such as C. W. Mills—see p. 84, "Significant Others"), underlined how political and economic elites and the organizations they controlled worked for their *own* benefit, rather than for the benefit of society as a whole. Structural functionalism came to be viewed as, at best, an old-fashioned tradition with a conservative bias, and at worst, a perspective that legitimated the exploiters, augmenting social problems rather than helping to correct them.[1]

In this chapter, we explore the basic premises of structural functionalism, an extremely important type of theory not only because it dominated American sociology

---

[1]Conflict theorists criticized structural functionalists for evoking a highly idealized image of society. While much of this criticism is valid, conflict theorists mistakenly interpreted the functionalist analogy of society as an organism to mean a *healthy* organism, but this is not necessarily the case. So, too, Parsons is commonly criticized for conflating his theory of society with value judgments as to what is desirable in societies; however, his intent was not to advocate for a particular system but rather to provide an analytical framework for analyzing it. Nevertheless, as you will see in Parsons's "empirical description" of the American family below, and as postmodernism (see Chapter 8) today makes eminently clear, social science is not at all a wholly objective, empirical enterprise, and a myriad of gender, racial, cultural, class, and other unacknowledged biases/lenses are readily apparent in the structural functionalism of the 1940s and 1950s.

throughout much of the twentieth century, but because it still informs sociological thinking today. As you will see later in this book, contemporary theorists, such as Harold Garfinkel (Chapter 6), Jürgen Habermas (Chapter 9), and Anthony Giddens (Chapter 9), to name a few, all draw extensively from and/or explicitly "talk back to" central functionalist figures (most important, Talcott Parsons). Sociologists still seek to explain the relations among various parts of society; the extent to which our social world is a product of preexisting structures and conditions as opposed to individual "free will"; and the relation between subjective emotions, symbols, and values and objective, strategic calculation—all vital issues at the heart of structural functionalism. In addition, understanding the basic premises of structural functionalism is necessary for understanding the approaches that sought to upend it in the 1970s.

In the first part of this chapter, we focus on the work of arguably the single most important theorist in the tradition of structural functionalism: Talcott Parsons. In the second part of this chapter, we turn to one of Parsons's most influential students, Robert Merton, who developed and extended Parsons's work.

TALCOTT PARSONS (1902–1979): A BIOGRAPHICAL SKETCH

Talcott Parsons was born in 1902 in Colorado Springs, Colorado. He was the fifth and last child of Mary Ingersol Parsons, a suffragist and backer of various progressive causes, and Edward Smith Parsons, an ordained Congregational minister who later became president of Marietta College in Ohio. Talcott Parsons acknowledged that his parents' values influenced him considerably. Theirs was a liberal household, in which morality, the modern industrial system, economic individualism, and exploitation of labor were topics of concern. After graduating from high school in 1920, Parsons attended Amherst College (as had his father and two older brothers). He studied the natural sciences, particularly biology, as well as philosophy and the social sciences, graduating magna cum laude in 1924. Thereafter he attended the London School of Economics as a graduate student, where he met another American economics student, Helen Walker, whom he married in 1927. It was at the London School of Economics that Parsons was introduced both to sociology and to the great functionalist anthropologist Bronislaw Malinowski, with whom he took two courses.

SOURCE: American Sociological Association; reprinted with permission.

During 1925–1926 Parsons studied at the University of Heidelburg, Germany, where he was exposed to and deeply influenced by the work of Max Weber (who had died in 1920). Following Weber, Parsons sought to explore the "relations between economic and sociological theory" (Camic 1991:xxii). He wrote his doctoral dissertation on the role of capitalism in German literature (highlighting both Weber and Marx), and he translated Weber's now-classic *The Protestant Ethic and the Spirit of Capitalism* (1930) into English, thereby introducing Weber to the English-speaking academic world.

In 1927, Parsons began teaching at Harvard University, where he would remain until his retirement in 1973. At first, Parsons taught in the Department of Economics since a sociology department was not founded until 1930. Parsons became a tenured professor of sociology in 1939; chair of the Harvard Sociology Department in 1944; and in 1949 was elected president of the American Sociological Association. Throughout the 1950s and 1960s, Parsons was a dominant figure in American sociology. He continued to teach and give lectures right up until his death in 1979, although by then an anti-Parsonian backlash was in full swing. C. Wright Mills and other critics charged Parsons with a conservative bias as well as academic elitism. The viciousness of these attacks make Parsons unique not only in terms of the profundity of his influence but also the extent to which his work has been disparaged. As former student Robin Williams, Jr. (1980:66), notes, "few sociologists of our time have been more subjected to stereotyping, to careless *ad hoc* readings, and to selectively distorted interpretations." By the late 1980s, however, the fervor of anti-Parsonianism had died down, and contemporary theorists—most important, Jeffrey C. Alexander, Jürgen Habermas (see Chapter 9), Anthony Giddens (see Chapter 9), and Richard Münch—began to field a new appreciation for Parsons's work.

INTELLECTUAL INFLUENCES AND CORE IDEAS

Between his first sole-authored publication in 1928 and his death in 1979, Talcott Parsons enjoyed a long and productive career during which he wrote seventeen books and more than two hundred articles. This illustrious career can be divided into three phases. In his "early period" (roughly 1928–1937), Parsons focused on bringing classical European theorists, particularly Émile Durkheim and Max Weber, into American sociology in order to upend the individualistic and rationalistic utilitarian models prevalent in American sociology at the time. Parsons sought to replace the pragmatic, "grounded" theory dominant in American sociology and most evident in the detailed microlevel work of the Chicago School (see Chapter 5) with an all-encompassing theory of action based on a synthesis of the works of classical European thinkers, particularly Émile Durkheim and Max Weber (see Chapter 1). This effort culminated in *The Structure of Social Action* (1937). Although it has since become a classic, initially, *The Structure of Social Action* was roundly criticized for its high level of abstraction. One empirically minded critic disparaged Parsons's theory of action as "about as scientifically useful as a sonnet to a skylark" (Bierstadt 1938:18, as cited by Gerhardt 2002:2). For that matter, Parsons's theory of action continues to be maligned for its high level of abstraction even today.

Parsons's second intellectual phase (roughly 1937–1950) is often termed "structural functionalism." It is during this period that Parsons wrote his most famous works, and it is for the ideas developed during this period that he is most well known. This period culminated in 1951 with the publication of two pivotal works: *Toward a Theory of Action* (coauthored with Edward A. Shils) and *The Social System*. In these works Parsons attempts to resolve the theoretical problems he himself had posed earlier. Specifically, fascinated by Freud and having read Freud thoroughly, Parsons integrated psychoanalytic theory into his general theory of action. Is so doing, Parsons added an individualistic bent to what had been a primarily collectivistic orientation (relying as it did on Durkheim and Weber). More generally, Parsons sought a conceptual convergence and synthesis in social psychology, sociocultural anthropology, and sociology. Indeed, *Toward a Theory of Action* is a collaborative work that originated in a grant from the Carnegie Corporation (a charitable educational trust) that brought social scientists from other universities, including the sociologist Edward Shils (1910–1955) from Chicago, to participate in a regular series of seminars with Parsons and his colleagues in the Department of Social Relations at Harvard in 1949.

In his third and final intellectual phase (roughly 1952–1979), Parsons developed his "interchange model" (dubbed by his students the "AGIL scheme") and focused on the evolution of societies. In this period, Parsons shifted back to his preoccupation with political and economic systems (recall his early interest in Max Weber), which was epitomized in his book *Politics and Social Structure* (1969).

Throughout these three periods, Parsons wrote on a wide variety of topics—including education, media, politics, and the family—and introduced into sociology a wide variety of terms, including norms, values, roles, social systems, social structures, and social institutions. However, Parsons (who called himself an "incurable theorist") never lost sight of his central theoretical concern (Rocher 1972/4:1). Parsons sought to devise a conceptual and theoretical framework with which to analyze the basis of all action and social organization. It is for this all-encompassing, overarching, metatheoretical framework that Parsons is most well known.

Action Systems and Social Systems

Perhaps Parsons's single most important idea is that action must not be viewed in isolation. Rather, action must be understood as a "process in time," or as a *system*. As Parsons and Shils (2001/1951:54) explicitly state, "actions are not empirically discrete but occur in constellations we call systems." To underscore this point, Parsons used the term **unit act** to refer to a hypothetical actor in a hypothetical situation bounded by an array of parameters and conditions (required effort, ends or goals, situation, norms). In other words, instead of construing action in terms of something concrete (such as a business or an individual), Parsons conceptualized action *systems* as a means for analyzing social phenomena. More generally, he saw social action as composed of four basic elements that distinguish it from isolated, individual behavior:

1. it is oriented toward attainment of *ends* or *goals*

2. it takes place in *situations*, consisting of the physical and social objects to which the actor relates

3. it is normatively regulated (i.e., regulated by *norms* that guide the orientation of action)

4. it involves expenditure of *effort* or energy[2]

This model of social action is illustrated in Figure 2.1.

Parsons (1937) and Parsons and Shils (2001/1951) further maintain that actions are *organized* into three modes or realms: social systems, personality systems, and cultural systems. These systems are analytically rather than empirically distinct. That is, these systems (and their subsystems) are not physically separate entities but rather a simplified model of society that Parsons and Shils use to explain the organization of action. Put in another way, social systems, personality systems, and cultural systems *undergird* all action and all social life.[3]

---

[2]Parsons and Shils (2001/1951:53). Elsewhere Parsons differentiates *symbols* (by which actors attribute meaning to situations) from *norms* (rules for behavior).

[3]Elsewhere Parsons includes a fourth system, the behavioral organism, which in contemporary terms is equivalent to the "body," or genetic composition. Here, however, he combines the biological (behavioral organism) and the psychological into the personality system, saying that the personality is organized by both "organic" and "emotional" needs.

Figure 2.1   Parsons's Model of Social Action

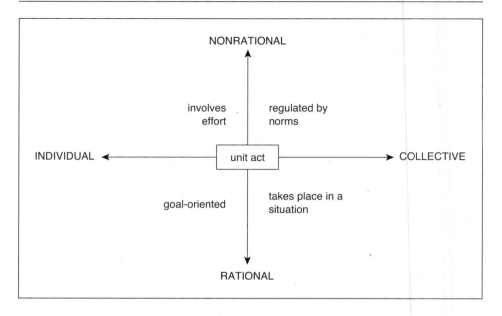

The **social system** refers to the level of integrated interaction between two or more actors. It also involves cognizance of the other actors' ideas and/or intentions (whether at a relatively conscious or unconscious level), as well as shared norms or expectations and interdependence (Parsons and Shils 2001/1951:55). In other words, social systems are not material structures or institutions (such as a university) but rather a complex arrangement of interconnected social roles (Alexander 1987:42). Parsons and Shils (2001/1951:23) define **roles** as complementary, detailed sets of obligations for interaction. Role-set theory begins with the idea that "each social status involves not a single associated role, but an array of roles." A **role-set** is that complement of interdependent social relationships in which persons are involved simply because they occupy a particular social status (ibid.). For instance, in an everyday situation such as buying groceries, you enter the store, walk around and pick out what you want, and go to the cashier to pay for it. Order and predictability ensue because you, as well as the other actors in the role-set (that is, other shoppers and store employees), know how to play your respective roles (e.g., shopper/cashier).

The **personality system** refers to a system of action organized by *need-dispositions*, both organic (e.g., "drives") and emotional, at the level of the individual. Although the personality system is the source of a distinctive and unique self, Parsons does not construe it as autonomous in the sense that psychologists typically do. Rather, for Parsons, the personality is a distinct level of social life; physical separateness of one's body never entails complete social or cultural differentiation, as personal uniqueness is itself a function of interaction and socialization (Alexander 1987:39). For instance, returning to our example of shopping for groceries, although there is an orderliness and predictability to the process, not everyone shops for food in exactly the same way. Some people are very organized and follow an exact list (perhaps even outlined according to sections of the grocery store), while others shop more spontaneously, buying more on impulse than a strict plan. In either case, the particular way that you shop reflects (to some extent) emotional as well as organic "need-dispositions" at the level of personality. That is, whether you are a very deliberate person celebrating a promotion by spontaneously

Figure 2.2   Parsons's Model of the Interpenetration of the Cultural, Social, and Personality Systems

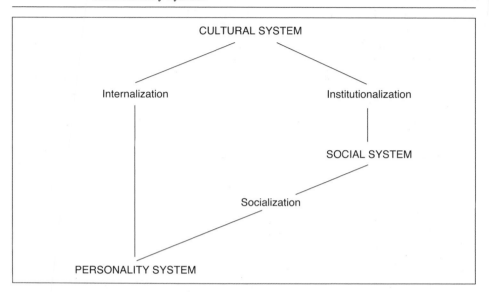

buying all your favorite foods, or an impulsive person restraining yourself by buying only "healthy" foods, your shopping reflects your emotional state.

The **cultural system** is made up of the "values, norms and symbols which guide the choices made by actors and which limit the type of interaction which may occur among actors" (Parsons and Shils 2001/1951:55). It is composed of intangible ideas and broad symbolic patterns of meaning that establish boundaries of social behavior. In the example of shopping for food, whether you help yourself to fruit or ask a clerk for assistance is not solely a "choice" at the level of personality, nor is it an issue of mere availability at the social system level. Rather, it is set by custom—as anyone who has tried to help themselves in a store in which you are not supposed to will know. So, too, even seemingly "personal" likes and dislikes are also a function of one's cultural environment; that is, they are rooted in specific systems of meaning of time and place. Whether your favorite ice cream flavor is *ube* (purple yam), green tea, or peanut butter and chocolate might reflect whether you grew up in Manila (the Philippines), Tokyo (Japan), or Los Angeles (U.S.), respectively. In sum, what we eat is determined, to a large extent, not only by instrumental concerns (e.g., price and convenience) and personal likes and dislikes, but by the taken-for-granted norms and symbols of the particular environment in which we are a part. While this is most evident in the case of sensationalistic regional variations (guinea pig in Ecuador, insects in Africa) and explicitly religious/philosophical variations (e.g., Orthodox Judaism), it is also true at a more routine, relatively unconscious, habitual level.

As shown in Figure 2.2, the personality, social, and cultural systems interpenetrate each other through socialization, internalization, and institutionalization. **Socialization** refers to the process by which individuals come to regard specific norms as binding. It necessarily involves a community, as it is a process of social learning. **Internalization** refers to the process by which the individual personality system incorporates some specific interpretation of cultural symbols into its need-dispositions. Finally, cultural values and norms are institutionalized at the level of the social system. **Institutionalization** refers to the long-standing processes of communal association that bind actors to particular meanings. Institutionalization privileges particular symbolic constructions and, at the same time, curtails resistance to social norms (Münch 1994:26–8).

Thus, for instance, children in a family of Orthodox Jews are taught, or *socialized* into, the rules for keeping kosher (kashrut). Consequently, they acquire, or *internalize*, a specific set of values and identity. However, what the practice entails is not hashed out anew in each and every Orthodox family. Rather, keeping kosher (which originates in the Torah and is further developed in later rabbinic literature) is *institutionalized* at the level of the social system; it is tradition and social and cultural codes that dictate what is involved in keeping kosher. As this example demonstrates, the processes of socialization, internalization, and institutionalization are intertwined: they involve the personality, cultural, and social realms at once.

One of the most contentious aspects of Parsons's systems theory is the supposition that the personality, social, and cultural systems function together to produce social order and stability. According to Parsons, system equilibrium ensues when the needs of the personality mesh with the resources available in the social system and cultural values and norms (Alexander 1987:47). Thus, for instance, in one essay you will read below, Parsons (1943/1954) describes the generation gap typical of contemporary American society as a time in which teenagers' need-dispositions are out of sync with the values of their family as well as the wider society. As such, there is a conflict (or gap) between the *personality* needs of the teenager (e.g., to stay out late, wear "weird" clothes, etc.) and the prevailing *cultural* values and norms (e.g., to respect authority, aspire toward educational and occupational success, etc.) as teenagers adopt identities, system of meanings, and social roles that contradict the expectations of parents and teachers.

Consequently, many critics contend that Parsons's model of societal equilibrium idealizes social conformity, that it suggests that the goal of society is complete institutionalization of norms and values, and that we should follow the rules for the "good of the system." In fact, however, Parsons argued that equilibrium is only a *theoretical* point of reference. The very notion of "action systems" suggests that systems are never completely stable; action itself is necessarily a disequilibrating factor, as by its very nature it involves change. In other words, although critics have long condemned Parsons for his "static" model of social order that emphasizes consensus, in fact, Parsons's main point is that, like a living organism, social systems are continuously in flux, adjusting, and changing as a result of environmental conditions. Parsons emphasized the continual *process* of managing discrepancies and conflicts between and within systems. He argued that, just as in biological organisms, social and personality systems continuously *seek* equilibrium, but that, as the old aphorism goes, the only thing constant is change. Complete and perfect institutionalization is an ideal; it refers to when role demands from the social system complement cultural ideals and when both, in turn, meet the needs of the personality system.

Thus, in the example of the generation gap, while the implication seems to be that this conflict (and conflict in general) is "bad," in fact, Parsons fully recognized that although the norms and values of youth culture may be in conflict with those of wider society, they may very well meet the need-dispositions of youth. As Parsons (1943/1954:189) states, among the functions of youth culture is "that of easing the difficult process of adjustment from childhood emotional dependency to full 'maturity.'" Put in another way, because Parsons maintains that each functional subsystem is itself a self-contained system that contains its own subsystems, it is inevitable that changes that are functional for one part of the system will produce changes that are not necessarily functional for other parts of the system. Parsons's student and colleague Robert Merton later deliberately developed this vital point, as is discussed further below.

The Pattern Variables

In *Toward a Theory of Action* (1951), Parsons and Shils develop a set of concepts called the **pattern variables** (see Table 2.1). The pattern variables are a set of five

Table 2.1   Parsons's Pattern Variables

PATTERN VARIABLE: a dichotomy that describes alternatives of action between which each person (or group) has to choose in every situation. The actions are shaped by the three systems: personality, cultural, and social.

1. **Affectivity/Affective-Neutrality**

   Affectivity: emotional impulses are gratified. For example, a child is allowed to show "love" for parent.

   Affective-neutrality: emotional impulses are inhibited. For example, a bureaucrat in an organization (such as the DMV) or a teacher grading papers is expected to be emotionally "neutral."

2. **Self-Orientation/Collectivity-Orientation**

   Self-orientation: action is based on the actor's own interests, needs, and goals. For example, a student decides what to study in college based on his or her own interests.

   Collectivity-orientation: action is based on what is best for the "collectivity." For example, a child quits school to work to support her family.

3. **Universalism/Particularism**

   Universalism: action is based on "general standards" or universal laws and moral rules. For example, the Supreme Court decides cases according to rules valid for the whole community.

   Particularism: action is based on the priority and attachment actors place on relationships and situations. For example, you give support to a friend without considering whether his or her actions were right or wrong.

4. **Ascription/Achievement**

   Ascription: action based on given attributes (race, sex, age). For instance, being eligible for the draft or allowed to buy alcohol or vote because you are a specified age.

   Achievement: action based on performance. For example, graduation from college based on completion of requirements for graduation.

5. **Specificity/Diffuseness**

   Specificity: action based on specific criteria/roles. For example, clerk/customer role, teacher/student role—there are narrowly and clearly defined criteria for interaction.

   Diffuseness: open guidelines for action. For example, becoming friends with a teacher, going beyond the clear boundaries of teacher/student relation.

"choices" that, akin to the AGIL scheme, apply not only to the individual level but to the collective level as well. They refer at once to the variant normative priorities of social systems, the dominant modes of orientation in personality systems, and the patterns of values in cultural systems (Coser 1977:569).

Though, as you will see, both ends of each pattern variable dichotomy are readily apparent in contemporary society at all three levels (social, cultural, and personality), in fact, the pattern variables are an extension of a renowned dichotomy first formulated by the German theorist Ferdinand Tönnies (1963/1935). Tönnies's distinction between *Gemeinschaft* (community) and *Gesellschaft* (purposive association) was later

Table 2.2   Parsons's Pattern Variables and Tönnies's Distinction Between *Gemeinschaft*
(Community) and *Gesellschaft* (Purposive Association)

	TRADITIONAL/*gemeinschaft*	MODERN/*gesellschaft*
PATTERN VARIABLE	Affectivity	Affective-neutrality
	Collectivity-orientation	Self-orientation
	Particularism	Universalism
	Ascription	Achievement
	Diffuseness	Specificity

reformulated by Émile Durkheim in his conceptualization of "mechanical" versus "organic solidarity." According to these classic dichotomies, modern societies are based on individualistic "purposiveness" and functional interdependence, while traditional societies are rooted in collectivistic "sameness" (or community) and an intense feeling of community. The relation between Parsons's pattern variables and Tönnies's distinction between *Gemeinschaft* and *Gesellschaft* is illustrated in Table 2.2.

As for Parson's pattern variables, as shown in Table 2.1, *affectivity* means that the emotions are considered legitimate in action ("gratification of impulse" in Parsons's terms), while *affective-neutrality* means that emotions are closed out of action ("discipline"; Münch 1994:32–3). For instance, in contemporary societies it is normative to display affectivity in personal relationships but not in bureaucratic relationships: you might kiss or hug a close friend upon greeting him on the street (affectivity), but you won't do the same to the next client in line in your job as a clerk at the Department of Motor Vehicles (affective-neutrality). Indeed, Parsons maintained that affective-neutrality was generally more pervasive in modern Western societies than in traditional societies—which parallels the shift noted by Tönnies as well as Weber from a more religiously oriented (nonrationalistic) society to a more rationalistic, scientifically oriented society.

This shift is particularly apparent when considering the contrast between traditional and modern scientific medicine. Modern medicine typically involves tests and procedures performed by a myriad of specialists who are often strangers to the patient. The relationship between patient and medical specialist (or medical technician) is typically marked by professionalism and affective-neutrality rather than affectivity and emotional involvement (see Photo 2.1a and 2.1b). At the other end of the spectrum, in a traditional society such as the Kamba, together shaman and patient might invoke a drug-induced state in order to complete a thorough spiritual and physical "cleansing" of the aggrieved soul. In this case, rather than being excluded from medical treatment, emotions are integral to the healing process.

Self-orientation means that the individual actor prioritizes the needs and goals of the "self," while conversely, the *collectivity-orientation* denotes the prioritization of the needs and goals of the collectivity or group as a whole. Following Tönnies, Parsons suggests that "self-orientation" is considered more legitimate in modern and postmodern than in traditional societies, while in traditional societies, the reverse is true. For instance, as shown in Table 2.1, in contemporary American society, college students typically choose their major based on their own interests and goals ("self-orientation"). So, too, most Americans choose their own marriage partner, a choice that is based primarily (if not strictly) on personal issues in which the central question is, "Is this the person *I* want to spend the rest of my life with?" Conversely, in many traditional

Photo 2.1a Traditional Shaman (Affectivity): Emotional
spontaneity is considered legitimate in shaman/patient interaction.
SOURCE: © Wendy Stone/CORBIS.

Affectivity vs. Affective
Neutrality

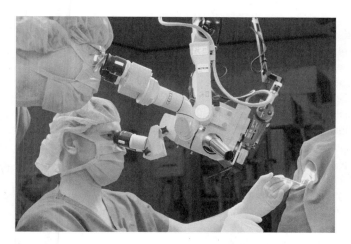

Photo 2.1b Modern Medicine (Affective-Neutrality): Emotional
spontaneity is usually not condoned.
SOURCE: © Lester Lefkowitz/CORBIS; used with permission.

societies, marriages are not so much an individual but, rather, a collective concern. In such societies, marriages are often arranged by elders, who focus on the economic and social benefits of the prospective new kinship formation (a collective consideration) rather than strictly the needs and wants of the bride and groom (who may or may not even know each other).

Universalism means that an action is based on impersonal, universal standards or general rules, such as queuing up, filling out a standardized job application, or having each person's vote count equally in an election. Conversely, *particularism* refers to actions that are guided by the uniqueness of that particular relationship, for instance, inviting only "really good friends" to your party. For example, if you stand by your sister even though she acted badly (or illegally), you are prioritizing the particular relationship you have with her over her action (even though you find it offensive). By contrast, if you turn your sister in to the police because what she did was illegal, you would be applying a universal standard. In this case, your particular relationship is not the central concern. Again, this dichotomy is related to Tönnies's differentiation between traditional and modern society. Action in modern bureaucratic societies typically relies on a myriad of universalistic standards and procedures (student grade point average or GPA, tax brackets, Supreme Court rulings), while action in traditional societies typically relies on more particularistic criteria (e.g., kinship bonds, rule of elders).

Ascription means that evaluations or interactions are guided by given personal attributes (e.g., race, gender, age), while *achievement* (performance) means that evaluations or interactions are based on an actor's performance with regard to established standards (e.g., college entrance examinations, physical endurance tests for firefighter trainees). Parsons maintained that the achievement orientation was increasingly important in modern Western societies, whereas in traditional societies, ascribed characteristics (e.g., clan, gender, age) were generally given greater priority. Thus, for instance, an individual's tenure and success in her career is determined more by her performance than by inheritance or privilege.

Of course, this is not to say that ascription is irrelevant in modern societies: in all of the pattern variables, the distinctions between traditional and modern society must not be taken too far. Obviously, upper-class children still inherit significant privileges, making class position one of the most vital attributes in today's world; and race and gender are, to a large extent, ascribed rather than achieved as well. Indeed, although his pattern variables explicitly follow Tönnies's dichotomy between traditional and modern societies, in fact, Parsons fully recognized that each pole of each pattern variable exists in both types of society.

The multivocality of the pattern variables is most readily apparent in Parsons's notion of *subsystems*, or systems within systems, because this means that the pattern-variable continuum is always apparent in full at another level. Thus, for instance, although affective-neutrality is generally considered more legitimate than affectivity in modern societies, as evidenced in economic relationships, affectivity is generally considered a more legitimate basis of action in the context of the family. At the same time, however, even within the economy, there are nevertheless times and places when affectivity is considered a legitimate basis for action; likewise, there are times and places in which affective-neutrality is prescribed within the family as well. So, too, at the level of the actor-ego (personality) as well as social roles, while it is generally considered more legitimate for women to display affectivity than for men, nevertheless, because actions always occur in systems (recall the concept of the unit act), there are situations in which affectivity is normative (or not) for both men and women (e.g., a funeral as opposed to a business conference).

Photo 2.2a Small Farmer (Diffuseness)
SOURCE: Photo courtesy of USDA Natural Resources Conservation Service.

Small farmers typically perform a wide range of tasks, from record-keeping to operating and servicing heavy machinery, to growing vegetables or raising animals. In Parsons's terms, role expectations are *diffuse*. By contrast, duties and role expectations for fast-food restaurant workers tend to be highly *specific*; indeed, workers are often mandated to follow finely-tuned scripts to maximize efficiency.

Photo 2.2b Fast-Food Restaurant Worker
SOURCE: Eleanor Desfor Edles.

Similarly, although achievement is generally prioritized in the public sector and ascription is prioritized in the family, even within one system (the family, the economy, the legal system), each dimension of the pattern variable invariably appears. For instance, parents might base a child's privileges on both achievement (e.g., grades,

Table 2.3   Four Functional Requirements of Action Systems: AGIL

Adapation: how well the system adapts to its material environment

Goal attainment: ability of individual or group to identify and pursue goals

Integration: dimensions of cohesion and solidarity

Latent pattern maintenance: sphere of general values

behavior) and ascription (e.g., age). So, too, ascription and achievement are both readily apparent in the legal system, for instance, in driving laws that say you must both pass a test to get a license (achievement) and be a certain age (ascription). Of course, traditional societies have a parallel continuum, too, in that there are explicit contests or competitions for particular social roles and rewards (achievement), but in order to participate you must possess specific ascribed traits (e.g., be a certain gender or age).

Finally, *diffuseness* means nothing is "closed out" in making a particular choice or undertaking a particular action, while *specificity* means that action is based on a *specific* criterion. For instance, in urban, bureaucratic societies, we are often expected to act within narrowly defined roles in order to maximize efficiency. Impersonal mechanisms, such as queuing up or taking a number, are intended to be based solely on *one* criterion (e.g., who got their first), thereby displaying affective-neutrality and universality (i.e., fairness) rather than emotion or favoritism. So, too, employees at banks, supermarkets, restaurants, insurance companies, and all sorts of other entities are often given a script to follow to ensure that dialogue follows the specific organizational goals for that interaction—and only that interaction (e.g., "Do you want to supersize that?"). By contrast, in smaller, slower-paced, rural, traditional communities in which speed and efficiency are not of such paramount importance, the criteria for action may be more diffuse; less is excluded from the interaction. For instance, a shopper might engage in a significant amount of small-talk before getting to the actual purchase, or a teacher might provide clothes or food for an impoverished student. Here, individuals are acting according to diffuse criteria, rather than to the specific demands of particular roles.

AGIL

This brings us to another central element in Parsons's theory. Parsons maintains that there are four "functional imperatives" or requirements encountered by all action systems. That is, there are four basic problems that a society, group, or individual must confront in order to survive as a system of action (Parsons 1971:4). Parsons called these four problems or functions adaptation, goal attainment, integration, and latent pattern maintenance (see Table 2.3). Parsons's students used the acronym "AGIL" to refer to this scheme. These four functions or requirements are evident at every level of every system, from entire social systems, to particular subsystems, to the level of the individual actor-ego.

Specifically, as shown in Table 2.3 (see above), *adaptation* (A) refers to responses to the physical environment. At the level of the actor-ego, the problem of adaptation is often managed by the behavioral or physiological organism. For example, the body adapts to heat by perspiring, thereby cooling itself down. At the level of the social

Table 2.4   Parsons's AGIL Scheme at the Level of the Social System

ADAPTATION (A)	GOAL ATTAINMENT (G)
Economic system (resources)	Polity (goals)
LATENT PATTERN MAINTENANCE (L)	INTEGRATION (I)
Cultural system (values)	Social system (norms, interaction)

system, the economy typically fulfills the requirement of adaptation (see Table 2.4). That is, the economy is the subsystem that adapts to the environment for social purposes (providing goods and services). For instance, a coastal island village might revolve around fishing while an inner-island village might revolve around farming, but in either case, it is the *economy* that is most central in adjusting to the environment. So, too, in the economic system of capitalism, the market is continually shifting based on supply and demand for goods and services (the environment).

Goal attainment (G) refers to the problem of resolving the discrepancies between "the inertial tendencies of the system and its 'needs' resulting from interchange with the situation" (Parsons 1961). At the level of the individual, goal attainment is met primarily by the personality system. As Parsons (1971:6) states, "the personality system is the primary *agency* of action processes," aimed at "the optimization of gratification or satisfaction." At the level of the social system, the requirement of goal attainment is typically met by the *polity*, as it is the realm in which goals and resources are prioritized, and discrepancies are resolved between "the inertial tendencies of the system and its 'needs' resulting from interchange with the situation" (Parsons 1961; see Table 2.4). The polity and government establish status and reward systems so that social goals can be attained.

Integration (I) refers to the coordination of a system's or subsystem's constituent parts, since "all social systems are differentiated and segmented into relatively independent units" (Parsons 1961). Within the four systems of action (behavioral organism, personality, social system, and cultural system), the function of integration is met primarily by the social system. Integration involves *solidarity*, that is the feeling of "we-ness" that develops in a social group as distinct roles are carried out; integration depends on interaction and the norms that guide interaction more so than abstract cultural values.

Latent pattern maintenance (L) refers to the "imperative of maintaining the stability of the patterns of institutionalized culture" (Parsons 1961). This function is carried out primarily by the cultural system, as it is through culture (made up of shared meanings and values) that specific patterns of behavior are maintained. Within the social system, the function of latent pattern maintenance, that is the maintaining of shared values, is most readily apparent in the realm of religion.

However, as indicated previously, the AGIL scheme refers to the dilemmas or problems faced by *all* systems of action. Thus, for instance, the need for latent pattern maintenance exists within all social units, including the economy, as the Great Depression attests. The great crash of 1929 was rooted in collective panic, a lack of faith in the banking system, or in Parsons's terms, a failure in latent pattern maintenance. So, too, although religion is intimately connected to the problems of latent pattern maintenance (L) and integration (I), nevertheless, religious organizations adapt to the environment (A) and set goals (G). Indeed, as the Protestant Reformation during the 1600s dramatically reflects, it is by adapting to external conditions and setting fresh goals that new religions and religious institutions are born.

PARSONS'S THEORETICAL ORIENTATION

As shown in Figure 2.1 and discussed above, Parsons explicitly sought to create a multidimensional metatheoretical model. Indeed, it is Parsons's ideas that gave rise to the "order" and "action" model that we use in this book. Parsons's multidimensionality is readily reflected in his conceptualization of the unit act. As we have seen, according to this model of social action, the hypothetical actor is at once guided by a strategic calculation of ends or goals (which indicates *rational* motivation), as well as *internalized* norms and values (which indicates *nonrational* motivation). At the level of the collective, a *situation* contains both normative (nonrational) and external or environmental (rational) dimensions. That is, it consists of both symbolic phenomena (e.g., societal norms and values) and more tangible constraints (e.g., economic conditions). At the level of the individual, social action involves the "*effort* to conform with *norms*" (1937/1969:76–7; emphasis added). "Effort" reflects both organic and nonorganic elements; it is a function of both internal (nonrational) biological constitution and (rational) strategic, conscious choice. Meanwhile, that individual effort is conditioned by norms reflects both the cultural (nonrational) and structural (rational) constraints placed on the individual by society at the collective level.

So, too, Parsons's conceptual trilogy of *institutionalization, internalization,* and *socialization* also explicitly integrates individual and collective approaches to order. Norms and values are *institutionalized* in the environment at the collective level in both culture and social structures (e.g., ideologies and organizations) and, at the same time, *internalized* at the level of the individual (nonrational/individual), while *socialization* is the mechanism that bridges these two realms.

Similarly, Parsons's integration of rational and nonrational forms of motivation is also apparent in his AGIL scheme: adaptation and goal attainment speak to the more rationalistic side of action and social systems, while integration and latent pattern maintenance speak to the more nonrational dimensions (see Table 2.4). That is, adaptation and goal attainment reflect how individuals or social groups adapt to, and set goals based on, the environment. At the other end of the action continuum, integration and latent pattern maintenance reflect how action is rooted in norms and ideas (e.g., feelings of belonging and shared values) *internal* to the individual. There is a *commitment* to the norms and ideas of the groups. Thus, from this point of view, of the four functions that every individual or social group must confront, two are largely internal and two are linked to strategic calculations or the environmental conditions to which the individual/social group must adapt.

Finally, Parsons's pattern variables also include both nonrational and rational forms of motivation at the individual and collective levels. Indeed, specific pattern variables speak directly to either action or order. For instance, affectivity versus affective-neutrality is an explicit reference to whether motivation for action is internal/nonrational (based on affectivity) or not; while the self versus collective pattern variable is a specific reference to whether individual decision-making or social patterns have priority. Moreover, as discussed previously and shown in Table 2.2, Parsons dichotomized traditional and modern societies along these same lines, construing modern Western societies as geared more toward rational and individualistic motivation and patterns and traditional societies as more nonrational and collectivistic. Thus, for instance, in traditional societies ascriptive factors, such as kinship ties, may have greater saliency than achievement criteria, such as test scores, in determining vocation and individual opportunity or success. So, too, as indicated previously, institutions such as marriage that tend to be considered intensely personal (individual) in modern societies are often rooted more in collective concerns in traditional societies. In this case, marrying someone on the basis of love bespeaks a self-orientation, while marrying for the good of the clan or family is indicative of a collective orientation.

That said, as indicated in Chapter 1 and shown in Figures 1.4 and 1.5, overall we situate Parsons and structural functionalism in the collective/nonrational quadrant of our theoretical model. That is because, above all, it is to the *moral* cohesion of the *system* to which structural functionalism and Parsons is most attuned. Perhaps, had Parsons achieved his goal and been *truly* multidimensional (for instance, had he acknowledged the organization and structural barriers to equality that so concerned conflict theorists such as C. W. Mills), he would not have suffered from the stigma of a conservative purveyor of the "status quo."

Readings

Two very different excerpts from Parsons's extensive oeuvre of works are provided below. The first selection, "Categories of the Orientation and Organization of Action," from *Toward a General Theory of Action* (2001/1951), written by Parsons and Edward Shils (1910–1955), a distinguished professor of sociology at the University of Chicago, in the United States, and Cambridge University in the United Kingdom, reflects the quintessence of structural functionalism. Considered "one of the most important theoretical statements in twentieth century sociology" (Smelser 2001:vii), Parsons and Shils set out a conceptual and theoretical framework with which to analyze the basis of all action and social organization. It is for this all-encompassing, overarching, metatheoretical framework that Parsons is most well known. In the second reading, "Sex Roles in the American Kinship System," Parsons applies his theory of action to the empirical topic of the American family.

Introduction to Parsons and Shils, "Categories of the Orientation and Organization of Action"

In this chapter from *Toward a General Theory of Action* (2001/1951), Parsons and coauthor Edward Shils delineate their groundbreaking theory of action; outline the basic elements of the social, cultural, and personality systems levels; and discuss the pattern variables. Specifically, in the first section of this reading, "Action and Its Orientation," Parsons and Shils explain their theory of action and the cultural, social, and personality systems. In the second and third sections of this reading, "Dilemmas of Orientation and the Pattern Variables" and "The Definitions of Pattern Variables," Parsons and Shils focus on the basic characteristics of the pattern variables as well as the relation between the pattern variables. In the fourth and fifth sections of this essay, "Classification of Need-Dispositions and Role-Expectations" and "The Basic Structure of the Interactive Relationship," the authors illuminate the basic structures of personalities and social systems. As noted above, "need-dispositions" refer to the allocative foci for personality systems, while "role-expectations" refer to the allocative foci for social systems. Need-dispositions and role-expectations are the connective tissue between systems of action and the pattern variables. As Parsons and Shils (p. 93) state, "*every* concrete need-disposition of personality, or every role-expectation of social structure, involves a combination of values of the five pattern variables" (emphasis in original).

❖

Categories of the
Orientation and Organization of Action (1951)

Talcott Parsons and Edward A. Shils

ACTION AND ITS ORIENTATION

The theory of action[i] is a conceptual scheme for the analysis of the behavior of living organisms. It conceives of this behavior as oriented to the attainment of ends in situations, by means of the normatively regulated expenditure of energy. There are four points to be noted in this conceptualization of behavior: (1) Behavior is oriented to the attainment of ends or goals or other anticipated states of affairs. (2) It takes place in situations. (3) It is normatively regulated. (4) It involves expenditure of energy or effort or "motivation" (which may be more or less organized independently of its involvement in action). Thus, for example, *a man driving his automobile to a lake to go fishing* might be the behavior to be analyzed. In this case, (1) *to be fishing* is the "end" toward which our man's behavior is oriented; (2) his situation is the road and the car and the place where he is; (3) his energy expenditures are normatively regulated—for example, this driving behavior is an *intelligent*[ii] means of getting to the lake; (4) but he does spend energy to get there; he holds the wheel, presses the accelerator, pays attention, and adapts his action to changing road and traffic conditions. When behavior can be and is so analyzed, it is called "action." This means that any behavior of a living organism might be called action; but to be so called, it must be analyzed in terms of the anticipated states of affairs toward which it is directed, the situation in which it occurs, the normative regulation (e.g., the intelligence) of the behavior, and the expenditure of energy or "motivation" involved. Behavior which is reducible to these terms, then, is action.

Each action is the action of an actor, and it takes place in a situation consisting of objects. The objects may be other actors or physical or cultural objects. Each actor has a system of relations-to-objects; this is called his "system of orientations." The objects may be goal objects, resources, means, conditions, obstacles, or symbols. They may become cathected (wanted or not wanted), and they may have different significances attached to them (that is, they may mean different things to different people). Objects, by the significances and cathexes attached to them, become organized into the actor's system of orientations.

The actor's system of orientations is constituted by a great number of specific orientations. Each of these "orientations of action" is a "conception" (explicit or implicit, conscious or unconscious) which the actor has of the situation in terms of what he wants (his ends), what he sees (how the situation looks to him), and how he intends to get from the objects he sees the things he wants (his explicit or implicit, normatively regulated "plan" of action).

Next, let us speak briefly about the sources of energy or motivation. These presumably

SOURCE: From Parsons, T., and Shils, E. A., *Toward a General Theory of Action,* © 2001 by Transaction Publishers. Reprinted by permission of the publisher.

[i]The present exposition of the theory of action represents in one major respect a revision and extension of the position stated in Parsons, *The Structure of Social Action* (pp. 43–51, 732–733), particularly in the light of psychoanalytic theory, of developments in behavior psychology, and of developments in the anthropological analysis of culture. It has become possible to incorporate these elements effectively, largely because of the conception of a system of action in both the social and psychological spheres and their integration with systems of cultural patterns has been considerably extended and refined in the intervening years.

[ii]Norms of intelligence are one set among several possible sets of norms that function in the regulation of energy expenditure.

lie ultimately in the energy potential of the physiological organisms. However, the manner in which the energy is expended is a problem which requires the explicit analysis of the orientation of action, that is, analysis of the normatively regulated relations of the actor to the situation. For, it is the system of orientations which establishes the modes in which this energy becomes attached and distributed among specific goals and objects; it is the system of orientations which regulates its flow and which integrates its many channels of expression into a system.

We have introduced the terms *action* and *actor*. We have said something about the goals of action, the situation of action, the orientation of action, and the motivation of action. Let us now say something about the *organization* of action into systems.

Actions are not empirically discrete but occur in constellations which we call systems. We are concerned with three systems, three modes of organization of the elements of action; these elements are organized as social systems, as personalities, and as cultural systems. Though all three modes are conceptually abstracted from concrete social behavior, the empirial referents of the three abstractions are not on the same plane. Social systems and personalities are conceived as modes of organization of motivated action (social systems are systems of motivated action organized about the relations of actors to each other; personalities are systems of *motivated* action organized about the living organism). Cultural systems, on the other hand, are systems of symbolic patterns (these patterns are created or manifested by individual actors and are transmitted among social systems by diffusion and among personalities by learning).

A social system is a system of action which has the following characteristics: (1) It involves a process of interaction between two or more actors; the interaction process as such is a focus of the observer's attention. (2) The situation toward which the actors are oriented includes other actors. These other actors (alters) are objects of cathexis. Alter's actions are taken

cognitively into account as data. Alter's various orientations may be either *goals* to be pursued or *means* for the accomplishment of goals. Alter's orientations may thus be objects for evaluative judgment. (3) There is (in a social system) interdependent and, in part, concerted action in which the concert is a function of collective goal orientation or common values,[iii] and of a consensus of normative and cognitive expectations.

A *personality system* is a system of action which has the following characteristics: (1) It is the system comprising the interconnections of the actions of an individual actor. (2) The actor's actions are organized by a structure of need-dispositions. (3) Just as the actions of a plurality of actors cannot be randomly assorted but must have a determinate organization of compatibility or integration, so the actions of the single actor have a determinate organization of compatibility or integration with one another. Just as the goals or norms which an actor in a social system will pursue or accept will be affected and limited by those pursued or accepted by the other actors, so the goals or norms involved in a single action of one actor will be affected and limited by one another and by other goals and norms of the same actor.

A *cultural system* is a system which has the following characteristics: (1) The system is constituted neither by the organization of interactions nor by the organization of the actions of a single actor (as such), but rather by the organization of the values, norms, and symbols which guide the choices made by actors and which limit the types of interaction which may occur among actors. (2) Thus a cultural system is not an empirical system in the same sense as a personality or social system, because it represents a special kind of abstraction of elements from these systems. These elements, however, may exist separately as physical symbols and be transmitted from one empirical action system to another. (3) In a cultural system the patterns of regulatory norms (and the other cultural elements which guide choices of concrete actors) cannot be made up of random or unrelated

---

[iii]A person is said to have "common values" with another when either (1) he wants the group in which he and the other belong to achieve a certain group goal which the other also wants, or (2) he intrinsically values conformity with the requirements laid down by the other.

elements. If, that is, a system of culture is to be manifest in the organization of an empirical action system it must have a certain degree of consistency. (4) Thus a cultural system is a pattern of culture whose different parts are interrelated to form value systems, belief systems, and systems of expressive symbols.

Social systems, personality systems, and cultural systems are critical subject matter for the theory of action. In the first two cases, the systems themselves are conceived to be actors whose action is conceived as oriented to goals and the gratification of need-dispositions, as occurring in situations, using energy, and as being normatively regulated. Analysis of the third kind of system is essential to the theory of action because systems of value standards (criteria of selection) and other patterns of culture, when *institutionalized* in social systems and *internalized* in personality systems, guide the actor with respect to both the *orientation to ends* and the *normative regulation* of means and of expressive activities, whenever the need-dispositions of the actor allow choices in these matters.

Components of the Frame of Reference of the Theory of Action

1. *The frame of reference of the theory of action* involves actors, a situation of action, and the orientation of the actor to that situation.

   a. One or more *actors* is involved. An actor is an empirical system of action. An actor is an individual or a collectivity which may be taken as a point of reference for the analysis of the modes of its orientation and of its processes of action in relation to objects. Action itself is a process of change of state in such empirical systems of action.

   b. A *situation* of action is involved. It is that part of the external world which means something to the actor whose behavior is being analyzed. It is only part of the whole realm of objects that might be seen. Specifically, it is that part to which the actor is oriented and in which the actor acts. The situation thus consists of objects of orientation.

   c. The *orientation of the actor to the situation* is involved. It is the set of cognitions, cathexes, plans, and relevant standards which relates the actor to the situation.

2. The *actor* is both a system of action and a point of reference. As a system of action the actor may be either an individual or a collectivity. As a point of reference the actor may be either an actor-subject (sometimes called simply *actor*) or a social object.

   a. The *individual-collectivity* distinction is made on the basis of whether the actor in question is a personality system or a social system (a society or subsystem).

   b. The *subject-object distinction* is made on the basis of whether the actor in question occupies a central position (as a point of reference) within a frame of reference or a peripheral position (as an object of orientation for an actor taken as the point of reference. When an actor is taken as the central point of reference, he is an actor-subject. (In an interaction situation, this actor is called *ego*.) When he is taken as an object of orientation for an actor-subject, he is a social object. (In an interaction situation, this actor is called *alter*.) Thus, the actor-subject (*the* actor) is an orienting subject; the social object is the actor who is oriented to. This distinction cross-cuts the individual-collectively distinction. Thus an individual or a collectivity may be either actor-subject or social object in a given analysis.

3. The situation of action may be divided into a class of social objects (individuals and collectivities) and a class of nonsocial (physical and cultural) objects.

   a. *Social objects* include actors as persons and as collectivities (i.e., systems of action composed of a plurality of individual actors in determinate relations to one another). The actor-subject may be oriented to himself as an object as well as to other social objects. A collectivity, when it is considered as a social object, is never constituted by all the action of the participating individual actors; it may, however, be constituted by anything from a specified segment of their actions—for example, their actions in a specific system of roles—to a very inclusive grouping of their actions—for example, all of their many roles in a society. . . .

Neither systems of value-orientation nor systems of culture as a whole are action systems in the same sense as are personalities and social systems. This is because neither motivation nor action is directly attributable to them. They may conjoin with motivation to evoke action in social systems or personalities, but they themselves cannot act, nor are they motivated. It seems desirable to treat them, however, because of the great importance of the particular ways in which they are involved in action systems. . . .

DILEMMAS OF ORIENTATION AND THE PATTERN VARIABLES

. . . An actor in a situation is confronted by a series of major dilemmas of orientation, a series of choices that the actor must make before the situation has a determinate meaning for him. The objects of the situation do not interact with the cognizing and cathecting organism in such a fashion as to determine automatically the meaning of the situation. Rather, the actor must make a series of choices before the situation will have a determinate meaning. Specifically, we maintain, the actor must make five specific dichotomous choices before any situation will have a determinate meaning. The five dichotomies which formulate these choice alternatives are called the *pattern variables* because any specific orientation (and consequently any action) is characterized by a pattern of the five choices.

Three of the pattern variables derive from the absence of any biologically given hierarchy of primacies among the various modes of orientation. In the first place, the actor must choose whether to accept gratification from the immediately cognized and cathected object or to evaluate such gratification in terms of its consequences for other aspects of the action system. (That is, one must decide whether or not the evaluative mode is to be operative at all in a situation.)[iv] In the second place, if the actor decides to evaluate, he must choose whether or not to give primacy to the moral standards of the social system or subsystem. In the third place, whether

or not he decides to grant primacy to such moral standards, he must choose whether cognitive or appreciative standards are to be dominant, the one set with relation to the other. If cognitive standards are dominant over appreciative standards, the actor will tend to locate objects in terms of their relation to some generalized frame of reference; if appreciative standards are dominant over cognitive, the actor will tend to locate objects in terms of their relation to himself, or to his motives.

The other pattern variables emerge from indeterminacies intrinsic to the object situation: social objects as relevant to a given choice situation are either quality complexes or performance complexes, depending on how the actor chooses to see them; social objects are either functionally diffuse (so that the actor grants them every feasible demand) or functionally specific (so that the actor grants them only specifically defined demands), depending on how the actor chooses to see them or how he is culturally expected to see them.

It will be noted now that the three pattern variables which derive from the problems of primacy among the modes of orientation are the first three of the pattern variables as these were listed in our introduction; the two pattern variables which derive from the indeterminacies in the object situation are the last two in that list.

. . . let us restate our definition: a *pattern variable* is a dichotomy, one side of which must be chosen by an actor before the meaning of a situation is determinate for him, and thus before he can act with respect to that situation. We maintain that there are only five *basic* pattern variables (i.e., pattern variables deriving directly from the frame of reference of the theory of action) and that, in the sense that they are *all* of the pattern variables which so derive, they constitute a system. Let us list them and give them names and numbers so that we can more easily refer to them in the future. They are:

1. Affectivity—Affective neutrality.

2. Self-orientation—Collectivity-orientation.

[iv]In a limited sense the evaluative mode is operative, even when no thought is given to the consequences of immediate gratification; this in the sense that aesthetic (appreciative) standards may be involved to determine the "appropriateness" of the form of gratification chosen. Only in this limited sense, however, does evaluation enter the immediate gratification picture.

3. Universalism—Particularism.

4. Ascription—Achievement.

5. Specificity—Diffuseness.

The first concerns the problem of whether or not evaluation is to take place in a given situation. The second concerns the primacy of moral standards in an evaluative procedure. The third concerns the relative primacy of cognitive and cathectic standards. The fourth concerns the seeing of objects as quality or performance complexes. The fifth concerns the scope of significance of the object.

These pattern variables enter the action frame of reference at four different levels. In the first place, they enter at the concrete level as five discrete choices (explicit or implicit) which every actor makes before he can act. In the second place, they enter on the personality level as habits of choice; the person has a set of habits of choosing, ordinarily or relative to certain types of situations, one horn or the other of each of these dilemmas. Since this set of habits is usually a bit of internalized culture, we will list it as a component of the actor's value-orientation standards. In the third place, the pattern variables enter on the collectivity level as aspects of role definition: the definitions of rights and duties of the members of a collectivity which specify the actions of incumbents of roles, and which often specify that the performer shall exhibit a habit of choosing one side or the other of each of these dilemmas. In the fourth place, the variables enter on the cultural level as aspects of value standards; this is because most value standards are rules or recipes for concrete action and thus specify, among other things, that the actor abiding by the standard shall exhibit a habit of choosing one horn or the other of each of the dilemmas.

From the foregoing paragraph, it should be obvious that, except for their integration in concrete acts as discrete choices, the pattern variables are most important as characteristics of value standards (whether these be the value standards of a personality, or the value standards defining the roles of a society, or just value standards in the abstract). In the sense that each concrete act is made up on the basis of a patterning of the choices formulated by the scheme, the pattern variables are not necessarily attributes of value standards, because any specific concrete choice may be a rather discrete and accidental thing. But as soon as a certain consistency of choosing can be inferred from a series of concrete acts, then we can begin to make statements about the value standards involved and the formulation of these standards in terms of the variables of the pattern-variable scheme.

What is the bearing of the pattern variables on our analysis of systems of action and cultural orientation? Basically, the pattern variables are the categories for the description of value-orientations which of course are in various forms integral to all three systems. A given value-orientation or some particular aspect of it may be interpreted as imposing a preference or giving a primacy to one alternative over the other *in a particular type of situation*. The pattern variables therefore delineate the alternative preferences, predispositions, or expectations; in all these forms the common element is the direction of selection in defined situations. In the personality system, the pattern variables describe essentially the predispositions or expectations as evaluatively defined in terms of what will below be called ego-organization[v] and superego-organization. In the case of the social system they are the crucial components in the definition of role-expectations. Culturally, they define patterns of value-orientation.

The pattern variables apply to the *normative* or ideal aspect of the structure of systems of action; they apply to one part of its culture. They are equally useful in the empirical description of the degree of conformity with or divergence of concrete action from the patterns of expectation or aspiration. When they are used to characterize differences of empirical structure of personalities or social systems, they contain an elliptical element. This element appears in such statements as, "The American occupational system is universalistic and achievement-oriented and specific." The more adequate, though still sketchy, statement would be: "Compared to other possible ways of organizing the division of labor, the predominant norms which are

---

[v]The term *ego* is here used in the sense current in the theory of personality, not as a point of reference.

institutionalized in the American society and which embody the predominant value-orientation of the culture give rise to expectations that occupational roles will be treated by their incumbents and those who are associated with them universalistically and specifically and with regard to proficiency of performance."

These categories could equally be employed to describe actual behavior as well as normative expectations and are of sufficient exactitude for first approximations in comparative analysis. For more detailed work, however, much more precise analysis of the degrees and incidence of deviance, with special reference to the magnitude, location, and forms of the tendencies to particularism, to ascriptiveness, and to diffuseness would have to be carried out.

We will now proceed to define the five pattern variables and the problems of alternative selection to which they apply. They are inherently patterns of cultural value-orientation, but they become integrated both in personalities and in social systems. Hence the general definitions will in each case be followed by definitions specific to each of the three types of systems. These definitions will be followed by an analysis of the places of the variables in the frame of reference of the theory of action, the reasons why this list seems to be logically complete on its own level of generality, and certain problems of their systematic interrelations and use in structural analysis.

THE DEFINITIONS OF PATTERN VARIABLES

1. *The dilemma of gratification of impulse versus discipline.* When confronted with situations in which particular impulses press for gratification, an actor faces the problem of whether the impulses should be released or restrained. He can solve the problem by giving primacy, at the relevant selection points, to evaluative considerations, at the cost of interests in the possibility of immediate gratification; or by giving primacy to such interests in immediate gratification, irrespective of evaluative considerations.

a. Cultural aspect. (1) *Affectivity*: the normative pattern which grants the permission for an actor, in a given type of situation, to take advantage of a given opportunity for immediate gratification without regard to evaluative considerations. (2) *Affective neutrality*: the normative pattern which prescribes for actors in a given type of situation renunciation of certain types of immediate gratification for which opportunity exists, in the interest of evaluative considerations regardless of the content of the latter.

b. Personality aspect. (1) *Affectivity*: a need-disposition on the part of the actor to permit himself, in a certain situation, to take advantage of an opportunity for a given type of immediate gratification and not to renounce this gratification for evaluative reasons. (2) *Affective neutrality*: a need-disposition on the part of the actor in a certain situation to be guided by evaluative considerations which prohibit his taking advantage of the given opportunity for immediate gratification; in this situation the gratification in question is to be renounced, regardless of the grounds adduced for the renunciation.

c. Social system aspect. (1) *Affectivity*: the role-expectation[vi] that the incumbent of the role may freely express certain affective reactions to objects in the situation and need not attempt to control them in the interest of discipline. (2) *Affective neutrality*: the role-expectation that the incumbent of the role in question should restrain any impulses to certain affective expressions and subordinate them to considerations of discipline. In both cases the affect may be positive or negative, and the discipline (or permissiveness) may apply only to certain qualitative types of affective expression (e.g., sexual).

2. *The dilemma of private versus collective interests*, or the distribution between private permissiveness and collective obligation. The high frequency of situations in which there is a disharmony of interests creates the problem of

---

[vi]A role-expectation is, in an institutionally integrated social system (or part of it), an expectation *both* on the part of ego and of the alters with whom he interacts. The same sentiments are shared by both. In a less than perfectly integrated social system, the concept is still useful for describing the expectations of each of the actors, even though they diverge.

choosing between action for private goals or on behalf of collective goals. This dilemma may be resolved by the actor either by giving primacy to interests, goals, and values shared with the other members of a given collective unit of which he is a member or by giving primacy to his personal or private interests without considering their bearing on collective interests.

    a. Cultural aspect. (1) *Self-orientation*: the normative pattern which prescribes a range of permission for an actor, in a given type of situation, to take advantage of a given opportunity for pursuing a private interest, regardless of the content of the interest or its direct bearing on the interests of other actors. (2) *Collectivity-orientation*: a normative pattern which prescribes the area within which an actor, in a given type of situation, is obliged to take directly into account a given selection of values which he shares with the other members of the collectivity in question. It defines his *responsibility* to this collectivity.

    b. Personality aspect. (1) *Self-orientation*: a need-disposition on the part of the actor to permit himself to pursue a given goal or interest of his own—regardless whether from his standpoint it is only cognitive-cathectic or involves evaluative considerations—but without regard to its bearing one way or another on the interests of a collectivity of which he is a member. (2) *Collectivity-orientation*: a need-disposition on the part of the actor to be guided by the obligation to take directly into account, in the given situation, values which he shares with the other members of the collectivity in question; therefore the actor must accept responsibility for attempting to realize those values in his action. This includes the expectation by ego that in the particular choice in question he will subordinate his private interests, whether cognitive-cathectic or evaluative, and that he will be motivated in superego terms.

    c. Social system aspect. (1) *Self-orientation*: the role-expectation by the relevant actors that it is *permissible* for the incumbent of the role in question to give priority in the given situation to his own private interests, whatever their motivational content or quality, independently of their bearing on the

interests or values of a given collectivity of which he is a member, or the interests of other actors. (2) *Collectivity-orientation*: the role-expectation by the relevant actors that the actor is *obliged*, as an incumbent of the role in question, to take directly into account the values and interests of the collectivity of which, in this role, he is a member. When there is a potential conflict with his private interests, he is expected in the particular choice to give priority to the collective interest. This also applies to his action in representative roles on behalf of the collectivity.

    3. *The dilemma of transcendence versus immanence*. In confronting any situation, the actor faces the dilemma whether to treat the objects in the situation in accordance with a general norm covering *all* objects in that class or whether to treat them in accordance with their standing in some particular relationship to him or his collectivity, independently of the objects' subsumibility under a general norm. This dilemma can be resolved by giving primacy to norms or value standards which are maximally generalized and which have a basis of validity transcending *any* specific system of relationships in which ego is involved, or by giving primacy to value standards which allot priority to standards *integral* to the *particular* relationship system in which the actor is involved with the object.

    a. Cultural aspect. (1) *Universalism*: the normative pattern which obliges an actor in a given situation to be oriented toward objects in the light of general standards rather than in the light of the objects' possession of properties (qualities or performances, classificatory or relational) which have a particular relation to the actor's own properties (traits or statuses). (2) *Particularism*: the normative pattern which obliges an actor in a given type of situation to give priority to criteria of the object's particular relations to the actor's own properties (qualities or performances, classificatory or relational) over generalized attributes, capacities, or performance standards.

    b. Personality aspect. (1) *Universalism*: a need-disposition on the part of the actor in a given situation to respond toward objects in conformity with a general standard rather than in the light of their possession of properties (qualities or performances, classificatory or relational) which have a particular relation to the actor's own. (2) *Particularism*: a need-disposition on the part of the actor to be guided by criteria of choice particular to his own and the object's position in an object-relationship system rather than by criteria defined in generalized terms.

c. Social system aspect. (1) *Universalism*: the role-expectation that, in qualifications for memberships and decisions for differential treatment, priority will be given to standards defined in completely generalized terms, independent of the particular relationship of the actor's own statuses (qualities or performances, classificatory or relational) to those of the object. (2) *Particularism*: the role-expectation that, in qualifications for memberships and decisions for differential treatment, priority will be given to standards which assert the primacy of the values attached to objects by their particular relations to the actor's properties (qualities or performances, classificatory or relational) as over against their general universally applicable class properties.

4. *The dilemma of object modalities.* When confronting an object in a situation, the actor faces the dilemma of deciding how to treat it. Is he to treat it in the light of what it is in itself or in the light of what it does or what might flow from its *actions*? This dilemma can be resolved by giving primacy, at the relevant selection points, to the "qualities" aspect of *social objects* as a focus of orientation, or by giving primacy to the objects' performances and their outcomes.

a. Cultural aspect. (1) *Ascription*: the normative pattern which prescribes that an actor in a given type of situation should, in his selections for differential treatment of social objects, give priority to certain attributes that they possess (including collectivity memberships and possessions) over any specific performances (past, present, or prospective) of the objects. (2) *Achievement*: the normative pattern which prescribes that an actor in a given type of situation should, in his selection and differential treatment of social objects, give priority to their specific

performances (past, present, or prospective) over their given attributes (including memberships and possessions), insofar as the latter are not significant as direct conditions of the relevant performances.

b. Personality aspect. (1) *Ascription*: the need-disposition on the part of the actor, at a given selection point, to respond to specific given attributes of the social object, rather than to their past, present, or prospective performances. (2) *Achievement*: a need-disposition on the part of the actor to respond, at a given selection point, to specific performances (past present, or prospective) of a social object, rather than to its attributes which are not directly involved in the relevant performances as "capacities," "skills," and so forth.

c. Social system aspect. (1) *Ascription*: the role-expectation that the role incumbent, in orienting himself to social objects in the relevant choice situation, will accord priority to the objects' given attributes (whether universalistically or particularistically defined) over their actual or potential performances. (2) *Achievement*: the role-expectation that the role incumbent, in orienting to social objects in the relevant choice situation, will give priority to the objects' actual or expected performances, and to their attributes only as directly relevant to these performances, over attributes which are essentially independent of the specific performances in question.

5. *The dilemma of the scope of significance of the object.* In confronting an object, an actor must choose among the various possible ranges in which he will respond to the object. The dilemma consists in whether he should respond to many aspects of the object or to a restricted range of them—how broadly is he to allow himself to be involved with the object? The dilemma may be resolved by accepting no inherent or prior limitation of the scope of the actor's "concern" with the object, either as an object of interest or of obligations, or by according only a limited and specific type of significance to the object in his system of orientation.

a. Cultural aspect. (1) *Diffuseness*: the normative pattern which prescribes that in a given situation the orientation of an actor to an object should contain no prior specification of the actor's interest in or concern with or for the object, but that the scope should vary with the exigencies of the situation as they arise. (2) *Specificity*: the normative pattern which prescribes that in a given type of situation an actor should confine his concern with a given type of object to a specific sphere and not permit other empirically possible concerns to enter.

b. Personality aspect. (1) *Diffuseness*: the need-disposition to respond to an object in any way which the nature of the actor and the nature of the object and its actual relation to ego require, actual significances varying as occasions arise. (2) *Specificity*: the need-disposition of the actor to respond to a given object in a manner limited to a specific mode or context of significance of a social object, including obligation to it, which is compatible with exclusion of other potential modes of significance of the object.

c. Social system aspect. (1) *Diffuseness*: the role-expectation that the role incumbent, at the relevant choice point, will accept any potential significance of a social object, including obligation to it, which is compatible with his other interests and obligations, and that he will give priority to this expectation over any disposition to confine the role-orientation to a specific range of significance of the object. (2) *Specificity*: the role-expectation that the role incumbent, at the relevant choice point, will be oriented to a social object only within a specific range of its relevance as a cathectic object or as an instrumental means or condition and that he will give priority to this expectation over any disposition to include potential aspects of significance of the object not specifically defined in the expectation pattern.

Of the five pattern variables defined above, the first three are determined by primacies among the interests inherently differentiated within the system of value-orientation itself and in the definition of the limits of its applicability; the other two are determined by the application of value-orientations to the alternatives which are inherent in the structure of the object system, and in the actor's relation to it. . . .

THE INTERRELATIONS OF THE PATTERN VARIABLES

We hold that the five pattern variables constitute a *system* covering all the fundamental alternatives which can arise directly out of the frame of reference for the theory of action. It should be remembered that the five pattern variables formulate five fundamental choices which must be made by an actor when he is confronted with a situation before that situation can have definitive (unambiguous) meaning for him. We have said that objects do not automatically determine the actors "orientation of action"; rather, a number of choices must be made before the meaning of the objects becomes definite. Now, we maintain that when the situation is social (when one actor is orienting to another), there are but five choices which are completely general (that is, which must always be made) and which derive directly from the action frame of reference; these choices must always be made to give the situation specific defined meaning. Other choices are often necessary to determine the meaning of a situation, but these may be considered accidents of content, rather than genuine alternatives intrinsic to the structure of *all* action. . . .

CLASSIFICATION OF NEED-DISPOSITIONS AND ROLE-EXPECTATIONS

The pattern variables are tools for the classification of need-dispositions and role-expectations, which, as has been pointed out, represent allocative foci for both personality and social systems. Before we go into the classification of these units, it might be wise to recapitulate briefly the way the allocative and integrative foci fit into the frame of reference of the theory of action. We have said that action systems, as either actors or social objects, may be personalities or collectivities, both of which are abstracted from the same concrete action. The different principles of abstraction used in locating the two systems derive directly from the notion that personalities and collectivities have different kinds of allocative and integrative foci. The integrative foci are, in some sense, the principles of abstraction used in locating or delimiting the system:

thus, the individual organism is the integrative focus of a personality system and the interacting social group is the integrative focus of a social system. The integrative foci are therefore used for abstracting social systems themselves from the total realm of possible subject matter.

The allocative foci, on the other hand, are the primary units used for analyzing the action system into elements or parts. The allocative foci of personality systems are need-dispositions. The personality system is in a sense composed of a variety of need-dispositions; each of these assures that some need of the personality system will be met. The referent of a need-disposition is, in a sense, a set of concrete orientations. That is, a need-disposition is an inferred entity; it is inferred on the basis of a certain consistency of choosing and cathecting in a wide variety of orientations. Thus, when we speak of a need-disposition, we will sometimes seem to be talking about a real entity, causally controlling a wide variety of orientations and rendering them consistent; other times we will seem to be talking about the consistent set of orientations (abstracted on the basis of the postulated entity) themselves. Logicians have shown that it is usually fair to use interchangeably the inferred entity postulated on the basis of a set of data and the whole set of data itself. The postulated entity is, in some sense, a shorthand for the set of data from which it is inferred.

The allocative foci of social systems are roles or role-expectations. The social system is in a sense composed of a variety of roles or role-expectations; each of these assures that some need of the social system will be met. The referent of a role, like that of a need-disposition, is a set of concrete orientations; the role or role-expectation is an inferred entity in exactly the same fashion as is the need-disposition. Each orientation, according to postulate, is a joint function of a role (which

partly controls it), a need-disposition (which also partly controls it), and probably of other factors not mentioned here.[vii] When orientations are grouped (or abstracted) according to the need-dispositions that control them, and according to the individual organisms who have these need-dispositions, we are dealing with personality systems. When orientations are grouped (or abstracted) according to the roles or roles-expectations that control them, and according to the interacting groups to which they belong, we are dealing with social systems.

Now, since none of the depth variables (allocative foci, etc.) are effective except as they influence the orientation of action (which is not necessarily either conscious or rational), and since all orientations tend to have not only the allocative foci of both social and personality systems as ingredients but also value standards (which, when internalized, are depth variables similar to need-dispositions and role-expectations), no need-disposition, nor any role-expectation, is effective except in conjunction with certain value-orientations with which it is systematically related (at least in the sense that both control the same orientation for the moment). Hence, in discussing personalities or social systems, using as the primary units of abstraction need-dispositions or role-expectations, we may regard the value-orientation components of the orientations so grouped to be the value-orientation components of the need-dispositions or role-expectations themselves. Thus we can classify the need-dispositions and role-expectations in terms of the value-orientations with which they tend to be linked.

In principle, therefore, *every* concrete need-disposition[viii] of personality, or every role-expectation of social structure, involves a combination of values of the five pattern variables. The cross-classification of each of the five against each of the others, yielding a table

---

[vii]As will be seen in a moment, each orientation is in some sense a function of the value standards which partly control it. Furthermore, each orientation is certainly partly a function of the present object situation.

[viii]A need-disposition as the term is used here always involves a set of dispositions toward objects. In abstraction from objects the concept becomes elliptical. Only for reasons of avoiding even greater terminological cumbersomeness is the more complex term "need-disposition toward objects" usually avoided. However, such a need-disposition and the *particular* objects of its gratification are independently variable. The mechanism of *substitution* links the need-disposition to various objects that are not its "proper" gratifiers.

of thirty-two cells, will, on the assumption that the list of pattern variables is exhaustive, produce a classification of the basic value patterns. Internalized in the personality system, these value patterns serve as a starting point for a classification of the possible types of need-dispositions; as institutionalized in the system of social action, they are a classification of components of role-expectation definitions.[ix]

It should be clear that the classification of the value components of need-dispositions and of role-expectations in terms of the pattern variables is a *first step* toward the construction of a dynamic theory of systems of action. To advance toward empirical significance, these classifications will have to be related to the functional problems of on-going systems of action.[x]

As a last word before taking up the problem of classification itself, we should mention that of the logically possible combinations of the pattern variables, not all are likely to be of equal empirical significance. Careful analysis of their involvement in a wide variety of phenomena shows that they are all in fact independently variable in some contexts and that there is no tautology in the scheme. Nonetheless there are certainly tendencies for certain combinations to cluster together. The uneven distribution of combinations and the empirical difficulty, or even perhaps impossibility, of the realization of some combinations in systems of action will raise important dynamic problems.

To classify need-dispositions and role-expectations, we must begin by making the cross-classification tables mentioned above. In constructing such tables we find that certain

of the pattern-variable dichotomies are of major importance with respect to need-dispositions (and hence personality systems). Similarly, certain pattern-variable dichotomies are of major importance with respect to role-expectations (and hence social systems). Furthermore, the pattern variables of major importance for classification of need-dispositions are not the same as those of major importance for classification of role-expectations. In fact, the two sets are more or less complementary; those of major importance for need-dispositions are the ones of minor importance for role-expectations, and vice versa.

The only one of the pattern variables equally applicable to both need-dispositions and role-expectations is the self-collectivity variable (number two). Of the other four, the first, affectivity-neutrality, and the fifth, specificity-diffuseness, are chiefly important with respect to need-dispositions. The third, universalism-particularism, and the fourth, ascription-achievement, are chiefly important with respect to role-expectations. . . .

THE BASIC STRUCTURE OF THE INTERACTIVE RELATIONSHIP

The interaction of ego and alter is the most elementary form of a social system. The features of this interaction are present in more complex form in all social systems.

In interaction ego and alter are each objects of orientation for the other. The basic differences from orientations to nonsocial objects are two.

[ix]The classification of role-expectations and need-dispositions according to value patterns is only a part of the larger problem of classifying concrete need-dispositions and role-expectations. Other components of action must enter the picture before a classification relevant and adequate to the problem of the analysis of systems is attainable. For example, one set of factors entering into need-dispositions, the constitutionally determined components, has been quite explicitly and deliberately excluded from the present analysis. So far as these are essential to an adequate classification of the need-disposition elements of personality, the classification in terms of pattern variables obviously requires adjustment.

[x]This means above all that the motivational *processes* of action must be analyzed as processes in terms of the laws governing them, and as mechanisms in terms of the significance of their outcomes for the functioning of the systems of which they are parts. In due course the attempt to do this will be made. Also, it should be noted that the necessary constitutional factors which are treated as residual in this conceptual scheme will find their place among the functional necessities of systems.

First, since the outcome of ego's action (e.g., success in the attainment of a goal) is contingent on alter's reaction to what ego does, ego becomes oriented not only to alter's probable *overt* behavior but also to what ego interprets to be alter's expectations relative to ego's behavior, since ego expects that alter's expectations will influence alter's behavior. Second, in an integrated system, this orientation to the expectations of the other is reciprocal or complementary.

Communication through a common system of symbols is the precondition of this reciprocity or complementarity of expectations. The alternatives which are open to alter must have some measure of stability in two respects: first, as realistic possibilities for alter, and second, in their meaning to ego. This stability presupposes generalization from the particularity of the given situations of ego and alter, both of which are continually changing and are never concretely identical over any two moments in time. When such generalization occurs, and actions, gestures, or symbols have more or less the *same* meaning for both ego and alter, we may speak of a common culture existing between them, through which their interaction is mediated.

Furthermore, this common culture, or symbol system, inevitably possesses in certain aspects a normative significance for the actors. Once it is in existence, observance of its conventions is a necessary condition for ego to be "understood" by alter, in the sense of allowing ego to elicit the type of reaction from alter which ego expects. This common set of cultural symbols becomes the medium in which is formed a constellation of the contingent actions of both parties, in such a way that there will simultaneously emerge a definition of a range of *appropriate* reactions on alter's part to each of a range of possible actions ego has taken and vice versa. It will then be a condition of the stabilization of such a system of complementary expectations, not only that ego and alter should *communicate*, but that they should *react appropriately* to each other's action.

A tendency toward consistent appropriateness of reaction is also a tendency toward conformity with a normative pattern. The culture is not only a set of symbols of communication but a *set of norms* for action.

The motivation of ego and alter become integrated with the normative patterns through interaction. The polarity of gratification and deprivation is crucial here. An appropriate reaction on alter's part is a gratifying one to ego. If ego conforms with the norm, this gratification is in one aspect a reward for his conformity with it; the converse holds for the case of deprivation and deviance. The reactions of alter toward ego's conformity with or deviance from the normative pattern thus become sanctions to ego. Ego's expectations vis-à-vis alter are expectations concerning the roles of ego and of alter; and sanctions reinforce ego's motivation to conform with these role-expectations. Thus the complementarity of expectations brings with it the reciprocal reinforcement of ego's and alter's motivation to conformity with the normative pattern which defines their expectations.

The interactive system also involves the process of generalization, not only in the common culture by which ego and alter communicate but in the interpretation of alter's discrete actions vis-à-vis ego as expressions of alter's *intentions* (that is, as indices of the cathectic-evaluative aspects of alter's motivational orientations toward ego). This "generalization" implies that ego and alter agree that certain actions of alter are indices of the *attitudes* which alter has acquired toward ego (and reciprocally, ego toward alter). Since these attitudes are, in the present paradigm, integrated with the common culture and the latter is internalized in ego's need-dispositions, ego is sensitive not only to alter's overt acts, but to his *attitudes*. He acquires a need not only to obtain specific *rewards* and avoid specific *punishments* but to enjoy the favorable attitudes and avoid the unfavorable ones of alter. Indeed, since he is integrated with the same norms, these are the same as his attitudes toward himself as an object. Thus violation of the norm causes him to feel shame toward alter, guilt toward himself.

It should be clear that as an ideal type this interaction paradigm implies *mutuality* of gratification in a certain sense, though not necessarily equal distribution of gratification. . . . This is also the paradigm of the process of the learning of generalized orientations. Even where special mechanisms of adjustment such as dominance and submission or alienation from normative expectations enter in, the process still must be described and analyzed in relation to the categories of this paradigm. It is thus useful both for the analysis of systems of normative expectations and for that of the actual conformity or deviation regarding these expectations in concrete action.

In summary we may say that this is the basic paradigm for the structure of a solidary interactive relationship. It contains all the fundamental elements of the role structure of the social system and the attachment and security system of the personality. It involves culture in both its communicative and its value-orientation functions. It is the nodal point of the organization of all systems of action.

THE CONCEPT OF SYSTEM AND THE CLASSIFICATION OF TYPES OF SYSTEMS

With our discussion of interaction we have entered upon the analysis of systems. Before we discuss more fully personality and social systems, it is desirable to state explicitly the principal properties of empirical systems which are relevant for the present analysis. The most general and fundamental property of a system is the interdependence of parts or variables. Interdependence consists in the existence of determinate relationships among the parts or variables as contrasted with randomness of variability. In other words, interdependence is *order* in the relationship among the components which enter into a system. This order must have a tendency to self-maintenance, which is very generally expressed in the concept of equilibrium.[xi] It need not, however, be a static self-maintenance or a stable equilibrium. It may be an ordered process of change—a process following a determinate pattern rather than random variability relative to the starting point. This is called a moving equilibrium and is well exemplified by growth. Furthermore, equilibrium, even when stable, by no means implies

that process is not going on; process is continual even in stable systems, the stabilities residing in the interrelations involved in the process.

A particularly important feature of all systems is the inherent limitation on the compatibility of certain parts or events within the same system. This is indeed simply another way of saying that the relations within the system are determinate and that not just anything can happen. Thus, to take an example from the solar system, if the orbit of one of the planets, such as Jupiter, is given, it is no longer possible for the orbits of the other planets to be distributed at random relative to this given orbit. Certain limitations are imposed by the fact that the value of one of the variables is given. This limitation may in turn be looked at from either a negative or a positive point of view. On the one hand, again using the solar system as example, if one of the planets should simply disappear, the fact that no mass was present in that particular orbit would necessitate a change in the equilibrium of the system. It would make necessary a readjustment of the orbits of the other planets in order to bring the system into equilibrium. This may also be expressed in the statement that there is a change in the structure of the system. On the other hand, the same problem may be treated from the standpoint of what would happen in the case of the coexistence of "incompatible" elements or processes within the same system. Incompatibility is always relative to a *given* state of the system. If, for example, the orbits of two of the planets should move closer to each other than is compatible for the maintenance of the current state of the system, one of two things would have to happen. Either processes would be set up which would tend to restore the previous relation by the elimination of the incompatibility; or if the new relation were maintained, there would have to be adjustments in *other* parts of the system, bringing the system into a new state of equilibrium.

These properties are inherent in all systems. A special additional property, however, is of primary significance for the theory of action. This is the tendency to maintain equilibrium, in

---

[xi]That is, if the system is to be permanent enough to be worth study, there must be a tendency to maintenance of order except under exceptional circumstances

the most general sense stated above, within certain boundaries relative to an environment—boundaries which are not imposed from outside but which are self-maintained by the properties of the constituent variables as they operate within the system. The most familiar example is the living organism, which is a physicochemical system that is not assimilated to the physicochemical conditions of the environment, but maintains certain distinct properties in relation to the environment. For example, the maintenance of the constant body temperature of the mammal necessitates processes which mediate the interdependence between the internal and the external systems in respect to temperature; these processes maintain constancy over a wide range of variability in environmental temperatures.

The two fundamental types of processes necessary for the maintenance of a given state of equilibrium of a system we call, in the theory of action, *allocation*[xii] and *integration*. By *allocation* we mean processes which maintain a distribution of the components or parts of the system which is compatible with the maintenance of a given state of equilibrium. By *integration*, we mean the processes by which relations to the environment are mediated in such a way that the distinctive internal properties and boundaries of the system as an entity are maintained in the face of variability in the external situation. It must be realized that self-maintenance of such a system is not only maintenance of boundaries but also maintenance of distinctive relationships of the parts of the system *within* the boundary. The system is in some sense a unity relative to its environment. Also, self-maintenance implies not only control of the environmental variations, but also control of tendencies to change—that is, to alteration of the distinctive state—coming from within the system.

The two types of empirical systems which will be analyzed in the subsequent chapters are personalities and social systems. These systems are, as will be repeatedly pointed out, *different* systems which are not reducible to each other. However, there are certain conceptual continuities or identities between them which derive from two sources. (1) They are both systems built out of the fundamental components of action as these have been discussed in the General Statement and in the present chapter. These components are differently organized to constitute systems in the two cases; nevertheless, they remain the same components. (2) They are both not only systems, but both are systems of the boundary-maintaining, self-maintenance type; therefore, they both have properties which are common to systems in general and the more special properties which are characteristic of this particular type of system. (3) A third basis of their intimate relation to each other is the fact that they *interpenetrate* in the sense that no personality system can exist without *participation* in a social system, by which we mean the integration of *part* of the actor's system of action as *part* of the social system. Conversely, there is no social system which is not from one point of view a mode of the integration of parts of the systems of action which constitute the personalities of the members. When we use the term *homology* to refer to certain formal identities between personalities and social systems which are to be understood in terms of the above considerations, it should be clear that we in no way intend to convey the impression that a personality is a microcosm of a social system, or that a social system is a kind of macrocosmic personality.

In spite of the formal similarities and the continuous empirical interdependencies and interpenetrations, both of which are of the greatest importance, personalities and social systems remain two distinct classes of systems.

[xii]The term *allocation* is borrowed from the usage of economics, where it has the general meaning here defined. Specifically, economists speak of the allocation of resources in the economy.

❖

Introduction to
"Sex Roles in the American Kinship System"

In "Sex Roles in the American Kinship System," Parsons applies his theory to the empirical topic of the American family. This descriptive essay did not incite much reaction when it was first published in the 1940s; however, in the 1970s it came to epitomize Parsons's conservatism, interpreted as it was as an explicit endorsement by Parsons of traditional gender roles and the dire consequences that would ensue should they be breeched. Feminists were particularly incensed by Parsons's assertion that "many women succumb to . . . dependency cravings through such channels as neurotic illness or compulsive domesticity" which leads them to "abdicate both their responsibilities and their opportunities for genuine independence" (1943:194). In addition, they found Parsons's assumption that "surely the pattern of romantic love which makes his relation to the 'woman he loves' the most important single thing in a man's life, is incompatible with the view that she is an inferior creature, fit only for dependency on him" especially naïve. Yet, interestingly, read in the context of the twenty-first century, one can see that in some respects Parsons got a "bad rap" for this essay. Although there is no question that his description of the ideal, typical, white middle-class family is told from an upper-middle-class white male's point of view, in fact, Parsons did capture important elements of this system. For instance, certainly his assertion that this traditional role structure "serves to concentrate the judgment and valuation of men on their occupational achievements, while the valuation of women is diverted into realms outside the occupationally relevant sphere" rings true. Indeed, one can even read this statement as an indictment of the traditional kinship system because of its demeaning effect on women. Parsons's most pivotal premise, however—that changes that are functional for one part of the system (e.g., the benefits to women and society as women enter the paid workforce) will produce changes that are not necessarily functional for other parts of the system (e.g., the schools, which relied on the free labor of female "volunteers" for essential tasks—see Dorothy Smith, Chapter 7; and hospitals, who relied heavily on low-paying female positions as nurses)—is not necessarily sexist at all, in the sense that what *is* sexist is the assumption (prevalent in the 1960s and 1970s) that women *could* enter the workforce without significant changes being made to other social structures and systems (e.g., families, schools, the workplace) and, at the least, without a major increase in quality day-care and child-care facilities.

❖

Sex Roles in the American Kinship System (1943)

Talcott Parsons

Much psychological research has suggested the very great importance to the individual of his affective ties, established in early childhood, to other members of his family of orientation. When strong affective ties have been formed, it seems reasonable to believe that situational pressures which force their drastic modification will impose important strains upon the individual.

Since all known kinship systems impose an incest tabu, the transition from asexual intrafamilial relationships to the sexual relation of marriage—generally to a previously relatively unknown person—is general. But with us this transition is accompanied by a process of "emancipation" from the ties both to parents and to siblings which is considerably more drastic than in most kinship systems, especially in that it applies to both sexes about equally, and includes emancipation from solidarity with *all* members of the family of orientation about equally, so that there is relatively little continuity with *any* kinship ties established by birth for anyone.

The effect of these factors is reinforced by two others. Since the effective kinship unit is normally the small conjugal family, the child's emotional attachments to kin are confined to relatively few persons instead of being distributed more widely. Especially important, perhaps, is the fact that no other adult woman has a role remotely similar to that of the mother. Hence the average intensity of affective involvement in family relations is likely to be high. Secondly, the child's relations outside the family are only to a small extent ascribed. Both in the play group and in the school he must to a large extent "find his own level" in competition with others. Hence the psychological significance of his security within the family is heightened.

We have then a situation where at the same time the inevitable importance of family ties is intensified and a necessity to become emancipated from them is imposed. This situation would seem to have a good deal to do with the fact that with us adolescence— and beyond—is, as has been frequently noted, a "difficult" period in the life cycle. In particular, associated with this situation is the prominence in our society of what has been called a "youth culture," a distinctive pattern of values and attitudes of the age groups between childhood and the assumption of full adult responsibilities. This youth culture, with its irresponsibility, its pleasure-seeking, its "rating and dating," and its intensification of the romantic love pattern, is not a simple matter of "apprenticeship" in adult values and responsibilities. It bears many of the marks of reaction to emotional tension and insecurity, and in all probability has among its functions that of easing the difficult process of adjustment from childhood emotional dependency to full "maturity." In it we find still a third element underlying the prominence of the romantic love complex in American society.

The emphasis which has here been placed on the multilineal symmetry of our kinship structure might be taken to imply that our society was characterized by a correspondingly striking assimilation of the roles of the sexes to each other. It is true that American society manifests a high level of the "emancipation" of women, which in important respects involves relative assimilation to masculine roles, in accessibility to occupational opportunity, in legal rights relative to property holding, and in various other respects. Undoubtedly the kinship system constitutes one of the important sets of factors underlying this emancipation since it does not, as do so many kinship systems, place a structural premium on the role of either sex in the maintenance of the continuity of kinship relations.

But the elements of sex-role assimilation in our society are conspicuously combined with elements of segregation which in many respects are even more striking than in other societies, as for instance in the matter of the much greater attention given by women to style and refinement of taste in dress and personal appearance. This and other aspects of segregation are connected with the structure of kinship, but not so much by itself as in its interrelations with the occupational system.

The members of the conjugal family in our urban society normally share a common basis of economic support in the form of money income, but this income is not derived from the co-operative efforts of the family as a unit—its principal source lies in the remuneration of occupational roles performed by individual members of the family. Status in an occupational role is generally, however, specifically segregated from kinship status—person holds a "job" as an individual, not by virtue of his status in a family.

Among the occupational statuses of members of a family, if there is more than one, much the most important is that of the husband and father, not only because it is usually the primary source of family income, but also because it is the most important single basis of the status of the family in the community at large. To be the main "breadwinner" of his family is a primary role of the normal adult man in our society. The corollary of this role is his far smaller participation than that of his wife in the internal affairs of the household. Consequently, "housekeeping" and the care of children is still the primary functional content of the adult feminine role in the "utilitarian" division of labor. Even if the married woman has a job, it is, at least in the middle classes, in the great majority of cases not one which in status or remuneration competes closely with those held by men of her own class. Hence there is a typically asymmetrical relation of the marriage pair to the occupational structure.

This asymmetrical relation apparently both has exceedingly important positive functional significance and is at the same time an important source of strain in relation to the patterning of sex roles.

On the positive functional side, a high incidence of certain types of patterns is essential to our occupational system and to the institutional complex in such fields as property and exchange which more immediately surround this system. In relatively commonsense terms it requires scope for the valuation of personal achievement, for equality of opportunity, for mobility in response to technical requirements, for devotion to occupational goals and interests relatively unhampered by "personal" consideration. In more technical terms it requires a high incidence of technical competence, of rationality, of universalistic norms, and of functional specificity. All these are drastically different from the patterns which are dominant in the area of kinship relations, where ascription of status by birth play a prominent part, and where roles are defined primarily in particularistic and functionally diffuse terms.

It is quite clear that the type of occupational structure which is so essential to our society requires a far-reaching structural segregation of occupational roles from the kinship roles of the *same* individuals. They must, in the occupational system, be treated primarily as individuals. This is a situation drastically different from that found in practically all non-literate societies and in many that are literate.

At the same time, it cannot be doubted that a solidary kinship unit has functional significance of the highest order, especially in relation to the socialization of individuals and to the deeper aspects of their psychological security. What would appear to have happened is a process of mutual accommodation between these two fundamental aspects of our social structure. On the one hand our kinship system is of a structural type which, broadly speaking, interferes least with the functional needs of the occupational system, above all in that it exerts relatively little pressure for the ascription of an individual's social status—through class affiliation, property, and of course particular "jobs"—by virtue of his kinship status. The conjugal unit can be mobile in status independently of the other kinship ties of its members, that is, those of the spouses to the members of their families of orientation.

But at the same time this small conjugal unit can be a strongly solidary unit. This is facilitated by the prevalence of the pattern that normally only *one* of its members has an occupational role which is of determinate significance for the status of the family as a whole. Minor children, that is, as a rule do not "work," and when they do, it is already a major step in the process of emancipation from the family of orientation. The wife and mother is either exclusively a "housewife" or at most has a "job" rather than a "career."

There are perhaps two primary functional aspects of this situation. In the first place, by confining the number of status-giving occupational roles of the members of the effective conjugal unit to one, it eliminates any competition for status, especially as between husband and wife, which might be disruptive of the solidarity of marriage. So long as lines of achievement are segregated and not directly comparable, there is less opportunity for jealousy, a sense of inferiority, etc, to develop. Secondly, it aids in clarity of definition of the situation by making the status of the family in the community relatively definite and unequivocal. There is much evidence that this relative definiteness of status is an important fact of in psychological security.

The same structural arrangements which have this positive functional significance also give rise to important strains. What has been said above about the pressure for thoroughgoing emancipation from the family of orientation is a case in point. But in connection with the sex-role problem there is another important source of strain.

Historically, in Western culture, it may perhaps be fairly said that there has been a strong tendency to define the feminine role psychologically as one strongly marked by elements of dependency. One of the best symbols perhaps was the fact that until rather recently the married woman was not *sui juris*, could not hold property, make contracts, or sue in her own right. But in the modern American kinship system, to say nothing of other aspects of the culture and social structure, there are at least two pressures which tend to counteract this dependency and have undoubtedly played a part in the movement for feminine emancipation.

The first, already much discussed, is the multilineal symmetry of the kinship system which gives no basis of sex discrimination, and which in kinship terms favors equal rights and responsibilities for both parties to a marriage. The second is the character of the marriage relationship. Resting as it does primarily on affective attachment for the other person as a concrete human individual, a "personality," rather than on more objective considerations of status, it puts a premium on a certain kind of mutuality and equality. There is no clearly structured superordination-subordination pattern. Each is a fully responsible "partner" with a claim to a voice in decisions, to a certain human dignity, to be "taken seriously." Surely the pattern of romantic love which makes his relation to the "woman he loves" the most important single thing in a man's life, is incompatible with the view that she is an inferior creature, fit only for dependency on him.

In our society, however, occupational status has tremendous weight in the scale of prestige values. The fact that the normal married woman is debarred from testing or demonstrating her fundamental equality with her husband in competitive occupational achievement, creates a demand for a functional equivalent. At least in the middle classes, however, this cannot be found in the utilitarian functions of the role of housewife since these are treated as relatively menial functions. To be, for instance, an excellent cook, does not give a hired maid a moral claim to a higher status than that of domestic servant.

This situation helps perhaps to account for a conspicuous tendency for the feminine role to emphasize broadly humanistic rather than technically specialized achievement values. One of the key patterns is that of "good taste," in personal appearance, house furnishings, cultural things like literature and music. To a large and perhaps increasing extent the more humanistic cultural traditions and amenities of life are carried on by women. Since these things are of high intrinsic importance in the scale of values of our culture, and since by virtue of the system of occupational specialization even many highly superior men are greatly handicapped in respect to them, there is some genuine redressing of the balance between the sexes.

There is also, however, a good deal of direct evidence of tension in the feminine role. In the "glamor girl" pattern, use of specifically feminine devices as an instrument of compulsive search for power and exclusive attention are conspicuous. Many women succumb to their dependency cravings through such channels as neurotic illness or compulsive domesticity and thereby abdicate both their responsibilities and their opportunities for genuine independence. Many of the attempts to excel in approved channels of achievement are marred by garishness of taste, by instability in response to fad and fashion, by a seriousness in community or club activities which is out of proportion to the intrinsic importance of the task. In all of these and other fields there are conspicuous signs of insecurity and ambivalence. Hence it may be concluded that the feminine role is a conspicuous focus of the strains inherent in our social structure, and not the least of the sources of these strains is to be found in the functional difficulties in the integration of our kinship system with the rest of the social structure.

Robert K. Merton (1910–2003): A Biographical Sketch

SOURCE: Columbia University.

Robert King Merton was born Meyer R. Schkolnick on July 4, 1910, in South Philadelphia, to working-class, Jewish immigrants from eastern Europe. After a rough-and-tumble early childhood—which allegedly included membership in the local street gang—the teenaged Schkolnick began to perform magic tricks around the neighborhood, at parties and social gatherings, using the stage name "Robert Merlin." After a young friend convinced him that borrowing King Arthur's mentor's name was clichéd, he changed it to "Robert King Merton."

From a very early age, Merton showed a passion for learning, and upon graduating from high school he earned a scholarship to Temple University. He graduated from Temple with a degree in sociology in 1931 and went on to earn his doctorate in sociology at Harvard University, where he was one of the first and most important students of Talcott Parsons. Merton first began publishing while still a graduate student, and by the time he was forty he was one of the most influential social scientists in the United States (Calhoun 2003:9). He developed the very idea of studying science sociologically (i.e., the sociology of science), and as early as 1942 his "ethos of science" challenged the common public perception of scientists as eccentric geniuses free of normal social constraints. It was primarily for this work that Merton became the first sociologist to be awarded a National Medal of Science in 1994. Merton continued to study the sociology of science, perhaps the field closest to his heart, publishing his masterpiece on this topic, *On the Shoulders of Giants* (which neatly captures his stance) in 1965. In 1949 (albeit revised and expanded in 1957 and 1968), Merton published what would become his magnus opus, *Social Theory and Social Structure*.

From 1941 until his death in 2003, Merton was a professor of sociology at Columbia University. He mentored an extraordinary number of students, many of whom would become prominent in their own right, including Robin Williams, Jr., Jesse Pitts, Peter Blau, James Coleman, Lewis Coser, Rose Coser, Alvin Gouldner, Seymour Martin Lipset, Alice Rossi, and Arthur Stinchcombe. Robert Merton is survived by his wife and collaborator Harriet Zuckerman, by three children, nine grandchildren, and nine great-grandchildren, and as Calhoun (2003:1) aptly notes, "by thousands of sociologists whose work is shaped every day by his."

Intellectual Influences and Core Ideas

Robert Merton is a major theorist who, as indicated above, coined several pivotal sociological concepts. However, Merton was also a prolific researcher who studied a wide variety of empirical areas and topics, including deviance, drug addiction, friendship formation, medical education, technology, media, and the history of science. In addition, Merton wrote extensively on the discipline of sociology, making vital methodological as well as empirical and theoretical contributions. (For instance, he developed the "focused interview," now called "focus group research.") Indeed, one could argue that Merton's single most important achievement has been to establish connections between theory and research, thereby charting the course of the discipline of sociology.

Merton was influenced by a broad array of theorists, philosophers, and social scientists. He read widely, and one can see traces of Durkheim, Weber, Simmel, and Marx, as well as the structural functionalist anthropologist Bronislaw Malinowski, in his work. Merton also drew inspiration from the work of William I. Thomas and Florian Znaniecki. Above all, however, Merton learned from Pitirim Sorokin, the first chair of the Department of Sociology at Harvard University, who recruited Merton for graduate school, and Sorokin's young colleague at Harvard, Talcott Parsons.

In contrast to Parsons, who sought to delineate a highly abstract, master conceptual schema, Merton favored what he called middle-range theory: theories that "lie between the minor but necessary working hypotheses that evolve in abundance during day-to-day research and the all-inclusive systematic efforts to develop a unified theory that will explain all the observed uniformities of social behavior, social organization, and social change" (1967:49, as cited in Sztompka 1986:41). Merton's middle-range reformulation of structural functionalism made it eminently more useful. Indeed, Merton has contributed numerous concepts that are now "staples" in sociology, and you will read about these concepts below. Yet, perhaps the single most important contribution that Merton made to functionalism—and sociology—is that he extended Parsons's point that society is a system of interrelated parts and reworked it in order to emphasize that the components of the system may or may not be "in sync," and that the results are not always predictable. This pivotal theoretical contribution is readily apparent not only in Merton's highly influential concepts of manifest and latent function and dysfunction, but also in his oft-cited theory of deviance, discussed below.

Perhaps the most well-known concepts to arise from functionalism are manifest and latent function. For Merton, **manifest function** refers to the overt or intended purpose of action. **Latent function**, on the other hand, refers to implicit or unintended purpose. As Merton readily notes, the terms "manifest" and "latent" come from Freud (1915), who emphasized that almost every behavior, including seemingly mundane ones such as gum chewing, have "latent" functions related to our sexual drive. From a Freudian perspective, gum chewing (and smoking, biting one's nails, etc.) is an "oral fixation" related to the "oral" period of child development (0–15 months), in which gratification for the child revolves around nursing, gumming, sucking, and mouth movement. Oral fixations reflect a failure to psychologically complete this stage, the behavior in question being a defense mechanism to avoid the anxiety produced from the conflict in and leaving that stage.

So, too, Merton argues, social actions sometimes have latent functions far more significant than their more manifest purpose. Consider, for instance, Merton's now classic example of the Hopi rain dance, which you will read about below. While the manifest, or overt, purpose of the dance is to produce rain, the latent function is to reaffirm group identity, solidarity, and/or cohesion. Thus, while from a strictly rationalist point of view, one might consider a rain dance that did not result in rain a failure, in fact, the latent function of the ritual may nevertheless have been fulfilled. Of course, this latent social function—the affirmation of social ties and celebration of shared identity—is among the most important latent functions in all of social life, undergirding a wide variety of social conventions and rituals, such as attending holiday celebrations, conferences, and/or weddings; writing thank-you notes; and joining a gang. (For a more recent discussion of this point, see Randall Collins 2004.) For instance, the "business lunch" often has this same latent function of reinforcing social bonds and asserting or celebrating group identity despite and/or alongside its more obvious (manifest) goals. And just as a rain dance may or may not immediately produce rain, so, too, a business lunch may not achieve immediate (manifest) results (e.g., a deal) but nevertheless fulfill its critical latent function.

In sum, Merton's concept of manifest and latent function greatly enhances the Parsonian notion of society as a system of interrelated parts, not only because it acknowledges that there are multiple functions for any one component, but because it underscores that the various functions within even a single component might not coincide with each other or that they might even conflict. Whereas Parsons's conceptualization of society as a system of interrelated parts seemed to imply that all social institutions were inherently functional—otherwise they would not exist—Merton emphasized that different parts of a system might be at odds with each other and, thus, that even functional or beneficial institutions or subsystems can produce *dysfunctions* or *unintended consequences* as well.

This is precisely the point of Merton's extraordinarily influential theory of **deviance**. In what is "arguably the most cited article" in sociology (Crothers 1987:120), Merton (1949/1957) seeks to explain variances in rates of deviance according to social structural location. In sociology, deviance refers to modes of action that do not conform to the dominant norms or values in a social group or society. Following the functionalist notion that society is a system of interrelated parts, Merton hypothesized that deviance results when there is a disconnect between the cultural and social realms. That is, deviance occurs when the *values* of a society are out of sync with the

Photo 2.4a Hopi Rain Dance

Photo 2.4b Business Lunch

The manifest function of the rain dance is to prove the Hopi worthy enough to receive the much needed thunderstorms, while the latent function is to reinforce group identity and social ties, and to celebrate the cosmic order in which rain and person all belong. So too, the manifest function of the business lunch is to discuss issues or make decisions, while the latent function is to reinforce group identity and social ties (e.g., to "network").

means available for achieving them. For Merton, this state of affairs exists when, for instance, an individual internalizes the notion that "success" means having lots of money but is not afforded the opportunity to earn a legitimate, well-paying living. Thus, the individual turns to illegal means (e.g., selling illegal drugs) in order to achieve economic success.

That unintended consequences occur because of a disconnect between the cultural and social realms brings us to the concept of **dysfunction**. It was Émile Durkheim (see Chapter 1) who first emphasized that while positive social changes, such as periods of economic prosperity, might alleviate certain problems, they may also produce significant unanticipated negative consequences (such as an increased likelihood for moral disorder). Merton not only elaborated on Durkheim's point that positive social institutions (or changes) may have unintended negative consequences; he went on to show that negative (or benign) social institutions (or social changes) might have unanticipated positive consequences as well. But it is for highlighting the "negative" unintended consequences and dysfunctions that Merton is most known.

Significantly, the concept of dysfunction is not incompatible with the functionalist metaphor of the body. The body is not a flawless machine; on the contrary, problems and irregularities often arise, as "subsystems" go awry. For instance, the body typically responds to infection by producing a fever. But while the fever has an important *function* as part of the body's defense, high fevers are dangerous or *dysfunctional* as they can result in brain damage. Similarly, a drug such as aspirin might be prescribed in order to reduce fever but have the undesirable side effect (or dysfunction) of producing stomach pain.

So, too, Merton points out, laws, social policies, norms, values, religions, and the like can all produce unintended consequences and dysfunctions. For instance, while most people today would not dispute that men and women should be allowed to enter any profession they choose and for which they are qualified, one of the unintended consequences of the rise in gender equality for women in employment has been that it has led to a shortage of nurses and teachers. Now that women have a wide variety of options for employment—many of which are more attractive and lucrative than teaching or nursing—hospitals and schools (especially in poor communities) are hard pressed to fill these extremely challenging, but still low-status, positions. Indeed, during the past thirty years the percentage of female physicians rose fivefold, from approximately 8 percent of physicians in 1970 to 34 percent in 2002 (© AMA's *Physician Masterfile*, http://www.phg.com/article_a057.htm); however, less than 6 percent of nurses today are male, an increase of only 2 percent in the last ten years (National Sample Survey of Registered Nurses, http://www.nursingworld.org/ajn/1998/sept/issu098f.htm).

Similarly, Merton made a significant contribution to role theory by demonstrating that "social status" and "role-sets" are organized in the social structure in a more complex way than Parsons initially supposed. Specifically, Merton (1996:43) defines *social status* as "a position in a social system, with its distinctive array of designated rights and obligations." That is, the status of a role is not fixed, but rather changes in conjunction with the particular role-set involved. Thus, for instance, the status of school teacher might be high in relation to the correlative (low) status of pupil, but low in relation to the school principal and superintendent and the Board of Education (ibid.:44). (see Photos 2.5a & 2.5b) Yet, the point is that not only role statuses but also role-expectations and role-obligations shift in interaction. What it means to be a "teacher" changes significantly based on the particular role-sets involved. Consequently, not only is role conflict inevitable because any one individual plays

Photo 2.5a   Teacher/Student   **Photo 2.5b**   Striking Teachers

Merton emphasized that the expectations, obligations, and status incumbent in roles is not static. Rather they change systematically depending on the particular *role-set* involved. For instance, the role of teacher may have high status in the teacher-student pair, but low status in relationship with the school board.

SOURCE: © CORBIS.   SOURCE: © Bettmann/CORBIS.

multiple roles (e.g., you are a little league coach on your way to the big game, when your elderly mother calls because she needs you to take her to the doctor); even within one role, conflict may occur because of the multiple role-sets involved.

These examples bring us to one of the most important criticisms of functionalism. Critics contend that functionalists rationalize or "explain away" *all* aspects of the social system, including social inequities. In contrast to critical explanations of inequality (which you will read about in the following chapter), functionalism does not expressly indict inequality. Rather, functionalists note that certain policies and institutions can be dysfunctional for entire groups of people but maintained because they are functional for a more powerful social group or the social system itself. For instance, in one of the most famous and controversial functionalist essays, Kingsley Davis and Wilbert E. Moore (1945) argued that a society develops an unequal distribution of rewards, such as money, power, or prestige, because it has to attract the most qualified people to fill its most vital positions. But critics read Davis and Moore's piece as an apology for the "system."

MERTON'S THEORETICAL ORIENTATION

Merton's work is far less abstract than Parsons's, but it is no less theoretically multidimensional. In terms of the question of order, Merton consistently argues that while individuals are constrained by social forces, alternative modes of action are

Figure 2.3   Merton's Basic Theoretical Orientation

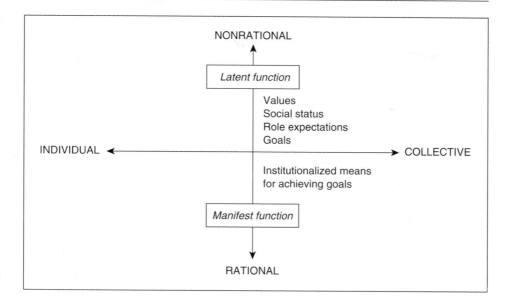

nevertheless possible. This is most readily apparent in Merton's theory of deviance, which is especially attuned to explaining the interchange between the individual and the collective levels. Merton integrates an appreciation for the (collective) structural impediments to acquiring money and status (which reflects a collective approach to order) with an acknowledgment that individuals nevertheless "choose" to follow or abandon specific means and goals (which reflects the level of the individual).

So, too, Merton's role theory reflects the level of the collective in that role-sets are composed of normative expectations and obligations that preexist the individual actor. On the other hand, however, the actor internalizes role-expectations, and he or she plays his or her role according to his or her own personality needs as well as the demands of the situation, thereby acknowledging agency at the level of the individual. In sum, individuals are socialized into roles, and they internalize role-expectations, which duly reflects and involves both the individual actor-ego and the social system.

In terms of action, on one hand, actors sometimes play their roles quite deliberately and strategically (e.g., in a job interview), and at the level of the *system*, positions and obligations in a highly rationalized society (e.g., the business model of capitalism, in which jobs are both created and dispensed with at the drop of a hat with respect to the "bottom line") reflect the rational realm. Above all, however, "role-sets" speak to the non-rational dimension of action in that even the most "strategic" playing of roles inevitably rests on symbols and values (e.g., the "tie" as a business emblem and sign of professionalism). Moreover, actors often take on roles unreflectively (such as gender roles) because they feel they are morally "right" or inevitable, which reflects both the nonrational/individual realm as well as that of the collective (since it is the collective level that creates gendered role expectations). This point is also duly reflected in Merton's theory of deviance, which, above all, emphasizes the moral forces and values of the cultural realm.

Significantly, then, as shown in Figure 2.3 (see above) and discussed previously, overall structural functionalism tends to emphasize the collective/nonrational realm. As indicated above, this point was forcefully taken up by the conflict theorists in the 1960s and 1970s who criticized structural functionalists for underemphasizing the influence of preexisting institutions and powerful social groups.

Reading

Introduction to "Manifest and Latent Functions"

"Manifest and Latent Functions" (1949) is a classic functionalist piece that introduces two of Merton's most famous and important sociological concepts: manifest and latent functions, discussed previously. While manifest and latent functions can be found in a wide variety of social situations, interestingly, this excerpt concludes with a pivotal example at the heart of American life: consumer activity. Following Thorsten Veblen (1857–1929), who coined the term "conspicuous consumption," Merton emphasizes that behind the obvious (manifest) purpose of buying goods in order to satisfy specific needs is the more significant latent function of "heightening or reaffirming social status." The result then is that "people buy expensive goods not so much because they are superior but because they are expensive" (69).

❖

Manifest and Latent Functions (1949)

Robert K. Merton

. . . The distinction between manifest and latent functions was devised to preclude the inadvertent confusion, often found in the sociological literature, between conscious *motivations* for social behavior and its *objective consequences*. Our scrutiny of current vocabularies of functional analysis has shown how easily, and how unfortunately, the sociologist may identify *motives* with *functions*. It was further indicated that the motive and the function vary independently and that the failure to register this fact in an established terminology has contributed to the unwitting tendency among sociologists to confuse the subjective categories of motivation with the objective categories of function. This, then, is the central purpose of our succumbing to the not-always-commendable practice of introducing new terms into the rapidly growing technical vocabulary of sociology, a practice regarded by many laymen as an affront to their intelligence and an offense against common intelligibility.

As will be readily recognized, I have adapted the terms "manifest" and "latent" from their use in another context by Freud (although Francis Bacon had long ago spoken of "latent process" and "latent configuration" in connection with processes which are below the threshold of superficial observation).

The distinction itself has been repeatedly drawn by observers of human behavior at irregular intervals over a span of many centuries. Indeed, it would be disconcerting to find that a distinction which we have come to regard as central to functional analysis had not been made by any of that numerous company who have in effect adopted a functional orientation. We need mention only a few of those who have, in recent decades, found it necessary to distinguish in their specific interpretations of behavior between the end-in-view and the functional consequences of action.

George H. Mead[i]: ". . . that attitude of hostility toward the law-breaker has the unique advantage [read: latent function] of uniting all members of the community in the emotional solidarity of aggression. While the most admirable of humanitarian efforts are sure to run counter to the individual interests of very many in the community, or fail to touch the interest and imagination of the multitude and to leave the community divided or indifferent, the cry of thief or murderer is attuned to profound complexes, lying below the surface of competing individual efforts, and citizens who have [been] separated by divergent interests stand together against the common enemy."

Émile Durkheim's[ii] similar analysis of the social functions of punishment is also focused on its latent functions (consequences for the community) rather than confined to manifest functions (consequences for the criminal).

W. G. Sumner[iii]: ". . . from the first acts by which men try to satisfy needs, each act stands by itself, and looks no further than the immediate satisfaction. From recurrent needs arise habits for the individual and customs for the group, but these results are consequences which were never conscious, and never foreseen or intended. They are not noticed until they have long existed, and it is still longer before they are appreciated." Although this fails to locate the latent functions of standardized social actions for a designated social structure, it plainly makes the basic distinction between ends-in-view and objective consequences.

R. M. MacIver[iv]: In addition to the direct effects of institutions, "there are further effects by way of control which lie outside the direct purposes of men . . . this type of reactive form of control . . . may, though unintended, be of profound service to society."

W. I. Thomas and F. Znaniecki[v]: "Although all the new [Polish peasant cooperative] institutions are thus formed with the definite purpose of satisfying certain specific needs, their social function is by no means limited to their explicit and conscious purpose . . . every one of these institutions—commune or agricultural circle, loan and savings bank, or theater—is not merely a mechanism for the management of certain values but also an association of people, each member of which is supposed to participate in the common activities as a living, concrete individual. Whatever is the predominant, official common interest upon which the institution is founded, the association as a concrete group of human personalities unofficially involves many other interests; the social contacts between its members are not limited to their common pursuit,

---

[i]George H. Mead, "The psychology of punitive justice," *American Journal of Sociology*, 1918, 23, 577–602, esp. 591.

[ii]As suggested earlier in this chapter, Durkheim adopted a functional orientation throughout his work, and he operates, albeit often without explicit notice, with concepts equivalent to that of latent function in all of his researches. The reference in the text at this point is to his "Deux lois de l'évolution penale," *L'année sociologique*, 1899–1900, 4, 55–95, as well as to his *Division of Labor in Society* (Glencoe, Illinois: The Free Press, 1947).

[iii]This one of his many such observations is of course from W. G. Sumner's *Folkways* (Boston: Ginn & Co., 1906), 3. His collaborator, Albert G. Keller, retained the distinction in his own writings; see, for example, his *Social Evolution* (New York: Macmillan, 1927), at 93–95.

[iv]This is advisedly drawn from one of MacIver's earlier works, *Community* (London: MacMillan, 1915). The distinction takes on greater importance in his later writings, becoming a major element in his *Social Causation* (Boston: Ginn & Co., 1942), esp. at 314–321, and informs the greater part of his *The More Perfect Union* (New York: Macmillan, 1948).

[v]The single excerpt quoted in the text is one of scores which have led to *The Polish Peasant in Europe and America* being deservedly described as a "sociological classic." See pages 1426–7 and 1523 ff. As will be noted later in this chapter, the insights and conceptual distinctions contained in this one passage, and there are many others like it in point of richness of content, were forgotten or never noticed by those industrial sociologists who recently came to develop the notion of "informal organization" in industry.

though the latter, of course, constitutes both the main reason for which the association is formed and the most permanent bond which holds it together. Owing to this combination of an abstract political, economic, or rather rational mechanism for the satisfaction of specific needs with the concrete unity of a social group, the new institution is also the best intermediary link between the peasant primary-group and the secondary national system."

These and numerous other sociological observers have, then, from time to time distinguished between categories of subjective disposition ("needs, interest, purposes") and categories of generally unrecognized but objective functional consequences ("unique advantages," "never conscious" consequences, "unintended . . . service to society," "function not limited to conscious and explicit purpose").

Since the occasion for making the distinction arises with great frequency, and since the purpose of a conceptual scheme is to direct observations toward salient elements of a situation and to prevent the inadvertent oversight of these elements, it would seem justifiable to designate this distinction by an appropriate set of terms. This is the rationale for the distinction between manifest functions and latent functions; the first referring to those objective consequences for a specified unit (person, subgroup, social or cultural system) which contribute to its adjustment or adaptation and were so intended; the second referring to unintended and unrecognized consequences of the same order.

There are some indications that the christening of this distinction may serve a heuristic purpose by becoming incorporated into an explicit conceptual apparatus, thus aiding both systematic observation and later analysis. In recent years, for example, the distinction between manifest and latent functions has been utilized in analyses of racial intermarriage,[vi] social stratification,[vii] affective frustration,[viii] Veblen's sociological theories,[ix] prevailing American orientations toward Russia,[x] propaganda as a means of social control,[xi] Malinowski's anthropological theory,[xii] Navajo witchcraft,[xiii] problems in the sociology of knowledge,[xiv] fashion,[xv] the dynamics of personality,[xvi] national security measures,[xvii] the internal social dynamics of bureaucracy,[xviii] and a great variety of other sociological problems.

The very diversity of these subject-matters suggests that the theoretic distinction between

---

[vi]Merton, "Intermarriage and the social structure," *op. cit.*

[vii]Kingsley Davis, "A conceptual analysis of stratification," *American Sociological Review*, 1942, 7, 309–321.

[viii]Thorner, *op. cit.*, esp. at 165.

[ix]A. K. Davis, *Thorstein Veblen's Social Theory*, Harvard Ph.D. dissertation, 1941, and "Veblen on the decline of the Protestant Ethic," *Social Forces*, 1944, 22, 282–86; Louis Schneider, *The Freudian Psychology and Veblen's Social Theory*, (New York: King's Crown Press, 1948), esp. Chapter 2.

[x]A. K. Davis, "Some sources of American hostility to Russia," *American Journal of Sociology*, 1947, 53, 174–183.

[xi]Talcott Parsons, "Propaganda and social control," in his *Essays in Sociological Theory*.

[xii]Clyde Kluckhohn, "Bronislaw Malinowski, 1884–1942," *Journal of American Folklore*, 1943, 56, 208–219.

[xiii]Clyde Kluckhohn, *Navaho Witchcraft, op. cit.*, esp. at 46–47 and ff.

[xiv]Merton, Chapter XII of this volume [*Social Theory and Social Structure*, 1957].

[xv]Bernard Barber and L. S. Lobel, "'Fashion' in women's clothes and the American social system," *Social Forces*, 1952, 31, 124–131.

[xvi]O. H. Mowrer and C. Kluckhohn, "Dynamic theory of personality," in J. M. Hunt, ed., *Personality and the Behavior Disorders* (New York: Ronald Press, 1944), 1, 69–135, esp. at 72.

[xvii]Marie Jahoda and S. W. Cook, "Security measures and freedom of thought: an exploratory study of the impact of loyalty and security programs," *Yale Law Journal*, 1952, 61, 296–333.

[xviii]Philip Selznick, *TVA and the Grass Roots* (University of California Press, 1949); A. W. Gouldner, *Patterns of Industrial Bureaucracy* (Glencoe, Illinois: The Free Press, 1954); P. M. Blau, *The Dynamics of Bureaucracy* (University of Chicago Press, 1955); A. K. Davis, "Bureaucratic patterns in Navy officer corps." *Social Forces* 1948, 27, 142–153.

manifest and latent functions is bound up with a limited and particular range of human behavior. But there still remains the large task of ferreting out the specific uses to which this distinction can be put, and it is to this large task that we devote the remaining pages of this chapter.

Heuristic Purposes of the Distinction

Clarifies the analysis of seemingly irrational social patterns. In the first place, the distinction aids the sociological interpretation of many social practices which persist even though their manifest purpose is clearly not achieved. The time-worn procedure in such instances has been for diverse, particularly lay, observers to refer to these practices as "superstitions," irrationalities," "mere inertia of tradition," *etc.* In other words, when group behavior does not—and, indeed, often cannot—attain its ostensible purpose there is an inclination to attribute its occurrence to lack of intelligence, sheer ignorance, survivals, or so-called inertia. Thus, the Hopi ceremonials designed to produce abundant rainfall may be labelled a superstitious practice of primitive folk and that is assumed to conclude the matter. It should be noted that this in no sense accounts for the group behavior. It is simply a case of name-calling; it substitutes the epithet "superstition" for an analysis of the actual role of this behavior in the life of the group. Given the concept of latent function, however, we are reminded that this behavior *may* perform a function for the group, although this function may be quite remote from the avowed purpose of the behavior.

The concept of latent function extends the observer's attention beyond the question of whether or not the behavior attains its avowed purpose. Temporarily ignoring these explicit purposes, it directs attention toward another range of consequences: those bearing, for example, upon the individual personalities of Hopi involved in the ceremony and upon the persistence and continuity of the larger group. Were one to confine himself to the problem of whether a manifest (purposed) function occurs, it becomes a problem, not for the sociologist, but for the meteorologist. And to be sure, our meteorologists agree that the rain ceremonial does not produce rain; but this is hardly to the point. It is merely to say that the ceremony does not have this technological use; that

this purpose of the ceremony and its actual consequences do not coincide. But with the concept of latent function, we continue our inquiry, examining the consequences of the ceremony not for the rain gods or for meteorological phenomena, but for the groups which conduct the ceremony. And here it may be found, as many observers indicate, that the ceremonial does indeed have functions—but functions which are non-purposed or latent.

Ceremonials may fulfill the latent function of reinforcing the group identity by providing a periodic occasion on which the scattered members of a group assemble to engage in a common activity. As Durkheim among others long since indicated, such ceremonials are a means by which collective expression is afforded the sentiments which, in a further analysis, are found to be a basic source of group unity. Through the systematic application of the concept of latent function, therefore, *apparently* irrational behavior may *at times* be found to be positively functional for the group. Operating with the concept of latent function, we are not too quick to conclude that if an activity of a group does not achieve its nominal purpose, then its persistence can be described only as an instance of "inertia," "survival," or "manipulation by powerful subgroups in the society."

In point of fact, some conception like that of latent function has very often, almost invariably, been employed by social scientists observing *a standardized practice designed to achieve an objective which one knows from accredited physical science cannot be thus achieved.* This would plainly be the case, for example, with Pueblo rituals dealing with rain or fertility. *But with behavior which is not directed toward a clearly unattainable objective, sociological observers are less likely to examine the collateral or latent functions of the behavior.*

Directs attention to theoretically fruitful fields of inquiry. The distinction between manifest and latent functions serves further to direct the attention of the sociologist to precisely those realms of behavior, attitude and belief where he can most fruitfully apply his special skills. For what is his task if he confines himself to the study of manifest functions? He is then concerned very largely with determining whether a practice instituted for a particular purpose does, in fact, achieve this purpose. He will then inquire, for example, whether a new system of wage-payment achieves its avowed purpose of reducing labor turnover or of increasing output. He will ask whether a propaganda campaign has indeed gained its objective of increasing "willingness to fight" or "willingness to buy war bonds," or "tolerance toward other ethnic groups." Now, these are important, and complex, types of inquiry. But, so long as sociologists *confine* themselves to the study of manifest functions, their inquiry is set for them by practical men of affairs (whether a captain of industry, a trade union leader, or, conceivably, a Navaho chieftain, is for the moment immaterial), rather than by the theoretic problems which are at the core of the discipline. By dealing primarily with the realm of manifest functions, with the key problem of whether deliberately instituted practices or organizations succeed in achieving their objectives, the sociologist becomes converted into an industrious and skilled recorder of the altogether familiar pattern of behavior. *The terms of appraisal are fixed and limited by the question put to him by the non-theoretic men of affairs, e.g., has the new wage-payment program achieved such-and-such purposes?*

But armed with the concept of latent function, the sociologist extends his inquiry in those very directions which promise most for the theoretic development of the discipline. He examines the familiar (or planned) social practice to ascertain the latent, and hence generally unrecognized, functions (as well, of course, as the manifest functions). He considers, for example, the consequences of the new wage plan for, say, the trade union in which the workers are organized or the consequences of a propaganda program, not only for increasing its avowed purpose of stirring up patriotic fervor, but also for making large numbers of people reluctant to speak their minds when they differ with official policies, *etc*. In short, it is suggested that the *distinctive* intellectual contributions of the sociologist are found primarily in the study of unintended consequences (among which are

latent functions) of social practices, as well as in the study of anticipated consequences (among which are manifest functions).[xix]

There is some evidence that it is precisely at the point where the research attention of sociologists has shifted from the plane of manifest to the plane of latent functions that they have made their *distinctive* and major contributions. . . .

The discovery of latent functions represents significant increments in sociological knowledge. There is another respect in which inquiry into latent functions represents a distinctive contribution of the social scientist. It is precisely the latent functions of a practice or belief which are not common knowledge, for these are unintended and generally unrecognized social and psychological consequences. As a result, findings concerning latent functions represent a greater increment in knowledge than findings concerning manifest functions. They represent, also, greater departures from "common-sense" knowledge about social life. Inasmuch as the latent functions depart, more or less, from the avowed manifest functions, the research which uncovers latent functions very often produces "paradoxical" results. The seeming paradox arises from the sharp modification of a familiar popular preconception which regards a standardized practice or belief *only* in terms of its manifest functions by indicating some of its subsidiary or collateral latent functions. The introduction of the concept of latent function in social research leads to conclusions which show that "social life is not as simple as it first seems." For as long as people confine themselves to *certain* consequences (*e.g.* manifest consequences), it is comparatively simple for them to pass moral judgments upon the practice or belief in question. Moral evaluations, generally based on these manifest consequences, tend to be polarized in terms of black or white. But the perception of further (latent) consequences often complicates the picture. Problems of moral evaluation (which are not our immediate concern) and problems of social engineering (which are our concern[xx]) both take

---

[xix]For a brief illustration of this general proposition, see Robert K. Merton, Marjorie Fiske, and Alberta Curtis, *Mass Persuasion* (New York: Harper, 1946), 185–189; Jahoda and Cook, *op. cit.*

[xx]This is not to deny that social engineering has direct moral implications or that technique and morality are inescapably intertwined, but I do not intend to deal with this range of problems in the present chapter. For some discussion of these problems see Merton, Fiske, and Curtis, *Mass Persuasion, op. cit.*

on the additional complexities usually involved in responsible social decisions.

An example of inquiry which implicitly uses the notion of latent function will illustrate the sense in which "paradox"—discrepancy between the apparent, merely manifest, function and the actual, which also includes latent functions—tends to occur as a result of including this concept. Thus, to revert to Veblen's well-known analysis of conspicuous consumption, it is no accident that he has been recognized as a social analyst gifted with an eye for the paradoxical, the ironic, the satiric. For these are frequent, if not inevitable, outcomes of applying the concept of latent function (or its equivalent).

The pattern of conspicuous consumption. The manifest purpose of buying consumption goods is, of course, the satisfaction of the needs for which these goods are explicitly designed. Thus, automobiles are obviously intended to provide a certain kind of transportation; candles to provide light; choice articles of food to provide sustenance; rare art products to provide aesthetic pleasure. Since these products *do* have these uses, it was largely assumed that these encompass the range of socially significant functions. Veblen indeed suggests that this was ordinarily the prevailing view (in the pre-Veblenian era, of course). "The end of acquisition and accumulation is conventionally held to be the consumption of the goods accumulated. . . . This is at least felt to be the economically legitimate end of acquisition, *which alone it is incumbent on the theory to take account of.*"[xxi]

However, says Veblen in effect, as sociologists we must go on to consider the latent functions of acquisition, accumulation and consumption, and these latent functions are remote indeed from the manifest functions. "But, it is only when taken in a sense far removed from its naive meaning [*i.e.* manifest function] that the consumption of goods can be said to afford the incentive from which accumulation invariably proceeds." And among these latent functions, which help explain the persistence and the social location of the pattern of conspicuous consumption, is its symbolization of "pecuniary strength and so of gaining or retaining a good name." The exercise of "punctilious discrimination" in the excellence of "food, drink, shelter, service, ornaments, apparel, amusements" results not merely in direct gratifications derived from the consumption of "superior" to "inferior" articles, but also, and Veblen argues, more importantly, it results in a *heightening or reaffirmation of social status.*

The Veblenian paradox is that people buy expensive goods not so much because they are superior but because they are expensive. For it is the latent equation ("costliness = mark of higher social status") which he singles out in his functional analysis, rather than the manifest equation ("costliness = excellence of the goods"). Not that he denies manifest functions *any* place in buttressing the pattern of conspicuous consumption. These, too, are operative. "What has just been said must not be taken to mean that there are no other incentives to acquisition and accumulation than this desire to excel in pecuniary standing and so gain the esteem and envy of one's fellowmen. The desire for added comfort and security from want is present as a motive at every stage. . . ." Or again: "It would be hazardous to assert that a useful purpose is ever absent from the utility of any article or of any service, however obviously its prime purpose and chief element is conspicuous waste" and derived social esteem.[xxii] It is only that *these*

[xxi]Veblen, *Theory of the Leisure Class, op. cit.,* p. 25.

[xxii]*Ibid.,* 32, 101. It will be noted throughout that Veblen is given to loose terminology. In the marked passages (and repeatedly elsewhere) he uses "incentive," "desire," "purpose," and "function" interchangeably. Since the context usually makes clear the denotation of these terms, no great harm is done. But it is clear that the expressed purposes of conformity to a culture pattern are by no means identical with the latent functions of the conformity. Veblen occasionally recognizes this. For example, "In strict accuracy nothing should be included under the head of conspicuous waste but such expenditure as is incurred on the ground of an invidious pecuniary comparison. But in order to bring any given item or element in under this head *it is not necessary that it should be recognized as waste in this sense by the person incurring the expenditure*" (*Ibid.* 99; italics supplied). Cf. A. K. Davis, "Veblen on the decline of the Protestant Ethic," *op. cit.*

direct, manifest functions do not fully account for the prevailing patterns of consumption. Otherwise put, if the latent functions of status-enhancement or status-reaffirmation were removed from the patterns of conspicuous consumption, these patterns would undergo severe changes of a sort which the "conventional" economist could not foresee.

In these respects, Veblen's analysis of latent functions departs from the common-sense notion that the end-product of consumption is "of course, the direct satisfaction which it provides": "People eat caviar because they're hungry; buy Cadillacs because they want the best car they can get; have dinner by candlelight because they like the peaceful atmosphere." The common-sense interpretation in terms of selected manifest motives gives way, in Veblen's analysis, to the collateral latent functions which are also, and perhaps more significantly, fulfilled by these practices. To be sure, the Veblenian analysis has, in the last decades, entered so fully into popular thought, that these latent functions are now widely recognized.

❖

Discussion Questions

1. Provide specific examples of each pattern variable in a particular social context, such as the military, church, or school. Then suggest which *system*—personality, social, and/or cultural—your example primarily reflects. Consider demonstrating the *interchange* between systems. For instance:

   "Affectivity": a soldier is taught that he should be willing to risk his life to save that of his fellow soldier. (CULTURAL SYSTEM—values)

   "Affective-neutrality": a soldier is taught to act according to military rules and codes rather than personal emotions. She is taught not to smile when she is saluting an officer. She rides through the streets of occupied territory exhibiting little or no sympathy for the enemy. (SOCIAL SYSTEM—institutionalized in norms)

2. Choose one *role* that you consistently play (e.g., mother, daughter, teacher, student) and discuss its relation to each pattern variable. For instance:

   MOTHER/FATHER ROLE:

   Affectivity/affective-neutrality:
   It used to be that mothers were expected to display more affectivity and fathers were expected to be more affectively neutral (relegated to the breadwinner role), but now emotional bonding/nurturing is expected/considered legitimate for both parents.

   Ascription/achievement:
   The mother/father role is mostly ascribed, although interestingly, the saying "It is easy to be a father, hard to be a dad" reflects the notion of performance. Also, because of complicated family situations, one's biological parent might not "perform" the role of parent.

   Individual/collective:
   Mostly collective, a "good" mother/father acts according to the best interests of the family, not him/herself. Gender is highly relevant, though, as expectation for collective orientation might be even higher for mothers today.

3. Discuss the manifest and latent functions behind everyday activities, using examples from three different aspects of your life: e.g., work, school, family, and/or social world. For example, discuss the manifest and latent functions of (1) doing your homework (school life), (2) visiting your parents on the weekend (family life), (3) going to clubs (social life), and/or (4) working.

4. Think about your own patterns of consumption and the extent that they reflect (latent) "status" as opposed to (manifest) "utility" functions. How does this reflect and interrelate with the issue of "rational" as opposed to "nonrational" motivation as well? Using concrete examples of popular advertising campaigns or prominent commercials, discuss the extent to which advertisers speak to rational and nonrational motivation, as well as the "manifest" and "latent" functions of advertising in general.

5. Discuss the extent to which you think that goals are determined by the overarching culture of a society as opposed to smaller social groups or subcultures. What are specific examples of different types of cultural and subcultural means and goals? Do you think that the means and goals of society are as easily identifiable or clear-cut as Merton seems to assume? How so or why not? If not, are there any cultural common denominators that you think transcend various subcultural means and goals? How would you go about researching the means and goals of particular social groups and/or subcultures?

3

CRITICAL THEORY

Culture is only true when implicitly critical, and the mind which forgets this revenges itself in the critics it breeds.

~Adorno (1967:23)

Many of us find living in a modern, industrial society to be pleasant. While such societies certainly are not without their problems, countries like the United States, France, England, and Japan offer their citizens many avenues for educational and occupational success as well as a seemingly unending supply of technological advances and modern conveniences. If ever there was a time and a place to enjoy the "good life," it is now and in democratic nations such as those noted above. For theorists in the critical tradition, however, life in the "land of opportunity" is not all that it is cracked up to be. On the contrary, critical theorists find in so-called progress a source of domination and dehumanization.[1] For them, culture, science, and technology are ideological forces that distort consciousness and, thus, prevent individuals from recognizing and satisfying their true human interests. So, the next time you tune in to your favorite show on your widescreen TV, download tunes to your MP3 player, or marvel over the easy access to your cash at the ATM, keep in mind that the pleasures such conveniences bring are not without potential pitfalls. In fact, these technological wonders are in part responsible for perpetuating the very dehumanizing conditions that they are advertised to alleviate.

In this chapter we outline the main arguments of critical theory by emphasizing the work of three of its leading exponents. Before turning to a discussion of the central theoretical ideas, however, we first provide a look into the personal lives of those who were most responsible for shaping their development. Doing so will offer a glimpse into the historical conditions that profoundly shaped their outlook as they crafted this branch of social theory.

HORKHEIMER, ADORNO, AND MARCUSE: BIOGRAPHICAL SKETCHES

SOURCE: © Getty Images; used with permission.

Max Horkheimer (1895–1973)

Max Horkheimer was born in Stuttgart, Germany, on February 14, 1895. His father was a successful businessman and owner of several textile factories. While his father intended for him to take over the family business, Max's radical political leanings and sympathies with the working class left him ill equipped for embracing the role of a capitalist. Instead, the younger Horkheimer pursued an academic career, taking up graduate studies in philosophy and psychology while attending the University of Frankfurt. During the course of his studies Horkheimer also spent a year at the University of Freiburg, where he worked with the preeminent philosopher Edmund Husserl and his assistant, Martin Heidegger, who would go on to become a leading intellectual in his own right.

After completing his doctorate in 1925, Horkheimer began work at the University of Frankfurt as an unsalaried lecturer, and then, in 1928, he was hired as a salaried member of the faculty. The start of his academic career also saw his marriage to Rose Riekher, with whom he had developed a ten-year relationship. Eight years his senior, Rose was the elder Horkheimer's private secretary. Father and son had clashed over the relationship from its beginning, not least of which because of Rose's humble family background. Yet, for Max, his attraction to Rose only confirmed his feelings of compassion for the plight of

---

[1]It is important to note that "critical" is not used here as a generic, derogative term. Critical theory, instead, refers to a specific theoretical tradition that first took shape in Frankfurt, Germany.

the working class and his distaste for "domineering businessmen like his father" (Wiggershaus 1994:44). His personal identification with the injustices suffered by those "without money" and sense of culpability on the part of the capitalist class is revealed in passages such as the following taken from his personal notes:

> Without money, without any economic security, we are at their mercy. It is certainly a dreadful punishment: having the daily grind wearing you down, being shackled to trivial business, having petty worries day and night, being dependent on the most despicable people. Not just we ourselves, but all of those we love and for whom we are responsible fall with us into this daily treadmill. We become victims of stupidity and sadism. (Quoted in Wiggershaus 1994:48)

Theodor Adorno (1903–1969)

Sharing Horkheimer's deeply felt concerns over social and economic inequalities was Theodor Adorno, whom he had met in the early 1920s. Adorno also shared his friend's comfortable family origins. He was born on September 11, 1903, in Frankfurt. Adorno's mother, who was descended from a member of the Corsican nobility, had been a successful singer before her marriage, while his father was the owner of a wholesale wine business. Following in his mother's footsteps (and his aunt's, a well-known pianist who lived with his family), the precocious Adorno began his formal studies of music composition at the age of sixteen. The following year he entered the University of Frankfurt, where he studied philosophy, psychology, sociology, and musicology. Although he earned his doctorate in philosophy in 1924, it was in the fields of music criticism and aesthetics that Adorno made his first mark. Indeed, he published nearly a hundred articles on the topics between 1921 and 1932, while his first publication in philosophy appeared

SOURCE: © Getty Images; used with permission.

only in 1933. Perhaps it should come as no surprise, then, that Adorno's original professional ambitions lay with becoming a composer and concert pianist (Wiggershaus 1994:70–72).

Adorno's interests in composing and performing music, however, were tied to his broader philosophy of aesthetics. For Adorno, music, or at least "real" music, offered an expression of truth itself, a truth defined in dialectic terms such that the value of music is measured by its freedom from conformity to existing forms. The rarified place Adorno held for music, and art more generally, stemmed from his view that it alone was capable of transcending the alienated, "soulless" world ushered in by the advance of capitalism and totalitarian political systems. In classic Marxist fashion, Adorno saw in dominant musical forms a reflection of existing material conditions or property relations that fueled the exploitation of one class by another. Thus, in order to perform its socially progressive function, music must escape the restraints imposed by previous forms. It is in this vein that Adorno lavished praise on the work of the pianist Arnold Schoenberg, in whose development of the twelve-tone scale and modernist compositions he saw a critique of corrupted bourgeois society. Meanwhile, he relentlessly attacked popular, "standardized" music for allegedly dumbing-down the masses and perpetuating oppressive social conditions.

Herbert Marcuse (1898–1979)

SOURCE: © Bettmann/CORBIS; used with permission.

The third figure to be considered in this section is Herbert Marcuse. Born in Berlin on July 19, 1898, Marcuse, like his counterparts, was raised in a well-to-do German family. His mother was the daughter of a factory owner, while his father had worked his way up to become part owner of a textile factory and a real estate entrepreneur. Marcuse served in the military during World War I, although because of vision problems he was spared from combat. As he witnessed the outbreak of strikes, riots, and general social unrest in Berlin during the war years, his views became increasingly politicized and he joined the Social Democratic Party (SPD), a socialist political party that represented working-class interests. Discontented with the actions and policies of the SPD, Marcuse dedicated himself to his studies at Humboldt University in Berlin, where he took up modern Germany history. Soon thereafter he left for Freiburg, where he studied philosophy and economics, completing his doctorate in 1922. It was here that Marcuse met Horkheimer and, with him, attended Husserl's lectures.

After earning his degree, Marcuse returned to Berlin, where for the next six years he worked in the book business, his father having provided him with a share in a publishing company. Active in literary and artistic circles, Marcuse's path took a fateful turn upon reading Martin Heidegger's newly published *Being and Time* (1927). He saw in Heidegger's work a crucial addition to Marxist theory, which had come to be the focal point of his intellectual outlook. Determined to pursue an academic career in philosophy, Marcuse abandoned the book business and returned to Freiburg with his wife and young son to study again with Husserl as well as with Heidegger, with whom he served as an assistant.

Having met one another during the course of their respective studies, these three figures' relationship was solidified through their association with the Institute of Social Research at the University of Frankfurt in Germany. The Institute was established on February 3, 1923, through the patronage of Felix Weil, the son of a wealthy grain merchant who, to his father's displeasure, sought to advance the ideals of socialism. It is here that the roots of critical theory, a Marxist-inspired social philosophy, were planted. While early on the Institute was home to a number of leading intellectuals, including the psychologist Erich Fromm (1900–1980), it would come to be dominated by Horkheimer, Adorno, and Marcuse. Together, they reshaped the direction of the Institute, changing what was initially a diverse, empirically oriented research program dedicated to reappraising Marxist theory in light of the defeat of the communist revolution throughout central Europe. With Horkheimer's appointment as director in 1930, a new course was established for the Institute. The study of history and economics was replaced with a critical social philosophy that attacked the scientific enterprise as a form of bourgeois ideology. Thus, the empirical sciences were regarded not only as incapable of revealing a true understanding of social life, but also of sanctioning the status quo and ushering in new forms of "technocratic" domination (Bottomore 1984:29). Far from leading to progress and the emancipation of humanity, science was leading civilization "into a new kind of barbarism" (Horkheimer and Adorno 2002/1944:xiv). Thus, the "critical" in critical theory ultimately refers to a critique of empirical sciences and the philosophy of positivism on which they are based.

To account for the critical theorists' rejection of science, and positivism more generally, we need to recall the broader social milieu in which the Institute was formed. Not only had the communist revolution, modeled on Marx's scientific prophecy, failed to turn Europe into a utopia, but the Bolsheviks' victory in Russia and Germany's defeat in World War I brought in their wake ruthless, totalitarian regimes. While the communist dream was turning into a nightmare under the dictatorship of Josef Stalin, the crippling of the German economy and sense of national humiliation left that nation vulnerable to the rise of fascism and with it, the rise of Hitler to political power. Moreover, the rampant anti-Semitism that spread through Germany and elsewhere in Europe had a profound impact on the Frankfurt School, for all of its leading members were Jewish.

Well aware of the impending danger the Nazis posed (his house had been occupied by Nazi storm-troops), Horkheimer left for Geneva, Switzerland, where he conducted the affairs of the Institute in exile. In the spring of 1933, the Gestapo (the secret police) closed the Institute and seized its possessions under the charge that it had "encouraged activities hostile to the state" (Wiggershaus 1994:128). Horkheimer was summarily expelled from his position in Frankfurt. Adorno was fired from his teaching position because he was "half-Jewish" (his father was Jewish), at which time he left for London, while Marcuse joined Horkheimer and the Institute in Geneva in 1933. The Institute's relocation to Geneva would be temporary, however. Concerned about the spread of fascism and anti-Semitism throughout Europe, Horkheimer immigrated to New York in May 1934, where he established a new home for the Institute at Columbia University. Marcuse arrived two months later, and Adorno in 1938.

During the next seven years, Horkheimer and his associates worked on a limited number of studies while publishing few essays and articles. Maintaining the academic independence of the Institute while meeting the expectations of the officials of Columbia University was proving to be a difficult task. For many of the Institute's members, affiliation with the University was a mixed blessing. Although it provided needed resources, the type of applied social research expected by the University was not fitting to the temperaments of the ideologically committed critical theorists. Moreover, increasing financial pressures as well as mounting personal and intellectual differences further jeopardized developing productive, collaborative research projects. Sensing the widening gap between his vision for the Institute and the realities that accompanied ties to external institutions, Horkheimer relocated to Pacific Palisades, just outside Los Angeles, in April 1941. Marcuse arrived the following month, and Adorno in November. Marcuse's stay would be short-lived, however. Receiving only a minimal stipend from the Institute's endowment, he returned to the East Coast, where he began work for the government in the Office of Strategic Services. Here he was assigned the task of determining ways of depicting foreign enemies in the press and in films.

Marcuse's move to Washington, D.C., marked the beginning of his permanent separation from the Institute. Although he desperately wanted to return to Los Angeles and continue his association with Horkheimer, his theoretical views were moving away from Horkheimer's and, even more so, Adorno's. Moreover, the need for steady income kept him working for the State Department until 1954, at which time, at the age of fifty-six, he was offered a full professorship from Brandeis University. In 1965 he took a position at the University of California, San Diego, where he remained until his retirement in 1976. His early years in San Diego sparked much controversy. Not surprisingly, his Marxist views were met with much resistance from the politically conservative community surrounding the University. With the Vietnam War intensifying fears over the spread of communism, some local organizations sought to have Marcuse, nearly seventy years old, expelled from the city, while other residents were content with sending him death threats. Meanwhile, then-governor Ronald Reagan, who regarded Marcuse as an enemy of the country, and the Board of Regents pressured the University to fire Marcuse, but to no avail. In an important sense, however, Marcuse was a real threat to conservative defenders of the status quo. By the late 1960s he had become the most widely read social theorist among those fighting for progressive change. (His books *Eros and Civilization* [1955] and *One-Dimensional Man* [1964], excerpted below, garnered the most attention.) With his fame spreading across Europe and America, antiwar activists, feminists, and disciples of the New Left and Black Power movements all saw in his writings an explanation of their discontent and a justification for their political action. And it was in the protests of "the outcasts and outsiders, the exploited and persecuted of other races and other colors, the unemployed and the unemployable" that Marcuse placed a guarded hope for the establishment of a truly democratic society (1964:256). He died of a stroke in 1979, with his hopes unfulfilled.

For their part, while in Los Angeles Horkheimer and Adorno produced several important works including *The Authoritarian Personality* (1950) and *Dialectic of Enlightenment* (2002/1944), a masterpiece of critical theory. The former was the product of a large-scale research project and appeared as part of the *Studies in Prejudice* series that was edited by Horkheimer and Samuel Flowerman. The series examined anti-Semitism from a range of perspectives including psychology, sociology, history, and psychoanalysis. In *The Authoritarian Personality*, Adorno and his coauthors administered extensive questionnaires and interviews in an effort to determine the personality traits of persons prone to harboring anti-Semitic views in particular and fascist attitudes more generally. In developing the "F-scale"(fascism scale), the authors concluded that socialization within the family as well as broader social conditions shape an individual's potential for developing a "fascist" personality—one that is characterized, among other things, by submissiveness, a rigid conformity to dominant values, and contempt for "outsiders" and "deviants."

In the *Dialectic of Enlightenment*, Horkheimer and Adorno developed a principal theme of critical theory, namely, that the Enlightenment had produced contradictory developments. Not only did it break the shackles of traditions and religious superstitions, ushering in an epoch of progress through the rise of science, technological advances, and the cultivation of individual freedom; the Age of Reason also created its own Frankenstein: the "irrationality of rationality." In other words, reason, far from offering a path to human liberation, had been transformed into an irresistible force for new forms of domination. "Enlightenment, understood in the widest sense as the advance of thought, has always aimed at liberating human beings from fear and installing them as masters. Yet the wholly enlightened earth is radiant with triumphant calamity" (Horkheimer and Adorno 2002/1944:1). Driven by reason and rationality, social life was becoming increasingly bureaucratized and dehumanized, while ever more efficient means of death and destruction were being deployed, as demonstrated by the horrors of World War II and the Nazi campaign of genocide.

With the book's translation into English in the 1970s, the authors of the *Dialectic of Enlightenment* became iconic figures among the New Left activists. Their claim that the Enlightenment, instead of fostering individual autonomy, "is totalitarian" struck a chord with those challenging the legitimacy of the existing social order. Yet, Horkheimer and Adorno's response to their newfound acclaim contrasted with that of Marcuse. As head of the Institute, Horkheimer had early on established a policy of political abstinence. Not only were associates to refrain from engaging in political activity or supporting the political efforts of others, but even their writings were to contain no direct references to ongoing political events or explicit condemnations of governmental or economic systems, whether fascist or capitalist (Wiggershaus 1994:133). No doubt Horkheimer's avoidance of activism was shaped, at least in part, by his "outsider" status, first as a Jew in Germany and later as an émigré living in the United States Nonetheless, Horkheimer would become increasingly pessimistic over the prospects for achieving truly progressive change and saw in the social movements of the 1960s no hope for realizing an end to repressive and dehumanizing social conditions. As for Adorno, his views on political engagement paralleled those of his friend and collaborator. Perhaps Adorno's opinion regarding those who invoked his ideas could be considered even bleaker as he saw in their actions and ambitions the very authoritarian tendencies that he himself had sought to expose.

Such were the views of two men who had returned to Frankfurt and reestablished the Institute of Social Research. Horkheimer resumed his duties at the University in 1950 and remained on the faculty until his retirement in 1959. He died in 1973. Adorno returned to Germany in 1953. Although the following decade saw his attitude toward the growing number of student radicals become increasingly hostile, he remained active at the University until his untimely death in 1969, at the age of sixty-six.

INTELLECTUAL INFLUENCES AND CORE IDEAS

In developing their theoretical perspective, the critical theorists drew from a number of scholars. In addition to those already mentioned (Edmund Husserl and Martin Heidegger), their works owe a debt to the idealist philosophies of Immanuel Kant and Georg Hegel, as well as to their contemporary Georg Lukács (1885–1971). Lukács's groundbreaking book *History and Class Consciousness* (1923) played a pivotal role in the critical theorists' reevaluation of Karl Marx's concept of class consciousness and ideology. In this chapter, however, we confine ourselves to a discussion of the three scholars who arguably made the most decisive impact on the central ideas of the Frankfurt School thinkers: Karl Marx (1818–1893), Max Weber (1864–1920), and Sigmund Freud (1856–1939). To be sure, the critical theorists' mining of the ideas of Marx, Freud, and Weber was by no means identical. Nevertheless, that their perspectives profoundly influenced the work of the critical theorists is undeniable.

Marx, Weber, and the Revolution That Wasn't

The critical theorists developed a framework that at once extends and departs from central Marxist ideas. Like Marx, the critical theorists saw in modern, industrial societies an oppressive, dehumanizing social order. And like Marx, their aim was not simply to construct a theory capable of explaining the real workings of society, but, in Horkheimer's words, the goal of critical theory "is man's emancipation from slavery" (Horkheimer 1972b:246). Yet, the critical theorists offered a picture of the sources of domination and the struggle to overcome them that was very different from that posited by Marx.

According to Marx's theoretical system, "historical materialism," "the history of all hitherto existing society is the history of class struggles" (1848/1978:473). In other words, the dynamics of historical changes are rooted in opposing class interests that are themselves a product of the distribution of private property. With private property comes economic classes—those who own the means of production and those who work for them—that necessarily are pitted against each other. While it is in the interest of the former to maintain the status quo, it is in the interest of the latter to radically transform the existing distribution of resources and thereby bring an end to their exploitation and subordination. History has evolved according to this dialectic process, wherein every stage of development contains within it the seeds of its own destruction, as private property perpetually ignites economic conflicts that inevitably will sweep away existing social arrangements and give birth to new classes of oppressors and the oppressed.

In the capitalist stage of development, society is divided into "two great classes": the bourgeoisie or capitalist and the proletariat or worker. However, the class conflict between these two factions was to be like no other previous struggle, for the proletariat heralded the redemption of humankind from the "wretchedness," exploitation, and alienation that, for Marx, characterized capitalism. As they made up a vast majority of the world's population, the victory of the proletariat over bourgeoisie was inevitable. In the wake of their victory, the proletariat would abolish private property—the catalyst of class conflict—and thus usher in "the end of prehistory." Marx maintained that once the means of production becomes collectively owned, exploitation of the worker is no longer possible. This is because the surplus value (i.e., profit) produced by the worker is not appropriated or siphoned off by an individual owner. Instead, it is distributed among the workers themselves. Alienation is also ended, as the worker, now a part owner of the enterprise, is able to direct the production process and maintain control over the products she creates. In turn, the worker is no longer estranged from herself and the "species being" (the creative essence of humanity). Finally, the competition for profit that characterizes bourgeois capitalism is brought to a close and, with it, recurring economic crises. Periods of "boom or bust" and their accompanying disruptions to employment are replaced by a more stable form of economic planning that produces according to the needs of the population and not the whims of an unpredictable market. Thus, the communist revolution was the historically necessary path to utopia.

This (albeit simplified) overview reveals the central role Marx assigned to economic relations. Indeed, for Marx the mode of economic production formed the "base" of society on which rests the "superstructure," or "the social, political, and intellectual life processes in general" (1859/1978:4). The superstructure, in short, consists of everything noneconomic in nature, such as a society's legal, political, and educational systems, as well as its stock of common-sense knowledge. As a result, an individual's very consciousness, how one views the world and defines one's interests, is determined not by one's own subjectivity. Instead, ideas about the world and one's place in it are structured by, or built into, the *objective* class position occupied, for "it is not the consciousness of men that determines their being, but, on the contrary, their social being that determines their consciousness" (1859/1978:4). This perspective, moreover, yields a radical conclusion: "The ideas of the ruling class are in every epoch the ruling ideas" (1846/1978:172). In other words, Marx maintains that the dominant economic class controls not only a society's means of material production, but the production of ideas as well.

This raises a vexing obstacle for prophesizing the downfall of capitalism. For how can the working class develop a revolutionary consciousness when a society's prevailing or dominant ideas (regarding private property rights or market competition, for example) serve to legitimate the very system that they are allegedly destined to overthrow? While Marx portended that historically necessary economic crises would instill the necessary class consciousness, later Marxists noted that changing economic circumstances alone are incapable of mechanically transforming the consciousness of the working class. Thus, Horkheimer concluded (following Lukács) that

> the situation of the proletariat is . . . no guarantee of correct knowledge. The proletariat may indeed have experience of meaninglessness in the form of continuing and increasing wretchedness and injustice in its own life. Yet this awareness is prevented from becoming a social force by the differentiation of social structure which is still imposed from above and by the opposition between personal class interests. . . . Even to the proletariat the world superficially seems quite different than it really is. (1972a:213, 214).

Given this state of affairs, Horkheimer and his colleagues looked elsewhere for the sources of emancipation, and, not surprisingly, they found them in critical theory. This signaled a major shift from orthodox Marxism, as the critical theorists abandoned analyses of economic conditions and no longer cast the working class in the role of savior of humanity. Moreover, in placing what limited hope they had for the establishment of a just society in the hands of critical theoreticians, they drew inspiration from the work of Georg Hegel and his followers—the Young Hegelians—whose philosophy Marx subjected to a scathing critique. In essence, the critical theorists turned away from Marx's doctrine of historical materialism to Hegelian idealism to better focus their analysis of culture and ideology, for it was not economic arrangements that were primarily responsible for the barbarism of humanity but ideas and the irrationality of reason. But if the critical theorists were skeptical of the revolutionary potential of the working class itself, or of the ability of a revolutionary communist party vanguard to advance "correct knowledge" of the proletariat's condition (as Lukács theorized), then it would be left to them to realize a free and peaceful society. For critical theory "was not just an extension of proletarian thought, but a means of thinking about the social totality that would aid in the movement from the empirical proletariat's necessarily still partial view of society from its own class position to the achievement of a classless society, one not structured on injustice" (Calhoun 1995:21).

Nevertheless, aside from asserting that the task of the critical theorist is "to reduce the tension between his own insight and oppressed humanity in whose service he thinks" (Horkheimer 1972:221) or claiming that "truth becomes clearly evident in the person of the theoretician" (ibid.:216), Horkheimer and his associates would fail to offer a specific account of the mechanisms for social change and who, precisely, the agents of such change would be.[2] Exactly how the critical theorist was to enlighten the class "in whose service he thinks" was a question that remained unanswered. This neglect would in turn heighten the sense of pessimism that pervaded the critical theorists' political outlook.

The bleak (if not realistic) picture of the future painted by the critical theorists was not simply a product of the shortcomings of their theoretical model. Instead, it stemmed more directly from what they saw as the changing nature of domination. It was not the exploitation inherent in capitalism that was responsible for the oppression of humanity but rather forms of thought, and in particular, the totalitarianism of reason and rationality. Here again the critical theorists draw from the work of Hegel as well as from Max Weber. For his part, Hegel argued that the essence of reality lies in thought or ideas, because it is only in and through the concepts that order our experiences that experiences, as such, are known. Thus, as our knowledge changes, so does the reality of experience. Moreover, Hegel combined aspects of Christian theology and Enlightenment philosophy to argue that as history evolves through a dialectical progression of ideas, humankind's knowledge comes ever closer to the perfected realization of "Spirit" or "Absolute Idea" as revealed by God. The perfectibility of humankind is reached once the utopia of "Truth" and "Reason" resolves the contradictions between ideas and reality. At this point in the evolution of consciousness or ideas, humankind will become truly free as we become fully self-conscious and able to recognize that the objective world is a product of human creation.

In suggesting that history is marked by a separation of the True from the real, it follows that we are alienated from Absolute Idea or Spirit. The alienation of humanity and the obstacles to realizing a perfected social order lie in distorted consciousness. As we noted earlier, the critical theorists located the source of distorted consciousness in the "irrationality of rationality." Reason itself had become corrupted, leaving individuals unable to **negate** or develop a critique of "objective truths," which alone enables us to resist the domination of the status quo. In short, the power of negative thinking to

---

[2]Jürgen Habermas (see Chapter 9), a sometime student of Adorno and leading contemporary theorist, addressed this very issue in his reworking of critical theory.

subvert the established social order and the oppressive conditions it fosters has been lost. Here, the critical theorists draw not only from Hegel but also from Weber. For it was Weber who offered a vision of the future in which "not summer's bloom lies ahead of us, but rather a polar night of icy darkness and hardness" (Weber 1958:128).

To what did Weber attribute his own pessimistic outlook? According to Weber, the development of capitalism in the West was predicated on an instrumental worldview that had ushered in an increasingly impersonal and bureaucratic society. This worldview was born out of the Protestant ethic that originally had promised individuals a path to religious salvation in the form of economic success. Eventually, the religious injunction to carry out one's worldly affairs on the basis of methodical and rational planning was shed. The ethical imperative to avoid idleness and enjoyment of luxuries while saving and investing one's wealth in service to God no longer stood as divinely granted proof of one's state of grace. Profit and efficiency were now twin demands that were pursued for their own sake. The rational and bureaucratic structures necessary to ignite the growth of modern capitalism rendered obsolete the religious spirit that first had imbued it with meaning. Unleashed from its religious moorings, the process of rationalization transformed the West into a disenchanted "iron cage" from which the modern individual is left with little power to escape. As it is one of the most compelling passages ever written in sociology, we quote Weber at length:

> The Puritan wanted to work in a calling; we are forced to do so. For when asceticism was carried out of monastic cells into everyday life, and began to dominate worldly morality, it did its part in building the tremendous cosmos of the modern economic order. This order is now bound to the technical and economic conditions of machine production which to-day [*sic*] determine the lives of all the individuals who are born into this mechanism, not only those directly concerned with economic acquisition, with irresistible force. . . .
>
> Since asceticism undertook to remodel the world and to work out its ideals in the world, material goods have gained an increasing and finally an inexorable power over the lives of men as at no previous period in history. To-day [*sic*.] the spirit of religious asceticism—whether finally, who knows?—has escaped from the cage. But victorious capitalism, since it rests on mechanical foundations, needs its support no longer. . . . For the last stage of this cultural development, it might well be truly said: "Specialists without spirit, sensualists without heart; this nullity images that it has attained a level of civilization never before achieved." (1904/1958:180, 181)

Along with this transition, "formal rationality" supplanted "substantive rationality" as the motivating force in human action. While substantive rationality provides for an ethic or value principle according to which actions are guided, formal rationality is grounded in rule-bound, matter-of-fact calculations. Thus, substantive rationality establishes ultimate ends that give meaning to our actions, while formal rationality is based on establishing impersonal, calculable procedures. Formal rationality is the lifeblood of the bureaucratic administration of human affairs. And for Weber, it is precisely the bureaucratic form of rationality that is most responsible for creating an oppressive, overly routinized, and depersonalized society. Bureaucracy is the "iron cage" that has stifled individual freedom.

This theme has formed the core of critical theory. For instance, Horkheimer drew a distinction between "subjective reason" and "objective reason."[3] Parallel to Weber's notion of formal or instrumental rationality, **subjective reason** is "essentially concerned with means and ends, with the adequacy of procedures for purposes more or less taken

---

[3]Horkheimer's distinction between subjective and objective reason parallels not only Weber's discussion of rationality but also the work of his contemporary Karl Mannheim (1893–1947), who drew a contrast between "functional rationality" and "substantial rationality." (See Karl Mannheim, *Man and Society in an Age of Reconstruction*, London: Routledge and Kegan.)

for granted and supposedly self-explanatory. It attaches little importance to the question whether the purposes as such are reasonable" (Horkheimer 1947:3). While subjective reason may allow us to determine the most efficient way of achieving our goals, it cannot in itself offer a guide for determining what is a "reasonable" goal. Subjective reason is the guiding force of the technician, the bureaucrat, who, while adept at carrying out functional, procedural rules, is blind to the ethical basis of them. It is the form of reason that at its most heinous allows for the callous torturing of others, demonstrated by the Holocaust during Horkheimer's time and today by the war with Iraq.

Conversely, **objective reason** speaks to the relative value of the *ends* of action and thus provides a basis for determining what is ethical, right, and just. It is premised on the notion that

> the existence of reason [is] a force not only in the individual mind but also in the objective world—in relations among human beings, between social classes, in social institutions, and in nature and its manifestations. . . . It aim[s] at evolving a comprehensive system, or hierarchy, of all beings, including man and his aims. The degree of reasonableness of a man's life could be determined according to its harmony with this totality. Its objective structure, and not just man and his purposes, was to be the measuring rod for individual thoughts and actions. (Horkheimer 1947:4)

For his part, Marcuse (1941) emphasized the distinction between "individualistic rationality" and "technological rationality." (The latter term was adopted by most of the Frankfurt theorists.) Analogous to Horkheimer's notion of objective reason, he defined **individualistic rationality** as "a critical and oppositional attitude that derived freedom of action from the unrestricted liberty of thought and conscience and measured all social standards and relations by the individual's rational self-interest" (1941:433). Individualistic rationality allows for negating all that is established in order to critically understand one's world, develop personal objectives, and achieve them through rational methods. The individual's ability to transcend the status quo was "liquidated," however, as the organization of society moved from the era of liberal, competitive capitalism to industrial, corporate capitalism. In the earlier stage, an individual's self-directed efforts enabled him to develop his unique identity and potential while contributing to the needs of society. In the modern era of mechanized, rationalized production, it is society that creates and "administers" all the individual's needs. And "with the disappearance of independent economic subjects, the subject as such disappears" (Horkheimer 1941:377).

This shift in the form of production altered individual consciousness, as technological rationality replaced individualistic forms of thought.[4] **Technological rationality** is marked by the scientific approach to all human affairs. Social relations as well as humanity's relationship to nature are now understood as "problems" to be efficiently solved. And with solutions comes control. While this form of reason has led to unprecedented material gains, under its sway "individuals are stripped of their individuality, not by external compulsion, but by the very rationality under which they live" (Marcuse 1941:421). As Marcuse notes:

> Autonomy of reason loses its meaning in the same measure as the thoughts, feelings and actions of men are shaped by the technical requirements of the apparatus which they have

---

[4]Marcuse's argument here recalls Marx's theory of the relationship between forms of economic production and consciousness. However, unlike Marx, Marcuse and the critical theorists did not contend that consciousness was tied to particular class positions, for no one can escape the numbing effects of technological rationality.

themselves created. Reason has found its resting place in the system of standardized control, production, and consumption. . . . Rationality here calls for unconditional compliance and coordination, and consequently, the truth values related to this rationality imply the subordination of thought to pregiven external standards. . . .

The point is that today the apparatus to which the individual is to adjust and adapt himself is so rational that individual protest and liberation appear not only as hopeless but as utterly irrational. The system of life created by modern industry is one of the highest expediency, convenience, and efficiency. Reason, once defined in these terms, becomes equivalent to an activity which perpetuates this world. Rational behavior becomes identical with a matter-of-factness which teaches reasonable submissiveness and thus guarantees getting along in the prevailing order. (ibid.: 421, 423)

Technological rationality represented a worldview that had come to dominate all spheres of life. Unquestioned conformity to the dictates of efficiency, convenience, and profit now "govern[s] performance not only in the factories and shops, but also in the offices, schools, assemblies, and finally, in the realm of relaxation and entertainment" (ibid.:421). For the critical theorists, this meant that "reason [had] liquidated itself as an agency of ethical, moral, and religious insight" (Horkheimer 1947:18). Scientific-technological progress had become the god of modern society, and only a "crank" would refuse to worship before its idols. Paradoxically, then, it was science itself—the bastion of reason—that had promoted the destruction of humanity. Indeed, the critical theorists maintained that science, in claiming that the empirical world can be objectively known, could at best produce a superficial understanding of the natural and social worlds. Based in "traditional theory" and "positivism," science mistook the world of appearances or "facts" for the world of essences. However, "the so-called facts ascertained by quantitative methods, which the positivists are inclined to regard as the only scientific ones, are often surface phenomena that obscure rather than disclose the underlying reality" (ibid.:82). Moreover, in treating "surface phenomena" as necessary, inescapable givens, science is unable to transcend the established order and thus reproduces an oppressive social system.

In contrast, the critical theorists claimed that all knowledge is finite; there are no timeless, empirical truths subject to scientific discovery and proof. Because objective knowledge is nothing but a fiction (albeit a comforting one), it is imperative for theorists to recognize that fact and value cannot be separated. Unlike the aloof intellectual who falsely proclaims the truth on the basis of his supposedly neutral and detached reflections on society, the critical theorist found truth "in personal thought and action, in concrete historical activity" (Horkheimer 1972:222). Departing from Weber's claim (and many others, including Karl Mannheim), the critical theorists argued that the notion of a free-floating intellectual, who somehow stands above or apart from the object of his investigation, is a self-aggrandizing myth. It serves to mask the real, although unintended, social consequences of the scientist's findings—perpetuation of a system of technological domination. For their part, the critical theorists recognized that their ideas were equally influenced by the conditions in which they lived and the concepts by which they thought. Thus, they abandoned all pretenses to objectivity and instead sought to develop a theoretical system morally committed to the emancipation of humanity. Their sword was Reason, for it alone cleared the path to the ultimate value: individual freedom.

Technology and science had reneged on their promise to usher in a just and reasonable world. While industrial and administrative advances had made possible the domination of nature and production of wealth on a scale that would have been unimaginable

Photo 3.4   Technological rationality at its best . . . or worst. Securing international peace through the threat of mutual annihilation.

SOURCE: Courtesy of the U.S. Marine Corp.; used with permission.

to the early prophets of the Enlightenment, modern society continued to be plagued by inequality, oppression, destruction, and poverty. While science has made it possible to feed, educate, and care for all the inhabitants of the world, many are left to starve, illiterate, poor, and ravaged by preventable illness. And for those whose "needs" are satisfied, "in the unjust state of society the powerless and pliability of the masses increase with the quantity of goods allocated to them" (Horkheimer and Adorno 2002/1944:xvii). It is no longer possible to justify—to find reasonable—the sacrifices of the many for the privileges of the few in the name of progress. The root of the inhumanity of the modern condition was not a result of a lack of economic or scientific development. Rather, it was the result of technological or instrumental rationality coming to form the basis of the dominant ideology. In other words, the logic of technological rationality, which emphasizes means and aims at answering the question "how?" was now the authority for determining legitimate courses of action. But this form of rationality is divorced from ethics and value judgments; it is not oriented to answering the question "why?" As the dominant ideology, however, the beliefs, concepts, and worldview that inform technological rationality serve as the taken-for-granted reality that shapes social life more generally. It provides the common-sense knowledge by which all groups understand the nature of society and the relationship between individuals. And it is this pervasive ideology, and not class-based exploitation as Marx contended, that is primarily responsible for sustaining oppression in modern society. Thus, it was to ideology that the critical theorists turned when attempting to articulate a theory of social change that envisioned a free and just society.

Significant Others | C. Wright Mills (1916–1962): An American Critic

While German philosophers planted the roots of critical theory, their influence was not confined within national boundaries. In America, the sociologist who most took up the charge of the critical theorists was C. Wright Mills. Born in Texas, Mills's foray into academics was launched when he won a research fellowship to attend the University of Wisconsin. After earning his doctorate, Mills went on to Columbia University, where he remained until his untimely death at the age of forty-six. Despite his passing at a young age, his penetrating analyses of American political, social, and intellectual life have led at least one reputable observer to consider Mills "the greatest sociologist the United States has ever produced" (Mills 1963:20).

To what did Mills owe such a reputation? Committed to a vision of a more just and moral society, he was throughout his career a relentless critic of the self-congratulatory hypocrisy that in his view pervaded American culture. His condemnation of the status quo, not surprisingly, made Mills his share of enemies in the "Establishment." For instance, in *The Power Elite* (1958), he detailed the undemocratic character of America's allegedly democratic governance. Far from being subject to the "will of the people," American politics is becoming dominated more and more by a small, interconnected group of political, economic, and military leaders. Power has become increasingly centralized within "the big three" institutions, while the public or *demos* has been transformed into an impotent "mass society," and elected representatives in Congress have become increasingly servile and ineffectual. In American society, important decisions are made by a more or less unified circle of individuals who move from leadership positions in one institutional domain to another. One need only look at the current roster of cabinet members in the executive branch to see how the revolving door works.

In *White Collar* (1951), Mills turns his attention to the plight of the American middle classes who, owing to their "status panic," are unable to realize a meaningful existence. A sense of powerlessness often characterizes the growing ranks of white-collar professionals as their daily lives have become increasingly routinized and regimented under the demands of bureaucratic efficiency. While white-collar professionals may have achieved a semblance of economic security, they have traded it for a sense of purpose and the ability to control their destiny. Alienated from their work and insecure about their status, white-collar professionals often turn to the world of leisure to provide succor. For Mills, this state of affairs has produced psychologically and politically fragmented individuals who are unable to recognize the true sources of their discontent. Reminiscent of the

Frankfurt School theorists, he feared that the malaise of the middle classes and their embracing of a vacuous mass culture left society vulnerable to the rise of authoritarianism.

Not one to avoid controversy, Mills turned his critical outlook onto his own peers. His classic introduction to sociology, *The Sociological Imagination* (1959), not only offers the definitive statement on the task of the discipline; it also reproaches those who are charged with carrying it out. First, Mills exalts sociology as uniquely able to "grasp history and biography and the relations between the two within society" (1959:6). In doing so, the sociological imagination enables its possessor to make the essential distinction between "the personal troubles of milieu" and "the public issues of social structure" (ibid.). Yet, to Mills's dismay, the promise of sociology was being lost, to the extent that academic research is rooted in an "abstracted empiricism" that concerns itself less with addressing pressing human needs than with uncovering scientific facts. Again recalling the misgivings of the critical theorists, Mills saw in his fellow sociologists' quest for facts an abdication of their social responsibility to advance a more humane, democratic society.

This ideology is disseminated primarily through the **culture industry**. This "industry" encompasses all those sectors involved in the creation and distribution of mass-culture products: television, film, radio, music, magazines, newspapers, books, and the advertisements that sell them. Geared toward entertaining and pacifying the masses, the culture industry administers "mass deception" by churning out a never-ending supply of mass-produced, standardized commodities that "aborts and silences criticism" (Bottomore 1984:19). Manufactured movie and television stars act as its leading spokespersons, promoting its superficial, conformist vision of the happy life both in their performances and in their revolving appearances on the cycle of vacuous, ever-the-same talk shows. Suggestive of the effectiveness of the culture industry, most people seem to prefer its familiar, predictable offerings to alternatives that require active contemplation. For instance, how many TV show theme songs can you hum? How many Mozart concertos?

Tied directly to the standardization of products is the "pseudo-individualization" that endows "cultural mass production with the halo of free choice or open market on the basis of standardization itself" (Adorno 1941:25). Here is the "parade of progress," the world of the "new and improved" that masks an eternal sameness. Deodorants and shampoos, hit songs and movie formulas, cars and soft drinks—each is made to closely resemble its competitors in order to conform to the consumer's pregiven expectations, but offers just the slightest difference in order to capture his attention:

> Although the consumer is, so to speak, given his choice, he does not get a penny's worth too much for his money, whatever the trademark he prefers to possess. The difference in quality between two equally priced popular articles is usually as infinitesimal as the difference in the nicotine content of two brands of cigarettes. Nevertheless, this difference, corroborated by "scientific tests," is dinned into the consumer's mind through posters illuminated by a thousand electric light bulbs, over the radio, and by use of entire pages of newspapers and magazines, as if it represented a revelation altering the entire course of the world rather than an illusory fraction that makes no real difference, even for a chain smoker. (Horkheimer 1947:99)

Despite, or perhaps because of, the superficial differences that distinguish one commodity from the next, the culture industry advertises its products with the promise of

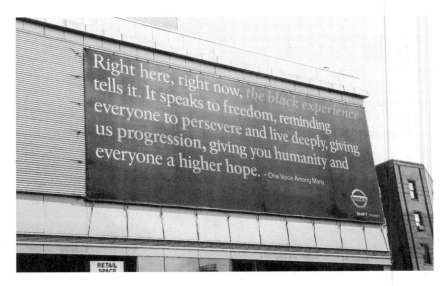

Photo 3.5 The culture industry fabricates a world where, in Marx's famous aphorism, "all that is solid melts into air." Nowhere is this condition more conspicuously promoted than in advertising. Above, Nissan, a Japanese auto maker, "sells" the values of freedom and hope to potential consumers in Harlem, New York, a predominately African-American neighborhood that for decades has been denied precisely what is being sold.

SOURCE: Scott Appelrouth; used with permission.

Photo 3.6 Advertising Happiness: Spirituality and Fashion—it's all the same.

SOURCE: Scott Appelrouth; used with permission.

an "escape from reality but it really offers an escape from the last thought of resisting that reality (Horkheimer and Adorno 2002/1944:116). Such are the movies where the audience can momentarily forget the drudgery and "defeat" of daily life through the ever-predictable triumph of the good guys; the commercials in which weight-loss pills, whitening toothpaste, and the latest clothing fashions will land you the object of your desires and everlasting happiness; car advertisements that pitch their mass-produced product to a mass audience with the slogan, "Engineered for those who never applaud conformity[5]"; and the music *industry* in which your favorite band's anti-establishment message can be bought for a mere $17. Yet, none of the offerings of the culture industry actually fulfills its promise. In fact, they are not designed to, and although we know this, we are unable to envision an alternative. And this, above all else, marks the power that the culture industry possesses. The essential lesson is that individuals are not to be treated as autonomous, freethinking persons. Rather, in the pursuit of efficient profit-making, individuals themselves are to be "created" in order to fit into a standardized model that mirrors the standardized products being sold to them.

> The culture industry endlessly cheats its consumers out of what it endlessly promises. . . . This principle requires that while all needs should be presented to individuals as capable of fulfillment by the culture industry, they should be so set up in advance that individuals experience themselves through their needs only as eternal consumers, as the culture industry's object. Not only does it persuade them that its fraud is satisfaction, it also gives them to understand that they must make do with what is offered, whatever it may be. . . . That is the triumph of advertising in the culture industry: the compulsive imitation by consumers of cultural commodities which, at the same time, they recognize as false. (Horkheimer and Adorno 2002/1944:111, 113, 136)

In the end, the culture industry combines with technological rationality to produce a totalitarian social order that transcends any particular economic or political arrangement. Whether a society is organized according to capitalist or socialist, fascist or democratic principles makes little difference, for *all* advanced, industrial societies are administered alike. Each is rooted to an all-encompassing culture industry that trumpets its conformist products as the avenue for individual success and happiness. No one, regardless of class position, is able to escape its ever more effective and "pleasant" method of control.

Significant Others | **Walter Benjamin (1892–1940): Art in the Age of Mechanical Reproduction**

Walter Benjamin was an associate of the Institute for Social Research, his main connection to the group coming in the form of freelance contributions to the Institute's *Journal of Social Research*. While his philosophical treatises addressed a range of topics, it is his studies on the nature of art in modern societies that have made the most enduring mark in the social sciences. Benjamin had met Adorno in 1923 while attending the University of Frankfurt, and the two established a close correspondence. However, despite the mutual respect each had for the other's ideas, Benjamin's profound influence on Adorno would be tempered as the two clashed over the revolutionary role assigned to works of art.

(Continued)

---

[5]This was the advertising slogan for Saab's 9-7X SUV, introduced in 2005.

(Continued)

> While Adorno saw in popular forms of musical and artistic expression a fetishized "standardization" that bred social conformity and the abandonment of reason, Benjamin perceived a potentially revolutionary form of politics. In his classic essay "The Work of Art in the Age of Mechanical Reproduction" (1936), Benjamin contended that technological advances promised to destroy the elitism of art (an elitism that Adorno was himself guilty of advocating). Specifically, lithography, photography, and film, in producing mechanical reproductions of works of art, had removed the distance or separateness that up to that point characterized the relationship between art and those who viewed it. In doing so, it undermined the source of art's aura or sacredness and, in turn, challenged conservative, elitist understandings and uses of art. (The work of Andy Warhol and the debates over its artistic merit illustrate well Benjamin's argument.) Authenticity, considered a hallmark of "true art," is rendered obsolete as images can be endlessly reproduced—popularized—and thus appropriated by "the masses." In Benjamin's own words:
>
> > . . . the technique of reproduction detaches the reproduced object from the domain of tradition. By making many reproductions it substitutes a plurality of copies for a unique existence. And in permitting the reproduction to meet the beholder or listener in his own particular situation, it reactivates the object reproduced. These two processes lead to a tremendous shattering of tradition which is the obverse of the contemporary crisis and renewal of mankind. (1936/1968:223)
>
> The intellectual dispute between Adorno and Benjamin would not be resolved. Tragically, Benjamin, a German of Jewish descent, took his own life when attempting to escape the Nazis through the Pyrenees Mountains.

Freud and the "Unhappy Consciousness"

The final influence on the critical theorists considered here is the work of Sigmund Freud, whose ideas had a particularly profound impact on Herbert Marcuse.[6] The critical theorists' turn to psychoanalysis is in large measure a reflection of their emphasis on consciousness, reason, and individual freedom and how ideology distorts human potential. Moreover, Marcuse saw in Freudian theory the basis of an explanation for the continuing repression and unhappiness of individuals and a pathway toward the end of human toil and suffering.

Central to the critical theorists' perspective is Freud's notion of the "pleasure principle" and the "reality principle." The pleasure principle refers to the individual's instinctual drive for the immediate and painless gratification of desires. According to Freud, this unconscious impulse is inimical to the development of civilization, because civilization demands cooperation between individuals in order to achieve social (as opposed to personal) aims, and cooperation entails the delay, if not denial, of

---

[6]See especially Marcuse's *Eros and Civilization* (1955) and *Five Lectures: Psychoanalysis, Politics, and Utopia* (1970).

self-gratification. Restraining the free play of the pleasure principle is the "reality principle." The reality principle serves as a precondition for entering into associations with others that alone are able to secure basic needs. Essentially, an unconscious trade-off is made as powerful—and at times destructive—instinctual pleasures are exchanged for less satisfying, sublimated pleasures that, nevertheless, make social life possible. As a result, the apparent freedom to do and think and say what one wants actually is based on an essential unfreedom. The necessary repression of the instincts that accompanies the transfer to the reality principle is a form of psychological domination as the socially imposed restraint of instinctual pleasures is internalized within one's own psyche. "The repressive transformation of the instincts becomes the biological constitution of the organism: history rules even in the instinctual structure; culture becomes nature as soon as the individual learns to affirm and to reproduce the reality principle from within himself" (Marcuse 1970:11).

For Freud, the domination of instincts is bound to the development of civilization. Humanity's struggle for existence amid scarcity compels the repression of selfish instincts if civilization is to progress beyond barbarism. Because the progress of civilization requires engaging in unpleasurable tasks and the denial of gratifications, the influence of the pleasure principle must be tamed. Herein lies the "discontent of civilization": the evolution of society is based on the redirecting of instinctual energies from unrestrained, immediate pleasure to the burden of socially useful labor that refuses instinctual desires. The "result is not only the conversion of the organism into an instrument of unpleasurable labor but also and above all the devaluation of happiness and pleasure as ends in themselves, the subordination of happiness and gratification to social productivity without which there is no progress in civilization" (Marcuse 1970:35). As Freud himself stated on the matter, "What we call our civilization is largely responsible for our misery" (Freud 1961:38).

This dynamic results in a "vicious circle of progress" (Marcuse 1970:36) in which the civilizing advances produced through the denial of instinctual satisfaction do not lead to individual happiness. For the very reason that such advances are achieved at the expense of psychological inhibitions, they cannot be fully enjoyed. Yet, frustrated, unfulfilling satisfactions lead to a rise in repressed instinctual energies that find release in ever more socially approved, although individually malign, forms of "progress." And so the vicious circle continues.

Over the course of evolution, however, civilization has now advanced to such a degree that the repression of instinctual energies in the name of progress is no longer necessary. Humanity's technical control over nature has increased the capacity to fulfill needs to the point where scarcity, not only in regard to life's essentials but also in terms of liberating "free play," is now a choice and not the result of technological obstacles. Enough wealth is produced to ensure the security and comfort of most, if not all, of humankind. Nevertheless, the world's population continues to toil unnecessarily in repressive, alienated labor that fails to provide satisfaction of individual needs and true happiness. Under conditions of increased productivity and enhanced intelligence, unfreedom in the form of instinctual denial is increasingly irrational, as scarcity and the struggle for existence can no longer justify the continued repression of individual happiness. To the extent that technology reduces the amount of labor time required to produce life's necessities, it creates the possibility for eliminating repression and satisfying needs beyond those of basic necessity. "But the closer the real possibility of liberating the individual from the constraints once justified by scarcity and immaturity, the greater the need for maintaining and streamlining these constraints lest the established order of domination dissolve. . . . If society cannot use its growing productivity for reducing repression (because such usage would upset the hierarchy of the *status quo*), productivity must be turned *against* the individuals; it becomes itself an instrument of universal control. Totalitarianism spreads over late industrial civilization wherever the interests of domination prevail upon productivity, arresting and diverting its potentialities" (Marcuse 1955:93; emphasis in the original). Such is a world dominated by the production of waste, where auto lots are filled with new cars that will never be driven and grocery stores are stocked with food that will rot before it's bought. Meanwhile, workers are left to live paycheck to paycheck, unable to purchase the very goods they produce.

A question arising from Freud's analysis is whether the conflict between the pleasure principle and the reality principle must inevitably lead to the repression of instinctual pleasure and thus the "misery" of humankind. While Freud himself ambivalently suggested that repression is an inescapable condition of civilization, Marcuse asserted the possibility of a world where "the expanding realm of freedom becomes truly a realm of play—of the free play of individual faculties" (Marcuse 1955:223). Indeed, the real mark of progress is measured by the extent to which the historically conditioned capacity to satisfy human needs is used to advance individual happiness or to meet technological demands for productivity. The degree of freedom and domination is thus not fixed or immutable, nor is it somehow limited by the psychological or instinctual makeup of individuals. In a sense, then, freedom can be "objectively" measured by comparing the needs of individuals to the productive capacity for satisfying such needs during a given period of development. The more the available means are organized so as to minimize instinctual repression in meeting the needs of the individual and of society, the freer a society is.

While the reality principle and the repressive control of instinctual energies that it demands are inherent in the continuing development of civilization, "the specific historical institutions of the reality principle and the specific interests of domination introduce *additional* controls over and above those indispensable for civilized human association" (Marcuse 1955:37; emphasis in original). These additional controls represent **surplus repression**: the portion of repression "which is the result of specific societal conditions sustained in the specific interest of domination" and that unnecessarily impedes the gratification of instinctual desires (ibid.:88). In other words, although the reality principle is intrinsically opposed to the pleasure principle, the specific form that it takes is determined by the prevailing method of social domination—the existing system of social institutions, norms, and values that guides the necessary control of the instincts. Thus, whether a society's mode of production is based on private or collective property, a market or planned economy, or whether all of its members work to secure their survival or only particular groups do so, the content of the reality principle will be affected and, thus, the scope and degree of instinctual repression. The extent of surplus repression, then, provides a standard of measurement according to which the repressiveness of a society can be gauged.

Given that repression is not "natural" but rather is socially conditioned, "psychology in its inner structure must reveal itself to be political" (Marcuse 1970:1). The politics of psychology are, for Marcuse, most evident in the spheres of free time and sexuality. As we noted above, technological progress has all but eliminated, at least in potential, scarcity and want as a necessary fate of the human condition. Consequently, advanced societies are objectively able to reduce the amount of time individuals spend in burdensome, alienated labor, without compromising the ability to provide the population with a "rational" level of comfort. Yet, advanced societies remain needlessly competitive, antagonistic, and enslaved to continued expansion. As a result, individuals needlessly spend the majority of their time engaged in labor "for an apparatus which they do not control, which operates as an independent power to which individuals must submit if they want to live. . . . Men do not live their own lives but perform pre-established functions . . . [L]abor time, which is the largest part of the individual's time, is painful time, for alienated labor is absence of gratification, negation of the pleasure principle" (Marcuse 1955:45).

Even when the individual is not laboring for the "apparatus," the limited free time available to him remains tightly controlled. As we discussed previously, the lifeblood of the culture industry is filling individuals' leisure with standardized, conformist commodities, including information. But more than this, leisure is controlled by the very length of the working day and the nature of the dulled, mechanized work experience. Too tired from the day's labor, the individual has only enough energy to passively consume mindless "entertainment" in preparation for the next day's work. If the status quo, the prevailing system of domination, is to be maintained, free time can serve no other purpose because "the individual is not to be left alone. For if left to itself, and supported by a free intelligence aware of the potentialities of liberation from the reality of repression" (Marcuse 1955:48), individuals may begin to challenge the legitimacy of the established social order. Herein lies the political dimension to free time: in the name of the sacred values of progress and productivity, humanity has become increasingly repressed and, thus, incapable of realizing true progress in the form of freedom. While earlier stages of civilization required for their development repressive labor, its persistence and the "need" for increasing material wealth lead not to human happiness but to technological unfreedom.

Like his perspective on repression and the politics of leisure, Marcuse's view of sexuality is deeply indebted to Freud. Individuals in their early developmental stages are dominated by the pleasure principle. Thus, before the reality principle is internalized, individuals are controlled by "sexual" instincts that seek polymorphous bodily pleasures. As part of their indoctrination into the repressive social order, individuals must be "desexualized"; that is, sexual energies must be densensualized in "love" in order to sustain the monogamous, patriarchal family structure. For this family structure is itself an essential accomplice to the administered, repressive society. Sex is now tolerated only so long as it furthers the propagation of the species and, thus, existing relations of domination. Meanwhile, sexuality is transformed from the experience of the entire body as a locus of pleasure to a constraining fixation on genitalia. Once tamed by repressive moral codes, the individual's sexuality is no longer a source of uninhibited, total pleasure as it is put into the service of society's needs and not one's own (Marcuse 1970:9).

Marcuse does recognize, however, that relative to the nineteenth century, sexual mores and behavior have been "desublimated" or liberalized. Yet, the modern liberation of sexuality provides only a false freedom. The conflict between sexuality (a central source of the pleasure principle) and society (the source of the reality principle) has produced a state of **repressive desublimation** or "institutionalized desublimation" as it "is managed by a controlled liberalization which increases satisfaction with the offerings of society" (Marcuse 1970:57). As Marcuse noted:

> [T]o the degree to which sexuality is sanctioned and even encouraged by society (not "officially," of course, but by the mores and behavior considered as "regular"), it loses the quality which, according to Freud, is its essentially erotic quality, that of freedom from social control. In this sphere was the surreptitious freedom, the dangerous autonomy of the individual under the pleasure principle. . . . Now, with the integration of this sphere into the realm of business and entertainment, the repression itself is repressed: society has enlarged not individual freedom, but its control over the individual. (ibid.)

Photo 3.7   A Truly Liberated Society or One that Offers "Convenient" Repression? Sex, Steaks, and "Everything" for Under a Buck.

SOURCE: Scott Appelrouth; used with permission.

Marcuse saw in the supposed loosening of sexual mores neither a threat to existing civilization, as conservatives may have feared, nor a mark of a freer society. Instead, sexual liberation was but another sign of "business as usual," a sign vividly illustrated today by the growing pornography industry in which "uninhibited" sex is bought and sold. Nevertheless, as an essential force of the pleasure principle, embracing non-repressive sexuality is necessary to the creation of an authentically liberated society.

CRITICAL THEORISTS THEORETICAL ORIENTATION

From our discussion to this point, it should be clear that critical theory possesses the elements of a multidimensional approach to the central issues of action and order. Drawing principally from Marx, Weber, and Freud, critical theory incorporates concepts that range from an emphasis on institutionalized class relations to the instinctual disposition of individuals. This range is suggested in Figure 3.1, which depicts a number of the concepts outlined in the previous section.

Despite the multidimensionality of their conceptual tool-kit, we consider the critical theorists primarily collectivist and rationalist in their theoretical orientation. This view is based on a distinction between the critical theorists' view of the world as it should be and how it actually is. Undoubtedly, the critical theorists yearn for the creation of a society in which social order is maintained according to dictates of individuals' true needs and desires, where society allows for the realization of goals and aspirations that are determined by the individual's own consciousness and autonomous capacity for reason. But the progress of civilization has not unfolded under such an individualistic dynamic. Instead, repressive, dehumanizing collectivist forces (the culture industry, technology,

Figure 3.1   Core Concepts in Critical Theory

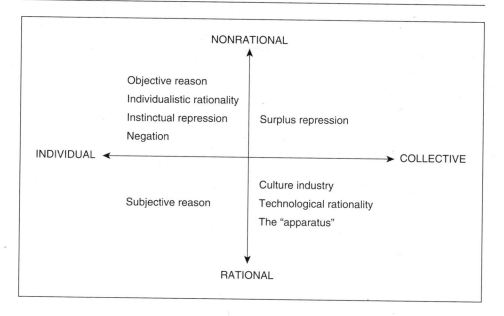

modes of economic production) have undermined the ability for individuals to develop a society free from domination. Although such forces are the products of human creativity, they have become reified or seemingly immutable. As such, they now confront their creators as alien, abstract powers that operate according to their own logic: the apparatus has a life of its own beyond the control of humans. Horkheimer points to this dynamic when he notes that "the substance of individuality itself, to which the idea of autonomy was bound, did not survive the process of industrialization. . . . With the decline of the ego and its reflective reason, human relationships tend to a point wherein the rule of economy over all personal relationships, the universal control of commodities over the totality of life, turns into a new and naked form of command and obedience" (1941:376, 379).

Ultimately, then, it is large-scale, institutional forces that account for the creation and re-creation of the social order, albeit in one that is founded on oppression. While the critical theorists focus on individual consciousness as the source of human liberation, their account of the social order rests on the broader cultural transformations that have distorted the individual's capacity to reason.

Concerning the issue of action, we again need to distinguish between the critical theorists' understanding of the world as it is and as it should be. In their view, modern society is fueled by a positivist, technological rationality that is incapable of providing an objectively meaningful source of human purpose. Driven by strategic calculations, individuals are motivated to pursue efficiency—a style—above all else in their everyday lives without exercising their own consciousness to determine what the purpose—a substance—of their life should be. While such motivations may prove "rational" insofar as they effectively coordinate means and ends, they fall short of being "reasonable." It is precisely this form of rationality that the critical theorists condemn for supplanting the primacy of morals and values in human affairs. For it is nonrational motivating factors that must guide consciousness and the act of reasoning if modern civilization is to stem the tide of "progress" and create a truly humane society as "the collapse of reason and the collapse of the individual are one and the same thing" (Horkheimer 1941:376).

Readings

The readings that follow explore the central theme of critical theory, namely, how progress has rendered the essence of individuality—negating—obsolete. This argument is based on the premise that individuals in advanced industrial societies live under a radically different set of conditions from those that prevailed during the previous period of competitive capitalism. During the era of "free" capitalism, the family was the center of economic and moral life. The survival of individuals was won and lost through the private family enterprise, which at the same time provided an avenue for them to express their own interests and abilities. Moreover, it was the family that trained youth and instilled in them the dominant social values. Thus, the process of socialization and the instinctual conflicts it created were tied to personal relationships between children and their parents. And it is the personal nature of this struggle that allows for the development of individuality.

Under the rule of economic, political, and cultural monopolies, however, the nature of the modern family has changed and with it the nature of the individual. The conflict between the child and the parents as authority figures and administrators of punishment and justice has been replaced. The child learns that it is not his parents that provide for his well being, but rather the "system" for which they labor. With the parents' loss of power and authority, it is no longer the family but external, standardizing forces to which the individual must adjust and submit. Yet, the reach of such forces is pervasive. The culture industry combines with the economic/political apparatus to erode the distinction between public and private domains. With no autonomous space from which to freely develop their own interests, individuals are unable to confront or oppose the established order. Individuals now identify themselves with and through the interests of the apparatus. Their very consciousness invaded by the apparatus, individuals become objects of technical administration as the whole of their existence has been absorbed by "pleasant" means of domination.

Introduction to Max Horkheimer's
Eclipse of Reason

In this reading, Horkheimer gives expression to the theme just outlined. In doing so, he argues that modern society is a "totality" that subjects all to its dehumanizing effects; worker and businessman alike are unable to escape the decline of individuality. This decline is most apparent in the modern form of consciousness that is unwilling and unable to image alternative truths. Indeed, "the very idea of truth has been reduced to the purpose of a useful tool in the control of nature, and the realization of the infinite potentialities inherent in man has been relegated to the status of a luxury. Thought that does not serve the interests of any established group or is not pertinent to the business of any industry has no place, is considered vain or superfluous" (1947:142, 143). This is a world in which "usefulness" is defined on technological grounds. Thinking in itself is useless or superfluous. Truth is found in "productivity" not critique. While "technocrats maintain that superabundance of goods produced on super-assembly lines will automatically eliminate all economic misery" (ibid.:151), human suffering continues. Yet, such misery and suffering are largely unnecessary, for the technological means to eliminate them are available. Without the ability to reason or find purpose in other than technological terms, humankind is destined to a future in which the "idolization of progress leads to the opposite of progress" (1947:153). For it is not technology or productivity in itself that makes for the decline of the individual, but loss of the ability to critically define humane principles according to which real progress must unfold. Perhaps, then, not all hope should be lost; the tide of "progress" may yet still be reversed. As Horkheimer desperately portends:

> Industrial discipline, technological progress, and scientific enlightenment, the very economic and cultural processes that are bringing about the obliteration of individuality, promise—though the augury is faint enough at present—to usher in a new era in which individuality may reemerge as an element in a less ideological and more humane form of existence. (ibid.:160, 161)

Eclipse of Reason (1947)

Max Horkheimer

RISE AND DECLINE OF THE INDIVIDUAL

The crisis of reason is manifested in the crisis of the individual, as whose agency it has developed. The illusion that traditional philosophy has cherished about the individual and about reason—the illusion of their eternity—is being dispelled. The individual once conceived of reason exclusively as an instrument of the self. Now he experiences the reverse of this self-deification. The machine has dropped the driver; it is racing blindly into space. At the moment of consummation, reason has become irrational and stultified. The theme of this time is self-preservation, while there is no self to preserve. In view of this situation, it behooves us to reflect upon the concept of the individual.

When we speak of the individual as a historical entity, we mean not merely the space-time and the sense existence of a particular member of the human race, but, in addition, his awareness of his own individuality as a conscious human being, including recognition of his own identity. This perception of the identity of the self is not equally strong in all persons. It is more clearly defined in adults than in children, who must learn to call themselves 'I'—the most elementary affirmation of identity. It is likewise weaker among primitive than among civilized men; indeed, the aborigine who has only recently been exposed to the dynamic of Western civilization often seems very uncertain of his identity. Living in the gratifications and frustrations of the moment, he seems but dimly aware that as an individual he must go on to face the hazards of tomorrow. This lag, it need hardly be said, partly accounts for the common belief that these people are lazy or that they are liars—a reproach that presupposes in the accused the very sense of identity they lack. The qualities found in extreme form among oppressed peoples, such as the Negroes, are also manifested, as a tendency, in persons of oppressed social classes that lack the economic fundament of inherited property. Thus, stunted individuality is found also among the poor white population of the American South. If these submerged people were not conditioned to imitation of their superiors, blatant advertising or educational appeals exhorting them to cultivation of personality would inevitably seem to them condescending, not to say hypocritical—an effort to lull them into a state of delusional contentment.

Individuality presupposes the voluntary sacrifice of immediate satisfaction for the sake of security, material and spiritual maintenance of one's own existence. When the roads to such a life are blocked, one has little incentive to deny oneself momentary pleasures. Hence, individuality among the masses is far less integrated and enduring than among the so-called elite. On the other hand, the elite have always been more preoccupied with the strategies of gaining and holding power. Social power is today more than ever mediated by power over things. The more intense an individual's concern with power over things, the more will things dominate him, the more will he lack any genuine individual traits, and the more will his mind be transformed into an automaton of formalized reason. . . .

In the era of free enterprise, the so-called era of individualism, individuality was most completely subordinated to self-preserving reason. In that era, the idea of individuality seemed to shake itself loose from metaphysical trappings and to become merely a synthesis of the individual's material interests. That it was not thereby saved from being used as a pawn by ideologists needs no proof. Individualism is the very heart of the theory and practice of bourgeois liberalism, which sees society as progressing through the automatic interaction of divergent interests in a free market. The individual could maintain himself as a social being only by pursuing his own long-term interests at the expense of ephemeral immediate gratifications. The qualities of individuality forged by the ascetic discipline of Christianity were thereby reinforced. The bourgeois individual did not necessarily see himself as opposed to the collectivity, but believed or was prevailed upon to believe himself to be a member of a society that could achieve the highest degree of harmony only through the unrestricted competition of individual interests.

Liberalism may be said to have considered itself the sponsor of a utopia that had come true, needing little more than the smoothing out of a few troublesome wrinkles. These wrinkles were not to be blamed on the liberalistic principle, but on the regrettable nonliberalistic obstacles that impeded its complete fruition. The principle of liberalism has led to conformity through the leveling principle of commerce and exchange which held liberalistic society together. The monad, a seventeenth-century symbol of the atomistic economic individual of bourgeois society, became a social type. All the monads, isolated though they were by moats of self-interest, nevertheless tended to become more and more alike through the pursuit of this very self-interest. In our era of large economic combines and mass culture, the principle of conformity emancipates itself from its individualistic veil, is openly proclaimed, and raised to the rank of an ideal *per se*.

Liberalism at its dawn was characterized by the existence of a multitude of independent entrepreneurs, who took care of their own property and defended it against antagonistic social forces. The movements of the market and the general trend of production were rooted in the economic requirements of their enterprises. Merchant and manufacturer alike had to be prepared for all economic and political eventualities. This need stimulated them to learn what they could from the past and to formulate plans for the future. They had to think for themselves, and although the much-vaunted independence of their thinking was to a certain extent nothing more than an illusion, it had enough objectivity to serve the interests of society in a given form and at a given period. The society of middle-class proprietors, particularly those who acted as middlemen in trade and certain types of manufacturers, had to encourage independent thinking, even though it might be at variance with their particular interests. The enterprise itself, which, it was assumed, would be handed down in the family, gave a businessman's deliberations a horizon that extended far beyond his own life span. His individuality was that of a provider, proud of himself and his kind, convinced that community and state rested upon himself and others like him, all professedly animated by the incentive of material gain. His sense of adequacy to the challenges of an acquisitive world expressed itself in his strong yet sober ego, maintaining interests that transcended his immediate needs.

In this age of big business, the independent entrepreneur is no longer typical. The ordinary man finds it harder and harder to plan for his heirs or even for his own remote future. The contemporary individual may have more opportunities than his ancestors had, but his concrete prospects have an increasingly shorter term. The future does not enter as precisely into his transactions. He simply feels that he will not be entirely lost if he preserves his skill and clings to his corporation, association, or union. Thus the individual subject of reason tends to become a shrunken ego, captive of an evanescent present, forgetting the use of the intellectual functions by which he was once able to transcend his actual position in reality. These functions are now taken over by the great economic and social forces of the era. The future of the individual depends less and less upon his own prudence and more and more upon the national and international struggles among the colossi of power. Individuality loses its economic basis.

There are still some forces of resistance left within man. It is evidence against social pessimism that despite the continuous assault of collective patterns, the spirit of humanity is still alive, if not in the individual as a member of social groups, at least in the individual as far as he is let alone. But the impact of the existing conditions upon the average man's life is such that the submissive type mentioned earlier has become overwhelmingly predominant. From the day of his birth, the individual is made to feel that there is only one way of getting along in this world—that of giving up his hope of ultimate self-realization. This he can achieve solely by imitation. He continuously responds to what he perceives about him, not only consciously but with his whole being, emulating the traits and attitudes represented by all the collectivities that enmesh him—his play group, his classmates, his athletic team, and all the other groups that, as has been pointed out, enforce a more strict conformity, a more radical surrender through complete assimilation, than any father or teacher in the nineteenth century could impose. By echoing, repeating, imitating his surroundings, by adapting himself to all the powerful groups to which he eventually belongs, by transforming himself from a human being into a member of organizations, by sacrificing his potentialities for the sake of readiness and ability to conform to and gain influence in such organizations, he manages to survive. It is survival achieved by the oldest biological means of survival, namely, mimicry.

Just as a child repeats the words of his mother, and the youngster the brutal manners of the elders at whose hands he suffers, so the giant loud-speaker of industrial culture, blaring through commercialized recreation and popular advertising—which become more and more indistinguishable from each other—endlessly reduplicates the surface of reality. All the ingenious devices of the amusement industry reproduce over and over again banal life scenes that are deceptive nevertheless, because the technical exactness of the reproduction veils the falsification of the ideological content or the arbitrariness of the introduction of such content. This reproduction has nothing in common with great realistic art, which portrays reality in order to judge it. Modern mass culture, although drawing freely upon stale cultural values, glorifies the world as it is. Motion pictures, the radio, popular biographies and novels have the same refrain: This is our grove, this is the rut of the great and the would-be great—this is reality as it is and should be and will be.

Even the words that could voice a hope for something besides the fruits of success have been pressed into this service. The idea of eternal bliss and everything relating to the absolute have been reduced to the function of religious edification, conceived as a leisure-time activity; they have been made part of the Sunday-school vernacular. The idea of happiness has similarly been reduced to a banality to coincide with leading the kind of normal life that serious religious thought has often criticized. The very idea of truth has been reduced to the purpose of a useful tool in the control of nature, and the realization of the infinite potentialities inherent in man has been relegated to the status of a luxury. Thought that does not serve the interests of any established group or is not pertinent to the business of any industry has no place, is considered vain or superfluous. Paradoxically, a society that, in the face of starvation in great areas of the world, allows a large part of its machinery to stand idle, that shelves many important inventions, and that devotes innumerable working hours to moronic advertising and to the production of instruments of destruction—a society in which these luxuries are inherent has made usefulness its gospel.

Because modern society is a totality, the decline of individuality affects the lower as well as the higher social groups, the worker no less than the businessman. One of the most important attributes of individuality, that of spontaneous action, which began to decline in capitalism as a result of the partial elimination of competition, played an integral part in socialist theory. But today the spontaneity of the working class has been impaired by the general dissolution of individuality. Labor is increasingly divorced from critical theories as they were formulated by the great political and social thinkers of the nineteenth century. . . . As a matter of fact not theory but its decline furthers surrender to the powers that be, whether they are represented by the controlling agencies of capital or those of labor. However, the masses, despite their pliability, have not capitulated completely to collectivization. Although, under the pressure of the pragmatic reality of today, man's self-expression has become identical with his function in the prevailing system, although he desperately represses any other impulse within himself as well as in others, the rage that seizes him whenever he becomes aware of an unintegrated longing that does not fit into the existing pattern is a sign of his smoldering resentment. This resentment, if repression were abolished, would be turned against the whole social order, which has an intrinsic tendency to prevent its members from gaining insight into the mechanisms of their own repression. Throughout history, physical, organizational, and cultural pressures have always had their role in the integration of the individual into a just or unjust order; today, the labor organizations, in their very effort to improve the status of labor, are inevitably led to contribute to that pressure.

There is a crucial difference between the social units of the modern industrial era and those of earlier epochs. The units of the older societies were totalities, in the sense that they had grown into hierarchically organized entities. The life of the totemistic tribe, the clan, the church of the Middle Ages, the nation in the era of the bourgeois revolutions, followed ideological patterns shaped through historical developments. Such patterns—magical, religious, or philosophical—reflected current forms of social domination. They constituted a cultural cement even after their role in production had become obsolete; thus they also fostered the idea of a common truth. This they did by the very fact that they had become objectified. Any system of ideas, religious, artistic, or logical, so far as it is articulated in meaningful language, attains a general connotation and necessarily claims to be true in a universal sense. . . .

The earlier totalities, which were supposed to conform to an abstract spiritual model, contained an element that is lacking in the purely pragmatistic totalities of industrialism. The latter likewise have a hierarchical structure; but they are thoroughly and despotically integrated. For example, promotion of their functionaries to higher ranks is not based on qualifications related to any spiritual ideals. Almost exclusively it is a matter of their ability to manipulate people; here purely administrative and technical skills determine the selection of governing personnel. Such capacities were by no means lacking in the hierarchical leadership of former societies; but the dissolution of relation between leadership capacities and an objectivized framework of spiritual ideals is what gives the modern totalities their distinctive character. . . .

Social theory—reactionary, democratic, or revolutionary—was the heir to the older systems of thought that were supposed to have set the patterns for past totalities. These older systems had vanished because the forms of solidarity postulated by them proved to be deceptive, and the ideologies related to them became hollow and apologetic. The latter-day critique of society for its part refrained from apologetics, and did not glorify its subject—not even Marx exalted the proletariat. He looked upon capitalism as the last form of social injustice; he did not condone the established ideas and superstitions of the dominated class whom his doctrine was supposed to guide. In contrast to the tendencies of mass culture, none of those doctrines undertook to 'sell' the people the way of life in which they are fixed and which they unconsciously abhor but overtly acclaim. Social theory offered a critical analysis of reality, including the workers' own warped thoughts. Under the conditions of modern industrialism, however, even political theory is infected with the apologetic trend of the total culture. . . .

As religious and moral ideologies fade, and political theory is abolished by the march of economic and political events, the ideas of the workers tend to be molded by the business ideology of their leaders. The idea of an intrinsic conflict between the laboring masses of the world and the existence of social injustice is superseded by the concepts relating to the strategy of conflicts between the several power groups. It is true that workers of earlier days did not have any conceptual knowledge of the mechanisms unveiled by social theory, and their minds and bodies bore the marks of oppression; yet their misery was still the misery of individual human beings, and therefore linked them with any miserable people in any country and in any sector of society. Their undeveloped minds were not continually being prodded by the techniques of mass culture that hammer the industrialistic behavior patterns into their eyes and ears and muscles during their leisure time as well as during working hours. Workers today, no less than the rest of the population, are intellectually better trained, better informed, and much less naive. They know the details of national affairs and the chicanery of political movements, particularly of those that live by propaganda against corruption. The workers, at least those who have not gone through the hell of fascism, will join in any persecution of a capitalist or politician who has been singled out because he has violated the rules of the game; but they do not question the rules in themselves. They have learned to take social injustice—even inequity within their own group—as a powerful fact, and to take powerful facts as the only things to be respected. Their minds are closed to dreams of a basically different world and to concepts that, instead of being mere classification of facts, are oriented toward real fulfillment of those dreams. Modern economic conditions make for a positivistic attitude in members as well as in leaders of labor unions, so that they resemble one another more and more. Such a trend, although constantly challenged by contrary tendencies, strengthens labor as a new force in social life.

It is not that inequality has decreased. To the old discrepancies between the social power of single members of different social groups, further differences have been added. While unions dealing in certain categories of labor have been able to raise their prices, the whole weight of oppressive social power is felt by other categories, organized or unorganized. There is, furthermore, the cleavage between members of unions and those who for any one of various reasons are excluded from unions, between the people of privileged nations and those who, in this contracting world, are dominated not only by their own traditional elite, but also by the ruling groups of the industrially more developed countries. The principle has not changed.

At the present time, labor and capital are equally concerned with holding and extending their control. The leaders in both groups contend to an increasing extent that theoretical critique of society has become superfluous as a result of the tremendous technological progress that promises to revolutionize the conditions of human existence. The technocrats maintain that superabundance of goods produced on super-assembly lines will automatically eliminate all economic misery. Efficiency, productivity, and intelligent planning are proclaimed the gods of modern man; so-called 'unproductive' groups and 'predatory' capital are branded as the enemies of society.

It is true that the engineer, perhaps the symbol of this age, is not so exclusively bent on profitmaking as the industrialist or the merchant. Because his function is more directly connected with the requirements of the production job itself, his commands bear the mark of greater objectivity. His subordinates recognize that at least some of his orders are in the nature of things and therefore rational in a universal sense. But at bottom this rationality, too, pertains to domination, not reason. The engineer is not interested in understanding things for their own sake or for the sake of insight, but in accordance with their being fitted into a scheme, no matter how alien to their own inner structure; this holds for living beings as well as for inanimate things. The engineer's mind is that of industrialism in its streamlined form. His purposeful rule would make men an agglomeration of instruments without a purpose of their own. . . .

It is not technology or the motive of self-preservation that in itself accounts for the decline of the individual; it is not production *per se*, but the forms in which it takes place—the interrelationships of human beings within the specific framework of industrialism. Human toil and research and invention is a response to the challenge of necessity. The pattern becomes absurd only when people make toil, research, and invention into idols. Such an ideology tends to supplant the humanistic foundation of the very civilization it seeks to glorify. While the concepts of complete fulfilment and unrestrained enjoyment fostered a hope that unshackled the forces of progress, the idolization of progress leads to the opposite of progress. Arduous labor for a meaningful end may be enjoyed and even loved. A philosophy that makes labor an end in itself leads eventually to resentment of all labor. The decline of the individual must be charged not to the technical achievements of man or even to man himself—people are usually much better than what they think or say or do—but rather to the present structure and content of the 'objective mind,' the spirit that pervades social life in all its branches. The patterns of thought and action that people accept ready-made from the agencies of mass culture act in their turn to influence mass culture as though they were the ideas of the people themselves. The objective mind in our era worships industry, technology, and nationality without a principle that could give sense to these categories; it mirrors the pressure of an economic system that admits of no reprieve or escape.

As for the ideal of productivity, it must be observed that economic significance today is measured in terms of usefulness with respect to the structure of power, not with respect to the needs of all. The individual must prove his value to one or other of the groups engaged in the struggle for a greater share of control over the national and the international economy. Moreover, the quantity and quality of the goods or services he contributes to society is merely one of the factors determining his success.

Nor is efficiency, the modern criterion and sole justification for the very existence of any individual, to be confused with real technical or managerial skill. It inheres in the ability to be 'one of the boys,' to hold one's own, to impress others, to 'sell' oneself, to cultivate the right connections—talents that seem to be transmitted through the germ cells of so many persons today. The fallacy of technocratic thinking from St. Simon to Veblen and his followers has lain in underestimating the similarity of the traits that make for success in the various branches of production and business, and in confusing rational use of the means of production with the rational proclivities of certain of its agents.

If modern society tends to negate all the attributes of individuality, are its members not compensated, it may be asked, by the rationality of its organization? The technocrats often maintain that when their theories are put into practice, depressions will become a thing of the past and basic economic disproportions will disappear; the whole productive mechanism will work smoothly according to blueprints. Actually, modern society is not so far from having realized the technocratic dream. The needs of the consumers as well as of the producers, which under the liberal market system made themselves felt in distorted and irrational forms, in a process culminating in depressions, can now to a great extent be forecast and satisfied or negated in accordance with the policies of economic and political leaders. The expression of human needs is no longer distorted by the dubious economic indicators of the market; instead, these needs are determined by statistics, and all kinds of engineers—industrial, technical, political—struggle to keep them under control. But if this new rationality is in one way closer to the idea of reason than the market system, it is in another way farther from it.

Dealings between the members of different social groups under the older system were really determined not by the market but by the unequal distribution of economic power; yet the transformation of human relations into objective economic mechanisms gave the individual, at least in principle, a certain independence. When unsuccessful competitors went to the wall or backward groups were reduced to misery under the liberalistic economy, they could preserve a sense of human dignity even though they were economically cast down, because responsibility for their plight could be thrown upon anonymous economic processes. Today individuals or entire groups may still suffer ruin through blind economic forces; but these are represented by better organized, more powerful elites. Although the interrelations of these dominant groups are subject to vicissitudes, they understand each other well in many respects. When concentration and centralization of industrial forces extinguish political liberalism in its turn, the victims are doomed in their entirety. Under totalitarianism, when an individual or group is singled out by the elite for discrimination, it is not only deprived of the means of livelihood, but its very human essence is attacked. American society may take a different course. However, the dwindling away of individual thinking and resistance, as it is brought about by the economic and cultural mechanisms of modern industrialism, will render evolution toward the humane increasingly difficult.

By making the watchword of production a kind of religious creed, by professing technocratic ideas and branding as 'unproductive' such groups as do not have access to the big industrial bastions, industry causes itself and society to forget that production has become to an ever greater extent a means in the struggle for power. The policies of economic leaders, on which society in its present stage more and more directly depends, are dogged and particularistic, and therefore perhaps even blinder with respect to the real needs of society than were the automatic trends that once determined the market. Irrationality still molds the fate of men. . . .

Every instrumentality of mass culture serves to reinforce the social pressures upon individuality, precluding all possibility that the individual will somehow preserve himself in the face of all the atomizing machinery of modern society. The accent on individual heroism and on the self-made man in popular biographics and pseudo-romantic novels and films does not invalidate this observation. These machine-made incentives to self-preservation actually accelerate the dissolution of individuality. Just as the slogans of rugged individualism are politically useful to large trusts in seeking exemption from social control, so in mass culture the rhetoric of individualism, by imposing patterns for collective imitation, disavows the very principle to which it gives lip service. . . .

The objection that the individual, despite everything, does not entirely disappear in the new impersonal institutions, that individualism is as rugged and rampant in modern society as ever before, seems to miss the point. The objection contains a grain of truth, namely, the consideration that man is still better than the world he lives in. Yet his life seems to follow a sequence that will fit any questionnaire he is asked to fill out. His intellectual existence is exhausted in the public opinion polls. Especially the so-called great individuals of today, the idols of the masses, are not genuine individuals, they are simply creatures of their own publicity, enlargements of their own photographs, functions of social processes. The consummate superman, against whom no one has warned more anxiously than Nietzsche himself, is a projection of the oppressed masses, King Kong rather than Caesar Borgia. The hypnotic spell that such counterfeit supermen as Hitler have exercised derives not so much from what they think or say or do as from their antics, which set a style of behavior for men who, stripped of their spontaneity by the industrial processing, need to be told how to make friends and influence people.

The tendencies described have already led to the greatest catastrophe in European history. Some of the causes were specifically European. Others are traceable to profound changes in man's character under the influence of international trends. Nobody can predict with certainty that these destructive tendencies will be checked in the near future. However, there is increasing awareness that the unbearable pressure upon the individual is not inevitable. It is to be hoped that men will come to see that it springs not directly from the purely technical requirements of the production, but from the social structure. Indeed, the intensification of repression in many parts of the world in itself testifies to fear in face of the imminent possibility of change on the basis of the present development of productive forces. Industrial discipline, technological progress, and scientific enlightenment, the very economic and cultural processes that are bringing about the obliteration of individuality, promise—though the augury is faint enough at present—to usher in a new era in which individuality may remerge as an element in a less ideological and more humane form of existence.

Fascism used terroristic methods in the effort to reduce conscious human beings to social atoms, because it feared that ever-increasing disillusionment as regards all ideologies might pave the way for men to realize their own and society's deepest potentialities; and indeed, in some cases, social pressure and political terror have tempered the profoundly human resistance to irrationality—a resistance that is always the core of true individuality.

The real individuals of our time are the martyrs who have gone through infernos of suffering and degradation in their resistance to conquest and oppression, not the inflated personalities of popular culture, the conventional dignitaries. These unsung heroes consciously exposed their existence as individuals to the terroristic annihilation that others undergo unconsciously through the social process. The anonymous martyrs of the concentration camps are the symbols of the humanity that is striving to be born. The task of philosophy is to translate what they have done into language that will be heard, even though their finite voices have been silenced by tyranny.

❖

Introduction to Theodor Adorno's "The Culture Industry Reconsidered"

In this selection, Adorno discusses how the culture industry has furthered the collapse of reason. Equating culture with the "high arts," Adorno describes culture as a form of protest "against the petrified relations" (1991:100) under which individuals live. The purpose of culture is to render the impossible possible, to offer alternatives to existing social conditions. To the extent that culture (art) is free from the profit-motive, it is able to develop according to its own internal logic and thus voice essential social critiques.

In advanced societies, however, culture has become synonymous with industry and hence subject to the rule of efficient production and standardization that is its hallmark. The relationship between mass culture and the individual is one akin to that of seller and buyer. However, "the customer is not king, as the culture industry would like to have us believe, not its subject but its object" (ibid.:99). Individuals, themselves objects of production, are left to consume mass-produced, prepackaged ideas that instill an uncritical consensus that strengthens established authority. Hit songs and movies are not the making of popular tastes but of marketing campaigns that predetermine what will be heard and seen while excluding potentially "disruptive" alternatives. Because culture is now a product of the machine and not the imagination, it is incapable of negating the oppressive conformity by the culture industry. Nor can mass culture critique prevailing patterns of social relations, for they, too, are a reflection of machine production. Culture no longer prods—it pacifies:

> The categorical imperative of the culture industry no longer has anything in common with freedom. It proclaims: You shall conform, without instruction as to what; conform to that which exists anyway, and to that which everyone thinks anyway as a reflex of its power and omnipresence. The power of the culture industry is that conformity has replaced consciousness. The order that springs from it is never confronted with what it claims to be or with the real interests of human beings. (ibid.:104)

While the culture industry claims to be a producer of choice, freedom, and individual identity, it instead provides its customers with a totalitarian, conformist social landscape. It thus "cheats its consumers out of the same happiness which it deceitfully projects" (ibid.:106). So while we are repeatedly instructed to "Just Do It," what "it" is is never truthfully revealed: BUY.

The Culture Industry Reconsidered (1975)

Theodore Adorno

The term culture industry was perhaps used for the first time in the book *Dialectic of Enlightenment*, which Horkheimer and I published in Amsterdam in 1947. In our drafts we spoke of 'mass culture.' We replaced that expression with 'culture industry' in order to exclude from the outset the interpretation agreeable to its advocates: that it is a matter of something like a culture that arises spontaneously from the masses themselves, the contemporary form of popular art. From the latter the culture industry must be distinguished in the extreme. The culture industry fuses the old and familiar into a new quality. In all its branches, products which are tailored for consumption by masses, and which to a great extent determine the nature of that consumption, are manufactured more or less according to plan. The individual branches are similar in structure or at least fit into each other, ordering themselves into a system almost without a gap. This is made possible by contemporary technical capabilities as well as by economic and administrative concentration. The culture industry intentionally integrates its consumers from above. To the detriment of both it forces together the spheres of high and low art, separated for thousands of years. The seriousness of high art is destroyed in speculation about its efficacy; the seriousness of the lower perishes with the civilizational constraints imposed on the rebellious resistance inherent within it as long as social control was not yet total. Thus, although the culture industry undeniably speculates on the conscious and unconscious state of the millions towards which it is directed, the masses are not primary, but secondary, they are an object of calculation; an appendage of the machinery. The customer is not king, as the culture industry would have us believe, not its subject but its object. The very word massmedia, specially honed for the culture industry, already shifts the accent onto harmless terrain. Neither is it a question of primary concern for the masses, nor of the techniques of communication as such, but of the spirit which sufflates them, their master's voice. The culture industry misuses its concern for the masses in order to duplicate, reinforce and strengthen their mentality, which it presumes is given and unchangeable. How this mentality might be changed is excluded throughout. The masses are not the measure but the ideology of the culture industry, even though the culture industry itself could scarcely exist without adapting to the masses.

The cultural commodities of the industry are governed, as Brecht and Suhrkamp expressed it thirty years ago, by the principle of their realization as value, and not by their own specific content and harmonious formation. The entire practice of the culture industry transfers the profit motive naked onto cultural forms. Ever since these cultural forms first began to earn a living for their creators as commodities in the market-place they had already possessed something of this quality. But then they sought after profit only indirectly, over and above their autonomous essence. New on the part of the culture industry is the direct and undisguised primacy of a precisely and thoroughly calculated efficacy in its most typical products. The autonomy of works of art, which of course rarely ever predominated in an entirely pure form, and was always permeated by a constellation of effects, is tendentially eliminated by the culture industry, with or without the conscious will of those in control. The latter include both those who carry out directives as well as those who hold the power. In economic terms they are or were in search of new opportunities for the realization of capital in the most economically developed countries. The old opportunities became increasingly more precarious as a result of the

SOURCE: From Adorno, T., *The Culture Industry Reconsidered,* New German Critique. Reprinted by permission of the Taylor & Francis Group.

same concentration process which alone makes the culture industry possible as an omni-present phenomenon. Culture, in the true sense, did not simply accommodate itself to human beings; but it always simultaneously raised a protest against the petrified relations under which they lived, thereby honouring them. In so far as culture becomes wholly assimilated to and integrated in those petrified relations, human beings are once more debased. Cultural entities typical of the culture industry are no longer *also* commodities, they are commodities through and through. This quantitative shift is so great that it calls forth entirely new phenomena. Ultimately, the culture industry no longer even needs to directly pursue everywhere the profit interests from which it originated. These interests have become objectified in its ideology and have even made themselves independent of the compulsion to sell the cultural commodities which must be swallowed anyway. The culture industry turns into public relations, the manufacturing of 'goodwill' per se, without regard for particular firms or saleable objects. Brought to bear is a general uncritical consensus, advertisements produced for the world, so that each product of the culture industry becomes its own advertisement.

Nevertheless, those characteristics which originally stamped the transformation of literature into a commodity are maintained in this process. More than anything in the world, the culture industry has its ontology, a scaffolding of rigidly conservative basic categories which can be gleaned, for example, from the commercial English novels of the late seventeenth and early eighteenth centuries. What parades as progress in the culture industry, as the incessantly new which it offers up, remains the disguise for an eternal sameness; everywhere the changes mask a skeleton which has changed just as little as the profit motive itself since the time it first gained its predominance over culture.

Thus, the expression 'industry' is not to be taken too literally. It refers to the standardization of the thing itself—such as that of the Western, familiar to every movie-goer—and to the rationalization of distribution techniques, but not strictly to the production process. Although in film, the central sector of the culture industry, the production process resembles technical modes of operation in the extensive division of labour, the employment of machines and the separation of the labourers from the means of production—expressed in the perennial conflict between artists active in the culture industry and those who control it—individual forms of production are nevertheless maintained. Each product affects an individual air; individuality itself serves to reinforce ideology, in so far as the illusion is conjured up that the completely reified and mediated is a sanctuary from immediacy and life. Now, as ever, the culture industry exists in the 'service' of third persons, maintaining its affinity to the declining circulation process of capital, to the commerce from which it came into being. Its ideology above all makes use of the star system, borrowed from individualistic art and its commercial exploitation. The more dehumanized its methods of operation and content, the more diligently and successfully the culture industry propagates supposedly great personalities and operates with heart-throbs. It is industrial more in a sociological sense, in the incorporation of industrial forms of organization even when nothing is manufactured—as in the rationalization of office work—rather than in the sense of anything really and actually produced by technological rationality. Accordingly, the misinvestments of the culture industry are considerable, throwing those branches rendered obsolete by new techniques into crises, which seldom lead to changes for the better.

The concept of technique in the culture industry is only in name identical with technique in works of art. In the latter, technique is concerned with the internal organization of the object itself, with its inner logic. In contrast, the technique of the culture industry is, from the beginning, one of distribution and mechanical reproduction, and therefore always remains external to its object. The culture industry finds ideological support precisely in so far as it carefully shields itself from the full potential of the techniques contained in its products. It lives parasitically from the extra-artistic technique of the material production of goods, without regard for the obligation to the internal artistic whole implied by its functionality (*Sachlichkeit*), but also without concern for the laws of form demanded by aesthetic autonomy. The result for the physiognomy of the culture industry is essentially a mixture of streamlining, photographic hardness and precision on the one hand, and individualistic residues, sentimentality and an already rationally disposed and adapted romanticism on the other. Adopting Benjamin's designation of the traditional work of art by the concept of aura, the presence of that which is not present, the culture industry is defined by the fact that it does not strictly counterpose another principle to that of aura, but rather by the fact that it conserves the decaying aura as a foggy mist. By this means the culture industry betrays its own ideological abuses.

It has recently become customary among cultural officials as well as sociologists to warn against underestimating the culture industry while pointing to its great importance for the development of the consciousness of its consumers. It is to be taken seriously, without cultured snobbism. In actuality the culture industry is important as a moment of the spirit which dominates today. Whoever ignores its influence out of scepticism for what it stuffs into people would be naive. Yet there is a deceptive glitter about the admonition to take it seriously. Because of its social role, disturbing questions about its quality, about truth or untruth, and about the aesthetic niveau of the culture industry's emissions are repressed, or at least excluded from the so-called sociology of communications. The critic is accused of taking refuge in arrogant esoterica. It would be advisable first to indicate the double meaning of importance that slowly worms its way in unnoticed. Even if it touches the lives of innumerable people, the function of something is no guarantee of its particular quality. The blending of aesthetics with its residual communicative aspects leads art, as a social phenomenon, not to its rightful position in opposition to alleged artistic snobbism, but rather in a variety of ways to the defence of its baneful social consequences. The importance of the culture industry in the spiritual constitution of the masses is no dispensation for reflection on its objective legitimation, its essential being, least of all by a science which thinks itself pragmatic. On the contrary: such reflection becomes necessary precisely for

this reason. To take the culture industry as seriously as its unquestioned role demands, means to take it seriously critically, and not to cower in the face of its monopolistic character.

Among those intellectuals anxious to reconcile themselves with the phenomenon and eager to find a common formula to express both their reservations against it and their respect for its power, a tone of ironic toleration prevails unless they have already created a new mythos of the twentieth century from the imposed regression. After all, those intellectuals maintain, everyone knows what pocket novels, films off the rack, family television shows rolled out into serials and hit parades, advice to the lovelorn and horoscope columns are all about. All of this, however, is harmless and, according to them, even democratic since it responds to a demand, albeit a stimulated one. It also bestows all kinds of blessings, they point out, for example, through the dissemination of information, advice and stress reducing patterns of behaviour. Of course, as every sociological study measuring something as elementary as how politically informed the public is has proven, the information is meagre or indifferent. Moreover, the advice to be gained from manifestations of the culture industry is vacuous, banal or worse, and the behaviour patterns are shamelessly conformist.

The two-faced irony in the relationship of servile intellectuals to the culture industry is not restricted to them alone. It may also be supposed that the consciousness of the consumers themselves is split between the prescribed fun which is supplied to them by the culture industry and a not particularly well-hidden doubt about its blessings. The phrase, the world wants to be deceived, has become truer than had ever been intended. People are not only, as the saying goes, falling for the swindle; if it guarantees them even the most fleeting gratification they desire a deception which is nonetheless transparent to them. They force their eyes shut and voice approval, in a kind of self-loathing, for what is meted out to them, knowing fully the purpose for which it is manufactured. Without admitting it they sense that their lives would be completely intolerable as soon as they no longer clung to satisfactions which are none at all.

The most ambitious defence of the culture industry today celebrates its spirit, which might be safely called ideology, as an ordering factor. In a supposedly chaotic world it provides human beings with something like standards for orientation, and that alone seems worthy of approval. However, what its defenders imagine is preserved by the culture industry is in fact all the more thoroughly destroyed by it. The colour film demolishes the genial old tavern to a greater extent than bombs ever could: the film exterminates its imago. No homeland can survive being processed by the films which celebrate it, and which thereby turn the unique character on which it thrives into an interchangeable sameness.

That which legitimately could be called culture attempted, as an expression of suffering and contradiction, to maintain a grasp on the idea of the good life. Culture cannot represent either that which merely exists or the conventional and no longer binding categories of order which the culture industry drapes over the idea of the good life as if existing reality were the good life, and as if those categories were its true measure. If the response of the culture industry's representatives is that it does not deliver art at all, this is itself the ideology with which they evade responsibility for that from which the business lives. No misdeed is ever righted by explaining it as such.

The appeal to order alone, without concrete specificity, is futile; the appeal to the dissemination of norms, without these ever proving themselves in reality or before consciousness, is equally futile. The idea of an objectively binding order, huckstered to people because it is so lacking for them, has no claims if it does not prove itself internally and in confrontation with human beings. But this is precisely what no product of the culture industry would engage in. The concepts of order which it hammers into human beings are always those of the status quo. They remain unquestioned, unanalysed and undialectically presupposed, even if they no longer have any substance for those who accept them. In contrast to the Kantian, the categorical imperative of the culture industry no longer has anything in common with freedom. It proclaims: you shall conform, without instruction as to what; conform to that which exists anyway, and to that which everyone thinks anyway as a reflex of its power and omnipresence. The power of the culture industry's ideology is such that conformity has replaced consciousness. The order that springs from it is never confronted with what it claims to be or with the real interests of human beings. Order, however, is not good in itself. It would be so only as a good order. The fact that the culture industry is oblivious to this and extols order *in abstracto*, bears witness to the impotence and untruth of the messages it conveys. While it claims to lead the perplexed, it deludes them with false conflicts which they are to exchange for their own. It solves conflicts for them only in appearance, in a way that they can hardly be solved in their real lives. In the products of the culture industry human beings get into trouble only so that they can be rescued unharmed, usually by representatives of a benevolent collective; and then in empty harmony, they are reconciled with the general, whose demands they had experienced at the outset as irreconcilable with their interests. For this purpose the culture industry has developed formulas which even reach into such non-conceptual areas as light musical entertainment. Here too one gets into a 'jam,' into rhythmic problems, which can be instantly disentangled by the triumph of the basic beat.

Even its defenders, however, would hardly contradict Plato openly who maintained that what is objectively and intrinsically untrue cannot also be subjectively good and true for human beings. The concoctions of the culture industry are neither guides for a blissful life, nor a new art of moral responsibility, but rather exhortations to toe the line, behind which stand the most powerful interests. The consensus which it propagates strengthens blind, opaque authority. If the culture industry is measured not by its own substance and logic, but by its efficacy, by its position in reality and its explicit pretensions; if the focus of serious concern is with the efficacy to which it always appeals, the potential of its effect becomes twice as weighty. This potential, however, lies in the promotion and exploitation of the ego-weakness to which the powerless members of contemporary society, with its concentration of power, are condemned. Their consciousness is further developed retrogressively. It is no coincidence that cynical American film producers are heard to say that their pictures must take into consideration the level of eleven-year-olds. In doing so they would very much like to make adults into eleven-year-olds.

It is true that thorough research has not, for the time being, produced an airtight case proving the regressive effects of particular products of the culture industry. No doubt an imaginatively designed experiment could achieve this more successfully than the powerful financial interests concerned would find comfortable. In any case, it can be assumed without hesitation that steady drops hollow the stone, especially since the system of the culture industry that surrounds the masses tolerates hardly any deviation and incessantly drills the same formulas on behaviour. Only their deep unconscious mistrust, the last residue of the difference between art and empirical reality in the spiritual make-up of the masses explains why they have not, to a person, long since perceived and accepted the world as it is constructed for them by the culture industry. Even if its messages were as harmless as they are made out to be—on countless occasions they are obviously not harmless, like the movies which chime in with currently popular hate campaigns against intellectuals by portraying them with the usual stereotypes—the attitudes which the culture industry calls forth are anything but harmless. If an astrologer urges his readers to drive carefully on a particular day, that certainly hurts no one; they will, however, be harmed indeed by the stupefication which lies in the claim that advice which is valid every day and which is therefore idiotic, needs the approval of the stars.

Human dependence and servitude, the vanishing point of the culture industry, could scarcely be more faithfully described than by the American interviewee who was of the opinion that the dilemmas of the contemporary epoch would end if people would simply follow the lead of prominent personalities. In so far as the culture industry arouses a feeling of well-being that the world is precisely in that order suggested by the culture industry, the substitute gratification which it prepares for human beings cheats them out of the same happiness which it deceitfully projects. The total effect of the culture industry is one of anti-enlightenment, in which, as Horkheimer and I have noted, enlightenment, that is the progressive technical domination of nature, becomes mass deception and is turned into a means for fettering consciousness. It impedes the development of autonomous, independent individuals who judge and decide consciously for themselves. These, however, would be the precondition for a democratic society which needs adults who have come of age in order to sustain itself and develop. If the masses have been unjustly reviled from above as masses, the culture industry is not among the least responsible for making them into masses and then despising them, while obstructing the emancipation for which human beings are as ripe as the productive forces of the epoch permit.

❖

Introduction to Herbert Marcuse's
One-Dimensional Man

Marcuse's *One-Dimensional Man* was one of the most widely read and influential books among advocates for social change during the 1960s. Although his message to the New Left was written more than forty years ago, Marcuse's insights ring just as powerfully today.

As we outlined previously, Marcuse describes contemporary, advanced societies—whether capitalist, communist, or socialist—as totalitarian social orders. For "totalitarian" does not refer only to a particular type of government. It "is not only a terroristic political coordination of society, but also a nonterroristic economic-political coordination which operates through the manipulation of needs by vested interests. It thus precludes the emergence of an effective opposition against the whole" (1964:3). Totalitarian societies are thus characterized by coordinated systems of domination that render all protest obsolete. Instead of being based on fear of external coercion or force, however, the methods of domination in advanced societies are based more on the manipulation of consciousness.

With the development of the industrial capacity to free individuals from want, the working class, the source of revolutionary change under Marxist theory, has been assimilated into the prevailing social order. Under the dominion of technological rationality and the benefits it offers, "the intellectual and emotional refusal 'to go along' appears neurotic and impotent" (ibid.:9). For why would anyone contest the satisfactions that the apparatus delivers through the progress of science and technology? The claim that the working class is alienated now becomes questionable as its members identify with, and literally buy into, the very system that is the source of their oppression. Once adversaries who harbored conflicting interests, capitalists and workers are united in their unquestioned, welcomed perpetuation of the status quo.

At the root of this social union lies the fabrication of new "needs" that maintain the existing way of life. Such needs do not spring from the consciousness of the individual; instead, they are a product of technological advances. (Do you really "need" a Blackberry or five-disc CD changer?) While the satisfaction of these false needs is advertised to be a path for happiness, they further the repression of true needs. Technology, then, is not neutral; rather it is a means for preserving domination. Indeed, its effectiveness as a dominating force resides in the fact that it appears to be neutral while it actually enslaves individuality. The creation of needs and the products dispensed to meet them serve to "indoctrinate and manipulate; they promote a false consciousness which is immune against its falsehood. And as these beneficial products become available to more individuals in more social classes, the indoctrination they carry ceases to be publicity; it becomes a way of life. It is a good way of life—much better than before—and as a good way of life it militates against qualitative change. Thus emerges a pattern of *one-dimensional thought and behavior* in which ideas, aspirations, and objectives that, by their content, transcend the established universe of discourse and action are either repelled or reduced to terms of this universe" (ibid.:12; emphasis in original).

This one-dimensional society intensifies repressive or institutionalized desublimation in which all opposition, whether political, cultural, or instinctual, is absorbed and thus defused by the very apparatus that it intended to oppose. With the range of alternative ideas and actions reduced to one, the indoctrination of the "Happy Consciousness" leaves individuals unable to grasp the essential unfreedom that characterizes advanced industrial society. Satisfied with the offerings and "liberties" of the established order, their loss of conscience leads to acceptance of the status quo and rampant conformity. As Marcuse argues:

> Under the rule of a repressive whole, liberty can be made into a powerful instrument of domination. The range of choice open to the individual is not the decisive factor in determining the degree of human freedom, but *what* can be chosen and what *is* chosen by the individual. . . . Free choice among a wide variety of goods and services does not signify freedom if these goods and services sustain social controls over a life of toil and fear. (ibid.:7, 8)

❖

One-Dimensional Man (1964)

Herbert Marcuse

THE NEW FORMS OF CONTROL

A comfortable, smooth, reasonable, democratic unfreedom prevails in advanced industrial civilization, a token of technical progress. Indeed, what could be more rational than the suppression of individuality in the mechanization of socially necessary but painful performances; the concentration of individual enterprises in more effective, more productive corporations; the regulation of free competition among unequally equipped economic subjects; the curtailment of prerogatives and national sovereignties which impede the international organization of resources. That this technological order also involves a political and intellectual coordination may be a regrettable and yet promising development.

The rights and liberties which were such vital factors in the origins and earlier stages of industrial society yield to a higher stage of this society: they are losing their traditional rationale and content. Freedom of thought, speech, and conscience were—just as free enterprise, which they served to promote and protect—essentially *critical* ideas, designed to replace an obsolescent material and intellectual culture by a more productive and rational one. Once institutionalized, these rights and liberties shared the fate of the society of which they had become an integral part. The achievement cancels the premises.

To the degree to which freedom from want, the concrete substance of all freedom, is becoming a real possibility, the liberties which pertain to a state of lower productivity are losing their former content. Independence of thought, autonomy, and the right to political opposition are being deprived of their basic critical function in a society which seems increasingly capable of satisfying the needs of the individuals through the way in which it is organized. Such

a society may justly demand acceptance of its principles and institutions, and reduce the opposition to the discussion and promotion of alternative policies *within* the status quo. In this respect, it seems to make little difference whether the increasing satisfaction of needs is accomplished by an authoritarian or a non-authoritarian system. Under the conditions of a rising standard of living, non-conformity with the system itself appears to be socially useless, and the more so when it entails tangible economic and political disadvantages and threatens the smooth operation of the whole. Indeed, at least in so far as the necessities of life are involved, there seems to be no reason why the production and distribution of goods and services should proceed through the competitive concurrence of individual liberties.

Freedom of enterprise was from the beginning not altogether a blessing. As the liberty to work or to starve, it spelled toil, insecurity, and fear for the vast majority of the population. If the individual were no longer compelled to prove himself on the market, as a free economic subject, the disappearance of this kind of freedom would be one of the greatest achievements of civilization. The technological processes of mechanization and standardization might release individual energy into a yet uncharted realm of freedom beyond necessity. The very structure of human existence would be altered; the individual would be liberated from the work world's imposing upon him alien needs and alien possibilities. The individual would be free to exert autonomy over a life that would be his own. If the productive apparatus could be organized and directed toward the satisfaction of the vital needs, its control might well be centralized; such control would not prevent individual autonomy, but render it possible.

This is a goal within the capabilities of advanced industrial civilization, the "end" of technological rationality. In actual fact, however, the contrary trend operates: the apparatus imposes its economic and political requirements for defense and expansion on labor time and free time, on the material and intellectual culture. By virtue of the way it has organized its technological base, contemporary industrial society tends to be totalitarian. For "totalitarian" is not only a terroristic political coordination of society, but also a non-terroristic economic-technical coordination which operates through the manipulation of needs by vested interests. It thus precludes the emergence of an effective opposition against the whole. Not only a specific form of government or party rule makes for totalitarianism, but also a specific system of production and distribution which may well be compatible with a "pluralism" of parties, newspapers, "countervailing powers," etc.

Today political power asserts itself through its power over the machine process and over the technical organization of the apparatus. The government of advanced and advancing industrial societies can maintain and secure itself only when it succeeds in mobilizing, organizing, and exploiting the technical, scientific, and mechanical productivity available to industrial civilization. And this productivity mobilizes society as a whole, above and beyond any particular individual or group interests. The brute fact that the machine's physical (only physical?) power surpasses that of the individual, and of any particular group of individuals, makes the machine the most effective political instrument in any society whose basic organization is that of the machine process. But the political trend may be reversed; essentially the power of the machine is only the stored-up and projected power of man. To the extent to which the work world is conceived of as a machine and mechanized accordingly, it becomes the *potential* basis of a new freedom for man.

Contemporary industrial civilization demonstrates that it has reached the stage at which "the free society" can no longer be adequately defined in the traditional terms of economic, political, and intellectual liberties, not because these liberties have become insignificant, but because they are too significant to be confined within the traditional forms. New modes of realization are needed, corresponding to the new capabilities of society.

Such new modes can be indicated only in negative terms because they would amount to the negation of the prevailing modes. Thus economic freedom would mean freedom *from* the economy—from being controlled by economic forces and relationships; freedom from the daily struggle for existence, from earning a living. Political freedom would mean liberation of the individuals *from* politics over which they have no effective control. Similarly, intellectual freedom would mean the restoration of individual thought now absorbed by mass communication and indoctrination, abolition of "public opinion" together with its makers. The unrealistic sound of these propositions is indicative, not of their utopian character, but of the strength of the forces which prevent their realization. The most effective and enduring form of warfare against liberation is the implanting of material and intellectual needs that perpetuate obsolete forms of the struggle for existence.

The intensity, the satisfaction and even the character of human needs, beyond the biological level, have always been preconditioned. Whether or not the possibility of doing or leaving, enjoying or destroying, possessing or rejecting something is seized as a *need* depends on whether or not it can be seen as desirable and necessary for the prevailing societal institutions and interests. In this sense, human needs are historical needs and, to the extent to which the society demands the repressive development of the individual, his needs themselves and their claim for satisfaction are subject to overriding critical standards.

We may distinguish both true and false needs. "False" are those which are superimposed upon the individual by particular social interests in his repression: the needs which perpetuate toil, aggressiveness, misery, and injustice. Their satisfaction might be most gratifying to the individual, but this happiness is not a condition which has to be maintained and protected if it serves to arrest the development of the ability (his own and others) to recognize the disease of the whole and grasp the chances of curing the disease. The result then is euphoria in unhappiness. Most of the prevailing needs to relax, to have fun, to behave and consume in accordance with the advertisements, to love and hate what others love and hate, belong to this category of false needs.

Such needs have a societal content and function which are determined by external powers over which the individual has no control; the development and satisfaction of these needs is heteronomous. No matter how much such needs may have become the individual's own, reproduced and fortified by the conditions of his existence; no matter how much he identifies himself with them and finds himself in their satisfaction, they continue to be what they were from the beginning—products of a society whose dominant interest demands repression.

The prevalence of repressive needs is an accomplished fact, accepted in ignorance and defeat, but a fact that must be undone in the interest of the happy individual as well as all those whose misery is the price of his satisfaction. The only needs that have an unqualified claim for satisfaction are the vital ones—nourishment, clothing, lodging at the attainable level of culture. The satisfaction of these needs is the prerequisite for the realization of *all* needs, of the unsublimated as well as the sublimated ones.

For any consciousness and conscience, for any experience which does not accept the prevailing societal interest as the supreme law of thought and behavior, the established universe of needs and satisfactions is a fact to be questioned—questioned in terms of truth and falsehood. These terms are historical throughout, and their objectivity is historical. The judgment of needs and their satisfaction, under the given conditions, involves standards of *priority*—standards which refer to the optimal development of the individual, of all individuals, under the optimal utilization of the material and intellectual resources available to man. The resources are calculable. "Truth" and "falsehood" of needs designate objective conditions to the extent to which the universal satisfaction of vital needs and, beyond it, the progressive alleviation of toil and poverty, are universally valid standards. But as historical standards, they do not only vary according to area and stage of development, they also can be defined only in (greater or lesser) *contradiction* to the prevailing ones. What tribunal can possibly claim the authority of decision?

In the last analysis, the question of what are true and false needs must be answered by the individuals themselves, but only in the last analysis; that is, if and when they are free to give their own answer. As long as they are kept incapable of being autonomous, as long as they are indoctrinated and manipulated (down to their very instincts), their answer to this question cannot be taken as their own. By the same token, however, no tribunal can justly arrogate to itself the right to decide which needs should be developed and satisfied. Any such tribunal is reprehensible, although our revulsion does not do away with the question: how can the people who have been the object of effective and productive domination by themselves create the conditions of freedom?

The more rational, productive, technical, and total the repressive administration of society becomes, the more un-imaginable the means and ways by which the administered individuals might break their servitude and seize their own liberation. To be sure, to impose Reason upon an entire society is a paradoxical and scandalous idea—although one might dispute the righteousness of a society which ridicules this idea while making its own population into objects of total administration. All liberation depends on the consciousness of servitude, and the emergence of this consciousness is always hampered by the predominance of needs and satisfactions which, to a great extent, have become the individual's own. The process always replaces one system of preconditioning by another; the optimal goal is the replacement of false needs by true ones, the abandonment of repressive satisfaction.

The distinguishing feature of advanced industrial society is its effective suffocation of those needs which demand liberation—liberation also from that which is tolerable and rewarding and comfortable—while it sustains and absolves the destructive power and repressive function of the affluent society. Here, the social controls exact the overwhelming need for the production and consumption of waste; the need for stupefying work where it is no longer a real necessity; the need for modes of relaxation which soothe and prolong this stupefication; the need for maintaining such deceptive liberties as free competition at administered prices, a free press which censors itself, free choice between brands and gadgets.

Under the rule of a repressive whole, liberty can be made into a powerful instrument of domination. The range of choice open to the individual is not the decisive factor in determining the degree of human freedom, but *what* can be chosen and what *is* chosen by the individual. The criterion for free choice can never be an absolute one, but neither is it entirely relative. Free election of masters does not abolish the masters or the slaves. Free choice among a wide variety of goods and services does not signify freedom if these goods and services sustain social controls over a life of toil and fear—that is, if they sustain alienation. And the spontaneous reproduction of superimposed needs by the individual does not establish autonomy; it only testifies to the efficacy of the controls.

Our insistence on the depth and efficacy of these controls is open to the objection that we overrate greatly the indoctrinating power of the "media," and that by themselves the people would feel and satisfy the needs which are now imposed upon them. The objection misses the point. The preconditioning does not start with the mass production of radio and television and with the centralization of their control. The people enter this stage as preconditioned receptacles of long standing; the decisive difference is in the flattening out of the contrast (or conflict) between the given and the possible, between the satisfied and the unsatisfied needs. Here, the so-called equalization of class distinctions reveals its ideological function. If the worker and his boss enjoy the same television program and visit the same resort places, if the typist is as attractively made up as the daughter of her employer, if the Negro owns a Cadillac, if they all read the same newspaper, then this assimilation indicates not the disappearance of classes, but the extent to which the needs and satisfactions that serve the preservation of the Establishment are shared by the underlying population.

Indeed, in the most highly developed areas of contemporary society, the transplantation of social into individual needs is so effective that the difference between them seems to be purely theoretical. Can one really distinguish between the mass media as instruments of information and entertainment, and as agents of manipulation and indoctrination? Between the automobile as nuisance and as convenience? Between the horrors and the comforts of functional architecture? Between the work for national defense and the work for corporate gain? Between the private pleasure and the commercial and political utility involved in increasing the birth rate?

We are again confronted with one of the most vexing aspects of advanced industrial civilization: the rational character of its irrationality. Its productivity and efficiency, its capacity to increase and spread comforts, to turn waste into need, and destruction into construction, the extent to which this civilization transforms the object world into an extension of man's mind and body makes the very notion of alienation questionable. The people recognize themselves in their commodities; they find their soul in their automobile, hi-fi set, split-level home, kitchen equipment. The very mechanism which ties the individual to his society has changed, and social control is anchored in the new needs which it has produced.

The prevailing forms of social control are technological in a new sense. To be sure, the technical structure and efficacy of the productive and destructive apparatus has been a major instrumentality for subjecting the population to the established social division of labor throughout the modern period. Moreover, such integration has always been accompanied by more obvious forms of compulsion: loss of livelihood, the administration of justice, the police, the armed forces. It still is. But in the contemporary period, the technological controls appear to be the very embodiment of Reason for the benefit of all social groups and interests—to such an extent that all contradiction seems irrational and all counteraction impossible.

No wonder then that, in the most advanced areas of this civilization, the social controls have been introjected to the point where even individual protest is affected at its roots. The intellectual and emotional refusal "to go along" appears neurotic and impotent. This is the socio-psychological aspect of the political event that marks the contemporary period: the passing of the historical forces which, at the preceding stage of industrial society, seemed to represent the possibility of new forms of existence.

But the term "introjection" perhaps no longer describes the way in which the individual by himself reproduces and perpetuates the external controls exercised by this society. Introjection suggests a variety of relatively spontaneous processes by which a Self (Ego) transposes the "outer" into the "inner." Thus introjection implies the existence of an inner dimension distinguished from and even antagonistic to the external exigencies—an individual consciousness and an individual unconscious *apart from* public opinion and behavior.[i] The idea of "inner freedom" here has its reality: it designates the private space in which man may become and remain "himself."

Today this private space has been invaded and whittled down by technological reality. Mass production and mass distribution claim the *entire* individual, and industrial psychology has long since ceased to be confined to the factory. The manifold processes of introjection seem to be ossified in almost mechanical reactions. The result is, not adjustment but *mimesis:* an immediate identification of the individual with *his* society and, through it, with the society as a whole.

This immediate, automatic identification (which may have been characteristic of primitive forms of association) reappears in high industrial civilization; its new "immediacy," however, is the product of a sophisticated, scientific management and organization. In this process, the "inner" dimension of the mind in which opposition to the status quo can take root is whittled down. The loss of this dimension, in which the power of negative thinking—the critical power of Reason—is at home, is the ideological counterpart to the very material process in which advanced industrial society silences and reconciles the opposition. The impact of progress turns Reason into submission to the facts of life, and to the dynamic capability of producing more and bigger facts of the same sort of life. The efficiency of the system blunts the individuals' recognition that it contains no facts which do not communicate the repressive power of the whole. If the individuals find themselves in the things which shape their life, they do so, not by giving, but by accepting the law of things—not the law of physics but the law of their society.

I have just suggested that the concept of alienation seems to become questionable when the individuals identify themselves with the existence which is imposed upon them and have in it their own development and satisfaction. This identification is not illusion but reality. However, the reality constitutes a more progressive stage of alienation. The latter has become entirely objective; the subject which is alienated is swallowed up by its alienated existence. There is only one dimension, and it is everywhere and in all forms. The achievements of progress defy ideological indictment as well as justification; before their tribunal, the "false consciousness" of their rationality becomes the true consciousness.

This absorption of ideology into reality does not, however, signify the "end of ideology." On the contrary, in a specific sense advanced industrial culture is *more* ideological than its predecessor, inasmuch as today the ideology is in the process of production itself. In a provocative form, this proposition reveals the political aspects of the prevailing technological rationality. The productive apparatus and the goods and services which it produces "sell" or impose the social system as a whole. The means of mass transportation and communication, the commodities of lodging, food, and clothing, the irresistible output of the entertainment and information industry carry with them prescribed attitudes and habits, certain intellectual and emotional reactions which bind the consumers more or less pleasantly to the producers and, through the latter, to the whole. The products indoctrinate and manipulate; they promote a false consciousness which is immune against its falsehood. And as these beneficial products become available to more individuals in more social classes, the indoctrination they carry ceases to be publicity; it becomes a way of life. It is a good way of life—much better than before—and as a good way of life, it militates against qualitative change. Thus emerges a pattern of *one-dimensional thought and behavior* in which ideas, aspirations, and objectives that, by their content, transcend the established universe of discourse and action are either repelled or reduced to terms of this universe. They are redefined by the rationality of the given system and of its quantitative extension. . . .

---

[i]The change in the function of the family here plays a decisive role: its "socializing" functions are increasingly taken over by outside groups and media.

One-dimensional thought is systematically promoted by the makers of politics and their purveyors of mass information. Their universe of discourse is populated by self-validating hypotheses which, incessantly and monopolistically repeated, become hypnotic definitions or dictations. For example, "free" are the institutions which operate (and are operated on) in the countries of the Free World; other transcending modes of freedom are by definition either anarchism, communism, or propaganda. "Socialistic" are all encroachments on private enterprises not undertaken by private enterprise itself (or by government contracts), such as universal and comprehensive health insurance, or the protection of nature from all too sweeping commercialization, or the establishment of public services which may hurt private profit. This totalitarian logic of accomplished facts has its Eastern counterpart. There, freedom is the way of life instituted by a communist regime, and all other transcending modes of freedom are either capitalistic, or revisionist, or leftist sectarianism. In both camps, non-operational ideas are non-behavioral and subversive. The movement of thought is stopped at barriers which appear as the limits of Reason itself.

Such limitation of thought is certainly not new. Ascending modern rationalism, in its speculative as well as empirical form, shows a striking contrast between extreme critical radicalism in scientific and philosophic method on the one hand, and an uncritical quietism in the attitude toward established and functioning social institutions. Thus Descartes' *ego cogitans* was to leave the "great public bodies" untouched, and Hobbes held that "the present ought always to be preferred, maintained, and accounted best." Kant agreed with Locke in justifying revolution *if and when* it has succeeded in organizing the whole and in preventing subversion.

However, these accommodating concepts of Reason were always contradicted by the evident misery and injustice of the "great public bodies" and the effective, more or less conscious rebellion against them. Societal conditions existed which provoked and permitted real dissociation from the established state of affairs; a private as well as political dimension was present in which dissociation could develop into effective opposition, testing its strength and the validity of its objectives.

With the gradual closing of this dimension by the society, the self-limitation of thought assumes a larger significance. The interrelation between scientific-philosophical and societal processes, between theoretical and practical Reason, asserts itself "behind the back" of the scientists and philosophers. The society bars a whole type of oppositional operations and behavior; consequently, the concepts pertaining to them are rendered illusory or meaningless. Historical transcendence appears as metaphysical transcendence, not acceptable to science and scientific thought. The operational and behavioral point of view, practiced as a "habit of thought" at large, becomes the view of the established universe of discourse and action, needs and aspirations. The "cunning of Reason" works, as it so often did, in the interest of the powers that be. The insistence on operational and behavioral concepts turns against the efforts to free thought and behavior *from* the given reality and *for* the suppressed alternatives. Theoretical and practical Reason, academic and social behaviorism meet on common ground: that of an advanced society which makes scientific and technical progress into an instrument of domination.

"Progress" is not a neutral term; it moves toward specific ends, and these ends are defined by the possibilities of ameliorating the human condition. Advanced industrial society is approaching the stage where continued progress would demand the radical subversion of the prevailing direction and organization of progress. This stage would be reached when material production (including the necessary services) becomes automated to the extent that all vital needs can be satisfied while necessary labor time is reduced to marginal time. From this point on, technical progress would transcend the realm of necessity, where it served as the instrument of domination and exploitation which thereby limited its rationality; technology would become subject to the free play of faculties in the struggle for the pacification of nature and of society.

Such a state is envisioned in Marx's notion of the "abolition of labor." The term "pacification of existence" seems better suited to designate the historical alternative of a world which—through an international conflict which transforms and suspends the contradictions within the established societies—advances on the brink of a global war. "Pacification of existence" means the development of man's struggle with man and with nature, under conditions where the competing needs, desires, and aspirations are no longer organized by vested interests in domination and scarcity—an organization which perpetuates the destructive forms of this struggle.

Today's fight against this historical alternative finds a firm mass basis in the underlying population, and finds its ideology in the rigid orientation of thought and behavior to the given universe of facts. Validated by the accomplishments of science and technology, justified by its growing productivity, the status quo defies all transcendence. Faced with the possibility of pacification on the grounds of its technical and intellectual achievements, the mature industrial society closes itself against this alternative. Operationalism, in theory and practice, becomes the theory and practice of *containment*. Underneath its obvious dynamics, this society is a thoroughly static system of life: self-propelling in its oppressive productivity and in its beneficial coordination. Containment of technical progress goes hand in hand with its growth in the established direction. In spite of the political fetters imposed by the status quo, the more technology appears capable of creating the conditions for pacification, the more are the minds and bodies of man organized against this alternative.

The most advanced areas of industrial society exhibit throughout these two features: a trend toward consummation of technological rationality, and intensive efforts to contain this trend within the established institutions. Here is the internal contradiction of this civilization: the irrational element in its rationality. It is the token of its achievements. The industrial society which makes technology and science its own is organized for the ever-more-effective domination of man and nature, for the ever-more-effective utilization of its resources. It becomes irrational when the success of these efforts opens new dimensions of human realization. Organization for peace is different from organization for war; the institutions which served the struggle for existence cannot serve the pacification of existence. Life as an end is qualitatively different from life as a means.

Such a qualitatively new mode of existence can never be envisaged as the mere by-product of economic and political changes, as the more or less spontaneous effect of the new institutions which constitute the necessary prerequisite. Qualitative change also involves a change in the *technical* basis on which this society rests—one which sustains the economic and political institutions through which the "second nature" of man as an aggressive object of administration is stabilized. The techniques of industrialization are political techniques; as such, they prejudge the possibilities of Reason and Freedom.

To be sure, labor must precede the reduction of labor, and industrialization must precede the development of human needs and satisfactions. But as all freedom depends on the conquest of alien necessity, the realization of freedom depends on the *techniques* of this conquest. The highest productivity of labor can be used for the perpetuation of labor, and the most efficient industrialization can serve the restriction and manipulation of needs.

When this point is reached, domination—in the guise of affluence and liberty—extends to all spheres of private and public existence, integrates all authentic opposition, absorbs all alternatives. Technological rationality reveals its political character as it becomes the great vehicle of better domination, creating a truly totalitarian universe in which society and nature, mind and body are kept in a state of permanent mobilization for the defense of this universe. . . .

THE CLOSING OF THE POLITICAL UNIVERSE

The new technological work-world thus enforces a weakening of the negative position of the working class: the latter no longer appears to be the living contradiction to the established society. This trend is strengthened by the effect of the technological organization of production on the other side of the fence: on management and direction. Domination is transfigured into administration.[ii] The capitalist bosses and owners

---

[ii]Is it still necessary to denounce the ideology of the "managerial revolution"? Capitalist production proceeds through the investment of private capital for the private extraction and appropriation of surplus value, and capital is a social instrument for the domination of man by man. The essential features of this process are in no way altered by the spread of stock-holdings, the separation of ownership from management, etc.

are losing their identity as responsible agents; they are assuming the function of bureaucrats in a corporate machine. Within the vast hierarchy of executive and managerial boards extending far beyond the individual establishment into the scientific laboratory and research institute, the national government and national purpose, the tangible source of exploitation disappears behind the façade of objective rationality. Hatred and frustration are deprived of their specific target, and the technological veil conceals the reproduction of inequality and enslavement. With technical progress as its instrument, unfreedom—in the sense of man's subjection to his productive apparatus—is perpetuated and intensified in the form of many liberties and comforts. The novel feature is the overwhelming rationality in this irrational enterprise, and the depth of the preconditioning which shapes the instinctual drives and aspirations of the individuals and obscures the difference between false and true consciousness. For in reality, neither the utilization of administrative rather than physical controls (hunger, personal dependence, force), nor the change in the character of heavy work, nor the assimilation of occupational classes, nor the equalization in the sphere of consumption compensate for the fact that the decisions over life and death, over personal and national security are made at places over which the individuals have no control. The slaves of developed industrial civilization are sublimated slaves, but they are slaves, for slavery is determined "neither by obedience nor by hardness of labor but by the status of being a mere instrument, and the reduction of man to the state of a thing."[iii] This is the pure form of servitude: to exist as an instrument, as a thing. And this mode of existence is not abrogated if the thing is animated and chooses its material and intellectual food, if it does not feel its being-a-thing, if it is a pretty, clean, mobile thing. Conversely, as reification tends to become totalitarian by virtue of its technological form, the organizers and administrators themselves become increasingly dependent on the machinery which they organize and administer. And this mutual dependence is no longer the dialectical relationship between Master and Servant, which has been broken in the struggle for mutual recognition, but rather a vicious circle which encloses both the Master and the Servant. Do the technicians rule, or is their rule that of the others, who rely on the technicians as their planners and executors?

. . . the pressures of today's highly technological arms race have taken the initiative and the power to make the crucial decisions out of the hands of responsible government officials and placed it in the hands of technicians, planners and scientists employed by vast industrial empires and charged with responsibility for their employers' interests. It is their job to dream up new weapons systems and persuade the military that the future of their military profession, as well as the country, depends upon buying what they have dreamed up.[iv]

As the productive establishments rely on the military for self-preservation and growth, so the military relies on the corporations "not only for their weapons, but also for knowledge of what kind of weapons they need, how much they will cost, and how long it will take to get them."[v] A vicious circle seems indeed the proper image of a society which is self-expanding and self-perpetuating in its own preestablished direction—driven by the growing needs which it generates and, at the same time, contains.

[iii]François Perroux, *La Coexistence pacifique* (Paris, Presses Universitaires, 1958), Vol. III, p. 600.

[iv]Stewart Meacham, *Labor and the Cold War* (American Friends Service Committee, Philadelphia 1959), p. 9.

[v]*Ibid.*

❖

Discussion Questions

1. Given the critical theorists' reservations regarding the scientific pursuit of knowledge, how might a sociologist conduct "valid" research? If the scientific method is rejected, what criteria can be used to assess a researcher's findings? More generally, if not science, what might serve as a basis for accepting anyone's claim to speak the "truth"?

2. Do you think that individuals living in advanced, capitalist societies are as "pacified" as the critical theorists argue? Has individuality been "liquidated" as the critical theorists suggest? What evidence can you point to in support of your view?

3. While the critical theorists presented here deride mass culture and technology for corrupting our ability to reason, what role, if any, might education play in promoting a "totally administered society"? Second, as a form of technology, do you consider the Internet a potential source of liberation or domination? Why?

4. According to the critical theorists, how, in modern industrial societies, does rationality lead to the oppression and/or alienation of the individual? Do you agree that the United States is a "totalitarian" society? Why or why not?

5. Many musical groups express in their songs a discontent with existing social conditions and a mistrust of those in positions of authority. What effect, if any, does such music have on the broader society? How might such "protest" songs paradoxically reinforce the very social order they aim to criticize?

4

EXCHANGE THEORY

Key Concepts

George Homans

- ❖ Elementary Social Behavior
- ❖ Costs
- ❖ Distributive Justice

Peter Blau

- ❖ Intrinsic/Extrinsic Rewards
- ❖ Power
- ❖ Imbalanced Exchange

A stable social relationship requires that individuals make some investments to bring it into being and maintain it in existence, and it is to the advantage of each party to have the other or others assume a disproportionate share of the commitments that secure their continuing association. Hence the common interest of individuals in sustaining a relation between them tends to be accompanied by conflicting interests as to whose investment should contribute most to its sustenance.

~Blau (1964:113)

W hat are the factors that motivate your choice of friends? What is it about you that induces others to strike up an acquaintanceship? Why do relationships—personal or professional—begin and end when they do? To these questions and countless others like it exchange theorists offer one fundamental answer: social behavior is guided by the *rational* calculation of an *exchange* of rewards and costs. Much like our economic calculations through which we determine whether the value (reward) of a good is worth its price (cost), so in our social interactions we decide to enter into or terminate a relationship (exchange) with another.

For example, why would a person join and remain in a peer group when he is the constant butt of jokes or pressured into conducting embarrassing or perhaps even dangerous acts? Certainly, any familiarity with college fraternities and sororities or even gangs would have introduced us to such a person. The explanation is straightforward: the rewards reaped for group membership (perhaps status or companionship) outweigh the costs associated with public humiliation or personal risk. And when the value or importance of the rewards diminishes below the costs incurred, the person will exit the group.

In what follows we outline the work of two sociologists, George Homans and Peter Blau, who arguably have made the most significant contributions to exchange theory. In doing so, we highlight their points of theoretical convergence and departure—points that are only hinted at in the simplified example drawn above. Equally important, outlining the central elements of their respective contributions will also provide a canvas for sketching the underlying theoretical and methodological assumptions that make exchange theory a distinct approach to understanding social life. For instance, both Homans and Blau (and exchange theorists more generally) portray individuals as strategic actors who use the resources they have at their disposal in an effort to optimize their rewards. Thus, they contend that individuals are motivated to act not on the basis of tradition, unconscious drives, or some type of structural imperative, but rather on the basis of rational considerations—namely, weighing the consequences of alternative lines of conduct in terms of the "profit" they will likely generate.

Despite such fundamental similarities, however, there are key differences in these theorists' work. Homans draws principally from behavioral psychology and neoclassical economics in developing his version of exchange theory. Blau's exchange theory, while sympathetic with economics, evinces a greater indebtedness to the German sociologist Georg Simmel. Consequently, each theorist provides a different pathway—and a different set of answers—to a related set of concerns. It is to a more thorough discussion of these issues and others that we now turn.

GEORGE HOMANS (1910–1989): A BIOGRAPHICAL SKETCH

Homans was born in Boston, Massachusetts, to one of the city's elite families. He attended Harvard College where, in 1932, he earned a degree in English literature. He was prepared to join the staff of a newspaper after graduating, but his career in journalism ended before it started. Like so many other jobs at the time, Homans's position with the newspaper vanished in the wake of the Depression. It was through this accident of circumstances that Homans would find his introduction to sociology. Remarking that he had nothing better to do, Homans attended a Harvard seminar on the work of the Italian sociologist Vilfredo Pareto (1848–1923). With another attendee to the seminar, Charles Curtis, he wrote *An Introduction to Pareto*, which in large measure helped earn him admission into the Harvard Society of Fellows in 1934. From that point forward, Homans's academic career would be spent entirely at Harvard, his alma mater. Yet, Homans did not commit himself full time to the sociology department until 1946 and would wait until 1953 to be appointed full professor—nearly twenty years after being elected to the Society of Fellows. Despite the accidental nature of his introduction into the field and the fact that he never earned a degree in sociology, Homans's work would come to make an important mark in the discipline. Certainly, his colleagues recognized the significance of his contributions when they elected him president of the American Sociological Association in 1964. During the next twenty-five years, Homans would go on to publish a number of articles and books, including *The Nature of the Social Sciences* (1967). The importance of his impact on the discipline was again affirmed with his awarding of the ASA's Distinguished Scholarship Award in 1988. Homans died the following year.

SOURCE: American Sociological Association; used with permission.

Intellectual Influences and Core Ideas

Homans developed his exchange theory with the ambition of creating a general framework for understanding individuals' behaviors in face-to-face dealings with one another. As we noted at the beginning of this chapter, his approach is based on a fusion of the principles of behavioral psychology with those of neoclassical economics. Here, we briefly outline the main elements of these two schools and their relevance to Homans's approach.

B. F. Skinner and Behavioral Psychology

In incorporating the insights of behavioral psychology, Homans turned to the work of his friend and colleague at Harvard B. F. Skinner (1904–1990). Skinner conducted experiments with pigeons in order to explore the effects of operant conditioning. This involves a process in which a particular behavior (operant) is reinforced through the use of rewards or punishments that, in turn, condition the likelihood that the behavior will be repeated or avoided. It is in this way, through the provision and removal of rewards and punishments, that all noninstinctual behaviors are learned. In one of the more remarkable examples of the techniques of operant conditioning and their effectiveness, Skinner trained his laboratory pigeons to play table tennis by reinforcing (rewarding) specific behaviors with food.

Skinner, however, was less interested in understanding how pigeons *learn* reinforced behaviors than in discovering the factors that account for *changes* in the frequency with which learned behaviors are exhibited. This led him to consider two conditions: the state of the pigeon (i.e., whether it is hungry or not) and the rate at which the behavior in question is reinforced. With regard to the former, Skinner noted that the longer a pigeon has gone without food and, thus, the hungrier it is, the more often it will perform a behavior that has been previously reinforced with food. Conversely, the more the pigeon's hunger has been satiated, the less often it will perform the behavior. As for the latter, the basic proposition suggests that the less frequently a behavior is reinforced, the less frequently it will be exhibited. On the other hand, the more frequent (and thus reliable) a reinforcement, the more often the conditioned behavior will be exhibited (Homans 1961:19–21).

A final consideration involves the role of punishments in determining the probability that a particular action will be performed. Punishments also take on two forms. First, in laboratory settings pigeons can be subjected to "aversive conditions," for instance, an electric shock. In such a setting, a given behavior will be reinforced if it enables the bird to escape from or avoid the punishment. Second, punishments also can come in the form of a withdrawal of positive reinforcements, such as the removal of food if a specified behavior is performed. Parents often resort to both forms of punishment when trying to correct (that is, eliminate) their children's disobedient behavior. Who has not heard "You're grounded!" or "No dessert for you!"

Photo 4.1 A Favored Form of Punishment by Today's Parents: The Time-Out
SOURCE: Scott Appelrouth; used with permission.

Skinner's work in behavioral psychology also highlighted a special class of punishments that would become central in Homans's theory on social exchange: **costs**. Costs are unavoidable punishments that are experienced when a behavior also elicits positive reinforcement. Costs have the effect of reducing the frequency of an otherwise rewarding behavior. Costs accompanying a given behavior also have the potential effect of increasing the frequency of an alternative behavior. Similarly, as the costs associated with a given behavior increase, the rewards reaped from pursuing an alternative behavior rise in kind. As a result, the costs entailed in performing a specific act involve the unavoidable punishment of losing or forgoing the rewards that would have been reaped had an alternative behavior been performed (Homans 1961:24–26).

As we noted previously, the preceding discussion of operant conditioning and its attendant concepts such as rewards, punishments, and costs is derived from Skinner's experimentation with pigeons. Thus, Homans had to first acknowledge some basic assumptions when transposing Skinner's work into his own theory, namely, that propositions regarding individual behavior could be adapted to social situations and, perhaps more controversial, that propositions on the behavior of pigeons could be generalized to the behavior of humans (Homans 1961:31). Taking these two assumptions into account, Homans sought to explain **elementary social behavior**, which he defined as "face-to-face contact between individuals, in which the reward [or punishment] each gets from the behavior of the others is relatively direct and immediate" (ibid.:7). While individual behavior (of pigeons or humans) involves an "exchange" between an animal and its physical environment, social behavior is based on the type of exchange "where the activity of each of at least two animals reinforces (or punishes) the activity of the other, and where accordingly each influences the other" (ibid.:30). However, it is noteworthy that Homans maintained that the laws of individual behavior developed by Skinner are identical to the laws of social behavior once the complications of mutual reinforcement are considered. Thus, there is nothing unique to social behavior that warrants the introduction of new propositions different from those that explain individual or psychological behavior. Not surprisingly, Homans's position on this issue was (and continues to be) met with much resistance on the part of many sociologists, for, in effect, he was giving over the discipline to psychology.

So what, specifically, are the psychological propositions that explain and predict social behavior? Homans offered five that, when taken together, are said to demonstrate how individuals profit from their actions. In other words, individuals design their conduct such that the value of the rewards gained in an exchange are greater than the costs incurred in forgoing the rewards associated with an alternative line of behavior. We summarize the propositions in Table 4.1 on the next page.

To illustrate the operation of these propositions, consider the following example adapted from Homans's (1961) work. Andrew is new to his job and needs help in order to complete his assigned tasks. Thus, he values help and finds it rewarding. Andrew turns to Emma, who is more experienced at the job and is able to take some amount of time from her own work in order to assist Andrew. Andrew rewards Emma for her efforts with thanks and expressions of approval, which Emma, we assume, finds worth receiving. In this scenario, help and approval are exchanged.

Considering proposition 1 ("stimulus"), we can first predict that Emma is more likely to provide Andrew with help if the present situation (i.e., stimulus) resembles previous ones in which her willingness to provide assistance has been rewarded. If in similar past experiences Emma has been "burned"—incurred the costs of taking time from her own work without receiving a sufficient reward for her time and expertise—then she would be less likely to risk her services.

Table 4.1   Homans's Behaviorist Propositions[1]

The Stimulus Proposition	If the previous occurrence of a particular stimulus has been the occasion on which an individual's action has been rewarded, then the more similar the current stimulus is to the past one, the more likely the person is to repeat the action.
The Success Proposition	The more often an action is followed by a reward, the more likely a person will repeat the behavior.
The Value Proposition	The more valuable a particular reward is to a person, the more often he will perform a behavior so rewarded.
The Deprivation-Satiation Proposition	The more often in the recent past an individual has received a particular reward, the less valuable any further unit of that reward becomes (and following the value proposition, the less likely the person is to perform the behavior for which he was so rewarded).
The Frustration-Aggression Proposition	If a person's action receives a punishment he did not expect, or if the person does not receive the reward he did expect, he will become angry and more likely to exhibit aggressive behavior, the results of which will become more valuable to him.

Taking together propositions 2 and 3 ("success" and "value"), we can predict that the more Andrew needs help and finds Emma's assistance valuable, the more he will ask for it, and the more approval he will offer in return. Likewise, the more Emma needs or values approval, the more often she will provide assistance to Andrew. As a result, the frequency of interaction or exchange between the two depends on the frequency with which each rewards the actions of the other and on the value of the reward each receives (1961:55). On the other hand, should either of the two begin to offer less valuable rewards (less than adequate help or a lackluster show of approval and thanks), then the frequency of their exchange will decrease and eventually end.

However, proposition 4 ("deprivation-satiation") argues that even if Andrew and Emma continue to exchange acceptable rewards, the value of such rewards will begin to decline. For just like the pigeon that stops pecking a lever once its hunger is satiated, at some point Andrew will find that he is no longer in need of help, while Emma will have had her fill of "thank you's." As a result, following the value proposition, the frequency of their exchange of approval and help will decrease. In short, as the profit of their activities begins to fall, each is more likely to pursue an alternative course of action, even if this simply means not asking for or supplying help.

While the value proposition tells us that both Andrew and Emma must have found their exchange more profitable than alternative courses of action (or else they would not have interacted), it does not provide the whole story. Asserting that individuals will enter into and maintain exchange relations so long as they are profitable says little about how the price of rewards and costs is established. In rounding out the account, the fifth proposition ("frustration-aggression") yields some interesting conclusions regarding evaluations of costs and rewards and, thus, the amount of profit an individual can justifiably expect from an exchange.

[1]Adapted from *Social Behavior: Its Elementary Forms*, Harcourt, Brace, and World, Inc., 1964, pp. 53–55, 75, and "Behaviorism and After," in *Social Theory Today*, edited by Anthony Giddens and Jonathan Turner, Stanford University Press, 1987, pp. 58–81.

To return to our example, when Andrew asks Emma for help, he pays a cost; for instance, he risks being judged incompetent or inferior in status. Accordingly, he forgoes the reward of appearing skilled had he pursued an alternative course and not asked for help. For her part, Emma incurs a cost in the exchange in the form of forgoing whatever rewards she may have reaped had she not spent her time helping Andrew. Perhaps she would have spent more time on her own tasks or used the time to schmooze her boss. The question each is faced with is, "What amount of cost should I expect to incur given the amount of reward I expect to receive?" Striking a fair balance between the rewards and costs each experience is a problem of **distributive justice**: each party to the exchange must perceive that they are not paying too high a cost relative to the rewards they are gaining. In other words, both Andrew and Emma must be convinced that the profit each derives from the exchange is just.

From where does one's sense of distributive justice arise? According to Homans, it is the history of an individual's past experiences that determines his or her present expectations regarding rewards and costs. Thus, "the more often in the past an activity emitted under particular stimulus-conditions has been rewarded, the more anger [an individual] will display at present when the same activity, emitted under similar conditions, goes without its reward: precedents are always turning into rights" (1961:73). If Emma is interrupted every twenty minutes with a request for help, she is likely to feel that she is being taken advantage of—that with merely a "thank you" in return, the costs are too high to continue the exchange, particularly if similar circumstances in her past required only the occasional interruption. In such a scenario, Emma is likely to feel angry that Andrew is seeking more of a reward than he has the right to expect.

For his part, Andrew is apt to appraise if the help he receives as reward is proportional to the costs that his submission entails. For instance, he may ask himself, "Is Emma expecting me to beg or grovel in order to get her assistance?" If so, then Andrew will gauge Emma's demands (i.e., her price) as unjust: the costs he is being expected to pay far exceed the value of the rewards Emma is able to supply. With exploitation comes the feeling of anger.

In all exchanges, each party evaluates whether he himself profited fairly as well as whether the other's profit likewise was just. In determining if the rewards gained were proportional (i.e., expected) to the costs incurred, a general, although often unstated, rule is applied: "The more valuable to the other (and costly to himself) an activity he gives the other, the more valuable to him (and costly to the other) an activity the other gives him" (1961:75). When a balance of expected profits is achieved, distributive justice exists. When either party judges profits to be unjust, then anger (or feelings of guilt if a person thinks he unfairly benefited from the exchange) will follow.

Classical Economics

While Homans draws explicitly on the fundamental principles of Skinner's behavioral psychology, his reliance on classical economics is more implicit. Homans does not turn to the propositions developed by any particular economist. Instead, he asserts that just as individuals exchange material goods for money in a market, they exchange, for instance, services or activities for social approval in a social market composed of "sellers" and "buyers." Like the propositions of behavioral psychology, classical economics depicts individual action as motivated by the pursuit of profit. In attempting to realize our goals, we enter a marketplace of others seeking to maximize our gains and minimize our costs, although in this case our profits are not measured by money.

Take, for instance, the economic Law of Supply, which states, in part, that the higher the price of a good, the more of it a supplier will seek to sell. This is akin to Homans's value proposition that states that the more valuable a particular reward is to a person, the more often he will perform a behavior so rewarded, and the less often he will perform an alternative activity. Similarly, consider the Law of Demand, which in turn states that the higher the price of a good, the less of it a consumer will purchase. This law is equivalent to the behaviorist principle that the higher the cost incurred by an activity, the less often an individual will perform it, and the more often he will engage in an alternative one (Homans 1961:69).

Although Homans did not incorporate economic analyses into his theory with the same pronouncedness as the principles of behavioral psychology, he was, nevertheless, convinced that economics could shed important light on social behavior. Indeed, Homans felt that his brand of exchange theory has the distinct advantage of "bring[ing] sociology closer to economics—that science of man most advanced, most capable of application, and, intellectually, most isolated" (1958:598).

HOMANS'S THEORETICAL ORIENTATION

Homans's approach to social life is avowedly individualistic and rationalist (see Figure 4.1). Holding himself to be "an ultimate psychological reductionist" (1958:597), he contends that all social behavior, including that which occurs in large-scale organizations and collectivities, is best explained on the basis of psychological principles. Such an argument is not without controversy, for it runs counter to the very raison d'être of sociology. Homans, himself, was quite aware of the critical nature of his theoretical position. Commenting on the state of theory, he remarked, "Much modern sociological theory seems to me to possess every virtue except that of explaining anything" (1961:10). This salvo was directed in particular toward the dominant sociological theorist of the period, his Harvard colleague Talcott Parsons (see Chapter 2). While Parsons was building abstract conceptual schemes of social systems, Homans was denying that social systems exist, at least not as *sui generis* social facts independent of the individuals that they comprise. Thus, Homans was not only dismissing structural functionalist theory at the height of its influence, he also was contesting the central ideas of one of the founding figures of the discipline, Émile Durkheim (1984:297–98, 323–25). On the relationship between individual action and social structures, Homans summed up his position as follows:

> Once [social] structures have been created, they have further effects on the behavior of persons who take part in them or come into contact with them. But these further effects are explained by the same [psychological] propositions as those used to explain the creation and maintenance of the structure in the first place. The structures only provide new given conditions to which the propositions are to be applied. My sociology remains fundamentally individualistic and not collectivistic. (Quoted in Ritzer and Goodman 2004:403)

For Homans, then, what accounts for the enduring patterns of behavior and social structures that make up society is basic behavioral psychology, "for structures do not act on individuals automatically. They do so because they establish some of the contingencies under which persons act: their stimuli, rewards and punishments. . . ." (1984:342).

Figure 4.1   Homans's Elementary Social Behavior

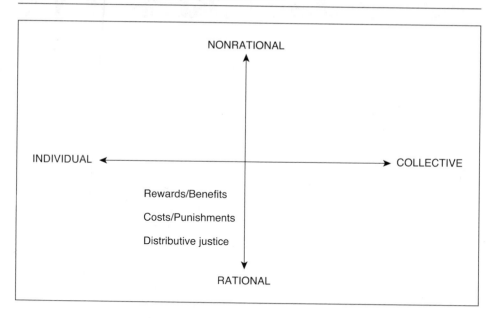

This leads us to Homans's approach to action. If social order is the product of individuals interacting with one another, on what basis is interaction itself motivated? As we noted above, individuals act with the same fundamental goal in mind: maximizing rewards and minimizing costs. In stressing the calculating, strategic aspect of interaction, Homans clearly aligns himself with a rationalist orientation to the problem of action. Yet, Homans acknowledges two limitations on his rationalist position. The first involves the role of values in the decision-making process. Homans assumes as a given the particular values that any individual may seek to maximize. His interest lies in explaining why people *behave* as they do in realizing their values, not why they value the things that they do. As he states it, "Our problem is not why they hold [particular] values, but given that they do hold them, what they do about them" (1961:48). However, this seeming simplification of the problem poses its own puzzles. While it may appear obvious to assume some values—a person new to a job will value the help co-workers can provide—others can confound an observer's expectations. It may well be the case that an individual values his sense of pride more than the help others can provide. Thus, while he is new to a job and in need of help, the cost in pride for asking outweighs the rewards for receiving it. Indeed, values that are their own reward, such as pride and altruism, greatly complicate the ability to predict and explain an individual's behavior (1961:45).

The second limitation involves the "bounded" nature of rationality attributed to actors (March and Simon 1958). The rational calculations that guide an individual's behaviors are by no means flawless. Thus, the rewards that are obtained are, more often than not, less than optimal. The ability to fully maximize the profit on one's values is limited by a number of conditions including the uniqueness of one's past experiences, the dependence on others for rewards, and the particularities of a given exchange situation. In short, there are boundaries to individuals' decision-making such that "[a]ll we impute to them in the way of rationality is that they know enough to come in out of the rain unless they enjoy getting wet" (1961:82).

Reading

Introduction to "Social Behavior as Exchange"

In this article, Homans introduces many of the central ideas discussed above. His individualistic orientation to understanding the basis of social order is made clear in the article's first paragraph. In it, he asserts that in studying elementary social behavior, we are studying "what happens when two or three persons are in a position to influence one another, the sort of thing of which those massive structures called 'classes,' 'firms,' 'communities,' and 'societies' must ultimately be composed" (1958:597). Similarly, he expresses his rationalist orientation to action and indebtedness to Skinner's behavioral psychology when describing interaction as an exchange of goods reinforced by the values that actors attach to rewards sought and costs endured.

After laying the theoretical groundwork, Homans turns to a discussion of a number of experiments and studies that shed empirical light on his behaviorist propositions. Given our own discussion of Homans's work, we will not review here the details of the article. Instead, we leave you to determine the validity of his argument and of the role he assigns to such matters as profit seeking, behavioral reinforcements, and distributive justice in interaction.

❖

Social Behavior as Exchange (1958)

George C. Homans

THE PROBLEMS OF SMALL-GROUP RESEARCH

What we are really studying in small groups is elementary social behavior: what happens when two or three persons are in a position to influence one another, the sort of thing of which those massive structures called "classes," "firms," "communities," and "societies" must ultimately be composed. . . .

[Analysis of elementary social behavior] would be furthered by our adopting the view that interaction between persons is an exchange of goods, material and non-material. This is one of the oldest theories of social behavior, and one that we still use every day to interpret our own behavior, as when we say, "I found so-and-so rewarding"; or "I got a great deal out of him"; or, even, "Talking with him took a great deal out of me." But, perhaps just because it is so obvious, this view has been much neglected by social scientists. . . .

An incidental advantage of an exchange theory is that it might bring sociology closer to economics—that science of man most advanced, most capable of application, and,

Excerpts from Homans, G. C., "Social behavior as exchange," in *The American Journal of Sociology* 63:6 (1958), pp. 597–606. Reprinted by permission of The University of Chicago Press.

intellectually, most isolated. Economics studies exchange carried out under special circumstances and with a most useful built-in numerical measure of value. What are the laws of the general phenomenon of which economic behavior is one class?

In what follows I shall suggest some reasons for the usefulness of a theory of social behavior as exchange and suggest the nature of the propositions such a theory might contain.

AN EXCHANGE PARADIGM

I start with the link to behavioral psychology and the kind of statement it makes about the behavior of an experimental animal such as the pigeon.[i] As a pigeon explores its cage in the laboratory, it happens to peck a target, whereupon the psychologist feeds it corn. The evidence is that it will peck the target again; it has learned the behavior, or, as my friend Skinner says, the behavior has been reinforced, and the pigeon has undergone *operant conditioning*. This kind of psychologist is not interested in how the behavior was learned: "learning theory" is a poor name for his field. Instead, he is interested in what determines changes in the rate of emission of learned behavior, whether pecks at a target or something else.

The more hungry the pigeon, the less corn or other food it has gotten in the recent past, the more often it will peck. By the same token, if the behavior is often reinforced, if the pigeon is given much corn every time it pecks, the rate of emission will fall off as the pigeon gets *satiated*. If, on the other hand, the behavior is not reinforced at all, then, too, its rate of emission will tend to fall off, though a long time may pass before it stops altogether, before it is *extinguished*. In the emission of many kinds of behavior the pigeon incurs *aversive stimulation*, or what I shall call "cost" for short, and this, too, will lead in time to a decrease in the emission rate. Fatigue is an example of a "cost." Extinction, satiation, and cost, by decreasing the rate of emission of a particular kind of behavior,

render more probable the emission of some other kind of behavior, including doing nothing. I shall only add that even a hard-boiled psychologist puts "emotional" behavior, as well as such things as pecking, among the unconditioned responses that may be reinforced in operant conditioning. As a statement of the propositions of behavioral psychology, the foregoing is, of course, inadequate for any purpose except my present one.

We may look on the pigeon as engaged in an exchange—pecks for corn—with the psychologist, but let us not dwell upon that, for the behavior of the pigeon hardly determines the behavior of the psychologist at all. Let us turn to a situation where the exchange is real, that is, where the determination is mutual. Suppose we are dealing with two men. Each is emitting behavior reinforced to some degree by the behavior of the other. How it was in the past that each learned the behavior he emits and how he learned to find the other's behavior reinforcing we are not concerned with. It is enough that each does find the other's behavior reinforcing, and I shall call the reinforcers—the equivalent of the pigeon's corn—*values*, for this, I think, is what we mean by this term. As he emits behavior, each man may incur costs, and each man has more than one course of behavior open to him.

This seems to me the paradigm of elementary social behavior, and the problem of the elementary sociologist is to state propositions relating the variations in the values and costs of each man to his frequency distribution of behavior among alternatives, where the values (in the mathematical sense) taken by these variable for one man determine in part their values for the other.

I see no reason to believe that the propositions of behavioral psychology do not apply to this situation, though the complexity of their implications in the concrete case may be great indeed. In particular, we must suppose that, with men as with pigeons, an increase in extinction, satiation, or aversive stimulation of any one kind of behavior will increase the probability of emission of some other kind. The problem

---

[i]B. F. Skinner, *Science and Human Behavior* (New York: Macmillan Co., 1953).

is not, as it is often stated, merely, what a man's values are, what he has learned in the past to find reinforcing, but how much of any one value his behavior is getting him now. The more he gets, the less valuable any further unit of that value is to him, and the less often he will emit behavior reinforced by it.

The Influence Process

We do not, I think, possess the kind of studies of two-person interaction that would either bear out these propositions or fail to do so. But we do have studies of larger numbers of persons that suggest that they may apply, notably the studies by Festinger, Schachter, Back, and their associates on the dynamics of influence. One of the variables they work with they call *cohesiveness*, defined as anything that attracts people to take part in a group. Cohesiveness is a value variable; it refers to the degree of reinforcement people find in the activities of the group. Festinger and his colleagues consider two kinds of reinforcing activity: the symbolic behavior we call "social approval" (sentiment) and activity valuable in other ways, such as doing something interesting.

The other variable they work with they call *communication* and others call *interaction*. This is a frequency variable; it is a measure of the frequency of emission of valuable and costly verbal behavior. We must bear in mind that, in general, the one kind of variable is a function of the other.

Festinger and his co-workers show that the more cohesive a group is, that is, the more valuable the sentiment or activity the members exchange with one another, the greater the average frequency of interaction of the members.[ii] With men, as with pigeons, the greater the reinforcement, the more often is the reinforced behavior emitted. The more cohesive a group,

too, the greater the change that members can produce in the behavior of other members in the direction of rendering these activities more valuable.[iii] That is, the more valuable the activities that members get, the more valuable those that they must give. For if a person is emitting behavior of a certain kind, and other people do not find it particularly rewarding, these others will suffer their own production of sentiment and activity, in time, to fall off. But perhaps the first person has found their sentiment and activity rewarding, and, if he is to keep on getting them, he must make his own behavior more valuable to the others. In short, the propositions of behavioral psychology imply a tendency toward a certain proportionality between the value to others of the behavior a man gives them and the value to him of the behavior they give him.

Schachter also studied the behavior of members of a group toward two kinds of other members, "conformers" and "deviates."[iv] I assume that conformers are people whose activity the other members find valuable. For conformity is behavior that coincides to a degree with some group standard or norm, and the only meaning I can assign to *norm* is "a verbal description of behavior that many members find it valuable for the actual behavior of themselves and others to conform to." By the same token, a deviate is a member whose behavior is not particularly valuable. Now Schachter shows that, as the members of a group come to see another member as a deviate, their interaction with him—communication addressed to getting him to change his behavior—goes up, the faster the more cohesive the group. The members need not talk to the other conformers so much; they are relatively satiated by the conformers' behavior: they have gotten what they want out of them. But if the deviate, by failing to change his behavior, fails to reinforce the members, they

[ii]K. W. Back, "The Exertion of Influence through Social Communication," in L. Festinger, K. Back, S. Schachter, H. H. Kelley, and J. Thibaut (eds.), *Theory and Experiment in Social Communication* (Ann Arbor: Research Center for Dynamics, University of Michigan, 1950), pp. 21–36.

[iii]S. Schachter, N. Ellertson, D. McBride, and D. Gregory, "An Experimental Study of Cohesiveness and Productivity," *Human Relations*, IV (1951), 229–38.

[iv]S. Schachter, "Deviation, Rejection, and Communication," *Journal of Abnormal and Social Psychology*, XLVI (1951), 190–207.

start to withhold social approval from him: the deviate gets low sociometric choice at the end of the experiment. And in the most cohesive groups—those Schachter calls "high cohesive-relevant"—interaction with the deviate also falls off in the end and is lowest among those members that rejected him most strongly, as if they had given him up as a bad job. But how plonking can we get? These findings are utterly in line with everyday experience.

PRACTICAL EQUILIBRIUM

. . . [Real-life small groups] often appear to be in practical equilibrium, and by this I mean nothing fancy. I do not mean that all real-life groups are in equilibrium. I certainly do not mean that all groups must tend to equilibrium. I do not mean that groups have built-in antidotes to change: there is no homeostasis here. I do not mean that we assume equilibrium. I mean only that we sometimes *observe* it, that for the time we are with a group—and it is often short—there is no great change in the values of the variables we choose to measure. If, for instance, person A is interacting with B more than with C both at the beginning and at the end of the study, then at least by this crude measure the group is in equilibrium.

Many of the Festinger-Schachter studies are experimental, and their propositions about the process of influence seem to me to imply the kind of proposition that empirically holds good of real-life groups in practical equilibrium. For instance, Festinger *et al.* find that, the more cohesive a group is, the greater the change that members can produce in the behavior of other members. If the influence is exerted in the direction of conformity to group norms, then, when the process of influence has accomplished all the change of which it is capable, the proposition should hold good that, the more cohesive a group is, the larger the number of members that conform to its norms. And it does hold good.[v]

Again, Schachter found, in the experiment I summarized above, that in the most cohesive

groups and at the end, when the effort to influence the deviate had failed, members interacted little with the deviate and gave him little in the way of sociometric choice. Now two of the propositions that hold good most often of real-life groups in practical equilibrium are precisely that the more closely a member's activity conforms to the norms the more interaction he receives from other members and the more liking choices he gets from them too. From these main propositions a number of others may be derived that also hold good.

Yet we must ever remember that the truth of the proposition linking conformity to liking may on occasion be masked by the truth of other propositions. If, for instance, the man that conforms to the norms most closely also exerts some authority over the group, this may render liking for him somewhat less than it might otherwise have been. . . .

PROFIT AND SOCIAL CONTROL

Though I have treated equilibrium as an observed fact, it is a fact that cries for explanation. I shall not, as structural-functional sociologists do, use an assumed equilibrium as a means of explaining, or trying to explain, why the other features of a social system should be what they are. Rather, I shall take practical equilibrium as something that is itself to be explained by the other features of the system.

If every member of a group emits at the end of, and during, a period of time much the same kinds of behavior and in much the same frequencies as he did at the beginning, the group is for that period in equilibrium. Let us then ask why any one member's behavior should persist. Suppose he is emitting behavior of value A_1. Why does he not let his behavior get worse (less valuable or reinforcing to the others) until it stands at $A_1 - \Delta A$? True, the sentiments expressed by others toward him are apt to decline in value (become less reinforcing to him), so that what he gets from them may be $S_1 - \Delta S$. But it is conceivable that, since most

[v]L. Festinger, S. Schachter, and K. Back, *Social Pressures in Informal Groups* (New York: Harper & Bros., 1950), pp. 72–100.

activity carries cost, a decline in the value of what he emits will mean a reduction in cost to him that more than offsets his losses in sentiment. Where, then, does he stabilize his behavior? This is the problem of social control.

Mankind has always assumed that a person stabilizes his behavior, at least in the short run, at the point where he is doing the best he can for himself under the circumstances, though his best may not be a "rational" best, and what he can do may not be at all easy to specify, except that he is not apt to think like one of the theoretical antagonists in the *Theory of Games*. Before a sociologist rejects this answer out of hand for its horrid profit-seeking implications, he will do well to ask himself if he can offer any other answer to the question posed. I think he will find that he cannot. Yet experiments designed to test the truth of the answer are extraordinarily rare.

I shall review one that seems to me to provide a little support for the theory, though it was not meant to do so. The experiment is reported by H. B. Gerard, a member of the Festinger-Schachter team, under the title "The Anchorage of Opinions in Face-to-Face Groups."[vi] The experimenter formed artificial groups whose members met to discuss a case in industrial relations and to express their opinions about its probable outcome. The groups were of two kinds: high-attraction groups, whose members were told that they would like one another very much, and low-attraction groups, whose members were told that they would not find one another particularly likable.

At a later time the experimenter called the members in separately, asked them again to express their opinions on the outcome of the case, and counted the number that had changed their opinions to bring them into accord with those of other members of their groups. At the same time, a paid participant entered into a further discussion of the case with each member, always taking, on the probable outcome of the case, a position opposed to that taken by the bulk of the other members of the group to which the person belonged. The experimenter counted the number of persons shifting toward the opinion of the paid participant.

The experiment had many interesting results, from which I choose only those summed up in Tables 1 and 2 below. The three different agreement classes are made up of people who, at the original sessions, expressed different degrees of agreement with the opinions of other members of their groups. And the figure 44, for instance, means that, of all members of high-attraction groups whose initial opinions were strongly in disagreement with those of other members, 44 per cent shifted their opinion later toward that of others.

Table 1   Percentage of Subjects Changing Toward Someone in the Group

	Agreement	Mild Disagreement	Strong Disagreement
High attraction. . . .	0	12	44
Low attraction. . . .	0	15	9

Table 2   Percentage of Subjects Changing Toward the Paid Participant

	Agreement	Mild Disagreement	Strong Disagreement
High attraction. . . .	7	13	25
Low attraction. . . .	20	38	8

[vi]*Human Relations*, VII (1954), 313–25.

In these results the experimenter seems to have been interested only in the differences in the sums of the rows, which show that there is more shifting toward the group, and less shifting toward the paid participant, in the high-attraction than in the low-attraction condition. This is in line with a proposition suggested earlier. If you think that the members of a group can give you much—in this case, liking—you are apt to give them much—in this case, a change to an opinion in accordance with their views—or you will not get the liking. And, by the same token, if the group can give you little of value, you will not be ready to give it much of value. Indeed, you may change your opinion so as to depart from agreement even further, to move, that is, toward the view held by the paid participant.

So far so good, but, when I first scanned these tables, I was less struck by the difference between them than by their similarity. The same classes of people in both tables showed much the same relative propensities to change their opinions, no matter whether the change was toward the group or toward the paid participant. We see, for instance, that those who change least are the high-attraction, agreement people and the low-attraction, strong-disagreement ones. And those who change most are the high-attraction, strong-disagreement people and the low-attraction, mild-disagreement ones.

How am I to interpret these particular results? Since the experimenter did not discuss them, I am free to offer my own explanation. The behavior emitted by the subjects is opinion and changes in opinion. For this behavior they have learned to expect two possible kinds of reinforcement. Agreement with the group gets the subject favorable sentiment (acceptance) from it, and the experiment was designed to give this reinforcement a higher value in the high-attraction condition than in the low-attraction one. The second kind of possible reinforcement is what I shall call the "maintenance of one's personal integrity," which a subject gets by sticking to his own opinion in the face of disagreement with the group. The experimenter does not mention this reward, but I cannot make sense of the results without something much like it. In different degrees for different subjects, depending on their initial positions, these rewards are in competition with one another:

they are alternatives. They are not absolutely scarce goods, but some persons cannot get both at once.

Since the rewards are alternatives, let me introduce a familiar assumption from economics—that the cost of a particular course of action is the equivalent of the foregone value of an alternative—and then add the definition: Profit = Reward–Cost.

Now consider the persons in the corresponding cells of the two tables. The behavior of the high-attraction, agreement people gets them much in the way of acceptance by the group, and for it they must give up little in the way of personal integrity, for their views are from the start in accord with those of the group. Their profit is high, and they are not prone to change their behavior. The low-attraction, strong-disagreement people are getting much in integrity, and they are not giving up for it much in valuable acceptance, for they are members of low-attraction groups. Reward less cost is high for them, too, and they change little. The high-attraction, strong-disagreement people are getting much in the way of integrity, but their costs in doing so are high, too, for they are in high-attraction groups and thus foregoing much valuable acceptance by the group. Their profit is low, and they are very apt to change, either toward the group or toward the paid participant, from whom they think, perhaps, they will get some acceptance while maintaining some integrity. The low-attraction, mild-disagreement people do not get much in the way of integrity, for they are only in mild disagreement with the group, but neither are they giving up much in acceptance, for they are members of low-attraction groups. Their rewards are low; their costs are low too, and their profit—the difference between the two—is also low. In their low profit they resemble the high-attraction, strong-disagreement people, and, like them, they are prone to change their opinions, in this case, more toward the paid participant. The subjects in the other two cells, who have medium profits, display medium propensities to change.

If we define profit as reward less cost, and if cost is value foregone, I suggest that we have here some evidence for the proposition that change in behavior is greatest when perceived profit is least. This constitutes no direct demonstration that change in behavior is least when profit is greatest, but if, whenever a man's behavior brought him a balance of reward and cost, he changed his behavior away from what got him, under the circumstances, the less profit, there might well come a time when his behavior would not change further. That is, his behavior would be stabilized, at least for the time being. And, so far as this were true for every member of a group, the group would have a social organization in equilibrium.

I do not say that a member would stabilize his behavior at the point of greatest conceivable profit to himself, because his profit is partly at the mercy of the behavior of others. It is a commonplace that the short-run pursuit of profit by several persons often lands them in positions where all are worse off than they might conceivably be. I do not say that the paths of behavioral change in which a member pursues his profit under the condition that others are pursuing theirs too are easy to describe or predict; and we can readily conceive that in jockeying for position they might never arrive at any equilibrium at all.

DISTRIBUTIVE JUSTICE

Yet practical equilibrium is often observed, and thus some further condition may make its attainment, under some circumstance, more probable than would the individual pursuit of profit left to itself. I can offer evidence for this further condition only in the behavior of subgroups and not in that of individuals. Suppose that there are two subgroups, working close together in a factory, the job of one being somewhat different from that of the other. And suppose that the members of the first complain and say: "We are getting the same pay as they are. We ought to get just a couple of dollars a week more to show that our work is more responsible." When you ask them what they mean by "more responsible," they say that, if they do their work wrong, more damage can result, and so they are under more pressure to take care.[vii] Something like this is a common feature of industrial behavior. It is at the heart of disputes not over absolute wages but over wage differentials—indeed, at the heart of disputes over rewards other than wages.

In what kind of proposition may we express observations like these? We may say that wages and responsibility give status in the group, in the sense that a man who takes high responsibility and gets high wages is admired, other things equal. Then, if the members of one group score higher on responsibility than do the members of another, there is a felt need on the part of the first to score higher on pay too. There is a pressure, which shows itself in complaints, to bring the *status factors*, as I have called them, into line with one another. If they are in line, a condition of *status congruence* is said to exist. In this condition the workers may find their jobs dull or irksome, but they will not complain about the relative position of groups.

But there may be a more illuminating way of looking at the matter. In my example I have considered only responsibility and pay, but these may be enough, for they represent the two kinds of thing that come into the problem. Pay is clearly a reward; responsibility may be looked on, less clearly, as a cost. It means constraint and worry—or peace of mind foregone. Then the proposition about status congruence becomes this: If the costs of the members of one group are higher than those of another, distributive justice requires that their rewards should be higher too. But the thing works both ways: If the rewards are higher, the costs should be higher too. This last is the theory of *noblesse oblige*, which we all subscribe to, though we all laugh at it, perhaps because the *noblesse* often fails to *oblige*. To put the matter in terms of profit: though the rewards and costs of two persons or the members of two groups may be different, yet the profits of the two—the excess of reward over cost—should tend to equality. And more than "should." The less-advantaged group will at least try to attain greater equality, as, in the example I have used, the first group tried to increase its profit by increasing its pay.

I have talked of distributive justice. Clearly, this is not the only condition determining the actual distribution of rewards and costs. At the same time, never tell me that notions of justice

[vii]G. C. Homans, "Status among Clerical Workers," *Human Organization*, XII (1953), 5–10.

are not a strong influence on behavior, though we sociologists often neglect them. Distributive justice may be one of the conditions of group equilibrium.

EXCHANGE AND SOCIAL STRUCTURE

I shall end by reviewing almost the only study I am aware of that begins to show in detail how a stable and differentiated social structure in a real-life group might arise out of a process of exchange between members. This is Peter Blau's description of the behavior of sixteen agents in a federal law-enforcement agency.[viii]

The agents had the duty of investigating firms and preparing reports on the firms' compliance with the law. Since the reports might lead to legal action against the firms, the agents had to prepare them carefully, in the proper form, and take strict account of the many regulations that might apply. The agents were often in doubt what they should do, and then they were supposed to take the question to their supervisor. This they were reluctant to do, for they naturally believed that thus confessing to him their inability to solve a problem would reflect on their competence, affect the official ratings he made of their work, and so hurt their chances for promotion. So agents often asked other agents for help and advice, and, though this was nominally forbidden, the supervisor usually let it pass.

Blau ascertained the ratings the supervisor made of the agents, and he also asked the agents to rate one another. The two opinions agreed closely. Fewer agents were regarded as highly competent than were regarded as of middle or low competence; competence, or the ability to solve technical problems, was a fairly scarce good. One or two of the more competent agents would not give help and advice when asked, and so received few interactions and little liking. A man that will not exchange, that will not give

you what he has when you need it, will not get from you the only thing you are, in this case, able to give him in return, your regard.

But most of the more competent agents were willing to give help, and of them Blau says:

A consultation can be considered an exchange of values: both participants gain something, and both have to pay a price. The questioning agent is enabled to perform better than he could otherwise have done, without exposing his difficulties to his supervisor. By asking for advice, he implicitly pays his respect to the superior proficiency of his colleague. This acknowledgment of inferiority is the cost of receiving assistance. The consultant gains prestige, in return for which he is willing to devote some time to the consultation and permit it to disrupt his own work. The following remark of an agent illustrates this: "I like giving advice. It's flattering, I suppose, if you feel that others come to you for advice."[ix]

Blau goes on to say: "All agents liked being consulted, but the value of any one of very many consultations became deflated for experts, and the price they paid in frequent interruptions became inflated."[x] This implies that, the more prestige an agent received, the less was the increment of value of that prestige; the more advice an agent gave, the greater was the increment of cost of that advice, the cost lying precisely in the foregone value of time to do his own work. Blau suggests that something of the same sort was true of an agent who went to a more competent colleague for advice: the more often he went, the more costly to him, in feelings of inferiority, became any further request. "The repeated admission of his inability to solve his own problems . . . undermined the self-confidence of the worker and his standing in the group."[xi]

The result was that the less competent agents went to the more competent ones for help less often than they might have done if the costs of repeated admissions of inferiority had been less

[viii]Peter M. Blau, *The Dynamics of Bureaucracy* (Chicago: University of Chicago Press, 1955), 99–116.
[ix]Ibid., p. 108.
[x]Ibid., p. 108.
[xi]Ibid., p. 109.

high and that, while many agents sought out the few highly competent ones, no single agent sought out the latter much. Had they done so (to look at the exchange from the other side), the costs to the highly competent in interruptions to their own work would have become exorbitant. Yet the need of the less competent for help was still not fully satisfied. Under these circumstances they tended to turn for help to agents more nearly like themselves in competence. Though the help they got was not the most valuable, it was of a kind they could themselves return on occasion. With such agents they could exchange help and liking, without the exchange becoming on either side too great a confession of inferiority.

The highly competent agents tended to enter into exchanges, that is, to interact with many others. But, in the more equal exchanges I have just spoken of, less competent agents tended to pair off as partners. That is, they interacted with a smaller number of people, but interacted often with these few. I think I could show why pair relations in these more equal exchanges would be more economical for an agent than a wider distribution of favors. But perhaps I have gone far enough. The final pattern of this social structure was one in which a small number of highly competent agents exchanged advice for prestige with a large number of others less competent and in which the less competent agents exchanged, in pairs and in trios, both help and liking on more nearly equal terms.

Blau shows, then, that a social structure in equilibrium might be the result of a process of exchanging behavior rewarding and costly in different degrees, in which the increment of reward and cost varied with the frequency of the behavior, that is, with the frequency of interaction. Note that the behavior of the agents seems also to have satisfied my second condition of equilibrium: the more competent agents took more responsibility for the work, either their own or others', than did the less competent ones, but they also got more for it in the way of prestige. I suspect that the same kind of explanation could be given for the structure of many "informal" groups.

SUMMARY

The current job of theory in small-group research is to make the connection between experimental and real-life studies, to consolidate the propositions that empirically hold good in the two fields, and to show how these propositions might be derived from a still more general set. One way of doing this job would be to revive and make more rigorous the oldest of theories of social behavior—social behavior as exchange.

Some of the statements of such a theory might be the following. Social behavior is an exchange of goods, material goods but also nonmaterial ones, such as the symbols of approval or prestige. Persons that give much to others try to get much from them, and persons that get much from others are under pressure to give much to them. This process of influence tends to work out at equilibrium to a balance in the exchanges. For a person engaged in exchange, what he gives may be a cost to him, just as what he gets may be a reward, and his behavior changes less as profit, that is, reward less cost, tends to a maximum. Not only does he seek a maximum for himself, but he tries to see to it that no one in his group makes more profit than he does. The cost and the value of what he gives and of what he gets vary with the quantity of what he gives and gets. It is surprising how familiar these propositions are; it is surprising, too, how propositions about the dynamics of exchange can begin to generate the static thing we call "group structure" and, in so doing, generate also some of the propositions about group structure that students of real-life groups have stated.

In our unguarded moments we sociologists find words like "reward" and "cost" slipping into what we say. Human nature will break in upon even our most elaborate theories. But we seldom let it have its way with us and follow up systematically what these words imply. Of all our many "approaches" to social behavior, the one that sees it as an economy is the most neglected, and yet it is the one we use every moment of our lives—except when we write sociology.

PETER BLAU (1918–2002): A BIOGRAPHICAL SKETCH

Peter Blau was born in Vienna, Austria, in 1918. As a teenager, he spoke out against the political repression exacted by Austria's fascist government, then controlled by the National Party. Writing for an underground journal associated with the Socialist Worker's Party, Blau was imprisoned when the Austrian authorities discovered the journal's circulation. He was convicted of high treason and faced a ten-year sentence until an agreement between Hitler and the Austrian government led to the release of political prisoners.

When Hitler seized control of Austria in 1938, Blau, of Jewish descent, attempted to secure a visa allowing him to emigrate to another country. Unsuccessful, he tried to escape to Czechoslovakia but was captured by Nazi border guards. For the next two months he faced torture and starvation. When he was released, he made his way to Prague. He was forced to leave only a year later when Hitler invaded Czechoslovakia. Fortunately, arrangements had been made for Blau to emigrate to the United States via France. As fate would have it, he caught what would be the last train out of the country. (His parents remained in Vienna and four years later died in Auschwitz, a Nazi concentration camp.)

SOURCE: American Sociological Association; used with permission.

Once in France, Blau, who held a German passport, "surrendered" to the Allied forces. The French Army responded by deporting him to a labor camp in Bordeaux. While he was imprisoned his visa was granted, so he left for the port city of Le Havre and a boat bound for the United States. As fate would again have it, he boarded what turned out to be the last civilian boat departing France. This trip proved doubly miraculous, for also waiting to board were representatives from Elmhurst College who were in Europe offering scholarships for Jewish refugees. Blau was given the address of the son of the college's president, and a remarkable academic career was born.

After receiving his bachelor's degree, Blau served four years in the army as an interrogation officer. With the end of the war, he began his graduate studies in sociology at Columbia University and, under the tutelage of Robert K. Merton (see Chapter 2), received his Ph.D. in 1952. During the next fifty years Blau would produce eleven books and more than one hundred articles, in the process becoming one of the leading scholars of his day. From 1953 to 1970 he was a professor at the University of Chicago and then, from 1970 to 1988, a professor at Columbia University. In addition to serving as president of the American Sociological Association in 1973, he was selected to a number of prominent positions. He was a Senior Fellow at King's College as well as a Fellow of the National Academy of Sciences, the American Philosophical Society, and the American Academy of Arts and Sciences. He was also Pitt Professor at Cambridge University and a Distinguished Honorary Professor at the Tianjin Academy of Social Sciences in China. Peter Blau died in March 2002 of adult respiratory distress syndrome.[2]

---

[2]This biographical account is adapted from the April 2002 edition of *Footnotes*, printed by the American Sociological Association.

INTELLECTUAL INFLUENCES AND CORE IDEAS

Like Homans, Blau was interested in examining the processes that guide face-to-face interaction. And like Homans, Blau argued that such interaction is shaped by a reciprocal exchange of rewards, both tangible and intangible. On these points, Homans was an important influence on Blau's work. However, the differences between the two exchange theorists outnumber the similarities. While Homans was interested in studying exchange relations in order to uncover the behaviorist principles that underlie interaction, Blau sought to derive from his analysis of social interaction a better understanding of the complex institutions and organizations that develop out of simpler exchange relations between individuals. Moreover, Blau not only abandoned Homans's brand of behavioral psychology, but in recognizing that imbalances of rewards and costs often pervade exchange relations, he also emphasized the role that power, inequality, and norms of legitimation play in interaction.

In extending the work of Homans and fashioning his own brand of exchange theory, Blau drew from a number of scholars. Perhaps most influential in shaping his views on interaction was the German sociologist and philosopher Georg Simmel (1858–1918). In charting a course for the newly created discipline, Simmel argued that sociology should concern itself above all with analyzing the *forms* in which interaction takes place; understanding the specific *content* of interactions—what people talk about and why—is of secondary importance. What is of sociological significance, then, is determining the uniformities or commonalities that exist between seemingly diverse social associations. For instance, while a husband and wife may share experiences and discuss issues quite different from those expressed among co-workers, both social relations may take on a common form of cooperation or conflict.

Simmel also noted that while the most dissimilar of contents (individual motivations) may be realized in an identical form of association, the same motivations or interests can be expressed in a range of forms of interaction. For instance, interactions within and between families, gangs, corporations, political organizations, and governments may all take the form of conflict. Thus, despite the varied interests or purposes that led to interaction in each of these cases, the individuals involved all may find themselves facing an opposing party that hinders the realization of their impulses or desires. Similarly, while giving a wedding present, paying for music lessons, and volunteering at the food co-op are motivated by different intentions or "contents," to the sociologist they all take the form of an exchange relation and thus share interaction properties. Conversely, the same drive or interest can be expressed through a number of forms. Attempts to gain economic advantage, for instance, can be asserted through cooperative agreements among parties as well as through relations of domination and subordination.

Like Simmel, Blau maintained that the central task of sociology is to uncover the basic forms of interaction through which individuals pursue their interests or satisfy their desires. For it is only in relating to others, acting both with them and against them, that we are able to satisfy our ambitions. Blau, moreover, would endorse Simmel's assertion that in exchange relations lie "the purest and most concentrated form of all human interactions" (1900/1971:43). Indeed, both maintained that every interaction (a performance, a conversation, or even a romantic affair) can be understood as a form of exchange in which the participants give the other "more than he had himself possessed" (ibid.:44).

As we noted above, Blau was interesting in building a theoretical bridge that would link sociological studies of everyday interactions between individuals and those that examined the collectivist or structural dimensions of society, such as economic systems, political institutions, or belief systems. While the work of Homans and Simmel (and to a lesser extent, Erving Goffman) informed the "interactionist" elements of his approach, his analysis of society's structural properties was most influenced by Max Weber (1864–1920) and Talcott Parsons (see Chapter 2). From them he developed his analysis of the role of power and norms of legitimation in shaping group processes.

While beginning with Weber's definition of power as "the probability that one actor within a social relationship will be in a position to carry out his own will despite resistance," Blau stressed the significance of rewards in inducing others to accede to one's wishes.[3] For Blau, then, an individual is able to exercise **power** over others when he alone is able to supply needed rewards to them. If the others are unable to receive the benefits from another source, *and* if they are unable to offer rewards to the individual, they become dependent on the individual. Their only option is to submit to his demands lest he withdraw the needed benefits. In short, power results from an unequal exchange stemming from an individual's or group's monopoly over a desired resource (1964:115, 118).[4]

In defining power in terms of an inequality of resources and the submission that an **imbalanced exchange** imposes, Blau is led to consider the processes that shape the exercise of power and the rise of opposition to it. These processes, in turn, account for both stability and change in interpersonal and group relations, as well as in more complex social institutions (see Figure 4.2 below). Of central importance is the role of social norms of fairness and the legitimacy they either confer on or deny those in dominant positions. Following the work of both Weber and Talcott Parsons, Blau argues that legitimate authority—a superior's right to demand compliance from subordinates and their willing obedience—is based on shared norms that constrain an individual's response to issued directives. Thus, imbalanced exchange relations are governed less by individual, rational calculations than by shared expectations and the cultural values that legitimate them. So long as the superior meets or exceeds the expectations for rewards

Figure 4.2   Blau's Model of Exchange and the Structure of Social Relations

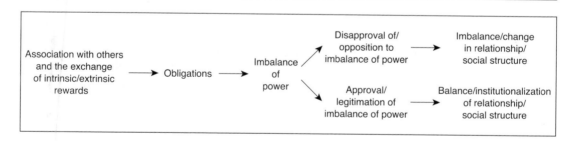

[3]Max Weber, *The Theory of Social and Economic Organization*, New York: Oxford University Press, 1947, p.152. Quoted in Blau (1964:115).

[4]In arguing that the dynamics of power and submission are tied to the availability of alternative exchange relations, Blau again draws on Simmel's insights. Of particular importance here is the latter's analysis of the patterns of interaction that distinguish dyads from triads and other larger groups. (See Georg Simmel, *The Sociology of Georg Simmel*, Glencoe: Free Press, 1950.)

deemed acceptable by the group, then the ensuing legitimacy conferred on the superior will foster the stability of the group. That is, the costs incurred by subordinates, both in the services they perform and in the very act of submission, must be judged fair relative to the benefits derived for obedience. Otherwise, opposition to the superior's exercise of power may arise and with it the potential for change in the structure of existing interpersonal or institutional relations. (See Figure 4.2.) Yet, this judgment rests, ultimately, on consensual, normative standards of fairness. Interestingly, Blau's emphasis on the normative dimension of group life and the exercise of power in it also represents a metatheoretical shift, a point that we discuss below.

| **Significant Others** | **James S. Coleman (1926–1996) and Rational Choice Theory** |

James S. Coleman graduated with a Ph.D. from Columbia University in 1955. While there he studied under the tutelage of some of the discipline's most influential figures of the day, most notably Robert Merton, Paul Lazarsfeld, and Seymor Martin Lipset. Coleman would go on to become one of the most distinguished sociologists in his own right, publishing more than twenty five books and three hundred articles and serving as president of the American Sociological Association in 1992. Moreover, for Coleman sociology was not to be an academic pursuit carried out by experts in a cloistered ivory tower; instead, it was a science with a unique capacity for informing crucial public policy issues. Much of his work examined the implications of public policy for America's educational system, including the "Coleman Report"(1966), a landmark study conducted for the federal government that helped set the stage for using busing to racially integrate schools and create equal educational opportunities for black children. However, it is Coleman's leading role in the development of rational choice theory, a perspective closely aligned with exchange theory, that establishes him as a key contemporary theorist. Indeed, in 1989 Coleman founded *Rationality and Society,* a journal dedicated to advancing theory and research grounded in a rational choice framework.

Rational choice theories share with exchange theories a view of the actor as a rational, purposive agent motivated by maximizing rewards. Beyond this similarity, however, a subtle yet important shift in emphasis distinguishes the two perspectives. While exchange theorists focus on the social *relationships* that develop as individuals strategically pursue optimum benefits, rational choice theorists focus on the *decisions* individuals make and, when combined with the decisions of others, their consequences both for the individuals and for the larger group of which they are a part.

For example, to the extent that education is linked to income and an individual is motivated to be economically secure, it is rational to pursue a college degree. However, as the opportunity to earn a bachelor's degree has expanded, and more and more people are rationally following this approved path to economic success, the value of a college degree has deteriorated. No longer is a college degree a "sure bet" to achieving a financially satisfying lifestyle.

Unfortunately, many college graduates find themselves employed in the types of clerical and service positions filled by high school graduates only a generation or two ago. In the end, decisions and behaviors that are individually rational can, when taken collectively, produce adverse effects.

In his nearly 1,000-page opus, *The Foundations of Social Theory* (1990), Coleman set out to elaborate the premises and promises of rational choice theory. To this end he introduced a number of concepts to explain and predict not only individual decision-making and behavior but also the formation of groups, or in Coleman's terms, "corporate actors," and the conditions that enable and affect group/corporate decision-making. Some of the concepts central to Coleman's theory are also integral to the work of exchange theorists. For instance, Coleman explores how norms emerge on the basis of recurring exchanges in which individuals partially give up the right to control their own actions while receiving in turn the authority to partially control the actions of others. The emergence of such "effective" norms requires that individuals subordinate some of their own interests—and thus forfeit some of their rights—to those of the group. Yet, it is the sanctions attached to effective norms that provide the incentive for individuals to coordinate their activities with others in the pursuit of collective goals. The possibility for, and patterning of, long-term group relations is thus established while limiting the domain of wholly self-interested (and potentially socially destructive) behavior.

In addition, Coleman emphasizes the role of "social capital" as an important resource that enables individuals to realize their interests. Social capital is derived from the *relations* between individuals, particularly those that are part of a "closed" social network in which most individuals either directly or indirectly (as in a friend of a friend) know one another. While social capital comes in many forms, Coleman emphasizes how authority, trustworthiness (and the obligations and expectations on which trust is based), information channels, and effective norms allow individuals to achieve goals that are otherwise unattainable. For instance, when you do a favor for a friend or colleague, it establishes an obligation on his or her part to repay the favor in order to uphold norms of trustworthiness and maintain the relationship. Much like a "credit slip," you can redeem the obligation owed in order to accomplish a task that might otherwise be impossible or too costly to undertake alone. Similarly, individuals often use their relationships with others in order to gain access to information such as the inside story on a job opening or the latest trends in music or fashion (Coleman 1990:300–21).

In examining the relationship between individual decisions and group action, Coleman (and many other rational choice theorists) turned his attention to the "free-rider" problem.[5] This refers to the individual's rational decision to not participate in group activity if the goals of the group cannot be denied to the individual. For instance, given that any one individual's efforts in the fight to protect the natural environment border on inconsequential, why should he spend his time and energy fighting for the cause? Surely one person's taking the time to distribute literature in his community or to write letters to his political representatives,

(Continued)

[5]See Mancur Olson, *The Logic of Collective Action* (1965); Russell Hardin, *Collective Action* (1982); and Michael Hechter (1987), *Principles of Group Solidarity* for foundational statements on the free-rider problem and its effects on goal-oriented group action.

(Continued)

or even to donate $50 to an environmental group, will not tip the balance in the fight one way or another. But this is not a matter of defeatism; rather, it makes sense (i.e., it's rational) to let others bear the costs of campaigning for cleaner air and water, because if the group is successful in achieving its goals, the individual will receive the benefits for free. After all, you cannot stop someone from breathing air or drinking water. The issue for rational choice theorists, then, is how to explain the formation and success of *groups* when it is rational for *individuals* not to pay the price of participation. (Similarly, it is rational not to vote in an election and avoid the cost of lost opportunities that come with standing in line considering that a given individual's vote will not affect the outcome. Yet, millions of people do vote.)

So, why do people participate in group actions when they cannot be excluded from consuming the benefits the group provides? Rational choice theorists typically offer three solutions to this seeming paradox. First, groups can reward individuals for their participation through "selective incentives"—benefits that are distributed exclusively to those who bear the costs for providing a good. Selective incentives can take on any number of forms, from winning a leadership position in a revolutionary movement to receiving a coffee mug or bumper sticker for making a contribution to a public television station. Second, individuals may work toward achieving a group goal for the intangible benefits that participation itself can provide. For instance, individuals may receive social approval from others or experience a sense of personal satisfaction for having altruistically participated in realizing a collective goal. Thus, a person might risk imprisonment in order to protest a chemical plant's environmental practices. Third, free-riding can be minimized by enforcing participation or negatively sanctioning individuals for not contributing to the public good. This is the rationale of government taxes and the penalties incurred for not paying them.

BLAU'S THEORETICAL ORIENTATION

Like Homans's, Blau's perspective is primarily individualistic and rationalist (see Figure 4.3). In his major work on exchange theory, *Exchange and Power in Social Life* (from which the following excerpt is taken), he states his position thusly:

> The [theoretical] problem is to derive the social processes that govern the complex structures of communities and societies from the simpler processes that pervade the daily intercourse among individuals and their interpersonal relations. (1964:2)

In other words, while acknowledging that complex social structures (a family, a university, manufacturing industries, the federal government, etc.) possess properties that are distinct from the individuals that live and work in and through them, such structures, nevertheless, emerge only through individual and group interactions. As such, any attempt to understand complex structures must begin with an analysis of the patterns of daily interactions that guide individual conduct.

Figure 4.3   Blau's Core Concepts

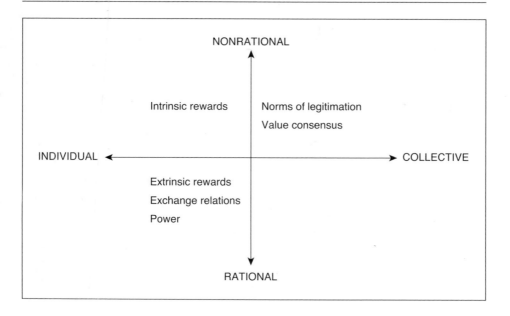

Although Blau's emphasis rested on examining the nature of interpersonal inter-action, his interests, unlike Homans's, did not lie in searching for the psychological roots of exchange behavior or the patterns of reinforcement that determine the future of such behavior. Instead, reminiscent of Simmel, his objective was to explain the dynam-ics of exchange *relations* that emerge *between* individuals and groups as they jointly pursue their interests. A simplified model of this dynamic is depicted in Table 4.2 on the next page. At their root, exchange relations present individuals with four basic interaction options. These options provide the context for an individual's calculation of the possible rewards and costs for initiating an exchange relation. Once an option is realized, it establishes the relational structure for subsequent exchange calculations that may, in turn, alter the very structure that shaped the individual's or group's decision. (You can see the logic of this model in the strategies devised by the participants in cur-rently popular "reality" shows such as *Survivor*. The players' efforts to prove their worth in the challenges and their use of deception and secret alliances are calculated attempts to create a favorable imbalance of power.)

As we alluded earlier, however, Blau would make a theoretical shift that incorpo-rated collectivist (and nonrational) aspects of social life. In attempting to build a theory of social structure on the basis of those "simpler processes" that shape face-to-face interaction, Blau saw in shared norms a generalized mechanism that defines the expec-tations and governs the reactions of those subjected to power imbalances. More broadly, Blau viewed "value consensus" as a crucial mediating link allowing for "inte-grative bonds and social solidarity among millions of people in society, most of whom have never met . . . [and] which alone make it possible to transcend personal transac-tions and develop complex networks of independent exchange" (1964:24). While originally an emergent product of simple exchange relations, norms and values become institutionalized in the broader social fabric as they are transmitted from one

Table 4.2   Exchange Relations and Interaction Options[6]

	A's Choice	
	Provide Rewards	*Withhold Rewards*
Provide Rewards	Peer relation (second choice of both)	A profits—imbalance of power (A's first choice)
B's Choice		
Withhold Rewards	B profits—imbalance of power (B's first choice)	No relation (last choice of both)

generation to the next. Despite this theoretical shift, however, Blau's argument in the following selection underscores the individualistic dimension of social order.[7]

Regarding his general position on the problem of action, Blau adopted a rational orientation. Although the incorporation of norms and values into his model suggests a nonrational perspective, Blau emphasized the goal-directed aspects of human behavior:

> Within the rather broad limits . . . norms impose on social relations, however, human beings tend to be governed in their associations with one another by the desire to obtain social rewards of various sorts, and the resulting exchanges of benefits shape the structure of social relations. (1964:18)

Yet, like Homans, he, too, assumed a restricted view on the nature of rational action, contending only that individuals "choose between alternative potential associates or courses of action by evaluating the experiences or expected experiences with each in terms of a preference ranking and then selecting the best alternative" (ibid.). Which objectives an individual pursues and how successful she will be in achieving them remains an open question, one that can be answered only inductively after the fact.[8]

As for the "rewards of various sorts," Blau distinguished two primary types: extrinsic and intrinsic. **Extrinsic rewards** are those that are "detachable" from the association in which they are acquired. In other words, extrinsic benefits are derived not from another's company itself, but from the external rewards his company will provide. Here, associating with others serves as a means to a further end.[9] Thus, a salesperson is considerate because she wants to make a commission, not because she values the relationship she initiates with any particular customer.

---

[6]Adapted from Peter Blau, *Exchange and Power in Social Life* (1964:45).

[7]Blau's theoretical shift also left him open to the charge of ad hoc theorizing. In other words, he resorted to logically inconsistent concepts to plug the holes in his essentially individualistic argument. Interestingly, Blau would later abandon his attempt to develop a theory of complex social structures on the basis of "simple" exchange relations.

[8]It is important to point out that our theoretical positioning of Blau is based primarily on the selection included in this volume. In fact, the totality of Blau's works spans into each quadrant of our map. For instance, in addition to his contributions to exchange theory, Blau also made a significant impact in the sociology of organizations and social stratification. See, for example, *Structural Contexts of Opportunities* (1994), *Inequality and Heterogeneity* (1977), and *The Dynamics of Bureaucracy* (1955).

[9]Blau saw his distinction between intrinsic and extrinsic rewards as a special case of Parsons's distinction between the pattern variables particularism and universalism, respectively (see Chapter 2).

Intrinsic rewards are those things we find pleasurable in and of themselves, not because they provide the means for obtaining other benefits. Examples of intrinsic rewards are celebrating a holiday with one's family, going on a walk with a friend, or love—the purest type of intrinsic reward. In cases such as these, rewards express one's commitment to the relationship and are exchanged in the interest of maintaining it.

Because linking intimate relations to exchange processes runs counter to our conventional understanding of such relations, some additional remarks on the topic are perhaps in order. As Blau notes, "Love appears to make human beings unselfish, since they themselves enjoy giving pleasure to those they love, but this selfless devotion generally rests on an interest in maintaining the other's love" (1964:76). Yet, it is often the case that in intimate relations one individual is more in love than the other. As a result, the "interests" in maintaining the relationship are not equal. This, in turn, creates an imbalance that advantages one partner while disadvantaging the other, as the costs for ending the relationship, as well as the willingness to endure costs to maintain it, are not proportionate. As is the case in other types of relationships, the individual who is less committed in an intimate relationship is able to exercise power over the other, whose greater interest in maintaining the relationship resigns him to a dependent position.

It is this dynamic that underlies "playing hard to get," where "the lover who does not express unconditional affection early gains advantages in the established interpersonal relationship. Indeed, the more restrained lover also seems to have a better chance of inspiring another's love for himself or herself" (ibid.:78). Like other benefits offered, affections that are given too freely depreciate their value. Moreover, the more freely one gives his affection, the more he signals that he has few options, thus reducing his value on the "market." From this perspective, dating is a "challenge of conquest" in which those "who are successful in making many conquests . . . validate their attractiveness in their own eyes as well as those of others" (ibid.:81). On the other hand, resisting conquests implies that one has many alternatives to choose from, which then enhances a person's desirability in the eyes of others. Just as relationships based on an exchange of extrinsic rewards involve a cost/benefit dilemma, so too do intimate relations, although in this instance the dilemma is one in which lovers must express affection for one another in order to maintain the relationship, while at the same time there is pressure to withhold such expressions in order to make oneself more attractive.

Reading

Introduction to *Exchange and Power in Social Life*

In the following selection you will encounter the themes discussed to this point: interaction as a reciprocal exchange of rewards, how an imbalance in exchanges can lead to an imbalance of power, and how this inequality can lead to a change in the structure of social relations depending on social norms of fairness that shape the exercise of legitimate authority. It is through such norms that subordinate individuals define the imbalances as just and beneficial or as oppressive and exploitative.

In addition to these themes, Blau also emphasizes the role of "social attraction" in exchange relations. For Blau, social attraction represents the fundamental "force that induces human beings to establish social associations" with others (1964:20). Such attraction rests on whether or not an individual expects to receive rewards for forming an association with another. Thus, it is what the other can offer us that determines whether we will find him "attractive." Our attraction to others often is motivated and sustained by a mix of extrinsic and intrinsic rewards. Indeed, associations we find intrinsically gratifying often were initiated for the extrinsic rewards they provided: the co-worker whose advice we sought last year is now a valued friend; the comparative (i.e., extrinsic) good looks and wit of another sparks a lasting courtship. Similarly, in addition to loving one another, spouses also may be attracted to the economic rewards that their marriage brings.

While the forms of social attraction may differ, the same basic exchange processes guide the relations they initiate. Whether the rewards exchanged are intrinsic or extrinsic in nature, the exchange itself produces a "strain toward reciprocity;" for individuals are interested in discharging their obligations to provide benefits to those from whom rewards were received. Failure to do so can jeopardize not only the continued supply of benefits, but also the conferring of social approval, a basic and important reward. Yet, the obligation to reciprocate, felt as a blessing or burden, also produces a strain toward imbalance in the relationship. For individuals seek not merely to stay out of "debt," but also to "accumulate credit that makes their status superior to that of others" (1964:26). As you will read below, even love relationships are not free from these twin strains and the power dynamics to which they give rise.

Exchange and Power in Social Life (1964)
Peter Blau

THE STRUCTURE OF SOCIAL ASSOCIATIONS

To speak of social life is to speak of the associations between people—their associating together in work and in play, in love and in war, to trade or to worship, to help or to hinder. It is in the social relations men establish that their interests find expression and their desires become realized. As Simmel put it: "Social association refers to the widely varying forms that are generated as the diverse interests of individuals prompt them to develop social units in which they realize these—sensual or ideal, lasting or fleeting, conscious or unconscious, casually impelling or teleologically inducing—interests."[i] Simmel's fundamental postulate, and also that of this book, is that the analysis of social associations, of the processes governing them, and of the forms they assume is the central task of sociology. . . .

The objectives of our investigation are to analyze social associations, the processes that sustain them and the forms they attain, and to proceed to inquire into the complex social forces and structures to which they give rise. Broad as this topic is, it is intended to provide a specific focus that explicitly excludes many sociological problems from consideration. Sociology is defined by Weber as "a science which attempts the interpretative understanding of social action in order thereby to arrive at a causal explanation of its course and effects. . . . Action is social insofar as, by virtue of the subjective meaning attached to it by the acting individual (or individuals), it takes account of the behavior of others and is thereby oriented in its course."[ii] A concern with social action, broadly conceived as any conduct that derives its impetus and meaning from social values, has characterized contemporary theory in sociology for some years. The resulting preoccupation with value orientations has diverted theoretical attention from the study of the actual

SOURCE: From *Exchange and Power in Social Life,* by Blau, P. Copyright © 1986 by Transaction Publishers; reprinted with permission.

[i]Georg Simmel, *Soziologie*, Leipzig: Duncker und Humblot, 1908, p. 6 (my translation).

[ii]Max Weber, *The Theory of Social and Economic Organization*, New York: Oxford University Press, 1947, p. 88.

associations between people and the structures of their associations. While structures of social relations are, of course, profoundly influenced by common values, these structures have a significance of their own, which is ignored if concern is exclusively with the underlying values and norms. Exchange transactions and power relations, in particular, constitute social forces that must be investigated in their own right, not merely in terms of the norms that limit and the values that reinforce them, to arrive at an understanding of the dynamics of social structures. If one purpose of the title of this chapter is to indicate a link with the theoretical tradition of Simmel, another purpose is to distinguish the theoretical orientation in this monograph from that of Weber and Parsons; not "the structure of social action" but the structure of social associations is the focal point of the present inquiry.

After illustrating the concept of social exchange and its manifestations in various social relations, this chapter presents the main theme of how more complex processes of social association evolve out of simpler ones. Forces of social attraction stimulate exchange transactions. Social exchange, in turn, tends to give rise to differentiation of status and power. Further processes emerge in a differentiated status structure that lead to legitimation and organization, on the one hand, and to opposition and change, on the other. Whereas the conception of reciprocity in exchange implies the existence of balancing forces that create a strain toward equilibrium, the simultaneous operations of diverse balancing forces recurrently produce imbalances in social life, and the resulting dialectic between reciprocity and imbalance gives social structures their distinctive nature and dynamics.

The Exchange of Social Rewards

Most human pleasures have their roots in social life. Whether we think of love or power, professional recognition or sociable companionship, the comforts of family life or the challenge of competitive sports, the gratifications experienced by individuals are contingent on actions of others. The same is true for the most selfless and spiritual satisfactions. To work effectively for a good cause requires making converts to it. Even the religious experience is much enriched by communal worship. Physical pleasures that can be experienced in solitude pale in significance by comparison. Enjoyable as a good dinner is, it is the social occasion that gives it its luster. Indeed, there is something pathetic about the person who derives his major gratification from food or drink as such, since it reveals either excessive need or excessive greed; the pauper illustrates the former, the glutton, the latter. To be sure, there are profound solitary enjoyments—reading a good book, creating a piece of art, producing a scholarly work. Yet these, too, derive much of their significance from being later communicated to and shared with others. The lack of such anticipation makes the solitary activity again somewhat pathetic: the recluse who has nobody to talk to about what he reads; the artist or scholar whose works are completely ignored, not only by his contemporaries but also by posterity.

Much of human suffering as well as much of human happiness has its source in the actions of other human beings. One follows from the other, given the facts of group life, where pairs do not exist in complete isolation from other social relations. The same human acts that cause pleasure to some typically cause displeasure to others. For one boy to enjoy the love of a girl who has committed herself to be his steady date, other boys who had gone out with her must suffer the pain of having been rejected. The satisfaction a man derives from exercising power over others requires that they endure the deprivation of being subject to his power. For a professional to command an outstanding reputation in his field, most of his colleagues must get along without such pleasant recognition, since it is the lesser professional esteem of the majority that defines his as outstanding. The joy the victorious team members experience has its counterpart in the disappointment of the losers. In short, the rewards individuals obtain in social associations tend to entail a cost to other individuals. This does not mean that most social associations involve zero-sum games in which the gains of some rest on the losses of others. Quite the contrary, individuals associate with one another because they all profit from their association. But they do not necessarily all profit equally, nor do they share the cost of providing the benefits equally, and even if there are no direct costs to participants, there are often indirect costs born by those excluded from the association, as the case of the rejected suitors illustrates.

Some social associations are intrinsically rewarding. Friends find pleasure in associating with one another, and the enjoyment of whatever they do together—climbing a mountain, watching a football game—is enhanced by the gratification that inheres in the association itself. The mutual affection between lovers or family members has the same result. It is not what lovers do together but their doing it *together* that is the distinctive source of their special satisfaction—not seeing a play but sharing the experience of seeing it. Social interaction in less intimate relations than those of lovers, family members, or friends, however, may also be inherently rewarding. The sociability at a party or among neighbors or in a work group involves experiences that are not especially profound but are intrinsically gratifying. In these cases, all associates benefit simultaneously from their social interaction, and the only cost they incur is the indirect one of giving up alternative opportunities by devoting time to the association.

Social associations may also be rewarding for a different reason. Individuals often derive specific benefits from social relations because their associates deliberately go to some trouble to provide these benefits for them. Most people like helping others and doing favors for them— to assist not only their friends but also their acquaintances and occasionally even strangers, as the motorist who stops to aid another with his stalled car illustrates. Favors make us grateful, and our expressions of gratitude are social rewards that tend to make doing favors enjoyable, particularly if we express our appreciation and indebtedness publicly and thereby help establish a person's reputation as a generous and competent helper. Besides, one good deed deserves another. If we feel grateful and obligated to an associate for favors received, we shall seek to reciprocate his kindness by doing things for him. He in turn is likely to reciprocate, and the resulting mutual exchange of favors strengthens, often without explicit intent, the social bond between us.

A person who fails to reciprocate favors is accused of ingratitude. This very accusation indicates that reciprocation is expected, and it serves as a social sanction that discourages individuals from forgetting their obligations to associates. Generally, people are grateful for favors and repay their social debts, and both their gratitude and their repayment are social rewards for the associate who has done them favors. The fact that furnishing benefits to others tends to produce these social rewards is, of course, a major reason why people often go to great trouble to help their associates and enjoy doing so. We would not be human if these advantageous consequences of our good deeds were not important inducements for our doing them.[iii] There are, to be sure, some individuals who selflessly work for others without any thought of reward and even without expecting gratitude, but these are virtually saints, and saints are rare. The rest of us also act unselfishly sometimes, but we require some incentive for doing so, if it is only the social acknowledgment that we are unselfish.

An apparent "altruism" pervades social life; people are anxious to benefit one another and to reciprocate for the benefits they receive. But beneath this seeming selflessness an underlying "egoism" can be discovered; the tendency to help others is frequently motivated by the expectation that doing so will bring social rewards. Beyond this self-interested concern with profiting from social associations, however, there is again an "altruistic" element or, at least, one that removes social transactions from simple egoism or psychological hedonism. A basic reward people seek in their associations is social approval, and selfish disregard for others makes it impossible to obtain this important reward.

The social approval of those whose opinions we value is of great significance to us, but its significance depends on its being genuine. We

---

[iii]Once a person has become emotionally committed to a relationship, his identification with the other and his interest in continuing the association provide new independent incentives for supplying benefits to the other. Similarly, firm commitments to an organization lead members to make recurrent contributions to it without expecting reciprocal benefits in every instance.

cannot force others to give us their approval, regardless of how much power we have over them, because coercing them to express their admiration or praise would make these expressions worthless. "Action can be coerced, but a coerced show of feeling is only a show."[iv] Simulation robs approval of its significance, but its very importance makes associates reluctant to withhold approval from one another and, in particular, to express disapproval, thus introducing an element of simulation and dissimulation into their communications. As a matter of fact, etiquette prescribes that approval be simulated in disregard of actual opinions under certain circumstances. One does not generally tell a hostess, "Your party was boring," or a neighbor, "What you say is stupid." Since social conventions require complimentary remarks on many occasions, these are habitually discounted as not reflecting genuine approbation, and other evidence that does reflect it is looked for, such as whether guests accept future invitations or whether neighbors draw one into further conversations.

In matters of morality, however, individuals have strong convictions that constrain them to voice their actual judgments more freely. They usually do not hesitate to express disapproval of or, at least, withhold approval from associates who have violated socially accepted standards of conduct. Antisocial disregard for the welfare of the ingroup meets universally with disapprobation regardless of how immoral, in terms of the mores of the wider community, the norms of a particular group may be. The significance of social approval, therefore, discourages conduct that is utterly and crudely selfish. A more profound morality must rest not merely on group pressure and long-run advantage but primarily on internalized normative standards. In the ideal case, an individual unerringly follows the moral commands of his conscience whatever the consequences. While such complete morality is attained only by the saint and the fool, and most men make some compromises, moral standards clearly do guide and restrain human conduct. Within the rather broad limits these norms impose on social relations,

however, human beings tend to be governed in their associations with one another by the desire to obtain social rewards of various sorts, and the resulting exchanges of benefits shape the structure of social relations.

The question that arises is whether a rationalistic conception of human behavior underlies this principle that individuals pursue social rewards in their social associations. The only assumption made is that human beings choose between alternative potential associates or courses of action by evaluating the experiences or expected experiences with each in terms of a preference ranking and then selecting the best alternative. Irrational as well as rational behavior is governed by these considerations, as Boulding has pointed out:

> All behavior, in so far as the very concept of behavior implies doing one thing rather than another, falls into the above pattern, even the behavior of the lunatic and the irrational or irresponsible or erratic person. The distinction between rational and irrational behavior lies in the degree of self-consciousness and the stability of the images involved rather than in any distinction of the principle of optimum.[v]

What is explicitly *not* assumed here is that men have complete information, that they have no social commitments restricting their alternatives, that their preferences are entirely consistent or remain constant, or that they pursue one specific ultimate goal to the exclusion of all others. These more restrictive assumptions, which are not made in the present analysis, characterize rationalistic models of human conduct, such as that of game theory. Of particular importance is the fact that men strive to achieve diverse objectives. The statement that men select the most preferred among available alternatives does not imply that they always choose the one that yields them the greatest material profit. They may, and often do, choose the alternative that requires them to make material sacrifices but contributes the most to the attainment of some lofty ideal, for *this* may be their objective. Even in this choice they may err and select

---

[iv]Erving Goffman, *Asylums*, Chicago: Aldine, 1962, p. 115.

[v]Kenneth Boulding, *Conflict and Defense*, New York: Harper, 1962, p. 151.

an alternative that actually is not the best means to realize their goal. Indeed, the need to anticipate in advance the social rewards with which others will reciprocate for favors in exchange relations inevitably introduces uncertainty and recurrent errors of judgment that make perfectly rational calculations impossible. Granted these qualifications, the assumption that men seek to adjust social conditions to achieve their ends seems to be quite realistic, indeed inescapable.

Basic Processes

The basic social processes that govern associations among men have their roots in primitive psychological processes, such as those underlying the feelings of attraction between individuals and their desires for various kinds of rewards. These psychological tendencies are primitive only in respect to our subject matter, that is, they are taken as given without further inquiry into the motivating forces that produce them, for our concern is with the social forces that emanate from them.

The simpler social processes that can be observed in interpersonal associations and that rest directly on psychological dispositions give rise to the more complex social processes that govern structures of interconnected social associations, such as the social organization of a factory or the political relations in a community. New social forces emerge in the increasingly complex social structures that develop in societies, and these dynamic forces are quite removed from the ultimate psychological base of all social life. Although complex social systems have their foundation in simpler ones, they have their own dynamics with emergent properties. In this section, the basic processes of social associations will be presented in broad strokes, to be analyzed subsequently in greater detail, with special attention to their wider implications.

Social attraction is the force that induces human beings to establish social associations on their own initiative and to expand the scope of their associations once they have been formed. Reference here is to social relations into which men enter of their own free will rather than to either those into which they are born (such as

kinship groups) or those imposed on them by forces beyond their control (such as the combat teams to which soldiers are assigned), although even in these involuntary relations the extent and intensity of the association depend on the degree of mutual attraction. An individual is attracted to another if he expects associating with him to be in some way rewarding for himself, and his interest in the expected social rewards draws him to the other. The psychological needs and dispositions of individuals determine which rewards are particularly salient for them and thus to whom they will be attracted. Whatever the specific motives, there is an important difference between the expectation that the association will be an intrinsically rewarding experience and the expectation that it will furnish extrinsic benefits, for example, advice. This difference calls attention to two distinct meanings of the term "attraction" and its derivatives. In its narrower sense, social attraction refers to liking another person *intrinsically* and having positive feelings toward him; in the broader sense, in which the term is now used, social attraction refers to being drawn to another person for any reason whatsoever. The customer is attracted in this broader sense to the merchant who sells goods of a given quality at the lowest price, but he has no intrinsic feelings of attraction for him, unless they happen to be friends.

A person who is attracted to others is interested in proving himself attractive to them, for his ability to associate with them and reap the benefits expected from the association is contingent on their finding him an attractive associate and thus wanting to interact with him. Their attraction to him, just as his to them, depends on the anticipation that the association will be rewarding. To arouse this anticipation, a person tries to impress others. Attempts to appear impressive are pervasive in the early stages of acquaintance and group formation. Impressive qualities make a person attractive and promise that associating with him will be rewarding. Mutual attraction prompts people to establish an association, and the rewards they provide each other in the course of their social interaction, unless their expectations are disappointed, maintain their mutual attraction and the continuing association.

Processes of social attraction, therefore, lead to processes of social exchange. The nature of the exchange in an association experienced as intrinsically rewarding, such as a love relationship, differs from that between associates primarily concerned with extrinsic benefits, such as neighbors who help one another with various chores, but exchanges do occur in either case. A person who furnishes needed assistance to associates, often at some cost to himself, obligates them to reciprocate his kindness. Whether reference is to instrumental services or to such intangibles as social approval, the benefits each supplies to the others are rewards that serve as inducements to continue to supply benefits, and the integrative bonds created in the process fortify the social relationship.

A situation frequently arises, however, in which one person needs something another has to offer, for example, help from the other in his work, but has nothing the other needs to reciprocate for the help. While the other may be sufficiently rewarded by expressions of gratitude to help him a few times, he can hardly be expected regularly to devote time and effort to providing help without receiving any return to compensate him for his troubles. (In the case of intrinsic attraction, the only return expected is the willingness to continue the association.) The person in need of recurrent services from an associate to whom he has nothing to offer has several alternatives. First, he may force the other to give him help. Second, he may obtain the help he needs from another source. Third, he may find ways to get along without such help. If he is unable or unwilling to choose any of these alternatives, however, there is only one other course of action left for him; he must subordinate himself to the other and comply with his wishes, thereby rewarding the other with power over himself as an inducement for furnishing the needed help. Willingness to comply with another's demands is a generic social reward, since the power it gives him is a generalized means, parallel to money, which can be used to attain a variety of ends. The power to command compliance is equivalent to credit, which a man can draw on in the future to obtain various benefits at the disposal of those obligated to him. The unilateral supply of important services establishes this kind of credit and thus is a source of power.

Exchange processes, then, give rise to differentiation of power. A person who commands services others need, and who is independent of any at their command, attains power over others by making the satisfaction of their need contingent on their compliance. This principle is held to apply to the most intimate as well as the most distant social relations. The girl with whom a boy is in love has power over him, since his eagerness to spend much time with her prompts him to make their time together especially pleasant for her by acceding her wishes. The employer can make workers comply with his directives because they are dependent on his wages. To be sure, the superior's power wanes if subordinates can resort to coercion, have equally good alternatives, or are able to do without the benefits at his disposal. But given these limiting conditions, unilateral services that meet basic needs are the penultimate source of power. Its ultimate source, of course, is physical coercion. While the power that rests on coercion is more absolute, however, it is also more limited in scope than the power that derives from met needs.

A person on whom others are dependent for vital benefits has the power to enforce his demands. He may make demands on them that they consider fair and just in relation to the benefits they receive for submitting to his power. On the other hand, he may lack such restraint and make demands that appear excessive to them, arousing feelings of exploitation for having to render more compliance than the rewards received justify. Social norms define the expectations of subordinates and their evaluations of the superior's demands. The fair exercise of power gives rise to approval of the superior, whereas unfair exploitation promotes disapproval. The greater the resources of a person on which his power rests, the easier it is for him to refrain from exploiting subordinates by making excessive demands, and consequently the better are the chances that subordinates will approve of the fairness of his rule rather than disapprove of its unfairness.

There are fundamental differences between the dynamics of power in a collective situation and the power of one individual over another. The weakness of the isolated subordinate limits the significance of his approval or disapproval of the superior. The agreement that emerges in a collectivity of subordinates concerning their judgment of the superior, on the other hand, has far-reaching implications for developments in the social structure.

Collective approval of power legitimates that power. People who consider that the advantages they gain from a superior's exercise of power outweigh the hardships that compliance with his demands imposes on them tend to communicate to each other their approval of the ruler and their feelings of obligation to him. The consensus that develops as the result of these communications finds expression in group pressures that promote compliance with the ruler's directives, thereby strengthening his power of control and legitimating his authority. "A feeling of obligation to obey the commands of the established public authority is found, varying in liveliness and effectiveness from one individual to another, among the members of any political society."[vi] Legitimate authority is the basis of organization. It makes it possible to organize collective effort to further the achievement of various objectives, some of which could not be attained by individuals separately at all and others that can be attained more effectively by coordinating efforts. Although power that is not legitimated by the approval of subordinates can also be used to organize them, the stability of such an organization is highly precarious.

Collective disapproval of power engenders opposition. People who share the experience of being exploited by the unfair demands of those in positions of power, and by the insufficient rewards they receive for their contributions, are likely to communicate their feelings of anger, frustration, and aggression to each other. There tends to arise a wish to retaliate by striking down the existing powers. "As every man doth, so shall it be done to him, and retaliation seems to be the great law that is dictated to us by nature."[vii] The social support the oppressed give each other in the course of discussing their common grievances and feelings of hostility justifies and reinforces their aggressive opposition against those in power. It is out of such shared discontent that opposition ideologies and movements

develop—that men organize a union against their employer or a revolutionary party against their government.

In brief, differentiation of power in a collective situation evokes contrasting dynamic forces: legitimating processes that foster the organization of individuals and groups in common endeavors; and countervailing forces that deny legitimacy to existing powers and promote opposition and cleavage. Under the influence of these forces, the scope of legitimate organization expands to include ever larger collectivities, but opposition and conflict recurrently redivide these collectivities and stimulate reorganization along different lines.

The distinctive characteristic of complex social structures is that their constituent elements are also social structures. We may call these structures of interrelated groups "macrostructures" and those composed of interacting individuals "microstructures." There are some parallels between the social processes in microstructures and macrostructures. Processes of social attraction create integrative bonds between associates, and integrative processes also unite various groups in a community. Exchange processes between individuals give rise to differentiation among them, and intergroup exchanges further differentiation among groups. Individuals become incorporated in legitimate organizations, and these in turn become part of broader bodies of legitimate authority. Opposition and conflict occur not only within collectivities but also between them. These parallels, however, must not conceal the fundamental differences between the processes that govern the interpersonal associations in microstructures and the forces characteristic of the wider and more complex social relations macrostructures.

First, *value consensus* is of crucial significance for social processes that pervade complex social structures, because standards commonly agreed upon serve as mediating links of social transactions between individuals and groups without any direct contact. Sharing basic values creates integrative bonds and solidarity among

---

[vi]Bertrand de Jouvenel, *Sovereignty*, University of Chicago Press, 1957, p. 87.

[vii]Adam Smith, *The Theory of Moral Sentiments* (2d ed.), London: A. Millar, 1761, p. 139.

millions of people in a society, most of whom have never met, and serves as functional equivalent for the feelings of personal attraction that unite pairs of associates and small groups. Common standards of valuation produce media of exchange—money being the prototype but not the only one—which alone make it possible to transcend personal transactions and develop complex networks of indirect exchange. Legitimating values expand the scope of centralized control far beyond the reach of personal influence, as exemplified by the authority of a legitimate government. Opposition ideals serve as rallying points to draw together strangers from widely dispersed places and unite them in a common cause. The study of these problems requires an analysis of the significance of social values and norms that must complement the analysis of exchange transactions and power relations but must not become a substitute for it.

A second emergent property of macrostructures is the complex interplay between the internal forces within substructures and the forces that connect the diverse substructures, some of which may be microstructures composed of individuals while others may themselves be macrostructures composed of subgroups. The processes of integration, differentiation, organization, and opposition formation in the various substructures, which often vary greatly among the substructures, and the corresponding processes in the macrostructure all have repercussions for each other. A systematic analysis of these intricate patterns . . . would have to constitute the core of a general theory of social structures.

Finally, enduring institutions typically develop in macrostructures. Established systems of legitimation raise the question of their perpetuation through time. The strong identification of men with the highest ideals and most sacred beliefs they share makes them desirous to preserve these basic values for succeeding generations. The investments made in establishing and expanding a legitimate organization create an interest in stabilizing it and assuring its survival in the face of opposition attacks. For this purpose, formalized procedures are instituted that make the organization independent of any individual member and permit it to persist beyond the life span or period of tenure

of its members. Institutionalization refers to the emergence of social mechanisms through which social values and norms, organizing principles, and knowledge and skills are transmitted from generation to generation. A society's institutions constitute the social matrix in which individuals grow up and are socialized, with the result that some aspects of institutions are reflected in their own personalities, and others appear to them as the inevitable external conditions of human existence. Traditional institutions stabilize social life but also introduce rigidities that make adjustment to changing conditions difficult. Opposition movements may arise to promote such adjustment, yet these movements themselves tend to become institutionalized and rigid in the course of time, creating needs for fresh oppositions.

Reciprocity and Imbalance

There is a strain toward imbalance as well as toward reciprocity in social associations. The term "balance" itself is ambiguous inasmuch as we speak not only of balancing our books but also of a balance in our favor, which refers, of course, to a lack of equality between inputs and outputs. As a matter of fact, the balance of the accounting sheet merely rests, in the typical case, on an underlying imbalance between income and outlays, and so do apparent balances in social life. Individuals and groups are interested in, at least, maintaining a balance between inputs and outputs and staying out of debt in their social transactions; hence the strain toward reciprocity. Their aspirations, however, are to achieve a balance in their favor and accumulate credit that makes their status superior to that of others; hence the strain toward imbalance.

Arguments about equilibrium—that all scientific theories must be conceived in terms of equilibrium models or that any equilibrium model neglects the dynamics of real life—ignore the important point that the forces sustaining equilibrium on one level of social life constitute disequilibrating forces on other levels. For supply and demand to remain in equilibrium in a market, for example, forces must exist that continually disturb the established patterns of exchange. Similarly, the circulation of the elite, an equilibrium model, rests on the operation of forces that create imbalances and disturbances in the various segments of society. The principle suggested is that balanced social states depend on imbalances in other social states; forces that restore equilibrium in one respect do so by creating disequilibrium in others. The processes of association described illustrate this principle.

A person who is attracted to another will seek to prove himself attractive to the other. Thus a boy who is very much attracted to a girl, more so than she is to him, is anxious to make himself more attractive to her. To do so, he will try to impress her and, particularly, go out of his way to make associating with him an especially rewarding experience for her. He may devote a lot of thought to finding ways to please her, spend much money on her, and do the things she likes on their dates rather than those he would prefer. Let us assume that he is successful and she becomes as attracted to him as he is to her, that is, she finds associating with him as rewarding as he finds associating with her, as indicated by the fact that both are equally eager to spend time together.

Attraction is now reciprocal, but the reciprocity has been established by an imbalance in the exchange. To be sure, both obtain satisfactory rewards from the association at this stage, the boy as the result of her willingness to spend as much time with him as he wants, and the girl as the result of his readiness to make their dates enjoyable for her. These reciprocal rewards are the sources of their mutual attraction. The contributions made, however, are in imbalance. Both devote time to the association, which involves giving up alternative opportunities, but the boy contributes in addition special efforts to please her. Her company is sufficient reward by itself, while his is not, which makes her "the more useful or otherwise superior" in terms of their own evaluations, and he must furnish supplementary rewards to produce "equality in a sense between the parties." Although two lovers may, of course, be equally anxious to spend time together and to please one another, it is rare for a perfect balance of mutual affection to develop spontaneously. The reciprocal attraction in most intimate relations—marriages and lasting friendships as well as more temporary attachments—is the result of some imbalance of contributions that compensates for inequalities in spontaneous affection, notably in the form of one partner's greater willingness to defer to the other's wishes. . . .

The theoretical principle that has been advanced is that a given balance in social associations is produced by imbalances in the same associations in other respects. This principle, which has been illustrated with the imbalances that underlie reciprocal attraction, also applies to the process of social differentiation. A person who supplies services in demand to others obligates them to reciprocate. If some fail to reciprocate, he has strong inducements to withhold the needed assistance from them in order to supply it to others who do repay him for his troubles in some form. Those who have nothing else to offer him that would be a satisfactory return for his services, therefore, are under pressure to defer to his wishes and comply with his requests in repayment for his assistance. Their compliance with his demands gives him the power to utilize their resources at his discretion to further his own ends. By providing unilateral benefits to others, a person accumulates a capital of willing compliance on which he can draw whenever it is to his interest to impose his will upon others, within the limits of the significance the continuing supply of his benefits has for them. The general advantages of power enable men who cannot otherwise repay for services they need to obtain them in return for their compliance; although in the extreme case of the person who has much power and whose benefits are in great demand, even an offer of compliance may not suffice to obtain them.

Here, an imbalance of power establishes reciprocity in the exchange. Unilateral services give rise to a differentiation of power that equilibrates the exchange. The exchange balance, in fact, rests on two imbalances: unilateral services and unilateral power. Although these two imbalances make up a balance or equilibrium in terms of one perspective, in terms of another, which is equally valid, the exchange equilibrium reinforces and perpetuates the imbalances of dependence and power that sustain it. Power differences not only are an imbalance by definition but also are actually experienced as such, as indicated by the tendency of men to escape from domination if they can. Indeed, a major impetus for the eagerness of individuals to discharge their obligations and reciprocate for services they receive, by providing services in return, is the threat of becoming otherwise subject to the power of the supplier of the services. While reciprocal services create an interdependence that balances power, unilateral dependence on services maintains an imbalance of power.

Differentiation of power evidently constitutes an imbalance in the sense of an inequality of power; but the question must be raised whether differentiation of power also necessarily constitutes an imbalance in the sense of a strain toward change in the structure of social relations. Power differences as such, analytically conceived and abstracted from other considerations, create such a pressure toward change, because it can be assumed that men experience having to submit to power as a hardship from which they would prefer to escape. The advantages men derive from their ruler or government, however, may outweigh the hardships entailed in submitting to his or its power, with the result that the analytical imbalance or disturbance introduced by power differences is neutralized. The significance of power imbalances for social change depends, therefore, on the reactions of the governed to the exercise of power.

Social reactions to the exercise of power reflect once more the principle of reciprocity and imbalance, although in a new form. Power over others makes it possible to direct and organize their activities. Sufficient resources to command power over large numbers enable a person or group to establish a large organization. The members recruited to the organization receive benefits, such as financial remuneration, in exchange for complying with the directives of superiors and making various contributions to the organization. The leadership exercises power within the organization, and it derives power from the organization for use in relation with other organizations or groups. The clearest illustration of this double power of organizational leadership is the army commander's power over his own soldiers and, through the force of their arms, over the enemy. Another example is the power business management exercises over its own employees and, through the strength of the concern, in the market. The

greater the external power of an organization, the greater are its chances of accumulating resources that put rewards at the disposal of the leadership for possible distribution among the members.

The normative expectations of those subject to the exercise of power, which are rooted in their social experience, govern their reactions to it. In terms of these standards, the benefits derived from being part of an organization or political society may outweigh the investments required to obtain them, or the demands made on members may exceed the returns they receive for fulfilling these demands. The exercise of power, therefore, may produce two different kinds of imbalance, a positive imbalance of benefits for subordinates or a negative imbalance of exploitation and oppression.

If the members of an organization, or generally those subject to a governing leadership, commonly agree that the demands made on them are only fair and just in view of the ample rewards the leadership delivers, joint feelings of obligation and loyalty to superiors will arise and bestow legitimating approval on their authority. A positive imbalance of benefits generates legitimate authority for the leadership and thereby strengthens and extends its controlling influence. By expressing legitimating approval of, and loyalty to, those who govern them subordinates reciprocate for the benefits their leadership provides, but they simultaneously fortify the imbalance of power in the social structure.

If the demands of the men who exercise power are experienced by those subject to its as exploitative and oppressive, and particularly if these subordinates have been unsuccessful in obtaining redress for their grievances, their frustrations tend to promote disapproval of existing powers and antagonism toward them. As the oppressed communicate their anger and aggression to each other, provided there are opportunities for doing so, their mutual support and approval socially justify and reinforce the negative orientation toward the oppressors, and their collective hostility may inspire them to organize an opposition. The exploitative use of coercive power that arouses active opposition is more prevalent in the relations between organizations and groups than within organizations. Two reasons for this are that the advantages of legitimating approval restrain organizational superiors and that the effectiveness of legitimate authority, once established, obviates the need for coercive measures. But the exploitative use of power also occurs within organizations, as unions organized in opposition to exploitative employers show. A negative imbalance for the subjects of power stimulates opposition. The opposition negatively reciprocates, or retaliates, for excessive demands in an attempt to even the score, but it simultaneously creates conflict, disequilibrium, and imbalance in the social structure.[viii]

Even in the relatively simple structures of social association considered here, balances in one respect entail imbalances in others. The interplay between equilibrating and disequilibrating forces is still more evident, if less easy to unravel, in complex macrostructures with their cross-cutting substructures, where forces that sustain reciprocity and balance have disequilibrating and imbalancing repercussions not only on other levels of the same substructure but also on other substructures.

[viii]Organized opposition gives expression to latent conflicts and makes them manifest.

Discussion Questions

1. Homans maintained that the motives behind the behavior of humans are analogous to that of pigeons. Do you find his claim credible? Why or why not? What aspects of human behavior might make it dissimilar to that of pigeons or other animals?

2. Homans claimed that the behaviorist propositions used to explain individual conduct are capable of explaining social or group behavior. Do you think that individual and group behaviors are rooted in the same set of processes? If not, what processes or mechanisms differentiate the two forms of conduct? Do you think that social systems or structures can produce behavioral effects independent of the individuals that compose them? If so, what might be some of these effects?

3. Compare Parsons's notion of system equilibrium to Blau's view of social interaction producing a strain toward reciprocity.

4. What role do favors and social approval play in Blau's model of social interaction?

5. Homans and Blau suggest that, in calculating the potential profits derived from interacting with others, individuals attempt to establish a position of dominance. As such, maximizing our own benefits is contingent upon having others dependent on us for the rewards they seek. Do you think this motive characterizes all relationships? If not, what other considerations might guide our interactions with others? What types of relationships are more likely to generate such considerations?

5

Symbolic Interactionism and Dramaturgy

Key Concepts

Herbert Blumer

- ❖ Meaning
- ❖ Significant Gestures
- ❖ Interpretation
- ❖ Joint Action

Arlie Russell Hochschild

- ❖ Feeling Rules
- ❖ Emotion Work
- ❖ Emotional Labor
- ❖ Commodification of Feeling

Erving Goffman

- ❖ Impression Management
- ❖ Definition of the Situation
- ❖ Front
- ❖ Backstage
- ❖ Self: Performer/Character
- ❖ Merchant of Morality
- ❖ Total Institutions
- ❖ Mortification of Self
- ❖ Secondary Adjustments
- ❖ Deference/Demeanor

A cardinal principle of symbolic interactionism is that any empirically oriented scheme of human society, however derived, must respect the fact that in the first and last instances human society consists of people engaging in action.

~Blumer (1969:7)

Consider the following commonplace scenario: You hop on a bus only to find that most of the seats are already taken. However, you notice an empty seat nearby on which a passenger has placed his briefcase. As you approach the seat, you try to make eye contact with the passenger seated next to it, only to find that he pretends not to notice you. Pausing for a moment, you spot another empty seat at the rear of the bus. What do you do?

A. Attempt to make eye contact, say, "Excuse me, may I sit here" and wait for the passenger to move his briefcase.

B. Pick up the passenger's briefcase and politely hand it to him as you proceed to sit down.

C. Stomp your feet and angrily blurt out, "Hey buddy, I paid for this ride—move your bag or I'll do it for you," and then sit down with a sigh of disdain next to the passenger.

D. Mutter some less-than-kind words as you pass the rider on your way to the back of the bus.

The purpose of this quiz lies not primarily in determining your answer but, rather, in calling your attention to the richness and complexity of social life that can be found under the surface of your response. Nothing short of a well-choreographed ballet is performed during this encounter. From determining the "definition of situation" as you read the meaning of the passenger's briefcase placed on the empty seat and his attempt to avoid eye contact, to controlling (or not) your emotional reaction, the scene is a give-and-take dance of gestures. While it may seem to unfold spontaneously, such an encounter illustrates the constructed and ritualized nature of everyday interaction. For no one answer above is "right," but each sheds light on how the meaning of gestures arises out of interaction and on the expectation that one's self is to be treated with ceremonial care.

In this chapter we take up such issues through the works of three sociologists who have made significant contributions to interactionist approaches to social life. Such approaches highlight how the self and society are created and recreated during the course of interaction. We begin with an overview of the work of Herbert Blumer. In addition to coining the term "symbolic interactionism," it was Blumer who set out the central theoretical and methodological principles that continue to shape much of the work in this field. We then turn to a discussion of Erving Goffman and his development of "dramaturgy," a perspective that is informed not only by symbolic interactionism but also by Émile Durkheim's insights into the ritual and moral realms of society. We conclude the chapter with a look at the work of Arlie Russell Hochschild, whose analyses of emotions expanded the theoretical and empirical terrain of symbolic interactionism. Moreover, Hochschild's examination of gender and family dynamics in contemporary American society has provided important insights into the relationship between self-identity and broader social conditions.

HERBERT BLUMER (1900–1987): A BIOGRAPHICAL SKETCH

Herbert Blumer was born in St. Louis, Missouri, and attended the nearby University of Missouri, where he completed his undergraduate education as well as his master's degree. After working for a couple of years as an instructor, he tried his hand at professional football, playing for the Chicago Cardinals (now the Arizona Cardinals). While with the Cardinals he enrolled at the University of Chicago, where he earned his doctorate in 1928. At that time the sociology department was solidifying its reputation as a leading voice in the discipline. Known as the "Chicago School," the department was at the forefront in developing a sociology that, through detailed, empirical studies, explores how individuals understand and negotiate their everyday life.[1] Blumer himself played a principal role in advancing the department's framework for the discipline while serving on the faculty from 1927 to 1952.

His next move took him to the University of California, Berkeley, where he was hired to chair the school's nascent sociology department. He spent the next twenty-five years at Berkeley, becoming a favorite professor among the students. His own reputation within the profession is revealed in part by his serving as secretary-treasurer and, in 1956, as president of the American Sociological Association (ASA). Blumer also served as editor of one of the discipline's leading journals, *American Journal of Sociology*, from 1941 to 1952. In addition, in 1983 the ASA presented him with the award for a Career of Distinguished Scholarship. Herbert Blumer died in April 1987.

SOURCE: American Sociological Association; used with permission.

INTELLECTUAL INFLUENCES AND CORE IDEAS

While at the University of Chicago as a student and as a professor, Blumer was in the company of many of the leading figures in American sociology. Yet, his greatest intellectual debt is owed not to a sociologist but to a philosopher, George Herbert Mead (1863–1931). In fact, Blumer's single most important contribution to sociology lies in his fashioning Mead's pragmatist philosophy into one of the discipline's major theoretical perspectives: symbolic interactionism. As such, this section focuses primarily on outlining Mead's work and the ideas stemming directly from it.

At the center of symbolic interactionism is Mead's view of the self. For Mead, the self does not passively react to its environment but, rather, actively creates the conditions to which it responds. Mead presented his views as a counter to those associated with behavioral psychology (an avowedly empirical branch of psychology committed

[1]There are a number of works that examine the Chicago School and its impact on sociology. Three such books that may be of interest to readers are Martin Bulmer's (1984) *The Chicago School of Sociology*, Robert Faris's (1967) *Chicago Sociology, 1920–1932*, and Lewis and Smith's (1980) *American Sociology and Pragmatism*. All are published by the University of Chicago Press.

to studying only observable actions) and its leading proponent John B. Watson (1878–1958).[2]

It is against this picture of a passive, nonreflexive self that Mead developed his own theoretical framework, which he labeled "social behaviorism." For Mead, an essential aspect of the self is the mind. Instead of an ephemeral "black box" that is inaccessible to investigation, however, Mead viewed the mind as a behavioral process that entails a "conversation of **significant gestures**," that is, an internal dialogue of words and actions whose meanings are shared by all those involved in a social act. In this internal conversation, the individual becomes an object to him- or herself through "taking the attitude of the other" and arouses in his or her own mind the same responses to one's potential action that are aroused in other persons.[3] Individuals then shape their actions on the basis of the imagined responses they attribute to others. Moreover, as we symbolically test alternative lines of conduct, we temporarily suspend our behaviors. Within the delay of responses produced by such testing lies the crux of intelligent behavior: controlling one's present action with reference to *ideas* about the future consequences. Yet, self-control of what we say and do is in actuality a form of social control, as we check our behaviors—discarding some options while pursuing others—against the responses that we anticipate will be elicited from others.

| Significant Others | Sheldon Stryker and Identity Theory |

Raised in St. Paul, Minnesota, Sheldon Stryker stayed close to home while pursuing his education. He earned his B.A. (1948), M.A. (1950), and Ph.D. (1955) from the University of Minnesota. In 1951, Stryker joined the faculty at Indiana University, where he would remain until his retirement in 2002. He served as director of the National Institute of Mental Health's training program in social psychology from 1977 to 2000. His contributions to the fields of social psychology and symbolic interactionism were officially recognized by his colleagues in the form of the Cooley-Mead Award for Lifetime Contributions to Social Psychology from the American Sociological Association (1986) and the George Herbert Mead Award for Lifetime Achievement from the Society for the Study of Symbolic Interaction (2000).

Much of Stryker's work is dedicated to developing and testing identity theory, a perspective that draws from and extends the ideas set out by George Herbert Mead. In fact, Stryker's theory offers a counter to the dominant strand of

---

[2]Behaviorists argue that understanding the self must be confined to studying the relationship between visible stimuli and the learned responses that are associated with them. This is tied to their assertion that human behavior differs little in principle from animal behavior: both can be explained and predicted on the basis of laws that govern the association of behavioral responses to external stimuli. Thus, as a learned response to a specific stimulus, a rabbit's retreat from the path of a snake is no different in kind from a person's efforts to perform well in her or his job. As you read in the chapter on exchange theory, this same view was expressed by B. F. Skinner, who was a disciple of Watson.

[3]Depending on the situation, "others" might be a specific person (a sibling or neighbor), an identifiable group (classmates or co-workers), or the community-at-large that Mead referred to as the "generalized other" (Southerners, Americans).

symbolic interactionism that was formulated by Blumer. As a critic of Blumer's views of interactionist theory and methods, Stryker's own perspective was ill received by many and created an antagonistic schism within the field (Stryker 2003).

Identity theory is centered on specifying the reciprocal relationship between self and society—how each is a product and producer of the other—which was a central theme in Mead's social psychology. Yet, Stryker intended to fashion a social structural version of symbolic interactionism. As he remarked, "A satisfactory theoretical framework must bridge social structure and person, must be able to move from the level of the person to that of large-scale social structure and back again" (1980:53). The "bridge" between these two levels is found in the concept of roles, or the behavioral expectations and meanings that are attached to positions located in the social structure. Roles allow us to predict the behavior of others and to orient our own conduct, thus making possible coordinated, organized interaction. Moreover, the concept of roles sheds light on the reciprocal relationship between self and society. "Asking how, or in what terms, society is patterned has led sociology to an image of society in terms of positions and roles. Given that the person is the other side of the society coin, then this view of society leads to an image of the person as a structure of positions and roles which, internalized, is the self" (ibid.:79).

This view leads to an understanding of the self that Mead (as well as Blumer) himself recognized but did not fully explore: a person has as many selves as he has patterned relations with others. To capture the complexity of the self and its connection to role-making, Stryker introduced three concepts: identity, identity salience, and commitment. An identity is a "part" of one's self that is "called up" in the course of interacting with others. The number of identities a person possesses corresponds to the number of structured role relationships he participates in. Thus, a person's self can be composed of multiple identities including child, parent, worker, friend, spouse, and so on (1980:60).

Identity salience refers to how the self is organized according to a hierarchy of identities. Not every identity has the same salience or importance to the individual, "such that the higher the identity in [the salience] hierarchy, the more likely that the identity will be invoked in a given situation or in many situations" (1980:61). When a situation structurally overlaps with other situations (for instance, your boss asks you to work a shift that conflicts with your class schedule), different identities are invoked. Which identity most influences an individual's subsequent behavior, and how, depends on its location in the salience hierarchy. As a result, social structural characteristics—the presence or absence of situational overlaps—are directly tied to the self that is called up during interaction.

Rounding out Stryker's identity theory and his attempt to explore the links between self and society is the concept of commitment. Here he notes that to the extent that a person's relationship to others is dependent on being a specific kind of person, "one is committed to being that kind of person" (1980:61). Moreover, to the extent that maintaining one's ties to a particular group of others is important to an individual, then he is committed to being a member of that group. In sum, because the forging of relationships with others is determined, in part, on the basis of identities and their salience for an individual, commitment is itself a reflection of identity salience (ibid.:61, 62). Yet, identities are themselves tied to socially structured role relationships that have been internalized as parts of one's self. Social structure (society) creates identities (self) that (re)create social structure that creates identities that (re)create. . .

This view of the mind as a process of thinking that entails both self- and social control can be illustrated through any number of commonplace examples, for it is something we all continually experience. Consider, for instance, the internal conversation you engage in before asking someone out for a date, going on a job interview, determining how you will resolve an argument with a friend, or deciding whether to ask a question in class. In each case, you take the attitude of the other, viewing your self as an object as other individuals do during interaction. So, you may ask yourself, "What type of movie should I take him or her to?" or "What music should we listen to when we're driving in the car?" Similarly, before raising your hand you may think, "Will I seem stupid if I ask the professor this question? Maybe it will seem like I'm trying to score 'brownie' points?" The answers to such questions, and hence the behavior you intend to undertake, are shaped by the responses evoked in your mind. The responses are not entirely your own, however. Instead, they reflect the assumed attitude that others take toward your behavior.

Our awareness of an object, gesture, or event makes it possible for us to form responses that indicate to others and ourselves how we are going to act in reference to the situation at hand. And in indicating our forthcoming responses we are at the same time indicating the meaning of the object, gesture, or event. Thus, Mead locates the source of meaning in social interaction. He defines **meaning** as a "threefold relationship" between (1) an individual's gesture, (2) the adjustive response by another to that gesture, and (3) the completion of the social act initiated by the gesture of the first individual. Meaning is thus not an idea, but a *response* to a gesture developed within a *social* act. In other words, meaning does not exist within one's consciousness, nor does it exist independently of the reality of interaction. One's gesture to another (for example, asking someone, "May I borrow a pencil?") refers to a desired result (getting a pencil) of the interaction. But an individual's gesture is meaningful, or significant, only if it elicits the desired response from the person to whom it is directed. That is, your gesture has meaning only if the other person responds as you responded in your mind. If a person hands you a book instead of the pencil you asked for, your gesture lacked meaning, as the other's behavior did not lead to the successful completion of the act. How many times have you said to someone, "You don't understand what I'm saying," when he did not respond as you had imagined he would. Such instances illustrate how meaning develops through a social process.

Blumer also contrasts symbolic interactionism with the views of psychological behaviorism by emphasizing **interpretation**. Interpretation entails *constructing* the meaning of another's actions as well as one's own, for meaning is not "released" by, or inherent in, the actions themselves, as the behaviorists would have us believe. As Blumer states,

> human beings interpret or "define" each other's actions instead of merely reacting to each other's actions. Their "response" is not made directly to the actions of one another but instead is based on the meaning which they attach to such actions. Thus, human interaction is mediated by the use of symbols, by interpretation, or by ascertaining the meaning of one another's actions. This interpretation is equivalent to inserting a process of interpretation between stimulus and response in the case of human behavior (1969:79).

Interpretation, then, is a behavioral process much like the mind, and, indeed, the two are closely related. Both are carried out through the conversation of gestures and symbols, and both are intertwined with the fundamental nature of the self: the consciousness of one's self as an object.

Thus, self-consciousness is experienced "not directly, but only indirectly, from the particular standpoints of other individual[s] . . . or from the generalized standpoint of the social group as a whole to which he belongs" (Mead 1934/1962:138). In turn, seeing our self as an object becomes possible only by taking the attitudes of others toward our self. Moreover, from the perspective of symbolic interaction, self-consciousness has a most profound impact on social life, for it makes possible group or **joint action**. Blumer defines joint action as "the larger collective form of action that is constituted by the fitting together of the lines of behavior of the separate participants. . . . Joint actions range from a simple collaboration of two individuals to a complex alignment of the acts of huge organizations or institutions" (1969:70). Yet, whether it is a family gathering, a corporate merger, or a nation conducting foreign policy, each is the outcome of a reflexive, interpretative process in which participants assign meaning to the separate acts that together constitute the joint action. In other words, in order to align their behaviors with one another, individuals must construct a shared interpretation—by becoming an object to one's self—of each other's gestures. This alone allows for the formation of joint action, the building block of society.

The preceding discussion highlights the significance of meaning, interaction, and interpretation to interactionist accounts of social life. Together, these three concepts form the basis of the theory's central premises. "The first premise is that human beings act toward things on the basis of the meanings that things have for them. . . . The second premise is that the meaning of such things is derived from, or arises out of, the social interaction that one has with one's fellows. The third premise is that these meanings are handled in, and modified through an interpretative process used by the person in dealing with the things he encounters" (Blumer 1969:2). Thus, your response to another's gesture—to copy your class notes, for instance—is dependent on how you define or give meaning to their request. But the meaning is not a product solely of your mind or inherent in the specific words used by the other person; instead, it is developed out of the interaction itself. While you may let some classmates copy your notes, you may refuse others depending on your interpretation of the motives (i.e., meaning) underlying their request. Was the person absent from class because of an illness, or is he trying to avoid doing the work? Perhaps he's asking for the notes as a way to strike up a friendship. Knowing the answer to such questions, however, does not determine the decision for each and every individual. For some, being sick is not a valid reason for missing class, while others are more than happy to help out a slacker.

BLUMER'S THEORETICAL ORIENTATION

Blumer's symbolic interactionism is individualistic and nonrationalist in orientation. His vision is one in which the social order—the patterning of social life—is continually constructed and reconstructed through the fitting together of acts by individuals (individualist) who are attempting to interpret and define the situations in which they find themselves (nonrationalist).

Turning first to the issue of order, Blumer's individualist approach was developed in large measure through his critique of the then-dominant structural-functionalist paradigm (see Chapter 2), which is rooted in a collectivist orientation to social order. In numerous passages he chides functionalists for presenting an unrealistically static view of social life. For instance, in comparing symbolic interactionism with the

Figure 5.1   Blumer's Core Concepts

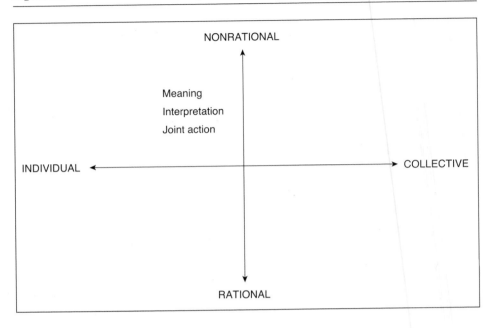

"conventional views of human society" (i.e., functionalism) on the question of social organization, Blumer remarks:

> From the standpoint of symbolic interactionism, social organization is a framework inside of which acting units develop their actions. Structural features, such as "culture," "social systems," "social stratification," or "social roles," set conditions for their action but do not determine their action. People—that is, acting units—do not act toward culture, social structure or the like; they act toward situations. Social organization enters into action only to the extent to which it shapes situations in which people act, and to the extent to which it supplies fixed sets of symbols which people use in interpreting their situations. (1969:87, 88)

One of Blumer's central theoretical objectives was to underscore the differences between symbolic interactionism and the more collectivist approaches such as functionalism that, to his mind, presented social structure as a "straitjacket" that determines the behavior of individuals and groups. While remarking that societal factors such as norms, values, culture, roles, and status positions (all collectivist concepts) play an important part in organizing social life, he nevertheless argued that they are significant "only as they enter into the process of interpretation and definition out of which joint actions are formed" (1969:75). Again quoting Blumer at some length on this point, he contended that symbolic interactionism

> sees human society not as an established structure but as people meeting their conditions of life; it sees social action not as an emanation of societal structure but as a formation made by human actors; it sees this formation of action not as societal factors coming to expression through the medium of human organisms but as constructions made by actors out of what they

take into account; it sees group life not as a release or expression of established structure but as a process of building up joint actions; . . . it sees the so-called interaction between parts of a society not as a direct exercising of influence by one part on another but as mediated throughout by interpretations made by people; accordingly, it sees society not as a system, whether in the form of a static, moving, or whatever kind of equilibrium, but as a vast number of occurring joint actions, many closely linked, many not linked at all, many prefigured and repetitious, others being carved out in new directions, and all being pursued to serve the purposes of the participants not the requirements of a system . . .

It is ridiculous, for instance, to assert, as a number of eminent sociologists have done, that social interaction is an interaction between roles. Social interaction is obviously an interaction between *people* and not between roles; the needs of the participants are to interpret and handle what confronts them—such as a topic of conversation or a problem—and not to give expression to their roles. (ibid.:74, 75; emphasis in the original)

Blumer's remarks reveal a clear picture of the problem of order. Social life is seen as a dynamic process in which actors, through interpreting the gestures of others as well as their own, are at every moment creating and recreating the patterns of behavior that form the basis for the social order. However, when we turn to the problem of action (what motivates individuals or groups to act), the same explicitness is, unfortunately, not to be found. Like Mead, who was "only casually and tangentially interested in the self as a source of motivational energy, or as an object of affective attachment" (Wrong 1994:65), Blumer's own "casual interest" on this issue leaves us with less to work with than we may like. Nevertheless, we can point out the general tendencies in Blumer's symbolic interactionist perspective.

Blumer's account of the self and interaction emphasizes the interpretive behaviors that individuals undertake when coordinating activities with others and assigning meaning to conduct and events. Moreover, in arguing that individuals approach situations pragmatically or as "problems" to be solved, he implies that we seek behaviors that "work." Such a cognitive focus, however, should not be confused with a rationalist orientation to motivation. As we discussed in Chapter 1, rationalist presuppositions portray actors and groups as *motivated* principally by their self-interested maximization of rewards and minimizing of costs. However, far from suggesting that our actions are primarily shaped by an attempt to strategically maximize rewards, Blumer notes that in modern societies individuals "may fit their acts to one another . . . on the basis of compromise, out of duress, because they may use one another in achieving their respective ends, because it is the sensible thing to do, or out of sheer necessity" (1969:76). In the end, uncovering the motivations that propel actors is considered an open matter that cannot be reduced to any single factor.

To further explain Blumer's theoretical orientation, briefly consider two of the core concepts of his theory discussed in the previous section. We focus on the issue of order as Blumer's position on this point is stated more clearly. Blumer contends that meanings (our responses to objects, gestures, and events) are not fixed or external to interaction. On the contrary, it is during the process of interaction that meanings are created and responses carried out. Moreover, developing shared meanings forms the basis of any social act; it allows us to coordinate our activities with one another, that is, to form joint actions. This is suggestive of an individualist orientation to order, as actors are the source of meaning production and, thus, the source of the patterns and routines of social life.

Reading

Introduction to "The Methodological Position of Symbolic Interactionism"

In the following chapter taken from *Symbolic Interactionism*, Blumer begins by outlining the three fundamental premises that characterize this theoretical perspective, underscoring the concepts that form the core of this approach: meaning, interaction, and interpretation. He then moves to an analysis of the "root images" or central ideas that together comprise a symbolic interactionist account of the nature of society, the self, and action. Throughout his discussion, Blumer emphasizes the emergent character of social interaction and of society itself. Nowhere does he more succinctly make this point than when he remarks, "It is the social process in group life that creates and upholds the rules, not the rules that create and uphold group life" (1969:19). That joint actions, and the institutions that they sustain, take on repetitive and stable forms is a function not of an organization's "inner dynamics" or "system requirements," but of the recurring use of schemes of interpretation and definition. Thus, even established patterns of group life are constantly "formed anew" as they are "just as much a result of an interpretive process as is a new form of joint action that is being developed for the first time" (1969:18). Whether the occasion of a joint action is a first-time collaboration between new co-workers or a weekly family dinner, fitting together lines of conduct is based on the shared meanings that participants ascribe to the situation. And as Blumer reminds us, meanings "are themselves subject to pressure as well as to reinforcement, to incipient dissatisfaction as well as to indifference; they may be challenged as well as affirmed, allowed to slip along without concern as well as subjected to infusions of vigor" (ibid.).

❖

The Methodological Position of Symbolic Interactionism (1969)

Herbert Blumer

The term "symbolic interactionism" has come into use as a label for a relatively distinctive approach to the study of human group life and human conduct.* The scholars who have used the approach or contributed to its intellectual foundation are many, and include such notable American figures as George Herbert Mead, John Dewey, W. I. Thomas, Robert E. Park, William James, Charles Horton Cooley, Florian Znaniecki, James Mark Baldwin, Robert

SOURCE: From Blumer, H., *Symbolic Interactionism: Perspective & Method, 1st ed.,* © 1969, pp. 1–21. Reprinted by permission of Pearson Education, Inc., Upper Saddle River, NJ.

Redfield, and Louis Wirth. Despite significant differences in the thought of such scholars, there is a great similarity in the general way in which they viewed and studied human group life. The concept of symbolic interactionism is built around this strand of general similarity. There has been no clear formulation of the position of symbolic interactionism, and above all, a reasoned statement of the methodological position of this approach is lacking. This essay is an effort to develop such a statement. . . .

The Nature of Symbolic Interactionism

Symbolic interactionism rests in the last analysis on three simple premises. The first premise is that human beings act toward things on the basis of the meanings that the things have for them. Such things include everything that the human being may note in his world—physical objects, such as trees or chairs; other human beings, such as a mother or a store clerk; categories of human beings, such as friends or enemies; institutions, such as a school or a government; guiding ideals, such as individual independence or honesty; activities of others, such as their commands or requests; and such situations as an individual encounters in his daily life. The second premise is that the meaning of such things is derived from, or arises out of, the social interaction that one has with one's fellows. The third premise is that these meanings are handled in, and modified through, an interpretative process used by the person in dealing with the things he encounters. I wish to discuss briefly each of these three fundamental premises.

It would seem that few scholars would see anything wrong with the first premise— that human beings act toward things on the basis of the meanings which these things have for them. Yet, oddly enough, this simple view is ignored or played down in practically all of the thought and work in contemporary social science and psychological science. Meaning is either taken for granted and thus pushed aside as unimportant or it is regarded as a mere neutral link between the factors responsible for human behavior and this behavior as the product of such factors. We can see this clearly in the

predominant posture of psychological and social science today. Common to both of these fields is the tendency to treat human behavior as the product of various factors that play upon human beings; concern is with the behavior and with the factors regarded as producing them. Thus, psychologists turn to such factors as stimuli, attitudes, conscious or unconscious motives, various kinds of psychological inputs, perception and cognition, and various features of personal organization to account for given forms or instances of human conduct. In a similar fashion sociologists rely on such factors as social position, status demands, social roles, cultural prescriptions, norms and values, social pressures, and group affiliation to provide such explanations. In both such typical psychological and sociological explanations the meanings of things for the human beings who are acting are either bypassed or swallowed up in the factors used to account for their behavior. If one declares that the given kinds of behavior are the result of the particular factors regarded as producing them, there is no need to concern oneself with the meaning of the things toward which human beings act; one merely identifies the initiating factors and the resulting behavior. Or one may, if pressed, seek to accommodate the element of meaning by lodging it in the initiating factors or by regarding it as a neutral link intervening between the initiating factors and the behavior they are alleged to produce. In the first of these latter cases the meaning disappears by being merged into the initiating or causative factors; in the second case meaning becomes a mere transmission link that can be ignored in favor of the initiating factors.

The position of symbolic interactionism, in contrast, is that the meanings that things have for human beings are central in their own right. To ignore the meaning of the things toward which people act is seen as falsifying the behavior under study. To bypass the meaning in favor of factors alleged to produce the behavior is seen as a grievous neglect of the role of meaning in the formation of behavior.

The simple premise that human beings act toward things on the basis of the meaning of such things is much too simple in itself to differentiate symbolic interactionism—there are several other approaches that share this premise.

A major line of difference between them and symbolic interactionism is set by the second premise, which refers to the source of meaning. There are two well-known traditional ways of accounting for the origin of meaning. One of them is to regard meaning as being intrinsic to the thing that has it, as being a natural part of the objective makeup of the thing. Thus, a chair is clearly a chair in itself, a cow a cow, a cloud a cloud, a rebellion a rebellion, and so forth. Being inherent in the thing that has it, meaning needs merely to be disengaged by observing the objective thing that has the meaning. The meaning emanates, so to speak, from the thing and as such there is no process involved in its formation; all that is necessary is to recognize the meaning that is there in the thing. It should be immediately apparent that this view reflects the traditional position of "realism" in philosophy— a position that is widely held and deeply entrenched in the social and psychological sciences. The other major traditional view regards "meaning" as a psychical accretion brought to the thing by the person for whom the thing has meaning. This psychical accretion is treated as being an expression of constituent elements of the person's psyche, mind, or psychological organization. The constituent elements are such things as sensations, feelings, ideas, memories, motives, and attitudes. The meaning of a thing is but the expression of the given psychological elements that are brought into play in connection with the perception of the thing; thus one seeks to explain the meaning of a thing by isolating the particular psychological elements that produce the meaning. One sees this in the somewhat ancient and classical psychological practice of analyzing the meaning of an object by identifying the sensations that enter into perception of that object; or in the contemporary practice of tracing the meaning of a thing, such as let us say prostitution, to the attitude of the person who views it. This lodging of the meaning of things in psychological elements limits the processes of the formation of meaning to whatever processes are involved in arousing and bringing together the given psychological elements that produce the meaning. Such processes are psychological in nature, and include perception, cognition, repression, transfer of feelings, and association of ideas.

Symbolic interactionism views meaning as having a different source than those held by the two dominant views just considered. It does not regard meaning as emanating from the intrinsic makeup of the thing that has meaning, nor does it see meaning as arising through a coalescence of psychological elements in the person. Instead, it sees meaning as arising in the process of interaction between people. The meaning of a thing for a person grows out of the ways in which other persons act toward the person with regard to the thing. Their actions operate to define the thing for the person. Thus, symbolic interactionism sees meanings as social products, as creations that are formed in and through the defining activities of people as they interact. This point of view gives symbolic interactionism a very distinctive position, with profound implications that will be discussed later.

The third premise mentioned above further differentiates symbolic interactionism. While the meaning of things is formed in the context of social interaction and is derived by the person from that interaction, it is a mistake to think that the use of meaning by a person is but an application of the meaning so derived. This mistake seriously mars the work of many scholars who otherwise follow the symbolic interactionist approach. They fail to see that the use of meanings by a person in his action involves an interpretative process. In this respect they are similar to the adherents of the two dominant views spoken of above—to those who lodge meaning in the objective makeup of the thing that has it and those who regard it as an expression of psychological elements. All three are alike in viewing the use of meaning by the human being in his action as being no more than an arousing and application of already established meanings. As such, all three fail to see that the use of meanings by the actor occurs through *a process of interpretation*. This process has two distinct steps. First, the actor indicates to himself the things toward which he is acting; he has to point out to himself the things that have meaning. The making of such indications is an internalized social process in that the actor is interacting with himself. This interaction with himself is something other than an interplay of psychological elements; it is an instance of the person engaging in a process of communication with himself. Second, by virtue of this process of communicating with himself, interpretation becomes a matter of handling meanings. The actor selects, checks, suspends, regroups, and transforms the meanings in the light of the situation in which he is placed and the direction of his action. Accordingly, interpretation should not be regarded as a mere automatic application of established meanings but as a formative process in which meanings are used and revised as instruments for the guidance and formation of action. It is necessary to see that meanings play their part in action through a process of self-interaction.

It is not my purpose to discuss at this point the merits of the three views that lodge meaning respectively in the thing, in the psyche, and in social action, nor to elaborate on the contention that meanings are handled flexibly by the actor in the course of forming his action. Instead, I wish merely to note that by being based on these three premises, symbolic interaction is necessarily led to develop an analytical scheme of human society and human conduct that is quite distinctive. It is this scheme that I now propose to outline.

Symbolic interactionism is grounded on a number of basic ideas, or "root images," as I prefer to call them. These root images refer to and depict the nature of the following matters: human groups or societies, social interaction, objects, the human being as an actor, human action, and the interconnection of the lines of action. Taken together, these root images represent the way in which symbolic interactionism views human society and conduct. They constitute the framework of study and analysis. Let me describe briefly each of these root images.

NATURE OF HUMAN SOCIETY OR HUMAN GROUP LIFE. Human groups are seen as consisting of human beings who are engaging in action. The action consists of the multitudinous activities that the individuals perform in their life as they encounter one another and as they deal with the succession of situations confronting them. The individuals may act singly, they may act collectively, and they may act on behalf of, or as representatives of, some organization or group of others. The activities belong to the acting individuals and are carried on by them always with regard to the situations in which they have to

act. The import of this simple and essentially redundant characterization is that fundamentally human groups or society *exists in action* and must be seen in terms of action. This picture of human society as action must be the starting point (and the point of return) for any scheme that purports to treat and analyze human society empirically. Conceptual schemes that depict society in some other fashion can only be derivations from the complex of ongoing activity that constitutes group life. This is true of the two dominant conceptions of society in contemporary sociology—that of culture and that of social structure. Culture as a conception, whether defined as custom, tradition, norm, value, rules, or such like, is clearly derived from what people do. Similarly, social structure in any of its aspects, as represented by such terms as social position, status, role, authority, and prestige, refers to relationships derived from how people act toward each other. The life of any human society consists necessarily of an ongoing process of fitting together the activities of its members. It is this complex of ongoing activity that establishes and portrays structure or organization. A cardinal principle of symbolic interactionism is that any empirically oriented scheme of human society, however derived, must respect the fact that in the first and last instances human society consists of people engaging in action. To be empirically valid the scheme must be consistent with the nature of the social action of human beings.

NATURE OF SOCIAL INTERACTION. Group life necessarily presupposes interaction between the group members; or, put otherwise, a society consists of individuals interacting with one another. The activities of the members occur predominantly in response to one another or in relation to one another. Even though this is recognized almost universally in definitions of human society, social interaction is usually taken for granted and treated as having little, if any, significance in its own right. This is evident in typical sociological and psychological schemes—they treat social interaction as merely a medium through which the determinants of behavior pass to produce the behavior. Thus, the typical sociological scheme ascribes behavior to such factors as status position, cultural prescriptions, norms, values, sanctions, role demands, and social system requirements; explanation in terms of such factors suffices without paying attention to the social interaction that their play necessarily pre-supposes. Similarly, in the typical psychological scheme such factors as motives, attitudes, hidden complexes, elements of psychological organization, and psychological processes are used to account for behavior without any need of considering social interaction. One jumps from such causative factors to the behavior they are supposed to produce. Social interaction becomes a mere forum through which sociological or psychological determinants move to bring about given forms of human behavior. I may add that this ignoring of social interaction is not corrected by speaking of an interaction of societal elements (as when a sociologist speaks of an interaction of social roles or an interaction between the components of a social system) or an interaction of psychological elements (as when a psychologist speaks of an interaction between the attitudes held by different people). Social interaction is an interaction between actors and not between factors imputed to them.

Symbolic interactionism does not merely give a ceremonious nod to social interaction. It recognizes social interaction to be of vital importance in its own right. This importance lies in the fact that social interaction is a process that *forms* human conduct instead of being merely a means or a setting for the expression or release of human conduct. Put simply, human beings in interacting with one another have to take account of what each other is doing or is about to do; they are forced to direct their own conduct or handle their situations in terms of what they take into account. Thus, the activities of others enter as positive factors in the formation of their own conduct; in the face of the actions of others one may abandon an intention or purpose, revise it, check or suspend it, intensify it, or replace it. The actions of others enter to set what one plans to do, may oppose or prevent such plans, may require a revision of such plans, and may demand a very different set of such plans. One has to *fit* one's own line of activity in some manner to the actions of others. The actions of others have to be taken into account and cannot be regarded as merely an arena for the expression of what one is disposed to do or sets out to do.

We are indebted to George Herbert Mead for the most analysis of social interaction—an analysis that squares with the realistic account just given. Mead identifies two forms or levels of social interaction in human society. He refers to them respectively as "the conversation of gestures" and "the use of significant symbols"; I shall term them respectively "non-symbolic interaction" and "symbolic interaction." Non-symbolic interaction takes place when one responds directly to the action of another without interpreting that action; symbolic interaction involves interpretation of the action. Non-symbolic interaction is most readily apparent in reflex responses, as in the case of a boxer who automatically raises his arm to parry a blow. However, if the boxer were reflectively to identify the forthcoming blow from his opponent as a feint designed to trap him, he would be engaging in symbolic interaction. In this case, he would endeavor to ascertain the meaning of the blow—that is, what the blow signifies as to his opponent's plan. In their association human beings engage plentifully in non-symbolic interaction as they respond immediately and unreflectively to each other's bodily movements, expressions, and tones of voice, but their characteristic mode of interaction is on the symbolic level, as they seek to understand the meaning of each other's action.

Mead's analysis of symbolic interaction is highly important. He sees it as a presentation of gestures and a response to the meaning of those gestures. A gesture is any part or aspect of an ongoing action that signifies the larger act of which it is a part—for example, the shaking of a fist as an indication of a possible attack, or the declaration of war by a nation as an indication of a posture and line of action of that nation. Such things as requests, orders, commands, cues, and declarations are gestures that convey to the person who recognizes them an idea of the intention and plan of forthcoming action of the individual who presents them. The person who responds organizes his response on the basis of what the gestures mean to him; the person who presents the gestures advances them as indications or signs of what he is planning to do as well as of what he wants the respondent to do or understand. Thus, the gesture has meaning for both the person who makes it and for the person to whom it is directed. When the gesture has the same meaning for both, the two parties understand each other. From this brief account it can be seen that the meaning of the gesture flows out along three lines (Mead's triadic nature of meaning): It signifies what the person to whom it is directed is to do; it signifies what the person who is making the gesture plans to do; and it signifies the joint action that is to arise by the articulation of the acts of both. Thus, for illustration, a robber's command to his victim to put up his hands is (a) an indication of what the victim is to do; (b) an indication of what the robber plans to do, that is, relieve the victim of his money; and (c) an indication of the joint act being formed, in this case a holdup. If there is confusion or misunderstanding along any one of these three lines of meaning, communication is ineffective, interaction is impeded, and the formation of joint action is blocked.

One additional feature should be added to round out Mead's analysis of symbolic interaction, namely, that the parties to such interaction must necessarily take each other's roles. To indicate to another what he is to do, one has to make the indication from the standpoint of that other; to order the victim to put up his hands the robber has to see this response in terms of the victim making it. Correspondingly, the victim has to see the command from the standpoint of the robber who gives the command; he has to grasp the intention and forthcoming action of the robber. Such mutual role-taking is the *sine qua non* of communication and effective symbolic interaction.

The central place and importance of symbolic interaction in human group life and conduct should be apparent. A human society or group consists of people in association. Such association exists necessarily in the form of people acting toward one another and thus engaging in social interaction. Such interaction in human society is characteristically and predominantly on the symbolic level; as individuals acting individually, collectively, or as agents of some organization encounter one another they are necessarily required to take account of the actions of one another as they form their own action. They do this by a dual process of indicating to others how to act and of interpreting the indications made by others. Human group

life is a vast process of such defining to others what to do and of interpreting their definitions; through this process people come to fit their activities to one another and to form their own individual conduct. Both such joint activity and individual conduct are formed *in* and *through* this ongoing process; they are not mere expressions or products of what people bring to their interaction or of conditions that are antecedent to their interaction. The failure to accommodate to this vital point constitutes the fundamental deficiency of schemes that seek to account for human society in terms of social organization or psychological factors, or of any combination of the two. By virtue of symbolic interaction, human group life is necessarily a formative process and not a mere arena for the expression of pre-existing factors.

NATURE OF OBJECTS. The position of symbolic interactionism is that the "worlds" that exist for human beings and for their groups are composed of "objects" and that these objects are the product of symbolic interaction. An object is anything that can be indicated, anything that is pointed to or referred to—a cloud, a book, a legislature, a banker, a religious doctrine, a ghost, and so forth. For purposes of convenience one can classify objects in three categories: (a) physical objects, such as chairs, trees, or bicycles; (b) social objects, such as students, priests, a president, a mother, or a friend; and (c) abstract objects, such as moral principles, philosophical doctrines, or ideas such as justice, exploitation, or compassion. I repeat that an object is anything that can be indicated or referred to. The nature of an object—of any and every object—consists of the meaning that it has for the person for whom it is an object. This meaning sets the way in which he sees the object, the way in which he is prepared to act toward it, and the way in which he is ready to talk about it. An object may have a different meaning for different individuals: a tree will be a different object to a botanist, a lumberman, a poet, and a home gardener; the President of the United States can be a very different object to a devoted member of his political party than to a member of the opposition; the members of an ethnic group may be seen as a different kind of object by members of other groups. The meaning of objects for a person arises fundamentally out of the way they are defined to him by others with whom he interacts. Thus, we come to learn through the indications of others that a chair is a chair, that doctors are a certain kind of professional, that the United States Constitution is a given kind of legal document, and so forth. Out of a process of mutual indications common objects emerge—objects that have the same meaning for a given set of people and are seen in the same manner by them.

Several noteworthy consequences follow from the foregoing discussion of objects. First, it gives us a different picture of the environment or milieu of human beings. From their standpoint the environment consists *only* of the objects that the given human beings recognize and know. The nature of this environment is set by the meaning that the objects composing it have for those human beings. Individuals, also groups, occupying or living in the same spatial location may have, accordingly, very different environments; as we say, people may be living side by side yet be living in different worlds. Indeed, the term "world" is more suitable than the word "environment" to designate the setting, the surroundings, and the texture of things that confront them. It is the world of their objects with which people have to deal and toward which they develop their actions. It follows that in order to understand the action of people it is necessary to identify their world of objects—an important point that will be elaborated later.

Second, objects (in the sense of their meaning) must be seen as social creations—as being formed in and arising out of the process of definition and interpretation as this process takes place in the action of people. The meaning of anything and everything has to be formed, learned, and transmitted through a process of indication—a process that is necessarily a social process. Human group life on the level of symbolic interaction is a vast process in which people are forming, sustaining, and transforming the objects of their world as they come to give meaning to objects. Objects have no fixed status except as their meaning is sustained through indications and definitions that people make of the objects. Nothing is more apparent than that objects in all categories can undergo change in their meaning. A star in the sky is a very different object to a modern astrophysicist

than it was to a sheepherder of biblical times; marriage was a different object to later Romans than to earlier Romans; the president of a nation who fails to act successfully through critical times may become a very different object to the citizens of his land. In short, from the standpoint of symbolic interactionism human group life is a process in which objects are being created, affirmed, transformed, and cast aside. The life and action of people necessarily change in line with the changes taking place in their world of objects.

THE HUMAN BEING AS AN ACTING ORGANISM. Symbolic interactionism recognizes that human beings must have a makeup that fits the nature of social interaction. The human being is seen as an organism that not only responds to others on the non-symbolic level but as one that makes indications to others and interprets their indications. He can do this, as Mead has shown so emphatically, only by virtue of possessing a "self." Nothing esoteric is meant by this expression. It means merely that a human being can be an object of his own action. Thus, he can recognize himself, for instance, as being a man, young in age, a student, in debt, trying to become a doctor, coming from an undistinguished family and so forth. In all such instances he is an object to himself; and he acts toward himself and guides himself in his actions toward others on the basis of the kind of object he is to himself. This notion of oneself as an object fits into the earlier discussion of objects. Like other objects, the self-object emerges from the process of social interaction in which other people are defining a person to himself. Mead has traced the way in which this occurs in his discussion of role-taking. He points out that in order to become an object to himself a person has to see himself from the outside. One can do this only by placing himself in the position of others and viewing himself or acting toward himself from that position. The roles the person takes range from that of discrete individuals (the "play stage"), through that of discrete organized groups (the "game stage") to that of the abstract community (the "generalized other"). In taking such roles the person is in a position to address or approach himself—as in the case of a young girl who in "playing mother" talks to herself as her mother would do, or in the case of a young priest who sees himself through the eyes of the priesthood. We form our objects of ourselves through such a process of role-taking. It follows that we see ourselves through the way in which others see or define us—or, more precisely, we see ourselves by taking one of the three types of roles of others that have been mentioned. That one forms an object of himself through the ways in which others define one to himself is recognized fairly well in the literature today, so despite its great significance I shall not comment on it further.

There is an even more important matter that stems from the fact that the human being has a self, namely that this enables him to interact with himself. This interaction is not in the form of interaction between two or more parts of a psychological system, as between needs, or between emotions, or between ideas, or between the id and the ego in the Freudian scheme. Instead, the interaction is social—a form of communication, with the person addressing himself as a person and responding thereto. We can clearly recognize such interaction in ourselves as each of us notes that he is angry with himself, or that he has to spur himself on in his tasks, or that he reminds himself to do this or that, or that he is talking to himself in working out some plan of action. As such instances suggest, self-interaction exists fundamentally as a process of making indications to oneself. This process is in play continuously during one's waking life, as one notes and considers one or another matter, or observes this or that happening. Indeed, for the human being to be conscious or aware of anything is equivalent to his indicating the thing to himself—he is identifying it as a given kind of object and considering its relevance or importance to his line of action. One's waking life consists of a series of such indications that the person is making to himself, indications that he uses to direct his action.

We have, then, a picture of the human being as an organism that interacts with itself through a social process of making indications to itself. This is a radically different view of the human being from that which dominates contemporary social and psychological science. The dominant prevailing view sees the human being as a complex organism whose behavior is a response to factors playing on the organization of the organism. Schools of thought in the social and psychological sciences differ enormously in which of such factors they regard as significant, as is shown in such a diverse array as stimuli, organic drives, need-dispositions, conscious motives, unconscious motives, emotions, attitudes, ideas, cultural prescriptions, norms, values, status demands, social roles, reference group affiliations, and institutional pressures. Schools of thought differ also in how they view the organization of the human being, whether as a kind of biological organization, a kind of psychological organization, or a kind of imported societal organization incorporated from the social structure of one's group. Nevertheless, these schools of thought are alike in seeing the human being as a responding organism, with its behavior being a product of the factors playing on its organization or an expression of the interplay of parts of its organization. Under this widely shared view the human being is "social" only in the sense of either being a member of social species, or of responding to others (social stimuli), or of having incorporated within it the organization of his group.

The view of the human being held in symbolic interactionism is fundamentally different. The human being is seen as "social" in a much more profound sense—in the sense of an organism that engages in social interaction with itself by making indications to itself and responding to such indications. By virtue of engaging in self-interaction the human being stands in a markedly different relation to his environment than is presupposed by the widespread conventional view described above. Instead of being merely an organism that responds to the play of factors on or through it, the human being is seen as an organism that has to deal with what it notes. It meets what it so notes by engaging in a process of self-indication in which it makes an object of what it notes, gives it a meaning, and uses the meaning as the basis for directing its action. Its behavior with regard to what it notes is not a response called forth by the presentation of what it notes but instead is an action that arises out of the interpretation made through the process of self-indication. In this sense, the human being who is engaging in self-interaction is not a mere responding organism but an acting organism—an organism that has to mold a line of action on the basis of what it takes into account instead of merely releasing a response to the play of some factor on its organization.

NATURE OF HUMAN ACTION. The capacity of the human being to make indications to himself gives a distinctive character to human action. It means that the human individual confronts a world that he must interpret in order to act instead of an environment to which he responds because of his organization. He has to cope with the situations in which he is called on to act, ascertaining the meaning of the actions of others and mapping out his own line of action in the light of such interpretation. He has to construct and guide his action instead of merely releasing it in response to factors playing on him or operating through him. He may do a miserable job in constructing his action, but he has to construct it.

This view of the human being directing his action by making indications to himself stands sharply in contrast to the view of human action that dominates current psychological and social science. This dominant view, as already implied, ascribes human action to an initiating factor or a combination of such factors. Action is traced back to such matters as motives, attitudes, need-dispositions, unconscious complexes, stimuli configurations, status demands, role require-ments, and situational demands. To link the action to one or more of such initiating agents is regarded as fulfilling the scientific task. Yet, such an approach ignores and makes no place for the process of self-interaction through which the individual handles his world and constructs his action. The door is closed to the vital process of interpretation in which the indi-vidual notes and assesses what is presented to him and through which he maps out lines of overt behavior prior to their execution.

Fundamentally, action on the part of a human being consists of taking account of various things that he notes and forging a line of conduct on the basis of how he interprets them. The things taken into account cover such matters as his wishes and wants, his objectives, the available means for their achievement, the actions and anticipated actions of others, his image of himself, and the likely result of a given line of action. His conduct is formed and guided through such a process of indication and interpretation. In this process, given lines of action may be started or stopped, they may be abandoned or postponed, they may be confined to mere planning or to an inner life of reverie, or if initiated, they may be transformed. My purpose is not to analyze this process but to call attention to its presence and operation in the formation of human action. We must recognize that the activity of human beings consists of meeting a flow of situations in which they have to act and that their action is built on the basis of what they note, how they assess and interpret what they note, and what kind of projected lines of action they map out. This process is not caught by ascribing action to some kind of fac-tor (for example, motives, need-dispositions, role requirements, social expectations, or social rules) that is thought to initiate the action and propel it to its conclusion; such a factor, or some expression of it, is a matter the human actor takes into account in mapping his line of action. The initiating factor does not embrace or explain how it and other matters are taken into account in the situation that calls for action. One has to get inside of the defining process of the actor in order to understand his action.

This view of human action applies equally well to joint or collective action in which numbers of individuals are implicated. Joint or collective action constitutes the domain of soci-ological concern, as exemplified in the behavior of groups, institutions, organizations, and social classes. Such instances of societal behavior, whatever they may be, consist of individuals fitting their lines of action to one another. It is both proper and possible to view and study such behavior in its joint or collective character instead of in its individual components. Such joint behavior does not lose its character of being constructed through an interpretative process in meeting the situations in which the collectivity is called on to act. Whether the col-lectivity be an army engaged in a campaign, a corporation seeking to expand its operations, or a nation trying to correct an unfavorable balance of trade, it needs to construct its action through an interpretation of what is happening in its area of operation. The interpretative process takes place by participants making indications to one another, not merely each to himself. Joint or col-lective action is an outcome of such a process of interpretative interaction.

INTERLINKAGE OF ACTION. As stated earlier, human group life consists of, and exists in, the fitting of lines of action to each other by the members of the group. Such articulation of lines of action gives rise to and constitutes "joint action"—a societal organization of conduct of different acts of diverse participants. A joint action, while made up of diverse component acts that enter into its formation, is different from any one of them and from their mere aggregation. The joint action has a distinctive character in its own right, a character that lies in the articulation or linkage as apart from what may be articulated or linked. Thus, the joint action may be identified as such and may be spoken of and handled without having to break it down into the separate acts that comprise it. This is what we do when we speak of such things as marriage, a trading transaction, war, a parliamentary discussion, or a church service. Similarly, we can speak of the collectivity that engages in joint action without having to identify the individual members of that collectivity, as we do in speaking of a family, a business corporation, a church, a university, or a nation. It is evident that the domain of the social scientist is constituted precisely by the study of joint action and of the collectivities that engage in joint action.

In dealing with collectivities and with joint action one can easily be trapped in an erroneous position by failing to recognize that the joint action of the collectivity is an interlinkage of the separate acts of the participants. This failure leads one to overlook the fact that a joint action always has to undergo a process of formation; even though it may be a well-established and repetitive form of social action, each instance of it has to be formed anew. Further, this career of formation through which it comes into being necessarily takes place through the dual process of designation and interpretation that was discussed above. The participants still have to guide their respective acts by forming and using meanings.

With these remarks as a background I wish to make three observations on the implications of the interlinkage that constitutes joint action. I wish to consider first those instances of joint action that are repetitive and stable. The preponderant portion of social action in a human society, particularly in a settled society, exists in the form of recurrent patterns of joint action. In most situations in which people act toward one another they have in advance a firm understanding of how to act and of how other people will act. They share common and pre-established meanings of what is expected in the action of the participants, and accordingly each participant is able to guide his own behavior by such meanings. Instances of repetitive and pre-established forms of joint action are so frequent and common that it is easy to understand why scholars have viewed them as the essence or natural form of human group life. Such a view is especially apparent in the concepts of "culture" and "social order" that are so dominant in social science literature. Most sociological schemes rest on the belief that a human society exists in the form of an established order of living, with that order resolvable into adherence to sets of rules, norms, values, and sanctions that specify to people how they are to act in their different situations.

Several comments are in order with regard to this neat scheme. First, it is just not true that the full expanse of life in a human society, in any human society, is but an expression of pre-established forms of joint action. New situations are constantly arising within the scope of group life that are problematic and for which existing rules are inadequate. I have never heard of any society that was free of problems nor any society in which members did not have to engage in discussion to work out ways of action. Such areas of unprescribed conduct are just as natural, indigenous, and recurrent in human group life as are those areas covered by pre-established and faithfully followed prescriptions of joint action. Second, we have to recognize that even in the case of pre-established and repetitive joint action each instance of such joint action has to be formed anew. The participants still have to build up their lines of action and fit them to one another through the dual process of designation and interpretation. They do this in the case of repetitive joint action, of course, by using the same recurrent and constant meanings. If we recognize this, we are forced to realize that the play and fate of meanings are what is important, not the joint action in its established form. Repetitive and stable joint action is just as much a result of an interpretative process as is a new form of joint action that is being developed for the first time. This is not an idle or pedantic point; the meanings that underlie established and recurrent joint action are themselves subject to pressure as well as to reinforcement, to incipient dissatisfaction as well as to indifference; they may be challenged as well as affirmed, allowed to slip along without concern as well as subjected to infusions of new vigor. Behind the facade of the objectively perceived joint action the set of meanings that sustains that joint action has a life that the social scientists can ill afford to ignore. A gratuitous acceptance of the concepts of norms, values, social rules, and the like should not blind the social scientist to the fact that any one of them is subtended by a process of social interaction—a process that is necessary not only for their change but equally well for their retention in a fixed form. It is the social process in group life that creates and upholds the rules, not the rules that create and uphold group life.

The second observation on the interlinkage that constitutes joint action refers to the extended connection of actions that make up so much of human group life. We are familiar with these large complex networks of action involving an interlinkage and interdependency of diverse actions of diverse people—as in the division of labor extending from the growing of grain by the farmer to an eventual sale of bread in a store, or in the elaborate chain extending from the arrest of a suspect to his eventual release from a penitentiary. These networks with their regularized participation of diverse people by diverse action at diverse points yields a picture of institutions that have been appropriately a major concern of sociologists. They also give substance to the idea that human group life has the character of a system. In seeing such a large complex of diversified activities, all hanging together in a regularized operation, and in seeing the complementary organization of participants in well-knit interdependent relationships, it is easy to understand why so many scholars view such networks or institutions as self-operating entities, following their own dynamics and not requiring that attention be given to the participants within the network. Most of the sociological analyses of institutions

and social organization adhere to this view. Such adherence, in my judgment, is a serious mistake. One should recognize what is true, namely, that the diverse array of participants occupying different points in the network engage in their actions at those points on the basis of using given sets of meanings. A network or an institution does not function automatically because of some inner dynamics or system requirements; it functions because people at different points do something, and what they do is a result of how they define the situation in which they are called on to act. A limited appreciation of this point is reflected today in some of the work on decision-making, but on the whole the point is grossly ignored. It is necessary to recognize that the sets of meanings that lead participants to act as they do at their stationed points in the network have their own setting in a localized process of social interaction—and that these meanings are formed, sustained, weakened, strengthened, or transformed, as the case may be, through a socially defining process. Both the functioning and the fate of institutions are set by this process of interpretation as it takes place among the diverse sets of participants.

A third important observation needs to be made, namely, that any instance of joint action, whether newly formed or long established, has necessarily arisen out of a background of previous actions of the participants. A new kind of joint action never comes into existence apart from such a background. The participants involved in the formation of the new joint action always bring to that formation the world of objects, the sets of meanings, and the schemes of interpretation that they already possess. Thus, the new form of joint action always emerges out of and is connected with a context of previous joint action. It cannot be understood apart from that context; one has to bring into one's consideration this linkage with preceding forms of joint action. One is on treacherous and empirically invalid grounds if he thinks that any given form of joint action can be sliced off from its historical linkage, as if its makeup and character arose out of the air through spontaneous generation instead of growing out of what went before. In the face of radically different and stressful situations people may be led to develop new forms of joint action that are markedly different from those in which they have previously engaged, yet even in such cases there is always some connection and continuity with what went on before. One cannot understand the new form without incorporating knowledge of this continuity into one's analysis of the new form. Joint action not only represents a horizontal linkage, so to speak, of the activities of the participants, but also a vertical linkage with previous joint action.

SUMMARY REMARKS. The general perspective of symbolic interactionism should be clear from our brief sketch of its root images. This approach sees a human society as people engaged in living. Such living is a process of ongoing activity in which participants are developing lines of action in the multitudinous situations they encounter. They are caught up in a vast process of interaction in which they have to fit their developing actions to one another. This process of interaction consists in making indications to others of what to do and in interpreting the indications as made by others. They live in worlds of objects and are guided in their orientation and action by the meaning of these objects. Their objects, including objects of themselves, are formed, sustained, weakened, and transformed in their interaction with one another. This general process should be seen, of course, in the differentiated character which it necessarily has by virtue of the fact that people cluster in different groups, belong to different associations, and occupy different positions. They accordingly approach each other differently, live in different worlds, and guide themselves by different sets of meanings. Nevertheless, whether one is dealing with a family, a boy's gang, an industrial corporation, or a political party, one must see the activities of the collectivity as being formed through a process of designation and interpretation.

❖

ERVING GOFFMAN (1922–1982): A BIOGRAPHICAL SKETCH

Erving Goffman was born in Mannville, Alberta, Canada, in 1922. He graduated with a B.A. from the University of Toronto in 1945. He than attended the University of Chicago, where he received his master's degree in 1949 and his Ph.D. in 1953. After completing his doctorate, Goffman spent the next three years as a visiting scientist at the National Institute of Mental Health (NIMH) in Bethesda, Maryland. During that period he conducted fieldwork at St. Elizabeth's Hospital in Washington, D.C., a federal mental institution with more than seven thousand patients in its charge. His research here led to one of the landmark books in sociology, *Asylums* (1961). Following his stint at the NIMH, Goffman took a position in the sociology department at the University of California, Berkeley, where he remained until 1968. He then left for the University of Pennsylvania, where he assumed an endowed chair, the Benjamin Franklin Professor of Anthropology and Psychology. He served on the

SOURCE: American Sociological Association; used with permission.

University of Pennsylvania faculty until his untimely death in 1982, at the age of sixty.

Goffman produced a number of works that have made their way into the canon of contemporary sociology. In addition to *Asylums*, his more notable books include *The Presentation of Self in Everyday Life* (1959), *Encounters* (1961), *Behavior in Public Places* (1963), *Stigma* (1965), *Interaction Ritual* (1967), *Strategic Interaction* (1969), *Frame Analysis* (1974), and *Gender Advertisements* (1979). His contributions to the discipline notwithstanding, Goffman maintained a reputation as an iconoclast; never content to be conventional, he chartered a rebellious intellectual course (Collins 1986; Lemert 1997). His unique, if not visionary, position within the profession was developed in several ways. For starters, Goffman refused to situate his perspective within a specific theoretical tradition, although that did not stop others from trying to do so. Indeed, while he is often considered a symbolic interactionist (and for good reason), Goffman himself found the label wanting. Denying an allegiance to that tradition or even to the more general label of "theorist," he was more prone to refer to himself as simply an "empiricist" or a "social psychologist" (Lemert 1997:xxi). In some respects, Goffman's self-description may be the more accurate, for his work drew from a number of distinct approaches that he fashioned together in forming his own novel account of everyday life.

Goffman's writing style also fueled his iconoclasm. Writing with the flair of a literary stylist, his was not the dry prose all too common among scientists. Instead of adopting the standard practice of situating one's analyses within a particular intellectual lineage or reigning contemporary debates, Goffman was busy inventing his own terminology, as he set out to "raise questions that no one else had ever asked and to look at data that no one had ever examined before" (Collins 1986:110). As a result, Goffman was at the forefront of important movements within sociology, for instance, doing ethnomethodology before the ethnomethodologists and exploring the central role of language in social life (the "linguistic turn") well ahead of most of his sociological brethren.

That Goffman stood with one foot in sociology and the other out can be read in his posthumously published article "The Interaction Order" (1983). Commenting on the state of the discipline, he remarked:

We have not been given the credence and weight that economists lately have acquired, but we can almost match them when it comes to the failure of rigorously calculated predictions. Certainly our systematic theories are every bit as vacuous as theirs: we manage to ignore almost as many critical variables as they do. We do not have the esprit that anthropologists have, but our subject matter at least has not been obliterated by the spread of the world economy. So we have an undiminished opportunity to overlook the relevant facts with our very own eyes. We can't get graduate students who score as high as those who go into Psychology, and at its best the training the latter gets seems more professional and more thorough than what we provide. So we haven't managed to produce in our students the high level of trained incompetence that psychologists have achieved in theirs, although, God knows, we're working on it. . . .

From the perspective of the physical and natural sciences, human life is only a small irregular scab on the face of nature, not particularly amenable to deep systematic analysis. And so it is. . . . I'm not one to think that so far our claims can be based on magnificent accomplishment. Indeed I've heard it said that we should be glad to trade what we've so far produced for a few really good conceptual distinctions and a cold beer. But there's nothing in the world we should trade for what we do have: the bent to sustain in regard to all elements of social life a spirit of unfettered, unsponsored inquiry, and the wisdom not to look elsewhere but ourselves and our discipline for this mandate. That is our inheritance and that so far is what we have to bequeath. (1983:2, 17)

Such were the words Goffman had written in 1982 for his address to the American Sociological Association. The occasion was his election to the office of president. However, he was unable to deliver his speech, too ill to attend the conference. He died from cancer shortly thereafter. But perhaps that is how it should have been, for the maverick had entered the mainstream.

INTELLECTUAL INFLUENCES AND CORE IDEAS

In this section and those that follow, we largely confine our discussion to Goffman's earlier works, for arguably they have had the most significant impact on the discipline. As we noted previously, Goffman resisted the typical tendency to position his work in one or another theoretical camps. For that matter, his citations and footnotes seemingly were designed to obscure the identities of those whose ideas he drew from, whether it was to champion or challenge their approaches (Collins 1986:108). Not surprisingly, this complicates efforts to trace connections to those whom Goffman is most indebted. Despite these obstacles, we nevertheless can identify a number of theorists whose work played a central role in the development of his dramaturgical perspective.

Symbolic Interactionism: George Herbert Mead and William I. Thomas

Notwithstanding his avoidance of the interactionist label, one figure who had an important impact on Goffman's work was George Herbert Mead, whose insights into the interconnectedness between the self and social experiences helped lay the foundation for symbolic interaction.

Mead envisioned the self as consisting of two principal "phases": the "I" and the "me." As the organized set of attitudes of others, the "me" is involved in thinking or reflexive role-taking during which individuals engage in an internal conversation. In this internal conversation, individuals "take the attitude of the other" whose imagined responses shape the course of one's conduct. As we project the possible implications of courses of action and attempt to elicit the desired responses from others, we in a sense split off from our self. In doing so, we become an "object" to ourselves by taking the attitudes of others toward our self. For Mead, then, the self exists as self-consciousness, that is, the capacity to be both subject and object to one's self.

Seeing ourselves as an object, or against the attitudes of others, is the phase of the self that Mead termed the "me." This phase represents a more or less stable sense of who we are that is created, sustained, and modified through our interaction with others. Thus, the individual self is essentially a social construct that is rooted in our perceptions of how others will interpret and respond to our behaviors. However, that we see ourselves and respond to our own conduct as others would is not the only way in which the self is a reflection of social interaction. According to Mead, "[w]e divide ourselves up in all sorts of different selves with reference to our acquaintances. . . . There are all sorts of different selves answering to all sorts of different social creations" (1934:142). In other words, it is interaction and the context within which it takes place that determines who we are, the "part" of the self that appears. We all have, in a sense, multiple personalities, as assuming the attitudes of a particular other often shapes our behavior. The self you experience as a sibling is different from the one you experience as a co-worker or student.

The notion that we see ourselves as an object, as others see us, forms the basis for one of Goffman's central concepts: **impression management**. Impression management refers to the verbal and nonverbal practices we employ in an attempt to present an acceptable image of our self to others. Much of Goffman's work is dedicated to describing the subtle ways in which we carry out such performances; for instance, concealing information about ourselves that is incompatible with the image we are trying to project, or ensuring "audience segregation" so that those for whom we play one of our parts will not be present for our performance of a different, potentially incompatible, role. It is this controlling of what we do and don't say and do, and how we do and don't say and do it, that speaks to taking the attitude of the other. For if our attempts to project an image of our self were not in some measure guided by the imagined responses of others to our actions, then we would be unable to coordinate our behavior with others and engage in relatively predictable and smoothly functioning interaction.

Yet, it is in the "some measure" clause that Goffman makes one of his breaks with the traditional symbolic interaction of Mead and Blumer. While he by no means denies that individuals see themselves as others see them, he is far less interested in exploring the internal conversations that individuals engage in as they map out their conduct. Instead, Goffman's genius lies in exploring how social arrangements themselves and the actual, physical copresence of individuals—the "interaction order"— shapes the organization of the self. Commenting on Mead's approach, Goffman remarks:

> The Meadian notion that the individual takes toward himself the attitude others take toward him seems very much an oversimplification. Rather the individual must rely on others to complete the picture of him of which he himself is allowed to paint only certain parts. Each individual is responsible for the demeanor image of himself and the deference image of others, so that for a complete man to be expressed, individuals must hold hands in a chain of ceremony, each giving deferentially with proper demeanor to the one on the right what will be received deferentially from the one on the left. While it may be true that the individual has a unique self all his own, evidence of this possession is thoroughly a product of joint ceremonial labor . . . (1967:84, 85)

While Mead contends that the central elements of social interaction are rooted in one's imagination, Goffman looks to the "scene" within which individuals orient their actions to one another. For Goffman, then, the essence of the self is found not in the interior, cognitive deliberations of the individual, but rather in interaction itself. In the end, both the dynamics of social encounters and the image of one's self are dependent on the willingness of others to "go along" with the particular impression that an individual is seeking to present.

The implications of these remarks extend beyond an attempt to capture the underpinnings of social interaction, to exposing the very nature of the self. But before addressing this latter issue, let us first turn to another concept central to Goffman's work. Closely connected to Goffman's notion of impression management is the **definition of the situation**, a concept derived from another early contributor to the Chicago School of symbolic interaction, William I. Thomas (1863–1947). Like many of the early interactionists, Thomas developed his perspective in part out of a critique of psychological behaviorism. His notion of the definition of the situation countered the view that individuals respond to stimuli on the basis of conditioned or instinctual reflexes. Instead, Thomas argued, in one of the most oft-cited concepts in sociology, that "preliminary to any self-determined act of behavior there is always a stage of examination and deliberation which we may call the definition of the situation" (1923:41). Thus, an individual's behavior or reaction to a situation is not automatic, but rather it is constructed on the basis of the meanings that are attributed to the situation. In turn, those interested in understanding individuals and their behaviors must attend to the subjective meanings that they attach to their actions.

There are two additional aspects to Thomas's notion that are noteworthy. First, Thomas points out that a person "is always born into a group of people among whom all the general types of situation which may arise have already been defined and corresponding rules of conduct developed, and where he has not the slightest chance of making his definitions and following his wishes without interference" (1923:42). More often than not, then, individuals do not create definitions of the situations so much as they select among preexisting definitions when determining the meaning of an event or encounter. Second, Thomas, in a phrase that would become one of the most famous in sociology, noted the link between meaning and action: "If men define situations as real, they are real in their consequences" (1928:571–72). In other words, behavior is fundamentally shaped by, or a consequence of, the definition of the situation assigned by an individual. Much like Mead, then, Thomas contended that we act on the basis of the meanings we ascribe to the situations or stimuli that we confront. Moreover, Thomas's dictum suggests that reality itself is created through the definition of the situation, for it lays the foundation on which individuals will interpret others' actions and their own. In short, individuals create reality as they define it. Thus, if you define a class as boring, then it will be, and your efforts will be different than if you had defined it as interesting.

So, how does Goffman's work connect with Thomas's insights? First, Goffman concurs that the act of defining the situation establishes the basis on which an encounter unfolds. He notes that

> When an individual enters the presence of others, they commonly seek to acquire information about him or to bring into play information about him already possessed. . . . Information about the individual helps to define the situation, enabling others to know in advance what he will expect of them and what they may expect of him. Informed in this way, the others will know how best to act in order to call forth a desired response from him. (1959:1)

In defining the situation, actors are then able to practice the arts of impression management more effectively, which, as we discussed previously, is a central ingredient of social interaction. For knowing which "self" a person is obliged to present and how to present—knowing what to say and how to say it, what to do and how to do it—is largely determined by defining what is going on in a situation. Knowing that you are, for the purposes of a given encounter, a student, a worker, or a friend, and whether you should present yourself as studious, compliant, or caring, requires knowing first what the situation itself demands of the actors. Goffman points to the relationship between the definition of the situation and impression management when he remarks:

> Regardless of the particular objective which the individual has in mind and of his motive for having this objective, it will be in his interests to control the conduct of others, especially their responsive treatment of him. This control is achieved largely by influencing the definition of the situation which the others come to formulate, and he can influence this definition by expressing himself in such a way as to give them the kind of impression that will lead them to act voluntarily in accordance with his own plans. (1959:3, 4)

While arguing that the definition of the situation plays a central role in interaction, particularly as it affects our attempts to manage impressions, Goffman nevertheless parts with Thomas's original understanding of the concept in important ways. In reference to Thomas's dictum that "if men define situations as real, they are real in their consequences," Goffman contends:

> This statement is true as it reads but false as it is taken. Defining situations as real certainly has consequences, but these may contribute very marginally to the events in question; in some cases only a slight embarrassment flits across the scene in mild concern for those who tried to define the situation wrongly. . . . Presumably, a "definition of the situation" is almost always to be found, but those who are in the situation ordinarily do not *create* this definition, even though their society often can be said to do so; ordinarily, all they do is to assess correctly what the situation ought to be for them and then act accordingly. (1974:1)

Goffman's point is that definitions are less a matter of an individual's efforts to assign meaning to a situation or to the subjective processes of "examination and deliberation" as Thomas maintains. Instead, definitions are largely a matter of convention that are given or built into situations themselves. Moreover, the definition of the situation also carries with it a "moral character" that structures the interaction between the participants in an encounter. As a structural (i.e., collectivist) component of encounters, definitions both constrain and enable actors to present themselves in particular ways. It is in his study of the structural and, more specifically, moral and ritual dimension of interaction that Goffman most clearly parts with the symbolic interactionists and takes up the charge of social anthropologists.

Social Anthropology: Émile Durkheim, A. R. Radcliffe-Brown, and W. Lloyd Warner

While he was earning his degree at the University of Chicago, one of Goffman's major influences was the anthropologist W. Lloyd Warner (1898–1970) (Collins 1986:109). For his part, Warner studied with the noted British social anthropologist A. R. Radcliffe-Brown (1881–1955), who, in turn, was largely responsible for introducing the work of Émile Durkheim (1858–1917) into British anthropology during the early decades of the twentieth century. While an extensive review of the works and legacy of these three figures is beyond the scope of this volume, we outline here the commonalties that span their approaches and their implications for Goffman's own approach to the study of social life.

It is Durkheim's classic study of tribal religions, *The Elementary Forms of Religious Life* (1912/1965), that arguably had the most impact on Goffman's unique view of social interaction. In this work, Durkheim sought to uncover the origins of religion and, in doing so, to demonstrate the inevitable presence of religion in all societies, including allegedly secular, modern ones. According to Durkheim, the worshipping of gods is, in fact, a worshipping of society itself. For while religious individuals experience and commune with a power greater than themselves, an external force that inspires awe and demands respect, this greater power is in fact society. The sacrifices we make in the name of gods, the feelings of dependence on their wisdom and mercy, the willingness to submit to their commands, are nothing other than our offerings of allegiance to the society of which we are a part and through which our individual nature and fate is determined. It is not a supernatural deity that we depend on for our well being and from which we draw our strength, but rather society and the benefits of civilization it provides.

If "the idea of society is the soul of religion" (Durkheim 1912/1965:466), then religious rituals do more than pay tribute to or placate the gods. Indeed, the importance of such rituals for Durkheim lies in their capacity to bind participants to a common experience. By unifying participants' focus through a shared practice, rituals reaffirm a society's collective conscience (the totality of beliefs and sentiments commonly held in a society) and thus play a central role in preserving social solidarity. Thus, in a very real sense the continued existence of any society requires that its members periodically reunite in ritual ceremonies in order to rekindle their adherence to the collective conscience and their commitment to upholding the moral order. In this way, not only are communions, baptisms, and bar mitzvahs religious rituals, but so too are college graduations, family reunions, annual professional meetings, July Fourth celebrations, and saying the Pledge of Allegiance at the start of the school day. Each marks an occasion during which time participants "reaffirm in common their common sentiments" and strengthen their ties to the community (ibid.:475).

That such secular ceremonies serve "religious" purposes raises an interesting question: what is sacred in a society, and how is this trait recognized? Neither objects nor animals are intrinsically sacred, yet every culture assigns to one or the other extraordinary qualities that set them apart from the everyday world of profane things. Above all else, such extraordinary qualities grant a moral authority to that which is deemed sacred. To those things that are sacred, that possess a moral authority or power, we yield unquestioningly our own interests and desires. And because, as Durkheim maintains, our interests are unlimited and we alone are incapable of restraining our passions and desires, we must obey something "bigger" than ourselves, lest life be "nasty, brutish, and short." Given that sacred objects and beings allegedly possess the power to make our lives possible and contented, it is no wonder that we celebrate them through ritual practices and ceremonies. For their part, rituals are designed to protect what is sacred and, in doing so, protect us.

Both Durkheim and Radcliffe-Brown confined their studies of rituals and their role in sustaining the stability of group life to "simple," traditional societies, primarily Australian aboriginal communities. However, Durkheim noted that as societies became larger and increasingly complex, what was imbued with sacred qualities changed as well. Inhabitants of small, traditional societies are tied together by "mechanical solidarity" or feelings of likeness or "oneness" that come with each member participating in the same round of activities and following the same system of beliefs. Indeed, the survival of such societies is dependent on each of its members engaging in a variety of tasks that contribute to the maintenance of the group. As a result, the collective conscience is marked by shared beliefs and sentiments that encompass the individual's entire existence, and what is sacred above all else is the group.

Modern, complex societies, by contrast, are bonded together by "organic solidarity" or interdependence that comes from its members performing specialized functions that, taken together, form a stable, cohesive whole. What is shared in societies such as our own are not similarities, but rather differences. Modern societies are populated by individuals who hold different occupations, who maintain different religious and political beliefs, and who affirm different ethnic and racial identities. And if specialization and cultivating individual differences marks modern societies, then that which is sacred must take on a different character, for likeness and "oneness" can no longer ensure the stability and survival of the society. The one thing we do share in modern societies, paradoxically, is our individuality. Thus, it is the individual who is deemed sacred, for he alone provides the common basis on which social solidarity can be maintained. Worshipping the group is replaced by the "cult of personality."

That the individual is sacred in modern societies can be seen in the plethora of laws that have been established to protect and to deny the "inalienable rights" of the individual. From the right to vote, the right to hold property, and the right to privacy, to incarceration and the denial of freedoms as a favored mode of punishment, the legal system is, in a sense, the church of the individual, while judges are its priests. For that matter, setting aside the veiled racism and sexism that underlies much of the backlash against affirmative action, those who are opposed to this policy could be seen as defending the sacredness of the individual who in their eyes has been profaned at the expense of group-based claims. Yet, it is not to the formal rule of law that Goffman sets his sights. Instead, it is to the interaction rituals that pervade everyday encounters, the ceremonial chain of "hello's" and "excuse me's," that he turns his perceptive eye. For it is through such perfunctory, conventionalized acts that the individual affirms the sacred status of others while receiving his due in kind.

Goffman's interest in exploring the rituals that structure social life in modern societies stems in part from the influence of W. Lloyd Warner, with whom he studied while earning his graduate degree at the University of Chicago. In his "Yankee City" series (1941–1959), Warner creatively adapted the anthropological study of tribal societies to the study of class and ethnic stratification in urban society. Conducted in a Massachusetts town, Warner's community studies examined the ritual practices that shape modern status systems and the inequalities they sustain. For instance, he argued that secular, patriotic ceremonies served not only to revivify group solidarity, as Durkheim maintained. In addition, such rituals reinforce class domination; "they suppress feelings of class conflict and dissension by emphasizing group unity, while implicitly conferring legitimacy on the class [WASPs in 'Yankee City'] that leads the rituals and exemplifies the culture expressed in them" (Collins 1994:217).

Goffman followed Warner's lead in applying the insights and methods of anthropology to urban society; however, he largely abandoned, at least overtly, his mentor's emphasis on stratification and turned to a Durkheimian-inspired, functionalist interpretation of the ritual practices that guide interaction (Collins 1986:109). Defining interaction rituals as "acts through whose symbolic component the actor shows how worthy he is of respect or how worthy he feels others are of it" (Goffman 1967:19), Goffman illuminated the significance of seemingly insignificant acts. Of particular import are a person's **demeanor** (conduct, dress) and the **deference** (honor, dignity, respect) it symbolically accords to others.

Consider the ritual act of wearing a suit for a job interview. Even if the employees do not wear suits at work, if you show up in more casual business attire for your interview you may ruin your chances of getting the job. Your failure to be hired in this case may have little to do with your abilities to fulfill the requirements of the position. More critical is the fact that your demeanor paid insufficient deference to the interviewer and the company. A strip of cloth tied in a knot under one's throat speaks volumes about one's character! By suggesting that the interviewer is unworthy of your donning "sacred" clothes, you likewise demonstrate a lack of commitment to or knowledge of basic rules of interaction, the most important of which is to allow others to tactfully present themselves as "gods." Reminiscent of Durkheim's "cult of personality," Goffman remarked on the connections between demeanor, displays of deference, and the self:

> [T]he self is in part a ceremonial thing, a sacred object which must be treated with proper ritual care and in turn must be presented in a proper light to others. As a means through which this self is established, the individual acts with proper demeanor while in contact with others and is treated by others with deference. . . . The implication is that in one sense this secular world is not so irreligious as we may think. Many gods have been done away with, but the individual himself stubbornly remains a deity of considerable importance. . . . Perhaps the individual is so viable a god because he can actually understand the ceremonial significance of the way he is treated, and quite on his own can respond dramatically to what is proffered him. In contacts between such deities there is no need for middlemen; each of these gods is able to serve as his own priest. (1967:91, 95)

Dramaturgy: A Synthesis

With his Durkheimian focus on rituals leaving him in, but not of, the symbolic interactionist tradition, Goffman developed his dramaturgical approach to the study of social life. Inspired in part by the literary critic and theorist Kenneth Burke (1897–1993), who viewed language as a symbolically enacted drama, Goffman analyzed interaction through analogy with the theater. For his part, Burke constructed a philosophy of rhetoric—"dramatism"—that sought to uncover the motives for action symbolically revealed in the formal structure underlying all instances of speech and writing. Goffman, however, claiming that "life itself is a dramatically enacted thing" (1959:72), turned his attention to the symbolic dimensions of social encounters in his effort to explore the nature of the self and its relation to the broader moral code that shapes interaction performances.

To this end, Goffman introduced a vocabulary normally associated with the world of the theater: front, backstage, setting, audience, performance, and perhaps most provocatively, performer and character, are all part of his repertoire of terms used to examine the often unspoken and taken-for-granted subtleties that structure the interaction order. Consider, for instance, Goffman's notion of the **front**, which he labels as

> that part of the individual's performance which regularly functions in a general and fixed fashion to define the situation for those who observe the performance. Front, then, is the expressive equipment of a standard kind intentionally or unwittingly employed by the individual during his performance. (1959:22)

Moreover, fronts tend to become "institutionalized" as performances conducted in similar settings and by similar actors give rise to "stereotyped expectations" that transcend and shape any particular presentation. Thus, "when an actor takes on an established social role, usually he finds that a particular front has already been established for it" (1959:27). As "facts in their own right," fronts, then, are typically selected, not created, by performers.

Goffman divides the front into two parts: the setting and the personal front. The setting consists of the scenery and props that make up the physical space where a performance is conducted. A professor needs a classroom and a lifeguard needs a swimming pool if they are to perform their roles. Presenting one's self as a high-powered executive, for instance, requires a spacious office, not a cubicle, adorned with expensive furniture, works of art, and a majestic view. It is much harder to convince an audience that you are an important "mover and shaker" if your office overlooks the dumpster in the back alley and the cushions on your furniture have tape or stains or them. The personal front, on the other hand, refers to those items of "expressive equipment" that the audience identifies with the performer himself. These items consist of "insignia of office or rank; clothing; sex, age, and racial characteristics; size and looks; posture; speech patterns; facial expressions; bodily gestures; and the like" (1959:24). Such things provide the resources that allow (or prevent) a person to carry himself and appear before others in a particular light. Certainly, audiences attribute traits, fairly or unfairly, to performers on the basis of their age, sex, race, and looks, and performers are often aware of this fact. For instance, all too often audiences equate intelligence with looks and personality traits with sex. Thus, males are seen as "naturally" aggressive and in turn have license to present themselves as such, while women are considered "naturally" passive and often face negative repercussions if they do not conform to gendered expectations.

The front is contrasted with the **backstage**, the region of the performance normally unobserved by, and restricted from, members of the audience. Backstage is

> where the impression fostered by a performance is knowingly contradicted as a matter of course . . . [where] illusions and impressions are openly constructed. . . . Here costumes and other parts of the personal front may be adjusted and scrutinized for flaws. . . . Here the performer can relax; he can drop his front, forgo speaking his lines, and step out of character. (1959:112)

Restaurants illustrate well the distinction between the front and backstage and their facilitation of performances. While managing his impression in the front region as a courteous, deft, and hygienic server, a waiter often can be found in the backstage of the kitchen cursing a customer, sneezing atop someone's meal, or assembling an assortment of previously tabled bread into a basket for the next diners.[4] Of course, the front and backstage are not solely the province of business establishments. Our homes are likewise divided up into distinct regions, the separation of which takes on particular import with the arrival of guests.

In addition to shedding light on how space functions in managing performances and impressions, the front and backstage also call attention to an issue that we alluded to earlier: the nature of the self. Implied in the passage above, Goffman draws a

---

[4]In one episode of *Seinfeld*, Jerry finds himself standing at the urinal next to the chef of a restaurant. After relieving himself, the chef heads back to the kitchen without first washing his hands. Upon his return to his table, Jerry watches as the chef energetically kneads the dough for a "special" pizza he is preparing for Jerry and his guest: the chef's daughter.

Before, During, and
After: The Dinner Party

Photo 5.3 Preparing for Guests. In anticipation of their arrival, we ceremoniously prepare the red carpet for our sacred guests—emptying trash cans, vacuuming the carpet, mopping the floors.

SOURCE: Scott Appelrouth; used with permission.

Photo 5.4 The Dinner Party. During the festive ritual, however, all the stress and glamorous-less labor that went into its preparation is momentarily forgotten as hosts and guests alike revel in the celebration of their solidarity.

SOURCE: © Royalty-Free/Corbis; used with permission.

Photo 5.5 The Cleanup. But afterward, it's back to more disheartening scut work.

SOURCE: Scott Appelrouth; used with permission.

distinction between the self as **performer** and as **character**, and in doing so he comes to a radical, antipsychological conclusion. As a character, the self

> is not an organic thing that has a specific location, whose fundamental fate is to be born, to mature and to die; it is a dramatic effect arising diffusely from a scene that is presented, and the characteristic issue, the crucial concern, is whether it will be credited or discredited. (1959:253)

In other words, the self is in reality an image, a managed impression, that is fabricated in concert with others during an encounter. While we typically see one's performed self as "something housed within the body of possessor . . . in the psychobiology of the personality" (1959:252), in actuality the self is imputed by others such that it "does not derive from its possessor but from the whole scene of his action. . . . [This] imputation—this self—is a *product* of a scene that comes off, and is not a *cause* of it" (ibid.). Goffman sums up his notion of self as character thusly:

> In analyzing the self . . . we are drawn from its possessor, from the person who will profit or lose most by it, for he and his body merely provide the peg on which something of collaborative manufacture will be hung for a time. And the means for producing and maintaining selves do not reside inside the peg; in fact these means are often bolted down in social establishments. (1959:253)

However, when we turn to the self as performer, Goffman offers a different view, one that suggests that the individual does indeed possess a self that is uniquely his own. For while we are presenting a contrived image to an audience in the front, in the backstage we can relax, forgo speaking our lines, and step out of character. But if we step out of character, to what do we step in? Here the self is not a fabrication, but rather as a performer "a fabricator of impressions . . . [who] has a capacity to learn, this being exercised in the task of training for a part" (1959:252, 253). The self as performer is more in keeping with our conventional understanding of selfhood, which maintains that behind whatever part may be played or impression cast, there lies a thinking, feeling "person," a core being that is *really* who we are. Yet, in the end, perhaps this self is really nothing more than an idea, a comforting myth. For if the front you present to audiences is what they know of you, and if you develop your sense of self through interaction with others, then is your self not an image realized in performances? Truth, in reality, is a fiction.

GOFFMAN'S THEORETICAL ORIENTATION

Goffman's theoretical orientation is particularly difficult to decipher. Not only is his overall approach multidimensional in the sense that it speaks to the different quadrants of our action/order framework, but in many instances the substance of specific concepts ranges across the presuppositions that inform them (see Figure 5.2). With that said, we begin our outline of Goffman's orientation by taking up first the issue of action, in which, far from positing a single motivating force, he asserts that when in the presence of others,

Figure 5.2   Goffman's Multidimensional Approach to Social Interaction and the
Presentation of Self

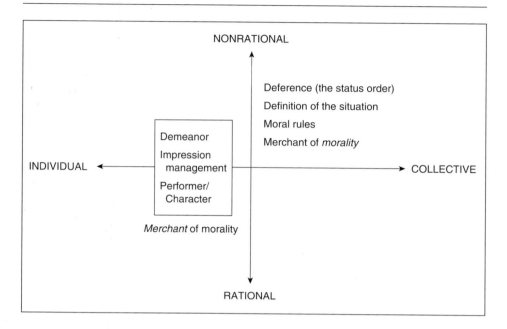

Sometimes the individual will act in a thoroughly calculating manner, expressing himself in a given way solely in order to give the kind of impression to others that is likely to evoke from them a specific response he is concerned to obtain. Sometimes the individual will be calculating in his activity but be relatively unaware that this is the case. Sometimes he will intentionally and consciously express himself in a particular way but chiefly because the tradition of his group or social status requires this kind of expression and not because of any particular response . . . that is likely to be evoked from those impressed by his expressions. Sometimes the traditions of an individual's role will lead him to give a well-designed impression of a particular kind and yet he may be neither consciously nor unconsciously disposed to create such an impression. (1959:6)

Here we clearly see that impression management, the fundamental dynamic underlying interaction, is carried out according to any number of motives. Thus, we can be motivated by rational, calculating self-interest, the nonrational commitment to tradition or status requirements, or even by purposes of which we are not consciously aware. (The multidimensionality of impression management is reflected in Figure 5.2 through its placement in two quadrants of our action/order framework.) This "having it both ways" approach can be unsatisfying if not frustrating, at least to the extent that the conditions are not specified under which we should expect rational or nonrational factors to be most salient.[5] On the other hand, Goffman's explicit inclusion of both

---

[5]Like his equivocal view on the nature of the self, his position on the issue of action says everything and thus arguably says nothing.

forms of motivating factors offers a more realistic portrayal of action. After all, behavior is rarely, if ever, motivated by a single consideration. This claim is all the more credible if we are interested in describing behavior in general and not a solitary slice of conduct.

To further illustrate Goffman's theoretical orientation, consider the following question: what is to prevent an individual from deceiving his audience into thinking that he is someone he is in fact not? Given that as sacred gods we have the moral "right" to present an image of our self and expect its acceptance without intrusive or violating questions from the audience, we have the freedom to be anything we want. Or do we? While it is true that we have license to portray who we "are" to our own advantage, this holds only so long as we abide by the moral rules of interaction. Foremost among these standards is that we are who we claim to be. Because the audience is left to infer traits to the individual on the basis of impressions, they have little choice but to accept a performance on faith. Thus, impressions are "treated as claims and promises that have implicitly been made, and claims and promises tend to have a moral character" (1959:249). This, too, accounts in part for the destructive nature of lies, for they breach the fundamental trust on which relationships are based.[6] This may also account for the legal challenges that often arise when law-enforcement agents pose as someone they are not to (en)trap a suspected criminal. And finally, notwithstanding the heinousness of the crime, perhaps this also accounts for the shock and feelings of betrayal that come with learning that your pillar-of-the-community, apple-pie-eating neighbor is in actuality a serial murderer.

This connection between impression management and the moral standards to which it is subject is captured in Goffman's notion of the **merchant of morality**. Here we see his dialectic understanding not only of rational and nonrational motivating forces, but also of the individualist and collectivist dimensions of social order.

> In their capacity as performers, individuals will be concerned with maintaining the impression that they are living up to the many standards by which they and their products are judged. Because these standards are so numerous and so pervasive, the individuals who are performers dwell more than we might think in a moral world. But, *qua* performers, individuals are concerned not with the moral issue of realizing these standards, but with the amoral issue of engineering a convincing impression that these standards are realized. Our activity, then, is largely concerned with moral matters, but as performers we do not have a moral concern with them. As performers we are merchants of morality . . . [T]he very obligation and profitability of appearing always in a steady moral light, of being a socialized character, forces one to be the sort of person who is practiced in the ways of the stage. (1959:251)

We present ourselves as well-demeaned persons in part because it is in our best interest to do so (a rationalist motivation), but in doing so, we announce our adherence to the moral standards that ritually organize social encounters. The notion that individuals are "merchants of morality" suggests that they are calculating in their attempts to "engineer" profits that may be earned from a properly enacted performance (*merchant*). However, actors are in an important sense compelled by the force of moral obligations (*morality*) to live up to the standards of propriety by which they will be judged. Yet, in the end, the social order is produced and reproduced not so much through the individual's

---

[6]An individual who knowingly presents a false impression runs the risk not only of losing face during the interaction but also of having his face destroyed. Once he is found guilty of being an imposter, mindful audiences may never again be willing to submit on his behalf to the moral vulnerability that is required of all interactions, leaving the individual in need of finding new ones (1959:62).

interaction with others, but rather through the moral rules around which interaction is itself organized (a collectivist approach to order). Like impression management, the multidimensionality of this concept is reflected in Figure 5.2 through its placement in two quadrants of our theoretical framework.

Figure 5.2 depicts a number of concepts central to Goffman's perspective in addition to those just discussed. (Again, several appear in more than one quadrant to reflect their multidimensional character.) Because we addressed the others in the previous section, we direct your attention to those earlier comments as you develop your understanding of Goffman's theoretical orientation. Yet from the figure it is clear that, despite his multidimensional approach, Goffman does not consider concepts that would be positioned in the rational/collective quadrant of our model. Here we might find an emphasis on such matters as political institutions, legal institutions, or economic systems. Instead, most of Goffman's central concepts are used to examine how *individuals* navigate their everyday life. Thus, we end this section with a question: what impact, if any, does the omission of these aspects of society have on Goffman's ability to construct a theory of interaction that accurately portrays social life?

Readings

In the following selections Goffman pursues three central themes. Taken from *The Presentation of Self in Everyday Life*, the first excerpts represent his most sustained use of theatrical metaphors as he advances his dramaturgical approach to impression management and its centrality to self and society. In the second selection, from "The Nature of Deference and Demeanor," Goffman's indebtedness to Durkheimian social anthropology is more pronounced as he sheds light on the ceremonial dimensions of interaction and the sacredness that envelops the individual. We end with an excerpt from *Asylums*, Goffman's study of total institutions, wherein he examines the ways in which social establishments produce the self.

Introduction to *The Presentation of Self in Everyday Life*

In this modern classic, Goffman develops his dramaturgical approach to social life and the self. It is in this work that Goffman introduces many of the central concepts discussed in the preceding sections: impression management, definition of the situation, front and backstage, and performer and character. In a sense, his book is an analysis of the familiar saying "actions speak louder than words," but after reading Goffman you will never be able to adjust the volume again.

He begins by distinguishing between two types of "sign-vehicles"—expressions one *gives* and expressions one *gives off*—that are used by actors and audiences as means for both managing impressions and defining the situation. The former refers to "verbal symbols or their substitutes which [the individual] uses admittedly and solely to convey the information that he and the others are known to attach to these symbols." The latter "involves a wide range of action that others can treat as symptomatic of the actor, the expectation being that the action was performed for reasons other than the information conveyed in this way" (1959:2). With this distinction, Goffman sets the backdrop for his analysis of the subtle techniques that actors and audiences strategically, if not manipulatively, employ as they go about the business of dramatically staging acceptable images of self. Yet, for all the deceit and feigning that may accompany a presentation, all participants in the encounter are obligated to abide by the moral rules that establish just what "acceptable" means. Here, participants in an interaction will establish a "working consensus" or surface agreement regarding the definition of the situation in which, in an effort to avoid conflict, embarrassment, or the discrediting of self-performances, each "is expected to suppress his immediate heartfelt feelings, conveying a view of the situation which he feels the others will be able to find at least temporarily acceptable" (1959:9). For often we find that in order to present a viable image of one's self, the definition of the situation compels us to tell "white lies." This explains our tactful refusals of invitations for interaction from people that we do not like: "Sorry, I'd love to come to your party but my cousin is visiting from out of town." You can only hope that on the night of the party no one sees you without your "cousin." Or, better yet, perhaps you can convince a friend to join your "team" for the evening and play the part of your favorite relative as you show them a night on the town.

❖

The Presentation of Self in Everyday Life (1959)

Erving Goffman

INTRODUCTION

When an individual enters the presence of others, they commonly seek to acquire information about him or to bring into play information about him already possessed. They will be interested in his general socio-economic status, his conception of self, his attitude toward them, his competence, his trustworthiness, etc. Although some of this information seems to be sought almost as an end in itself, there are usually quite practical reasons for acquiring it. Information about the individual helps to define the situation, enabling others to know in advance what he will expect of them and what they may expect of him. Informed in these ways, the others will know how best to act in order to call forth a desired response from him.

For those present, many sources of information become accessible and many carriers (or "sign-vehicles") become available for conveying this information. If unacquainted with the individual, observers can glean clues from his conduct and appearance which allow them to apply their previous experience with individuals roughly similar to the one before them or, more important, to apply untested stereotypes to him. They can also assume from past experience that only individuals of a particular kind are likely to be found in a given social setting. They can rely on what the individual says about himself or on documentary evidence he provides as to who and what he is. If they know, or know of, the individual by virtue of experience prior to the interaction, they can rely on assumptions as to the persistence and generality of psychological traits as a means of predicting his present and future behavior.

However, during the period in which the individual is in the immediate presence of the others, few events may occur which directly provide the others with the conclusive information they will need if they are to direct wisely their own activity. Many crucial facts lie beyond the time and place of interaction or lie concealed within it. For example, the "true" or "real" attitudes, beliefs, and emotions of the individual can be ascertained only indirectly, through his avowals or through what appears to be involuntary expressive behavior. Similarly, if the individual offers the others a product or service, they will often find that during the interaction there will be no time and place immediately available for eating the pudding that the proof can be found in. They will be forced to accept some events as conventional or natural signs of something not directly available to the senses. In Ichheiser's terms,[i] the individual will have to act so that he intentionally or unintentionally *expresses* himself, and the others will in turn have to be *impressed* in some way by him.

The expressiveness of the individual (and therefore his capacity to give impressions) appears to involve two radically different kinds of sign activity: the expression that he *gives*, and the expression that he *gives off*. The first involves verbal symbols or their substitutes which he uses admittedly and solely to convey the information that he and the others are known to attach to these symbols. This is communication in the traditional and narrow sense. The second involves a wide range of action that others can treat as symptomatic of the actor, the expectation being that the action was performed for reasons other than the information conveyed in this way. As we shall have to see, this distinction has an only initial validity. The individual does of course intentionally convey misinformation by means of both of these types of communication, the first involving deceit, the second feigning.

Taking communication in both its narrow and broad sense, one finds that when the individual is in the immediate presence of others, his activity will have a promissory character. The others are likely to find that they must accept the individual on faith, offering him a just return while he is present before them in exchange for something whose true value will not be established until after he has left their presence. (Of course, the others also live by inference in their dealings with the physical world, but it is only in the world of social interaction that the objects about which they make inferences will purposely facilitate and hinder this inferential process.) The security that they justifiably feel in making inferences about the individual will vary, of course, depending on such factors as the amount of information they already possess about him, but no amount of such past evidence can entirely obviate the necessity of acting on the basis of inferences. As William I. Thomas suggested:

> It is also highly important for us to realize that we do not as a matter of fact lead our lives, make our decisions, and reach our goals in everyday life either statistically or scientifically. We live by inference. I am, let us say, your guest. You do not know, you cannot determine scientifically, that I will not steal your money or your spoons. But inferentially I will not, and inferentially you have me as a guest.[ii]

Let us now turn from the others to the point of view of the individual who presents himself before them. He may wish them to think highly of him, or to think that he thinks highly of them, or to perceive how in fact he feels toward them, or to obtain no clear-cut impression; he may wish to ensure sufficient harmony so that the interaction can be sustained, or to defraud, get rid of, confuse, mislead, antagonize, or insult them. Regardless of the particular objective which the individual has in mind and of his motive for having this objective, it will be in his interests to control the conduct of the others, especially their responsive treatment of him. This control is achieved largely by influencing the definition of the situation which the others come to formulate, and he can influence this

[i]Gustav Ichheiser, "Misunderstandings in Human Relations," Supplement to *The American Journal of Sociology*, LV (September, 1949), pp. 6–7.

[ii]Quoted in E. H. Volkart, editor, *Social Behavior and Personality*, Contributions of W. I. Thomas to Theory and Social Research (New York: Social Science Research Council, 1951), p. 5.

definition by expressing himself in such a way as to give them the kind of impression that will lead them to act voluntarily in accordance with his own plan. Thus, when an individual appears in the presence of others, there will usually be some reason for him to mobilize his activity so that it will convey an impression to others which it is in his interests to convey. Since a girl's dormitory mates will glean evidence of her popularity from the calls she receives on the phone, we can suspect that some girls will arrange for calls to be made, and Willard Waller's finding can be anticipated:

> It has been reported by many observers that a girl who is called to the telephone in the dormitories will often allow herself to be called several times, in order to give all the other girls ample opportunity to hear her paged.[iii]

Of the two kinds of communication—expressions given and expressions given off—this report will be primarily concerned with the latter, with the more theatrical and contextual kind, the non-verbal, presumably unintentional kind, whether this communication be purposely engineered or not. As an example of what we must try to examine, I would like to cite at length a novelistic incident in which Preedy, a vacationing Englishman, makes his first appearance on the beach of his summer hotel in Spain:

> But in any case he took care to avoid catching anyone's eye. First of all, he had to make it clear to those potential companions of his holiday that they were of no concern to him whatsoever. He stared through them, round them, over them—eyes lost in space. The beach might have been empty. If by chance a ball was thrown his way, he looked surprised; then let a smile of amusement lighten his face (Kindly Preedy), looked round dazed to see that there *were* people on the beach, tossed it back with a smile to himself and not a smile *at* the people, and then resumed carelessly his nonchalant survey of space.
>
> But it was time to institute a little parade, the parade of the Ideal Preedy. By devious handlings

he gave any who wanted to look a chance to see the title of his book—a Spanish translation of Homer, classic thus, but not daring, cosmopolitan too—and then gathered together his beach-wrap and bag into a neat sand-resistant pile (Methodical and Sensible Preedy), rose slowly to stretch at ease his huge frame (Big-Cat Preedy), and tossed aside his sandals (Carefree Preedy, after all).

> The marriage of Preedy and the sea! There were alternative rituals. The first involved the stroll that turns into a run and a dive straight into the water, thereafter smoothing into a strong splashless crawl towards the horizon. But of course not really to the horizon. Quite suddenly he would turn on to his back and thrash great white splashes with his legs, somehow thus showing that he could have swum further had he wanted to, and then would stand up a quarter out of water for all to see who it was.
>
> The alternative course was simpler, it avoided the cold-water shock and it avoided the risk of appearing too high-spirited. The point was to appear to be so used to the sea, the Mediterranean, and this particular beach, that one might as well be in the sea as out of it. It involved a slow stroll down and into the edge of the water—not even noticing his toes were wet, land and water all the same to *him!*—with his eyes up at the sky gravely surveying portents, invisible to others, of the weather (Local Fisherman Preedy).[iv]

The novelist means us to see that Preedy is improperly concerned with the extensive impressions he feels his sheer bodily action is giving off to those around him. We can malign Preedy further by assuming that he has acted merely in order to give a particular impression, that this is a false impression, and that the others present receive either no impression at all, or, worse still, the impression that Preedy is affectedly trying to cause them to receive this particular impression. But the important point for us here is that the kind of impression Preedy thinks he is making is in fact the kind of impression that others correctly and incorrectly glean from someone in their midst.

I have said that when an individual appears before others his actions will influence the

---

[iii]Willard Waller, "The Rating and Dating Complex," *American Sociological Review*, II, p. 730.

[iv]William Sansom, *A Contest of Ladies* (London: Hogarth, 1956), pp. 230–32.

definition of the situation which they come to have. Sometimes the individual will act in a thoroughly calculating manner, expressing himself in a given way solely in order to give the kind of impression to others that is likely to evoke from them a specific response he is concerned to obtain. Sometimes the individual will be calculating in his activity but be relatively unaware that this is the case. Sometimes he will intentionally and consciously express himself in a particular way, but chiefly because the tradition of his group or social status require this kind of expression and not because of any particular response (other than vague acceptance or approval) that is likely to be evoked from those impressed by the expression. Sometimes the traditions of an individual's role will lead him to give a well-designed impression of a particular kind and yet he may be neither consciously nor unconsciously disposed to create such an impression. The others, in their turn, may be suitably impressed by the individual's efforts to convey something, or may misunderstand the situation and come to conclusions that are warranted neither by the individual's intent nor by the facts. In any case, in so far as the others act *as if* the individual had conveyed a particular impression, we may take a functional or pragmatic view and say that the individual has "effectively" projected a given definition of the situation and "effectively" fostered the understanding that a given state of affairs obtains.

There is one aspect of the others' response that bears special comment here. Knowing that the individual is likely to present himself in a light that is favorable to him, the others may divide what they witness into two parts; a part that is relatively easy for the individual to manipulate at will, being chiefly his verbal assertions, and a part in regard to which he seems to have little concern or control, being chiefly derived from the expressions he gives off. The others may then use what are considered to be the ungovernable aspects of his expressive behavior as a check upon the validity of what is conveyed by the governable aspects. In this a fundamental asymmetry is demonstrated in the communication process, the individual presumably being aware of only one stream of his communication, the witnesses of this stream and one other. For example, in

Shetland Isle one crofter's wife, in serving native dishes to a visitor from the mainland of Britain, would listen with a polite smile to his polite claims of liking what he was eating; at the same time she would take note of the rapidity with which the visitor lifted his fork or spoon to his mouth, the eagerness with which he passed food into his mouth, and the gusto expressed in chewing the food, using these signs as a check on the stated feelings of the eater. The same woman, in order to discover what one acquaintance (A) "actually" thought of another acquaintance (B), would wait until B was in the presence of A but engaged in conversation with still another person (C). She would then covertly examine the facial expressions of A as he regarded B in conversation with C. Not being in conversation with B, and not being directly observed by him, A would sometimes relax usual constraints and tactful deceptions, and freely express what he was "actually" feeling about B. This Shetlander, in short, would observe the unobserved observer.

Now given the fact that others are likely to check up on the more controllable aspects of behavior by means of the less controllable, one can expect that sometimes the individual will try to exploit this very possibility, guiding the impression he makes through behavior felt to be reliably informing. For example, in gaining admission to a tight social circle, the participant observer may not only wear an accepting look while listening to an informant, but may also be careful to wear the same look when observing the informant talking to others; observers of the observer will then not as easily discover where he actually stands. A specific illustration may be cited from Shetland Isle. When a neighbor dropped in to have a cup of tea, he would ordinarily wear at least a hint of an expectant warm smile as he passed through the door into the cottage. Since lack of physical obstructions outside the cottage and lack of light within it usually made it possible to observe the visitor unobserved as he approached the house, islanders sometimes took pleasure in watching the visitor drop whatever expression he was manifesting and replace it with a sociable one just before reaching the door. However, some visitors, in appreciating that this examination was occurring, would blindly adopt a social face a long distance from the house, thus ensuring the projection of a constant image.

This kind of control upon the part of the individual reinstates the symmetry of the communication process, and sets the stage for a kind of information game—a potentially infinite cycle of concealment, discovery, false revelation, and rediscovery. It should be added that since the others are likely to be relatively unsuspicious of the presumably unguided aspect of the individual's conduct, he can gain much by controlling it. The others of course may sense that the individual is manipulating the presumably spontaneous aspects of his behavior, and seek in this very act of manipulation some shading of conduct that the individual has not managed to control. This again provides a check upon the individual's behavior, this time his presumably uncalculated behavior, thus re-establishing the asymmetry of the communication process. Here I would like only to add the suggestion that the arts of piercing an individual's effort at calculated unintentionality seem better developed than our capacity to manipulate our own behavior, so that regardless of how many steps have occurred in the information game, the witness is likely to have the advantage over the actor, and the initial asymmetry of the communication process is likely to be retained.

When we allow that the individual projects a definition of the situation when he appears before others, we must also see that the others, however passive their role may seem to be, will themselves effectively project a definition of the situation by virtue of their response to the individual and by virtue of any lines of action they initiate to him. Ordinarily the definitions of the situation projected by the several different participants are sufficiently attuned to one another so that open contradiction will not occur. I do not mean that there will be the kind of consensus that arises when each individual present candidly expresses what he really feels and honestly agrees with the expressed feelings of the others present. This kind of harmony is an optimistic ideal and in any case not necessary for the smooth working of society. Rather, each participant is expected to suppress his immediate heartfelt feelings, conveying a view of the situation which he feels the others will be able to find at least temporarily acceptable. The

maintenance of this surface of agreement, this veneer of consensus, is facilitated by each participant concealing his own wants behind statements which assert values to which everyone present feels obliged to give lip service. Further, there is usually a kind of division of definitional labor. Each participant is allowed to establish the tentative official ruling regarding matters which are vital to him but not immediately important to others, e.g., the rationalizations and justifications by which he accounts for his past activity. In exchange for this courtesy he remains silent or non-committal on matters important to others but not immediately important to him. We have then a kind of interactional *modus vivendi*. Together the participants contribute to a single over-all definition of the situation which involves not so much a real agreement as to what exists but rather a real agreement as to whose claims concerning what issues will be temporarily honored. Real agreement will also exist concerning the desirability of avoiding an open conflict of definitions of the situation. I will refer to this level of agreement as a "working consensus." It is to be understood that the working consensus established in one interaction setting will be quite different in content from the working consensus established in a different type of setting. Thus, between two friends at lunch, a reciprocal show of affection, respect, and concern for the other is maintained. In service occupations, on the other hand, the specialist often maintains an image of disinterested involvement in the problem of the client, while the client responds with a show of respect for the competence and integrity of the specialist. Regardless of such differences in content, however, the general form of these working arrangements is the same.

In noting the tendency for a participant to accept the definitional claims made by the others present, we can appreciate the crucial importance of the information that the individual *initially* possesses or acquires concerning his fellow participants, for it is on the basis of this initial information that the individual starts to define the situation and starts to build up lines of responsive action. The individual's initial projection commits him to what he is proposing to be and requires him to drop all pretenses of being other things. As the interaction among the participants progresses, additions and modifications in this initial informational state will of course occur, but it is essential that these later developments be related without contradiction to, and even built up from, the initial positions taken by the several participants. It would seem that an individual can more easily make a choice as to what line of treatment to demand from and extend to the others present at the beginning of an encounter than he can alter the line of treatment that is being pursued once the interaction is underway.

In everyday life, of course, there is a clear understanding that first impressions are important. Thus, the work adjustment of those in service occupations will often hinge upon a capacity to seize and hold the initiative in the service relation, a capacity that will require subtle aggressiveness on the part of the server when he is of lower socio-economic status than his client. W. F. Whyte suggests the waitress as an example:

> The first point that stands out is that the waitress who bears up under pressure does not simply respond to her customers. She acts with some skill to control their behavior. The first question to ask when we look at the customer relationship is, "Does the waitress get the jump on the customer, or does the customer get the jump on the waitress?" The skilled waitress realizes the crucial nature of this question. . . .
>
> The skilled waitress tackles the customer with confidence and without hesitation. For example, she may find that a new customer has seated himself before she could clear off the dirty dishes and change the cloth. He is now leaning on the table studying the menu. She greets him, says, "May I change the cover, please?" and, without waiting for an answer, takes his menu away from him so that he moves back from the table, and she goes about her work. The relationship is handled politely but firmly, and there is never any question as to who is in charge.[v]

When the interaction that is initiated by "first impressions" is itself merely the initial interaction in an extended series of interactions involving the same participants, we speak of "getting off on the right foot" and feel that it is crucial that we do so. Thus, one learns that some teachers take the following view:

> You can't ever let them get the upper hand on you or you're through. So I start out tough. The first day I get a new class in, I let them know who's boss. . . . You've got to start off tough, then you can ease up as you go along. If you start out easy-going, when you try to get tough, they'll just look at you and laugh.[vi]

Similarly, attendants in mental institutions may feel that if the new patient is sharply put in his place the first day on the ward and made to see who is boss, much future difficulty will be prevented.

Given the fact that the individual effectively projects a definition of the situation when he enters the presence of others, we can assume that events may occur within the interaction which contradict, discredit, or otherwise throw doubt upon this projection. When these disruptive events occur, the interaction itself may come to a confused and embarrassed halt. Some of the assumptions upon which the responses of the participants had been predicated become untenable, and the participants find themselves lodged in an interaction for which the situation has been wrongly defined and is now no longer defined. At such moments the individual whose presentation has been discredited may feel ashamed while the others present may feel hostile, and all the participants may come to feel ill at ease, nonplussed, out of countenance, embarrassed, experiencing the kind of anomy that is generated when the minute social system of face-to-face interaction breaks down.

In stressing the fact that the initial definition of the situation projected by an individual tends to provide a plan for the co-operative activity that follows—in stressing this action point of view—we must not overlook the crucial fact

---

[v]W. F. Whyte, "When Workers and Customers Meet," Chap. VII, *Industry and Society*, ed. W. F. Whyte (New York: McGraw-Hill, 1946), pp. 132–33.

[vi]Teacher interview quoted by Howard S. Becker, "Social Class Variations in the Teacher-Pupil Relationship," *Journal of Educational Sociology*, XXV, p. 459.

that any projected definition of the situation also has a distinctive moral character. It is this moral character of projections that will chiefly concern us in this report. Society is organized on the principle that any individual who possesses certain social characteristics has a moral right to expect that others will value and treat him in an appropriate way. Connected with this principle is a second, namely that an individual who implicitly or explicitly signifies that he has certain social characteristics ought in fact to be what he claims he is. In consequence, when an individual projects a definition of the situation and thereby makes an implicit or explicit claim to be a person of a particular kind, he automatically exerts a moral demand upon the others, obliging them to value and treat him in the manner that persons of his kind have a right to expect. He also implicitly forgoes all claims to be things he does not appear to be and hence forgoes the treatment that would be appropriate for such individuals. The others find, then, that the individual has informed them as to what is and as to what they *ought* to see as the "is."

One cannot judge the importance of definitional disruptions by the frequency with which they occur, for apparently they would occur more frequently were not constant precautions taken. We find that preventive practices are constantly employed to avoid these embarrassments and that corrective practices are constantly employed to compensate for discrediting occurrences that have not been successfully avoided. When the individual employs these strategies and tactics to protect his own projections, we may refer to them as "defensive practices"; when a participant employs them to save the definition of the situation projected by another, we speak of "protective practices" or "tact." Together, defensive and protective practices comprise the techniques employed to safeguard the impression fostered by an individual during his presence before others. It should be added that while we may be ready to see that no fostered impression would survive if defensive practices were not employed, we are less ready perhaps to see that few impressions could survive if those who received the impression did not exert tact in their reception of it.

In addition to the fact that precautions are taken to prevent disruption of projected definitions, we may also note that an intense interest in these disruptions comes to play a significant role in the social life of the group. Practical jokes and social games are played in which embarrassments which are to be taken unseriously are purposely engineered. Fantasies are created in which devastating exposures occur. Anecdotes from the past—real, embroidered, or fictitious—are told and retold, detailing disruptions which occurred, almost occurred, or occurred and were admirably resolved. There seems to be no grouping which does not have a ready supply of these games, reveries, and cautionary tales, to be used as a source of humor, a catharsis for anxieties, and a sanction for inducing individuals to be modest in their claims and reasonable in their projected expectations. The individual may tell himself through dreams of getting into impossible positions. Families tell of the time a guest got his dates mixed and arrived when neither the house nor anyone in it was ready for him. Journalists tell of times when an all-too-meaningful misprint occurred, and the paper's assumption of objectivity or decorum was humorously discredited. Public servants tell of times a client ridiculously misunderstood form instructions, giving answers which implied an unanticipated and bizarre definition of the situation. Seamen, whose home away from home is rigorously he-man, tell stories of coming back home and inadvertently asking mother to "pass the fucking butter." Diplomats tell of the time a near-sighted queen asked a republican ambassador about the health of his king.

To summarize, then, I assume that when an individual appears before others he will have many motives for trying to control the impression they receive of the situation. This report is concerned with some of the common techniques that persons employ to sustain such impressions and with some of the common contingencies associated with the employment of these techniques. The specific content of any activity presented by the individual participant, or the role it plays in the interdependent activities of an ongoing social system, will not be at issue; I shall be concerned only with the participant's dramaturgical problems of presenting the activity before others. The issues dealt with by stagecraft and stage management are sometimes trivial but they are quite general; they seem to occur everywhere in social life, providing a clear-cut dimension for formal sociological analysis.

It will be convenient to end this introduction with some definitions that are implied in what has gone before and required for what is to follow. For the purpose of this report, interaction (that is, face-to-face interaction) may be roughly defined as the reciprocal influence of individuals upon one another's actions when in one another's immediate physical presence. *An* interaction may be defined as all the interaction which occurs throughout any one occasion when a given set of individuals are in one another's continuous presence; the term "an encounter" would do as well. A "performance" may be defined as all the activity of a given participant on a given occasion which serves to influence in any way any of the other participants. Taking a particular participant and his performance as a basic point of reference, we may refer to those who contribute the other performances as the audience, observers, or co-participants. The pre-established pattern of action which is unfolded during a performance and which may be presented or played through on other occasions may be called a "part" or "routine." These situational terms can easily be related to conventional structural ones. When an individual or performer plays the same part to the same audience on different occasions, a social relationship is likely to arise. Defining social role as the enactment of rights and duties attached to a given status, we can say that a social role will involve one or more parts and that each of these different parts may be presented by the performer on a series of occasions to the same kinds of audience or to an audience of the same persons.

PERFORMANCES

Belief in the Part One Is Playing

When an individual plays a part he implicitly requests his observers to take seriously the impression that is fostered before them. They are asked to believe that the character they see actually possesses the attributes he appears to possess, that the task he performs will have the consequences that are implicitly claimed for it, and that, in general, matters are what they appear to be. In line with this, there is the popular view that the individual offers his performance and puts on his show "for the benefit of other people." It will be convenient to begin a consideration of performances by turning the question around and looking at the individual's own belief in the impression of reality that he attempts to engender in those among whom he finds himself.

At one extreme, one finds that the performer can be fully taken in by his own act; he can be sincerely convinced that the impression of reality which he stages is the real reality. When his audience is also convinced in this way about the show he puts on—and this seems to be the typical case—then for the moment at least, only the sociologist or the socially disgruntled will have any doubts about the "realness" of what is presented.

At the other extreme, we find that the performer may not be taken in at all by his own routine. This possibility is understandable, since no one is in quite as good an observational position to see through the act as the person who puts it on. Coupled with this, the performer may be moved to guide the conviction of his audience only as a means to other ends, having no ultimate concern in the conception that they have of him or of the situation. When the individual has no belief in his own act and no ultimate concern with the beliefs of his audience, we may call him cynical, reserving the term "sincere" for individuals who believe in the impression fostered by their own performance. It should be understood that the cynic, with all his professional disinvolvement, may obtain unprofessional pleasures from his masquerade, experiencing a kind of gleeful spiritual aggression from the fact that he can toy at will with something his audience must take seriously.[vii]

[vii]Perhaps the real crime of the confidence man is not that he takes money from his victims but that he robs all of us of the belief that middle-class manners and appearance can be sustained only by middle-class people. A disabused professional can be cynically hostile to the service relation his clients expect him to extend to them, the confidence man is in a position to hold the whole "legit" world in this contempt.

It is not assumed, of course, that all cynical performers are interested in deluding their audiences for purposes of what is called "self-interest" or private gain. A cynical individual may delude his audience for what he considers to be their own good, or for the good of the community, etc. . . . We know that in service occupations practitioners who may otherwise be sincere are sometimes forced to delude their customers because their customers show such a heartfelt demand for it. Doctors who are led into giving placebos, filling station attendants who resignedly check and recheck tire pressures for anxious women motorists, shoe clerks who sell a shoe that fits but tell the customer it is the size she wants to hear—these are cynical performers whose audiences will not allow them to be sincere. Similarly, it seems that sympathetic patients in mental wards will sometimes feign bizarre symptoms so that student nurses will not be subjected to a disappointingly sane performance. So also, when inferiors extend their most lavish reception for visiting superiors, the selfish desire to win favor may not be the chief motive; the inferior may be tactfully attempting to put the superior at ease by simulating the kind of world the superior is thought to take for granted.

I have suggested two extremes: an individual may be taken in by his own act or be cynical about it. These extremes are something a little more than just the ends of a continuum. Each provides the individual with a position which has its own particular securities and defenses, so there will be a tendency for those who have traveled close to one of these poles to complete the voyage. Starting with lack of inward belief in one's role, the individual may follow the natural movement described by Park:

> It is probably no mere historical accident that the word person, in its first meaning, is a mask. It is rather a recognition of the fact that everyone is always and everywhere, more or less consciously, playing a role. . . . It is in these roles that we know each other; it is in these roles that we know ourselves.[viii]

In a sense, and in so far as this mask represents the conception we have formed of ourselves—the role we are striving to live up to—this mask is our truer self, the self we would like to be. In the end, our conception of our role becomes second nature and an integral part of our personality. We come into the world as individuals, achieve character, and become persons.[ix]

. . . While we can expect to find natural movement back and forth between cynicism and sincerity, still we must not rule out the kind of transitional point that can be sustained on the strength of a little self-illusion. We find that the individual may attempt to induce the audience to judge him and the situation in a particular way, and he may seek this judgment as an ultimate end in itself, and yet he may not completely believe that he deserves the valuation of self which he asks for or that the impression of reality which he fosters is valid. . . .

Front

I have been using the term "performance" to refer to all the activity of an individual which occurs during a period marked by his continuous presence before a particular set of observers and which has some influence on the observers. It will be convenient to label as "front" that part of the individual's performance which regularly functions in a general and fixed fashion to define the situation for those who observe the performance. Front, then, is the expressive equipment of a standard kind intentionally or unwittingly employed by the individual during his performance. For preliminary purposes, it will be convenient to distinguish and label what seem to be the standard parts of front.

First, there is the "setting," involving furniture, décor, physical layout, and other background items which supply the scenery and stage props for the spate of human action played out before, within, or upon it. A setting tends to stay put, geographically speaking, so that those who would use a particular setting as part of their performance cannot begin their act until

---

viiiRobert Ezra Park, *Race and Culture* (Glencoe, Ill.: The Free Press, 1950), p. 249.

ixIbid., p. 250.

they have brought themselves to the appropriate place and must terminate their performance when they leave it. It is only in exceptional circumstances that the setting follows along with the performers; we see this in the funeral cortège, the civic parade, and the dreamlike processions that kings and queens are made of. In the main, these exceptions seem to offer some kind of extra protection for performers who are, or who have momentarily become, highly sacred. These worthies are to be distinguished, of course, from quite profane performers of the peddler class who move their place of work between performances, often being forced to do so. In the matter of having one fixed place for one's setting, a ruler may be too sacred, a peddler too profane. . . .

If we take the term "setting" to refer to the scenic parts of expressive equipment, one may take the term "personal front" to refer to the other items of expressive equipment, the items that we most intimately identify with the performer himself and that we naturally expect will follow the performer wherever he goes. As part of personal front we may include: insignia of office or rank; clothing; sex, age, and racial characteristics; size and looks; posture; speech patterns; facial expressions; bodily gestures; and the like. Some of these vehicles for conveying signs, such as racial characteristics, are relatively fixed and over a span of time do not vary for the individual from one situation to another. On the other hand, some of these sign vehicles are relatively mobile or transitory, such as facial expression, and can vary during a performance from one moment to the next.

It is sometimes convenient to divide the stimuli which make up personal front into "appearance" and "manner," according to the function performed by the information that these stimuli convey. "Appearance" may be taken to refer to those stimuli which function at the time to tell us of the performer's social statuses. These stimuli also tell us of the individual's temporary ritual state, that is, whether he is engaging in formal social activity, work, or informal recreation, whether or not he is celebrating a new phase in the season cycle or in his life-cycle. "Manner" may be taken to refer to those stimuli which function at the time to warn us of the interaction role the performer will expect to play

in the oncoming situation. Thus a haughty, aggressive manner may give the impression that the performer expects to be the one who will initiate the verbal interaction and direct its course. A meek, apologetic manner may give the impression that the performer expects to follow the lead of others, or at least that he can be led to do so. . . .

In order to explore more fully the relations among the several parts of social front, it will be convenient to consider here a significant characteristic of the information conveyed by front, namely, its abstractness and generality.

However specialized and unique a routine is, its social front, with certain exceptions will tend to claim facts that can be equally claimed and asserted of other, somewhat different routines. For example many service occupations offer their clients a performance that is illuminated with dramatic expressions of cleanliness, modernity, competence, and integrity. While in fact these abstract standards have a different significance in different occupational performances the observer is encouraged to stress the abstract similarities. For the observer this is a wonderful, though sometime disastrous, convenience. Instead of having to maintain a different pattern of expectation and responsive treatment for each slightly different performer and performance he can place the situation in a broad category around which it is easy for him to mobilize his past experience and stereo-typical thinking. Observers then need only be familiar with a small and hence manageable vocabulary of fronts, and know how to respond to them, in order to orient themselves in a wide variety of situations. . . .

In addition to the fact that different routines may employ the same front, it is to be noted that a given social front tends to become institutionalized in terms of the abstract stereotyped expectations to which it gives rise, and tends to take on a meaning and stability apart from the specific tasks which happen at the time to be performed in its name. The front becomes a "collective representation" and a fact in its own right.

When an actor takes on an established social role, usually he finds that a particular front has already been established for it. Whether his acquisition of the role was primarily motivated by a desire to perform the given task or by a desire to maintain the corresponding front, the actor will find that he must do both.

Further, if the individual takes on a task that is not only new to him but also unestablished in the society, or if he attempts to change the light in which his task is viewed, he is likely to find that there are already several well-established fronts among which he must choose. Thus, when a task is given a new front we seldom find that the front it is given is itself new. . . .

Reality and Contrivance

In our own Anglo-American culture there seems to be two common-sense models according to which we formulate our conceptions of behavior: the real, sincere, or honest performance; and the false one that thorough fabricators assemble for us, whether meant to be taken unseriously, as in the work of stage actors, or seriously, as in the work of confidence men. We tend to see real performances as something not purposely put together at all, being an unintentional product of the individual's unselfconscious response to the facts in his situation. And contrived performances we tend to see as something painstakingly pasted together, one false item on another, since there is no reality to which the items of behavior could be a direct response. It will be necessary to see now that these dichotomous conceptions are by way of being the ideology of honest performers, providing strength to the show they put on, but a poor analysis of it.

First, let it be said that there are many individuals who sincerely believe that the definition of the situation they habitually project is the real reality. In this report I do not mean to question their proportion in the population but rather the structural relation of their sincerity to the performances they offer. If a performance is to come off, the witnesses by and large must be able to believe that the performers are sincere. This is the structural place of sincerity in the drama of events. Performers may be sincere—or be insincere but sincerely convinced of their own sincerity—but this kind of affection for one's part is not necessary for its convincing performance. There are not many French cooks who are really Russian spies, and

perhaps there are not many women who play the part of wife to one man and mistress to another but these duplicities do occur, often being sustained successfully for long periods of time. This suggests that while persons usually are what they appear to be, such appearances could still have been managed. There is, then, a statistical relation between appearances and reality, not an intrinsic or necessary one. In fact, given the unanticipated threats that play upon a performance, and given the need . . . to maintain solidarity with one's fellow performers and some distance from the witnesses, we find that a rigid incapacity to depart from one's inward view of reality may at times endanger one's performance. Some performances are carried off successfully with complete dishonesty, others with complete honesty; but for performances in general neither of these extremes is essential and neither, perhaps, is dramaturgically advisable.

The implication here is that an honest, sincere, serious performance is less firmly connected with the solid world than one might first assume. And this implication will be strengthened if we look again at the distance usually placed between quite honest performances and quite contrived ones. In this connection take, for example, the remarkable phenomenon of stage acting. It does take deep skill, long training, and psychological capacity to become a good stage actor. But this fact should not blind us to another one: that almost anyone can quickly learn a script well enough to give a charitable audience some sense of realness in what is being contrived before them. And it seems this is so because ordinary social intercourse is itself put together as a scene is put together, by the exchange of dramatically inflated actions, counteractions, and terminating replies. Scripts even in the hands of unpracticed players can come to life because life itself is a dramatically enacted thing. All the world is not, of course, a stage, but the crucial ways in which it isn't are not easy to specify. . . .

When the individual does move into a new position in society and obtains a new part to perform, he is not likely to be told in full detail how to conduct himself, nor will the facts of his new situation press sufficiently on him from the start to determine his conduct without his further giving thought to it. Ordinarily he will be given only a few cues, hints, and stage directions, and it will be assumed that he already has in his repertoire a large number of bits and pieces of performances that will be required in the new setting. The individual will already have a fair idea of what modesty, deference, or righteous indignation looks like, and can make a pass at playing these bits when necessary. He may even be able to play out the part of a hypnotic subject or commit a "compulsive" crime on the basis of models for these activities that he is already familiar with.

A theatrical performance or a staged confidence game requires a thorough scripting of the spoken content of the routine; but the vast part involving "expression given off" is often determined by meager stage directions. It is expected that the performer of illusions will already know a good deal about how to manage his voice, his face, and his body, although he—as well as any person who directs him—may find it difficult indeed to provide a detailed verbal statement of this kind of knowledge. And in this, of course, we approach the situation of the straightforward man in the street. Socialization may not so much involve a learning of the many specific details of a single concrete part—often there could not be enough time or energy for this. What does seem to be required of the individual is that he learn enough pieces of expression to be able to "fill in" and manage, more or less, any part that he is likely to be given. The legitimate performances of everyday life are not "acted" or "put on" in the sense that the performer knows in advance just what he is going to do, and does this solely because of the effect it is likely to have. The expressions it is felt he is giving off will be especially "inaccessible" to him. But as in the case of less legitimate performers, the incapacity of the ordinary individual to formulate in advance the movements of his eyes and body does not mean that he will not express himself through these devices in a way that is dramatized and preformed in his repertoire of actions. In short, we all act better than we know how. . . .

[W]hen we observe a young American middle-class girl playing dumb for the benefit of her boy friend, we are ready to point to items of guile and contrivance in her behavior. But like herself and her boy friend, we accept as an unperformed fact that this performer *is* a young American middle-class girl. But surely here we neglect the greater part of the performance. It is commonplace to say that different social groupings express in different ways such attributes as age, sex, territory, and class status, and that in each case these bare attributes are elaborated by means of a distinctive complex cultural configuration of proper ways of conducting oneself. To *be* a given kind of person, then, is not merely to possess the required attributes, but also to sustain the standards of conduct and appearance that one's social grouping attaches thereto. The unthinking ease with which performers consistently carry off such standard-maintaining routines does not deny that a performance has occurred, merely that the participants have been aware of it.

A status, a position, a social place is not a material thing, to be possessed and then displayed; it is a pattern of appropriate conduct, coherent, embellished, and well articulated. Performed with ease or clumsiness, awareness or not, guile or good faith, it is none the less something that must be enacted and portrayed, something that must be realized. . . .

CONCLUSION

The Role of Expression Is Conveying Impressions of Self

Underlying all social interaction there seems to be a fundamental dialectic. When one individual enters the presence of others, he will want to discover the facts of the situation. Were he to possess this information, he could know, and make allowances for, what will come to happen and he could give the others present as much of their due as is consistent with his enlightened self-interest. To uncover fully the factual nature of the situation, it would be necessary for the individual to know all the relevant social data about the others. It would also be necessary for the individual to know the actual outcome or end product of the activity of the others during the interaction, as well as their innermost feelings concerning him. Full information of this order is rarely available; in its absence, the individual tends to employ substitutes—cues, tests, hints, expressive gestures, status symbols, etc.—as predictive devices. In short, since the reality that the individual is concerned with is unperceivable at the moment, appearances must be relied upon in its stead. And, paradoxically, the more the individual is concerned with the reality that is not available to perception, the more must he concentrate his attention on appearances.

The individual tends to treat the others present on the basis of the impression they give now about the past and the future. It is here that communicative acts are translated into moral ones. The impressions that the others give tend to be treated as claims and promises they have implicitly made, and claims and promises tend to have a moral character. In his mind the individual says: "I am using these impressions of you as a way of checking up on you and your activity, and you ought not to lead me astray." The peculiar thing about this is that the individual tends to take this stand even though he expects the others to be unconscious of many of their expressive behaviors and even though he may expect to exploit the others on the basis of the information he gleans about them. Since the sources of impression used by the observing individual involve a multitude of standards pertaining to politeness and decorum, pertaining both to social intercourse and task-performance, we can appreciate afresh how daily life is enmeshed in moral lines of discrimination.

Let us shift now to the point of view of the others. If they are to be gentlemanly, and play the individual's game, they will give little conscious heed to the fact that impressions are being formed about them but rather act without guile or contrivance, enabling the individual to receive valid impressions about them and their efforts. And if they happen to give thought to the fact that they are being observed, they will not allow this to influence them unduly, content in the belief that the individual will obtain a correct impression and give them their due because of it. Should they be concerned with influencing the treatment that the individual gives them, and this is properly to be expected, then a gentlemanly means will be available to them. They need only guide their action in the present so that its future consequences will be the kind that would lead a just individual to treat them now in a way they want to be treated; once this is done,

they have only to rely on the perceptiveness and justness of the individual who observes them.

Sometimes those who are observed do, of course, employ these proper means of influencing the way in which the observer treats them. But there is another way, a shorter and more efficient way, in which the observed can influence the observer. Instead of allowing an impression of their activity to arise as an incidental by-product of their activity, they can reorient their frame of reference and devote their efforts to the creation of desired impressions. Instead of attempting to achieve certain ends by acceptable means, they can attempt to achieve the impression that they are achieving certain ends by acceptable means. It is always possible to manipulate the impression the observer uses as a substitute for reality because a sign for the presence of a thing, not being that thing, can be employed in the absence of it. The observer's need to rely on representations of things itself creates the possibility of misrepresentation.

There are many sets of persons who feel they could not stay in business, whatever their business, if they limited themselves to the gentlemanly means of influencing the individual who observes them. At some point or other in the round of their activity they feel it is necessary to band together and directly manipulate the impression that they give. The observed become a performing team and the observers become the audience. Actions which appear to be done on objects become gestures addressed to the audience. The round of activity becomes dramatized.

We come now to the basic dialectic. In their capacity as performers, individuals will be concerned with maintaining the impression that they are living up to the many standards by which they and their products are judged. Because these standards are so numerous and so pervasive, the individuals who are performers dwell more than we might think in a moral world. But, *qua* performers, individuals are concerned not with the moral issue of realizing these standards, but with the amoral issue of engineering a convincing impression that these standards are being realized. Our activity, then, is largely concerned with moral matters, but as performers we do not have a moral concern with them. As performers we are merchants of morality. Our day is given over to intimate contact with the goods we display and our minds are filled with intimate understandings of them; but it may well be that the more attention we give to these goods, then the more distant we feel from them and from those who are believing enough to buy them. To use a different imagery, the very obligation and profitability of appearing always in a steady moral light, of being a socialized character, forces one to be the sort of person who is practiced in the ways of the stage.

Staging and the Self

The general notion that we make a presentation of ourselves to others is hardly novel; what ought to be stressed in conclusion is that the very structure of the self can be seen in terms of how we arrange for such performances in our Anglo-American society.

In this report, the individual was divided by implication into two basic parts: he was viewed as a *performer*, a harried fabricator of impressions involved in the all-too-human task of staging a performance; he was viewed as a *character*, a figure, typically a fine one, whose spirit, strength, and other sterling qualities the performance was designed to evoke. The attributes of a performer and the attributes of a character are of a different order, quite basically so, yet both sets have their meaning in terms of the show that must go on.

First, character. In our society the character one performs and one's self are somewhat equated, and this self-as-character is usually seen as something housed within the body of its possessor, especially the upper parts thereof, being a nodule, somehow, in the psychobiology of personality. I suggest that this view is an implied part of what we are all trying to present, but provides, just because of this, a bad analysis of the presentation. In this report the performed self was seen as some kind of image, usually creditable, which the individual on stage and in character effectively attempts to induce others to hold in regard to him. While this image is entertained *concerning* the individual, so that a self is imputed to him, this self itself does not derive from its possessor, but from the whole scene of his action, being generated by that attribute of local events which renders them interpretable by witnesses. A correctly staged and performed scene leads the audience to impute a self to a performed character, but this imputation—this self—is a *product* of a scene that comes off, and is not a *cause* of it. The self, then, as a performed character, is not an organic thing that has a specific location, whose fundamental fate is to be born, to mature, and to die; it is a dramatic effect arising diffusely from a scene that is presented, and the characteristic issue, the crucial concern, is whether it will be credited or discredited.

In analyzing the self then we are drawn from its possessor, from the person who will profit or lose most by it, for he and his body merely provide the peg on which something of collaborative manufacture will be hung for a time. And the means for producing and maintaining selves do not reside inside the peg; in fact these means are often bolted down in social establishments. There will be a back region with its tools for shaping the body, and a front region with its fixed props. There will be a team of persons whose activity on stage in conjunction with available props will constitute the scene from which the performed character's self will emerge, and another team, the audience, whose interpretive activity will be necessary for this emergence. The self is a product of all of these arrangements, and in all of its parts bears the marks of this genesis.

The whole machinery of self-production is cumbersome, of course, and sometimes breaks down, exposing its separate components: back region control; team collusion; audience tact; and so forth. But, well oiled, impressions will flow from it fast enough to put us in the grips of one of our types of reality—the performance will come off and the firm self accorded each performed character will appear to emanate intrinsically from its performer.

Let us turn now from the individual as character performed to the individual as performer. He has a capacity to learn, this being exercised in the task of training for a part. He is given to having fantasies and dreams, some that pleasurably unfold a triumphant performance, others full of anxiety and dread that nervously deal with vital discreditings in a public front region. He often manifests a gregarious desire for teammates and audiences, a tactful considerateness for their concerns; and he has a capacity for deeply felt shame, leading him to minimize the chances he takes of exposure.

These attributes of the individual *qua* performer are not merely a depicted effect of particular performances; they are psychobiological in nature, and yet they seem to arise out of intimate interaction with the contingencies of staging performances.

And now a final comment. In developing the conceptual framework employed in this report, some language of the stage was used. I spoke of performers and audiences; of routines and parts; of performances coming off or falling flat; of cues, stage settings and backstage; of dramaturgical needs, dramaturgical skills, and dramaturgical strategies. Now it should be admitted that this attempt to press a mere analogy so far was in part a rhetoric and a maneuver.

The claim that all the world's a stage is sufficiently commonplace for readers to be familiar with its limitations and tolerant of its presentation, knowing that at any time they will easily be able to demonstrate to themselves that it is not to be taken too seriously. An action staged in a theater is a relatively contrived illusion and an admitted one; unlike ordinary life, nothing real or actual can happen to the performed characters—although at another level of course something real and actual can happen to the reputation of performers *qua* professionals whose everyday job is to put on theatrical performances.

And so here the language and mask of the stage will be dropped. Scaffolds, after all, are to build other things with, and should be erected with an eye to taking them down. This report is not concerned with aspects of theater that creep into everyday life. It is concerned with the structure of social encounters—the structure of those entities in social life that come into being whenever persons enter one another's immediate physical presence. The key factor in this structure is the maintenance of a single definition of the situation, this definition having to be expressed, and this expression sustained in the face of a multitude of potential disruptions.

A character staged in a theater is not in some ways real, nor does it have the same kind of real consequences as does the thoroughly contrived character performed by a confidence man; but the *successful* staging of either of these types of false figures involves use of *real* techniques—the same techniques by which everyday persons sustain their real social situations. Those who conduct face to face interaction on a theater's stage must meet the key requirement of real situations; they must expressively sustain a definition of the situation: but this they do in circumstances that have facilitated their developing an apt terminology for the interactional tasks that all of us share.

Introduction to "The Nature of Deference and Demeanor"

Goffman's focus in this work is on the ritual dimensions of social interaction. Evincing the influence of Durkheim, he explores the role of ceremonial shows of deference and demeanor in shaping the structure of encounters and in symbolically affirming the sacred status of all those present. Thus, the ritual code of behavior not only structures well-demeaned displays of deference, it also forms the basis for the production of the self.

The ceremonial rules to which Goffman speaks in this selection are more commonly described as manners or rules of etiquette. In his hands, however, the perfunctory acts through which politeness is expressed are seen in an entirely new light. The greetings and salutations we offer others, the disclosure or concealment of personal information, the tactful "nonobservance" we display in response to another's gaffe, the closing or granting of physical space we afford others, and countless other acts, if carried out properly, all serve as ceremonial indulgences that mark an individual as a well-demeaned person and thus deserving of the deference only others can provide him. We rely on such "avoidance" and "presentational" rituals to steer our way through the potentially hazardous conditions that always lurk beneath the surface of an encounter. For much of interaction is guided by an attempt to avoid embarrassment and the discrediting of one another's self as an object worthy of receiving deference. In a way, interaction is like driving a car. In both, the object is to get where you want to be without having an accident.

❖

The Nature of Deference and Demeanor (1956)

Erving Goffman

Under the influence of Durkheim and Radcliffe-Brown, some students of modern society have learned to look for the symbolic meaning of any given social practice and for the contribution of the practice to the integrity and solidarity of the group that employs it. However, in directing their attention away from the individual to the group, these students seem to have neglected a theme that is presented in Durkheim's chapter on the soul.[i] There he suggests that the individual's personality can be seen as one apportionment of the collective *mana*, and that (as he implies in later chapters), the rites performed to representations of the social collectivity will sometimes be performed to the individual himself.

In this paper I want to explore some of the senses in which the person in our urban secular world is allotted a kind of sacredness that is displayed and confirmed by symbolic acts. An attempt will be made to build a conceptual scaffold by stretching and twisting some common anthropological terms. This will be used to support two concepts which I think are central to this area: deference and demeanor. Through these reformulations I will try to show that a version of Durkheim's social psychology can be effective in modern dress.

Data for the paper are drawn chiefly from a brief observational study of mental patients in a modern research hospital. I use these data on the assumption that a logical place to learn about personal properties is among persons who have been locked up for spectacularly failing to maintain them. Their infractions of propriety occur in the confines of a ward, but the rules broken are quite general ones, leading us outward from the ward to a general study of our Anglo-American society.

INTRODUCTION

A rule of conduct may be defined as a guide for action, recommended not because it is pleasant, cheap, or effective, but because it is suitable or just. . . . Attachment to rules leads to a constancy and patterning of behavior; while this is not the only source of regularity in human affairs it is certainly an important one. Of course, approved guides to conduct tend to be covertly broken, side-stepped, or followed for unapproved reasons, but these alternatives merely add to the occasions in which rules constrain at least the surface of conduct.

Rules of conduct impinge upon the individual in two general ways: directly, as *obligations*, establishing how he is morally constrained to conduct himself; indirectly, as *expectations*,

SOURCE: From Erving Goffman, "The Nature of Deference and Demeanor," *American Anthropologist 58* (3): 473–499, 1956.

[i]Émile Durkheim, *The Elementary Forms of the Religious Life*, tr. J. W. Swain (Free Press, Glencoe, Ill., 1954), pp. 240–72.

establishing how others are morally bound to act in regard to him. A nurse, for example, has an obligation to follow medical orders in regard to her patients; she has the expectation, on the other hand, that her patients will pliantly co-operate in allowing her to perform these actions upon them. This pliancy, in turn, can be seen as an obligation of the patients in regard to their nurse, and points up the interpersonal, actor-recipient character of many rules: what is one man's obligation will often be another's expectation. . . .

When an individual becomes involved in the maintenance of a rule, he tends also to become committed to a particular image of self. In the case of his obligations, he becomes to himself and others the sort of person who follows this particular rule, the sort of person who would naturally be expected to do so. In the case of his expectations, he becomes dependent upon the assumption that others will properly perform such of their obligations as affect him, for their treatment of him will express a conception of him. In establishing himself as the sort of person who treats others in a particular way and is treated by them in a particular way, he must make sure that it will be possible for him to act and be this kind of person. For example, with certain psychiatrists there seems to be a point where the obligation of giving psychotherapy to patients, *their* patients, is transformed into something they must do if they are to retain the image they have come to have of themselves. The effect of this transformation can be seen in the squirming some of them may do in the early phases of their careers when they may find themselves employed to do research, or administer a ward, or give therapy to those who would rather be left alone.

In general then, when a rule of conduct is broken we find that two individuals run the risk of becoming discredited: one with an obligation, who should have governed himself by the rule; the other with an expectation, who should have been treated in a particular way because of this governance. Both actor and recipient are threatened.

An act that is subject to a rule of conduct is, then, a communication, for it represents a way in which selves are confirmed—both the self for which the rule is an obligation and the self for which it is an expectation. An act that is subject to rules of conduct but does not conform to them is also a communication—often even more

so—for infractions make news and often in such a way as to disconfirm the selves of the participants. Thus rules of conduct transform both action and inaction into expression, and whether the individual abides by the rules or breaks them, something significant is likely to be communicated. For example, in the wards under study, each research psychiatrist tended to expect his patients to come regularly for their therapeutic hours. When patients fulfilled this obligation, they showed that they appreciated their need for treatment and that their psychiatrist was the sort of person who could establish a "good relation" with patients. When a patient declined to attend his therapeutic hour, others on the ward tended to feel that he was "too sick" to know what was good for him, and that perhaps his psychiatrist was not the sort of person who was good at establishing relationships. Whether patients did or did not attend their hours, something of importance about them and their psychiatrist tended to be communicated to the staff and to other patients on the ward. . . .

In dealing with rules of conduct it is convenient to distinguish two classes, symmetrical and asymmetrical. A symmetrical rule is one which leads an individual to have obligations or expectations regarding others that these others have in regard to him. For example, in the two hospital wards, as in most other places in our society, there was an understanding that each individual was not to steal from any other individual, regardless of their respective statuses, and that each individual could similarly expect not to be stolen from by anyone. What we call common courtesies and rules of public order tend to be symmetrical, as are such biblical admonitions as the rule about not coveting one's neighbor's wife. An asymmetrical rule is one that leads others to treat and be treated by an individual differently from the way he treats and is treated by them. For example, doctors give medical orders to nurses, but nurses do not give medical orders to doctors. Similarly, in some hospitals in America nurses stand up when a doctor enters the room, but doctors do not ordinarily stand up when a nurse enters the room.

Students of society have distinguished in several ways among types of rules, as for example, between formal and informal rules; for this paper, however, the important distinction is that between substance and ceremony. A substantive rule is one which guides conduct in regard to matters felt to have significance in their own right, apart from what the infraction or maintenance of the rule expresses about the selves of the persons involved. Thus, when an individual refrains from stealing from others, he upholds a substantive rule which primarily serves to protect the property of these others and only incidentally functions to protect the image they have of themselves as persons with proprietary rights. The expressive implications of substantive rules are officially considered to be secondary; this appearance must be maintained, even though in some special situations everyone may sense that the participants were primarily concerned with expression.

A ceremonial rule is one which guides conduct in matters felt to have secondary or even no significance in their own right, having their primary importance—officially anyway—as a conventionalized means of communication by which the individual expresses his character or conveys his appreciation of the other participants in the situation.[ii] This usage departs from the everyday one, where "ceremony" tends to imply a highly specified, extended sequence of symbolic action performed by august actors on solemn occasions when religious sentiments are likely to be invoked. . . .

The acts or events, that is, the sign-vehicles or tokens which carry ceremonial messages, are remarkably various in character. They may be linguistic, as when an individual makes a statement of praise or depreciation regarding self or other, and does so in a particular language and intonation; gestural, as when the physical bearing of an individual conveys insolence or obsequiousness; spatial, as when an individual precedes another through the door, or sits on his right instead of his left; task-embedded, as when an individual accepts a task graciously and performs it in the presence of others with aplomb and dexterity; part of the communication structure, as when an individual speaks more frequently than the others, or receives more attentiveness than they do. The important point is that ceremonial activity, like substantive activity, is an analytical element referring to a component or function of action, not to concrete empirical action itself. While some activity that has a ceremonial component does not seem to have an appreciable substantive one, we find that all activity that is primarily substantive in significance will nevertheless carry some ceremonial meaning, provided that its performance is perceived in some way by others. The manner in which the activity is performed, or the momentary interruptions that are allowed so as to exchange minor niceties, will infuse the instrumentally-oriented situation with ceremonial significance. . . .

Ceremonial activity seems to contain certain basic components. As suggested, a main object of this paper will be to delineate two of these components, deference and demeanor, and to clarify the distinction between them.

DEFERENCE

By deference I shall refer to that component of activity which functions as a symbolic means by which appreciation is regularly conveyed to a recipient of this recipient, or of something of which this recipient is taken as a symbol, extension, or agent. These marks of devotion represent ways in which an actor celebrates and confirms his relation to a recipient. In some cases, both actor and recipient may not really be individuals at all, as when two ships greet each other with four short whistle blasts when passing. In some

---

[ii]While the substantive value of ceremonial acts is felt to be quite secondary it may yet be quite appreciable. Wedding gifts in American society provide an example. It is even possible to say in some cases that if a sentiment of a given kind is to be conveyed ceremonially it will be necessary to employ a sign-vehicle which has a given amount of substantive value. Thus in the American lower-middle class, it is understood that a small investment in an engagement ring, as such investments go, may mean that the man places a small value on his fiancee as these things go, even though no one may believe that women and rings are commensurate things. In those cases where it becomes too clear that the substantive value of a ceremonial act is the only concern of the participants, as when a girl or an official receives a substantial gift from someone not interested in proper relations, then the community may respond with a feeling that their symbol system has been abused.

cases, the actor is an individual but the recipient is some object or idol, as when a sailor salutes the quarterdeck upon boarding ship, or when a Catholic genuflects to the altar. I shall only be concerned, however, with the kind of deference that occurs when both actor and recipient are individuals, whether or not they are acting on behalf of something other than themselves. Such ceremonial activity is perhaps seen most clearly in the little salutations, compliments, and apologies which punctuate social intercourse, and may be referred to as "status rituals" or "interpersonal rituals." I use the term "ritual" because this activity, however informal and secular, represents a way in which the individual must guard and design the symbolic implications of his acts while in the immediate presence of an object that has a special value for him. . . .

The individual may desire, earn, and deserve deference, but by and large he is not allowed to give it to himself, being forced to seek it from others. In seeking it from others, he finds he has added reason for seeking them out, and in turn society is given added assurance that its members will enter into interaction and relationships with one another. If the individual could give himself the deference he desired there might be a tendency for society to disintegrate into islands inhabited by solitary cultish men, each in continuous worship at his own shrine.

The appreciation carried by an act of deference implies that the actor possesses a sentiment of regard for the recipient, often involving a general evaluation of the recipient. Regard is something the individual constantly has for others, and knows enough about to feign on occasion; yet in having regard for someone, the individual is unable to specify in detail what in fact he has in mind.

Those who render deference to an individual may feel, of course, that they are doing this merely because he is an instance of a category, or a representative of something, and that they are giving him his due not because of what they think of him "personally" but in spite of it. Some organizations, such as the military, explicitly stress this sort of rationale for according deference, leading to an impersonal bestowal of something that is specifically directed toward the person. By easily showing a regard that he does not have, the actor can feel that he is preserving a kind of inner autonomy, holding off the ceremonial order by the very act of upholding it. And of course in scrupulously observing the proper forms he may find that he is free to insinuate all kinds of disregard by carefully modifying intonation, pronunciation, pacing, and so forth. . . .

In addition to a sentiment of regard, acts of deference typically contain a kind of promise, expressing in truncated form the actor's avowal and pledge to treat the recipient in a particular way in the on-coming activity. The pledge affirms that the expectations and obligations of the recipient, both substantive and ceremonial, will be allowed and supported by the actor. Actors thus promise to maintain the conception of self that the recipient has built up from the rules he is involved in. (Perhaps the prototype here is the public act of allegiance by which a subject officially acknowledges his subservience in certain matters to his lord.) Deferential pledges are frequently conveyed through spoken terms of address involving status-identifiers, as when a nurse responds to a rebuke in the operating room with the phrase, "yes, Doctor," signifying by term of address and tone of voice that the criticism has been understood and that, however unpalatable, it has not caused her to rebel. When a putative recipient fails to receive anticipated acts of deference, or when an actor makes clear that he is giving homage with bad grace, the recipient may feel that the state of affairs which he has been taking for granted has become unstable, and that an insubordinate effort may be made by the actor to reallocate tasks, relations, and power. To elicit an established act of deference, even if the actor must first be reminded of his obligations and warned about the consequence of discourtesy, is evidence that if rebellion comes it will come slyly; to be pointedly refused an expected act of deference is often a way of being told that open insurrection has begun.

A further complication must be mentioned. A particular act of deference is something an actor, acting in a given capacity, owes a recipient, acting in a given capacity. But these two individuals are likely to be related to one another through more than one pair of capacities, and these additional relationships are likely to receive ceremonial expression too. Hence the same act of deference may show signs of different kinds of regard, as when a doctor by a paternal gesture shows authority over a nurse in her capacity as subordinate technician but affection for her as a young female who is dependent on him in his capacity as a supportive older male. Similarly, an attendant in cheerfully addressing a doctor as "doc" may sometimes show respect for the medical role and yet male-solidarity with the person who fills it. Throughout this paper we must therefore keep in mind that a spate of deferential behavior is not a single note expressing a single relationship between two individuals active in a single pair of capacities, but rather a medley of voices answering to the fact that actor and recipient are in many different relations to one another, no one of which can usually be given exclusive and continuous determinacy of ceremonial conduct. . . .

Deference can take many forms, of which I shall consider only two broad groupings, avoidance rituals and presentational rituals.

Avoidance rituals, as a term, may be employed to refer to those forms of deference which lead the actor to keep at a distance from the recipient and not violate what Simmel has called the "ideal sphere" that lies around the recipient:

> Although differing in size in various directions and differing according to the person with whom one entertains relations, this sphere cannot be penetrated, unless the personality value of the individual is thereby destroyed. A sphere of this sort is placed around man by his honor. Language poignantly designates an insult to one's honor as "coming to close;" the radius of this sphere marks, as it were, the distance whose trespassing by another person insults one's honor.[iii]

. . . Here, it should be said, is one of the important differences between social classes in our society: not only are some of the tokens different through which consideration for the privacy of others is expressed, but also, apparently, the higher the class the more extensive and elaborate are the taboos against contact. For example, in a study of a Shetlandic community the writer found that as one moves from middle-class urban centers in Britain to the rural lower-class islands, the distance between chairs at table decreases, so that in the outermost Shetland Islands actual bodily contact during meals and similar social occasions is not considered an invasion of separateness and no effort need be made to excuse it. And yet, whatever the rank of the participants in an action, the actor is likely to feel that the recipient has some warranted expectation of inviolability. . . .

There appear to be some typical relations between ceremonial distance and other kinds of sociological distance. Between status equals we may expect to find interaction guided by symmetrical familiarity. Between superordinate and subordinate we may expect to find asymmetrical relations, the superordinate having the right to exercise certain familiarities which the subordinate is not allowed to reciprocate. Thus, in the research hospital, doctors tended to call nurses by their first names, while nurses responded with "polite" or "formal" address. Similarly, in American business organizations the boss may thoughtfully ask the elevator man how his children are, but this entrance into another's life may be blocked to the elevator man, who can appreciate the concern but not return it. Perhaps the clearest form of this is found in the psychiatrist-patient relations, where the psychiatrist has a right to touch on aspects of the patient's life that the patient might not even allow himself to touch upon, while of course this privilege is not reciprocated. . . . Patients, especially mental ones, may not even have the right to question their doctor about his opinion of their own case; for one thing, this would bring them into too intimate a contact with an area of knowledge in which doctors invest their special apartness from the lay public which they serve. . . .

In general, it would seem, one avoids a person of high status out of deference to him and avoids a person of lower status than one's own out of a self-protective concern. Perhaps the social distance sometimes carefully maintained between equals may entail both kinds of avoidance on both their parts. In any case, the similarity in the two kinds of avoidance is not deep. . . . In addition, the distances an actor keeps out of deference to others decline when he rises in status, but the self-protective one's increase.

Avoidance rituals have been suggested as one main type of deference. A second type, termed *presentational rituals*, encompasses acts through

[iii]Simmel, Georg. *The Sociology of Georg Simmel*, trans. and ed. Kurt Wolff (Glencoe, Ill.: Free Press, 1950), p. 321.

which the individual makes specific attestations to recipients concerning how he regards them and how he will treat them in the on-coming interaction. Rules regarding these ritual practices involve specific prescriptions, not specific proscriptions; while avoidance rituals specify what is not to be done, presentational rituals specify what is to be done. Some illustrations may be taken from social life on Ward A as maintained by the group consisting of patients, attendants, and nurses. These presentational rituals will not, I think, be much different from those found in many other organizations in our society.

When members of the ward passed by each other, salutations would ordinarily be exchanged, the length of the salutation depending on the period that had elapsed since the salutation and the period that seemed likely before the next. At table, when someone left for the weekend, a farewell involving a pause in on-going activity and a brief exchange of words would be involved. In any case, there was the understanding that when members of the ward were in a physical position to enter into eye-to-eye contact of some kind, this contact would be effected. It seemed that anything less would not have shown proper respect for the state of relations that existed among the members of the ward.

Associated with salutations were practices regarding the "noticing" of any change in appearance, status, or repute, as if these changes represented a commitment on the part of the changed individual which had to be underwritten by the group. New clothes, new hairdos, occasions of being "dressed up" would call forth a round of compliments, whatever the group felt about the improvement. Similarly, any effort on the part of a patient to make something in the occupational therapy room or to perform in other ways was likely to be commended by others. Staff members who participated in the hospital amateur theatricals were complimented, and when one of the nurses was to be married, pictures of her fiancé and his family were viewed by all and approved. In these ways a member of the ward tended to be saved from the embarrassment of presenting himself to others as someone who had risen in value, while receiving a response as someone who had declined, or remained the same. . . .

Two main types of deference have been illustrated: presentational rituals through which the actor concretely depicts his appreciation of the recipient; and avoidance rituals, taking the form of proscriptions, interdictions, and taboos, which imply acts the actor must refrain from doing lest he violate the right of the recipient to keep him at a distance. We are familiar with this distinction from Durkheim's classification of ritual into positive and negative rites.[iv]

In suggesting that there are things that must be said and done to a recipient, and things that must not be said and done, it should be plain that there is an inherent opposition and conflict between these two forms of deference. To ask after an individual's health, his family's well-being, or the state of his affairs, is to present him with a sign of sympathetic concern; but in a certain way to make this presentation is to invade the individual's personal reserve, as will be made clear if an actor of wrong status asks him these questions, or if a recent event has made such a question painful to answer. As Durkheim suggested, "The human personality is a sacred thing; one dare not violate it nor infringe its bounds, while at the same time the greatest good is in communion with others."[v]

[iv]Durkheim, *The Elementary Forms*, p. 299.

[v]Émile Durkheim, "The Determination of Moral Facts," In *Sociology and* Philosophy, trans. D. F. Popcock, pp. 35-62. Glencoe, Ill., Free Press p. 37. Durkheim provides a fuller statement (1953:48):

"The sacred object inspires us, if not with fear, at least with respect that keeps us at a distance; at the same time it is an object of love and aspiration that we are drawn towards. Here then, is a dual sentiment which seems to be self-contradictory but does not for all that cease to be real. "The human personality presents a notable example of this apparent duality which we have just distinguished. On the one hand, it inspires us with a religious respect that keeps us at some distance. Any encroachment upon the legitimate sphere of action of our fellow beings we regard as sacrilege. It is, as it were, sacrosanct and thus set apart. But at the same time human personality is the outstanding object of our sympathy, and we endeavour to develop it."

... As an implication of this dilemma, we must see that social intercourse involves a constant dialectic between presentational rituals and avoidance rituals. A peculiar tension must be maintained, for those opposing requirements of conduct must somehow be held apart from one another and yet realized together in the same interaction: the gestures which carry an actor to a recipient must also signify that things will not be carried too far.

DEMEANOR

It was suggested that the ceremonial component of concrete behavior has at least two basic elements, deference and demeanor. Deference, defined as the appreciation an individual shows of another to that other, whether through avoidance rituals or presentational rituals, has been discussed and demeanor may now be considered.

By demeanor I shall refer to that element of the individual's ceremonial behavior typically conveyed through deportment, dress, and bearing, which serves to express to those in his immediate presence that he is a person of certain desirable or undesirable qualities. In our society, the "well" or "properly" demeaned individual displays such attributes as: discretion and sincerity; modesty in claims regarding self; sportsmanship; command of speech and physical movements; self-control over his emotions, his appetites, and his desires; poise under pressure; and so forth.

When we attempt to analyze the qualities conveyed through demeanor, certain themes become apparent. The well-demeaned individual possesses the attributes popularly associated with "character training" or "socialization," these being implanted when a neophyte of any kind is housebroken. Rightly or wrongly, others tend to use such qualities diagnostically, as evidence of what the actor is generally like at other times and as a performer of other activities. In addition, the properly demeaned individual is someone who has closed off many avenues of perception and penetration that others might take to him, and is therefore unlikely to be contaminated by them. Most importantly, perhaps, good demeanor is what is required of an actor if he is to be transformed into someone who can

be relied upon to maintain himself as an interactant, poised for communication, and to act so that others do not endanger themselves by presenting themselves as interactants to him.

It should be noted once again that demeanor involves attributes derived from interpretations others make of the way in which the individual handles himself during social intercourse. The individual cannot establish these attributes for his own by verbally avowing that he possesses them, though sometimes he may rashly try to do this. (He can, however, contrive to conduct himself in such a way that others, through their interpretation of his conduct, will impute the kinds of attributes to him he would like others to see in him.) In general, then, through demeanor the individual creates an image of himself, but properly speaking this is not an image that is meant for his own eyes. Of course this should not prevent us from seeing that the individual who acts with good demeanor may do so because he places an appreciable value upon himself, and that he who fails to demean himself properly may be accused of having "no self-respect" or of holding himself too cheaply in his own eyes. ...

Rules of demeanor, like rules of deference, can be symmetrical or asymmetrical. Between social equals, symmetrical rules of demeanor seem often to be prescribed. Between unequals many variations can be found. For example, at staff meetings on the psychiatric units of the hospital, medical doctors had the privilege of swearing, changing the topic of conversation, and sitting in undignified positions; attendants, on the other hand, had the right to attend staff meetings and to ask questions during them (in line with the milieu-therapy orientation of these research units) but were implicitly expected to conduct themselves with greater circumspection than was required of doctors. (This was pointed out by a perceptive occupational therapist who claimed she was always reminded that a mild young female psychiatrist was really an M.D. by the fact that this psychiatrist exercised these prerogatives of informal demeanor.) The extreme here perhaps is the master-servant relation as seen in cases where valets and maids are required to perform in a dignified manner services of an undignified kind. Similarly, doctors had the right to saunter into the nurses' station, lounge on the station's dispensing counter, and engage in joking with the nurses; other ranks participated in this informal interaction with doctors, but only after doctors had initiated it. . . .

DEFERENCE AND DEMEANOR

Deference and demeanor are analytical terms; empirically there is much overlapping of the activities to which they refer. An act through which the individual gives or withholds deference to others typically provides means by which he expresses the fact that he is a well or badly demeaned individual. Some aspects of this overlapping may be cited. First, in performing a given act of presentational deference, as in offering a guest a chair, the actor finds himself doing something that can be done with smoothness and aplomb, expressing self-control and poise, or with clumsiness and uncertainty, expressing an irresolute character. This is, as it were, an incidental and adventitious connection between deference and demeanor. It may be illustrated from recent material on doctor-patient relationships, where it is suggested that one complaint a doctor may have against some of his patients is that they do not bathe before coming for an examination; while bathing is a way of paying deference to the doctor it is at the same time a way for the patient to present himself as a clean, well demeaned person. A further illustration is found in acts such as loud talking, shouting, or singing, for these acts encroach upon the right of others to be let alone, while at the same time they illustrate a badly demeaned lack of control over one's feelings. . . .

A second connection between deference and demeanor turns upon the fact that a willingness to give others their deferential due is one of the qualities which the individual owes it to others to express through his conduct, just as a willingness to conduct oneself with good demeanor is in general a way of showing deference to those present.

In spite of these connections between deference and demeanor, the analytical relation between them is one of "complementarity," not identity. The image the individual owes to others to maintain of himself is not the same type of image these others are obliged to maintain of him. Deference images tend to point to the wider society outside the interaction, to the place the individual has achieved in the hierarchy of this society. Demeanor images tend to point to qualities which any social position gives its incumbents a chance to display during interaction, for these qualities pertain more to the way in which the individual handles his position than to the rank and place of that position relative to those possessed by others.

Further, the image of himself the individual owes it to others to maintain through his conduct is a kind of justification and compensation for the image of him that others are obliged to express through their deference to him. Each of the two images in fact may act as a guarantee and check upon the other. In an interchange that can be found in many cultures, the individual defers to guests to show how welcome they are and how highly he regards them; they in turn decline the offering at least once, showing through their demeanor that they are not presumptuous, immodest, or over-eager to receive favor. Similarly, a man starts to rise for a lady, showing respect for her sex; she interrupts and halts his gesture, showing she is not greedy of her rights in this capacity but is ready to define the situation as one between equals. In general, then, by treating others deferentially one gives them an opportunity to handle the indulgence with good demeanor. Through this differentiation in symbolizing function the world tends to be bathed in better images than anyone deserves, for it is practical to signify great appreciation of others by offering them deferential indulgences, knowing that some of these indulgences will be declined as an expression of good demeanor.

There are still other complementary relations between deference and demeanor. If an individual feels he ought to show proper demeanor in order to warrant deferential treatment, then he must be in a position to do so. He must, for example, be able to conceal from others aspects of himself which would make him unworthy in their eyes, and to conceal himself from them when he is in an indignified state, whether of dress, mind, posture, or action. The avoidance rituals which others perform in regard to him give him room to maneuver, enabling him to present only a self that is worthy of deference; at the same time, this avoidance makes it easier for them to assure themselves that the deference they have to show him is warranted.

To show the difference between deference and demeanor, I have pointed out the complementary relation between them, but even this kind of relatedness can be overstressed. The failure of an individual to show proper deference to others does not necessarily free them from the obligation to act with good demeanor in his presence, however disgruntled they may be at having to do this. Similarly, the failure of an individual to conduct himself with proper demeanor does not always relieve those in his presence from treating him with proper deference. It is by separating deference and demeanor that we can appreciate many things about ceremonial life, such as that a group may be noted for excellence in one of these areas while having a bad reputation in the other. . . .

We are to see, then, that there are many occasions when it would be improper for an individual to convey about himself what others are ready to convey about him to him, since each of these two images is a warrant and justification for the other, and not a mirror image of it. The Meadian notion that the individual takes toward himself the attitude others take to him seems very much an oversimplification. Rather the individual must rely on others to complete the picture of him of which he himself is allowed to paint only certain parts. Each individual is responsible for the demeanor image of himself and the deference image of others, so that for a complete man to be expressed, individuals must hold hands in a chain of ceremony, each giving deferentially with proper demeanor to the one on the right what will be received deferentially from the one on the left. While it may be true that the individual has a unique self all his own, evidence of this possession is thoroughly a product of joint ceremonial labor, the part expressed through the individual's demeanor being no more significant than the part conveyed by others through their deferential behavior toward him. . . .

CONCLUSIONS

The rules of conduct which bind the actor and the recipient together are the bindings of society. But many of the acts which are guided by these rules occur infrequently or take a long time for their consummation. Opportunities to affirm the moral order and the society could therefore be rare. It is here that ceremonial rules play their social function, for many of the acts which are guided by these rules last but a brief moment, involve no substantive outlay, and can be performed in every social interaction. Whatever the activity and however profanely instrumental, it can afford many opportunities for minor ceremonies as long as other persons are present. Through these observances, guided by ceremonial obligations and expectations, a constant flow of indulgences is spread through society, with others who are present constantly reminding the individual that he must keep himself together as a well demeaned person and affirm the sacred quality of these others. The gestures which we sometimes call empty are perhaps in fact the fullest things of all.

It is therefore important to see that the self is in part a ceremonial thing, a sacred object which must be treated with proper ritual care and in turn must be presented in a proper light to others. As a means through which this self is established, the individual acts with proper demeanor while in contact with others and is treated by others with deference. It is just as important to see that if the individual is to play this kind of sacred game, then the field must be suited to it. The environment must ensure that the individual will not pay too high a price for acting with good demeanor and that deference will be accorded him. Deference and demeanor practices must be institutionalized so that the individual will be able to project a viable, sacred self and stay in the game on a proper ritual basis.

An environment, then, in terms of the ceremonial component of activity, is a place where it is easy or difficult to play the ritual game of having a self. Where ceremonial practices are thoroughly institutionalized, as they were on Ward A, it would appear easy to be a person. Where these practices are not established, as to a degree they were not in Ward B, it would appear difficult to be a person. Why one ward comes to be a place in which it is easy to have a self and another ward comes to be a place where this is difficult depends in part on the type of patient that is recruited and the type of regime the staff attempts to maintain.

One of the bases upon which mental hospitals throughout the world segregate their patients is degree of easily apparent "mental illness." By and large this means that patients are graded according to the degree to which they violate ceremonial rules of social intercourse. There are very good practical reasons for sorting patients into different wards in this way, and in fact that institution is backward where no one bothers to do so. This grading very often means, however, that individuals who are desperately uncivil in some areas of behavior are placed in the intimate company of those who are desperately uncivil in others. Thus, individuals who are the least ready to project a sustainable self are lodged in a milieu where it is practically impossible to do so.

It is in this context that we can reconsider some interesting aspects of the effect of coercion and constraint upon the individual. If an individual is to act with proper demeanor and show proper deference, then it will be necessary for him to have areas of self-determination. He must have an expendable supply of the small indulgences which his society employs in its idiom of regard—such as cigarettes to give, chairs to proffer, food to provide, and so forth. He must have freedom of bodily movement so that it will be possible for him to assume a stance that conveys appropriate respect for others and appropriate demeanor on his own part; a patient strapped to a bed may find it impractical not to befoul himself, let alone to stand in the presence of a lady. He must have a supply of appropriate clean clothing if he is to make the sort of appearance that is expected of a well demeaned person. To look seemly may require a tie, a belt, shoe laces, a mirror, and razor blades—all of which the authorities may deem unwise to give him. He must have access to the eating utensils which his society defines as appropriate ones for use, and may find that meat cannot be circumspectly eaten with a cardboard spoon. And finally, without too much cost to himself he must be able to decline certain kinds of work, now sometimes classified as "industrial therapy," which his social group considers *infra dignitatem*.

When the individual is subject to extreme constraint he is automatically forced from the circle of the proper. The sign vehicles or physical tokens through which the customary ceremonies are performed are unavailable to him. Others may show ceremonial regard for him, but it becomes impossible for him to reciprocate the show or to act in such a way as to make himself worthy of receiving it. The only ceremonial statements that are possible for him are improper ones.

The history of the care of mental cases is the history of constricting devices: constraining gloves, camisoles, floor and seat chains, handcuffs, "biter's mask," wet-packs, supervised toileting, hosing down, institutional clothing, forkless and knifeless eating, and so forth. The use of these devices provides significant data on the ways in which the ceremonial grounds of selfhood can be taken away. By implication we can obtain information from this history about the conditions that must be satisfied if individuals are to have selves. . . .

Throughout this paper I have assumed we can learn about ceremony by studying a contemporary secular situation—that of the individual who has declined to employ the ceremonial idiom of his group in an acceptable manner and has been hospitalized. In a crosscultural view it is convenient to see this as a product of our complex division of labor which brings patients together instead of leaving each in his local circle. Further, this division of labor also brings together those who have the task of caring for these patients.

We are thus led to the special dilemma of the hospital worker: as a member of the wider society he ought to take action against mental patients, who have transgressed the rules of ceremonial order; but his occupational role obliges him to care for and protect these very people. When "milieu therapy" is stressed, these obligations further require him to convey warmth in response to hostility; relatedness in response to alienation. . . .

In summary, then, modern society brings transgressors of the ceremonial order to a single place, along with some ordinary members of society who make their living there. These dwell in a place of unholy acts and unholy understandings, yet some of them retain allegiance to the ceremonial order outside the hospital setting. Somehow ceremonial people must work out mechanisms and techniques for living without certain kinds of ceremony.

In this paper I have suggested that Durkheimian notions about primitive religion can be translated into concepts of deference and demeanor, and that these concepts help us to grasp some aspects of urban secular living. The implication is that in one sense this secular world is not so irreligious as we might think. Many gods have been done away with, but the individual himself stubbornly remains as a deity of considerable importance. He walks with some dignity and is the recipient of many little offerings. He is jealous of the worship due him, yet, approached in the right spirit, he is ready to forgive those who may have offended him. Because of their status relative to his, some persons will find him contaminating while others will find they contaminate him, in either case finding that they must treat him with ritual care. Perhaps the individual is so viable a god because he can actually understand the ceremonial significance of the way he is treated, and quite on his own can respond dramatically to what is proffered him. In contacts between such deities there is no need for middlemen; each of these gods is able to serve as his own priest.

Introduction to *Asylums*

In *Asylums*, Goffman again takes up the issue of the social sources of this self. However, in this study he reports on daily life as it transpires in mental hospitals and prisons. Yet his aim is not solely to understand how these specific establishments shape the self, but also to explore how such places shed light on the nature of the self as it is experienced in more ordinary, civilian settings.

Mental hospitals, prisons, monasteries, convents, the military, and boarding schools all have one thing in common: they are all total institutions. **Total institutions** are places of "residence and work where a large number of like-situated individuals, cut off from the wider society for an appreciable period of time, together lead an enclosed, formally administered round of life" (1961:xiii). It is here where "under one roof and according to one rational plan, all spheres of individuals' lives—sleeping, eating, playing, and working—are regulated" (Branaman 1997:lv). To one degree or another, inhabitants of such facilities are stripped of the freedoms and resources to manage their self-presentation that are normally provided by social arrangements. As a result, they are subjected to **mortifications of self**, processes of "killing off" the multiple selves possessed prior to one's entrance into the total institution and replacing them with one totalizing identity over which the person exercises little, if any, control. Here is the life of the prison inmate or military recruit: shaven head, dressed in institutional clothing, substitution of a number or insult for one's name, dispossessed of personal property, endless degradation, and complete loss of privacy over intimate information and matters of personal hygiene. All work together to construct a self radically different from the one that entered the establishment.

To counteract this profanation of self, inhabitants of total institutions engage in the types of practices we all do when we sense that our sacredness is threatened, only here they appear more extreme. Thus, when patients in a mental institution repeatedly bang a chair against the floor or smear their feces on the wall of the ward, their "recalcitrance" is less a symptom of their psychosis and more a sign of the conditions under which they are forced to live. Such actions serve the function of preserving one's self-autonomy, as do our calling in sick to work or devising (unconvincing) excuses for missing an exam in order to recuperate from a "festive" weekend, or the sarcastic enthusiasm we display in response to our boss's directives. The failure to cooperate with institutional demands that is expressed in each case is a "normal" attempt to preserve control over one's self. Each represents a **secondary adjustment** or a way "of taking leave of a place without moving from it" (1961:308). Secondary adjustments, then, are "ways in which the individual stands apart from the role and the self that were taken for granted for him by the institution" (ibid.:189). They are oppositional practices through which we refuse the "official" view of what we should be and thus distance ourselves from an organization.

Goffman's notion of secondary adjustments recalls the distinction he made in *The Presentation of Self in Everyday Life* between the "performer" and "character." While he arguably emphasized the "fictional" nature of the self in that work, here he contends that behind the performer's mask lies a solid, "stance-taking entity." Nevertheless, the self, contrary to the claims of psychologists and psychiatrists, is realized only in and through the social arrangements that alone create the conditions for its expression. And contrary to the claims of sociologists, the self is much more than a simple reflection of the groups to which it belongs:

> Without something to belong to, we have no stable self, and yet total commitment and attachment to any social unit implies a kind of selflessness. Our sense of being a person can come from being drawn into a wider social unit; our sense of selfhood can rise through the little ways we resist the pull. Our status is backed by the solid building of the world, while our sense of personal identity often resides in the cracks. (1961:320)[7]

---

[7]Georg Simmel (1858–1918), a German sociologist and philosopher whose ideas influenced the development of the Chicago School of symbolic interactionism, as well as Goffman's own perspective on the social order, made a similar observation half a century before. Commenting on the relationship between self and society, Simmel noted that while who you are as an individual is in an important sense defined and made possible by the groups to which you belong, preserving your individuality demands that your identity not be completely submerged into or engulfed by group membership. Otherwise, you have no self that you can call your own. Society, in his words, is:

> a structure which consists of beings who stand inside and outside of it at the same time. This fact forms the basis for one of the most important sociological phenomena, namely, that between a society and its component individuals a relation may exist as if between two parties. . . . [T]he individual can never stay within a unit which he does not at the same time stay outside of, that he is not incorporated into any order without also confronting it (1908:14, 15). (See also Edles and Appelrouth 2005, Chapter 6.)

Asylums (1961)

Erving Goffman

CHARACTERISTICS OF TOTAL INSTITUTIONS

I

A basic social arrangement in modern society is that the individual tends to sleep, play, and work in different places, with different co-participants, under different authorities, and without an over-all rational plan. The central feature of total institutions can be described as a breakdown of the barriers ordinarily separating these three spheres of life. First, all aspects of life are conducted in the same place and under the same single authority. Second, each phase of the member's daily activity is carried on in the immediate company of a large batch of others, all of whom are treated alike and required to do the same thing together. Third, all phases of the day's activities are tightly scheduled, with one activity leading at a prearranged time into the

---

next, the whole sequence of activities being imposed from above by a system of explicit formal rulings and a body of officials. Finally, the various enforced activities are brought together into a single rational plan purportedly designed to fulfill the official aims of the institution.

Individually, these features are found in places other than total institutions. For example, our large commercial, industrial, and educational establishments are increasingly providing cafeterias and free-time recreation for their members; use of these extended facilities remains voluntary in many particulars, however, and special care is taken to see that the ordinary line of authority does not extend to them. Similarly, housewives or farm families may have all their major spheres of life within the same fenced-in area, but these persons are not collectively regimented and do not march through the day's activities in the immediate company of a batch of similar others.

The handling of many human needs by the bureaucratic organization of whole blocks of people—whether or not this is a necessary or effective means of social organization in the circumstances—is the key fact of total institutions. From this follow certain important implications.

When persons are moved in blocks, they can be supervised by personnel whose chief activity is not guidance or periodic inspection (as in many employer-employee relations) but rather surveillance—a seeing to it that everyone does what he has been clearly told is required of him, under conditions where one person's infraction is likely to stand out in relief against the visible, constantly examined compliance of the others. Which comes first, the large blocks of managed people, or the small supervisory staff, is not here at issue; the point is that each is made for the other.

In total institutions there is a basic split between a large managed group, conveniently called inmates, and a small supervisory staff. Inmates typically live in the institution and have restricted contact with the world outside the walls; staff often operate on an eight-hour day and are socially integrated into the outside world. Each grouping tends to conceive of the other in terms of narrow hostile stereotypes, staff often seeing inmates as bitter, secretive,

and untrustworthy, while inmates often see staff as condescending, highhanded, and mean. Staff tends to feel superior and righteous; inmates tend, in some ways at least, to feel inferior, weak, blameworthy, and guilty.

Social mobility between the two strata is grossly restricted; social distance is typically great and often formally prescribed. Even talk across the boundaries may be conducted in a special tone of voice.... Just as talk across the boundary is restricted, so, too, is the passage of information, especially information about the staff's plans for inmates. Characteristically, the inmate is excluded from knowledge of the decisions taken regarding his fate. Whether the official grounds are military, as in concealing travel destination from enlisted men, or medical, as in concealing diagnosis, plan of treatment, and approximate length of stay from tuberculosis patients, such exclusion gives staff a special basis of distance from and control over inmates....

The total institution is a social hybrid, part residential community, part formal organization; therein lies its special sociological interest. There are other reasons for being interested in these establishments, too. In our society, they are the forcing houses for changing persons; each is a natural experiment on what can be done to the self.

II

The recruit comes into the establishment with a conception of himself made possible by certain stable social arrangements in his home world. Upon entrance, he is immediately stripped of the support provided by these arrangements. In the accurate language of some of our oldest total institutions, he begins a series of abasements, degradations, humiliations, and profanations of self. His self is systematically, if often unintentionally, mortified. He begins some radical shifts in his *moral career*, a career composed of the progressive changes that occur in the beliefs that he has concerning himself and significant others.

The processes by which a person's self is mortified are fairly standard in total institutions;[i] analysis of these processes can help us to see the arrangements that ordinary establishments

[i]An example of the description of these processes may be found in Gresham M. Sykes, *The Society of Captives* (Princeton: Princeton University Press, 1958), ch. iv, "The Pains of Imprisonment," pp. 63–83.

must guarantee if members are to preserve their civilian selves.

The barrier that total institutions place between the inmate and the wider world marks the first curtailment of self. In civil life, the sequential scheduling of the individual's roles, both in the life cycle and in the repeated daily round, ensures that no one role he plays will block his performance and ties in another. In total institutions, in contrast, membership automatically disrupts role scheduling, since the inmate's separation from the wider world lasts around the clock and may continue for years. Role dispossession therefore occurs. In many total institutions the privilege of having visitors or of visiting away from the establishment is completely withheld at first, ensuring a deep initial break with past roles and an appreciation of role dispossession. A report on cadet life in a military academy provides an illustration:

> This clean break with the past must be achieved in a relatively short period. For two months, therefore, the swab is not allowed to leave the base or to engage in social intercourse with non-cadets. This complete isolation helps to produce a unified group of swabs, rather than a heterogeneous collection of persons of high and low status. Uniforms are issued on the first day, and discussions of wealth and family background are taboo. Although the pay of the cadet is very low, he is not permitted to receive money from home. The role of the cadet must supersede other roles the individual has been accustomed to play. There are few clues left which will reveal social status in the outside world.[ii]

I might add that when entrance is voluntary, the recruit has already partially withdrawn from his home world; what is cleanly severed by the institution is something that had already started to decay. . . .

The inmate, then, finds certain roles are lost to him by virtue of the barrier that separates him from the outside world. The process of entrance typically brings other kinds of loss and mortification as well. We very generally find staff employing what are called admission procedures, such as taking a life history, photographing, weighing, fingerprinting, assigning numbers, searching, listing personal possessions for storage, undressing, bathing, disinfecting, haircutting, issuing institutional clothing, instructing as to rules, and assigning to quarters. Admission procedures might better be called "trimming" or "programming" because in thus being squared away the new arrival allows himself to be shaped and coded into an object that can be fed into the administrative machinery of the establishment, to be worked on smoothly by routine operations. Many of these procedures depend upon attributes such as weight or fingerprints that the individual possesses merely because he is a member of the largest and most abstract of social categories, that of human being. Action taken on the basis of such attributes necessarily ignores most of his previous bases of self-identification. . . .

The admission procedure can be characterized as a leaving off and a taking on, with the midpoint marked by physical nakedness. Leaving off of course entails a dispossession of property, important because persons invest self feelings in their possessions. Perhaps the most significant of these possessions is not physical at all, one's full name; whatever one is thereafter called, loss of one's name can be a great curtailment of the self.

Once the inmate is stripped of his possessions, at least some replacements must be made by the establishment, but these take the form of standard issue, uniform in character and uniformly distributed. These substitute possessions are clearly marked as really belonging to the institution and in some cases are recalled at regular intervals to be, as it were, disinfected of identifications. With objects that can be used up—for example, pencils—the inmate may be required to return the remnants before obtaining a reissue. Failure to provide inmates with individual lockers and periodic searches and confiscations of accumulated personal property reinforce property dispossession. Religious orders have appreciated the implications for self of such separation from belongings. Inmates may be required to change their cells once a year so as not to become attached to them. . . .

[ii]Sanford M. Dornbusch, "The Military Academy as an Assimilating Institution," *Social Forces*, XXXIII (1955), p. 317.

One set of the individual's possessions has a special relation to self. The individual ordinarily expects to exert some control over the guise in which he appears before others. For this he needs cosmetic and clothing supplies, tools for applying, arranging, and repairing them, and an accessible, secure place to store these supplies and tools—in short, the individual will need an "identity kit" for the management of his personal front. He will also need access to decoration specialists such as barbers and clothiers.

On admission to a total institution, however, the individual is likely to be stripped of his usual appearance and of the equipment and services by which he maintains it, thus suffering a personal defacement. Clothing, combs, needle and thread, cosmetics, towels, soap, shaving sets, bathing facilities—all these may be taken away or denied him, although some may be kept in inaccessible storage, to be returned if and when he leaves. In the words of St. Benedict's Holy Rule:

> Then forthwith he shall, there in the oratory, be divested of his own garments with which he is clothed and be clad in those of the monastery. Those garments of which he is divested shall be placed in the wardrobe, there to be kept, so that if, perchance, he should ever be persuaded by the devil to leave the monastery (which God forbid), he may be stripped of the monastic habit and cast forth.[iii]

. . . At admission, loss of identity equipment can prevent the individual from presenting his usual image of himself to others. After admission, the image of himself he presents is attacked in another way. Given the expressive idiom of a particular civil society, certain movements, postures, and stances will convey lowly images of the individual and be avoided as demeaning. Any regulation, command, or task that forces the individual to adopt these movements or postures may mortify his self. In total institutions, such physical indignities abound. In mental hospitals, for example, patients may be forced to eat all food with a spoon. In military

prisons, inmates may be required to stand at attention whenever an officer enters the compound. In religious institutions, there are such classic gestures of penance as the kissing of feet, and the posture recommended to an erring monk that he

> . . . lie prostrate at the door of the oratory in silence; and thus, with his face to the ground and his body prone, let him cast himself at the feet of all as they go forth from the oratory.[iv]

In some penal institutions we find the humiliation of bending over to receive a birching.

Just as the individual can be required to hold his body in a humiliating pose, so he may have to provide humiliating verbal responses. An important instance of this is the forced deference pattern of total institutions; inmates are often required to punctuate their social interaction with staff by verbal acts of deference, such as saying "sir." Another instance is the necessity to beg, importune, or humbly ask for little things such as a light for a cigarette, a drink of water, or permission to use the telephone.

Corresponding to the indignities of speech and action required of the inmate are the indignities of treatment others accord him. The standard examples here are verbal or gestural profanations: staff or fellow inmates call the individual obscene names, curse him, point out his negative attributes, tease him, or talk about him or his fellow inmates as if he were not present.

Whatever the form or the source of these various indignities, the individual has to engage in activity whose symbolic implications are incompatible with his conception of self. A more diffuse example of this kind of mortification occurs when the individual is required to undertake a daily round of life that he considers alien to him—to take on a disidentifying role. In prisons, denial of heterosexual opportunities can induce fear of losing one's masculinity. In military establishments, the patently useless make-work forced on fatigue details can make men feel their time and effort are worthless. In religious institutions

---

[iii]*The Holy Rule of Saint Benedict*, Ch. 58.

[iv]*The Holy Rule of Saint Benedict*, Ch. 44.

there are special arrangements to ensure that all inmates take a turn performing the more menial aspects of the servant role. An extreme is the concentration-camp practice requiring prisoners to administer whippings to other prisoners.

There is another form of mortification in total institutions; beginning with admission a kind of contaminative exposure occurs. On the outside, the individual can hold objects of self-feeling—such as his body, his immediate actions, his thoughts, and some of his possessions—clear of contact with alien and contaminating things. But in total institutions these territories of the self are violated; the boundary that the individual places between his being and the environment is invaded and the embodiments of self profaned.

There is, first, a violation of one's informational preserve regarding self. During admission, facts about the inmate's social statuses and past behavior—especially discreditable facts—are collected and recorded in a dossier available to staff. Later, in so far as the establishment officially expects to alter the self-regulating inner tendencies of the inmate, there may be group or individual confession—psychiatric, political, military, or religious, according to the type of institution. On these occasions the inmate has to expose facts and feelings about self to new kinds of audiences. . . .

New audiences not only learn discreditable facts about oneself that are ordinarily concealed but are also in a position to perceive some of these facts directly. Prisoners and mental patients cannot prevent their visitors from seeing them in humiliating circumstances. Another example is the shoulder patch of ethnic identification worn by concentration-camp inmates. Medical and security examinations often expose the inmate physically, sometimes to persons of both sexes; a similar exposure follows from collective sleeping arrangements and door-less toilets. An extreme here, perhaps, is the situation of a self-destructive mental patient who is stripped naked for what is felt to be his own protection and placed in a constantly lit seclusion room, into whose Judas window any person passing on the ward can peer. In general, of course, the inmate is never fully alone; he is always within sight and often earshot of someone, if only his fellow inmates. Prison cages with bars for walls fully realize such exposure.

Perhaps the most obvious type of contaminative exposure is the directly physical kind—the besmearing and defiling of the body or of other objects closely identified with the self. Sometimes this involves a breakdown of the usual environmental arrangements for insulating oneself from one's own source of contamination, as in having to empty one's own slops or having to subject one's evacuation to regimentation. . . . A very common form of physical contamination is reflected in complaints about unclean food, messy quarters, soiled towels, shoes and clothing impregnated with previous users' sweat, toilets without seats, and dirty bath facilities. . . . Finally, in some total institutions the inmate is obliged to take oral or intravenous medications, whether desired or not, and to eat his food, however unpalatable. When an inmate refuses to eat, there may be forcible contamination of his innards by "forced feeding."

I have suggested that the inmate undergoes mortification of the self by contaminative exposure of a physical kind, but this must be amplified: when the agency of contamination is another human being, the inmate is in addition contaminated by forced interpersonal contact and, in consequence, a forced social relationship. (Similarly, when the inmate loses control over who observes him in his predicament or knows about his past, he is being contaminated by a forced relationship to these people—for it is through such perception and knowledge that relations are expressed.) . . .

THE MORAL CAREER OF THE MENTAL PATIENT

I

In general . . . mental hospitals systematically provide for circulation about each patient the kind of information that the patient is likely to try to hide. And in various degrees of detail this information is used daily to puncture his claims. At the admission and diagnostic conferences, he will be asked questions to which he must give wrong answers in order to maintain his self-respect, and then the true answer may be shot back at him. An attendant whom he tells a version of his past and his reason for being in the hospital may smile disbelievingly, or say, "That's not the way I heard it," in line with the practical psychiatry of bringing the patient down to reality. When he accosts a physician or nurse on the ward and presents his claims for more privileges or for discharge, this may be countered by a question which he cannot answer truthfully without calling up a time in his past when he acted disgracefully. When he gives his view of his situation during group psychother-apy, the therapist, taking the role of interrogator, may attempt to disabuse him of his face-saving interpretations and encourage an interpretation suggesting that it is he himself who is to blame and who must change. When he claims to staff or fellow patients that he is well and has never been really sick, someone may give him graphic details of how, only one month ago, he was prancing around like a girl, or claiming that he was God, or declining to talk or eat, or putting gum in his hair.

Each time the staff deflates the patient's claims, his sense of what a person ought to be and the rules of peer-group social intercourse press him to reconstruct his stories; and each time he does this, the custodial and psychiatric interests of the staff may lead them to discredit these tales again. . . .

Learning to live under conditions of immi-nent exposure and wide fluctuation in regard, with little control over the granting or withhold-ing of this regard, is an important step in the socialization of the patient, a step that tells something important about what it is like to be an inmate in a mental hospital. Having one's past mistakes and present progress under con-stant moral review seems to make for a special adaptation consisting of a less than moral atti-tude to ego ideals. One's shortcomings and suc-cesses become too central and fluctuating an issue in life to allow the usual commitment of concern for other persons' views of them. It is not very practicable to try to sustain solid claims about oneself. The inmate tends to learn that degradations and reconstructions of the self need not be given too much weight, at the same time learning that staff and inmates are ready to

view an inflation or deflation of a self with some indifference. He learns that a defensible picture of self can be seen as something outside oneself that can be constructed, lost, and rebuilt, all with great speed and some equanimity. He learns about the viability of taking up a standpoint—and hence a self—that is outside the one which the hospital can give and take away from him.

The setting, then, seems to engender a kind of cosmopolitan sophistication, a kind of civic apathy. In this unserious yet oddly exaggerated moral context, building up a self or having it destroyed becomes something of a shameless game, and learning to view this process as a game seems to make for some demoralization, the game being such a fundamental one. In the hospital, then, the inmate can learn that the self is not a fortress, but rather a small open city; he can become weary of having to show pleasure when held by troops of his own, and weary of having to show displeasure when held by the enemy. Once he learns what it is like to be defined by society as not having a viable self, this threatening definition—the threat that helps attach people to the self society accords them—is weakened. The patient seems to gain a new plateau when he learns that he can survive while acting in a way that society sees as destructive of him.

[An] . . . illustration of this moral loosen-ing and moral fatigue might be given. . . . On the worst ward level, discreditings seem to occur the most frequently, in part because of lack of facilities, in part through the mockery and sarcasm that seem to be the occupational norm of social control for the attendants and nurses who administer these places. At the same time, the paucity of equipment and rights means that not much self can be built up. The patient finds himself constantly toppled, therefore, but with very little distance to fall. A kind of jaunty gallows humor seems to develop in some of these wards, with considerable freedom to stand up to the staff and return insult for insult. While these patients can be punished, they cannot, for example, be easily slighted, for they are accorded as a matter of course few of the niceties that people must enjoy before they can suffer subtle abuse. Like prostitutes in connec-tion with sex, inmates on these wards have very little reputation or rights to lose and can therefore take certain liberties. As the person moves up the ward system, he can manage more and more to avoid incidents which discredit his claim to be a human being, and acquire more and more of the varied ingredients of self-respect; yet when eventually he does get toppled—and he does—there is a much farther distance to fall. For instance, the privileged patient lives in a world wider than the ward, containing recreation workers who, on request, can dole out cake, cards, table-tennis balls, tickets to the movies, and writing materials. But in the absence of the social control of payment which is typically exerted by a recipient on the outside, the patient runs the risk that even a warmhearted functionary may, on occasion, tell him to wait until she has finished an informal chat, or teasingly ask why he wants what he has asked for, or respond with a dead pause and a cold look of appraisal.

Moving up and down the ward system means, then, not only a shift in self-constructive equipment, a shift in reflected status, but also a change in the calculus of risks. Appreciation of risks to his self-conception is part of everyone's moral experience, but an appreciation that a given risk level is itself merely a social arrangement is a rarer kind of experience, and one that seems to help to disenchant the person who undergoes it. . . .

Each moral career, and behind this, each self, occurs within the confines of an institutional system, whether a social establishment such as a mental hospital or a complex of personal and professional relationships. The self, then, can be seen as something that resides in the arrangements prevailing in a social system for its members. The self in this sense is not a property of the person to whom it is attributed, but dwells rather in the pattern of social control that is exerted in connection with the person by himself and those around him. This special kind of institutional arrangement does not so much support the self as constitute it. . . .

In the usual cycle of adult socialization one expects to find alienation and mortification followed by a new set of beliefs about the world and a new way of conceiving of selves. In the case of the mental-hospital patient, this rebirth does sometimes occur, taking the form of a strong belief in the psychiatric perspective, or, briefly at least, a devotion to the social cause of better treatment for mental patients. The moral career of the mental patient has unique interest, however; it can illustrate the possibility that in casting off the raiments of the old self—or in having this cover torn away—the person need not seek a new robe and a new audience before which to cower. Instead he can learn, at least for a time, to practise before all groups the amoral arts of shamelessness.

THE UNDERLIFE OF A PUBLIC INSTITUTION

I

In every social establishment, there are official expectations as to what the participant owes the establishment. Even in cases where there is no specific task, as in some night-watchman jobs, the organization will require some presence of mind, some awareness of the current situation, and some readiness for unanticipated events; as long as an establishment demands that its participants not sleep on the job, it asks them to be awake to certain matters. And where sleeping is part of the expectation, as in a home or a hotel, then there will be limits on where and when the sleeping is to occur, with whom, and with what bed manners. And behind these claims on the individual, be they great or small, the managers of every establishment will have a widely embracing implicit conception of what the individual's character must be for these claims on him to be appropriate.

Whenever we look at a social establishment, we find a counter to this first theme: we find that participants decline in some way to accept the official view of what they should be putting into and getting out of the organization and, behind this, of what sort of self and world they are to accept for themselves. Where enthusiasm is expected, there will be apathy; where loyalty, there will be disaffection; where attendance, absenteeism; where robustness, some kind of illness; where deeds are to be done, varieties of inactivity. We find a multitude of homely little histories, each in its way a movement of liberty. Whenever worlds are laid on, underlives develop.

II

The study of underlife in restrictive total institutions has some special interest. When existence is cut to the bone, we can learn what people do to flesh out their lives. Stashes, means of transportation, free places, territories, supplies for economic and social exchange—these apparently are some of the minimal requirements for building up a life. Ordinarily these arrangements are taken for granted as part of one's primary adjustment; seeing them twisted out of official existence through bargains, wit, force, and cunning, we can see their significance anew. The study of total institutions also suggests that formal organizations have standard places of vulnerability, such as supply rooms, sick bays, kitchens, or scenes of highly technical labor. These are the damp corners where secondary adjustments breed and start to infest the establishment.

The mental hospital represents a peculiar instance of those establishments in which underlife is likely to proliferate. Mental patients are persons who caused the kind of trouble on the outside that led someone physically, if not socially, close to them to take psychiatric action against them. Often this trouble was associated with the "prepatient" having indulged in situational improprieties of some kind, conduct out of place in the setting. It is just such misconduct that conveys a moral rejection of the communities, establishments, and relationships that have a claim to one's attachment.

Stigmatization as mentally ill and involuntary hospitalization are the means by which we answer these offenses against propriety. The individual's persistence in manifesting symptoms after entering the hospital, and his tendency to develop additional symptoms during his initial response to the hospital, can now no longer serve him well as expressions of disaffection. From the patient's point of view, to decline to exchange a word with the staff or with his fellow patients may be ample evidence of

rejecting the institution's view of what and who he is; yet higher management may construe this alienative expression as just the sort of symptomatology the institution was established to deal with and as the best kind of evidence that the patient properly belongs where he now finds himself. In short, mental hospitalization outmaneuvers the patient, tending to rob him of the common expressions through which people hold off the embrace of organizations—insolence, silence, *sotto voce* remarks, uncooperativeness, malicious destruction of interior decorations, and so forth; these signs of disaffiliation are now read as signs of their maker's proper affiliation. Under these conditions all adjustments are primary.

Furthermore, there is a vicious-circle process at work. Persons who are lodged on "bad" wards find that very little equipment of any kind is given them—clothes may be taken from them each night, recreational materials may be withheld, and only heavy wooden chairs and benches provided for furniture. Acts of hostility against the institution have to rely on limited, ill-designed devices, such as banging a chair against the floor or striking a sheet of newspaper sharply so as to make an annoying explosive sound. And the more inadequate this equipment is to convey rejection of the hospital, the more the act appears as a psychotic symptom, and the more likely it is that management feels justified in assigning the patient to a bad ward. When a patient finds himself in seclusion, naked and without visible means of expression, he may have to rely on tearing up his mattress, if he can, or writing with feces on the wall—actions management takes to be in keeping with the kind of person who warrants seclusion.

We can also see this circular process at work in the small, illicit, talisman-like possessions that inmates use as symbolic devices for separating themselves from the position they are supposed to be in. What I think is a typical example may be cited from prison literature:

Prison clothing is anonymous. One's possessions are limited to toothbrush, comb, upper or lower cot, half the space upon a narrow table, a razor. As in jail, the urge to collect possessions is carried to preposterous extents. Rocks, string, knives—anything made by man and forbidden in man's institution—anything,—a red comb, a different kind of toothbrush, a belt—these things are assiduously gathered, jealously hidden or triumphantly displayed.[v]

But when a patient, whose clothes are taken from him each night, fills his pockets with bits of string and rolled up paper, and when he fights to keep these possessions in spite of the consequent inconvenience to those who must regularly go through his pockets, he is usually seen as engaging in symptomatic behavior befitting a very sick patient, not as someone who is attempting to stand apart from the place accorded him.

Official psychiatric doctrine tends to define alienative acts as psychotic ones—this view being reinforced by the circular processes that lead the patient to exhibit alienation in a more and more bizarre form—but the hospital cannot be run according to this doctrine. The hospital cannot decline to demand from its members exactly what other organizations must insist on; psychiatric doctrine is supple enough to do this, but institutions are not. Given the standards of the institution's environing society, there have to be at least the minimum routines connected with feeding, washing, dressing, bedding the patients, and protecting them from physical harm. Given these routines, there have to be inducements and exhortations to get patients to follow them. Demands must be made, and disappointment is shown when a patient does not live up to what is expected of him. Interest in seeing psychiatric "movement" or "improvement" after an initial stay on the wards leads the staff to encourage "proper" conduct and to express disappointment when a patient backslides into "psychosis." The patient is thus re-established as someone whom others are depending on, someone who ought to know enough to act correctly. Some improprieties, especially ones like muteness and apathy

that do not obstruct and even ease ward routines, may continue to be perceived naturalistically as symptoms, but on the whole the hospital operates semi-officially on the assumption that the patient ought to act in a manageable way and be respectful of psychiatry, and that he who does will be rewarded by improvement in life conditions and he who doesn't will be punished by a reduction of amenities. Within this semi-official reinstatement of ordinary organizational practices, the patient finds that many of the traditional ways of taking leave of a place without moving from it have retained their validity; secondary adjustments are therefore possible.

III

Of the many different kinds of secondary adjustment, some are of particular interest because they bring into the clear the general theme of involvement and disaffection, characteristic of all these practices.

One of these special types of secondary adjustment is "removal activities" (or "kicks"), namely, undertakings that provide something for the individual to lose himself in, temporarily blotting out all sense of the environment which, and in which, he must abide. In total institutions a useful exemplary case is provided by Robert Stroud, the "Birdman," who, from watching birds out his cell window, through a spectacular career of finagling and make-do, fabricated a laboratory and became a leading ornithological contributor to medical literature, all from within prison. Language courses in prisoner-of-war camps and art courses in prisons can provide the same release.

Central Hospital provided several of these escape worlds for inmates.[vi] One, for example, was sports. Some of the baseball players and a few tennis players seemed to become so caught

---

[v]Cantine and Rainer, *op. cit.*, p. 78. Compare the things that small boys stash in their pockets; some of these items also seem to provide a wedge between the boy and the domestic establishment.

[vi]Behind informal social typing and informal group formation in prisons there is often to be seen a removal activity. Caldwell, *op. cit.*, pp. 651–53, provides some interesting examples of prisoners on such kicks: those involved in securing and using drugs; those focused on leatherwork for sale; and "Spartans," those involved in the glorification of their bodies, the prison locker room apparently serving as a muscle beach; the homosexuals; the gamblers, etc. The point about these activities is that each is world-building for the person caught up in it, thereby displacing the prison.

up in their sport, and in the daily record of their efforts in competition, that at least for the summer months this became their overriding interest. In the case of baseball this was further strengthened by the fact that, within the hospital, parole patients could follow national baseball as readily as could many persons on the outside. For some young patients, who never failed to go, when allowed, to a dance held in their service or in the recreation building, it was possible to live for the chance of meeting someone "interesting" or remeeting someone interesting who had already been met—in much the same way that college students are able to survive their studies by looking forward to the new "dates" that may be found in extracurricular activities. The "marriage moratorium" in Central Hospital, effectively freeing a patient from his marital obligations to a non-patient, enhanced this removal activity. For a handful of patients, the semi-annual theatrical production was an extremely effective removal activity: tryouts, rehearsals, costuming, scenery-making, staging, writing and rewriting, performing— all these seemed as successful as on the outside in building a world apart for the participants. Another kick, important to some patients—and a worrisome concern for the hospital chaplains— was the enthusiastic espousal of religion. Still another, for a few patients, was gambling.

Portable ways of getting away were much favored in Central Hospital, paper-back murder mysteries, cards, and even jigsaw puzzles being carried around on one's person. Not only could leave be taken of the ward and grounds be taken leave of through these means, but if one had to wait for an hour or so upon an official, or the serving of a meal, or the opening of the recreation building, the self-implication of this subordination could be dealt with by immediately bringing forth one's own world-making equipment. . . .

IV

If a function of secondary adjustments is to place a barrier between the individual and the social unit in which he is supposed to be participating, we should expect some secondary adjustments to be empty of intrinsic gain and to function solely to express unauthorized distance—a self-preserving "rejection of one's rejectors."[vii] This seems to happen with the very common forms of ritual insubordination, for example, griping or bitching, where this behavior is not realistically expected to bring about change. Through direct insolence that does not meet with immediate correction, or remarks passed half out of hearing of authority, or gestures performed behind the back of authority, subordinates express some detachment from the place officially accorded them. . . . Some of these ways of openly but safely taking a stand outside the authorized one are beautiful, especially when carried out collectively. Again, prisons provide ready examples:

> . . . When the sky pilot got up in the pulpit to give us our weekly pep talk each Sunday he would always make some feeble joke which we always laughed at as loud and as long as possible, although he must have known that we were sending him up. He still used to make some mildly funny remark and every time he did the whole church would be filled with rawcous [*sic*] laughter, even though only half the audience had heard what had been said.[viii]

> . . . Beyond irony, however, there is an even more subtle and telling kind of ritual insubordination. There is a special stance that can be taken to alien authority; it combines stiffness, dignity, and coolness in a particular mixture that conveys insufficient insolence to call forth immediate punishment and yet expresses that one is entirely one's own man. Since this communication is made through the way in which the body and face are held, it can be constantly conveyed wherever the inmate finds himself. Illustrations can be found in prison society:

> "Rightness" implies bravery, fearlessness, loyalty to peers, avoidance of exploitation, adamant refusal to concede the superiority of the official

---

[vii]Lloyd W. McCorkle and Richard Korn, "Resocialization Within Walls," *The Annals*, CCXCIII (1954), p. 88.
[viii]J. F. N., *op. cit.*, pp. 15–16. See also Goffman, *Presentation of Self*, "derisive collusion," pp. 186–88.

value system, and repudiation of the notion that the inmate is of a lower order. It consists principally in the reassertion of one's basic integrity, dignity, and worth in an essentially degrading situation, and the exhibition of these personal qualities regardless of any show of force by the official system.[ix]

Similarly, in Central Hospital, in the "tough" punishment wards of maximum security, where inmates had very little more to lose, fine examples could be found of patients not going out of their way to make trouble but by their very posture conveying unconcern and mild contempt for all levels of the staff, combined with utter self-possession.

V

It would be easy to account for the development of secondary adjustments by assuming that the individual possessed an array of needs, native or cultivated, and that when lodged in a milieu that denied these needs the individual simply responded by developing makeshift means of satisfaction. I think this explanation fails to do justice to the importance of these undercover adaptations for the structure of the self.

The practice of reserving something of oneself from the clutch of an institution is very visible in mental hospitals and prisons but can be found in more benign and less totalistic institutions, too. I want to argue that this recalcitrance is not an incidental mechanism of defense but rather an essential constituent of the self.

Sociologists have always had a vested interest in pointing to the ways in which the individual is formed by groups, identifies with groups, and wilts away unless he obtains emotional support from groups. But when we closely observe what goes on in a social role, a spate of sociable interaction, a social establishment—or in any other unit of social organization—embracement of the unit is not all that we see. We always find the individual employing methods to keep some distance, some elbow room, between himself and that with which others assume he should be identified. No doubt a state-type mental hospital provides an overly lush soil for the growth of these secondary adjustments, but in fact, like weeds, they spring up in any kind of social organization. If we find, then, that in all situations actually studied the participant has erected defenses against his social bondedness, why should we base our conception of the self upon how the individual would act were conditions "just right"?

The simplest sociological view of the individual and his self is that he is to himself what his place in an organization defines him to be. When pressed, a sociologist modifies this model by granting certain complications: the self may be not yet formed or may exhibit conflicting dedications. Perhaps we should further complicate the construct by elevating these qualifications to a central place, initially defining the individual, for sociological purposes, as a stance-taking entity, a something that takes up a position somewhere between identification with an organization and opposition to it, and is ready at the slightest pressure to regain its balance by shifting its involvement in either direction. It is thus *against something* that the self can emerge. . . .

Without something to belong to, we have no stable self, and yet total commitment and attachment to any social unit implies a kind of selflessness. Our sense of being a person can come from being drawn into a wider social unit; our sense of selfhood can arise through the little ways in which we resist the pull. Our status is backed by the solid buildings of the world, while our sense of personal identity often resides in the cracks.

[ix]Richard Cloward, "Social Control in the Prison," S.S.R.C. Pamphlet No. 15, *op. cit.*, p. 40. See also Sykes and Messinger, *op. cit.*, pp. 10–11.

Arlie Russell Hochschild (1940–): A Biographical Sketch

Born and raised in a Maryland suburb, Arlie Russell's interest in "emotion management" was kindled at the age of twelve when her parents joined the U.S. Foreign Service. As her family hosted parties for foreign diplomats, she became precociously attuned to the subtleties of emotional displays and the importance of controlling, if not manipulating, them. This led her to question early on whether the "self" we present to others is a reality or fiction, as she found herself wondering, "Had I passed the peanuts to a person . . . or to an actor?" (1983:ix). The insightfulness of her innocent childhood musings has been confirmed, as today Hochschild has earned an international audience as a leading social psychologist.

Hochschild completed her M.A. and Ph.D. at the University of California, Berkeley. While a student she became increasingly attuned to the struggles women faced as they attempted to straddle two worlds: the "male" world of professional life and the "female" world of caregiver. Moreover, her studies led her to the conclusion that sociology was a patently male discipline whose points of reference, theories, and methods were derived from men's experiences. This realization would, along with her fleeting childhood encounters with diplomats, inspire her to develop a branch of sociology that addressed not only the experiences of men but also the experiences of women; that informed the public not through "objective," statistical facts but through stories of everyday life told by those living it; and that sought to explore not only what people *think* but also how people *feel*: the sociology of emotions.

SOURCE: UC Berkeley.

During the past thirty years, Hochschild has written five books, coedited another, and has published more than fifty scholarly articles, book chapters, and reviews. Her academic works have been translated into ten languages. The American Sociological Association has twice recognized her contributions to the discipline by presenting her with both a Lifetime Achievement Award and the Award for Public Understanding of Sociology. Hochschild has also contributed significantly as a public intellectual. She established the Center for Working Families at the University of California, Berkeley, for which she currently serves as the director, and her expertise on the impact of government policy and business/employee relations on the family has led her into the political arena as well. She has presented her work to the State of California's Child Development Policy Advisory Committee and, on the national level, to the Democratic Leadership Council, the National Council on Family Relations, and the White House's Domestic Policy Council. She also advised former vice president Al Gore on the development of work-family policies. Hochschild currently teaches at the University of California, Berkeley.

Intellectual Influences and Core Ideas

In developing her theory of emotions, Hochschild draws from two distinct approaches. The first, which she labels the "organismic model," focuses on how emotions are rooted in an individual's biological or psychological makeup. The second, the "interactional model," stresses the role of social processes in shaping self-consciousness. As you will shortly see, Hochschild fashions a third approach, "emotion-management perspective," by weaving together the insights of these two approaches, and in doing so she significantly expands the terrain of symbolic interactionism (Hochschild, 2003).

The Organismic Model

The organismic model is derived primarily from the writings of Charles Darwin (1809–1882), Sigmund Freud (1856–1939), and William James (1842–1910). For instance, Darwin argues that emotive "gestures" are vestiges of humankind's earlier, direct experiences. Thus, baring one's teeth in an expression of rage is a vestige of the instinctual act of biting used by primitive humans to attack, or defend themselves against, another. Similarly, our expression of love is a holdover from what was once a direct act of sexual intercourse. For Darwin, then, emotive gestures—that is, emotional expressions—are largely universal, as we all can be traced to the same ancestral gene pool. Biology, not social factors, is said to shape emotions, which, in turn, accounts for why there allegedly is little cross-cultural variation in emotive experience. Here, emotions are instinctual or automatic responses to a stimulus that produces physiological changes in our bodies. Our conscious awareness of such changes or the meanings we attribute to them are considered extrinsic to the emotions themselves. For example, from this perspective the emotion we call fear is fundamentally a biologically driven response marked by an increased heart rate, heightened adrenaline levels, and a constriction of muscles.

For his part, Freud connects emotions to instinctual drives, namely Eros (love or creation) and Thanatos (death or destruction). When our ability to directly satisfy the demands of these two psychobiological instincts is hindered, we experience anxiety, the single most powerful emotion. Yet, civilization itself is predicated on the individual repressing or sublimating these basic drives. Anxiety is thus inescapably part of the human condition, tied as it is to the necessary denial of instinctual gratification.[8] In our attempt to avoid or minimize unpleasant or painful psychological distress, we develop defense mechanisms through which we unconsciously repress and redefine the real source of our anxiety. While shielding the ego by displacing unwanted thoughts and feelings, such mechanisms, however, can lead to inappropriate or neurotic behavior. For the psychoanalyst, then, an individual's misfitted emotional expressions and behaviors (for instance, laughing at a funeral or feeling depressed at one's wedding) are held to be a reflection of unconscious or involuntary psychic processes.

Freud also assigns an important "signal function" to anxiety, a function that would become central to Hochschild's theory of emotions. Here, Freud asserts that the experience of anxiety serves to alert the individual to impending dangers emanating either from the immediate environment or from inside the individual's own psychic state. For instance, anxiety is likely to increase when we find ourselves in a potentially embarrassing situation or when we feel as though we are emotionally "flooded out" from a particularly intense situation and unable to control our behaviors. However, what Freud reserves primarily for anxiety, Hochschild extends to all emotions, arguing that the entire range of emotive experiences—from joy to sadness, pride to shame—serve as signals through which we fit our prior expectations to our present situation. Envy, for

---

[8]For additional comments on Freud's theory, see our discussion of his influence on critical theory in Chapter 3.

example, is the name for the "signal" we receive when our expectations regarding what we think we deserve are not met while another person has what it is we desire.

The Interactional Model

The "interactional model" is expressed in the work of a number of figures including John Dewey (1859–1952), George Herbert Mead, Hans Gerth (1908–1978) and C. Wright Mills (1916–1962), Herbert Blumer, and Erving Goffman. These theorists all share a conception of the individual as an active, conscious participant in the production and reproduction of social life—a view that provides a critical point of departure for Hochschild's own emotion-management perspective. Moreover, although they pursued different lines of inquiry, each called attention to the relationship between thinking (a social act rooted in taking the attitude of others toward our own conduct) and feeling. Here, emotive experiences thus are not tied to biologically driven responses or to the unconscious workings of the psyche. Emotions are viewed, instead, as intimately connected to our conscious perceptions and interpretations of the situations in which we are involved. In other words, the act of assigning meaning to an emotion is intrinsic to—not an aftereffect of—the emotive experience itself. Importantly, the active production of emotions is itself a social process, as the interpretation and labeling of feeling is based both on our reaction to the imagined responses of others as well as on our awareness of the normative expectations that infuse a given situation. Thus, we are sad at funerals not only because of the loss of a loved one, but also because we are *supposed* to be sad. Similarly, we feel a sense of pride in our accomplishments in part because we reflect back on the obstacles confronted along the path to our successes and realize that we deserve to feel proud.

The model of the actor and her relation to the broader society posed by the interactional perspective is instructive on several fronts. Emphasizing the social dimensions of self-consciousness provides a vantage point for linking emotive experiences to cognitive awareness and recognizing the connections between self- and social-control mechanisms. From this perspective, emotions can be understood as something other than irrational, displaced, or instinctual physiological responses to events. Moreover, recognizing that an individual's "private" emotions are produced and shaped within a public context opens the door for examining how broader social structures can impinge on emotive experiences: for instance, how the institutionalization of class and gender relations shapes both the inner experience and outer expression of emotions, an issue that Hochschild addresses in the readings that follow.

Goffman and Impression Management

Above all, it is Erving Goffman who had the greatest impact on Hochschild's conceptualization of emotions. Although Goffman did not explore explicitly the full range of emotions, his notion of impression management is central to Hochschild's own emotion management model. As we discussed earlier in connection to Goffman's dramaturgical perspective, impression management refers to the technique of controlling one's behavior in order to present an acceptable image of one's self to others. But, according to Hochschild, Goffman's singular focus on outward expressions, or "surface acting," leads to a blind spot in his analysis. The notion that individuals have inner feelings that, like outward appearances, must be actively managed as they plot their course of projected impressions is scarcely entertained by Goffman. This assumption, however, is fundamental to Hochschild's own model. Indeed, Goffman's ambivalent position on the nature of self (whether it is primarily an imputed "dramatic effect" arising from a scene, or whether a "psychobiological" organism stands behind the mask donned for the performance) makes it difficult to determine how *inner* feelings might be managed or shaped.

While Goffman did not make the study of emotions a cornerstone to his approach, he did devote attention to embarrassment and its role in sustaining both the informal rules that govern social encounters and the self-identity of the actors involved (1967). In his analysis, we can glimpse the blind spot that Hochschild sought to rectify. Goffman defines embarrassment as a feeling that arises when one or more actors in an encounter are unable to fulfill the expectations required to project an acceptable self-image to others. Certainly no one has fully escaped the feeling of embarrassment (or "flustering") that signals an interaction gone awry. Goffman's description will no doubt ring familiar:

> [A] completely flustered individual is one who cannot for the time being mobilize his muscular and intellectual resources for the task at hand, although he would like to; he cannot volunteer a response to those around him that will allow them to sustain the conversation smoothly. He and his flustered actions block the line of activity the others have been pursuing. He is present with them, but he is not "in play." The others may be forced to stop and turn their attention to the impediment; the topic of conversation is neglected, and energies are directed to the task of re-establishing the flustered individual, of studiously ignoring him, or of withdrawing from his presence . . . [F]lustering threatens the encounter itself by disrupting the smooth transmission and reception by which encounters are sustained. (1967:100–02)

Here, embarrassment is studied less as an inner emotional state and more for what it contributes to the flow of interaction. The point is not that Goffman ignores the play and power of emotions, but rather, that his situationalism leads him to view emotions as something "done" to the actor; embarrassment happens *to* him. Thus, essential features of emotions are not to be found in the mind or body of the individual as the organismic and emotion-management models contend, but rather, in their ramifications for the encounter and the actor's attempt to maintain a viable presentation of self. As Goffman puts it:

> By showing embarrassment . . . [the individual's] role in the current interaction may be sacrificed, and even the encounter itself, but he demonstrates that, while he cannot present a sustainable and coherent self on this occasion, he is at least disturbed by the fact and may prove worthy another time. To this extent, embarrassment is not an irrational impulse breaking through socially prescribed behavior but part of the orderly behavior itself. (1967:111)

Hochschild's Emotion-Management Model

Having presented in broad strokes the models from which Hochschild draws, we turn now to a brief overview of her own emotion-management perspective. To begin, Hochschild (1983), borrowing from Darwin, defines emotion as a "biologically-given sense," much like hearing, sight, and smell, that communicates information about the world around us. Thus, emotions are fundamentally connected to biological processes. Unlike our other senses, however, emotions are directly tied to behavior; they are experienced as the body physiologically readies itself to engage in action. In addition to providing an orientation toward action, emotions also possess a cognitive component in the form of a "signal function." In this way, emotions spring from our attempts to reconcile our prior expectations with the actuality of events.

Yet, emotions are not biological or psychological givens that are immune to social and cultural influences, a picture that is painted by the organismic model. Emotions are actively produced and managed by individuals in the context of interaction: they are not simply experienced, they are created. In an important sense, we "do" emotions in the form of **emotion work**. This refers to efforts to alter (i.e., manage) the intensity or type of feelings one is experiencing. Emotion work can involve conscious attempts to either evoke or shape particular feelings as well as attempts to suppress them. Here we see both Hochschild's indebtedness to, and extension of, Goffman's dramaturgical perspective. For while Goffman's notion of impression management emphasizes surface acting—the *outward* behavioral and verbal expressions we "put on" in order to convincingly play a role—Hochschild's emotion management focuses on "deep acting"— our *inner* efforts to produce not the appearance of feeling but, rather, a "real feeling that has been self-induced" (1983:35). Thus, after a stressful day we *try* to be happy at our friend's birthday party. Similarly, we often must work to suppress the nervousness or anxiety we experience during a job interview or on a first date.

Directly related to the notion of emotion work is **emotional labor**, in which one's deep acting is sold for a wage. Thus, inner feelings are managed in order to produce an outward display as part of one's job. For example, in her research on flight attendants, Hochschild found that manufacturing feelings of caring and cheerfulness while suppressing anger or boredom was a common feature of the job. Of course, emotional labor does not pertain only to flight attendants. Rather, Hochschild points out that it is required by an array of jobs that share three characteristics: (1) face-to-face or voice-to-voice interaction with the public, (2) employees are directed to produce specified emotional states in clients, and (3) through training and supervision, employers are able to exercise control over the emotional activities of workers (1983:147). From this description, it's easy to see that emotional labor is a pervasive feature in a service economy such as ours in the United States Waiters and waitresses, front desk attendants in hotels, and just about anyone who works in a retail store are all subject to the supervised control of their own emotions, as a major component of their job is to produce a sense of satisfaction or self-importance in their customers. Likewise, police officers engage in emotional labor in their dealings with the public. Trained to keep their emotions in check under dangerous and threatening conditions—and subject to a range of penalties if they fail to do so—police officers are also instructed in techniques designed to produce specified emotional states in suspects and witnesses. Indeed, emotional labor is essential to performing the often-used "good cop/bad cop" routine and eliciting the required emotions, such as fear or trust, from those they are questioning.

Emotional labor, however, often exacts a high cost from the worker. Following the work of Gerth and Mills (and through them, the work of Karl Marx and Max Weber), Hochschild draws a parallel between the alienation experienced by the factory worker and that experienced by those employed in service industries. While the factory worker's body is bought and controlled by his employer, it is the service worker's feelings that are subject to the dictates of another, although in different ways, both are detached or alienated from something that is vital to their self. As Hochschild describes it:

> Those who perform emotional labor in the course of giving service are like those who perform physical labor in the course of making things: both are subject to the demands of mass production. But when the product—the thing to be engineered, mass-produced, and subjected to speed-up and slow-down—is a smile, a mood, a feeling, or a relationship, it comes to belong more to the organization and less to the self. (1983:198)

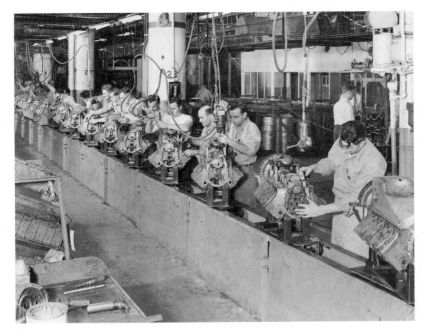

Equally alienated? The factory worker (Photo 5.7) sells his physical labor, finding its embodiment in a tangible commodity. The flight attendant (Photo 5.8) sells her emotions and smile to produce desired feeling-states (contentment, safety) in others.

Photo 5.7 Factory Workers

SOURCE: © Bettmann/CORBIS; used with permission.

When our natural capacity to engage in emotion work is sold for a wage and bought to serve the profit motive, our feelings become engineered to further corporate and organizational interests. "Transmuted" from a private act controlled by the individual herself to one that is publicly administered by a supervisor and codified in training manuals and company policies, emotion work becomes rationalized to better serve instrumental purposes. However, the commercial reshaping of emotions, or **commodification of feelings**, is not experienced alike by all. As you will read in the selections that follow, gender and class differences leave women and middle-class workers more susceptible to the commodification of their emotive experiences.

HOCHSCHILD'S THEORETICAL ORIENTATION

In the preceding discussion, we introduced several concepts that suggest the contours of Hochschild's theoretical orientation. Given the theoretical wells from which she draws and the influence of Goffman's work in particular, it is not surprising that Hochschild has developed a multidimensional approach to the study of emotion that spans the four quadrants of our framework (see Figure 5.3). Consider first the twin concepts of emotion work and deep acting that, in speaking to the actor's inner experiences, are rooted in individualist and nonrational presuppositions. Here, Hochschild focuses on the efforts of individuals to actively shape their *real* feelings in the course of interacting with others. Thus, we may find ourselves trying to get excited about a concert we've been invited to or trying to suppress our feelings of disappointment over

Photo 5.8   Flight Attendant
SOURCE: © Royalty-Free/Corbis; used with permission.

Figure 5.3   Hochschild's Multidimensional Approach to Emotions

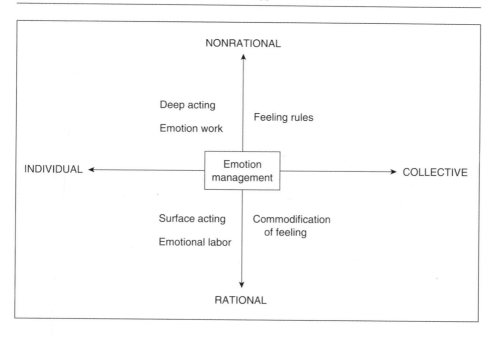

not getting a promotion. Together these two concepts emphasize the role that individuals play in creating their emotive experiences.

In contrast, surface acting refers to the individual's managing of her outward appearance in order to present a convincing image of one's self. The emphasis is less on emotions, per se, and more on the actor's interest in maintaining an acceptable impression, which may involve faking feelings. For instance, we may pretend to thoroughly enjoy another's company, when in actuality we are more interested in having him help us with our work. Thus, a more strategic or calculating motive often forms the backdrop of surface acting. This rationalist dimension of action is carried one step further with the notion of emotional labor, where an employee tries to evoke or suppress real emotions not because she wants to, but because she is paid to. While the feelings experienced may be real, they are nevertheless manufactured for "artificial" rational purposes, namely, to keep one's job.

Closely related to emotional labor is the concept of the commodification of feelings, a concept that points to the collectivist and rational dimension of emotive experience. In this case, the instrumental, strategic stance toward emotions is adopted and executed through corporate design. It is not the interests of the individual that are being served here, but rather, those of the company. Like a car or a pair of shoes, emotions are bought and sold under the logic of the profit motive and the impersonal market forces it infuses. The notion of the commodification of feelings thus turns our attention to the institutional or structural pressures that shape the individual's experience of emotions.

Hochschild's multidimensional approach is rounded out by her notion of feeling rules, which captures the collectivist, nonrational dimension of emotions. **Feeling rules** are the shared, social (collectivist) conventions that determine what we should feel in a given situation, how intensely we should feel it, and how long we should feel. They form the taken-for-granted backdrop (nonrational) according to which we manage our emotions and assess the emotive expressions of others. Feeling rules account for the social patterning of emotive experiences and in doing so establish the "standards used in emotional conversation to determine what is rightly owed and owing in the currency of feeling" (1983:18). It is on the basis of feeling rules, and the sense of emotional entitlement or obligation they establish, that we guide our private emotion work (ibid.:56). For just as there are social expectations that set the boundaries of acceptable behavior, so, too, there are rules that set limits to our feelings. In extreme cases, feeling rules may even have the power of life and death over the individual. Consider a court trial where the defendant is found guilty of a crime in part because he expressed the "wrong amount" of grief, thus providing a clue to his guilt.

Readings

In the selections that follow, you will first find Hochschild explicating her general approach to emotions. Next, she goes on to discuss the everyday implications of her perspective, in particular how emotive experiences are connected to gender identity and the unequal distribution of resources, power, and authority along gendered lines.

Introduction to "Working on Feeling"

In her essay "Working on Feeling," Hochschild outlines her emotion management model. Here you will encounter many of the key concepts discussed in the previous section. After laying out the theoretical lineage of her perspective, Hochschild moves to a discussion of two of her central ideas: emotion work and feeling rules. In doing so, Hochschild evinces her multidimensional model of emotive experiences by exploring the links between our awareness of our feelings and the social rules that shape our personal efforts to manage them. Moreover, feeling rules are themselves embedded in a broader structural context. Most significant, Hochschild here claims, are existing class relations, which subject middle-class workers more than others to the commodification of feelings. For it is the middle-class job that is more likely to entail personal interaction with the public, the requirement to produce specific feeling-states in others, and the surveillance of their emotional labor by superiors.

❖

Working on Feeling (2003)

Arlie Russell Hochschild

Why is the emotive experience of normal adults in daily life as orderly as it is? Why, generally speaking, do people feel gay at parties, sad at funerals, happy at weddings? This question leads us to examine not conventions of appearance or outward comportment, but conventions of *feeling*. Conventions of feeling become surprising only when we imagine, by contrast, what totally unpatterned, unpredictable emotive life might actually be like at parties, funerals, weddings, and in all of normal adult life. Indeed, when novelists set out to create poignant scenes they evoke the full weight of a feeling rule. In *Lie Down in Darkness*, for example, William Styron describes a confused and desperately unhappy bride on the "happy" day of her wedding:

When she spoke the vows her lips parted not like all the brides he'd ever seen—exposing their clean, scrubbed teeth in a little eager puff of rapture—but rather with a kind of wry and somber resignation. It had been a brief shadow of a mood, just a flicker, but enough for him to tell her "I will" had seemed less an avowal than a

confession, like the tired words of some sad, errant nun. Not any of her put-on gaiety could disguise this.[i]

Against the chaotic flow of feeling that emerges from real relationships are more abiding (though also changeable) rules of feeling. In a culture of freely chosen love matches, the bride *should* feel like saying "I will" with an "eager puff of rapture."

But what, then, is a feeling or emotion? I define "emotion" as bodily cooperation with an image, a thought, a memory—a cooperation of which the individual is usually aware. I will use the terms "emotion" and "feeling" interchangeably, although the term "emotion" denotes a state of being overcome that "feeling" does not. The term "emotion management" I use synonymously with "emotion work" and "deep acting."

What happens to these emotions? Erving Goffman suggests both the surprise to be explained and part of the explanation: "We find that participants will hold in check certain psychological states and attitudes, for after

SOURCE: From The *Commercialization of Intimate Life: Notes from Home and Work* by Hochschild, A., reprinted with permission from University of California Press via Copyright Clearance Center.

[i]Styron 1951, p. 291.

all, the very general rule that one enter into the prevailing mood in the encounter carries the understanding that contradictory feelings will be in abeyance. . . . So generally, in fact, does one suppress unsuitable affect, that we need to look at offenses to this rule to be reminded of its usual operation."[ii]

The key—and curiously bureaucratic—word here is "unsuitable." In light of the passage from William Styron above, we could also add "disturbing" or even, in the emotional sense, "dangerous." "So why is she at the altar at all? And why in this way?" we ask. And, from the viewpoint of the guests and surely the groom, what is wrong with how—beneath the put-on gaiety—she is really feeling? This very line of questioning suggests that we have in mind a right way for her to feel. How are we to understand such a thing?

We can take two possible approaches. One is to study the situation that would seem to cause her to feel as she does. The other is to study secondary acts performed *upon* the ongoing nonreflective stream of primary emotive experience, that is, how she is or isn't trying to alter her state of feeling. The first approach focuses on how social factors affect what people feel, the second on how social factors affect what people think and do about what they feel or sense they are going to feel (i.e., acts of assessment and management). Those who take the first approach might regard those who take the second as being "overly cognitive," while those who take the second approach see the "stimulate primary emotions" people as simplistic. But we need both approaches, and indeed the second, taken here, relies on some understanding of the first.

If we take as our object of focus what it is people think or do about feelings, several questions emerge. What is an emotion? How responsive is emotion to deliberate attempts to suppress or evoke it? What are the links among social structure, ideology, feeling rules, and emotion management? To begin with, *are* there feeling rules? How do we *know* about them? How are these rules used as baselines in social exchanges? What in the nature of word and child-rearing might account for different ways adults of varying social classes and ethnic or religious cultures manage their feelings?

TWO ACCOUNTS OF EMOTION AND FEELING

So what do we assume is true about emotion? There is the *organismic* account and there is the *interactive* account. They differ in what they imply about our capacity to manage emotion, and thus in what they imply about the importance of rules about managing it. According to the organismic view, the paramount questions concern the relation of emotion to biologically given *instinct* or *impulse*. In large part, biological factors account for the questions the organismic theorist poses. The early writings of Sigmund Freud, Charles Darwin, and, in some though not all respects, William James fit this model. The concept "emotion" refers mainly to strips of experience in which there is no conflict between one and another aspect of self: the individual "floods out," is "overcome." The image that comes to mind is that of a sudden, automatic reflex syndrome—Darwin's instant snarl expression, Freud's tension discharge at a given breaking point of tension overload, James and Lange's notion of an instantaneous unmediated visceral reaction to a perceived stimulus, the perception of which is also unmediated by social influences.

In this first model, social factors enter in only in regard to how emotions are stimulated and expressed (and even here Darwin took the universalist position). Social factors are not seen as an influence on how emotions are actively suppressed or evoked. Indeed, emotion is seen as fixed and universal, much like a knee-jerk reaction or a sneeze. In this view, one could as easily manage an emotion as one could manage a knee jerk or a sneeze. If the organismic theorist were to be presented with the concept of feeling rules, he or she would be hard put to elucidate what these rules impinge *on*, or what capacity of the self could *be called on* to try to obey a feeling rule. Recent attempts to link an organismic notion of emotion to social structure, such as Randall Collins's wonderfully bold

[ii]Goffman 1961, p. 23.

attempt, suffer from the problems that were implicit in the organismic account to begin with. Collins, like Darwin, on whom he draws, sees emotions as capacities (or susceptibilities) within a person, to be automatically triggered, as Collins develops it, by one or another group in control of the ritual apparatus that does the triggering.[iii] A wholly different avenue of social control, that of feeling rules, is bypassed because the individual's capacity to try to—or try not to—feel that to which the rule applies is not suggested by the organismic model with which Collins begins.

In the interactive account, social influences permeate emotion more insistently, more effectively, and at more junctures. In large part, socio-psychological factors account for the questions the interactive theorist poses. The writings of Hans Gerth and C. Wright Mills, Erving Goffman, Richard Lazarus, James Averill, Stanley Schachter, Jerome Singer, Thomas Kemper, Judith Katz, and aspects of late Freudian and neo-Freudian thought fit this model. To invoke the Freudian vocabulary, the image here is not that of a runaway id, but of an ego and superego, acting in union, shaping and nagging the id, however ineffectively, temporarily, or consciously. Emotion is sometimes posited as a psychobiological means of adaptation—an analogue to other adaptive mechanisms, such as shivering when cold or perspiring when hot. But emotion differs from these other adaptive mechanisms, in that thinking, perceiving, and imagining—themselves subject to social influence—enter in.

As in the first model, social factors affect how emotions are elicited and expressed. But here we also notice how social factors guide the ways we *label*, interpret, and manage emotion. These actions *reflect back*, in turn, on that which is labeled, interpreted, and managed. They are, finally, intrinsic to what we call emotion. Emotion, in this second school of thought, is seen as more deeply social. Lazarus's work in particular lends empirical weight to the interactive model. It shows how normal adults, like the university students on whom he conducted experiments, can control their emotions. Their

capacity is far greater than what we expect from a small child, an insane adult, or an animal, from all of which Freud and Darwin drew inspiration. But since we're trying to understand the emotional experience of normal adults, we would do well to explore the model that fits them best—the interactive account.

If emotions and feelings can to some degree be managed, how might we get a conceptual grasp of the managing act from a social perspective? The interactive account of emotion leads us into a conceptual arena "between" the Goffmanian focus on consciously designed appearances, on the one hand, and the Freudian focus on unconscious intrapsychic events, on the other. The focus of A. H. Mead and Herbert Blumer on conscious, active, and responsive gestures might have been most fruitful had not their focus on deeds and thought almost entirely obscured the importance of feeling. The self as emotion manager is an idea that borrows from both sides—Goffman and Freud—but squares completely with neither. Here I sketch only the basic borrowings and departures—and these begin with Goffman.

Erving Goffman Goffman catches an important irony: moment to moment, the individual is actively, consciously negotiating a personal and apparently unique course of action, but in the long run all the action often seems like passive acquiescence to some unconscious social convention. But the conserving of convention is not a passive business. We can extend and deepen Goffman's approach by showing how people not only try to conform outwardly, but do so inwardly as well. "When they issue uniforms, they issue skins," Goffman says. And, we can add, "two inches of flesh."[iv] But how can we understand these two inches of flesh? . . .

Goffman proposed an intermediate level of conceptual elaboration, *between* social structure and personality. He focused one by one on situations, episodes, encounters. The emergent encounters he evoked were not only nearly divorced from social structure and from personality; he even seems to intend his situationism as an analytic substitute for these concepts. Structure, he seems to say, can be not only transposed but

[iii]Collins 1975, p. 59.

[iv]Goffman 1974.

reduced "in and down," while personality can be reduced "up and out" to the here-now, gone-then interactional moment. The resulting perspective removes the determinisms of institution and personality. It illuminates the room there is between them to slide around.

But each episode—a card game, a party, a greeting on the street—takes on the character of a government. It exacts from us certain "taxes" in the form of appearances we "pay" for the sake of sustaining the encounter. We are repaid in the currency of safety from disrepute.

This model of the situation qua minigovernment illuminates something. But, to study how and why "participants . . . hold in check certain psychological states,"[v] we are forced out of the here-now, gone-then situationism and back, in part at least, to the social structure and personality model. We are led to appreciate the importance of Goffman's work, as it seems he didn't, *as the critical set of conceptual connecting tissues by which structure and personality, real in their own right, are more precisely joined*. For if we are to understand the origin and causes of change in feeling rules—this underside of ideology—we are forced back out of a study of the immediate situations in which they show up, to a study of such things as the changing relations between classes, sexes, races, and nations, in order to see why they're changing. . . .

The characters in Goffman's books actively manage outer impressions, but they do not actively manage inner feelings. The very topic, sociology of emotion, presupposes a human capacity for, if not the actual habit of, reflecting on and shaping inner feelings, a habit itself distributed variously across time, age, class, and locale. This variation would quickly drop from sight were we to adopt an exclusive focus on the actor's attentiveness to behavioral facade and assume a uniform passivity vis-à-vis feelings. . . .

Sigmund Freud The need to replace Goffman's "black-box psychology" with some theory of self, in the full sense of the term, might seem to lead to Freudian or neo-Freudian theory. Yet, here, as with Goffman, only some

aspects of the Freudian model seem useful to my understanding of conscious, deliberate efforts to suppress or evoke feeling.

Freud dealt with emotions, of course, but for him they were always secondary to *drive*. He proposed a general theory of sexual and aggressive drives. Anxiety, as a derivative of aggressive and sexual drives, was of paramount importance, while a wide range of other emotions, including joy, jealousy, and depression, were given relatively little attention. He developed, and many others have since elaborated, the concept of ego defense as a generally unconscious, involuntarily means of avoiding painful or unpleasant affect. The notion of "inappropriate affect" is then used to point to aspects of the individual's ego functioning, not the social rules according to which a feeling is or is not deemed appropriate to a situation.

The emotion-management perspective is indebted to Freud for the general notion of what resources individuals of different sorts possess for accomplishing the task of emotion work and for the notion of unconscious involuntary emotion management. The emotion-management perspective differs from the Freudian model in its focus on the full range of emotions and feelings and its focus on conscious and deliberate efforts to shape feeling.

How do we understand inappropriate emotion? . . . To the psychiatrist, which circumstances warrant which degree and type of feeling seems relatively unproblematic. A doctor intuitively knows what inappropriate affect is; one should be happy at occupational success. The main problem is not so much to discern the rich variety of kinds of misfit of feeling to situation as to cure the patient of whatever interferes with feeling that "right" feeling. From the emotion-management perspective, on the other hand, the warranting function of circumstances is a real problem. How does the psychiatrist decide what the patient should feel? The way he decides may well be the same for a psychiatrist as for a salesclerk or school disciplinarian. For in a sense, we all act as lay psychiatrists using unexamined means of arriving at a determination about just *which* circumstances warrant *that much* feeling of *that sort*.

---

[v]Goffman 1961, p. 23.

What the psychiatrist, the salesclerk, and the school disciplinarian share is a habit of comparing situation (e.g., high opportunity, associated with an accomplishment at work) with role (e.g., hopes, aspirations, expectations typical of, and expected from, those enacting the role). Social factors alter how we expect a person to play—or shall we say encounter—a role. If, for example, the patient were a "sober, technically minded and active" *woman*, and if the observer (rightly or wrongly) assumed or expected her to value family and personal ties over worldly success, ambivalence at the prospect of advance might seem perfectly appropriate. Lack of enthusiasm would have a warrant of that social sort. Again, if the patient were an antinuclear activist and his discovery had implications for nuclear energy, that would alter his hopes and aspirations and might warrant dismay. Or if an immigrant is, by virtue of enormous family sacrifice, sent off to succeed in America, his or her enthusiasm might be infused with a sense of indebtedness to those left back home.

We assess the "appropriateness" of a feeling by making a comparison between feeling and situation, not by examining the feeling in the abstract. This comparison lends the assessor a "normal" yardstick—a *socially* normal one—with which to factor out the personal meaning systems that may lead a worker to distort his view of "the" situation and feel inappropriately with regard to it. The psychiatrist holds constant the socially normal yardstick and focuses on what we have just factored out. The student of emotion management holds constant what is factored out and studies variations in socially normal yardsticks. . . .

In sum, the emotion-management perspective fosters attention on how people try to feel, not, as for Goffman, on how people try to appear to feel. It leads us to attend to how people consciously feel and not, as for Freud, to how people feel unconsciously. The interactive account of emotion points to alternate theoretical junctures—between consciousness of feeling and consciousness of feeling rules, between feeling rules and emotion work, between feeling rules and social structure.

By "emotion work" I refer to the act of trying to change in degree or quality an emotion or feeling. To "work on" an emotion or feeling is, for our purposes, the same as "to manage" an emotion or to do "deep acting." Note that "emotion work" refers to the effort—the act of trying—and not to the outcome, which may or may not be successful. Failed acts of management still indicate what ideal formulations guide the effort, and on that account are no less interesting than emotion management that works.

The very notion of an attempt suggests an active stance vis-à-vis feeling. In my exploratory study respondents characterized their emotion work by a variety of active verb forms: "I *psyched myself up* . . . I *squashed* my anger down . . . I *tried hard* not to feel disappointed . . . I *made* myself have a good time . . . I *tried* to feel grateful . . . I *killed* the hope I had burning." There was also the actively passive form, as in "I *let myself* finally feel sad."

Emotion work differs from emotion "control" or "suppression." The latter two terms suggest an effort merely to stifle or prevent feeling. "Emotion work" refers more broadly to the act of evoking or shaping, as well as suppressing feeling. I avoid the term "manipulate" because it suggests a shallowness I do not want to imply. We can speak, then, of two broad types of emotion work: *evocation*, in which the cognitive focus is on a desired feeling that is initially absent, and *suppression*, in which the cognitive focus is on an undesired feeling that is initially present. One respondent, going out with a priest twenty years her senior, exemplifies the problems of evocative emotion work:

> Anyway, I started to try and make myself like him. I made myself focus on the way he talked, certain things he'd done in the past. . . . When I was with him I did like him, but I would go home and write in my journal how much I couldn't stand him. I kept changing my feeling and actually thought I really liked him while I was with him, but a couple of hours after he was gone, I reverted back to different feelings.[vi]

[vi]The illustrations of emotion work come from a content analysis of 261 protocols given to students in two classes at the University of California, Berkeley, in 1974.

Another respondent exemplifies the work not of working feeling up, but of working feeling down:

> Last summer I was going with a guy often, and I began to feel very strongly about him. I knew, though, that he had just broken up with a girl a year ago because she had gotten too serious about him, so I was afraid to show any emotion. I also was afraid of being hurt, so I attempted to change my feelings. *I talked myself into not caring about Mike* . . . but I must admit it didn't work for long. *To sustain this feeling I had to almost invent bad things about him and concentrate on them or continue to tell myself he didn't care. It was a hardening of emotions,* I'd say. It took a lot of work and was unpleasant, because I had to concentrate on anything I could find that was irritating about him.

Often emotion work is aided by setting up an emotion-work system—for example, telling friends all the worst faults of the person one wanted to fall out of love with and then going to those friends for reinforcement of this view of the ex-beloved. This suggests another point: emotion work can be done by the self upon the self, by the self upon others, and by others upon oneself.

In each case the individual is conscious of a moment of "pinch," or discrepancy, between what one does feel and what one wants to feel (which is, in turn, affected by what one thinks one ought to feel in such a situation). In response, the individual may try to eliminate the pinch by working on feeling. Both the sense of discrepancy and the response to it can vary in time. The managing act, for example, can be a five-minute stopgap measure, or it can be a decade-long effort suggested by the term "working through."

There are various techniques of emotion work. One is *cognitive:* the attempt to change images, ideas, or thoughts in the service of changing the feelings associated with them. A second is *bodily:* the attempt to change somatic or other physical symptoms of emotion (e.g., trying to breathe slower, trying not to shake). Third, there is *expressive* emotion work: trying to change expressive gestures in the service of changing inner feeling (e.g., trying to smile or cry). This differs from simple display in that it is directed toward change in feeling. It differs from bodily emotion work in that the individual tries to alter or shape one or another of the classic public channels for the expression of feeling.

These three techniques are distinct theoretically, but often go together in practice. For example:

> I was a star halfback in high school. Before games I didn't feel the upsurge of adrenalin—in a word I wasn't "psyched up." (This was due to emotional difficulties I was experiencing and still experience—I was also an A student whose grades were dropping.) Having been in the past a fanatical, emotional, intense player, a "hitter" recognized by coaches as a very hard worker and a player with "desire," this was very upsetting. *I did everything I could to get myself "up." I would try to be outwardly "rah rah" or get myself scared of my opponent—anything to get the adrenalin flowing.* I tried to look nervous and intense before games, so at least the coaches wouldn't catch on. . . . When actually I was mostly bored, or in any event, not "up." I recall before one game wishing I was in the stands watching my cousin play for his school, rather than "out here."

Emotion work becomes an object of awareness most often, perhaps, when the individual's feelings do not fit the situation, that is, when the latter does not account for or legitimate feelings in the situation. A situation (such as a funeral) often carries with it a proper definition of itself ("this is a time of facing loss"). This official frame carries with it a sense of what it is fitting to feel (sadness). It is when this tripartite consistency among situation, conventional frame, and feeling is somehow ruptured, as when the bereaved feels an irrepressible desire to laugh delightedly at the thought of an inheritance, that rule and management come into focus. It is then that the more normal flow of deep convention—the more normal fusion of situation, frame, and feeling—seems like an enormous accomplishment.

The smoothly warm airline hostess, the ever-cheerful secretary, the unirritated complaint clerk, the undisgusted proctologist, the teacher who likes every student equally, and Goffman's unflappable poker player may all have to engage in deep acting, an acting that goes well beyond the mere ordering of display. Work to make feeling and frame consistent with situation is work in which individuals continually and privately engage. But they do so in obeisance to rules not completely of their own making.

FEELING RULES

We feel. We try to feel. We want to try to feel. The social guidelines that direct how we want to try to feel may be describable as a set of socially shared, albeit often latent (not thought about unless probed at), rules. In what way, we may ask, are these rules themselves known and how are they developed?

To begin with, let us consider several common forms of evidence for feeling rules. In common parlance, we often talk about our feelings or those of others as if rights and duties applied directly to them. For example, we speak of "having the right" to feel angry at someone. Or we say we "should feel more grateful" to a benefactor. We chide ourselves that a friend's misfortune, a relative's death, "should have hit us harder," or that another's good luck, or our own, should have inspired more joy. We know feeling rules, too, from how others react to what they infer from our emotive display. Someone may say to us, "You *shouldn't* feel so guilty: it wasn't your fault," or "You *don't have a right* to feel jealous, given our agreement." Another may simply declare an opinion as to the fit of feeling to situation and attach authority to his opinion. Others may question or call for an account of a particular feeling in a situation, whereas they do not ask for an accounting of some other situated feeling. Claims and callings for an account can be seen as *rule reminders*. At other times, a person may, in addition, chide, tease, cajole, scold, shun—in a word, sanction—us for "misfeeling." Such sanctions are a clue to the rules they are meant to enforce.

Rights and duties set out the proprieties as to the *extent* (one can feel "too" angry or "not angry enough"), the *direction* (one can feel sad when one should feel happy), and the *duration* of a feeling, given the situation against which it is set. These rights and duties of feeling are a clue to the depth of social convention, to one final reach of social control.

There is a distinction, in theory at least, between a feeling rule as it is known by our sense of what we can *expect* to feel in a given situation and a rule as it is known by our sense of what we *should* feel in that situation. For example, one may realistically expect (knowing oneself and one's neighbor's parties) to feel bored at a large New Year's Eve party and at the same time acknowledge that it would be more fitting to feel exuberant.

In any given situation, we often invest what we expect to feel with idealization. To a remarkable extent these realizations vary socially, as is shown by a woman recalling her experiences as a "flower child":

> When I was living down south, I was involved with a group of people, friends. We used to spend most evenings after work or school together. We used to do a lot of drugs, acid, coke or just smoke dope, and we had this philosophy that we were very communal and did our best to share everything—clothes, money, food, and so on. I was involved with this one man—and thought I was "in love" with him. He in turn had told me that I was very important to him. Anyway, this one woman who was a very good friend of mine at one time and this man started having a sexual relationship, supposedly without my knowledge. I knew though and had a lot of mixed feelings about it. I thought intellectually that I had no claim to the man, and believed in fact that no one should ever try to *own* another person. I believed also that it was none of my business and I had no reason to worry about their relationship together, for it had nothing really to do with my friendship with either of them. I also believed in sharing. But I was horribly hurt, alone and lonely, depressed, and I couldn't shake the depression and on top of those feelings I felt guilty for having those possessively jealous feelings. And so I would continue going out with these people every night and try to suppress my feelings. My ego was shattered. I got to the point where I couldn't even laugh around them. So finally I confronted my friends and left for the summer and traveled with a new friend. I realized later what a heavy situation it was, and it took me a long time to get myself together and feel whole again.

Whether the convention calls for trying joyfully to possess, or trying casually not to, the individual compares and measures experience against an expectation that is often idealized. It is left for motivation ("what I want to feel") to mediate between feeling rule ("what I should feel") and emotion work ("what I try to feel"). Much of the time we live with a certain dissonance between "ought" and "want," and between "want" and "try to." But the attempts to reduce emotive dissonance are our periodic clues to rules of feeling.

A feeling rule shares some formal properties with other sorts of rules, such as rules of etiquette, rules of bodily comportment, and those of social interaction in general. A feeling rule is like these other kinds of rules in the following ways: It delineates a zone within which one has permission to be free of worry, guilt, or shame with regard to the situated feeling. A feeling rule sets down a metaphoric floor, walls, and ceiling, there being room for motion and play within boundaries. Like other rules, feeling rules can be obeyed halfheartedly or boldly broken, the latter at varying costs. A feeling rule can be in varying proportions external or internal. Feeling rules differ curiously from other types of rules in that they do not apply to action but to what is *often taken as a precursor to action.* Therefore they tend to be latent and resistant to formal codification.

Feeling rules reflect patterns of social membership. Some rules may be nearly universal, such as the rule that one should not enjoy killing or witnessing the killing of a human being. Other rules are unique to particular social groups and can be used to distinguish among them as alternate governments or colonizers of individual internal events.

FRAMING RULES AND
FEELING RULES: ISSUES IN IDEOLOGY

Rules for managing feeling are implicit in any ideological stance: they are the "bottom side" of ideology. Ideology has often been construed as a flatly cognitive framework, lacking implications for how we feel. Yet, drawing on Emile Durkheim, Clifford Geertz, and Erving Goffman, we can think of ideology as an interpretive framework that can be described in terms of framing rules and feeling rules. By

"framing rules" I refer to the rules according to which we ascribe definitions or meanings to situations. For example, a man who just got fired can see it as a result of personal failure or heartless capitalism. According to another, one can't. Framing and feeling rules mutually imply each other. They stand back to back.

It follows that when an individual changes an ideological stance, he or she drops old rules and assumes new ones for reacting to situations, cognitively and emotively. A sense of rights and duties applied to feelings in situations is also changed. One uses emotional sanctions differently and accepts different sanctioning from others. For example, feeling rules in American society have differed for men and women because of the assumption that their natures differ basically. The feminist movement brings with it a new set of rules for framing the work and family life of men and women: the same balance of priorities in work and family now ideally applies to men as to women. This carries with it implications for feeling. A woman can now as legitimately as a man become angry (as opposed to disappointed) over abuses at work, since her heart is supposed to be in that work and she has the right to hope for advancement as much as a man would. Or a man has the right to feel angry at the loss of custody if he has shown himself the fitter parent. Old-fashioned feelings are now as subject to new chidings and cajolings as are old-fashioned perspectives on the same array of situations.

One can defy an ideological stance not simply by maintaining an alternative frame on a situation but by maintaining an alternative set of feeling rights and obligations. One can defy an ideological stance by inappropriate affect and by refusing to perform the emotion management necessary to feel what, according to the official frame, it would seem fitting to feel. Deep acting is a *form of obeisance* to a given ideological stance and lax emotion management a clue to a lapsed ideology.

As some ideologies gain acceptance and others dwindle, contending sets of feeling rules rise and fall. Sets of feeling rules contend for a place in people's minds as a governing standard with which to compare the actual lived experience of, say, the first kiss, the abortion, the wedding, the birth, the first job, the first layoff, the divorce. What we call the changing climate of opinion partly involves a changed framing of the same sorts of events. For example, each of two mothers may feel guilty about leaving her small child at daycare while working all day. One mother, a feminist, may feel that she should not feel as guilty as she does. The second, a traditionalist, may feel that she should feel more guilty than she does.

Part of what we refer to as the psychological effects of "rapid social change," or unrest, is a change in the relation of feeling rule to feeling and a lack of clarity about what the rule actually is, owing to conflicts and contradictions between contending rules and between rules and feelings. Feelings are taken out of their conventional frames but not set into new ones. We may, like the marginal man, say, "I don't know how I should feel."

It remains to note that ideologies can function, as Randall Collins rightly notes, as weapons in the conflict between contending elites and social strata.[vii] Collins suggests that elites try to gain access to the emotive life of adherents by gaining legitimate access to ritual, which for him is a form of emotive technology. Developing his view, we can add that elites, and indeed social groups in general, struggle to assert the legitimacy of their framing rules and their feeling rules. Not simply the evocation of emotion but the rules governing it become the objects of political struggle.

FEELING RULES AND SOCIAL EXCHANGE

Any gesture—a cool greeting, an appreciative laugh, the apology for an outburst—is measured against a prior sense of what is reasonably owed another, given the sort of bond involved. Against this background measure, some gestures will seem more than ample, others less. The exchange of gestures has in turn two aspects. It is an exchange of display acts—of surface acting—and an exchange of emotion work—of deep acting. In either case, rules (display rules or feeling rules), once agreed upon, *establish the worth of a gesture and are thus used in social exchange to measure the worth of emotional gestures*. Feeling rules thus establish the basis of worth to be ascribed to a range of gestures, including emotion work. Emotion work is a gesture in a social exchange; it has a function there and is not to be understood merely as a facet of personality.

There seem to be two ways in which feeling rules come into play in social exchange. In the first, the individual takes the "owed" feeling to heart, takes it seriously. For example, a young woman on the eve of her college graduation felt anxious and depressed but thought that she "ought to feel happy," and that she "owed this happiness" to her parents for making her graduation possible.

> To my parents and friends, graduation was a really big deal, especially for my parents, since I'm the oldest in the family. For some reason, however, I couldn't get excited about it. I had had a good time at college and all, but I was ready to get out and I knew it. Also, we had practiced the ceremony so many times that it had lost its meaning to me. I put on an act, though, and tried to act real emotional and hug my friends and cry, but I knew inside I didn't really feel it.[viii]

The young graduate "paid" her parents, we might say, in surface acting dissociated from her "real" definition of the situation. Going one step further, she could pay them with a gesture of deep acting—of trying to feel. A most generous gesture of all is the act of successful self-persuasion, of genuine feeling and frame change, a deep acting that jells, that works, that becomes what the emotion *is*, though it is nonetheless not a "natural" gift. The best gift, the gift the parents wish for, is, of course, their daughter's real joy.

The second way feeling rules come into play in exchange is shown when the individual does not take the affective convention seriously but

---

[vii]Collins suggests that elite groups contend not only for access to the means of economic production or the means of violence but also for access to the means of "emotion production" (1975, p. 59). Rituals are seen as useful tools for forging emotional solidarity (that can be used against others) and for setting up status hierarchies (that can dominate those who find that the new ideals have denigrating effects on themselves).

[viii]Hochschild 1983, p. 82.

instead plays with it. For example, an airport observation: There are two airline ticket agents, one experienced, one new on the job. The new agent is faced with the task of rewriting a complex ticket (involving change of date, lower fare, and credit of the difference between the previous and present fare to be made toward an air travel card, etc.). The new ticket agent looks for the "old hand," who is gone, while the customers in line shift postures and stare intently at the new agent. The old hand finally reappears after ten minutes, and the following conversation takes place: "I was looking for you. You're supposed to be my instructor." Old hand: "Gee," with an ironic smile, "I am *really* sorry, I feel *so* bad I wasn't here to help out" (they both laugh). The inappropriate feeling (lack of guilt, or sympathy) can be played upon in a way that says, "Don't take my nonpayment in emotion work or display work personally. I don't want to work here. You can understand that." The laughter at an ironic distance from the affective convention suggests also an intimacy: we do not need these conventions to hold us together. We share our defiance of them.

COMMODIFICATION OF FEELING

In the beginning I asked how feeling rules might vary in salience across social classes. One possible approach to this question is via the connections among social exchange, commodification of feeling, and the premium, in many middle-class jobs, on the capacity to manage meanings.

Conventionalized feeling may come to assume the properties of a commodity. When deep gestures of exchange enter the market sector and are bought and sold as an aspect of labor power, feelings are commodified. When the manager gives the company his enthusiastic faith, when the airline stewardess gives her passengers her psyched-up but quasi-genuine reassuring warmth, what is sold as an aspect of labor power is deep acting.

But commodification of feeling may not have equal salience for people in every social class or occupational sector. When I speak of social class, it is not strictly income, education, or occupational status that I refer to, but to something roughly correlated to these—the on-the-job task of creating and sustaining

appropriate meanings. The bank manager or the IBM executive may be required to sustain a definition of self, office, and organization as "up-and-coming" or "on the go," "caring," or "reliable," meanings most effectively sustained through acts upon feeling. Feeling rules are of utmost salience in jobs such as these; rule reminders and sanctions are more in play. It is not, as Erich Fromm and C. Wright Mills suggest, that the modern middle-class man "sells" his personality but that many jobs call for an appreciation of display rules, feeling rules, and a capacity for deep acting.

Working-class jobs more often call for the individual's external behavior and the products of it—a car part assembled, a truck delivered 500 miles away, a road repaired. The creation and the sustaining of meanings go on of course, but it is not what the boss pays for. Some working- or lower-class jobs do require emotion work—the jobs of prostitute, servant, nanny, and eldercare worker, for example. Such workers are especially important as a source of insight about emotion management. Being less rewarded for their work than their superiors, they are, perhaps, more detached from, and perceptive about it. Just as we can learn more about "appropriate situation-feeling fits" by studying misfits, we can probably understand commodification of feeling better from those who more often have to ask themselves: Is this what I *do* feel or what I *have* to feel?

Why, I asked, do we feel in ways appropriate to the situation as much of the time as we do? One answer is because we *try* to manage what we feel in accordance with latent rules. In order to elaborate this suggestion I considered first the responsiveness of emotion to acts of management as it is treated in the organismic and interactive account of emotion.

Still, occasionally emotions come over us like an uncontrollable flood. We feel overcome with grief, anger, or joy. Insofar as emotion is, as Darwin suggests, a substitute for action, or *action-manqué*, we may become enraged instead of killing, envious instead of stealing, depressed instead of dying. Or, yet again, emotion can be a prelude to action—and we become so enraged that we kill, so envious that we steal, so depressed that we die. Newspapers make a business of recording emotions of this sort. But the other half of the human story concerns how people calm down before they kill someone, how people want something but don't steal it, how people put the bottle of sleeping pills away and call a friend. Just how it is we hold, shape, and—to the extent we can—direct feeling is not what we read about in the newspaper. But it may be the really important news.

Introduction to *The Managed Heart*

While in the previous reading Hochschild singled out class position as a central determinate of the commodification of feelings, in this chapter from *The Managed Heart* she turns her attention to the effects of gender relations on emotion management. If members of the lower and working classes tend more to things than to people, and thus are less practiced in the skills of emotional labor, the hierarchical patterning of managing emotions is reversed when it comes to gender. In other words, while the occupations associated with the more advantaged classes (flight attendants, sales workers, teachers, lawyers, health care providers, etc.) are more likely to require the manipulation of personal feelings, it is women, the less advantaged gender, who more often find it necessary to be skilled emotion managers and are thus more susceptible to the commodification of their feelings. As you will read, Hochschild attributes these differences to the unequal distribution of money, power, authority, and status. As a result, in their private life "women make a resource out of feeling and offer it to men as a gift in return for the more material resources they lack" (1983:163). Emotion work becomes central to how to be, and what it means to be, a wife, a mother, and a woman. Meanwhile, men and women are typically called on to perform different types of emotional labor because of the gendered nature of occupations. This, too, carries with it a number of consequences that make the managing of feelings a different business for women and men.

The Managed Heart (1983)

Arlie Russell Hochschild

GENDER, STATUS, AND FEELING

More emotion management goes on in the families and jobs of the upper classes than in those of the lower classes. That is, in the class system, social conditions conspire to make it more prevalent at the top. In the gender system, on the other hand, the reverse is true: social conditions make it more prevalent, and prevalent in different ways, for those at the bottom—women. In what sense is this so? And why?

Both men and women do emotion work, in private life and at work. In all kinds of ways, men as well as women get into the spirit of the party, try to escape the grip of hopeless love, try to pull themselves out of depression, try to

SOURCE: From *The Managed Heart* by Hochschild, A., reprinted with permission from University of California Press via Copyright Clearance Center.

allow grief. But in the whole realm of emotional experience, is emotion work as important for men as it is for women? And is it important in the same ways? I believe that the answer to both questions is No. The reason, at bottom, is the fact that women in general have far less independent access to money, power, authority, or status in society. They are a subordinate social stratum, and this has four consequences.

First, lacking other resources, women make a resource out of feeling and offer it to men as a gift in return for the more material resources they lack. . . . Thus their capacity to manage feeling and to do "relational" work is for them a more important resource. Second, emotion work is important in different ways for men and for women. This is because each gender tends to be called on to do different kinds of this work. . . . This specialization of emotional labor in the marketplace rests on the different childhood training of the heart that is given to girls and to boys. ("What are little girls made of? Sugar and spice and everything nice. What are little boys made of? Snips and snails and puppy dog tails.") Moreover, each specialization presents men and women with different emotional tasks. Women are more likely to be presented with the task of mastering anger and aggression in the service of "being nice." To men, the socially assigned task of aggressing against those that break rules of various sorts creates the private task of mastering fear and vulnerability.

Third, and less noticed, the general subordination of women leaves every individual woman with a weaker "status shield" against the displaced feelings of others. . . . The fourth consequence of the power difference between the sexes is that for each gender a different portion of the managed heart is enlisted for commercial use. Women more often react to subordination by making defensive use of sexual beauty, charm, and relational skills. For them, it is these capacities that become most vulnerable to commercial exploitation, and so it is these capacities that they are most likely to become estranged from. For male workers in "male" jobs, it is more often the capacity to wield anger and make threats that is delivered over to the company, and so it is this sort of capacity that they are more likely to feel estranged from. After the

great transmutation, then, men and women come to experience emotion work in different ways. . . .

Women as Emotion Managers

Middle-class American women, tradition suggests, feel emotion more than men do. The definitions of "emotional" and "cogitation" in the *Random House Dictionary of the English Language* reflect a deeply rooted cultural idea. Yet women are also thought to command "feminine wiles," to have the capacity to premeditate a sigh, an outburst of tears, or a flight of joy. In general, they are thought to *manage* expression and feeling not only better but more often than men do. How much the conscious feelings of women and men may differ is an issue I leave aside here. However, the evidence seems clear that women do *more* emotion managing than men. And because the well-managed feeling has an outside resemblance to spontaneous feeling, it is possible to confuse the condition of being more "easily affected by emotion" with the action of willfully managing emotion when the occasion calls for it.

Especially in the American middle class, women tend to manage feeling more because in general they depend on men for money, and one of the various ways of repaying their debt is to do extra emotion work—*especially emotion work that affirms, enhances, and celebrates the well-being and status of others.* When the emotional skills that children learn and practice at home move into the marketplace, the emotional labor of women becomes more prominent because men in general have not been trained to make their emotions a resource and are therefore less likely to develop their capacity for managing feeling.

There is also a difference in the kind of emotion work that men and women tend to do. Many studies have told us that women adapt more to the needs of others and cooperate more than men do. These studies often imply the existence of gender-specific characteristics that are inevitable if not innate. But do these characteristics simply exist passively in women? Or are they signs of a social work that women *do*—the work of affirming, enhancing, and celebrating the well-being and status of others? I believe that much of the time, the adaptive, cooperative woman is actively working at showing deference. This deference requires her to make an outward display of what Leslie Fiedler has called the "seriously" good girl in her and to support this effort by evoking feelings that make the "nice" display seem natural.[i] Women who want to put their own feelings less at the service of others must still confront the idea that if they do so, they will be considered less "feminine."

. . . The emotional arts that women have cultivated are analogous to the art of feigning that Lionel Trilling has noted among those whose wishes outdistance their opportunities for class advancement. As for many others of lower status, it has been in the woman's interest to be the better actor.[ii] As the psychologists would say, the techniques of deep acting have unusually high "secondary gains." Yet these skills have long been mislabeled "natural," a part of woman's "being" rather than something of her own making.[iii]

Sensitivity to nonverbal communication and to the micropolitical significance of feeling gives women something like an ethnic language, which men can speak too, but on the whole less well. It is a language women share offstage in their talk "about feelings." This talk is not, as it is for men offstage, the score-keeping of conquistadors. It is the talk of the artful prey, the language of tips on how to make him want her, how to psyche him out, how to put him on or turn him off. Within the traditional female subculture, subordination at close quarters is understood, especially in adolescence, as a "fact of life." Women accommodate, then, but not passively. They actively adapt feeling to a need or a purpose at hand, and they do it so that it *seems* to express a passive state of agreement, the chance occurrence of coinciding needs. Being becomes a way of doing. Acting is the needed art, and emotion work is the tool. . . .

Almost everyone does the emotion work that produces what we might, broadly speaking, call deference. But women are expected to do more of it. A study by Wikler (1976) comparing male with female university professors found that students expected women professors to be warmer and more supportive than male professors; given these expectations, proportionally more women professors were perceived as cold. In another study, Broverman, Broverman, and Clarkson (1970) asked clinically trained psychologists, psychiatrists, and social workers to match various characteristics with "normal adult men" and "normal adult women"; they more often associated "very tactful, very gentle, and very aware of feelings of others" with their ideas of the normal adult woman. In being adaptive, cooperative, and helpful, the woman is on a private stage behind the public stage, and as a consequence she is often seen as less good at arguing, telling jokes, and teaching than she is at expressing appreciation of these activities. She is the conversational cheerleader. She actively enhances other people—usually men, but also other women to whom she plays woman. The more she seems natural at it, the more her labor does not show as labor, the more successfully it is disguised as the *absence* of other, more prized qualities. As a *woman* she may be praised for out-enhancing the best enhancer, but as a *person* in comparison with comics, teachers, and argument-builders, she usually lives outside the climate of enhancement that men tend to inhabit. Men, of course, pay court to certain other men

---

[i]Fiedler (1960) suggests that girls are trained to be "seriously" good and to be ashamed of being bad whereas boys are asked to be good in formalistic ways but covertly invited to be ashamed of being "too" good. Oversocialization into "sugar-and-spice" demeanor produces feminine skills in delivering deference.

[ii]Other researchers have found men to have a more "romantic" orientation to love, women a more "realistic" orientation. That is, males may find cultural support for a passive construction of love, for seeing themselves as "falling head over heels," or "walking on air." According to Kephart, "the female is not pushed hither and yon by her romantic compulsions. On the contrary, she seems to have a greater measure of rational control over her romantic inclinations than the male" (1967, p. 473).

[iii]The use of feminine wiles (including flattery) is felt to be a psychopolitical style of the subordinate; it is therefore disapproved of by women who have gained a foothold in the man's world and can afford to disparage what they do not need to use.

and women and thus also do the emotion work that keeps deference sincere. The difference between men and women is a difference in the psychological effects of having or not having power.

Racism and sexism share this general pattern, but the two systems differ in the avenues available for the translation of economic inequality into private terms. The white manager and the black factory worker leave work and go home, one to a generally white neighborhood and family and the other to a generally black neighborhood and family. But in the case of women and men, the larger economic inequality is filtered into the intimate daily exchanges between wife and husband. Unlike other subordinates, women seek *primary* ties with a supplier. In marriage, the principle of reciprocity applies to wider arenas of each self: there is more to choose from in how we pay and are paid, and the paying between economically unequal parties goes on morning, noon, and night. The larger inequities find intimate expression.

Wherever it goes, the bargain of wages-for-other-things travels in disguise. Marriage both bridges and obscures the gap between the resources available to men and those available to women.[iv] Because men and women do try to love one another—to cooperate in making love, making babies, and making a life together—the very closeness of the bond they accept calls for some disguise of subordination. There will be talk in the "we" mode, joint bank accounts and joint decisions, and the idea among women that they are equal in the ways that "really count." But underlying this pattern will be *different potential futures outside the marriage* and the effect of that on the patterning of life.[v] The woman may thus become especially assertive about certain secondary decisions, or especially active in certain limited domains, in order to experience a sense of equality that is missing from the overall relationship.

Women who understand their ultimate disadvantage and feel that their position cannot change may jealously guard the covertness of their traditional emotional resources, in the understandable fear that if the secret were told, their immediate situation would get worse. For to confess that their social charms are the product of secret work might make them less valuable, just as the sexual revolution has made sexual contact less "valuable" by lowering its bargaining power without promoting the advance of women into better-paying jobs. In fact, of course, when we redefine "adaptability" and "cooperativeness" as a form of shadow labor, we are pointing to a hidden cost for which some recompense is due and suggesting that a general reordering of female-male relationships is desirable.

There is one further reason why women may offer more emotion work of this sort than men: more women at all class levels do unpaid labor of a highly interpersonal sort. They nurture, manage, and befriend children. More "adaptive" and "cooperative," they address themselves better to the needs of those who are not yet able to adapt and cooperate much themselves. Then, according to Jourard (1968), because they are seen as members of the category from which mothers come, women in general are asked to look out for psychological needs more than men are. The world turns to women for mothering, and this fact silently attaches itself to many a job description.

Women at Work

With the growth of large organizations calling for skills in personal relations, the womanly art of status enhancement and the emotion work that it requires has been made more public, more systematized, and more standardized. It is performed by largely middle-class women in largely public-contact jobs. . . . Jobs involving emotional labor comprise over a third of all jobs.

[iv]Because women have less access to money and status than their male class peers do, they are more motivated than men to marry in order to win access to a much higher "male wage."

[v]Zick Rubin's study of young men and women in love relationships (generally middle-class persons of about the same age) found that the women tended to admire their male loved ones more than they were, in turn, admired by them. The women also felt "more like" their loved ones than the men did. (See Rubin 1970; Reiss 1960.)

But they form only a *quarter* of all jobs that men do, and over *half* of all jobs that women do.

Many of the jobs that call for public contact also call for giving service to the public. Richard Sennett and Jonathan Cobb, in *The Hidden Injuries of Class*, comment on how people tend to rank service jobs in relation to other kinds of jobs: "At the bottom end of the scale are found not factory jobs but service jobs where the individual has to perform personally for someone else. A bartender is listed below a coal miner, a taxi driver below a truck driver; we believe this occurs because their functions *are felt to be more dependent on and more at the mercy of others*" [my emphasis].[vi] Because there are more women than men in service jobs (21 percent compared with 9 percent), there are "hidden injuries" of gender attached to those of class.

Once women are at work in public-contact jobs, a new pattern unfolds: they receive less basic deference. That is, although some women are still elbow-guided through doors, chauffeured in cars, and protected from rain puddles, they are not shielded from one fundamental consequence of their lower status: their feelings are accorded less weight than the feelings of men. . . .

How, then, does a woman's lower status influence how she is treated by others? More basically, what is the prior link between status and the treatment of feeling? High-status people tend to enjoy the privilege of having their feelings noticed and considered important. The lower one's status, the more one's feelings are not noticed or treated as inconsequential. H. E. Dale, in *The Higher Civil Service of Great Britain*, reports the existence of a "doctrine of feelings":

The doctrine of feelings was expounded to me many years ago by a very eminent civil servant.

. . . He explained that the importance of feelings varies in close correspondence with the importance of the person who feels. If the public interest requires that a junior clerk should be removed from his post, no regard need be paid to his feelings; if it is the case of an assistant secretary, they must be carefully considered, within reason; if it is a permanent secretary, feelings are a principal element in the situation, and only imperative public interest can override their requirements.[vii]

Working women are to working men as junior clerks are to permanent secretaries. Between executive and secretary, doctor and nurse, psychiatrist and social worker, dentist and dental assistant, a power difference is reflected as a gender difference. The "doctrine of feelings" is another double standard between the two sexes.[viii]

The feelings of the lower-status party may be discounted in two ways: by considering them rational but unimportant or by considering them irrational and hence dismissable. An article entitled "On Aggression in Politics: Are Women Judged by a Double Standard?" presented the results of a survey of female politicians. All those surveyed said they believed there was an affective double standard. As Frances Farenthold, the president of Wells College in Aurora, New York, put it: "You certainly see to it that you don't throw any tantrums. Henry Kissinger can have his scenes—remember the way he acted in Salzburg? But for women, we're still in the stage that if you don't hold in your emotions, you're pegged as emotional, unstable, and all those terms that have always been used to describe women."[ix] These women in public life were agreed on the following points. When a man expresses anger, it is deemed "rational" or understandable anger, anger that indicates not

[vi]Sennett and Cobb (1973), p. 236.

[vii]Quoted in Goffman (1967), p. 10.

[viii]The code of chivalry is said to require protection of the weaker *by* the stronger. Yet a boss may bring flowers to his secretary or open the door for her only to make up for the fact that he gets openly angry at her more often than he does at a male equal or superior, and more often than she does at him. The flowers symbolize redress, even as they obscure the basic maldistribution of respect and its psychic cost.

[ix]*New York Times*, February 12, 1979.

weakness of character but deeply held conviction. When women express an equivalent degree of anger, it is more likely to be interpreted as a sign of personal instability. It is believed that women are more emotional, and this very belief is used to invalidate their feelings. That is, the women's feelings are seen not as a response to real events but as reflections of themselves as "emotional" women.

Here we discover a corollary of the "doctrine of feelings": the lower our status, the more our manner of seeing and feeling is subject to being discredited, and the less believable it becomes. An "irrational" feeling is the twin of an invalidated perception. A person of lower status has a weaker claim to the right to define what is going on; less trust is placed in her judgments; and less respect is accorded to what she feels. Relatively speaking, it more often becomes the burden of women, as with other lower-status persons, to uphold a minority viewpoint, a discredited opinion.

Medical responses to male and female illness provide a case in point. One study of how doctors respond to the physical complaints of back pain, headache, dizziness, chest pain, and fatigue—symptoms for which a doctor must take the patient's word—showed that among fifty-two married couples, the complaints of the husbands elicited more medical response than those of the wives. The authors conclude: "The data may bear out . . . that the physicians . . . tend to take illness more seriously in men than in women."[x] Another study of physician interactions with 184 male and 130 female patients concluded that "doctors were more likely to consider the psychological component of the patient's illness important when the patient was a woman."[xi] The female's assertion that she was physically sick was more likely to be invalidated as something "she just imagined," something "subjective," not a response to anything real.

To make up for either way of weighing the feelings of the two sexes unequally, many women urge their feelings forward, trying to express them with more force, so as to get them treated with seriousness. But from there the spiral moves down. For the harder women try to oppose the "doctrine of feeling" by expressing their feelings more, the more they come to fit the image awaiting them as "emotional." Their efforts are discounted as one more example of emotionalism. The only way to counter the doctrine of feelings is to eliminate the more fundamental tie between gender and status.

The Status Shield at Work

Given this relation between status and the treatment of feeling, it follows that persons in low-status categories—women, people of color, children—lack a status shield against poorer treatment of their feelings. This simple fact has the power to utterly transform the content of a job. The job of flight attendant, for example, is not the *same job* for a woman as it is for a man. A day's accumulation of passenger abuse for a woman differs from a day's accumulation of it for a man. Women tend to be more exposed than men to rude or surly speech, to tirades against the service, the airline, and airplanes in general. As the company's main shock absorbers against "mishandled" passengers, their own feelings are more frequently subjected to rough treatment. In addition, a day's exposure to people who resist authority in women is a different experience for a woman than it is for a man. Because her gender is accorded lower status, a woman's shield against abuse is weaker, and the importance of what she herself might be feeling—when faced with blame for an airline delay, for example—is correspondingly reduced. Thus the job for a man differs in essential ways from the same job for a woman.

In this respect, it is a disadvantage to be a woman—as 85 percent of all flight attendants are. And in this case, they are not simply women in the biological sense. They are also a highly visible distillation of middle-class American

---

[x]More women than men go to doctors, and this might seem to explain why doctors take them less seriously. But here it is hard to tell cause from effect, for if a woman's complaints are not taken seriously, she may have to make several visits to doctors before a remedy is found (Armitage et al. 1979).

[xi]Wallens et al. (1979), p. 143.

notions of femininity. They symbolize Woman. Insofar as the category "female" is mentally associated with having less status and authority, female flight attendants are more readily classified as "really" female than other females are. And as a result their emotional lives are even less protected by the status shield.

More than female accountants, bus drivers, or gardeners, female flight attendants mingle with people who expect them to *enact* two leading roles of Womanhood: the loving wife and mother (serving food, tending the needs of others) and the glamorous "career woman" (dressed to be seen, in contact with strange men, professional and controlled in manner, and literally very far from home). They do the job of symbolizing the transfer of homespun femininity into the impersonal marketplace, announcing, in effect, "I work in the public eye, but I'm still a woman at heart."

Passengers borrow their expectations about gender biographies from home and from the wider culture and then base their demands on this borrowing. The different fictive biographies they attribute to male and female workers make sense out of what they expect to receive in the currency of caretaking and authority. One male flight attendant noted:

They always ask about my work plans. "Why are you doing this?" That's one question we get all the time from passengers. "Are you planning to go into management?" Most guys come in expecting to do it for a year or so and see how they like it, but we keep getting asked about the management training program. I don't know any guy that's gone into management from here.

In contrast, a female flight attendant said:

Men ask me why I'm not married. They don't ask the guys that. Or else passengers will say, "Oh, when you have kids, you'll quit this job. I know you will." And I say, "Well, no, I'm not going to have kids." "Oh yes you will," they say. "No I'm not," I say, and I don't want to get more personal than that. They may expect me to have kids because of my gender, but I'm not, no matter what they say.

If a female flight attendant is seen as a protomother, then it is natural that the work of nurturing should fall to her. As one female attendant said: "The guys bow out of it more and we pick up the slack. I mean the handling of babies, the handling of children, the coddling of the old folks. The guys don't get involved in that quite as much." Confirming this, one male flight attendant noted casually, "Nine times out of ten, when I go out of my way to talk, it will be to attractive gal passengers." In this regard, females generally appreciated gay male flight attendants who, while trying deftly to sidestep the biography test, still gravitate more toward nurturing work than straight males are reputed to do.

Gender makes two jobs out of one in yet another sense. Females are asked more often than males to appreciate jokes, listen to stories, and give psychological advice. Female specialization in these offerings takes on meaning only in light of the fact that flight attendants of both sexes are required to be both deferential and authoritative; they have to be able to appreciate a joke nicely, but they must also be firm in enforcing the rules about oversized luggage. But because more deference is generally expected from a woman, she has a weaker grasp on passenger respect for her authority and a harder time enforcing rules.

In fact, passengers generally assume that men have *more* authority than women and that men exercise authority *over* women. For males in the corporate world to whom air travel is a way of life, this assumption has more than a distant relation to fact. As one flight attendant put it: "Say you've got a businessman sitting over there in aisle five. He's got a wife who takes his suite to the cleaners and makes the hors d'oeuvres for his business guests. He's got an executive secretary with horn-rimmed glasses who types 140 million words a minute and knows more about his airline ticket than he does. There's no woman in his life over him." This assumption of male authority allows ordinary twenty-year-old male flight attendants to be mistaken for the "managers" or "superintendents" of older female flight attendants. A uniformed male among women, passengers assume, must have authority over women. In fact, because males were excluded from this job until after a long "discrimination" suit in the mid-1960s and few were hired until the early 1970s, most male flight attendants are younger and have less seniority than most female attendants.

The assumption of male authority has two results. First, authority, like status, acts as a shield against scapegoating. Since the women workers on the plane were thought to have less authority and therefore less status, they were more susceptible to scapegoating. When the plane was late, the steaks gone, or the ice out, frustrations were vented more openly toward female workers. Females were expected to "take it" better, it being more their role to absorb an expression of displeasure and less their role to put a stop to it.

In addition, both male and female workers adapted to this fictional redistribution of authority. Both, in different ways, made it more real. Male flight attendants tended to react to passengers *as if they had more authority* than they really did. This made them less tolerant of abuse and firmer in handling it. They conveyed the message that *as authorities* they expected compliance without loud complaint. Passengers sensing this message were discouraged from pursuing complaints and stopped sooner. Female flight attendants, on the other hand, assuming that passengers would honor their authority less, used more tactful and deferential means of handling abuse. They were more deferential toward male passengers (from whom they expected less respect) than toward female passengers (whose own fund of respect was expected to be lower). And they were less successful in preventing the escalation of abuse. As one male flight attendant observed: "I think the gals tend to get more intimidated if a man is crabby at them than if a woman is."

Some workers understood this as merely a difference of style. As one woman reflected:

The guys have a low level of tolerance and their own male way of asserting themselves with the passenger that I'm not able to use. I told a guy who had a piece of luggage in front of him that wouldn't fit under the seat, I told him, "It won't fit, we'll have to do something with it." He came back with, "Oh, but it's been here the whole trip, I've had it with me all the time, blah, blah, blah." He gave me some guff. I thought to myself, I'll

finish this later, I'll walk away right now. I intended to come back to him. A flying partner of mine, a young man, came by this passenger, without knowing about our conversation, and said to him, "Sir, that bag is too big for your seat. We're going to have to take it away." "Oh, here you are," the guy says, and he hands it over to him. . . . You don't see the male flight attendants being physically abused or verbally abused nearly as much as we are.

The females' supposed "higher tolerance for abuse" amounted to a combination of higher exposure to it and less ammunition—in the currency of respect—to use against it.

This pattern set in motion another one: female workers often went to their male co-workers to get them to "cast a heavier glance." As one woman who had resigned herself to this explained wearily: "I used to fight it and assert myself. Now I'm just too overworked. It's simpler to just go get the male purser. One look at him and the troublemaker shuts up. Ultimately it comes down to the fact that I don't have time for a big confrontation. The job is so stressful these days, you don't go out of your way to make it more stressful. A look from a male carries more weight." Thus the greater the respect males could command, the more they were called on to claim it.

This only increased the amount of deference that male workers felt their female co-workers owed them, and women found it harder to supervise junior males than females. One young male attendant said that certain conditions had to be met—and deference offered—before he would obey a woman's orders: "If it's an order without a human element to it, then I'll balk. I think sometimes it's a little easier for a man to be an authority figure and command respect and cooperation. I think it depends on how the gal handles herself. If she doesn't have much confidence or if she goes the other way and gets puffed out of shape, then in that case I think she could have more trouble with the stewards *than with the gals*" [my emphasis]. Workers tended to agree that females took orders better than males, no matter how "puffed out of shape" the attendant in charge might be, and that women in charge had to be nicer in exercising their authority than men did.

This attitude toward status and authority inspired compensatory reactions among some female workers. One response was to adopt the crisply cheerful but no-nonsense style of a Cub Scout den mother—a model of female authority borrowed from domestic life and used here to make it acceptable for women to tell adult men what to do. In this way a woman might avoid being criticized as "bossy" or "puffed out of shape" by placing her behavior within the boundaries of the gender expectations of passengers and co-workers.

Another response to displaced anger and challenged authority was to make small tokens of respect a matter of great concern. Terms of address, for example, were seen as an indicator of status, a promise of the right to politeness which those deprived of status unfortunately lack. The term, "girl," for example, was recognized by female workers as the moral equivalent of calling black men "boys." Although in private and among themselves, the women flight attendants I knew usually called themselves "girls," many were opposed to the use of the term in principle. They saw it not only as a question of social or moral importance but as a *practical matter*. To be addressed as a "girl" was to be subjected to more on-the-job stress. The order, "Girl, get me some cream" has a different effect than the request "Oh miss, could I please have some cream?" And if the cream has run out because the commissary didn't provide enough, it will be the "girls" who get the direct expressions of disappointment, exasperation, and blame. Tokens of respect can be exchanged to make a bargain: "I'll manage my unpleasant feelings for you if you'll manage yours for me." When outrageously rude people occasionally enter a plane, it reminds all concerned why the flimsy status shield against abuse is worth struggling over.

Schooled in emotion management at home, women have entered in disproportionate numbers those jobs that call for emotional labor outside the home. Once they enter the marketplace, a certain social logic unfolds. Because of the division of labor in the society at large, women *in any particular job* are assigned lower status and less authority than men. As a result, they lack a shield against the "doctrine of feelings." Much more often than men, they become the complaint department, the ones to whom dissatisfaction is fearlessly expressed. Their own feelings tend to be treated as less important. In ways that the advertising smiles obscure, the job has different contents for women and men.

Estrangement From Sexual Identity

Regardless of gender, the job poses problems of identity. What is my work role and what is "me"? How can I do deep acting without "feeling phony" and losing self-esteem? How can I redefine the job as "illusion making" without becoming cynical?

But there are other psychological issues a flight attendant faces if she is a woman. In response to her relative lack of power and her exposure to the "doctrine of feelings," she may seek to improve her position by making use of two traditionally "feminine" qualities—those of the supportive mother and those of the sexually desirable mate. Thus, some women *are* motherly; they support and enhance the well-being and status of others. But in *being* motherly, they may also *act* motherly and may sometimes experience themselves using the motherly act to win regard from others. In the same way, some women are sexually attractive and may act in ways that are sexually alluring. For example, one flight attendant who played the sexual queen—swaying slowly down the aisle with exquisitely understated suggestiveness—described herself as using her sexual attractiveness to secure interest and favors from male passengers. In each case, the woman is using a feminine quality for private purposes. But it is also true, for the flight attendant, that both "motherly" behavior and a "sexy" look and manner are partly an achievement of corporate engineering—a result of the company's emphasis on the weight and (former) age requirements, grooming classes, and letters from passengers regarding the looks and demeanor of flight attendants. In its training and supervisory roles, the company may play the part of the protective duenna. But in its commercial role as an advertiser of sexy and glamorous service, it acts more like a backstage matchmaker. Some early

United Airlines ads said, "And she might even make a good wife." The company, of course, has always maintained that it does not meddle in personal affairs.

Thus the two ways in which women traditionally try to improve their lot—by using their motherly capacity to enhance the status and well-being of others, and by using their sexual attractiveness—have come under company management. Most flight attendants I spoke with agreed that companies used and attached profit to these qualities. . . .

Estrangement from aspects of oneself are, in one light, a means of defense. On the job, the acceptance of a division between the "real" self and the self in a company uniform is often a way to avoid stress, a wise realization, a saving grace. But this solution also poses serious problems. For in dividing up our sense of self, in order to save the "real" self from unwelcome intrusions, we necessarily relinquish a healthy sense of wholeness. We come to accept as normal the tension we feel between our "real" and our "on-stage" selves.

More women than men go into public-contact work and especially into work in which status enhancement is the essential social-psychological task. In some jobs, such as that of the flight attendant, women may perform this task by playing the Woman. Such women are more vulnerable, on this account, to feeling estranged from their capacity to perform and enjoy two traditional feminine roles—offering status enhancement and sexual attractiveness to others. These capacities are now under corporate as well as personal management.

Perhaps this realization accounts for the laughter at a joke I heard surreptitiously passed around the Delta Training Office, as if for an audience of insiders. It went like this: A male passenger came across a woman flight attendant seated in the galley, legs apart, elbows on knees, her chin resting in one hand and a lighted cigarette in the other—held between thumb and forefinger. "Why are you holding your cigarette like that?" the man asked. Without looking up or smiling, the woman took another puff and said, "If I had balls, I'd be driving this plane." Inside the feminine uniform and feminine "act" was a would-be man. It was an estrangement joke, a poignant behind-the-scenes protest at a commercial logic that standardizes and trivializes the dignity of women.

❖

Discussion Questions

1. Symbolic interactionism emphasizes the constructed and negotiated aspects of the self and social life more generally. As a result, it shifts attention from analyses of the structural/institutional features of society. How might some of the key concepts in this framework (for instance, meaning, impression management, definition of the situation, interaction rituals, front and backstage, secondary adjustments, feeling rules, emotion work) be used to explore stratification systems and the relations of domination/subordination they sustain?

2. Symbolic interactionism is an inductive theoretical perspective that examines the interpretive nature of social life. For their part, symbolic interactionists are themselves inescapably engaged in an interpretation of their observations (as all observers are). As a result, their findings are, in a sense, interpretations of interpretations. What implications might this have on producing generalizable conclusions and, with them, theory itself? For that matter, how does one empirically study the self, which, after all, is the central concept within this theoretical tradition? Similarly, how might you observe and scientifically analyze the operation of feeling rules?

3. Following Blumer's argument, discuss how language is the fundamental basis of the self and social life.

4. Frederick Wiseman's *Titicut Follies*, Ken Kesey's *One Flew Over the Cuckoo's Nest*, and Philip Zimbardo's *Stanford Prison Experiment* are classic works that explore the psychological effects of being confined within total institutions. View one of these films and discuss its implications for Goffman's analysis of the relationship between the self and social arrangements. In what way does the film confirm and/or challenge Goffman's perspective?

5. In general, how important do you think emotions are in shaping an individual's (or your own) experiences and decisions? To what extent are emotions seen as a legitimate basis for action? In which domains of life (work, school, family, religion, politics, etc.) are emotive experiences encouraged or discouraged? Following Hochschild's insights, what factors might account for the differing types and intensity of emotions that are experienced within particular domains?

6

PHENOMENOLOGY AND ETHNOMETHODOLOGY

It is the meaning of our experiences, and not the ontological structure of the objects, which constitutes reality.

~Alfred Schutz,
On Phenomenology and Social Relations

Have you ever thought about just how many intricate habits, rules, and principles there are in everyday life? For instance, have you ever been talking to an acquaintance on the phone, trying to end the conversation by saying things like, "So, well, thanks for calling . . . " but he just prattles on as if you hadn't said anything (or, even worse, starts a whole new topic of conversation)? Or have you ever said your good-byes at a party and left, only to get to your car and realize you forgot your keys? Why does it feel so extremely awkward to go back in the door? These small, unexpected disruptions to routine social interactions exemplify just how nuanced social life is—and how many aspects of it are taken for granted. One classic example of this is elevator-riding: everyone everywhere rides an elevator in pretty much the same way (by turning around and facing the door through which you just entered). How would people react if you were to get on an elevator and then face someone already riding in the elevator, looking straight at him or her, rather than at the door? Ethnomethodologists actually do experiments like this and see the results.

In this chapter, we explore two different (albeit interrelated) traditions that focus on the *phenomena* of everyday life: phenomenology and ethnomethodology. Phenomenologists and ethnomethodologists analyze the taken-for-granted everyday world that is the basis for all human conduct. We begin with phenomenology, which is a philosophy, method, and approach that has deeply influenced psychology and psychiatry as well as sociology. Focusing particularly on the work of Alfred Schutz and his students Peter Berger and Thomas Luckmann, we will see that phenomenologists seek to explain how people actively produce and sustain meaning. We then turn to ethnomethodology, which is a more recent tradition developed principally by Harold Garfinkel. Ethnomethodologists focus less on meaning and subjectivity and more on the actual *methods* people use to accomplish their everyday lives. In contrast to phenomenology, which as indicated above has close ties to psychology and philosophy, ethnomethodology has close ties to linguistics and mainstream sociology. Ethnomethodologists are more interested in how actors assure each other that meaning is shared than the actual meaning structures themselves, although obviously the subject matter of phenomenology and ethnomethodology is very much intertwined.

ALFRED SCHUTZ (1899–1959): A BIOGRAPHICAL SKETCH

SOURCE: Used with permission of Evelyn Shutz Lang.

Alfred Schutz was born in Vienna, Austria, in 1899 to an upper-middle-class Jewish family. He studied law and the social sciences at the University of Vienna and after graduating began a career in banking. Although he was not an academic by profession, Schutz was intrigued by phenomenological sociology and participated in informal lecture and discussion circles. He was particularly interested in the work of the German sociologist Max Weber (1864–1920; see Edles and Appelrouth 2005, Chapter 3, and Chapter 1 of this book) and philosopher Edmund Husserl (1859–1938), who Schutz often visited in Freiburg and who even invited Schutz to be his assistant. Although he was only informally connected to academic life, in 1932 Schutz published what would come to be an essential work in the field: *Phenomenology of the Social World*. This groundbreaking work was not widely appreciated at first, however, both because Schutz was not an established academic with a university position and because it would not be translated into English until more than thirty-five years later. With the outbreak of World War II, Schutz fled to Paris and then to the United States shortly thereafter. Although he continued to work in banking, he also began teaching at the New School for Social Research in New York City in 1943, an institution that became home to a number of exiled German intellectuals. Among those he met in the United States and whose work significantly influenced his was the eminent pragmatist philosopher George Herbert Mead (see Chapter 5 of this book). Schutz finally gave up his banking career in 1956 and devoted himself full time to teaching and research. At the time of his death in 1959, Schutz was working on a comprehensive statement as to the development of his ideas since publication of *Phenomenology of the Social World*. This work (discussed below) was finished by Schutz's student Thomas Luckmann and published as *The Structures of the Life World* (*Strukturen der Lebenswelt*) by Schutz and Luckmann (1973).

INTELLECTUAL INFLUENCES AND CORE IDEAS

Above all, two key thinkers were pivotal in shaping the work of Alfred Schutz: Edmund Husserl and Max Weber.[1] As indicated previously, Edmund Husserl is commonly considered the founder of phenomenology. A student of mathematics, physics, and philosophy and influenced himself by Rene Descartes, David Hume, and Immanuel Kant, Husserl developed what he called "transcendental phenomenology," which holds that there is no pure subjective subject or pure objective object. Rather, all consciousness is consciousness of something, and objects do not have appearances independent of the beings that perceive them. Thus, the human experience in the world is as "a world of *meaningful* objectives and relations" (Wagner 1973:14; emphasis in original). Husserl used the term **lifeworld** (*Lebenswelt*) to refer to the world of existing assumptions as they are experienced and made meaningful in consciousness (Wagner 1973:63). Husserl (1913) explains how intentional consciousness, that is, directing our attention in one way or another, enables the phenomenologist to reconstruct or bracket his basic views on the world and himself and explore their interconnections. In doing so, Husserl made the lifeworld, or "thinking as usual" in everyday life situations, a legitimate object of investigation. Phenomenology investigates the systematic **bracketing** of all existing assumptions regarding the external world.

Following Husserl, Schutz emphasized that humans do not experience the world as an "objective" reality; rather, they experience the world as made of meaningful objects and relations. Understanding and explaining "reality," then, requires paying attention to the meaning structures by and through which individuals perceive the world. Extending Husserl's idea that the human actor, as a socialized member of society, operates within a lifeworld that is pregiven and already organized, Schutz emphasized that this taken-for-granted world includes whatever prejudices and typical interpretations may derive from it. Within the standpoint of this "natural attitude," the individual does not question the structures of meaning that comprise her lifeworld. Instead, the individual is guided by practical concerns, and her task is to live in rather than to reflect on the lifeworld. As Schutz (1970:136) states, the lifeworld is "the unproblematic ground for the emergence of all possible problems, the prerequisite for transforming any unclarified situation into warranted ascertainability." The lifeworld is the taken-for-granted backdrop within which all situations are measured and given meaning.

---

[1]Schutz was also particularly influenced by the sociologist and philosopher Max Scheler (1874–1928), who wrote on intersubjectivity, the intentionality of the Other, and sympathy (see *The Nature of Sympathy*, 1954/1922), as well as the French philosopher Henri Bergson, whose conception of *durée* provided the recognition of subjective experience of time in distinction from the mechanical notion of clock time (Wagner 1973:61).

Most important, the lifeworld is an intersubjective world, known and experienced by others. **Intersubjectivity** refers not so much to the fact that we share the same empirical or material world as others, but that we share the same consciousness. It is intersubjectivity—that you know that I know that you know—that allows human beings from a wide variety of personal and social backgrounds to function and interact.

On one hand, this emphasis on shared consciousness and meaning recalls Émile Durkheim's conceptualization of "collective conscience." Durkheim used this term to refer to the "totality of beliefs and sentiments common to average citizens of the same society" that "forms a determinate system which has its own life" (1893/1984:38–39).[2] However, in contrast to Durkheim, Schutz does not conceptualize the preorganized and pregiven elements of the lifeworld as acting on the individual with the external power of constraint. Rather, in accordance with the basic premises of symbolic interactionism (see Chapter 5), Schutz views one's "natural attitude" as based on the acceptance, interpretation, redefinition, and modification of cultural elements by the individual (Wagner 1973:64). That is, the individual gives the elements of the lifeworld a personal note and subtly changes, enlarges, or reduces their meaning in distinctive ways. A unique accumulation of lived experiences results, as the individual goes from situation to situation that makes up her everyday world.

This brings us to another important influence on Schutz: Max Weber, one of the leading figures in the development of modern sociology. Weber was one of the first to differentiate sociology from philosophy by proclaiming that the social sciences must abstain from value judgments. He envisioned sociology as the science of human behavior and its consequences, and he sought a method that would prevent the intrusion of political and moral ideologies that all too easily influence the judgment of the social scientist (whether this influence is conscious or not). However, Weber was not a crass positivist who simply ignored subjectivity in the quest for objectivity and timeless truths. His position on the proper method and subject of sociology is laid out in his definition of the discipline: sociology is "a science which attempts the *interpretive understanding* of social action in order thereby to arrive at a causal explanation of its course and effects" (1947:88; emphasis added). In casting interpretive understanding, or *Verstehen,* as the principal objective of sociology, Weber offered a distinctive counter to those who sought to base sociology on the effort to uncover universal laws applicable to all societies. In short, Weber sought to explain both the objective dimensions of social life (e.g., historical conditions, politico-economic structures, etc.) and the subjective dimension of social life, particularly the states of mind or motivations that guide individuals' behavior.

Schutz sought to expand on Weber's conceptualization of *Verstehen* and interpretive sociology (*verstedhende Soziologie*) by formulating his own concept of meaning. Starting with Weber's conceptualization of action as behavior to which a subjective meaning is attached, and drawing heavily on Husserl (as well as Bergson), Schutz envisions social action as an action oriented toward the past, present, or future behavior of another person or persons. In other words, while agreeing with Weber that social science must be interpretive, Schutz finds that Weber had failed to state clearly the essential characteristics of understanding (*Verstehen*), of subjective meaning (*gemeinter Sinn*), or of action (*Handeln*) (Walsh:xxi). As Schutz (1967:8) maintains:

> Weber makes no distinction between the *action*, considered as something in progress, and the completed *act*, between the meaning of the producer of a cultural object and the meaning of the object produced, between the meaning of my own action and the meaning of another's

---

[2]For Durkheim, the task of sociology is to analyze "social facts," that is, the conditions and circumstances external to the individual that, nevertheless, determine one's course of action. See Edles and Appelrouth (2005:82–86).

action, between my own experience and that of someone else, between my self-understanding and my understanding of another person. He does not ask how an actor's meaning is constituted or what modifications this meaning undergoes for his partners in the social world or for a nonparticipating observer. He does not try to identify the unique and fundamental relation existing between the self and the other self, that relation whose clarification is essential to a precise understanding of what it is to know another person. (emphasis in original)

Schutz sets out several interrelated concepts that help clarify the Weberian notion of social action and interpretive understanding. These concepts include lifeworld and intersubjectivity, discussed above, and **stocks of knowledge**, **recipes**, and **typifications**.

Stocks of knowledge (*Erfahrung*) provide actors with rules for interpreting interactions, social relationships, organizations, institutions, and the physical world. This is the "lower strata" of consciousness that does not receive a "reflective glance"; it consists of what has already been experienced and is thus taken for granted (Schutz 1967:80). For instance, the actor has a stock of knowledge about physical things and fellow creatures and artifacts, including cultural objects. She likewise has a stock of knowledge made up of "syntheses of inner experience." As Schutz (1973:81) states:

> The ordinary man in every moment of his lived experience lights upon past experiences in the storehouse of his consciousness. He knows about the world and he knows what to expect. With every moment of conscious life a new item is filed away in this vast storehouse. At a minimum, this is due to the fact that, with the arrival of a new moment, things are seen in a slightly different light. All of this is involved in the conception of a duration that is manifold, continuous, and irreversible in direction.

Moreover, it is only with a stock of knowledge that one is able to imaginatively explore courses of action other than those he already knows (Schutz 1964:229); although, to be sure, Schutz insists that it is only when the unexpected happens or new situations occur and the taken-for-granted is thrown into question that one is forced to consider alternative schemes of interpretation.

Schutz (1970:98) also refers to stocks of knowledge as "cookery-book knowledge." Just as a cookbook has recipes and lists of ingredients and formulas for making something to eat, so, too, we all have a "cookbook" of recipes, or implicit instructions, for accomplishing everyday life. Indeed, according to Schutz (1970:99), most of our daily activities, from rising to going to bed, "are performed by following recipes reduced to automatic habits or unquestioned platitudes."

Although Schutz sometimes uses the terms "recipe" and "typification" interchangeably, typification is the process of constructing personal "ideal-types" based on the typical function of people or things rather than their unique features. On one hand, typifications are akin to stereotypes (or stereotypes can be considered a form of typification). In both cases, perceptions are formed based on preconceived categories rather than on all possible information. However, Schutz's conceptualization of typification is more individualistic and interactive than the collectivistic sociological notion of "stereotype." While stereotypes are, by definition, pregiven and somewhat stagnant or fixed, building on Weber's notion of "ideal-type," Schutz emphasizes that typification is a process through which actors isolate the generic characteristics that are relevant for their particular interactive goal. As Schutz (1970:107) states:

> We typify in daily life, human activities which interest us only as appropriate means of bringing about intended effects, but not as emanations of the personality of our fellow-men. . . . In short, the ideal type is but a model of a conscious mind without the faculty of spontaneity and without a will of its own. In typical situations of our daily life, we too, assume certain typical roles. By isolating one of our activities from its interrelations with all the other manifestations

of our personality, we disguise ourselves as consumers or taxpayers, citizens, members of a church or of a club, clients, smokers, bystanders, etc. The traveler, for instance, has to behave in the specific way he believes the type "railway agent" to expect from a typical passenger.

Thus, for instance, we use typifications and recipes to know who and how to ask for help in the grocery store. We look around for a "kind-and-knowledgeable-looking shopper" or a "sales clerk," and then we initiate an interaction by saying, "Excuse me, do you know where I can find . . . " (as opposed to just blurting out the item that we need). Most important, the point is that the successful accomplishment of this everyday interaction relies not only on an abstract perception and knowledge of who and how to ask for help, but on our own actualization of recipes and typification as well. That is, we "bracket" or set aside other aspects of our personality, life, and experience in order to carry out the typified role of the "generic" shopper looking for an item in the store. For instance, if I can't find something in the store, I don't begin an interaction by saying, "Hi, I'm Laura, and I teach sociology"—even though that is an important biographical element of my life. I "bracket" that information and dimension of myself in order to carry out the shopper role.

Schutz's point is not only that typifications and recipes are economical and efficient, but that typification is vital to the very accomplishment of social life. Conscious life (as well as social life) itself relies on us having relatively unreflexive or routine typifications and recipes at our disposal. We cannot "carry on" without bracketing certain features of the social world because otherwise our consciousness would be overloaded. Indeed, Asperger syndrome (a type of autism) can be viewed as an example of the painful consequences that ensue for people unable to typify and/or bracket irrelevant information and stimuli. Asperger syndrome is a neurological disorder marked by deficiencies in social skills. Individuals with Asperger syndrome are often sensitive to sounds, tastes, smells, and sights that seem not to affect others. They often have a great deal of difficulty reading nonverbal cues and determining proper body space. In social interaction, people with Asperger syndrome may demonstrate gaze avoidance or turn away at the same moment as greeting another. They often want to interact with others, but they have trouble knowing how to make it work. From the perspective of a person with Asperger syndrome, the world is an inconstant, chaotic place, a deafening cacophony of overwhelming sound and an unintelligible jumble of symbols, as Alison Hale, in her autobiography, *My World Is Not Your World* (1998), makes clear:

> My first vivid memories of life are the senseless confusion at play school and the terror of being unable to make sense of my surroundings. I was bewildered by "the vast place of deafening, confusing mush of sound" where "the multi-coloured blurs [children] rushed past sometimes knocking into me" . . .
>
> I spent my primary school life tormented by confusion, bemused by the shapes on a page of printed text "should I read the black bits or the white bits?", puzzled by the riddle of "Why high notes on a piano are not further from the ground than low notes" and baffled by the way people treated me and why I was considered unintelligent. (http://www.hale.ndo.co.uk/alison/index.htm)

Hale eventually learned basic social skills in the same way that other people learn to play the piano: with effort and practice. She consciously learned to "make sense" of the world, that is, to decipher and respond to social cues that people without Asperger syndrome pick up intuitively (reflexively) and take for granted simply by being a member of the social group.[3]

In sum, the language we learn and the social structures within which we live provide us with a stockpile of typifications and recipes that make the world both intelligible and

_____

[3]See Barbara L. Kirby, *What Is Asperger Syndrome?* Founder of the OASIS Web site (www.asperger syndrome.org), coauthor of *The Oasis Guide to Asperger Syndrome* (Crown, 2001, revised 2005).

manageable. This does not mean, however, that specific elements of the cultural realm are the same for every person. Rather, stocks of knowledge are "biographically articulated"; every individual has a unique stock of knowledge because no two individuals have the same biographical or subjective experience. Thus, for instance, even identical twins, whom obviously have significant genetic and environmental commonalities, have distinct stocks of knowledge and subjectivity.

It is important to note, too, that not only does each of us have our own biographically articulated stock of knowledge, but the elements in our stock of knowledge do not contain the same weight or value in every situation. Schutz uses the terms *umwelt* and *mitwelt* to differentiate various realms of social experience, based on the level of intimacy/immediacy. Specifically, the umwelt is the realm of directly experienced social reality. Umwelt experiences (we relations) are a product of face-to-face relationships and are defined by a high degree of intimacy, as actors are in one another's immediate copresence. Because the pure umwelt (or we relation) is rooted in intimate interaction, it includes indicators of the subjectivity of the other. That is, each person must be aware of the other's body as a field of expression of inner processes of consciousness in a face-to-face situation (Psathas 1989:55). This, in turn, fosters the development of intersubjectivity.

By contrast, the mitwelt (world of contemporaries) is the realm of indirectly experienced social reality. In mitwelt relations, people are experienced only as "types," or within larger social structures, rather than individual actors (e.g., the postal worker who we've never met who delivers our mail). As people grow together (from mitwelt to umwelt relations), typifications and recipes are modified as they are infused with intimate bits of knowledge and actual experience. Conversely, as people grow apart (from mitwelt to umwelt relations), they move from less anonymous to more anonymous interactions, and as a result they become less able to know what goes on in the other person's mind.[4]

Another way to discuss the relationship between our biographically articulated stock of knowledge, typifications, and recipes is to say that individuals do not actually have identical experiences, but rather we act as if our experiences are, for all practical purposes, equivalent. For instance, even though you and I may go to the same football game, our actual experience of the game (i.e., what we actually see and experience) is different. First, since we inhabit different bodies, it is impossible for us to look at exactly the same things at each and every moment. Moreover, even if we both happen to look at exactly the same thing at exactly the same moment, we are not in the same seat or physical location, thus we are actually seeing the "same" thing but from slightly different perspectives. Most important, however, we do not have the same experience of the game because each of us brings our own biographically articulated stock of knowledge with us to the game. Thus, even if we were to look at exactly the same thing at the same moment from exactly the same vantage point, we would not in fact "see" exactly the same thing. Rather, we would be interpreting and bracketing the action we are witnessing in different ways, based on our unique biographically articulated life-world. This is most readily apparent in the difference between how experts and novices view the "same" phenomenon. The individual who really knows the game of football (and who perhaps has actually played football himself) will "see" entirely different categories of phenomena than the uninitiated spectator. While the experienced fan sees attempted versus actualized plays, standard versus unexpected formations, and the like the unversed spectator sees only who's on what side (based on the color of the uniforms) or who has the ball. So, too, the professional musician hears individual instruments, errors, interpretive styles, and patterns of syncopation that the inexperienced listener does not, even though they might be sitting side by side at the "same" recital.

---

[4]As you saw in Chapter 5, Erving Goffman (1961, 1963, 1969) brilliantly describes and analyzes the characteristics of "face-to-face" versus less personal interaction.

Photo 6.2   Individuals do not have identical experiences of even the "same" phenomena because stocks of knowledge are biographically articulated. Thus, for instance, a dedicated connoisseur will often see (or hear) entirely different categories of phenomena than the uninitiated viewer. Here, an opera connoisseur literally sees more with the help of opera glasses.

SOURCE: © Royalty-Free/CORBIS; used with permission.

Despite the fact that individuals never experience exactly the same thing, it is still possible to develop intersubjectivity, or shared meaning. Indeed, the very existence of society is dependent on individuals developing a shared meaning of their environment, for this alone allows for the fitting together of actions. In short, intersubjectivity is itself made possible through the process of typification, intercommunication, and language. As Schutz (1962:53) states:

> From the outset, we, the actors on the social scene, experience the world we live in as a world both of nature and of culture, not as private but as an intersubjective one, that is, as a world common to all of us, either actually given or potentially accessible to everyone; and this involves intercommunication and language.

In sum, this is the importance of language and shared interpretive schemes: they unite individuals who inevitably have their own experiences into a cohesive whole. In other words, because we cannot access other people's experiences or get inside each other's heads, social life is possible only via shared interpretive schemes and language.

SCHUTZ'S THEORETICAL ORIENTATION

As shown in Figure 6.1, Schutz pointedly seeks to illuminate the relationship between the individual and collective levels. On one hand, in the spirit of Durkheim, Schutz emphasizes the pregiven nature of the lifeworld, which reflects a collective approach to order. Schutz maintains that the elements of the lifeworld exist long before our birth, that we are born into particular cultural systems, such that, for instance, our "native language" and "natural attitude" are somewhat predetermined. As Schutz (1973:329) states, "I find myself in my everyday life within a world not of my own making . . . I was born into a pre-organized social world which will survive me, a world shared from the outset with fellow-men who are organized in groups."

Figure 6.1   Schutz's Basic Concepts and Theoretical Orientation

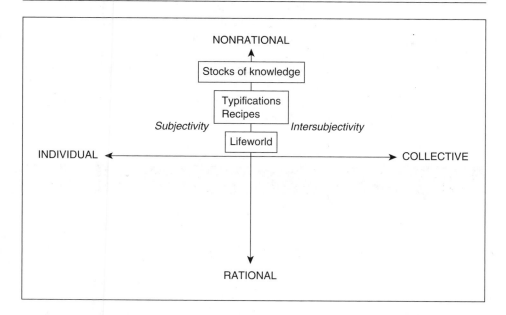

On the other hand, however, Schutz emphasizes that we do not merely "internalize" elements of the lifeworld, rather, we experience them; we interpret them, thereby reflecting an individual approach regarding order. We are not simply "vessels" for pre-given cultural forms. In other words, while the intersubjective dimension of the life-world is essential for social relationships and interaction, it nevertheless possesses a "private component." This dual collectivistic/individualistic bent regarding the question of order is also readily apparent in Schutz's notion that stocks of knowledge are "biographically articulated," that is, they vary from individual to individual because personal and subjective experiences are never exactly the same.

As shown in Figure 6.1, in emphasizing that social life is accomplished only via the intersubjective nature of stocks of knowledge, Schutz takes a primarily nonrational approach regarding action. Schutz stresses how each biographically articulated experience is part of a relatively unconscious, taken-for-granted (and thereby nonrational) lifeworld. We experience the world as one of common and shared objects, events, values, goals, and recipes for acting, and it is this taken-for-granted intersubjectivity that sustains social life, as well as each of our biographically articulated lifeworlds.

To be sure, in addition to the unreflective, habitual nature of everyday action is the problem-solving aspect of stocks of knowledge. There is a strategic (and thereby rational) dimension to typifications and recipes in that they enable us to "save face" and effectively manage new developments and situations. In short, we use our existing stocks of knowledge to muddle through life. Indeed, as you will shortly see, understanding the methods at our disposal for muddling through everyday situations is a central point taken up by ethnomethodologists such as Harold Garfinkel. For instance, even if we make mistakes in using recipes (e.g., we embrace someone as a greeting when they are not expecting or prepared for that because we are in, for instance, Japan), typifications and recipes enable us to do *something* in new situations.

Nevertheless, overall Schutz clearly emphasizes the taken-for-granted character of the lifeworld much more than the ability of actors to use the elements of the lifeworld to max-imize rewards and minimize costs. Indeed, as indicated above, Schutz suggests that it is only when taken-for-granted recipes and typifications don't work that new and creative ideas are then applied. Moreover, Schutz's understanding of rational motivation remains at the level of the individual and not the collective. In fact, Schutz does not have much to say about the collective/rational dimensions of social life at all. As you will see in the following section, this theoretical lacuna (the collective/rational quadrant) is to some extent taken up by Peter Berger and Thomas Luckmann, who add the concept of **institutionalization** to the phenomenological focus on **habitualization** and consciousness in order to address social structural concerns. Nevertheless, one of the most important criticisms of both ethnomethodology and phenomenology is that they ignore the social structural constraints that impact both collective cultural life and biographically articulated lifeworlds.

Reading

Introduction to *The Phenomenology of the Social World*

The following selection from *The Phenomenology of the Social World* begins with a discussion of intersubjectivity. Here Schutz explains how it is that we can come to "know" another person even though their "stream of consciousness" is not open to us. How is it that we can come to say that we "understand" him or her? Schutz's answer is twofold. First, he points out how we "put ourselves in the place of the actor and identify our lived experiences with his." Second, he notes that we interpret our own and others' experience using shared signs and interpretive schemes. (As you read in the previous chapter, these two themes are central to symbolic interactionism as well.) In the second part of this excerpt, Schutz focuses on the distinctive characteristics of face-to-face (we) relations versus indirect (they) relations. He argues that the pure "they-orientation" is based on the supposition of characteristics "in the form of a type," and hence actions between contemporaries are only mutually related. By contrast, in the pure "we" relation, actions are mutually interlocked, rooted as they are not in "types" but in immediate experience.

❖

The Phenomenology of the Social World (1967)

Alfred Schutz

INTERSUBJECTIVE UNDERSTANDING

Your whole stream of lived experience is *not* open to me. To be sure, your stream of lived experience is also a continuum, but I can catch sight of only disconnected segments of it. We have already made this point. If I could be aware of your whole experience, you and I would be the same person. But we must go beyond this. You and I differ from each other not merely with respect to how

SOURCE: From Schutz, A., *The Phenomenology of the Social World,* translated by George Walsh and Frederick Lehnert, Northwestern University Press, 1967. Reprinted with permission.

much of each other's lived experiences we can observe. We also differ in this: When I become aware of a segment of your lived experience, I arrange what I see within my own meaning-context. But meanwhile you have arranged it in yours. Thus I am always interpreting your lived experiences from my own standpoint. Even if I had ideal knowledge of all your meaning-contexts at a given moment and so were able to arrange your whole supply of experience, I should still not be able to determine whether the particular meaning-contexts of yours in which *I* arranged your lived experiences were the same as those which *you* were using. This is because your manner of attending to your experiences would be different from my manner of attending to them. However, if I look at my whole stock of knowledge of your lived experiences and ask about the structure of this knowledge, one thing becomes clear: *This is that everything I know about your conscious life is really based on my knowledge of my own lived experiences. My* lived experiences of you are constituted in simultaneity or quasisimultaneity with *your* lived experiences, to which they are intentionally related. It is only because of this that, when I look backward, I am able to synchronize *my* past experiences of you with *your* past experiences. . . .

BEFORE WE PROCEED FURTHER, it would be well to note that there are ambiguities in the ordinary notion of understanding another person. Sometimes what is meant is intentional Acts directed toward the other self; in other words, my lived experiences of you. At other times what is in question is *your* subjective experiences. Then, the arrangements of all such experiences into meaning-contexts (Weber's comprehension of intended meaning) is sometimes called "understanding of the other self," as is the classification of others' behavior into motivation contexts. The number of ambiguities associated with the notion of "understanding another person" becomes even greater when we bring in the question of understanding the signs he is using. On the one hand, what is understood is the sign itself, then again *what* the other person means by using this sign, and finally the significance of the fact *that* he is using the sign, here, now, and in this particular context. . . .

The man in the natural attitude, then, understands the world by interpreting his own lived

experiences of it, whether these experiences be of inanimate things, of animals, or of his fellow human beings. And so our initial concept of the understanding of the other self is simply the concept "our explication of our lived experiences *of* our fellow human beings as such." The fact that the Thou who confronts me is a fellow man and not a shadow on a movie screen—in other words, that he has duration and consciousness—is something I discover by explicating my own lived experiences of him.

Furthermore, the man in the natural attitude perceives changes in that external object which is known to him as the other's body. He interprets these changes just as he interprets changes in inanimate objects, namely, by interpretation of his own lived experiences of the events and processes in question. Even this second phase does not go beyond the bestowing of meaning within the sphere of the solitary consciousness.

The transcending of this sphere becomes possible only when the perceived processes come to be regarded as lived experiences belonging to another consciousness, which, in accordance with the general thesis of the other self, exhibits the same structure as my own. The perceived bodily movements of the other will then be grasped not merely as *my* lived experience of these movements within *my* stream of consciousness. Rather it will be understood that, simultaneous with *my* lived experience of you, there is *your* lived experience which belongs to you and is part of your stream of consciousness. Meanwhile, the specific nature of your experience is quite unknown to me, that is, I do not know the meaning-contexts you are using to classify those lived experiences of yours, provided, indeed, you are even aware of the movements of your body.

However, I can know the meaning-context into which I classify my own lived experiences of you. We have already seen that this is not your intended meaning in the true sense of the term. What can be comprehended is always only an "approximate value" of the limiting concept "the other's intended meaning." . . .

But, of course, by "understanding the other person" much more is meant, as a rule. This additional something, which is really the only strict meaning of the term, involves grasping what is really going on in the other person's mind, grasping those things of which the external manifestations are mere indications. To be sure, interpretation of such external indications and signs in terms of interpretation of one's own experiences must come first. But the interpreter will not be satisfied with this. He knows perfectly well from the total context of his own experience that, corresponding to the outer objective and public meaning which he has just deciphered, there is this other, inner, subjective meaning. He asks, then, . . . "What does this person mean by speaking to me in this manner, at this particular moment? For the sake of what does he do this (what is his in-order-to motive)? What circumstance does he give as the reason for it (that is, what is his genuine because-motive)? What does the choice of these words indicate?" Questions like these point to the other person's *own* meaning-contexts, to the complex ways in which his own lived experiences have been constituted polythetically and also to the monothetic glance with which he attends to them. . . .

HAVING ESTABLISHED THAT all genuine understanding of the other person must start out from acts of explication performed by the observer on his own lived experience, we must now proceed to a precise analysis of this genuine understanding itself. From the examples we have already given, it is clear that our inquiry must take two different directions. First we must study the genuine understanding of actions which are performed *without any communicative intent*. . . . Second we would examine cases where such communicative intent was present. The latter type of action involves a whole new dimension, the using[i] and interpreting of signs.

Let us first take actions performed without any communicative intent. We are watching a man in the act of cutting wood and wondering what is going on in his mind. Questioning him is ruled out, because that would require entering into a social relationship[ii] with him, which in turn would involve the use of signs.

Let us further suppose that we know nothing about our woodcutter except what we see before our eyes. By subjecting our own perceptions to interpretation, we know that we are in the presence of a fellow human being and that his bodily movements indicate he is engaged in an action which we recognize as that of cutting wood.

Now how do we know what is going on in the woodcutter's mind? Taking this interpretation of our own perceptual data as a starting point, we can plot out in our mind's eye exactly how *we* would carry out the action in question. Then we can actually imagine ourselves doing so. In cases like this, then, we project the other person's goal as if it were our own and fancy ourselves carrying it out. Observe also that we here project the action in the future perfect tense as completed and that our imagined execution of the action is accompanied by the usual retentions and reproductions of the project, although, of course, only in fancy. Further, let us note that the imagined execution may fulfill or fail to fulfill the imagined project.

Or, instead of imagining for ourselves an action wherein we carry out the other person's goal, we may recall in concrete detail how we once carried out a similar action ourselves. Such a procedure would be merely a variation on the same principle.

In both these cases, we put ourselves in the place of the actor and identify our lived experiences with his. It might seem that we are here repeating the error of the well-known "projective" theory of empathy. For here we are reading our own lived experiences into the other person's mind and are therefore only discovering our own experiences. But, if we look more closely, we will see that our theory has nothing in common with the empathy theory except for one point. This is the general thesis of the Thou as the "other I," the one whose experiences are constituted in the same fashion as mine. But even this similarity is only apparent, for we start out from the general thesis of the other person's flow of duration, while the projective theory of empathy jumps from the mere fact of empathy to the belief in other minds by an act of blind faith. Our theory only brings out the implications of what

---

[i][*Setzung*; literally, "positing" or "establishing."]

[ii]The term "social relationship" is here being used in Weber's vague colloquial sense.

is already present in the self-explicative judgment "I am experiencing a fellow human being." We know with certainty that the other person's subjective experience of his own action is in principle different from our own imagined picture of what we would do in the same situation. The reason, as we have already pointed out, is that the intended meaning of an action is always in principle subjective and accessible only to the actor. The error in the empathy theory is two-fold. First, it naïvely tries to trace back the constitution of the other self within the ego's consciousness to empathy, so that the latter becomes the direct source of knowledge of the other.[iii] Actually, such a task of discovering the constitution of the other self can only be carried out in a transcendentally phenomenological manner. Second, it pretends to a knowledge of the other person's mind that goes far beyond the establishment of a structural parallelism between that mind and my own. In fact, however, when we are dealing with actions having no communicative intent, all that we can assert about their meaning is already contained in the general thesis of the alter ego.

It is clear, then, that we imaginatively project the in-order-to motive of the other person as if it were our own and then use the fancied carrying-out of such an action as a scheme in which to interpret his lived experiences. However, to prevent misunderstanding, it should be added that what is involved here is only a reflective analysis of another person's completed act. It is an interpretation carried out after the fact. When an observer is directly watching someone else to whom he is attuned in simultaneity, the situation is different. Then the observer's living intentionality carries him along without having to make constant playbacks of his own past or imaginary experiences. The other person's action unfolds step by step before his eyes. In such a situation, the identification of the observer with the observed person is not carried out by starting with the goal of the act as already given and then proceeding to reconstruct the lived experiences which must have accompanied it. Instead, the observer keeps pace, as it were, with each step of the observed person's action, identifying himself with the latter's experiences within a

common "we-relationship." We shall have much more to say about this later.

So far we have assumed the other person's bodily movement as the only datum given to the observer. It must be emphasized that, if the bodily movement is taken by itself in this way, it is necessarily isolated from its place within the stream of the observed person's living experience. And this context is important not only to the observed person but to the observer as well. He can, of course, if he lacks other data, take a mental snapshot of the observed bodily movement and then try to fit it into a phantasied filmstrip in accordance with the way he thinks he would act and feel in a similar situation. However, the observer can draw much more reliable conclusions about his subject if he knows something about his past and something about the over-all plan into which this action fits. To come back to Max Weber's example, it would be important for the observer to know whether the woodcutter was at his regular job or just chopping wood for physical exercise. An adequate model of the observed person's subjective experiences calls for just this wider context. We have already seen, indeed, that the unity of the action is a function of the project's span. From the observed bodily movement, all the observer can infer is the single course of action which has directly led to it. If, however, I as the observer wish to avoid an inadequate interpretation of what I see another person doing, I must "make my own" all those meaning-contexts which make sense of this action on the basis of my past knowledge of this particular person. We shall come back later on to this concept of "inadequacy" and show its significance for the theory of the understanding of the other person. . . .

At this point we shall . . . try to recapitulate the complex structures involved in understanding another person insofar as these bear on communication and the use of signs. For to say, as we do, that for the user of the sign the sign stands in a meaning-context involves a number of separate facts which must be disentangled.

First of all, whenever I make use of a sign, those lived experiences signified by that sign stand for me in a meaning-context. For they

---

[iii]For a critique of the empathy theory see Scheler, *Wesen und Formen der Sympathie*, pp. 277 ff. [E.T., Heath, p. 241].

have already been constituted into a synthesis, and I look upon them as a unit.

In the second place, for me the sign must already be part of a sign system. Otherwise I would not be able to use it. A sign must already have been interpreted before it can be used. But the understanding of a sign is a complicated synthesis of lived experiences resulting in a special kind of meaning-context. This meaning-context is a configuration involving two elements: the sign as object in itself and the *signatum*, each of which, of course, involves separate meaning-contexts in its own right. The total new meaning-context embracing them both we have called the "coordinating scheme" of the sign.

Third, the act of selecting and using the sign is a special meaning-context for the sign-user to the extent that each use of a sign is an expressive action. Since every action comprises a meaning-context by virtue of the fact that the actor visualizes all the successive lived experiences of that action as one unified act, it follows that every expressive action is therefore a meaning-context. This does not mean that every case of sign-using is *ipso facto* a case of communication. A person may, talking to himself for instance, use a sign purely as an act of self-expression without any intention of communication.

Fourth, the meaning-context "sign-using as act" can serve as the basis for a superimposed meaning-context "sign-using as communicative act" without in any way taking into account the particular person addressed.

Fifth, however, this superimposed meaning-context can enter into a still higher and wider meaning-context in which the addressee *is* taken into account. In this case the communicating act has as its goal not merely that someone take cognizance of it but that its message should motivate the person cognizing to a particular attitude or piece of behavior.

Sixth, the fact that this particular addressee is communicated with *here, now*, and *in this way* can be placed within a still broader context of meaning by finding the in-order-to motive of that communicative act.

All these meaning-contexts are in principle open to the interpreter and can be uncovered systematically by him. Just which ones he does seek to inquire into will depend upon the kind of interest he has in the sign.

However, the statement that all these meaning-contexts in principle lie open to interpretation requires some modification. As we have said repeatedly, the structure of the social world is by no means homogeneous. Our fellow men and the signs they use can be given to us in different ways. There are different approaches to the sign and to the subjective experience it expresses. Indeed, we do not even need a sign in order to gain access to another person's mind; a mere indication can offer us the opening. This is what happens, for instance, when we draw inferences from artifacts concerning the experiences of people who lived in the past. . . .

THE STRUCTURE OF THE SOCIAL WORLD

In the face-to-face situation, directness of experience is essential, regardless of whether our apprehension of the Other is central or peripheral and regardless of how adequate our grasp of him is. I am still "Thou-oriented" even to the man standing next to me in the subway. When we speak of "pure" Thou-orientation or "pure" We-relationship, we are ordinarily using these as limiting concepts referring to the simple givenness of the Other in abstraction from any specification of the degree of concreteness involved. But we can also use these terms for the lower limits of experience obtainable in the face-to-face relationship, in other words, for the most peripheral and fleeting kind of awareness of the other person.

We make the transition from direct to indirect social experience simply by following this spectrum of decreasing vividness. The first steps beyond the realm of immediacy are marked by a decrease in the number of perceptions I have of the other person and a narrowing of the perspectives within which I view him. At one moment I am exchanging smiles with my friend, shaking hands with him, and bidding him farewell. At the next moment he is walking away. Then from the far distance I hear a faint good-by, a moment later I see a vanishing figure give a last wave, and then he is gone. It is quite impossible to fix the exact instant at which my friend left the world of my direct experience and entered the shadowy realm of those who are merely my contemporaries. As another example, imagine a face-to-face conversation, followed by a telephone call, followed by an exchange of letters, and finally messages exchanged through a third party. Here too we have a gradual progression from the world of immediately experienced social reality to the world of contemporaries. In both examples the total number of the other person's reactions open to my observation is progressively diminished until it reaches a minimum point. It is clear, then, that the world of contemporaries is itself a variant function of the face-to-face situation. They may even be spoken of as two poles between which stretches a continuous series of experiences. . . .

We tend to picture marriage or friendship as primarily face-to-face relationships, especially intimate ones at that. We do this because of a tendency we have to conceive the actions of the partners as integrated into the larger unity of the relationship and goal-directed toward that unity.

In actual life, however, a marriage or a friendship is made up of many separate events occurring over a long period of time. Some of these events involve face-to-face situations, in others the partners simply exist side by side as contemporaries. To call such social relationships as these "continuous" is erroneous in the extreme,[iv] since discontinuity and repeatability are included in their very definition. What, then, do friends mean when they speak of their "friendship"? We can distinguish three different meanings they may have in mind.

1. When *A* speaks of his friendship with *B*, he may be thinking of a series of past face-to-face relationships which he shared with *B*. We say "series," because *A* does remember that during the course of his friendship with *B* he did spend some time alone or with other people.

2. When *A* speaks of his friendship with *B*, he may mean that, over and above such face-to-face

situations, his behavior is oriented to *B*'s expected behavior or to the fact that *B* exists—that he is the kind of man he is. In this case, *A* is oriented toward *B* as a contemporary, and their relationship is the kind that exists between contemporaries. This relationship can be either one of orientation or of social interaction.[v] For instance, *A* may perform a certain action because he thinks it will please *B* as soon as the latter finds out about it. Whereas in the face-to-face situation he would literally see *B*'s reaction, here he is confined to merely imagining it. Within the "friendship" such contemporary-oriented acts are inserted between consociate-oriented acts. Face-to-face interaction involves mutual engagement in which the partners can witness the literal coming-to-birth of each other's experiences. Interaction between contemporaries, however, merely involves the expectation on the part of each partner that the other will respond in a relevant way. But this expectation is always a shot in the dark compared to the knowledge one has of one's consociate in the face-to-face situation. Actions between contemporaries are only mutually *related*, whereas actions between consociates are mutually *interlocked*.[vi] The being related to each other of contemporaries occurs in imagination, whereas the interlocking mutual engagement of the We-relationship is a matter of immediate experience. Between these two situations we find many intermediate degrees. For instance, think of the gradually decreasing immediacy of the following: (a) carrying on an imagined conversation with a friend, (b) wondering what my friend would say if I were to do such and such, (c) doing something "for him."

3. When *A* speaks of his friendship with *B*, he may be referring to the fact that, external obstacles aside, they can always get together again and begin where they have left off. This is

---

[iv][There is an unfortunate linguistic ambiguity here. A friendship, it is true, is (happily) not a continu*ous* series of contacts in the Cantorian sense that between any two contacts there is another. It is a series of continu*al* or recurring contacts. But, although it is not a continuous series, it can be spoken of as a continu*ous relationship* unless every *au revoir* is a temporary "breaking-off" of the friendship.]

[v]The different forms of orientation relationships and social interaction in the world of contemporaries remain to be described exactly.

[vi]["Aufeinanderbezogen . . . aufeinander eingestellt."]

parallel to what happens in the sphere of judgment. We showed in our analysis of the concept "knowledge" that the latter refers to a sum of already constituted objectified judgments [or judgment-objectivities—*Urteilsgegen ständlichkeiten*]. Knowledge, then, is a storehouse which can be drawn on at any time by the reactivation of the judgments in question. In the same way, when *A* speaks of his friendship with *B*, he is referring to a storehouse of past experiences of *B*. But he is assuming at the same time that these experiences can be reactivated in a revived We-relationship and that, on that basis, both parties can proceed as before. What is here revived, of course, is not so much the specific lived experiences that previously occurred within the We-relationship but the lived experience of the We-relationship itself.

In the last few pages we have been describing the intermediate zone between the face-to-face situation and the situation involving mere contemporaries. Let us continue our journey. As we approach the outlying world of contemporaries, our experience of others becomes more and more remote and anonymous. Entering the world of contemporaries itself, we pass through one region after another: (1) the region of those whom I once encountered face to face and could encounter again (for instance, my absent friend); then (2) comes the region of those once encountered by the person I am now talking to (for instance, your friend, whom you are promising to introduce to me); next (3) the region of those who are as yet *pure* contemporaries but whom I will soon meet (such as the colleague whose books I have read and whom I am now on my way to visit); then (4) those contemporaries of whose existence I know, not as concrete individuals, but as points in social space as defined by a certain function (for instance, the postal employee who will process my letter); then (5) those collective entities whose function and organization I know while not being able to name any of their members, such as the Canadian Parliament; then (6) collective entities which are by their very nature anonymous and of which I could never in principle have direct experience, such as "state" and "nation"; then (7) objective configurations of meaning which have been instituted in the

world of my contemporaries and which live a kind of anonymous life of their own, such as the interstate commerce clause and the rules of French grammar; and finally (8) artifacts of any kind which bear witness to the subjective meaning-context of some unknown person. The farther out we get into the world of contemporaries, the more anonymous its inhabitants become, starting with the innermost region, where they can almost be seen, and ending with the region where they are by definition forever inaccessible to experience. . . .

MY MERE CONTEMPORARY (or "contemporary"), then, is one whom I know coexists with me in time but whom I do not experience immediately. This kind of knowledge is, accordingly, always indirect and impersonal. I cannot call my contemporary "Thou" in the rich sense that this term has within the We-relationship. Of course, my contemporary may once have been my consociate or may yet become one, but this in no way alters his present status.

Let us now examine the ways in which the world of contemporaries is constituted and the modifications which the concepts "Other-orientation" and "social relationship" undergo in that world. These modifications are necessitated by the fact that the contemporary is only indirectly accessible and that his subjective experiences can only be known in the form of *general types* of subjective experience.

That this should be the case is easy to understand if we consider the difference between the two modes of social experience. When I encounter you face to face I know you as a person in one unique moment of experience. While this We-relationship remains unbroken, we are open and accessible to each other's intentional Acts. For a little while we grow older together, experiencing each other's flow of consciousness in a kind of intimate mutual possession.

It is quite otherwise when I experience you as my contemporary. Here you are not prepredicatively given to me at all. I do not even directly apprehend your existence (*Dasein*). My whole knowledge of you is mediate and descriptive. In this kind of knowledge your "characteristics" are established for me by inference. From such knowledge results the indirect We-relationship. . . .

THE THEY-ORIENTATION is the pure form[vii] of understanding the contemporary in a predicative fashion, that is, in terms of his typical character-istics. Acts of They-orientation are, therefore, intentionally directed toward another person imagined as existing at the same time as oneself but conceived in terms of an ideal type. And just as in the cases of the Thou-orientation and the We-relationship, so also with the They-orientation can we speak of different *stages of concretization* and *actualization*.

In order to distinguish from one another the various stages of concretization of the We-relationship, we established as our crite-rion the degree of closeness to direct experi-ence. We cannot use this criterion within the They-orientation. The reason is that the latter possesses by definition a high degree of remote-ness from direct experience, and the other self which is its object possesses a correspondingly higher degree of anonymity.

It is precisely this degree of anonymity which we now offer as the criterion for dis-tinguishing between the different levels of concretization and actualization that occur in the They-orientation. The more anonymous the per-sonal ideal type applied in the They-orientation, the greater is the use made of objective meaning-contexts instead of subjective ones, and likewise, we shall find, the more are lower-level personal ideal types and objective meaning-contexts

pregiven. (The latter have in turn been derived from other stages of concretization of the They-orientation.)

Let us get clear as to just what we mean by the anonymity of the ideal type in the world of con-temporaries. The pure Thou-orientation consists of mere awareness of the existence of the other person, leaving aside all questions concerning the characteristics of that person. On the other hand, the pure They-orientation is based on the presup-position of such characteristics in the form of a type. Since these characteristics are genuinely typical, they can in principle be presupposed again and again. Of course, whenever I posit such typical characteristics, I assume that they now exist or did once exist. However, this does not mean that I am thinking of them as existing in a particular person in a particular time and place. The contemporary alter ego is therefore anony-mous in the sense that its existence is only the individuation of a type, an individuation which is merely supposable or possible. Now since the very existence of my contemporary is always less than certain, any attempt on my part to reach out to him or influence him may fall short of its mark, and, of course, I am aware of this fact.

The concept which we have been analyzing is the concept of the anonymity of the partner in the world of contemporaries. It is crucial to the understanding of the nature of the indirect social relationship.

[vii][*Die Leerform*, literally, "the empty form."]

BERGER (1929–) AND LUCKMANN (1927–): BIOGRAPHICAL SKETCHES

Peter, Berger (1929–)

Peter Berger was born in Vienna in 1929. He studied for a short time in London and then emigrated to the United States shortly after World War II. He received his bachelor's degree in philosophy from Wagner College on Staten Island, New York, in 1949, and both his master's and doctorate degrees in sociology from the New School for Social Research. The New School faculty included at the time a number of illustrious German expatriates including Alfred Schutz. These men were not only well versed in the works of Karl Marx and Max Weber but also fluent in a number of languages and an array of fields that stretched from classical to modern thought (Fernandez 2003:237). In addition to his exposure to a broad liberal arts education, Berger was a fervent student of religion.

SOURCE: ISEC.

He continuously contemplated his own Christian beliefs and spent a "very happy" year at the Lutheran Theological Seminary in Philadelphia, where he studied to be a minister (ibid.). Indeed, Berger is just as well known for his work in the sociology of religion as in phenomenology and the sociology of knowledge.[5] His now classic *Invitation to Sociology* (1963) continues to be one of the most acclaimed and inspiring introductions to the discipline of sociology today. Professor Berger has taught at a number of universities including The New School; Evangelische Akademie in Bad Boll, Germany; the University of North Carolina; the Hartford Theological Seminary; Rutgers University; and Boston College. Since 1981, Professor Berger has been professor of sociology and theology at Boston University. He is also currently director of the Institute on Culture, Religion and World Affairs at Boston University.

Thomas Luckmann (1927–)

Reprinted with permission.

Thomas Luckmann was born in 1927 in Slovenia. He was educated both in Europe and in the United States, studying at the Universities of Vienna and Innsbruck and the New School for Social Research. Luckmann's first major sole-authored publication, *The Invisible Religion* (original title *Das problem der Religion*, 1963), did not appear in English until the year after the publication of Berger and Luckmann's groundbreaking *The Social Construction of Reality* (1966), and he never became quite as well known in the United States as either his teacher, Alfred Schutz, or his collaborator, Peter Berger. Luckmann's "unequal" relationship with Schutz is duly noted by Luckmann himself in the preface to *The Structures of the Life World* (Schutz and Luckmann 1973), which he finished editing after Schutz's death:

> The completion of the *Strukturen der Lebenswelt* combined the difficulties of the posthumous editing of the manuscript of a great teacher by his student with the problems of collaboration between two unequal authors (one dead, the other living), one looking back at the results of many years of singularly concentrated efforts devoted to the resolution of the problems that were to be dealt with in the book, the other the beneficiary of these efforts; one a master, always ready to revise his analyses but now incapable of doing so, the other a pupil, hesitant to revise what the master had written but forced by the exigencies of the analyses that he continued in the direction indicated by the master to go back, occasionally, to the beginning. (1973:xvii ff. cited in Luckmann 2001:24)

Like Berger, Luckmann has taught at a variety of universities throughout the world, including in New York, Massachusetts, California, Frankfurt, and Constance, Germany. Almost thirty years after Peter Berger and Thomas Luckmann wrote *The Social*

---

[5]Among Berger's prodigious work in the sociology of religion are *The Precarious Vision* (1961), *The Sacred Canopy* (1967), *A Far Glory* (1992), *The Desecularization of the World* (1999), and *Questions of Faith* (2003).

Construction of Reality, they coauthored a second book, *Modernity, Pluralism and the Crisis of Meaning* (1995).

INTELLECTUAL INFLUENCES AND CORE IDEAS

Berger and Luckmann extend Schutz's phenomenology by melding it with the pivotal ideas of Émile Durkheim, Max Weber, Karl Marx, and George Herbert Mead. Berger and Luckmann also draw extensively from philosophical anthropology, especially the work of Arnold Gehlen and Helmuth Plessner. The result is a theoretically multidimensional and provocative phenomenological sociology, captured, above all, in Berger and Luckmann's (1966:61; emphasis in original) famous assertion that "*society is a human product. Society is an objective reality. Man is a social product.*"

From Gehlen and Plessner, Berger and Luckmann borrow the idea that humans, unlike other animals, are "instinctually deprived" or biologically underdeveloped (Berger and Luckmann 1966:48). Important organismic developments that take place in the womb in other animals take place in humans' first year of life. This means not only that the survival of the human infant is dependent on certain social arrangements, but that lacking an instinctual basis for action, human beings have to create a world that ensures social stability. Common-sense knowledge and social institutions compensate for biological underdevelopment. They provide a "base" that operates "automatically" (analogous to the instincts that guide other animals' behavior). "Commonsense knowledge is the knowledge that I share with others in the normal, self-evident routines of everyday life" (Berger and Luckmann 1966:23). It is what allows us to perceive the reality of everyday life as "reality," to suspend our doubts so that we can act in the world. Social institutions are the bridges between humans and their physical environments (Turner 2001:109). Following Schutz, Berger and Luckmann emphasize that it is the intersubjective character of common-sense knowledge that enables human institutions and culture to produce stability. It is because "most of the time, my encounters with others in everyday life are typical in a double sense—I apprehend the other *as* a type and I interact with him in a situation that is itself typical" that social interaction is successful (Berger and Luckmann 1966:31; emphasis in original). Without intersubjectivity—that you know that I know that we both know—social order and interaction would break down, as we would be left to doubt the most fundamental aspects of communication.

This brings us to the issue of **habitualization**, that is, the process by which the flexibility of human actions is limited. All activity is subject to habitualization, as repeated actions inevitably become routinized. Habitualization carries with it the psychological advantage that choices are narrowed. That an action may be "performed again in the future in the same manner and with the same economical effort" provides a stable background from which human activity can proceed (Berger and Luckmann 1966:53–4). In other words, from the time we wake up in the morning until we go to bed at night, we can direct our minds and bodies to constructive action only because we take most actions for granted.

Moreover, habitualized actions set the stage for **institutionalization**, for "institutionalization occurs whenever there is a reciprocal typification of habitualized action by types of actors" (Berger and Luckmann 1966:54). That is, it is when habitualized actions are shared and/or "available to all members of the particular social group" (ibid.) that institutions are born. Akin to habits that function at the level of the individual, then, institutions control human conduct by setting up predefined patterns of conduct that channel in one direction as opposed to another theoretically possible direction. Of course, institutions are not created instantaneously, but rather are "built up in the course of a shared history" (ibid.). In other words, over time, shared habitualized actions become institutions that are taken for granted and therefore limiting for the individuals who are subject to them. Thus, it is through institutions that human life becomes coherent, meaningful, and continuous (ibid.).

Thus, it is through the dual processes of habitualization and institutionalization that the systems of meaning and social institutions that humans create act back on them as a fixed "objective reality." Interestingly, however, we seldom ponder the fact that our institutions are arbitrarily rooted in shared typifications; it is only when the taken-for-granted elements of our lifeworld are disrupted (e.g., when we travel abroad) that we think about them at all. Most often, the system appears to us (and we act) as if it is a fixed, "objective" reality.

Consider, for instance, driving a car. At the level of the individual, learning to drive entails learning to habitualize specific actions, one of the most important of which is knowing which pedal is the gas and which is the brake, and where the brake is in the car. You must automatically know this, for if you had to stop and think "Which pedal is the brake?" every time you needed to brake, or if you had to stop and think "Where is the brake?" (and consider all theoretically possible locations for the brake in the vehicle), you would most certainly crash, for you don't have time for hemming and hawing and contemplation while driving a car. Of course, in terms of institutionalization, if we each had our own solitary driving habits that shared no common features, the result would be chaos. It is only to the extent that our typifications and recipes for driving are shared (or "reciprocal") that the traffic system works and that order is maintained at all.

Berger and Luckmann use the terms **externalization, objectivation,** and **reification** to refer to the process by which human activity and society attain the character of objectivity. Externalization and objectivation enable the actor to confront the social world as something outside of herself. Institutions appear external to the individual, as historical and objective facticities. They confront the individual as undeniable facts (Berger and Luckmann 1966:60). Reification is "an extreme step" in the process of objectivation. In reification, "the real relationship between man and his world is reversed in consciousness. Man, the producer of a world, is apprehended as its product, and human activity as an epiphenomenon of non-human processes." That is, reification is the apprehension of human phenomena as if they were "non-human or possibly suprahuman" things (Berger and Luckmann 1966:89). For instance, we reify our social roles in such a way that we say, "I have no choice in the matter. I have to act this way" (ibid.:91). This is what Berger refers to as "bad faith." Of course, history is full of examples of the horrendous consequences that ensue from such reification. The Nazi concentration camps relied on guards who are said to have merely "taken orders." A parallel also can be drawn with the recent example of torture in the Abu Ghraib prison.

Objectivation and reification are related to the Marxist concept of alienation (Berger and Luckmann 1966:197, 200). Here Berger and Luckmann are consciously drawing on Marx in order to underscore the dialectical relationship between substructure and superstructure, that is, the intimate relationship between the material and ideal realms. For instance, in a famous passage in *The German Ideology* (1845), Marx maintains that the material or economic basis of religious systems is obscured for believers much like "the inversion of objects on the retina."[6] For Marx, religion is rooted in material processes (namely, the ruling class's interest in maintaining its dominance) that are

---

[6]Marx states, "If in all ideology men and their circumstances appear upside-down as in a camera obscura, this phenomenon arises just as much from historical life-process as the inversion of objects on the retina does from their physical life-process" (in Robert C. Tucker, ed., *The Marx-Engels Reader*, 2nd ed. NY: Norton, 1978:154).

experienced as reified "Facts" and fixed "Truths" by the proletariat. Similarly, Berger and Luckmann emphasize that human beings create systems of meaning and ideologies that they then experience as "objective" and "suprahuman." And just as Marx perceived religious beliefs as having the same effect as an opiate—providing the masses with "comfort" and a cushion to shield them from the harsh realities of everyday life—so, too, Berger and Luckmann argue that "human actors prefer reification to anomie, because the former offers comfort through amnesia"; the "burden of the homeless mind cannot be easily endured" (Turner 2001:111).

However, in stark contrast to Marx, Berger and Luckmann perceive the process of reification as not necessarily alienating. While Marx likened reification to a delusion that must be dispelled in order to create a fully human, liberated society, Berger and Luckmann view reification as inherent to the human condition. Institutionalization, objectivation, and reification are simply the processes by which man becomes "capable of producing a world that he then experiences as something other than a human product" (Turner 2001:61). They are what enable social life to be both meaningful and continuous.

The notion that objectivation is tied to shared cultural systems vital to social life reflects Berger and Luckmann's indebtedness to Durkheim (rather than to Marx). Durkheim (1895/1966:13) used the term "social fact" to refer to any manner of action capable of exercising "exterior constraint" over the individual, that is, "*every way of acting which is general throughout a given society, while at the same time existing in its own right independent of its individual manifestations*" (ibid.; emphasis in original), and he defined sociology as the study of social facts. In other words, just as a game has rules that are "coercive" for its players, so, too, societies are made up of "social facts" that are "coercive." In the process of participating in society (or playing a game), the rules/social structures are iterated and learned and unwittingly upheld. Thus, for instance, in the case of learning to drive a car discussed above, once we learn to drive we take the rules of the road (e.g., which side of the road to drive on) for granted as we go about our business (e.g., where it is we're going). However, if we ever do "forget" and get a ticket for not following the law, this rule/law for us is again reaffirmed.

Indeed, in his later work, Durkheim (1912/1965) maintains that the primary function of religion is to encode the system of relations of the group, and that through the dual processes of ritualization and symbolization collective sentiments are reaffirmed. As Durkheim (1912/1965:474–5) states:

> There can be no society which does not feel the need of upholding and reaffirming at regular intervals the collective sentiments and the collective ideas which make its unity and personality. Now this moral remaking cannot be achieved except by the means of reunions, assemblies, and meetings where the individuals, being closely united to one another, reaffirm in common their common sentiments.

Thus, highly routinized acts, such as taking communion or saluting the flag, are rituals through which participants are bound together and their collective beliefs and sentiments are reaffirmed. In addition, collective sentiments and beliefs are reaffirmed through symbolization. Symbols (defined as something that stands for something else), such as the Christian cross, are markers that are capable of calling up and reaffirming shared meaning and the feeling of community in between periodic ritual acts (such as religious celebrations and church services). As Durkheim (1912/1965:232) states, "without symbols, social sentiments could have only a precarious existence."

In the spirit of Durkheim, Berger and Luckmann underscore that shared meanings and categories are a "sacred canopy" vital to social existence (Berger 1967). And just as Durkheim emphasized how systems of meaning tie individuals together in a system that they experience as "objective" reality (i.e., social facts), so, too, Berger and Luckmann (1966:58) emphasize that institutions are "experienced as possessing a reality of their own, a reality that confronts the individual as an external and coercive fact." Moreover, akin to Durkheim's emphasis on symbolization, so, too, Berger and Luckmann (1966:35) stress that signification (the human production of signs) is simply one of the most important examples of objectivation. As Berger (1967:18–19) states:

> Language confronts the individual as an objective facticity. He subjectively appropriates it by engaging in linguistic interaction with others. In the course of this interaction, however, he inevitably modifies the language. . . . Furthermore, his continuing participation in the language is part of the human activity that is the only ontological base for the language in question. The language exists because he, along with others, continues to employ it. In other words, both with regard to language and to the socially objectivated world as a whole, it may be said that the individual keeps "talking back" to the world that formed him and thereby continues to maintain the latter as reality.

Nevertheless, as this discussion of language reflects, in contrast to both Marx and Durkheim, Berger and Luckmann stress that "the individual is not molded as an inert and passive thing" (Berger 1967:18). They emphasize the active role that individuals take in maintaining the world that they experience as an objective reality; that is, they stress the experience of institutions over their external, empirical "reality." This focus on everyday life reflects Berger and Luckmann's indebtedness not only to Schutz but to symbolic interactionism, particularly to the work of George Herbert Mead (see the previous chapter). In conjunction with the microlevel emphasis of Mead, Berger and Luckmann focus on the dynamics of face-to-face interaction. They explain, for instance, how during interaction actors "A and B . . . play roles vis-à-vis each other. . . . That is, A will inwardly appropriate B's reiterated roles and make them the models for his own role-playing." As Berger and Luckmann (1966:22) state, "The reality of everyday life is organized around the 'here' of my body and the 'now' of my present. This 'here' and 'now' is the focus of my attention to the reality of everyday life."

This brings us to the final step in the process of externalization, objectivation, and institutionalization: **internalization**. Internalization is "the immediate apprehension or interpretation of an objective event as expressing meaning" (1966:129), that is, the process through which individual subjectivity is attained. Internalization means that "the objectivated social world is retrojected into consciousness in the course of social-ization" (ibid.:61). As such, internalization is the "beginning point" in the process of becoming a member of society (ibid.:129), as well as the "end point" in institutional-ization (see Figure 6.2).

The three moments of externalization, objectivation, and internalization are not to be understood "as occurring in a temporal sequence," but rather as a simultaneous, dialec-tical process. Nevertheless, it is in intergenerational transmission that the process of internalization is complete. As Berger and Luckmann (1966:61) maintain:

> only with the transmission of the social world to a new generation (that is, internalization as effectuated in socialization) does the fundamental social dialectic appear in its totality. To repeat, only with the appearance of a new generation can one properly speak of a social world.

In other words, every individual is born into an environment within which she encounters the significant others who are in charge of her socialization. One does not choose one's own significant others; rather, they are imposed on her. In the process of socialization, the stocks of knowledge that the individual experiences as a preexisting objective reality are imposed on her. The individual is thereby "born into not only an objective social structure but also an objective social world" (1966:131).

Berger and Luckmann differentiate two types of socialization based on the extent to which individuals are active and conscious of the process of internalization. **Primary socialization** refers to "the first socialization an individual undergoes in childhood, through which he becomes a member of society" (1966:130–1). On the other hand, **secondary socialization** refers to subsequent processes of socialization that induct "an already socialized individual into new sectors of the objective world of his society" (ibid.). Whereas primary socialization is predefined and taken for granted, secondary socialization is acquired in a more conscious way (e.g., training for a new job). It is for this reason that primary socialization has so much more of an impact on the individual than secondary socialization. As Berger and Luckmann (1966:134; emphasis in original) state:

> The child does not internalize the world of his significant others as one of many possible worlds. He internalizes it as *the* world, the only existent and only conceivable world, the world *tout court*. It is for this reason that the world internalized in primary socialization is so much more firmly entrenched in consciousness than worlds internalized in secondary socialization.

Furthermore, primary socialization is distinguished by the fact that it cannot take place without an emotionally shared identification of the child with his significant others: you have to love your mother, but not your teacher (1966:141). This distinction between the more intimate (primary) and less intimate (secondary) types of socialization recalls Schutz's more abstract discussion of umwelt versus mitwelt relations. Each type of relationship is distinguished by a different level of intersubjectivity and typification. Primary socialization and significant others (essential to "we relations") are far more central to the maintenance of "identity" than are secondary relationships/socialization (Berger and Luckmann 1966:151).

Figure 6.2   Berger and Luckmann's Basic Concepts and Theoretical Orientation

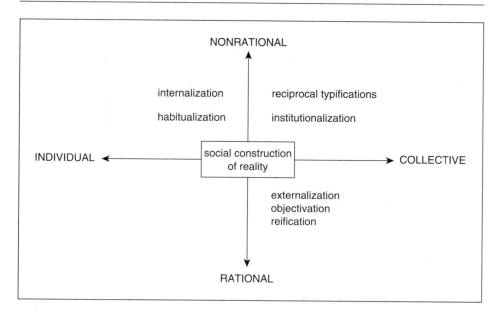

BERGER AND LUCKMANN'S THEORETICAL ORIENTATION

Berger and Luckmann (1966:18) explicitly seek to illuminate "the dual character of society in terms of objective facticity *and* subjective meaning" (emphasis in original). In so doing, they move back and forth between individual and collective approaches to order. Specifically, as shown in Figure 6.2, Berger and Luckmann emphasize both how individual actors shape social patterns and how social patterns structure individual behavior and consciousness. They argue that institutions "control human conduct by setting up predefined patterns of conduct" (ibid.:55), but at the same time, they assert that it is only to the extent that such patterns of conduct are internalized and taken for granted by the individual that they shape consciousness and behavior.

Of course, this dual approach to order is a function of Berger and Luckmann's reliance both on Schutz's phenomenology and on the classical sociologists Marx, Weber, Durkheim, and Mead (see Figure 1.5 in Chapter 1). While as we have seen, Schutz and Mead are most attuned to the level of the individual, Durkheim, Marx, and Weber are particularly attuned to the collective realm. In addition, from Mead and symbolic inter-actionism, Berger and Luckmann borrow an appreciation for the pragmatic dimensions of everyday consciousness and action, which also reflects a more individualistic approach, as it emphasizes individuals' attempts to make sense of or give meaning to the situations that comprise their everyday life.

In terms of action, above all Berger and Luckmann emphasize the *taken-for-granted* workings of society, which reflects a primarily nonrational theoretical approach. As discussed above, at the level of the individual, this emphasis on nonrational motivation reflects Berger and Luckmann's indebtedness to Schutz and symbolic interactionism. Rather than stress the strategic, calculative aspects of human behavior, they assert the extent to which we act according to internalized typifications, recipes, and lifeworlds (see Figure 6.2). At the level of the collective, Berger and Luckmann emphasize the shared, intersubjective dimensions of symbolic life (à la Durkheim). Indeed, Berger and Luckmann insist that it is only by using the preexisting, intersubjective elements of language and culture that individuals are able to act at all. This emphasis on preexisting, taken-for-granted systems of meaning can be said to reflect a primary interest in the collective/nonrational realm.

This is not to say that Berger and Luckmann ignore the rational dimension of action entirely, however. As shown in Figure 6.2, objectivation and reification are concepts rooted in Marx that exude a rationalistic bent at the collective level. That is, Berger and Luckmann's whole point is that the power and force of social as well as culture structures is that they are perceived as forces outside and external to the individual.

Reading

Introduction to *The Social Construction of Reality*

Berger and Luckmann's *The Social Construction of Reality* (1966) is one of the most widely read and influential books in contemporary sociology. In the following excerpts, you will see many of the themes discussed above, including the Schutzian concepts of intersubjectivity, typification, and language, as well as Berger and Luckmann's own analyses of habitualization, institutionalization, externalization, objectivation, reification, internalization, and socialization. The selection begins with Berger and Luckmann's fundamental point that "the reality of everyday life appears already objectified" (ibid.:21) and that this objectivation is *intersubjective*, as is most readily apparent in language and sign systems. In the next section, Berger and Luckmann focus on the dual processes of habitualization and institutionalization, emphasizing that it is the lack of human instinctual parameters that necessitates the development of sociocultural limits on social behavior. Berger and Luckmann then move on to viewing society as "subjective reality," emphasizing the processes of internalization and socialization at the level of the individual. Here Berger and Luckmann stress that "no individual internalizes the totality of what is objectivated as reality in his society . . . [and that] there are always elements of subjective reality that have not originated in socialization, such as the awareness of one's own body prior to and apart from any socially learned apprehension of it" (ibid.:134). Here Berger and Luckmann also insist that "the symmetry between objective and subjective reality is never a static, one-for-all state of affairs. It must always be produced and reproduce *in actu*" (ibid.), which reflects their dual individualistic and collectivistic approach.

❖

The Social Construction of Reality (1966)

Peter L. Berger and Thomas Luckmann

FOUNDATIONS OF
KNOWLEDGE IN EVERYDAY LIFE

I apprehend the reality of everyday life as an ordered reality. Its phenomena are prearranged in patterns that seem to be independent of my apprehension of them and that impose themselves upon the latter. The reality of everyday life appears already objectified, that is, constituted by an order of objects that have been designated *as* objects before my appearance on the scene. The language used in everyday life continuously provides me with the necessary objectifications and posits the order within which these make sense and within which everyday life has meaning for me. I live in a place that is geographically designated; I employ tools, from can openers to sports cars, which are designated in the technical vocabulary of my society; I live within a web of human relationships, from my chess club to the United States of America, which are also ordered by means of vocabulary. In this manner language marks the co-ordinates of my life in society and fills that life with meaningful objects.

The reality of everyday life is organized around the "here" of my body and the "now" of my present. This "here and now" is the focus of my attention to the reality of everyday life. What is "here and now" presented to me in everyday life is the *realissimum* of my consciousness. The reality of everyday life is not, however, exhausted by these immediate presences, but embraces phenomena that are not present "here and now." This means that I experience everyday life in terms of differing degrees of closeness and remoteness, both spatially and temporally. Closest to me is the zone of everyday life that is directly accessible to my bodily manipulation. This zone contains the world within my reach, the world in which I act so as to modify its reality, or the world in which I work. In this world of working my consciousness is dominated by the pragmatic motive, that is, my attention to this world is mainly determined by what I am doing, have done or plan to do in it. In this way it is *my* world par excellence. I know, of course, that the reality of everyday life contains zones that are not accessible to me in this manner. But either I have no pragmatic interest in these zones or my interest in them is indirect insofar as they may be, potentially, manipulative zones for me. Typically, my interest in the far zones is less intense and certainly less urgent. I am intensely interested in the cluster of objects involved in my daily occupation—say, the world of the garage, if I am a mechanic. I am interested, though less directly, in what goes on in the testing laboratories of the automobile industry in Detroit—I am unlikely ever to be in one of these laboratories, but the work done there will eventually affect my everyday life. I may also be interested in what goes on at Cape Kennedy or in outer space, but this interest is a matter of private, "leisure-time" choice rather than an urgent necessity of my everyday life.

The reality of everyday life further presents itself to me as an intersubjective world, a world that I share with others. This intersubjectivity sharply differentiates everyday life from other realities of which I am conscious. I am alone in the world of my dreams, but I know that the world of everyday life is as real to others as it is to myself. Indeed, I cannot exist in everyday life without continually interacting and communicating with others. I know that my natural attitude to this world corresponds to the natural attitude of others, that they also comprehend the objectifications by which this world is ordered, that they also organize this world around the "here and now" of *their* being in it and have projects for working in it. I also know, of course, that the others have a perspective on this common world that is not identical with mine. My "here" is their "there." My "now" does not fully overlap with theirs. My projects differ from and may even conflict with theirs. All the same, I know that I live with them in a common world. Most importantly, I know that there is an ongoing correspondence between *my* meanings and *their* meanings in this world, that we share a common sense about its reality. The natural attitude is the attitude of commonsense consciousness precisely because it refers to a world that is common to many men. Commonsense knowledge is the knowledge I share with others in the normal, self-evident routines of everyday life.

The reality of everyday life is taken for granted *as* reality. It does not require additional verification over and beyond its simple presence. It is simply *there*, as self-evident and compelling facticity. I *know* that it is real. While I am capable of engaging in doubt about its reality, I am obliged to suspend such doubt as I routinely exist in everyday life. This suspension of doubt is so firm that to abandon it, as I might want to do, say, in theoretical or religious contemplation, I have to make an extreme transition. The world of everyday life proclaims itself and, when I want to challenge the proclamation, I must engage in a deliberate, by no means easy effort. The transition from the natural attitude to the theoretical attitude of the philosopher or scientist illustrates this point. But not all aspects of this reality are equally unproblematic. Everyday life is divided into sectors that are apprehended routinely, and others that present me with problems of one kind or another. Suppose that I am an automobile mechanic who is highly knowledgeable about all American-made cars. Everything that pertains to the latter is a routine, unproblematic facet of my everyday life. But one day someone appears in the garage and asks me to repair his Volkswagen. I am now compelled to enter the problematic world of foreign-made cars. I may do so reluctantly or with professional curiosity, but in either case I am now faced with problems that I have not yet routinized. At the same time, of course, I do not leave the reality of everyday life. Indeed, the latter becomes enriched as I begin to incorporate into it the knowledge and skills required for the repair of foreign-made cars. The reality of everyday life encompasses both kinds of sectors, as long as what appears as a problem does not pertain to a different reality altogether (say, the reality of theoretical physics, or of nightmares). As long as the routines of everyday life continue without interruption they are apprehended as unproblematic.

But even the unproblematic sector of everyday reality is so only until further notice, that is, until its continuity is interrupted by the appearance of a problem. When this happens, the reality of everyday life seeks to integrate the problematic sector into what is already unproblematic. Commonsense knowledge contains a variety of instructions as to how this is to be done. . . .

SOCIAL INTERACTION IN EVERYDAY LIFE

The reality of everyday life is shared with others. But how are these others themselves experienced in everyday life? Again, it is possible to differentiate between several modes of such experience.

The most important experience of others takes place in the face-to-face situation, which is the prototypical case of social interaction. All other cases are derivatives of it.

In the face-to-face situation the other is appresented to me in a vivid present shared by both of us. I know that in the same vivid present I am appresented to him. My and his "here and now" continuously impinge on each other as long as the face-to-face situation continues. As a result, there is a continuous interchange of my expressivity and his. I see him smile, then react to my frown by stopping the smile, then smiling again as I smile, and so on. Every expression of mine is oriented toward him, and vice versa, and this continuous reciprocity of expressive acts is simultaneously available to both of us. This means that, in the face-to-face situation, the other's subjectivity is available to me through a maximum of symptoms. To be sure, I may misinterpret some of these symptoms. I may think that the other is smiling while in fact he is smirking. Nevertheless, no other form of social relating can reproduce the plenitude of symptoms of subjectivity present in the face-to-face situation. Only here is the other's subjectivity emphatically "close." All other forms of relating to the other are, in varying degrees, "remote."

In the face-to-face situation the other is fully real. This reality is part of the overall reality of everyday life, and as such massive and compelling. To be sure, another may be real to me without my having encountered him face to face—by reputation, say, or by having corresponded with him. Nevertheless, he becomes real to me in the fullest sense of the word only when I meet him face to face. Indeed, it may be argued that the other in the face-to-face situation is more real to me than I myself. Of course I "know myself better" than I can ever know him. My subjectivity is accessible to me in a way his can never be, no matter how "close" our relationship. My past is available to me in memory in a fullness with which I can never reconstruct

his, however much he may tell me about it. But this "better knowledge" of myself requires reflection. It is not immediately appresented to me. The other, however, *is* so appresented in the face-to-face situation. "What he is," therefore, is ongoingly available to me. This availability is continuous and prereflective. On the other hand, "What I am" is *not* so available. To make it available requires that I stop, arrest the continuous spontaneity of my experience, and deliberately turn my attention back upon myself. What is more, such reflection about myself is typically occasioned by the attitude toward me that *the other* exhibits. It is typically a "mirror" response to attitudes of the other.

It follows that relations with others in the face-to-face situation are highly flexible. Put negatively, it is comparatively difficult to impose rigid patterns upon face-to-face interaction. Whatever patterns are introduced will be continuously modified through the exceedingly variegated and subtle interchange of subjective meanings that goes on. For instance, I may view the other as someone inherently unfriendly to me and act toward him within a pattern of "unfriendly relations" as understood by me. In the face-to-face situation, however, the other may confront me with attitudes and acts that contradict this pattern, perhaps up to a point where I am led to abandon the pattern as inapplicable and to view him as friendly. In other words, the pattern cannot sustain the massive evidence of the other's subjectivity that is available to me in the face-to-face situation. By contrast, it is much easier for me to ignore such evidence as long as I do not encounter the other face to face. Even in such a relatively "close" relation as may be maintained by correspondence I can more successfully dismiss the other's protestations of friendship as not actually representing his subjective attitude to me, simply because in correspondence I lack the immediate, continuous and massively real presence of his expressivity. It is, to be sure, possible for me to misinterpret the other's meanings even in the face-to-face situation, as it is possible for him "hypocritically" to hide his meanings. All the same, both misinterpretation and "hypocrisy" are more difficult to sustain in face-to-face interaction than in less "close" forms of social relations.

On the other hand, I apprehend the other by means of typificatory schemes even in the face-to-face situation, although these schemes are more "vulnerable" to his interference than in "remoter" forms of interaction. Put differently, while it is comparatively difficult to impose rigid patterns on face-to-face interaction, even it is patterned from the beginning if it takes place within the routines of everyday life. (We can leave aside for later consideration cases of interaction between complete strangers who have no common background of everyday life.) The reality of everyday life contains typificatory schemes in terms of which others are apprehended and "dealt with" in face-to-face encounters. Thus I apprehend the other as "a man," "a European," "a buyer," "a jovial type," and so on. All these typifications ongoingly affect my interaction with him as, say, I decide to show him a good time on the town before trying to sell him my product. Our face-to-face interaction will be patterned by these typifications as long as they do not become problematic through interference on his part. Thus he may come up with evidence that, although "a man," "a European" and "a buyer," he is also a self-righteous moralist, and that what appeared first as joviality is actually an expression of contempt for Americans in general and American salesmen in particular. At this point, of course, my typificatory scheme will have to be modified, and the evening planned differently in accordance with this modification. Unless thus challenged, though, the typifications will hold until further notice and will determine my actions in the situation.

The typificatory schemes entering into face-to-face situations are, of course, reciprocal. The other also apprehends me in a typified way—as "a man," "an American," "a salesman," "an ingratiating fellow," and so on. The other's typifications are as susceptible to my interference as mine are to his. In other words, the two typificatory schemes enter into an ongoing "negotiation" in the face-to-face situation. In everyday life such "negotiation" is itself likely to be prearranged in a typical manner—as in the typical bargaining process between buyers and salesmen. Thus, most of the time, my encounters with others in everyday life are typical in a double sense—I apprehend the other *as* a type and I interact with him in a situation that is itself typical.

The typifications of social interaction become progressively anonymous the farther away they are from the face-to-face situation. Every typification, of course, entails incipient anonymity. If I typify my friend Henry as a member of category X (say, as an Englishman), I *ipso facto* interpret at least certain aspects of his conduct as resulting from this typification—for instance, his tastes in food are typical of Englishmen, as are his manners, certain of his emotional reactions, and so on. This implies, though, that these characteristics and actions of my friend Henry appertain to *anyone* in the category of Englishman, that is, I apprehend these aspects of his being in anonymous terms. Nevertheless, as long as my friend Henry is available in the plenitude of expressivity of the face-to-face situation, he will constantly break through my type of anonymous Englishman and manifest himself as a unique and therefore atypical individual—to wit, as my friend Henry. The anonymity of the type is obviously less susceptible to this kind of individualization when face-to-face interaction is a matter of the past (my friend Henry, *the Englishman*, whom I knew when I was a college student), or is of a superficial and transient kind (the Englishman with whom I have a brief conversation on a train), or has never taken place (my business competitors in England).

An important aspect of the experience of others in everyday life is thus the directness or indirectness of such experience. At any given time it is possible to distinguish between consociates with whom I interact in face-to-face situations and others who are mere contemporaries, of whom I have only more or less detailed recollections, or of whom I know merely by hearsay. In face-to-face situations I have direct evidence of my fellowman, of his actions, his attributes, and so on. Not so in the case of contemporaries—of them I have more or less reliable knowledge. Furthermore, I must take account of my fellowmen in face-to-face situations, while I may, but need not, turn my thoughts to mere contemporaries. Anonymity increases as I go from the former to the latter, because the anonymity of the typifications by means of which I apprehend fellowmen in face-to-face situations is constantly "filled in" by the multiplicity of vivid symptoms referring to a concrete human being.

This, of course, is not the whole story. There are obvious differences in my experiences of mere contemporaries. Some I have experienced again and again in face-to-face situations and expect to meet again regularly (my friend Henry); others I *recollect* as concrete human beings from a past meeting (the blonde I passed on the street), but the meeting was brief and, most likely, will not be repeated. Still others I *know* of as concrete human beings, but I can apprehend them only by means of more or less anonymous intersecting typifications (my British business competitors, the Queen of England). Among the latter one could again distinguish between likely partners in face-to-face situations (my British business competitors), and potential but unlikely partners (the Queen of England).

The degree of anonymity characterizing the experience of others in everyday life depends, however, upon another factor too. I see the newspaper vendor on the street corner as regularly as I see my wife. But he is less important to me and I am not on intimate terms with him. He may remain relatively anonymous to me. The degree of interest and the degree of intimacy may combine to increase or decrease anonymity of experience. They may also influence it independently. I can be on fairly intimate terms with a number of the fellow-members of a tennis club and on very formal terms with my boss. Yet the former, while by no means completely anonymous, may merge into "that bunch at the courts" while the latter stands out as a unique individual. And finally, anonymity may become near-total with certain typifications that are not intended ever to become individualized—such as the "typical reader of the London *Times*." Finally, the "scope" of the typification—and thereby its anonymity—can be further increased by speaking of "British public opinion."

The social reality of everyday life is thus apprehended in a continuum of typifications, which are progressively anonymous as they are removed from the "here and now" of the face-to-face situation. At one pole of the continuum are those others with whom I frequently and intensively interact in face-to-face situations—my "inner circle," as it were. At the other pole are highly anonymous abstractions, which by their very nature can never be available in face-to-face interaction. Social structure is the sum total of these typifications and of the recurrent patterns of interaction established by means of them. As such, social structure is an essential element of the reality of everyday life.

One further point ought to be made here, though we cannot elaborate it. My relations with others are not limited to consociates and contemporaries. I also relate to predecessors and successors, to those others who have preceded and will follow me in the encompassing history of my society. . . .

LANGUAGE AND KNOWLEDGE IN EVERYDAY LIFE

The reality of everyday life is not only filled with objectivations; it is only possible because of them. I am constantly surrounded by objects that "proclaim" the subjective intentions of my fellowmen, although I may sometimes have difficulty being quite sure just what it is that a particular object is "proclaiming," especially if it was produced by men whom I have not known well or at all in face-to-face situations. Every ethnologist or archaeologist will readily testify to such difficulties, but the very fact that he *can* overcome them and reconstruct from an artifact the subjective intentions of men whose society may have been extinct for millennia is eloquent proof of the enduring power of human objectivations.

A special but crucially important case of objectivation is significant, that is, the human production of signs. A sign may be distinguished from other objectivations by its explicit intention to serve as an index of subjective meanings. . . .

Language, which may be defined here as a system of vocal signs, is the most important sign system of human society. Its foundation is, of course, in the intrinsic capacity of the human organism for vocal expressivity, but we can begin to speak of language only when vocal expressions have become capable of detachment from the immediate "here and now" of subjective states. It is not yet language if I snarl, grunt, howl, or hiss, although these vocal expressions are capable of becoming linguistic insofar as they are integrated into an objectively available sign system. The common objectivations of everyday life are maintained primarily by linguistic signification. Everyday life is, above all, life with and by means of the language I share with my fellowmen. An understanding of language is thus essential for any understanding of the reality of everyday life. . . .

As a sign system, language has the quality of objectivity. I encounter language as a facticity external to myself and it is coercive in its effect on me. Language forces me into its patterns. I cannot use the rules of German syntax when I speak English; I cannot use words invented by my three-year-old son if I want to communicate outside the family; I must take into account prevailing standards of proper speech for various occasions, even if I would prefer my private "improper" ones. Language provides me with a ready-made possibility for the ongoing objectification of my unfolding experience. Put differently, language is pliantly expansive so as to allow me to objectify a great variety of experiences coming my way in the course of my life. Language also typifies experiences, allowing me to subsume them under broad categories in terms of which they have meaning not only to myself but also to my fellowmen. As it typifies, it also anonymizes experiences, for the typified experience can, in principle, be duplicated by anyone falling into the category in question. For instance, I have a quarrel with my mother-in-law. This concrete and subjectively unique experience is typified linguistically under the category of "mother-in-law trouble." In this typification it makes sense to myself, to others, and, presumably, to my mother-in-law. The same typification, however, entails anonymity. Not only I but *anyone* (more accurately, anyone in the category of son-in-law) can have "mother-in-law trouble." In this way, my biographical experiences are ongoingly subsumed under general orders of meaning that are both objectively and subjectively real.

Because of its capacity to transcend the "here and now," language bridges different zones within the reality of everyday life and integrates them into a meaningful whole. The transcendences have spatial, temporal and social dimensions. Through language I can transcend the gap between my manipulatory zone and that of the other; I can synchronize my biographical time sequence with his; and I can converse with him about individuals and collectivities with whom we are not at present in face-to-face interaction. As a result of these transcendences language is capable of "making present" a variety of objects that are spatially, temporally and socially absent from the "here and now." *Ipso facto* a vast accumulation of experiences and meanings can become objectified in the "here and now." Put

simply, through language an entire world can be actualized at any moment. This transcending and integrating power of language is retained when I am not actually conversing with another. Through linguistic objectification, even when "talking to myself" in solitary thought, an entire world can be appresented to me at any moment. As far as social relations are concerned, language "makes present" for me not only fellowmen who are physically absent at the moment, but fellowmen in the remembered or reconstructed past, as well as fellowmen projected as imaginary figures into the future. All these "presences" can be highly meaningful, of course, in the ongoing reality of everyday life.

Moreover, language is capable of transcending the reality of everyday life altogether. It can refer to experiences pertaining to finite provinces of meaning, and it can span discrete spheres of reality. For instance, I can interpret "the meaning" of a dream by integrating it linguistically within the order of everyday life. Such integration transposes the discrete reality of the dream into the reality of everyday life by making it an enclave within the latter. The dream is now meaningful in terms of the reality of everyday life rather than of its own discrete reality. Enclaves produced by such transposition belong, in a sense, to both spheres of reality. They are "located" in one reality, but "refer" to another. . . .

SOCIETY AS OBJECTIVE REALITY

Man's instinctual organization may be described as underdeveloped, compared with that of the other higher mammals. Man does have drives, of course. But these drives are highly unspecialized and undirected. This means that the human organism is capable of applying its constitutionally given equipment to a very wide and, in addition, constantly variable and varying range of activities. This peculiarity of the human organism is grounded in its ontogenetic development. Indeed, if one looks at the matter in terms of organismic development, it is possible to say that the fetal period in the human being extends through about the first year after birth. Important organismic developments, which in the animal are completed in the mother's body, take place in the human infant after its separation from the womb. At this time, however, the human infant is not only *in* the outside world, but interrelating with it in a number of complex ways.

The human organism is thus still developing biologically while already standing in a relationship to its environment. In other words, the process of becoming man takes place in an interrelationship with an environment. This statement gains significance if one reflects that this environment is both a natural and a human one. That is, the developing human being not only interrelates with a particular natural environment, but with a specific cultural and social order, which is mediated to him by the significant others who have charge of him. Not only is the survival of the human infant dependent upon certain social arrangements, the direction of his organismic development is socially determined. From the moment of birth, man's organismic development, and indeed a large part of his biological being as such, are subjected to continuing socially determined interference.

Despite the obvious physiological limits to the range of possible and different ways of becoming man in this double environmental interrelationship the human organism manifests an immense plasticity in its response to the environmental forces at work on it. This is particularly clear when one observes the flexibility of man's biological constitution as it is subjected to a variety of socio-cultural determinations. It is an ethnological commonplace that the ways of becoming and being human are as numerous as man's cultures. Humanness is socio-culturally variable. In other words, there is no human nature in the sense of a biologically fixed substratum determining the variability of socio-cultural formations. There is only human nature in the sense of anthropological constants (for example, world-openness and plasticity of instinctual structure) that delimit and permit man's socio-cultural formations. But the specific shape into which this humanness is molded is determined by those socio-cultural formations and is relative to their numerous variations. While it is possible to say that man has a nature, it is more significant to say that man constructs his own nature, or more simply, that man produces himself.

The plasticity of the human organism and its susceptibility to socially determined interference is best illustrated by the ethnological evidence concerning sexuality. While man possesses sexual drives that are comparable to those of the other higher mammals, human sexuality is characterized by a very high degree of pliability. It is not only relatively independent of temporal rhythms, it is pliable both in the objects toward which it may be directed and in its modalities of expression. Ethnological evidence shows that, in sexual matters, man is capable of almost anything. . . .

Social order is not part of the "nature of things," and it cannot be derived from the "laws of nature." Social order exists *only* as a product of human activity. No other ontological status may be ascribed to it without hopelessly obfuscating its empirical manifestations. Both in its genesis (social order is the result of past human activity) and its existence in any instant of time (social order exists only and insofar as human activity continues to produce it) it is a human product. . . .

All human activity is subject to habitualization. Any action that is repeated frequently becomes cast into a pattern, which can then be reproduced with an economy of effort and which, *ipso facto*, is apprehended by its performer *as* that pattern. Habitualization further implies that the action in question may be performed again in the future in the same manner and with the same economical effort. This is true of non-social as well as of social activity. Even the solitary individual on the proverbial desert island habitualizes his activity. When he wakes up in the morning and resumes his attempts to construct a canoe out of matchsticks, he may mumble to himself. "There I go again," as he starts on step one of an operating procedure consisting of, say, ten steps. In other words, even solitary man has at least the company of his operating procedures.

Habitualized actions, of course, retain their meaningful character for the individual although the meanings involved become embedded as routines in his general stock of knowledge, taken for granted by him and at hand for his projects into the future. Habitualization carries with it the important psychological gain that choices are narrowed. While in theory there may be a hundred ways to go about the project of building a canoe out of matchsticks, habitualization narrows these down to one. This frees the individual from the burden of "all those decisions," providing a psychological relief that has its basis in man's undirected instinctual structure. Habitualization provides the direction and the specialization of activity that is lacking in man's biological equipment, thus relieving the accumulation of tensions that result from undirected drives. And by providing a stable background in which human activity may proceed with a minimum of decision-making most of the time, it frees energy for such decisions as may be necessary on certain occasions. In other words, the background of habitualized activity opens up a foreground for deliberation and innovation.

In terms of the meanings bestowed by man upon his activity, habitualization makes it unnecessary for each situation to be defined anew, step by step. A large variety of situations may be subsumed under its predefinitions. The activity to be undertaken in these situations can then be anticipated. Even alternatives of conduct can be assigned standard weights.

These processes of habitualization precede any institutionalization, indeed can be made to apply to a hypothetical solitary individual detached from any social interaction. The fact that even such a solitary individual, assuming that he has been formed as a self (as we would have to assume in the case of our matchstick-canoe builder), will habitualize his activity in accordance with biographical experience of a world of social institutions preceding his solitude need not concern us at the moment. Empirically, the more important part of the habitualization of human activity is coextensive with the latter's institutionalization. The question then becomes how do institutions arise.

Institutionalization occurs whenever there is a reciprocal typification of habitualized actions by types of actors. Put differently, any such typification is an institution. What must be stressed is the reciprocity of institutional typifications and the typicality of not only the actions but also the actors in institutions. The typifications of habitualized actions that constitute institutions are always shared ones. They are *available* to all the members of the particular social group in question, and the institution itself typifies individual actors as well as individual actions. The institution posits that actions of type X will be performed by actors of type X. For example, the institution of the law posits that heads shall be chopped off in specific ways under specific circumstances, and that specific types of individuals shall do the chopping (executioners, say, or members of an impure caste, or virgins under a certain age, or those who have been designated by an oracle).

Institutions further imply historicity and control. Reciprocal typifications of actions are built up in the course of a shared history. They cannot be created instantaneously. Institutions always have a history, of which they are the products. It is impossible to understand an institution adequately without an understanding of the historical process in which it was produced. Institutions also, by the very fact of their existence, control human conduct by setting up predefined patterns of conduct, which channel it in one direction as against the many other directions that would theoretically be possible. It is important to stress that this controlling character is inherent in institutionalization as such, prior to or apart from any mechanisms of sanctions specifically set up to support an institution. These mechanisms (the sum of which constitute what is generally called a system of social control) do, of course, exist in many institutions and in all the agglomerations of institutions that we call societies. Their controlling efficacy, however, is of a secondary or supplementary kind. As we shall see again later, the primary social control is given in the existence of an institution as such. To say that a segment of human activity has been institutionalized is already to say that this segment of human activity has been subsumed under social control. Additional control mechanisms are required only insofar as the processes of institutionalization are less than completely successful. Thus, for instance, the law may provide that anyone who breaks the incest taboo will have his head chopped off. This provision may be necessary because there have been cases when individuals offended against the taboo. It is unlikely that this sanction will have to be invoked continuously (unless the institution delineated by the incest taboo is itself in the course of disintegration, a special case that we need not elaborate here). It makes little sense, therefore, to say that human sexuality is socially controlled by beheading certain individuals. Rather, human sexuality is socially controlled by its institutionalization in the course of the particular history in question. One may add, of course, that the incest taboo itself is nothing but the negative side of an assemblage of typifications, which define in the first place which sexual conduct is incestuous and which is not. . . .

An institutional world, then, is experienced as an objective reality. It has a history that antedates the individual's birth and is not accessible to his biographical recollection. It was there before he was born, and it will be there after his death. This history itself, as the tradition of the existing institutions, has the character of objectivity. The individual's biography is apprehended as an episode located within the objective history of the society. The institutions, as historical and objective facticities, confront the individual as undeniable facts. The institutions are *there*, external to him, persistent in their reality, whether he likes it or not. He cannot wish them away. They resist his attempts to change or evade them. They have coercive power over him, both in themselves, by the sheer force of their facticity, and through the control mechanisms that are usually attached to the most important of them. The objective reality of institutions is not diminished if the individual does not understand their purpose or their mode of operation. He may experience large sectors of the social world as incomprehensible, perhaps oppressive in their opaqueness, but real nonetheless. Since institutions exist as external reality, the individual cannot understand them by introspection. He must "go out" and learn about them, just as he must to learn about nature. This remains true even though the social world, as a humanly produced reality, is potentially understandable in a way not possible in the case of the natural world.

It is important to keep in mind that the objectivity of the institutional world, however massive it may appear to the individual, is a humanly produced, constructed objectivity. The process by which the externalized products of human activity attain the character of objectivity is objectivation. The institutional world is objectivated human activity, and so is every single institution. In other words, despite the objectivity that marks the social world in human experience, it does not thereby acquire an ontological status apart from the human activity that produced it. The paradox that man is capable of producing a world that he then experiences as something other than a human product will concern us later on. At the moment, it is important to emphasize that the relationship between man, the producer, and the social world, his product, is and remains a dialectical one. That is, man (not, of course, in isolation but in his collectivities) and his social world interact with each other. The product acts back upon the producer. Externalization and objectivation are moments in a continuing dialectical process. The third moment in this process, which is internalization constitution of subject (by which the objectivated social world is retrojected into consciousness in the course of socialization), will occupy us in considerable detail later on. It is already possible, however, to see the fundamental relationship of these three dialectical moments in social reality. Each of them corresponds to an essential characterization of the social world. *Society is a human product. Society is an objective reality. Man is a social product.* It may also already be evident than an analysis of the social world that leaves out any one of these three moments will be distortive. One may further add that only with the transmission of the social world to a new generation (that is, internalization as effectuated in socialization) does the fundamental social dialectic appear in its totality. To repeat, only with the appearance of a new generation can one properly speak of a social world.

At the same point, the institutional world requires legitimation, that is, ways by which it can be "explained" and justified. This is not because it appears less real. As we have seen, the reality of the social world gains in massivity in the course of its transmission. This reality, however, is a historical one, which comes to the new generation as a tradition rather than as a biographical memory. . . .

A final question of great theoretical interest arising from the historical variability of institutionalization has to do with the manner in which the institutional order is objectified: To what extent is an institutional order, or any part of it, apprehended as a non-human facticity? This is the question of the reification of social reality.

Reification is the apprehension of human phenomena as if they were things, that is, in non-human or possibly supra-human terms. Another way of saying this is that reification is the apprehension of the products of human activity *as if* they were something else than human products—such as facts of nature, results of cosmic laws, or manifestations of divine will. Reification implies that man is capable of forgetting his own authorship of the human world, and further, that the dialectic between man, the producer, and his products is lost to consciousness.

The reified world is, by definition, a dehumanized world. It is experienced by man as a strange facticity, an *opus alienum* over which he has no control rather than as the *opus proprium* of his own productive activity.

It will be clear from our previous discussion of objectivation that, as soon as an objective social world is established, the possibility of reification is never far away. The objectivity of the social world means that it confronts man as something outside of himself. The decisive question is whether he still retains the awareness that, however objectivated, the social world was made by men—and, therefore, can be remade by them. In other words, reification can be described as an extreme step in the process of objectivation, whereby the objectivated world loses its comprehensibility as a human enterprise and becomes fixated as a non-human, non-humanizable, inert facticity. Typically, the real relationship between man and his world is reversed in consciousness. Man, the producer of a world, is apprehended as its product, and human activity as an epiphenomenon of non-human processes. Human meanings are no longer understood as world-producing but as being, in their turn, products of the "nature of things." It must be emphasized that reification is a modality of consciousness, more precisely, a modality of man's objectification of the human world. Even while apprehending the world in reified terms, man continues to produce it. That is, man is capable paradoxically of producing a reality that denies him.

Reification is possible on both the pretheoretical and theoretical levels of consciousness. Complex theoretical systems can be described as reifications, though presumably they have their roots in pretheoretical reifications established in this or that social situation. Thus it would be an error to limit the concept of reification to the mental constructions of intellectuals. Reification exists in the consciousness of the man in the street and, indeed, the latter presence is more practically significant. It would also be a mistake to look at reification as a perversion of an originally non-reified apprehension of the social world, a sort of cognitive fall from grace, On the contrary, the available ethnological and psychological evidence seems to indicate the opposite, namely, that the original apprehension of the social world is highly reified both phylogenetically and ontogenetically. This implies that an apprehension of reification *as* a modality of consciousness is dependent upon an at least relative dereification of consciousness, which is a comparatively late development in history and in any individual biography.

Both the institutional order as a whole and segments of it may be apprehended in reified terms. For example, the entire order of society may be conceived of as a microcosm reflecting the macrocosm of the total universe as made by the gods. Whatever happens "here below" is but a pale reflection of what takes place "up above." Particular institutions may be apprehended in similar ways. The basic "recipe" for the reification of institutions is to bestow on them an ontological status independent of human activity and signification. Specific reifications are variations on this general theme. Marriage, for instance, may be reified as an imitation of divine acts of creativity, as a universal mandate of natural law, as the necessary consequence of biological or psychological forces, or, for that matter, as a functional imperative of the social system. What all these reifications have in common is their obfuscation of marriage as an ongoing human production. As can be readily seen in this example, the reification may occur both theoretically and pretheoretically. Thus the mystagogue can concoct a highly sophisticated theory reaching out from the concrete human event to the farthest corners of the divine cosmos, but an illiterate peasant couple being married may apprehend the event with a similarly reifying shudder of metaphysical dread. Through reification, the world of institutions appears to merge with the world of nature. It becomes necessity and fate, and is lived through as such, happily *or* unhappily as the case may be.

Roles may be reified in the same manner as institutions. The sector of self-consciousness that has been objectified in the role is then also apprehended as an inevitable fate, for which the individual may disclaim responsibility. The paradigmatic formula for this kind of reification is the statement "I have no choice in the matter, I have to act this way because of my position"—as husband, father, general, archbishop, chairman of the board, gangster, or hangman, as the case may be. This means that the reification of roles narrows the subjective distance that the individual may establish between himself and his role-playing. The distance implied in all objectification remains, of course, but the distance brought about by disidentification shrinks to the vanishing point. Finally, identity itself (the total self, if one prefers) may be reified, both one's own and that of others. There is then a total identification of the individual with his socially assigned typifications. He is apprehended as *nothing but* that type. This apprehension may be positively or negatively accented in terms of values or emotions. The identification of "Jew" may be equally reifying for the anti-Semite and the Jew himself, except that the latter will accent the identification positively and the former negatively. Both reifications bestow an ontological and total status on a typification that is humanly produced and that, even as it is internalized, objectifies but a segment of the self. Once more, such reifications may range from the pretheoretical level of "what everybody knows about Jews" to the most complex theories of Jewishness as a manifestation of biology ("Jewish blood"), psychology ("the Jewish soul") or metaphysics ("the mystery of Israel"). . . .

SOCIETY AS SUBJECTIVE REALITY

Since society exists as both objective and subjective reality, any adequate theoretical understanding of it must comprehend both these aspects. As we have already argued, these aspects receive their proper recognition if society is understood in terms of an ongoing dialectical process composed of the three moments of externalization, objectivation, and internalization. As far as the societal phenomenon is concerned, these moments are *not* to be thought of as occurring in a temporal sequence. Rather society and each part of it are simultaneously characterized by these three moments, so that any analysis in terms of only one or two of them falls short. The same is true of the individual member of society, who simultaneously externalizes his own being into the social world and internalizes it as an objective reality. In other words, to be in society is to participate in its dialectic.

The individual, however, is not born a member of society. He is born with a predisposition toward sociality, and he becomes a member of society. In the life of every individual, therefore, there *is* a temporal sequence, in the course of which he is inducted into participation in the societal dialectic. The beginning point of this process is internalization: the immediate apprehension or interpretation of an objective event as expressing meaning, that is, as a manifestation of another's subjective processes which thereby becomes subjectively meaningful to myself. . . .

Only when he has achieved this degree of internalization is an individual a member of society. The ontogenetic process by which this is brought about is socialization, which may thus be defined as the comprehensive and consistent induction of an individual into the objective world of a society or a sector of it. Primary socialization is the first socialization an individual undergoes in childhood, through which he becomes a member of society. Secondary socialization is any subsequent process that inducts an already socialized individual into new sectors of the objective world of his society. We may leave aside here the special question of the acquisition of knowledge about the objective world of societies other than the one of which we first became a member, and the process of internalizing such a world as reality—a process that exhibits, at least superficially, certain similarities with both primary and secondary socialization, yet is structurally identical with neither.

It is at once evident that primary socialization is usually the most important one for an individual, and that the basic structure of all secondary socialization has to resemble that of primary socialization. Every individual is born into an objective social structure within which he encounters the significant others who are in charge of his socialization. These significant others are imposed upon him. Their definitions of his situation are posited for him as objective reality. He is thus born into not only an objective social structure but also an objective social world. The significant others who mediate this world to him modify it in the course of mediating it. They select aspects of it in accordance with their own location in the social structure, and also by virtue of their individual, biographically rooted idiosyncrasies. The social world is "filtered" to the individual through this double selectivity. Thus the lower-class child not only absorbs a lower-class perspective on the social world, he absorbs it in the idiosyncratic coloration given it by his parents (or whatever other individuals are in charge of his primary socialization). The same lower-class perspective may induce a mood of contentment, resignation, bitter resentment, or seething rebelliousness. Consequently, the lower-class child will not only come to inhabit a world greatly different from that of an upper-class child, but may do so in a manner quite different from the lower-class child next door. . . .

The formation within consciousness of the generalized other marks a decisive phase in socialization. It implies the internalization of society as such and of the objective reality established therein, and, at the same time, the subjective establishment of a coherent and continuous identity. Society, identity *and* reality are subjectively crystallized in the same process of internalization. This crystallization is concurrent with the internalization of language. Indeed, for reasons evident from the foregoing observations on language, language constitutes both the most important content and the most important instrument of socialization.

When the generalized other has been crystallized in consciousness, a symmetrical relationship is established between objective and subjective reality. What is real "outside" corresponds to what is real "within." Objective reality can readily be "translated" into subjective reality, and vice versa. Language, of course, is the principal vehicle of this ongoing translating process in both directions. It should, however, be stressed that the symmetry between objective and subjective reality cannot be complete. The two realities correspond to each other, but they are not coextensive. There is always more objective reality "available" than is actually internalized in any individual consciousness, simply because the contents of socialization are determined by the social distribution of knowledge. No individual internalizes the totality of what is objectivated as reality in his society, not even if the society and its world are relatively simple ones. On the other hand, there are always elements of subjective reality that have not originated in socialization, such as the awareness of one's own body prior to and apart from any socially learned apprehension of it. Subjective biography is not fully social. The individual apprehends himself as being both inside *and* outside society. This implies that the symmetry between objective and subjective reality is never a static, once-for-all state of affairs. It must always be produced and reproduced *in actu*. In other words, the relationship between the individual and the objective social world is like an ongoing balancing act. The anthropological roots of this are, of course, the same as those we discussed in connection with the peculiar position of man in the animal kingdom.

In primary socialization there is no *problem* of identification. There is no choice of significant others. Society presents the candidate for socialization with a predefined set of significant others, whom he must accept as such with no possibility of opting for another arrangement. *Hic Rhodus, hic salta*. One must make do with the parents that fate has regaled one with. This unfair disadvantage inherent in the situation of being a child has the obvious consequence that, although the child is not simply passive in the process of his socialization, it is the adults who set the rules of the game. The child can play the game with enthusiasm or with sullen resistance. But, alas, there is no other game around. This has an important corollary. Since the child has no choice in the selection of his significant others, his identification with them is quasi-automatic. For the same reason, his internalization of their particular reality is quasi-inevitable. The child does not internalize the world of his significant others as one of many possible worlds. He internalizes it as *the* world, the only existent and only conceivable world, the world *tout court*. It is for this reason that the world internalized in primary socialization is so much more firmly entrenched in consciousness than worlds internalized in secondary socializations. However much the original sense of inevitability may be weakened in subsequent disenchantments, the recollection of a never-to-be-repeated certainty—the certainty of the first dawn of reality—still adheres to the first world of childhood. Primary socialization thus accomplishes what (in hindsight, of course) may be seen as the most important confidence trick that society plays on the individual—to make appear as necessity what is in fact a bundle of contingencies, and thus to make meaningful the accident of his birth.

HAROLD GARFINKEL (1917–): A BIOGRAPHICAL SKETCH

Harold Garfinkel was born on October 29, 1917, in Newark, New Jersey. His father, Abraham Garfinkel, owned a small furniture business, and after Harold graduated from high school the family decided that he would take business courses at the University of Newark and go into the furniture business as well. According to Garfinkel, the business courses he took in college—particularly one called "theory of accounts"—influenced his later work as much as or more than, did the work of C. Wright Mills and Kenneth Burke, whose social theories he would later study (Rawls 2002:10). As you will shortly see, ethnomethodologists are particularly intrigued by **accounting practices**, that is, by the way in which actors "offer accounts" in order to make sense out of events. Throughout his long and illustrious career, Garfinkel was most interested in how formal analytic theorizing creates an orderly social world out of "indicators," that is, how actors use signs and categories methodically to make sense of the world (Rawls 2002:10).

SOURCE: Reprinted from www.workpractice.com. Photographers: Andrew Clement and Jeannette Blomberg.

After he graduated from the University of Newark in 1939, Garfinkel decided to not join the family's furniture business. Instead, he enrolled in graduate school at the University of North Carolina at Chapel Hill. In 1942, Garfinkel completed a master's thesis on intraracial and interracial homicide. This was a sophisticated investigation into the institutional production of statistics and accounts and the social construction of racial differences (Rawls 2002:12). Based on observations in court cases and court records on homicides, Garfinkel concluded that the formulation and processing of cases within races was different from that between races (ibid.). Garfinkel's education was interrupted by World War II and his enlisting in the air force. After the war, Garfinkel decided to attend Harvard to study with Talcott Parsons (see Chapter 2) rather than go back to Chapel Hill. In 1952, Garfinkel completed his doctoral thesis, which was essentially an extended debate with Parsons as to the relative importance of empirical detail versus conceptual categories and generalizations. From 1954 to 1987, Garfinkel served on the faculty at the University of California, Los Angeles where today he remains active as an emeritus professor (Rawls 2002:17). Garfinkel and his wife of more than sixty years, Arlene, continue to live in Pacific Palisades, California.

INTELLECTUAL INFLUENCES AND CORE IDEAS

Ethnomethodology literally means the study of the methods people use to accomplish their everyday lives. The basic premise of ethnomethodology is that "people do what they do, right there and then, to be reasonable and effective and they do so for pervasively practical reasons and under unavoidably local conditions of knowledge, action and material resources" (Boden 1990:189).

Like phenomenology, ethnomethodology is concerned with how individuals make sense of their everyday circumstances. Both emphasize that "we accept as *unquestionable* the world of facts which surrounds us" (Schutz 1970:58; emphasis added), and both pay attention to the methods or procedures that individuals use to interpretively produce the recognizable, intelligible forms of action that, paradoxically, they treat as "facts." In short, both are intrigued by the "suspension of doubt" that sustains our everyday world.

The central difference between phenomenology and ethnomethodology is that while phenomenology has deeply influenced and been influenced by psychology, ethnomethodology is resolutely sociological. Indeed, as the subtitle of one of Garfinkel's books—*Ethnomethodology's Program: Working Out Durkheim's Aphorism* (2002)— makes clear, this perspective is based on a direct response to Durkheim's famous dictum discussed above, that the concreteness of social facts is sociology's most fundamental phenomenon (Rawls 2002:2). Ethnomethodologists seek to explain how "people make joint sense of their social world *together* and [how] they do so *methodically using social procedures or methods* that they share" (Heritage 1998:176, emphasis in original). In other words, instead of focusing on the cognitive or psychological aspects of sense-making and perceptions, ethnomethodologists attribute the very existence of an apparently real world to the interactional and interpretive skills of individual actors. In so doing, they shift the focus from "the real world" to "reality-constituting procedures" that are carried out during social interaction (Gubrium and Holstein 1997:39–41).

Consider, for instance, a visit to the doctor. When the doctor comes in, she may begin with a friendly hello and chat about the upcoming holiday. Then she asks, "So, what brings you here today?" and you begin to describe your stomach pains. This completely routine, but nevertheless complex, interaction involves much more than a simple internalization and acting out of preprogrammed norms or an automatic exchange of gestures. Rather, the success of this interaction depends on both actors' ability to read and respond to verbal and nonverbal cues on the spot. In this way everyday interaction is more like a dance using shared methods (or steps) than an instance of predetermined socialization. For instance, you (and the doctor) must gain a sense of exactly how much small talk in which to engage before getting to the point. (You won't spend twenty minutes answering the doctor's question about the holidays.) So, too, your response is based on a quick implicit assessment as to whether the doctor seems friendly and sincere or rushed and mechanical.

While ethnomethodologists focus on social interaction and behavior rather than abstract mental phenomenon, and thus share much with other sociologists, they are highly critical of work associated with "conventional" forms of sociological theory. First, ethnomethodologists reject the fundamental sociological conceit (especially apparent in structural functionalism and the Frankfurt School—see Chapters 2 and 3) that actors' views of their social worlds are somehow flawed or marginal to a full understanding of social phenomena (Cicourel 1964). In other words, ethnomethodologists condemn those perspectives that construe actors as "judgmental dopes" (Garfinkel 1967). Second, ethnomethodologists criticize conventional approaches for naïvely taking for granted the same skills, practices, and suppositions as the "unenlightened" members of the society they are studying (Pollner 1987:xi). Ethnomethodologists strive for "ethnomethodological indifference," an attitude of detachment that is rooted in neither intellectual naïveté nor condescension (Garfinkel and Sacks 1970:346). They seek to suspend belief in a rule-governed order in order to observe how the regular, coherent, connected patterns of social life are described and explained in ways that create that order itself (Zimmerman and Wieder 1970:289). That is, they seek to understand how people see, describe, and jointly develop a definition of the situation (ibid.).

This brings us to **breaching experiments**. Garfinkel's method for identifying the building blocks of everyday interaction was to formulate experiments that disrupt normal procedures in order to expose them. The point of breaching experiments is to "modify the *objective* structure of the familiar, known-in-common environment by rendering the background expectancies inoperative"(Garfinkel 1967:54; emphasis in original). An effective breaching experiment (1) makes it impossible for the subject to interpret the situation as a game or experiment or deception, (2) makes it necessary for the actor to reconstruct the "natural facts" of the encounter, and (3) deprives the actor of consensual support for an alternative definition of the situation (ibid.:58). In short, breaching experiments work much in the same way that "culture shock" does: by thrusting into consciousness the basic elements of a previously taken-for-granted world.

For instance, in one experiment you will read about below, Garfinkel asked his students to spend fifteen minutes to an hour interacting with their family members as if they were boarders and not intimates. "They were instructed to conduct themselves in a circumspect and polite fashion. They were to avoid getting personal, to use formal address, to speak only when spoken to" (1967:47). Garfinkel reports that in four-fifths of the cases, "family members were stupefied. They vigorously sought to make the strange actions intelligible and to restore the situation to normal appearances" (ibid.). The point is that the families were stupefied because their taken-for-granted world was challenged, and as such, their normal procedures for making sense of things were rendered useless or at least questionable, which produced more than a little anxiety. Indeed, while always controversial, today such stress-inducing experiments are no longer considered ethical.

Comedy "reality" shows such as *Punk'd* and *Boiling Point* and, long before that, *Candid Camera* have no compunction carrying out their own versions of Garfinkel's stress-inducing breaching experiments, however. *Candid Camera*, which first premiered in 1948, used hidden cameras to catch unsuspecting guests trying to figure out and deal with hoaxes such as mailboxes that talked or moved.[7] Similarly, the short-lived cable show *Boiling Point* placed unsuspecting victims in situations that tried their patience (such as a florist who kept on cutting and cutting flowers out of an already-paid-for bouquet). The television audience watched as the clock ticked down, and if the victim was still involved in the interaction (without using profanity) after a given time limit, their patience was rewarded with $100. In the spirit of Garfinkel's breaching experiments, these shows are based on observing how unsuspecting victims respond to slight (or not so slight) disruptions in their taken-for-granted world.

Yet, it is not only reality-based comedy that is related to ethnomethodology. Identifying the intricate, taken-for-granted elements of everyday life—and then commenting on, satirizing, or subverting them—is central to many stand-up comedians and slapstick comedians as well. For example, comedian George Carlin's famous routine on the "seven words you can't say on television" epitomizes how comedians expose and then violate core but unspoken recipes. As Carlin quips, "I think it's the duty of the comedian to find out where the line is drawn and cross it deliberately" (http://www.quotationspage.com/quotes/George_Carlin).[8] So, too, *Saturday Night Live*'s "Weekend Update" is based on an exact imitation of newscasters' actual comments, mannerisms, demeanor, and so on coupled with an unexpected jolt from not following the "script," as in Chevy Chase's famous recurring

---

[7]Interestingly, *Candid Camera* (which is considered to be the first and longest running reality-based comedy program) was inspired in part by host Allen Funt's background as a research assistant at Cornell University. Funt aided psychologist Kurt Lewin in experiments on the behaviors of mothers and children (http://www.museum.tv/archives/etv/C/htmlC/candidcamera/candidcamera.htm, maintained by Amy Loomis).

[8]Akin to many comedians, Carlin is a student of language and words. Here is the beginning of the original "Seven Dirty Words" routine that caused such a fracas:

"I love words. I thank you for hearing my words. I want to tell you something about words that I uh, I think is important. I love . . . as I say, they're my work, they're my play, they're my passion. Words are all we have, really. We have thoughts, but thoughts are fluid. You know, [humming]. And, then we assign a word to a thought, [clicks tongue]. And we're stuck with that word for that thought. So be careful with words. I like to think, yeah, the same words that hurt can heal. It's a matter of how you pick them . . . " (http://www.erenkrantz.com/Humor/SevenDirtyWords.shtml).

Photo 6.6a "Normal" Elevator Riding

SOURCE: Laura Desfor Edles; used with permission.

Photo 6.6b "Deviant" Elevator Riding

SOURCE: Laura Desfor Edles; used with permission.

A common breaching experiment is to stand in an elevator facing the back wall rather than the door. Other passengers often will "account" for such deviation by attributing it to mental illness.

line, "Good evening, I'm Chevy Chase, and you're not." Comedy Central's *The Daily Show with Jon Stewart* and *The Colbert Report* hosted by Stephen Colbert, are rooted in a similar tack, parodying both newscasters and cocky "correspondents in the field," as well as political pundit programs.

One of the central methods that actors use to order and make sense of their everyday world (and that breaching experiments were explicitly designed to expose) is **accounting practices.** For instance, in Garfinkel's experiment discussed above, parents typically responded to the unexpected behavior of their child by constructing and attributing motives that looked to the past to explain the present: "the student was 'working too hard' in school; the student was 'ill'; there had been 'another fight' with a fiancée" (Garfinkel 1967:48). Here, parents are trying to make "account-able" the behavior observed. Garfinkel emphasizes that the process of accounting is vital to the sustenance of reality because it is what enables us to believe that social life is coherent and that meaning is shared.

One of the most important features of accounting practices is **indexicality**. Taken from linguistics, the term "indexical" refers to the fact that just as words have different meanings in different contexts, so, too, all expressions and practical actions are interpreted in a particular context.

Consider, for instance, the following conversation:

A: I have a fourteen-year-old son.

B: Well, that's all right.

A: I also have a dog.

B: Oh, I'm sorry. (Sacks 1984, as cited in Heritage 1984:237)

At first glance this conversation appears incoherent or nonsensical. However, once we are told that "A" is a would-be tenant of an apartment and "B" is the landlord, the conversation makes perfect sense. Then we recognize that the conversation is an exchange about issues that might disqualify the potential tenant from the rental. This is indexicality.

The centrality of both accounting practices and indexicality to ethnomethodology is evident in Garfinkel's very definition of ethnomethodology as "the investigation of the rational properties of indexical expressions and other practical actions as contingent on ongoing accomplishments of organized artful practices of everyday life" (1967:11). Everyday life is made up of not only determining the meaning of objects or practices within a given context, but also inferring meaning by creating or attributing a context or "index" when one is not readily apparent (as the experiment above makes clear). Thus, for example, staring out at pouring rain, a speaker observes: "What a wonderful summer we're having!" and the hearer concludes that the remark was intended to be ironical (Heritage 1984:152).

In sum, the everyday world is created and sustained by our ability to make "definite sense with indefinite resources" (Heritage 1984:144). Human descriptive resources, our abilities to understand the situations that we face, are only "approximate"; they do not reflect or correspond directly to "real" states of affairs, but rather provide a field of possibilities. Individuals must actively perform contextualizing work in order to see what the descriptions used in encounters mean (ibid.:148).

This brings us back to the concept of typification. Recall that for Schutz (1962: 14), language is the principal tool for typifying the elements in all encounters; that is, it is a kind of "treasure house of ready-made pre-constituted types and characteristics all socially derived and carrying along an open horizon of unexplored content." As John Heritage (1984:145) states:

> Language is the medium through which . . . common-sense equivalence classes are constituted and communicated. It embodies a continual compromise between generality and specificity. There is thus an inherently approximate relationship between a descriptor and the range of states of affairs it may be used to describe.

In the 1960s, ethnomethodologists' emphasis on language as a constituting practice combined with new technology to produce a new direction in the field, called **conversation analysis**. Conversation analysis infuses the ethnomethodological interest in the details of mundane everyday action and the production of order with a rigorous methodology and focus on the fundamental, taken-for-granted structures of conversational interaction. Using audio- and videotape for recording conversations as they naturally occur, and linguistic conventions for meticulously coding and analyzing them, conversation analysts investigate not only the use of words, but also "the hesitations, cut-offs, restarts, silences, breathing noises, throat clearings, sniffles, laughter and laughterlike noises, prosody, and the like, not to mention the 'nonverbal' behaviors available on video records that are usually closely integrated with the stream of activity captured on the audiotape" (Zimmerman 1988:413). Conversation analysts have been quite prolific in the last thirty years, successfully uncovering the characteristic features of such phenomena as conversational openings and closings, turn-taking, interruptions, as well as applause and booing (Sacks, Schlegoff, and Jefferson 1974; Jefferson 1978; Heritage and Greatbatch 1986; Clayman 1993).

Yet, ironically, by taking a more positivistic approach to conversational structures, conversation analysts have veered from ethnomethodology's phenomenological roots. In contrast to Berger and Luckmann and Schutz, conversation analysts are not interested in studying the actor's consciousness or a community of "shared understandings," but rather only studying observable, measurable behaviors. Put in another way, conversation analysts are interested in the "architecture of intersubjectivity" (Heritage 1984:254)—rather than intersubjectivity itself.

GARFINKEL'S THEORETICAL ORIENTATION

In terms of action, akin to phenomenology, ethnomethodology's emphasis on the taken-for-granted world reflects a primarily nonrational approach, since the taken-for-granted world is not open to conscious, cost/benefit (i.e., rational) analysis. For ethnomethodologists, even the seemingly "rational" ways in which we seek to "save face" and "strategically" negotiate through everyday life rely on a bevy of typifications, recipes, and other cognitive resources that we do not question (until they are breached or exposed or proven inadequate). This nonrational bent is illustrated in Figure 6.3.

In terms of order, ethnomethodologists confer on actors a great deal of agency, which reflects a prioritization of the level of the individual. They attribute the very existence of an apparently real world to the interactional and interpretive skills of individual actors, and they emphasize that social order is maintained only by individuals in interaction and that preexisting symbolic patterns are themselves created and recreated

Figure 6.3   Garfinkel's Basic Concepts and Theoretical Orientation

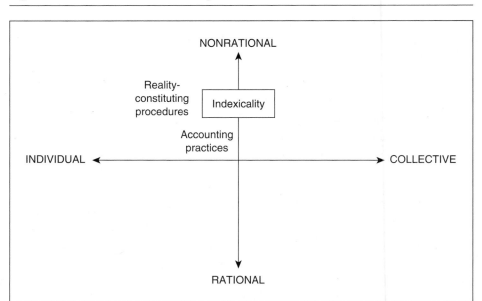

in everyday interaction. To be sure, this emphasis on agency and practical action should not be mistaken for a view of action as infinite or open to all possibilities. For like phenomenologists (particularly Berger and Luckmann), ethnomethodologists fully recognize the role played by preexisting symbolic structures in shaping accounting practices, that is, the significance of the collective/nonrational realm. However, parallel to phenomenology, ethnomethodologists are routinely criticized for ignoring the collective/ rational dimensions of society. They are perceived as obsessed with the trivial, microlevel details of everyday life at the expense of larger social structural concerns (e.g., inequality, globalization).

Reading

Introduction to *Studies in Ethnomethodology*

This excerpt from Garfinkel's groundbreaking work in ethnomethodology features his famous breaching experiments. As indicated previously, the purpose of breaching experiments is to make the underlying assumptions that guide commonplace scenes visible and to illuminate "background understandings and social affects" (Garfinkel 1967:49). Breaching experiments highlight the common denominators between phenomenology and ethnomethodology as well as Garfinkel's reliance on Schutz, because while they focus on behavior, breaching experiments uncover the basic, taken-for-granted elements of the "attitude of daily life" as well. Put in another way, breaching experiments make individuals suspend the "suspension of doubt" that sustains our everyday world (Schutz 1967).

❖

Studies in Ethnomethodology (1967)

Harold Garfinkel

For Kant the moral order "within" was an awesome mystery; for sociologists the moral order "without" is a technical mystery. From the point of view of sociological theory the moral order consists of the rule governed activities of everyday life. A society's members encounter and know the moral order as perceivedly normal courses of action—familiar scenes of everyday affairs, the world of daily life known in common with others and with others taken for granted.

They refer to this world as the "natural facts of life" which, for members, are through and through moral facts of life. For members not only are matters so about familiar scenes, but they are

SOURCE: From Garfinkel, H., "*Studies in Ethnomethodology,* Prentice-Hall, 1967, pp. 35–38; 44–58.

so because it is morally right or wrong that they are so. Familiar scenes of everyday activities, treated by members as the "natural facts of life," are massive facts of the members' daily existence both as a real world and as the product of activities in a real world. They furnish the "fix," the "this is it" to which the waking state returns one, and are the points of departure and return for every modification of the world of daily life that is achieved in play, dreaming, trance, theater, scientific theorizing, or high ceremony.

In every discipline, humanistic or scientific, the familiar common sense world of everyday life is a matter of abiding interest. In the social sciences, and in sociology particularly, it is a matter of essential preoccupation. It makes up sociology's problematic subject matter, enters the very constitution of the sociological attitude, and exercises an odd and obstinate sovereignty over sociologists' claims to adequate explanation.

Despite the topic's centrality, an immense literature contains little data and few methods with which the essential features of socially recognized "familiar scenes" may be detected and related to dimensions of social organization. Although sociologists take socially structured scenes of everyday life as a point of departure they rarely see,[i] as a task of sociological inquiry in its own right, the general question of how any such common sense world is possible. Instead, the possibility of the everyday world is either settled by theoretical representation or merely assumed. As a topic and methodological ground for sociological inquiries, the definition of the common sense world of everyday life, though it is appropriately a project of sociological inquiry, has been neglected. My purposes in this paper are to demonstrate the essential relevance, to sociological inquiries, of a concern for common sense activities as a topic of inquiry in its own right and, by reporting a series of studies, to urge its "rediscovery."

MAKING COMMONPLACE SCENES VISIBLE

In accounting for the stable features of everyday activities sociologists commonly select familiar settings such as familial households or work places and ask for the variables that contribute to their stable features. Just as commonly, one set of considerations are unexamined: the socially standardized and standardizing, "seen but unnoticed," expected, background features of everyday scenes. The member of the society uses background expectancies as a scheme of interpretation. With their use actual appearances are for him recognizable and intelligible as the appearances-of-familiar-events. Demonstrably he is responsive to this background, while at the same time he is at a loss to tell us specifically of what the expectancies consist. When we ask him about them he has little or nothing to say.

For these background expectancies to come into view one must either be a stranger to the "life as usual" character of everyday scenes, or become estranged from them. As Alfred Schutz pointed out, a "special motive" is required to make them problematic. In the sociologists' case this "special motive" consists in the programmatic task of treating a societal member's practical circumstances, which include from the member's point of view the morally necessary character of many of its background features, as matters of theoretic interest. The seen but unnoticed backgrounds of everyday activities are made visible and are described from a perspective in which persons live out the lives they do, have the children they do, feel the feelings, think the thoughts, enter the relationships they do, all in order to permit the sociologist to solve his theoretical problems.

Almost alone among sociological theorists, the late Alfred Schutz, in a series of classical studies[ii] of the constitutive phenomenology of the world of everyday life, described many of

---

[i]The work of Alfred Schutz, cited in footnote 2, is a magnificent exception. Readers who are acquainted with his writings will recognize how heavily this paper is indebted to him.

[ii]Alfred Schutz, *Der Sinnhafte Aufbau Der Sozialen Welt* (Wein: Verlag von Julius Springer, 1932); *Collected Papers I: The Problem of Social Reality*, ed. Maurice Natanson (The Hague: Martinus Nijhoff, 1962); *Collected Papers II: Studies in Social Theory*, ed. Arvid Broderson (The Hague: Martinus Nijhoff, 1964); *Collected Papers III: Studies in Phenomenological Philosophy*, ed. I. Schutz (The Hague: Martinus Nijhoff, 1966).

these seen but unnoticed background expectancies. He called them the "attitude of daily life." He referred to their scenic attributions as the "world known in common and taken for granted." Schutz' fundamental work makes it possible to pursue further the tasks of clarifying their nature and operation, of relating them to the processes of concerted actions, and assigning them their place in an empirically imaginable society.

The studies reported in this paper attempt to detect some expectancies that lend commonplace scenes their familiar, life-as-usual character, and to relate these to the stable social structures of everyday activities. Procedurally it is my preference to start with familiar scenes and ask what can be done to make trouble. The operations that one would have to perform in order to multiply the senseless features of perceived environments; to produce and sustain bewilderment, consternation, and confusion; to produce the socially structured affects of anxiety, shame, guilt, and indignation; and to produce disorganized interaction should tell us something about how the structures of everyday activities are ordinarily and routinely produced and maintained.

A word of reservation. Despite their procedural emphasis, my studies are not properly speaking experimental. They are demonstrations, designed, in Herbert Spiegelberg's phrase, as "aids to a sluggish imagination." I have found that they produce reflections through which the strangeness of an obstinately familiar world can be detected. . . .

BACKGROUND UNDERSTANDINGS AND "ADEQUATE" RECOGNITION OF COMMONPLACE EVENTS

What kinds of expectancies make up a "seen but unnoticed" background of common understandings, and how are they related to persons' recognition of stable courses of interpersonal transactions? Some information can be obtained if we first ask how a person will look at an ordinary and familiar scene and what will he see in it if we require of him that he do no more than look at it as something that for him it "obviously" and "really" is not.

Undergraduate students were assigned the task of spending from fifteen minutes to an hour in their homes viewing its activities while assuming that they were boarders in the household. They were instructed not to act out the assumption. Thirty-three students reported their experiences.

In their written reports students "behaviorized" the household scenes. Here is an excerpt from one account to illustrate my meaning.

> A short, stout man entered the house, kissed me on the cheek and asked, "How was school?" I answered politely. He walked into the kitchen, kissed the younger of the two women, and said hello to the other. The younger woman asked me, "What do you want for dinner, honey?" I answered, "Nothing." She shrugged her shoulders and said no more. The older woman shuffled around the kitchen muttering. The man washed his hands, sat down at the table, and picked up the paper. He read until the two women had finished putting the food on the table. The three sat down. They exchanged idle chatter about the day's events. The older woman said something in a foreign language which made the others laugh.

Persons, relationships, and activities were described without respect for their history, for the place of the scene in a set of developing life circumstances, or for the scenes as texture of relevant events for the parties themselves. References to motives, propriety, subjectivity generally, and the socially standardized character of the events were omitted. Descriptions might be thought of as those of a keyhole observer who puts aside much of what he knows in common with subjects about the scenes he is looking at, as if the writer had witnessed the scenes under a mild amnesia for his common sense knowledge of social structures.

Students were surprised to see the ways in which members' treatments of each other were personal. The business of one was treated as the business of the others. A person being criticized was unable to stand on dignity and was prevented by the others from taking offense. One student reported her surprise at how freely she had the run of the house. Displays of conduct and feeling occurred without apparent concern for the management of impressions. Table manners were bad, and family members showed each other little politeness. An early casualty in the scene was the family news of the day which turned into trivial talk.

Students reported that this way of looking was difficult to sustain. Familiar objects—persons obviously, but furniture and room arrangements as well—resisted students' efforts to think of themselves as strangers. Man became uncomfortably aware of how habitual movements were being made; of *how* one was handling the silverware, or *how* one opened a door or greeted another member. Many reported that the attitude was difficult to sustain because with it quarreling, bickering, and hostile motivations became discomfitingly visible. Frequently an account that recited newly visible troubles was accompanied by the student's assertion that his account of family problems was not a "true" picture; the family was *really* a very happy one. Several students reported a mildly oppressive feeling of "conforming to a part." Several students attempted to formulate the "real me" as activities governed by rules of conduct but gave it up as a bad job. They found it more convincing to think of themselves in "usual" circumstances as "being one's real self." Nevertheless one student was intrigued with how deliberately and successfully he could predict the other's responses to his actions. He was not troubled by this feeling.

Many accounts reported a variation on the theme: "I was glad when the hour was up and I could return to the real me."

Students were convinced that the view from the boarder's attitude was not their real home environment. The boarder's attitude produced appearances which they discounted as interesting incongruities of little and misleading practical import. How had the familiar ways of looking at their home environments been altered? How did their looking differ from usual?

Several contrasts to the "usual" and "required" way of looking are detectable from their accounts. (1) In looking at their homes as boarders they replaced the mutually recognized texture of events with a rule of interpretation which required that this mutual texture be *temporarily* disregarded. (2) The mutually recognized texture was brought under the jurisdiction

of the new attitude as a definition of the essential structures of this texture. (3) This was done by engaging in interaction with others with an attitude whose nature and purpose only the user knew about, that remained undisclosed, that could be either adopted or put aside at a time of the user's own choosing, and was a matter of willful election. (4) The attitude as an intention was sustained as a matter of personal and willed compliance with an explicit and single rule, (5) in which, like a game, the goal of the intention was identical with looking at things under the auspices of the single rule itself. (6) Above all, looking was not bound by any necessity for gearing one's interests within the attitude to the actions of others. These were the matters that students found strange.

When students used these background expectancies not only as ways of looking at familial scenes but as grounds for acting in them, the scenes exploded with the bewilderment and anger of family members.

In another procedure students were asked to spend from fifteen minutes to an hour in their homes imagining that they were boarders and acting out this assumption. They were instructed to conduct themselves in a circumspect and polite fashion. They were to avoid getting personal, to use formal address, to speak only when spoken to.

In nine of forty-nine cases students either refused to do the assignment (five cases) or the try was "unsuccessful" (four cases). Four of the "no try" students said they were afraid to do it; a fifth said she preferred to avoid the risk of exciting her mother who had a heart condition. In two of the "unsuccessful" cases the family treated it as a joke from the beginning and refused despite the continuing actions of the student to change. A third family took the view that something undisclosed was the matter, but what it might be was of no concern to them. In the fourth family the father and mother remarked that the daughter was being "extra nice" and undoubtedly wanted something that she would shortly reveal.

In the remaining four-fifths of the cases family members were stupefied. They vigorously sought to make the strange actions intelligible and to restore the situation to normal appearances. Reports were filled with accounts of astonishment, bewilderment, shock, anxiety, embarrassment, and anger, and with charges by various family members that the student was mean, inconsiderate, selfish, nasty, or impolite. Family members demanded explanations: What's the matter? What's gotten into you? Did you get fired? Are you sick? What are you being so superior about? Why are you mad? Are you out of your mind or are you just stupid? One student acutely embarrassed his mother in front of her friends by asking if she minded if he had a snack from the refrigerator. "Mind if you have a little snack? You've been eating little snacks around here for years without asking me. What's gotten into you?" One mother, infuriated when her daughter spoke to her only when she was spoken to, began to shriek in angry denunciation of the daughter for her disrespect and insubordination and refused to be calmed by the student's sister. A father berated his daughter for being insufficiently concerned for the welfare of others and of acting like a spoiled child.

Occasionally family members would first treat the student's action as a cue for a joint comedy routine which was soon replaced by irritation and exasperated anger at the student for not knowing when enough was enough. Family members mocked the "politeness" of the students—"Certainly Mr. Herzberg!"—or charged the student with acting like a wise guy and generally reproved the "politeness" with sarcasm.

Explanations were sought in previous, understandable motives of the student: the student was "working too hard" in school; the student was "ill"; there had been "another fight" with a fiancee. When offered explanations by family members went unacknowledged, there followed withdrawal by the offended member, attempted isolation of the culprit, retaliation, and denunciation. "Don't bother with him, he's in one of his moods again"; "Pay no attention but just wait until he asks me for something"; "You're cutting me, okay I'll cut you and then some"; "Why must you always create friction in our family harmony?" Many accounts reported versions of the following confrontation. A father followed his son into the bedroom. "Your Mother is right. You don't look well and you're not talking sense. You had better get another job that doesn't require such late hours." To this the student replied that he appreciated the consideration, but that he felt fine and only wanted a little privacy. The father responded in a high rage, "I don't want any more of *that* out of *you* and if you can't treat your mother decently you'd better move out!"

There were no cases in which the situation was not restorable upon the student's explanation. Nevertheless, for the most part family members were not amused and only rarely did they find the experience instructive as the student argued that it was supposed to have been. After hearing the explanation a sister replied coldly on behalf of a family of four, "Please, no more of these experiments. We're not rats, you know." Occasionally an explanation was accepted but still it added offense. In several cases students reported that the explanations left them, their families, or both wondering how much of what the student had said was "in character" and how much the student "really meant."

Students found the assignment difficult to complete. But in contrast with on-lookers' accounts students were likely to report that difficulties consisted in not being treated as if they were in the role that they were attempting to play, and of being confronted with situations but not knowing how a boarder would respond.

There were several entirely unexpected findings. (1) Although many students reported extensive rehearsals in imagination, very few mentioned anticipatory fears or embarrassment. (2) On the other hand, although unanticipated and nasty developments frequently occurred, in only one case did a student report serious regrets. (3) Very few students reported heartfelt relief when the hour was over. They were much more likely to report partial relief. They frequently reported that in response to the anger of others they became angry in return and slipped easily into subjectively recognizable feelings and actions.

In contrast to the reports of the on-looking "boarders" very few reports "behaviorized" the scene.

Background Understandings and Social Affects

Despite the interest in social affects that prevails in the social sciences, and despite the extensive concern that clinical psychiatry pays them, surprisingly little has been written on the socially structured conditions for their production. The role that a background of common understandings plays in their production, control, and recognition is, however, almost *terra incognita*. This lack of attention from experimental investigators is all the more remarkable if one considers that it is precisely this relationship that persons are concerned with in their common sense portrayals of how to conduct one's daily affairs so as to solicit enthusiasm and friendliness or avoid anxiety, guilt, shame, or boredom. The relationship between the common understandings and social affects may be illustrated by thinking of the acting out student-boarders' procedure as one that involved the production of bewilderment and anger by treating an important state of affairs as something that it "obviously," "naturally," and "really," is not.

The existence of a definite and strong relationship between common understandings and social affects can be demonstrated and some of its features explored by the deliberate display of distrust, a procedure that for us produced highly standardized effects. The rationale was as follows:

One of the background expectancies Schutz described concerns the sanctioned use of doubt as a constituent feature of a world that is being understood in common. Schutz proposed that for the *conduct of his everyday affairs* the person assumes, assumes the other person assumes as well, and assumes that as he assumes it of the other person, the other person assumes it of him, that a relationship of undoubted correspondence is the sanctioned relationship between the actual appearances of an object and the intended object that appears in a particular way. For the person conducting his everyday affairs, objects, for him

as he expects for others, are as they appear to be. To treat this relationship under a *rule* of doubt requires that the necessity and motivation for such a rule be justified.

We anticipated that because of the differing relationship of an exhibited rule of doubt (distrust)[iii] that the other person was as he appeared to be to the legitimate texture of common expectancies, there should be different affective states for the doubter and the doubted. On the part of the person distrusted there should be the demand for justification, and when it was not forthcoming, as "anyone could see" it could not be, anger. For the experimenter we expected embarrassment to result from the disparity, under the gaze of his victim, between the lesser thing that the experimenter's challenges of "what anyone could see" made him out to be and the competent person he with others knew himself "after all" to be but which the procedure required that he could not claim.

Like Santayana's clock, this formulation was neither right nor wrong. Although the procedure produced what we anticipated, it also furnished us and the experimenters with more than we had bargained for.

Students were instructed to engage someone in conversation and to imagine and act on the assumption that what the other person was saying was directed by hidden motives which were his real ones. They were to assume that the other person was trying to trick them or mislead them.

In only two of thirty-five accounts did students attempt the assignment with strangers. Most students were afraid that such a situation would get out of hand so they selected friends, roommates, and family members. Even so they reported considerable rehearsal in imagination,

---

[iii]The concepts of "trust" and "distrust" are elaborated in my paper, "A Conception of and Experiments with 'Trust' as a Condition of Stable Concerted Actions," in *Motivation and Social Interaction*, ed. O. J. Harvey (New York: The Ronald Press Company, 1963, pp. 187–238). The term "trust" is used there to refer to a person's compliance with the expectancies of the attitude of daily life as a morality. Acting in accordance with a rule of doubt directed to the correspondence between appearances and the objects that appearances are appearances of is only one way of specifying "distrust." Modifications of each of the other expectancies that make up the attitude of everyday life, as well as their various sub-sets, furnish variations on the central theme of treating a world that one is required to know in common and take for granted as a problematic matter. See footnote 2 for references to Schutz' discussion of the attitude of daily life. The attitude's constituent expectancies are briefly enumerated on pages 55–56.

much review of possible consequences, and deliberate selections among persons.

The attitude was difficult to sustain and carry through. Students reported acute awareness of being "in an artificial game," of being unable "to live the part," and of frequently being "at a loss as to what to do next." In the course of listening to the other person, experimenters would lose sight of the assignment. One student spoke for several when she said she was unable to get any results because so much of her effort was directed to maintaining an attitude of distrust that she was unable to follow the conversation. She said she was unable to imagine how her fellow conversationalists might be deceiving her because they were talking about such inconsequential matters.

With many students the assumption that the other person was not what he appeared to be and was to be distrusted was the same as the attribution that the other person was angry with them and hated them. On the other hand many victims, although they complained that the student had no reason to be angry with them, offered unsolicited attempts at explanation and conciliation. When this was of no avail there followed frank displays of anger and "disgust."

Anticipated and acute embarrassment swiftly materialized for the two students who attempted the procedure with strangers. After badgering a bus driver for assurances that the bus would pass the street that she wanted and receiving several assurances in return that indeed the bus did pass the street, the exasperated bus driver shouted so that all passengers overheard, "Look lady, I told you once, didn't I? How many times do I have to tell you!" She reported, "I shrank to the back of the bus to sink as low as I could in the seat. I had gotten a good case of cold feet, a flaming face, and a strong dislike for my assignment."

There were very few reports of shame or embarrassment from students who tried it with friends and family. Instead they were surprised, and so were we, to find as one student reported that "once I started acting the role of a hated person I actually came to feel somewhat hated and by the time I left the table I was quite angry." Even more surprising to us, many reported that they found the procedure enjoyable and this included the real anger not only of others but their own.

Although students' explanations easily restored most situations, some episodes "turned serious" and left a residue of disturbance for one or both parties that offered explanation did not resolve. This can be illustrated in the report of a student housewife who, at the conclusion of dinner, and with some trepidation, questioned her husband about having worked late the night before and raised a question about his actually having played poker as he claimed on an evening of the week before. Without asking him what he had actually done she indicated an explanation was called for. He replied sarcastically, "You seem to be uneasy about something. Do you know what it might be? This conversation would no doubt make more sense if I knew too." She accused him of deliberately avoiding the subject, although the subject had not been mentioned. He insisted that *she* tell *him* what the *subject* was. When she did not say, he asked directly, "Okay, what's the joke?" Instead of replying, "I gave him a long, hurt look." He became visibly upset, became very solicitous, gentle, and persuasive. In response she acknowledged the experiment. He stalked off obviously unhappy and for the remainder of the evening was sullen and suspicious. She, in the meanwhile, remained at the table piqued and unsettled about the remarks that her statements had drawn forth about his not being bored at work "with all the insinuations it might or could mean," particularly the insinuation that he was not bored at work but he *was* bored with her and at home. She wrote, "I was actually bothered by his remarks. . . . I felt more upset and worried than he did throughout the experiment. . . . about how imperturbable he seemed to be." Neither one attempted nor wanted to discuss the matter further. The following day the husband confessed that he had been considerably disturbed and had the following reactions in this order: determination to remain calm; shock at his wife's "suspicious nature"; surprise to find that cheating on her was liable to be hard; a determination to make her figure out her own answers to her questions without any denial or help from him; extreme relief when the encounter was revealed to have been experimentally contrived; but finally a residue of uneasy feelings which he characterized as "his shaken ideas of my (the wife's) nature which remained for the rest of the evening."

BACKGROUND UNDERSTANDINGS AND BEWILDERMENT

Earlier the argument was made that the possibility of common understanding does not consist in demonstrated measures of shared knowledge of social structure, but consists instead and entirely in the enforceable character of actions in compliance with the expectancies of everyday life as a morality. Common sense knowledge of the facts of social life for the members of the society is institutionalized knowledge of the real world. Not only does common sense knowledge portray a real society for members, but in the manner of a self fulfilling prophecy the features of the real society are produced by persons' motivated compliance with these background expectancies. Hence the stability of concerted actions should vary directly with whatsoever are the real conditions of social organization that guarantee persons' motivated compliance with this background texture of relevances as a legitimate order of beliefs about life in society seen "from within" the society. Seen from the person's point of view, his commitments to motivated compliance consist of his grasp of and subscription to the "natural facts of life in society."

Such considerations suggest that the firmer a societal member's grasp of What Anyone Like Us Necessarily Knows, the more severe should be his disturbance when "natural facts of life" are impugned for him as a depiction of his real circumstances. To test this suggestion a procedure would need to modify the *objective* structure of the familiar, known-in-common environment by rendering the background expectancies inoperative. Specifically, this modification would consist of subjecting a person to a breach of the background expectancies of everyday life while (a) making it difficult for the person to interpret his situation as a game, an experiment, a deception, a play, *i.e.*, as something other than the one known according to the attitude of everyday life as a matter of enforceable morality and action, (b) making it necessary that he reconstruct

the "natural facts" but giving him insufficient time to manage the reconstruction with respect to required mastery of practical circumstances for which he must call upon his knowledge of the "natural facts," and (c) requiring that he manage the reconstruction of the natural facts by himself and without consensual validation.

Presumably he should have no alternative but to try to normalize the resultant incongruities within the order of events of everyday life. Under the developing effort itself, events should lose their perceivedly normal character. The member should be unable to recognize an event's status as typical. Judgments of likelihood should fail him. He should be unable to assign present occurrences to similar orders of events he has known in the past. He should be unable to assign, let alone to "see at a glance," the conditions under which the events can be reproduced. He should be unable to order these events to means-ends relationships. The conviction should be undermined that the moral authority of the familiar society compels their occurrence. Stable and "realistic" matchings of intentions and objects should dissolve, by which I mean that the ways, otherwise familiar to him, in which the objective perceived environment serves as both the motivating grounds of feelings and is motivated by feelings directed to it, should become obscure. In short, the members' real perceived environment on losing its known-in-common background should become "specifically senseless."[iv] Ideally speaking, behaviors directed to such a senseless environment should be those of bewilderment, uncertainty, internal conflict, psycho-social isolation, acute, and nameless anxiety along with various symptoms of acute depersonalization. Structures of interaction should be correspondingly disorganized.

This is expecting quite a lot of a breach of the background expectancies. Obviously we would settle for less if the results of a procedure for their breach was at all encouraging about this formulation. As it happens, the procedure produced convincing and easily detected bewilderment and anxiety.

[iv]The term is borrowed from Max Weber's essay, "The Social Psychology of the World Religions," in *From Max Weber: Essays in Sociology*, trans. H. H. Gerth and C. Wright Mills (New York: Oxford University Press, 1946), pp. 267–301. I have adapted its meaning.

To begin with, it is necessary to specify just what expectancies we are dealing with. Schutz reported that the feature of a scene, "known in common with others," was compound and consisted of several constituents. Because they have been discussed elsewhere[v] I shall restrict discussion to brief enumeration.

According to Schutz, the person assumes, assumes that the other person assumes as well, and assumes that as he assumes it of the other person the other person assumes the same for him:

1. That the determinations assigned to an event by the witness are required matters that hold on grounds that specifically disregard personal opinion or socially structured circumstances of particular witnesses, *i.e.*, that the determinations are required as matters of "objective necessity" or "facts of nature."

2. That a relationship of undoubted correspondence is the sanctioned relationship between the-presented-appearance-of-the-object and the-intended-object-that-presents-itself-in-the-perspective-of-the-particular-appearance.

3. That the event that is known in the manner that it is known can actually and potentially affect the witness and can be affected by his action.

4. That the meanings of events are products of a socially standardized process of naming, reification, and idealization of the user's stream of experience, *i.e.*, are the products of a language.

5. That present determinations of an event, whatsoever these may be, are determinations that were intended on previous occasions and that may be again intended in identical fashion on an indefinite number of future occasions.

6. That the intended event is retained as the temporally identical event throughout the stream of experience.

7. That the event has as its context of interpretation: (a) a commonly entertained scheme of interpretation consisting of a standardized system of symbols, and (b) "What Anyone Knows," *i.e.*, a preestablished corpus of socially warranted knowledge.

8. That the actual determinations that the event exhibits for the witness are the potential determinations that it would exhibit for the other person were they to exchange positions.

9. That to each event there corresponds its determinations that originate in the witness's and in the other person's particular biography. From the witness's point of view such determinations are irrelevant for the purposes at hand of either, and both he and the other have selected and interpreted the actual and potential determinations of events in an empirically identical manner that is sufficient for all their practical purposes.

10. That there is a characteristic disparity between the publicly acknowledged determinations and the personal, withheld determinations of events, and this private knowledge is held in reserve, *i.e.*, that the event means for both the witness and the other more than the witness can say.

11. That alterations of this characteristic disparity remain within the witness's autonomous control.

It is *not* the case that what an event exhibits as a distinctive determination is a condition of its membership in a known-in-the-manner-of-common-sense-environment. Instead the conditions of its membership are the attributions that its determinations, *whatever they might substantively consist of*, could be seen by the other person if their positions were exchanged, or that its features are not assigned as matters of personal preference but are to be seen by anyone, *i.e.*, the previously enumerated features. These and only these enumerated features *irrespective* of any other determinations of an event define the common sense character of an event.

[v]Schutz, "Common Sense and Scientific Interpretations of Human Action," in *Collected Papers I: The Problem of Social Reality*, pp. 3–96; and "On Multiple Realities," pp. 207–259. Garfinkel, Chapter Eight, and "Common Sense Knowledge of Social Structures," *Transactions of the Fourth World Congress of Sociology*, 4 (Milan, 1959), 51–65.

Whatever other determinations an event of everyday life may exhibit—whether its determinations are those of persons' motives, their life histories, the distributions of income in the population, kinship obligations, the organization of an industry, or what ghosts do when night falls—if and only if the event has for the witness the enumerated determinations is it an event in an environment "known in common with others."

Such attributions are features of witnessed events that are seen without being noticed. They are demonstrably relevant to the common sense that the actor makes of what is going on about him. They inform the witness about any particular appearance of an interpersonal environment. They inform the witness as to the real objects that actual appearances are the appearances of, but without these attributed features necessarily being recognized in a deliberate or conscious fashion.

Since each of the expectancies that make up the attitude of daily life assigns an expected feature to the actor's environment, it should be possible to breach these expectancies by deliberately modifying scenic events so as to disappoint these attributions. By definition, surprise is possible with respect to each of these expected features. The nastiness of surprise should vary directly with the extent to which the person as a matter of moral necessity complies with their use as a scheme for assigning witnessed appearances their status as events in a perceivedly normal environment. In short, the realistic grasp by a collectivity member of the natural facts of life, and his commitment to a knowledge of them as a condition of self-esteem as a bona-fide and competent collectivity member,[vi] is the condition that we require in order to maximize his confusion upon the occasion that the grounds of this grasp are made a source of irreducible incongruity.

[vi] I use the term "competence" to mean the claim that a collectivity member is entitled to exercise that he is capable of managing his everyday affairs without interference. That members can take such claims for granted I refer to by speaking of a person as a "bona-fide" collectivity member. More extensive discussion of the relationships between "competence" and "common sense knowledge of social structures" will be found in the Ph.D. dissertation by Egon Bittner, "Popular Interests in Psychiatric Remedies: A Study in Social Control," University of California, Los Angeles, 1961. The terms, "collectivity" and "collectivity membership" are intended in strict accord with Talcott Parsons' usage in *The Social System* (New York: The Free Press of Glencoe, Inc., 1951) and in the general introduction to *Theories of Society*, by Talcott Parsons, Edward Shils, Kaspar D. Naegele, and Jesse R. Pitts (New York: the Free Press of Glencoe, Inc., 1961).

Discussion Questions

1. What would happen if you got on an elevator and then faced the person already riding in the elevator (looking straight at him or her) rather than the door? Try it a few times. Report your findings to the class. Most important, you should not only explain exactly what you did and how the other person responded, but also analyze and explain how you felt during this experiment.

2. Discuss three specific recipes that you use in a typical classroom situation. Be as precise as possible about the exact conditions under which you use these recipes (indexicality) and how you acquired them.

3. According to Berger and Luckmann, "Habitualization carries with it the important psychological gain that choices are narrowed." Discuss this point using a concrete example from your everyday life. How does this process result in objectivation?

4. What impact might the insights of phenomenology and ethnomethodology have on doing cross-cultural research? More generally, what types of research questions do you think these two perspectives can address? To what types are they not well suited?

5. Ethnomethodologists explore the methods people use to construct their everyday world. What methods do we use to construct such things as race or gender? In other words, how do we "do" race or gender? For instance, how does an individual act like a "white" person or a woman? How, or on what basis, do you "read" such behaviors?

7

FEMINIST THEORY

Key Concepts

Dorothy Smith

- ❖ Relations of Ruling
- ❖ Bifurcation of Consciousness
- ❖ Institutional Ethnography
- ❖ Standpoint Theory

Nancy Chodorow

- ❖ Object Relations Theory

Patricia Hill Collins

- ❖ Standpoint Epistemology
- ❖ Black Feminist Thought
- ❖ Matrix of Domination

Judith Butler

- ❖ Queer Theory
- ❖ Heterosexual Matrix
- ❖ Performativity

There is no original or primary gender a drag imitates, but gender is a kind of imitation for which there is no original.

~Judith Butler

A Brief History of Women's Rights in the United States

1700s

American colonial law held that "by marriage, the husband and wife are one person in the law. The very being and legal existence of the woman is suspended during the marriage, or at least is incorporated into that of her husband under whose wing and protection she performs everything."

By 1777, women are denied the right to vote in all states in the United States.

1800s

In *Missouri v. Celia* (1855), a slave, a black woman, is declared to be property without the right to defend herself against a master's act of rape.

In 1866, the Fourteenth Amendment is passed by Congress (ratified by the states in 1868). It is the first time "citizens" and "voters" are defined as male in the U.S. Constitution.

1900s

In 1920, the Nineteenth Amendment to the U.S. Constitution is ratified. It declares, "The right of citizens of the United States to vote shall not be denied or abridged by the United States or by any State on account of sex."

In 1923, the Equal Rights Amendment is introduced in Congress in the United States.

In 1963, the Equal Pay Act is passed by the U.S. Congress, promising equitable wages for the same work, regardless of the race, color, religion, national origin, or sex of the worker. In 1982, the Equal Rights Amendment (which had languished in Congress for fifty years) is defeated, falling three states short of the thirty-eight needed for ratification.

SOURCE: http://www.legacy98.org/timeline.html; Jo Freeman, *AJS*, in Goodwin and Jasper 2004.

The brief timeline above underscores an obvious but all too often overlooked point: the experience of women in society is not the same as that of men. In the United States, women's rights have expanded considerably since the nineteenth century, when women were denied access to higher education and the right to own property and vote. Despite major advances, there are still some troubling gender gaps in the United States, however. Women still suffer disproportionately, leading to what sociologists refer to as the "feminization of poverty," where two out of every three poor adults are women. In addition, in contrast to countries such as Sweden where more than 45 percent of elected officials in the national parliament are women, in the United States only about 15 percent of the politicians in the House or Senate are women, placing the United States a lowly sixtieth worldwide in the global ranking of women in politics (http://www.iwdc.org/resources/factsheet.htm; http://www.ipu.org/wmn-e/classif.htm).

Yet, it was not until 2005 that women in Kuwait were granted the right to vote and stand for election (see Table 7.1), and sadly, as of this writing, women in Saudi Arabia do not yet have those political freedoms. Indeed, in a recent study by Freedom House,

Photo 7.1 Kuwaiti women press for their full political rights amid crucial parliamentary meeting in March 2005.

SOURCE: Stephanie McGehee/Reuters/CORBIS; used with permission.

Saudi Arabia ranked dead last in all five categories analyzed in terms of women's equality, although in none of the seventeen societies of the Arab Middle East and Northern Africa (MEDA) studied do women enjoy the same citizenship and national- ity rights as men.[1] In Saudi Arabia, women are segregated in public places, cannot drive cars, and must be covered from head to toe when in public. Men are entitled to divorce without explanation simply by registering a statement to the court and repeating it three times. By contrast, most women not only lack the right of divorce, but because their children legally belong to the father, to leave their husband means giving up their children (http://www.freedomhouse.org and http://www.pbs.org/wgbh/globalconnections/ mideast/timeline/text/qwomen.html).

What these latter cases also demonstrate is that the expansion of women's rights does not proceed automatically and must not be taken for granted. Laws that discriminate against women were instituted in the United States in the nineteenth century that had not existed in the previous decades. On a global scale, nowhere was the precariousness of women's rights more evident than when the Taliban radically rescinded them in Afghanistan (1996–2002). Under the rule of the Taliban, women who had previously enjoyed many rights were banished from the workforce, forbidden an education, and prohibited from leaving their homes unless accompanied by a close male relative (http:// www.pbs.org/wgbh/globalconnections/mideast/timeline/text/qwomen.html).

In this chapter, we explore the works of four different analysts who take seriously the distinct social situation of women and examine it from a variety of theoretical view- points. We begin with the Canadian sociologist Dorothy Smith, who provocatively blends neo-Marxist, phenomenological, and ethnomethodological concepts and ideas. We then turn to the work of African American sociologist Patricia Hill Collins, who

---

[1] For instance, in no country in the region is domestic violence outlawed, and some laws, such as those that encourage men who rape women to marry their victims, even condone violence against women.

Table 7.1   International Women's Suffrage Timeline

• 1893 New Zealand	• 1950 India
• 1902 Australia[1]	• 1954 Colombia
• 1906 Finland	• 1957 Malaysia, Zimbabwe
• 1913 Norway	• 1962 Algeria
• 1915 Denmark	• 1963 Iran, Morocco
• 1917 Canada[2]	• 1964 Libya
• 1918 Austria, Germany, Poland, Russia	• 1967 Ecuador
• 1919 Netherlands	• 1971 Switzerland
• 1920 United States	• 1972 Bangladesh
• 1921 Sweden	• 1974 Jordan
• 1928 Britain, Ireland	• 1976 Portugal
• 1931 Spain	• 1989 Namibia
• 1944 France	• 1990 Western Samoa
• 1945 Italy	• 1993 Kazakhstan, Moldova
• 1947 Argentina, Japan, Mexico, Pakistan	• 1994 South Africa
• 1949 China	• 2005 Kuwait

NOTE: Two countries do not allow their people, male or female, to vote: Brunei and the United Arab Emirates. Saudi Arabia is the only country with suffrage that does not allow its women to vote.
1. Australian women, with the exception of aboriginal women, won the vote in 1902. Aboriginals, male and female, did not have the right to vote until 1962.
2. Canadian women, with the exception of Canadian Indian women, won the vote in 1917. Canadian Indians, male and female, did not win the vote until 1960. *Source: The New York Times,* May 22, 2005.

SOURCE: Information Please® Database, © 2005 Pearson Education, Inc. All rights reserved. (http://www .info please.com/ipa/A0931343.html)

extends the work of Smith by formally situating the variable of race into the critical/ phenomenological exploration of class and gender, while also borrowing significantly from postmodernism and recent work on the body and sexuality. We then turn to the psychoanalytic feminist Nancy Chodorow, who draws on both the Frankfurt School and Freud to explore various factors that serve to perpetuate sexism. We conclude this chapter with an examination of the work of American philosopher Judith Butler, who, in accordance with postmodernist lines of thought, challenges the very binary categories that we use to think about both gender and sexual orientation.[2]

---

[2]To be sure, feminism has never been a unified body of thought, and there are various ways that feminisms and feminist theorists can be contemplated. One of the most common is according to political/ideological orientation. According to this approach (which typically equates "feminism" with "feminist theory"), "liberal feminists," such as Betty Friedan (see Significant Others, p. 318), focus on how political, economic, and social rights can be fully extended to women within contemporary society; while "radical feminists," such as Andrea Dworkin (1946–2005) and Catharine MacKinnon (1946–), most famous for their proposal for a law that defined pornography as a violation of women's civil rights (thereby allowing women to sue the producers and distributors of pornography in a civil court for damages), view women as an oppressed group, who, like other oppressed peoples, must struggle for their liberation against their oppressors—in this case, men. However, here we consider feminists largely in terms of their theoretical orientation rather than political/ideological commitment, because we view the former as *prior to* the latter (Alexander 1987:7). As discussed in Chapter 1, theoretical presuppositions are, by definition, simply the most basic assumptions that theorists make as they go about thinking and writing about the world (ibid.:12).

This brings us to the question: why not discuss each of these theorists in the chapter on the theoretical tradition of which they are a part? Although this is certainly an option for professors and students, as you will see, the feminists whose works you will read in this chapter do not fit very neatly into a single theoretical tradition; rather, they provocatively draw from a variety of theoretical and disciplinary wells in order to fully address feminist concerns. In addition, grouping feminist theorists together in this chapter better enables us to compare and contrast these various approaches to gender.

Significant Others — Simone de Beauvoir (1908–1986): The Second Sex

---

Simone de Beauvoir was born in Paris to a bourgeois family. Like her famous companion, Jean-Paul Sartre, who she met at the Ecole Normale Superieure, she was an acclaimed French existentialist philosopher, who wrote fiction and memoirs, as well as philosophy. In her most influential book, *The Second Sex* (1949), de Beauvoir argued that women have been defined by men and that if they attempt to break with this then they risk alienating themselves. Specifically, following Hegel, de Beauvoir maintained that "otherness is a fundamental category of human thought" (xvii). Women are defined and differentiated with reference to man and not he with reference to her; she is incidental, the inessential as opposed to the essential. He is the Subject, he is the Absolute; she is the "Other." De Beauvoir links woman's identity as Other and her fundamental alienation to her body—especially her reproductive capacity. Childbearing, childbirth, and menstruation are draining physical events that tie women to their bodies and to immanence. The male, however, is not tied down by such inherently physical events (pp. 19–29, as cited in Donovan 2000/1985, p. 137). In the struggle described by Sartre as that between *pour-soi* and *en-soi,* men are cast in the role of the pour-soi (for itself), that is, the continual process of self-realization, or creative freedom; while women are cast in the role of en-soi (in-itself), i.e. who instead of choosing to engage in the authenticating project of self-realization, consent to become an object, to exist as en-soi (Donovan, p. 136). De Beauvoir urged women "to decline to be the Other, to refuse to be a party to the deal" (p. xx). Akin to earlier feminists such as Charlotte Perkins-Gilman (see Edles and Appelrouth 2005, chapter 5), de Beauvoir encouraged women to strengthen their "masculine" rational faculties and critical powers, to exist as a pour soi, that is, a transcendent subject who constitutes her own future by means of creative projects (Donovan, p. 130). However, de Beauvoir fully recognized that this moral choice was fraught with anxiety, since "women's independent successes are in contradiction with her femininity, since the 'true woman' is required to make herself object, to be the Other" (p. 246). De Beauvoir died on April 14, 1986.

Significant Others	Betty Friedan (1921–2006): The Feminine Mystique

Betty Friedan was born Betty Naomi Goldstein in Peoria, Illinois, in 1921. She graduated from Smith College in 1942 with a B.A. in psychology. In 1958 she circulated a questionnaire among her Smith classmates which suggested that a great many of them were, like her, deeply dissatisfied with their lives. She turned her findings into a book, *The Feminine Mystique* (1963), which became an immediate and controversial best-seller. It sold over a million copies, was translated into a number of foreign languages, and ushered in a new era of consciousness-raising. Friedan's central thesis was that women suffered under a pervasive system of delusions and false values under which they were urged to find personal fulfillment, even identity, vicariously through the husbands and children to whom they were expected cheerfully to devote their lives. This restricted role of wife-mother, whose spurious glorification by advertisers and others was suggested by the title of the book, led almost inevitably to a sense of unreality or general spiritual malaise in the absence of genuine, creative, self-defining work. In effect, then, Friedan extended de Beauvoir's writing in a more popular form. In 1966 Friedan co-founded the National Organization for Women, a civil-rights group dedicated to achieving equality of opportunity for women. It became the largest and probably the most effective organization in the women's movement. Friedan also helped found the National Association for the Repeal of Abortion Laws in 1969, and the National Women's Political Caucus in 1971. Friedan's other major works include *It Changed My Life: Writings on the Women's Movement* (1976); *The Second Stage* (1981); and *The Fountain of Age* (1993), which focuses on the psychology of old age and urged a revision of society's view that aging means loss and depletion. Betty Friedan died on February 5, 2006, in Washington, D.C.

DOROTHY SMITH (1926–): A BIOGRAPHICAL SKETCH

Dorothy E. Smith was born in Great Britain in 1926. She worked at a variety of jobs and was a secretary at a publishing company before she decided to enhance her employment prospects by attaining a college degree. She began college at the London School of Economics in 1951, and she received her bachelor's degree in sociology from the London School of Economics in 1955. She and her husband then decided to both go on to graduate school at the University of California, Berkeley. Smith maintains that although her years at Berkeley were in many ways the unhappiest of her life, she learned a lot, both inside and outside the classroom (http://sociology.berkeley.edu/alumni/). Through "the experience of marriage . . . and the arrival of children, and the departure of her husband rather early one morning," she learned about the discrepancy between social scientific description and lived experience (1979:151). Through courses in survey methods and mathematical sociology, she learned a type of sociological methodology that she would come to reject, but with which would come to formulate her own opposing methodology. Through a wonderful course taught by Tamotsu Shibutani, she gained a deep appreciation for George Herbert Mead, which "laid the groundwork for a later deep involvement with the phenomenology of Maurice Merleau-Ponty" (http://faculty.maxwell.syr .edu/mdevault/dorothy_smith.htm).

Reprinted with permission.

After completing her doctorate in sociology in 1963, Smith worked as a research sociologist and lecturer at the University of California, Berkeley. At times, she was the only woman in the U.C. Berkeley Department of Sociology. Deeply moved by the newly emerging women's movement, Smith organized a session for graduate students to "tell their stories" about gender inequities in academia (of which "there were many") (http:// faculty.maxwell.syr.edu/mdevault/dorothy_smith.htm).

By the late 1960s, Smith's marriage had fallen apart, and lacking day care and family support, she returned home to England to raise her children and teach. She became a lecturer in sociology at the University of Essex, Colchester. Several years later, Smith accepted a full-time position at the University of British Columbia, and it was here that Smith's feminist transformation (which had begun in Berkeley) deepened. Smith taught one of the first women's studies courses, and the lack of existing materials gave her impetus to "go from the kind of deep changes in my psyche that accompanied the women's movement to writing those changes into the social" (ibid.). Smith also helped create a women's action group that worked to improve the status of women "at all levels of the university," and she was involved in establishing a women's research center in Vancouver outside the university that would provide action-relevant research to women's organizations (ibid.). Smith also edited a volume providing a feminist critique of psychiatry (*Women Look at Psychiatry: I'm Not Mad, I'm Angry*, 1975), and she began to reread Marx and integrate Marxist ideas into her work, as is reflected in her pamphlet *Feminism and Marxism, a Place to Begin, a Way to Go* (1977).[3]

In 1977, Smith became a professor in the Department of Sociology and Equity Studies in Education at the Ontario Institute for Studies in Education at the University of Toronto. Here Smith published the works for which she is most well known, including *A Sociology for Women* (1979), *The Everyday World as Problematic* (1987), *The Conceptual Practices of Power* (1990), *Texts, Facts, and Femininity* (1990), *Writing the Social* (1999), and most recently, *Institutional Ethnography: A Sociology for People* (2005). In these works, Smith exhorts a powerful feminist theory of what she calls relations of ruling, and she sets out her own approach, which she calls institutional ethnography, as a means for building knowledges as to how the relations of ruling operate from the standpoints of the people participating in them. These pivotal ideas will be discussed further below.

Smith continues to be an active teacher and scholar. As professor emerita in the Department of Sociology and Equity Studies in Education at the Ontario Institute for Studies in Education at the University of Toronto and an adjunct professor in the Department of Sociology, University of Victoria, British Columbia, she continues to

---

[3]Interestingly, Smith (1977:9) maintains that although she worked as a socialist when she was a young woman in England, it was not until she reread Marx in the 1970s that she came to really understand what Marx meant.

educate and inspire a new generation of scholars dedicated to institutional ethnography (see, for instance, Marie Campbell and Ann Manicom, eds., *Experience, Knowledge and Ruling Relations: Explorations in the Social Organization of Knowledge*, University of Toronto Press, 1995).

INTELLECTUAL INFLUENCES AND CORE IDEAS

Although Dorothy Smith has written on a wide variety of topics, including education, Marxism, the family, mental illness, and textual analysis, she is most well known as one of the originators of **standpoint theory**.[4] Smith uses the notion of **standpoint** to emphasize that what one knows is affected by where one stands (one's subject position) in society. We begin from the world as we actually experience it, and what we know of the world and of the "other" is conditional upon that location (Smith 1987). Yet, Smith's argument is not that we cannot look at the world in any way other than our given standpoint. Rather, her point is that (1) no one can have complete, objective knowledge; (2) no two people have exactly the same standpoint; and (3) we must not take the standpoint from which we speak for granted. Instead, we must recognize it, be reflexive about it, and problematize it. Our situated, everyday experience should serve as a "point of entry" of investigation (Smith 2005:10).

Put in another way, the goal of Smith's feminist sociology is to explicitly reformulate sociological theory by fully accounting for the standpoint of gender and its effects on our experience of reality. Interestingly, it was Smith's particular standpoint as a female in a male-dominated world, and specifically as simultaneously a wife and mother and a sociology graduate student in the 1960s, that led her to the formulation of her notion of standpoint. By overtly recognizing the particular standpoint from which she spoke, Smith was bringing to the fore the extent to which the issue of standpoint had been unacknowledged in sociology. This point is quite ironic, really. Sociology was explicitly set out as the "scientific" and "objective" study of society when it first emerged as a discipline in the nineteenth century; but because its first practitioners were almost exclusively men, it implicitly assumed and reflected the relevancies, interests, and perspectives of (white, middle-class) European males.[5] "Its method, conceptual schemes and theories had been based on and built up within the male social universe" (Smith 1990a:23).

The failure to recognize the particular standpoints from which they spoke not only left sociologists unaware of the biases inherent to their position. In addition, by implicitly making the discipline of sociology a masculine sociology—that is, by focusing on the world of paid labor, politics, and formal organizations (spheres of influence from which women have historically been excluded) and erasing or ignoring women's world of sexual reproduction, children, household labor, and affective ties—sociology unwittingly

[4]The term "feminist standpoint theory" was actually not coined by Smith. Rather, feminist standpoint theory (and hence "standpoint theory") is traced to Sandra Harding (1986), who, based on her reading of the work of feminist theorists—most important, Dorothy Smith, Nancy Hartstock, and Hilary Rose—used the term to describe a feminist critique beyond the strictly empirical one of claiming a special privilege for women's knowledge, and emphasizing that knowledge is always rooted in a particular position and that women are privileged epistemologically by being members of any oppressed group (Smith 2005:8). See also Harding (2004).

[5]Although Smith did not focus on race, as you will shortly see, Patricia Hill Collins built on Smith's work by illuminating how race is intertwined with gender and class standpoints.

served as a vehicle for alienating women from their own lives (Seidman 1994:212–3). This is the irony mentioned previously: at the same time that sociology emerged as provocative new discipline dedicated to explaining the inequalities and systems of stratification at the heart of various societies (especially apparent, for instance, in Marx and Weber), it created its own version of domination by shifting attention almost exclusively to one particular dimension of human social life—the masculine-dominated macrolevel public sphere—at the expense of another (the world of women).

In short, Smith underscores not only that the standpoint of men is consistently privileged and that of women devalued, but that the standpoint of the (white) male upper-class pervades and *dominates* other worldviews. This idea, that not all standpoints are equally valued and accessed in society, clearly reflects Smith's critical/Marxist roots. As discussed previously, beginning with her pamphlet *Feminism and Marxism* (1977), Smith explicitly links her feminism with Marxism. She explains how "objective social, economic and political relations . . . shape and determine women's oppression" (ibid.:12). She focuses on "the relations between patriarchy and class in the context of the capitalist mode of production" (1985:1) and emphasizes how "the inner experiences which also involved our exercise of oppression against ourselves were ones that had their location in the society outside and originated there" (1977:10).

Yet, Smith's feminist theory is not just derived from an application of Marx to the issue of gender; rather, it reflects Smith's phenomenological roots (see Chapter 6) as well. Specifically, Smith links a neo-Marxist concern about structures of domination with a phenomenological emphasis on consciousness and the active construction of the taken-for-granted world. She explicitly demonstrates the extent to which men and women bracket and view the world in distinctive ways, in conjunction with their distinct, biographically articulated lifeworlds. In her own case, for instance, Smith recognizes that she experienced "two subjectivities, home and university" that could not be blended, for "they ran on separate tracks with distinct phenomenal organization" (Smith 2005:11). "Home was organized around the particularities of my children's bodies, faces, movements, the sound of their voices, the smell of their hair . . . and the multitudes of the everyday that cannot be enumerated," while the "practice of subjectivity in the university excluded the local and bodily from its field" (ibid.:12). In this way, Smith (1987:83–4) notes that female-dominated work in the concrete world of the everyday demands one to be attuned to the sensory experiences of the body. "Here there are textures and smells. . . . It has to happen here somehow if she is to experience it at all" (1987:82). The abstract world of the professions, on the other hand, requires an individual to take this level of experience for granted.

Smith is particularly indebted to the phenomenologist Alfred Schutz (see Chapter 6). Recall that it was Schutz (1970:11, as cited in Smith 1987:83) who argued that we put various levels of our personality "in play" in various provinces of reality. Schutz used the term mitwelt relations to refer to relations in which individuals are experienced as "types" (e.g., the relationship between you and the person who delivers your mail), and he used the term umwelt relations to refer to more intimate face-to-face relations. According to Schutz, in contrast to mitwelt relations, in umwelt relations each person must be aware of the other's body as a field of expression that fosters the development of intersubjectivity.

Smith (1987:83) extends Schutz's distinction between umwelt and mitwelt relations by asserting that "if men are to participate fully in the abstract mode of action, they must be liberated from having to attend to their needs in the concrete and particular." That is, traditionally not only are umwelt relations more central in women's lives, but men *relegate* their umwelt relations to women (for instance, a boss has his secretary shop for an anniversary present for his wife and make his personal calls). Thus, Smith argues that "women's work conceals from men the actual concrete forms on which their work depends" (ibid.:83–4).

This brings us to Smith's concept of **bifurcation of consciousness**. Smith uses this term to refer to a separation or split between the world as you actually experience it and the dominant view to which you must adapt (e.g., a masculine point of view). The notion of bifurcation of consciousness underscores that subordinate groups are conditioned to view the world from the perspective of the dominant group, since the perspective of the latter is *embedded* in the institutions and practices of that world, while the dominant group, on the other hand, enjoys the privilege of remaining oblivious to the worldview of the Other, or subordinate group, since the Other is fully expected to accommodate to them. The "governing mode" of the professions, then, creates a bifurcation of consciousness in the actor: "It establishes two modes of knowing, experiencing, and acting—one located in the body and in the space that it occupies and moves into, the other passing beyond it" (1987:82).

Of course, bifurcation of consciousness reflects Smith's own experience of living in "two worlds": the dominant, masculine-oriented, "abstract" world of the sociologist and the "concrete" world of wife and mother. The key point, as Smith (2005:11) notes, is that "the two subjectivities, home and university, could not be blended." In this way, Smith's concept of bifurcation of consciousness recalls W. E. B. Du Bois's concept of "double consciousness," which he used to describe the experiential condition of black Americans.[6] In both cases, it is the oppressed person who must adapt to the "rules of the game" that do not reflect her interests or desires, even though, in both cases, the dual subjectivities provide a uniquely "clairvoyant" vantage point (in Du Bois's terms). Thus, for instance, women in male-dominated professions (e.g., law enforcement, construction) acclimate themselves to sexist and even misogynistic talk about the female body that is a normal part of their everyday work environment. Not only do they learn to ignore the banter, indeed, they might even chime in. However, because they must continually accommodate themselves to the dominant group in order to gain acceptance in a world that is not theirs, members of oppressed or minority groups become alienated from their "true" selves.

Thus far we have discussed Smith's dual neo-Marxist and phenomenological roots. There is also an important discursive bent in Smith's work that has become especially apparent in the last decade, however. In conjunction with the poststructuralist turn (see Chapter 8), Smith emphasizes that in modern, Western societies social domination operates through *texts* (such as medical records, census reports, psychiatric evaluations, employment files) that facilitate social control. Thus, Smith (1990b:6) describes **relations of ruling** as including not only forms such as "bureaucracy, administration, management, professional organization and media" but also "the complex of discourses, scientific, technical, and cultural, that intersect, interpenetrate, and coordinate" them. Smith (1987:4) maintains that behind and within the "apparently neutral and impersonal rationality of the ruling apparatus" is concealed a "male subtext." Women are "excluded from the practices of power within textually mediated relations of ruling" (ibid.). Thus, for instance, official psychiatric evaluations replace the individual's actual lived experience with a means for interpreting it; the individual becomes a case history, a type, a disease, a syndrome, and a treatment possibility (Seidman 1994:216).

Smith goes on to suggest that because sociology too relies on these same kinds of texts, it too is part and parcel of the relations of ruling. The subject matter and topics of sociology are those of the ruling powers. Sociological knowledge receives its shape

---

[6] See Edles and Appelrouth (2005:323–5).

less from actualities and the lived experiences of real individuals than from the interests in control and regulation, by the state, professional associations, and bureaucratization (Seidman 1994:216).

Most important, Smith does not just criticize modern, "masculinist" sociology; she provides an alternative to it. Inspired by Marx's historical realism but also drawing on ethnomethodology—which, as discussed in Chapter 6, considers that practical activities, practical circumstances, and practical sociological reasoning must not be taken for granted but rather be topics of empirical study (Garfinkel 1967:1)—Smith advocates a "sociology for women" that begins "where women are situated": in the "particularities of an actual, everyday world" (1987:109). Smith's sociology for women aims not to "transform people into objects" but to "preserve their presence as subjects" (1987:151). Smith (1987:143) argues that the "only route to a faithful telling that does not privilege the perspectives arising in the sites of her sociological project and her participation in a sociological discourse is to commit herself to an inquiry that is ontologically faithful, faithful to the presence and activity of her subjects and faithful to the actualities of the world that arises for her, for them, for all of us, in the ongoing co-ordering of our actual practices."[7]

Smith calls her particular approach **institutional ethnography**. Institutional ethnography is a method of elucidating and examining the relationship between everyday activities and experiences and larger institutional imperatives. Interestingly, the very term "institutional ethnography" explicitly couples an emphasis on structures of power ("institutions") with the microlevel practices that make up everyday life ("ethnography"). Smith's point, of course, is that it is in microlevel, everyday practices at the level of the individual that collective, hierarchical patterns of social structure are experienced, shaped, and reaffirmed. For instance, in one passage you will read, Smith explains how the seemingly benign, everyday act of walking her dog actually reaffirms the class system. As Smith "keeps an eye on her dog" so that it does its business on some lawns as opposed to others, she is, in fact, "observing some of the niceties of different forms of property ownership" (renters versus owners) (1987:155); she is participating in the existing relations of ruling. This point is illustrated in Figure 7.1.

SMITH'S THEORETICAL ORIENTATION

Smith's theoretical approach is explicitly multidimensional, as can be readily seen in her central concepts (see Figures 7.1 and 7.2). For instance, as discussed above, the term "institutional ethnography" explicitly reflects Smith's dual emphasis on collective structures of ruling and the institutionalization of power and their actual workings at the level of the individual in everyday life. In terms of action, as shown in Figure 7.1, institutional ethnography can be said to reflect a rationalistic emphasis on practical action both at the level of the individual and at the collective level of the institution; however,

---

[7]In her most recent book, Smith (2005) updates her terminology by replacing the notion of "a sociology for women" with that of "a sociology for people." In other words, the notion of "a sociology for women" can be understood as reflecting a particular historical era in which feminists called attention to the fact that the standpoint of women was absent in the academy; however, today the more pertinent (and more postmodern) point is that we must begin wherever we are, that is, not only in terms of "gender," but also class, race, sexual orientation, ablebodiedness, and so on. This is institutional ethnography.

Figure 7.1   Smith's Concept of Institutional Ethnography: Walking the Dog

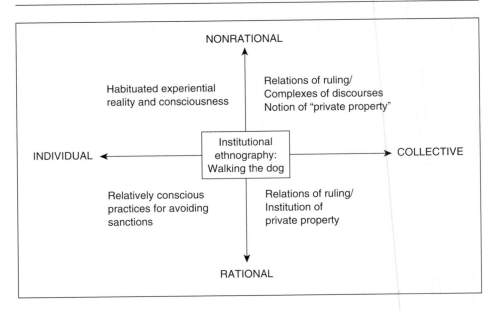

Figure 7.2   Smith's Concepts of "Standpoint" and "Relations of Ruling"

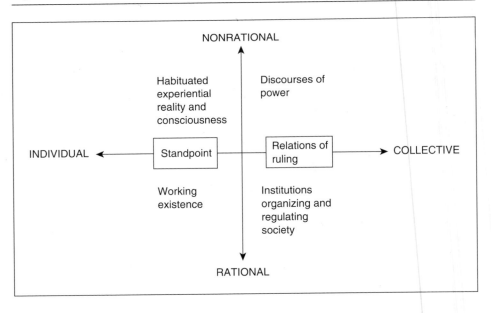

clearly Smith's phenomenological roots lead her to appreciate the nonrational motivation for action as well. Above all, Smith emphasizes that taken-for-granted, subjective categories provide the backdrop for the pragmatic performances that constitute the everyday world and, in doing so, reaffirm the existing structural order. For instance, in the example above, it is only because of her internalization of taken-for-granted notions of class and private property that Smith knows how and where to walk her dog. In Schutz's terms, she uses specific "recipes" (see Chapter 6) and taken-for-granted habits, which, by definition, work at the individual/nonrational level.

So, too, the term "standpoint" reflects Smith's dual rational and nonrational approach to action and individual and collective approach to order, in that "standpoint" refers both to our objective (rational) position and subjective (nonrational) position in the (collective) social hierarchy, and to our unique biographical (individual) situation. For instance, as shown in Figure 7.2, my "standpoint" as a mother is rooted at once in the *meaning* (including social status or honor) accorded to "mothers" in general in our society, as determined by the complexes of discourses that are part of relations of ruling (collective/nonrational), and the specific reward structure accrued to that position by the (collective/rational) institutions organizing and regulating society (collective/ rational) as well. That said, above all, "standpoint" reflects the specific attitudes, emotions, and values that I experience and internalize at the level of the individual (individual/nonrational) as well as the habituated day-to-day experience, and the particular strategic advantages and disadvantages I am able to accrue through this position and my mundane working existence (individual/rational).

Put in another way, Smith articulates not only how individuals unthinkingly "do" gender (and class) in daily life at the individual/nonrational level, but also the subjective categories that make this possible, that is, the taken-for-granted subjective understandings of what it means to be a "boy" or a "girl" that reflect the collective, nonrational realm. Akin to Schutz and Berger and Luckmann (see Chapter 6) as well as the poststructuralists who emphasize discourse and are discussed in the next chapter, Smith continually emphasizes that gender cannot be "done" at the individual level in everyday life without taken-for-granted conceptualizations at the collective level.

In a similar vein, that Smith's concept "relations of ruling" encompasses both such forms as "bureaucracy, administration, management, professional organization and media" and scientific, technical, and cultural discourses reflects the collective/rational and collective/nonrational realms, respectively (see Figure 7.2). Specifically, that Smith (2005:227; emphasis added) defines ruling relations as "objectified forms of consciousness and organization, *constituted externally to particular places and people*" clearly reflects her collectivistic orientation to order. And although Smith also underscores that ruling relations refer to "that total complex of activities, differentiated into many spheres . . . through which we are ruled and through which we, and I emphasize this *we,* participate in ruling" (Smith 1990a, as cited in Calhoun 2003:316), which indicates an acknowledgment of individual agency, that "forms of consciousness are created that are properties of organization or discourse *rather than of individual subjects*" (1987:3, emphasis added) clearly reflects a collectivistic approach to order. This dual rational/nonrational approach to action and collectivistic approach to order inherent in Smith's concept of relations of ruling is illustrated in Figure 7.2. Interestingly, then, taken together Figures 7.1 and 7.2 illustrate that the multidimensionality of the concept of institutional ethnography is a function of its incorporation of the more individualistic concept of standpoint and the more collectivistic concept of ruling relations.

Readings

Introduction to *Institutional Ethnography*

In this excerpt from her most recent book, *Institutional Ethnography* (2005), Smith explicitly defines "institutional ethnography" and explains how she came to formulate this unique method of inquiry. In addition, Smith explains the historical trajectory of gender and relations of ruling, that is, how the radical division between spheres of action and of consciousness of middle-class men and women came to emerge. As indicated previously, it is precisely this conceptualization of relations of ruling (or ruling relations) as not simply modes of domination but also forms of *consciousness* that forms the crux of Smith's work.

❖

Institutional Ethnography (2005)

Dorothy Smith

WOMEN'S STANDPOINT: EMBODIED KNOWING VS THE RULING RELATIONS

It's hard to recall just how radical the experience of the women's movement was at its inception for those of us who had lived and thought within the masculinist regime against which the movement struggled. For us, the struggle was a much within ourselves, with what we knew how to do and think and feel, as with that regime as an enemy outside us. Indeed we ourselves had participated however passively in that regime. There was no developed discourse in which the experiences that were spoken originally as everyday experience could be translated into a public language and become political in the ways distinctive to the women's movement. We learned in talking with other women about experiences that we had and about others that we had not had. We began to name "oppression," "rape," "harassment," "sexism," "violence," and others. These were terms that did more than name. They gave shared experiences a political presence.

Starting with our experiences as we talked and thought about them, we discovered depths of alienation and anger that were astonishing. Where had all these feelings been? How extraordinary were the transformations we experienced as we discovered with other women how to speak with one another about such experiences and then how to bring them forward publicly, which meant exposing them to men. Finally, how extraordinary were the transformations of ourselves in this process. Talking our experience was a means of discovery. What we did not know and did not know how to think about, we could examine as we found what we had in common. The approach that I have taken in developing an alternative sociology takes up women's standpoint in a way that is modeled on these early adventures of the women's movement. It takes up women's standpoint not as a given and finalized form of knowledge but as a ground in experience from which discoveries are to be made.

It is this active and shared process of speaking from our experience, as well as acting and organizing to change how those experiences had been created, that has been translated in feminist thinking into the concept of a feminist standpoint—or, for me, women's standpoint. However the concept originated, Sand Harding (1988) drew together the social scientific thinking by feminists, particularly Nancy Hartsock, Hilary Rose, and myself, that had as a common project taking up a standpoint in women's experience. Harding argued that feminist empiricists who claimed both a special privilege for women's knowledge and an objectivity were stuck in an irresolvable paradox. Those she described as "feminist standpoint theorists" moved the feminist critique a step beyond feminist empiricism by claiming that knowledge of society must always be from a position in it and that women are privileged epistemologically by being members of an oppressed group. Like the slave in Hegel's parable of the master-slave relationship, they can see more, further, and better than the master precisely because of their marginalized and oppressed condition. She was, however, critical of the way in which experience in the women's movement had come to hold authority as a ground for speaking, and claiming to speak truly, that challenged the rational and objectified forms of knowledge and their secret masculine subject (123). Furthermore, feminist standpoint theory, according to Harding, implicitly reproduced the universalized subject and claims to objective truth of traditional philosophical discourse, an implicit return to the empiricism we claimed to have gone beyond.

The notion of women's standpoint–or indeed the notion that women's experience has special authority–has also been challenged by feminist theorists. It fails to take into account diversities of class and race as well as the various forms and modulations of gender. White middleclass heterosexual women dominated the early phases of the women's movement in the 1960s and 1970s, but soon our, and I speak as one, assumptions about what would hold for women in general were challenged and undermined, first by working-class women and lesbians, then by African-North American, Hispanic, and Native women. The implicit presence of class, sexuality, and colonialism began to be exposed. Our assumptions were also challenged by women in other societies who experience wasn't North American, By women such as those with disabilities and older women who experience was not adequately represented and, as the women's movement evolved over time, by younger women who have found the issues of older feminists either alien or irrelevant.

The theoretical challenge to the notion of women's standpoint has been made in terms of its alleged essentialism. It has been seen as essentialist because it excludes other bases of oppression and inequity that intersect with the category "women." The critique of essentialism, however, assumes the use of the category "women" or "woman" to identify shared and defining attributes. While essentialism has been a problem in the theorizing of *woman,* it cannot be extended to all uses of such categories. In practice in the women's movement, the category has worked politically rather than referentially.

As a political concept, it coordinates struggle against the masculinist forms of oppressing women that those forms themselves explicitly or implicitly universalize. Perhaps most important, it creates for women what had been missing, a subject position in the public sphere and, more generally, one in the political, intellectual, and cultural life of the society.

Claiming a subject position within the public sphere in the name of women was a central enterprise of the women's movement in its early days in the 1970s and 1980s. A powerful dynamic was created. While those making the claim first were white middle-class women, the new subject position in public discourse opened the way for others who had found themselves excluded by those who'd gone before. Their claims were positioned and centered differently, and their own experience became authoritative. It is indeed one of the extraordinary characteristics of the women's movement that its continual disruption, its internal struggles against racism and white cultural dominance, its internal quarrels and angers, have been far from destructive to the movement. On the contrary, these struggles in North America and Europe have expanded and diversified the movement as women other than those with whom it originated gave their own experiences voice.

WOMEN'S STANDPOINT AND THE RULING RELATIONS

Standpoint is a term lifted out of the vernacular, largely through Harding's innovative thinking and her critique (1988), and it is used for doing new discursive work. Harding identifies standpoint in terms of the social positioning of the subject of knowledge, the knower and creator of knowledge. Her own subsequent work develops an epistemology that relies on a diversity of subject positions in the sociopolitical-economic regimes of colonialism and imperialism. The version of standpoint that I have worked with, after I had adopted the term from Harding (previously I'd written of "perspective"; D. E. Smith (1974a), is rather different. It differs also from the concept of a feminist standpoint that has been put forward by Nancy Hartsock (1998) in that it does not identify a socially determined position or category of position in society (or political economy).[i] Rather, my notion of women's (rather than feminist) standpoint is integral to the design of what I originally called "a sociology for women," which has necessarily been transformed into "a sociology for people." It does not identify a position or a category of position, gender, class, or race within the society, but it does establish as a subject position for institutional ethnography as a method of inquiry, a site for the knower that is open to anyone.

As a method of inquiry, institutional ethnography is designed to create an alternate to the objectified subject of knowledge of established social scientific discourse. The latter conforms to and is integrated with what I have come to call the "ruling relations"—that extraordinary yet ordinary complex of relations that are textually mediated, that connect us across space and time and organize our everyday lives—the corporations, government bureaucracies, academic and professional discourses, mass media, and the complex of relations that interconnect them. AT the inception of this early stage of late-twentieth-century women's movement, women were excluded from appearing as agents or subjects with the ruling relations. However we might have been at work in them, we were subordinates. We were women whose work as mothers reproduced the same gendered organization that subordinated us; we were the support staff, store clerks, nurses, social workers doing casework and not administration, and so on. In the university itself, we were few and mostly marginal (two distinguished women in the department where I first worked in Canada had never had more than annual lectureships).

"Standpoint" as the design of a subject position in institutional ethnography creates a point of entry into discovering the social that does not subordinate the knowing subject to objectified forms of knowledge of society or political economy. It is a method of inquiry that works from the actualities of people's everyday lives and experience to discover the social as it extends beyond experience. A standpoint in people's everyday lives is integral to that method. It is integral to a sociology creating a subject position within its discourse, which anyone can occupy. The institutional ethnographer works from the social in people's experience to discover its presence and organization in their lives and to explicate or map that organization beyond the local of the everyday.

EXAMINING SOCIOLOGY FROM A WOMAN'S STANDPOINT

The project of developing a sociology that does not objectify originated, as did so much in the women's movement, in exploring experiences in my life as a woman. That exploration put into question the fundamentals of the sociology I had learned at length and sometimes painfully as an undergraduate and graduate school student. I was, in those early times, a sociologist teaching at the University of British Columbia, on the west coast of Canada, and a single parent with two small boys. My experience was of contradictory modes of working existence: on the one hand was he work of the home and of being a mother; on the other, the work of the academy, preparing for classes, teaching, faculty meetings,

---

[i] Hartsock's concern is to reframe historical materialism so that women's experience and interests are fully integrated. Of particular importance to her is the adequate recognition of the forms of power that the women's movement has named "patriarchal." Women's marginal position, structured as it is around the work associated with reproduction and the direct production of subsistence, locates women distinctively in the mode of production in general. For her, taking a feminist standpoint introduces a dimension into historical materialism neglected by Marx and his successors. She designs a feminist standpoint that has a specifically political import. It might, I suppose, be criticized as essentialist, but, if we consider not just North America and not just white middle-class professional North America, it's hard to deny that Hartsock is characterizing a reality for women worldwide. In Canada a recent census report shows that while women's participation in the paid labor force has increased substantially over the past thirty years, "women remain more than twice as likely as men to do at least 30 hours a week of cooking and cleaning" (Andersen 2003, A7) and are move involved in child care than men, particularly care of younger children.

writing papers, and so on. I could not see my work at home I relation to the sociology I taught, in part, of course, because that sociology had almost nothing to say about it.

I learned from the women's movement to begin in my own experience and start there in finding the voice that asserted the buried woman. I started to explore what it might mean to think sociologically from the place where I was in-body, living with my children in my home and with those cares and consciousness that are integral to that work. Here were the particularities of my relationships with my children, my neighbors, my friends, their friends, our rabbit (surprisingly fierce and destructive—my copy of George Herbert Mead's *Mind, Self, and Society* bars scores inflicted by our long-eared pet's teeth an claws), our two dongs, and an occasional hamster. In this mode, I was attentive to the varieties of demands that housekeeping, cooking, child care, and the multiple minor tasks of our local settings made on me. When I went to work in the university, I did not, of course, step our of my body, but the focus of my work was not on the local particularities of relationships and setting but on sociological discourse read and taught or on the administrative work of a university department. Body, of course, was there as it had to be to get the work done, but the work was not organized by and in relation to it.

The two subjectivities, home and university, could not be blended. They ran on separate tracks with distinct phenomenal organization. Memory, attention, reasoning, and response were organized quite differently. Remembering a dental appointment for one of the children wasn't part of my academic consciousness, and if I wasn't careful to find some way of reminding myself that didn't depend on memory, I might have well forgot it. My experiences uncovered radical differences between home and academy in how they were situated, and how they situated me, in the society. Home was organized around the particularities of my children's bodies, faces, movements, the sounds of their voices, the smell of their hair, the arguments, the play, the evening rituals of reading, the stress of getting them off to school in the morning, cooking, and serving meals, and the multitudes of the everyday that cannot be enumerated, an intense, preoccupying world of work that also cannot really be defined. My work at the university was quite differently articulated; the sociology I thought and taught was embedded in the texts that linked me into a discourse extending indefinitely into only very partially known networks of others, some just names of the dead; some the heroes and masters of the contemporary discipline; some just names on books or articles; and others known as teachers, colleagues, and contemporaries in graduate school. The administrative work done by faculty tied into the administration of the university, know at that time only vaguely as powers such as dean or president or as offices such as the registrar, all of whom regulated the work we did with students. My first act on arriving in the department office, after greeting the secretaries, was to open my mail and thus to enter a world of action in texts.

I knew a practice of subjectivity in the university that excluded the local and moodily from its field. Learning from the women's movement to start from where I was as a woman, I began to attend to the university and my work there from the standpoint of "home" subjectivity. I started to notice what I had not seen before. How odd, as I am walking down the central mall of that university that opens up to the dark blue of the humped islands and the further snowy mountains to the north, to see on my left a large hole where before there had been a building! In the mode of the everyday you can find the connections, though you may not always understand them. In a house with children and dogs and rabbits, the connection between the destruction of the spine of my copy of *Mind, Self, and Society* and that rabbit hanging around in my workspace was obvious. But the hole where once there'd been a building couldn't be connected to any obvious agent. The peculiar consciousness I practiced in the university began to emerge for me as a puzzlingly strange form of organization. If I traced the provenance of that hole, I'd be climbing up into an order of relations linking administrative process with whatever construction company was actually responsible for the making of the hole; I'd be climbing into a web of budgets, administrative decisions, provincial and federal government funding, and so on and so on. I'd be climbing into that order of relations that institutional ethnographers call the "ruling relations." These could be seen as relations that divorced the subject from the particularized settings and relationships of her life and work as mother and housewife. They created subject positions that elevated consciousness into a universalized mode, whether of the social relations mediated by money or of those organized as objectivity in academic or professional discourse. Practicing embodiment on the terrain of the disembodied of those relations brought them into view. I became aware of them as I became aware of their presence and power in the everyday, and, going beyond that hole in the ground, I also began to think of the sociology I practiced in the everyday working world of the university as an organization of discursive relations fully integrated with them.

THE HISTORICAL TRAJECTORY OF GENDER AND THE RULING RELATIONS

My experience when I examined it as a woman, an act in and of the women's movement of that time, brought into view an order of social relations that enter into and may be observed in the everyday world of our experience but cannot be fully explored there. The objectified relations of ruling coordinate multiple local everyday worlds trans-or extralocally. The organization that was the matrix both of my experiences and my reflections on them itself arose in a historical trajectory of gender and the ruling relations.

The concept of ruling relations (D. E. Smith 1987, 199c) doesn't refer to modes of domination but to a new and distinctive mode of organizing society that comes into prominence during the latter part of the nineteenth century in Europe and North America. The ruling relations are forms of consciousness and organization that are objectified in the sense that they are constituted externally to particular people and places.

The transformations that were accelerating rapidly at the turn of the nineteenth and twentieth centuries began earlier, with the invention of movable type and of the possibilities of widespread access to words from beyond those spoken locally. The availability of the Bible as a text printed in the vernacular and hence readable

by people without the mediation of priests transformed not just the substance but the organization of Christianity in Europe. Government pronouncements could be replicated and distributed widely in the same form; news media emerged; opinion was vested in print; the novel emerged as a distinctive genre of storytelling (McKeon 1987); political and social thought took on the generalized form of ideology. Complementing and transforming the rapid development of capitalism as a mode of production were forms of consciousness and agency that were no longer identified with individuals. Marx, writing in the first two-thirds of the nineteenth century, theorized capital in terms of individual ownership. His conceptions of "consciousness" were also identified with individuals and what goes on in our heads (1973). By contrast, the ruling relations objectify consciousness: these new forms of social relations had not developed in Marx's time; hence, he did not incorporate into this thinking forms of social consciousness that were (a) differentiated and specialized as specific social relations and (b) objectified in the sense of being produced as independent of particular individuals and particularized relations.

Leonore Davidoff and Catherine Hall (1987) have described how, during the seventeenth and eighteenth centuries in England, the domestic sphere of the middle classes became increasingly isolated from the more and more exclusively male worlds of business, politics, and science. While women remained at work in the particularities of domesticity, men of the middle classes were active in businesses that connected them to the impersonal, extralocal dynamic of the market; they were also active in the public discourse that emerged in talk with other men in the clubs and coffee houses of Britain and Europe and in the saloons and places of public assembly in North America where the topics of journals, newspapers, and books were discussed (Habermas (1992; Ryan 1993). A radical division between the spheres of action and of consciousness of middle-class men and women emerged. The peculiar out-of-body modes of consciousness of the nascent ruling relations required a specialization of subject and agency. The formation of the middle-class male subject in education and ideology aimed at creating that extraordinary form of modern consciousness that is capable of agency in modes that displace or subdue a local bodily existence.[ii]

According to Joan Landes (1996), women's exclusion from the emerging public discourse, associated with the Enlightenment and with the rise of capitalism as a general economic form of life, was essential to men's capacity to sustain what she calls "the masquerade of universality." The public sphere was defined by a gender order that excluded women. During the French Revolution and later, women's attempts to organize in public "risked violating the constitutive principles of the bourgeois public sphere. . . . [They] risked disrupting the gendered organization of nature, truth, and opinion that assigned them to a place in the private, domestic but not the public realm" (97–88). Men confronting men did not raise the specter of particularity whereas women bore particularity as their social being. Hence men associating exclusively with men could avoid recognizing "the masquerade through while the (male) particular was able to posture behind the veil of the universal" (Landes, 1996, 98).

From the mid-nineteenth century and accelerating rapidly into the early twentieth century, the new forms of social organization enabled by printed and other technologies for reproducing words and images expanded rapidly (Beniger 1986; Yates 1989). Developments in the bureaucratization of the state, familiar in sociological literature from the writings of Max Weber (1978),[iii] were accompanied by radical innovations in the management of business enterprises (Beniger 1986; Waring 1991; Yates 1989). The direct connection between individual owner and the capitalist enterprise largely taken for granted by Marx is progressively displaced by the invention of corporate ownership and control (Chandler 1977; Noble 1977; Roy 1997), which not only separates ownership from control, creating management as a distinct function, but also

leads to the creation of what Alfred Sloan (1964) of General Motors called "objective" as contrasted with "subjective" organization. Objective organization relied on procedures for rendering the performance of the different divisions systematically accountable in terms of a financial accounting system oriented to the quarterly reporting periods of the stock exchange. The knowledge on which decisions were made were no longer in the individual manager's or owner's head; decisions were made on grounds warranted by the data rather than on the basis of guesswork and forms of reporting that had no objective basis in calculations. Relationships were no longer as they had been, for example, in the DuPont Company, where in the latter part of the nineteenth century the sons and sons-in-law of the patriarch lived in one house, ran the various plants, and wrote daily letters to the patriarch reporting on the day's doings (Yates 1989). The importance of the personal trust that familial relationships supplied, along with creating a community of interest in the family business, was displaced by regimes of written rules and administrative practices, combined with systems of data collection, enabling managers' performance to be evaluated objectively.

The trajectory of the ruling relations since the late nineteenth century, at least in North America, has been one that progressively expropriates locally developed forms of social organization embedded in particularized relationships, changing relations among women and men as well as among men. In his major study of the emergence of what he calls "the visible hand," Chandler (1977) directs attention to the progressive incorporation of the local organization of economic functions and their coordination through networks of market relations into the large-scale corporation. The unregulated processes of the market became integrated into the administration of the corporation. Problems of financing and

---

[ii]Rousseau's *Emile* (1966) designs an educational regime aimed at creating the autonomous male subject of civil society. His complement is a woman equally highly trained but not for autonomy; it's her role to sop up the bodily needs that are residual to the masculine project; she is never to appear for herself or as herself in the zone of civil society that is Emile's preserve.

[iii]Indeed Weber is one of the few sociologists who theorized organization to recognize the significance of texts and documents in bureaucracy.

credit that dogged systems of exchange based on sequences of transactions among small local businesses came to be regulated under the administrative umbrella of a corporation's managerial and accounting systems. Uncertainties in sources of supplies were resolved by vertical integration with manufacturing. For example, General Motors (Sloan 1964) first expanded in a process of vertical integration of independent craft firms that were suppliers of parts, in an attempt to secure a coordination of supplies with expanding production; a second kind of acquisition was of firms making automobiles occupying different market segments from General Motors but potentially in competition with it. Similarly, the expansion of mail-order retailing and department stores appropriated and displaced the local organization of jobbers, incorporating their functions into a single administrative system (Beniger 1986; Chandler 1977; Mills 1951, 25–26).

Complementing Chandler's account is Thorstein Veblen's (1954) earlier observation of the transformation of the country town with the expansion of what he calls "Big Business." He describes the country town as a "retail trading-station" in which townsmen competed to buy the product of farms or to sell to farmers the means of production (144). The coming of Big Business transformed this. Smaller retail and wholesale businesses became subordinated to the new, large-scale forms of organizing business:

> Increased facilities of transport and communication; increased size and combination of the business concerns engaged in the wholesale trade, as packers, jobbers, warehouse-concerns handling farm products; increased resort to package-goods, brands, and trade-marks, advertised on a liberal plan which runs over the heads of the retailers; increased employment of chain-store methods and agencies; increased dependence of local bankers on the greater credit establishments of the financial centers. (154)

"The country town," Veblen writes, "is no longer what it once was," a local habitation in which a man might "bear his share in the control of affairs without being accountable to any master-concern 'higher up' in the hierarchy of business" (155; see also, Mills 1951).

The progressive appropriation of organization and control, the objectification of consciousness in Marx's sense of the term, is also an expropriation of the kinds of organization that developed among people as individuals. The changed organization of ownership and control of capital emerged in and may indeed have been promoted by changes of the same kind in other institutional area. The governance of cities began to be transformed from forms of patronage to bureaucratic administrations. Public schooling came to be organized through the administrative apparatus of school districts and a professional educational staff of college- or university-trained teachers. Generally speaking, professions came into new prominence as a method of guaranteeing training, credentials, and standards of practice in the dispersed settings of professional practice (Collins 1979; Larson 1977; Noble 1977), a development of special importance in the geography of North America.[iv]

An important dimension of the ruling relations is that identified by Michel Foucault (1970) in his conception of discourse. He used the term to pry thinking away from that of the traditional history of ideas that interpreted works in terms of the intentional thought of their authors. The concept of discourse located systems of knowledge and knowledge making independent of particular individuals. Rather than trace continuities and influences, he directed inquiry to discursive events–that is, spoken or written effective statements that happen and have happened (1972, 28)–and to the distinctive forms of power that discourse represents. He ascribed to discourse an order prior to any given moment of the making of a statement.

[iv]Harold Perkin's study (1989) of the history of "professional society" in England from 1880 to the present is, I think, locating a parallel phenomenon to the emergence of what I am calling the "ruling relations" in the North American context. His study, however, adopts social class as its major framework, focusing largely on the emergence of a professional class, and it does not therefore focus on those aspects of the ruling relations that locate the objectification of organization and consciousness.

The speaker's or writer's intention is never purely expressed. What can be said or written is subject to the regulation of the discourse within which it is framed.

Foucault's conception of discourse displaces the traditional basis of knowledge in individual perception and locates it externally to particular subjectivities as an order that imposes on and coerces them. In his account of the order of discourse (1972), he describes it as regulating how people's subjectivities are coordinated, what can be uttered, what must be excluded, what is simply not made present. What can be spoken or written and heard and understood by others is discursively determined (a term not to be misread as "caused"). As women learned in the women's movement, there are experiences that discourse will not speak.

The development of new textual technologies radically expanded the sphere of public discourse: to the existing newspaper industry, radio was added and then television. These transformed public discourse profoundly. What we had ordinarily called "culture" was objectified: A massive cultural industry emerged. Instead of people making their own stories and songs, drawing or carving their own pictures, and acting their own dramas; instead of people passing on news from mouth to ear and waiting to hear about distant places from travelers, we watch television news, dramas, games, talk shows, and so on, which no one individual created and the sources of which are many.

In general, instead of being ruled directly by individuals whom we've known (and perhaps hated) for years and who were known before us by our parents, we are ruled by people who are at work in corporation, government, professional settings and organizations, universities, public schools, hospitals and clinics, and soon and so on. Though they are, of course, individuals, their capacities to act derive from the organizations and social relations that they both produce and are produced by. The relations and organizations in which they are active are also those that organize our lives and in which we in various ways participate. Watching television, reading the

newspaper, going to the grocery store, taking a child to school, taking on a mortgage for a home, walking down a city street, switching on a light, plugging in a computer—these daily acts articulate us into social relations of the order I have called *ruling* as well as those of the economy; what we pick up when we're out shopping will likely have been produced by people living far away from us whom we'll never know. And so on. These transactions aren't with people we know as particular individuals, such as family members or neighbors. It doesn't matter whether the taxman or the supermarket clerk is someone we have a personal relationship with; it's their job that is the basis on which we interact with them. It doesn't matter that we'll never know—except as screen images—the people who tell us news stories on CNN or CBC.[v] The functions of "knowledge, judgment, and will" have become built into a specialized complex of objectified forms of organization and consciousness that organize and coordinate people's everyday lives.

The progress of the ruling relations toward their present comprehensive extension into almost all aspects of our everyday lives created contradictions in women's situations, particularly for middle-class women. On the one hand, the gender divide that emerged among the white middle classes widened and deepened as the powers, technologies, and scope of the extralocal organization of the relations of the economy, the state, and public discourse increased from the late nineteenth century on. The domestic sphere of the middle classes became increasingly ancillary to the translocal organization of power, knowledge, and opportunity in which men were at work as subjects and agents, a period culminating in the gender relationships described in William H. Whyte's study (1956) of "organization man." This was the gender order of which Betty Friedan wrote her celebrated critique of suburban women's way of life (1963).

During the nineteenth century and into the twentieth, print and the consequent replication of texts provided the technological foundation of a reading public in which women participated both

---

[v]CBC stands for the Canadian Broadcasting Corporation, a national government-funded broadcaster of radio and television.

as writers and as readers. Though women were largely excluded from the public sphere as it has been specified by Habermas (1992), the consciousness of middleclass women as being transformed by the emergence of novels written by women and featuring women as the leading characters. New forms of subjectivity were made possible by the same basic technologies that expanded the arenas and powers in which men of the white middle classes were absorbed. Expanding railroads in North America expedited the distributions of news, literature, traveling speakers, and less formal kinds of news, creating new bases of organization among women. African American women, for example, in the late nineteenth century used the news media circulating in African American communities to mobilize opposition to lynching beyond the local communities in which it was used to enforce white dominance. In general, women's movements of the late nineteenth century were based on the reading circles, on pamphlets and other resources enabling organization that did not rely exclusively on networks of geographically localized connection. They were supplemented, as in the Women's Christian Temperance Movement, by traveling organizers and speakers.

Women, particularly middle-class women, were deeply engaged in the emerging educational system at all levels. They were successful in gaining at first marginal access to universities; they were active in establishing child development as a university offering; they were involved in the creation of a mothering discourse that mobilized the efforts and thought of middle-class women in North America across racial and ethnic boundaries to secure for their children the advantages of the public educational system (Dehli 1988, Griffith 1984; Griffith 1986; Griffith and D.E. Smith 1987; Griffith and D.E. Smith 2004; Rothman 1978; D.E. Smith 1997). A new form of middle-class family emerged in which the earnings of the husband/father enabled the wife/mother to specialize not just in housewifery (nothing new there) but in socializing the couple's children based on knowledge produced by experts and in supporting their children through the schooling process to secure for them the class status of their parents. And, after the Second World War, in the period of economic growth known sometimes as Fordism,

working-class families too could begin to work with and through the public educational system to enable their children to move into higher education with the possibility of professional and managerial occupations. Though in the earlier period, middle-class white women's participation in higher education tended to focus in the fields traditionally associated with the domestic, they became, particularly after the Second World War, concentrated in the liberal arts. However, at all class levels and among whatever racial differences, women remained marginal within the ruling relations, playing the subordinate roles, lacking agency, producing their work for men's appropriation.

LOCATING WOMEN'S STANDPOINT IN THE TRAJECTORY

In my life and in the lives of many women from those early years of the women's movement during the 1960s through the 1980s, the differentiated social relations and modes of subjectivity of the domestic sphere and those of the world of intellect, business, and politics coexisted. The gendered division laid down over the previous three or more centuries was being eroded through the very print-based media that had been the foundation of the ruling relations. The work of housewifery and the working consciousness of housewives must have been among the conditions that enabled men to avoid the distractions of thinking about the pragmatics of the working world so far as their personal needs were concerned. Indeed, Alfred Schutz (1962b) identifies as a necessary corollary of participation in that domain the exclusion from consciousness of the personal and pragmatics of the everyday world. These are precisely those encumberments of consciousness from which women could not divest themselves or from which they might divest themselves only by becoming unwomanly or going mad. Correlatively, the function of housewifery on which masculine freedom depended in order to engage in the extralocal relations of capitalism, the public sphere, and eventually the ruling relations required a consciousness continually attentive to the multiple, minute-by-minute demands that bring an orderly household into daily being. It is a mode of consciousness that is itself at odds with that of the domain of scientific theorizing as Schutz (1962b) has described it, and yet here, in my life and in the lives of other women like myself who were at work both in the home and in the academic world, these two modes of subjectivity and activity coexisted.

The women's movement made me aware of the disjuncture between my participation in the "masquerade of universality" (Landes 1996) of academic life and my everyday life with children and home as daily organization and reorganization of subjectivity. I became actively implicated in that masquerade when I went to the university as an undergraduate at the age of twenty-six. I thought I had entered a realm of mind in which I was no longer limited by my sex—fool that I was. It is hard to describe how deep the alienation of intellect and imagination had gone in me. I became aware of it only in what was at first the work of finding out how to resituate my self as an intellectual subject in my alienated being as a woman at home with her children. I discovered that I did not cease to be present and active in the everyday world when I went to work. Alfred Schutz's domain of the theoretical consciousness, stripped of local and biographical particularities, was also anchored in the specific locally created conditions (libraries, offices, and such) designed to insulate the subject's consciousness from particularity, enabling consciousness to be swallowed up in the universalities that texts make possible—including, of course, computer texts. Discovering these necessary anchors entailed by my bodily existence, I began to reconstruct how I connected with the world of intellect, which meant also reconstructing those aspects of it in which I was active, namely, the sociology I had been trained in, had taught, and, very occasionally, had written.

Once started, the process of unraveling the intellectual nets that trapped me could not be stopped. At the time, I thought of it as like being in labor. In childbirth, your body is taken over by a massive muscular activity, unwilled and controllable; you can ride it, but you don't manage it. This deeply muscular period of transformation lasted, I think, for about three years. I worked with it by trying to be true to it and, beyond the period of major transformation, by continually engaging with the problem of how

to tell the truth from where I was, whatever that meant, and how not to be afraid to do so. Above all, I had to avoid assenting to or recreating the division between intellect and my being as a woman, a sexually and motherly being, anchored in her bodily being, in her everyday life and inside the society she meant to explore.

In taking up what I'm now calling "women's standpoint" in the local actualities of her everyday world, I learned that sociological discourse replicated the contours of the ruling relations that I was discovering. The issue wasn't sexism; it wasn't even the assumptions built into its theories or the lack of attention to women and women's issues and concerns. It was how its discursive practices created for knowers a universalized subject transcending the local actualities of people's lives. For the knower positioned as such, people became the *objects* of investigation and explanation (D.E. Smith 1987); we are not its subjects, its knowers.

Thus, the division I experienced in my working life was one that was replicated and reinforced in the sociology I practiced. I could not escape it; I could not find how to reassembly myself as a woman without changing it. I had to find a sociological practice that could begin in the actualities of people's lives so that I could explore the social from there on, as it is brought into being in that same actuality.

My own experience was located at a distinctive moment in the historical trajectory of the expansion of the ruling relations and the changing technological bases of household organization, including the extensive labor of food preparation now provided, at least in Western industrialized societies, before purchase. The concept of women's standpoint that I work with has evolved from the conjuncture of the local and embodied work of mothering, immediate subsistence, and household care and the locally transcending work of participating in the extralocal relations of sociological discourse and the institutional regime of the university. I recognize the historical specificity of this intersection in the lives of women like myself. It locates a contradiction fundamental to our society between, on the one hand, forms of ruling (including discourse) mediated by texts and organized extra- or translocally in objectified modes of the ruling relations and, on the other, the traditional particularizations of both locale and relationships that still characterize family households.

It has been the exclusion of women as subjects from the objectified relations of discourse and ruling that situate my formulation of women's standpoint. We do not have to look for it in what women otherwise may or may not have in common. "I think, therefore I am" has been spoken by men; "I do sex, I give birth, I care for children, I clean house, I cook, therefore I am not" has been the unspoken of women since the emergence of these extraordinary new forms of ruling—at least until the women's movement began our work of eroding the barriers excluding us from agency within these forms of organization. What has been repugnant, dangerous to the purity of the world of enlightened intellect,[vi] has been the presence of the mortal body that women's presence inserts, our breach of the divide that insulates mind's recognition that it has, dwells in, is not separable from, a body.

The concealed masculinity of the subject claiming the formal universality that is foundational to objectified forms of knowledge became visible in the women's movement somewhat indirectly. Perhaps it should have been obvious to us right off that when women claimed a subject position, it directly undermined the dichotomy of mind and discarded body on which universality depends. It wasn't just that subjects had bodies. Indeed phenomenology had been at work trying to ensure the cogency of a universal subject that was definitely embodied by bracketing embodiment. But women's claims to speak were not just as new members of the club; the starting point of the women's movement refused the separation of body and mind. Speaking from the experience of women, however diverse our experience and however refined and elaborated in feminist theory, was always and necessarily from sites of bodily being. Speaking from women's standpoint did not permit the constitutional separation between mind and body built into Western philosophy since Descartes and incorporated into sociology.

Women's standpoint, as I've taken it up to remake sociology, does not permit that separation.

As feminist thinking has developed, theorists have moved toward developing a theorizing of the body that breaks with the Cartesian dichotomy, one reproduced in the everyday organization of my life. Here, for example, is Elizabeth Grosz (1995):

> For a number of years I have been involved in research on how to reconceived the body as a sociocultural artifact. I have been interested in trying to refine and transform traditional notions of corporeality so that the oppositions by which the body has usually been understood (mind and body, inside and outside, experience, and social context, subject and object, self and other—and underlying them, the opposition between male and female) can be problematized. Corporeality can be seen as the material condition of subjectivity, and the subordinated term in the opposition, can move to its rightful place in the very heart of the dominant term, mind. (103)

Grosz uses Derrida's analysis of the binary interdependence of two terms, one the dominant and the other its complement or supplement, often unrecognized but essential to the dominant. Her aim is to change the relation of these two so that the corporeal can be recognized as "in the very heart" of mind. Both Derrida's binary and Grosz's rearrangement of the two terms are, in my view, expressions of social relations underlying the text. The dominance of mind is more than conceptual; it is a local achievement of people who are active in the social relations that rule; these relations are also those of the gender regime that women of my generation inherited. The very notion of turning toward the body as a philosopher's move is one that relies on a deep and foundational division that people are bringing into being daily in their local practices.

The strategy of beginning from women's standpoint in the local actualities of the everyday/everynight world does not bridge this

---

[vi]I am referring here to Mary Douglas's remarkable study, *Purity and Danger* (1966).

division. It collapses it. The embodied knower begins in her experience. Here she is an expert. I mean by this simply that when it comes to knowing her way around in it, how things get done, where the bus top for the B-line bus is, at which supermarket she can pickup both organic vegetables and lactate-reduced milk, and all the unspecifiables of her daily doings and the local conditions on which she relies—when it comes to knowing these matters, she is an expert. It is another matter altogether when it comes to the forms of organization that authenticate the organic status of the vegetables; that brings the supermarket or the bus company into daily existence; or that constitute the responsibility of the municipal government for the state of the streets, the sidewalks, the standards of waste disposal, and so on. And going deeper into the complex of relations into which these locally visible and effective forms are tied are the social relations of the economy.

Such are the ordinary realities of our contemporary world in North America. There are people at work elsewhere whom we don't know and will never know whose doings are coordinated with ours, whether it's when we go to the corner store to pickup a laundry detergent after hours, or when we turn on the television to listen to the latest news on the catastrophic present, or when we pick up a book about the cumulation of sociological theory to connect with the work of others done at who knows what times and places. Social relations coordinating across time and distance are present but largely unseen within the everyday/everynight worlds of people's experience. A sociology from women's standpoint makes this reality a problematic, a project of research and discovery.

The project of inquiry form women's standpoint begins in the local actualities of people's lives. In a sense it reverses the traditional relationship between mind and body wherein mind may examine, explore, and reflect on what is of the body. Body isn't something to be looked at or even theorized. It is rather the site of consciousness, mind, thought, subjectivity, and agency as particular people's local doings. By pulling mind back into body, phenomena of mind and discourse—ideology, beliefs, concepts, theory, ideas and so on—are recognized as themselves the doings of actual people situated in particular local sites at particular times. They are no longer treated as if they were essentially inside people's heads. They become observable insofar as they are produced in language as talk and/or text. Discourse itself is among people's doings; it is the actualities of people's lives; it organizes relations among people; and while it speaks of and from and in people's activities, it does not exhaust them.

❖

Introduction to *The Everyday World as Problematic*

In this reading taken from *The Everyday World as Problematic* (1987), Smith further elucidates institutional ethnography using concrete examples from her own experience. As you will see, by starting from her own experience Smith does *not* mean that she engages only in a self-indulgent inner exploration with herself as sole focus and object. Rather, Smith means that she begins from her own original but tacit knowledge as well as from the acts by which she brings this knowledge into her grasp (Calhoun 2003: 320). As Smith states, "we can never escape the circles of our own heads if we accept that as our territory . . . We aim not at a reiteration of what we already (tacitly) know, but at an exploration of what passes beyond that knowledge and is deeply implicated in how it is" (ibid).

❖

The Everyday World as Problematic (1987)
Dorothy Smith

INSTITUTIONAL ETHNOGRAPHY: A FEMINIST RESEARCH STRATEGY

Institutional Relations as Generalizers of Actual Local Experience

Let me give an everyday example of what I mean by the "problematic of the everyday world." When I take my dog for a walk in the morning, I observe a number of what we might call "conventions." I myself walk on the sidewalk; I do not walk on the neighbors' lawns. My dog, however, freely runs over the lawns. My dog also, if I am not careful, may shit on a neighbor's lawn, and there are certainly some neighbors who do not like this. I am, of course, aware of this problem, and I try to arrange for my dog to do his business in places that are appropriate. I am particularly careful to see that he avoids the well-kept lawns because those are the ones I know I am most likely to be in trouble over should I/he slip up—which does happen occasionally. The neighborhood I live in is a mixture of single-family residences and rental units, and the differences between the well- and ill-kept lawns are related to this. On the whole, those living in rental units do not care so much about the appearance of their front lawn, whereas those who own their own residences are more likely to give care and attention to the grass and sometimes to the flower beds in front of the house.

So as I walk down the street keeping an eye on my dog I am observing some of the niceties of different forms of property ownership. I try to regulate my dog's behavior with particular scrupulousness in relation to the property rights of the owners of single-family dwellings and am a little more casual where I know the house consists of rented apartments or bachelor units, or, as in one case, a fraternity house.[i]

Customarily in sociology we talk about this behavior in terms of norms. Then we see my selection of a path of behavior for my dog as guided by certain norms held in common by myself and my neighbors. But something important escapes this. The notion of "norm" provides for the surface properties of my behavior, what I can be seen to be doing—in general preventing my dog from shitting on others' lawns and being particularly careful where negative sanctions are more likely to be incurred. A description of the kind I have given is in this way transposed into a normative statement.

As a norm it is represented as governing the observed behavior. What is missing, however, is an account of the constitutive work that is going on. This account arises from a process of practical reasoning. How I walk my dog attends to and constitutes in an active way different forms of property as a locally realized organization. The normative analysis misses how this local course of action is articulated to social relations. Social relations here mean concerted sequences or courses of social action implicating more than one individual whose participants are not necessarily present or known to one another. There are social relations that are not encompassed by the setting in which my dog is walked, but they nonetheless enter in and organize it. The existence of single-family dwellings, of rental units, and the like has reference to and depends upon the organization of the state at various levels, its local by-laws, zoning laws, and so forth determining the "real estate" character of the neighborhood; it has reference to and depends upon the organization of a real estate market in houses

[i]The more tender and civic-minded of my readers may like to know that two things have changed in my life since I wrote this. One is that I no longer have a dog of my own. I do, however, sometimes dog-sit my two sons' dogs. The second is that we now have "poop 'n' scoop" laws in Toronto, so I have learned to overcome my rural-bred tendencies to let the shit lie where it falls.

and apartments, and the work of the legal profession and others; it has reference to and organizes the ways in which individual ownership is expressed in local practices that maintain the value of the property both in itself and as part of a respectable neighborhood. Thus this ordinary daily scene, doubtless enacted by many in various forms and settings, has an implicit organization tying each particular local setting to a larger generalized complex of social relations. . . .

The language of the everyday world as it is incorporated into the description of that world is rooted in social relations beyond it and expresses relations not peculiar to the particular setting it describes. In my account of walking the dog, there are categories anchored in and depending for their meaning on a larger complex of social relations. The meaning of such terms as "single-family residence" and "rental units," for example, resides in social relations organizing local settings but not fully present in them. The particularizing description gives access to that which is not particular since it is embedded in categories whose meaning reaches into the complex of social relations our inquiry would explicate. Ordinary descriptions, ordinary talk, trail along with them as a property of the meaning of their terms, the extended social relations they name as phenomena.

Thus taking the everyday world as problematic does not confine us to particular descriptions of local settings without possibility of generalization. This has been seen to be the problem with sociological ethnographies, which, however fascinating as accounts of people's lived worlds, cannot stand as general or typical statements about society and social relations. They have been seen in themselves as only a way station to the development of systematic research procedures that would establish the level of generality or typicality of what has been observed of such-and-such categories of persons. Or they may be read as instances of a general sociological principle. This procedure has been turned on its head in an ingenious fashion in "grounded theory," which proposes a method of distilling generalizing concepts from the social organization of the local setting observed whereupon the latter becomes an instance of the general principles distilled from it.[ii] The popularity of this device testifies to the extent to which the problem of generalizability is

felt by sociologists. The single case has no significance unless it can in some way or another be extrapolated to some general statement either about society or some subgroup represented methodologically as a population of individuals, or connecting the local and particular with a generalizing concept of sociological discourse.

Beginning with the everyday world as problematic bypasses this issue. The relation of the local and particular to generalized social relations is not a conceptual or methodological issue, it is a property of social organization. The particular "case" is not particular in the aspects that are of concern to the inquirer. Indeed, it is not a "case" for it presents itself to us rather as a point of entry, the locus of an experiencing subject or subjects, into a larger social and economic process. The problematic of the everyday world arises precisely at the juncture of particular experience, with generalizing and abstracted forms of social relations organizing a division of labor in society at large . . .

I am using the terms "institutional" and "institution" to identify a complex of relations forming part of the ruling apparatus, organized around a distinctive function—education, health care, law, and the like. In contrast to such concepts as bureaucracy, "institution" does not identify a determinate form of social organization, but rather the intersection and coordination of more than one relational mode of the ruling apparatus. Characteristically, state agencies are tied in with professional forms of organization, and both are interpenetrated by relations of discourse of more than one order. We might imagine institutions as nodes or knots in the relations of the ruling apparatus to class, coordinating multiple strands of action into a functional complex. Integral to the coordinating process are ideologies systematically developed to provide categories and concepts expressing the relation of local courses of action to the institutional function (a point to be elaborated later), providing a currency or currencies enabling interchange between different specialized parts of the complex and a common conceptual organization coordinating its diverse sites. The notion of ethnography is introduced to commit us to an exploration, description, and analysis of such a complex of relations, not conceived in the abstract but from the entry point of

[ii]Barney Glaser and Anselm L. Strauss, *The Discovery of Grounded Theory: Strategies for Qualitative Research* (Chicago: Aldine Press, 1967).

some particular person or persons whose everyday world of working is organized thereby . . .

Institutional ethnography explores the social relations individuals bring into being in and through their actual practices. Its methods, whether of observation, interviewing, recollection of work experience, use of archives, textual analysis, or other, are constrained by the practicalities of investigation of social relations as actual practices. Note however that the institutional ethnography as a way of investigating the problematic of the everyday world does not involve substituting the analysis, the perspectives and views of subjects, for the investigation by the sociologist. Though women are indeed the expert practitioners of their everyday worlds, the notion of the everyday world as problematic assumes that disclosure of the extralocal determinations of our experience does not lie within the scope of everyday practices. We can see only so much without specialized investigation, and the latter should be the sociologist's special business.

Ideology, Institutions, and the Concept of Work as Ethnographic Ground

The coordination of institutional processes is mediated ideologically. The categories and concepts of ideology express the relation of member's actual practices—their work—to the institutional function. Ethnomethodology has developed the notion of accountability to identify members' methods accomplishing the orderliness and sense of local processes.[iii] Members themselves and for themselves constitute the observability and reportability of what has happened or is going on, in how they take it up as a matter for anyone to find and recognize. Members make use of categories and concepts to analyze settings for features thus made observable. The apparently referential operation of locally applied categories and concepts is constitutive of the reference itself.[iv] When applied to the institutional context, the notion of accountability locates practices tying local settings to the nonlocal organization of the ruling apparatus. Indeed, the institutional

process itself can be seen as a dialectic between what members do intending the categories and concepts of institutional ideology and the analytic and descriptive practices of those categories and concepts deployed in accomplishing the observability of what is done, has happened, is going on, and so forth. Thus local practices in their historical particularity and irreversibility are made accountable in terms of categories and concepts expressing the function of the institution. Members' interpretive practices analyzing the work processes that bring the institutional process into being in actuality constitute those work processes as institutional courses of action.[v]

Institutional ideologies are acquired by members as methods of analyzing experiences located in the work process of the institution. Professional training in particular teaches people how to recycle the actualities of their experience into the forms in which it is recognizable within institutional discourse. For example, when teachers are in training they learn a vocabulary and analytic procedures that accomplish the classroom in the institutional mode. They learn to analyze and name the behavior of students as "appropriate" or "inappropriate" and to analyze and name their own (and others') responses. In responding to "inappropriate" behavior, they have been taught to avoid "undermining the student's ego" and hence to avoid such practices as "sarcasm." They should, rather, be "supportive." This ideological package provides a procedure for subsuming what goes on in the classroom under professional educational discourse, making classroom processes observable-reportable within an institutional order.[vi] In this way the work and practical reasoning of individuals and the locally accomplished order that is their product become an expression of the non-local relations of the professional and bureaucratic discourse of the ruling apparatus.

The accountability procedures of institutions make some things visible, while others as much a part of the overall work organization that performs the institution do not come into view at all

---

[iii]Harold Garfinkel, *Studies in Ethnomethodology* (Englewood Cliffs, NJ: Prentice-Hall, 1967).

[iv]D.L. Wieder, *Language and Social Reality: The Case of Telling the Convict Code* (The Hague: Moulton, 1974).

[v]Dorothy E. Smith, "No one commits suicide: Textual analyses of ideological practices," *Human Studies* 6 (1983): 309–359.

[vi]See Garfinkel, *Studies in Ethnomethodology.*

or as other than themselves. Local practices glossed by the categories of the discourse are provided with boundaries of observability beneath which a subterranean life continues. What is observable does not appear as the work of individuals, and not all the work and practices of individuals become observable. When my son was in elementary school, his homework one day was to write up an experiment he had done in science class that day. He asked me how to do it and I replied (not very helpfully), "Well, just write down everything you did." He told me not to be so stupid. "Of course," he said, "they don't mean you write about *everything,* like about filling the jar with water from the tap and taking it to the bench." Clearly there were things

done around the doing of an experiment that were essential to, but not entered into or made accountable within, the "experimental procedure." Its boundaries were organized conceptually to select from a locally indivisible work process, some aspects to be taken as part of the experiment and others to be discounted. All were done. All were necessary. But only some were to be made observable-reportable within the textual mode of the teaching of science. In like ways, institutional ideologies analyze local settings, drawing boundaries and the like. They provide analytic procedures for those settings that attend selectively to work processes, thus making only selective aspects of them accountable within the institutional order.

❖

PATRICIA HILL COLLINS (1948–): A BIOGRAPHICAL SKETCH

Patricia Hill Collins was born in 1948 and grew up in a working-class family in Philadelphia. She earned her B.A. from Brandeis University in 1969 and her M.A.T. from Harvard University in 1970. Collins worked as a school teacher and curriculum specialist before returning to graduate school and receiving her Ph.D. in sociology from Brandeis University in 1984. It was in teaching a course called "The Black Woman" to middle-school girls in 1970 that Collins realized not only the dearth of teaching materials by and about black women, but the *significance* of this dearth. The exclusion of black women from intellectual discourses became the subject of her first book, *Black Feminist Thought: Knowledge, Consciousness, and the Politics of Empowerment* (1990), which won the Jessie Bernard Award of the American Sociological Association for significant schol-

Reprinted with permission.

arship in gender as well as the C. Wright Mills Award from the Society for the Study of Social Problems. In this highly acclaimed book (excerpts from which you will read below), Collins illuminates the rich, self-defined intellectual tradition of black women, which, she argues, has persisted despite formal discursive exclusion. By positioning itself as documenting a tradition or canon, *Black Feminist Thought* legitimates black women's intellectual production as critical social theory (Collins 1998:8).

Collins further explores black feminist thought in *Fighting Words: Black Women and the Search for Justice* (1998) and *Black Sexual Politics* (2004). In *Fighting Words,* Collins shows not only how elite discourses present a view of social reality that elevates the ideas and actions of highly educated white men as normative and superior (ibid.:45), but how black feminist thought has remained dynamic and oppositional under changing social conditions. In *Black Sexual Politics* (2004), Collins continues to firmly situate black feminist thought in the critical tradition by underscoring that antiracist African American politics in the post–civil rights era must soundly address questions of gender and sexuality.

Collins has taught at a number of universities, including Northern Kentucky University, Tufts University, Boston College, and the University of Cincinnati, where she is Charles Phelps Taft Emeritus Professor of Sociology within the Department of African American Studies. Since 2005, she has also been a professor of sociology at the University of Maryland. Collins's most recent book, *From Black Power to Hip Hop: Essays on Racism, Nationalism, and Feminism* (2006), explores how black nationalism works today in the wake of changing black youth identity.

INTELLECTUAL INFLUENCES AND CORE IDEAS

Patricia Hill Collins's work integrates elements of feminist theory, standpoint theory, critical theory, Afrocentrism, poststructuralism, and postmodernism. Collins was particularly influenced by Dorothy Smith, as is evident in her concept of **standpoint epistemology**, which she defines as the philosophic viewpoint that what one knows is affected by the standpoint (or position) one has in society ("epistemology" means how we know what we know, how we decide what is valid knowledge). Collins extends the critical/phenomenological/feminist ideas of Dorothy Smith by illuminating the particular epistemological standpoint of black women. Yet, Collins does not merely add the empirical dimension of "race" to Smith's feminist, critical/phenomenological framework. Rather, taking a poststructural/postmodern turn, Collins emphasizes the "interlocking" nature of the wide variety of statuses—for example, race, class, gender, nationality, sexual orientation—that make up our standpoint, and, in the spirit of Foucault (see Chapter 8), she stresses that where there are sites of domination, there are also potential sites of resistance.

Specifically, Collins (1998, 2004) explicitly situates her work within the critical tradition (indeed, she conceptualizes standpoint theory and postmodernism as "*examples* of critical theory," 1998:254; emphasis added).[8] For Collins (2004:350), what makes critical theory "critical" is its commitment to "justice, for one's own group and/or for that of other groups." Critical social theory illuminates the "bodies of knowledge and sets of institutional practices that actively grapple with the central questions facing groups of people differently placed in specific political, social, and historical contexts characterized by injustice" (ibid.). Yet, Collins rejects "additive" models of oppression that reflect a dichotomous ("top-down") way of thinking about domination rooted specifically in European masculinist thought. Rather than simply elevate one group's suffering over that of another, Collins maps "differences in penalty and privilege that accompany race, class, gender and similar systems of social injustice" (2004:3).

Collins uses the term **matrix of domination** to underscore that one's position in society is made up of multiple contiguous standpoints rather than just one essentialist standpoint. Thus, in contrast to earlier critical accounts (e.g., the Frankfurt School—see Chapter 3) that assume that power operates from the top down by forcing and controlling unwilling victims to bend to the will of more powerful superiors, Collins (1990:226) asserts that "depending on the context, an individual may be an oppressor, a member of an oppressed group, or simultaneously oppressor and oppressed. . . . Each

---

[8]By following Craig Calhoun (1995) in considering postmodernism and standpoint theory as "examples of critical theory," Collins (1998:254, n. 4) is rejecting the narrower (but perhaps more well known) definition of critical theory as simply the Frankfurt School tradition (see Chapter 3) or the style of theorizing of Jürgen Habermas (see Chapter 9).

individual derives varying amounts of penalty and privilege from the multiple systems of oppression which frame everyone's lives."[9]

In addition, Collins emphasizes "that people simultaneously experience and resist oppression on three levels: the level of personal biography; the group or community level of the cultural context created by race, class, and gender; and the systemic level of social institutions." (Collins 1990:227). At the level of the individual, she insists on "the power of the self-definition" (Collins 2004:306) and "self-defined standpoint" (1998:47), and that "each individual has a unique personal biography made up of concrete experiences, values, motivations, and emotions," thereby reasserting both the subjectivity and agency absent in earlier critical models (e.g., the Frankfurt School). For Collins (1998:50), breaking silence represents a moment of insubordination in relations of power—"a direct, blatant insult delivered before an audience."

The group or community level of the cultural context created by race, class, and gender is vital to Collins's conceptualization of **black feminist thought,** which like all specialized thought reflects the interests and standpoint of its creators. Collins locates black feminist thought in the unique literary traditions forged by black women such as bell hooks, Audre Lorde, and Alice Walker, as well as in the everyday experience of ordinary black women. In addition, black feminist thought is rooted in black women's intellectual tradition nurtured by black women's community. As Collins (1990/2000:253) maintains:

> When white men control the knowledge validation process, both political criteria (contextual credibility and evaluation of knowledge claims) can work to suppress Black feminist thought. Therefore, Black women are more likely to choose an alternative epistemology for assessing knowledge claims, one using different standards that are consistent with Black women's criteria for substantiated knowledge and with our criteria for methodology adequacy. . . .

In other words, Collins maintains that the experience of multiple oppressions makes black women particularly skeptical of and vulnerable to dominant paradigms of knowledge and thus more reliant on their own experiential sources of information. Black women "come to voice" and break the silence of oppression by drawing both from their own experience and from the "collective secret knowledge generated by groups on either side of power," that is, the black community and the black female community in particular (Collins 1998:48–9). Black feminist thought offers individual African American women the conceptual tools to resist oppression. Black women have historically resisted, and continue to resist, oppression at individual, community, and institutional levels. A women's blues tradition, the voices of contemporary African American woman writers and thinkers, and women's everyday relationships with each other speak to the outpouring of contemporary black feminist thought in history and literature despite exclusion and/or marginalization in the hegemonic framework.[10]

---

[9]In her recent *Black Sexual Politics* (2004:9–10), Collins takes an even more radical postmodern stance. Here she sees the complexity of "mutually constructing," intertwined dimensions of race, class, gender, and sexuality as so great that she sets her sights not on "untangling the effects" of race, class, gender, sexuality, ethnicity, age, and the like, but rather on simply illuminating them. The point of *Black Sexual Politics*, she says, is not "to tell readers what to think," but rather "it examines what we might think about" (ibid.).

[10]For instance, Alice Walker's *The Color Purple* epitomizes black feminist thought. Told from the perspective of the fourteen-year-old Celie, a semiliterate black girl brutalized first by her father then by her husband, *The Color Purple* supplants the typical patriarchal concerns of the historical novel—"the taking of lands, or the birth, battles, and deaths of Great Men"—with the scene of "one woman asking another for her underwear" (Berlant 2000:4).

By articulating the powerful but hidden dynamics of black feminist thought, Collins highlights the underlying assumed whiteness of both feminism and academia and reminds white women in particular that they are not the only feminists. In addition, however, black feminist thought disrupts the masculinist underpinnings of Afrocentrism. Collins maintains that in the same way that European theorists have historically prioritized class over race or gender, and feminists have prioritized gender over either race or class, Afrocentric scholarship, although formally acknowledging the significance of gender, relegates it secondary to the more pressing fight against racism.

To be sure, Collins (1998:174) readily appreciates the guiding principles at the heart of Afrocentrism—most important, the emphases on reconstructing black culture, reconstituting black identity, using racial solidarity to build black community, and fostering an ethic of service to black community development. Yet, she is highly critical of the "unexamined yet powerful" gender ideology in black nationalist projects, particularly that of Afrocentrists such as Molefi Kete Asante (1942–) who seek to replace Eurocentric systems of knowledge with African-centered ways of knowing.[11]

COLLINS'S THEORETICAL ORIENTATION

As indicated above, the terms "matrix of domination" and "standpoint epistemology" are explicitly devised so as to reflect a multidimensional approach to order; that is, they pointedly work at the level of the social structure or group and the individual. However, above all, in the spirit of the critical tradition, it is to the collective level that Collins's work is most attuned. For instance, while on one hand Collins's term

Figure 7.3   Collins's Black Feminist Thought

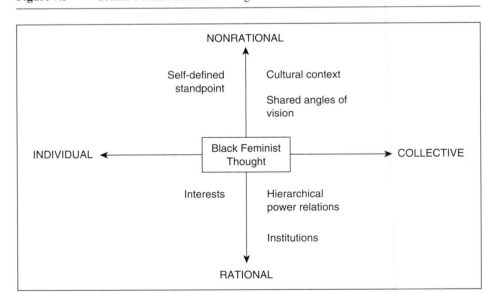

---

[11]Asante asserts that Afrocentricity can be done only via complete separation, and that Afrocentrism is vital to combat the Eurocentric arrogance that necessarily obliterates others, for Eurocentrism is nothing less than "symbolic imperialism." However, Collins identifies several specific ways in which gender assumptions undergird black cultural nationalism.

"self-defined standpoint" seems to readily reflect agency at the level of the individual, interestingly, Collins (1998:47) maintains that she favors this term over bell hooks's term "self-reflexive speech" because self-defined standpoint "ties Black women's speech communities much more closely to institutionalized power relations." Clearly, that "standpoint" refers to "historically shared *group-based* experiences" and that "groups have a degree of permanence over time such that group realities transcend individual experiences" reflects a prioritization of the collective realm (2000:247; emphasis in original). As Collins (2000:249) states:

> Groups who share common placement in hierarchical power relations also share common experiences in such power relations. Shared angles of vision lead those in similar social locations to be predisposed to interpret in comparable fashion.

To be sure, Collins readily acknowledges that the individual has "unique" experiences that are rooted in her inimitable social location, which reflects her cognizance of the level of the individual (see Figure 7.3). Here we see that the individual is not a proxy for the group, that in contrast to what Marx supposed, oppressed groups do not possess a fixed or stagnant (or "essential") identity. As Collins (1998:249) contends, "using the group as the focal point provides space for individual agency." Nevertheless, Collins never loses sight of the "collective secret knowledge generated by groups on either side of power" from within which individual self-definition ensues (1998:49).

In terms of action, overall Collins's theory reflects a collective/rationalistic view of power characteristic of critical theory, in that relations of power are perceived as a preexisting hierarchical structure external to the individual. However, at the same time, by emphasizing that these are *relations* of power and that this involves both collective, discursive codes and their internalization at the nonrational/individual level, Collins presents a nonrational approach to action as well. Of course, her emphasis on "shared angles of vision" as well as "self-defined standpoint" reflects the collective/nonrational realm and the individual/nonrational realms, respectively. Here we see the significance of "group consciousness, group self-definition and 'voice'" (ibid.:251), that is, the collective/nonrational realm. Explicitly challenging the materialist, structural Marxist point of view, standpoint theorists such as Collins argue that "ideas matter in systems of power" (ibid.:252). This multidimensional approach is illustrated in Figure 7.3.

Reading

Introduction to *Black Feminist Thought*

In the following selection from Collins's most highly acclaimed book, *Black Feminist Thought*, Collins exposes and discusses the tension for black women as agents of knowledge, acknowledging that "Black culture and many of its traditions oppress women" (p. 230). However, she also warns against portraying black women either "solely as passive, unfortunate recipients of racial and sexual abuses" or "heroic figures who easily engage in resisting oppression" (p. 238). In sum, Collins continually emphasizes the complexity of both systems of domination and resistance.

❖

Black Feminist Thought (1990/2000)

Patricia Hill Collins

DISTINGUISHING FEATURES OF BLACK FEMINIST THOUGHT

Widely used yet increasingly difficult to define, U.S. Black feminist thought encompasses diverse and often contradictory meanings . . .

Rather than developing definitions and arguing over naming practices—for example, whether this thought should be called Black feminism, womanism, Afrocentric feminism, Africana womanism, and the like—a more useful approach lies in revisiting the reasons why Black feminist thought exists at all. Exploring six distinguishing features that characterize Black feminist thought may provide the common ground that is so sorely needed both among African-American women, and between African-American women and all others whose collective knowledge or thought has a similar purpose. Black feminist thought's distinguishing features need not be unique and may share much with other bodies of knowledge. Rather, it is the *convergence* of these distinguishing features that gives U.S. Black feminist thought its distinctive contours.

Why U.S. Black Feminist Thought?

Black feminism remains important because U.S. Black women constitute an oppressed group. As a collectivity, U.S. Black women participate in a *dialectical* relationship linking African-American women's oppression and activism. Dialectical relationships of this sort mean that two parties are opposed and opposite. As long as Black women's subordination within intersecting oppressions of race, class, gender, sexuality, and nation persists, Black feminism as an activist response to that oppression will remain needed.

In a similar fashion, the overarching purpose of U.S. Black feminist thought is also to resist oppression, both its practices and the ideas that justify it. If intersecting oppressions did not exist, Black feminist thought and similar oppositional knowledges would be unnecessary. As a critical social theory, Black feminist thought aims to empower African-American women within the context of social injustice sustained by intersecting oppressions. Since Black women cannot be fully empowered unless intersecting oppressions themselves are eliminated, Black feminist thought supports broad principles of social justice that transcend U.S. Black women's particular needs.

Because so much of U.S. Black feminism has been filtered through the prism of the U.S. context, its contours have been greatly affected by the specificity of American multiculturalism (Takaki 1993). In particular, U.S. Black feminist thought and practice respond to a fundamental contradiction of U.S. society. On the one hand, democratic promises of individual freedom, equality under the law, and social justice are made to all American citizens. Yet on the other hand, the reality of differential group treatment based on race, class, gender, sexuality, and citizenship status persists. Groups organized around race, class, and gender in and of themselves are not inherently a problem. However, when African-Americans, poor people, women, and other groups discriminated against see little hope for group-based advancement, this situation constitutes social injustice.

Within this overarching contradiction, U.S. Black women encounter a distinctive set of social practices that accompany our particular history within a unique matrix of domination characterized by intersecting oppressions. Race is far from being the only significant marker of group difference—class, gender, sexuality, religion, and citizenship status all matter greatly in the United States (Andersen and Collins 1998). Yet for African-American women, the effects of institutionalized racism remain visible and palpable. Moreover, the institutionalized racism that African-American women encounter relies heavily on racial segregation and accompanying discriminatory practices designed to deny U.S. Blacks equitable treatment. Despite important strides to desegregate U.S. society since 1970, racial segregation remains deeply entrenched in housing, schooling, and employment (Massey and Denton 1993). For many African-American women, racism is not something that exists in the distance. We encounter racism in everyday situations in workplaces, stores, schools, housing, and daily social interaction (St. Jean and Feagin 1998). Most Black women do not have the opportunity to befriend White women and men as neighbors, nor do their children attend school with White children. Racial segregation remains a fundamental feature of the U.S. social landscape, leaving many African-Americans with the belief that "the more things change, the more they stay the same" (Collins 1998a, 11–43). Overlaying these persisting inequalities is a rhetoric of color blindness designed to render these social inequalities invisible. In a context where many believe that to talk of race fosters racism, equality allegedly lies in treating everyone the same. Yet as Kimberle Crenshaw (1997) points out, "it is fairly obvious that treating different things the same can generate as much inequality as treating the same things differently" (p. 285).

Although racial segregation is now organized differently than in prior eras (Collins 1998a, 11–43), being Black and female in the United States continues to expose African-American women to certain common experiences. U.S. Black women's similar work and family experiences as well as our participation in diverse expressions of African-American culture mean that, overall, U.S. Black women as a group live in a different world from that of people who are not Black and female. For individual women, the particular experiences that accrue to living as a Black woman in the United States can stimulate a distinctive consciousness concerning our own experiences and society overall. Many African-American women grasp this connection between what one does and how one thinks. Hannah Nelson, an elderly Black domestic worker, discusses how work shapes the perspectives of African-American and White women: "Since I have to work, I don't really have to worry about most of the things that most of the white women I have worked for are worrying about. And if these women did their own work, they would think just like I do—about this, anyway" (Gwaltney 1980, 4). Ruth Shays, a Black inner-city resident, points out how variations in men's and women's experiences lead to differences in perspective. "The mind of the man and the mind of the woman is the same" she notes, "but this business of living makes women use their minds in ways that men don't even have to think about" (Gwaltney 1980, 33).

A recognition of this connection between experience and consciousness that shapes the everyday lives of individual African-American women often pervades the works of Black women activists and scholars. In her autobiography, Ida B. Wells-Barnett describes how the lynching of her friends had such an impact on her worldview that she subsequently devoted much of her life to the anti-lynching cause (Duster 1970). Sociologist Joyce Ladner's discomfort with the disparity between the teachings of mainstream scholarship and her experiences as a young Black woman in the South led her to write *Tomorrow's Tomorrow* (1972), a groundbreaking study of Black female adolescence. Similarly, the transformed consciousness experienced by Janie, the light-skinned heroine of Zora Neale Hurston's (1937) classic *Their Eyes Were Watching God*, from obedient granddaughter and wife to a self-defined African-American woman, can be directly traced to her experiences with each of her three husbands. In one scene Janie's second husband, angry because she served him a dinner of scorched rice, underdone fish, and soggy bread, hits her. That incident stimulates Janie to stand "where he left her for unmeasured time" and think. And in her thinking "her image of Jody tumbled down and shattered. . . . [S]he had an inside and an outside now and suddenly she knew how not to mix them" (p. 63).

Overall, these ties between what one does and what one thinks illustrated by *individual* Black women can also characterize Black women's experiences and ideas as a *group*. Historically, racial segregation in housing, education, and employment fostered group commonalities that encouraged the formation of a group-based, collective standpoint. For example, the heavy concentration of U.S. Black women in domestic work coupled with racial segregation in housing and schools meant that U.S. Black women had common organizational networks that enabled them to share experiences and construct a collective body of wisdom. This collective wisdom on how to survive as U.S. Black women constituted a distinctive Black women's standpoint on gender-specific patterns of racial segregation and its accompanying economic penalties.

The presence of Black women's collective wisdom challenges two prevailing interpretations of the consciousness of oppressed groups. One approach claims that subordinate groups identify with the powerful and have no valid independent interpretation of their own oppression. The second assumes the oppressed are less human than their rulers, and are therefore less capable of interpreting their own experiences (Rollins 1985; Scott 1985). Both approaches see any independent consciousness expressed by African-American women and other oppressed groups as being either not of our own making or inferior to that of dominant groups. More importantly, both explanations suggest that the alleged lack of political activism on the part of oppressed groups stems from our flawed consciousness of our own subordination.

Historically, Black women's group location in intersecting oppressions produced commonalities among individual African-American women. At the same time, while common experiences may predispose Black women to develop a distinctive group consciousness, they guarantee neither that such a consciousness will develop among all women nor that it will be articulated as such by the group. As historical conditions change, so do the links among the types of experiences Black women will have and any ensuing group consciousness concerning those experiences. Because group standpoints are situated in, reflect, and help shape unjust power relations, standpoints are not static (Collins 1998a, 201–28). Thus, common challenges may foster similar angles of vision leading to a group knowledge or standpoint among African-American women. Or they may not.

Diverse Responses to Common Challenges Within Black Feminism

A second distinguishing feature of U.S. Black feminist thought emerges from a tension linking experiences and ideas. On the one hand, all African-American women face similar challenges that result from living in a society that historically and routinely derogates women of African descent. Despite the fact that U.S. Black women face common challenges, this neither means that individual African-American women have all had the same experiences nor that we agree on the significance of our varying experiences. Thus, on the other hand, despite the common challenges confronting U.S. Black women as a group, diverse responses to these core themes characterize U.S. Black women's group knowledge or standpoint.

Despite differences of age, sexual orientation, social class, region, and religion, U.S. Black women encounter societal practices that restrict us to inferior housing, neighborhoods, schools, jobs, and public treatment and hide this differential consideration behind an array of common beliefs about Black women's intelligence, work habits, and sexuality. These common challenges in turn result in recurring patterns of experiences for individual group members. For example, African-American women from quite diverse backgrounds report similar treatment in stores. Not every *individual* Black woman consumer need experience being followed in a store as a potential shoplifter, ignored while others are waited on first, or seated near restaurant kitchens and rest rooms, for African-American women as a collectivity to recognize that differential *group* treatment is operating.

Since standpoints refer to group knowledge, recurring patterns of differential treatment such as these suggest that certain themes will characterize U.S. Black women's group knowledge or standpoint. For example, one core theme concerns multifaceted legacies of struggle, especially in response to forms of violence that accompany intersecting oppressions (Collins 1998d). Katie Cannon observes, "[T]hroughout the history of the United States, the interrelationship of white supremacy and male superiority has characterized the Black woman's reality as a situation of struggle—a struggle to survive in two contradictory worlds simultaneously, one white, privileged, and oppressive, the other black, exploited, and oppressed" (1985, 30). Black women's vulnerability to assaults in the workplace, on the street, at home, and in media representations has been one factor fostering this legacy of struggle.

Despite differences created by historical era, age, social class, sexual orientation, skin color, or ethnicity, the legacy of struggle against the violence that permeates U.S. social structures is a common thread binding African-American women. Anna Julia Cooper, an educated, nineteenth-century Black woman intellectual, describes Black women's vulnerability to sexual violence:

> I would beg . . . to add my plea for the *Colored Girls* of the South:—that large, bright, promising fatally beautiful class . . . so full of promise and possibilities, yet so sure of destruction; often without a father to whom they dare apply the loving term, often without a stronger brother to espouse their cause and defend their honor with his life's blood; in the midst of pitfalls and snares, waylaid by the lower classes of white men, with no shelter, no protection. (Cooper 1892, 240)

Yet during this period Cooper and other middle-class U.S. Black women built a powerful club movement and numerous community organizations (Giddings 1984, 1988; Gilkes 1985).

Stating that a legacy of struggle exists does not mean that all U.S. Black women share its benefits or even recognize it. For example, for African-American girls, age often offers little protection from assaults. Far too many young Black girls inhabit hazardous and hostile environments (Carroll 1997). In 1975 I received an essay titled "My World" from Sandra, a sixth-grade student who was a resident of one of the most dangerous public housing projects in Boston. Sandra wrote, "My world is full of people getting rape. People shooting on another. Kids and grownups fighting over girlsfriends. And people without jobs who can't afford to get a education so they can get a job . . . winos on the streets raping and killing little girls." Her words poignantly express a growing Black feminist sensibility that she may be victimized by racism, misogyny, and poverty. They reveal her awareness that she is vulnerable to rape as a form of sexual violence. Despite her feelings about her neighborhood, Sandra not only walked the streets daily but managed safely to deliver three siblings to school. In doing so she participated in a Black women's legacy of struggle. Sandra prevailed, but at a cost. Unlike Sandra, others simply quit.

This legacy of struggle constitutes one of several core themes of a Black women's standpoint. Efforts to reclaim U.S. Black women's intellectual traditions have revealed Black women's long-standing attention to additional core themes first recorded by Maria W. Stewart (Richardson 1987). Stewart's perspective on intersecting oppressions, her call for replacing derogated images of Black womanhood with self-defined images, her belief in Black women's activism as mothers, teachers, and Black community leaders, and her sensitivity to sexual politics are all core themes advanced by a variety of Black feminist intellectuals.

Despite the common challenges confronting African-American women as a group, individual Black women neither have identical experiences nor interpret experiences in a similar fashion. The existence of core themes does not mean that African-American women respond to these themes in the same way. Differences among individual Black women produce different patterns of experiential knowledge that in turn shape individual reactions to the core themes. For example, when faced with controlling images of Black women as being ugly and unfeminine, some women—such as Sojourner Truth—demand, "Ain't I a woman?" By deconstructing the conceptual apparatus of the dominant group, they challenge notions of Barbie-doll femininity premised on middle-class White women's experiences (duCille 1996, 8–59). In contrast, other women internalize the controlling images and come to believe that they are the stereotypes (Brown-Collins and Sussewell 1986). Still others aim to transgress the boundaries that frame the images themselves. Jaminica, a 14-year-old Black girl, describes her strategies: "Unless you want to get into a big activist battle, you accept the stereotypes given to you and just try and reshape them along the way. So in a way, this gives me a lot of freedom. I can't be looked at any worse in society than I already am—black and female is pretty high on the list of things not to be" (Carroll 1997, 94–95).

Many factors explain these diverse responses. For example, although all African-American women encounter institutionalized racism, social class differences among African-American women influence patterns of racism in housing, education, and employment. Middle-class Blacks are more likely to encounter a pernicious form of racism that has left many angry and disappointed (Cose 1993; Feagin and Sikes 1994). A young manager who graduated with honors from the University of Maryland describes the specific form racism can take for middle-class Blacks. Before she flew to Cleveland to explain a marketing plan for her company, her manager made her go over it three or four times in front of him so that she would not forget *her* marketing plan. Then he explained how to check luggage at an airport and how to reclaim it. "I just sat at lunch listening to this man talking to me like I was a monkey who could remember but couldn't think," she recalled. When she had had enough, "I asked him if he wanted to tie my money up in a handkerchief and put a note on me saying that I was an employee of this company. In case I got lost I would be picked up by Traveler's Aid, and Traveler's Aid would send me back" (Davis and Watson 1985, 86). Most middle-class Black women do not encounter such blatant incidents, but many working-class Blacks do. Historically, working-class Blacks have struggled with forms of institutionalized racism directly organized by White institutions and by forms mediated by some segments of the Black middle class. Thus, while it shares much with middle-class Black women, the legacy of struggle by working-class Blacks (Kelley 1994) and by working-class Black women in particular will express a distinctive character (Fordham 1993).

Sexuality signals another important factor that influences African-American women's varying responses to common challenges. Black lesbians have identified heterosexism as a form of oppression and the issues they face living in homophobic communities as shaping their interpretations of everyday events (Shockley 1974; Lorde 1982, 1984; Clarke et al. 1983; Barbara Smith 1983, 1998; Williams 1997). Beverly Smith describes how being a lesbian affected her perceptions of the wedding of one of her closest friends: "God, I wish I had one friend here. Someone who knew me and would understand how I feel. I am masquerading as a nice, straight, middle-class Black 'girl'" (1983, 172). While the majority of those attending the wedding saw only a festive event, Beverly Smith

felt that her friend was being sent into a form of bondage. In a similar fashion, varying ethnic and citizenship statuses within the U.S. nation-state as well also shape differences among Black women in the United States. For example, Black Puerto Ricans constitute a group that combines categories of race, nationality, and ethnicity in distinctive ways. Black Puerto Rican women thus must negotiate a distinctive set of experiences that accrue to being racially Black, holding a special form of American citizenship, and being ethnically Latino.

Given how these factors influence diverse response to common challenges, it is important to stress that no homogeneous Black *woman's* standpoint exists. There is no essential or archetypal Black woman whose experiences stand as normal, normative, and thereby authentic. An essentialist understanding of a Black woman's standpoint suppresses differences among Black women in search of an elusive group unity. Instead, it may be more accurate to say that a Black *women's* collective standpoint does exist, one characterized by the tensions that accrue to different responses to common challenges. Because it both recognizes and aims to incorporate heterogeneity in crafting Black women's oppositional knowledge, this Black *women's* standpoint eschews essentialism in favor of democracy. Since Black feminist thought both arises within and aims to articulate a Black *women's* group standpoint regarding experiences associated with intersecting oppressions, stressing this group standpoint's heterogeneous composition is significant.

Moreover in thinking through the contours of a Black women's standpoint it is equally important to recognize that U.S. Black women also encounter the same challenges (and correspondingly different expressions) as women of African descent within a Black diasporic context. This context in turn is situated within a transnational, global context. The term *diaspora* describes the experiences of people who, through slavery, colonialism, imperialism, and migration, have been forced to leave their native lands (Funani 1998, 417). For U.S. Black women and other people of African descent, a diasporic framework suggests a dispersal from Africa to societies in the Caribbean, South America, North America, and Europe. Understandings of African-American womanhood thus reflect a distinctive pattern of dispersal associated with forced immigration to the United States and subsequent enslavement (Pala 1995). Since a diasporic framework is not normative, it should not be used to assess the authenticity of people of African descent in reference to an assumed African norm. Rather, Black diasporic frameworks center analyses of Black women within the context of common challenges experienced transnationally.

The version of Black feminism that U.S. Black women have developed certainly must be understood in the context of U.S. nation-state politics. At the same time, U.S. Black feminism as a social justice project shares much with comparable social justice projects advanced not only by other U.S. racial/ethnic groups (see, e.g., Takaki 1993), but by women of African descent across quite diverse societies. In the context of an "intercontinental Black women's consciousness movement" (McLaughlin 1995, 73), women of African descent are dispersed globally, yet the issues we face may be similar. Transnationally, women encounter recurring social issues such as poverty, violence, reproductive concerns, lack of education, sex work, and susceptibility to disease (*Rights of Women* 1998). Placing African-American women's experiences, thought, and practice in a transnational, Black diasporic context reveals these and other commonalities of women of African descent while specifying what is particular to African-American women.

Black Feminist Practice and Black Feminist Thought

A third distinguishing feature of Black feminist thought concerns the connections between U.S. Black women's experiences as a heterogeneous collectivity and any ensuing group knowledge or standpoint . . .

As members of an oppressed group, U.S. Black women have generated alternative practices and knowledges that have been designed to foster U.S. Black women's group empowerment. In contrast to the dialectical relationship linking oppression and activism, a *dialogical* relationship characterizes Black women's collective experiences and group knowledge. On both the individual and the group level, a

dialogical relationship suggests that changes in thinking may be accompanied by changed actions and that altered experiences may in turn stimulate a changed consciousness. For U.S. Black women as a collectivity, the struggle for a self-defined Black feminism occurs through an ongoing dialogue whereby action and thought inform one another.

U.S. Black feminism itself illustrates this dialogical relationship. On the one hand, there is U.S. Black feminist practice that emerges in the context of lived experience. When organized and visible, such practice has taken the form of overtly Black feminist social movements dedicated to the empowerment of U.S. Black women. Two especially prominent moments characterize Black feminism's visibility. Providing many of the guiding ideas for today, the first occurred at the turn of the century via the Black women's club movement. The second or modern Black feminist movement was stimulated by the antiracist and women's social justice movements of the 1960s and 1970s and continues to the present. However, these periods of overt political activism where African-American women lobbied in our own behalf remain unusual. They appear to be unusual when juxtaposed to more typical patterns of quiescence regarding Black women's advocacy.

Given the history of U.S. racial segregation, Black feminist activism demonstrates distinctive patterns. Because African-Americans have long been relegated to racially segregated environments, U.S. Black feminist practice has often occurred within a context of Black community development efforts and other Black nationalist-inspired projects. Black nationalism emerges in conjunction with racial segregation—U.S. Blacks living in a racially integrated society would most likely see less need for Black nationalism. As a political philosophy, Black nationalism is based on the belief that Black people constitute a people or "nation" with a common history and destiny. Black solidarity, the belief that Blacks have common interests and should support one another, has long permeated Black women's political philosophy. Thus, Black women's path to a "feminist" consciousness often occurs within the context of antiracist social justice projects, many of them influenced by Black nationalist ideologies. In describing how this phenomenon affects

Black women in global context, Andree Nicola McLaughlin contends, "[A]mong activist Black women, it is generally recognized that nationalist struggle provides a rich arena for developing a woman's consciousness" (McLaughlin 1995, 80). To look for Black feminism by searching for U.S. Black women who self-identify as "Black feminists" misses the complexity of how Black feminist practice actually operates (Collins 1993a). . . .

As critical social theory, Black feminist thought encompasses bodies of knowledge and sets of institutional practices that actively grapple with the central questions facing U.S. Black women as a group. Such theory recognizes that U.S. Black women constitute one group among many that are differently placed within situations of injustice. What makes critical social theory "critical" is its commitment to justice, for one's own group and for other groups.

Within these parameters, knowledge for knowledge's sake is not enough—Black feminist thought must both be tied to Black women's lived experiences and aim to better those experiences in some fashion. When such thought is sufficiently grounded in Black feminist practice, it reflects this dialogical relationship. Black feminist thought encompasses general knowledge that helps U.S. Black women survive in, cope with, and resist our differential treatment. It also includes more specialized knowledge that investigates the specific themes and challenges of any given period of time. Conversely, when U.S. Black women cannot see the connections among themes that permeate Black feminist thought and those that influence Black women's everyday lives, it is appropriate to question the strength of this dialogical relationship. Moreover, it is also reasonable to question the validity of that particular expression of Black feminist thought. For example, during slavery, a special theme within Black feminist thought was how the institutionalized rape of enslaved Black women operated as a mechanism of social control. During the period when Black women worked primarily in agriculture and service, countering the sexual harassment of live-in domestic workers gained special importance. Clear connections could be drawn between the content and purpose of Black feminist thought and important issues in Black women's lives.

The potential significance of Black feminist thought goes far beyond demonstrating that African-American women can be theorists. Like Black feminist practice, which it reflects and which it seeks to foster, Black feminist thought can create collective identity among African-American women about the dimensions of a Black women's standpoint. Through the process of *rearticulation,* Black feminist thought can offer African-American women a different view of ourselves and our worlds (Omi and Winant 1994, 99). By taking the core themes of a Black women's standpoint and infusing them with new meaning. Black feminist thought can stimulate a new consciousness that utilizes Black women's everyday, taken-for-granted knowledge. Rather than raising consciousness, Black feminist thought affirms, rearticulates, and provides a vehicle for expressing in public a consciousness that quite often already exists. More important, this rearticulated consciousness aims to empower African-American women and stimulate resistance. . . .

Dialogical Practices and Black Women Intellectuals

A fourth distinguishing feature of Black feminist thought concerns the essential contributions of African-American women intellectuals. The existence of a Black women's standpoint does not mean that African-American women, academic or otherwise, appreciate its content, see its significance, or recognize its potential as a catalyst for social change. One key task for Black women intellectuals of diverse ages, social classes, educational backgrounds, and occupations consists of asking the right questions and investigating all dimensions of a Black women's standpoint with and for African-American women. Historically, Black women intellectuals stood in a special relationship to the larger community of African-American women, a relationship that framed Black feminist thought's contours as critical social theory . . .

This special relationship of Black women intellectuals to the community of African-American women parallels the existence of two interrelated levels of knowledge (Berger and Luckmann 1966). The commonplace, taken-for-granted knowledge shared by

African-American women growing from our everyday thoughts and actions constitutes a first and most fundamental level of knowledge. The ideas that Black women share with one another on an informal, daily basis about topics such as how to style our hair, characteristics of "good" Black men, strategies for dealing with White folks, and skills of how to "get over" provide the foundations for this taken-for-granted knowledge.

Experts or specialists who participate in and emerge from a group produce a second, more specialized type of knowledge. Whether working-class or middle-class, educated or not, famous or everyday, the range of Black women intellectuals discussed in Chapter 1 are examples of these specialists. Their theories that facilitate the expression of a Black women's standpoint form the specialized knowledge of Black feminist thought. The two types of knowledge are interdependent. While Black feminist thought articulates the often taken-for-granted knowledge shared by African-American women as a group, the consciousness of Black women may be transformed by such thought. Many Black women blues singers have long sung about taken-for-granted situations that affect U.S. Black women. Through their music, they not only depict Black women's realities, they aim to shape them.

Because they have had greater opportunities to achieve literacy, middle-class Black women have also had greater access to the resources to engage in Black feminist scholarship. Education need not mean alienation from this dialogical relationship. The actions of educated Black women within the Black women's club movement typify this special relationship between one segment of Black women intellectuals and the wider community of African-American women:

> It is important to recognize that black women like Frances Harper, Anna Julia Cooper, and Ida B. Wells were not isolated figures of intellectual genius; they were shaped by and helped to shape a wider movement of Afro-American women. This is not to claim that they were representative of all black women; they and their counterparts formed an educated, intellectual elite, but an elite that tried to develop a cultural and historical perspective that was organic to the wider condition of black womanhood. (Carby 1987, 115)

The work of these women is important because it illustrates a tradition of joining scholarship and activism. Because they often lived in the same neighborhoods as working-class Blacks, turn-of-the-century club women lived in a Black civil society where this dialogical relationship was easier to establish. They saw the problems. They participated in social institutions that encouraged solutions. They fostered the development of a "cultural and historical perspective that was organic to the wider condition of black womanhood." Contemporary Black women intellectuals face similar challenges of fostering dialogues, but do so under greatly changed social conditions. Whereas racial segregation was designed to keep U.S. Blacks oppressed, it fostered a form of racial solidarity that flourished in all-Black neighborhoods. In contrast, now that Blacks live in economically heterogeneous neighborhoods, achieving the same racial solidarity raises new challenges. . . .

Black Feminism as Dynamic and Changing

A fifth distinguishing feature of U.S. Black feminist thought concerns the significance of change. In order for Black feminist thought to operate effectively within Black feminism as a social justice project, both must remain dynamic. Neither Black feminist thought as a critical social theory nor Black feminist practice can be static; as social conditions change, so must the knowledge and practices designed to resist them. For example, stressing the importance of Black women's centrality to Black feminist thought does not mean that all African-American women desire, are positioned, or are qualified to exert this type of intellectual leadership. Under current conditions, some Black women thinkers have lost contact with Black feminist practice. Conversely, the changed social conditions under which U.S. Black women now come to womanhood—class-segregated neighborhoods, some integrated, far more not—place Black women of different social classes in entirely new relationships with one another. . . .

The changing social conditions that confront African-American women stimulate the need for new Black feminist analyses of the common differences that characterize U.S.

Black womanhood. Some Black women thinkers are already engaged in this process. Take, for example, Barbara Omolade's (1994) insightful analysis of Black women's historical and contemporary participation in mammy work. Most can understand mammy work's historical context, one where Black women were confined to domestic service, with Aunt Jemima created as a controlling image designed to hide Black women's exploitation. Understanding the limitations of domestic service, much of Black women's progress in the labor market has been measured by the move out of domestic service. Currently, few U.S. Black women work in domestic service in private homes. Instead, a good deal of this work in private homes is now done by undocumented immigrant women of color who lack U.S. citizenship; their exploitation resembles that long visited upon African-American women (Chang 1994). But, as Omolade points out, these changes do not mean that U.S. Black women have escaped mammy work. Even though few Aunt Jemimas exist today, and those that do have been cosmetically altered, leading to the impression that mammy work has disappeared, Omolade reminds us that mammy work has assumed new forms. Within each segment of the labor market—the low-paid jobs at fast-food establishments, nursing homes, day-care centers, and dry cleaners that characterize the secondary sector, the secretaries and clerical workers of the primary lower tier sector, or the teachers, social workers, nurses, and administrators of the primary upper tier sector—U.S. Black women still do a remarkable share of the emotional nurturing and cleaning up after other people, often for lower pay. In this context the task for contemporary Black feminist thought lies in explicating these changing relationships and developing analyses of how these commonalities are experienced differently.

The changing conditions of Black women's work overall has important implications for Black women's intellectual work. Historically, the suppression of Black feminist thought has meant that Black women intellectuals have traditionally relied on alternative institutional locations to produce specialized knowledge about a Black women's standpoint. Many Black women scholars, writers, and artists have worked either alone, as was the case with Maria W. Stewart, or within African-American community organizations, the case for Black women in the club movement and in Black churches. The grudging incorporation of work on Black women into curricular offerings of historically White colleges and universities, coupled with the creation of a critical mass of African-American women writers such as Toni Morrison, Alice Walker, and Gloria Naylor within these institutional locations, means that Black women intellectuals can now find employment within academia. Black women's history and Black feminist literary criticism constitute two focal points of this renaissance in Black women's intellectual work (Carby 1987). Moreover, U.S. Black women's access to the media remains unprecedented, as talk show hostess Oprah Winfrey's long-running television show and forays into film production suggest.

The visibility provided U.S. Black women and our ideas via these new institutional locations has been immense. However, one danger facing African-American women intellectuals working in these new locations concerns the potential isolation of individual thinkers from Black women's collective experiences—lack of access to other U.S. Black women and to Black women's communities. Another is the pressure to separate thought from action—particularly political activism—that typically accompanies training in standard academic disciplines or participating in allegedly neutral spheres like the "free" press. Yet another involves the inability of some Black women "superstars" to critique the terms of their own participation in these new relations. Blinded by their self-proclaimed Black feminist diva aspirations, they feel that they owe no one, especially other Black women. Instead, they become trapped within their own impoverished Black feminist universes. Despite these dangers, these new institutional locations provide a multitude of opportunities for enhancing Black feminist thought's visibility. In this new context, the challenge lies in remaining dynamic, all the while keeping in mind that a moving target is more difficult to hit.

U.S. Black Feminism and Other Social Justice Projects

A final distinguishing feature of Black feminist thought concerns its relationship to other projects for social justice. A broad range of African-American women intellectuals have advanced the view that Black women's struggles are part of a wider struggle for human dignity, empowerment, and social justice. In an 1893 speech to women, Anna Julia Cooper cogently expressed this worldview:

We take our stand on the solidarity of humanity, the oneness of life, and the unnaturalness and injustice of all special favoritisms, whether of sex, race, country, or condition. . . . The colored woman feels that woman's cause is one and universal; and that. . . not till race, color, sex, and condition are seen as accidents, and not the substance of life; not till the universal title of humanity to life, liberty, and the pursuit of happiness is conceded to be inalienable to all; not till then is woman's lesson taught and woman's cause won—not the white woman's nor the black woman's, not the red woman's but the cause of every man and of every woman who has writhed silently under a mighty wrong. (Loewenberg and Bogin 1976, 330–31)

Like Cooper, many African-American women intellectuals embrace this perspective regardless of particular political solutions we propose, our educational backgrounds, our fields of study, or our historical periods. Whether we advocate working through autonomous Black women's organizations, becoming part of women's organizations, running for political office, or supporting Black community institutions, African-American women intellectuals repeatedly identify political actions such as these as a *means* for human empowerment rather than ends in and of themselves. Thus one important guiding principle of Black feminism is a recurring humanist vision (Steady 1981, 1987) . . .

Perhaps the most succinct version of the humanist vision in U.S. Black feminist thought is offered by Fannie Lou Hamer, the daughter of sharecroppers and a Mississippi civil rights activist. While sitting on her porch, Ms. Hamer observed, "Ain' no such thing as I can hate anybody and hope to see God's face" (Jordan 1981, xi).

❖

NANCY CHODOROW (1944–): A BIOGRAPHICAL SKETCH

Nancy Chodorow was born in 1944. She earned her B.A. in social anthropology from Radcliffe University in 1966 and her Ph.D. in sociology from Brandeis University in 1974. She first taught women's studies at Wellesley College in 1973 and then taught at the University of California, Santa Cruz, from 1974 to 1986. Since 1986 she has been teaching at the University of California, Berkeley. From 1985 to 1993, Chodorow undertook training at the San Francisco Psychoanalytic Institute. Arguably the most important psychoanalytic feminist and reinterpreter of Freud, Chodorow is a practicing clinical psychoanalyst and psychotherapist as well as a sociologist. Her most highly acclaimed book, *The Reproduction of Mothering*, first published in 1978, has won numerous awards. Chodorow's more recent books include *Feminism and Psychoanalytic Theory* (1989), *Femininities Masculinities, Sexualities: Freud and Beyond* (1994), and *The Power of Feelings: Personal Meaning in Psychoanalysis, Gender and Culture* (1999).

SOURCE: Photo courtesy of UC Berkeley; used with permission.

INTELLECTUAL INFLUENCES AND CORE IDEAS

Most students do not associate Sigmund Freud with feminist theory. This is for good reason. After all, it was Freud who developed such concepts as "penis envy"—the idea that women are, by nature, "envious" of men's physiological superiority; and "double orgasm"—the idea that orgasm achieved by transferring the center of orgasm to the vagina is a more "mature" form of orgasm than that achieved through stimulation of the clitoris.

In recent decades, Freud's concepts of "penis envy" and "double orgasm" have been soundly discredited. Scientists concur that the center of female sexuality is the clitoris; hence, there can be no such thing as "vaginal orgasm" or "double orgasm." So, too, the notion that a woman's personality is inevitably determined by her lack of a penis has no basis in fact. Indeed, as Chodorow points out, Freud's concept of "penis envy" violates a fundamental rule of psychoanalytic interpretation—that traumas need explaining. Freud does not seek to find the *source* of penis envy in previous individual history; that is, he does not explain *why* females want a penis. He simply argues that "she sees one and she knows she wants one" (Chodorow 1989:173).

Thus, feminists routinely condemn Freud not merely for the scientific inaccuracy of his ideas, but also because of their sexist and misogynistic origins and implications. Phallocentric thinking, which focuses on the penis and assumes that women need men for sexual arousal and satisfaction, is simply self-evident to Freud because he takes female "passivity" as a given. Moreover, scholars such as Chodorow (1989:175) point out that "Freud did not content himself with simply making *ad hominem* claims about women. He actively threw down the political gauntlet at feminists." When women psychoanalysts started to object to his characterizations of women, Freud answered with a subtle antiwoman put-down: women psychoanalysts were not afflicted with the negative characteristics of femininity but were the "exception." Women psychoanalysts were not like other women, but were more "masculine" (ibid.:176).

Yet, feminist psychoanalysts such as Chodorow have not given up entirely on either Freud or psychoanalysis. On the contrary, Chodorow (1989:174) maintains that psychoanalysis is "first and foremost a theory of femininity and masculinity, a theory of gender inequality, and a theory of the development of heterosexuality." She maintains that psychoanalytic theory and feminism coincide in that both presuppose that women and men are "made" not "born," that is, that biology alone does not explain sexual orientation or gender personality. In short, although intensely critical of Freud, psychoanalytic feminists such as Chodorow accept the basic Freudian idea that unconscious and innate erotic and aggressive drives do exist. But in contrast to Freud, they situate innate erotic drives in the context of interpersonal relations; they focus not so much on sexuality per se as on intimacy and separation, primarily in the family and especially between mother and child.

These revised Freudian ideas, broadly known as **object relations theory**, replace Freud's emphasis on "pleasure-seeking" with an emphasis on "relationship-seeking." Freud used the term "object relation" to emphasize that bodily drives are satisfied through a medium, or object. Object relations theory extends this point, emphasizing that the psychological life of the individual is created in and through relations with other human beings. Object relations theorists contend that humans have an innate drive to form and maintain relationships and that this is the fundamental human need that forms a context against which other drives, such as libidinal and aggressive drives, gain meaning. In sum, the term "object relations" refers to the self-structure that we internalize in early childhood, which functions as a blueprint for establishing and maintaining future relationships (http://www.objectrelations.org/orkey.htm).[12]

Object relations theorists emphasize that during the first few years of life, certain innate potentials and character traits (e.g., the ability to walk and talk) develop in the presence of good object relations. The quality of these relations affects the quality of one's linguistic and motor skills (http://www.objectrelations.org/orkey.htm). In addition, in stark contrast to traditional Freudian thought, object relations theorists emphasize that the child's gender identity has little to do with the child's own awareness of sexuality and reproduction (whether conscious or unconscious). Rather, gender identity is developed through a process involving (1) the establishment of a close, symbiotic relationship to the primary caretaker (which is generally the mother) in the first three years of life, followed by (2) the subsequent dissolution of that relationship through *separation* (differentiating oneself from one's primary caretaker) and *individuation* (establishing one's own skills and personality traits). Of course, this newly developed gender identity reflects and expresses not merely personal traits, but also the gender-specific ideals and inequities of the family/community into which s/he is born.

In this way, psychoanalytic feminists tackle one of the enduring conundrums that feminists face: the resiliency of gender roles. Especially in the 1960s and 1970s, many feminists were profoundly optimistic about the power of socialization to change gendered patterns of behavior. They assumed that if boys and girls were socialized in similar ways (i.e., if girls were not trained to do "girl" things and boys not to do "boy" things), stereotypical gender roles would not persist. Gender roles would become obsolete, and

Photo 7.5 Mother and Child: For Chodorow, the mother-child relationship is central to the formation of the child's personality.

SOURCE: Mitch Dickerman; used with permission.

---

[12]Klee (2005) notes that while object relations theory might well be called "human-relations theory" because of its prioritization of human relationships, in fact, in childhood, we form relationships with "transitional objects," such as stuffed animals, toys, and pets, and later in life, some people form intense and even self-destructive relationships with food and alcohol, as well as with other people. "So the term object is more inclusive for our understanding of how humans form and preserve a sense of self, as well as relationships with others" (http://www.objectrelations.org/orkey.htm).

sexism at the microlevel would be largely eliminated. However, this has not been the case. Despite significant changes in socialization (e.g., the rise in girls' sports and more gender-neutral activities in school), and much to the chagrin of many parents and teachers, there are still strongly gendered preferences among both boys and girls. Thus, psychoanalytic feminists seek to explain how gender patterns are reproduced independent of our conscious intentions (Chodorow 1978:34; Williams 1993:134).

Chodorow begins by noting that because of the allocation of work roles, infants usually originally identify with the female parent. That is, the infant first develops a sense of his/her own selfhood in a close, one-on-one relationship with the mother, and qualities possessed by the mother are internalized by the infant to form the beginnings of the child's personality.

However, the particularly strong bonds formed with the mother and the relative absence of the father have important implications for the development of "normal" adult heterosexual identity. Boys achieve their adult sexual identity (i.e., become "men") only by separating themselves from their mothers. This separation entails denying the world of emotional intimacy that she represents. That is, boys become men by defining themselves in opposition to the femininity of their mother. According to Chodorow, the consequence of this is that men have difficulty in dealing with emotional matters: they see acknowledgment of emotions as a sign of vulnerability and weakness. Moreover, social contempt for women (and, in its extreme form, misogyny) arises as boys deny their earliest emotional experiences with their mother and particularly the sexually charged nature of their oedipal love for their mothers. The acknowledgment of emotions, in particular feelings of vulnerability, is considered "femininizing" and is threatening to their status as "real" men (Alsop, Fitzsimons, and Lennon 2002:59).

Girls, on the other hand, are never required to make a complete break with their mothers in order to achieve their adult sexual identity (become "women"). Rather, society fosters the continuation of intense mother-daughter bonds into adulthood.

Photo 7.6 Teenage Boy at Video Arcade: According to Chodorow, boys become "men" by separating themselves from the emotional intimacy that the mother represents.

SOURCE: © Reuters/CORBIS; used with permission.

However, not having been forced to emotionally separate from their mothers, women continue to long for the emotional intimacy provided by close relationships. This unconscious desire to form attachments to others leads women to suffer greater dependency needs, as their self-identity is tied to their relationships with others. According to Chodorow, this lack of differentiation explains why women become preoccupied with the very relational issues at the heart of motherhood: intimacy and a lack of ego separation. Women find their self-in-relation (in intimate relations with others), but because of their socialization into adult heterosexuality men lack the emotional capabilities that women need in order to be fulfilled in relationships. Because masculinity is defined by separation and distance, women turn not to men but to motherhood to fulfill their unconscious desire for intimacy; they recreate the early infant-mother relationship by becoming mothers themselves. Of course, as women again mother (and fathers continue to eschew intimacy), the cycle continues on in another generation: a female self that is fundamentally a self-in-relation and a male self that is fundamentally a self in denial of relations (Gerhenson and Williams 2001:282).

To be sure, Chodorow is not the first sociologist to suggest that gender personality is shaped within the psychodynamics of the family. Talcott Parsons (see Chapter 2) also borrowed this idea from Freud. But, in contrast to Parsons, who Chodorow (1978:38) maintains, "always sounds as though he wants to understand order to contribute to its maintenance," Chodorow examines the family critically. She maintains that the strains in the family that Parsons (1943) describes (e.g., the "asymmetrical relation of the marriage pair" in the occupational structure, which leads men to oppress and dominate women, and women to "succumb to their dependency cravings through such channels as neurotic illness or compulsive domesticity"—see Chapter 2) are actually deep distortions that, far from being a pathological exception to mostly harmonious family relations, "undermine the sex-gender system even while reproducing it" (1978:211).

This critical strain in Chodorow's examination of the traditional family coincides with that of the Frankfurt School (see Chapter 3). Also inspired by Freud, the Frankfurt School described the central "strain" within the family as the masculine urge to dominate and oppress women. In conjunction with their Marxist roots (and in sharp

Figure 7.4   Chodorow's Basic Theoretical Orientation

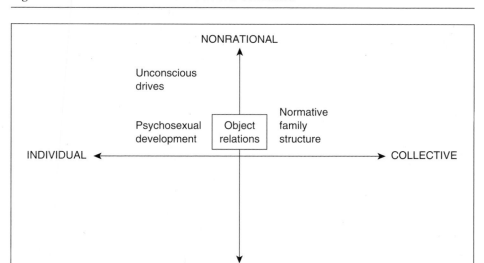

contrast to functionalism), the Frankfurt School tied the disruptive effects in the family to the decline of paternal authority because of the spread of industrial capitalism.

Chodorow provocatively extends this Frankfurt School emphasis on the oppressive elements within the family structure by rooting the masculine urge to dominate women in the dynamics of psychosexual development. In other words, in contrast to the masculinist standpoint of the Frankfurt School theorists (as well as functionalism), which emphasizes "the way the family and women socialize *men* into capitalist society" (ibid.:37; emphasis in original), Chodorow takes an explicitly feminist and psychoanalytic standpoint, replacing the study of paternal authority with a study of mothering and situating the root of the problem not in the capitalist economy, but in object relations (see Figure 7.4).

CHODOROW'S THEORETICAL ORIENTATION

As both a psychoanalyst and a sociologist, Chodorow can be said to incorporate both individualistic and collectivistic approaches to order in her work, explicitly melding the more individualistic tradition of psychoanalysis with the more collectivistic tradition of sociology. Specifically, Chodorow explicitly combines an individualistic emphasis on the psychological hurdles that a child must overcome in order to become an able "man" or "woman," with an emphasis on the social and cultural milieu that preexists the individual and shapes the gender roles to which he or she conforms. So, too, in conjunction with object relations theory, Chodorow emphasizes the importance of the significant persons who are the object or target of another's feelings of intentions (at the level of the individual); but as a sociologist she recognizes that the objects to which individuals attach themselves are sanctioned in preexisting social patterns (at the collective level).

In terms of action, Chodorow is primarily nonrationalistic in orientation. As a psychoanalyst, she underscores that people attach themselves to particular things because of unconscious desires, which, by definition, reflects the nonrational realm, since the unconscious is not open to strategic or other cost/benefit calculations. In addition, however, the normative gender patterns that children internalize in the process of social interaction also speak primarily to the nonrational realm.

In sum, as shown in Figure 7.4, it is Chodorow's psychoanalytic framework that sets her apart from other feminists and results in her individualistic/nonrationalistic theoretical orientation. However, there are sociological roots to this theoretical orientation as well. Akin to symbolic interactionists (see Chapter 5) who also exhibit a primarily individualistic and nonrationalistic approach, her theory emphasizes how we learn to direct our desires in socially appropriate ways in social interaction (see Figure 7.4).

Of course, it is precisely this individualistic and nonrationalistic approach that infuriates nonpsychoanalytic feminists, particularly neo-Marxist feminists. These folks have no truck with *either* the individualistic or the nonrationalistic orientation that psychoanalytic feminism exhibits, for they see the (individualistic) emphasis on (nonrationalistic) unconscious motivation and psychic structures as an irritatingly long way from the (rationalistic/collectivistic) politico-economic roots of gender inequality and oppression. They consider macrolevel social structures, power dynamics, and the political and economic basis of gender inequality far more important than "unconscious desires" and psychological developmental concerns. Collins (1990/2000:6) also criticizes Chodorow for relying so heavily on white, middle-class samples and promoting the notion of "a generic woman who is White and middle-class."

Reading

Introduction to *The Reproduction of Mothering*

The following selection is extracted from Chodorow's most highly acclaimed book, *The Reproduction of Mothering* (1978). The selection begins with a brief excerpt on the effects of early mothering and the pre-oedipal period. In this section, Chodorow outlines how the infant's early relation to its mother profoundly affects not only its sense of self and its later object relationships, but also its feeling about women in general (ibid.:77). The next excerpt you will read focuses on mothering, masculinity, and capitalism. Here Chodorow explains how women's mothering in isolated nuclear families in contemporary capitalist societies both "prepares men for participation in a male-dominant family and society [and] for their lesser emotional participation in family life" (ibid.:180–1). The final excerpt you will read is from the conclusion of the book. Chodorow criticizes conventional feminist and social psychological theories for relying too much on conscious intention and recaps her particular version of psychoanalytic theory, highlighting psychic organization and orientation.

The Reproduction of Mothering (1978)

Nancy Chodorow

THE RELATION TO THE MOTHER AND THE MOTHERING RELATION

The Effects of Early Mothering

The character of the infant's early relation to its mother profoundly affects its sense of self, its later object-relationships, and its feelings about its mother and about women in general. The continuity of care enables the infant to develop a self—a sense that "I am." The quality of any particular relationship, however, affects the infant's personality and self-identity. The experience of self concerns *who* "I am" and not simply *that* "I am."

In a society where mothers provide nearly exclusive care and certainly the most meaningful relationship to the infant, the infant develops its sense of self mainly in relation to her. Insofar as the relationship with its mother has continuity,

the infant comes to define aspects of its self (affectively and structurally) in relation to internalized representations of aspects of its mother and the perceived quality of her care. (As I have indicated, to call this quality "perceived" brackets the variety of fantasies and transformations the infant may engage in to deal with its anxiety and ambivalence.) For instance, the experience of satisfactory feeding and holding enables the child to develop a sense of loved self in relation to a loving and caring mother. Insofar as aspects of the maternal relationship are unsatisfactory, or such that the infant feels rejected or unloved, it is likely to define itself as rejected, or as someone who drives love away. In this situation, part of infantile attention, and then the infantile ego, remains preoccupied with this negatively experienced internal relationship. Because this situation is unresolvable, and interferes with the ongoing need for love, the infant represses its preoccupation. Part of its definition of self and its affective energy thus splits off experientially from its central self, drawing to an internal object energy and commitment which would otherwise be available for ongoing external relationships. The growing child's psychic structure and sense of self thus comes to consist of unconscious, quasi-independent, divided experiences of self in affective (libidinal-attached, aggressive, angry, ambivalent, helpless-dependent) relation with an inner object world, made up originally of aspects of its relation to its mother.

The infant's mental and physical existence depends on its mother, and the infant comes to feel that it does. It experiences a sense of oneness with her and develops a self only by convincing itself that it is in fact a separate being from her. She is the person whom it loves with egoistic primary love and to whom it becomes attached. She is the person who first imposes on it the demands of reality. Internally she is also important. The infant comes to define itself as a person through its relationship to her, by internalizing the most important aspects of their relationship. Its stance toward itself and the world—its emotions, its quality of self-love (narcissism), or self-hate (depression)—all derive in the first instance from this earliest relationship.

In later life a person's early relation to her or his mother leads to a preoccupation with issues of primary intimacy and merging. On one psychological level, all people who have experienced primary love and primary identification have some aspect of self that wants to recreate these experiences, and most people try to do so. Freud talks about the turn to religion as an attempt to recreate the lost feeling of oneness. Michael Balint suggests that adult love relationships are an attempt to recreate primary intimacy and merging, and that the "tranquil sense of well-being" is their ultimate goal: "This primary tendency, I shall be loved always, everywhere, in every way, my whole body, my whole being—without any criticism, without the slightest effort on my part—is the final aim of all erotic striving."

The preoccupation with issues of intimacy and merging, however, can also lead to avoidance. Fear of fusion may overwhelm the attraction to it, and fear of loss of a love object may make the experience of love too risky. When a person's early experience tells him or her that only one unique person can provide emotional gratifications—a realistic expectation when they have been intensely and exclusively mothered—the desire to recreate that experience has to be ambivalent . . .

Children wish to remain one with their mother, and expect that she will never have different interests from them; yet they define development in terms of growing away from her. In the face of their dependence, lack of certainty of her emotional permanence, fear of merging, and overwhelming love and attachment, a mother looms large and powerful. Several analytic formulations speak to this, and to the way growing children come to experience their mothers. Mothers, they suggest, come to symbolize dependence, regression, passivity, and the lack of adaptation to reality. Turning from mother (and father) represents independence and individuation, progress, activity, and participation in the real world: "It is by turning away from our mother that we finally become, by our different paths, grown men and women."

These attitudes, and the different relations to mother and father, are generalized as people grow up. During most of the early period, gender is not salient to the child (nor does it know gender categories). However, the fact that the child's earliest relationship is with a woman becomes exceedingly important for the object-relations of subsequent developmental periods; that women mother and men do not is projected back by the child *after* gender comes to count. Women's early mothering, then, creates specific conscious and unconscious attitudes or expectations in children. Girls and boys expect and assume women's unique capacities for sacrifice, caring, and mothering, and associate women with their own fears of regression and powerlessness. They fantasize more about men, and associate them with idealized virtues and growth. . . .

GENDER DIFFERENCES IN THE PREOEDIPAL PERIOD

Family structure produces crucial differentiating experiences between the sexes in oedipal object-relations and in the way these are psychologically appropriated, internalized, and transformed. Mothers are and have been the child's primary caretaker, socializer, and inner object; fathers are secondary objects for boys and girls. My interpretation of the oedipus complex, from a perspective centered on object-relations, shows that these basic features of family structure entail varied modes of differentiation for the ego and its internalized object-relations and lead to the development of different relational capacities for girls and boys.

The feminine oedipus complex is not simply a transfer of affection from mother to father and a giving up of mother. Rather, psychoanalytic research demonstrates the continued importance of a girl's external and internal relation to her mother, and the way her relation to her father is added to this. This process entails a relational complexity in feminine self-definition and personality which is not characteristic of masculine self-definition or personality. Relational capacities that are curtailed in boys as a result of the masculine oedipus complex are sustained in girls.

Because of their mothering by women, girls come to experience themselves as less separate than boys, as having more permeable ego boundaries. Girls come to define themselves more in relation to others. Their internalized object-relational structure becomes more complex, with more ongoing issues. These personality features are reflected in superego development.

My investigation, then, does not focus on issues at the center of the traditional psychoanalytic account of the oedipus complex—superego formation, gender identity, the attainment of gender role expectations, differential valuations of the sexes, and the genesis of sexual orientation. It takes other issues as equally central. I will be concerned with traditional issues only insofar as my analysis of oedipal object-relations of boys and girls sheds new insight on the different nature of male and female heterosexual object-relations . . .

The clinical and cultural examples I have discussed all point to the conclusion that preoedipal experiences of girls and boys differ. The girl's preoedipal mother-love and preoccupation with preoedipal issues are prolonged in a way that they are not for the boy. With the exception of Whiting's cross-cultural analysis, all the examples I cite are cases which their authors

have taken to be noteworthy for their "abnormality" or "pathology." However, the extent of such pathology varies (from preoccupation to mild neurosis to psychosis). More important, there is systematic variation in the form it takes depending on whether a person is female or male—on whether we are talking about mother-daughter or mother-son relationships. In all cases the pathology reflects, in exaggerated form, differences in what are in fact normal tendencies. The cases give us, as Freud suggests about neurosis in general, insight into what we would otherwise miss just because it is subtle, typical, and familiar. These cases, then, point to typical gender differences in the preoedipal period, differences that are a product of the asymmetrical organization of parenting which founds our family structure.

Because they are the same gender as their daughters and have been girls, mothers of daughters tend not to experience these infant daughters as separate from them in the same way as do mothers of infant sons. In both cases, a mother is likely to experience a sense of oneness and continuity with her infant. However, this sense is stronger, and lasts longer, vis-à-vis daughters. Primary identification and symbiosis with daughters tend to be stronger and cathexis of daughters is more likely to retain and emphasize narcissistic elements, that is, to be based on experiencing a daughter as an extension or double of a mother herself, with cathexis of the daughter as a sexual other usually remaining a weaker, less significant theme.

Other accounts also suggest that mothers normally identify more with daughters and experience them as less separate. Signe Hammer's book, *Daughters and Mothers: Mothers and Daughters,* based on interviews with over seventy-five mothers, daughters, and grandmothers, describes how issues of primary identification, oneness, and separateness follow mother-daughter pairs from a daughter's earliest infancy until she is well into being a mother or even grandmother herself:

> Most of the daughters in this book have received enough support from their mothers to emerge from the stage of complete symbiosis in early infancy. But for the vast majority of mothers and daughters, this emergence remains only partial. At

some level mothers and daughters tend to remain emotionally bound up with each other in what might be called a semisymbiotic relationship, in which neither ever quite sees herself or the other as a separate person.

Hammer's study is certainly confirmed by my own discussions with a number of mothers of daughters and sons, first in a women's group devoted to the discussion and analysis of mother-daughter relationships in particular and family relationships in general, and later with individual acquaintances. Finally, the resurfacing and prevalence of preoedipal mother-daughter issues in adolescence (anxiety, intense and exclusive attachment, orality and food, maternal control of a daughter's body, primary identification) provide clinical verification of the claim that elements of the preoedipal mother-daughter relationship are maintained and prolonged in both maternal and filial psyche.

Because they are of different gender than their sons, by contrast, mothers experience their sons as a male opposite. Their cathexis of sons is more likely to consist from early on in an object cathexis of a sexual other, perhaps in addition to narcissistic components. Sons tend to be experienced as differentiated from their mothers, and mothers push this differentiation (even while retaining, in some cases, a kind of intrusive controlling power over their sons). Maternal behavior, at the same time, tends to help propel sons into a sexualized, genitally toned relationship, which in its turn draws the son into triangular conflicts.

Early psychoanalytic findings about the special importance of the preoedipal mother-daughter relationship describe the first stage of a general process in which separation and individuation remain particularly female developmental issues. The cases I describe suggest that there is a tendency in women toward boundary confusion and a lack of sense of separateness from the world. Most women do develop ego boundaries and a sense of separate self. However, women's ego and object-relational issues are concerned

with this tendency on one level (of potential conflict, of experience of object-relations), even as on another level (in the formation of ego boundaries and the development of a separate identity) the issues are resolved.

That these issues become more important for girls than for boys is a product of children of both genders growing up in families where women, who have a greater sense of sameness with daughters than sons, perform primary parenting functions.[i] As long as women mother, we can expect that a girl's preoedipal period will be longer than that of a boy and that women, more than men, will be more open to and preoccupied with those very relational issues that go into mothering—feelings of primary identification, lack of separateness or differentiation, ego and body-ego boundary issues and primary love not under the sway of the reality principle. A girl does not simply identify with her mother or want to be like her mother. Rather, mother and daughter maintain elements of their primary relationship which means they will feel alike in fundamental ways. Object-relations and conflicts in the oedipal period build upon this preoedipal base . . .

OBJECT RELATIONS AND THE FEMALE OEDIPAL CONFIGURATION

Mothering, Masculinity, and Capitalism

Women's mothering in the isolated nuclear family of contemporary capitalist society creates specific personality characteristics in men that reproduce both an ideology and psychodynamic of male superiority and submission to the requirements of production. It prepares men for participation in a male-dominant family and society, for their lesser emotional participation in family life, and for their participation in the capitalist world of work.

Masculine development takes place in a family in which women mother and fathers are relatively uninvolved in child care and family

---

[i] I must admit to fudging here about the contributory effect in all of this of a mother's sexual orientation—whether she is heterosexual or lesbian. Given a female gender identity, she is "the same as" her daughter and "different from" her son, but part of what I am talking about also presumes a different kind of cathexis of daughter and son deriving from heterosexuality. Nancy Chodorow, *The Reproduction of Mothering*. Berkeley: NC Press, 1978.

life, and in a society characterized by sexual inequality and an ideology of masculine superiority. This duality expresses itself in the family. In family ideology, fathers are usually important and considered the head of the household. Wives focus energy and concern on their husbands, or at least think and say that they do. They usually consider, or at least claim, that they love these husbands. Mothers may present fathers to children as someone important, someone whom the mother loves, and may even build up their husbands to their children to make up for the fact that these children cannot get to know their father as well as their mother. They may at the same time undercut their husband in response to the position he assumes of social superiority or authority in the family.

Masculinity is presented to a boy as less available and accessible than femininity, as represented by his mother. A boy's mother is his primary caretaker. At the same time, masculinity is idealized or accorded superiority, and thereby becomes even more desirable. Although fathers are not as salient as mothers in daily interaction, mothers and children often idealize them and give them ideological primacy, precisely because of their absence and seeming inaccessibility, and because of the organization and ideology of male dominance in the larger society.

Masculinity becomes an issue in a way that femininity does not. Masculinity does not become an issue because of some intrinsic male biology, nor because masculine roles are inherently more difficult than feminine roles, however. Masculinity becomes an issue as a direct result of a boy's experience of himself in his family—as a result of his being parented by a woman. For children of both genders, mothers represent regression and lack of autonomy. A boy associates these issues with his gender identification as well. Dependence on his mother, attachment to her, and identification with her represent that which is not masculine; a boy must reject dependence and deny attachment and identification. Masculine gender role training becomes much more rigid than feminine. A boy represses those qualities he takes to be feminine inside himself, and rejects and devalues women and whatever he considers to be feminine in the social world.

Thus, boys define and attempt to construct their sense of masculinity largely in negative terms. Given that masculinity is so elusive, it becomes important for masculine identity that certain social activities are defined as masculine and superior, and that women are believed unable to do many of the things defined as socially important. It becomes important to think that women's economic and social contribution cannot equal men's. The secure possession of certain realms, and the insistence that these realms are superior to the maternal world of youth, become crucial both to the definition of masculinity and to a particular boy's own masculine gender identification.

Freud describes the genesis of this stance in the masculine oedipal crisis. A boy's struggle to free himself from his mother and become masculine generates "the contempt felt by men for a sex which is the lesser"—"What we have come to consider the normal male contempt for women."

Both sexes learn to feel negatively toward their mother during the oedipal period. A girl's negative feelings, however, are not so much contempt and devaluation as fear and hostility: "The little girl, incapable of such contempt because of her own identical nature, frees herself from the mother with a degree of hostility far greater than any comparable hostility in the boy." A boy's contempt serves to free him not only from his mother but also from the femininity within himself. It therefore becomes entangled with the issue of masculinity and is generalized to all women. A girl's hostility remains tied more to her relationship to her mother (and/or becomes involved in self-depreciation).

A boy's oedipus complex is directly tied to issues of masculinity, and the devaluation of women is its "normal" outcome. A girl's devaluation of or hostility toward her mother may be a part of the process, but its "normal" outcome, by contrast, entails acceptance of her own femininity and identification with her mother. Whatever the individual resolution of the feminine oedipus complex, however, it does not become institutionalized in the same way.

Freud "explains" the development of boys' contempt for mothers as coming from their perception of genital differences, particularly their mother's "castration." He takes this perception to be unmediated by social experience, and not in need of explanation. As many commentators have pointed out, it did not occur to Freud that such differential valuation and ensuing contempt were not in the natural order of things. However, the analysis of "Little Hans," which provides the most direct (reported) evidence that Freud had for such an assumption, shows that in fact Hans's father perpetuated and created such beliefs in his son—beliefs about the inferiority of female genitalia, denial of the feminine role in gestation and parturition, views that men have something and women have nothing, rather than having something different.

Karen Horney, unlike Freud, does take masculine contempt for and devaluation of women as in need of interactive and developmental explanation. According to her, these phenomena are manifestations of a deeper "dread of women"—a masculine fear and terror of maternal omnipotence that arises as one major consequence of their early caretaking and socialization by women. Psychoanalysts previously had stressed boys' fears of their fathers. Horney argues that these fears are less severe and therefore less in need of being repressed. Unlike their fears of a mother, boys do not react to a father's total and incomprehensible control over his child's life at a time when the child has no reflective capacities for understanding: "Dread of the father is more actual and tangible, less uncanny in quality." Moreover, since their father is male like them, boys' fears of men do not entail admission of feminine weakness or dependency on women: "Masculine self-regard suffers less in this way."

Dread of the mother is ambivalent, however. Although a boy fears her, he also finds her seductive and attractive. He cannot simply dismiss and ignore her. Boys and men develop psychological and cultural/ideological mechanisms to cope with their fears without giving up women altogether. They create folk legends, beliefs, and poems that ward off the dread by externalizing and objectifying women: "It is not . . . that I dread her; it is that she herself is malignant, capable of any crime, a beast of prey, a vampire, a witch, insatiable in her desires . . . the very personification of what is sinister." They deny dread at the expense of realistic views of women. On the one hand, they glorify and adore: "There is no need for me to dread a being so wonderful, so beautiful, nay, so saintly." On the other, they disparage: "It would be too ridiculous to dread a creature who, if you take her all round, is such a poor thing." . . .

PSYCHODYNAMICS OF THE FAMILY

Gender Personality and the Reproduction of Mothering

In spite of the apparently close tie between women's capacities for childbearing and lactation on the one hand and their responsibilities for child care on the other, and in spite of the probable prehistoric convenience (and perhaps survival necessity) of a sexual division of labor in which women mothered, biology and instinct do not provide adequate explanations for how women come to mother. Women's mothering as a feature of social structure requires an explanation in terms of social structure. Conventional feminist and social psychological explanations for the genesis of gender roles—girls and boys are "taught" appropriate behaviors and "learn" appropriate feelings—are insufficient both empirically and methodologically to account for how women become mothers.

Methodologically, socialization theories rely inappropriately on individual intention. Ongoing social structures include the means for their own reproduction—in the regularized repetition of social processes, in the perpetuation of conditions which require members' participation, in the genesis of legitimating ideologies and institutions, and in the psychological as well as physical reproduction of people to perform necessary roles. Accounts of socialization help to explain the perpetuation of ideologies about gender roles. However, notions of appropriate behavior, like coercion, cannot in themselves produce parenting. Psychological capacities and a particular object-relational stance are central and definitional to parenting in a way that they are not to many other roles and activities.

Women's mothering includes the capacities for its own reproduction. This reproduction consists in the production of women with, and men without, the particular psychological capacities and stance which go into primary parenting.

Psychoanalytic theory provides us with a theory of social reproduction that explains major features of personality development and the development of psychic structure, and the differential development of gender personality in particular. Psychoanalysts argue that personality both results from and consists in the ways a child appropriates, internalizes, and organizes early experiences in their family—from the fantasies they have, the defenses they use, the ways they channel and redirect drives in this object-relational context. A person subsequently imposes this intrapsychic structure, and the fantasies, defenses, and relational modes and preoccupations which go with it, onto external social situations. This reexternalization (or mutual reexternalization) is a major constituting feature of social and interpersonal situations themselves.

Psychoanalysis, however, has not had an adequate theory of the reproduction of mothering. Because of the teleological assumption that anatomy is destiny, and that women's destiny includes primary parenting, the ontogenesis of women's mothering has been largely ignored, even while the genesis of a wide variety of related disturbances and problems has been accorded widespread clinical attention. Most psychoanalysts agree that the basis for parenting is laid for both genders in the early relationship to a primary caretaker. Beyond that, in order to explain why *women* mother, they tend to rely on vague notions of a girl's subsequent identification with her mother, which makes her and not her brother a primary parent, or on an unspecified and uninvestigated innate femaleness in girls, or on logical leaps from lactation or early vaginal sensations to caretaking abilities and commitments.

The psychoanalytic account of male and female development, when reinterpreted, gives us a developmental theory of the reproduction of women's mothering. Women's mothering reproduces itself through differing object-relational experiences and differing psychic outcomes in women and men. As a result of having been parented by a woman, women are more likely than men to seek to be mothers, that is, to relocate themselves in a primary mother-child relationship, to get gratification from the mothering relationship, and to have psychological and relational capacities for mothering.

The early relation to a primary caretaker provides in children of both genders both the basic capacity to participate in a relationship with the features of the early parent-child one, and the desire to create this intimacy. However, because women mother, the early experience and preoedipal relationship differ for boys and girls. Girls retain more concern with early childhood issues in relation to their mother, and a sense of self involved with these issues. Their attachments therefore retain more preoedipal aspects. The greater length and different nature of their preoedipal experience, and their continuing preoccupation with the issues of this period, mean that women's sense of self is continuous with others and that they retain capacities for primary identification, both of which enable them to experience the empathy and lack of reality sense needed by a cared-for infant. In men, these qualities have been curtailed, both because they are early treated as an opposite by their mother and because their later attachment to her must be repressed. The relational basis for mothering is thus extended in women, and inhibited in men, who experience themselves as more separate and distinct from others.

The different structure of the feminine and masculine oedipal triangle and process of oedipal experience that results from women's mothering contributes further to gender personality differentiation and the reproduction of women's mothering. As a result of this experience, women's inner object world, and the affects and issues associated with it, are more actively sustained and more complex than men's. This means that women define and experience themselves relationally. Their heterosexual orientation is always in internal dialogue with both oedipal and preoedipal mother-child relational issues. Thus, women's heterosexuality is triangular and requires a third person—a child—for its structural and emotional completion. For men, by contrast, the heterosexual relationship alone recreates the early bond to their mother; a child interrupts it. Men, moreover, do not define themselves in relationship and have come to suppress relational capacities and repress relational needs. This prepares them to participate in the affect-denying world of alienated work, but not to fulfill women's needs for intimacy and primary relationships.

The oedipus complex, as it emerges from the asymmetrical organization of parenting, secures a psychological taboo on parent-child incest and pushes boys and girls in the direction of extra-familial heterosexual relationships. This is one step toward the reproduction of parenting. The creation and maintenance of the incest taboo and of heterosexuality in girls and boys are different, however. For boys, superego formation and identification with their father, rewarded by the superiority of masculinity, maintain the taboo on incest with their mother, while heterosexual orientation continues from their earliest love relation with her. For girls, creating them as heterosexual in the first place maintains the taboo. However, women's heterosexuality is not so exclusive as men's. This makes it easier for them to accept or seek a male substitute for their fathers. At the same time, in a male-dominant society, women's exclusive emotional heterosexuality is not so necessary, nor is her repression of love for her father. Men are more likely to initiate relationships, and women's economic dependence on men pushes them anyway into heterosexual marriage.

Male dominance in heterosexual couples and marriage solves the problem of women's lack of heterosexual commitment and lack of satisfaction by making women more reactive in the sexual bonding process. At the same time, contradictions in heterosexuality help to perpetuate families and parenting by ensuring that women will seek relations to children and will not find heterosexual relationships alone satisfactory. Thus, men's lack of emotional availability and women's less exclusive heterosexual commitment help ensure women's mothering.

Women's mothering, then, produces psychological self-definition and capacities appropriate to mothering in women, and curtails and inhibits these capacities and this self-definition in men. The early experience of being cared for by a woman produces a fundamental structure of expectations in women and men concerning mothers' lack of separate interests from their infants and total concern for their infants' welfare. Daughters grow up identifying with these mothers, about whom they have such expectations. This set of expectations is generalized to the assumption that women naturally take care of children of all ages and the belief that women's "maternal" qualities can and should be extended to the nonmothering work that they do. All these results of women's mothering have ensured that women will mother infants and will take continuing responsibility for children.

The reproduction of women's mothering is the basis for the reproduction of women's location and responsibilities in the domestic sphere. This mothering, and its generalization to women's structural location in the domestic sphere, links the contemporary social organization of gender and social organization of production and contributes to the reproduction of each. That women mother is a fundamental organizational feature of the sex-gender system: It is basic to the sexual division of labor and generates a psychology and ideology of male dominance as well as an ideology about women's capacities and nature. Women, as wives and mothers, contribute as well to the daily and generational reproduction, both physical and psychological, of male workers and thus to the reproduction of capitalist production.

Women's mothering also reproduces the family as it is constituted in male-dominant society. The sexual and familial division of labor in which women mother creates a sexual division of psychic organization and orientation. It produces socially gendered women and men who enter into asymmetrical heterosexual relationships; it produces men who react to, fear, and act superior to women, and who put most of their energies into the nonfamilial work world and do not parent. Finally, it produces women who turn their energies toward nurturing and caring for children—in turn reproducing the sexual and familial division of labor in which women mother.

Social reproduction is thus asymmetrical. Women in their domestic role reproduce men and children physically, psychologically, and emotionally. Women in their domestic role as houseworkers reconstitute themselves physically on a daily basis and reproduce themselves as mothers, emotionally and psychologically, in the next generation. They thus contribute to the perpetuation of their own social roles and position in the hierarchy of gender.

Institutionalized features of family structure and the social relations of reproduction reproduce themselves. A psychoanalytic investigation shows that women's mothering capacities and commitments, and the general psychological capacities and wants which are the basis of women's emotion work, are built developmentally into feminine personality. Because women are themselves mothered by women, they grow up with the relational capacities and needs, and

psychological definition of self-in-relationship, which commits them to mothering. Men, because they are mothered by women, do not. Women mother daughters who, when they become women, mother.

❖

JUDITH BUTLER (1957–): A BIOGRAPHICAL SKETCH

Judith Butler was born in 1956. She received her B.A. in philosophy from Bennington College in 1978 and her Ph.D. in philosophy from Yale University in 1984. Butler has taught at Wesleyan and Johns Hopkins Universities and is currently professor of rhetoric and comparative literature at the University of California at Berkeley. Butler's books include *Subjects of Desire* (1987), *Gender Trouble: Feminism and the Subversion of Identity* (1989), *Bodies That Matter: On the Discursive Limits of "Sex"* (1993), and *Excitable Speech: Politics of the Performance* (1997), which analyzes name-calling as both a social injury and the way in which individuals are called into action for political purposes.

Reprinted with permission.

INTELLECTUAL INFLUENCES AND CORE IDEAS

Whereas feminists committed to modern ideas about gender ask the question "And what about women?" postmodern feminists, such as Judith Butler, ask "And what do you *mean* by 'women'?" Butler (1990:145–7) rejects the very idea that "women" can be understood as a concrete category at all, construing gender identity instead as an unstable "fiction." She criticizes modern feminists for remaining within the confines of traditional binary categories that in her view necessarily perpetuate sexism. In keeping with Foucault (see Chapter 8), Butler provides a "critical genealogy of gender categories in . . . different discursive domains" (1999/1990:xxx). In short, while modern feminists had in separating (biologically determined) "sex" from (socially constructed) "gender" helped rupture the idea of a stable or essential self, Butler takes this rupture to an extreme by upending the alleged "biological" dimensions of sexuality. Far from seeing "desire" as a biological given, Butler (1990:70) maintains that "which pleasures shall live and which shall die is often a matter of which serve the legitimating practices of identity formation that take place within the matrix of gender norms."

Specifically, Butler conceptualizes gendered subjectivity as a fluid identity and contends that the individual subject is never exclusively "male" or "female" but rather, is always in a state of contextually dependent flux. That is, gendered subjectivity is not something "fixed" or "essential," but a continual performance. Gender is not "a singular act, but a representation and a ritual" (1999:xv). Consequently, Butler (1993) seeks to explain the conditions of performances; that is, she seeks to explain "the practice by which gendering occurs," for the embodying of norms is "a compulsory practice, a forcible production," repeated, although "not fully determining."

Indeed, it is the sustained, continual nature of gender performance that compels Butler to use the term **performativity** rather than "performance." Performativity contests the very notion of a subject. Whereas the noun "performance" implies distinct, concrete, finished events, the term "performativity" reflects "culturally sustained temporal duration." As Butler (1999:xv) states:

> The view that gender is performative show[s] that what we take to be an internal essence of gender is manufactured through a sustained set of acts, posited through the gendered stylization of the body. In this way, it show[s] that what we take to be a in "internal" feature of ourselves is one that we anticipate and produce through certain bodily acts, at an extreme, an hallucinatory effect of naturalized gestures.

So, too, the "culturally sustained" (rather than essentialist) nature of gender performances is evident in Butler's discussion of performative *acts,* which she conceptualizes as "forms of authoritative speech . . . [or] statements that, "*in uttering* . . . exercise a binding power" (1993:224; emphasis added); as Butler maintains:

> Implicated in a network of authorization and punishment, performatives tend to include legal sentences, baptisms, inaugurations, declarations of ownership, statements which not only perform an action, but confer a binding power on the action performed. If the power of discourse to produce that which it names is linked with the question of performativity, then the performative is one domain in which power acts *as* discourse. (1993:224; emphasis added)

In other words, for Butler, "what we take to be an internal essence of gender is manufactured through a sustained set of acts, posited through the gendered stylization of the body" (ibid.:xv). "Gender is a kind of persistent impersonation that passes as the real" (ibid.:xxviii). Just as in Kafka's "Before the Law," where one sits before the door of the law awaiting that authority to be distributed, so, too, gender is "an expectation that ends up producing the very phenomenon that it anticipates" (1999:xiv).

This brings us to the issue of **queer theory.** In addition to being a leading feminist theorist, Butler is one of the most important figures in queer theory. Queer theory emerged from gay/lesbian studies (which emerged from gender studies) in the 1980s. Up until the 1980s, the term "queer" had a derogatory connotation, meaning "odd" or "peculiar" or "out of the ordinary." However, queer theorists, including Butler, appropriated this term, insisting that all sexual behaviors, all concepts linking sexual behaviors to sexual identities, and all categories of normative and deviant sexualities are social constructs, which create certain types of social meaning. In short, "sex is a norm" (Osborne and Segel, Interview with Judith Butler, http://www.theory.org.uk/but-int1.htm).

Thus, the undergirding emphasis in all these projects (gay/lesbian, queer, feminist) is that the categories of normative and deviant sexual behavior are not biologically but rather socially constructed. In contrast to those who see sexuality as biological and gender as a social construction, Butler sees sex as no more a natural category than gender. She conceptualizes gender norms as structuring biology and not the reverse, which informs the more conventional view.

Butler does not deny certain kinds of biological differences, but she seeks to explain under what discursive and institutional conditions do certain arbitrary biological differences become salient characteristics of sex (ibid.). She emphasizes that sexuality is a complex array of individual activity and institutional power, of social codes and forces, which interact to shape the ideas of what is normative and what is deviant at any particular moment, and which then result in categories as to "natural," "essential," "biological," or "god-given." She seeks to show how a norm can actually materialize a

Photo 7.8 Harris Glenn Milstead (1945–1988), better known by his drag persona, Divine, who starred in several of John Waters's films, including *Hairspray,* exemplifies performativity.

SOURCE: © Getty Images; used with permission.

body, that is, how the body is not only invested with a norm but in some sense animated by a norm or contoured by a norm (ibid.).

Specifically, Butler describes a **heterosexual matrix** in which "proper men" and "proper women" are identified as heterosexual. She shows that the essential unity between biological sex, gender identification, and heterosexuality is not dictated by nature; indeed, this unity is an illusion mediated through cultural systems of meaning that underlie our understanding of material, anatomical differences. According to Butler, heterosexual normativity "ought *not* to order gender" (1999/1990:xiv; emphasis in original). The subversion of gender performances (e.g., drag performances) indicates nothing about sexuality or sexual practice. "Gender can be rendered ambiguous without disturbing or reorientating normative sexuality at all" (ibid.).

Thus, for instance, Butler points out that discrimination against gays is a function not of their sexuality but of their failure to perform heterosexual gender norms. Because heterosexuality is based on a binary difference between male and female (a person is either one or the other), there is a socially constructed gender in which heterosexuality is central, which informs our understanding of biology.

Interestingly, then, akin to Harold Garfinkel's "breaching" experiments, which exposed taken-for-granted normative expectations (see Chapter 6), cross-dressing, "kiss-ins," gender parodies, and so on can be used to transgress and rebel against existing sexual categories. In short, queer politics seeks to explicitly challenge gender norms to show their lack of naturalness and inevitability and to celebrate transgressions from them (Alsop, Fitzsimons, and Lennon 2002:96), while postmodern queer theorists seek to upend and "resignify" our gender expectations.

Figure 7.5   Butler's Basic Theoretical Orientation

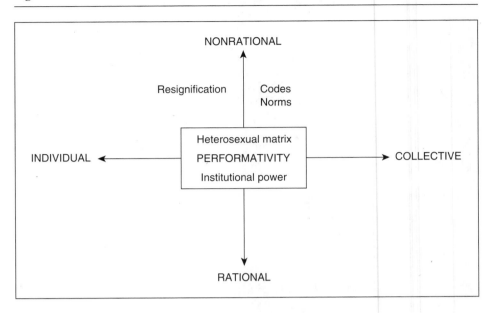

BUTLER'S THEORETICAL ORIENTATION

As will be discussed further in the next chapter, postmodernists tend to eschew meta-theoretical frameworks as "essentializing." However, it is difficult not to see postmodernists, including Butler, as nonrationalistic in their approach to action. That "there is no reality" anymore (only "hyperreality"—Baudrillard—see Chapter 8); that sex is not a "natural" category but constituted through social discourse; that performances create subjectivities (see Butler, above) seems a profoundly nonrationalistic orientation to action. In contrast to Goffman, who, as we have seen (see Chapter 5), also at times used the term "performance" in a more rationalistic way (wittingly constructed, via calculation and even rehearsal), Butler argues that we become subjects *from* our performances. Subjectivity is a process of submitting ourselves to socially constituted norms and practices (Alsop, Fitzsimons, and Lennon 2002:98). This speaks to the nonrational realm.

In terms of order, on one hand postmodernists such as Butler emphasize the role of structured "scripts," discourses, and preexisting symbolic patterns that reflect a collective orientation. In addition, Butler exudes a neo-Marxist emphasis on hierarchical (class, gender, racial) structures, oppression, and corporate control, which also speaks to the collective realm (see Chapter 3). She shows how gender performances are tied to relations of ruling, in Smith's terms. On the other hand, however, like Foucault (see Chapter 8), Butler insists that regulatory norms and discourses are never wholly determining. One could argue that in the end, Butler's work seems individualistic because she emphasizes that it is in interaction that subjectivities are formed. Moreover, in contrast to cultural Marxists (e.g., the Frankfurt School), Butler optimistically asserts that because of the multiplicity of symbols that cannot all be obeyed coherently, we can "reconfigure" and "redeploy" symbols. However, again it must be emphasized that Butler would undoubtedly chafe at this label. First, because Butler goes to great lengths to show that performances are never isolated acts, but occur only *within* specific discursive contexts, and second, because she would chafe at any sort of metatheoretical label at all. The whole point of postmodernism is to do away with this kind of academic theoretical scaffolding. In keeping with the spirit of Butler, then, we place the notion of "performativity" at the center of our theoretical map, thereby indicating its fluid, multidimensional nature, while nevertheless acknowledging its nonrational bent.

Reading

Introduction to "Subjects of Sex/Gender/Desire"

The following excerpt is from Butler's most widely read and celebrated book, *Gender Trouble* (1990), which has sold more than 100,000 copies. Here you will see Butler challenge the presumed universality and unity of the concept of "woman" in feminist theory and, drawing on Foucault, dispute the predominant binary opposition of sex as a "biological" and gender as a "cultural" category.

Subjects of Sex/Gender/Desire (1990)

Judith Butler

One is not born a woman, but rather becomes one.

— Simone de Beauvoir

Strictly speaking, "women" cannot be said to exist.

— Julia Kristeva

Woman does not have a sex.

— Luce Irigaray

The deployment of sexuality . . . established this notion of sex.

— Michel Foucault

The category of sex is the political category that founds society as heterosexual.

— Monique Wittig

I. "Women" as the Subject of Feminism

For the most part, feminist theory has assumed that there is some existing identity, understood through the category of women, who not only initiates feminist interests and goals within discourse, but constitutes the subject for whom political representation is pursued. But *politics* and *representation* are controversial terms. On the one hand, *representation* serves as the operative term within a political process that seeks to extend visibility and legitimacy to women as political subjects; on the other hand, representation is the normative function of a language which is said either to reveal or to distort what is assumed to be true about the category of women. For feminist theory, the development of a language that fully or adequately represents women has seemed necessary to foster the political visibility of women. This has seemed obviously important considering the pervasive cultural condition in which women's lives were either misrepresented or not represented at all.

Recently, this prevailing conception of the relation between feminist theory and politics has come under challenge from within feminist discourse. The very subject of women is no longer understood in stable or abiding terms. There is a great deal of material that not only questions the viability of "the subject" as the ultimate candidate for representation or, indeed, liberation, but there is very little agreement after all on what it is that constitutes, or ought to constitute, the category of women. The domains of political and linguistic "representation" set out in advance the criterion by which subjects themselves are formed, with the result that representation is extended only to what can be acknowledged as a subject. In other words, the qualifications for being a subject must first be met before representation can be extended.

Foucault points out that juridical systems of power *produce* the subjects they subsequently come to represent. Juridical notions of power appear to regulate political life in purely negative terms—that is, through the limitation, prohibition, regulation, control, and even "protection" of individuals related to that political structure through the contingent and retractable operation of choice. But the subjects regulated by such structures are, by virtue of being subjected to them, formed, defined, and reproduced in accordance with the requirements of those structures. If this analysis is right, then the juridical formation of language and politics that represents women as "the subject" of feminism is itself a discursive formation and effect of a given version of representational politics. And the feminist subject turns out to be discursively constituted by the very political system that is supposed to facilitate its emancipation. This becomes politically problematic if that system can be shown to produce gendered subjects along a differential axis of domination or to produce subjects who are presumed to be masculine. In such cases, an uncritical appeal to such a system for the emancipation of "women" will be clearly self-defeating.

The question of "the subject" is crucial for politics, and for feminist politics in particular, because juridical subjects are invariably produced through certain exclusionary practices that do not "show" once the juridical structure of politics has been established. In other words, the political construction of the subject proceeds with certain legitimating and exclusionary aims, and these political operations are effectively concealed and naturalized by a political analysis that takes juridical structures as their foundation. Juridical power inevitably "produces" what it claims merely to represent; hence, politics must be concerned with this dual function of power: the juridical and the productive. In effect, the law produces and then conceals the notion of "a subject before the law" in order to invoke that discursive formation as a naturalized foundational premise that subsequently legitimates that law's own regulatory hegemony. It is not enough to inquire into how women might become more fully represented in language and politics. Feminist critique ought also to understand how the category of "women," the subject of feminism, is produced and restrained by the very structures of power through which emancipation is sought.

Indeed, the question of women as the subject of feminism raises the possibility that there may not be a subject who stands "before" the law, awaiting representation in or by the law. Perhaps the subject, as well as the invocation of a temporal "before," is constituted by the law as the fictive foundation of its own claim to legitimacy. The prevailing assumption of the ontological integrity of the subject before the law might be understood as the contemporary trace of the state of nature hypothesis, that foundationalist fable constitutive of the juridical structures of classical liberalism. The performative invocation of a nonhistorical "before" becomes the foundational premise that guarantees a presocial ontology of persons who freely consent to be governed and, thereby, constitute the legitimacy of the social contract.

Apart from the foundationalist fictions that support the notion of the subject, however, there is the political problem that feminism encounters in the assumption that the term *women* denotes a common identity. Rather than a stable signifier that commands the assent of those whom it purports to describe and represent, *women*, even in the plural, has become a troublesome term, a site of contest, a cause for anxiety. As Denise Riley's title suggests, *Am I That Name?* is a question produced by the very possibility of the name's multiple significations. If one "is" a woman, that is surely not all one is; the term fails to be exhaustive, not because a pregendered "person" transcends the specific paraphernalia of its gender, but because gender is not always constituted coherently or consistently in different historical contexts, and because gender intersects with racial, class, ethnic, sexual, and regional modalities of discursively constituted identities. As a result, it becomes impossible to separate out "gender" from the political and cultural intersections in which it is invariably produced and maintained.

The political assumption that there must be a universal basis for feminism, one which must be found in an identity assumed to exist cross-culturally, often accompanies the notion that the oppression of women has some singular form discernible in the universal or hegemonic structure of patriarchy or masculine domination. The notion of a universal patriarchy has been widely criticized in recent years for its failure to account for the workings of gender oppression in the concrete cultural contexts in which it exists. Where those various contexts have been consulted within such theories, it has been to find "examples" or "illustrations" of a universal principle that is assumed from the start. The form of feminist theorizing has come under criticism for its efforts to colonize and appropriate non-Western cultures to support highly Western notions of oppression, but because they tend as well to construct a "Third World" or even an "Orient" in which gender oppression is subtly explained as symptomatic of an essential, non-Western barbarism. The urgency of feminism to establish a universal status for patriarchy in order to strengthen the appearance of feminism's own claims to be representative has occasionally motivated the shortcut to a categorial or fictive universality of the structure of domination, held to produce women's common subjugated experience.

Although the claim of universal patriarchy no longer enjoys the kind of credibility it once did, the notion of a generally shared conception of "women," the corollary to that framework, has been much more difficult to displace. Certainly, there have been plenty of debates: Is there some commonality among "women" that preexists their oppression, or do "women" have a bond by virtue of their oppression alone? Is there a

specificity to women's cultures that is independent of their sub-ordination by hegemonic, masculinist cultures? Are the specificity and integrity of women's cultural or linguistic practices always specified against and, hence, within the terms of some more dominant cultural formation? Is there is a region of the "specifically feminine," one that is both differentiated from the masculine as such and recognizable in its difference by an unmarked and, hence, presumed universality of "women"? The masculine/feminine binary constitutes not only the exclusive framework in which that specificity can be recognized, but in every other way the "specificity" of the feminine is once again fully decontextualized and separated off analytically and politically from the constitution of class, race, ethnicity, and other axes of power relations that both constitute "identity" and make the singular notion of identity a misnomer.

My suggestion is that the presumed universality and unity of the subject of feminism is effectively undermined by the constraints of the representational discourse in which it functions. Indeed, the premature insistence on a stable subject of feminism, understood as a seamless category of women, inevitably generates multiple refusals to accept the category. These domains of exclusion reveal the coercive and regulatory consequences of that construction, even when the construction has been elaborated for emancipatory purposes. Indeed, the fragmentation within feminism and the paradoxical opposition to feminism from "women" whom feminism claims to represent suggest the necessary limits of identity politics. The suggestion that feminism can seek wider representation for a subject that it itself constructs has the ironic consequence that feminist goals risk failure by refusing to take account of the constitutive powers of their own representational claims. This problem is not ameliorated through an appeal to the category of women for merely "strategic" purposes, for strategies always have meanings that exceed the purposes for which they are intended. In this case, exclusion itself might qualify as such an unintended yet consequential meaning. By conforming to a requirement of representational politics that feminism articulate a stable subject, feminism thus opens itself to charges of gross misrepresentation.

Obviously, the political task is not to refuse representational politics—as if we could. The juridical structures of language and politics constitute the contemporary field of power; hence, there is no position outside this field, but only a critical genealogy of its own legitimating practices. As such, the critical point of departure is *the historical present*, as Marx put it. And the task is to formulate within this constituted frame a critique of the categories of identity that contemporary juridical structures engender, naturalize, and immobilize.

Perhaps there is an opportunity at this juncture of cultural politics, a period that some would call "postfeminist," to reflect from within a feminist perspective on the injunction to construct a subject to feminism. Within feminist political practice, a radical rethinking of the ontological constructions of identity appears to be necessary in order to formulate a representational politics that might revive feminism on other grounds. On the other hand, it may be time to entertain a radical critique that seeks to free feminist theory from the necessity of having to construct a single or abiding ground which is invariably contested by those identity positions or anti-identity positions that it invariably excludes. Do the exclusionary practices that ground feminist theory in a notion of "women" as subject paradoxically undercut feminist goals to extend its claims to "representation"?

Perhaps the problem is even more serious. Is the construction of the category of women as a coherent and stable subject an unwitting regulation and reification of gender relations? And is not such a reification precisely contrary to feminist aims? To what extent does the category of women achieve stability and coherence only in the context of the heterosexual matrix? If a stable notion of gender no longer proves to be the foundational premise of feminist politics, perhaps a new sort of feminist politics is now desirable to contest the very reifications of gender and identity, one that will take the variable construction of identity as both a methodological and normative prerequisite, if not a political goal.

To trace the political operations that produce and conceal what qualifies as the juridical subject of feminism is precisely the task of *a feminist genealogy* of the category of women. In the course of this effort to question "women" as the subject of feminism, the unproblematic invocation of that category may prove to *preclude* the possibility of feminism as a representational politics. What sense does it make to extend representation to subjects who are constructed through the exclusion of those who fail to conform to unspoken normative requirements of the subject? What relations of domination and exclusion are inadvertently sustained when representation becomes the sole focus of politics? The identity of the feminist subject ought not to be foundation of feminist politics, if the formation of the subject takes place within a field of power regularly buried through the assertion of that foundation. Perhaps, paradoxically, "representation" will be shown to make sense for feminism only when the subject of "women" is nowhere presumed.

II. The Compulsory Order of Sex/Gender/Desire

Although the unproblematic unity of "women" is often invoked to construct a solidarity of identity, a split is introduced in the feminist subject by the distinction between sex and gender. Originally intended to dispute the biology-is-destiny formulation, the distinction between sex and gender serves the argument that whatever biological intractability sex appears to have, gender is culturally constructed: hence, gender is neither the causal result of sex nor as seemingly fixed as sex. The unity of the subject is thus already potentially contested by the distinction the permits of gender as a multiple interpretation of sex.

If gender is the cultural meanings that the sexed body assumes, then a gender cannot be said to follow from a sex in any one way. Taken to its logical limit, the sex/gender distinction suggests a radical discontinuity between sexed bodies and culturally constructed genders. Assuming for the moment the stability of binary sex, it does not follow that the construction of "men" will accrue exclusively to the bodies of males or that "women" will interpret only female bodies. Further, even if the sexes appear to be unproblematically binary in their morphology and constitution (which will become a question), there is no reason to assume that genders ought also to remain as two. The presumption of a binary gender system implicitly retains the belief in a mimetic relation of gender to sex whereby gender mirrors sex or is otherwise restricted by it. When the constructed status of gender is theorized as radically independent of sex, gender itself becomes a free-floating artifice, with the consequence that *man* and *masculine* might just as easily signify a female body as a male one, and *woman* and *feminine* a male body as easily as a female one.

This radical splitting of the gendered subject poses yet another set of problems. Can we refer to a "given" sex or a "given" gender without first inquiring into how sex and/or gender is given, through what means? And what is "sex" anyway? Is it natural, anatomical, chromosomal, or hormonal, and how is a feminist critic to assess the scientific discourses which purport to establish such "facts" for us? Does sex have a history? Does each sex have a different history, or histories? Is there a history of how the duality of sex was established, a genealogy that might expose the binary options as a variable construction? Are the ostensibly natural facts of sex discursively produced by various scientific discourses in the service of other political and social interests? If the immutable character of sex is contested, perhaps this construct called "sex" is as culturally constructed as gender; indeed, perhaps it was always already gender, with the consequence that the distinction between sex and gender turns out to be no distinction at all.

It would make no sense, then, to define gender as the cultural interpretation of sex, if sex itself is a gendered category. Gender ought not to be conceived merely as the cultural inscription of meaning on a pregiven sex (a juridical conception); gender must also designate the very apparatus of production whereby the sexes themselves are established. As a result, gender is not to culture as sex is to nature; gender is also the discursive/cultural means by which "sexed nature" or "a natural sex" is produced and established as "prediscursive," prior to culture, a politically neutral surface *on which* culture acts. This construction of "sex" as the radically unconstructed will concern us again in the discussion of Lévi-Strauss and structuralism in chapter 2. At this juncture it is already clear that one way the internal stability and binary frame for sex is effectively secured is by casting the duality of sex in a prediscursive domain. This production of sex as the prediscursive ought to be understood as the effect of the apparatus of cultural construction designated by *gender*. How, then, does gender need to be reformulated to encompass the power relations that produce the effect of a prediscursive sex and so conceal that very operation of discursive production?

Discussion Questions

1. Smith (1987:64) states, "So as I walk down the street keeping an eye on my dog I am observing some of the niceties of different forms of property ownership." In what ways do you "do class" in your everyday life? In what ways do you "do gender"? How do your class and gender performances reaffirm forms of domination? To what extent do your gender performances reflect, reaffirm, and/or challenge normative heterosexuality or what Butler calls the heterosexual matrix?

2. According to Smith (1987:68), "The role of women is central both in the work that is done and in the management of its routine daily order . . . whatever the relations between school achievement, career success, and the 'intricate psychosocial processes' of the family, the conscious, planned thoughtful work of women as mothers has been part of its actuality." Discuss the extent to which "behind-the-scenes" women's work is still taken for granted in both schools and the workplace today. Do you think that this aspect of gender roles has changed in the last twenty years? How so or why not? Do you think full gender equality can be achieved? Why or why not?

3. According to Collins (1990:228), "A matrix of domination contains few pure victims or oppressors. Each individual derives varying amounts of penalty and privilege from the multiple systems of oppression which frame everyone's lives." Give concrete examples of moments or situations in which you have found yourself a "victim" and concrete examples of moments or situations in which you found yourself an "oppressor." Explain how your examples reflect the matrix of domination at the level of personal biography, the community, and the systemic level of social institutions.

4. Discuss the neo-Marxist or critical dimensions of Smith, Collins, Chodorow, and Butler. In addition to critical theory, what other traditions and concepts does each draw from to produce their own distinct perspective?

5. Compare and contrast Butler's conceptualization of "performativity" with Goffman's dramaturgical theory (Chapter 5).

8

POSTSTRUCTURAL AND POSTMODERN THEORIES

WITH DAVID BOYNS

Key Concepts

Michel Foucault

- ❖ Archaeology
- ❖ Discipline/Disciplinary Society
- ❖ Epistemes
- ❖ Genealogy
- ❖ Panopticon
- ❖ Power/Knowledge
- ❖ Sign
- ❖ Surveillance
- ❖ Metanarratives

Jean Baudrillard

- ❖ Hyperreality
- ❖ Simulation/Simulacrum

Jean-François Lyotard

- ❖ Mercantilization of Knowledge
- ❖ Computerization of Society

The judges of normality are present everywhere. We are in the society of the teacher-judge, the doctor-judge, the educator-judge, the "social worker" judge.

~Michel Foucault

Television knows no night. It is perpetual day. TV embodies our fear of the dark, of night, of the other side of things.

~Jean Baudrillard

379

Have you ever felt that you were being watched—imagined that unbeknownst to you, someone, somewhere was inspecting you, maybe through the lens of a camera or through some information tracking system, monitoring your purchases, collecting information on your "identity," measuring your rate of speed, observing your every move? Such is the alarming experience of computer programmer Thomas Anderson ("Neo"), the central character in the popular film *The Matrix*. Through a series of cryptic messages from a computer hacker named Trinity, Neo discovers that someone is monitoring his computer activities. As he learns more about this surveillance from Trinity, Neo's ordinary life begins to unravel. He finds that a group of mysterious "agents" have him under observation and that technologies of surveillance are being used to record and scrutinize his daily activities. Neo soon recognizes that these are just the beginning of his problems. Rescued from the agents by Trinity and a faction of rogue revolutionaries from the "real world," Neo discovers that the entirety of his life experiences has been false, that he has been "living" inside a simulated world generated by an elaborate computer program. All of his memories and relationships, loves and fears, have been delusions designed to keep him unaware of the reality of his virtual deception. Bewildered by these discoveries, Neo is forced to confront two overwhelming contemporary truths. First, he lives in a social world that is saturated with technologies of **surveillance** that monitor his daily activities. Second, the authenticity of his experiences is distorted by the existence of **simulations** of reality. "Simulation" means a model or reproduction, and in postmodernism simulation refers particularly to when an image or model becomes more "real" than "reality" itself.

While Neo's story is certainly the invention of science fiction, the film *The Matrix* and other films like it[1] bring into awareness some important changes in the contemporary social world. We are increasingly both the objects of surveillance and the inhabitants of a world permeated by simulations. Like Neo, our daily lives are increasingly monitored. We are watched by cameras in our workplaces and as we patronize shopping centers; our consumer activities are "recorded" to document our spending habits; we are monitored by police radar guns and photo-radar cameras as we drive our cars; our financial history is recorded and scrutinized. Such processes allow a great deal of information about us to be gathered; they allow our lives to be documented and recorded in very personal ways. Strangely, and perhaps frighteningly, we have no real idea who has access to this information, what they are doing with it, and exactly what is known about us. Also like Neo, we increasingly find that our daily experiences are fused with simulations. Think for a moment about what you know about the world in which you live, and more important, *how* you have come to know what you know. If we take an honest inventory of our knowledge about the world, many of us would discover that much of what we "know" we haven't directly experienced for ourselves. Instead, we "know" much of our world secondhand, through conversation, books, television, radio, newspaper, and the Internet. Reflect on all the people that you know of but have never actually met—celebrities, newscasters, political figures, athletes, cartoon characters, and pop stars; or consider to how many places—even fictional places—you have traveled only through photographs, film, and television. Increasingly, as the French postmodern theorist Jean Baudrillard argues, the social world we inhabit has become **hyperreal**, filled with simulations of reality that replace "reality" itself.

Neo's world is one of ubiquitous surveillance and simulation. The key poststructural and postmodern theorists profiled in this chapter—Michel Foucault, Jean Baudrillard, and Jean-François Lyotard—all develop these two central themes, exploring them as a dominant condition of the contemporary world. The ideas of these three writers have

---

[1]For instance, *Matrix 3*, *Existenz*, *The Thirteenth Floor*, *Blade Runner*, *The Truman Show*, *Edtv*, and *Donnie Darko*.

Photo 8.1   *The Matrix* exemplifies two critical features of the postmodern world: technological surveillance and simulation.

SOURCE: © Yuriko Nakao/Reuters/CORBIS.

become greatly influential in the development of poststructural and postmodern theories. As mentioned previously, Jean Baudrillard, who is one of the first and most important sociological theorists to be associated with postmodern theory, is particularly concerned about the issue of simulation. Michel Foucault, who is commonly identified as a chief progenitor of poststructuralist theory as well as one of the most influential intellectuals of the twentieth century, has written extensively on the issue of surveillance. Although Foucault died in 1984, his work still reverberates throughout many scholarly fields (e.g., history, philosophy, literary criticism, feminist studies, psychology, gay and lesbian studies, and sociology) and has become an important reference point for activists around the world. The final theorist whose works you will read in this chapter, Jean-François Lyotard, is a philosopher and self-conscious proponent of the postmodern position, whose writings span from philosophical and political treatises to critical discussions of art, literature, and aesthetics. Although his work covers a broad range of topics and disciplines, there is one central theme that tends to dominate Lyotard's work—the ability of "difference" to undermine established forms of knowledge. In place of an acceptance of established knowledge and conventional truth, Lyotard explores the limitations of knowledge and the margins of truth, analyzing the means by which knowledge collapses under multiple perspectives.

Before we turn to the specific ideas of Foucault, Baudrillard, and Lyotard, however, it is essential to define the two terms that frame this chapter: poststructuralism and postmodernism. Poststructuralism and postmodernism are among the most controversial and puzzling theories within sociology. These "post" theories radically oppose many of the established understandings of sociology and call for social thinkers to interpret the world in new, and often startling, ways. Indeed, they attack the ability of sociology to develop claims to the truth of social reality, as well as the very idea of the "social" upon which sociology is based. It should come as no surprise, then, that not all sociologists accept the legitimacy of poststructural and postmodern analysis. Many see these "post" theories as academic fads created by social theorists who have sought to carve new intellectual territory by making wild and exaggerated claims. Moreover, even among those who do recognize their validity, clear, consistent, and succinct definitions of poststructuralism and postmodernism are rarely offered. In fact, many of the theorists primarily identified with poststructuralism and postmodernism—including the theorists profiled in this chapter—never, or at least rarely, use the terms in their own work. Thus, before we go any further, it is essential to clarify these ambiguous and controversial terms.

DEFINING POSTSTRUCTURALISM

Poststructuralism is not so much a coherent theory as an assemblage of converging themes developed by theorists in the 1960s. These common themes (to be discussed shortly) include the fragmentation of meaning, the localization of politics, the decline of the idea of Truth, and the decentering of the subject. Put in another way, poststructuralism is better understood as a theoretical trend, as a loosely articulated set of ideas that find common expression in the works of influential French writers of the second-half of the 20th century.[2]

Poststructuralism is so named because it represents a challenge to the central European and American tradition of theory dominant in the mid-twentieth century—structuralism. Structuralist thought emphasizes that there are forces in social life that emerge out of human activity but stand outside of human agency or intervention. Often called "emergent properties," these social forces are the external and constraining "social facts" that the classical sociological theorist Émile Durkheim described in his work, and a similar structuralist emphasis is echoed in many of the works of other classical theorists in sociology, particularly Karl Marx and Max Weber. Indeed, it was by drawing from these classical sources that Talcott Parsons would crystallize his structural functionalist theory that dominated American sociology during the middle years of the twentieth century (see Chapter 2).

A different version of structuralism emerged during the mid-twentieth century in France.[3] French structuralism is most distinct from American structural functionalism in its particular emphasis on language. In contrast to Parsons's structural functionalism which emphasizes the patterns of human social organization, French structuralism focuses on meaning and the role of language in the organization of systems of ideas. French structuralists seek to demonstrate how language has formal properties (such as

---

[2]In addition to Foucault, whose work is profiled in this chapter, these writers include Roland Barthes, Jacques Derrida, Julia Kristeva, Jacques Lacan, Gilles Deleuze, and Felix Guattari. Interestingly, although most of the writers identified with poststructuralism are French, poststructuralism has its general origins in American traditions of literary criticism (Poster 1989:6). It is the way in which American literary scholars adopted and unified the ideas of French thinkers that created what is known today as poststructural theory. Ironically but not surprisingly, then, most of those French theorists who were canonized and identified as "poststructuralists" do not write under the label of "poststructuralism," and they do not identify themselves with poststructuralism as a theoretical movement.

[3]French structuralism emerged throughout a variety of disciplines and theoretical traditions, including the anthropology of Claude Lévi-Strauss, the Marxist sociology of Louis Althusser, the psychoanalytic psychology of Jacques Lacan, the literary criticism of Roland Barthes, and the linguistics of Ferdinand de Saussure.

grammar) that provide the structure not only for communication but also for broader aspects of human existence. For French structuralists, myths, kinship systems, religious rituals, advertising messages, fashion, class relationships, and the human psyche all have formal elements that can be understood through an analysis of the structures of meaning, especially those organized by the properties of language. That is, just as there are grammatical rules and linguistic structures in our native language that speakers follow without being cognizant of them, there is a rigid formula for virtually every aspect of social life that structures understanding, although social actors are not necessarily cognizant of its impact.

In most accounts, the story of French structuralism begins with Swiss linguist Ferdinand de Saussure's (1857–1913) development of what is today known as *semiotics*.[4] Semiotics is the study of signs, those aspects of human communication that are used to indicate and convey meaning. In *A Course in General Linguistics* (1966), Saussure develops his theory by making a key distinction between the formal structure of language (*langue*) and the everyday use of speech (*parole*). For Saussure, *langue* is the structural dimension of language that is institutionalized and patterned through the establishment of social conventions. According to Saussure, language has several characteristics: it is collective, well defined, concrete, composed of systems of shared meanings, and subject to objective study. Speech (*parole*), on the other hand, is the active use of language in everyday interaction and is more transitory and individualized.

From this distinction, Saussure developed a description of the formal structure of the **sign**. For Saussure, a sign is that which is socially designated to represent the meaning of objects and experiences. Anything that carries meaning—language, nonverbal gestures, street signs, clothing, pictures—can function as a sign. Each sign in turn is constructed out of two interrelated elements, the *signified* and the *signifier*. The signified is that idea, object, experience, belief, concept, or feeling that one individual wishes to express to another (e.g., greeting a person upon meeting them). The signifier is that deeply inculcated representation designated to stand for the signified (e.g., shaking hands, kissing on both cheeks, or saying "hello"). The *signified-signifier* pair combines to form two inseparable dimensions of a sign that has two fundamental characteristics. First, the relationship that connects a signifier to a signified is essentially arbitrary, produced only through social conventions established by a community of speakers. Second, the signifier-signified pair has a relatively stable meaning because signs exist only in the context of a stable, institutionalized structure of language. Thus, for Saussure language has both static and dynamic properties, as it embodies the structured nature of a social institution but is also subject to shifts and changes as a consequence of its arbitrary nature.

The semiotic model developed by Saussure is the foundation for the development of French structuralism and for the poststructural critique of the sign. While structuralist theorists are inclined to develop theories based on the assumption of formal, patterned, and commonly shared meaning, the poststructural position expresses extreme doubt about the existence of universal patterns of meaning and culture. Thus, one of the guiding themes that unify the various poststructural thinkers is their general skepticism toward the universality of shared meaning as conveyed by signs. Instead, in one of their most influential arguments, poststructuralists argue that the meaning of signs has fragmented, resulting in "floating signifiers." They contend that the links between signifieds and their signifiers have become destabilized. Signifiers are no longer connected to only one signified, nor are signifieds represented by only one signifier. The internal structure of the sign has collapsed, with signifiers disconnected from any stable signified, making meaning multiplicative, open-ended, and fragmented.

---

[4] A parallel set of ideas is found in the works of American philosopher Charles Sanders Peirce, who is credited with coining the term "semiotics." Saussure preferred the term "semiology."

The cultural world described by the poststructuralists is one of inherent fragmentation, instability and confusion. But language, meaning, and signs are not the only objects of the poststructuralist critique. The notions of Truth, knowledge, power, and identity also are challenged. From the perspective of poststructuralism, social life is chaotic and radically relative without any potential for unity, consensus, or coherent analysis. This extreme relativism is one of the primary reasons that poststructural theories are thus named: the analysis of the social world is based on the assumption that the patterns, routines, and conventions of social life are inherently unstable and thus only temporarily structured. As a result, existing notions of truth and knowledge are not seen as universal claims to a total understanding of reality, but instead are seen as derived from the perspective of individuals who inhabit positions of privilege (such as high levels of status and power). Truth, with a capital "T," is no longer seen as "the Truth" but is instead "a truth" resulting from a particular, privileged point of view. The poststructuralists contend that the importance of social structures as constraining forces upon individual action has been reduced and replaced by a more fluid exercise of power that manifests itself in multiple forms within local contexts, and without the coercive force of overarching social institutions. In short, from the perspective of poststructuralism, a sociological understanding of contemporary societies requires moving beyond the analysis of structures and unified perspectives and toward an investigation of local, everyday practices.

DEFINING POSTMODERNISM

Like poststructuralism, there are many definitions of postmodernism and many approaches to understanding what is described as "postmodern." Unlike poststructuralism, however, the term "postmodern" has achieved wide public use, especially in popular forms of culture. Newscasters, talk-show hosts, pop-song lyricists, magazine and newspaper columnists, and television program script-writers have all been conspicuous in their use of the term. MTV even ran a "Postmodern Hour" in the early 1990s. Despite its pervasive use, however, there is considerable ambiguity and range in the meaning of the term "postmodern."[5]

As the name suggests, postmodernism questions the adequacy of the designation "modern" with reference to contemporary societies, engaging in debates on the importance and sense of the changes in the surrounding world. In very general terms, "postmodernism" points to a basic skepticism about the methods, goals, and ideals of modern society. The advent of modern society, typically considered to be an outgrowth of the Industrial Revolution and the eighteenth-century Enlightenment period in Europe, was premised upon the potential for scientific knowledge, the universal emancipation and institution of dignity of the individual, democratic equality, the economic effectiveness of a capitalist division of labor, and the security of the rational organization of society (see Chapter 1). Looking back over the last three centuries of human

---

[5]While there is some debate over the true origins of the term "postmodern," Best and Kellner (1991) trace initial uses to the late nineteenth and early twentieth centuries. They find that the first applications of the term "post-modern" were used by the English painter John Watkins Chapman in the 1870s to describe a burgeoning artistic movement in painting, and by Arnold Toynbee (1957) in his study of history to describe a new stage of social development beginning with the rise of an urbanized industrial working class in the late nineteenth century. However, as Bertens (1995:20) appropriately points out, there is little in the way of continuity between these early uses of the term and its appearance in social and cultural theory today.

history and especially over the twentieth century, postmodern theorists have arrived at a profoundly skeptical attitude toward the promises of modern society. The emergence of international conflict, weapons of mass destruction, environmental threats, fascism and totalitarianism, hyperrationalization, global inequality, and rampant consumerism all incline to pessimism about the prospects of the modern world.

However, while some postmodernists see the postmodern shift in contemporary societies as harkening a new type of sociocultural environment that represents a firm rupture with, and implosion of, the modern, others argue that the postmodern is a natural extension and development of the modern world, an intensive expansion of advanced (or "high") modern tendencies. Yet, both positions in this debate are premised upon the idea that the contemporary world is significantly different from what preceded it and thus requires novel theoretical approaches to capture the dynamics of the new social order.

One of the most important changes giving rise to postmodernism as a historical moment is the rise of new media and interactive technology.[6] While media in the modern period was understood as having clear boundaries between "fact" and "fiction," postmodernism is characterized by a complex *fusion* of "reality" and "unreality." Instead of television programs being labeled *either* "drama" or "documentary" we now have a preponderance of "docudramas" (based on or inspired by a true story), "reality" shows with all their staged enactments and simulations, and "live" crimes in action such as car chases and shoot-outs. In the postmodern era, *virtual reality* and *simulation* are the order of the day.[7]

Postmodernism, as a more or less coherent perspective, became most visible in the artistic and cultural criticism of the 1960s. Its early uses were in the field of American literary criticism. In these works, the possibility for arriving at transcendental truths and unbiased readings, indicative of a "modernist" approach to art, were denied and replaced by an emphasis on antirationality, antirepresentation, and the visceral experience of art. In general, localized and idiosyncratic meaning and interpretation were celebrated over transcendent and objective truth. The cut-up literature of William S. Burroughs, the jump-cut fragmentation of Jean Luc Goddard's "French New Wave" films, and the "found object" collages of Robert Rauschenberg were seen to be exemplars of these antimodern aesthetics. These artistic forms emphasized discontinuity, multivocality, indeterminacy, and the immanence of consciousness as its own reality. Ihab Hassan's (1987) famous definition of postmodernism is a useful tool for clarifying this distinction between modernism and postmodernism. An abbreviated and modified version of Hassan's table can be found in Table 8.1.

---

[6]Traditionally, media analysts have used the term "mass media" to describe a one-way dissemination of information to a mass, anonymous audience (e.g., newspapers) and "interpersonal media" to describe a two-way process between specific individuals (e.g., the telephone). However, today "mass" and "interpersonal" media are merged: one can respond to mass-generated messages, set up one's own Web site for a mass, anonymous audience, or engage in virtual relationships and even virtual sex, which clearly epitomizes the melding of intimate, personal worlds and mass communications (see Edles 2002:57).

[7]For instance, on the Internet site voyeurdorm.com you can watch live pictures of "college women" as they go about their daily lives, twenty-four hours a day. For merely $34 a month, subscribers can see women take showers, put on their makeup, study, sleep, and (so the advertising promises) sunbathe nude and have lingerie parties (see Edles 2002:80–88). Interestingly, however, although the site describes the women as "sexy, young college girls," none of those interviewed for a story in the *LA Times* about the site was in fact a college student. See *LA Times* (Sept. 16, 1999:E2).

Table 8.1   Distinctions Between Modernism and Postmodernism

Modernism	Postmodernism
romanticism/symbolism	paraphysics/dadaism
form (conjunctive, closed)	antiform (disjunctive, open)
purpose	play
design	chance
hierarchy	anarchy
mastery/logos	exhaustion/silence
art object/finished work	process/performance/happening
distance	participation
creation/totalization/synthesis	decreation/deconstruction/antithesis
presence	absence
centering	dispersal
genre/boundary	text/intertext
semantics	rhetoric
paradigm	syntagm
hypotaxis	parataxis
metaphor	metonymy
selection	combination
root/depth	rhizome/surface
interpretation/reading	against interpretation/misreading
signified	signifier
lisible (readerly)	scriptable (writerly)
narrative/grand histoire	anti-narrative/petite histoire
master code	idiolect
symptom	desire
type	mutant
genital/phallic	polymorphous/androgynous
paranoia	schizophrenia
god the father	the holy ghost
metaphysics	irony
determinacy	indeterminacy
transcendence	immanence

SOURCE: Hassan (1987); used with permission.

Whereas criticism within the artistic and literary worlds would announce the emergence of postmodernism, it would really be the field of architecture that ensconced postmodernism as a field of cultural inquiry. Beginning in the 1970s, a substantial body of work emerged that introduced the term "postmodernism" as an analytical construct used to describe a new, iconoclastic architectural movement characterized not only by bric-a-brac forms but also by its playful appropriation of existing stylistic conventions. Postmodern architecture threw out the design principles of modernism altogether in favor of a collagelike eclecticism. Perhaps the best large-scale example of postmodern architecture is Las Vegas (Venturi, Scott Brown, and Izenour 1977), where a patchwork

Photo 8.2 Las Vegas architecture epitomizes postmodernism, a patchwork of simulated styles ranging from Ancient Egypt to classical Rome, to the early American West, to the streets of New York and Monte Carlo.

of architectural styles—ranging from ancient Egypt, to classical Rome, to the early American Southwest, to the streets of New York and Monte Carlo—are combined to create a discontinuous architectural landscape. Many other architectural examples have been recognized as postmodern: for example, Philip Johnson's AT&T (Sony) building in New York City, Charles Moore's Piazza d'Italia in New Orleans, shopping malls like Horton Plaza in San Diego, Marriott's Bonaventure Hotel in Los Angeles, and the Mall of America in Minneapolis.

With the development of postmodernist analyses of literature, art, and architecture, it was not long before social scientists began developing an interest in the theme of postmodernism. In fact, early sociological uses of the term "postmodern" can be found in the works of several prominent sociological theorists: C. Wright Mills (1959), Talcott Parsons (1971), and Ralf Dahrendorf (1979). In his famous work *The Sociological Imagination*, C. Wright Mills (1959:165–167) argues that the "Modern Age is being succeeded by a post-modern period" in which the liberating notion of progress celebrated by the Enlightenment is challenged and that "the ideas of freedom and reason have become moot." This point would be later contested by Talcott Parsons (1971:143) in his claim that "anything like a 'culminating' phase of modern development is a good way off—very likely a century or more. Talk of 'postmodern' society is thus decidedly premature . . . the main trend of the next century or more will be toward completion of the type of society we have called 'modern.'" Debates of this nature would come to the surface during the 1950s and 1960s but with little impact on sociology. It would not be until the 1980s that the idea of postmodernism would make important inroads into the discipline with the incorporation of elements of French poststructuralism.

MICHEL FOUCAULT (1926–1984): A BIOGRAPHICAL SKETCH

SOURCE: © CORBIS; used with permission.

Paul-Michel Foucault was born on October 15, 1926, in the town of Poitiers in central France. The son of a prominent surgeon, it was hoped that the younger Foucault would follow his father in his occupational aspirations. Michel, however, found himself drawn toward philosophy, history, and the social sciences. After graduating from the Jesuit College Saint-Stanislaus, Foucault enrolled in the prestigious *lycée* Henri-IV in Paris, where he studied under the well-known French philosopher Jean Hyppolite (1907–1968), a noted Hegelian scholar. In 1946, Foucault passed the entrance exams for the *École Normale Supérieure,* one of the most prestigious universities in France, and entered as the fourth-highest ranked student in his class. His time at the *École* was difficult as he suffered from acute depression and even attempted suicide. However, Foucault was able to recover, and studying under the famous French phenomenologist Maurice Merleau-Ponty (1908–1961) he completed his studies in 1950, earning diplomas in both philosophy and psychology. He would receive an additional academic degree in psychopathology in 1952 from the *Institute de Psychologie* in Paris.

Strongly influenced by the structuralist Marxism of Louis Althusser (1918–1990), Foucault became politically radicalized during the 1950s and joined the *Parti Communiste Français* (the French Communist Party). (He would later leave the Party in 1953.) At the invitation of Althusser, Foucault became a member of the faculty at the *École Normale Supérieure,* where he taught psychology. Between 1952 and 1969, Foucault would be invited to teach at a number of universities throughout Europe (in France, Sweden, and Germany and in Tunisia in Northern Africa. It was also during this time, in 1960, that Foucault met Daniel Defert, the man who would become his lover and companion throughout the rest of his life. In 1969, at the age of forty-three, Foucault was elected to the *Collège de France,* France's most prestigious research university, and accepted the chair of the newly developed "History of Systems of Thought."

As Foucault established himself as an eminent lecturer and scholar during the 1960s, the publication of a number of works secured him considerable intellectual prominence. The first of these, *Madness and Civilization: A History of Insanity in the Age of Reason*, published in 1960, was a historical account of the rise of Western conceptualizations of mental illness and the means by which systems of knowledge increasingly served to socially construct "madness." This work was followed by *The Birth of the Clinic: An Archaeology of Medical Perception* (1963), an analysis of the institutionalization of clinical practices and the medical "gaze." Foucault's most celebrated book came with the publication of *The Order of Things: An Archaeology of the Human Sciences* (1966), a historical treatment of the socially constituted basis of knowledge, a work that surprisingly became a national best-seller in France. Foucault closed the 1960s with the publication of the *Archaeology of Knowledge and the Discourse on Language* (1969), investigating the links between systems of discourse and the production of knowledge.

The 1970s marked a notable shift in Foucault's lifestyle and work. After his election to the *Collège de France,* Foucault became a sought-after lecturer and traveled widely throughout Europe, North and South America, and the Far East. His political activities increased, especially in the area of prison reform. Throughout his travels, Foucault had visited many prison facilities, including Attica State Prison in New York State, which was the site of a massive prison riot in 1971. In an effort to initiate prison reforms, Foucault helped to establish the *Groupe d'Information sur les Prisons* (the Prison Information Group) and called for a radical reorganization of the care and treatment of prisoners. Also during this period, Foucault began to incorporate personal experiences into his philosophical investigations. Foucault experimented with LSD on a trip to Death Valley, California, in 1975 and described the experience as one of the most profound of his life.[8] In addition, he immersed himself in anonymous sex in San Francisco's S and M and gay subcultures, creating experiential ground for the exploration of their theoretical possibilities.

In the mid-1970s, Foucault published two of his most influential works, *Discipline and Punish: The Birth of the Prison* (1975) and the first volume of his trilogy on sexuality, *The History of Sexuality* (1976). These two works incorporated a new dimension to Foucault's analysis: the interpenetration of knowledge, discourse, and, most important, power. Foucault published the second and third volumes of his study of sexuality, *The Use of Pleasure* and *The Care of the Self*, shortly before his death in 1984. At the time of his death, Foucault was at work on a fourth volume in his history of sexuality.

In his life and in his work, Foucault pushed the boundaries of conventional worldviews. He succumbed to AIDS-related illness in a Paris hospital on June 24, 1984, at the age of fifty-seven.

INTELLECTUAL INFLUENCES AND CORE IDEAS

Michel Foucault emerged on the French intellectual scene amid an intense debate between two mid-twentieth-century philosophical perspectives: existentialism and French structuralism. Rather than taking a side in this debate, however, Foucault sought to simultaneously challenge them both. On the one hand, existentialism—spearheaded by one of France's most famous intellectuals, Jean-Paul Sartre (1905–1980)—emphasized the importance of individual autonomy and personal responsibility. Premised upon the idea that individual human activity is a more potent and meaningful force than any underlying and determining structure, existentialism argues that human beings are charged with discovering the significance of their lives while confronted with the finality of their own death. In short, as Sartre puts it, human beings are "condemned to be free," responsible for their every action and left alone with the daunting task of providing meaning to their own lives. In contrast, French structuralism emphasized the latent social, psychological, and linguistic structures that shape and mold human existence and activity.

In challenging these reigning perspectives, Foucault adopted two distinct methodologies: **archaeology** and **genealogy**. As Foucault uses the term, "archaeology" is a historical method whereby discursive practices are "unearthed" much like the artifacts of past civilizations. This makes it possible to expose the evolution or history of human understanding. By excavating forms of discourse, the knowledge that is embedded in them can be revealed along with the means by which humans have come to construct particular meanings about reality and themselves. Central here are Foucault's works of the 1960s in which he systematically investigated the origins of madness (1960), medical

---

[8]This account is taken from one of Foucault's biographers, James Miller (1993). Although it is clear that Foucault did experiment with psychedelic drugs and heightened sexual experiences, Miller claims that these events fundamentally shifted the course of Foucault's philosophical investigations. The importance of Foucault's experimentation with drugs and sexual experience on his philosophical work has been met with some controversy. See Halperin (1995) for a critical engagement of these ideas.

practices (1963), and the human sciences (1966). Foucault argues that the pattern of knowledge changes over time via discursive shifts in what he calls *epistemes*. For Foucault, an **episteme** is a framework of knowledge (such as religion or science) that shapes discourse, that collection of linguistic tools, rules, descriptions, and habits of logic that make possible specific understandings of the world. Guided by his archaeological investigations, Foucault seeks to uncover the development of epistemes and the social practices that they set in motion. Thus, for example, in *Madness and Civilization* Foucault explores how the emergence of psychiatric labels and treatments served not to cure or increase the knowledge of mental illness, but to define and refine definitions of insanity and the identities of those who allegedly suffered from the affliction.

The mid-1970s reflects a notable shift in Foucault's methodology. Now, his investigations borrow heavily from the nineteenth-century German philosopher Friedrich Nietzsche (1844–1900) and his method of "genealogy." The move from archaeology to genealogy does not simply involve a terminological change but primarily reflects an important shift in Foucault's focus of analysis. For Foucault, **genealogy** is a method of sociohistorical analysis of the impact of power on discourse. Unlike archaeology, which seeks to examine the role of discourse in the production of knowledge, genealogy articulates the dependence of the production of knowledge on relationships of power. Nietzsche had used the term "genealogy" to explore the changing nature of moral norms and value standards, revealing the intersection of ethics and power in the formation of morals and law.[9] Foucault explores similar correlations focusing on the topics of punishment and sexuality, continuing and expanding Nietzschean motifs with sociological analyses.

Popular understanding of the interrelationship between knowledge and power is frequently expressed through the phrase "knowledge is power." Foucault, in his genealogical studies, reverses the logic of this expression. He contends that it is not the acquisition of knowledge that gives one power. Instead, knowledge is already always deeply invested with power in such a way that it must be said that "power is knowledge." Thus, in Foucault's analysis, knowledge is never separate from power but is instead a specific means for exercising power. In this way, power is not simply something embodied within an individual or a social structure and expressed by brute coercion or punishment. Power appears in its most potent form when successfully translated into systems of "knowledge" and thus removed from reflection under the veil of obvious truths. The inseparability of power and knowledge is so thoroughgoing, according to Foucault, that he often conjoins the two into the phrase **power/knowledge**.

Discipline and Punish (1975)—from which reading selections in this chapter are drawn—is Foucault's first, and perhaps best, genealogical investigation. In what is among the most memorable openings of any academic work, Foucault begins *Discipline and Punish* with a description of the gruesome 1757 execution of Frenchman Robert-François Damiens (1715–1757). Damiens, who was commonly known during his day as "Robert the Devil," was condemned to death for the attempted assassination of the French monarch Louis XV. Although he failed in his attempt, inflicting only a single stab wound, Damiens was mercilessly and publicly tortured, dismembered, and finally burned—all to the delight and appreciation of the crowd that had gathered to watch.

Foucault contends that public executions like that of Damiens, although condoned in eighteenth-century Europe as an established form of punishment, are today considered abhorrent not because they violate the boundaries of moral acceptability. Rather, it is because punishment and the power that guides it have taken new, more acceptable forms. Specifically, in his analysis of penal practices, Foucault argues that punishment

---

[9]Nietzsche's genealogical method is especially illustrated in his works *Beyond Good and Evil* (1886) and *On the Genealogy of Morals* (1887).

has moved through three stages since the eighteenth century. The first stage of punishment, according to Foucault, is characterized by corporal practices such as torture, bodily mutilation, and disfigurement, such as those exemplified in the grisly execution of Damiens. Here, punishment is orchestrated and meted out by a centralized authority, like a king, and is clearly visible among, and given legitimacy by, the general population. In addition, there are explicit social structures and hierarchies through which the exercise of power is channeled. In short, the first phase of punishment is characterized by the existence of clear and unambiguous sources of power that adopt severe physical punitive practices typically performed for public demonstration and repressive in intent.

The second phase of punishment moves Foucault's investigation into the nineteenth century and toward the contemporary era. Foucault presents this phase of punishment as marked by a noted decline in the ferocity and publicity of penal force accompanied by the rise of humanistic concerns surrounding the implementation of punishment. However, Foucault suggests that the contemporary decline of torture and corporal punishment is much less an indication of a growing humaneness concerning penal practices than a transformation in the technologies of power. This new stage is marked by the introduction of penal practices based on **surveillance** and **discipline**. The physical harm as the central focus of punishment is replaced by technologies of observation and discipline aimed at the mind rather than the body. While surveillance-based systems of punishment are certainly less physically severe, Foucault argues that they actually may be more insidious and sinister. In an era where penal practices are organized by surveillance and discipline, there is no longer a need for a sole, centralized authority around which punishment is legitimized and carried out. Instead, surveillance and discipline become penal techniques integral to a wide range of social institutions— schools, hospitals, military camps, asylums, workplaces, churches, and, most notably, prisons. (For instance, a dossier or record follows a student throughout his or her scholastic career.) Foucault contends that such social institutions do not need to rely on external forms of authority, like the state, in order to surveil and discipline their members and thus produce punishment. On the contrary, institutions have come to increasingly develop and incorporate technologies of surveillance and discipline into their own operations as normalized and taken-for-granted operating procedures. For instance, students and workers are routinely kept in line by the possibility of notes or warnings being placed in their files/records regarding violations of school or workplace policy or unsatisfactory progress in their work.

Pivotal in Foucault's investigation of surveillance and discipline is his analysis of the architectural form of an ideal prison called the **Panopticon**. The blueprint for the Panopticon was designed by the British philosopher Jeremy Bentham (1748–1832) in the 1790s and was intended to be the model for a perfectly rational and efficient prison. The architecture of the Panopticon was based on two unique elements: a central guard tower surrounded by a circular gallery of cells. The inward faces of each cell within the Panopticon were barred but left unobstructed, such that their contents could be completely visible from a single vantage point in the central tower. Thus, while hundreds of inmates might be confined within the circular architecture of the Panopticon, only a single, watchful guard would be required to surveil the inmates at any given time. However, with a bit of architectural ingenuity, Bentham added an important element to the design: he made it impossible for inmates to see the guard in the central tower, making it difficult to discern at any given moment whether or not they were being observed or whether or not a guard was even present in the tower. Thus, in the Panopticon it was simply the threat of surveillance that provided the basis for the self-sanctioning of behavior, where inmates would develop a psychology of self-discipline motivated by the fear of being under constant observation.

Photo 8.4a   Foucault's First Phase in Punishment: Public Torture

Photo 8.4b   The Second Phase: The Panopticon

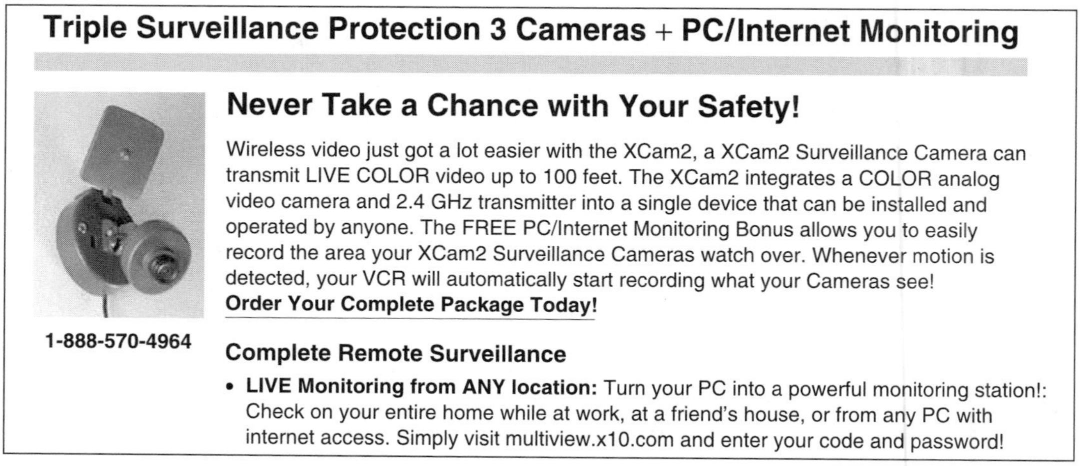

Photo 8.4c   The Third Phase: Disciplinary Society—A Virtual Fortress

Table 8.2   Foucault's Three Phases of Punishment

Phase	Time Period	Basis of Authority/Power	Methods
1st	18th C	Orchestrated by a central authority, e.g., king	Public corporal punishment, e.g., torture
2nd	19th – 20th C	Orchestrated by decentralized institutions	Surveillance, discipline e.g., Panopticon
3rd	21st C	Diffuse, multiple self-regulation	Surveillance, disciplinary individuals

Foucault argues that the architecture of the Panopticon is a metaphor for the general emergence of a new type of penal system that he calls the **disciplinary society**. Because the anxiety produced by being continually watched tends to put one on his "best behavior"—as Foucault suggests, to be "visible" is to be "trapped"—the intimidation created by possible surveillance tends to normalize human activity and create a self-induced complicity with the rules. Foucault suggests, however, that surveillance need not take the form of the continual observation exemplified by the Panopticon. Instead, he argues that there are many methods by which the unrelenting "gaze" of surveillance has been operationalized in the contemporary world: routine inspections in the workplace, rigorous training in procedures and protocol, registration and credentialing, self-reports of daily activities, standardized work quotas, measurement of effort, grades, performance evaluations, and so on. Such technologies of surveillance have become part and parcel of normal and routine daily activity. In fact, Panopticonesque surveillance has become so effective that individuals now sanction and normalize their own behavior without any prompting, surveilling and disciplining themselves as if they were simultaneously the inmate and guard of their own self-produced Panopticon.

The systematic internalization of the Panopticon, where individuals continually surveil and discipline themselves, has resulted in the third and most recent phase of punishment. Foucault characterizes this phase by its increasingly diffuse and polymorphic locations of power. While the first phase of punishment was based on the centralization of power within a specific social institution, the second phase witnessed the expansion of power into surveillance and disciplinary practices of manifold institutions. This trend is intensified in the third phase of punishment, which is exemplified by a generalized and multiple physics of "micro-power" creating what Foucault describes as a "disciplinary individual." No longer are social structures or specific institutions necessary for the exercise of power and the meting out of punishment. Power has become destructured and individualized, free-floating within society in multiple manifestations. These three distinct phases of power are summarized in Table 8.2 above.

It is with this last phase of punishment that Foucault makes an intriguing connection between knowledge and power. He argues that while the development of new forms of knowledge (through scientific investigations, educational practices, psychotherapeutic techniques, pharmacological and medical discoveries, etc.) creates broader and deeper understandings of the social and physical world, it simultaneously generates new locations for the application of power. As that knowledge expands, so does the number of sites in which power is exercised. Thus, as knowledge grows, the techniques of discipline and surveillance multiply such that power takes on an ever-increasing number of forms and circulates throughout society everywhere without originating in any single location or source.

Figure 8.1   Foucault's Basic Concepts, Intellectual Influences, and Theoretical Orientation

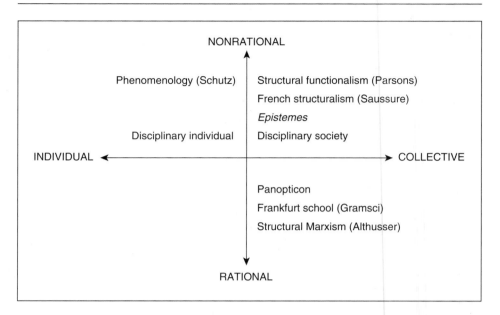

FOUCAULT'S THEORETICAL ORIENTATION

As shown in Figure 8.1, Foucault's provocative poststructural approach can be understood as explicitly confronting and seeking to correct the theoretical weaknesses of structuralism. That is, whereas structuralism is predominantly collectivistic and nonrationalistic, Foucault's theory adds both individualistic and rationalistic dimensions to this theoretical orientation without undermining it. The emphasis on how preexisting social patterns shape individual behavior reflects the collective approach to order in structuralism. This is most evident in French structuralists' analysis of language and sign systems as pregiven structures that shape and mold (or work *down* on) human activity and behavior; in contrast, the ethnomethodologists and phenomenologists, highlighted in Chapter 6, focus on individual agency and the creativity entailed in interpretation. In terms of action, French structuralists emphasize that language works in a relatively unconscious and habitual, rather than a strategically calculative, way. For the most part, we do not manipulate linguistic codes to maximize our self-interest; rather, we simply use them in a taken-for-granted, unreflective way.[10]

In sum, Foucault's theoretical approach is best understood not as subverting the structuralist approach but as making it more multidimensional. In terms of order, Foucault does not at all abandon structuralists' emphasis on the determining force of linguistic, social, and psychological codes; instead, he emphasizes that, in addition, in the process of *using* these codes, the codes themselves are reshaped and changed. Thus,

[10]As foreign-language students well know, trying to construe your thoughts in a language that you have to consciously think about and manipulate in order to use is exhausting. One of the most important cognitive leaps in language acquisition occurs when one stops translating from one's first language into one's second language and can automatically use the new one. Many people recognize having made this transition by noting that they have begun to dream in their new tongue.

rather than adopting a unidimensional conceptualization of preexisting codes working down on individuals as French structuralists do, like the phenomenologists outlined in Chapter 6, Foucault emphasizes that it is *only* in their use at the level of the individual that their existence takes form. In this sense, codes do not really "preexist" the subject at all.

In terms of action, as his work on punishment makes clear, Foucault emphasizes not only the relatively unconscious, and thereby nonrational, workings of semiotic, social, and psychological codes, but their strategic and thereby rational dimensions as well. Thus, Foucault identifies a historical shift in the methods of punishment from external (e.g., physical torture) to unconscious and internal (e.g., self-regulation of the disciplinary society), which reflects a shift in emphasis from the rational to the nonrational realm. Yet, Foucault never loses sight of the strategic, manipulative premises of both discipline and punishment. Discipline and punishment suit the interests of power and governability.

So, too, Foucault's power/knowledge problematic reflects his stimulating multidimensional approach. Power is not something embodied within either an individual or a social structure and executed in a singularly coercive manner; rather, power is most potent when appearing in the guise of knowledge at both the individual and the collective levels. Power is at once profoundly strategic and manipulative (i.e., rational) and relatively unconscious and unreflective (i.e., nonrational). Power is not so much structured (collectivistic) or unstructured (individualistic) as *de*-structured.

Reading

Introduction to *Discipline and Punish*

The following excerpts from *Discipline and Punish* (1975) highlight the distinction between the first and third phases of punishment discussed above (see Table 8.2). In the first excerpt taken from the "body of the condemned," we see Foucault dramatically enticing the reader with voyeuristic descriptions of the torture spectacle. Here scintillating images of the tearing and burning of flesh, the pulling away of limbs, and so on, are contrasted with placid descriptions from a mere eighty years later describing a prisoner's typical day. Foucault's point, of course, is that this shift in the methods of punishment reflects a profound cultural as well as social change. Rather than being based on physical, brute force, discipline and punishment are managed in a discursive, but from Foucault's perspective, no less insidious, way.

In the second excerpt, titled "Panopticism," Foucault develops his ideas regarding surveillance. Here Foucault draws a parallel between the aggressive mechanisms used by plague-stricken cities in the late seventeenth century and Bentham's Panopticon, which was intended to be the model for the perfectly rational and efficient prison, and the unrelenting "gaze" of surveillance in the contemporary world. The point of this genealogical investigation is that although surveillance-based regulatory systems are certainly physically less severe than earlier methods of punishment, they actually may be more insidious and effective. Foucault's theme, so popular in science fiction, is the internalization of the Panopticon. The fear of being "watched" in contemporary disciplinary society normalizes and "traps" complicity within the individual's own psyche.

❖

Discipline and Punish (1975)

Michel Foucault

TORTURE

The Body of the Condemned

On 2 March 1757 Damiens the regicide was condemned "to make the *amende honorable* before the main door of the Church of Paris," where he was to be "taken and conveyed in a cart, wearing nothing but a shirt, holding a torch of burning wax weighing two pounds"; then, "in the said cart, to the Place de Grève, where, on a scaffold that will be erected there, the flesh will be torn from his breasts, arms, thighs and calves with red-hot pincers, his right hand, holding the knife with which he committed the said parricide, burnt with sulphur, and, on those places where the flesh will be torn away, poured molten lead, boiling oil, burning resin, wax and sulphur melted together and then his body drawn and quartered by four horses and his limbs and body consumed by fire, reduced to ashes and his ashes thrown to the winds" (*Pièces originales. . .* , 372–4).

"Finally, he was quartered," recounts *the Gazette d'Amsterdam* of 1 April 1757. "This last operation was very long, because the horses used were not accustomed to drawing; consequently, instead of four, six were needed; and when that did not suffice, they were forced, in order to cut off the wretch's thighs, to sever the sinews and hack at the joints. . . .

"It is said that, though he was always a great swearer, no blasphemy escaped his lips; but the excessive pain made him utter horrible cries, and he often repeated: 'My God, have pity on me! Jesus, help me!' The spectators were all edified by the solicitude of the parish priest of St Paul's who despite his great age did not spare himself in offering consolation to the patient."

Bouton, an officer of the watch, left us his account: "The sulphur was lit, but the flame was so poor that only the top skin of the hand was burnt, and that only slightly. Then the executioner, his sleeves rolled up, took the steel pincers, which had been especially made for the occasion, and which were about a foot and a half long, and pulled first at the calf of the right leg, then at the thigh, and from there at the two fleshy parts of the right arm; then at the breasts. Though a strong, sturdy fellow, this executioner found it so difficult to tear away the pieces of flesh that he set about the same spot two or three times, twisting the pincers as he did so, and what he took away formed at each part a wound about the size of a six-pound crown piece.

"After these tearings with the pincers, Damiens, who cried out profusely, though without swearing, raised his head and looked at himself; the same executioner dipped an iron spoon in the pot containing the boiling potion, which he poured liberally over each wound. Then the ropes that were to be harnessed to the horses were attached with cords to the patient's body; the horses were then harnessed and placed alongside the arms and legs, one at each limb.

"Monsieur Le Breton, the clerk of the court, went up to the patient several times and asked him if he had anything to say. He said he had not; at each torment, he cried out, as the damned in hell are supposed to cry out, 'Pardon, my God! Pardon, my Lord.' Despite all this pain, he raised his head from time to time and looked at himself boldly. The cords had been tied so tightly by the men who pulled the ends that they

SOURCE: From Foucalt, M., *Discipline and Punish*. English trans. copyright © 1977 by Alan Sheridan (New York: Pantheon). Originally published in French as *Surveiller et Punir*, copyright © 1975 by Editions Gallimard. Reprinted by permission of George Borchardt, Inc., for Editions Gallimard.

caused him indescribable pain. Monsieur le [sic] Breton went up to him again and asked him if he had anything to say; he said no. Several confessors went up to him and spoke to him at length; he willingly kissed the crucifix that was held out to him; he opened his lips and repeated: 'Pardon, Lord.'

"The horses tugged hard, each pulling straight on a limb, each horse held by an executioner. After a quarter of an hour, the same ceremony was repeated and finally, after several attempts, the direction of the horses had to changed, thus: those at the arms were made to pull towards the head, those at the thighs towards the arms, which broke the arms at the joints. This was repeated several times without success. He raised his head and looked at himself. Two more horses had to be added to those harnessed to the thighs, which made six horses in all. Without success.

"Finally, the executioner, Samson, said to Monsieur Le Breton that there was no way or hope of succeeding, and told him to ask their Lordships if they wished him to have the prisoner cut into pieces. Monsieur Le Breton, who had come down from the town, ordered that renewed efforts be made, and this was done; but the horses gave up and one of those harnessed to the thighs fell to the ground. The confessors returned and spoke to him again. He said to them (I heard him): 'Kiss me, gentlemen.' The parish priest of St Paul's did not dare to, so Monsieur de Marsilly slipped under the rope holding the left arm and kissed him on the forehead. The executioners gathered round and Damiens told them not to swear, to carry out their task and that he did not think ill of them; he begged them to pray to God for him, and asked the parish priest of St Paul's to pray for him at the first mass.

"After two or three attempts, the executioner Samson and he who had used the pincers each drew out a knife from his pocket and cut the body at the thighs instead of severing the legs at the joints; the four horses gave a tug and carried off the two thighs after them, namely, that of the right side first, the other following; then the same was done to the arms, the shoulders, the arm-pits and the four limbs; the flesh had to be cut almost to the bone, the horses pulling hard carried off the right arm first and the other afterwards.

"When the four limbs had been pulled away, the confessors came to speak to him; but his executioner told them that he was dead, though the truth was that I saw the man move, his lower jaw moving from side to side as if he were talking. One of the executioners even said shortly afterwards that when they had lifted the trunk to throw it on the stake, he was still alive. The four limbs were untied from the ropes and thrown on the stake set up in the enclosure in line with the scaffold, then the trunk and the rest were covered with logs and faggots, and fire was put to the straw mixed with this wood.

". . . In accordance with the decree, the whole was reduced to ashes. The last piece to be found in the embers was still burning at half-past ten in the evening. The pieces of flesh and the trunk had taken about four hours to burn. The officers of whom I was one, as also was my son, and a detachment of archers remained in the square until nearly eleven o'clock.

"There were those who made something of the fact that a dog had lain the day before on the grass where the fire had been, chased away several times, and had always returned. But it is not difficult to understand that an animal found this place warmer than elsewhere" (quoted in Zevaes, 201–14).

Eighty years later, Léon Faucher drew up his rules "for the House of young prisoners in Paris":

"Art. 17. The prisoners' day will begin at six in the morning in winter and at five in summer. They will work for nine hours a day throughout the year. Two hours a day will be devoted to instruction. Work and the day will end at nine o'clock in winter and at eight in summer.

Art. 18. *Rising*. At the first drum-roll, the prisoners must rise and dress in silence, as the supervisor opens the cell doors. At the second drum-roll, they must be dressed and make their beds. At the third, they must line up and proceed to the chapel for morning prayer. There is a five-minute interval between each drum-roll.

Art. 19. The prayers are conducted by the chaplain and followed by a moral or religious reading. This exercise must not last more than half an hour.

Art. 20. *Work*. At a quarter to six in the summer, a quarter to seven in winter, the prisoners go down into the courtyard where they must wash their hands and faces, and receive their first ration of bread. Immediately afterwards, they form into work-teams and go off to work, which must begin at six in summer and seven in winter.

Art. 21. *Meal.* At ten o'clock the prisoners leave their work and go to the refectory; they wash their hands in their courtyards and assemble in divisions. After the dinner, there is recreation until twenty minutes to eleven.

Art. 22. *School.* At twenty minutes to eleven, at the drum-roll, the prisoners form into ranks, and proceed in divisions to the school. The class lasts two hours and consists alternately of reading, writing, drawing and arithmetic.

Art. 23. At twenty minutes to one, the prisoners leave the school, in divisions, and return to their courtyards for recreation. At five minutes to one, at the drum-roll, they form into workteams.

Art. 24. At one o'clock they must be back in the workshops: they work until four o'clock.

Art. 25. At four o'clock the prisoners leave their workshops and go into the courtyards where they wash their hands and form into divisions for the refectory.

Art. 26. Supper and the recreation that follows it last until five o'clock: the prisoners then return to the workshops.

Art. 27. At seven o'clock in the summer, at eight in winter, work stops; bread is distributed for the last time in the workshops. For a quarter of an hour one of the prisoners or supervisors reads a passage from some instructive or uplifting work. This is followed by evening prayer.

Art. 28. At half-past seven in summer, half-past eight in winter, the prisoners must be back in their cells after the washing of hands and the inspection of clothes in the courtyard; at the first drum-roll, they must undress, and at the second get into bed. The cell doors are closed and the supervisors go the rounds in the corridors, to ensure order and silence" (Faucher, 274, 82).

We have, then, a public execution and a time-table. They do not punish the same crimes or the same type of delinquent. But they each define a certain penal style. Less than a century separates them. It was a time when, in Europe and in the United States, the entire economy of punishment was redistributed. It was a time of great "scandals" for traditional justice, a time of innumerable projects for reform. It saw a new theory of law and crime, a new moral or political justification of the right to punish; old laws were abolished, old customs died out. "Modern" codes were planned or drawn up: Russia, 1769; Prussia, 1780; Pennsylvania and Tuscany, 1786; Austria, 1788; France, 1791, Year IV, 1808 and 1810. It was a new age for penal justice.

Among so many changes, I shall consider one: the disappearance of torture as a public spectacle. Today we are rather inclined to ignore it; perhaps, in its time, it gave rise to too much inflated rhetoric; perhaps it has been attributed too readily and too emphatically to a process of "humanization", thus dispensing with the need for further analysis. And, in any case, how important is such a change, when compared with the great institutional transformations, the formulation of explicit, general codes and unified rules of procedure; with the almost universal adoption of the jury system, the definition of the essentially corrective character of the penalty and the tendency, which has become increasingly marked since the nineteenth century, to adapt punishment to the individual offender? Punishment of a less immediately physical kind, a certain discretion in the art of inflicting pain, a combination of more subtle, more subdued sufferings, deprived of their visible display, should not all this be treated as a special case, an incidental effect of deeper changes? And yet the fact remains that a few decades saw the disappearance of the tortured, dismembered, amputated body, symbolically branded on face or shoulder, exposed alive or dead to public view. The body as the major target of penal repression disappeared.

DISCIPLINE

Panopticism

The following, according to an order published at the end of the seventeenth century, were the measures to be taken when the plague appeared in a town.

First, a strict spatial partitioning: the closing of the town and its outlying districts, a prohibition to leave the town on pain of death, the killing of all stray animals; the division of the town into distinct quarters, each governed by an intendant. Each street is placed under the authority of a syndic, who keeps it under surveillance; if he leaves the street, he will be condemned to death. On the appointed day, everyone is ordered to stay indoors: it is forbidden to leave on pain of death. The syndic himself comes to lock the door of each house from the outside; he takes the key with him and hands it over to the intendant of the quarter; the intendant keeps it until the end of the quarantine. Each family will have made its own provisions; but, for bread and wine, small wooden canals are set up between the street and the interior of the houses, thus allowing each person to receive his ration without communicating with the suppliers and other residents; meat, fish and herbs will be hoisted up into the houses with pulleys and baskets. If it is absolutely necessary to leave the house, it will be done in turn, avoiding any meeting. Only the intendants, syndics and guards will move about the streets and also, between the infected houses, from one corpse to another, the 'crows,' who can be left to die: these are 'people of little substance who carry the sick, bury the dead, clean and do many vile and abject offices.' It is a segmented, immobile, frozen space. Each individual is fixed in his place. And, if he moves, he does so at the risk of his life, contagion or punishment.

Inspection functions ceaselessly. The gaze is alert everywhere: 'A considerable body of militia, commanded by good officers and men of substance,' guards at the gates, at the town hall and in every quarter to ensure the prompt obedience of the people and the most absolute authority of the magistrates, 'as also to observe all disorder, theft and extortion.' At each of the town gates there will be an observation post; at the end of each street sentinels. Every day, the intendant visits the quarter in his charge, inquires whether the syndics have carried out their tasks, whether the inhabitants have anything to complain of; they 'observe their actions.' Every day, too, the syndic goes into the street for which he is responsible; stops before each house: gets all the inhabitants to appear at the windows (those who live overlooking the courtyard will be allocated a window looking

onto the street at which no one but they may show themselves); he calls each of them by name; informs himself as to the state of each and every one of them—'in which respect the inhabitants will be compelled to speak the truth under pain of death'; if someone does not appear at the window, the syndic must ask why: 'In this way he will find out easily enough whether dead or sick are being concealed.' Everyone locked up in his cage, everyone at his window, answering to his name and showing himself when asked—it is the great review of the living and the dead.

This surveillance is based on a system of permanent registration: reports from the syndics to the intendants, from the intendants to the magistrates or mayor. At the beginning of the 'lock up,' the role of each of the inhabitants present in the town is laid down, one by one; this document bears 'the name, age, sex of everyone, notwithstanding his condition': a copy is sent to the intendant of the quarter, another to the office of the town hall, another to enable the syndic to make his daily roll call. Everything that may be observed during the course of the visits— deaths, illnesses, complaints, irregularities—is noted down and transmitted to the intendants and magistrates. The magistrates have complete control over medical treatment; they have appointed a physician in charge; no other practitioner may treat, no apothecary prepare medicine, no confessor visit a sick person without having received from him a written note 'to prevent anyone from concealing and dealing with those sick of the contagion, unknown to the magistrates.' The registration of the pathological must be constantly centralized. The relation of each individual to his disease and to his death passes through the representatives of power, the registration they make of it, the decisions they take on it.

Five or six days after the beginning of the quarantine, the process of purifying the houses one by one is begun. All the inhabitants are made to leave; in each room 'the furniture and goods' are raised from the ground or suspended from the air; perfume is poured around the room; after carefully sealing the windows, doors and even the keyholes with wax, the perfume is set alight. Finally, the entire house is closed while the perfume is consumed; those who have carried out the work are searched, as they were on entry, 'in the presence of the residents of the house, to see that they did not have something on their persons as they left that they did not have on entering.' For hours later, the residents are allowed to re-enter their homes.

This enclosed, segmented space, observed at every point, in which the individuals are inserted in a fixed place, in which the slightest movements are supervised, in which all events are recorded, in which an uninterrupted work of writing links the centre and periphery, in which power is exercised without division, according to a continuous hierarchical figure, in which each individual is constantly located, examined and distributed among the living beings, the sick and the dead—all this constitutes a compact model of the disciplinary mechanism. The plague is met by order; its function is to sort out every possible confusion: that of the disease, which is transmitted when bodies are mixed together; that of the evil, which is increased when fear and death overcome prohibitions. It lays down for each individual his place, his body, his disease and his death, his well-being, by means of an omnipresent and omniscient power that subdivides itself in a regular, uninterrupted way even to the ultimate determination of the individual, of what characterizes him, of what belongs to him, of what happens to him. Against the plague, which is a mixture, discipline brings into play its power, which is one of analysis. A whole literary fiction of the festival grew up around the plaque: suspended laws, lifted prohibitions, the frenzy of passing time, bodies mingling together without respect, individuals unmasked, abandoning their statutory identity and the figure under which they had been recognized, allowing a quite different truth to appear. But there was also a political dream of the plague, which was exactly its reverse: not the collective festival, but strict divisions; not laws transgressed, but the penetration of regulation into even the smallest details of everyday life through the mediation of the complete hierarchy that assured the capillary functioning of power; not masks that were put on and taken off, but the assignment to each individual of his 'true' name, his 'true' place, his 'true' body, his 'true' disease. The plague as a form, at once real and imaginary, of disorder had as its medical

and political correlative discipline. Behind the disciplinary mechanisms can be read the haunting memory of 'contagions,' of the plague, of rebellions, crimes, vagabondage, desertions, people who appear and disappear, live and die in disorder.

If it is true that the leper gave rise to rituals of exclusion, which to a certain extent provided the model for and general form of the great Confinement, then the plague gave rise to disciplinary projects. Rather than the massive, binary division between one set of people and another, it called for multiple separations, individualizing distributions, an organization in depth of surveillance and control, an intensification and a ramification of power. The leper was caught up in a practice of rejection, of exile-enclosure; he was left to his doom in a mass among which it was useless to differentiate; those sick of the plague were caught up in a meticulous tactical partitioning in which individual differentiations were the constricting effects of a power that multiplied, articulated and subdivided itself; the great confinement on the one hand; the correct training on the other. The leper and his separation; the plague and its segmentations. The first is marked; the second analysed and distributed. The exile of the leper and the arrest of the plague do not bring with them the same political dream. The first is that of a pure community, the second that of a disciplined society. Two ways of exercising power over men, of controlling their relations, of separating out their dangerous mixtures. The plague-stricken town, traversed throughout with hierarchy, surveillance, observation, writing; the town immobilized by the functioning of an extensive power that bears in a distinct way over all individual bodies—this is the utopia of the perfectly governed city. The plague (envisaged as a possibility at least) is the trial in the course of which one may define ideally the exercise of disciplinary power. In order to make rights and laws function according to pure theory, the jurists place themselves in imagination in the state of nature; in order to see perfect disciplines functioning, rulers dreamt of the state of plague. Underlying disciplinary projects the image of the plague stands for all forms of confusion and disorder; just as the image of the leper, cut off from all human contact, underlies projects of exclusion.

They are different projects, then, but not incompatible ones. We see them coming slowly together, and it is the peculiarity of the nineteenth century that it applied to the space of exclusion of which the leper was the symbolic inhabitant (beggars, vagabonds, madmen and the disorderly formed the real population) the technique of power proper to disciplinary partitioning. Treat 'lepers' as 'plague victims,' project the subtle segmentations of discipline onto the confused space of internment, combine it with the methods of analytical distribution proper to power, individualize the excluded, but use procedures of individualization to mark exclusion—this is what was operated regularly by disciplinary power from the beginning of the nineteenth century in the psychiatric asylum, the penitentiary, the reformatory, the approved school and, to some extent, the hospital. Generally speaking, all the authorities exercising individual control function according to a double mode; that of binary division and branding (mad/sane; dangerous/harmless; normal/abnormal); and that of coercive assignment of differential distribution who he is; where he must be; how he is to be characterized; how he is to be recognized; how a constant surveillance is to be exercised over him in an individual way, etc.). On the one hand, the lepers are treated as plaque victims; the tactics of individualizing disciplines are imposed on the excluded; and, on the other hand, the universality of disciplinary controls makes it possible to brand the 'leper' and to bring into play against him the dualistic mechanisms of exclusion. The constant division between the normal and the abnormal, to which every individual is subjected, brings us back to our own time, by applying the binary branding and exile of the leper to quite different objects; the existence of a whole set of techniques and institutions for measuring, supervising and correcting the abnormal brings into play the disciplinary mechanisms to which the fear of the plague gave rise. All the mechanisms of power which, even today, are disposed around the abnormal individual, to brand him and to alter him, are composed of those two forms from which they distantly derive.

Bentham's Panopticon is the architectural figure of this composition. We know the principle on which it was based: at the periphery, an annular building; at the centre, a tower; this tower is pierced with wide windows that open onto the inner side of the ring; the peripheric building is divided into cells, each of which extends the whole width of the building; they have two windows, one on the inside, corresponding to the windows of the tower; the other, on the outside, allows the light to cross the cell from one end to the other. All that is needed, then, is to place a supervisor in a central tower and to shut up in each cell a madman, a patient, a condemned man, a worker or a schoolboy. By the effect of backlighting, one can observe from the tower, standing out precisely against the light, the small captive shadows in the cells of the periphery. They are like so many cages, so many small theatres, in which each actor is alone, perfectly individualized and constantly visible. The panoptic mechanism arranges spatial unities that make it possible to see constantly and to recognize immediately. In short, it reverses the principle of the dungeon; or rather of its three functions—to enclose, to deprive of light and to hide—it preserves only the first and eliminates the other two. Full lighting and the eye of a supervisor capture better than darkness, which ultimately protected. Visibility is a trap.

To begin with, this made it possible—as a negative effect—to avoid those compact, swarming, howling masses that were to be found in places of confinement, those painted by Goya or described by Howard. Each individual, in his place, is securely confined to a cell from which he is seen from the front by the supervisor; but the side walls prevent him from coming into contact with his companions. He is seen, but he does not see; he is the object of information, never a subject in communication. The arrangement of his room, opposite the central tower, imposes on him an axial visibility; but the divisions of the ring, those separated cells, imply a lateral invisibility. And this invisibility is a guarantee of order. If the inmates are convicts, there is no danger of a plot, an attempt at collective escape, the planning of new crimes for the future, bad reciprocal influences; if they are patients, there is no danger of contagion; if they are madmen there is no risk of their committing violence upon one another; if they are schoolchildren, there is no copying, no noise, no chatter, no waste of time; if they are workers, there are no disorders, no theft, no coalitions, none of those distractions that slow down the rate of work, make it less perfect or cause accidents. The crowd, a compact mass, a locus of multiple exchanges, individualities merging together, a collective effect, is abolished and replaced by a collection of separated individualities. From the point of view of the guardian, it is replaced by a multiplicity that can be numbered and supervised; from the point of view of the inmates, by a sequestered and observed solitude (Bentham, 60–64).

Hence the major effect of the Panopticon: to induce in the inmate a state of conscious and permanent visibility that assures the automatic functioning of power. So to arrange things that the surveillance is permanent in its effects, even if it is discontinuous in its action; that the perfection of power should tend to render its actual exercise unnecessary; that this architectural apparatus should be a machine for creating and sustaining a power relation independent of the person who exercises it; in short, that the inmates should be caught up in a power situation of which they are themselves the bearers. To achieve this, it is at once too much and too little that the prisoner should be constantly observed/by an inspector: too little, for what matters is that he knows himself to be observed; too much, because he has no need in fact of being so. In view of this, Bentham laid down the principle that power should be visible and unverifiable. Visible: the inmate will constantly have before his eyes the tall outline of the central tower from which he is spied upon. Unverifiable: the inmate must never know whether he is being looked at any one moment; but he must be sure that he may always be so. In order to make the presence or absence of the inspector unverifiable, so that the prisoners, in their cells, cannot even see a shadow, Bentham envisaged not only venetian blinds on the windows of the central observation hall, but, on the inside, partitions that intersected the hall at right angles and, in order to pass from one quarter to the other, not doors but zig-zag openings; for the slightest noise, a gleam of light, a brightness in a half-opened door would betray the presence of the guardian. The Panopticon is a machine for dissociating the see/being seen dyad: in the peripheric ring, one is totally seen, without ever seeing; in the central tower, one sees everything without ever being seen.

It is an important mechanism, for it automatizes and disindividualizes power. Power has its principle not so much in a person as in a certain concerted distribution of bodies, surfaces, lights, gazes; in an arrangement whose internal mechanisms produce the relation in which individuals are caught up. The ceremonies, the rituals, the marks by which the sovereign's surplus power was manifested are useless. There is a machinery that assures dissymmetry, disequilibrium, difference. Consequently, it does not matter who exercises power. Any individual, taken almost at random, can operate the machine: in the absence of the director, his family, his friends, his visitors, even his servants (Bentham, 45). Similarly, it does not matter what motive animates him: the curiosity of the indiscreet, the malice of a child, the thirst for knowledge of a philosopher who wishes to visit this museum of human nature, or the perversity of those who take pleasure in spying and punishing. The more numerous those anonymous and temporary observers are, the greater the risk for the inmate of being surprised and the greater his anxious awareness of being observed. The Panopticon is a marvellous machine which, whatever use one may wish to put it to, produces homogeneous effects of power.

A real subjection is born mechanically from a fictitious relation. So it is not necessary to use force to constrain the convict to good behaviour, the madman to calm, the worker to work, the schoolboy to application, the patient to the observation of the regulations. Bentham was surprised that panoptic institutions could be so light: there were no more bars, no more chains, no more heavy locks; all that was needed was that the separations should be clear and the openings well arranged. The heaviness of the old 'houses of security,' with their fortress-like architecture, could be replaced by the simple, economic geometry of a 'house of certainty.' The efficiency of power, its constraining force have, in a sense, passed over to the other side—to the side of its surface of application. He who is subjected to a field of visibility, and who knows it, assumes responsibility for the constraints of power; he makes them play spontaneously upon himself; he inscribes in himself the power relation which he simultaneously plays both roles; he becomes the principle of his own subjection. By this very fact, the external power may throw off its physical weight; it tends to the non-corporal; and, the more it approaches this limit, the more constant, profound and permanent are its effects: it is a perpetual victory that avoids any physical confrontation and which is always decided in advance.

Bentham does not say whether he was inspired, in his project, by Le Vaux's menagerie at Versailles: the first menagerie in which the different elements are not, as they traditionally were, distributed in a park (Loisel, 104–7). At the centre was an octagonal pavilion which, on the first floor, consisted of only a single room, the king's salon; on every side large windows looked out onto seven cages (the eighth side was reserved for the entrance), containing different species of animals. By Bentham's time, this menagerie had disappeared. But one finds in the programme of the Panopticon a similar concern with individualizing observation, with characterization and classification, with the analytical arrangement of space. The Panopticon is a royal menagerie; the animal is replaced by man, individual distribution by specific grouping and the king by the machinery of a furtive power. With this exception, the Panopticon also does the work of a naturalist. It makes it possible to draw up differences: among patients, to observe the symptoms of each individual, without the proximity of beds, the circulation of miasmas, the effects of contagion confusing the clinical tables; among school-children, it makes it possible to observe performances (without there being any imitation or copying), to map aptitudes, to assess characters, to draw up rigorous classifications and, in relation to normal development, to distinguish 'laziness and stubbornness' from 'incurable imbecility'; among workers, it makes it possible to note the aptitudes of each worker, compare the time he takes to perform a task, and if they are paid by the day, to calculate their wages (Bentham, 60–64).

So much for the question of observation. But the Panopticon was also a laboratory; it could be used as a machine to carry out experiments, to alter behaviour, to train or correct individuals. To experiment with medicines and monitor their effects. To try out different punishments on prisoners, according to their crimes and character,

and to seek the most effective ones. To teach different techniques simultaneously to the workers, to decide which is the best. To try out pedagogical experiments—and in particular to take up once again the well-debated problem of secluded education, by using orphans. One would see what would happen when, in the sixteenth or eighteenth year, they were presented with other boys or girls; one could verify whether, as Helvetius thought, anyone could learn anything; one would follow 'the genealogy of every observable idea'; one could bring up different children according to different systems of thought, making certain children believe that two and two do not make four or that the moon is a cheese, then put them together when they are twenty or twenty-five years old; one would then have discussions that would be worth a great deal more than the sermons or lectures on which so much money is spent; one would have at least an opportunity of making discoveries in the domain of metaphysics. The Panopticon is a privileged place for experiments on men, and for analysing with complete certainty the transformations that may be obtained from them. The Panopticon may even provide an apparatus for supervising its own mechanisms. In this central tower, the director may spy on all the employees that he has under his orders: nurses, doctors, foremen, teachers, warders; he will be able to judge them continuously, alter their behaviour, impose upon them the methods he thinks best; and it will even be possible to observe the director himself. An inspector arriving unexpectedly at the centre of the Panopticon will be able to judge at a glance, without anything being concealed from him, how the entire establishment is functioning. And, in any case, enclosed as he is in the middle of this architectural mechanism, is not the director's own fate entirely bound up with it? The incompetent physician who has allowed contagion to spread, the incompetent prison governor or workshop manager will be the first victims of an epidemic or a revolt.' 'By every tie I could devise,' said the master of the Panopticon, 'my own fate had been bound up by me with theirs' (Bentham, 177). The Panopticon functions as a kind of laboratory of power. Thanks to its mechanisms of observation, it gains in efficiency and in the ability to penetrate into men's behaviour; knowledge follows the advances of power, discovering new objects of knowledge over all the surfaces on which power is exercised.

The plague-stricken town, the panoptic establishment—the differences are important. They mark, at a distance of a century and a half, the transformations of the disciplinary programme. In the first case, there is an exceptional situation: against an extraordinary evil, power is mobilized; it makes itself everywhere present and visible; it invents new mechanisms; it separates, it immobilizes, it partitions constructs for a time what is both a counter-city and the perfect society; it imposes an ideal functioning, but one that is reduced, in the final analysis, like the evil that it combats, to a simple dualism of life and death: that which moves brings death, and one kills that which moves. The Panopticon, on the other hand, must be understood as a generalizable model of functioning; a way of defining power relations in terms of the everyday life of men. No doubt Bentham presents it as a particular institution, closed in upon itself. Utopias, perfectly closed in upon themselves, are common enough. As opposed to the ruined prisons, littered with mechanisms of torture, to be seen in Piranese's engravings, the Panopticon presents a cruel, ingenious cage. The fact that it should have given rise, even in our own time, to so many variations, projected or realized, is evidence of the imaginary intensity that it has possessed for almost two hundred years. But the Panopticon must not be understood as a dream building: it is the diagram of a mechanism of power reduced to its ideal form; its functioning, abstracted from any obstacle, resistance or friction, must be represented as a pure architectural and optical system: it is in fact a figure of political technology that may and must be detached from any specific use.

It is polyvalent in its applications; it serves to reform prisoners, but also to treat patients, to instruct schoolchildren, to confine the insane, to supervise workers, to put beggars and idlers to work. It is a type of location of bodies in space, of distribution of individuals in relation to one another, of hierarchical organization, of disposition of centres and channels of power, of definition of the instruments and modes of intervention of power, which can be implemented in

hospitals, workshops, schools, prisons. Whenever one is dealing with a multiplicity of individuals on whom a task or a particular form of behaviour must be imposed, the panoptic schema may be used. It is—necessary modifications apart—applicable 'to all establishments whatsoever, in which, within a space not too large to be covered or commanded by buildings, a number of persons are meant to be kept under inspection' (Bentham, 40; although Bentham takes the penitentiary house as his prime example, it is because it has many different functions to fulfill—safe custody, confinement, solitude, forced labour and instruction).

In each of its applications, it makes it possible to perfect the exercise of power. It does this in several ways: because it can reduce the number of those who exercise it, while increasing the number of those on whom it is exercised. Because it is possible to intervene at any moment and because the constant pressure acts even before the offences, mistakes or crimes have been committed. Because, in these conditions, its strength is that it never intervenes, it is exercised spontaneously and without noise, it constitutes a mechanism whose effects follow from one another. Because, without any physical instrument other than architecture and geometry, it acts directly on individuals; it gives 'power of mind over mind.' The panoptic schema makes any apparatus of power more intense: it assures its economy (in material, in personnel, in time); it assures its efficacity by its preventative character, its continuous functioning and its automatic mechanisms. It is a way of obtaining from power 'in hitherto unexampled quantity,' 'a great and new instrument of government . . . ; its great excellence consists in the great strength it is capable of giving to any institution it may be thought proper to apply it to' (Bentham, 66).

It's a case of 'it's easy once you've thought of it' in the political sphere. It can in fact be integrated into any function (education, medical treatment, production, punishment); it can increase the effect of this function, by being linked closely with it; it can constitute a mixed mechanism in which relations of power (and of knowledge) may be precisely adjusted, in the smallest detail, to the processes that are to be supervised; it can establish a direct proportion between 'surplus power' and 'surplus production.' In short, it arranges things in such a way that the exercise of power is not added on from the outside, like a rigid, heavy constraint to the functions it invests, but is so subtly present in them as to increase their efficiency by itself increasing its own points of contact. The panoptic mechanism is not simply a hinge, a point of exchange between a mechanism of power and a function; it is a way of making power relations function in a function, and of making a function through these power relations. Bentham's Preface to Panopticon opens with a list of the benefits to be obtained from his 'inspection-house': 'Morals reformed—health preserved—industry invigorated—instruction diffused—public burthens lightened—Economy seated, as it were, upon a rock—the gordian knot of the Poor-Laws not cut, but untied—all by a simple idea in architecture!' (Bentham, 39)

Furthermore, the arrangement of this machine is such that its enclosed nature does not preclude a permanent presence from the outside: we have seen that anyone may come and exercise in the central tower the functions of surveillance, and that, this being the case, he can gain a clear idea of the way in which the surveillance is practised. In fact, any panoptic institution, even if it is as rigorously closed as a penitentiary, may without difficulty be subjected to such irregular and constant inspections: and not only by the appointed inspectors, but also by the public; any member of society will have the right to come and see with his own eyes how the schools, hospitals, factories, prisons function. There is no risk, therefore, that the increase of power created by the panoptic machine may degenerate into tyranny; the disciplinary mechanism will be democratically controlled, since it will be constantly accessible 'to the great tribunal committee of the world.' This Panopticon, subtly arranged so that an observer may observe, at a glance, so many different individuals, also enables everyone to come and observe any of the observers. The seeing machine was once a sort of dark room into which individuals spied; it has become a transparent building in which the exercise of power may be supervised by society as a whole.

The panoptic schema, without disappearing as such or losing any of its properties, was destined to spread throughout the social body; its

vocation was to become a generalized function. The plague-stricken town provided an exceptional disciplinary model: perfect, but absolutely violent; to the disease that brought death, power opposed its perpetual threat of death; life inside it was reduced to its simplest expression; it was, against the power of death, the meticulous exercise of the right of the sword. The Panopticon, on the other hand, has a role of amplification; although it arranges power, although it is intended to make it more economic and more effective, it does so not for power itself, nor for the immediate salvation of a threatened society: its aim is to strengthen the social forces—to increase production, to develop the economy, spread education, raise the level of public morality; to increase and multiply. . . .

There are two images, then, or discipline. At one extreme, the discipline-blockade, the enclosed institution, established on the edges of society, turned inwards towards negative functions: arresting evil, breaking communications, suspending time. At the other extreme, with panopticism, is the discipline-mechanism: a functional mechanism that must improve the exercise of power by making it lighter, more rapid, more effective, a design of subtle coercion for a society to come. The movement from one project to the other, from a schema of exceptional discipline to one of a generalized surveillance, rests on a historical transformation: the gradual extension of the mechanisms of discipline throughout the seventeenth and eighteenth centuries, their spread throughout the whole social body, the formation of what might be called in general the disciplinary society.

A whole disciplinary generalization—the Benthamite physics of power represents an acknowledgement of this—had operated throughout the classical age. The spread of disciplinary institutions, whose network was beginning to cover an ever larger surface and occupying above all a less and less marginal position, testifies to this: what was an islet, a privileged place, a circumstantial measure, or a singular model, became a general formula; the regulations characteristic of the Protestant and pious armies of William of Orange or of Gustavus Adolphus were transformed into regulations for all the armies of Europe; the model colleges of the Jesuits, or the schools of Batencour or Demia, following the example set by Sturm, provided the outlines for the general forms of educational discipline; the ordering of the naval and military hospitals provided the model for the entire reorganization of hospitals in the eighteenth century.

But this extension of the disciplinary institutions was no doubt only the most visible aspect of various, more profound processes.

1. The functional inversion of the disciplines. At first, they were expected to neutralize dangers, to fix useless or disturbed populations, to avoid the inconveniences of over-large assemblies; now they were being asked to play a positive role, for they were becoming able to do so, to increase the possible utility of individuals. Military discipline is no longer a mere means of preventing looting, desertion or failure to obey orders among the troops; it has become a basic technique to enable the army to exist, not as an assembled crowd, but as a unity that derives from this very unity an increase in its forces; discipline increases the skill of each individual, coordinates these skills, accelerates movements, increases fire power, broadens the fronts of attack without reducing their vigour, increases the capacity for resistance, etc. The discipline of the workshop, while remaining a way of enforcing respect for the regulations and authorities, of preventing thefts or losses, tends to increase aptitudes, speeds, output and therefore profits: it still exerts a moral influence over behaviour, but more and more it treats actions in terms of their results, introduces bodies into a machinery, forces into an economy. When, in the seventeenth century, the provincial schools or the Christian elementary schools were founded, the justifications given for them were above all negative: those poor who were unable to bring up their children left them 'in ignorance of their obligations: given the difficulties they have in earning a living, and themselves having been badly brought up, they are unable to communicate a sound upbringing that they themselves never had'; this involves three major inconveniences: ignorance of God, idleness (with its consequent drunkenness, impurity, larceny, brigandage); and the formation of those gangs of beggars, always ready to stir up public disorder and 'virtually to exhaust the funds of the Hotel-Dieu' (Demia, 60–61). Now, at the

beginning of the Revolution, the end laid down for primary education was to be, among other things, to 'fortify,' to 'develop the body,' to prepare the child 'for a future in some mechanical work,' to give him 'an observant eye, a sure hand and prompt habits' (Talleyrand's Report to the Constituent Assembly, 10 September 1791, quoted by Leon, 106). The disciplines function increasingly as techniques for making useful individuals. Hence their emergence from a marginal position on the confines of society, and detachment from the forms of exclusion or expiation, confinement or retreat. Hence the slow loosening of their kinship with religious regularities and enclosures. Hence also their rooting in the most important, most central and most productive sectors of society. They become attached to some of the great essential functions: factory production, the transmission of knowledge, the diffusion of aptitudes and skills, the war-machine. Hence, too, the double tendency one sees developing throughout the eighteenth century to increase the number of disciplinary institutions and to discipline the existing apparatuses.

2. The swarming of disciplinary mechanisms. While, on the one hand, the disciplinary establishments increase, their mechanisms have a certain tendency to become 'de-institutionalized,' to emerge from the closed fortresses in which they once functioned and to circulate in a 'free' state; the massive, compact disciplines are broken down into flexible methods of control, which may be transferred and adapted. Sometimes the closed apparatuses add to their internal and specific function a role of external surveillance, developing around themselves a whole margin of lateral controls. Thus the Christian School must not simply train docile children; it must also make it possible to supervise the parents, to gain information as to their way of life, their resources, their piety, their morals. The school tends to constitute minute social observatories that penetrate even to the adults and exercise regular supervision over them: the bad behaviour of the child, or his absence, is a legitimate pretext, according to Demia, for one to go and question the neighbours, especially if there is any reason to believe that the family will not tell the truth; one can

then go and question the parents themselves, to find out whether they know their catechism and the prayers, whether they are determined to root out the vices of their children, how many beds there are in the house and what the sleeping arrangements are; the visit may end with the giving of alms, the present of a religious picture, or the provision of additional beds (Demia, 39–40). . . .

3. The state-control of the mechanisms of discipline. In England, it was private religious groups that carried out, for a long time, the functions of social discipline (cf. Radzinovitz, 203–14); in France, although a part of this role remained in the hands of parish guilds or charity associations, another—and no doubt the most important part—was very soon taken over by the police apparatus.

The organization of a centralized police had long been regarded, even by contemporaries, as the most direct expression of absolutism; the sovereign had wished to have 'his own magistrate to whom he might directly entrust his orders, his commissions, intentions, and who was entrusted with the execution of orders and orders under the King's private seal' (a note by Duval, first secretary at the police magistrature, quoted in Funck-Brentano, 1). In effect, in taking over a number of pre-existing functions— the search for criminals, urban surveillance, economic and political supervision—the police magistratures and the magistrature-general that presided over them in Paris transposed them into a single, strict, administrative machine: 'All the radiations of force and information that spread from the circumference culminate in the magistrate-general. . . . It is he who operates all the wheels that together produce order and harmony. The effects of his administration cannot be better compared than to the movement of the celestial bodies' (Des Essarts, 344 and 528).

But, although the police as an institution were certainly organized in the form of a state apparatus, and although this was certainly lined directly to the centre of political sovereignty, the type of power that it exercises, the mechanisms it operates and the elements to which it applies them are specific. It is an apparatus that must be coextensive with the entire social body and not only by the extreme limits that it embraces, but by the minuteness of the details it is concerned with. Police power must bear 'over everything': it is not however the totality of the state nor of the kingdom as visible and invisible body of the monarch; it is the dust of events, actions, behaviour, opinions—'everything that happens'; the police are concerned with 'those things of every moment,' those 'unimportant things,' of which Catherine II spoke in her Great Instruction (Supplement to the Instruction for the drawing up of a new code, 1769, article 535). With the police, one is in the indefinite world of a supervision that seeks ideally to reach the most elementary particle, the most passing phenomenon of the social body: 'The ministry of the magistrates and police officers is of the greatest importance; the objects that it embraces are in a sense definite, one may perceive them only by a sufficiently detailed examination' (Delamare, unnumbered Preface): the infinitely small of political power.

And, in order to be exercised, this power had to be given the instrument of permanent, exhaustive, omnipresent surveillance, capable of making all visible, as long as it could itself remain invisible. It had to be like a faceless gaze that transformed the whole social body into a field of perception: thousands of eyes posted everywhere, mobile attentions ever on the alert, a long, hierarchized network which, according to Le Maire, comprised for Paris the forty-eight commissaires, the twenty inspecteurs, then the 'observers,' who were paid regularly, the 'basses mouches,' or secret agents, who were paid by the day, then the informers, paid according to the job done, and finally the prostitutes. And this unceasing observation had to be accumulated in a series of reports and registers; throughout the eighteenth century, an immense police text increasingly covered society by means of a complex documentary organization (on the police registers in the eighteenth century, cf. Chassaigne). And, unlike the methods of judicial or administrative writing, what was registered in this way were forms of behaviour, attitudes, possibilities, suspicions—a permanent account of individuals' behaviour.

Now, it should be noted that, although this police supervision was entirely 'in the hands of the king,' it did not function in a single direction. It was in fact a double-entry system: it had to correspond, by manipulating the machinery of justice, to the immediate wishes of the king, but it was also capable of responding to solicitations from below; the celebrated lettres de cachet, or orders under the king's private seal, which were long the symbol of arbitrary royal rule and which brought detention into disrepute on political grounds, were in fact demanded by families, masters, local notables, neighbours, parish priests; and their function was to punish by confinement a whole infra-penality, that of disorder, agitation, disobedience, bad conduct; those things that Ledoux wanted to exclude from his architecturally perfect city and which he called 'offences of non-surveillance.' In short, the eighteenth-century police added a disciplinary function to its role as the auxiliary of justice in the pursuit of criminals and as an instrument for the political supervision of plots, opposition movements or revolts. It was a complex function since it linked the absolute power of the monarch to the lowest levels of power disseminated in society; since, between these different, enclosed institutions of discipline (workshops, armies, schools), it extended an intermediary network, acting where they could not intervene, disciplining the non-disciplinary spaces; but it filled in the gaps, linked them together, guaranteed with its armed forces an interstitial discipline and a meta-discipline. 'By means of a wise police, the sovereign accustoms the people to order and obedience' (Vattel, 162).

The organization of the police apparatus in the eighteenth century sanctioned a generalization of the disciplines that became co-extensive with the state itself. Although it was linked in the most explicit way with everything in the royal power that exceeded the exercise of regular justice, it is understandable why the police offered such slight resistance to the rearrangement of the judicial power; and why it has not ceased to impose its prerogatives upon it, with everincreasing weight, right up to the present day; this is no doubt because it is the secular arm of the judiciary; but it is also because to a far greater degree than the judicial institution, it is identified, by reason of its extent and mechanisms, with a society of the disciplinary type. Yet it would be wrong to believe that the

disciplinary functions were confiscated and absorbed once and for all by a state apparatus.

'Discipline' may be identified neither with an institution nor with an apparatus; it is a type of power, a modality for its exercise, comprising a whole set of instruments, techniques, procedures, levels of application, targets; it is a 'physics' or an 'anatomy' of power, a technology. And it may be taken over either by 'specialized' institutions (the penitentiaries or 'houses of correction' of the nineteenth century), or by institutions that use it as an essential instrument for a particular end (schools, hospitals), or by pre-existing authorities that find in it a means of reinforcing or reorganizing their internal mechanisms of power (one day we should show how intra-familial relations, essentially in the parents-children cell, have become 'disciplined,' absorbing since the classical age external schemata, first educational and military, then medical, psychiatric, psychological, which have made the family the privileged locus of emergence for the disciplinary question of the normal and the abnormal); or by apparatuses that have made discipline their principle of internal functioning (the disciplinarization of the administrative apparatus from the Napoleonic period), or finally by state apparatuses whose major, if not exclusive, function is to assure that discipline reigns over society as a whole (the police).

On the whole, therefore, one can speak of the formation of a disciplinary society in this movement that stretches from the enclosed disciplines, a sort of social 'quarantine,' to an indefinitely generalizable mechanism of 'panopticism.' Not because the disciplinary modality of power has replaced all the others; but because it has infiltrated the others, sometimes undermining them, but serving as an intermediary between them, linking them together, extending them and above all making it possible to bring the effects of power to the most minute and distant elements. It assures an infinitesimal distribution of the power relations. . . .

The formation of the disciplinary society is connected with a number of broad historical processes—economic, juridico-political and, lastly, scientific—of which it forms part.

1. Generally speaking, it might be said that the disciplines are techniques for assuring the

ordering of human multiplicities. It is true that there is nothing exceptional or even characteristic in this; every system of power is presented with the same problem. But the peculiarity of the disciplines is that they try to define in relation to the multiplicities a tactics of power that fulfils three criteria: firstly, to obtain the exercise of power at the lowest possible cost (economically, by the low expenditure it involves; politically, by its discretion, its low exteriorization, its relative invisibility, the little resistance it arouses); secondly, to bring the effects of this social power to their maximum intensity and to extend them as far as possible, without either failure or interval; thirdly, to link this 'economic' growth of power with the output of the apparatuses (educational, military, industrial or medical) within which it is exercised; in short, to increase both the docility and the utility of all the elements of the system. This triple objective of the disciplines corresponds to a well-known historical conjuncture. One aspect of this conjuncture was the large demographic thrust of the eighteenth century; an increase in the floating population (one of the primary objects of discipline is to fix; it is an anti-nomadic technique); a change of quantitative scale in the groups to be supervised or manipulated (from the beginning of the seventeenth century to the eve of the French Revolution, the school population had been increasing rapidly, as had no doubt the hospital population; by the end of the eighteenth century, the peace-time army exceeded 200,000 men). The other aspect of the conjuncture was the growth in the apparatus of production, which was becoming more and more extended and complex, it was also becoming more costly and its profitability had to be increased. The development of the disciplinary methods corresponded to these two processes, or rather, no doubt, to the new need to adjust their correlation. . . .

In short, to substitute for a power that is manifested through the brilliance of those who exercise it, a power that insidiously objectifies those on whom it is applied; to form a body of knowledge about these individuals, rather than to deploy the ostentatious signs of sovereignty. In a word, the disciplines are the ensemble of minute technical inventions that made it possible to increase the useful size of multiplicities

by decreasing the inconveniences of the power which, in order to make them useful, must control them. A multiplicity, whether in a workshop or a nation, an army or a school, reaches the threshold of a discipline when the relation of the one or the other becomes favourable. . . .

2. The panoptic modality of power—at the elementary, technical, merely physical level at which it is situated—is not under the immediate dependence or a direct extension of the great juridico-political structures of a society; it is nonetheless not absolutely independent. Historically, the process by which the bourgeoisie became in the course of the eighteenth century the politically dominant class was masked by the establishment of an explicit, coded and formally egalitarian juridical framework, made possible by the organization of a parliamentary, representative regime. But the development and generalization of disciplinary mechanisms constituted the other, dark side of these processes. The general juridical form that guaranteed a system of rights that were egalitarian in principle was supported by these tiny, everyday, physical mechanisms, by all those systems of micro-power that are essentially non-egalitarian and asymmetrical that we call the disciplines. And although, in a formal way, the representative regime makes it possible, directly or indirectly, with or without relays, for the will of all to form the fundamental authority of sovereignty, the disciplines provide, at the base, a guarantee of the submission of forces and bodies. The real, corporal disciplines constituted the foundation of the formal, juridical liberties. The contract may have been regarded as the ideal foundation of law and political power; panopticism constituted the technique, universally widespread, of coercion. It continued to work in depth on the juridical structures of society, in order to make the effective mechanisms of power function in opposition to the formal framework that it had acquired. The 'Enlightenment,' which discovered the liberties, also invented the disciplines.

In appearance, the disciplines constitute nothing more than an infra-law. They seem to extend the general forms defined by law to the infinitesimal level of individual lives; or they appear as methods of training that enable individuals to become integrated into these general demands. They seem to constitute the same type of law on a different scale, thereby making it more meticulous and more indulgent. The disciplines should be regarded as a sort of counter-law. They have the precise role of introducing insuperable asymmetries and excluding reciprocities. First, because discipline creates between individuals a 'private' link, which is a relation of constraints entirely different from contractual obligation; the acceptance of a discipline may be underwritten by contract; the way in which it is imposed, the mechanisms it brings into play, the non-reversible subordination of one group of people by another, the 'surplus' power that is always fixed on the same side, the inequality of position of the different 'partners' in relation to the common regulation, all these distinguish the disciplinary link from the contractual link, and make it possible to distort the contractual link systematically from the moment it has as its content a mechanism of discipline. We know, for example, how many real procedures undermine the legal fiction of the work contract: workshop discipline is not the least important. Moreover, whereas the juridical systems define juridical subjects according to universal norms, the disciplines characterize, classify, specialize; they distribute along a scale, around a norm, hierarchize individuals in relation to one another and, if necessary, disqualify and invalidate. In any case, in the space and during the time in which they exercise their control and bring into play the asymmetries of their power, they effect a suspension of the law that is never total, but is never annulled either. Regular and institutional as it may be, the discipline, in its mechanism, is a 'counter-law.' And, although the universal juridicism of modern society seems to fix limits on the exercise of power, its universally widespread panopticism enables it to operate, on the underside of the law, a machinery that is both immense and minute, which supports, reinforces, multiplies the asymmetry of power and undermines the limits that are traced around the law. The minute disciplines, the panopticisms of every day may well be below the level of emergence of the great apparatuses and the great political struggles. But, in the genealogy of modern society, they have been, with the class domination that traverses it, the political counterpart of the juridical norms

according to which power was redistributed. Hence, no doubt, the importance that has been given for so long to the small techniques of discipline, to those apparently insignificant tricks that it has invented, and even to those 'sciences' that give it a respectable face; hence the fear of abandoning them if one cannot find any substitute; hence the affirmation that they are at the very foundation of society, and an element in its equilibrium, whereas they are a series of mechanisms for unbalancing power relations definitively and everywhere; hence the persistence in regarding them as the humble, but concrete form of every morality, whereas they are a set of physico-political techniques.

To return to the problem of legal punishments, the prison with all the corrective technology at its disposal is to be resituated at the point where the codified power to punish turns into a disciplinary power to observe; at the point where the universal punishments of the law are applied selectively to certain individuals and always the same ones; at the point where the redefinition of the juridical subject by the penalty becomes a useful training of the criminal; at the point where the law is inverted and passes outside itself, and where the counter-law becomes the effective and institutionalized content of the juridical forms. What generalizes the power to punish, then, is not the universal consciousness of the law in each juridical subject; it is the regular extension, the infinitely minute web of panoptic techniques.

3. Taken one by one, most of these techniques have a long history behind them. But what was new, in the eighteenth century, was that, by being combined and generalized, they attained a level at which the formation of knowledge and the increase of power regularly reinforce one another in a circular process. At this point, the disciplines crossed the 'technological' threshold. First the hospital, then the school, then, later, the workshop were not simply 'reordered' by the disciplines; they became, thanks to them, apparatuses such that any mechanism of objectification could be used in them as an instrument of subjection, and any growth of power could give rise in them to possible branches of knowledge; it was this link, proper to the technological systems, that made possible within the disciplinary element the formation of

clinical medicine, psychiatry, child psychology, educational psychology, the rationalization of labour. It is a double process, then: an epistemological 'thaw' through a refinement of power relations; a multiplication of the effects of power through the formation and accumulation of new forms of knowledge. . . .

In the Middle Ages, the procedure of investigation gradually superseded the old accusatory justice, by a process initiated from above; the disciplinary technique, on the other hand, insidiously and as if from below, has invaded a penal justice that is still, in principle, inquisitorial. All the great movements of extension that characterize modern penality—the problematization of the criminal behind his crime, the concern with a punishment that is a correction, a therapy, a normalization, the division of the act of judgment between various authorities that are supposed to measure, assess, diagnose, cure, transform individuals—all this betrays the penetration of the disciplinary examination into the judicial inquisition.

What is now imposed on penal justice as its point of application, its 'useful' object, will no longer be the body of the guilty man set up against the body of the king; nor will it be the juridical subject of an ideal contract; it will be the disciplinary individual. The extreme point of penal justice under the Ancien Regime was the

infinite segmentation of the body of the regicide: a manifestation of the strongest power over the body of the greatest criminal, whose total destruction made the crime explode into its truth. The ideal point of penalty today would be an indefinite discipline: an interrogation without end, an investigation that would be extended without limit to a meticulous and ever more analytical observation, a judgment that would at the same time be the constitution of a file that was never closed, the calculated leniency of a penalty that would be interlaced with the ruthless curiosity of an examination, a procedure that would be at the same time the permanent measure of a gap in relation to an inaccessible norm and the asymptotic movement that strives to meet in infinity. The public execution was the logical culmination of a procedure governed by the Inquisition. The practice of placing individuals under 'observation' is a natural extension of a justice imbued with disciplinary methods and examination procedures. Is it surprising that the cellular prison, with its regular chronologies, forced labour, its authorities of surveillance and registration, its experts in normality, who continue and multiply the functions of the judge, should have become the modern instrument of penalty? Is it surprising that prisons resemble factories, schools, barracks, hospitals, which all resemble prisons?

Jean Baudrillard (1929–): A Biographical Sketch

Jean Baudrillard was born in France in Reims, the capital of the Champagne region, on July 20, 1929. The son of civil servants, Baudrillard was the first in his family to attend the university, where he studied German. After graduation, he taught German in a high school from 1958 to 1966 before completing his doctoral work in sociology under the advisement of Henri Lefebvre. In 1966, Baudrillard completed his doctoral thesis "Thèse de Troisième Cycle: Le Système des Objets" ("Third Cycle Thesis: The System of Objects"), which would later be published as his first major book, *The System of Objects*. He began his university career as an assistant professor in 1966 at University of Paris X, Nanterre. He would stay at Nanterre until 1987.

SOURCE: © Eric Fougere/VIP Images/CORBIS; used with permission.

The turmoil of the 1950s and 1960s politicized Baudrillard's outlook. Of particular import was the rising opposition to the Algerian War voiced by Jean-Paul Sartre and other French intellectuals. At Nanterre, Baudrillard became embroiled in the student revolts in 1968 and began contributing essays to the Marxist-inspired journal *Utopie*. While many of his early writings were works of literary criticism and translations of German playwrights into French, the Marxist influence on Baudrillard's early work is nevertheless clear. But with the rise of the "poststructural" movement in France, he would become critical of the economic focus of Marxist theory and later abandoned Marxism altogether. In the mid-1970s and continuing into the late 1980s, Baudrillard's work would move away from economic analyses almost entirely and toward the study of culture, particularly the examination of semiotics and the changing nature of signs in late-twentieth-century consumer capitalism. It is during this period that Baudrillard developed his central ideas of *hyperreality* and *simulations* that have become widely influential in postmodern theory.

In 1987, Baudrillard left Nanterre University to become the scientific director of the *Institut de Recherche et d'Information Socio-Économique* at the University of Paris IX in Dauphine. During the 1980s and 1990s, Baudrillard increasingly gained both academic and public celebrity. In *America* (1988) and the *Cool Memories* series (1990), Baudrillard chronicled his travels throughout Europe, Australia, and the United States, expressing a cynical attitude toward consumer culture, especially as he witnessed it in America. In the early 1990s, during the first U.S.-Iraq conflict, Baudrillard published a series of widely contested essays about why the Gulf War would, could, and did not take place (Baudrillard 1995). Baudrillard proclaimed that the Gulf War "did not take place"; rather, what took place was a carefully scripted media event, the outcome of which was predetermined. In this media spectacle, Saddam Hussein emerged as a villain of extravagant, exaggerated proportions; equally inflated were American media constructs of an effortless victory (see Dixon 1997:54; Edles 2002:81). These essays brought him much criticism but also served to increase his stature as a controversial intellectual. His November 1996 appearance at Whiskey Pete's Hotel and Casino in Nevada at the event "Chance: 3 Days in the Desert," an eclectic mixture of an academic conference and celebratory rave, increased his currency as an eccentric scholar and public icon. However, perhaps the pinnacle of Baudrillard's claim to fame is the use of several of his key ideas in the storyline for the film *The Matrix* (1999). Not only are passages of his text *Simulacra and Simulation* (1981) referenced verbatim in the film, but a copy of the book is shown in a key early sequence.

Today, Baudrillard continues to write, having produced numerous books on a wide range of subjects—including terrorism, politics, television, symbolic exchange, and virtual reality. Baudrillard is currently a professor in the division of media and communications at the European Graduate School.

INTELLECTUAL INFLUENCES AND CORE IDEAS

Jean Baudrillard is arguably the most prominent postmodern theorist. He assumes a unique position in the debates over postmodernism because his ideas provide much of the groundwork for the discussion. His conceptions of **simulacra**—or copies of objects for which there is no true original—and **hyperreality**—"reality" that has always already been reproduced—are among the most important contributions to postmodern theory. While Baudrillard did not begin to write explicitly under the label "postmodern" until the late 1980s, it is the works of the late 1970s and early 1980s that have become central to the theory of postmodernism.

Baudrillard began his career influenced by Marxist theory, but his early writing investigated the capitalist mode of consumption rather than the mode of production emphasized by Marx. His first book, *The System of Objects* (1968), initiated a series of studies in which Baudrillard developed a critique of consumerism and commodity fetishism. In this first book, Baudrillard explores everyday home furnishings and their role in the creation of domestic environments. He examines how mundane elements of home decor create environments of "modern" functionality (through furnishings like the "kitchen set" or the "living room set"), signify "keeping up" with technological progress (through the increasing accumulation of "gadgets"), and contribute to the overall process of conspicuous consumption (especially through the accumulation of "collections"). Baudrillard's indebtedness to Saussure and semiotics is clear as he explores the systems of signs through which everyday objects are attributed cultural meaning and symbolic value.

Baudrillard expanded this line of analysis in his next series of books, *Consumer Society* (1970), *For a Critique of the Political Economy of the Sign* (1972), and *The Mirror of Production* (1973), in which he developed a critique of the Marxist analytical framework, moving away from an emphasis on capitalist economic production toward the increasing relevance of consumption practices. These works are representative of an important shift in his approach to cultural analysis. Baudrillard no longer investigates the obvious, overt meaning of household objects but instead analyzes the multiple meanings attached to objects of consumption. For example, Baudrillard explores department stores, shopping malls, television programs, and leisure activities and the role they play in creating a culture of consumption. With a theoretical perspective that parallels that developed by the Frankfurt School (see Chapter 3), Baudrillard is critical of mass consumption and its ability to create false needs and to tie individual identities to commodities.

In these works Baudrillard also adumbrated the ideas underlying the theory of simulations. What marks this development is Baudrillard's shift in the way he explores the role of the sign in conveying meaning. Gone, he argues, are the days when signs conveyed simple and clear meaning. Today, consumer goods, and in particular mass media, have created a uniquely complex cultural world where signs routinely take on multiple meanings or have no stable meaning at all.

However, in postmodern society meaning is obscured not only because of the multiplicity of connotations but also because symbols no longer refer directly to a concrete reality. Nowhere is this trend more readily apparent than in the rise of "imagistic" advertising. Today, statements of explicit value (buy this car because it is well made) have given way to statements regarding implicit values and lifestyle images (buy this car because it will make you "cool"). Rather than focus on clear-cut evaluations as to the price and quality of a particular product, imagistic advertising encourages emotional engagement as well as unconscious desires and compels consumers to organize and find identity in cultural products. We come to understand who we (and you) are via symbols in the same way we come to understand the commercial products at hand. Thus, we docilely observe and order our lives using symbols (do they sport baggy pants or Armani; drive a Honda CRX or a Hummer). The result is not only that the world of true needs has been subordinated to the world of false needs but that "the realm of needing has become a function of the field of communication" (Kline and Leiss 1978:18).

Consider, for instance, a favorite object of postmodern analysis: the Nike "swoosh." While you are probably familiar with this symbol, you might have a difficult time identifying its specific meaning. What makes the semiotics of the "swoosh" so interesting is that it doesn't have any particular denotative meaning. In fact, the "swoosh" means multiple things: a powerful company, athleticism, status, sweatshop labor, and connections to celebrities like Tiger Woods, Mia Hamm, and Michael Jordan. It is difficult to pin down the clear, denotative meaning of the Nike "swoosh" because it does not have *one*; instead, it has multiple connotative associations and in some ways no real meaning at all. In Baudrillard's terms, the "swoosh" has meaning not through its specific connections to any particular signified; instead, its meaning stems from its multiplicity as a signifier. The Nike "swoosh" is a "floating signifier" that is able to move from one signified to another.

As we have seen, Baudrillard uses the term "hyperreality" to refer to this state when the distinction between "reality" and the model or simulation is completely dissolved. In the condition of hyperreality, simulations stand in for—they are more "real" than—reality; the map of the territory is taken for the territory itself. Baudrillard argues that the development of hyperreality can be seen through history. He suggests that the last six centuries can be described by changes in the strategies with which human beings have come to simulate reality. He argues that prior to the fifteenth-century Renaissance

Photo 8.6   Nike "Swoosh": The Epitome of a Floating Signifier

SOURCE: Reprinted with permission from www.adbusters.org.

in Europe, the symbolic order of society was built upon the obligation of signs to represent an authentic reality. This was particularly true for feudal societies in which the nature and number of signs were extremely limited. The meaning of such signs was hierarchically bound by the obligations of a rigid social structure, an effect of religious and politic hegemony. In other words, it was not only perfectly clear who was a lord and who was a serf, but which markers (clothing, style, language, etc.) connoted each position. The meaning of signs was "sure," nonarbitrary, and denotative, as it was based on what was considered to be an irrefutable social order.

The first true order of simulacra, Baudrillard suggests, began with the Renaissance and culminated with the birth of the Industrial Revolution. Here, the order of obligated signs is replaced by the first "modern signs" in an era of the "counterfeit," where the meaning of signs is no longer bound to the obligations of a feudal order. In this phase, signs begin to multiply with the expansion of strategies by which human beings come to represent the world (primarily painting and the printing press). Nevertheless, although signs remain largely unrestricted during this phase, they are still tied to representations of the natural world. Thus, this order of signs is based on what Baudrillard calls a "natural law of value," as signs acquire their value based on their ability, or inability, to represent the natural world. In this order, signs do not have to represent directly the material world; they may be flagrantly counterfeit, but their meaning is judged with respect to an empirical reality. An example of this order of simulacra is an artistic reproduction of a famous painting that confirms rather than calls into question the value of the "original" piece.

Baudrillard's second order of simulacra begins with the Industrial Revolution and ends in the early part of the twentieth century. A newfound logic of technological reproduction creates a mass proliferation of signs serially produced on a massive scale (through photography, film, print, etc.). A novel order of signs emerges not only because of increases in quantitative scale, but also as a result of the production of signs as reproductions of other signs. Mass advertising not only represents products and their uses, but also begins to refer to lifestyles that are found only in other ads. The value of objects is now determined by the logic of the marketplace of signs, where they take on a second-order of signification and their meaning is severed (!) from their commodity-like "exchange value."

The third order of simulacra, beginning in the late twentieth century, is the order of simulation proper and describes the contemporary period. The dominant scheme is one in which signs no longer have any contact with material reality but, instead, are completely liberated from objective signifieds. Pure simulacra emerge as copies of things that have always only been copies. For Baudrillard, this order is organized around what he calls a "structural law of value," where the meaning of a particular sign is not derived from a connection to a real signified but instead to its structural relationship to a semiotic code that is divorced from reality. For instance, the popularity of Nike shoes is based on an emulation of a "street style," an attitude of self-assertion and even rebellion associated with African American inner-city culture, a "prestige from below." However, not only is this nothing more than *hyperreality* since Nike is a multinational corporation *not* rooted in inner-city street culture at all, paradoxically, inner-city youth who buy Nike themselves are victims of this imaging. In a sense, they "buy themselves back" by sporting the expensive, popular Nike brand (see Lipsitz 1994:123; Edles 2002:88).

Baudrillard's description of the historical progression of simulacra has become widely influential and is frequently recounted as a seminal statement on postmodern culture. A summary of Baudrillard's "order of simulacra" is presented in Table 8.3.

Table 8.3   Baudrillard's Theory of the "Orders of Simulacra"

Dominant Scheme	Law of Value	Nature of Semiotic Value	Semiotic Focus	Historical Era
Obligation	Prestige	Non-arbitrary	Sure-signs	Pre-Renaissance
Counterfeit	Natural	Use-value	Natural object	Renaissance to Industrial
Production	Market	Exchange-value	Logic of commodity	Industrial to early 20th century
Simulation	Structural	Sign-value	Codes and models	Late 20th century to contemporary period

Throughout his works, Baudrillard offers many examples of the simulacra he describes. Below we summarize a few of these examples:

- Theme parks like Disneyland now simulate the experiences of space travel, submarine voyages, driving on the Autobahn, strolling through the French Quarter in New Orleans, expeditions through the "Western Frontier," nostalgic walks down "Main Street" America, and journeys into fairy tales and children's stories. Baudrillard argues that Disneyland is a perfect model of a simulation. Disneyland is not just simply a simulated fantasyland, but instead it is presented as fantasy, which, ironically, leads us to believe that the rest of America is real. Thus for Baudrillard, in contrast to the simulated malls and theme restaurants of everyday "*real*" life, Disneyland is more authentic than "reality" because it does not purport to be "real."

- Television, which invites viewers into a counterfeit world rich with the intimate and personal details of the lives of "fictional" and "nonfictional" characters, delivers individuals into a fantasy world of consumerism and consumer goods, allows masses of people to simultaneously attend public events without leaving the couch, and ultimately simulates travel through both time and space. There is perhaps no better example of the role of television as a simulation than the way that television actors and their characters are confused by the viewing public. It is often reported that television characters (not the actors) will receive "get well" cards from viewers when they (the *character*) become sick, and that television actors will be chastised in public for something their *character* has done on the show. The "Trekkies" phenomenon, those devoted fans of *Star Trek* who are passionately committed to the show, is another characteristic example of the role of television in producing simulations.

- The first Gulf War, which Baudrillard claims did not really occur, was more of a simulation of the much-feared nuclear war between the Soviet Union and the United States. In addition, the war was entirely simulated for viewers through highly regulated news reports and tightly controlled military briefings. For Americans, Baudrillard claims, much of the actual experience of the war resembled a flight simulation video game in which planes dropped bombs on targets marked by crosshairs and casualties were largely removed from the equation.

- Watergate, Baudrillard argues, was a simulated political scandal in which reporters and government officials revived a dying political process by creating an indignity as a reminder of the existence of American politics. Baudrillard argues that the Watergate scandal was a hyperreal event created in order to simulate political credibility in an era of political cynicism.

Demographic polls, statistical research, and voting have become simulated attempts to represent the idea of "the social" in the era of the "mass" society. Borrowing a phrase used by Richard Nixon to manufacture consensus as a political tool, Baudrillard argues that the social is now "in the shadow of the silent majorities." He suggests that contemporary mass society is "frozen," as individuals demonstrate their social connections only "silently" in simulated forms, through surveys, demographic counts, and political polls. This has a dual effect: on the one hand, it continually reproduces a simulation of the social; and on the other hand, it neutralizes the need for real social relationships (i.e., "we have been counted, therefore we exist").

Additional examples of simulations abound in our contemporary world—flight simulators, interactive video games, virtual-reality technology, IMAX films, robotic pets, virtual celebrities, computer-generated animation, Barbie dolls, museums, zoos, aquariums, and so on. There are even copies of Disneyland in France and Japan. For Baudrillard, it is the mass media with its endless ability to create and reproduce images and signs that drives this process, becoming the great simulation-producing machine of the twentieth and twenty-first centuries. The result is that ours is a thoroughly hyperreal world, as images and signs become our primary references. For instance, Disneyland's Main Street has become the benchmark for what America *is*, such that new towns are created emulating *it*. Indeed, Disney "opened" its own neotraditional town of "Celebration" in the swamplands of Florida in 1996. In addition to an instantly functioning downtown modeled after Disneyland's Main Street, the town sports a man-made lake and cutting-edge technology. Disney expects Celebration to grow to a population of 20,000 (Ehrenhalt, 1999: 8; Edles, 2002:87).

Photo 8.7   Picture Perfect: Downtown Celebration

SOURCE: Photo taken by Bobak Ha'Eri February 23, 2006; used with permission.

Figure 8.2   Baudrillard's Basic Concepts and Theoretical Orientation

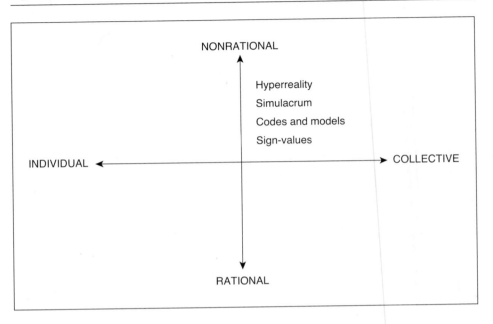

BAUDRILLARD'S THEORETICAL ORIENTATION

As discussed above, Baudrillard seeks to complement Marxist theories of economic production with parallel studies of consumerism. Theoretically, Baudrillard's orientation can best be understood as preserving the Frankfurt School's collectivistic approach to order while moving it in a nonrationalistic direction (see Figure 8.2). Theoretically, this means that Baudrillard's collectivist and nonrationalist approach parallels both American structural functionalism (see Chapter 2) and French structuralism—which is no surprise. As discussed above, both these versions of structuralism emphasize the salience of culture, as does Baudrillard; and of course, Baudrillard's work is explicitly based on the semiotic model. In other words, by definition, theoretical approaches that emphasize how *systems of meaning* shape action necessarily prioritize the nonrational realm.

In terms of order, Baudrillard's emphasis is almost entirely collectivist. He has little to say about individuals and their social interaction, except the degree to which they are ensconced in a system of hyperreality saturated by simulations. Like the theories associated with functionalism, the Frankfurt School, and French structuralism, his analytical focus is at the level of the collective, underscoring the role of simulations and their transformative effects on culture. Individuals are entirely absent as producers of simulations; instead they are simply subject to the ability of simulations to distort reality. In Baudrillard's analysis, it is culture that reigns supreme, filled with simulacra that construct an artificial world and minimize the efficacy of individual agency.

In terms of action, although Baudrillard shares with structural functionalists an emphasis on the nonrationalist workings of the cultural realm, his emphasis on the changing nature of culture in the contemporary era of mass media–generated simulations, and the blurring of the boundaries of reality and unreality, make his conceptualization of culture far less coherent and integrative than that of Parsons (see Chapter 2). Instead, culture is depicted as a cacophony of signs and symbols that circulate without any necessarily rational logic. Despite its transcendence over individuals, culture is not seen as a standardized system of domination created by a culture industry, as described by the theorists of the Frankfurt School (see Chapter 3). For Baudrillard, the signs that circulate through culture are ever fluctuating, unstable, and potentially incoherent. Without a concrete, empirical reality from which to draw, even an allegedly "strategic" calculation of "costs" and "benefits" is itself an illusion.

Reading

Introduction to *Simulacra and Simulations*

In the following essay from *Simulacra and Simulations* (1981), Baudrillard sets out his key terms "simulacra" and "hyperreality" and explains how today the circulation of signs within the mass media creates a semiotic "code" that is based not on "reality" but, rather, on a symbolic logic of its own. To help us understand this idea, Baudrillard begins by borrowing an allegory from the Argentinean writer Jorge Luis Borges. Borges describes an imaginary empire where a group of cartographers set out to construct a map with so much detail that it becomes a perfect replication of the original territory it charts. This map is such a seamless simulation of the territory that it is mistaken for the real territory itself. However, as fate would have it, the map begins to disintegrate and the citizens of the empire who inhabit the map, mistaking it for the territory itself, find themselves disoriented and uncertain of the authenticity of their reality.

Baudrillard suggests that a similar condition of confusion is present in contemporary societies today. We have increasingly filled our world with simulations of reality and, mistaking them for reality itself, cannot distinguish between the simulation and the real. Such is the condition of hyperreality. In semiotic terms, Baudrillard argues that hyperreality is a product of the separation of signifiers from signifieds. If signifieds are some object, thought, or feeling that one wishes to represent, and a signifier is that symbol chosen to stand for the signified, then, drawing a parallel to Borges's allegory, signifieds are like the territory and signifiers are like the map. In Baudrillard's theory of the simulation, we have increasingly come to create and use signifiers (i.e., maps) that have lost their connection to a stable signified (i.e., the territory). In short, simulations now stand in for reality, where the map of the territory is taken for the territory itself, the signifier is mistaken for the signified, and reproductions are experienced as real—all creating a condition of hyperreality . . . a "reality" that is rooted in reproduction rather than in "reality" itself. In this essay, Baudrillard gives several other examples of this "divine irreference of images" characteristic of contemporary society, including Disneyland and Watergate discussed above. Most provocatively, in the final section of this essay Baudrillard reiterates that since "reality" does not exist anymore (only hyperreality) neither does "illusion" and, in accordance with Foucault's conceptualization of disciplinary society, he emphasizes that power has been replaced by *signs* of power.

❖

Simulacra and Simulations (1981)

Jean Baudrillard

The simulacrum is never that which conceals the truth—it is the truth which conceals that there is none.

The simulacrum is true.

Ecclesiastes

If we were able to take as the finest allegory of simulation the Borges tale where the cartographers of the Empire draw up a map so detailed that it ends up exactly covering the territory (but where, with the decline of the Empire this map becomes frayed and finally ruined, a few shreds still discernible in the deserts—the metaphysical beauty of this ruined abstraction, bearing witness to an imperial pride and rotting like a carcass, returning to the substance of the soil, rather as an aging double ends up being confused with the real thing), this fable would then have come full circle for us, and now has nothing but the discrete charm of second-order simulacra.[i]

Abstraction today is no longer that of the map, the double, the mirror or the concept.

Simulation is no longer that of a territory, a referential being or a substance. It is the generation by models of a real without origin or reality: a hyperreal. The territory no longer precedes the map, nor survives it. Henceforth, it is the map that precedes the territory—*precession of simulacra*—it is the map that engenders the territory and if we were to revive the fable today, it would be the territory whose shreds are slowly rotting across the map. It is the real, and not the map, whose vestiges subsist here and there, in the deserts which are no longer those of the Empire, but our own. *The desert of the real itself.*

In fact, even inverted, the fable is useless. Perhaps only the allegory of the Empire remains. For it is with the same imperialism that present-day simulators try to make the real, all the real, coincide with their simulation models. But it is no longer a question of either maps or territory. Something has disappeared: the sovereign difference between them that was the abstraction's charm. For it is the difference which forms the poetry of the map and

SOURCE: From Baudrillard, J., *Simulacra and Simulations,* Edited by Sylvère Lotringer and translated by Paul Foss, Paul Patton and Philip Beitchman, copyright © 1983. Reprinted with permission from Semiotext(e), Inc.

[i]Counterfeit and reproduction imply always an anguish, a disquieting foreignness: the uneasiness before the photograph, considered like a witch's trick—and more generally before any technical apparatus, which is always an apparatus of reproduction, is related by Benjamin to the uneasiness before the mirror-image. There is already sorcery at work in the mirror. But how much more so when this image can be detached from the mirror and be transported, stocked, reproduced at will (cf. The Student of Prague, where the devil detaches the image of the student from the mirror and harrasses him to death by the intermediary of this image). All reproduction implies therefore a kind of black magic, from the fact of being seduced by one's own image in the water, like Narcissus, to being haunted by the double and, who knows, to the mortal turning back of this vast technical apparatus secreted today by man as his own image (the narcissistic mirage of technique, McLuhan) and that returns to him, cancelled and distorted-endless reproduction of himself and his power to the limits of the world. Reproduction is diabolical in its very essence; it makes something fundamental vacillate. This has hardly changed for us: simulation (that we describe here as the operation of the code) is still and always the place of a gigantic enterprise of manipulation, of control and of death, just like the imitative object (primitive statuette, image of photo) always had as objective an operation of black image.

the charm of the territory, the magic of the concept and the charm of the real. This representational imaginary, which both culminates in and is engulfed by the cartographer's mad project of an ideal coextensivity between the map and the territory, disappears with simulation, whose operation is nuclear and genetic, and no longer specular and discursive. With it goes all of metaphysics. No more mirror of being and appearances, of the real and its concept; no more imaginary coextensivity: rather, genetic miniaturization is the dimension of simulation. The real is produced from miniaturized units, from matrices, memory banks and command models—and with these it can be reproduced an indefinite number of times. It no longer has to be rational, since it is no longer measured against some ideal or negative instance. It is nothing more than operational. In fact, since it is no longer enveloped by an imaginary, it is no longer real at all. It is a hyperreal: the product of an irradiating synthesis of combinatory models in a hyperspace without atmosphere.

In this passage to a space whose curvature is no longer that of the real, nor of truth, the age of simulation thus begins with a liquidation of all referentials—worse: by their artificial resurrection in systems of signs, which are a more ductile material than meaning, in that they lend themselves to all systems of equivalence, all binary oppositions and all combinatory algebra. It is no longer a question of imitation, nor of reduplication, nor even of parody. It is rather a question of substituting signs of the real for the real itself; that is, an operation to deter every real process by its operational double, a metastable, programmatic, perfect descriptive machine which provides all the signs of the real and short-circuits all its vicissitudes. Never again will the real have to be produced: this is the vital function of the model in a system of death, or rather of anticipated resurrection which no longer leaves any chance even in the event of death. A hyperreal henceforth sheltered from the imaginary, and from any distinction between the real and the imaginary, leaving room only for the orbital recurrence of models and the simulated generation of difference.

THE DIVINE IRREFERENCE OF IMAGES

To dissimulate is to feign not to have what one has. To simulate is to feign to have what one hasn't. One implies a presence, the other an absence. But the matter is more complicated, since to simulate is not simply to feign: "Someone who feigns an illness can simply go to bed and pretend he is ill. Someone who simulates an illness produces in himself some of the symptoms" (Littre). Thus, feigning or dissimulating leaves the reality principle intact: the difference is always clear, it is only masked; whereas simulation threatens the difference between "true" and "false," between "real" and "imaginary." Since the simulator produces "true" symptoms, is he or she ill or not? The simulator cannot be treated objectively either as ill, or as not ill. Psychology and medicine stop at this point, before a thereafter undiscoverable truth of the illness. For if any symptom can be "produced," and can no longer be accepted as a fact of nature, then every illness may be considered as simulatable and simulated, and medicine loses its meaning since it only knows how to treat "true" illnesses by their objective causes. Psychosomatics evolves in a dubious way on the edge of the illness principle. As for psychoanalysis, it transfers the symptom from the organic to the unconscious order: once again, the latter is held to be real, more real than the former; but why should simulation stop at the portals of the unconscious? Why couldn't the "work" of the unconscious be "produced" in the same way as any other symptom in classical medicine? Dreams already are.

The alienist, of course, claims that "for each form of the mental alienation there is a particular order in the succession of symptoms, of which the stimulator is unaware and in the absence of which the alienist is unlikely to be deceived." This (which dates from 1865) in order to save at all cost the truth principle, and to escape the specter raised by simulation: namely that truth, reference and objective causes have ceased to exist. What can medicine do with something which floats on either side of illness, on either side of health, or with the reduplication of illness in a discourse that is no longer true or false? What can psychoanalysis do with the reduplication of the discourse of the unconscious in a discourse of simulation that can never be unmasked, since it isn't false either?[ii]

What can the army do with simulators? Traditionally, following a direct principle of identification, it unmasks and punishes them. Today, it can reform an excellent simulator as though he were equivalent to a "real" homosexual, heart-case or lunatic. Even military psychology retreats from the Cartesian clarifies and hesitates to draw the distinction between true and false, between the "produced" symptom and the authentic symptom. "If he acts crazy so well, then he must be mad." Nor is it mistaken: in the sense that all lunatics are simulators, and this lack of distinction is the worst form of subversion. Against it, classical reason armed itself with all its categories. But it is this today which again outflanks them, submerging the truth principle.

Outside of medicine and the army, favored terrains of simulation, the affair goes back to religion and the simulacrum of divinity: "I forbade any simulacrum in the temples because the divinity that breathes life into nature cannot be represented." Indeed it can. But what becomes of the divinity when it reveals itself in icons, when it is multiplied in simulacra? Does it remain the supreme authority, simply incarnated in images as a visible theology? Or is it volatilized into simulacra which alone deploy their pomp and power of fascination—the visible machinery of icons being substituted for the pure and intelligible Idea of God? This is precisely what was feared by the Iconoclasts, whose millennial quarrel is still with us today.[iii] Their rage to destroy images rose precisely because they sensed this omnipotence of simulacra, this facility they have of erasing God from the consciousnesses of people, and the overwhelming, destructive truth which they suggest: that ultimately there has never been any God; that only simulacra exist; indeed that God himself has only ever been his own simulacrum. Had they been able to believe that images only occulted or masked the Platonic idea of God, there would have been no reason to destroy them. One can live with the idea of a distorted truth. But their metaphysical despair came from the idea that the images concealed nothing at all, and that in fact they were not images, such as the original model would have made them, but actually perfect simulacra forever radiant with their own fascination. But this death of the divine referential has to be exorcised at all cost.

It can be seen that the iconoclasts, who are often accused of despising and denying images, were in fact the ones who accorded them their actual worth, unlike the iconolaters, who saw in them only reflections and were content to venerate God at one remove. But the converse can also be said, namely that the iconolaters possessed the most modern and adventurous minds, since, underneath the idea of the apparition of God in the mirror of images, they already enacted his death and his disappearance in the epiphany of his representations (which they perhaps knew no longer represented anything, and that they were purely a game, but that this was precisely the greatest game—knowing also that it is dangerous to unmask images, since they dissimulate the fact that there is nothing behind them).

This was the approach of the Jesuits, who based their politics on the virtual disappearance of God and on the worldly and spectacular manipulation of consciences—the evanescence of God in the epiphany of power—the end of

---

[ii]There is furthermore in Monod's book a flagrant contradiction, which reflects the ambiguity of all current science. His discourse concerns the code, that is the third-order simulacra, but it does so still according to "scientific" schemes of the second-order—objectiveness, "scientific" ethic of knowledge, science's principle of truth and transcendence. All things incompatible with the indeterminable models of the third-order.

[iii]"It's the feeble 'definition' of TV which condemns its spectator to rearranging the few points retained into a kind of abstract work. He participates suddenly in the creation of a reality that was only just presented to him in dots: the television watcher is in the position of an individual who is asked to project his own fantasies on inkblots that are not supposed to represent anything." TV as perpetual Rorschach test. And furthermore: "The TV image requires each instant that we 'close' the spaces in the mesh by a convulsive sensuous participation that is profoundly kinetic and tactile."

transcendence, which no longer serves as alibi for a strategy completely free of influences and signs. Behind the baroque of images hides the grey eminence of politics.

Thus perhaps at stake has always been the murderous capacity of images: murderers of the real; murderers of their own model as the Byzantine icons could murder the devine identity. To this murderous capacity is opposed the dialectical capacity of representations as a visible and intelligible mediation of the real. All of Western faith and good faith was engaged in this wager on representation: that a sign could refer to the depth of meaning, that a sign could exchange for meaning and that something could guarantee this exchange God, of course. But what if God himself can be simulated, that is to say, reduced to the signs which attest his existence? Then the whole system becomes weightless; it is no longer anything but a gigantic simulacrum: not unreal, but a simulacrum, never again exchanging for what is real, but exchanging in itself, in an uninterrupted circuit without reference or circumference.

So it is with simulation, insofar as it is opposed to representation. Representation starts from the principle that the sign and the real are equivalent (even if this equivalence is Utopian, it is a fundamental axiom). Conversely, simulation starts from the Utopia of this principle of equivalence, *from the radical negation of the sign as value,* from the sign as reversion and death sentence of every reference. Whereas representation tries to absorb simulation by interpreting it as false representation, simulation envelops the whole edifice of representation as itself a simulacrum.

These would be the successive phases of the image:

1. It is the reflection of a basic reality.

2. It masks and perverts a basic reality.

3. It masks the *absence* of a basic reality.

4. It bears no relation to any reality whatever: it is its own pure simulacrum.

In the first case, the image is a *good* appearance: the representation is of the order of sacrament. In the second, it is an evil appearance: of the order of malefice. In the third, it *plays at being* an appearance: it is of the order of sorcery. In the fourth, it is no longer in the order of appearance at all, but of simulation.

The transition from signs which dissimulate something to signs which dissimulate that there is nothing, marks the decisive turning point. The first implies a theology of truth and secrecy (to which the notmn of ideology still belongs). The second inaugurates an age of simulacra and simulation, in which there is no longer any God to recognize his own, nor any last judgment to separate truth from false, the real from its artificial resurrection, since everything is already dead and risen in advance.

When the real is no longer what it used to be, nostalgia assumes its full meaning. There is a proliferation of myths of origin and signs of reality; of second-hand truth, objectivity and authenticity. There is an escalation of the true, of the lived experience; a resurrection of the figurative where the object and substance have disappeared. And there is a panic-stricken production of the real and the referential, above and parallel to the panic of material production. This is how simulation appears in the phase that concerns us: a strategy of the real, neo-real and hyperreal, whose universal double is a strategy of deterrence.

HYPERREAL AND IMAGINARY

Disneyland is a perfect model of all the entangled orders of simulation. To begin with it is a play of illusions and phantasms: pirates, the frontier, future world, etc. This imaginary world is supposed to be what makes the operation successful. But, what draws the crowds is undoubtedly much more the social microcosm, the miniaturized and *religious* revelling in real America, in its delights and drawbacks. You park outside, queue up inside, and are totally abandoned at the exit. In this imaginary world the only phantasmagoria is in the inherent warmth and affection of the crowd, and in that auffi-ciently excessive number of gadgets used there to specifically maintain the multitudinous affect. The contrast with the absolute solitude of the parking lot—a veritable concentration camp—is total. Or rather: inside, a whole range of gadgets magnetize the crowd into direct flows; outside, solitude is directed onto a single gadget: the automobile. By an extraordinary coincidence (one that undoubtedly belongs to the peculiar enchantment of this universe), this deep-frozen infantile world happens to have been conceived and realized by a man who is himself now cryogenized; Walt Disney, who awaits his resurrection at minus 180 degrees centigrade.

The objective profile of the United States, then, may be traced throughout Disneyland, even down to the morphology of individuals and the crowd. All its values are exalted here, in miniature and comic-strip form. Embalmed and pacified. Whence the possibility of an ideological analysis of Disneyland (L. Marin does it well in Utopies, jeux d'espaces): digest of the American way of life, panegyric to American values, idealized transposition of a contradictory reality. To be sure. But this conceals something else, and that "ideological" blanket exactly serves to cover over a third-order simulation: Disneyland is there to conceal the fact that it is the "real" country, all of "real" America, which is Disneyland (just as prisons are there to conceal the fact that it is the social in its entirety, in its banal omnipresence, which is carceral). Disneyland is presented as imaginary in order to make us believe that the rest is real, when in fact all Los Angeles and the America surrounding it are no longer real, but of the order of the hyperreal and of simulation. It is no longer a question of a false representation of reality (ideology), but of concealing the fact that the real is no longer real, and thus of saving the reality principle.

The Disneyland imaginary is neither true nor false: it is a deterrence machine set up in order to rejuvenate in reverse the fiction of the real. Whence the debility, the infantile degeneration of this imaginary. It's meant to be an infantile world, in order to make us believe that the adults are elsewhere, in the "real" world, and to conceal the fact that real childishness is everywhere, particularly among those adults who go there to act the child in order to foster illusions of their real childishness.

Moreover, Disneyland is not the only one. Enchanted Village, Magic Mountain, Marine World: Los Angeles is encircled by these "imaginary stations" which feed reality, reality-energy, to a town whose mystery is precisely that it is nothing more than a network of endless, unreal circulation: a town of fabulous proportions, but without space or dimensions. As much as electrical and nuclear power stations, as much as film studios, this town, which is nothing more than an immense script and a perpetual motion picture, needs this old imaginary made up of childhood signals and faked phantasms for its sympathetic nervous system. . . .

STRATEGY OF THE REAL

Of the same order as the impossibility of rediscovering an absolute level of the real, is the impossibility of staging an illusion. Illusion is no longer possible, because the real is no longer possible. It is the whole *political* problem of the parody, of hypersimulation or offensive simulation, which is posed here.

For example: it would be interesting to see whether the repressive apparatus would not react more violently to a simulated hold up than to a real one? For a real hold up only upsets the order of things, the right of property, whereas a simulated hold up interferes with the very principle of reality. Transgression and violence are less serious, for they only contest the *distribution* of the real. Simulation is infinitely more dangerous since it always suggests, over and above its object, that *law and order themselves might really be nothing more than a simulation.*

But the difficulty is in proportion to the peril. How to feign a violation and put it to the test? Go and simulate a theft in a large department store: how do you convince the security guards that it is a simulated theft? There is no "objective" difference: the same gestures and the same signs exist as for a real theft; in fact the signs incline neither to one side nor the other. As far as the established order is concerned, they are always of the order of the real.

Go and organize a fake hold up. Be sure to check that your weapons are harmless, and take the most trustworthy hostage, so that no life is in danger (otherwise you risk committing an offence). Demand ransom, and arrange it so that the operation creates the greatest commotion possible. In brief, stay close to the "truth," so as to test the reaction of the apparatus to a perfect simulation. But you won't succeed: the web of artificial signs will be inextricably mixed up with real elements (a police officer will really shoot on sight; a bank customer will faint and die of a heart attack; they will really turn the phoney ransom over to you). In brief, you will unwittingly find yourself immediately in the real, one of whose functions is precisely to devour every attempt at simulation, to reduce everything to some reality: that's exactly how the established order is, well before institutions and justice come into play.

In this impossibility of isolating the process of simulation must be seen the whole thrust of an order that can only see and understand in terms of some reality, because it can function nowhere else. The simulation of an offence, if it is patent, will either be punished more lightly (because it has no "consequences") or be punished as an offence to public office (for example, if one triggered off a police operation "for nothing")—but *never as simulation*, since it is precisely as such that no equivalence with the real is possible, and hence no repression either. The challenge of simulation is irreceivable by power. How can you punish the simulation of virtue? Yet as such it is as serious as the simulation of crime. Parody makes obedience and transgression equivalent, and that is the most serious crime, since it *cancels out the difference upon which the law is based*. The established order can do nothing against it, for the law is a

second-order simulacrum whereas simulation is a third-order simulacrum, beyond true and false, beyond equivalences, beyond the rational distinctions upon which function all power and the entire social stratum. Hence, *failing the real*, it is here that we must aim at order.

This is why order always opts for the real. In a state of uncertainty, it always prefers this assumption (thus in the army they would rather take the simulator as a true madman). But this becomes more and more difficult, for it is practically impossible to isolate the process of simulation; through the force of inertia of the real which surrounds us, the inverse is also true (and this very reversibility forms part of the apparatus of simulation and of power's impotency): namely, *it is now impossible to isolate the process of the real,* or to prove the real.

Thus all hold ups, hijacks and the like are now as it were simulation hold ups, in the sense that they are inscribed in advance in the decoding and orchestration rituals of the media, anticipated in their mode of presentation and possible consequences. In brief, where they function as a set of signs dedicated exclusively to their recurrence as signs, and no longer to their "real" goal at all. But this does not make them inoffensive. On the contrary, it is as hyperreal events, no longer having any particular contents or aims, but indefinitely refracted by each other (for that matter like so-called historical events: strikes, demonstrations, crises, etc.[iv]),

[iv]The entire current "psychological" situation is characterized by this shortcircuit.

Doesn't emancipation of children and teenagers, once the initial phase of revolt is passed and once there has been established the principle of the right to emancipation, seem like the real emancipation of parents? And the young (students, high-schoolers, adolescents) seem to sense it in their always more insistent demand (though still as paradoxical) for the presence and advice of parents or of teachers. Alone at least, free and responsible, it seemed to them suddenly that other people possibly have absconded with their true liberty. Therefore, there is no question of "leaving them be." They're going to hassle them, not with any emotional or material spontaneous demand, but with an exigency that has been premediated and corrected by an implicit oedipal knowledge. Hyperdependence (much greater than before) distorted by irony and refusal, parody of libidinous original mechanisms. Demand without content, without referent, unjustified, but for all that all the more severe—naked demand with no possible answer. The contents of knowledge (teaching) or of affective relations, the pedagogical or familial referent having been eliminated in the act of emancipation, there remains only a demand linked to the empty form of the institution—perverse demand, and for that reason all the more obstinate. "Transferable" desire (that is to say non-referential, un-referential), desire that has been fed by lack, by the place left vacant, "liberated," desire captured in its own vertiginous image, desire of desire, as pure form, hyperreal. Deprived of that they are precisely unverifiable by an order which can only exert itself on the real and the rational, on ends and means: a referential order which can only dominate referentials, a determinate power which can only dominate a determined world, but which can do nothing about that indefinite recurrence of simulation, about that weightless nebula no longer obeying the law of gravitation of the real—power itself eventually breaking apart in this space and becoming a simulation of power (disconnected from its aims and objectives, and dedicated to *power effects* and mass simulation).

The only weapon of power, its only strategy against this defection, is to reinject realness and referentiality everywhere, in order to convince us of the reality of the social, of the gravity of the economy and the finalities of production. For that purpose it prefers the discourse of crisis, but also—why not?—the discourse of desire. "Take your desires for reality!" can be understood as the ultimate slogan of power, for in a nonreferential world even the confusian of the reality principle with the desire principle is less dangerous than contagious hyperreality. One remains among principles, and there power is always right.

Hyperreality and simulation are deterrents of every principle and of every objective; they turn against power this deterrence which is so well

---

iv(Continued)

symbolic substance, it doubles back upon itself, draws its energy from its own reflection and its disappointment with itself. This is literally today the "demand," and it is obvious that unlike the "classical" objective or transferable relations this one here is insoluble and interminable.

Simulated Oedipus.

Francois Richard: "Students asked to be seduced either bodily or verbally. But also they are aware of this and they play the game, ironically. 'Give us your knowledge, your presence, you have the word, speak, you are there for that.' Contestation certainly, but not only: the more authority is contested, vilified, the greater the need for authority as such. They play at Oedipus also, to deny it all the more vehemently. The 'teach', 'he's Daddy, they say' it's fun, you play at incest, malaise, the untouchable, at being a tease—in order to de-sexualize finally." Like one under analysis who asks for Oedipus back again, who tells the "oedipal" stories, who has the "analytical" dreams to satisfy the supposed request of the analyst, or to resist him? In the same way the student goes through his oedipal number, his seduction number, gets chummy, close, approaches, dominates—but this isn't desire, it's simulation. Oedipal psychodrama of simulation (neither less real nor less dramatic for all that). Very difference from the real libidinal stakes of knowledge and power or even of a real mourning for the absence of same (as could have happened after 1968 in the universities). Now we've reached the phase of desperate reproduction, and where the stakes are nil, the simulacrum is maximal—exacerbated and parodied simulation at one and the same time—as interminable as psychoanalysis and for the same reasons.

The interminable psychoanalysis.

There is a whole chapter to add to the history of transference and countertransference: that of their liquidation by simulation, of the impossible psychoanalysis because it is itself, from now on, that produces and reproduces the unconscious as its institutional substance. Psychoanalysis dies also of the exchange of the signs of the unconscious. Just as revolution dies of the exchange of the critical signs of political economy. This short-circuit was well known to Freud in the form of the gift of the analytic dream, or with the "uninformed" patients, in the form of the gift of their analytic knowledge. But this was still interpreted as resistance, as detour, and did not put fundamentally into question either the process of analysis or the principle of transference. It is another thing entirely when the unconscious itself, the discourse of the unconscious becomes unfindable—according to the same scenario of simulative anticipation that we have seen at work on all levels with the machines of the third order. The analysis then can no longer end, it becomes logically and historically interminable, since it stabilizes on a puppetsubstance of reproduction, an unconscious programmed on demand—an impossible-to-breakthrough point around which the whole analysis is rearranged. The messages of the unconscious have been short-circuited by the psychoanalysis "medium." This is libidinal hyperrealism. To the famous categories of the real, the symbolic and the imaginary, it is going to be necessary to add the hyperreal, which captures and obstructs the functioning of the three orders.

utilized for a long time itself. For, finally, it was capital which was the first to feed throughout its history on the destruction of every referential, of every human goal, which shattered every ideal distinction between true and false, good and evil, in order to establish a radical law of equivalence and exchange, the iron law of its power. It was the first to practice deterrence, abstraction, disconnection, deterritorialization, etc.; and if it was capital which fostered reality, the reality principle, it was also the first to liquidate it in the extermination of every use value, of every real equivalence, of production and wealth, in the very sensation we have of the unreality of the stakes and the omnipotence of manipulation. Now, it is this very logic which is today hardened even more *against* it. And when it wants to fight this catastrophic spiral by secreting one last glimmer of reality, on which to found one last glimmer of power, it only multiplies the *signs* and accelerates the play of simulation.

As long as it was historically threatened by the real, power risked deterrence and simulation, disintegrating every contradiction by means of the production of equivalent signs. When it is threatened today by simulation (the threat of vanishing in the play of signs), power risks the real, risks crisis, it gambles on remanufacturing artificial, social, economic, political stakes. This is a question of life or death for it. But is too late.

Whence the characteristic hysteria of our time: the hysteria of production and reproduction of the real. The other production, that of goods and commodities, that of *la belle epoque* of political economy, no longer makes any sense of its own, and has not for some time. What society seeks through production, and overproduction, is the restoration of the real which escapes it. That is why *contemporary "material" production is itself hyperreal*. It retains all the features, the whole discourse of traditional production, but it is nothing more than its scaled-down refraction (thus the hyperrealists fasten in a striking resemblance a real from which has fled all meaning and charm, all the profundity and energy of representation). Thus the hyperrealism of simulation is expressed everywhere by the real's striking resemblance to itself.

Power, too, for some time now produces nothing but signs of its resemblance. And at the same time, another figure of power comes into play: that of a collective demand for *signs* of power—a holy union which forms around the disappearance of power. Everybody belongs to it more or less in fear of the collapse of the political. And in the end the game of power comes down to nothing more than the *critical* obsession with power: an obsession with its death; an obsession with its survival which becomes greater the more it disappears. When it has totally disappeared, logically we will be under the total spell of power—a haunting memory already foreshadowed everywhere, manifesting at one and the same time the satisfaction of having got rid of it (nobody wants it any more, everybody unloads it on others) and grieving its loss. Melancholy for societies without power: this has already given rise to fascism, that overdose of a powerful referential in a society which cannot terminate its mourning.

But we are still in the same boat: none of our societies know how to manage their mourning for the real, for power, for the *social itself*, which is implicated in this same breakdown. And it is by an artificial revitalization of all this that we try to escape it. *Undoubtedly this will even end up in socialism.* By an unforeseen twist of events and an irony which no longer belongs to history, it is through the death of the social that socialism will emerge—as it is through the death of God that religions emerge. A twisted coming, a perverse event, an unintelligible reversion to the logic of reason. As is the fact that power is no longer present except to conceal that there is none. A simulation which can go on indefinitely, since—unlike "true" power which is, or was, a structure, a strategy, a relation of force, a stake—this is nothing but the object of a social *demand*, and hence subject to the law of supply and demand, rather than to violence and death. Completely expunged from the *political* dimension, it is dependent, like any other commodity, on production and mass consumption. Its spark has disappeared; only the fiction of a political universe is saved.

Likewise with work. The spark of production, the violence of its stake no longer exists. Everybody still produces, and more and more, but work has subtly become something else: a need (as Marx ideally envisaged it, but not at all in the same sense), the object of a social "demand," like leisure, to which it is equivalent in the general run of life's options. A demand exactly proportional to the loss of stake in the work process.[v] The same change in fortune as for power: the *scenario* of work is there to conceal the fact that the work-real, the production-real, has disappeared. And for that matter so has the strike-real too, which is no longer a stoppage of work, but its alternative pole in the ritual scansion of the social calendar. It is as if everyone has "occupied" their work place or work post, after declaring the strike, and resumed production, as is the custom in a "self-managed" job, in exactly the same terms as before, by declaring themselves (and virtually being) in a state or permanent strike.

This isn't a science-fiction dream: everywhere it is a question of a doubling of the work process. And of a double or locum for the strike process—strikes which are incorporated like obsolescence in objects, like crises in production. Then there are no longer any strikes or work, but both simultaneously, that is to say something else entirely: a wizardry of work, a trompe l'oeil, a scenodrama (not to say melodrama) of production, collective dramaturgy upon the empty stage of the social.

It is no longer a question of the *ideology* of work—of the traditional ethic that obscures the "real" labour process and the "objective" process of exploitation—but of the scenario of work. Likewise, it is no longer a question of the ideology of power, but of the *scenario* of power. Ideology only corresponds to a betrayal of reality by signs; simulation corresponds to a short-circuit of reality and to its reduplication by signs. It is always the aim of ideological analysis to restore the objective process; it is always a false problem to want to restore the truth beneath the simulacrum.

This is ultimately why power is so in accord with ideological discourses and discourses on ideology, for these are all discourses of *truth*—always good, even and especially if they are revolutionary, to counter the mortal blows of simulation.

---

[v]Athenian democracy, much more advanced than our own, had reached the point where the vote was considered as payment for a service, after all other repressive solutions had been tried and found wanting in order to insure a quorum.

❖

Jean-François Lyotard (1924–1998): A Biographical Sketch

Jean-François Lyotard was born on August 10, 1924, in Vincennes, France. The son of a sales representative, the younger Lyotard had multiple aspirations, including interests in becoming a novelist, a historian, or a Dominican monk. Schooled at a *lycée* in Paris, Lyotard eventually elected to study philosophy and literature at the Sorbonne. It is here that he would strike up a friendship with Giles Deleuze (1925–1995), a thinker who would also come to play a significant role in the development of poststructural and postmodern debates. At the Sorbonne, Lyotard wrote his master's dissertation entitled "Indifference as an Ethical Notion," addressing a theme that would become central to his lifelong philosophical investigations—the theme of difference in systems of politics and philosophy.

During World War II, Lyotard became heavily politicized and volunteered his time as a first-aid worker in Paris. This was among the first of the political activities in which he would engage throughout the 1940s and 1950s. After the war, Lyotard married Andrée May in 1948, with whom he would have two children. In 1950, he received his French teaching license and began teaching philosophy at a *lycée* in French-occupied Eastern Algeria. While in Algeria, Lyotard began to read Marx and was animated by the French-Algerian political conflict that, as with many young French intellectuals, would provide the inspiration for his left-leaning political orientation. He left Algeria in 1952 and taught at the French military college *La Flèche* in Paris until 1959. While teaching at *La Flèche*, Lyotard joined the socialist group *Socialisme ou Barbarie* (Socialism or Barbarism) and became an advocate, author, and journal editor for the group until 1964, when, under internal tension, the group splintered. Disillusioned, not only with socialist politics but with Marxism altogether, Lyotard left the group and began to move away from Marxist thought in general.

Between 1959 and 1966, Lyotard was a lecturer at the Sorbonne, gaining a faculty position at the University of Paris X, Nanterre, in the department of philosophy. In conjunction with his disenchantment with Marxism, Lyotard returned to the study of philosophy and became particularly inspired by the structural psychoanalysis of Jacques Lacan (1901–1981), attending several of his seminars in Paris in the mid-1960s. Exposure to Lacan's ideas provided the foundation for Lyotard's first major work of philosophy, *Discours, figure* (1971), for which Lyotard would receive his doctorate degree. In 1968, Lyotard was appointed to a research position at the *Centre National de la Recherche Scientifique*, a position he held until 1970 when he became a professor at the University of Paris VIII at Vincennes.

During the 1970s, Lyotard authored dozens of articles and several books, the most famous of which was the commissioned report *The Postmodern Condition: A Report on Knowledge* (1979), which Lyotard developed on behalf of the *Conseil des Universities* of the government of Quebec, Canada. The publication of *The Postmodern Condition*— from which the excerpts included in this chapter are drawn—earned Lyotard worldwide acclaim and laid the groundwork for key developments in postmodern theory. As Lyotard's reputation grew, so, too, did his academic prominence. In 1987, Lyotard became a professor emeritus at the University of Paris VIII at Vincennes, and throughout the late 1980s and the 1990s he accepted professorships at universities in the United States, Canada, Brazil, Germany, and France. In 1993, Lyotard married his second wife, Dolorès Djidzek, with whom he had a son. Suffering from leukemia, Jean-François Lyotard died in Paris on April 21, 1998.

INTELLECTUAL INFLUENCES AND CORE IDEAS

The development of Lyotard's work can be divided into three periods. The first comprises his early philosophical and political writings from the late 1940s through the mid-1960s. It is during the early part of this period that Lyotard's work, inspired by the French phenomenologist Maurice Merleau-Ponty (1908–1961), had a decisively phenomenological emphasis.[12] As Lyotard became more politicized, however, motivated doubly by his interest in the Algerians' fight for independence from France and his

---

[12]The French philosopher Maurice Merleau-Ponty emphasized the centrality of perception in the process of accessing the "real." However, in contrast to many phenomenologists, Merleau-Ponty stressed the physical and the biological (or vital) levels of conceptualization that preconditioned all mental concepts as well. This emphasis led him to sympathy for Karl Marx's historical materialism, although he differed from most Marxists in regarding history as irreducibly plural and contingent (http://www.answers.com/topic/maurice-merleau-ponty).

membership in the socialist organization *Socialisme ou Barbarie*, his work began to embrace a more thoroughgoing Marxist orientation.

The second phase in the development of Lyotard's work is represented by the publication of *Discours, figure* (1971) and *The Libidinal Economy* (1974). These works reflect a turn to the psychoanalysis of Jacques Lacan (1901–1981) and a parting with the Marxist position.[13] They constitute a critical engagement with both French structuralism and psychoanalysis rooted in the exploration of the theoretical scope of the concept of "difference," as well as a growing preoccupation with "singularities," those events, forces, and desires that cannot be located within conventionalized political processes or understood in the categories of legitimized discourse. Lyotard argues that there are always outlying instances of human activity and knowledge that elude uniform interpretation and do not fit in a legitimized system of representations. As the potential for universal discourse is discredited, political structures succumb to fragmentation and inconsistencies accumulate in systems of meaning subjected to contradiction and change; the "difference" cannot be nullified, sublimated, or explained away. This period of intellectual development sets the stage for Lyotard's most celebrated work, *The Postmodern Condition: A Report on Knowledge* (1979).

The third period of Lyotard's work, represented by *The Postmodern Condition*, is his most influential contribution to postmodern theory. Now we see a number of themes already developing in Lyotard's writing begin to converge. As its subtitle suggests, *The Postmodern Condition: A Report on Knowledge* is primarily concerned with knowledge and its changing organization in contemporary societies. With the increasing **computerization of society**, computers have come to play a major role in the development, manipulation, storage, and rationalization of knowledge. Consequently, what is considered "knowledge" depends primarily on translatability into rational and cybernetic systems of information. That computer-based information processing is the criterion of knowledge systems has far-reaching implications for the organization of social institutions, like politics, education, science, economics, and systems of justice, all of which depend on institutionalized knowledge

Lyotard argues that the structure of knowledge has changed dramatically since the second World War. Prior to World War II, knowledge was legitimized by reference to what Lyotard calls **metanarratives**. Metanarratives, or grand narratives, are paradigmatic systems of knowledge that contain established and credible worldviews and describe a total picture of society; they provide the basis on which truth claims are made and through which the validity of knowledge is judged. Examples of modern metanarratives are Marxism and its socialist variants, the democratic and progressive ideologies of the European Enlightenment, science and the quest for empirical truth, and systems of religious thought like Christianity. Lyotard suggests that changes in the structure of contemporary societies have initiated a profound skepticism toward the legitimacy of metanarratives—not only the dominant metanarratives of the Western world (Marxism, science, Christianity, Enlightenment progress, etc.) but *all* metanarratives. Lyotard argues that this suspicious attitude toward metanarratives is the hallmark of the postmodern condition, defining postmodernism simply and famously as "incredulity toward metanarratives" (1979:xxiv).

Lyotard contends that with the advent of computer-based information technology knowledge can no longer be legitimized by metanarratives held unquestionably true

[13]Jacques Lacan was a French psychiatrist and early adherent and interpreter of Freud. However, Lacan diverged from Freud in that he argued that the constant conflict between the ego and the unconscious mind could not be resolved; the ego could not be "healed." Thus, the true intention of psychoanalysis was analysis and not cure (http://www.answers.com/JacquesLacan).

and valid. Instead, knowledge is legitimized by its ability to enhance the performance and efficiency of rationalized social institutions. The rational functionality of contemporary societies—what Lyotard refers to as "performativity"—is now of central concern because the legitimacy of social order is based on its organization through rational means. Consistent with Weber's metaphor of the "iron cage of rationality," Lyotard contends that rationality is now a dominant force in the contemporary world. But, unlike Weber, Lyotard argues that the rationalization of society is inherently limited because of the decline of legitimizing metanarratives capable of providing it with foundational support. Instead, knowledge is commercialized, subjected to the whims of the capitalist marketplace, easily fragmented, and often sold piecemeal. With knowledge circumscribed by economic forces, it is no longer important what one knows but whether one can afford to buy what one needs to know. It is astonishing how much knowledge is today collected, how frequently it is traded as a commodity, and to what extent its importance is assessed by its price. This **mercantilization of knowledge** should be of great concern, suggests Lyotard, even though by his own analysis not much could be done about it.

As an example, consider the role of scientific knowledge in the field of medical research. It is true that much of scientific research is undertaken with the goal of discovering new knowledge about the underlying workings of physical and social reality and developing innovative technologies for their investigation. However, in scientific fields like medicine, discoveries are evaluated not only by how much they contribute to our base of knowledge and the degree to which they can be used for social, and even political, benefit. Medical innovations have increasingly succumbed to the dynamics of the marketplace, as pharmaceutical companies compete to be the first to develop new treatments and cures for physical and psychological ailments, thus capitalizing on the economic profits of medical research. For instance, critics charge that today drug companies are far more preoccupied with the research and development of potentially superprofitable drugs (such as the antidepressant drug Prozac, the anti-impotence drug Viagra, and the antibaldness drug Propecia) that enhance the lives of relatively healthy, middle-class consumers than they are with much less profitable drugs that can cure life-threatening illnesses.[14] Such a perspective on contemporary medicine reflects a cynicism toward the legitimacy of the scientific pursuit of "truth," instead emphasizing the colonization of scientific research by the mercantilization of knowledge.

According to Lyotard, the Western metanarratives that supported the modern world collapsed, and a postmodern world emerged that pivots on pluralism and multivocality. Gone are the days when knowledge was cumulative and consisted of the simple "truths" validated by scientific discovery. In the postmodern condition, "scientific knowledge" (and all metanarratives, for that matter) has been replaced by a new structure of knowing in which the truth claims are deeply intertwined with power. Lyotard contends that the legitimacy of science does not derive from its truth, but derives from the support it obtains from the state or the corporation, which saturate the public with narratives hailing them as the chief bastions of knowledge. Thus, in Lyotard's analysis, scientific knowledge has become a form of "narrative knowledge," a story that is told to affirm a local and particularistic point of view.

Lyotard further points out that science is able to gain a monopoly on knowledge only by excluding voices other than those produced through the privileged perspective of the scientific method. That is, the narratives that scientists produce, such as research

---

[14]Indeed, in 1995, Prozac became the first prescription mental-health drug to bring in more than $2 billion in annual receipts (T. Burton, "Lilly sales rise as use of Prozac keeps growing," *Wall Street Journal*, 1/31/96).

papers, hypotheses, and histories, are always governed by the protocols of the field in which they work. Each discipline has a special terminology that makes sense only within its own boundaries. Thus, in practice, a theorist or researcher is not faced with infinite possibilities to explore; rather, he or she can only play within the limits of a system of permissible moves. The scope of permissible moves is determined by the power structure of the particular branch of science in which the scientist is working, which is just as political and unscientific as any other human activity (Denning 2004).

Ironically, then, science has come to increasingly rely on its ability to articulate itself as an "epic narrative" for its own legitimation. In this way, science does not simply represent a quest for the "truth"; instead, it has become just another story, a particularistic means of generating an understanding of the world. While this might suggest that the days of science are over, Lyotard argues that science is not to be abandoned; it has simply lost its legitimacy as a privileged and hegemonic means of acquiring knowledge about the world. Science has become delegitimated, and the knowledge it provides is just another story among many.

To help support his argument, Lyotard borrows the concept of "language games" from the Austrian philosopher Ludwig Wittgenstein (1889–1951). By language games, Wittgenstein sought to convey the idea that meaning is determined by a set of rules governing the contextual use of words. Every expression is like a move in a game; it can only be understood and responded to within the rules of the given game. The greater the particularity and specificity of the rules, the harder it is for those unfamiliar with the game to learn to play.

Lyotard draws a parallel between the state of knowledge in the postmodern condition and the "language games" described by Wittgenstein. Following Lyotard, all forms of knowledge have rules that prescribe both their use and their meaning. Thus, metanarratives are not established systems of "truth" but "language games" bounded by particular rules accessible only to the initiated. Postmodernism represents an era in which systems of knowledge that had once achieved metanarrative status—like science, religion, political ideologies, and so on—are delegitimated and retranslated into forms of narrative discourse with their own logic and rules of play. Because all knowledge has been reduced to particularized narratives, and the comprehension of and participation in any given narrative requires an understanding of the rules of its "game," it is now impossible for a local narrative to claim a privileged access to truth. Because the narrative making of any given perspective is organized around a distinctive set of rules, it is likely that the rules of particular language games will be inconsistent with one another such that players in a game cannot engage in effective dialogue and develop a working consensus. This situation is much like two players meeting at a gaming board, one trying to play checkers and another trying to play backgammon (and there is always someone waiting on the side who wants to play chess).

As an illustration of Lyotard's notion of the collapse of metanarratives, one needs only to examine the manifestation of "language games" in the current interpretations of history. For example, it is true that Europeans long celebrated the narrative of the "discovery" of a "new" world in the late fifteenth century. The voyages of Christopher Columbus and his predecessors did, in fact, reveal to Europeans a world that was new to them. The colonial expansion of European nations into this "new" world, the appropriation of "new" land and resources, and the enslavement and exploitation of a "newly discovered" indigenous population was seen by Europeans as their divine right. This historical account, however, is only one perspective on these events. What did this "discovery" look like from the standpoint of the indigenous population? From their own perspective, the native populations of the "new" world couldn't be discovered; they already knew they were there and had no need of their own "discovery." Instead of a discovery, the indigenous population undoubtedly experienced this period of history as one of invasion, domination, cultural displacement, and genocide. With these two conflicting stories from opposing points of view, which account can be said to carry the truth? On the one hand, the "discovery narrative" certainly was true from the perspective of fifteenth-century Europeans. On the other hand, the "invasion narrative" bears the undeniable truth of the experiences of the indigenous population of the Americas. In fact, the rules of the "language games" by which these narratives are constructed are irreconcilable. Because these narratives cannot sufficiently speak to one another, a final truth of the events is difficult, if not impossible, to establish.

For Lyotard, this inability to form universal or "totalizing" truth is the *sine qua non* of the postmodern condition. Knowledge is forced to take refuge in localized forms with only limited possibilities for consensual understanding and collective politics. Lyotard applies his argument directly to the revisionist theories of Jürgen Habermas (see Chapter 9). Lyotard criticizes Habermas's emphasis on the role of language and communication in the development of a universal discourse. Lyotard contends that such a project necessarily entails the development of shared rules for a singular "language game" and, in effect, the reinscription of a new metanarrative. In sum, Lyotard finds a return to metanarratives not only largely unfeasible but also undesirable in the postmodern condition, attainable as it is only through force and the suppression of alternative voices.

LYOTARD'S THEORETICAL ORIENTATION

Postmodern theories are sometimes called "antitheories" because they eschew the very idea of "theory," that is, grand narratives, metanarratives, or any kind of overarching theoretical framework or scaffolding such as the one used in this book. Postmodernism represents an era in which all knowledge has been reduced to particularized narratives such that it is difficult to make definitive truth claims about any of them. In other words,

Figure 8.3   Lyotard's Basic Concepts and Theoretical Orientation

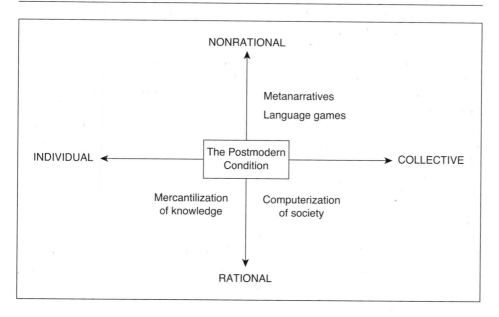

from a postmodern point of view, there are only multiple "truth claims" rather than definitive "truths" regarding the theoretical orientation of any theorist, but this position would especially hold true for postmodern theorists.

Not surprisingly, then, there are multiple ways to portray postmodernism theoretically. On one hand, the notion that narratives are inescapably particular implies an individualistic approach to order, as does the idea that meaning is devoid of "structure," that it is unfixed and fluid rather than determined by pregiven social structural or cultural conditions. In contrast to the Frankfurt School (see Chapter 3), which portrayed mass culture as homogeneous and monolithic, and French structuralists and structural functionalists, who viewed culture as rooted in shared semiotic codes and/or values, Lyotard's assertion that the postmodern condition is one devoid of transcendent values and narratives suggests an absence of shared, collective culture structures or intersubjectivity (that works *down* on the individual) and in that way can be said to be primarily individualistic. Lyotard portrays the postmodern condition as one of multivocality and pluralism, and he conceptualizes individuals as subverting and redeploying symbols in sometimes startling ways.

So, too, the fluidity of symbols at the heart of postmodernism implies little space for strategic calculations of interests and, hence, a nonrationalistic approach to action. One might think from reading Lyotard that rational action is inherently impossible in postmodern society, since the games being played are multiple and the rules constantly changing. In short, how can one determine and achieve one's strategic interests when the playing field is forever in a state of flux? Rather than being motivated by a strategic calculation of interests, we are caught in a web of fluctuating illusions of truth as we move from one idea and meaning to the next, making the attempt to follow a strategic path useless in the midst of multivocality and continuous change.

On the other hand, Lyotard's concepts of the "mercantilization of knowledge" and "computerization of society" clearly reflect his (neo-Marxist) notion that knowledge in postmodern society is circumscribed by economic forces, which reflects a more collectivistic approach to order and rationalistic approach to action (see Figure 8.3). In keeping with the neo-Marxist tradition and particularly the Frankfurt School, Lyotard here emphasizes the strategic maximization of interests (rather than transcendent values) as the underlying motivation in the accumulation of knowledge, as our example regarding the pharmaceutical companies makes clear. Here the patterns of social life are seen as a function of preexisting structures, namely, the corporation or the state, rather than autonomous individuals.

Nevertheless, Lyotard's concept of the "mercantilization of knowledge" can be understood in an individualistic economic sense as well. That knowledge is subject to the whims of the capitalist marketplace and sold piecemeal (rather than reflecting totalizing cultural structures) is more in keeping with the notion of laissez-faire capitalism than the views of the Frankfurt School. From this more individualistic/rationalistic point of view, the nature of the postmodern era prevents knowledge from becoming "fixed" in a single ideology. For instance, while within the scientific metanarrative, Truth is based on objective inquiry and new discoveries; in fact in the postmodern condition science itself has become delegitimated. Scientific stories are just one of many stories that are told.

Of course, as indicated previously in regard to the postmodern feminist Judith Butler, that we can see postmodernism from multiple theoretical standpoints is precisely the point that postmodernists seek to emphasize. They do not want to be pigeonholed and said to be, for instance, "collectivistic and rationalistic" or aligned with any other orientation. Rather, they seek to be "both" and "neither" all at once. They are, after all, part and parcel of the postmodern condition that they seek to explain.

Reading

Introduction to *The Postmodern Condition*

The following excerpts from Lyotard's most famous work, *The Postmodern Condition*, are divided into several different sections. In the first section, Lyotard explains his diagnosis of the computerization of society and transformations in the nature of knowledge. In the second section, Lyotard discusses legitimation. In the third section, Lyotard discusses his notion of language games. In the fourth section, Lyotard talks back to the cultural determinism dominant in social theory, particularly as espoused by Parsons and the Frankfurt School. In the final section, Lyotard sets out his postmodern alternative for understanding contemporary social life.

❖

The Postmodern Condition (1979)

Jean-François Lyotard

1. The Field: Knowledge in Computerised Societies

Our working hypothesis is that the status of knowledge is altered as societies enter what is known as the postindustrial age and cultures enter what is known as the postmodern age. This transition has been under way since at least the end of the 1950s, which for Europe marks the completion of reconstruction. The pace is faster or slower depending on the country, and within countries it varies according to the sector of activity: the general situation is one of temporal disjunction which makes sketching an overview difficult. A portion of the description would necessarily be conjectural. At any rate, we know that it is unwise to put too much faith in futurology.

Rather than painting a picture that would inevitably remain incomplete, I will take as my point of departure a single feature, one that immediately defines our object of study. Scientific knowledge is a kind of discourse. And it is fair to say that for the last forty years the "leading" sciences and technologies have had to do with language: phonology and theories of linguistics, problems of communication and cybernetics, modern theories of algebra and informatics, computers and their languages, problems of translation and the search for areas of compatibility among computer languages, problems of information storage and data banks, telematics and the perfection of intelligent terminals, to paradoxology. The facts speak for themselves (and this list is not exhaustive).

SOURCE: From Lyotard, J., *The Postmodern Condition*, trans. by Geoff Benningham and Brian Massumi (University of Minnesota Press, 1984), pp. 3–17. English translation and Foreword, copyright © 1984 by the University of Minnesota. Original French-language edition copyright © 1979 by Les Editions de Minuit.

These technological transformations can be expected to have a considerable impact on knowledge. Its two principal functions—research and the transmission of acquired learning—are already feeling the effect, or will in the future. With respect to the first function, genetics provides an example that is accessible to the layman: it owes its theoretical paradigm to cybernetics. Many other examples could be cited. As for the second function, it is common knowledge that the miniaturisation and commercialisation of machines is already changing the way in which learning is acquired, classified, made available, and exploited. It is reasonable to suppose that the proliferation of information-processing machines is having, and will continue to have, as much of an effect on the circulation of learning as did advancements in human circulation (transportation system) and later, in the circulation of sounds and visual images (the media).

The nature of knowledge cannot survive unchanged within this context of general transformation. It can fit into the new channels, and become operational, only if learning is translated into quantities of information. We can predict that anything in the constituted body of knowledge that is not translatable in this way will be abandoned and that the direction of new research will be dictated by the possibility of its eventual results being translatable into computer language. The "producers" and users of knowledge must now, and will have to, possess the means of translating into these languages whatever they want to invent or learn. Research on translating machines is already well advanced. Along with the hegemony of computers comes a certain logic, and therefore a certain set of prescriptions determining which statements are accepted as "knowledge" statements.

We may thus expect a thorough exteriorisation of knowledge with respect to the "knower," at whatever point he or she may occupy in the knowledge process. The old principle that the acquisition of knowledge is indissociable from the training (Bildung) of minds, or even of individuals, is becoming obsolete and will become ever more so. The relationships of the suppliers and users of knowledge to the knowledge they supply and use is now tending, and will increasingly tend, to assume the form already taken by the relationship of commodity producers and consumers to the commodities they produce and consume—that is, the form of value. Knowledge is and will be produced in order to be sold, it is and will be consumed in order to be valorised in a new production: in both cases, the goal is exchange.

Knowledge ceases to be an end in itself, it loses its "use-value."

It is widely accepted that knowledge has become the principal force of production over the last few decades; this has already had a noticeable effect on the composition of the work force of the most highly developed countries and constitutes the major bottleneck for the developing countries. In the postindustrial and postmodern age, science will maintain and no doubt strengthen its preeminence in the arsenal of productive capacities of the nation-states. Indeed, this situation is one of the reasons leading to the conclusion that the gap between developed and developing countries will grow ever wider in the future.

But this aspect of the problem should not be allowed to overshadow the other, which is complementary to it. Knowledge in the form of an informational commodity indispensable to productive power is already, and will continue to be, major—perhaps the major—stake in the worldwide competition for power. It is conceivable that the nation-states will one day fight for control of information, just as they battled in the past for control over territory, and afterwards for control of access to and exploitation of raw materials and cheap labor. A new field is opened for industrial and commercial strategies on the one hand, and political and military strategies on the other.

However, the perspective I have outlined above is not as simple as I have made it appear. For the merchantilisation of knowledge is bound to affect the privilege the nation-states have enjoyed, and still enjoy, with respect to the production and distribution of learning. The notion that learning falls within the purview of the State, as the brain or mind of society, will become more and more outdated with the increasing strength of the opposing principle, according to which society exists and progresses only if the messages circulating within it are rich in information and easy to decode.

The ideology of communicational "transparency," which goes hand in hand with the commercialisation of knowledge, will begin to perceive the State as a factor of opacity and "noise." It is from this point of view that the problem of the relationship between economic and State powers threatens to arise with a new urgency.

Already in the last few decades, economic powers have reached the point of imperilling the stability of the state through new forms of the circulation of capital that go by the generic name of *multi-national corporations*. These new forms of circulation imply that investment decisions have, at least in part, passed beyond the control of the nation-states. The question threatens to become even more thorny with the development of computer technology and telematics. Suppose, for example, that a firm such as IBM is authorised to occupy a belt in the earth's orbital field and launch communications satellites or satellites housing data banks. Who will have access to them? Who will determine which channels or data are forbidden? The State? Or will the State simply be one user among others? New legal issues will be raised, and with them the question: "who will know?"

Transformation in the nature of knowledge, then, could well have repercussions on the existing public powers, forcing them to reconsider their relations (both *de jure* and *de facto*) with the large corporations and, more generally, with civil society. The reopening of the world market, a return to vigorous economic competition, the breakdown of the hegemony of American capitalism, the decline of the socialist alternative, a probable opening of the Chinese market—these and many other factors are already, at the end of the 1970s, preparing States for a serious reappraisal of the role they have been accustomed to playing since the 1930s: that of, guiding, or even directing investments. In this light, the new technologies can only increase the urgency of such a re-examination, since they make the information used in decision making (and therefore the means of control) even more mobile and subject to piracy.

It is not hard to visualise learning circulating along the same lines as money, instead of for its "educational" value or political (administrative, diplomatic, military) importance; the pertinent distinction would no longer be between knowledge and ignorance, but rather, as is the case with money, between "payment knowledge" and "investment knowledge"—in other words, between units of knowledge exchanged in a daily maintenance framework (the reconstitution of the work force, "survival") versus funds of knowledge dedicated to optimising the performance of a project.

If this were the case, communicational transparency would be similar to liberalism. Liberalism does not preclude an organisation of the flow of money in which some channels are used in decision making while others are only good for the payment of debts. One could similarly imagine flows of knowledge travelling along identical channels of identical nature, some of which would be reserved for the "decision makers," while the others would be used to repay each person's perpetual debt with respect to the social bond.

2. THE PROBLEM: LEGITIMATION

That is the working hypothesis defining the field within which I intend to consider the question of the status of knowledge. This scenario, akin to the one that goes by the name "the computerisation of society" (although ours is advanced in an entirely different spirit), makes no claims of being original, or even true. What is required of a working hypothesis is a fine capacity for discrimination. The scenario of the computerisation of the most highly developed societies allows us to spotlight (though with the risk of excessive magnification) certain aspects of the transformation of knowledge and its effects on public power and civil institutions—effects it would be difficult to perceive from other points of view. Our hypotheses, therefore, should not be accorded predictive value in relation to reality, but strategic value in relation to the question raised.

Nevertheless, it has strong credibility, and in that sense our choice of this hypothesis is not arbitrary. It has been described extensively by the experts and is already guiding certain decisions by the governmental agencies and private firms most directly concerned, such as those managing the telecommunications industry. To some extent, then, it is already a part of observable reality. Finally, barring economic stagnation or a general recession (resulting, for example, from a continued failure to solve the world's energy problems), there is a good chance that this scenario will come to pass: it is hard to see what other direction contemporary technology could take as an alternative to the computerisation of society.

This is as much as to say that the hypothesis is banal. But only to the extent that it fails to challenge the general paradigm of progress in science and technology, to which economic growth and the expansion of sociopolitical power seem to be natural complements. That scientific and technical knowledge is cumulative is never questioned. At most, what is debated is the form that accumulation takes—some picture it as regular, continuous, and unanimous, others as periodic, discontinuous, and conflictual.

But these truisms are fallacious. In the first place, scientific knowledge does not represent the totality of knowledge; it has always existed in addition to, and in competition and conflict with, another kind of knowledge, which I will call narrative in the interests of simplicity (its characteristics will be described later). I do not mean to say that narrative knowledge can prevail over science, but its model is related to ideas of internal equilibrium and conviviality next to which contemporary scientific knowledge cuts a poor figure, especially if it is to undergo an exteriorisation with respect to the "knower" and an alienation from its user even greater than has previously been the case. The resulting demoralisation of researchers and teachers is far from negligible; it is well known that during the 1960s, in all of the most highly developed societies, it reached such explosive dimensions among those preparing to practice these professions—the students—that there was noticeable decrease in productivity at laboratories and universities unable to protect themselves from its contamination. Expecting this, with hope or fear, to lead to a revolution (as was then often the case) is out of the question: it will not change the order of things in postindustrial society overnight. But this doubt on the part of scientists must be taken into account as a major factor in evaluating the present and future status of scientific knowledge.

It is all the more necessary to take it into consideration since—and this is the second point—the scientists' demoralisation has an impact on the central problem of legitimation. I use the word in a broader sense than to contemporary German theorists in their discussions of the question of authority. Take any civil law as an example: it states that a given category of citizens must perform a specific kind of action. Legitimation is the process by which a legislator is authorised to promulgate such a law as a norm. Now take the example of a scientific statement: it is subject to the rule that a statement must fulfill a given set of conditions in order to be accepted as scientific. In this case, legitimation is the process by which a "legislator" dealing with scientific discourse is authorised to prescribe the stated conditions (in general, conditions of internal consistency and experimental verification) determining whether a statement is to be included in that discourse for consideration by the scientific community.

The parallel may appear forced. But as we will see, it is not. The question of the legitimacy of science has been indissociably linked to that of the legitimation of the legislator since the time of Plato. From this point of view, the right to decide what is true is not independent of the right to decide what is just, even if the statements consigned to these two authorities differ in nature. The point is that there is a strict interlinkage between the kind of language called science and the kind called ethics and politics: they both stem from the same perspective, the same "choice" if you will—the choice called the Occident.

When we examine the current status of scientific knowledge at a time when science seems more completely subordinated to the prevailing powers than ever before and, along with the new technologies, is in danger of becoming a major stake in their conflicts—the question of double legitimation, far from receding into the background, necessarily comes to the fore. For it appears in its most complete form, that of reversion, revealing that knowledge and power are simply two sides of the same question: who decides what knowledge is, and who knows what needs to be decided? In the computer age, the question of knowledge is now more than ever a question of government.

3. The Method: Language Games

The reader will already have noticed that in analysing this problem within the framework set forth I have favoured a certain procedure: emphasising facts of language and in particular their pragmatic aspect. To help clarify what follows it would be useful to summarise, however briefly, what is meant here by the term *pragmatic*.

A denotative utterance such as "The university is sick," made in the context of a conversation or an interview, positions its sender (the person who utters the statement), its addressee (the person who receives it), and its referent (what the statement deals with) in a specific way: the utterance places (and exposes) the sender in the position of "knower" (he knows what the situation is with the university), the addressee is put in the position of having to give or refuse his assent, and the referent itself is handled in a way unique to denotatives, as something that demands to be correctly identified and expressed by the statement that refers to it.

If we consider a declaration such as "The university is open," pronounced by a dean or rector at convocation, it is clear that the previous specifications no longer apply. Of course, the meaning of the utterance has to be understood, but that is a general condition of communication and does not aid us in distinguishing the different kinds of utterances or their specific effects. The distinctive feature of this second, "performative," utterance is that its effect upon the referent coincides with its enunciation. The university is open because it has been declared open in the above-mentioned circumstances. That this is so is not subject to discussion or verification on the part of the addressee, who is immediately placed within the new context created by the utterance. As for the sender, he must be invested 'with the' authority to make such a statement. Actually, we could say it the other way around: the sender is dean or rector that is, he is invested with the authority to make this kind of statement—only insofar as he can directly affect both the referent (the university) and the addressee (the university staff) in the manner I have indicated.

A different case involves utterances of the type, "Give money to the university"; these are prescriptions. They can be modulated as orders, commands, instructions, recommendations, requests, prayers, pleas, etc. Here, the sender is clearly placed in a position of authority, using the term broadly (including the authority of a sinner over a god who claims to be merciful): that is, he expects the addressee to perform the action referred to. The pragmatics of prescription entail concomitant changes in the posts of addressee and referent.

Of a different order again is the efficiency of a question, a promise, a literary description, a narration, etc. I am summarising. Wittgenstein, taking up the study of language again from scratch, focuses his attention on the effects of different modes of discourse; he calls the various types of utterances he identifies along the way (a few of which I have listed) *language games*. What he means by this term is that each of the various categories of utterance can be defined in terms of rules specifying their properties and the uses to which they can be put—in exactly the same way as the game of chess is defined by a set of rules determining the properties of each of the pieces, in other words, the proper way to move them.

It is useful to make the following three observations about language games. The first is that their rules do not carry within themselves their own legitimation, but are the object of a contract, explicit or not, between players (which is not to say that the players invent the rules). The second is that if there are no rules, there is no game, that even an infinitesimal modification of one rule alters the nature of the game, that a "move" or utterance that does not satisfy the rules does not belong to the game they define. The third remark is suggested by what has just been said: every utterance should be thought of as a "move" in a game.

This last observation brings us to the first principle underlying our method as a whole: to speak is to fight, in the sense of playing, and speech acts fall within the domain of a general agonistics. This does not necessarily mean that one plays in order to win. A move can be made for the sheer pleasure of its invention: what else is involved in that labor of language harassment undertaken by popular speech and by literature? Great joy is had in the endless invention of turns of phrase, of words and meanings, the process behind the evolution of language on the level of *parole*. But undoubtedly even this pleasure depends on a feeling of success won at the expense of an adversary—at least one adversary, and a formidable one: the accepted language, or connotation.

This idea of an agonistics of language should not make us lose sight of the second principle, which stands as a complement to it and governs our analysis: that the observable social bond is composed of language "moves." An elucidation of this proposition will take us to the heart of the matter at hand.

4. THE NATURE OF THE SOCIAL BOND: THE MODERN ALTERNATIVE

If we wish to discuss knowledge in the most highly developed contemporary society, we must answer the preliminary question of what methodological representation to apply to that society. Simplifying to the extreme, it is fair to say that in principle there have been, at least over the last half-century, two basic representational models for society: either society forms a functional whole, or it is divided in two. An illustration of the first model is suggested by Talcott Parsons (at least the postwar Parsons) and his school, and of the second, by the Marxist current (all of its component schools, whatever differences they may have, accept both the principle of class struggle and dialectics as a duality operating within society).

This methodological split, which defines two major kinds of discourse on society, has been handed down from the nineteenth century. The idea that society forms an organic whole, in the absence of which it ceases to be a society (and sociology ceases to have an object of study), dominated the minds of the founders of the French school. Added detail was supplied by functionalism; it took yet another turn in the 1950s with Parsons's conception of society as a self-regulating system. The theoretical and even material model is no longer the living organism; it is provided by cybernetics, which, during and after the Second World War, expanded the model's applications.

In Parsons's work, the principle behind the system is still, if I may say so, optimistic: it corresponds to the stabilisation of the growth economies and societies of abundance under the aegis of a moderate welfare state. In the work of contemporary German theorists, *systemtheorie* is technocratic, even cynical, not to mention despairing: the harmony between the needs and hopes of individuals or groups and the functions guaranteed by the system is now only a secondary component of its functioning. The true goal of the system, the reason it programs itself like a computer, is the optimisation of the global relationship between input and output, in other words, performativity. Even when its rules are in the process of changing and innovations are occurring, even when its dysfunctions (such as strikes, crises, unemployment, or political revolutions) inspire hope and lead to belief in an alternative, even then what is actually taking place is only an internal readjustment, and its result can be no more than an increase in the system's "viability." The only alternative to this kind of performance improvement is entropy, or decline.

Here again, while avoiding the simplifications inherent in a sociology of social theory, it is difficult to deny at least a parallel between this "hard" technocratic version of society and the ascetic effort that was demanded (the fact that it was done in name of "advanced liberalism" is beside the point) of the most highly developed industrial societies in order to make them competitive—and thus optimise their "irrationality"—within the framework of the resumption of economic world war in the 1960s.

Even taking into account the massive displacement intervening between the thought of a man like Comte and the thought of Luhmann, we can discern a common conception of the social: society is a unified totality, a "unicity." Parsons formulates this clearly: "The most essential condition of successful dynamic analysis is a continual and systematic reference of every problem to the state of the system as a whole. . . A process or set of conditions either 'contributes' to the maintenance (or development) of the system or it is 'dysfunctional' in that it detracts from the integration, effectiveness, etc., of the 'system.'" The "technocrats" also subscribe to this idea. Whence its credibility: it has the means to become a reality, and that is all the proof it needs. This is what Horkheimer called the "paranoia" of reason.

But this realism of systemic self-regulation, and this perfectly sealed circle of facts and interpretations, can be judged paranoid only if one has, or claims to have, at one's disposal a viewpoint that is in principle immune from their allure. This is the function of the principle of class struggle in theories of society based on the work of Marx.

"Traditional" theory is always in danger of being incorporated into the programming of the social whole as a simple tool for the optimisation of its performance; this is because its desire for a unitary and totalising truth lends itself to the unitary and totalising practice of the system's managers. "Critical" theory, based on a principle of dualism and wary of syntheses and reconciliations, should be in a position to avoid this fate. What guides Marxism, then, is a different model of society, and a different conception of the function of the knowledge that can be produced by society and acquired from it. This model was born of the struggles accompanying the process of capitalism's encroachment upon traditional civil societies. There is insufficient space here to chart the vicissitudes of these struggles, which fill more than a century of social, political, and ideological history. We will have to content ourselves with a glance at the balance sheet, which is possible for us to tally today now that their fate is known: in countries with liberal or advanced liberal management, the struggles and their instruments have been transformed into regulators of the system; in communist countries, the totalising model and its totalitarian effect have made a comeback in the name of Marxism itself, and the struggles in question have simply been deprived of the right to exist. Everywhere, the Critique of political economy (the subtitle of Marx's *Capital*) and its correlate, the critique of alienated society, are used in one way or another as aids in programming the system.

Of course, certain minorities, such as the Frankfurt School or the group *Socialisme ou barbarie*, preserved and refined the critical model in opposition to this process. But the social foundation of the principle of division, or class struggle, was blurred to the point of losing all of its radicality; we cannot conceal the fact that the critical model in the end lost its theoretical standing and was reduced to the status of a "utopia" or "hope," a token protest raised in the name of man or reason or creativity, or again of some social category such as the Third World or the students—on which is conferred in extremes the henceforth improbable function of critical subject.

The sole purpose of this schematic (or skeletal) reminder has been to specify the problematic in which I intend to frame the question of knowledge in advanced industrial societies. For it is impossible to know what the state of knowledge is—in other words, the problems its development and distribution are facing today—without knowing something of the society within which it is situated. And today more than ever, knowing about that society involves first of all choosing what approach the inquiry will take, and that necessarily means choosing how society can answer. One can decide that the principal role of knowledge is as an indispensable element in the functioning of society, and act in accordance with that decision, only if one has already decided that society is a giant machine.

Conversely, one can count on its critical function, and orient its development and distribution in that direction, only after it has been decided that society does not form an integrated whole, but remains haunted by a principle of oppositions. The alternative seems clear: it is a choice between the homogeneity and the intrinsic duality of the social, between functional and critical knowledge. But the decision seems difficult, or arbitrary.

It is tempting to avoid the decision altogether by distinguishing two kinds of knowledge. One, the positivist kind, would be directly applicable to technologies bearing on men and materials, and would lend itself to operating as an indispensable productive force within the system. The other—the critical, reflexive, or hermeneutic kind—by reflecting directly on values or aims, would resist any such "recuperation."

5. THE NATURE OF THE SOCIAL BOND: THE POSTMODERN PERSPECTIVE

I find this partition solution unacceptable. I suggest that the alternative it attempts to resolve, but only reproduces, is no longer relevant for the societies with which we are concerned and that the solution itself is still caught within a type of oppositional thinking that is out of step with the most vital modes of postmodern knowledge.

As I have already said, economic "redeployment" in the current phase of capitalism, aided by a shift in techniques, goes hand in hand with a change in the function of the State: the image of society this syndrome suggests necessitates a serious revision of the alternate approaches considered. For brevity's sake, suffice it to say that functions of regulation, and therefore of reproduction, are being and will be further withdrawn from administrators and entrusted to machines. Increasingly, the central question is becoming who will have access to the information these machines must have in storage to guarantee that the right decisions are made. Access to data is, and will continue to be, the prerogative of experts of all stripes. The ruling class is and will continue to be the class of decision makers. Even now it is no longer composed of the traditional political class, but of a composite layer of corporate leaders, high-level administrators, and the heads of the major professional, labor, political, and religious organisations.

What is new in all of this is that the old poles of attraction represented by nation-states, parties, professions, institutions, and historical traditions are losing their attraction. And it does not look as though they will be replaced, at least not on their former scale, The Trilateral Commission is not a popular pole of attraction. "Identifying" with the great names, the heroes of contemporary history, is becoming more and more difficult. Dedicating oneself to "catching up with Germany," the life goal the French president [Giscard d'Estaing at the time this book was published in France] seems to be offering his countrymen, is not exactly exciting. But then again, it is not exactly a life goal. It depends on each individual's industriousness. Each individual is referred to himself. And each of us knows that our *self* does not amount to much.

This breaking up of the grand Narratives (discussed below, sections 9 and 10) leads to what some authors analyse in terms of the dissolution of the social bond and the disintegration of social aggregates into a mass of individual atoms thrown into the absurdity of Brownian motion. Nothing of the kind is happening: this point of view, it seems to me, is haunted by the paradisaic representation of a lost organic" society.

A *self* does not amount to much, but no self is an island; each exists in a fabric of relations that is now more complex and mobile than ever before. Young or old, man or woman, rich or poor, a person is always located at "nodal points" of specific communication circuits, however tiny these may be. Or better: one is always located at a post through which various kinds of messages pass. No one, not even the least privileged among us, is ever entirely powerless over the messages that traverse and position him at the post of sender, addressee, or referent. One's mobility in relation to these language game effects (language games, of course, are what this is all about) is tolerable, at least within certain limits (and the limits are vague); it is even solicited by regulatory mechanisms, and in particular by the self-adjustments the system undertakes in order to improve its performance. It may even be said that the system can and must encourage such movement to the extent that it combats its own entropy, the novelty of an unexpected "move," with its correlative displacement of a partner or group of partners, can supply the system with that increased performativity it forever demands and consumes.

It should now be clear from which perspective I chose language games as my general methodological approach. I am not claiming that the *entirety* of social relations is of this nature—that will remain an open question. But there is no need to resort to some fiction of social origins to establish that language games are the minimum relation required for society to exist: even before he is born, if only by virtue of the name he is given, the human child is already positioned as the referent in the story recounted by those around him, in relation to which he will inevitably chart his course. Or more simply still, the question of the social bond, insofar as it is a question, is itself a language game, the game of inquiry. It immediately positions the person who asks, as well as the addressee and the referent asked about: it is already the social bond.

On the other hand, in a society whose communication component is becoming more prominent day by day, both as a reality and as an issue, it is clear that language assumes a new importance. It would be superficial to reduce its significance to the traditional alternative between manipulatory speech and the unilateral transmission of messages on the one hand, and free expression and dialogue on the other.

A word on this last point. If the problem is described simply in terms of communication theory, two things are overlooked: first, messages have quite different forms and effects depending on whether they are, for example, denotatives, prescriptives, evaluatives, performatives, etc. It is clear that what is important is not simply the fact that they communicate information. Reducing them to this function is to adopt an outlook which unduly privileges the system's own interests and point of view. A cybernetic machine does indeed run on information, but the goals programmed into it, for example, originate in prescriptive and evaluative statements it has no way to correct in the course of its functioning—for example, maximising its own performance, how can one guarantee that performance maximisation is the best goal for the social system in every case. In any case the "atoms" forming its matter are competent to handle statements such as these—and this question in particular.

Second, the trivial cybernetic version of information theory misses something of decisive importance, to which I have already called attention: the agonistic aspect of society. The atoms are placed at the crossroads of pragmatic relationships, but they are also displaced by the messages that traverse them, in perpetual motion. Each language partner, when a "move" pertaining to him is made, undergoes a "displacement," an alteration of some kind that not only affects him in his capacity as addressee and referent, but also as sender. These moves necessarily provoke "countermoves"—and everyone knows that a countermove that is merely reactional is not a "good" move. Reactional countermoves are no more than programmed effects in the opponent's strategy; they play into his hands and thus have no effect on the balance of power. That is why it is important to increase displacement in the games, and even to disorient it, in such a way as to make an unexpected "move" (a new statement).

What is needed if we are to understand social relations in this manner, on whatever scale we choose, is not only a theory of communication, but a theory of games which accepts agonistics as a founding principle. In this context, it is easy to see that the essential element of newness is not simply "innovation." Support for this approach can be found in the work of a number of contemporary sociologists, in addition to linguists and philosophers of language.

This "atomisation" of the social into flexible networks of language games may seem far removed from the modern reality, which is depicted, on the contrary, as afflicted with bureaucratic paralysis. The objection will be made, at least, that the weight of certain institutions imposes limits on the games, and thus restricts the inventiveness of the players in making their moves. But I think this can be taken into account without causing any particular difficulty.

In the ordinary use of discourse—for example, in a discussion between two friends—the interlocutors use any available ammunition, changing games from one utterance to the next: questions, requests, assertions, and narratives are launched pell-mell into battle. The war is not without rules, but the rules allow and encourage the greatest possible flexibility of utterance.

From this point of view, an institution differs from a conversation in that it always requires supplementary constraints for statements to be declared admissible within its bounds. The constraints function to filter discursive potentials, interrupting possible connections in the communication networks: there are things that should not be said. They also privilege certain classes of statements (sometimes only one) whose predominance characterises the discourse of the particular institution: there are things that should be said, and there are ways of saying them. Thus: orders in the army, prayer in church, denotation in the schools, narration in families, questions in philosophy, performativity in businesses. Bureaucratisation is the outer limit of this tendency.

However, this hypothesis about the institution is still too "unwieldy": its point of departure is an overly "reifying" view of what is institutionalised. We know today that the limits the institution imposes on potential language "moves" are never established once and for all (even if they have been formally defined). Rather, the limits are themselves the stakes and provisional results of language strategies, within the institution and without. Examples: Does the university have a place for language experiments (poetics)? Can you tell stories in a cabinet meeting? Advocate a cause in the barracks? The answers are clear: yes, if the university opens creative workshops; yes, if the cabinet works with prospective scenarios; yes, if the limits of the old institution are displaced. Reciprocally, it can be said that the boundaries only stabilise when they cease to be stakes in the game.

This, I think, is the appropriate approach to contemporary institutions of knowledge.

❖

Discussion Questions

1. Compare and contrast critical theories/the Frankfurt School (see Chapter 3) and post-structural and postmodern theories, paying particular attention to the themes of standardization, rationality, power, and the impact of media in contemporary social life. How are the respective theoretical orientations reflected in their similarities and differences?

2. In her famous essay, "Foucault on Power: A Theory for Women?" (1990: 163–164), feminist Nancy Hartsock criticizes both Foucault and postmodernism in the following way:

   > Why is it that just at the moment when so many of us who have been silenced begin to demand the right to name ourselves, to act as subjects rather than objects of history, that just then the concept of subjecthood becomes problematic? Just when we are forming our own theories about the world, uncertainty emerges about whether the world can be theorized. Just when we are talking about the changes we want, ideas of progress and the possibility of systematically and rationally organizing human society become dubious and suspect. Why is it only now that critiques are made of the will to power inherent in the effort to create theory? I contend that these intellectual moves are no accident (but no conspiracy either). They represent the transcendental voice of the Enlightenment attempting to come to grips with the social and historical changes of the middle-to-late twentieth century.

   What are the essential issues Hartsock raises in this eloquent critique? To what extent do you agree and/or disagree with her position?

3. Discuss Foucault's genealogy of punishment with an emphasis on contemporary society. Do you think that the continued existence of torture in contemporary societies today (e.g., the Abu Ghraib scandal) undermines Foucault's historical trajectory of discipline and punishment? Or do you think that the contemporary prohibitions against torture and the moral attitude toward it confirm his position? To what extent do you think that Foucault's notion of a disciplinary society rings true? Using concrete examples, discuss the effect of surveillance in your own life and in contemporary society as a whole.

4. Keep a twenty-four-hour log documenting the extent to which your life is mediated. That is, write down *every* instance of your use of media, including radio, newspapers, television, Internet, telephone, and so on, over a twenty-four-hour period. Then analyze your log and discuss the extent to which your life reflects postmodern "hyperreality" as opposed to modern "reality." To what extent is your knowledge of the world a function of representations and the media rather than personal experience? Do you think the fact that contemporary life is experienced *via* representations (going to the movies, watching TV, etc.) negates Baudrillard's point that representations *replace* experience? Why not or how so?

5. Discuss the methodological implications of postmodernism. If there are no "objective" truths to be uncovered, if sociology is always told from a particular perspective, can sociologists "document" particular social phenomena or uncover "new" information? What kinds of claims *can* sociologists make in the postmodern condition?

9

CONTEMPORARY THEORETICAL SYNTHESES

Key Concepts

Pierre Bourdieu

- ❖ Habitus
- ❖ Field
- ❖ Cultural Capital
- ❖ Social Capital
- ❖ Economic Capital
- ❖ Symbolic Capital
- ❖ Symbolic Violence

Jürgen Habermas

- ❖ System
- ❖ Lifeworld
- ❖ Colonization of the Lifeworld
- ❖ Communicative Action
- ❖ Public Sphere
- ❖ Steering Mechanisms
  - – Money/Power

Anthony Giddens

- ❖ Agency
- ❖ Structure
  - – Rules/Resources
- ❖ System
- ❖ Duality of Structure
- ❖ Discursive Consciousness
- ❖ Practical Consciousness
- ❖ Trust
- ❖ Time-Space Distanciation
- ❖ Ontological Security

Of all the oppositions that artificially divide social science, the most fundamental, and the most ruinous, is the one that is set up between subjectivism and objectivism.

~Bourdieu (1990b:25), from *The Logic of Practice*

In this chapter we consider the work of the three leading theorists in contemporary sociology: Pierre Bourdieu, Jürgen Habermas, and Anthony Giddens. Each is engaged in a similar project, namely, developing a multidimensional theoretical approach to understanding social life. While most of the theorists whose work we have discussed thus far emphasize one or another approach to the questions of order and action, the theorists examined here all seek to bridge the divide between individualist (subjectivist) and collectivist (objectivist) and rational and nonrational orientations in social theory. This long-standing theoretical divide was tempered for some thirty years when Parsonian structural-functionalism (see Chapter 2) dominated sociological theorizing. The period of the "orthodox consensus," however, was fractured during the 1960s as theorists began to incorporate ideas from an array of disciplines and perspectives—psychoanalysis, economics, comparative literature, linguistics, Marxism, phenomenology, and anthropology, to name but a few. While the injection of various approaches ushered in a period of astounding creativity, it also left many in the field to talk past one another. The proliferation of competing approaches made for little common ground between those who emphasized one aspect of social order and action and those who emphasized another dimension of these fundamental theoretical questions. Equally important, this division necessarily produced incomplete portraits of social life, as the unidimensional theoretical models were ill equipped to capture the complexities of the relationship between the individual and society.

Addressing this state of the field, each of the three theorists discussed in this chapter has developed a perspective that explicitly incorporates elements from all sides of the theoretical divide. As each uniquely melds the work of a host of scholars, their approaches cast different shades of light on their common effort to bridge the oppositions separating the different theoretical dimensions. Along the way they also introduce a unique set of concerns. While Bourdieu develops his project through an emphasis on the reproduction of class relations, Habermas examines the prospects for democracy in the modern world. For his part, Giddens explores the effects of modern society on the nature of trust, risk, and the self.

PIERRE BOURDIEU (1930–2002): A BIOGRAPHICAL SKETCH

Pierre Bourdieu was born in 1930 in Denguin, a small village in southwestern France. Bourdieu was raised in a family of modest means, his father being a farmer turned town postman. Bourdieu proved to be a talented and hardworking student, enabling him to gain entry into the elite *lycées* (public secondary schools) in Paris. In 1951 Bourdieu entered the prestigious *École Normale Supérieure* (ENS), long a training ground for French intellectuals, including Maurice Merleau-Ponty, Michel Foucault, Jean-Paul Sartre, and Louis Althusser, all of whom developed a decidedly Marxist orientation to their studies, as would Bourdieu. However, as a provincial outsider to the Parisian intellectual and cultural elite, Bourdieu became acutely aware of the advantages that his upper-class schoolmates possessed. This fostered within Bourdieu an anti-establishment sentiment that some have construed as an "extraordinary desire for revenge" against the Parisian intellectual world (Dufay and Dufort 1993:196, cited in Swartz 1997:18). Even though he himself was a successful product of it, Bourdieu would become a relentless critic of the French educational establishment and the aura of meritocracy with which it legitimated itself. He wrote extensively about the hostility harbored by the upper classes toward the middle and lower classes, a hostility that was embedded not only in the educational system but in matters such as the arts, sports, and food. In a number of his works including *The Inheritors* (1964), *Distinction* (1979), and *The State Nobility* (1989), Bourdieu makes clear that education and cultural tastes are central to creating differences between social classes and to the reproduction of those class differences.

SOURCE: © CORBIS.

Bourdieu completed his *agregation* (a highly competitive exam for teachers) in philosophy in 1955 and began teaching philosophy in the French provinces at the secondary level. Three years later, however, he was called into military service and sent to Algeria to combat the Algerians' armed struggle to end French rule. Like many French intellectuals, Bourdieu opposed the French colonial war effort, and his military experience had a profound effect on him, leading to his lifelong commitment to producing socially relevant empirical research. After completing his military duties, Bourdieu remained in Algeria to lecture at the University of Algiers and to carry out ethnographic studies of tribal life, farming communities, and industrial laborers. Conducting extensive interviews with local inhabitants and migrant workers and taking hundreds of photographs, Bourdieu left for Algeria as a philosopher and returned to France in 1960 as a self-taught anthropologist.

Upon his return to France, Bourdieu attended the Sorbonne, where he studied anthropology and sociology under the direction of Raymond Aron, one of France's leading sociologists. In 1962, he took a position at the University of Lille, and two years later he joined the faculty of the *École pratique des Hautes Etudes* in Paris. Ever the *agent provocateur*,[1] Bourdieu refused to complete the state doctorate degree, which is the standard requirement for those seeking chairs in French universities (Swartz and Zolberg 2004:19).

In 1968, in the midst of the student political protests that swept through much of Western Europe, Bourdieu split with Aron and set up his own research center (*Centre de Sociologie de l'education et de la Culture*). Thereafter followed a spate of groundbreaking publications. In 1970, Bourdieu coauthored with Jean-Claude Passeron *Reproduction: In Education, Society and Culture*, now considered a classic in the sociology of education. This was followed by *Distinction* (1979), which was named the sixth most important social scientific work of the twentieth century in a survey by the International Sociological Association (Swartz and Zolberg 2004:17), while his *The Logic of Practice* (1980) placed fourth in the same survey. In addition, he published *Outline of a Theory of Practice* (1972), *Sociology in Question* (1980), *Language and Symbolic Power* (1982), *Homo Academicus* (1984), and dozens of articles addressing a wide variety of methodological, philosophical, and other issues. Meanwhile, in 1975, Bourdieu founded the review journal *actes de la recherché en sciences socials*, and in

---

[1]Grenfell (2004) subtitles his intellectual biography of Bourdieu "agent provocateur" because this "term seems best to sum up Bourdieu as iconoclast, as someone who was ready to challenge established orthodoxies and incite action against the violence (both symbolic and real) of the world."

1981 he was elected chair in sociology at the *College de France*, a position formerly held by Aron.

Bourdieu dominated French public intellectual life during the 1980s and 1990s. He continued to produce work at a prolific pace, publishing *The Rules of Art* and the widely read *An Invitation to Reflexive Sociology* (coauthored with Loïc Wacquant) in 1992. Two more books were published in 1993, *The Field of Cultural Production* and *The Weight of the World*. In 1993 he was awarded the Gold Medal from the *Centre National de Recherche Scientifique* (CNRS) in France—the highest accolade to be awarded to an intellectual (Grenfell 2004:8). His last publications dealt with such topics as masculine domination, neoliberal newspeak, globalization, and television. Apt to be recognized in the streets or cafés throughout France, particularly after he was featured in the documentary film *Sociology is a Martial Art* (2000), Bourdieu's fame was unusual for an intellectual (Calhoun and Wacquant 2002). Although he died from cancer in January 2002, with more than forty books and hundreds of articles published in a variety of languages, Bourdieu's influence on sociology will undoubtedly be felt for years to come.

INTELLECTUAL INFLUENCES AND CORE IDEAS

Bourdieu's work largely can be understood as an attempt to overcome the "dualism" that plagues much of social theory. Indeed, he notes, "I can say that all of my thinking started from this point: how can behaviour be regulated without being the product of obedience to rules?" (quoted in Swartz 1997:95). In seeking to answer this question, he has developed an approach that takes into consideration the objective or external social forces that shape attitudes and behaviors as well as an individual's subjectivity or perception of and action in the world. Along the way he has introduced a number of concepts into the lexicon of sociology: cultural and symbolic capital, fields, habitus, and symbolic violence, to name but a few. Moreover, his conceptual vocabulary evinces his cross-disciplinary influences, as he draws not only from sociology but also from anthropology and philosophy. In addition to Marx, Durkheim, and Weber, his work bears the imprint of Durkheim's nephew, the anthropologist Marcel Mauss (1872–1950); the structural anthropologist Claude Lévi-Strauss (1908–); and a range of philosophers, including the "father" of phenomenology Edmund Husserl (1859–1938, see Chapter 6) and many of his intellectual descendents, most notably Martin Heidegger (1889–1976), Alfred Schutz (1899–1959, see Chapter 6), Maurice Merleau-Ponty (1908–1961), and the existentialist Jean-Paul Sartre (1905–1980). Finally, important aspects of Bourdieu's work were developed in reaction to the structural Marxist philosophy of Louis Althusser (1918–1990), his teacher at the *École Normale Superiéure*.[2]

Bourdieu draws from these scholars but avoids adopting their ideas wholesale, opting instead to extend the themes they addressed by way of his own set of conceptual tools. In this way, the concepts he devises often fuse together those aspects of others' ideas that he finds most fruitful for his own empirical analyses, while casting off those ideas deemed least instructive or useful. The result is a highly creative and complex approach to the study of social life that defies easy summary. Nevertheless, in the remainder of this section we attempt the impossible, discussing several of the concepts

---

[2]Because Bourdieu, Habermas, and Giddens draw from numerous perspectives, discussing their intellectual influences at any length would exceed the space limitations of this chapter. However, we have outlined the work of many of their influences in previous chapters. Thus, to help readers better situate the approaches of the three theorists examined here, we will reference the relevant chapters whenever possible.

that are central to Bourdieu's unique perspective while pointing to the intellectual sources from which he drew inspiration.

Habitus

The cornerstone of Bourdieu's efforts to link objectivist and subjectivist approaches is his notion of **habitus**, a concept he began to develop during his anthropological studies of Kabyle society in Algeria. The habitus is a mental filter that structures an individual's perceptions, experiences, and practices such that the world takes on a taken-for-granted, common-sense appearance. It refers to an individual's "dispositions" or "mental structures" through which the social world is apprehended and expressed through both verbal and bodily language (Bourdieu 1990a:131). "As an acquired system of generative schemes, the habitus makes possible the free production of all the thoughts, perceptions and actions inherent in the condition of its production" (1990b:55). In short, it is through the habitus that one acquires a "sense of one's place" in the world or a "point of view" from which one is able to interpret one's own actions as well as the actions of others. As a "way of being," however, the habitus shapes not only interpretive schemes and thoughts—the mind—but also the body, by molding one's "natural propensity" for a wide range of movements including posture, gait, and agility.[3]

Bourdieu's notion of habitus draws from Husserl's phenomenological philosophy and thus speaks to an understanding of social life that emphasizes its active construction as part and parcel of individuals' attempts to navigate their everyday world. Yet, Bourdieu goes to great lengths to demonstrate that individuals do not create their dispositions, rather, they *acquire* them. In this way, his notion of habitus offers a critique of not only Husserl's work but also that of Jean-Paul Sartre, a towering figure in French intellectual and political life. A Marxist philosopher, novelist, and playwright, Sartre's work and political activism made him the model "total intellectual," for which he served as a standard for some three decades. Most noted for his existentialist philosophy, Sartre maintained that "man is condemned to be free" (Sartre 1947:27) as a result of living in a world without meaning or design. However, this inherent meaninglessness provided the opportunity for the individual to develop an "authentic" self, a potential that he notes as the "first principle of existentialism": "Man is nothing else but what he makes of himself" (ibid.:18). For Sartre, consciousness is not determined by one's social environment; rather, individuals possess the capacity to will themselves an existence that is freely chosen. Ultimately, individuals are solely responsible for being what they have willed themselves to be.

While drawing on phenomenology and existentialism, Bourdieu maintains that the habitus is not simply a mental or internal compass that shapes one's attitudes, perceptions, tastes, and "inclinations," nor does it refer to one's will or undetermined consciousness; it is instead an "internalization of externality" (1990b:55). Rather, Bourdieu introduces an objectivist or structural element into the workings of the habitus by critically incorporating the insights of Marx, Weber, Durkheim, and Claude Lévi-Strauss (1908–), whose structural anthropology was a landmark in the social sciences. Developed in part out of a critique of Sartre's subjectivist orientation and emphasis on free will, Lévi-Strauss sought to uncover the "fundamental structures of the human mind" in the binary codes that structure a society's cultural system. In essence,

---

[3]Bourdieu's emphasis on the corporeal dimensions of the habitus stems from the work of Maurice Merleau-Ponty, whose phenomenology emphasized the centrality of embodied practice to everyday experience. See Jeremy Lane (2000), *Pierre Bourdieu: A Critical Introduction*.

Lévi-Strauss was expanding Ferdinand de Saussure's structural linguistics (see Chapter 8) to explain what he took as the universal foundation of human society, namely, the binary opposites (good/evil, weak/strong, masculine/feminine, etc.) that structure all human ways of thinking, kinship systems, and myths. On the basis of his richly detailed anthropological studies, Lévi-Strauss created quasi-mathematical formulas to map out the structural relations according to which all cultures are said to be organized like so many variations on a common theme.

Lévi-Strauss's commitment to a scientific, as opposed to a philosophical, examination of social life had a major impact on Bourdieu's empirical research. It was in the "confrontation" between the works of Sartre and Lévi-Strauss that he saw the possibility "of reconciling theoretical and practical intentions, bringing together the scientific and the ethical or political vocation . . . in a humbler and more responsible way of performing [one's] task as researcher" (Bourdieu 1990b:2). Nevertheless, Bourdieu did not adopt Lévi-Strauss's structuralism wholesale. Most troubling for Bourdieu is structuralism's "mechanical" view of action whereby individuals' consciousness or reasons for acting are of secondary interest, as they are held to be reflections of underlying cultural codes of which they are unaware. Through his conception of the habitus, Bourdieu sought "to reintroduce agents that Lévi-Strauss and the structuralists . . . tended to abolish, making them into simple epiphenomena of structure" (1990a:9). Contrary to the structuralists' portrayal of conduct, Bourdieu contended that "action is not the mere carrying out of a rule, or obedience to a rule. Social agents . . . are not automata regulated like clocks, in accordance with laws they do not understand" (ibid.).

Despite Bourdieu's criticism of the mechanistic nature of Lévi-Strauss's structural anthropology, there is a decidedly structuralist element in Bourdieu's notion of the habitus, as an individual's dispositions are a product of the "internalization of externality." The externality that shapes the habitus is readily apparent if we compare it to a "point of view." As the term itself suggests, points of view "are views taken from a certain point, that is, from a given position within social space. And we know too that there will be different or even antagonistic points of view, since points of view depend on the point from which they are taken, since the vision that every agent has of space depends on his or her position in that space" (Bourdieu 1990a:131). For example, your vision of geographic space is dependent on your position or the point you occupy within that same space. If you were to stand facing north, your surroundings would appear to you in a particular way that is quite different from one who is facing south. You each will see things that the other is unaware of, as it is outside of his field of vision. Moreover, those things that you both see will not look the same, as your distinctive points of view will determine their appearance. Nevertheless, both of you will perceive the world as natural or self-evident despite the fact that your perceptions are dependent not on the world but, rather, on the point of view from which you apprehend the world.

Now extend the notion of geographic space to social space. In this case, your point of view or disposition is determined by your position within a space that is structured by two "principles of differentiation": economic capital and cultural capital (Bourdieu 1998:6). **Economic capital** refers to the material resources—wealth, land, money—that one controls or possesses. **Cultural capital** refers to nonmaterial goods such as educational credentials, types of knowledge and expertise, verbal skills, and aesthetic preferences that can be converted into economic capital. It is these two forms of capital that constitute the "externality" that is internalized via the habitus by forming the social space within which points of view are taken. Within this social space, individuals are positioned relative to one another first according to the overall volume of the capital they possess and, second, according to the relative amount of economic and cultural capital they possess. Moreover, the closer individuals are to one another in terms of the amount and types of capital they possess, the more they have in common (the more their lifestyles, tastes, and aspirations coincide), while the further apart they are in social space (that is, the less similar the composition of their capital), the less they have in common (ibid.:6, 7). Thus, you are more apt to see "eye to eye" or "hit it off" with someone the more your position in social space overlaps. But this is not a direct result of possessing similar amounts of money and types of educational credentials, per se, but rather because of the similarity of the habitus each has acquired by virtue of being similarly positioned in social space.

The habitus, then, is a structured structure that structures how one views and acts in the world. First, as a scheme or structure of perceptions, dispositions, and actions, the habitus "generates and organizes practices and representations"—it *structures* an individual's experience of and orientation to the social world. An individual's early childhood socialization has a particularly strong effect in this regard as it provides the basis for apprehending and structuring all future experiences. As Bourdieu notes, the habitus is a system of durable dispositions that "tends to ensure its own constancy and defence against change through the selection it makes within new information by rejecting information capable of calling into question its accumulated information. . . . Through the systematic 'choices' it makes among the places, events and people that might be frequented, the habitus tends to protect itself from crises and critical challenges by providing itself with a milieu to which it is as pre-adapted as possible, that is, a relatively constant universe of situations tending to reinforce its dispositions" (1990b:60, 61).

However, as a structure, the habitus is itself *structured* by one's position in social space, which is determined by the volume and types of capital possessed. As a product of an objective position within social space, the habitus encompasses a system of objectively determined practices that reflect the possibilities or "life chances" that are tied to a given social position. In this way, the habitus is an "embodiment of history" or a "present past" born out of the long accumulation of life experiences distinctive to a given social position.

Bourdieu sees in the habitus the union of structures and practices: "objective structures tend to produce structured subjective dispositions that produce structured actions which, in turn, tend to reproduce objective structure" (Bourdieu and Passeron 1977: 203, quoted in Swartz 1997:103). For Bourdieu, however, a central unintended consequence of this circular process is the legitimation and reproduction of a stratified social order that advantages some groups while disadvantaging others. Insofar as an individual's habitus is structured by the existing social distribution of economic and cultural capital, the aspirations and expectations it engenders will conform to what is objectively accessible given one's class position. Objective probabilities for success or failure are translated into a subjective appraisal of a "sense of one's place." A person whose parents are successful, college-educated professionals or corporate executives will grow up expecting to be a successful, college-educated professional or corporate executive; more than likely he will not aspire to be a worker in a furniture assembly plant. On the other hand, a person whose family has worked as manual laborers for generations will be more likely to expect to do the same while assuming that a career as a corporate executive or physician is outside of his reach. As a result, an individual's internalized estimation of what is objectively possible or impossible, reasonable or unreasonable to accomplish fosters aspirations and practices that reproduce the objective structures that generate the world of unequal possibilities. Like a self-fulfilling prophecy, the habitus perpetuates structural inequality across generations by adapting individuals' expectations and behaviors to a social space that is constructed on an unequal distribution of resources (Swartz 1997:103–107).

The discriminatory effects of the habitus apply not only to life chances and career aspirations but also to a wide range of lifestyle "choices." For example, persons who possess relatively little economic capital but possess a relatively high volume of cultural capital (the "dominated fraction of the dominant class," in Bourdieu's terms) are

SOCIOLOGICAL THEORY IN THE CONTEMPORARY ERA

likely to enjoy the same types of food, read the same types of books, listen to the same types of music, speak with a similar vocabulary and accent, participate in the same types of sports, and share similar political views. These affinities are the product of a shared point of view that enables those who occupy this space to acquire the code necessary for understanding, for example, the distinctions that make Beethoven different from Mozart, James Joyce's novels different from Joseph Conrad's, a Monet different from a Manet, or one bottle of red wine different from any other. Those situated differently in social space, for instance, those who possess little in the way of economic and cultural capital, are unlikely to be exposed to the necessary socialization that would endow them with the categorical schemes required to appreciate these distinctions. Being unable to "understand" such types of music, books, paintings, or wines, those so situated would be little interested in partaking of them.

In his groundbreaking book, *Distinction*, Bourdieu analyzed the schemes of perception individuals bring to bear on the social world including works of art. Based on interviews and questionnaires, he documented distinctive modes of apprehending art that corresponded to the class position of respondents. For instance, when asked to comment on the photo of an old woman's hands (see Photo 9.2), working-class respondents, those who possessed little economic and cultural capital, replied in everyday terms that lacked an explicitly aesthetic judgment: "Oh, she's got terribly deformed hands! . . . Looks like she's got arthritis. . . . I really feel sorry seeing that poor old woman's hands, they're all knotted." On the other hand, respondents from the more privileged classes described the photograph in abstract terms that reflect their own distance from the necessities of everyday life and their possession of the aesthetic code required for properly appreciating art: "I find this a very beautiful photograph. It's the very symbol of toil. It puts me in mind of Flaubert's old servant-woman. . . . That woman's gesture, at once very humble. . . . It's terrible that work and poverty are so deforming" (Bourdieu 1984:44, 45).

On the other hand, when responding to a "modernist" photo similar to Photo 9.3, those possessing little cultural capital were unable to apply an aesthetic code to the photograph that would allow them to perceive it as a form of artistic expression. Neither, however, could the image be decoded through common, "realist" perceptual schemes. Perplexed and defeated, manual workers offered the following descriptions: "At first sight it's a construction in metal but I can't make head or tail of it. It might be something used in an electric power station. . . . I can't make out what it really is, it's a mystery to me." "Now, that one really bothers me, I haven't got anything to say about it. . . . I can't see what it could be, apart from lighting. It isn't car headlights, it wouldn't be all straight lines like that." "That's something to do with electronics, I don't

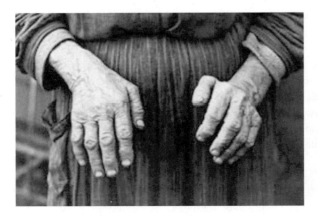

Photo 9.2 An Old Woman's Hands
SOURCE: Library of Congress.

Photo 9.3 Nighttime Industrial Scene
SOURCE: © CORBIS; used with permission.

know anything about that." Similarly situated in social space, small shopkeepers and craftsmen offered similar verdicts: "That is of no interest, it may be all very fine, but not for me. . . . Personally that stuff leaves me cold." " I wouldn't know what to do with a photo like that. Perhaps it suits modern tastes." By contrast, members of the dominant class were able to "appreciate" the image by applying an abstract, aesthetic code in which judgments of form are freed from judgments of contents: "It's inhuman but aesthetically beautiful because of the contrasts" (Bourdieu 1984:46, 47) .

Bourdieu's analysis reveals how possessing the code—that is, the cultural capital—to properly understand works of art, haute cuisine, or the finer points of golf is not simply a matter of an individual's aesthetic preferences and tastes. Because differences in lifestyles and knowledge are the product of hierarchically ordered positions within social space, they, too, are ordered hierarchically. In class-based societies, it matters whether or not an individual prefers to visit museums or watch wrestling on TV, read *The New Yorker or the National Inquirer*, attend a tennis match or a stock car race. While the former are considered "highbrow" and refined, the latter are "lowbrow" and vulgar. As a result, tastes symbolically mark the social positions they are connected to—and the individuals who inhabit them—as either dignified or inferior and serve to legitimate existing social inequalities. Even how a person handles his silverware at mealtime can signify the cultural capital he possesses, and "cultured" parents who are attuned to the symbolic significance of such behavior often stress to their young children the need to refrain from holding their forks and spoons like a "caveman."

Social Reproduction

While Bourdieu's notion of the habitus speaks to a central debate that has long framed the social sciences—namely, the relationship between agency and structure—he combines the concept of the habitus with his discussion of cultural capital to shed light on another longstanding problematic: how are societies reproduced from one generation to the next such that social stability is preserved? In answering this question, Bourdieu draws heavily from Marx, Durkheim, and Weber to fashion a novel account of the process of social reproduction. The resulting analyses of cultural capital and its accumulation through socialization and education represent one of his most important contributions to social theory.

Like Marx, Bourdieu sees modern societies as based fundamentally on relations of power. Arguing that "economic capital is at the root of all the other types of capital" (Bourdieu 1990a:252), Bourdieu shares with Marx's work, and Marxism more generally, an emphasis on class-based forms of dominance. Economic capital (money/ property) provides the means for acquiring other forms of capital, including cultural capital, by providing an escape from "necessity." The more wealth a person possesses, the more he is able to remove himself from the necessary daily concerns over physical survival. When freed from pressing concerns over one's material existence, economic capital grants opportunities for traveling to foreign lands, frequenting the bastions of high culture (museums, operas, etc.), and otherwise indulging one's tastes. In short, economic capital affords an individual the possibility for becoming "worldly"—that is, "knowing" the world—and thus deserving of the privileged status that is bestowed upon him by others. Most important for the purposes of social reproduction, economic capital can be readily transferred to succeeding generations through inheritance. Certainly it is easier to give your money to your family members than your cultural capital in the form of knowledge and aesthetic preferences, no matter how "superior" they may be. Moreover, the value of specific tastes can fluctuate within a relatively short period of time, while the value of money remains an enduring feature of advanced societies.

Although Bourdieu contends that class relations form the basis of modern, hierarchical societies and that economic capital is the most valuable form of capital, his analysis of social reproduction parts in significant ways from traditional Marxist interpretations. Marxist social theory typically assigns a derivative role to noneconomic domains. Thus, political, legal, and cultural systems compose a "superstructure" that reflects the organization of production within the more primary economic "base." However, as our discussion of cultural capital suggests, Bourdieu contends that economic resources alone do not form the social space of positions. Nor are money and property the only avenues for expressing and sustaining relations of domination. Moreover, in addition to cultural capital, social positions are also endowed with varying degrees of **social capital** or networks of contacts and acquaintances that can be used to secure or advance one's position. For instance, a friend's father may write a letter of recommendation on your behalf to attend a prestigious university of which he is an alumnus, or perhaps you know someone who knows someone who can arrange an interview for you at a highly coveted software firm. Of course, irrespective of the amount of economic and cultural capital we may possess, we all have friends and acquaintances that can help us in one way or another. Bourdieu's point, however, is that social capital circulates within defined boundaries of social space and thus serves to reproduce existing relations of domination. If one is raised in a poor family living in a rural community, it is unlikely that one will have connections to corporate executives working in a major metropolitan center. Thus, social capital promotes the perpetuation of class position across generations by providing access to opportunities denied to those who do not possess such resources.

Social reproduction, then, essentially consists of the reproduction of stratified, hierarchical relations that deflect or resist calls for radical change by those positioned in dominated positions in social space. Typically, this requires that dominated social groups sanction the legitimacy of the existing system of relations, thus perpetuating their own domination. Like Marx, who argued that "the ruling ideas are the ideas of the ruling class," Bourdieu sees relations of domination disguised through a false consciousness that renders the social system immune from challenges. This is made possible once the real sources of individuals' domination are "misrecognized" as stemming from personal failings or from causes beyond the control of their society and its leaders.

According to Bourdieu, no institution does more to ensure the reproduction of class relations than education. Misrecognized as a meritocratic institution that rewards individual aptitudes over hereditary privileges, the educational system "maintains the preexisting social order, that is, the gap between pupils endowed with unequal amounts of cultural capital. More precisely, by a series of selection operations, the system separates holders of inherited cultural capital from those who lack it. Differences of aptitude being inseparable from social differences according to inherited capital, the system thus tends to maintain preexisting social differences" (Bourdieu 1998:20). As guardians of the dominant culture—what is worth knowing and what the worthy should know—universities are charged with separating the cultured from the uncultured. Their mission is effected through an application process and competitive entrance exams (e.g., SATs) that establish a "true magical threshold separating the last candidate to have passed from the first to have failed" and thus a boundary separating the sacred from the profane (ibid.:21). Applicants are judged, and once admitted, grades are assigned, as much, if not more, on the basis of what students already know than on what they will learn. And what successful students already know is the "feel for the game" that comes with possessing the same types of cultural capital that are enshrined in institutions of higher education. Success in school is not simply tied to writing and speaking well; rather, it is a matter of writing and speaking in a particular way. Similarly, knowing how to install home plumbing, repair a television, or provide emotional support to those who are distressed is of little value in university classrooms unless it is coupled with an understanding of, and ability to articulate, the *science* that underlies such skills. What the best schools do best—the *Grande Écoles* in France or the Ivy League in the United States—is conceal the links between scholastic aptitude and inherited cultural capital in a diploma that consecrates a social difference in the guise of a technical competence (ibid.:22). Ostensibly, impersonally defined qualifications serve to perpetuate social inequalities by transforming their effects into the fate of personal traits.

Symbolic Struggles

While economic, cultural, and social capital are crucial resources that shape an individual's position in social space and thus his life chances, Bourdieu argues that these forms of capital are not directly responsible for charting one's destiny or for the reproduction of social relations more generally. Instead, these forms of capital are realized symbolically through a "war of words," the stakes of which are establishing a monopoly over the "legitimate principle of vision and division" on which social reality is constructed (Bourdieu 1990a:134). In this "war," opposing sides struggle to define what is just and unjust, good and bad, right and wrong, pure and corrupt. Both the stability of, and challenges to, the prevailing social order are the consequence of individuals and groups strategically marshalling the capital at their disposal in an effort to advance their particular interests.

However, the struggle to impose a particular vision of the world in the name of a universal "truth" cannot be waged through naked coercion or under the banner that "might makes right" if that vision is to retain its legitimacy. To be effective, capital must be deployed in a "disinterested" fashion such that all strategies, interests, and calculations appear to be untainted by self-serving ambition. This requires that individuals and groups possess **symbolic capital**. Commonly labeled prestige, honor, reputation, or charisma, symbolic capital is converted economic or cultural capital denied as capital, "recognized as legitimate, that is, misrecognized as capital" (Bourdieu 1990b:118). Here, Bourdieu is extending Weber's insights into charisma as a source of legitimacy and authority (Swartz 1997:43). In his studies of world religions, Weber examined how the charisma of prophets served as a basis for exercising authority over their followers. Charisma—a state of "grace"—endows religious prophets with a virtual magical power that instills in believers an unquestioned obedience to their commands. While Weber confined his discussion of charisma to the religious field, Bourdieu argues that charisma operates within the secular world as well. Artists, scientists, politicians, university professors, journalists, and others can use their charisma or reputation, accumulated within their respective areas of expertise, as a source of power to legitimately demand obedience from others. Those who possess symbolic capital possess the authority to make the world through a "magical power" that transforms and disguises what is the result of the self-interested exercise of economic and political domination into the naturally inevitable.

Bourdieu uses the term **symbolic violence** to refer to acts leading to the misrecognition of reality or distortion of underlying power relations. "Symbolic violence rests on the adjustment between the structures constitutive of the habitus of the dominated and the structure of the relation of domination to which they apply: the dominated perceive the dominant through the categories that the relation of domination has produced and which are thus identical to the interests of the dominant" (Bourdieu 1998:121). In this way, relations of domination take on a "naturalness" that is inscribed in the habitus, the schemes of perception and apprehension, of both the dominant and the dominated. Through committing acts of symbolic violence, a misrecognized vision of the social world is legitimated—a vision that reproduces, with the complicity of the dominated, a stratified social order. Thus, for instance, through acts of symbolic violence the beneficiaries of the educational system appear intrinsically worthy of their success, while the less successful appear intrinsically unworthy (Bourdieu 1991:24, 25).

The struggle to impose the legitimate categories according to which social life is understood is, for Bourdieu, at the root of all action. These struggles take place within "fields," a concept central in Bourdieu's theoretical scheme. **Fields** are relatively autonomous arenas within which actors and institutions mobilize their capital in an effort to capture the stakes—the distribution of capital—that are specific to it. Examples of fields include art, literature, science, religion, the family, and education. The evolving history of each of these arenas is determined by the struggles that take place between its dominant and subordinate factions as each attempts to either defend or subvert the legitimacy of existing practices—the status quo—and the meanings assigned to them. For instance, painters and critics within the field of art are engaged in a continual struggle over what qualifies as "art" and whose works deserve to be so consecrated. As is the case in all such struggles, participants here adopt strategies that correspond to the amount and types of capital they possess. Thus, artists, critics, dealers, and gallery owners whose interests and positions are aligned with established, orthodox styles will put into play their symbolic capital to denounce avant-garde or heretical works as "pretentious," "undisciplined," or, the worst of all charges in the artistic field, "commercial." For their part, the "newcomers" will challenge the legitimacy of the establishment by classifying works associated with it as "stale," "dated," or "hackneyed." While the former seeks to fix the current boundaries of the field, the latter, who can make a name for themselves only by being different or distinctive from consecrated producers, seeks to rupture them (Bourdieu 1993).

No matter the field, those who have an interest or stake in it take a position, that is, they pursue a strategy that corresponds to the position they occupy in that field. In this light all action is self-interested, although in order to be perceived as legitimate it must be misrecognized as disinterested. Because strategies of misrecognition are carried out symbolically, the words used to classify or assign meaning to acts and others are instruments of power. Symbolic power is a power of "worldmaking," "a power of creating things with words" exercised in the struggle to impose the legitimate vision of the social world (Bourdieu 1990 a or b:137, 138). Of course, not every individual or group is able to exercise symbolic power and define the "truth." The power to name the world—to "make people see and believe"—is dependent on the amount of symbolic capital (charisma, authority, recognition) one possesses, which, in turn, is dependent on the outcome of previous struggles as well as one's position within the relevant field.

Consider the controversies surrounding the definition of obscenity, attempts to form an employee union in a retail store chain, or efforts to redraw electoral districts. In each instance, the interested parties (artists and religious leaders, workers and business owners, politicians and community activists) seek to impose their particular vision on the issue as the universal, and thus legitimate, truth. When is a painting or song lyric a form of artistic expression or an obscenity? What is the best way to strike balance between workers' rights and a corporation's ability to turn a profit? When does redistricting serve to enhance democratic representation or unfairly distort the voting process? Seldom do such questions yield a simple, obvious answer. Nevertheless, they are answered, as one fraction in the controversy is able to mobilize belief in the legitimacy of its words through "an almost magical power which enables [it] to obtain the equivalent of what is obtained through force (whether physical or economic)," namely, the ability to establish the social order (Bourdieu 1991:170).

We conclude this section by briefly noting several of the influences Bourdieu draws on in developing his analyses of symbolic struggles and their relevance to the reproduction of social relations. Like Durkheim and Lévi-Strauss, Bourdieu views all symbolic systems as grounded in fundamental binary categories.[4] Evincing the imprint of both scholars, he notes:

All the agents in a given social formation share a set of basic perceptual schemes, which receive the beginnings of objectification in the pairs of antagonistic adjectives commonly used to classify and qualify persons or objects in the most varied areas of practice. The network of oppositions between high (sublime, elevated, pure) and low (vulgar, low, modest), spiritual and material, fine (refined, elegant) and coarse (heavy, fat, crude, brutal), light (subtle, lively, sharp, adroit) and heavy (slow, thick, blunt, laborious, clumsy), free and forced, broad and narrow, or, in another dimension, between unique (rare, different, distinguished, exclusive, exceptional, singular, novel) and common (ordinary, banal, commonplace, trivial, routine), brilliant (intelligent) and dull (obscure, grey, mediocre), is the matrix of all the commonplaces which find such ready acceptance because behind them lies the whole social order. (1984:468)

Bourdieu parts company with Durkheim and Lévi-Strauss, however, when he argues that binary classifications, while serving as the foundation for appending the everyday world and creating shared meaning and social solidarity, also provide the conceptual basis for social domination (Swartz 1997). The world of common sense produced by the logic of binary opposites is a world in which only some individuals and groups are entitled to the privileged axis of opposing terms. The binary categories we use to distinguish practices and things classify at the same time those individuals and groups associated with them. As an outcome of symbolic struggles, what is consecrated as sacred, pure, strong, or brilliant reflects and legitimates the underlying hierarchical social order that pits the dominant against the dominated (Swartz 1997:85, 86).

This leads us to consider the influence of Weber's work on Bourdieu. Like Weber, Bourdieu sees interests and power as deriving from a number of sources, and his analyses of multiple forms of capital represent an important extension of Weber's earlier

---

[4]Durkheim saw in the early religious distinction drawn between the sacred and the profane the basis for all other systems of thought (1912). This distinction was born out of focused group activity in tribal societies that produced in participants an altered state of consciousness. Durkheim referred to this group energy as "mana" or "collective effervescence" and argued that tribal members attributed their newly found feelings of efficacy to the influence of supernatural spirits and gods. These feelings, in turn, provided the foundation for group solidarity and a sense of community. Lévi-Strauss would later develop Durkheim's ideas regarding binary classifications into the basis for his structural anthropology.

work in this regard.[5] Bourdieu's analyses of lifestyle patterns as signs of distinction that disguise class-based domination are particularly indebted to Weber's conceptualization of class and status groups (Swartz 1997:45). Bourdieu also adopts a view similar to Weber's regarding the existence of social classes. For Weber, classes, contrary to Marxian definitions of the concept, are not real groups whose composition reflects existing property relations. Instead, classes refer to individuals who share life chances that are determined by "economic interests in the possession of goods and opportunity for income" (1925/1978:927). As you will read in the first selection excerpted below, Bourdieu argues that classes exist only "on paper," as individuals who are "related" to one another in social space, and not as real groups. This view has important ramifications for understanding how the social order and relations of domination are maintained and challenged, particularly by calling attention to the shortcomings of Marxist perspectives.

BOURDIEU'S THEORETICAL ORIENTATION

As noted at the outset, Bourdieu developed his theoretical model with the intention of overcoming the theoretical dualism that, in his estimation, is responsible for producing only partial understandings of social life. Bourdieu's concerns in this matter speak directly to both the questions of action and order. Specifically, with regard to the question of order, Bourdieu's concept of the habitus is a theoretical device that makes

Figure 9.1   Some Central Concepts in Bourdieu's Theory of Practice and Social Reproduction

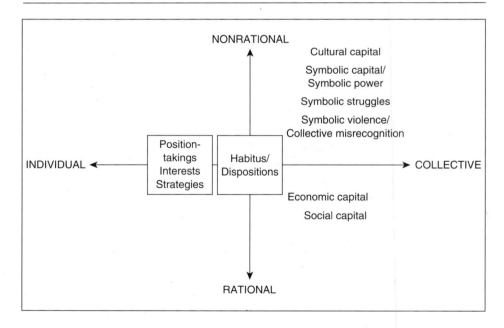

---

[5]In his essay "Class, Status, Party," Weber (1925/1978) explored how interests and the power to realize them flow not only from one's class position but from one's position in the status hierarchy as well. Moreover, Weber notes that "parties" can be formed in an effort to strategically pursue group goals or otherwise influence communal action that is not directly tied to specific class or status group interests.

| Significant Others | Randall Collins (1941–): Bridging the Micro and Macro |

Randall Collins was born in 1941. His father was a foreign service officer who at various times was stationed in Moscow, South America, and Germany. Among Collins's earliest memories are seeing bomb craters and dead bodies in Berlin at the end of the second World War. His childhood experiences were central to the emergence of his sociological imagination. As Collins notes:

> this experience made [me] receptive toward the ideas of Erving Goffman, because there's nothing like the diplomatic world for this stark contrast between what happens on the very formal idealized front stage and what happens back stage. I can remember my mother being wonderfully polite to people who were coming to visit in this tremendous round of sociability in the diplomatic world, and then she'd shut the door and it was like she took off a mask and became a different person. (Interview with Randall Collins, by Alair Maclean and James Yocom, September 20, 2000)

Collins's neo-Marxist and neo-Weberian conflict sociology combines his early understanding of the world as being full of large-scale, violent power conflicts, with the microlevel ideas of Goffman and Mead and a Durkheimian emphasis on social solidarity. This multidimensional theoretical orientation is also a product of Collins's educational training. As an undergraduate at Harvard University, Collins was influenced by the work of Talcott Parsons (see Chapter 2). Although there are many points on which Parsons and Collins sharply disagree, they both share an interest in building a comprehensive sociological theory that works on both the micro and macro levels, as well as a particular appreciation for the works of Durkheim and Weber. Later, as a graduate student in sociology at the University of California, Berkeley, in the 1960s, Collins worked with Goffman and Blumer, both of whom helped to further refine his interests in microsociology. Meanwhile, the turbulent political climate prevailing at that time and place also shaped his views by making clear the continuing real-world relevance of the works of Marx and Weber.

The central premise of Collins's conflict theory is that social life is based on individuals seeking to satisfy their own needs and wants through using whatever material or cultural resources they have at their disposal. As Collins (1975:59) succinctly states the matter, "the basic insight [of conflict theory] is that human beings are sociable but conflict-prone animals. . . . The simultaneous existence of emotional bases for solidarity—which may well be the basis of cooperation, as Durkheim emphasized—only adds group divisions and tactical resources to be used in these conflicts" with one another.

In his most recent book, *Interaction Ritual Chains* (1994), Collins continues to draw on Durkheim, Mead, and Goffman to further develop his version of microsociology. Describing the book as interpreting the theory of Durkheim "through the eyes of Goffman and the microsociological movement, that is . . . in the spirit of symbolic interaction, ethnomethodology, social constructionism, and sociology of emotions" (1994:xi), Collins investigates variations in the emotional intensity of social rituals in order to explain patterns of group membership. Here he argues that successful rituals create feelings of group membership and "pump up" individuals

(Continued)

(Continued)

with emotional energy, while failed rituals drain emotional energy, making continued interaction between the individuals involved less likely. Moreover, indicative of his conflict approach to understanding social life, Collins emphasizes that privilege and power are not only tied to an unequal distribution of material and cultural resources; they are derived also from a "flow of emotional energy across situations that makes some individuals more impressive, more attractive or dominant" while narrowing the sources of emotional energy for others (1994:xiii). Describing the emotional and symbolic exchanges at the heart of such activities as sex and smoking, Collins argues that individuals are drawn to interactions in which their economic and cultural capital promises them the best emotional payoff.

Collins has also written extensively on the "credential society" (see *The Credential Society*, 1979). For Collins, educational credentials (university degrees) not only serve as barriers to the labor market that lead to further inflationary effects (the need for more and more degrees); they are also mired in inequality. In order for individuals to receive fair treatment in the labor market, then, this system of barriers would have to be removed. Collins argues that "credential abolitionism" is necessary because "the prospects of continuing to expand the credential system indefinitely, to let job requirements inflate to the point where 4 years of college is needed for a manual laborer or 20 years of postdoctoral study is required for a technical profession, would be exceedingly alienating to all concerned. Moreover, it would not affect the rate of mobility, nor change the order of stratification among ethnic groups; it would simply reproduce their order at higher and higher levels of education" (Collins 1979:197). Evidencing his disdain for the credential society, at various points in his life Collins has quit the academic world because of his disapproval of the credential-seeking process.

During his time away from academia, Collins wrote textbooks and novels, such as *The Case of the Philosopher's Ring* (1979). Drawn back into the profession by the appeal of working with interesting colleagues, Collins has taught at a number of universities, including the University of California, San Diego; the University of California, Riverside; and the University of Virginia. Since 1997, he has been professor of sociology at the University of Pennsylvania.

possible an encompassing answer to the question, "What accounts for the patterns of behavior that lead us to experience social life as routine and predictable?" Bourdieu's response is centered on the notion that the habitus, as the "internalization of externality," structures an individual's perception of the social world at the same time that it is itself a product of social and historical conditions.

Understood as "schemes of perception, thought and action," the habitus incorporates both individualist and collectivist dimensions of the nature of social order (see Figure 9.1). The habitus both enables and constrains our actions that then reproduce the very social conditions that structure the habitus. On the one hand, Bourdieu goes to great lengths to argue that the system of dispositions produced by the habitus does not lead to "mechanical" conduct that simply reflects the external conditions that structure the habitus. In this light, individuals actively make and remake the social order as they "take positions" or advance particular points of view, constructing their vision of the world in the process. However, position-taking is not unconstrained; individuals are not free to adopt any stance they choose. Points of view and the "strategies" individuals construct as they go about fitting their conduct to others' are structured by the point they occupy in the space of social positions. The distribution of capital, in particular economic and cultural capital, structures the relation of positions within social space as well as within the specific fields in which individuals seek to impose the legitimate categories of perception. This is crucial, as the distribution of capital, in defining the space of positions, defines the space of possible position-takings, that is, the dispositions or habitus that is internalized by those who are located in one point or another.

Concerning the question of action, Bourdieu has developed a framework that likewise seeks to incorporate both rational and nonrational dimensions. (This is indicated by the boxed terms that span the rational/nonrational axis in Figure 9.1.) His efforts are based on adopting a conceptual language linked to economic and utilitarian perspectives ("interests," "strategies," "calculation," "profit") that underscores the rational aspects of motivation while arguing that action is typically carried out in a prereflective, nonrational manner. Bourdieu argues that all action is "interested" and thus oriented to the maximization of profit. Indeed, Bourdieu extends the notion of interests and profits to incorporate economic or material gains and advantages as well as the pursuit of symbolic "goods" (Swartz 1997:42). Thus, Bourdieu contends that actors adopt strategies that maximize their economic, cultural, social, and symbolic capital. In this light, we might take Bourdieu to mean that action is motivated by a conscious, rational calculation of costs and benefits. Yet, this is the very interpretation of action he means to dispel. Action is not guided by the logic of profit; it is driven by a *practical* logic that Bourdieu likens to a prereflective "feel for the game." Similar to how a good tennis player will position himself "not where the ball is but where it will be, one invests oneself and one invests not where the profit is but where it will be" (Bourdieu 1998:79). Bourdieu argues that the habitus embodies actors with a "know how" that enables them to strategically orient their conduct without necessarily having a strategic intention or goal that can be put into words. Actions are more adaptive than purposive in nature (Robbins 2000:29).

Put in another way, in taking a position, actors deploy their capital so as to realize their interests. However, conduct is not consciously chosen as if alternative means were weighed in terms of their potential for achieving specific ends. Rather, conduct is inscribed in the very nature of the "game" in which actors are involved and in the habitus through which a taken-for-granted world is constructed. Although the strategies that actors pursue are rational—that is, fitting to the field in which they are "absorbed"—they are not pursued rationally. While a politician may find it "natural" to publicly express his religious commitments on the campaign trail, a scientist would not be predisposed to such a strategy when trying to convince the public of the significance of her findings.

Readings

In the first selection, "Social Space and the Genesis of Groups," Bourdieu outlines his relational model for the study of social life. He conceptualizes social space as an arena in which individuals and groups are positioned in relation to one another based on the amount and types of capital they have at their disposal. It is on the basis of such relations that struggles are waged to classify the world. In the second selection, "Outline of a Sociological Theory of Art Perception," Bourdieu argues that artistic competence, far from being the product of an individual's natural aesthetic preferences, is dependent on the possession of cultural capital. Unrecognized as such, artistic tastes function as a sign of distinction that legitimates the dominance of those who possess the code for deciphering works of art.

Introduction to
"Social Space and the Genesis of Groups"

In this reading Bourdieu addresses many of the themes discussed above. After describing social space as structured according to the distribution of capital, he embarks on a critique of "substantialist" approaches to social classes by emphasizing the space of relations within which ongoing struggles are waged to name the social world. In particular, Bourdieu takes aim at Marxist theory for treating classes as real groups mobilized solely on the basis of the conditions of economic production. He counters by presenting the view that classes and groups do not "exist"; rather, they are an outcome of symbolic struggles that seek to pronounce a reality that exists only because it is pronounced by those in an authorized position to declare its existence, that is, by those who possess the necessary symbolic capital. It is above all the spokesperson "who, speaking about a group, speaking on behalf of a group, surreptitiously posits the existence of the group in question, institutes the group, through that magical operation which is inherent in any act of naming" (Bourdieu 1991:250).

Yet, the struggle for the "monopoly of legitimate naming" is not an entirely symbolic affair. Imposing the legitimate vision of the social world reproduces the relations of power that structure the social world. Thus, to fully understand the classifications, the principles of vision and division, according to which the world is named, one must account for the positions occupied by those engaged in the struggle to establish meaning. For the categories through which the world is perceived "are the product of the incorporation of the very structures to which they are applied" (ibid.:238). Different points of view, and the categories of perception that are used to express them, are but expressions, mediated through the habitus, of different points or positions within the space of objective relations. Any "science of classifications" must acknowledge this fundamental reality if it is to offer sound analyses of social life.

❖

Social Space and the Genesis of Groups (1985)

Pierre Bourdieu

Constructing a theory of the social space presupposes a series of breaks with Marxist theory. First, a break with the tendency to privilege substance—here, the real groups, whose number, limits, members, etc., one claims to define—at the expense of *relationships*; and with the intellectualist illusion which leads one to consider the theoretical class, constructed by the sociologist, as a real class, an effectively mobilized group. Secondly, there has to be a

SOURCE: "Social Space and Genesis of 'Classes'" reprinted by permission of the publisher from *Language and Symbolic Power* by Pierre Bourdieu, p. 229–250, edited and introduced by John B. Thompson, trans. by Gino Raymond and Matthew Adamson, Cambridge, MA: Harvard University Press. Copyright © 1991 by Polity Press.

break with the economism which leads one to reduce the social field, a multi-dimensional space, solely to the economic field, to the relations of economic production, which are thus constituted as coordinates of social position. Finally, there has to be a break with the objectivism which goes hand-in-hand with intellectualism and which leads one to ignore the symbolic struggles of which the different fields are the site, where what is at stake is the very representation of the social world and, in particular, the hierarchy within each of the fields and among the different fields. . . .

THE SOCIAL SPACE

Initially, sociology presents itself as a *social topology*. Thus, the social world can be represented as a space (with several dimensions) constructed on the basis of principles of differentiation or distribution constituted by the set of properties active within the social universe in question, i.e. capable of conferring strength, power within that universe, on their holder. Agents and groups of agents are thus defined by their relative positions within that space. Each of them is assigned to a position or a precise class of neighbouring positions (i.e. a particular region in this space) and one cannot really—even if one can in thought—occupy two opposite regions of the space. Inasmuch as the properties selected to construct this space are active properties, one can also describe it as a field of forces, i.e. as a set of objective power relations which impose themselves on all who enter the field and which are irreducible to the intentions of the individual agents or even to the direct *interactions* among the agents.

The active properties which are selected as principles of construction of the social space are the different kinds of power or capital which are current in the different fields. Capital, which may exist in objectified form—in the form of material properties—or, in the case of cultural capital, in the embodied state, and which may be legally guaranteed, represents a power over the field (at a given moment) and, more precisely, over the accumulated products of past labour (in particular over the set of instruments of production) and thereby over the mechanisms tending to ensure the production of a particular

category of goods and so over a set of incomes and profits. The kinds of capital, like the aces in a game of cards, are powers which define the chances of profit in a given field (in fact, to each field or sub-field there corresponds a particular kind of capital, which is current, as a power or stake, in that game). For example, the volume of cultural capital (the same thing would be true, *mutatis mutandis*, of the economic game) determines the aggregate chances of profit in all the games in which cultural capital is effective, thereby helping to determine position in social space (to the extent that this is determined by success in the cultural field).

The position of a given agent within the social space can thus be defined by the positions he occupies in the different fields, that is, in the distribution of the powers which are active within each of them. These are, principally, economic capital (in its different kinds), cultural capital and social capital, as well as symbolic capital, commonly called prestige, reputation, renown, etc., which is the form in which the different forms of capital are perceived and recognized as legitimate. One can thus construct a simplified model of the social field as a whole which makes it possible to conceptualize, for each agent, his position in all possible spaces of competition (it being understood that, while each field has its own logic and its own hierarchy, the hierarchy which prevails among the different kinds of capital and the statistical link between the different types of assets tends to impose its own logic on the other fields).

The social field can be described as a multi-dimensional space of positions such that every actual position can be defined in terms of a multi-dimensional system of co-ordinates whose values correspond to the values of the different pertinent variables. Thus, agents are distributed within it, in the first dimension, according to the overall volume of the capital they possess and, in the second dimension, according to the composition of their capital—i.e. according to the relative weight of the different kinds of assets within their total assets. . . .

Thus, in the first dimension, which is undoubtedly the most important, the holders of a great volume of overall capital, such as industrial employers, members of liberal professions, and university professors are opposed, in the mass, to those who are most deprived of economic and cultural capital, such as unskilled workers. But from another point of view, that is, from the point of view of the relative weight of economic capital and cultural capital in their patrimony, professors (relatively wealthier in cultural capital than is economic capital) are strongly opposed to industrial employers (relatively wealthier in economic capital than in cultural capital). . . . The second opposition, like the first, is the source of differences in dispositions and, therefore, in position-takings. This is the case of the opposition between intellectuals and industrial employers or, on a lower level of the social hierarchy, between, [for instance,] primary school teachers and small merchants. . . .

In a more general sense, the space of social positions is retranslated into a space of position-takings through the mediation of the space of dispositions (or habitus). In other words, the system of differential deviations which defines the different positions in the two major dimensions of social space corresponds to the system of differential deviations in agents' properties (or in the properties of constructed classes of agents), that is, in their practices and in the goods they possess. To each class of positions there corresponds a class of habitus (or *tastes*) produced by the social conditioning associated with the corresponding condition and, through the mediation of the habitus and its generative capability, a systematic set of goods and properties, which are united by an affinity of style.

One of the functions of the notion of habitus is to account for the unity of style, which unites the practices and goods of a single agent or a class of agents (this is what writers such as Balzac or Flaubert have so finely expressed through their descriptions of settings—such as the Pension Vauquer in *Le Père Goriot* or the elegant dishes and drinks consumed in the homes of different protagonists of *L'Education sentimentale*—which are at the same time descriptions of the characters who live in them). The habitus is this generative and unifying principle which retranslates the intrinsic and relational characteristics of a position into a unitary lifestyle, that is, a unitary set of choices of persons, goods, practices.

Like the positions of which they are the product, habitus are differentiated, but they are also differentiating. Being distinct and distinguished, they are also distinction operators, implementing different principles of differentiation of using differently the common principles of differentiation.

Habitus are generative principles of distinct and distinctive practices—what the worker eats, and especially the way he eats it, the sport he practices and the way he practices it, his political opinions and the way he expresses them are systematically different from the industrial owner's corresponding activities. But habitus are also classificatory schemes, principles of classification, principles of vision and division, different tastes. They make distinctions between what is good and what is bad, between what is right and what is wrong, between what is distinguished and what is vulgar, and so forth, but the distinctions are not identical. Thus, for instance, the same behavior or even the same good can appear distinguished to one person, pretentious to someone else, and cheap or showy to yet another.

But the essential point is that, when perceived through these social categories of perception, these principles of vision and division, the differences in practices, in the goods possessed, or in the opinions expressed become symbolic differences and constitute a veritable *language*. Differences associated with different positions, that is, goods, practices, and especially *manners*, function, in each society, in the same way as differences which constitute symbolic systems, such as the set of phonemes of a language or the set of distinctive features and of differential "*écarts*" that constitute a mythical system, that is, as *distinctive signs*. . . .

The form that is taken, at every moment, in each social field, by the set of distributions of the different kinds of capital (embodied or materialized), as instruments for the appropriation of the objectified product of accumulated social labour, defines the state of the power relations, institutionalized in long-lasting social statuses, socially recognized or legally guaranteed, between social agents objectively defined by their position in these relations; it determines the actual or potential powers within the different fields and the chances of access to the specific profits that they offer.[i]

Knowledge of the position occupied in this space contains information as to the agents' intrinsic properties (their condition) and their relational properties (their position). This is seen particularly clearly in the case of the occupants of the intermediate or middle positions, who, in addition to the average or median values of their properties, owe a number of their most typical properties to the fact that they are situated *between* the two poles of the field, in the *neutral* point of the space, and that they are balanced between the two extreme positions.

CLASSES ON PAPER

On the basis of knowledge of the space of positions, one can separate out *classes*, in the logical sense of the word, i.e. sets of agents who occupy similar positions and who, being placed in similar conditions and subjected to similar conditionings, have every likelihood of having similar dispositions and interests and therefore of producing similar practices and adopting similar stances. This "class on paper" has the *theoretical* existence which is that of theories: insofar as it is the product of an explanatory classification, entirely similar to those of zoologists or botanists, it makes it possible to *explain* and predict the practices and properties of the things classified—including their group-forming practices. It is not really a class, an *actual* class, in the sense of a group, a group mobilized for struggle; at most, it might be called a *probable class*, inasmuch as it is a set of agents which will present fewer hindrances to efforts at mobilization than any other set of agents.

Thus, contrary to the *nominalist relativism* which cancels out social differences by reducing

them to pure theoretical artefacts, one must therefore assert the existence of an objective space determining compatibilities and incompatibilities, proximities and distances. Contrary to the *realism of the intelligible* (or the reification of concepts), one must assert that the classes which can be separated out in social space (for example, for the purposes of the statistical analysis which is the only means of manifesting the structure of the social space) do not exist as real groups although they explain the probability of individuals constituting themselves as practical groups, in families (homogamy), clubs, associations and even trade-union or political "movement." What does exist is a *space of relationships* which is as real as a geographical space, in which movements are paid for in work, in efforts and above all in time (moving up means raising oneself, climbing, and acquiring the marks, the stigmata, of this effort). Distances within it are also measured in time (time taken to rise or to convert capital, for example). And the probability of mobilization into organized movements, equipped with an apparatus and spokesmen, etc. (precisely that which leads one to talk of a "class") will be inverse ratio to distance in this space. While the probability of assembling a set of agents, really or nominally—through the power of the delegate—rises when they are closer in social space and belong to a more restricted and therefore more homogeneous constructed class, alliance between those who are closest is never *necessary*, inevitable (because the effects of immediate competition may act as a screen), and alliance between those most distant from each other is never *impossible*. Though there is more chance of mobilizing the set of workers than the set composed of workers and bosses, it is possible, in an international crisis, for example, to provoke a grouping

---

[i]In some social universes, the principles of division which, like volume and structure of capital, determine the structure of the social space, are reinforced by principles of division relatively independent of economic or cultural properties, such as ethnic or religious affiliation. In such cases, the distribution of the agents appears as the product of the intersection of two spaces which are partially independent: an ethnic group situated in a lower position in the space of the ethnic groups may occupy positions in all the fields, including the highest, but with rates of representation inferior to those of an ethnic group situated in a higher position. Each ethnic group may thus be characterized by the social positions of its members, by the rate of dispersion of these positions, and by its degree of social integration despite this dispersion. (Ethnic solidarity may have the effect of ensuring a form of collective mobility.)

on the basis of links of national identity (partly because, by virtue of its specific history, each national social space has its specific structure—e.g. as regards hierarchical distances within the economic field).

Like "being," according to Aristotle, the social world can be uttered and constructed in different ways. It may be practically perceived, uttered, constructed, according to different principles of vision and division—for example, ethnic division. But groupings grounded in the structure of the space constructed in terms of capital distribution are more likely to be stable and durable, while other forms of grouping are always threatened by the splits and oppositions linked to distances in social space. To speak of a social space means that one cannot group just *anyone* with *anyone* while ignoring the fundamental differences, particularly economic and cultural ones. But this never entirely excludes the possibility of organizing agents in accordance with other principles of division—ethnic or national ones, for example,—though it has to be remembered that these are generally linked to the fundamental principles, with ethnic groups themselves being at least roughly hierarchized in the social space, in the USA for example (through seniority in immigration).[ii]

This marks a first break with the Marxist tradition. More often than not, Marxism either summarily identifies constructed class with real class (in other words, as Marx complained about Hegel, it confuses the things of logic with the logic of things); or, when it does make the distinction, with the opposition between "class-in-itself," defined in terms of a set of objective conditions, and "class-for-itself," based on subjective factors, it describes the movement from one to the other (which is always celebrated as nothing less than an ontological promotion) in terms of a logic which is either totally determinist or totally voluntarist. In the former case, the transition is seen as a logical, mechanical or organic necessity (the transformation of the proletariat from class-in-itself to class-for-itself is presented as an inevitable effect of time, of the "maturing of the objective conditions"); in the latter case, it is seen as the effect of an "awakening of consciousness" (*prise de conscience*) conceived as a "taking cognizance" (*prise de connaissance*) of theory, performed under the enlightened guidance of the Party. In all cases, there is no mention of the mysterious alchemy whereby a "group in struggle," a personalized collective, a historical agent assigning itself its own ends, arises from the objective economic conditions.

A sleight of hand removes the most essential questions. First, the very question of the political, of the specific action of the agents who, in the name of a theoretical definition of the "class," assign to its members the goals *officially* best matching their "objective"—i.e. theoretical—interests; and of the work whereby they manage to produce, if not the mobilized class, then belief in the existence of the class, which is the basis of the authority of its spokesmen. Secondly, the question of the relationship between the would-be scientific classifications produced by the social scientist (in the same way as a zoologist) and the classifications that the agents themselves constantly produce in their ordinary existence, and through which they seek to modify their position within the objective classifications or to modify the very principles which underlie these classifications.

PERCEPTION OF THE SOCIAL WORLD AND POLITICAL STRUGGLE

The most resolutely objectivist theory has to integrate the agents' representation of the social world; more precisely, it must take account of the contribution that agents make towards constructing the view of the social world, and through this, towards constructing this world, by means of the *work of representation* (in all

[ii]The same thing would be true of the relationship between geographical space and social space. These two spaces never coincide completely, but a number of differences that are generally attributed to the effect of geographical space, e.g. the opposition between centre and periphery, are the effect of distance in social space, i.e. the unequal distribution of the different kinds of capital in geographical space.

senses of the word) that they constantly perform in order to impose their view of the world or the view of their own position in this world—their social identity. Perception of the social world is the product of a double social structuration: on the "objective" side, it is socially structured because the properties attached to agents or institutions do not offer themselves independently to perception, but in combinations that are very unequally probable (and, just as animals with feathers are more likely to have wings than are animals with fur, so the possessors of a substantial cultural capital are more likely to be museum-goers than those who lack such capital); on the "subjective" side, it is structured because the schemes of perception and appreciation available for use at the moment in question, especially those that are deposited in language, are the product of previous symbolic struggles and express the state of the symbolic power relations, in a more or less transformed form. The objects of the social world can be perceived and uttered in different ways because, like objects in the natural world, they always include a degree of indeterminacy and fuzziness— owing to the fact, for example, that even the most constant combinations of properties are only founded on statistical connections between interchangeable features; and also because, as historical objects, they are subject to variations in time so that their meaning, insofar as it depends on the future, is itself in suspense, in waiting, dangling, and therefore relatively indeterminate. This element of play, or uncertainty, is what provides a basis for the plurality of world views, itself linked to the plurality of points of view, and to all the symbolic struggles for the power to produce and impose the legitimate world view and, more precisely, to all the cognitive "filling-in" strategies which produced the meaning of the objects of the social world by going beyond the directly visible attributes by reference to the future or the past. This reference may be implicit and tacit, through what Husserl calls protention and retention, practical forms of prospection or retrospection without a positing of the future and the past as such; or it may be explicit, as in political struggles, in which the past—with retrospective reconstruction of a past tailored to the needs of the present—and especially the future, with creative forecasting, are endlessly invoked, to determine, delimit and define the always open meaning of the present.

To point out that perception of the social world implies an act of construction in no way entails acceptance of an intellectualist theory of knowledge: the essential part of the experience of the social world and of the act of construction that is implies takes place in practice, below the level of explicit representation and verbal expression. More like a class unconscious than a "class consciousness" in the Marxist sense, the sense of the position occupied in social space (what Erving Goffman calls the "sense of one's place") is the practical mastery of the social structure as a whole that reveals itself through the sense of the position occupied within that structure. The categories of perception of the social world are, as regards their most essential features, the product of the internalization, the incorporation, of the objective structures of social space. Consequently, they incline agents to accept the social world as it is, to take it for granted, rather than to rebel against it, to counterpose to it different, even antagonistic, possibles. The sense of one's place as a sense of what one can or cannot "permit oneself," implies a tacit acceptance of one's place, a sense of limits ("that's not for the likes of us," etc.), or, which amounts to the same thing, a sense of distances, to be marked and kept, respected or expected. It does so all the more strongly where the conditions of existence are most rigorous and where the reality principle most rigorously asserts itself. (Hence the profound realism which generally characterizes the world view of the dominated; functioning as a sort of socially constituted instinct of conservation, it can be seen as conservative only in terms of an external, and therefore normative, representation of the "objective interest" of those whom it helps to live, or survive.)

If objective power relations tend to reproduce themselves in views of the social world which contribute to the permanence of these relations, this is therefore because the structuring principles of a world view are rooted in the objective structures of the social world: power relations are also present in people's minds, in the form of the categories of perception of these relations.

However, the degree of indeterminacy and fuzziness in the objects of the social world, together with the practical, pre-reflexive and implicit nature of the schemes of perception and appreciation that are applied to them, is the Archimedean leverage point that is objectively offered for political action proper. Knowledge of the social world and, more precisely, the categories which make it possible, are the stakes, par excellence, of political struggle, the inextricably theoretical and practical struggle for the power to conserve or transform the social world by conserving or transforming the categories through which it is perceived.

The capacity to make entities exist in the explicit state, to publish, make public (i.e. render objectified, visible, and even official) that which had not previously attained objective and collective existence and had therefore remained in the state of individual or serial existence— people's malaise, anxiety, disquiet, expectations— represents a formidable social power, the power to make groups by making the *common sense*, the explicit consensus, of the whole group. In fact, this work of categorization, i.e. of making-explicit and of classification, is performed incessantly, at every moment of ordinary existence, in the struggles in which agents clash over the meaning of the social world and of their position within it, the meaning of their social identity, through all the forms of benediction or malediction, eulogy, praise, congratulations, compliments, or insults, reproaches, criticisms, accusations, slanders, etc. . . .

It becomes clear why one of the elementary forms of political power, in many archaic societies, consisted in the quasi-magical power to *name* and to make-exist by virtue of naming. Thus in traditional Kabylia, the function of making-explicit and the work of symbolic production that the poets performed, particularly in crisis situations, when the meaning of the world slips away, conferred on them major political functions, those of the warlord or ambassador. But with the growing differentiation of the social world and the constitution of relatively autonomous fields, the work of producing and imposing meaning is carried on in and through the struggles within the field of cultural production (particularly the political sub-field); it becomes the particular concern, the specific interest, of the professional producers of objectified representations of the social world or, more precisely, of methods of objectification.

If the legitimate mode of perception is such an important prize at stake in social struggles, this is partly because the shift from the implicit to the explicit is in no way automatic: the same experience of the social may be uttered in very different expressions. And partly it is because the most marked objective differences may be masked by more immediately visible differences (e.g. those between ethnic groups). It is true that perceptual configurations, social *Gestalten*, exist objectively, and that the proximity of conditions, and therefore of dispositions, tends to be translated into durable linkages and groupings, immediately perceptible social units, such as socially distinct regions or neighbourhoods (with spatial segregation), or sets of agents endowed with entirely similar visible properties, such as Weber's *Stände*. But the fact remains that socially known and recognized differences only exist for a subject capable not only of perceiving differences but of recognizing them as significant, interesting, i.e. only for a subject endowed with the capacity and inclination to *make* the distinctions that are regarded as significant in the social universe in question.

Thus, particularly through properties and their distributions, the social world achieves, objectively, the status of a *symbolic system*, which, like the system of phonemes, is organized according to the logic of difference, differential deviation, thereby constituted as significant *distinction*. The social space, and the differences that "spontaneously" emerge within it, tends to function symbolically as a *space of life-styles* or as a set of *Stände*, of groups characterized by different life-styles.

Distinction does not necessarily imply the pursuit of distinction, as is often supposed, following Veblen and his theory of conspicuous consumption. All consumption and, more generally, all practice, is "conspicuous," visible, whether or not it is performed *in order to be seen*; it is distinctive, whether or not it springs from the intention of being "conspicuous," standing out, or distinguishing oneself or behaving with distinction. As such, it inevitably functions as a *distinctive sign* and, when the difference is recognized, legitimate and approved, as a *sign of distinction* (in all senses of the phrase). However, because social agents are capable of perceiving as significant distinctions the "spontaneous" distinctions that their categories of perception lead them to regard as pertinent, it follows that they are also capable of intentionally underscoring these spontaneous differences in life-style by what Weber calls "the stylization of life" (*die Stilisierung des Lebens*). The pursuit of distinction—which may be expressed in ways of speaking or the refusal of misalliances—produces separations intended to be perceived or, more precisely, known and recognized, as legitimate differences, which most often means differences in nature ("natural distinction").

Distinction—in the ordinary sense of the word—is the difference inscribed in the very structure of the social space when perceived through categories adapted to that structure; and the Weberian *Stände*, which is often contrasted with the Marxist class, is the class constructed by an adequate division of social space, when perceived through categories derived from the structure of that space. Symbolic capital—another name for distinction—is nothing other than capital, in whatever form, when perceived by an agent endowed with categories of perception arising from the internalization (embodiment) of the structure of its distribution, i.e., when it is known and recognized as self-evident. Distinctions, as symbolic transfigurations of de facto differences and, more generally, ranks, orders, grades, and all other symbolic hierarchies, are the product of the application of schemes of construction which, like (for example) the pairs of adjectives used to utter most social judgements, are the product of the internalization of the structures to which they are applied; and the most absolute recognition of legitimacy is nothing other than the apprehension of the everyday world as self-evident which results from the quasi-perfect coincidence of objective structures and embodied structures.

It follows, among other things, that symbolic capital goes to symbolic capital, and that the—real—autonomy of the field of symbolic production does not prevent it being dominated, in its functioning, by the constraints which dominate the social field, so that objective power relations tend to reproduce themselves in symbolic power relations, in views of the social world which help to ensure the permanence of these power relations. In the struggle to impose the legitimate view of the social world, in which science itself is inevitably involved, agents wield a power proportionate to their symbolic capital, i.e. to the recognition they receive from a group. The authority which underlies the performative efficacy of discourse about the social world, the symbolic strength of the views and forecasts aimed at imposing principles of vision and division of the social world, is a *percipi*, a being-known and being-recognized (this is the etymology of *nobilis*), which makes it possible to impose a *percipere*. Those most *visible* in terms of the prevailing categories of perception are those best placed to change the vision by changing the categories of perception. But also, on the whole, those least inclined to do so.

THE SYMBOLIC ORDER AND THE POWER TO NAME

In the symbolic struggle over the production of common sense or, more precisely, for the monopoly of legitimate *naming*, that is to say, official—i.e. explicit and public—imposition of the legitimate vision of the social world, agents engage the symbolic capital they have acquired in previous struggles, in particular, all the power they possess over the instituted taxonomies, inscribed in minds or in objectivity, such as qualifications. Thus, all the symbolic strategies through which agents seek to impose their vision of the divisions of the social world and their position within it, can be located between two extremes: the insult, and *idios logos* with which an individual tries to impose his point of view while taking the risk of reciprocity, and *official nomination*, an act of symbolic imposition which has behind it all the strength of the collective, the consensus, the common sense, because it is performed by a delegated agent of the state, the holder of the *monopoly of legitimate symbolic violence*. On the one hand, there is the world of particular perspectives, singular agents who, from their individual viewpoint, their personal position, produce particular, self-interested namings of themselves and others (nicknames, by-names, insults, even accusations, slanders) that lack the capacity to force recognition, and therefore to exert a symbolic effect, to the extent that their authors are less authorized and have a more direct interest in forcing recognition of the viewpoint they seek to impose. On the other hand, there is the authorized viewpoint of an agent authorized, in his personal capacity, such as a "major critic," a prestigious prefacer or a consecrated author (cf. Zola's *J'accuse*); and, above all, the legitimate viewpoint of the authorized spokesman of the mandated representative of the state, the "plane of all perspectives," in Leibniz's phrase—official nomination, the "entitlement" (*titre*) which, like the academic qualification (*titre scolaire*) is valid on all markets and which, as an official definition of official identity, rescues its holders from the symbolic struggle of all against all, by uttering the authorized, university recognized perspective on all social agents. The state, which produces the official classifications, is in a sense the supreme tribunal to which Kafka was referring in *The Trial* when he had Block say of the advocate and his claim to be one of the "great advocates": "Naturally anyone can call himself 'great' if he wants to, but in such matters it is the practices of the court that decide." The fact is that scientific analysis does not have to choose between perspectivism and what has to be called absolutism; the truth of the social world is the stake in a struggle between agents very unequally equipped to achieve absolute, i.e. self-fulfilling, vision and pre-vision.

One could analyse in this light the functioning of an institution like the French national statistics office, INSEE, a state institute which produces official taxonomies, invested with quasi-legal authority, particularly, in relations between employers and employees, that of the *title*, capable of conferring rights independent of actual productive activity. In so doing, it tends to fix the hierarchies and thus to sanction and consecrate a power relationship between the agents with respect to the names of trades and occupations, an essential component of social identity. The management of names is one of the ways of managing material scarcity, and the names of groups, especially occupational groups, record a state of the struggles and bargaining over official designations and the material and symbolic advantages associated with them. The occupational name which is conferred on agents, the title they are given, is one of the positive or negative retributions (on the same footing as their salary), inasmuch as it is a *distinctive mark* (an emblem or stigma) which receives its *value* from its position in a hierarchically organized system of titles and which thereby helps to determine the relative positions of agents and groups. Consequently, agents have recourse to practical or symbolic strategies aimed at maximizing the symbolic profit of naming: for example, they may decline the economic gratifications provided by one job in order to occupy a less well-paid but more prestigiously named position; or they may try to move towards positions whose designation is less precise and so escape the effects of symbolic devaluation. Similarly, in stating their personal identity, they may give themselves a name which includes them in a class sufficiently broad to include agents occupying positions superior to their own: for example, in France, a primary school teacher, an *instituteur*, may refer to himself as an *enseignant*, thereby implying that he might be a *lycée* teacher or a university teacher. More generally, they always have a choice between several names and they can play on the uncertainties and the effects of vagueness linked to the plurality of perspectives so as to try to escape the verdict of the official taxonomy.

But the logic of official naming is most clearly seen in the case of all the symbolic property rights which in French are called *titres*—titles of nobility, educational qualifications, professional titles. Titles are symbolic capital, socially and even legally recognized. The noble is not just someone who is known (*nobilis*), noteworthy, well-regarded, recognized, he is someone recognized by an *official*, "universal" tribunal, in other words known and recognized by all. The professional or academic title is a kind of legal rule of social perception, a "being-perceived" guaranteed as a right. It is symbolic capital in an institutionalized, legal (and no longer merely legitimate) form. Increasingly inseparable from the academic qualification, since the educational system increasingly tends to represent the ultimate and only guarantee of professional titles, it has a value in itself and, although it is a "common noun," it functions like a "great name" (the name of a great family or a proper name), securing all sorts of symbolic profits (and assets that cannot be obtained directly with money).[iii] It is the symbolic scarcity of the title in the space of the names of professions that tends to govern the rewards of the occupation (and not the relationship between the supply of and demand for a particular form of labour). It follows from this that the rewards of the title tend to acquire autonomy with respect to the rewards of labour. Thus the same work may receive different remuneration depending on the titles of the person who does it (e.g. tenured, official post-holder (*titulaire*) as opposed to a part-timer (*intérimaire*) or someone "acting" (*faisant fonction*) in that capacity, etc.). Since the title is in itself an institution (like language) that is more durable than the intrinsic characteristics of the work, the rewards of the title may be maintained despite changes in the work and its relative value. It is not relative value of the work that determines the value of the name, but the institutionalized value of the title that can be used as a means of defending or maintaining the value of the work.[iv]

This means that one cannot conduct a science of classifications without conducting a science of the struggle over classifications and without taking account of the position occupied, in this struggle over the power of knowledge, for power through knowledge, for the monopoly of legitimate symbolic violence, by each of the agents or groups of agents who are involved in it, whether they be ordinary individuals, exposed to the vicissitudes of the everyday symbolic struggle, or authorized (and full-time) professionals, which includes all those who speak or write about the social classes, and who are distinguished according to the greater or lesser extent to which their classifications commit the authority of the state, the holder of the monopoly of *official naming*, correct classification, the correct order.

While the structure of the social world is defined at every moment by the structure of the distribution of the capital and profits characteristic of the different particular fields, the fact remains that in each of these arenas, the very definition of the stakes and of the "trump cards" can be called into question. Every field is the site of more or less overt struggle over the definition of the legitimate principles of division of the field. The question of legitimacy arises from the very possibility of this questioning, of a break with the *doxa* which takes the ordinary order for granted. Having said this, the symbolic strength of the participants in this struggle is never completely independent of their position in the game, even if the specifically symbolic power of nomination constitutes a strength relatively independent of the other forms of social power. The constraints of the necessity inscribed in the very structure of the different fields continue to bear on the symbolic struggles aimed at conserving or transforming that structure. The social world is, to a large extent, what the agents make of it, at each moment; but they have no chance of un-making and re-making it except on the basis of realistic knowledge of what it is and of what they can do with it from the position they occupy within it.

In short, scientific work aims to establish adequate knowledge both of the space of objective relations between the different positions constituting the field and of the necessary relations set up, through the mediation of the *habitus* of their occupants, between these positions and their corresponding stances (*prises de position*), that is to say, between the points occupied within that space and the points of view on that very space, which play a part in the reality and the evolution of that space. In other words, the objective delimitation of constructed classes, i.e. of *regions* of the constructed space of positions, makes it possible to understand the principle and the efficacy of the classificatory strategies by

---

[iii]Entry into an occupation endowed with a title is increasingly subordinated to possession of an educational qualification (*titre scolaire*), and there is a close relationship between educational qualifications and remuneration, in contrast to untitled occupations in which agents doing the same work may have very different qualifications.

[iv]The possessors of the same title tend to constitute themselves into a group and to equip themselves with permanent organizations—medical associations, alumni associations, etc. intended to ensure the group's cohesion—periodic meetings, etc. and to promote its material and symbolic interests.

means of which agents seek to conserve or modify this space, in the forefront of which is the constituting of groups organized with a view to defending their members' interests.

Analysis of the struggle over classifications brings to light the political ambition which pervades the epistemic ambition of producing the correct classification—the ambition which defines the rex, to whom it falls, according to Emile Benveniste, to *regere fines* and *regere sacra*, to set forth the frontier between the sacred and the profane, good and evil, the vulgar and the distinguished. If he is not to make social science merely a way of pursuing politics by other means, the sociologist must take as his object the intention of assigning others to classes and of telling them thereby what they are and what they have to be (this is the whole ambiguity of forecasting); he must analyse, in order to repudiate, the ambition of the creative world view, a kind of *intuitus originarius* that would make things exist in accordance with its vision (this is the whole ambiguity of the Marxist conception of class, which is inextricably an "is" and an "ought"). He must objectify the ambition of objectifying, of classifying from outside, objectively, agents who struggle to classify others and to classify themselves. If he does classify—by making divisions, for the purposes of statistical analysis, in the continuous space of social positions—he does so precisely so as to be able to objectify *all* forms of objectification, from the particular insult to the official nomination, not forgetting the claim, characteristic of science in its positivist, bureaucratic, definition, to arbitrate in these struggles in the name of "axiological neutrality." The symbolic power of agents, understood as the power to make things seen—*theorein*—and to make things believed, to produce and impose the legitimate or legal classification, in fact depends, as the case of the *rex* reminds us, on the position occupied in the space (and in the classifications potentially inscribed in it). But objectifying objectification means, above all, objectifying the field of production of objectified representations of the social world, in particular, of the law-making taxonomies, in a word, the field of cultural or ideological production, a space and a game in which the social scientist himself is caught, like all those who argue about the social classes (and who else talks about them?).

THE POLITICAL FIELD AND THE EFFECT OF THE HOMOLOGIES

It is this field of political struggles, in which the professional practitioners of representation, in all senses of the word, clash with one another over another field of struggles, that has to be analysed if one wants to understand (without subscribing to the mythology of the "awakening of consciousness") the shift from the practical sense of the position occupied, itself amenable to being made explicit in different ways, to specifically political manifestations. Those who occupy the dominated positions within the social space are also located in dominated positions in the field of symbolic production, and it is not clear where they could obtain the instruments of symbolic production that are needed in order to express their specific viewpoint on the social space, were it not that the specific logic of the field of cultural production, and the particular interests that are generated within it, have the effect of inclining a fraction of the professionals involved in this field to supply the dominated, on the basis of homology of position, with the means of challenging the representations that arise from the immediate complicity between social structures and mental structures, and which tend to ensure the continuous reproduction of the distribution of symbolic capital. . . .

The inadequacies of the Marxist theory of classes, in particular its inability to explain the set of objectively observed differences, stems from the fact that, in reducing the social world solely to the economic field, it is forced to define social position solely in terms of position in the relations of economic production and consequently ignores positions in the different fields and sub-fields, particularly in the relations of cultural production, as well as all the oppositions that structure the social field, which are irreducible to the opposition between owners and non-owners of the means of economic production. It thereby secures a one-dimensional social world, simply organized around the opposition between two blocs (and one of the major questions is then that of the *boundary* between these two blocs, with all the associated, endlessly debated, questions of the "labour aristocracy," the "embourgeoisement" of the working class, etc.). In reality, the social space is a multi-dimensional space, an open set of fields that are relatively autonomous, i.e. more or less strongly and directly subordinated, in their functioning and their transformations, to the field of the economic production. Within each of these sub-spaces, the occupants of the dominated positions are constantly engaged in struggles of different forms (without necessarily constituting themselves into antagonistic groups).

But the most important thing, from the standpoint of the problem of breaking the circle of symbolic production, is the fact that, on the basis of the homologies between positions within different fields (and the invariant, or indeed universal, content of the relationship between the dominant and the dominated), *alliances* can be set up which are more or less lasting and always based on a more or less conscious misunderstanding. Homology of position between intellectuals and industrial workers—with the former occupying within the field of power, i.e. vis-à-vis industrial and commercial employers, positions which are homologous to those which industrial workers occupy within the social space as a whole—is the basis of an ambiguous alliance, in which the cultural producers, dominated agents among the dominant, divert their accumulated cultural capital so as to offer to the dominated the means of objectively constituting their view of the world and the representation of their interest in an explicit theory and in institutionalized instruments of representation—trade-union organizations, parties, social technologies for mobilization and demonstration, etc. . . .

But above all it would become clear that the effect of the specific interests associated with the position they occupy in the field and in the competition to impose views of the social world, inclines professional theoreticians and spokesmen, i.e. all those who are called in everyday language "full-time" or "permanent" officials, to produce differentiated, distinctive products which, because of the homology between the field of professional producers and the field of the consumers of opinions, are quasi-automatically adjusted to the different forms of demand—this demand being defined, especially in this case, as a demand for difference, for opposition, which they actually help to produce by helping it to find expression. It is the structure of the

political field, in other words the objective relationship to the occupants of the other positions, and the relationship to the competing stances which they offer, which, as much as the direct relationship to their mandators, determines the stances they take, i.e. the supply of political products. Because the interests directly involved in the struggle for the monopoly of the legitimate expression of the truth of the social world tend to be the specific equivalent of the interests of the occupants of homologous positions in the social field, political discourses have a sort of structural duplicity. They seem to be directly addressed to the mandators, but in reality they are and aimed at competitors within the field. . . .

CLASS AS REPRESENTATION AND AS WILL

But to establish how the power to constitute and institute that is held by the authorized spokesman—a party leader or trade-union leader, for example—is itself constituted and instituted, it is not sufficient to give an account of the specific interests of the theoreticians or spokesmen and of the structural affinities that link them to their mandators. One must also analyze the logic of the process of institution, which is ordinarily perceived and described as a process of delegation, in which the mandated representative receives from the group the power to make the group. Here, making the necessary transpositions, we may follow the historians of law (Kantorowicz, Post and others), when they describe the mystery of "ministry"—the *mysterium* of *ministerium*, a play on words much favoured by the canonists. The mystery of the process of transubstantiation whereby the spokesman becomes the group that he expresses can only be understood through a historical analysis of the genesis and functioning of *representation*, through which the representative makes the group he represents. The spokesman endowed with full power to speak and act in the name of the group, and first of all to act on the group through the magic of the slogan, the password (*mot d'ordre*), is the substitute of the group which exists only through this surrogacy. Personifying a fictitious person, a social fiction, he raises those whom he represents from the state of separate individuals, enabling them to act and speak, through him, as one man. In exchange, he receives the right to take himself for the group, to speak and act as if he were the group made man: "*status est magistratus,*" "*l'etat c'est moi,*" "the union thinks that . . . ," etc.

The mystery of ministry is one of those cases of social magic in which a thing or a person becomes something other than what it or he is, so that a man (a government minister, a bishop, a delegate, a member of parliament, a general secretary, etc.) can identify himself, and be identified, with a set of men, the People, the Workers, etc. or a social entity, the Nation, the State, the Church, the Party. The mystery of ministry culminates when the group can only exist through delegation to a spokesman who will make it exist by speaking for it, i.e. on its behalf and in its place. The circle is then complete: the group is made by the man who speaks in its name, who thus appears as the source of the power which he exerts on those who are its real source. This circular relationship is the root of the charismatic illusion in which, extreme cases, the spokesman can appear to himself and other as *causa sui.* Political alienation arises from the fact that isolated agents—the more so the less strong they are symbolically—cannot constitute themselves as a group, i.e. as a force capable of making itself heard in the political field, except by dispossessing themselves in favour of an apparatus; in other words from the fact that one always has to risk political dispossession in order to escape political dispossession. Fetishism, according to Marx, is what happens when "the products of the human brain appear as autonomous figures endowed with a life of their own"; political fetishism lies precisely in the fact that the value of the hypostatized individual, a product of the human brain, appears as charisma, a mysterious objective property of the person, an impalpable charm, an unnameable mystery. The minister—a minister of religion or a minister of state—is related metonymically to the group; a part of the group, he functions as a sign in place of the whole of the group. It is he who, as an entirely real for an entirely symbolic being, induces a "category mistake," as Ryle would have said, rather like that of the child who, after seeing the soldiers composing a regiment march past, asks where the regiment is. By his mere visible existence, he constitutes the pure serial diversity of

the separate individuals (*collectio personarum plurium*) into an "artificial person" (*une personne morale*), a *corporatio,* a constituted body, and, through the effect of mobilization and demonstration, he may even make it appear as a social agent.

Politics is the site par excellence of symbolic efficacy, the action that is performed through signs capable of producing social things and, in particular, groups. Through the potency of the oldest of the metaphysical effects linked to the existence of a symbolism, the one which enables one to regard as a really existing everything that can be *symbolized* (God or non-being), political representation produces and reproduces at every moment a derived form of the case of the bald king of France, so dear to the logicians: any predicative proposition having "the working class" as its subject disguises an existential proposition (*there* is a working class). More generally, all utterances which have as their subject a collective noun—people, class, university, school, state, etc.—presuppose the existence of the group in question and conceal the same sort of metaphysical boot-strapping that was denounced in the ontological argument. The spokesman is he who, in speaking of a group, on behalf of a group, surreptitiously posits the existence of the group in question, institutes the group, through the magical operation that is inherent in any act of naming. That is why one must perform a critique of political reason, which is intrinsically inclined to abuses of language that are also abuses of power, if one wants to pose the question with which all sociology ought to begin, that of the existence and the mode of existence of collectives.

A class exists insofar—and only insofar— as mandated representatives endowed with *plena potestas agendi* can be and feel authorized to speak in its *name*—in accordance with the question "the Party is the working class," or "the working class is the Party," a formula which reproduces the canonists' equation: "The Church is the Pope (or the Bishops), the Pope is (or the Bishops are) the Church"—and so to make it exist as a real force within the political field. The mode of existence of what is nowadays called, in many societies (with variations, of course), "the working class," is entirely paradoxical: it is a sort of *existence in thought*, an existence in the thinking of a large proportion of those whom the taxonomies designate as workers, but also in the thinking of the occupants of the positions remotest from the workers in the social space. This almost universally recognized existence is itself based on the existence of a *working class in representation*, i.e. of political and trade-union apparatuses and professional spokesmen, vitally interested in believing that it exists and in having this believed both by those who identify with it and those who exclude themselves from it, and capable of making the "working class" *speak,* and with one voice, of invoking it, as one invokes gods or patron saints, even of symbolically manifesting it through *demonstration*, a sort of theatrical deployment of the class-in-representation, with on the one hand the corps of professional representatives and all the symbolism constitutive of its existence, and on the other the most convinced fraction of the believers who, through their presence, enable the representatives to manifest their representativeness. This working class "as will and representation" (in the words of Schopenhauer's famous title) is not the self-enacting class, a real group really mobilized, which is evoked in the Marxist tradition. But it is no less real, with the magical reality which

(as Durkheim and Mauss maintained) defines institutions as social fictions. It is a "mystical body," created through an immense historical labour of theoretical and practical invention, starting with that of Marx himself, and endlessly re-created through the countless, constantly renewed, efforts and energies that are needed to produce and reproduce belief and the institution designed to ensure the reproduction of belief. It exists in and through the corps of mandated representatives who give it material speech and visible presence, and in the belief in its existence which this corps of plenipotentiaries manages to enforce, by its sheer existence and by its representations, on the basis of the affinities objectively uniting the members of the same "class on paper" as a probable group.

The historical success of Marxist theory, the first would-be scientific social theory to have realized itself so fully in the social world, thus helps to bring about a paradoxical situation: the theory of the social world least capable of integrating the *theory effect*—which Marxism has exerted more than any other—nowadays no doubt represents the most powerful obstacle to the progress of the adequate theory of the social world, to which it has, in other times, contributed more than any other.

❖

Introduction to "Outline of a Sociological Theory of Art Perception"

In this essay Bourdieu examines artistic competence as a symbolic asset that legitimates relations of social domination. As an asset, the ability to appropriately decipher and appreciate works of art functions as a sign of distinction that separates those who possess the ability from those who do not. Individuals are not born with this competence; rather, they acquire it through exposure to and internalization of uniquely artistic interpretive schemes. These schemes allow the viewer to understand works of art in an aesthetic manner that is freed from the "necessities" of everyday reality. However, the connection between "being" cultured and "acquiring" culture is seldom recognized. Instead, the link between artistic competence and education is denied by a "charismatic ideology" that misrecognizes social privilege as a gift of nature. Thus, while art is made accessible to all, not everyone is equally comfortable in its presence. To the extent that we understand the "unfortunate" as simply being born without the blessings of grace that allow an individual's spirit to be touched by works of art, we fail to uncover the ideological functions of culture. Bourdieu speaks directly to the ideological or political dimensions of art when he notes:

By symbolically shifting the essential of what sets them apart from other classes from the economic field to that of culture, or rather, by adding to strictly economic differences, namely those created by the simple possession of material wealth, differences created by the possession of symbolic wealth such as works of art, or by the pursuit of symbolic distinctions in the manner of using such wealth (economic or symbolic) . . . the privileged members of bourgeois society replace the difference between two cultures, historic products of social conditions, by the essential difference between two natures, a naturally cultivated nature and a naturally natural nature. Thus, the sacrilization of culture and art fulfills a vital function of contributing to the consecration of the social order: to enable educated people to believe in barbarism and persuade the barbarians within the gates of their own barbarity, all they must and need do is manage to conceal themselves and to conceal the social conditions which render possible not only culture as a second nature in which society recognizes human excellence or "good form" as the "realization" in a habitus of the aesthetics of the ruling classes, but also the legitimized dominance . . . of a particular definition of culture. (Bourdieu 1993:236)

To reproduce their privileged position, the "civilized" need only to convince the "barbarians" that the conditions that produce the culturally gifted and ungifted are but the expression of a state of nature that condemns both to their destiny.

❖

Outline of a Sociological Theory of Art Perception (1968)

Pierre Bourdieu

I

Any art perception involves a conscious or unconscious deciphering operation.

An act of deciphering *unrecognized as such*, immediate and adequate 'comprehension,' is possible and effective only in the special case in which the cultural code which makes the act of deciphering possible is immediately and completely mastered by the observer (in the form of cultivated ability or inclination) and merges with the cultural code which has rendered the work perceived possible. . . .

The question of the conditions that make it possible to experience the work of art (and, in a more general way, all cultural objects) as at once endowed with meaning is totally excluded from the experience itself, because the recapturing of the work's objective meaning (which may have nothing to do with the author's intention) is completely adequate and immediately effected in the case—and only in the case—where the culture that the originator puts into the work is identical with the culture or, more accurately, the *artistic competence* which the beholder brings to the deciphering of the work. In this case, everything is a matter of course and the question of the meaning, of the deciphering of the meaning and of the conditions of this deciphering does not arise.

Whenever these specific conditions are not fulfilled, misunderstanding is inevitable: the illusion of immediate comprehension leads to an illusory comprehension based on a mistaken code. In the absence of the perception that the works are coded, and coded in another code, one unconsciously applies the code which is good for everyday perception, for the deciphering of familiar objects, to works in a foreign tradition. There is no perception which does not involve an unconscious code and it is essential to dismiss the myth of the 'fresh eye,' considered a virtue attributed to naïveté and innocence. One of the reasons why the less educated beholders in our societies are so strongly inclined to demand a realistic representation is that, being devoid of specific categories of perception, they cannot apply any other code to works of scholarly culture than that which enables them to apprehend as meaningful objects of their everyday environment. Minimum, and apparently immediate, comprehension, accessible to the simplest observers and enabling them to recognize a house or a tree, still presupposes partial (unconscious) agreement between artist and beholder concerning categories that define the representation of the real that a historic society holds to be 'realistic.' . . .

The spontaneous theory of art perception is founded on the experience of familiarity and immediate comprehension—an unrecognized special case.

Educated people are at home with scholarly culture. They are consequently carried towards that kind of ethnocentrism which may be called class-centrism and which consists in considering as natural (in other words, both as a matter of course and based on nature) a way of perceiving which is but one among other possible ways and which is acquired through education that may be diffuse or specific, conscious or unconscious, institutionalized or non-institutionalized. 'When, for instance, a man wears a pair of spectacles which are so close to him physically that they are "sitting on his nose," they are environmentally more remote from him than the picture on the opposite wall. Their proximity is normally so weakly perceived as to go unnoticed.' Taking Heidegger's analysis metaphorically, it can be said that the illusion of the 'fresh eye' as a 'naked eye' is an attribute of those who wear the spectacles of culture and who do not see that which enables them to see, any more than they see what they would not see if they were deprived of what enables them to see.

Conversely, faced with scholarly culture, the least sophisticated are in a position identical with that of ethnologists who find themselves in a foreign society and present, for instance, at a ritual to which they do not hold the key. The disorientation and cultural blindness of the less-educated beholders are an objective reminder of the objective truth that art perception is a mediate deciphering operation. Since the information presented by the works exhibited exceeds the deciphering capabilities of the beholder, he perceives them as devoid of signification—or, to be more precise, of structuration and organization—because he cannot 'decode' them, i.e. reduce them to an intelligible form.

Scientific knowledge is distinguished from naïve experience (whether this is shown by disconcertment or by immediate comprehension) in that it involves an awareness of the conditions permitting adequate perception. The object of the science of the work of art is that which renders possible both this science and the immediate comprehension of the work of art, that is, culture. It therefore includes, implicitly at least, the science of the difference between scientific knowledge and naïve perception. 'The naïve "beholder" differs from the art historian in that the latter is conscious of the situation.'[i] . . .

II

The work of art considered as a symbolic good (and not as an economic asset, which it may also be) only exists as such for a person who has the means to appropriate it, or in other words, to decipher it.[ii]

---

[i]Panofsky, 'The History of Art as Humanistic Discipline,' *Meaning in the Visual Arts*, p. 17.

[ii]The laws governing the reception of works of art are a special case of the laws of cultural diffusion: whatever may be the nature of the message—religious prophecy, political speech, publicity image, technical object—reception depends on the categories of perception, thought and action of those who receive it. In a differentiated society, a close relationship is therefore established between the nature and quality of the information transmitted and the structure of the public, its 'readability' and its effectiveness being all the greater when it meets as directly as possible the expectations, implicit or explicit, which the receivers owe chiefly to their family upbringing and social circumstances (and also, in the matter of scholarly culture at least, to their school education) and which the diffuse pressure of the reference group maintains, sustains and reinforces by constant recourse to the norm.

The degree of an agent's art competence is measured by the degree to which he or she masters the set of instruments for the appropriation of the work of art, available at a given time, that is to say, the interpretation schemes which are the prerequisite for the appropriation of art capital or, in other words, the prerequisite for the deciphering of works of art offered to a given society at a given moment.

Art competence can be provisionally defined as the preliminary knowledge of the possible divisions into complementary classes of a universe of representations. A mastery of this kind of system is necessarily determined in relation to another class, itself constituted by all the art representations consciously or unconsciously taken into consideration which do not belong to the class in question. The *style* proper to a period and to a social group is none other than such a class defined in relation to all the works of the same universe which it excludes and which are complementary to it. The *recognition* (or, as the art historians say when using the vocabulary of logic, the *attribution*) proceeds by *successive elimination* of the possibilities which the class is—negatively—related and to which the possibility which has become a reality in the work concerned belongs. It is immediately evident that the uncertainty concerning the different characteristics likely to be attributed to the work under consideration (authors, schools, periods, styles, subjects, etc.) can be removed by employing different codes, functioning as classification systems; it may be a case of a properly artistic code which, by permitting the deciphering of specifically stylistic characteristics, enables the work concerned to be assigned to the class formed by the whole of the works of a period, a society, a school or an author ('that's a Cézanne'), or a code from everyday life which, in the form of previous knowledge of the possible divisions into complementary classes of the universe of signifiers and of the universe of signifieds, and of the correlations between the divisions of the one and the divisions of the other, enables the particular representation, treated as a sign, to be assigned to a class of signifiers and consequently makes it possible to know, by means of the correlations with the universe of signifieds, that the corresponding signified belongs to a certain class of signifieds ('that's a forest'). In the first case the beholder is paying attention to the manner of treating the leaves or the clouds, that is to say to the stylistic indications, locating the possibility realized, characteristic of one class of works, by reference to the universe of stylistic possibilities; in the other case, she is treating the leaves or the clouds as indications or signals associated, according to the logic set forth above, with significations transcendent to the representation itself ('that's a poplar,' 'that's a storm').

Artistic competence is therefore defined as the previous knowledge of the strictly artistic principles of division which enable a representation to be located, through the classification of the stylistic indications which it contains, among the possibilities of representation constituting the universe of art and not among the possibilities of representation constituting the universe of everyday objects or the universe of signs, which would amount to treating it as a mere monument, i.e. as a mere means of communication used to transmit a transcendent signification. The perception of the work of art in a truly aesthetic manner, that is, as a signifier which signifies nothing other than itself, does not consist of considering it 'without connecting it with anything other than itself, either emotionally or intellectually,' in short of giving oneself up to the work apprehended in its irreducible singularity, but rather of noting its *distinctive stylistic features* by relating it to the ensemble of the works forming the class to which it belongs, and to these works only. On the contrary, the taste of the working classes is determined, after the manner of what Kant describes in his *Critique of Judgement* as 'barbarous taste,' by the refusal or the impossibility (one should say the impossibility-refusal) of operating the distinction between 'what is liked' and 'what pleases' and, more generally, between 'disinterestedness,' the only guarantee of the aesthetic quality of contemplation, and 'the interest of the senses' which defines 'the agreeable' or 'the interest of reason': it requires that every image shall fulfil a function, if only that of a sign. This 'functionalist' representation of the work of art is based on the refusal of gratuitousness, the idolatry of work or the placing of value on what is 'instructive' (as opposed to what is 'interesting') and also on the impossibility of placing each individual work in the universe of representations, in the absence of strictly stylistic principles of classification. . . .

The art code as a system of possible principles of division into complementary classes of the universe of representations offered to a particular society at a given time is in the nature of a social institution.

Being an historically constituted system, founded on social reality, this set of instruments of perception whereby a particular society, at a given time, appropriates artistic goods (and, more generally, cultural goods) does not depend on individual wills and consciousnesses and forces itself upon individuals, often without their knowledge, defining the distinctions they can make and those which escape them. Every period arranges artistic representations as a whole according to an institutional system of classification of its own, bringing together works which other periods separated, or distinguishing between works which other periods placed together, and individuals have difficulty in imagining differences other than those which the available system of classification allows them to imagine. . . .

III

Since the work of art only exists as such to the extent that it is perceived, or, in other words, deciphered, it goes without saying that the satisfactions attached to this perception—whether it be a matter of purely aesthetic enjoyment or of more indirect gratification, such as the *effect of distinction*—are only accessible to those who are disposed to appropriate them because they *attribute a value to them*, it being understood that they can do this only if they have the means to appropriate them. Consequently, the need to appropriate goods which, like cultural goods, only exist as such for those who have received the means to appropriate them from their family environment and school, can appear only in those who can satisfy it, and it can be satisfied as soon as it appears. . . .

The disposition to appropriate cultural goods is the product of general or specific education, institutionalized or not, which creates (or cultivates) art competence as a mastery of the instruments for appropriation of these goods, and which creates the 'cultural need' by giving the means to satisfy it.

The repeated perception of works of a certain style encourages the unconscious internalization of the rules that govern the production of these works. Like rules of grammar, these rules are not apprehended as such, and are still less explicitly formulated and capable of being formulated; for instance, lovers of classical music may have neither awareness nor knowledge of the laws obeyed by the sound-making art to which they are accustomed, but their auditive education is such that, having heard a dominant chord, they are induced urgently to await the tonic which seems to him the 'natural' resolution of this chord, and they have difficulty in apprehending the internal coherence of music founded on other principles. The unconscious mastery of the instruments of appropriation which are the basis of familiarity with cultural works is acquired by slow familiarization, a long succession of 'little perceptions,' in the sense in which Leibniz uses the expression. Connoisseurship is an 'art' which, like the art of thinking or the art of living, cannot be imparted entirely in the form of precepts or instruction, and apprenticeship to it presupposes the equivalent of prolonged contact between disciple and initiate in traditional education, i.e. repeated contact with the work (or with works of the same class). And, just as students or disciples can *unconsciously* absorb the rules of the art—including those which are not explicitly known to the initiates themselves—by giving themselves up to it, excluding analysis and the selection of elements of exemplary conduct, so art-lovers can, by abandoning themselves in some way to the work, internalize the principles and rules of its construction without there ever being brought to their consciousness and formulated as such. This constitutes the difference between the art theorist and the connoisseur, who is usually incapable of explicating the principles on which his judgements are based. In this field as in others (learning the grammar of one's native tongue, for instance), school education tends to encourage the conscious reflection of patterns of thought, perception or expression which have already been mastered unconsciously by formulating explicitly the principles of the creative grammar, for example, the laws of harmony and counterpoint or the rules of pictorial composition, and by providing the verbal and conceptual material essential for naming differences previously experienced in a purely intuitive way. The danger of academicism is obviously inherent in any rationalized teaching which tends to mint, within one doctrinal body, precepts, prescriptions and formulae, explicitly described and taught, more often negative than positive, which a traditional education imparts in the form of a habitus, directly apprehended *uno intuitu*, as a global style not susceptible to analytical breakdown. . . .

Even when the educational institution makes little provision for art training proper (as is the case in France and many other countries), even when, therefore, it gives neither specific encouragement to cultural activities nor a body of concepts specifically adapted to the plastic arts, it tends on the one hand to inspire a certain *familiarity*—conferring a feeling of belonging to the cultivated class—with the world of art, in which people feel at home and among themselves as the appointed addressees of works which do not deliver their message to the first-comer; and on the other to inculcate (at least in France and in the majority of European countries, at the level of secondary education) a *cultivated disposition* as a durable and generalized attitude which implies recognition of the value of works of art and the ability to appropriate them by means of generic categories.[iii] Although it deals almost exclusively with literary works, in-school learning tends to create on the one hand a transposable inclination to admire works approved by the school and a duty to admire and to love certain works or, rather, certain classes of works which gradually seem to become linked to a certain educational and social status; and, on the other hand, an equally generalized and transposable aptitude for categorizing by authors, by genres, by schools and by periods, for the handling of educational categories of literary analysis and for the mastery of the code which governs the use of the different codes, giving at least a tendency to acquire equivalent categories in other fields and to store away the typical knowledge which, even though

extrinsic and anecdotal, makes possible at least an elementary form of apprehension, however inadequate it may be. Thus, the first degree of strictly pictorial competence shows itself in the mastery of an arsenal of words making it possible to name differences and to apprehend them while naming them: these are the proper names of famous painters—da Vinci, Picasso, Van Gogh—which function as generic categories, because one can say about any painting or non-figurative object 'that suggests Picasso,' or, about any work recalling nearly or distantly the manner of the Florentine painter, 'that looks like a da Vinci'; there are also broad categories, like 'the Impressionists' (a school commonly considered to include Gaugin, Cézanne and Degas), 'the Dutch School,' 'the Renaissance.' It is particularly significant that the proportion of subjects who think in terms of schools very clearly grows as the level of education rises and that, more generally, generic knowledge which is required for the perception of differences and consequently for memorizing—proper names and historical, technical or aesthetic concepts—becomes increasingly specific as we go towards the more educated beholders, so that the most adequate perception differs only from the least adequate in so far as the specificity, richness and subtlety of the categories employed are concerned. By no means contradicting these arguments is the fact that the less educated visitors to museums—who tend to prefer the most famous paintings and those sanctioned by school teaching, whereas modern painters who have the least chance of being mentioned in schools are quoted only by those with the highest educational qualifications—live in large cities. To be able to form discerning or so-called 'personal' opinions is again a result of the education received: the ability to go beyond school constraints is the privilege of those who have sufficiently assimilated school education to make their own the free attitude towards scholastic culture taught by a school so deeply impregnated with the values of the ruling classes that it accepts the fashionable depreciation of school instruction. The contrast between

---

[iii]School instruction always fulfils a function of legitimation, if only by giving its blessing to works which it sets up as worthy of being admired, and thus helps to define the hierarchy of cultural goods valid in a particular society at a given time.

accepted, stereotyped and, as Max Weber would say, 'routinized' culture, and genuine culture, freed from school discourse, has meaning only for an infinitely small minority of educated people for whom culture is second nature, endowed with all the appearances of talent, and the full assimilation of school culture is a prerequisite for going beyond it towards this 'free culture'—free, that is to say, from its school origins—which the bourgeois class and its school regard as the value of values.

But the best proof that the general principles for the transfer of training also hold for school training lies in the fact that the practices of one single individual and, *a fortiori*, of individuals belonging to one social category or having a specific level of education, tend to constitute a system, so that a certain type of practice in any field of culture very probably implies a corresponding type of practice in all the other fields; thus, frequent visits to museums are almost necessarily associated with an equal amount of theatre-going and, to a lesser degree, attendance at concerts. Similarly, everything seems to indicate that knowledge and preferences tend to form into constellations that are strictly linked to the level of education, so that a typical structure of preferences in painting is most likely to be linked to a structure of preferences of the same type in music or literature.

Owing to the particular status of the work of art and the specific logic of the training which it implies, art education which is reduced to a discourse (historical, aesthetic or other) on the works is necessarily at a secondary level; like the teaching of the native tongue, literary or art education (that is to say 'the humanities' of traditional education) necessarily presupposes, without ever, or hardly ever, being organized in the light of this principle, that individuals are endowed with a previously acquired competence and with a whole capital of experience unequally distributed among the various social classes (visits to museums or monuments, attending concerts, lectures, etc.).

In the absence of a methodical and systematic effort, involving the mobilization of all available means from the earliest years of school onwards, to procure for all those attending school a direct contact with the works or, at least, an approximate

substitute for that experience (by showing reproductions or reading texts, organizing visits to museums or playing records, etc.), art education can be of full benefit only to those who owe the competence acquired by slow and imperceptible familiarization to their family milieu, because it does not explicitly give to all what it implicitly demands from all. While it is true that only the school can give the continuous and prolonged, methodical and uniform training capable of *mass production*, if I may use that expression, of competent individuals, provided with schemes of perception, thought and expression which are prerequisites for the appropriation of cultural goods, and endowed with that generalized and permanent inclination to appropriate them which is the mark of devotion to culture, the fact remains that the effectiveness of this formative action is directly dependent upon the degree to which those undergoing it fulfil the preliminary conditions for adequate reception: the influence of school activity is all the stronger and more lasting when it is carried on for a longer time (as is shown by the fact that the decrease of cultural activity with age is less marked when the duration of schooling was longer), when those upon whom it is exercised have greater previous competence, acquired through early and direct contact with works (which is well known to be more frequent always as one goes higher up the social scale) and finally when a propitious cultural atmosphere sustains and relays its effectiveness. Thus, humanities students who have received a homogeneous and homogenizing training for a number of years, and who have been constantly selected according to the degree to which they conform to school requirements, remain separated by systematic differences, both in their pursuit of cultural activities and in their cultural preferences, depending upon whether they come from a more or less cultivated milieu and for how long this has been so; their knowledge of the theatre (measured according to the average number of plays that they have seen on the stage) or of painting is greater if their father or grandfather (or, *a fortiori*, both of them) belongs to a higher occupational category; and, furthermore, if one of these variables (the category of the father or of the grandfather) has a fixed value, the other tends, by itself, to hierarchize the scores. Because of the slowness of the acculturation process, subtle differences linked with the length of time that they have been in contact with culture thus continue to separate individuals who are apparently equal with regard to social success and even educational success. Cultural nobility also has its quarterings.

Only an institution like the school, the specific function of which is methodically to develop or create the dispositions which produce an educated person and which lay the foundations, quantitatively and consequently qualitatively, of a constant and intense pursuit of culture, could offset (at least partially) the initial disadvantage of those who do not receive from their family circle the encouragement to undertake cultural activities and the competence presupposed in any discourse on works, on the condition—and only on the condition—that it employs every available means to break down the endless series of cumulative processes to which any cultural education is condemned. For if the apprehension of a work of art depends, in its intensity, its modality and in its very existence, on the beholders' mastery of the generic and specific code of the work, i.e. on their competence, which they owe partly to school training, the same thing applies to the pedagogic communication which is responsible, among its other functions, for transmitting the code of works of scholarly culture (and also the code according to which it effects this transmission). Thus the intensity and modality of the communication are here again a function of culture (as a system of schemes of perception, expression and historically constituted and socially conditioned thinking) which the receiver owes to his or her family milieu and which is more or less close to scholarly culture and the linguistic and cultural models according to which the school effects the transmission of this culture. Considering that the direct experience of works of scholarly culture and the institutionally organized acquisition of culture which is a prerequisite for adequate experience of such works are subject to the same laws, it is obvious how difficult it is to break the sequence of the cumulative effects which cause cultural capitol to attract cultural capital. In fact, the school has only to give free play to the objective machinery of cultural diffusion without working systematically to give to all, in and through the pedagogical message itself, what is given to some through family inheritance—that is, the instruments which condition the adequate reception of the school message—for it to redouble and consecrate by its approval the socially conditioned inequalities of cultural competence, by treating them as natural inequalities or, in other words, as inequalities of gifts or natural talents.

Charismatic ideology is based on parenthesizing the relationship, evident as soon as it is revealed, between art competence and education, which alone is capable of creating both the disposition to recognize a value in cultural goods and the competence which gives a meaning to this disposition by making it possible to appropriate such goods. Since their art competence is the product of an imperceptible familiarization and an automatic transferring of aptitudes, members of the privileged classes are naturally inclined to regard as a gift of nature a cultural heritage which is transmitted by a process of unconscious training. But, in addition, the contradictions and ambiguities of the relationship which the most cultured among them maintain with their culture are both encouraged and permitted by the paradox which defines the 'realization' of culture as *becoming natural*. Culture is thus achieved only by negating itself as such, that is, as artificial and artificially acquired, so as to become second nature, a habitus, a possession turned into being; the virtuosi of the judgement of taste seem to reach an experience of aesthetic grace so completely freed from the constraints of culture and so little marked by the long, patient training of which it is the product that any reminder of the conditions and the social conditioning which have rendered it possible seems to be at once obvious and scandalous. It follows that the most experienced connoisseurs are the natural champions of charismatic ideology, which attributes to the work of art a magical power of conversion capable of awakening the potentialities latent in a few of the elect, and which contrasts authentic experience of a work of art as an 'affection' of the heart or immediate enlightenment of the intuition with the laborious proceedings and cold comments of the intelligence, ignoring the social and cultural conditions underlying such an experience, and at the same time treating as a birthright the virtuosity acquired through long familiarization or through the exercises of a methodical training; silence concerning the social prerequisites for the appropriation of culture or, to be more exact, for the acquisition of art competence in the sense of mastery of all the means for the specific appropriation of works of art is a self-seeking silence because it is what makes it possible to legitimatize a social privilege by pretending that it is a gift of nature.

To remember that culture is not what one is but what one has, or rather, what one has become; to remember the social conditions which render possible aesthetic experience and the existence of those beings—art lovers or 'people of taste'—for whom it is possible; to remember that the work of art is given only to those who have received the means to acquire the means to appropriate it and who could not seek to possess it if they did not already possess it, in and through the possession of means of possession as an actual possibility of effecting the taking of possession; to remember, finally, that only a few have the real possibility of benefitting from the theoretical possibility, generously offered to all, of taking advantage of the works exhibited in museums—all this is to bring to light the hidden force of the effects of the majority of culture's social uses.

The parenthesizing of the social conditions which render possible culture and culture become nature, cultivated nature, having all the appearances of grace or a gift and yet acquired, so therefore 'deserved,' is the precedent condition of charismatic ideology which makes it possible to confer on culture and in particular on 'love of art' the all-important place which they occupy in bourgeois 'sociodicy.' The bourgeoisie find naturally in culture as cultivated nature and culture that has become nature the only possible principle for the legitimation of their privilege. Being unable to invoke the right of birth (which their class, through the ages, has refused to the aristocracy) or nature which,

according to 'democratic' ideology, represents universality, i.e. the ground on which all distinctions are abolished, or the aesthetic virtues which enabled the first generation of bourgeois to invoke their merit, they can resort to cultivated nature and culture become nature, to what is sometimes called 'class,' through a kind of tell-tale slip, to 'education,' in the sense of a product of education which seems to owe nothing to education,[iv] to distinction, grace which is merit and merit which is grace, an unacquired merit which justifies unmerited acquisitions, that is to say, inheritance. To enable culture to fulfil its primary ideological function of class co-optation and legitimation of this mode of selection, it is necessary and sufficient that the link between culture and education, which is simultaneously obvious and hidden, be forgotten, disguised and denied. The unnatural idea of inborn culture, of a gift of culture, bestowed on certain people by nature, is inseparable from blindness to the functions of the institution which ensures the profitability of the cultural heritage and legitimizes its transmission while concealing that it fulfils this function. The school in fact is the institution which, through its outwardly irreproachable verdicts, transforms socially conditioned inequalities in regard to culture into inequalities of success, interpreted as inequalities of gifts which are also inequalities of merit. Plato records, towards the end of *The Republic*, that the souls who are to begin another life must themselves choose their lot among 'patterns of life' of all kinds and that, when the choice has been made, they must drink of the water of the river Lethe before returning to earth. The function which Plato attributes to the water of forgetfulness falls, in our societies, on the university which, in its impartiality, through pretending to recognize students as equal in rights and duties, divided only by inequalities of gifts and of merit, in fact confers on individuals degrees judged according to their cultural heritage, and therefore according to their social status.

By symbolically shifting the essence of what sets them apart from other classes from the economic field to that of culture, or rather,

---

[iv]It was understood thus by a very cultivated old man who declared during a conversation: 'Education, Sir, is inborn.'

by adding to strictly economic differences, namely those created by the simple possession of material goods, differences created by the possession of symbolic goods such as works of art, or by the pursuit of symbolic distinctions in the manner of using such goods (economic or symbolic), in short, by turning into a fact of nature everything which determines their 'value,' or to take the word in the linguistic sense, their *distinction*—a mark of difference which, according to the Littré, sets people apart from the common herd 'by the characteristics of elegance, nobility and good form'—the privileged members of bourgeois society replace the difference between two cultures, historic products of social conditions, by the essential difference between two natures, a naturally cultivated nature and a naturally natural nature. Thus, the sacralization of culture and art fulfils a vital function by contributing to the consecration of the social order: to enable educated people to believe in barbarism and persuade the barbarians within the gates of their own barbarity, all they must and need do is to manage to conceal themselves and to conceal the social conditions which render possible not only culture as a second nature in which society recognizes human excellence or 'good form' as the 'realization' in a habitus of the aesthetics of the ruling classes, but also the legitimized dominance (or, if you like, the legitimacy) of a particular definition of culture. And in order that the ideological circle may be completely closed, all they have to do is to find in an essentialist representation of the bipartition of society into barbarians and civilized people the justification of their right to conditions which produce the possession of culture and the dispossession of culture, a state of 'nature' destined to appear based on the nature of the men who are condemned to it.

If such is the function of culture and if it is love of art which really determines the choice that separates, as by an invisible and insuperable barrier, those who have from those who have not received this grace, it can be seen that museums betray, in the smallest details of their morphology and their organization, their true function, which is to strengthen the feeling of belonging in some and the feeling of exclusion in others.[v] Everything, in these civic temples in which bourgeois society deposits its most sacred possessions, that is, the relics inherited from a past which is not its own, in these holy places of art, in which the chosen few come to nurture a faith of virtuosi while conformists and bogus devotees come and perform a class ritual, old palaces or great historic homes to which the nineteenth century added imposing edifices, built often in the Greco-Roman style of civic sanctuaries, everything combines to indicate that the world of art is as contrary to the world of everyday life as the sacred is to the profane. The prohibition against touching the objects, the religious silence which is forced upon visitors, the puritan asceticism of the facilities, always scarce and uncomfortable, the almost systematic refusal of any instruction, the grandiose solemnity of the decoration and the decorum, colonnades, vast galleries, decorated ceilings, monumental staircases both outside and inside, everything seems done to remind people that the transition from the profane world to the sacred world presupposes, as Durkheim says, 'a genuine metamorphosis,' a radical spiritual change, that the bringing together of the worlds 'is always, in itself, a delicate operation which calls for precaution and a more or less complicated initiation,' that 'it is not even possible unless the profane lose their specific characteristics, unless they themselves become sacred to some extent

---

[v]It is not infrequent that working-class visitors explicitly express the feeling of exclusion which, in any case, is evident in their whole behaviour. Thus, they sometimes see in the absence of any indication which might facilitate the visit—arrows showing the direction to follow, explanatory panels, etc.—the signs of a deliberate intention to exclude the uninitiated. The provision of teaching and didactic aids would not, in fact, really make up for the lack of schooling, but it would at least proclaim the right not to know, the right to be there in ignorance, the right of the ignorant to be there, a right which everything in the presentation of works and in the organization of the museum combines to challenge, as this remark overheard in the Chateau of Versailles testifies: 'This chateau was not made for the people, and it has not changed.'

and to some degree.'[vi] Although the work of art, owing to its sacred character, calls for particular dispositions or predispositions, it brings in return its consecration to those who satisfy its demands, to the small elite who are self-chosen by their aptitude to respond to its appeal.

The museum gives to all, as a public legacy, the monuments of a splendid past, instruments of the sumptuous glorification of the great figures of bygone ages, but this is false generosity, because free entrance is also optional entrance, reserved for those who, endowed with the ability to appropriate the works, have the privilege of using this freedom and who find themselves consequently legitimized in their privilege, that is, in the possession of the means of appropriating cultural goods or, to borrow an expression of Max Weber, in the *monopoly* of the handling of cultural goods and of the institutional signs of cultural salvation (awarded by the school). Being the keystone of a system which can function only by concealing its true function, the charismatic representation of art experience never fulfills its function of mystifying so well as when it resorts to a 'democratic' language: to claim that works of art have power to awaken the grace of aesthetic enlightenment in anyone, however culturally uninitiated he or she may be, to presume in all cases to ascribe to the unfathomable accidents of grace or to the arbitrary bestowal of 'gifts' aptitudes which are always the product of unevenly distributed education, and therefore to treat inherited aptitudes as personal virtues which are both natural and meritorious. Charismatic ideology would not be so strong if it were not the only outwardly irreproachable means of justifying the right of the heirs to the inheritance without being inconsistent with the ideal of formal democracy, and if, in this particular case, it did not aim at establishing in nature the sole right of the bourgeoisie to appropriate art treasures to itself, to appropriate them to itself *symbolically*, that is to say, in the only legitimate manner, in a society which pretends to yield to all, 'democratically,' the relics of an aristocratic past.

[vi]E. Durkheim, *Les formes élémentaires de la vie religieuse*, 6th edn (Paris: Presses Universitaires de France, 1960), 55–6. The holding of a Danish exhibition showing modern furniture and utensils in the old ceramic rooms of the Lille museum brought about such a 'conversion' in the visitors as can be summarized in the following contrasts, the very ones which exist between a department store and a museum: noise/silence; touch/see; quick, haphazard exploration, in no particular order/leisurely, methodical inspection, according to a fixed arrangement; freedom/constraint; economic assessment of works which may be purchased/aesthetic appreciation of 'priceless' works. However, despite these differences, bound up with the things exhibited, the solemnizing (and distancing) effect of the museum no less continued to be felt, contrary to expectations, for the structure of the public at the Danish exhibition was more 'aristocratic' (in respect of level of education) than the ordinary public of the museum. The mere fact that works are consecrated by being exhibited in a consecrated place is sufficient, in itself, profoundly to change their signification and, more precisely, to raise the level of their emission; were they presented in a more familiar place, a large emporium for instance, they would be more accessible.

❖

JÜRGEN HABERMAS (1929–): A BIOGRAPHICAL SKETCH

Jürgen Habermas was born in Dusseldorf, Germany, in 1929. He grew up in the small town of Gummersbach, where his father, a successful businessman, was the head of the Chamber of Industry and Commerce. Ten years old at the outbreak of World War II, Habermas served in the Hitler Youth, a compulsory organization that trained young boys for military service and young girls for motherhood. With the

defeat of Germany and fall of Nazism, however, Habermas was forced to confront the atrocities committed under the Nazis' reign of terror. Horrified by the genocide carried out under Hitler's rule, Habermas viewed the end of the war as "a liberation, both historical and personal," as he came to realize that "it was a politically criminal system in which we lived" (interview, cited in Horster 1992:78–9).

Between 1949 and 1954, Habermas studied philosophy, history, and psychology at the Universities of Göttingen, Zurich, and Bonn. In 1953 he published a provocative critique of the influential philosopher Martin Heidegger (1889–1976) that questioned how Heidegger's allegiance to the Nazi effort shaped his development of existential philosophy (Lalonde 1999:37, 38). The following year he completed his dissertation, "The Absolute in History," on the work of Friedrich Wilhelm Schelling (1775–1854), a renowned German idealist philosopher. Toward the end of his studies, Habermas turned his attention to the writings of Marx and developed a fervent interest in the work associated with the Frankfurt School of critical theory. Greatly influenced by Georg Lukács' *History and Class Consciousness* and Horkheimer and Adorno's *Dialectic of Enlightenment* (see Chapter 3), Habermas served as Adorno's assistant from 1956 to 1959 at the Institute for Social Research (ISR), which by then had relocated to Frankfurt, Germany.

Despite his interests in critical theory, Habermas's intellectual position began to shift away from key tenets espoused by his mentors. He was particularly disillusioned by the earlier critical theorists' rejection of the public sphere of debate as a possible arena for democratic, progressive change and their despairing view of modern society more generally. In 1959, Habermas left the ISR and began a second doctorate ("Habilitation") at the University of Marburg. The following year he joined the faculty at the University of Heidelberg, where he served as a professor of philosophy until 1964. He then returned to Frankfurt as professor of philosophy and sociology. He would eventually leave Frankfurt after disagreements with the student protest movement over what he believed to be its politically and intellectually extremist positions. Between 1971 and 1981, he lived in Starnberg, Bavaria, where he served as director of the Max Planck Institute for the Study of the Conditions of Life in the Scientific-Technical World. During this time, he wrote several highly acclaimed works, including *Knowledge and Human Interests* (1971) and *Legitimation Crisis* (1975). In 1980 Habermas won the Adorno Prize from the city of Frankfurt, and in 1982 he was named Extraordinary Professor of Philosophy in Heidelberg. That same year, he accepted a professorship at the University of Frankfurt, where he would remain until his retirement in 1994.

Considered one of Europe's most important public intellectuals and described by *Der Spiegel* magazine as "the most intellectually powerful" philosopher in Germany (Horster 1992:3), Habermas is read not only by sociologists, philosophers, and political scientists, but also by politicians throughout the world. His most important works, *The Theory of Communicative Action, v. 1: Reason and the Rationalization of Society* (1984) and *The Theory of Communicative Action, v. 2: Lifeworld and System* (1987), continue to inspire democratic activists who seek to increase the scope and power of the public sphere.

INTELLECTUAL INFLUENCES AND CORE IDEAS

Jürgen Habermas is commonly regarded as one of sociology's greatest synthetic thinkers (McCarthy 1978). He is also the most celebrated inheritor of the tradition of thought developed by the Frankfurt School (Kellner 2000; McCarthy 1978; Seidman 1989). As a student of two of its founders—Max Horkheimer and Theodor Adorno (see Chapter 3)—his work is centrally informed by critical theory and the issues with which its leading figures grappled, particularly their inquiries into the role of reason in promoting a free and just society. However, Habermas's influences run much deeper into German intellectual history, for, like the critical theorists, he draws on the legacy of German Enlightenment thinkers whose roots date back to the eighteenth century. Incorporating the insights of Kant, Hegel, and Marx, he fashions a contemporary approach to the emancipatory project of social philosophy. This project envisions the creation of a social order in which reason and rationality provide the pathway for establishing economic equality, political democracy, and the liberation of the individual from systems of domination. These themes form the core of Habermas's own theoretical perspective, a perspective that, in addition to Marxist-inspired writers, incorporates the insights of a range of additional scholars including Weber, Durkheim, Mead, Husserl, Schutz, and Parsons, as well as linguistic philosophers and developmental psychologists.

Like Weber and the Frankfurt School theorists, Habermas (1984) contends that the modern world is characterized by increasing instrumental rationalization, that is, by the spread of methodical procedures and calculable rules into more and more domains of social and personal life. However, whereas the earlier critical theorists saw rationalization leading only to the corruption of the human spirit and the decay of civilization, Habermas finds modernity yielding mixed results. For while it is true that the possibilities for democracy and human emancipation have been distorted in modern societies, modernity has also brought the rule of law, the expansion of political and civil rights, and, if not the full realization of democracy, at least the hallowing of democratic principles of government. Moreover, rationalizing processes have led to advances in a variety of fields, from medical sciences and food production to architecture and the arts. Nevertheless, the growth of bureaucratic structures of social organization, complex political processes, sophisticated economic systems, and rationalized means of mass-mediated communication has not been without its drawbacks. It is precisely this duality embodied in the rationalization of society—both facilitating and restricting the development of human knowledge, democratic organization, and ultimately liberation—that Habermas seeks to address.

In stark contrast to the Frankfurt School theorists, whose antimodernist stance and loss of faith in reason led them to abandon Marx's utopian commitment to emancipation, Habermas holds out great hope for the power of reason to combat the dehumanizing consequences stemming from the rationalization of society. His rekindled utopian vision, however, does not mark a return to "orthodox" Marxism's emphasis on capitalism as the primary cause for humanity's unfreedom. Instead, drawing from phenomenology, Habermas reconstructs Marxism to examine the *intersubjective* and *normative* dimensions of social life that Marx had largely ignored. For according to Habermas, it is not the form of *economic* or material reproduction of society (the relationship between individuals and their physical environment) but, rather, the form of its *symbolic* reproduction (processes of socialization, identity formation, and social integration) that poses the greatest threat to freedom and progress in modern society.

Lifeworld and System

Habermas's efforts to chart the historical development of societies and the course for emancipation begins with his discussion of the lifeworld and system. Drawing from and extending the work of Husserl and Schutz (see Chapter 6), Habermas conceives of the **lifeworld** as a prereflexive framework of background assumptions, a "network of shared meanings that individuals draw from to construct identities, to negotiate situational definitions, or to create social solidarity" (Seidman 1989:18). It consists of taken-for-granted cultural know-how, customs, and norms through which we are able to construct common understandings of our social world. In addition, the lifeworld provides for the socialization of society's members and the internalization of the norms and values essential to the stability of the social order.

The lifeworld serves as the backdrop for social integration, identity formation, and the construction of meaning in two domains: the private sphere of the family and the public sphere of open civic debate (see Figure 9.2 below). (We address the issue of the public sphere more fully later in this Chapter.) Interaction within these domains is mediated through language and the development of shared meanings that in turn serves to reinforce or challenge the legitimacy of existing social norms and values.

A key component of modern societies, however, is the ongoing *rationalization* of the lifeworld in which the discourses regarding "truth, goodness, and beauty" are differentiated into separate spheres of knowledge (Seidman 1989:24). Rationalization produces a greater potential to question our actions and the actions of others and to question more generally the conditions of the world around us. In the process, highly abstract concepts like democracy, equality, freedom, and universal rights circulate in debates that, in turn, create the conditions for a consensual understanding of the forces that shape social life.

Habermas maintains that his notion of the lifeworld helps correct Marx's reductive, one-sided theory of society. According to Habermas, Marx and his successors failed to recognize the significance of the symbolic and communicative domains of society, opting instead to emphasize the role of economic production and property relations both in generating conditions of exploitation and in sparking the eventual communist revolution. Nevertheless, to avoid developing his own one-sided, and thus incomplete, theory, Habermas (1984, 1987) introduces the notion of the "system" to address some of the concerns that Marx had earlier studied. The **system** comprises a society's political and economic structures that are responsible for the organization of power relations and the production and distribution of material resources. As societies evolve, both the state and the economy develop their own formal structure and mechanisms for

Figure 9.2   The Domains of Lifeworld and System

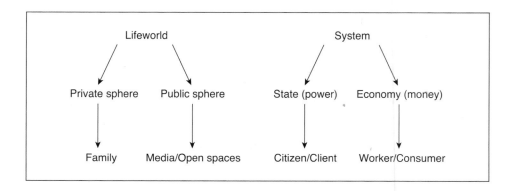

self-organization. Habermas calls these organizational mechanisms **steering media** and argues that two primary forms emerge: **power** and **money**. As shown in Figure 9.2, while the state is organized around the distribution of power, the economy is organized around the circulation of money. What makes both power and money unique is that they are abstract, "delinguistified" media; they operate according to a goal-oriented, instrumental logic that lies outside of language and norm-confirming, consensus-producing debate.

In modern societies, individuals are related to the system in their roles as formal citizens/clients of the state and as economic workers/consumers. To the extent that the state (power) and the economy (money) shape social relations, they do so without the benefit of negotiated, consensual understandings of their impact on individuals and the broader society. This is because such understandings are made possible only through interactions that are grounded in the norm- and value-rich environment of the lifeworld. That power and money are impersonal, "meaningless" steering mechanisms without normative value is of crucial significance both for the maintenance of social stability and for the emancipation of individuals from domination. In advanced capitalist societies, families are linked to the economy through the medium of money: wages are paid for work that are then spent to consume goods and services. At no point during this process do families exercise significant control over the terms of these exchanges. Meanwhile, individuals are related to the state less as informed citizens capable of effectively influencing political decisions than as "clients" who use the services (education, health care, social security, etc.) it provides. This client relation is reinforced as the state enters into more domains that formerly were free from political interference. Not only does the state intervene in the economy to minimize destabilizing fluctuations in the market (e.g., by creating a public sector or raising interest rates); it also increasingly penetrates into private matters ordinarily addressed in the lifeworld. The state now regulates virtually every aspect of personal "choice," from marriage and biological reproduction to euthanasia.

In exchange for the goods and services purchased in the economy and the benefits provided by the state, individuals offer their obedience to the system. Mass loyalty is thus secured at the cost of forestalling genuine democratic participation in decisions that profoundly affect the most fundamental aspects of one's life. However, because mass loyalty can never be completely assured, "legitimation crises" are endemic to the system. These crises are prone to erupt when the class biases of the political system are revealed. While the state is charged with promoting the general well-being of all its citizens, it often effects policies that further the interests of only the most privileged; indeed, it must do so to ensure the continued growth of the economy. Nevertheless, such policies run counter to the democratic principles of egalitarianism underlying the political system; principles that are necessary to uphold in order to confer legitimacy on state actions. To avoid such crises, the state provides its clients with material rewards in the form of various social welfare programs. And by restricting the political participation of citizens to periodic voting, state officials are afforded "substantial freedom from public accountability" while securing the legitimacy of the state (Seidman 1989: 21, 22).

The relationship between lifeworld and system thus represents for Habermas the crucial dynamic shaping the development of human society. Although the system has its origins in the lifeworld, highly differentiated and complex societies have developed a set of emergent structures that become increasingly segmented from the communicative and integrative processes of the lifeworld. In smaller and less differentiated societies, the system and lifeworld are closely coupled in a tight, mutual interrelationship. In such societies the weight of tradition presents its members with a world that is unquestioned. Marriage arrangements, productive tasks, and the distribution of wealth and power confront members as natural and unchanging conditions of social life. However, as societies become larger and more complex, system and lifeworld begin to grow increasingly detached. Economic and political institutions become functionally independent of kinship structures that previously provided the basis for societal organization (Seidman 1989:19). On the one hand, this "uncoupling" is an essential condition for the development of modern societies and the greater potential for individual freedom they offer. It enables societies to more efficiently organize and control their productive and administrative requirements. Moreover, with the growing rationalization of the lifeworld, individuals come to possess the symbolic resources enabling them to question the legitimacy of the existing social conditions and to demand that they be explicitly justified according to shared principles and standards for action. Indeed, for Habermas, the rationalization of the lifeworld is the "pacesetter" of social evolution.

On the other hand, as the complexity, power, and differentiation of the system grows, it eventually becomes sealed off from the lifeworld and ultimately comes to engulf it. In one of his more famous expressions, Habermas (1987) describes this process as the **colonization of the lifeworld**. In this process, system steering media (money and power) and technical/instrumental logic come to replace the consensual negotiation of shared meanings as the foundation for social integration and the reproduction of the lifeworld. The result is a "totally administered" society in which social relationships are increasingly mediated by power and money and the interpersonal debates and discussions within the lifeworld come to have less and less impact on the constitution of the system. Thus, while modern societies have witnessed a phenomenal expansion of productive capacity and material wealth, they have yet to fulfill the promise of the Enlightenment. To more fully understand Habermas's ambivalent view of modernity, we must explore his conception of rationality. It is to this task that we now turn.

Habermas and Rational Action

Like that of the critical theorists, Habermas's work is grounded in an investigation of the increasing rationalization of society, a subject first explored by Max Weber. Habermas's discussion of modern forms of rationality parallels the "moments of reason" outlined by Weber. To Weber's three moments of reason—science, law, and art—Habermas posits three complementary modes of rationality—instrumental, moral-practical, and aesthetic-expressive—that individuals use to give meaning to their everyday life. As illustrated in Table 9.1, each form of rationality corresponds to a specific mode of reasoning; addresses specific philosophical, ethical, or interpersonal questions; speaks to a unique dimension of the world of experience; and has distinct consequences for sociocultural reproduction.

Following Weber, Habermas conceptualizes instrumental rationality as a purposive and goal-oriented attitude underlying the pursuit of objective truth and technical, empirical knowledge. Instrumental rationality reflects the moment of reason captured by science as it serves to quantify, organize, and systematically control the *objective* or *external* world of physical objects. Moral-practical rationality is a form of reasoning that shapes our understanding of cultural norms and values, ethics and law, justice, and the exercise of authority—in short, the "rightness" and legitimacy of action. Tied to law, it serves as a normative and moral guide within the *social* world of interpersonal relations. Finally, aesthetic-expressive rationality informs our evaluations of taste and the sincerity or deceitfulness of managed self-presentations and expressions (Goffman

Table 9.1   Summary of Habermas's Theory of Action

Rationality	*Moment of Reason*	*Questions Addressed*	*World*	*Action*
Instrumental	Science	Truth/Knowledge	Objective	Teleological
Moral-Practical	Law	Justice/Morality	Social	Normatively regulated
Aesthetic-Expressive	Art	Aesthetics/Sincerity	Subjective	Dramaturgical
Communicative	Critical	Mutual understanding Coordination of action Socialization	Lifeworld	Transmission of cultural knowledge Social integration Formation of identity

1959). It is oriented to the *subjective* or *internal* world of personal experience and artistic judgment. (See Table 9.1)

While Habermas's analysis of rationality shares much with Weber's moments of reason, he nevertheless contends that Weber (as well as Marx, the earlier critical theorists, and Parsons, all of whose ideas he incorporates in some fashion) failed to recognize a vital dimension of human rationality, one which is embodied in intersubjective communication. To fill this gap, Habermas draws on the work of symbolic interactionists and phenomenologists (most notably George Herbert Mead and Alfred Schutz) and linguistic philosophers to develop his notion of "communicative rationality" or "communicative action." Habermas defines **communicative action** as the process in which individuals come to mutual understanding and consensus through open, noncoercive debate and discussion freed from the corrosive effects of money, power, and manipulation. Encompassing the other forms of rationality and addressing simultaneously the worlds of objective, social, and subjective experience, communicative action embodies a critical stance that allows for the negotiation of shared meanings, the coordination of action, and the socialization of individuals. In the process, communicative action—itself an outgrowth of the evolutionary rationalization of the lifeworld—reproduces the lifeworld by transmitting the cultural stock of knowledge, integrating individuals into the community, and securing the formation of personal and social identities. For Habermas, then, the rationality embedded within communicative action provides the foundation for renewing the social order according to the simultaneous demands for proof, justice, and authenticity.

Significantly, communicative rationality is achieved only when individuals are confident that the claims being made by others meet the criteria for proof specific to the other worlds. For instance, while a person may convince us of the truth of her statements (objective world), we may still doubt the sincerity of her intentions (subjective world) or the normative appropriateness, the "rightness," of what she says (social world). Indeed, determining whether someone is attempting to reach a shared understanding or trying to manipulate us is a crucial aspect of communication. Communicative action is the crucial means through which technical, moral, and aesthetic critiques can be advanced, providing in turn the basis for mutual agreement and a thriving democracy.

To shed light on how these forms of rationality and the worlds they connect to shape interaction, consider the following set of statements that could come up in a discussion. "Did you know that in America, women are paid less than men for performing the same work? I think America is a sexist country; otherwise we wouldn't accept this. We must do something to change gender relations and stop the discriminatory treatment of women." To these statements we would apply the various forms of rationality in order to determine whether or not an agreement can be reached on the issues at hand. The first statement primarily addresses the objective world of facts. Here we might seek relevant scientific statistics in order to be convinced of the truth of the claim. The second statement does not address the world of facts; rather, it speaks to the social world of normative expectations that regulate behavior and interpersonal relations in American society. This statement implies that the truth is not "right," that in a society that promises equality for all, such treatment is not morally legitimate and "ought" not exist. In response we would consider whether or not the person is entitled or justified to assert this claim given our understanding of society's normative code. The third statement is directed toward the subjective world and leads us to consider whether or not the speaker is being sincere or deceitful in making her claim. In determining if she really means what she says, we would gauge her self-presentation and management of expressions to assess whether ulterior motives might be at play. Communicative rationality is obtained when uncoerced, mutual agreement is reached in each "world" of interaction and the truth, rightness, and sincerity of all claims are established.

Faith in Reason: The Public Sphere and "New" Social Movements

One of the more controversial elements of Habermas's theory is his enduring faith in the power of reason and critical reflection to rescue humanity from systems of domination and oppression. His conviction not only places him at odds with the founders of critical theory, but also runs against the most basic claims of postmodern theorists. While postmodern theory (see Chapter 8) challenges the very existence of truth and contends that all knowledge is inherently relative, Habermas asserts that universal standards for establishing both facts and normative judgments are not only possible, but mark the road toward advancing individual freedom and creating a progressive society. In order to win the mantle of "truth," universal standards must be born out of the democratic expression of communicative rationality. In modern society, communicative action that is directed toward broad social issues is most visible in the public sphere and in the protests mounted by new social movements.

Habermas (1962) argues that the world of public discussion and debate that first emerged within European bourgeois social circles in the eighteenth and nineteenth centuries held great promise for the rise of democratic government. The **public sphere** is composed of an array of social spaces where, ideally, private individuals can publicly congregate and freely debate political, ethical, and social issues in a noncoercive and "undistorted" manner. The public sphere is not an institution, an organization, or a system; rather, it is:

a network for communicating information and points of view (i.e., opinions expressing affirmative or negative attitudes); the streams of communication are, in the process, filtered and synthesized in such a way that they coalesce into bundles of topically specified *public* opinions. Like the lifeworld as a whole, so, too, the public sphere is reproduced through communicative action. . . .

The public sphere is differentiated into levels according to the density of communication, organizational complexity, and range—from the *episodic* publics found in taverns, coffee houses, or on the streets; through the *occasional* or "arranged" publics of particular presentations and events, such as theater performances, rock concerts, party assemblies, or church congresses; up to the *abstract* public sphere of isolated readers, listeners, and viewers scattered across large geographic areas, or even around the globe, and brought together only through the mass media. (Habermas 1996:360, 374)

If left free from distorting influences and guided by its own logic of communicative rationality, the public sphere makes possible the vigorous, compelling debate necessary for the unrestricted growth of democratic processes and the legitimation of the political system. In the public sphere, debate ideally is won on the merits of the best argument, and opinions are formed without consideration of the status or power of speakers or the intrusions of manipulation or coercion.

While Habermas's notion of the public sphere has been roundly criticized for being overly idyllic (e.g., see Calhoun 1992; Kellner 2000; McCarthy 1978), he nevertheless maintains that the potential for creating a truly democratic society based on universal reason lies within this domain. He is, however, not entirely blind to his critics. He notes that the public sphere of open debate was deformed by the scale of its growth over the last century and by the rationalization of economic and political institutions whose technical requirements and forms of rationality have seeped into the public sphere. With the extension of democratic rights, more citizens demanded inclusion in the public sphere, and the resulting "structural transformation" impeded its own rational development. "Social decisions were increasingly removed from the rational-critical discourse of citizens in the political public sphere and made the province of negotiation (rather than discourse proper) among bureaucrats, credentialed experts, and interest group elites" (Calhoun 1995:31). This is particularly evident in commercial mass media, whose dissemination of *public* news and information has been altered by "an influx of *private* interests that achieved privileged representation within it" (Habermas 1989:235; emphasis added). It is likewise evident in the manufacturing of "publicity" on the part of organized interest groups that manipulate the public sphere to carry out their "secret policies" (ibid.:236). The public sphere is now less a space for free debate than a market for the sale of prepackaged opinions.

Habermas's argument reflects real concerns that we encounter every day. Think for a moment about the last time that you had a rigorous political or philosophical debate. This debate may have occurred within any number of arenas: your family; a friendship network; your school, workplace, or neighborhood; a community association devoted to sociopolitical concerns or leisure activities; or perhaps the Internet. Yet, consider how much impact this debate may have had on the political processes that shape your social world. For many of us, such encounters happen infrequently, and when they do it is rarer that they have anything but a trivial impact on the political and economic life of our society. Habermas's theory helps us understand why public debate seldom occurs and why it has little influence on the institutions that most dramatically affect our lives. He contends that the space for open, democratic, public discussion is limited to the extent that resources like money and power interfere in the process of opinion formation. Public debates have become all too infrequent because, in the face of political and economic processes that seem to be beyond our control, we recognize the limitations of their efficacy. Thus, we experience a type of communicative alienation within a public sphere that has become increasingly dominated by powerful and rationalized social forces (like political and economic interest groups) that are largely divorced from the influence of public deliberation. The result is that the public sphere idealized by Habermas has been deformed, making it all the more essential to reconstruct the vision of the emancipatory project that began with the Enlightenment.

Nevertheless, Habermas refuses to give up on the promise of communicative rationality and its expression in the public sphere. He places his hopes for freedom and progress in "new" social movements whose efforts signal a resistance to the colonization of the lifeworld and the deformation of the public sphere. New social movements are composed of an array of groups whose disparate aims are united by the "critique of growth." They emerge from the margins of established economic and political structures to give voice to a "crisis consciousness" that calls attention to the social and environmental pathologies created in the wake of advanced industrial capitalism. Theirs are not the struggles of class-based, labor movements seeking to effect a more egalitarian distribution of wealth or to secure more humane working conditions: the movements in which Marxist theorists placed their hopes and disappointments are no longer the vanguard for progressive change. It is not economic interests or issues concerning material reproduction that form the nucleus of their causes; rather, it is "quality of life" issues that are embedded in the symbolic reproduction of the lifeworld. These concerns are expressed in the form of "green" groups fighting to stop the destruction of timberlands or reduce the reliance on polluting energy sources, antinuclear movements, squatters protesting the commercial buyout of affordable residential housing, efforts to end discrimination against homosexuals, protests against the consolidation of the media, and demands for greater personal control over decisions regarding one's health and life.

These movements are potentially effective avenues for invigorating the public sphere because they inject claims into the political process that are largely peripheral to the interests of bureaucratic political organizations and their leaders. New social movements and their counter-institutional political tactics, like civil disobedience, are indicators that the emancipatory project of the Enlightenment is as of yet "unfinished." By nurturing the mechanisms for communicative action, new social movements hold out the promise for democracy and social equality that can be fulfilled only through struggles to defend the lifeworld against the intrusion of money and power and the corrupting influences of instrumental rationality.

Photo 9.5 New Social Movements and the Struggle Over the "Grammar of Forms of Life": Protesting for Civil Rights.

SOURCE: © Patrice Latron/CORBIS; used with permission.

Figure 9.3   Habermas's Central Concepts and Theoretical Orientation

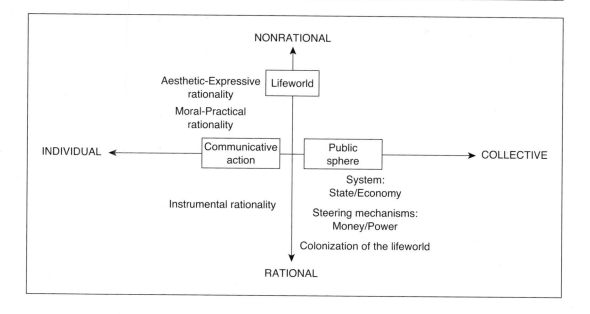

HABERMAS'S THEORETICAL ORIENTATION

Like Bourdieu, Habermas draws from a diverse array of influences to create a system of thought that is broad, complex, and theoretically multidimensional. His work bears the imprint not only of classical sociological theorists (particularly Marx, Weber, Durkheim, and Mead) but also of more contemporary thinkers in sociology, psychology, political science, phenomenology, and philosophy. The result of this synthesis is a theoretical system that blends individualist and collectivist levels of analysis, addresses concerns of individual agency and social structures, and explores issues of rational and nonrational dimensions of social life. (See Figure 9.3.)

With regard to the issue of action, Habermas's multidimensional approach is most apparent in his discussion of rationality (see Table 9.1). This model clearly reflects that action can be motivated by a number of factors. First, instrumental rationality refers to the means/ends calculations in which individuals seek to optimize the benefits that are likely to be reaped from pursuing a particular course of action. This entails a rational or technical approach to the social and physical world that asks *how* a given goal can be achieved most efficiently. Conversely, Habermas's discussion of moral-practical rationality and aesthetic-expressive rationality speaks to nonrational motivating forces. A different set of motivating questions is raised to the extent that these forms of reasoning guide our actions. Instead of asking "how" or "if" a line of action can be profitably pursued, our behaviors are governed by normative considerations that lead us to ask *why* we should carry out a course of action. Our determinations of whether or not we *ought* to pursue a given line of conduct are grounded not in an evaluation of facts, but rather in normative prescriptions for behavior that are not subject to empirical proof. Such prescriptions are instead embedded in the traditions and customs of a given culture.

Habermas's notion of communicative action is premised on the conviction that human emancipation is not possible so long as one form of reasoning dominates another. In an ideal, democratic society, both rational and nonrational forms of reasoning would motivate an individual's actions. That is, in order to be truly progressive our actions must satisfy technical requirements for efficiency as well as normative requirements for "rightness" and authenticity. Yet, modern societies have fallen short of the democratic ideal of mutual understanding based on the full range of motivating forces. Individuals remain dominated by seemingly autonomous forces that have corrupted their capacity to reason.

In terms of the question of order (that is, "what accounts for the routines and patterns of behavior through which social life appears, and is experienced as, orderly and predictable?"), Habermas again devises a multidimensional approach. While he holds onto the promise of a future society ordered on the basis of individually negotiated communication action, this condition, as well as all other forms of interaction, is dependent on the evolutionary stage of the relationship between the system and lifeworld. Thus, Habermas contends that the distortion of consciousness, the unfreedom, that plagues modern individuals is a result of the steering mechanisms of economic and political systems colonizing the lifeworld and its framework of shared meanings and norms. Economic and political systems operate according to their own impersonal logic that confronts individuals as an abstract, amorphous force that largely defies their ability to control their own destinies. In short, modern society is ordered less by the ongoing negotiation of meanings through which the world is made and remade than by the imperatives of collectivist structures that shape the nature of social interaction. Indeed, it is this very condition that Habermas seeks to dismantle through his reviving of critical theory and reinvigorating of the public sphere.

It is important to note, however, that Habermas's perspective by no means overlooks the individualist dimension. Incorporating both collectivist and individualist dimensions is an essential element in his theoretical system. His twin notions of system integration and social integration and his emphasis on the lifeworld are aimed precisely at understanding the (distorted) ways in which individuals construct their personal and collective identities, negotiate meanings, and, in the process, create and recreate the social order. The social order is produced and reproduced as individuals coordinate their actions through processes of reaching understanding mediated within the lifeworld. In providing the symbolic resources for making sense of the world, the lifeworld establishes a horizon of possibilities that places "internal limitations" on the reproduction of society. Such interpretive possibilities and limitations are formed within the minds of individuals and thus are not determined by the functional "needs" of the system. At the same time, however, actions are interconnected by system mechanisms that "are not intended by [individuals] and are usually not even perceived within the horizon of everyday practice" (ibid.).

Readings

In the selections that follow, you are presented with two key works from Jürgen Habermas. The first is an essay entitled "Civil Society, Public Opinion, and Communicative Power" in which Habermas outlines the key characteristics of the public sphere, its role in promoting discussion and debate, and the forces that impair its efficacy and corrupt the communicative processes ushering from the lifeworld. The second selection, "The Tasks of a Critical Theory of Society," finds Habermas extending these ideas, exploring the growing tensions that emerge between the system and lifeworld and the colonization of the latter by delinguistified steering mechanisms rooted in the system. Together, these selections offer a set of ideas that examine the obstacles that jeopardize the realization of the emancipatory project embraced by Enlightenment thinkers, and a vision of hope for democracy in contemporary societies.

Introduction to "Civil Society,
Public Opinion, and Communicative Power"

In the essay "Civil Society, Public Opinion, and Communicative Power," Habermas investigates the connections between the public sphere, the formation of public opinion, and the effectiveness of democratic politics. The public sphere serves as a "sounding board" or "warning system" that alerts the political system to pressing social problems. It is not an organization or institution per se, and neither does it refer to the functions or contents of communication. Rather, the public sphere is a "social space" that is created out of communicative action. These spaces can take the form of "episodic" publics found, for instance, in cafés and on the street; "occasional" publics that meet for specific events, such as church meetings or music concerts; or "abstract" publics consisting of isolated individuals who are "brought together" through their shared consumption of mass media.

As a space for opinion formation, the public sphere is not itself invested with political power. Thus, within the public sphere actors engage in a struggle over influence, that is, over the ability to shape public opinion in order to catapult an issue into official, institutionalized political bodies. In order for public influence to be transformed into effective political power, however, it must first pass "through the filters of institutionalized *procedures* of democratic opinion- and will-formation and [enter] through parliamentary debates into legitimate lawmaking" (1996:371). The structure of public opinion is thus governed by "rules of a *shared* practice of communication" that determine the "quality" or "success" of public opinion. These rules require that consensus on an issue "*develops* only as a result of more or less exhaustive controversy in which proposals, information, and reasons can be more or less rationally dealt with" (ibid.:362). As a result, not all opinion is equally qualified to *convince* the public of its relevance. The public sphere is thus a central space for fostering democracy, as its egalitarian public alone possesses the final authority to certify the salience and comprehensibility of publicly voiced opinions.

The democratic potential inherent in the public sphere is, however, subject to distortion from at least two sources. First, money and organizational power are capable of manipulating the process of public opinion formation so long as their use remains hidden from public view. Once the general public becomes aware of a previously undeclared infusion of money and power, however, public opinions made visible by such resources lose their credibility. Certainly, the public outcry in the wake of news stories detailing the illicit action of interest groups and lobbyists and the behind-the-scene efforts of corporations and government officials attempting to shape public opinion reminds us that "public opinion can be manipulated, but neither publicly bought nor publicly blackmailed" (ibid.: 364).

A second threat to the democratically formed public sphere stems from journalism and the mass media. In a mass-media–dominated public sphere such as our own, members of the press and media executives act as gatekeepers for the flow of information. Through their decisions about what is newsworthy, they determine the topics and the perspectives that are disseminated to the mass audience. Moreover, as the mass media become increasingly complex and expensive, avenues of communication become more centralized. As a result, their control over the selection of topics and viewpoints allows the mass media to become increasingly powerful in the world of public opinion formation. Groups who are peripheral to the organized political system or who do not possess significant resources have become less able to influence media programming. As Habermas notes, this problem is compounded for those groups whose messages "do not fall inside the 'balanced,' that is, the centrist and rather narrowly defined, spectrum of 'established opinions' dominating the programs of the electronic media" (1996:377). In addition, the profit-driven market strategies that steer media programming lead to an oversimplification or watering down of information—infotainment—that "works to depoliticize public communication" (ibid.). Yet, despite the public sphere's apparent undermining, as soon as a "crises consciousness" develops within the public sphere the balance of power shifts as actors press for solutions to relevant social problems.

❖

Civil Society, Public Opinion, and Communicative Power (1994)

Jürgen Habermas

Up to now, I have generally dealt with the public sphere as a communication structure rooted in the lifeworld through the associational network of civil society. I have described the political public sphere as a sounding board for problems that must be processed by the political system because they cannot be solved elsewhere. To this extent, the public sphere is a warning system with sensors that, though unspecialized, are sensitive throughout society. From the perspective of democratic theory, the public sphere must, in addition, amplify the pressure of problems, that is not only detect and identify problems but also convincing and *influentially* thematize them, furnish them with possible solutions, and dramatize them in such a way that they are taken up and dealt with by parliamentary complexes. Besides the "signal" function, there must be an effective problematization. The capacity of the public sphere to solve problems *on its own* is limited. But this capacity must be utilized to oversee the further treatment of problems that takes place inside the political system. . . .

I

The public sphere is a social phenomenon just as elementary as action, actor, association, or collectivity, but it eludes the conventional sociological concepts of "social order." The public sphere cannot be conceived as an institution and certainly not as an organization. It is not even a framework of norms with differentiated competences and roles, membership regulations, and so on. Just as little does it represent a system; although it permits one to draw international boundaries, outwardly it is characterized by open, permeable, and shifting horizons. The public sphere can best be described as a network for communicating information and points of view (i.e., opinions expressing affirmative or negative attitudes); the streams of communication are, in the process, filtered and synthesized in such a way that they coalesce into bundles of topically specified *public* opinions. Like the lifeworld as a whole, so, too, the public sphere is reproduced through communicative action, for which mastery of a natural language suffices; it is tailored to the *general comprehensibility* of everyday communicative practice. We have become acquainted with the "lifeworld" as a reservoir for simple interactions; specialized systems of action and knowledge that are differentiated within the lifeworld remain tied to these interactions. These systems fall into one of two categories. Systems like religion, education, and the family become associated with general reproductive functions of the lifeworld (that is, with cultural reproduction, social integration, or socialization). Systems like science, morality, and art take up different validity aspects of everyday communicative action (truth, rightness, or veracity). The public sphere, however, is specialized in neither of these two ways; to the extent that it extends to politically relevant questions, it leaves their specialized treatment to the political system. Rather, the public sphere distinguishes itself through a *communication structure* that is related to a third feature of communicative action: it refers neither to the *functions* nor to the *contents* of everyday communication but to the *social space* generated in communicative action.

Unlike success-oriented actors who mutually observe each other as one observes something in the objective world, persons acting communicatively encounter each other in a *situation* they at the same time constitute with their cooperatively negotiated interpretations. The intersubjectively shared space of a speech situation is disclosed when the participants enter into interpersonal relationships by taking positions on mutual speech-act offers and assuming illocutionary obligations. Every encounter in which actors do not just observe each other but take a second-person attitude, reciprocally attributing communicative freedom to each other, unfolds in a linguistically constituted public space. This space stands open, in principle, for potential dialogue partners who are present as bystanders or could come on the scene and joint those present. That is, special measures would be required to prevent a third party from entering such a linguistically constituted space. Founded in communicative action, this spatial structure of simple and episodic encounters can be expanded and rendered more permanent in an abstract form for a larger public of present persons. For the public infrastructure of such *assemblies*, performances, presentations, and so on, architectural metaphors of structured spaces recommend themselves: we speak of forums, stages, arenas, and the like. These public spheres still cling to the concrete locales where an audience is physically gathered. The more they detach themselves from the public's physical presence and extend to the virtual presence of scattered readers, listeners, or viewers linked by public media, the clearer becomes the abstraction that enters when the spatial structure of simple interactions is expanded into a public sphere.

When generalized in this way, communication structures contract to informational content and points of view that are uncoupled from the thick context of simple interactions, from specific persons, and from practical obligations. At the same time, context generalization, inclusion, and growing anonymity demand a higher degree of explication that must dispense with technical vocabularies and special codes. Whereas the *orientation to laypersons* implies a certain loss in differentiation, uncoupling communicated opinions from concrete practical obligations tends to have an *intellectualizing* effect. Processes of opinion-formation, especially when they have to do with political questions, certainly cannot be separated from the transformation of the participants' preferences and attitudes, but they can be separated from putting these dispositions into action. To this extent, the communication structures of the public sphere *relieve* the public *of the burden of decision making*; the postponed decisions are reserved for the institutionalized political process. In the public sphere, utterances are sorted according to issue and contribution, whereas the contributions are weighted by the affirmative versus negative responses they receive. Information and arguments are thus worked into focused opinions. What makes such "bundled" opinions into *public opinion* is both the controversial way it comes about and the amount of approval that "carries" it. Public opinion is not representative in the statistical sense. It is not an aggregate of individually gathered, privately expressed opinions held by isolated persons. Hence it must not be confused with survey results. Political opinion polls provide a certain reflection of "public opinion" only if they have been preceded by a focused public debate and a corresponding opinion-formation in a mobilized public sphere.

The diffusion of information and points of view via effective broadcasting media is not the only thing that matters in public processes of communication, nor is it the most important. True, only the broad circulation of comprehensible, attention-grabbing messages arouses a sufficiently inclusive participation. But the rules of a *shared* practice of communication are of greater significance for structuring public opinion. Agreement on issues and contributions develops only as the result of more or less exhaustive controversy in which proposals, information, and reasons can be more or less rationally dealt with. In general terms, the *discursive level* of opinion-formation and the "quality" of the outcome vary with this "more or less" in the "rational" processing of "exhaustive" proposals, information, and reasons. Thus the success of public communication is not intrinsically measured by the requirement of inclusion either but by the formal criteria governing how a qualified public opinion comes about. The structures of a power-ridden, oppressed public sphere exclude fruitful and clarifying discussions. The "quality" of public opinion, insofar as it is measured by the procedural properties of its process of generation, is an empirical variable. From a normative perspective, this provides a basis for measuring the legitimacy of the influence that public opinion has on the political system. Of course, actual influence coincides with legitimate influence just as little as the belief in legitimacy coincides with legitimacy. But conceiving things this way at least opens a perspective from which the relation between actual influence and the procedurally grounded quality of public opinion can be empirically investigated.

Parsons introduced "influence" as a symbolically generalized form of communication that facilitates interactions in virtue of conviction or persuasion. For example, persons or institutions can enjoy a reputation that allows their utterances to have an influence on others' beliefs without having to demonstrate authority or to give explanations in the situation. "Influence" feeds on the resource of mutual understanding, but it is based on advancing trust in beliefs that are not currently tested. In this sense, public opinion represents political potentials that can be used for influencing the voting behavior of citizens or the will-formation in parliamentary bodies, administrative agencies, and courts. Naturally, political *influence* supported by public opinion is converted into political *power*—into a potential for rendering binding decisions—only when it affects the beliefs and decisions of *authorized* members of the political system and determines the behavior of voters,

legislators, officials, and so forth. Just like social power, political influence based on public opinion can be transformed into political power only through institutionalized procedures.

Influence develops in the public sphere and becomes the object of struggle there. This struggle involves not only the political influence that has already been acquired (such as that enjoyed by experienced political leaders and officeholders, established parties, and well-known groups like Greenpeace and Amnesty International). The reputation of groups of persons and experts who have acquired their influence in special public spheres also comes into play (for example, the authority of religious leaders, the public visibility of literary figures and artists, the reputation of scientists, and the popularity of sports figures and movie stars). For as soon as the public space has expanded beyond the context of simple interactions, a differentiation sets in among organizers, speakers, and hearers; arenas and galleries; stage and viewing space. The *actors' roles* that increasingly professionalize and multiply with organizational complexity and range of media are, of course, furnished with unequal opportunities for exerting influence. But the political influence that the actors gain through public communication must *ultimately* rest on the resonance and indeed the approval of a lay public whose composition is egalitarian. The public of citizens must be *convinced* by comprehensible and broadly interesting contributions to issues it finds relevant. The public audience possesses final authority, because it is *constitutive* for the internal structure and reproduction of the public sphere, the *only* place where actors can appear. There can be no public sphere without a public.

To be sure, we must distinguish the actors who, so to speak, emerge from the public and take part in the reproduction of the public sphere itself from actors who occupy an already constituted public domain in order to use it. This is true, for example, of the large and well-organized interest groups that are anchored in various social subsystems and affect the political system *through* the public sphere. They cannot make any manifest use in the public sphere of the sanctions and rewards they rely on in bargaining or in nonpublic attempts at pressure. They can capitalize on their social power and convert it into political power only insofar as they can advertise their interests in a language that can mobilize convincing reasons and shared value orientations—as, for example, when parties to wage negotiations inform the public about demands, strategies, or outcomes. The contributions of interest groups are, in any case, vulnerable to a kind of criticism to which contributions from other sources are not exposed. Public opinions that can acquire visibility only because of an undeclared infusion of money or organizational power lose their credibility as soon as these sources of social power are made public. Public opinion can be manipulated but neither publicly bought nor publicly blackmailed. This is due to the fact that a public sphere cannot be "manufactured" as one pleases. Before it can be captured by actors with strategic intent, the public sphere together with its public must have developed as a structure that stands on its own and reproduces itself *out of itself.* This lawlike regularity governing the formation of a public sphere remains latent in the constituted public sphere—and takes effect again only in moments when the public sphere is mobilized.

The political public sphere can fulfill its function of perceiving and thematizing encompassing social problems only insofar as it develops out of the communication taking place among *those who are potentially affected.* It is carried by a public recruited from the entire citizenry. But in the diverse voices of this public, one hears the echo of private experiences that are caused throughout society by the externalities (and internal disturbances) of various functional systems—and even by the very state apparatus on whose regulatory activities the complex and poorly coordinated sub-systems depend. Systemic deficiencies are experienced in the context of individual life histories; such burdens accumulate in the lifeworld. The latter has the appropriate antennae, for in its horizon are intermeshed the private life histories of the "clients" of functional systems that might be failing in their delivery of services. It is only for those who are immediately affected that such services are paid in the currency of "use values." Besides religion, art, and literature, only the spheres of "private" life have an existential language at their disposal, in which such socially

generated problems can be *assessed in terms of one's own life history.* Problems voiced in the public sphere first become visible when they are mirrored in personal life experiences. To the extent that these experiences find their concise expression in the languages of religion, art, and literature, the "literary" public sphere in the broader sense, which is specialized for the articulation of values and world disclosure, is intertwined with the political public sphere.

As both bearers of the political public sphere and as *members of society*, citizens occupy two positions at once. As members of society, they occupy the roles of employees and consumers, insured persons and patients, taxpayers and clients of bureaucracies, as well as the roles of students, tourists, commuters, and the like; in such complementary roles, they are especially exposed to the specific requirements and failures of the corresponding service systems. Such experiences are first assimilated "privately," that is are interpreted within the horizon of a life history intermeshed with other life histories in the contexts of shared lifeworlds. The communication channels of the public sphere are linked to private spheres—to the thick networks of interaction found in families and circles of friends as well as to the looser contacts with neighbors, work colleagues, acquaintances, and so on— and indeed they are linked in such a way that the spatial structures of simple interactions are expanded and abstracted but not destroyed. Thus the orientation to reaching understanding that is predominant in everyday practice is also preserved for a *communication among strangers* that is conducted over great distances in public spheres whose branches are quite complex. The threshold separating the private sphere from the public is not marked by a fixed set of issues or relationships but by *different conditions of communication.* Certainly these conditions lead to differences in the accessibility of the two spheres, safeguarding the intimacy of the one sphere and publicity of the other. However, they do not seal off the private from the public but only channel the flow of topics from the one sphere into the other. For the public sphere draws its impulses from the private handling of social problems that resonate in life histories. It is symptomatic of this close connection, incidentally, that a modern bourgeois public sphere developed in the European societies of the seventeenth and eighteenth centuries as the "sphere of private persons come together as a public." Viewed historically, the connection between the public and the private spheres is manifested in the clubs and organizational forms of a reading public composed of bourgeois private persons and crystallizing around newspapers and journals.

II

This sphere of civil society has been rediscovered today in wholly new historical constellations. The expression "civil society" has in the meantime taken on a meaning different from that of the "bourgeois society" of the liberal tradition, which Hegel conceptualized as a "system of needs," that is, as a market system involving social labor and commodity exchange. What is meant by "civil society" today, in contrast to its usage in the Marxist tradition, no longer includes the economy as constituted by private law and steered through markets in labor, capital, and commodities. Rather, its institutional core comprises those nongovernmental and noneconomic connections and voluntary associations that anchor the communication structures of the public sphere in the society component of the lifeworld. Civil society is composed of those more or less spontaneously emergent associations, organizations, and movements that, attuned to how societal problems resonate in the private life spheres, distill and transmit such reactions in amplified form to the public sphere. The core of civil society comprises a network of associations that institutionalizes problem-solving discourses on questions of general interest inside the framework of organized public spheres. These "discursive designs" have an egalitarian, open form of organization that mirrors essential features of the kind of communication around which they crystallize and to which they lend continuity and permanence.

Such associations certainly do not represent the most conspicuous element of a public sphere dominated by mass media and large agencies, observed by market and opinion research, and

inundated by the public relations work, propaganda, and advertising of political parties and groups. All the same, they do form the organizational substratum of the general public of citizens. More or less emerging from the private sphere, this public is made of citizens who seek acceptable interpretations for their social interests and experiences and who want to have an influence on institutionalized opinion- and will-formation.

One searches the literature in vain for clear definitions of civil society that would go beyond such descriptive characterizations. . . . Jean Cohen and Andrew Arato, who have presented the most comprehensive study on this topic, provide a catalog of features characterizing the civil society that is demarcated from the state, the economy, and other functional systems but coupled with the core private spheres of the lifeworld:

> (1) *Plurality*: families, informal groups, and voluntary associations whose plurality and autonomy allow for a variety of forms of life; (2) *Publicity*: institutions of culture and communication; (3) *Privacy*: a domain of individual self-development and moral choice; (4) *Legality*: structures of publicity from at least the state and, tendentially, the economy. Together, these structures secure the institutional existence of a modern differentiated civil society.[i]

The *constitution of this sphere through basic rights* provides some indicators for its social structure. Freedom of assembly and freedom of association, when linked with freedom of speech, define the scope for various types of associations and societies: for voluntary associations that intervene in the formation of public opinion, push topics of general interest, and act as advocates for neglected issues and underrepresented groups; for groups that are difficult to organize or that pursue cultural, religious, or humanitarian aims; and for ethnical communities, religious denominations, and so on. Freedom of the press, radio, and television, as well as the right to engage in these areas, safeguards the media infrastructure of public

[i]J. L. Cohen and A. Arato, *Civil Society and Political Theory* (Cambridge, Mass., 1992), p. 346.

communication; such liberties are thereby supposed to preserve an openness for competing opinions and a representative diversity of voices. The political system, which must remain sensitive to the influence of public opinion, is intertwined with the public sphere and civil society through the activity of political parties and general elections. This intermeshing is guaranteed by the right of parties to "collaborate" in the political will-formation of the people, as well as by the citizens' and passive voting rights and other participatory rights. Finally, the network of associations can assert its autonomy and preserve its spontaneity only insofar as it can draw support from a mature pluralism of forms of life, subcultures, and worldviews. The constitutional protection of "privacy" promotes the integrity of private life spheres: rights of personality, freedom of belief and of conscience, freedom of movement, the privacy of letters, mail, and telecommunications, the inviolability of one's residence, and the protection of families circumscribe an untouchable zone of personal integrity and independent judgment.

The tight connection between an autonomous civil society and an integral private sphere stands out even more clearly when contrasted with totalitarian societies of bureaucratic socialism. Here a panoptic state not only directly controls the bureaucratically desiccated public sphere, it also undermines the private basis of this public sphere. Administrative intrusions and constant supervision corrode the communicative structure of everyday contacts in families and schools, neighborhoods and local municipalities. The destruction of solidary living conditions and the paralysis of initiative and independent engagement in overregulated yet legally uncertain sectors go hand in hand with the crushing of social groups, associations, and networks: with indoctrination and the dissolution of cultural identities; with the suffocation of spontaneous public communication. Communicative rationality is thus destroyed *simultaneously* in both public and private contexts of communication. The more the bonding force of communicative action wanes in private life spheres and the embers of communicative freedom die out, the easier it is for someone who monopolizes the public sphere to align the mutually estranged and isolated

actors into a mass that can be directed and mobilized in a plebiscitarian manner.

Basic constitutional guarantees alone, of course, cannot preserve the public sphere and civil society from deformations. The communication structures of the public sphere must rather be kept intact by an energetic civil society. That the political public sphere must in a certain sense reproduce and stabilize itself from its own resources is shown by the odd *self-referential character of the practice of communication in civil society*. Those actors who are the carriers of the public sphere put forward "texts" that always reveal the same subtext, which refers to the critical function of the public sphere in general. Whatever the manifest content of their public utterances, the performative meaning of such public discourse at the same time actualizes the function of an undistorted political public sphere as such. Thus, the institutions and legal guarantees of free and open opinion-formation rest on the unsteady ground of the political communication of actors who, in making use of them, at the same time interpret, defend, and radicalize their normative content. Actors who know they are involved in the *common* enterprise of reconstituting and maintaining structures of the public sphere as they contest opinions and strive for influence differ from actors who merely use forums that already exist. More specifically, actors who support the public sphere are distinguished by the *dual orientation* of their political engagement: with their programs, they directly influence the political system, but at the same time they are also reflexively concerned with revitalizing and enlarging civil society and the public sphere as well as with confirming their own identifies and capacities to act.

Cohen and Arato see this kind of "dual politics" especially in the "new" social movements that simultaneously pursue offensive and defensive goals. "Offensively," these movements attempt to bring up issues relevant to the entire society, to define ways of approaching problems, to propose possible solutions, to supply new information, to interpret values differently, to mobilize good reasons and criticize bad ones. Such initiatives are intended to produce a broad shift in public opinion, to alter the parameters of organized political will-formation, and to exert pressure on parliaments, courts, and administrations in favor of specific policies. "Defensively," they attempt to maintain existing structures of association and public influence, to generate subcultural counterpublics and counterinstitutions, to consolidate new collective identities, and to win new terrain in the form of expanded rights and reformed institutions:

> On this account, the "defensive" aspect of the movements involves preserving *and developing* the communicative infrastructure of the lifeworld. This formulation captures the dual aspect of movements discussed by Touraine as well as Habermas' insight that movements can be the carriers of the potentials of cultural modernity. This is the sine qua non for successful efforts to redefine identities, to reinterpret norms, and to develop egalitarian, democratic associational forms. The expressive, normative and communicative modes of collective action . . . [also involve] efforts to secure *institutional* changes within civil society that correspond to the new meanings, identities, and norms that are created.[ii]

In the self-referential mode of reproducing the public sphere, as well as in the Janus-faced politics aimed at the political system and the self-stabilization of public sphere and civil society, the space is provided for the extension and radicalization of existing rights: "The combination of associations, publics, and rights, when supported by a political culture in which independent initiatives and movements represent an ever-renewable, legitimate, political option, represents, in our opinion, an effective set of bulwarks around civil society within whose limits much of the program of radical democracy can be reformulated.[iii]

In fact, the *interplay* of a public sphere based in civil society with the opinion- and will-formation institutionalized in parliamentary bodies and courts offers a good starting point for translating the concept of deliberative politics into sociological terms. However, we must not look on civil society as a focal point where the lines of societal self-organization as a whole would converge. Cohen and Arato rightly emphasize the *limited scope for action* that civil society and the public sphere afford to noninstitutionalized political movements and forms of political expression. They speak of a structurally necessary "self-limitation" of radical-democratic practice:

First, a robust civil society can develop only in the context of a liberal political culture and the corresponding patterns of socialization, and on the basis of an integral private sphere; it can blossom only in an already rationalized lifeworld. Otherwise, populist movements arise that blindly defend the frozen traditions of a lifeworld endangered by capitalist modernization. In their forms of mobilization, these fundamentalist movements are as modern as they are antidemocratic.

Second, within the boundaries of the public sphere, or at least of a liberal public sphere, actors can acquire only influence, not political power. The influence of a public opinion generated more or less discursively in open controversies is certainly an empirical variable that can make a difference. But public influence is transformed into communicative power only after it passes through the filters of the institutionalized *procedures* of democratic opinion- and will-formation and enters through parliamentary debates into legitimate lawmaking. The informal flow of public opinion issues in beliefs that have been *tested* from the standpoint of the generalizability of interests. Not influence per se, but influence transformed into communicative power legitimates political decisions. The popular sovereignty set communicatively aflow cannot make itself felt *solely* in the influence of informal public discourses—not even when these discourses arise from autonomous public spheres. To generate political power, their influence must have an effect on the democratically regulated deliberations of democratically elected assemblies and assume an authorized form in formal decisions. This also holds, mutatis mutandis, for courts that decide politically relevant cases.

Third, and finally, the instruments that politics have available in law and administrative

---

[ii]Cohen and Arato, *Civil Society*, p. 531.

[iii]Cohen and Arato, *Civil Society*, p. 474.

power have limited effectiveness in functionally differentiated societies. Politics indeed continues to be the addressee for all unmanaged integration problems. But political steering can often take only an indirect approach and must, as we have seen, leave intact the modes of operation internal to functional systems and other highly organized spheres of action. As a result, democratic movements emerging from civil society must give up holistic aspirations to a self-organizing society, aspirations that also undergirded Marxist ideas of social revolution. Civil society can directly transform only itself, and it can have at most an indirect effect on the self-transformation of the political system; generally, it has an influence only on the personnel and programming of this system. But in no way does it occupy *the position* of a macrosubject supposed to bring society as a whole under control and simultaneously act for it. Besides these limitations, one must bear in mind that the administrative power deployed for purposes of social planning and supervision is not suitable medium for fostering emancipated forms of life. These can *develop* in the wake of democratization processes but they cannot be *brought about* through intervention. . . .

III

The concepts of the political public sphere and civil society introduced above are not mere normative postulates but have empirical relevance. However, additional assumptions must be introduced if we are to use these concepts to translate the discourse-theoretic reading of radical democracy into sociological terms and reformulate it in empirically falsifiable manner. I would like to defend the claim that *under certain circumstances* civil society can acquire influence in the public sphere, have an effect on the parliamentary complex (and the courts) through its own public opinions, and compel the political system to switch over to the official circulation of power. . . . Social movements, citizen initiatives and forums, political and other associations, in short, the groupings of civil society, are indeed sensitive to problems, but the signals they send out and the impulses they give are generally too weak to initiate learning processes

or redirect decision making in the political system in the short run.

In complex societies, the public sphere consists of an intermediary structure between the political system, on the one hand, and the private sectors of the lifeworld and functional systems, on the other. It represents a highly complex network that branches out into a multitude of overlapping international, national, regional, local, and subcultural arenas. Functional specifications, thematic foci, policy fields, and so forth, provide the points of reference for a substantive differentiation of public spheres that are, however, still accessible to laypersons (for example, popular science and literary publics, religious and artistic publics, feminist and "alternative" publics, publics concerned with health-care issues, social welfare, or environmental policy). Moreover, the public sphere is differentiated into levels according to the density of communication, organizational complexity, and range—from the *episodic* publics found in taverns, coffee houses, or on the streets; through the *occasional* or "arranged" publics of particular presentations and events, such as theater performances, rock concerts, party assemblies, or church congresses; up to the *abstract* public sphere of isolated readers, listeners, and viewers scattered across large geographic areas, or even around the globe, and brought together only through the mass media. Despite these manifold differentiations, however, all the partial publics constituted by ordinary language remain porous to one another. The one text of "the" public sphere, a text continually extrapolated and extending radially in all directions, is divided by internal boundaries into arbitrarily small texts for which everything else is context; yet one can always build hermeneutical bridges from one text to the next. Segmented public spheres are constituted with the help of exclusion mechanisms; however, because publics cannot harden into organizations or systems, there is no exclusion rule without a proviso for its abolishment. . . .

The more the audience is widened through mass communications, the more inclusive and the more abstract in form it becomes. Correspondingly, the *roles of the actors* appearing in the arenas are, to an increasing degree, sharply separated from the roles of the spectators in the galleries. Although the "success of the actors in the arena is ultimately decided in the galleries, the question arises of how autonomous the public is when it takes a position on an issue, whether its affirmative or negative stand reflects a process of becoming informed or in fact only a more or less concealed game of power. Despite the wealth of empirical investigations, we still do not have a well-established answer to this cardinal question. But one can at least pose the question more precisely by assuming that public processes of communication can take place with less distortion the more they are left to the internal dynamic of a civil society that emerges from the lifeworld.

One can distinguish, at least tentatively, the more loosely organized actors who "emerge from" the public, as it were, from other actors merely "appearing before" the public. The latter have organizational power, resources, and sanctions available *from the start*. Naturally, the actors who are more firmly anchored in civil society and participate in the reproduction of the public sphere also depend on the support of "sponsors" who supply the necessary resources of money, organization, knowledge, and social capital. But patrons or "like-minded" sponsors do not necessarily reduce the authenticity of the public actors they support. By contrast, the collective actors who merely enter the public sphere from, and utilize it for, a specific organization or functional system have *their own* basis of support. Among these political and social actors who do not have to obtain their resources from other spheres, I primarily include the large interest groups that enjoy social power, as well as the established parties that have largely become arms of the political system. They draw on market studies and opinion surveys and conduct their own professional public-relations campaigns.

In and of themselves, organizational complexity, resources, professionalization, and so on, are admittedly insufficient indicators for the difference between "indigenous" actors and mere users. Nor can an actor's pedigree be read directly from the interests actually represented. Other indicators are more reliable. Thus actors differ in how they can be identified. Some actors one can easily identify from their functional background; that is, they represent political parties or pressure groups; unions or professional associations; consumer-protection groups or rent-control organizations, and so on. Other actors, by contrast, must first *produce* identifying features. This is especially evident with social movements that initially go through a phase of self-identification and self-legitimation; even after that, they still pursue a self-referential "identity politics" parallel to their goal-directed politics—they must continually reassure themselves of their identity. Whether actors merely use an already constituted public sphere or whether they are involved in reproducing its structures is, moreover, evident in the above-mentioned sensitivity to threats to communication rights. It is also shown in the actors' willingness to go beyond an interest in self-defense and take a universalist stand against the open or concealed exclusion of minorities or marginal groups. The very existence of social movements, one might add, depends on whether they find organizational forms that produce solidarities and publics, forms that allow them to fully utilize and radicalize existing communication rights and structures as they pursue special goals.

A third group of actors are the journalists, publicity agents, and members of the press (i.e., in the broad sense of *Publizisten*) who collect information, make decisions about the selection and presentation of "programs," and to a certain extent control the entry of topics, contributions, and authors into the mass-media-dominated public sphere. As the mass media become more complex and more expensive, the effective channels of communication become more centralized. To the degree this occurs, the mass media face an increasing pressure of selection, on both the supply side and the demand side. These selection processes become the source of a new sort of power. This *power of the media* is not sufficiently reined in by professional standards, but today, by fits and starts, the "fourth branch of government" is being subjected to constitutional regulation. In the Federal Republic, for example, it is both the legal form and the institutional structure of television networks that determine whether they depend more on the influence of political parties and public interest groups or more on private firms with large advertising outlays. In general, one can say that the image of politics presented on television is predominantly made up of issues and contributions that are professionally produced as media input and then fed in via press conferences, news agencies, public-relations campaigns, and the like. These official producers of information are all the more successful the more they can rely on trained personnel, on financial and technical resources, and in general on a professional infrastructure. Collective actors operating outside the political system or outside large organizations normally have fewer opportunities to influence the content and views presented by the media. This is especially true for messages that do not fall inside the "balanced," that is, the centrist and rather narrowly defined, spectrum of "established options" dominating the programs of the electronic media.

Moreover, before messages selected in this way are broadcast, they are subject to *information-processing strategies* within the media. These are oriented by reception conditions as perceived by media experts, program directors, and the press. Because the public's receptiveness, cognitive capacity, and attention represent unusually scarce resources for which the programs of numerous "stations" compete, the presentation of news and commentaries for the most part follows market strategies. Reporting facts as human-interest stores, mixing information with entertainment, arranging material episodically, and breaking down complex relationships into smaller fragments—all of this comes together to form a syndrome that works to depoliticize public communication. This is the kernel of truth in the theory of the culture industry. The research literature provides fairly reliable information on the institutional framework and structure of the media, as well as on the way they work, organize programs, and are utilized. But, even a generation after Paul Lazarsfeld, propositions concerning the *effects of the media* remain controversial. The research on effect and reception has at least done away with the image of passive consumers as "cultural dopes" who are manipulated by the programs offered to them. It directs our attention to the *strategies of interpretation* employed by viewers, who communicate with one another, and who in fact can be provoked to criticize or reject what programs offer or to synthesize it with judgments of their own.

Even if we know something about the internal operation and impact of the mass media, as well as about the distribution of roles among the public and various actors, and even if we can make some reasonable conjectures about who has privileged access to the media and who has a share in media power, it is by no means clear how the mass media intervene in the diffuse circuits of communication in the political public sphere. The *normative reactions* to the relatively new phenomenon of the mass media's powerful position in the competition for public influence are clearer. Michael Gurevitch and Jay G. Blumler have summarized the tasks that the media *ought* to fulfill in democratic political systems:

1. surveillance of the sociopolitical environment, reporting developments likely to impinge, positively or negatively, on the welfare of citizens;

2. meaningful agenda-setting, identifying the key issues of the day, including the forces that have formed and may resolve them:

3. platforms for an intelligible and illuminating advocacy by politicians and spokespersons of other causes and interest groups;

4. dialogue across a diverse range of views, as well as between power-holders (actual and prospective) and mass publics;

5. mechanisms for holding officials to account for how they have exercised power;

6. incentives for citizens to learn, choose, and become involved, rather than merely to follow and kibitz over the political process;

7. a principled resistance to the efforts of forces outside the media to subvert their independence, integrity and ability to serve the audience;

8. a sense of respective for the audience member, as potentially concerned and able to make sense of his or her political environment.[iv]

[iv]M. Gurevitch and J. G. Blumler, "Political Communication Systems and Democratic Values," in J. Lichtenberg, ed., *Democracy and the Mass Media* (Cambridge, Mass., 1990), p. 270.

Such principles orient the professional code of journalism and the profession's ethical self-understanding, on the one hand, and the formal organization of a free press by laws governing mass communication, on the other. In agreement with the concept of deliberative politics, these principles express a simple idea: the mass media ought to understand themselves as the mandatary of an enlightened public whose willingness to learn and capacity for criticism they at once presuppose, demand, and reinforce; like the judiciary, they ought to preserve their independence from political and social pressure; they ought to be receptive to the public's concerns and proposals, take up these issues and contributions impartially, augment criticisms and, and confront the political process with articulate demands for legitimation. The power of the media should thus be neutralized and the tacit conversion of administrative or social power into political influence blocked. According to this idea, political and social actors would be allowed to "use" the public sphere only insofar as they make convincing contributions to the solution of problems that have been perceived by the public or have been put on the public agenda with the public's consent. In a similar vein, political parties would have to participate in the opinion- and will-formation from the public's own perspective, rather than patronizing the public and extracting mass loyalty from the public sphere for the purposes of maintaining their own power.

The sociology of mass communication depicts the public sphere as infiltrated by administrative and social power and dominated by the mass media. If one places this image, diffuse though it might be, alongside the above normative expectations, then one will be rather cautious in estimating the chances of civil society having an influence on the political system. To be sure, this estimate pertains only to a *public sphere at rest*. In periods of mobilization, the structures that actually support the authority of a critically engaged public begin to vibrate. The balance of power between civil society and the political system then shifts.

IV

With this I return to the central question of who can place issues on the agenda and determine what direction the lines of communication take. Roger Cobb, Jennie-Keith Ross, and Marc Howard Ross have constructed models that depict how new and compelling issues develop, from the first initiative up to formal proceedings in bodies that have the power to decide.[v] If one suitably modifies the proposed models-inside access model, mobilization model, outside initiative model-from the viewpoint of democratic theory, they present basic alternatives in how the public sphere and the political system influence each other. In the first case, the initiative comes from office holders or political leaders, and the issue continues to circulate inside the political system all the way to its formal treatment, while the broader public is either excluded from the process or does not have any influence on it. In the second case, the initiative again starts inside the political system, but the proponents of the issue must mobilize the public sphere, because they need the support of certain groups, either to obtain formal consideration or to implement an adopted program successfully. Only in the third case does the initiative lie with forces at the periphery, outside the purview of the political system. With the help of the mobilized public sphere, that is, the pressure of public opinion, such forces compel formal consideration of the issue:

> The outside initiative model applies to the situation in which a group outside the government structure 1) articulates a grievance, 2) tries to expand interest in the issue enough to other groups in the population to gain a place on the public agenda, in order to 3) create sufficient pressure on decision makers to force the issue onto the formal agenda for their serious consideration. This model of agenda building is likely to predominate in more egalitarian societies. Formal agenda status, . . . however, does not necessarily mean that the final decisions of the authorities or the actual

---

[v] R. Cobb, J. K. Ross, and M. H. Ross, "Agenda Building as a Comparative Political Process," *American Political Science Review* 70 (1976): 126–38; R. Cobb and C. Elder, "The Politics of Agenda-Building," *Journal of Politics* (1971): 892–915.

policy implementation will be what the grievance group original sought.[vi]

In the normal case, issues and proposals have a history whose course corresponds more to the first or second model than to the third. As long as the informal circulation of power dominates the political system, the initiative and power to put problems on the agenda and bring them to a decision lies more with the Government leaders and administration than with the parliamentary complex. As long as in the public sphere the mass media prefer, contrary to their normative self-understanding, to draw their material from powerful, well-organized information producers and as long as they prefer media strategies that lower rather than raise the discursively level of public communication, issues will tend to start in, and be managed from, the center, rather than follow a spontaneous course originating in the periphery. At least, the skeptical findings on problem articulation in public arenas accord with this view. In the present context, of course, there can be no question of a conclusive empirical evaluation of the mutual influence that politics and public have on each other. For our purposes, it suffices to make it plausible that in a perceived crisis situation, the *actors in civil society* thus far neglected in our scenario *can* assume a surprisingly active and momentous role. In spite of a lesser organizational complexity and a weaker capacity for action, and despite the structural disadvantages mentioned earlier, at the critical moments of an accelerated history, these actors get the chance to *reverse* the normal circuits of communication in the political system and the public sphere. In this way they can shift the entire system's mode of problem solving.

The communication structures of the public sphere are linked with the private life spheres in a way that gives the civil-social periphery, in contrast to the political center, the advantage of greater sensitivity in detecting and identifying new problem situations. The great issues of the last decades give evidence for this. Consider, for example, the spiraling nuclear-arms race; consider the risks involved in the peaceful use of atomic energy or in other large-scale technological projects and scientific experimentation, such

as genetic engineering; consider the ecological threats involved in an overstrained natural environment (acid rain, water pollution, species extinction, etc.); consider the dramatically progressing impoverishment of the Third World and problems of the world economic order; or consider such issues as feminism, increasing immigration, and the associated problems of multiculturalism. Hardly any of these topics were *initially* brought up by exponents of the state apparatus, large organizations, or functional systems. Instead, they were broached by intellectuals, concerned citizens, radical professionals, self-proclaimed "advocates," and the like. Moving in from this outermost periphery, such issues force their way into newspapers and interested associations, clubs, professional organizations, academies, and universities. They find forums, citizen initiatives, and other platforms before they catalyze the growth of social movements and new subcultures. The latter can in turn dramatize contributions, presenting them so effectively that the mass media take up the matter. Only through their controversial presentation in the media do such topics reach the larger public and subsequently gain a place on the "public agenda." Sometimes the support of sensational actions, mass protests, and incessant campaigning is required before an issue can make its way via the surprising election of marginal candidates or radical parties, expanded platforms of "established" parties, important court decisions, and so on, into the core of the political system and there receive formal consideration.

Naturally, there are other ways in which issues develop, other paths from the periphery to the center, and other patterns involving complex branchings and feedback loops. But, in general, one can say that even in more or less power-ridden public spheres, the power relations shift as soon as the perception of relevant social problems evokes a *crisis consciousness* at the periphery. If actors from civil society then join together, formulate the relevant issue, and promote it in the public sphere, their efforts can be successful, because the endogenous mobilization of the public sphere activates an otherwise latent dependency built into the internal structure of every public sphere, a dependency also present

---

[vi]Cobb, Ross, and Ross, "Agenda Building as a Comparative Political Process," p. 132.

in the normative self-understanding of the mass media: the players in the arena owe their influence to the approval of those in the gallery. At the very least, one can say that insofar as a rationalized lifeworld supports the development of a liberal public sphere by furnishing it with a solid foundation in civil society, the authority of a position-taking public is strengthened in the course of escalating public controversies. Under the conditions of a *liberal* public sphere, informal public communication accomplishes two things in cases in which mobilization depends on crisis. On the one hand, it prevents the accumulation of indoctrinated masses that are seduced by populist leaders. On the other hand, it pulls together the scattered critical potentials of a public that was only abstractly held together through the public media, and it helps this public have a political influence on institutionalized opinion- and will-formation. Only in *liberal* public spheres, of course, do subinstitutional political movements—which abandon the conventional paths of interest politics in order to boost the constitutionally regulated circulation of power in the political system—take this direction. By contrast, an authoritarian, distorted public sphere that is brought into alignment merely provides a forum for plebiscitary legitimation.

This sense of reinforced demand for legitimation becomes especially clear when subinstitutional protest movements reach a high point by escalating their protests. The last means for obtaining more of a hearing and greater media influence for oppositional arguments are acts of civil disobedience. These acts of nonviolent, symbolic rule violation are meant as expressions of protest against binding decisions that, their legality notwithstanding, the actors consider illegitimate in the light of valid constitutional principles. Acts of civil disobedience are directed simultaneously to two addressees. On the one hand, they appeal to officeholders and parliamentary representatives to reopen formally concluded political deliberations so that their decisions may possibly be revised in view of the continuing public criticism. On the other hand, they appeal "to the sense of justice of the majority of the community," as Rawls puts it,[vii] and thus to the critical judgment of a public of citizens that is to be mobilized with exceptional means. Independently of the current object of controversy, civil disobedience is also always an implicit appeal to connect organized political will-formation with the communicative processes of the public sphere. The message of this subtext is aimed at a political system that, as constitutionally organized, may not detach itself from civil society and make itself independent vis-à-vis the periphery. Civil disobedience thereby refers to its own origins in a civil society that in crisis situations actualizes the normative contents of constitutional democracy in the medium of public opinion and summons it against the systemic inertia of institutional politics.

This *self-referential character* is emphasized in the definition that Cohen and Arato have proposed, drawing on considerations raised by Rawls, Dworkin, and me:

> Civil disobedience involves illegal acts, usually on the part of collective actors, that are public, principled, and symbolic in character, involved primarily nonviolent means of protest, and appeal to the capacity for reason and the sense of justice of the populace. The aim of civil disobedience is to persuade public opinion in civil and political society . . . that a particular law or policy is illegitimate and a change is warranted. Collective actors involved in civil disobedience invoke the utopian principles of constitutional democracies, appealing to the ideas of fundamental rights or democratic legitimacy. Civil disobedience is thus a means for reasserting the link between civil and political society . . . when legal attempts at exerting the influence of the former on the latter have failed and other avenues have been exhausted.[viii]

This interpretation of civil disobedience manifests the self-consciousness of a civil society confident that at least in a crisis it can increase the pressure of a mobilized public on the political system to the point where the latter switches into the conflict mode and neutralizes the unofficial countercirculation of power.

[vii]J. Rawls, *A Theory of Justice* (Cambridge, Mass., 1971), p. 364.

[viii]Cohen and Arato, *Civil Society*, pp. 587ff.

Beyond this, the justification of civil disobedience relies on a *dynamic understanding* of the constitution as an unfinished project. From this long-term perspective, the constitutional state does not represent a finished structure but a delicate and sensitive—above all fallible and revisable—enterprise, whose purpose is to realize the system of rights *anew* in changing circumstances, that is, to interpret the system of rights better, to institutionalize it more appropriately, and to draw out its contents more radically. This

is the perspective of citizens who are actively engaged in realizing the system of rights. Aware of, and referring to, changed contexts, such citizens want to overcome in practice the tension between social facticity and validity. Although legal theory cannot adopt this participant perspective as its own, it can reconstruct the paradigmatic *understanding* of law and democracy that guides citizens whenever they form an idea of the structural constraints on the self-organization of the legal community in their society.

❖

Introduction to
"The Tasks of a Critical Theory of Society"

In this selection, Habermas extends his analysis of the public sphere into a more general theory of communication in modern societies. Central to the essay are several key concepts: system, lifeworld, uncoupling, the colonization of the lifeworld, and communicative action. In Habermas's account, all societies can be understood theoretically as composed of two primary components—the system and the lifeworld. The system is that set of interrelated social structures, like the state and economy, that form the primary basis for the organization of social life. The lifeworld is the arena of everyday, human interaction carved out of ongoing and negotiated interpersonal communication.

Habermas suggests that an optimally functioning society is one in which systemic processes are neatly coupled with the lifeworld dynamics of everyday communication and consensus formation. Such interrelations allow for rationalized and differentiated system-level structures to emerge that are grounded in and guided by the critical and communicative demands of the lifeworld. Habermas argues, however, that in the modern world, system and lifeworld have become "uncoupled," resulting in the emergence of "steering crises" and "pathologies in the lifeworld." The most striking disturbance has been within the lifeworld, which has been "colonized" by reified and increasingly self-insulated systemic processes. The result of this "colonization of the lifeworld" is that system-level institutions, most notably economic institutions and governments, operate with virtual autonomy from the normative checks and balances that can only emanate from the lifeworld, and that the lifeworld itself has become radically deformed. Here, the "steering media" that guide systemic institutional processes (money and power) penetrate the lifeworld and displace meaningful social interaction and symbolic communication as a primary basis for social relationships. It is the "task of a critical theory of society" to critique existing social structures in order to rebalance the relationship between system and lifeworld and thus create the conditions necessary for producing a free and democratic social order.

Habermas places his hopes for the emancipation of humanity in the counterweight of social movements and, in particular, the power of communicative action. While the system is steered by money and power and a form of instrumental rationality that emphasizes efficiency and means over ends, communicative action emanates from within the lifeworld. As such, communicative action is grounded in a distinct form of rationality (i.e., "communicative rationality") that makes possible a discourse capable of generating social solidarity, mutual understandings, and personal and collective identities. For their part, new social movements mount protests and give air to public opinion in an effort to defend and restore "endangered ways of life" that cannot be secured through money and power. Rather, the conflicts they give voice to "arise in domains of cultural reproduction, social integration, and socialization." Their aims speak not to economic or political transformations but, rather, to reestablishing control over "the grammar of forms of life."

❖

The Tasks of a Critical Theory of Society (1987)

Jürgen Habermas

In respects a theory of capitalist modernization developed by some means of a theory of communicative action does follow the Marxian model. It is *critical* both of contemporary social sciences and of the social reality they are supposed to grasp. It is critical of the reality of developed societies inasmuch as they do not make full use of the learning potential culturally available to them, but deliver themselves over to an uncontrolled growth of complexity. . . . This increasing system complexity encroaches upon nonrenewable supplies like a quasinatural force; not only does it out-flank traditional forms of life, it attacks the communicative infrastructure of largely rationalized lifeworlds. But the theory is also critical of social-scientific approaches that are incapable of deciphering the paradoxes of societal rationalization because they make complex social systems their object only from one or another abstract point of view, without accounting for the historical constitution of their object domain (in the sense of a reflexive sociology). Critical social theory does not relate to established lines of research as a competitor; starting from its concept of the rise of modern societies, it attempts to explain the specific limitations and the relative rights of those approaches.

If we leave to one side the insufficiently complex approach of behaviorism, there are today three main lines of inquiry occupied with the phenomenon of modern societies. We cannot even say that they are in competition, for they scarcely have anything to say to one another.

Efforts at theory comparison do not issue in reciprocal critique; fruitful critique that might foster a common undertaking can hardly be developed across these distances, but at most within one or another camp. There is a good reason for this mutual incomprehension: the object domains of the competing approaches do not come into contact, for they are the result of one-sided abstractions that unconsciously cut the ties between system and lifeworld constitutive for modern societies.

Taking as its point of departure the work of Max Weber, and also in part Marxist historiography, an approach—sometimes referred to as the history of society [*Gesellschaftsgeschichte*]—has been developed that is comparative in outlook, typological in procedure, and, above all, well informed about social history. The dynamics of class struggle are given greater or lesser weight according to the positions of such different authors as Reinhard Bendix, R. Lepsius, C. Wright Mills, Barrington Moore, and Hans-Ulrich Wehler; however, the theoretical core is always formed by assumptions about the structural differentiation of society in functionally specified systems of action. Close contact with historical research prevents the *theory of structural differentiation* from issuing in a more strongly theoretical program, for instance, in some form of systems functionalism. Rather, analysis proceeds in such a way that modernization processes are referred to the level of institutional differentiation. The functionalist

SOURCE: From *The Theory of Communicative Action, Volume 1: Reason and Rationalization of Society* by Jurgen Habermas. Introduction and English translation copyright © 1984 by Beacon Press. German text: copyright © 1981 by Suhrkamp Verlag, Frankfurt am Main. Reprinted by permission of Beacon Press, Boston.

mode of investigation is not so widely separated from the structuralist mode that the potential competition between the two conceptual strategies could develop. The modernization of society is, to be sure, analyzed in its various ramifications, but a one-dimensional idea of the whole process of structural differentiation predominates. It is not conceived as a second-order differentiation process, as an uncoupling of system and lifeworld that, when sufficiently advanced, makes it possible for media-steered subsystems to react back on structurally differentiated lifeworlds. As a result, the pathologies of modernity do not come into view as such from this research perspective; it lacks the conceptual tools to distinguish adequately between (*a*) the structural differentiation of the lifeworld, particularly of its societal components, (*b*) the growing autonomy of action systems that are differentiated out via steering media, as well as the internal differentiation of these subsystems, and finally (*c*) those differentiation processes that simultaneously dedifferentiate socially integrated domains of action in the sense of colonizing the lifeworld.

Taking as its point of departure neoclassical theory, on the one hand, and social-scientific functionalism, on the other, a *systems-theoretical approach* has established itself above all in economics and in the sciences of administration. These system sciences have, so to speak, grown up in the wake of the two media-steered subsystems. As long as they were occupied chiefly with the internal complexity of the economic and administrative systems, they could rest content with sharply idealized models. To the extent that they had to bring the restrictions of the relevant social environments into their analyses, however, there arose a need for an integrated theory that would also cover the interaction between the two functionally intermeshed subsystems of state and economy.

It is only with the next step in abstraction, which brought society as a whole under systems-theoretical concepts, that the system sciences over drew their account. The systems theory of society first developed by Parsons and consistently carried further by Luhmann views the rise and development of modern society solely in the functionalist perspective of growing system complexity. Once systems functionalism is cleansed of the dross of the sociological tradition, it becomes insensitive to

social pathologies that can be discerned chiefly in the structural features of socially integrated domains of action. It hoists the vicissitudes of communicatively structured lifeworlds up to the level of media dynamics; by assimilating them, from the observer perspective, to disequilibria in intersystemic exchange relations, it robs them of the significance of identity-threatening deformations, which is how they are experienced from the participant perspective.

Finally, from phenomenology, hermeneutics, and symbolic interactionism there has developed an *action-theoretical approach*. To the extent that the different lines of *interpretive sociology* proceed in a generalizing manner at all, they share an interest in illuminating structures of worldviews and forms of life. The essential part is a theory of everyday life, which can also be linked up with historical research, as it is in the work of E. P. Thompson. To the extent that is done, modernization processes can be presented from the viewpoint of the lifeworlds specific to different strata and groups; the everyday life of the subcultures dragged into these processes are disclosed with the tools of anthropological research. Occasionally these studies condense to fragments of history written from the point of view of its victims. Then modernization appears as the sufferings of those who had to pay for the establishment of the new mode of production and the new system of states in the coin of disintegrating traditions and forms of life. Research of this type sharpens our perception of historical asynchronicities; they provide a stimulus to critical recollection in Benjamin's sense. But it has a little place for the internal systemic dynamics of economic development, of nation and state building, as it does for the structural logics of rationalized lifeworlds. As a result, the subcultural mirrorings in which the sociopathologies of modernity are refracted and reflected retain the subjective and accidental character of *uncomprehended* events.

Whereas the theory of structural differentiation does not sufficiently separate systemic and lifeworld aspects, systems theory and action theory, each isolates and overgeneralizes one of the two aspects. The methodological abstractions have the same result in all three cases. The theories of modernity made possible by these approaches remain insensitive to what Marx called "real abstractions"; the latter can be gotten at through an analysis that at once traces the rationalization of lifeworlds *and* the growth in complexity of media-steered subsystems, and that keeps the paradoxical nature of their interference in sight. As we have seen, it is possible to speak in a nonmetaphorical sense of paradoxical conditions of life if the structural differentiation of lifeworlds is described as rationalization. Social pathologies are not to be measured against "biological" goal states but in relation to the contradictions in which communicatively intermeshed interaction can get caught because deception and self-deception can gain objective power in an everyday practice reliant on the facticity of validity claims.

By "real abstractions" Marx was referring not only to paradoxes experienced by those involved as deformations of their lifeworld, but above all to paradoxes that could be gotten at only through an analysis of reification (or of rationalization). It is in this latter sense that we call "paradoxical" those situations in which systemic relief mechanisms made possible by the rationalization of the lifeworld turns around and overburden the communicative infrastructure of the lifeworld. After attempting to render a fourth approach to inquiry—the *genetic structuralism* of developmental psychology—fruitful for appropriating Weber's sociology of religion, Mead's theory of communication, and Durkheim's theory of social integration, I proposed that we read the Weberian rationalization thesis in that way. The basic conceptual framework I developed by these means was, naturally, not meant to be an end in itself; rather, it has to prove itself against the task of explaining those pathologies of modernity that other approaches pass right by for methodological reasons. . . .

With these illustrative remarks I also intend to emphasize the fully open character and the flexibility of an approach to social theory whose fruitfulness can be confirmed only in the ramifications of social and philosophical research. As to what social theory can accomplish in and of itself—it resembles the focusing power of a magnifying glass. Only when the social sciences no longer sparked a single thought would the time for social theory be past.

(a) On the forms of integration in postliberal societies. Occidental rationalism arose within the framework of bourgeois capitalist societies.

For this reason, following Marx and Weber I have examined the initial conditions of modernization in connection with societies of this type and have traced the capitalist path of development. In postliberal societies there is a fork in this path: modernization pushes forward in one direction through endogenously produced problems of economic accumulation, in the other through problems arising from the state's efforts at rationalization. Along the developmental path of organized capitalism, a political order of welfare-state mass democracy took shape. In some places, however, under the pressure of economic crises, the mode of production, threatened by social disintegration, could be maintained for a time only in the political form of authoritarian or fascist orders. Along the developmental path of bureaucratic socialism a political order of dictatorship by state parties took shape. In recent years Stalinist domination by force has given way to more moderate, post-Stalinist regimes; the beginnings of a democratic workers' movement and of democratic decision-making processes within the Party are for the time visible only in Poland. Both the fascist and the democratic deviations from the two dominant patterns depend rather strongly, it seems, on national peculiarities, particularly on the political culture of the countries in question. At any rate, these branchings make historical specifications necessary even at the most general level of types of societal integration and of corresponding social pathologies. If we permit ourselves to simplify in an ideal-typical manner and limit ourselves to the two dominant variants of postliberal societies, and if we start from the assumption that alienation phenomena arise as systemically induced deformations of the lifeworld, then we can take a few steps toward a comparative analysis of principles of societal organizations, kinds of crisis tendencies, and forms of social pathology.

On our assumption, a considerably rationalized lifeworld is one of the initial conditions for modernization processes. It must be possible to anchor money and power in the lifeworld as media, that is, to institutionalize them by means of positive law. If these conditions are met, economic and administrative systems can be differentiated out, systems that have a complementary relation to one another and enter into interchanges with their environments via steering media. At this level of system differentiation modern societies arise, first capitalist societies, and later—setting themselves off from those— bureaucratic-socialist societies. A capitalist path of modernization opens up as soon as the economic system develops its own intrinsic dynamic of growth and, with its endogenously produced problems, takes the lead, that is, the evolutionary primacy, for society as a whole. The path of modernization runs in another direction when, on the basis of state ownership of most of the means of production and an institutionalized one-party rule, the administrative action system gains a like autonomy in relation to the economic system.

To the extent that these organizational principles are established, there arise interchange relations between the two functionally interlocked subsystems and the societal components of the lifeworld in locked subsystems and the societal components of the lifeworld in which the media are anchored. The lifeworld, more or less relieved of tasks of material reproduction, can in turn become more differentiated in its symbolic structures and can set free the inner logic of development of cultural modernity. At the same time, the private and public spheres are now set off as the environments of the system. According to whether the economic system or the state apparatus attains evolutionary primacy, either private households or politically relevant memberships are the points of entry for crises that are shifted from the subsystems to the lifeworld. In modernized societies disturbances in the material reproduction of the lifeworld take the form of stubborn systemic disequilibria; the latter either take effect directly as *crises* or they call forth *pathologies* in the lifeworld.

Steering crises were first studied in connection with the business cycle of market economies. In bureaucratic socialism, crisis tendencies spring from self-blocking mechanisms in planning administrations, as they do on the other side from endogenous interruptions of accumulation processes. Like the paradoxes of exchange rationality, the paradoxes of planning rationality can be explained by the fact that rational action orientations come into contradiction with themselves through unintended systemic effects. These crisis tendencies are worked through not only in the subsystem in which they arise, but also in the complementary action system into which they can be shifted. Just as the capitalist economy relies on organizational performances of the state, the socialist planning bureaucracy has to rely on self-steering performances of the economy. Developed capitalism swings between the contrary policies of "the market's self-healing powers" and state interventionism. The structural dilemma is even clearer on the other side, where policy oscillates hopelessly between increased central planning and decentralization, between orienting economic programs toward investment and toward consumption.

These *systemic disequilibria* become *crises* only when the performances of economy and state remain manifestly below an established level of aspiration and harm the symbolic reproduction of the lifeworld by calling forth conflicts and reactions of resistance there. It is the societal components of the lifeworld that are directly affected by this. Before such conflicts threaten core domains of social integration, they are pushed to the periphery—periphery—before anomic conditions arise there are appearances of withdrawal of legitimation or motivation. But when steering crises—that is, perceived disturbances of material reproduction—are successfully intercepted by having recourse to lifeworld resources, pathologies arise in the lifeworld. These resources appear as contributions to cultural reproduction, social integration, and socialization. For the continued existence of the economy and the state, it is the resources that contribute to the maintenance of society that are relevant, for it is here, in the institutional orders of the lifeworld, that subsystems are anchored.

We can represent the replacement of steering crises with lifeworld pathologies as follows: anomic conditions are avoided, and legitimations and motivations important for maintaining institutional orders are secured, at the expense of, and through the ruthless exploitation of, other resources. Culture and personality come under attack for the sake of warding off crises and stabilizing society. Instead of manifestations of anomie (and instead of the withdrawal of legitimation and motivation in place of anomie), phenomena of alienation and the unsettling of collective identity emerge. I have traced such phenomena back to a colonization of the lifeworld and characterized them as a reification of the communicative practice of everyday life.

However, deformations of the lifeworld take the form of a reification of communicative relations only in capitalist societies, that is, only where the private household is the point of incursion for the displacement of crises into the lifeworld. This is not a question of the overextension of a single medium but of the monetarization and bureaucratization of the sphere of action of employees and of consumers, of citizens and of clients of state bureaucracies. Deformations of the lifeworld take a different form in societies in which the points of incursion for the penetration of crises into the lifeworld are politically relevant memberships. There too, in bureaucratic-socialist societies, domains of action that are dependent on social integration are switched over to mechanisms of system integration. But instead of the reification of communicative relations we find the shamming of communicative relations in bureaucratically desiccated, forcibly "humanized" domains of pseudopolitical intercourse in an overextended and administered public sphere. This pseudopoliticization is symmetrical to reifying privatization in certain respects. The lifeworld is not directly assimilated to the system, that is, to legally regulated, formally organized domains of action; rather, systemically self-sufficient organizations are fictively put back into a simulated horizon of the lifeworld. While the system is draped out as the lifeworld, the lifeworld is absorbed by the system.

(b) Family socialization and ego development. The diagnosis of an uncoupling of system and lifeworld also offers a different perspective for judging the structural change in family, education, and personality development. For a psychoanalysis viewed from a Marxist standpoint, the theory of the Oedipus complex, interpreted sociologically, was pivotal for explaining how the functional imperatives of the economic system could establish themselves in the superego structures of the dominant social character. Thus, for example, Löwenthal's studies of drama and fiction in the nineteenth century served to show in detail that the constraints of the economic system—concentrated in status hierarchies, occupational roles, and gender stereotypes—penetrated into the innermost aspects of life history via intra-familial dependencies and patterns of socialization. The intimacy of highly personalized relations merely concealed the blind force of economic interdependencies that had become autonomous in relation to the private sphere—a force that was experienced as "fate."

Thus the family was viewed as the agency through which systemic imperatives influenced our instinctual vicissitudes; its communicative internal structure was not taken seriously. Because the family was always viewed only from functionalist standpoints and was never given its own weight from structuralist points of view, the epochal changes in the bourgeois family could be misunderstood; in particular, the results of the leveling out of paternal authority could be interpreted wrongly. It seemed as if systemic imperatives now had the chance—by way of a mediatized family—to take hold directly of intrapsychic events, as process that the soft medium of mass culture could at most slow down. If, by contrast, we *also* recognize in the structural transformation of the bourgeois family the inherent rationalization of the lifeworld; if we see that, in egalitarian patterns of relationship, in individual forms of intercourse, and in liberalized child-rearing practices, some of the potential for rationality ingrained in communicative action is *also* released; then the changed conditions of socialization in the middle-class nuclear family appear in a different light.

Empirical indicators suggest the growing autonomy of a nuclear family in which socialization processes take place through the medium of largely deinstitutionalized communicative action. Communicative infrastructures are developing that have freed themselves from latent entanglements in systemic dependencies. The contrast between the *homme* who is educated to freedom and humanity in the intimate sphere and the *citoyen* who obeys functional necessities in the sphere of social labor was always an ideology. But it has now taken on a different meaning. Familial lifeworlds see the imperatives of the economic and administrative systems coming at them from outside, instead of being mediated by them from behind. In the families and their environments we can observe a polarization between communicatively structured and formally organized domains of action; this places socialization processes under different conditions and exposes them to a different type of danger. This view is supported by two rough sociopsychological clues: the diminishing significance of the Oedipal problematic and the growing significance of adolescent crises.

For some time now, psychoanalytically trained physicians have observed a symptomatic change in the typical manifestations of illness. Classical hysterias have almost died out; the number of compulsion neuroses is drastically reduced; on the other hand, narcissistic disturbances are on the increase. Christopher Lasch has taken this symptomatic change as the occasion for a diagnosis of the times that goes beyond the clinical domain.[i] It confirms the fact that the significant changes in the present escape sociopsychological explanations that start from the Oedipal problematic, from an internalization of societal repression which is simply masked by parental authority. The better explanations start from the premise that the communications structures that have been set free in the family provide conditions for socialization that are as demanding as they are vulnerable. The potential for irritability grows, and with it the probability that instabilities in parental behavior will have a comparatively strong effect—a subtle neglect.

The other phenomenon, a sharpening of the adolescence problematic, also speaks for the socializatory significance of the uncoupling of system and lifeworld. Systemic imperatives do not so much insinuate themselves into the family, establish themselves in systematically distorted communication, and inconspicuously intervene in the formation of the self as, rather, openly come at the family from outside. As a result, there is a tendency toward disparities between competences, attitudes, and motives, on the one hand, and the functional requirements of adult roles on the other. The problem of detaching oneself from the family and forming one's own identity have in any case turned adolescent development (which is scarcely safeguarded by institutions anymore) into a critical test for the ability of the coming generation to connect up with the preceding one. When the

conditions of socialization in the family are no longer functionally in tune with the organizational membership conditions that the growing child will one day have to meet, the problems that young people have to solve in their adolescence become insoluble for more and more of them. One indication of this is the social and even political significance that youth protest and withdrawal cultures have gained since the end of the 1960s.

This new problem situation cannot be handled with the old theoretical means. If we connect the epochal changes in family socialization with the rationalization of the lifeworld, socializatory interaction becomes the point of reference for the analysis of ego development, and systematically distorted communication— the reification of interpersonal relations—the point of reference for investigating pathogenesis. The theory of communicative action provides a framework within which the structural model of ego, id, and superego can be recast. Instead of an instinct theory that represents the relation of ego to inner nature in terms of a philosophy of consciousness—on the model of relations between subject and object—we have a theory of socialization that connects Freud with Mead, gives structures of intersubjectivity their due, and replaces hypotheses about instinctual vicissitudes with assumptions about identity information. This approach can (i) appropriate more recent developments in psychoanalytic research, particularly the theory of object relations and ego psychology, (ii) take up the theory of defense mechanisms in such a way that the interconnections between intrapsychic communication barriers and communication disturbances at the interpersonal level become comprehensible, and (iii) use the assumptions about mechanisms of conscious and unconscious mastery to establish a connection between orthogenesis and pathogenesis. The cognitive and sociomoral development studied in the Piagetian tradition takes place in accord with structural patterns that provide a reliable foil for intuitively recorded clinical deviations.

(c) Mass media and mass culture. With its distinction between system and lifeworld, the theory of communicative action brings out the

---

[i] Christopher Lasch, *The Culture of Narcissism* (New York, 1978).

independent logic of socializatory interaction; the corresponding distinction between two contrary types of communication media makes us sensitive to the ambivalent potential of mass communications. The theory makes us skeptical of the thesis that the essence of the public sphere has been liquidated in postliberal societies. According to Horkheimer and Adorno, the communication flows steered via mass media *take the place of* those communication structures that had once made possible public discussion and self-understanding by citizens and private individuals. With the shift from writing to images and sounds, the electronic media—first film and radio, later television—present themselves as an apparatus that completely permeates and dominates the language of everyday communication. On the one hand, it transforms the authentic content of modern culture into the sterilized and ideologically effective stereotypes of a mass culture that merely replicates what exists; on the other hand, it uses up a culture cleansed of all subversive and transcending elements for an encompassing system of social controls, which is spread over individuals, in part reinforcing their weakened internal behavioral controls, in part replacing them. The mode of functioning of the culture industry is said to be a mirror image of the psychic apparatus, which, as long as the internalization of paternal authority was still functioning, had subjected instinctual nature to the control of the superego in the way that technology had subjected outer nature to its domination.

Against this theory we can raise the empirical objections that can always be brought against stylizing oversimplifications—that it proceeds ahistorically and does not take into consideration the structural change in the bourgeois public sphere; that it is not complex enough to take account of the marked national differences—from differences between private, public-legal, and state-controlled organizational structures of broadcasting agencies, to differences in programming, viewing practices, political culture, and so forth. But there is an even more serious objection, and objection in principle, that can be derived from the dualism of media discussed above.

I distinguished two sorts of media that can ease the burden of the (risky and demanding) coordinating mechanism of reaching understanding: on the one hand, steering media, via which subsystems are differentiated out of the lifeworld, on the other hand, generalized forms of communication, which do not replace reaching agreement in language but merely condense it, and thus remain tied to lifeworld contexts. Steering media uncouple the coordination of action from building consensus in language altogether and neutralize it in regard to the alternative of coming to an agreement or failing to do so. In the other case we are dealing with a specialization of linguistic processes of consensus formation that remains dependent on recourse to the resources of the lifeworld background. The mass media belong to these generalized forms of communication. They free communication processes from the provinciality of spatiotemporally restricted contexts and permit public spheres to emerge, through establishing the abstract simultaneity of a virtually present network of communication contents far removed in space and time and through keeping messages available for manifold contexts.

These media publics hierarchize and at the same time remove restrictions on the horizon of possible communication. The one aspect cannot be separated from the other—and therein lies their ambivalent potential. Insofar as mass media one-sidedly channel communication flows in a centralized network—from the center to the periphery or from above to below—they considerably strengthen the efficiency of social controls. But tapping this authoritarian potential is always precarious because there is a counterweight of emancipatory potential built into communication structures themselves. Mass media can simultaneously contextualize and concentrate processes of reaching understanding, but it is only in the first instance that they relieve interaction from yes/no responses to criticizable validity claims. Abstracted and clustered though they are, these communications cannot be reliably shielded from the possibility of opposition by responsible actors.

When communications research is not abridged in an empiricist manner and allows for dimensions of reification in communicative everyday practice, it confirms this ambivalence. Again and again reception research and program analysis have provided illustrations of the theses in culture criticism that Adorno, above all, developed with a certain overstatement. In the meantime, the same energy has been put into working out the contradictions resulting from the facts that

- the broadcasting networks are exposed to competing interests; they are not able to smoothly integrate economic, political and ideological, professional and aesthetic viewpoints;
- normally the mass media cannot, without generating conflict, avoid the obligations that accrue to them from their journalistic mission and the professional code of journalism;
- the programs do not only, or even for the most part, reflect the standards of mass culture; even when they take the trivial forms of popular entertainment, they may contain critical messages— "popular culture as popular revenge";[ii]
- ideological messages miss their audience because the intended meaning is turned into its opposite under conditions of being received against a certain subcultural background;
- the inner logic of everyday communicative practice sets up defenses against the direct manipulative intervention of the mass media; and
- the technical development of electronic media does not necessarily move in the direction of centralizing networks, even though "video pluralism" and "television democracy" are at the moment not much more than anarchist visions.

(d) Potentials for protest. My thesis concerning the colonization of the lifeworld, for which Weber's theory of societal rationalization served as a point of departure, is based on a critique of functionalist reason, which agrees with the critique of instrumental reason only in its intention and in its ironic use of the word reason. One major difference is that the theory of communicative action conceives of the lifeworld as a sphere in which processes of reification do not appear as mere reflexes—as manifestations of a repressive integration emanating from an oligopolistic economy and an authoritarian state. In this respect, the earlier critical theory merely repeated the errors of Marxist functionalism. My references to the socializatory relevance of the uncoupling of system and lifeworld and my

remarks on the ambivalent potentials of mass media and mass culture show the private and public spheres in the light of a rationalized lifeworld in which system imperatives *clash with* independent communication structures. The transposition of communicative action to media-steered interactions and the deformation of the structures of a damaged intersubjectivity are by no means predecided processes that might be distilled from a few global concepts. The analysis of lifeworld pathologies calls for an (unbiased) investigation of tendencies *and* contradictions. The fact that in welfare-state mass democracies class conflict has been institutionalized and thereby pacified does not mean that protest potential has been altogether laid to rest. But the potentials for protest emerge now along different lines of conflict—just where we would expect them to emerge if the thesis of the colonization of the lifeworld were correct.

In the past decade or two, conflicts have developed in advanced Western societies that deviate in various ways from the welfare-state pattern of institutionalized conflict over distribution. They no longer flare up in domains of material reproduction; they are no longer channeled through parties and associations; and they can no longer be allayed by compensations. Rather, these new conflicts arise in domains of cultural reproduction, social integration, and socialization; they are carried out in subinstitutional— or at least extraparliamentary—forms of protest; and the underlying deficits reflect a reification of communicatively structure domains of action that will not respond to the media of money and power. The issue is not primarily one of compensations that the welfare state can provide, but of defending and restoring endangered ways of life. In short, the new conflicts are not ignited by distribution problems but by questions having to do with the grammar of forms of life.

This new type of conflict is an expression of the "silent revolution" in values and attitudes that R. Inglehart has observed in entire populations. Studies by Hildebrandt and Dalton, and by Barnes Kaase, confirm the change in themes from the "old politics" (which turns on questions of economic and social security, internal and military security) to a "new politics." The

---

[ii]D. Kellner, "TV, Ideology and Emancipatory Popular Culture," *Socialist Review* 45 (1979): 13ff.

new problems have to do with quality of life, equal rights, individual self-realization, participation, and human rights. In terms of social statistics, the "old politics" is more strongly supported by employers, workers, and middle-class tradesmen, whereas the new politics finds stronger support in the new middle classes, among the younger generation, and in groups with more formal education. These phenomena tally with my thesis regarding internal colonization.

If we take the view that the growth of the economic-administrative complex sets off processes of erosion in the lifeworld, then we would expect old conflicts to be overlaid with new ones. A line of conflict forms between, on the one hand, a center composed of strata *directly* involved in the production process and interested in maintaining capitalist growth as the basis of the welfare-state compromise, and, on the other hand, a periphery composed of a variegated array of groups that are lumped together. Among the latter are those groups that are further removed from the "productivist core of performance" in late capitalist societies, that have been more strongly sensitized to the self-destructive consequences of the growth in complexity or have been more strongly affected by them. The bond that unites these heterogeneous groups is the critique of growth. Neither the bourgeois emancipation movements nor the struggles of the organized labor movement can serve as a model for this protest. Historical parallels are more likely to be found in the social-romantic movements of the early industrial period, which were supported by craftsmen, plebians, and workers, in the defensive movements of the populist middle class, in the escapist movements (nourished by bourgeois critiques of civilization) undertaken by reformers, the *Wandervögel*, and the like.

The current potentials for protest are very difficult to classify, because scenes, grouping, and topics change very rapidly. To the extent that organizational nuclei are formed at the level of parties or associations, members are recruited from the same diffuse reservoir. The following catchphrases serve at the moment to identify the various currents in the Federal Republic of Germany: the antinuclear and environmental movements; the peace movement (including the theme of north-south conflict); single-issue and local movements; the alternative movement (which encompasses the urban "scene," with its squatters and alternative projects, as well as the rural communes); the minorities (the elderly, gays, handicapped, and so forth); the psychoscene, with support groups and youth sects; religious fundamentalism; the tax-protest movement, school protest by parents' associations, resistance to "modernist" reforms; and, finally, the women's movement. Of international significance are the autonomy movements struggling for regional, linguistic, cultural, and also religious independence.

In this spectrum I will differentiate emancipatory potentials from potentials for resistance and withdrawal. After the American civil rights movement—which has since issued in a particularistic self-affirmation of black subcultures—only the feminist movement stands in the tradition of bourgeois-socialist liberation movements. The struggle against patriarchal oppression and for the redemption of a promise that has long been anchored in the acknowledged universalistic foundations of morality and law gives feminism the impetus of an offensive movement, whereas the other movements have a more defensive character. The resistance and withdrawal movements aim at stemming formally organized domains of action for the sake of communicatively structured domains, and not a conquering new territory. There is an element of particularism that connects feminism with these movements; the emancipation of women means not only establishing formal equality and eliminating male privilege, but overturning concrete forms of life marked by male monopolies. Furthermore, the historical legacy of the sexual division of labor to which women were subjected in the bourgeois nuclear family has given them access to contrasting virtues, to a register of values complementary to those of the male world and opposed to a one-sidedly rationalized everyday practice.

Within resistance movements we can distinguish further between the defense of traditional and social rank (based on property) and a defense that already operates on the basis of a rationalized lifeworld and tries out new ways of cooperating and living together. This criterion makes it possible to demarcate the protest of the traditional middle classes against threats to neighborhoods by large technical projects, the protest of parents against comprehensive schools, the protest against taxes (patterned after the movement in support of Proposition 13 in California), and most of the movements for autonomy, on the one side, from the core of a new conflict potential, on the other: youth and alternative movements for which a critique of growth sparked by themes of ecology and peace is the common focus. It is possible to conceive of these conflicts in terms of resistance to tendencies toward a colonization of the lifeworld, as I hope now to indicate, at least in a cursory way. The objectives, attitudes, and ways of acting prevalent in youth protest groups can be understood, to begin with, as reactions to certain problem situations that are perceived with great sensitivity.

"Green" problems. The intervention of large-scale industry into ecological balances, the growing scarcity of nonrenewable natural resources, as well as demographic developments present industrially developed societies with major problems; but these challenges are abstract at first and call for technical and economic solutions, which must in turn be globally planned and implemented by administrative means. What sets off the protest is rather the tangible destruction of the urban environment; the despoliation of the countryside through housing developments, industrialization, and pollution; the impairment of health through the ravages of civilization, pharmaceutical side-effects, and the like—that is, developments that noticeably affect the organic foundations of the lifeworld and make us drastically aware of standards of livability, of inflexible limits to the deprivation of sensual-aesthetic background needs.

Problems of excessive complexity. There are certainly good reasons to fear military potentials for destruction, nuclear power plants, atomic waste, genetic engineering, the storage and central utilization of private data, and the like. These real anxieties are combined, however, with the terror of a new category of risks that are literally invisible and are comprehensible only from the perspective of the system. These risks invade the lifeworld and at the same time burst its dimensions. The anxieties function as catalysts for a feeling of being overwhelmed in view

of the possible consequences of processes for which we are morally accountable—since we do set them in motion technically and politically—and yet for which we can no longer take moral responsibility—since their scale has put them beyond our control. Here resistance is directed against abstractions that are forced upon the lifeworld, although they go beyond the spatial, temporal, and social limits of complexity of even highly differentiated lifeworlds, centered as these are around the senses.

Overburdening the communicative infrastructure. Something that is expressed rather blatantly in the manisfestations of the psychomovement and renewed religious fundamentalism is also a motivating force behind most alternative projects and many citizens' action groups—the painful manifestations of deprivation in a culturally impoverished and one-sidedly rationalized practice of everyday life. For this reason, ascriptive characteristics such as gender, age, skin color, neighborhood or locality, and religious affiliation serve to build up and separate off communities, to establish subculturally protected communities supported of the search for personal and collective identity. The revaluation of the particular, the natural, the provincial, of social spaces that are small enough to be familiar, of decentralized forms of commerce and despecialized activities, of segmented pubs, simple interactions and dedifferentiated public spheres—all this is meant to foster the revitalization of possibilities for expression and communication that have been buried alive. Resistance to reformist interventions that turn into their opposite, because the means by which they are implemented run counter to the declared aims of social integration, also belongs in this context.

The new conflicts arise along the seams between system and life-world. Earlier I described how the interchange between the private and public spheres, on the one hand, and the economic and administrative action systems, on the other, takes place via the media of money and power, and how it is institutionalized in the roles of employees and consumers, citizens and clients of the state. It is just these roles that are the targets of protest. Alternative practice is directed against the profit-dependent instrumentalization of work in one's vocation, the market-dependent mobilization of labor power, against the extension of pressures of competition and performance all the way down into elementary school. It also takes aim at the monetarization of services, relationships, and time, at the consumerist redefinition of private spheres of life and personal life-styles. Furthermore, the relation of clients to public service agencies is to be opened up and reorganized in a participatory mode, along the lines of self-help organizations. It is above all in the domains of social policy and health policy (e.g., in connection with psychiatric care) that models of reform point in this direction. Finally, certain forms of protest negate the definitions of the role of citizen and the routines for pursuing interests in a purposive-rational manner—forms ranging from the undirected explosion of disturbances by youth ("Zurich is burning!"), through calculated or surrealistic violations of rules (after the pattern of the American civil rights movement and student protests), to violent provocation and intimidation.

According to the programmatic conceptions of some theoreticians, a partial disintegration of the social roles of employees and consumers, of clients and citizens of the state, is supposed to clear the way for counterinstitutions that develop from within the lifeworld in order to set limits to the inner dynamics of the economic and political-administrative action systems. These institutions are supposed, on the one hand, to divert out of the economic system a second, informal sector that is no longer oriented to profit and, on the other hand, to oppose to the party system new forms of a "politics in the first person," a politics that is expressive and at the same time has a democratic base. Such institutions would reverse just those abstractions and neutralizations by which in modern societies labor and political will-formation have been tied to media-steered interaction. The capitalist enterprise and the mass party (as an "ideology-neutral organization for acquiring power") generalize their points of social entry via labor markets and manufactured public spheres; they treat their employees and voters as abstract labor power and voting subjects; and they keep at a distance—as environments of the

system—those spheres in which personal and collective identities can alone take shape. By contrast, the counterinstitutions are intended to dedifferentiate some parts of the formally organized domains of action, remove them from the clutches of the steering media, and return these "liberated areas" to the action-coordinating mechanisms of reaching understanding.

However unrealistic these ideas may be, they are important for the polemical significance of the new resistance and withdrawal movements reacting to the colonization of the lifeworld. This significance is obscured, both in the self-understanding of those involved and in the ideological imputations of their opponents, if the communicative rationality of cultural modernity is rashly equated with the functionalist rationality of self-maintaining economic and administrative action systems—that is, whenever the rationalization of the lifeworld is not carefully distinguished from the increasing complexity of the social system. This confusion explains the fronts—which are out of place and obscure the real political oppositions—between the anti-modernism of the Young Conservatives and the neoconservative defense of postmodernity that robs a modernity at variance itself of its rational content and its perspectives on the future. . . .

The theory of modernity that I have here sketched in broad strokes permits us to recognize the following: In modern societies there is such an expansion of the scope of contingency for interaction loosed from normative contexts that the inner logic of communicative action "becomes practically true" in the deinstitutionalized forms of intercourse of the familial private sphere as well as in a public sphere stamped by the mass media. At the same time, the systemic imperatives of autonomous subsystems penetrate into the lifeworld and, through monetarization and bureaucratization, force an assimilation of communicative action to formally organized domains of action—even in areas where the action-coordinating mechanism of reaching understanding is functionally necessary. It may be that this provocative threat, this challenge that places the symbolic structures of the lifeworld as a whole in question, can account for why they have become accessible to us.

❖

ANTHONY GIDDENS (1938–): A BIOGRAPHICAL SKETCH

Anthony Giddens was born in 1938 in Edmonton, a suburb of London. His father was a clerk who worked for London Transport, and his mother was a housewife. Theirs was a typical middle-class family, and Giddens graduated from grammar school with below-average marks. Nevertheless, he would later attend the University of Hull, where he originally went to study philosophy. However, Giddens found that he excelled in psychology and sociology. Inspired by a lively sociology department led by Peter Worsley, Giddens graduated with a first-class honors degree in sociology in 1959 (Kaspersen 2000:1). He then went on to study at the prestigious London School of Economics (LSE), where he wrote a Weber-inspired master's thesis on the development of sport in England in the nineteenth century. Unfortunately for Giddens, sport was a marginal topic in sociology at the time, leaving him to feel that his supervisors did not take his work all that seriously (Elliot 2001:293).

SOURCE: Used with permission.

From 1961 to 1969, Giddens worked as a lecturer at the University of Leicester alongside several of Europe's top sociologists, including Norbert Elias and Ilya Neustadt. He also held guest lectureships at Simon Fraser University near Vancouver, Canada, and the University of California, Los Angeles. During this time, Giddens began to focus on the connections and divergences between the core classical figures in sociology (Marx, Weber, and Durkheim) and drew up plans for his first book, *Capitalism and Modern Social Theory* (1971). This book was followed by a spate of others, including *New Rules of Sociological Method*[6] (1976), *Studies in Social and Political Theory* (1977), *Central Problems in Social Theory* (1979), and *A Contemporary Critique of Historical Materialism* (1981). His most ambitious work, *The Constitution of Society*, was published in 1984. In this book, Giddens outlined his theory of "structuration," which has made a lasting impact on the field.

In 1970, Giddens became a lecturer at King's College Cambridge and attained a professorship there in 1985. During this time, he continued to focus on structuration theory and historical sociology in such works as *The Nation-State and Violence* (1985) and *Social Theory and Modern Sociology* (1987). In *The Consequences of Modernity* (1990), he turned his attention to the debates over postmodern theory while examining the effects of contemporary society on social relations and the role of trust in everyday life. In 1992, Giddens was named winner of the prestigious Spanish prize, the Prince of Asturias Award for Social Sciences, which recognizes the "scientific, technical, cultural, social and humanistic work performed by individuals, groups or institutions worldwide." In 1996, Giddens left Cambridge to become director of the London School of Economics and Political Science, a position that he still holds.

In the mid-1990s, Giddens's career took a striking new turn as he became an advisor to British Prime Minister Tony Blair, helping popularize the ideas of left-of-center politics known as the "Third Way." His recent books, *The Third Way* (Polity Press 1998) and *Beyond Left and Right* (Polity Press 1994), have influenced debates about the future of democracy in many countries across the world. In the 1990s, his work also

---

[6]The title of Giddens's book connotes the influence of Émile Durkheim, whose book *The Rules of Sociological Method* (1895) was one of the first systematic statements outlining sociology as a distinct field of scientific study.

took a decidedly social psychological turn, as Giddens addressed such issues as the self, identity, intimacy, and sexuality in *Modernity and Self-Identity* (1991) and *The Transformation of Intimacy* (1992). Although Giddens's ongoing political and publishing activities (he is cofounder of Polity Press and consulting editor for two publishing companies) reflect a departure from more formal theoretical concerns, his query into the sociology of the self is not necessarily inconsistent with his earlier work. For Giddens has always held that sociology is "not only about the big institutions, such as government organizations, business firms or societies as a whole. It is very much about the individual and our individual experiences. We come to understand ourselves much better through grasping the wider social forces that influence our lives" (an interview with Anthony Giddens, 1999, http://www.polity.co.uk/giddens/interview.htm).

INTELLECTUAL INFLUENCES AND CORE IDEAS

In this section we provide an overview of Giddens's general theory of social action: the theory of structuration. In developing his approach, Giddens creatively combines the insights of linguistic philosophy, phenomenology, ethnomethodology, psychoanalysis, hermeneutics, structuralism, post-structuralism, dramaturgy, and existentialism (Craib 1992: Chapter 2) to fashion a multidimensional account of social life. At the heart of his theory is the notion that the individual and society form an interdependent duality that he terms the **duality of structure**. By this Giddens means that social structures are both the "medium and outcome" of the practices they organize. To understand what Giddens means by the duality of structure, consider the use of language. Every time an individual communicates with someone, she relies on language to convey the information she wishes to impart. In this way, language serves as the medium or structure that allows the individual to communicate. Moreover, in intentionally using language to communicate, the language itself and the rules that govern its use are unintentionally reproduced as an outcome or consequence of the process of communication (Giddens 1981:171, 172). The significance of Giddens's notion of the duality of structure lies in his attempt to overcome the dualism that plagues social theory, the divide between subjectivist/individualist and objectivist/collectivist approaches that, in fostering either/or views of social life, presents only half of the story.

To more fully appreciate Giddens's position, we must define several core ideas that inform his structuration theory. First is **structure**. Giddens defines structure as rules and resources drawn upon by individuals "in the production and reproduction of social action" (Giddens 1984:19). Evidencing his indebtedness to the work of Alfred Schutz and Harold Garfinkel (see Chapter 6, "Phenomenology and Ethnomethodology"), **rules** are defined as "techniques or generalizable procedures applied in the enactment/ reproduction of social practices" (ibid.:21). Rules are common-sense social recipes that allow us to make sense of the words and conduct of others as well as to form our own words and behavior. **Resources** refer to "'the capabilities of making things happen,' of bringing about particular states of affairs" (Giddens 1981:170). Often this capability is tied to an individual's command over objects, goods, or other persons that then allows him to affect the world around him. In this light, resources are "bases" or "vehicles" for exercising power (Giddens 1979:69) and are by no means equally shared.

Drawing on the work of Ferdinand de Saussure, the founder of linguistic structuralism (see Chapter 8), Giddens argues that structures are properties that exist only in the moment of their use by actors. They have no existence outside of the time and space in which they draw on during social encounters, save as "know how" or "memory traces" on the part of actors. Yet, structures are reproduced at the very moment individuals draw on them to make sense of, and act in, the social world—thus the duality of structure. Recalling de Saussure's distinction between speech (*parole*) and language (*langue*), the duality of structure illustrates how "just as each speech act implies and draws upon the whole structure of language, so each social action implies and draws upon the structure it instantiates" (Craib 1992:42).

Giddens's understanding of structure is a significant departure from conventional sociological uses of the term, particularly those uses that are aligned with functionalist modes of analysis. Functionalist approaches view social structures as external forces that determine or constrain individual action.[7] Like the scaffolding of a building or the anatomy of an organism that is invisible to the observer, social structures are said to work "behind the backs" of individuals, as such structures exist to fulfill the needs of larger social systems. From this viewpoint, functionalists emphasize how the patterned actions of individuals have the unintended consequence or "latent function" of preserving the stability of the existing social order. What is of importance here is not understanding the motives and reasons individuals themselves may possess for carrying out certain behaviors, but rather, uncovering "society's reasons" for requiring such behavior on the part of its members (Giddens 1979:210–215). Ultimately, such reasons entail a society's need to survive and to reproduce the structures—or parts—that compose it.

For Giddens, this account of structure is problematic on a number of fronts. Most important, it ignores the fact that individuals more often than not "know what they are doing and why they are doing it" (Giddens 1981:163). Individuals are "purposeful" actors who draw on the rules and resources at their disposal in order to make their way through everyday life. Structure, then, is both constraining *and* enabling, for while it establishes limitations on action, it is also the medium through which one is able to affect their surroundings. Returning to our example of language, without the words (resources) and the know-how to use them correctly (rules) to describe an event or object, we cannot communicate its meaning to others. In this way structure is constraining; it prevents us from acting. On the other hand, structure is enabling to the extent that possessing both the words and the recipes for their use allows us to communicate the meaning of situations and things to others.

Claiming that individuals are "purposeful" and that they "know what they are doing" regarding their use of rules and resources leads Giddens to consider the issue of **agency**. Agency refers to a person's capability or power to act, to "make a difference," or to intentionally intervene in her world. "Agency concerns events of which an individual is the perpetrator, in the sense that the individual could, at any phase in a given sequence of conduct, have acted differently" (1984:9). This notion of agency likewise entails assumptions regarding the "knowledgeability" or consciousness of actors. Here Giddens draws an important distinction between what we "know" about our actions and our ability to put this knowledge into words—that is, our ability to explain or give

---

[7]In *The Rules of Sociological Method* (1895), Émile Durkheim offered an early functionalist account of the constraints imposed on individual action by society. He noted:

> When I fulfill my obligations as brother, husband, or citizen, when I execute my contracts, I perform duties which are defined, externally to myself and my acts, in law and custom. Even if they conform to my own sentiments and I feel their reality subjectively, such reality is still objective, for I did not create them. . . . The system of signs I use to express my thought, the system of currency I employ to pay my debts, the instruments of credit I utilize in my commercial relations, the practices followed in my profession, etc., function independently of my own use of them. . . . These types of conduct or thought are not only external to the individual but are, moreover, endowed with coercive power, by virtue of which they impose themselves upon him, independent of his individual will.

Figure 9.4   Modes of Consciousness[8]

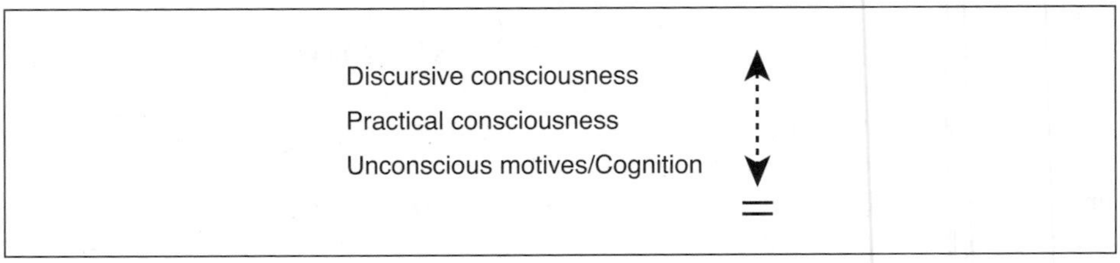

Discursive consciousness
Practical consciousness
Unconscious motives/Cognition

reasons for our conduct. This distinction represents different modes of consciousness that Giddens depicts in Figure 9.4.

Drawing again on phenomenology and ethnomethodology, as well as on Freudian psychoanalysis and Goffman's dramaturgy, Giddens notes that although we often are unable to explicitly state the reasons for our behaviors, it does not necessarily follow that we do not know why we carried them out. Thus, much of our conduct is carried out with only our tacit, unspoken awareness of how and why we do what we do. This tacit awareness is lodged in "practical consciousness" and consists of shared stocks of knowledge, or "mutual knowledge," on the basis of which we are able to coordinate our actions with others. Parallel to Bourdieu's notion of the habitus, **practical consciousness** refers to what individuals know "about social conditions, including especially the conditions of their own action, but cannot express" in words (Giddens 1984:375). For instance, when conversing we employ any number of rules regarding turn-taking, eye contact, body positioning, choice of topics, and speed and volume of speech. Typically these behaviors are simply done; we are not asked to supply explicit reasons or explanations for doing them, nor would it be easy for us to do so should we be asked. The knowledge that informs these behaviors is not immediately accessible to the individual's consciousness; rather, it is practical in nature, "inherent in the capability to 'go on' within the routines of social life" (ibid.:1984:4). While social interaction is shaped largely by tacit adherence to rules governing behaviors such as these, that does not mean that individuals do not understand why they act as they do, nor does it suggest that such behaviors are unintentional.

Discursive consciousness, on the other hand, refers to the capacity to explicitly state reasons or explanations for our conduct. It is "what actors are able to say . . . about social conditions, including especially the conditions of their own action" (ibid.:374). Thus, if you were asked why you gave someone a gift, you might reply, "Because it's his birthday." Or when asked to explain why you refused to lend your notes to another student, you might respond, "Because the last time I did, I never got them back." Yet as Giddens points out, there is no "bar" between discursive and practical consciousness such that one is impermeable to the other. The only differences between the two consist in "what can be said and what is characteristically done," a difference that can be modified through ongoing socialization (ibid.:7).

While no rigid boundary exists between discursive and practical consciousness, there are barriers between discursive consciousness and the individual's unconscious motives for action (represented by the double line in Figure 9.4). By definition, unconscious motives are repressed from conscious awareness or seep into consciousness only in distorted form. Actors, then, typically are unable to offer a discursive account of their unconscious motivations. Nevertheless, Giddens maintains that a complete theory of

---

[8]Figure reproduced from Giddens (1984:7).

action must incorporate an analysis of the unconscious, as it is the source of our wishes and desires that in turn often moves us to pursue particular lines of action.

Giddens's discussion of the conscious/unconscious is offered as a corrective to structural-functionalist and psychoanalytic accounts of agency. From the perspective of the former, individuals' actions stem from system imperatives, and thus their significance lies in how they serve societal purposes of which the individuals themselves are unaware. Learning what individuals say or think about their conduct is of little importance, given that the impetus for action operates behind the backs of individuals who are seen as vessels for the play of larger social forces. For their part, psychoanalytic theories, while focusing on the individual and related concepts such as personality and identity, likewise suggest that conduct often is not consciously guided; in this case it is driven by unknown psychic forces. For Giddens, both accounts underestimate the degree to which individuals are aware of and control their conduct.

To counter these approaches, Giddens offers a "stratification model of action" (1979:53–59, 1984:5–14), which is graphically represented in Figure 9.5. In this model, Giddens combines his perspective on consciousness with a reworking of key structural-functionalist ideas. During social encounters, individuals routinely and continuously monitor their own activity, the behavior of others with whom they are interacting, and the setting in which the interaction is taking place. Moreover, during social encounters individuals routinely maintain a taken-for-granted practical (that is, nondiscursive) understanding or rationalization of the interaction. The motivation of action refers to the wants and desires—often unconsciousness—that impel us to act. Yet, the individual's intentional action is bounded by two dimensions of conduct that remain largely outside of his awareness but that nevertheless profoundly shape the ability to act. Giddens notes that actions are situated within unacknowledged conditions and produce unintended consequences that, in turn, reproduce the unacknowledged conditions. In other words, our intentional actions are often motivated by unconscious wants of which we are unaware, while these same actions often have the unintended consequence of reproducing the social institutions in which they are embedded. As such, the unintended consequences "loop back" to create the unacknowledged conditions of action. Thus, "every process of action is a production of something new, a fresh act; but at the same time all action exists in continuity with the past, which supplies the means of its initiation" (Giddens 1979:70).

As we noted above, Giddens's view of agency and structure is developed out of a critique of structural-functionalist analyses represented by the work of notable scholars such as Talcott Parsons, Robert Merton, and the structural Marxism of Louis Althusser.

Figure 9.5   Giddens's Stratification Model of Action[9]

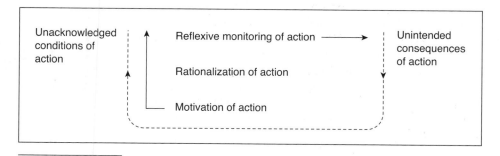

---

[9]Figure reproduced from Giddens (1984:5).

Figure 9.6   Agency and Structure[10]

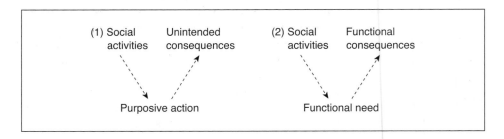

In Figure 9.6, Giddens contrasts his version of agency and structure with that put forward by functionalist interpretations.

Aligned with structuration theory, the first version (1) views social activities (for instance, attending religious services) as purposive action intentionally initiated by individuals for reasons of which they are aware (for instance, searching for moral and spiritual guidance). However, while a degree of rationality is imputed to the actors, this version recognizes that actors' knowledgeability of the conditions of their conduct and its consequences is not perfect or total. This presents the sociologist with an opportunity to uncover unintended consequences that stem from the actors' intentional conduct. Thus, attending religious services does more than provide a sense of moral or spiritual direction to worshippers. For example, it may reinforce feelings of community or solidarity among participants while producing tensions or hostilities directed toward those who do maintain similar beliefs. Yet, whatever the unintended consequences may be, they do not exist as a result of societal "needs" that somehow filter down into the behavior of individuals. Instead, they are a result of intentional activity pursued, albeit, for different purposes.

Giddens associates the second version (2) with functionalist analysis, which does posit the existence of system needs that operate independently of the individuals who fulfill them. Giddens illustrates this version through a critique of Robert Merton's analysis of the Hopi rain dance in which Merton asks us to consider why a rain dance ceremony (social activity) would persist when it fails to produce its manifest or intended function—to make rain. Merton's answer is that, far from a mere "superstition" or "irrational" practice, the rain dance serves crucial societal needs, namely, to ensure the survival of the group by providing an occasion for its members to participate in a common activity and thereby rekindle their attachment to the group. From this perspective, to understand the significance of social activities, it is less important to examine the manifest or intended consequences of the actors involved because such activities are driven by functional needs unknown to the individuals but, nevertheless, accomplished through their conduct. While Merton is right to point out that unintended consequences often usher from social activities, Giddens maintains that he is wrong to suggest that they do so because of "society's reasons" or some "invisible" social need. Thus, while participation in a religious ceremony may produce the unintended consequence of fostering group unity, this consequence does not explain why such activity persists, for societies have no needs, only people do. Social activities, "irrational" or otherwise, persist only because they satisfy the desires or interests of the individuals who engage in them.

[10]Figure reproduced from Giddens (1984:294).

Giddens's understanding of structure and agency is rounded out with his notion of **system**. Here again Giddens is attempting to separate his theory from varieties of structuralism and functionalism that, he argues, in defining a system as a "functioning structure" (Giddens 1981:169) fail to adequately distinguish between the two concepts. In Giddens's structuration theory, social systems are patterned or "reproduced relations between individuals or collectivities, organized as regular social practices" (Giddens 1984:25). As recurring patterns of interaction, social systems do not consist of structures, but rather have "structural properties" that are reproduced across time and space as an unintended consequence of interaction (ibid.:17). Unlike structures, which exist only in the moment of their instantiation (that is, the moment of their use or appearance in interaction) or as enabling and constraining memory traces possessed by actors, social systems do stretch beyond the time and space of a given interaction. Social systems, then, exist "outside" of the particular interactions they shape and are shaped by. Any ongoing, patterned social relation constitutes a social system. Thus, a friendship between two individuals, a family, a hospital, or a university are all forms of systems, as are recurring relations that exist between two or more nations. As Craib notes, "[t]he scope of a system has to do with the amount of time-space that it binds, or rather the extent of its ability to bind time and space" (1992:60, 61). In other words, in "binding" time and space (what Giddens terms "time-space distanciation"), social systems consist of similar practices that are repeated at different times and in different places. Social systems thus make for experiencing social life as orderly and predictable. When two friends meet after not having seen each other for a month, they do not have to remake their relationship anew. Likewise, the system of market relations provides for recurring, predictable practices that bind the activities of individuals and groups across large expanses of time and space. From my home, I can invest in the future profitability of a Russian corporation or purchase a car manufactured with parts from four different countries. In both cases, my activities are embedded in a larger system of relations and practices that extends far beyond the time and space of my involvement.

To illustrate the foregoing discussion, consider the example of writing a check. The ability to write a check is dependent on our common-sense understanding or know-how of the rules regarding the uses of them. More often than not, this knowledge is part of our practical consciousness. When asked, few of us can articulate exactly how a slip of paper can be converted into a monetary value, which is then transferred to the business to which we are giving the slip of paper. What we do know is that the process "works." However, should we take a course in economics or read a few books on the subject, that know-how can become explicit and "converted" to our discursive consciousness. In addition, the rules that govern check-writing structure the activity in ways that make it predictable and orderly. These rules, or structure, are both constraining and enabling. We cannot use just any scrap of paper to write a check, and without a bank account from which the funds can be withdrawn, checks are of little use (unless one is willing to pay a penalty for overdrawing funds—another rule). On the other hand, if we possess the necessary *resources*, the rules governing the use of checks can enable us to purchase goods and services that we would otherwise have to do without. Here we see the duality of structure operating as well, for not only do the rules provide the medium for our action, they are also an unintended outcome, as they are reproduced at the same moment we draw on them. This unintended consequence is not the product of a structural need working behind our back that must be met in order to ensure the stability of the economy. Rather, it is the unintended consequence of actions purposively pursued for reasons of which we are consciously aware. Finally, each instance of writing a check involves a practice that is reproduced countless times and in countless places. As a "regular social practice," check-writing is a structural property of a broader system of economic relations that binds the activities of numerous individuals and groups across time and space. The recurring interactions (either face-to-face or by mail) that involve check-writing are patterned by the system of economic relations that is reproduced each time a check is written.

Photo 9.7   The Duality of Structure: There's More Than Meets the Eye in Writing a Check.
SOURCE: Scott Appelrouth; used with permission.

GIDDENS'S THEORETICAL ORIENTATION

As discussed above and as illustrated in Figure 9.7, Giddens's theory of structuration is an overt attempt to overcome the theoretical dualism that has divided individualist from collectivist perspectives. In doing so, he has created a synthetic general theory of social action that seeks to incorporate elements from each of the quadrants making up our action/order framework. Taking up the issue of action first, Giddens draws from the work of Erving Goffman, phenomenology and ethnomethodology (see Chapters 5 and 6), to develop a view of agency that highlights how individuals make sense of their everyday world. While he by no means rules out the rational dimension of action (indicated by the "agency box" spanning both dimensions), his emphasis lies in exploring the practical knowledgeability of actors, that is, how actors put their common-sense know-how to use as they go about constructing their daily lives. Perhaps, to the extent that Giddens defines resources in terms of the power that actors are capable of exercising over people and things, conduct can then be understood as motivated by calculated attempts to secure advantages. However, Giddens's view of rational motivation speaks less to a strategic weighing of costs and benefits and more to an individual's pragmatic and routine interventions in the world. It is not that an individual is seen as acting in an unreflexive or unthinking manner. Rather, the thinking that guides an individual's conduct is prefaced on the ability to "go on" with the routines making up everyday life.

Figure 9.7   Basic Theoretical Orientation of Giddens's Theory of Structuration

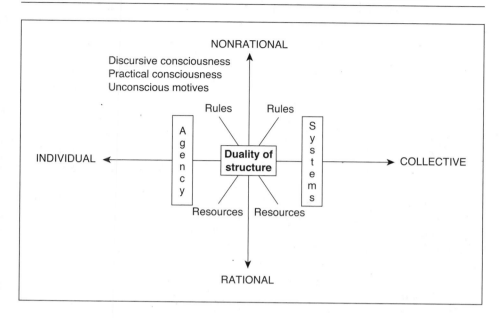

As for the issue of order, Giddens again develops a number of concepts that incorporate both dimensions of the continuum. Consider first his notion of the duality of structure. Giddens defines rules as shared (i.e., collective) recipes of know-how that enable individuals to meaningfully navigate their everyday lives. As generalized procedures for "getting on," rules are not the creation or "property" of isolated individuals. Instead, their existence transcends individuals, as we are born into a culture whose rules and procedures for making sense of the world predate our birth. Yet, these recipes do not exist outside of their use by individuals; they exist only insofar as people apply them. On the other hand, because they are not of our own making, rules constrain, as well as enable, our ability to act. Moreover, an unintended consequence of our individual conduct is the reproduction of the very rules that both enable and constrain our actions. And in reproducing the rules, we are at the same time reproducing the broader social systems in which these rules are embedded and in which our action takes place.

Further insight into Giddens's perspective on the relationship between agency and structure and the theoretical question of order is provided in his discussion of the limits or constraints on freedom of choice and action. Giddens identifies three forms of limits: material constraints, sanctions, and structural constraints. *Material constraints* refer to limitations on choice and action imposed by the "physical capacities of the human body, plus relevant features of the physical environment" (Giddens 1984:174). There are some things we cannot do simply because our bodies have finite abilities. For instance, we cannot live 175 years or survive without food or water for more than one month.

Sanctions refer to constraints on choice and action that are derived from another's exercise of power. (As noted previously, the exercise of power is itself tied to control over resources.) Sanctions range from "the direct application of force or violence, or the threat of such application, to the mild expression of disapproval" (Giddens 1984:175). However, because Giddens maintains that resistance to power is almost always an option, the effectiveness of sanctions, regardless of how oppressive they may be, rests on the compliance of those who are subjected to them. As Giddens remarks:

> Even the threat of death carries no weight unless it is the case that the individual so threatened in some way values life. To say that an individual "had no choice but to act in such and such a way," in a situation of this sort evidently means "Given his/her desire not to die, the only alternative open was to act in the way he or she did." (1984:175)

More often than not, sanctions are "implied" in power relations that are themselves "often most profoundly embedded in modes of conduct which are taken for granted by those who follow them, most especially in routinized behavior, which is only diffusely motivated" (ibid.:175).

Finally, limits on action also take the form of *structural constraints*. Such constraints derive from the fact that individuals are born into preexisting societies possessing structural properties. As we noted previously, although structural properties possess an "objectivity" that constrains (and enables) the conduct of individuals, this objectivity does not imply that individuals "have no choice" but to pursue a particular line of action in a given circumstance. On the contrary, structural constraints "do not operate independently of the motives and reasons that agents have for what they do. . . . The structural properties of social systems do not act, or 'act on,' anyone like forces of nature to 'compel' him or her to behave in a particular way" (Giddens 1984:181). To argue that individuals cannot resist or alter the course of a structural constraint only means "that they are unable to do anything other than conform to whatever the trends in question are, given the motives or goals which underlie their action" (ibid.:178).

Thus, for Giddens the relation between agency and structure is understood best not as an either/or—a dualism—but rather, as a duality in which the individual and society are seen as two sides of one and the same coin. Nevertheless, in emphasizing matters such as consciousness, knowledgeability, intentionality, and choice, his analysis privileges the role of the individual in shaping and reshaping the social world. For Giddens, social life does not move according to some mechanical formula, despite the efforts of those sociologists who seek to locate general laws of social behavior in one or another variant of structural constraint that allegedly governs conduct. For in the end, "the only moving objects in human social relations are individual agents, who employ resources to make things happen, intentionally or otherwise" (Giddens 1984:181).

Readings

In the first excerpt you will read, taken from *The Constitution of Society*, Giddens lays out his general theory of action: the theory of structuration. In the second selection, taken from *The Consequences of Modernity*, Giddens explores the nature of modern society. Here he outlines a number of concepts including trust, risk, the transformation of intimacy, and ontological security. In doing so, he examines how the development of modern institutions has radically changed our relationship with others and our experience of the world around us.

Introduction to *The Constitution of Society*

In this selection from *The Constitution of Society*, "Elements of the Theory of Structuration," you will encounter the key concepts discussed in previous sections. Giddens begins by outlining the "empire-building endeavors" associated with two opposing theoretical traditions: structuralism and interpretative sociology. He then moves to an explication of the theory of structuration, offering his framework as a corrective to the one-sided portraits presented by approaches that unduly emphasize either collectivist or individualist dimensions of social life. To this end, he provides an account of individual agency taking into consideration the different layers of consciousness and the role of intention in action. He then introduces the central concepts of structuration theory, "structure," "system," and the "duality of structure": rules and resources that are both the medium and the outcome of the behavior they recursively organize. The reading concludes with Giddens's discussion of "forms of institution." Here he considers how interaction is linked to structures via the paired "modalities" of communication/signification, power/domination, and sanction/legitimation. The first term in each pair refers to the modalities that shape everyday interaction, while the second term refers to structural dimensions of various institutional orders that are produced in the course of interaction.

❖

The Constitution of Society (1984)

Anthony Giddens

ELEMENTS OF THE THEORY OF STRUCTURATION

In offering a preliminary exposition of the main concepts of structuration theory it will be useful to begin from the divisions which have separated functionalism (including systems theory) and structuralism on the one hand from hermeneutics and the various forms of 'interpretative sociology' on the other. Functionalism and structuralism have some notable similarities, in spite of the otherwise marked contrasts that exist between them. Both tend to express a naturalistic standpoint, and both are inclined towards objectivism. Functionalist thought, from Comte onwards, has looked particularly towards biology as the science providing the closest and most compatible model for social science. Biology has been taken to provide a guide to conceptualizing the structure and the functioning of social systems and to analysing

processes of evolution via mechanisms of adaptation. Structuralist thought, especially in the writings of Lévi-Strauss, has been hostile to evolutionism and free from biological analogies. Here the homology between social and natural science is primarily a cognitive one in so far as each is supposed to express similar features of the overall constitution of mind. Both structuralism and functionalism strongly emphasize the pre-eminence of the social whole over its individual parts (i.e., its constituent actors, human subjects).

In hermeneutic traditions of thought, of course, the social and natural sciences are regarded as radically discrepant. Hermeneutics has been the home of that 'humanism' to which structuralists have been so strongly and persistently opposed. In hermeneutic thought, such as presented by Dilthey, the gulf between subject and social object is at its widest. Subjectivity is the preconstituted centre of the experience of culture and history and as such provides the basic foundation of the social or human sciences. Outside the realm of subjective experience, and alien to it, lies the material world governed by impersonal relations of cause and effect. Whereas for those schools of thought which tend towards naturalism subjectivity has been regarded as something of a mystery, or almost a residual phenomenon, for hermeneutics it is the world of nature which is opaque—which, unlike human activity, can be grasped only from the outside. In interpretative sociologies, action and meaning are accorded primacy in the explication of human conduct; structural concepts are not notably prominent, and there is not much talk of constraint. For functionalism and structuralism, however, structure (in the divergent senses attributed to that concept) has primacy over action, and the constraining qualities of structure are strongly accentuated.

The differences between these perspectives on social science have often been taken to be epistemological, whereas they are in fact also ontological. What is at issue is how the concepts of action, meaning and subjectivity should be specified and how they might relate to notions of structure and constraint. If interpretative sociologies are founded, as it were, upon an imperialism of the subject, functionalism and structuralism propose an imperialism of the social object. One of my principal ambitions in the formulation of structuration theory is to put an end to each of these empire-building endeavours. The basic domain of study of the social sciences, according to the theory of structuration, is neither the experience of the individual actor, nor the existence of any form of society totality, but social practices ordered across space and time. Human social activities, like some self-reproducing items in nature, are recursive. That is to say, they are not brought into being by social actors but continually recreated by them via the very means whereby they express themselves *as* actors. In and through their activities agents reproduce the conditions that make these activities possible. However, the sort of 'knowledgeability' displayed in nature, in the form of coded programmes, is distant from the cognitive skills displayed by human agents. It is in the conceptualizing of human knowledgeability and its involvement in action that I seek to appropriate some of the major contributions of interpretative sociologies. In structuration theory a hermeneutic starting-point is accepted in so far as it is acknowledged that the description of human activities demands a familiarity with the forms of life expressed in those activities.

It is the specifically reflexive form of the knowledgeability of human agents that is most deeply involved in the recursive ordering of social practices. Continuity of practices presumes reflexivity, but reflexivity in turn is possible only because of the continuity of practices that makes them distinctively 'the same' across space and time. 'Reflexivity' hence should be understood not merely as 'self-consciousness' but as the monitored character of the ongoing flow of social life. To be a human being is to be a purposive agent, who both has reasons for his or her activities and is able, if asked, to elaborate discursively upon those reasons (including lying about them). But terms such as 'purpose' or 'intention,' 'reason,' 'motive' and so on have to be treated with caution, since their usage in the philosophical literature has very often been associated with a hermeneutical voluntarism, and because they extricate human action from the contextuality of time-space. Human action occurs as a durée, a continuous flow of conduct, as does cognition. Purposive action is not composed of an aggregate or series of separate intentions, reasons and motives. Thus it is useful to speak of reflexivity as grounded in the continuous monitoring of action which human beings display and expect others to display the reflexive monitoring of action depends upon rationalization, understood here as a process rather than a state and as inherently involved in the competence of agents. An ontology of time-space as constitutive of social practices is basic to the conception of structuration, which *begins* from temporality and thus, in one sense, 'history.' . . .

Structure, Structuration

Let me now move to the core of structuration theory: the concepts of 'structure,' 'system' and 'duality of structure.' The notion of structure (or 'social structure'), of course, is very prominent in the writings of most functionalist authors and has lent its name to the traditions of 'structuralism.' But in neither instance is this conceptualized in a fashion best suited to the demands of social theory. Functionalist authors and their critics have given much more attention to the idea of 'function' than to that of 'structure,' and consequently the latter has tended to be used as a received notion. But there can be no doubt about how 'structure' is usually understood by functionalists and, indeed, by the vast majority of social analysts—as some kind of 'patterning' of social relations or social phenomena. This is often naively conceived of in terms of visual imagery, akin to the skeleton or morphology of an organism or to the girders of a building. Such conceptions are closely connected to the dualism of subject and social object: 'structure' here appears as 'external' to human action, as a source of constraint on the free initiative of the independently constituted subject. As conceptualized in structuralist and post-structuralist thought, on the other hand, the notion of structure is more interesting. Here it is characteristically thought of not as a patterning of presences but as an intersection of presence and absence; underlying codes have to be inferred from surface manifestations.

These two ideas of structure might seem at first sight to have nothing to do with one another, but in fact each relates to important aspects of the structuring of social relations, aspects which, in the theory of structuration, are grasped by recognizing a differentiation between the concepts of 'structure' and 'system.' In analysing social relations we have to acknowledge both a syntagmatic dimension, the patterning of social relations in time-space involving the reproduction of situated practices, and a paradigmatic dimension involving a virtual order of 'modes of structuring' recursively implicated in such reproduction. In structuralist traditions there is usually ambiguity over whether structures refer to a matrix of admissible transformations within a set or to rules of transformation governing the matrix. I treat structure, in its most elemental meaning at least, as referring to such rules (and resources). It is misleading, however, to speak of 'rules of transformation' because all rules are inherently transformational. Structure thus refers, in social analysis, to the structuring properties allowing the 'binding' of time-space in social systems, the properties which make it possible for discernibly similar social practices to exist across varying spans of time and space and which lend them 'systemic' form. To say that structure is a 'virtual order' of transformative relations means that social systems, as reproduced social practices, do not have 'structures' but rather exhibit 'structural properties' and that structure exists, as time-space presence, only in its instantiations in such practices and as memory traces orienting the conduct of knowledgeable human agents. This does not prevent us from conceiving of structural properties as hierarchically organized in terms of the time-space extension of the practices they recursively organize. The most deeply embedded structural properties, implicated in the reproduction of societal totalities, I call *structural principles*. Those practices which have the greatest time-space extension within such totalities can be referred to as *institutions*.

To speak of structure as 'rules' and resources, and of structures as isolable sets of rules and resources, runs a distinct risk of misinterpretation because of certain dominant uses of 'rules' in the philosophical literature.

1. Rules are often thought of in connection with games, as formalized prescriptions. The rules implicated in the reproduction of social systems are not generally like this. Even those which are codified as laws are characteristically subject to a far greater diversity of contestations than the rules of games. Although the use of the rules of games such as chess, etc. as prototypical of the rule-governed properties of social systems is frequently associated with Wittgenstein, more relevant is what Wittgenstein has to say about children's play as exemplifying the routines of social life.

2. Rules are frequently treated in the singular, as if they could be related to specific instances or pieces of conduct. But this is highly misleading if regarded as analogous to the operation of social life, in which practices are sustained in conjunction with more or less loosely organized sets.

3. Rules cannot be conceptualized apart from resources, which refer to the modes whereby transformative relations are actually incorporated into the production and reproduction of social practices. Structural properties thus express forms of *domination* and *power*.

4. Rules imply 'methodical procedures' of social interaction, as Garfinkel in particular has made clear. Rules typically intersect with practices in the contextuality of situated encounters: the range of 'ad hoc' considerations which he identifies are chronically involved with the instantiation of rules and are fundamental to the form of those rules. Every competent social actor, it should be added, is *ipso facto* a social theorist on the level of discursive consciousness and a 'methodological specialist' on the levels of both discursive and practical consciousness.

5. Rules have two aspects to them, and it is essential to distinguish these conceptually, since a number of philosophical writers (such as Winch) have tended to conflate them. Rules relate on the one hand to the constitution of *meaning*, and on the other to the *sanctioning* of modes of social conduct.

I have introduced the above usage of 'structure' to help break with the fixed or mechanical character which the term tends to have in orthodox sociological usage. The concepts to system and structuration do much of the work that 'structure' is ordinarily called upon to perform. In proposing a usage of 'structure' that might appear at first sight to be remote from conventional interpretations of the term, I do not mean to hold that looser versions be abandoned altogether. 'Society,' 'culture' and a range of other forms of sociological terminology can have double usages that are embarrassing only in contexts where a difference is made in the nature of the statements employing them. Similarly, I see no particular objection to speaking of 'class structure,' 'the structure of the industrialized societies' and so on, where these terms are meant to indicate in a general way relevant institutional features of a society or range of societies.

One of the main propositions of structuration theory is that the rules and resources drawn upon in the production and reproduction of social action are at the same time the means of system reproduction (the duality of structure). But how is one to interpret such a claim? In what sense is it the case that when I go about my daily affairs my activities incorporate and reproduce, say, the overall institutions of modern capitalism? What rules are being invoked here in any case? Consider the following possible instances of what rules are:

1. 'The rule defining checkmate in chess is . . .';

2. A formula: $^a n = n^2 + n - 1$;

3. 'As a rule R gets up at 6:00 every day';

4. 'It is a rule that all workers must clock in at 8:00 a.m.'

Many other examples could of course be offered, but these will serve in the present context. In usage (3) 'rule' is more or less equivalent to habit or routine. The sense of 'rule' here is fairly weak, since it does not usually presuppose some sort of underlying precept that the individual is following or any sanction which applies to back up the precept; it is simply something that the person habitually does. Habit is part of routine, and I shall strongly emphasize the importance of routine in social life. 'Rules,' as I understand them, certainly impinge upon numerous aspects of routine practice, but a routine practice is not as such a rule.

Cases (1) and (4) have seemed to many to represent two types or rule, constitutive and regulative. To explain the rule governing checkmate in chess is to say something about what goes into the very making of chess as a game. The rule that workers must clock in at a certain hour, on the other hand, does not help define what work is; it specifies how work is to be carried on. As Searle puts it, regulative rules can usually be paraphrased in the form 'Do X,' or 'If Y, do X.' Some constitutive rules will have this character, but most will have the form 'X counts as Y,' or 'X counts as Y in context C.' That there is something suspect in this distinction, as referring to two types of rule, is indicated by the etymological clumsiness of the term 'regulative rule.' After all, the word 'regulative' already implies 'rule': its dictionary definition is 'control by rules.' I would say of (1) and (4) that they express two aspects of rules rather than two variant types of rule. (1) is certainly part of what chess is, but for those who play chess it has sanctioning or 'regulative' properties; it refers to aspects of play that must be observed. But (4) also has constitutive aspects. It does not perhaps enter into the definition of what 'work' is, but it does enter into that of a concept like 'industrial bureaucracy.' What (1) and (4) direct our attention to are two aspects of rules: their role in the constitution of meaning, and their close connection with sanctions.

Usage (2) might seem the least promising as a way of conceptualizing 'rule' that has any relation to 'structure.' In fact, I shall argue, it is the most germane of all of them. I do not mean to say that social life can be reduced to a set of mathematical principles, which is very far from what I have in mind. I mean that it is in the nature of formulae that we can best discover what is the most analytically effective sense of 'rule' in social theory. The formula $^a n = n^2 + n - 1$ is from Wittgenstein's example of number games. One person writes down a sequence of numbers; a second works out the formula supplying the numbers which follow. What is a formula of this kind, and what is it to understand one? To understand the formula is not to utter it. For someone could utter it and not understand the series; alternatively, it is possible to understand the series without being able to give verbal expression to the formula. Understanding is not a mental process accompanying the solving of the puzzle that the sequence of numbers presents—at least, it is not a mental process in the sense in which the hearing of a tune or a spoken sentence is. It is simply being able to apply the formula in the right context and way is order to continue the series.

A formula is a generalizable procedure—generalizable because it applies over a range of contexts and occasions, a procedure because it allows for the methodical continuation of an established sequence. Are linguistic rules like this? I think they are—much more than they are like the sorts of rule of which Chomsky speaks. And this seems also consonant with Wittgenstein's arguments, or a possible construal of them at any rate. Wittgenstein remarks, 'To understand a language means to be a master of a technique.' This can be read to mean that language use is primarily methodological and that rules of language are methodically applied procedures implicated in the practical activities of day-to-day life. This aspect of language is very important, although not often given much prominence by most followers of Wittgenstein.

Rules which are 'stated,' as (1) and (4) above, are interpretations of activity as well as relating to specific sorts of activities: all codified rules take this form, since they give verbal expression to what is supposed to be done. But rules are procedures of action, aspects of *praxis*. It is by reference to this that Wittgenstein resolves what he first of all sets up as a 'paradox' or rules and rule-following. This is that no course of action can be said to be guided by a rule because every course of action can be made to accord with that rule. However, if such is the case, it is also true that every course of action can be made to conflict with it. There is a misunderstanding here, a confusing of the interpretation or verbal expression of a rule with following the rule.

Let us regard the rules of social life, then, as techniques or generalizable procedures applied in the enactment/reproduction of social practices. Formulated rules—those that are given verbal expression as canons of law, bureaucratic rules, rules of games and so on—are thus codified interpretations of rules rather than rules as such. They should be taken not as exemplifying rules in general but as specific types of formulated rule, which, by virtue of their overt formulation, take on various specific qualities.

So far these considerations offer only a preliminary approach to the problem. How do formulate relate to the practices in which social actors engage, and what kinds of formulae are we most interested in for general purposes of social analysis? As regards the first part of the question, we can say that awareness of social rules, expressed first and foremost in practical consciousness, is the very core of that 'knowledgeability' which specifically characterizes human agents. As social actors, all human beings are highly 'learned' in respect of knowledge which they possess, and apply, in the production and reproduction of day-to-day social encounters; the vast bulk of such knowledge is practical rather than theoretical in character. As Schutz and many others have pointed out, actors employ typified schemes (formulae) in the course of their daily activities to negotiate routinely the situations of social life. Knowledge of procedure, or mastery of the techniques of 'doing' social activity, is by definition methodological. That is to say, such knowledge does not specify all the situations which an actor might meet with, nor could it do so; rather, it provides for the generalized capacity to respond to and influence an indeterminate range of social circumstances.

Those types of rule which are of most significance for social theory are locked into the reproduction of institutionalized practices, that is, practices most deeply sedimented in time-space. The main characteristics of rules relevant to general questions of social analysis can be described as follows:

intensive	tacit	informal	weakly sanctioned
:	:	:	
shallow	discursive	formalized	strongly sanctioned

By rules that are intensive in nature, I mean formulae that are constantly invoked in the course of day-to-day activities, that enter into the structuring of much of the texture of everyday life. Rules of language are of this character. But so also, for example, are the procedures utilized by actors in organizing turn-taking in conversations or in interaction. They may be contrasted with rules which, although perhaps wide in scope, have only a superficial impact upon much of the texture of social life. The contrast is an important one, if only because it is commonly taken for granted among social analysts that the more abstract rules—e.g., codified law—are the most influential in the structuring of social activity. I would propose, however, that many seemingly trivial procedures followed in daily life have a more profound influence upon the generality of social conduct. The remaining categories should be more or less self-explanatory. Most of the rules implicated in the production and reproduction of social practices are only tacitly grasped by actors: they know how to 'go on.' *The discursive formulation of a rule is already an interpretation of it*, and, as I have noted, may in and of itself alter the form of its application. Among rules that are not just discursively formulated but are formally codified, the type case is that of laws. Laws, of course, are among the most strongly sanctioned types of social rules and in modern societies have formally prescribed gradations of retribution. However, it would be a serious mistake to underestimate the strength of informally applied sanctions in respect of a variety of mundane daily practices. Whatever else Garfinkel's

'experiments with trust' might be thought to demonstrate, they do show the extraordinarily compelling force with which apparently minor features of conversational response are invested.

The structuring qualities of rules can be studied in respect, first of all, of the forming, sustaining, termination and reforming of encounters. Although a dazzling variety of procedures and tactics are used by agents in the constitution and reconstitution of encounters, probably particularly significant are those involved in the sustaining of ontological security. Garfinkel's 'experiments' are certainly relevant in this respect. They indicate that the prescriptions involved in the structuring of daily interaction are much more fixed and constraining than might appear from the ease with which they are ordinarily followed. This is surely because the deviant responses or acts that Garfinkel instructed his 'experimenters' to perform disturbed the sense of ontological security of the 'subjects' by undermining the intelligibility of discourse. Breaking or ignoring rules is not, of course, the only way in which the constitutive and sanctioning properties of intensively invoked rules can be studied. But there is no doubt that Garfinkel has helped to disclose a remarkably rich field of study—performing the 'sociologist's alchemy,' the 'transmutation of any patch of ordinary social activity into an illuminating publication.'

I distinguish 'structure' as a generic term from 'structures' in the plural and both from the 'structural properties of social systems.' 'Structure' refers not only to rules implicated in the production and reproduction of social systems but also to resources (about which I have so far not said much but will do so shortly). As ordinarily used in the social sciences, 'structure' tends to be employed with the more enduring aspects of social systems in mind, and I do not want to lose this connotation. The most important aspects of structure are rules and resources recursively involved in institutions. Institutions by definition are the more enduring features of social life. In speaking of the structural properties of social systems I mean their institutionalized features, giving 'solidity' across time and space. I use the concept of 'structures' to get at relations of transformation and mediation which are the 'circuit switches' underlying observed conditions of system reproduction.

Let me now answer the question I originally posed: in what manner can it be said that the conduct of individual actors reproduces the structural properties of larger collectivities? The question is both easier and more difficult to answer than it appears. On a logical level, the answer to it is nothing more than a truism. That is to say, while the continued existence of large collectivities or societies evidently does not depend upon the activities of any particular individual, such collectivities or societies manifestly would cease to be if all the agents involved disappeared. On a substantive level, the answer to the question depends upon issues yet to be broached—those concerning the mechanisms of integration of different types of societal totality. It is always the case that the day-to-day activity of social actors draws upon and reproduces structural features of wider social systems. But 'societies'—as I shall make clear—are not necessarily unified collectivities. 'Social reproduction' must not be equated with the consolidation of social cohesion. The location of actors and of collectivities in different sectors or regions of more encompassing social systems strongly influences the impact of even their habitual conduct upon the integration of societal totalities. Here we reach the limits of linguistic examples which might be used to illustrate the concept of the duality of structure. Considerable illumination of problems of social analysis can be derived from studying the recursive qualities of speech and language. When I produce a grammatical utterance, I draw upon the same syntactical rules as those that utterance helps to produce. But I speak the 'same' language as the other speakers in my language community; we all share the same rules and linguistic practices, give or take a range of relatively minor variations. Such is not necessarily the case with the structural properties of social systems in general. But this is not a problem to do with the concept of the duality of structure as such. It is to do with how social systems, especially 'societies,' should be conceptualized.

The Duality of Structure

Let me summarize the argument thus far [see figure below]. Structure, as recursively organized sets of rules and resources, is out of time and space, save in its instantiations and co-ordination as memory traces, and is marked by an 'absence of the subject.' The social systems in which structure is recursively implicated, on the contrary, comprise the situated activities of human agents, reproduced across time and space. Analysing the structuration of social systems means studying the modes in which such systems, grounded in the knowledgeable activities of situated actors who draw upon rules and resources in the diversity of action contexts, are produced and reproduced in interaction. Crucial to the idea of structuration is the theorem of the duality of structure, which is logically implied in the arguments portrayed above. The constitution of agents and structures are not two independently given sets of phenomena, a dualism, but represent a duality. According to the notion of the duality of structure, the structural properties of social systems are both medium and outcome of the practices they recursively organize. Structure is not 'external' to individuals: as memory traces, and as instantiated in social practices, it is in a certain sense more 'internal' than exterior to their activities in a Durkheimian sense. Structure is not to be equated with constraint but is always both constraining and enabling. This, of course, does not prevent the structured properties of social systems from stretching away, in time and space, beyond the control of any individual actors. Nor does it compromise the possibility that actors' own theories of the social systems which they help to constitute and reconstitute in their activities may reify those systems. The reification of social relations, or the discursive 'naturalization' of the historically contingent circumstances and products of human action, is one of the main dimensions of ideology in social life.

Even the crudest forms of reified thought, however, leave untouched the fundamental

Structure(s)	*System(s)*	*Structuration*
Rules and resources, or sets of transformation relations, organized as properties of social systems	Reproduced relations between actors or collectivities, organized as regular social practices	Conditions governing the continuity of transmutation of structures, and therefore the reproduction of social systems

significance of the knowledgeability of human actors. For knowledgeability is founded less upon discursive than practical consciousness. The knowledge of social conventions, of oneself and of other human beings, presumed in being able to 'go on' in the diversity of contexts of social life is detailed and dazzling. All competent members of society are vastly skilled in the practical accomplishments of social activities and are expert 'sociologists.' The knowledge they possess is not incidental to the persistent patterning of social life but is integral to it. This stress is absolutely essential if the mistakes of functionalism and structuralism are to be avoided, mistakes which, suppressing or discounting agents' reasons—the rationalization of action as chronically involved in the structuration of social practices—look for the origins of their activities in phenomena of which these agents are ignorant. But it is equally important to avoid tumbling into the opposing error of hermeneutic approaches and of various versions of phenomenology, which tend to regard society as the plastic creation of human subjects. Each of these is an illegitimate form of reduction, deriving from a failure adequately to conceptualize the duality of structure. According to structuration theory, the moment of the production of action is also one of reproduction in the contexts of the day-to-day enactment of social life. This is so even during the most violent upheavals or most radical forms of social change. It is not accurate to see the structural properties of social systems as 'social products' because this tends to imply that pre-constituted actors somehow come together to create them. In reproducing structural properties to repeat a phrase used earlier, agents also reproduce the conditions that make such action possible. Structure has no existence independent of the knowledge that agents have about what they do in their day-to-day activity. Human agents always know what they are doing on the level of discursive consciousness under some description. However, what they do may be quite unfamiliar under other descriptions, and they may know little of the ramified consequences of the activities in which they engage.

The duality of structure is always the main grounding of continuities in social reproduction across time-space. It in turn presupposes the reflexive monitoring of agents in, and as

constituting, the durée of daily social activity. But human knowledgeability is always bounded. The flow of action continually produces consequences which are unintended by actors, and these unintended consequences also may form unacknowledged conditions of action in a feedback fashion. Human history is created by intentional activities but is not an intended project; it persistently eludes efforts to bring it under conscious direction. However, such attempts are continually made by human beings, who operate under the threat and the promise of the circumstance that they are the only creatures who make their 'history' in cognizance of that fact.

The theorizing of human beings about their action means that just as social theory was not an invention of professional social theorists, so the ideas produced by those theorists inevitably tend to be fed back into social life itself. One aspect of this is the attempt to monitor, and thereby control, highly generalized conditions of system reproduction—a phenomenon of massive importance in the contemporary world. To grasp such monitored processes of reproduction conceptually, we have to make certain distinctions relevant to what social systems 'are' as reproduced practices in interaction settings. The relations implied or actualized in social systems are, of course, widely variable in terms of their degree of 'looseness' and permeability. But, this being accepted, we can recognize two levels in respect of the means whereby some element of 'systemness' is achieved in interaction. One is that generally prominent in functionalism, as referred to earlier, where interdependence is conceived of as a homeostatic process akin to mechanisms of self-regulation operating within an organism. There can be no objection to this as long as it is acknowledged that the 'looseness' of most social systems makes the organic parallel a very remote one and that this relatively 'mechanized' mode of system reproduction is not the only one found in human societies. Homeostatic system reproduction in human society can be regarded as involving the operation of causal loops, in which a range of unintended consequences of action feed back to reconstitute the initiating circumstances. But in many contexts of social life there occur processes of selective 'information filtering' whereby strategically placed actors seek reflexively to regulate the overall conditions of system reproduction either to keep things as they are or to change them.

The distinction between homeostatic causal loops and reflexive self-regulation in system reproduction must be complemented by one further, and final, one: that between social and system integration. 'Integration' may be understood as involving reciprocity of practices (of autonomy and dependence) between actors or collectivities. Social integration then means systemness on the level of face-to-face interaction. System integration refers to connections with those who are physically absent in time or space. The mechanisms of system integration certainly presuppose those of social integration, but such mechanisms are also distinct in some key respects from those involved in relations of co-presence.

Social Integration	System Integration
Reciprocity between actors in contexts of co-presence	Reciprocity between actors or collectivities across extended time-space

Forms of Institution

The division of rules into modes of signifying or meaning constitution and normative sanctions,

together with the concept of resources—fundamental to the conceptualization of power—carries various implications which need to be spelled out. What I call the 'modalities' of structuration serve to clarify the main dimensions of the duality of structure in interaction, relating the knowledgeable capacities of agents to structural features. Actors draw upon the modalities of structuration in the reproduction of systems of interaction, by the same token reconstituting their structural properties. The communication of meaning in interaction, it should be stressed, is separable only analytically from the operation of normative sanctions. This is obvious, for example, in so far as language use is itself sanctioned by the very nature of its 'public' character. The very identification of acts or of aspects of interaction—their accurate description, as grounded hermeneutically in the capability of an observer to 'go on' in a form of life—implies the interlacing of meaning, normative elements and power. This is most evident in the not infrequent contexts of social life where what social phenomena 'are,' how they are aptly described, is contested. Awareness of such contestation, of divergent and overlapping characterizations of activity, is an essential part of 'knowing a form of life.' . . .

The dimensions of the duality of structure are portrayed in [Figure 1 below]. Human actors are

Figure 1

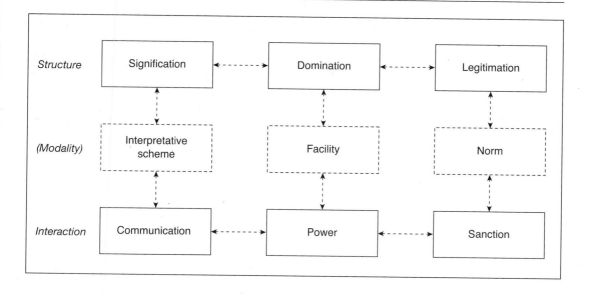

not only able to monitor their activities and those of others in the regularity of day-to-day conduct; they are also able to 'monitor that monitoring' in discursive consciousness. 'Interpretative schemes' are the modes of typification incorporated within actors' stocks of knowledge, applied reflexively in the sustaining of communication. The stocks of knowledge which actors draw upon in the production and reproduction of interaction are the same as those whereby they are able to make accounts, offer reasons, etc. The communication of meaning, as with all aspects of the contextuality of action, does not have to be seen merely as happening 'in' timespace. Agents routinely incorporate temporal and spatial features of encounters in processes of meaning constitution. Communication, as a general element of interaction, is a more inclusive concept than communicative intent (i.e. what an actor 'means' to say or do). There are once more two forms of reductionism to be avoided here. Some philosophers have tried to derive overall theories of meaning or communication from communicative intent; others, by contrast, have supposed that communicative intent is at best marginal to the constitution of the meaningful qualities of interaction, 'meaning' being governed by the structural ordering of sign systems. In the theory of structuration, however, these are regarded as of equivalent interest and importance, aspects of a duality rather than a mutually exclusive dualism.

The idea of 'accountability' in everyday English gives cogent expression to the intersection of interpretative schemes and norms. To be 'accountable' for one's activities is both to explicate the reasons for them and to supply the normative grounds whereby they may be 'justified.' Normative components of interaction always centre upon relations between the rights and obligations 'expected' of those participating in a range of interaction contexts. Formal codes of conduct, as, for example, those enshrined in law (in contemporary societies at least), usually express some sort of claimed symmetry between rights and obligations, the one being the justification of the other. But no such symmetry necessarily exists in practice, a phenomenon which it is important to emphasize, since both the

'normative functionalism' of Parsons and the 'structuralist Marxism' of Althusser exaggerates the degree to which normative obligations are 'internalized' by the members of societies. Neither standpoint incorporates a theory of action which recognizes human beings as knowledgeable agents, reflexively monitoring the flow of interaction with one another. When social systems are conceived of primarily from the point of view of the 'social object,' the emphasis comes to be placed upon the pervasive influence of a normatively co-ordinated legitimate order as an overall determinant or 'programmer' of social conduct. Such a perspective masks the fact that the normative elements of social systems are contingent claims which have to be sustained and 'made to count' through the effective mobilization of sanctions in the contexts of actual encounters. Normative sanctions express structural asymmetries of domination, and the relations of those nominally subject to them may be of various sorts other than expressions of the commitments those norms supposedly engender.

Concentration upon the analysis of the structural properties of social systems, it should be stressed, is a valid procedure only if it is recognized as placing an *epoché* upon—holding in suspension—reflexively monitored social conduct. Under such an *epoché* we may distinguish three structural dimensions of social systems: signification, domination and legitimation. The connotations of the analysis of these structural properties are indicated in the table below. The theory of coding presumed in the study of structures of signification must look to the extraordinary advances in semiotics which have been pioneered in recent decades. At the same time we have to guard against the association of semiotics with structuralism and with the shortcomings of the latter in respect of the analysis of human agency. Signs 'exist' only as the medium and outcome of communicative processes in interaction. Structuralist conceptions of language, in common with similar discussions of legitimation, tend to take signs as the given properties of speaking and writing rather than examining their recursive grounding in the communication of meaning. . . .

Structure(s)	Theoretical Domain	Institutional Order
Signification	Theory of coding	Symbolic orders/modes of discourse
Domination	Theory of resource authorization	Political institutions
	Theory of resource allocation	Economic institutions
Legitimation	Theory of normative regulation	Legal institutions

'Domination' and 'power' cannot be thought of only in terms of asymmetries of distribution but have to be recognized as inherent in social association (or, I would say, in human action as such). Thus . . . power is not an inherently noxious phenomenon, not just the capacity to 'say no'; nor can domination be 'transcended' in some kind of putative society of the future, as has been the characteristic aspiration of at least some strands of socialist thought. . . .

In the terminology indicated in the table above the 'signs' implied in 'signification' should not be equated with 'symbols.' Many writers treat the two terms as equivalent, but I regard symbols, interpolated within symbolic orders, as one main dimension of the 'clustering' of institutions. Symbols coagulate the 'surpluses of meaning' implied in the polyvalent character of signs; they conjoin those intersections of codes which are especially rich in diverse forms of meaning association, operating along the axes of metaphor and metonymy. Symbolic orders and associated modes of discourse are a major institutional locus of ideology. However, in the theory of structuration ideology is not a particular 'type' of symbolic order or form of discourse. One cannot separate off 'ideological discourse' from 'science,' for example. 'Ideology' refers only to those asymmetries of domination which connect signification to the legitimation of sectional interests.

We can see from the case of ideology that structures of signification are separable only analytically either from domination and from legitimation. Domination depends upon the mobilization of two distinguishable types of resource. Allocative resources refer to capabilities—or, more accurately, to forms of transformative capacity—generating command over objects, goods or material phenomena. Authoritative resources refer to types of transformative capacity generating command over persons or actors. Some forms of allocative resources (such as raw materials, land, etc.) might seem to have a 'real existence' in a way which I have claimed that structural properties as a whole do not. In the sense of having a time-space 'presence,' in a certain way such is obviously the case. But their 'materiality' does not affect the fact that such phenomena become resources, in the manner in which I apply that term here, only when incorporated within processes of structuration. The transformational character of resources is logically equivalent to, as well as inherently bound up with the instantiation of, that of codes and normative sanctions.

The classification of institutional orders offered above depends upon resisting what has sometimes been called 'substantivist' concepts of 'economic,' 'political' and other institutions. We can conceive of the relationships involved as follows:

S-D-L   Symbolic orders /modes of discourse

D (auth)-S-L   Political institutions

D (alloc)-S-L   Economic institutions

L-D-S   Legal institutions

where S = signification, D = domination,

L = legitimation

'Substantivist' conceptions presume concrete institutional differentiation of these various orders. That is to say, it is held, for example, that 'politics' exists only in societies having distinct forms of state apparatus and so on. But the work of anthropologists demonstrates effectively enough that there are 'political' phenomena—to do with the ordering of authority relations—in all societies. The same applies to the other institutional orders. We have to be particularly careful in conceptualizing the 'economic,' even having made the point that this does not presuppose the existence of a clearly differentiated 'economy.' There has been a strong tendency in some of the literature of economics to 'read back' into traditional cultures concepts that have meaning only in the context of market economies. The 'economic' cannot properly be defined, in a generic way at least, as concerning struggles for scarce resources. This is somewhat like defining power solely by reference to sectional struggles. It is not scarcity of resources as such, far less struggles or sectional divisions centred upon distribution, that is the main feature of the 'economic.' Rather, the sphere of the 'economic' is given by the inherently constitutive role of allocative resources in the structuration of societal totalities. Other cautionary notes should be added here. If it is held that all societies are haunted by the possibility of material scarcity, it is only a short step to the supposition that conflicts over scarce resources make up the fundamental motor of social change, as is presumed in at least some versions of historical materialism and in many non-Marxist theories also. But his presumption is both logically wanting, usually depending upon a specious form of functional reasoning, and empirically false.

❖

Introduction to *The Consequences of Modernity*

In addition to developing his theory of structuration, Giddens has undertaken a number of investigations into the nature of modern society and the interpersonal relationships that are forged within the context of everyday, modern life. In the excerpt provided below, taken from *The Consequences of Modernity*, Giddens argues that modern societies are marked by two paradoxical developments: *security* versus *danger* and *trust* versus *risk*. Relative to premodern or traditional societies, inhabitants in modern society, by and large, are able to avoid the disease, famine, and harsh realities of daily life that were all too common in civilizations past. While not everyone is able to enjoy all the conveniences modern society has to offer, what we now consider basic necessities would be unfathomable for the vast majority of the populations in traditional societies. On the other hand, the security that modernity affords us is offset by the unparalleled dangers that we face today. Ongoing destruction of our ecology, the rise of totalitarian regimes, the outbreak of horrific wars, and the proliferation of nuclear and biological weapons have all played their part in creating a world that is more dangerous than ever before.

The interplay between trust and risk is also novel to modern societies. Giddens defines **trust** as "confidence in the reliability of a person or system, regarding a given set of outcomes or events, where that confidence expresses a faith in the probity [honor] or love of another, or in the correctness of abstract principles (technical knowledge)" (1990:34). Trust inevitably involves risk: the people and systems in which we place our trust may not perform as we had anticipated; chance, incompetence, or unforeseen events can all lead to undesired outcomes. Nevertheless, trust is an inescapable feature of modern society, in large measure because **time-space distanciation**—system and social integration linking individuals across large spans of time and space—has "disembedded" or "lifted out" social relations from the immediate contexts of face-to-face interaction (ibid.:21). As Giddens notes, "There would be no need to trust anyone whose activities were continually visible and whose thought processes were transparent, or to trust any system whose workings were wholly known or understood . . . [T]he prime condition of requirements for trust is . . . lack of full information" (ibid.:33). Because we do not "know" the pilot of the airplane we are flying in or understand how planes can defy gravity, we have little choice but to trust the expertise of the pilot and all those whose efforts make air travel a manageable risk. The same can be said for those who monitor the systems that purify our drinking water or that deliver highly combustible natural gas to our homes. From the car mechanic, traffic engineer, and architect, to the electrician, doctor, and nuclear power plant technician, modern life is predicated on trust in the expertise of others and the abstract systems whose workings we do not fully understand.

Disembedding mechanisms are of two types: "symbolic tokens" and "expert systems" (sometimes referred to as "abstract systems," as above). Giddens defines the former as "media of interchange which can be 'passed around' without regard to the specific characteristics of individuals or groups that handle them at any particular juncture" (Giddens 1990:22). Drawing on the work of Georg Simmel (1858–1918), Giddens finds in money the paramount symbolic token, as it makes possible transactions between individuals who are distanced from another in terms of both time and space. Expert systems are "systems of technical accomplishment or professional expertise that organize large areas of the material and social environments in which we live" (ibid.:27). Despite the fact that we do not regularly seek expert knowledge, our lives are continuously linked to the expert or abstract systems in which that knowledge is integrated. Given that individuals are linked across increasing spans of time and space, a hallmark of modern society is our routine placing of trust or faith in such abstract, disembedding mechanisms and the expertise that defines them. Yet, expert knowledge, like scientific knowledge more generally, is never certain but instead always open to refutation and revision.

Giddens next considers how the spreading of abstract systems and our trust in them has led to a "transformation of intimacy." Here he notes the impact of modernity on our personal relationships with others, particularly how in modern society trust is a "project" that requires work in the form of self-disclosure in order to be "won." The need for self-disclosure is itself bound up with a reflexive search for self-identity in which the construction of the self and a concern for self-fulfillment likewise become ongoing projects. However, these projects are carried out in an environment fraught with risks of unprecedented proportions. The disembedding mechanisms associated with modernity have altered both the scope and the types of risks that currently confront individuals. The potential for global catastrophe is now part of everyday life. The threat of nuclear war, the collapse of the global economy, destruction of the planet's resources, and global warming are just a few of the risks that are forever looming on the horizon. No one can completely escape the effects of these modern global dangers, almost all of which are the product of humans' intervention in the world. Living daily with the knowledge that risks of high consequence are always present affects feelings of ontological security. **Ontological security** refers to unconscious feelings regarding the continuity of one's self-identity and of the broader social and physical world. It is a sense of security rooted in a trust that people and the surrounding world are as they appear. Yet, precisely because modern society poses an array of catastrophic risks of which individuals are aware, and because the experts and abstract systems charged with controlling the sources of potential danger are known to be imperfect, the sense of confidence, reliability, and trust that is basic to feelings of ontological security is jeopardized (Giddens 1990:92). Such is the "juggernaut of modernity."

❖

The Consequences of Modernity (1990)

Anthony Giddens

THE DISCONTINUITIES OF MODERNITY

The modes of life brought into being by modernity have swept us away from *all* traditional types of social order, in quite unprecedented fashion. In both their extensionality and their intensionality the transformations involved in modernity are more profound than most sorts of change characteristic of prior periods. On the extensional plane they have served to establish forms of social interconnection which span the globe; in intensional terms they have come to alter some of the most intimate and personal features of our day-to-day existence. Obviously there are continuities between the traditional and the modern, and neither is cut of whole cloth; it is well known how misleading it can be to contrast these two in too gross a fashion. But the changes occurring over the past three or four centuries—a tiny period of historical time—have been so dramatic and so comprehensive in their impact that we get only limited assistance from our knowledge of prior periods of transition in trying to interpret them. . . .

How should we identify the discontinuities which separate modern social institutions from the traditional social orders? Several features are involved. One is the sheer *pace of change* which the era of modernity sets into motion. Traditional civilisations may have been considerably more dynamic than other pre-modern systems, but the rapidity of change in conditions of modernity is extreme. If this is perhaps most obvious in respect of technology, it also pervades all other spheres. A second discontinuity is the *scope of change*. As different areas of the globe are drawn into interconnection with one another, waves of social transformation crash across virtually the whole of the earth's surface. A third feature concerns the intrinsic *nature of modern institutions*. Some modern social forms are simply not found in prior historical periods—such as the political system of the nation-state, the wholesale

dependence of production upon inanimate power sources, or the thoroughgoing commodification of products and wage labour. Others only have a specious continuity with pre-existing social orders. An example is the city. Modern urban settlements often incorporate the sites of traditional cities, and it may look as though they have merely spread out from them. In fact, modern urbanism is ordered according to quite different principles from those which set off the pre-modern city from the countryside in prior periods.

SECURITY AND DANGER, TRUST AND RISK

In pursuing my enquiry into the character of modernity, I want to concentrate a substantial portion of the discussion upon the themes of *security versus danger* and *trust versus risk*. Modernity, as everyone living in the closing years of the twentieth century can see, is a double-edge phenomenon. The development of modern social institutions and their worldwide spread have created vastly greater opportunities for human beings to enjoy a secure and rewarding existence than any type of pre-modern system. But modernity also has a sombre side, which has become very apparent in the present century.

On the whole, the "opportunity side" of modernity was stressed most strongly by the classical founders of sociology. Marx and Durkheim both saw the modern era as a troubled one. But each believed that the beneficent possibilities opened up by the modern era outweighed its negative characteristics. Marx saw class struggle as the source of fundamental schisms in the capitalistic order, but at the same time envisaged the emergence of a more humane social system. Durkheim believed the further expansion of industrialism would establish a harmonious and fulfilling social life, integrated through a combination of the division of labour and moral individualism. Max Weber was the most pessimistic among the three founding fathers, seeing the modern world as a paradoxical one in which material progress was obtained only at the cost of an expansion of bureaucracy that crushed individual creativity and autonomy. Yet even he did not fully anticipate how extensive the darker side of modernity would turn out to be.

To take an example, all three authors saw that modern industrial work had degrading consequences, subjecting many human beings to the discipline of dull, repetitive labour. But it was not foreseen that the furthering of the "forces of production" would have large-scale destructive potential in relation to the material environment. Ecological concerns do not brook large in the traditions of thought incorporated into sociology, and it is not surprising that sociologists today find it hard to develop a systematic appraisal of them.

A second example is the consolidated use of political power, particularly as demonstrated in episodes of totalitarianism. The arbitrary use of political power seemed to the sociological founders to belong primarily to the past (although sometimes having echoes in the present, as indicated in Marx's analysis of the rule of Louis Napoleon). "Despotism" appeared to be mainly characteristic of pre-modern states. In the wake of the rise of fascism, the Holocaust, Stalinism, and other episodes of twentieth-century history, we can see that totalitarian possibilities are contained within the institutional parameters of modernity rather than being foreclosed by them. Totalitarianism is distinct from traditional despotism, but is all the more frightening as a result. Totalitarian rule connects political, military, and ideological power in more concentrated form than was ever possible before the emergence of modern nation-states.

The development of military power as a general phenomenon provides a further case in point. Durkheim and Weber both lived to witness the horrendous events of the First World War, although Durkheim died before the war reached its conclusion. The conflict shattered the anticipation Durkheim has previously held that a pacific, integrated industrial order would naturally be promoted by industrialism and proved impossible to accommodate within the intellectual framework he had developed as the basis of his sociology. Weber gave more attention to the role of military power in past history than did either Marx or Durkheim. Yet he did not elaborate an account of the military in modern times, shifting the burden of his analysis towards rationalisation and bureaucratisation. None of the classical founders of sociology gave systematic attention to the phenomenon of the "industrialisation of war."

Social thinkers writing in the late nineteenth and early twentieth centuries could not have foreseen the invention of nuclear weaponry.* But the connecting of industrial innovation and organisation to military power is a process that dates back to the early origins of modern industrialisation itself. That this went largely unanalysed in sociology is an indication of the strength of the view that the newly emergent order of modernity would be essentially pacific, in contrast to the militarism that had characterised previous ages. Not just the threat of nuclear confrontation, but the actuality of military conflict, form a basic part of the "dark side" of modernity in the current century. The twentieth century is the century of war, with the number of serious military engagements involving substantial loss of life being considerably higher than in either of the two preceding centuries. In the present century thus far, over 100 million people have been killed in wars, a higher proportion of the world's population than in the nineteenth century, even allowing for overall population increase. Should even a limited nuclear engagement be fought, the loss of life would be staggering, and a full superpower conflict might eradicate humanity altogether.

---

*Yet, writing in 1914, just before the outbreak of the Great War, H. G. Wells did make such a prediction, influenced by the physicist Frederick Soddy, a collaborator of Ernest Rutherford. Wells's book, *The World Set Free*, recounts the story of a war which erupts in Europe in 1958, from there spreading throughout the world. In the war, a terrible weapon is used, constructed from a radioactive substance called Carolinum. Hundreds of these bombs, which Wells called "atomic bombs," are dropped on the world's cities, causing immense devastation. A time of mass starvation and political chaos follows, after which a new world republic is set up, in which war is forever prohibited.

The world in which we live today is a fraught and dangerous one. This has served to do more than simply blunt or force us to qualify the assumption that the emergence of modernity would lead to the formation of a happier and more secure social order. Loss of a belief in "progress," of course, is one of the factors that underlies the dissolution of "narratives" of history. Yet there is much more at stake here than the conclusion that history "goes nowhere." We have to develop an institutional analysis of the double-edged character of modernity. In so doing, we must make good some of the limitations of the classical sociological perspectives, limitations which have continued to affect sociological thought in the present day. . . .

ABSTRACT SYSTEMS AND THE TRANSFORMATION OF INTIMACY

Abstract systems have provided a great deal of security in day-to-day life which was absent in pre-modern orders. A person can board a plane in London and reach Los Angeles some ten hours later and be fairly certain that not only will the journey be made safely, but that the plane will arrive quite close to a predetermined time. The passenger may perhaps only have a vague idea of where Los Angeles is, in terms of a global map. Only minimal preparations need to be made for the journey (obtaining passport, visa, air-ticket, and money)—no knowledge of the actual trajectory is necessary. A large amount of "surrounding" knowledge is required to be able to get on the plane, and this is knowledge which has been filtered back from expert systems to lay discourse and action. One has to know what an airport is, what an air-ticket is, and very many other things besides. But security on the journey itself does not depend upon mastery of the technical paraphernalia which make it possible.

Compare this with the task of an adventurer who undertook the same journey no more than three or four centuries ago. Although he would be the "expert," he might have little idea of where he was traveling *to*—and the very notion of "traveling" sounds oddly inapplicable. The journey would be fraught with dangers, and the risk of disaster or death very considerable. No one could participate in such an expedition who was not physically tough, resilient, and possessed of skills relevant to the conduct of the voyage.

Every time someone gets cash out of the bank or makes a deposit, casually turns on a light or a tap, sends a letter or makes a call on the telephone, she or he implicitly recognises the large areas of secure, coordinated actions and events that make modern social life possible. Of course, all sorts of hitches and breakdowns can also happen, and attitudes of scepticism or antagonism develop which produce the disengagement of individuals from one or more of these systems. But most of the time the taken-for-granted way in which everyday actions are geared into abstract systems bears witness to the effectiveness with which they operate (within the contexts of what is expected from them, because they also produce many kinds of unintended consequences).

Trust in abstract systems is the condition of time-space distanciation and of the large areas of security in day-to-day life which modern institutions offer as compared to the traditional world. The routines which are integrated with abstract systems are central to ontological security in conditions of modernity. Yet this situation also creates novel forms of psychological vulnerability, and trust in abstract systems is not psychologically rewarding in the way in which trust in person is. I shall concentrate on the second of these points here, returning to the first later. To begin, I want to advance the following theorems: that there is a direct (although dialectical) connection between the globalising tendencies of modernity and what I shall call the *transformation of intimacy* in contexts of day-to-day life; that the transformation of intimacy can be analysed in terms of the building of trust mechanisms; and that personal trust relations, in such circumstances, are closely bound up with a situation in which the construction of the self becomes a reflexive project. . . .

TRUST AND PERSONAL IDENTITY

With the development of abstract systems, trust in impersonal principles, as well as in anonymous others, becomes indispensable to social existence. Nonpersonalized trust of this sort is discrepant from basic trust. There is a strong psychological need to find others to trust, but institutionally organised personal connections are lacking, relative to pre-modern social situations. The point here is *not* primarily that many social characteristics which were previously part of everyday life or the "life-world" become drawn off and incorporated into abstract systems. Rather, the tissue and form of day-to-day life become reshaped in conjunction with wider social changes. Routines which are structured by abstract systems have an empty, unmoralised character—this much is valid in the idea that the impersonal increasingly swamps the personal. But this is not simply a diminishment of personal life in favour of impersonally organized systems—it is a genuine transformation of the nature of the personal itself. Personal relations whose main objective is sociability, informed by loyalty and authenticity, become as much a part of the social situations of modernity as the encompassing institutions of time-space distanciation.

It is quite wrong, however, to set off the impersonality of abstract systems against the intimacies of personal life as most existing sociological accounts tend to do. Personal life and the social ties it involves are deeply intertwined with the most far-reaching of abstract systems. It has long been the case, for example, that Western diets reflect global economic interchanges: "every cup of coffee contains within it the whole history of Western imperialism." With the accelerating globalisation of the past fifty years or so, the connections between personal life of the most intimate kind and disembedding mechanisms have intensified. As Ulrich Beck has observed, "The most intimate—say, nursing a child—and the most distant, most general— say a reactor accident in the Ukraine, energy politics—are now suddenly *directly* connected."

What does this mean in terms of personal trust? The answer to this question is fundamental to the transformation of intimacy in the twentieth century. Trust in persons is not focused by personalised connections within the local community and kinship networks. Trust on a personal level becomes a project, to be "worked at" by the parties involved, and demands the *opening out of the individual to the other*. Where it cannot be controlled by fixed normative codes, trust has to be *won*, and the means of doing this is demonstrable warmth and openness. Our peculiar concern with "relationships," in the sense which that word has now taken on, is expressive of this phenomenon. Relationships are ties based upon trust, where trust is not pre-given but worked upon, and where the work involved means a *mutual process of self-disclosure*.

Given the strength of the emotions associated with sexuality, it is scarcely surprising that erotic involvements become a focal point for such self-disclosure. The transition to modern forms of erotic relations is generally thought to be associated with the formation of an ethos of romantic love, or with what Lawrence Stone calls "affective individualism." The ideal of romantic love is aptly described by Stone in the following way:

> the notion that there is only one person in the world with whom one can unite at all level; the personality of that person is so idealised that the normal faults and follies of human nature disappear from view; love is like a thunderbolt and strikes at first sight; love is the most important thing in the world, to which all other considerations, particularly material ones, should be sacrificed; and lastly, the giving of full rein to personal emotions is admirable, no matter how exaggerated and absurd the resulting conduct might appear to others.[i]

Characterised in this way, romantic love incorporates a cluster of values scarcely ever realisable in their totality. Rather than being an ethos associated in a continuous way with the rise of modern instructions, it seems essentially to have been a transitional phenomenon, bound up with a relatively early phase in the dissolution of the older forms of arranged marriage. Aspects of the "romantic love complex" as described by Stone have proved quite durable, but these have become increasingly meshed with the dynamics of personal trust described above. Erotic relations involve a progressive path of mutual discovery, in which a process of self-realisation on the part of the lover is as much a

---

[i]Lawrence Stone, *The Family, Sex and Marriage in England 1500–1800*, London: Weidenfeld 1977, p. 282.

part of the experience as increasing intimacy with the loved one. Personal trust, therefore, has to be established through the process of self-enquiry; the discovery of oneself becomes a project directly involved with the reflexivity of modernity.

Interpretations of the quest for self-identity tend to divide in much the same way as views of the decline of community, to which they are often linked. Some see a preoccupation with self-development as an offshoot of the fact that the old communal orders have broken down, producing a narcissistic, hedonistic concern with the ego. Others reach much the same conclusion, but trace this end result to forms of social manipulation. Exclusion of the majority from the arenas where the most consequential policies are forged and decisions taken forces a concentration upon the self; this is a result of the powerlessness most people feel. In the words of Christopher Lasch:

> As the world takes on a more and more menacing appearance, life becomes a never-ending search for health and well-being through exercise, dieting, drugs, spiritual regimens of various kinds, psychic self-help, and psychiatry. For those who have withdrawn interest from the outside world except in so far as it remains a source of gratification and frustration, the state of their own health becomes an all-absorbing concern.[ii]

Is the search for self-identity a form of somewhat pathetic narcissism, or is it, in some part at least, a subversive force in respect of modern institutions? Most of the debate about the issue has concentrated upon this question, . . . but for the moment we should see that there is something awry in Lasch's statement. A "search for health and well-being" hardly sounds compatible with a "withdrawal of interest in the outside world." The benefits of exercise or dieting are not personal discoveries but came from the lay reception of expert knowledge, as does the appeal of therapy or psychiatry. The spiritual regimens in question may be an electric assemblage, but include religions and cults from around the world. The outside world not only enters in here; it is an outside world vastly more

extensive in character than anyone would have had contact with in the pre-modern era.

To summarise all this, the transformation of intimacy involves the following:

1. An intrinsic relation between the *globalising tendencies* of modernity and *localised events* in day-to-day life—a complicated, dialectical connection between the "extensional" and the "intensional."

2. The construction of the self as a *reflexive project*, an elemental part of the reflexivity of modernity; an individual must find her or his identity and amid the strategies and options provided by abstract systems.

3. A drive towards self-actualisation, founded upon *basic trust*, which in personalised contexts can only be established by an "opening out" of the self to the other.

4. The formation of personal and erotic ties as "relationships," guided by the *mutuality of self-disclosure*.

5. *A concern for self-fulfillment*, which is not just a narcissistic defense against an externally threatening world, over which individuals have little control, but also in part a *positive appropriation* of circumstances in which globalised influences impinge upon everyday life.

RISK AND DANGER IN THE MODERN WORLD

How should we seek to analyse the "menacing appearance" of the contemporary world of which Lasch speaks? To do so means looking in more detail at the specific risk profile of modernity, which may be outlined in the following way:

1. *Globalisation of risk* in the sense of *intensity*: for example, nuclear war can threaten the survival of humanity.

2. *Globalisation of risk* in the sense of the *expanding number of contingent events* which affect everyone or at least large numbers of people on the planet: for example, changes in the global division of labour.

[ii]Christopher Lasch, *Haven in a Heartless World,* New York: Basic Books 1977, p. 140.

3. Risk stemming from the *created environment*, or *socialised nature*; the infusion of human knowledge into the material environment.

4. The development of *institutionalised risk environments* affecting the life-chances of millions: for example, investment markets.

5. *Awareness of risk as risk*: the "knowledge gaps" in risks cannot be converted into "certainties" by religious or magical knowledge.

6. The *well-distributed awareness of risk*: many of the dangers we face collectively are known to wide publics.

7. *Awareness of the limitations of expertise*: no expert system can be wholly expert in terms of the consequences of the adoption of expert principles.

If the disembedding mechanisms have provided large areas of security in the present-day world, the new array of risks which have thereby been brought into being are truly formidable. The main forms I have listed can be separated out into those that alter the objective distribution of risks (the first four items listed) and those that alter the experience of risk or the perception of perceived risk (the remaining three items).

What I have termed the intensity of risk is surely the basic element in the "menacing appearance" of the circumstances in which we live today. The possibility of nuclear war, ecological calamity, uncontainable population explosion, the collapse of global economic exchange, and other potential global catastrophes provide an unnerving horizon of dangers for everyone. As Beck has commented, globalised risks of this sort do not respect divisions between rich and poor or between regions of the world. The fact that "Chernobyl is everywhere" spells what he calls "the end of 'others'"—boundaries between those who are privileged and those who are not. The global intensity of certain kinds of risk transcends all social and economic differentials. (Of course, this should not blind us to the fact that, in conditions of modernity, as in the pre-modern world, many risks are differentially distributed between the privileged and the underprivileged. Differential risk—in relation, for example, to levels of nutrition and susceptibility to illness—is a large part of what is actually meant by "privilege" and "underprivilege.")

Nuclear war is plainly the most potentially immediate and catastrophic of all current global dangers. Since the early 1980's it has been recognised that the climatic and environmental effects of a quite limited nuclear engagement could be very far-reaching. The detonation of a small number of warheads might produce irreversible environmental damage which could threaten the life of all complex animal species. The threshold for the occurrence of a "nuclear winter" has been calculated at between 500 and 2,000 warheads—less than 10 percent of the total held by the nuclear nations. It is even below the number possessed during the 1950's. This circumstance wholly justifies the assertion that in such a context, there are no longer "others": the combatants and those uninvolved would all suffer.

The second category of globalised risks concerns the world-wide extension of risk environments, rather than the intensification of risk. All disembedding mechanisms take things out of the hands of any specific individuals or groups; and the more such mechanisms are of global scope, the more this tends to be so. Despite the high levels of security which globalised mechanisms can provide, the other side of the coin is that novel risks come into being: resources or services no longer under local control and therefore cannot be locally refocused to meet unexpected contingencies, and there is a risk that the mechanism as a whole can falter, thus affecting everyone who characteristically makes use of it. Thus someone who has oilfired central heating and no fireplaces is particularly vulnerable to changes in the price of oil. In circumstances such as the "oil crisis" of 1973, produced as a result of the actions of the OPEC cartel, all consumers of petroleum products are affected.

The first two categories in the risk profile concern the scope of risk environments; the next two are to do with changes in the type of risk environment. The category of the created environment, or "socialised nature" refers to the altered character of the relation between human beings and the physical environment. The variety of ecological dangers in such a category derive from the transformation of nature by human knowledge systems. The sheer number of serious risks in respect of socialised nature is quite daunting: radiation from major accidents at nuclear power-stations or from nuclear waste; chemical pollution of the seas sufficient to destroy the phytoplankton that renews much of the oxygen in the atmosphere; a "greenhouse effect" deriving from atmospheric pollutants which attack the ozone layer, melting part of the ice caps and flooding vast areas; the destruction of large areas of rain forest which are a basic source of renewable oxygen; and the exhaustion of millions of acres of topsoil as a result of widespread use of artificial fertilizers. . . .

In terms of the experience of risk, far more could be said than I have the opportunity to analyse here. The three aspects of the awareness of risk indicated in the risk profile above, however, are immediately relevant to the arguments developed in this study thus far and to subsequent sections. The fact that risks—including in this regard many different forms of activity— are generally accepted by the lay population to *be* risks is a major aspect of the disjuncture between the pre-modern and the modern worlds. High-risk enterprises undertaken in traditional cultures may sometimes have occurred in a secular domain, but more typically were carried out under the auspices of religion or magic. How far individuals may have been prepared to vest trust in particular religious or magical prescriptions in specific risk domains was no doubt widely variable. But religion and magic very often provided a way of sealing over the uncertainties entailed in risky endeavours, thus translating the experience of risk into feelings of relative security. Where risk is known *as* risk, this mode of generating confidence in hazardous actions is by definition unavailable. In a predominantly secular milieu, there are various ways of trying to transmute risk into providential *fortuna*, but they remain half-hearted superstitions rather than truly effective psychological supports. People in occupations entailing life-threatening risk, such as steeplejacks, or in enterprises where the outcome is structurally indetermined, like sports players, quite often have recourse to charms or superstitious rituals, to "influence" the outcomes of what they do. But they might very well be scorned by others if they make these practices too public.

We can take the final two points in the risk profile together. Widespread lay knowledge of modern risk environments leads to awareness of the limits of expertise and forms one of the "public relations" problems that has to be faced by those who seek to sustain lay trust in expert systems. The faith that supports trust in expert systems involves a blocking off of the ignorance of the lay person when faced with the claims of expertise; but realisation of the areas of ignorance which confront the experts themselves, as individual practitioners and in terms of overall fields of knowledge, may weaken or undermine that faith on the part of lay individuals. Experts often take risks "on behalf" of lay clients while concealing, or fudging over, the true nature of those risks or even the fact that there are risks at all. More damaging than the lay discovery of this kind of concealment is the circumstance where the full extent of a particular set of dangers and the risks associated with them is not realised by the experts. For in this case what is in question is not only the limits of, or the gaps in, expert knowledge, but an inadequacy which compromises the very idea of expertise.

RISK AND ONTOLOGICAL SECURITY

In what ways does this array of risks impinge upon lay trust in expert systems and feelings of ontological security? The baseline for analysis has to be the *inevitability* of living with dangers which are *remote* from the control not only of individuals, but also of large organisations, including states; and which are of *high intensity* and *life-threatening* for millions of human beings and potentially for the whole of humanity. The facts that these are not risks anyone *chooses* to run and that there are, in Beck's terms, no "others" who could be held responsible, attacked, or blamed reinforce the sense of foreboding which so many have noted as a characteristic of the current age. Nor is it surprising that some of those who hold to religious beliefs are inclined to see the potential for global disaster as an expression of the wrath of God. For the high consequence global risks which we all now run are key elements of the runaway, juggernaut character of modernity, and no specific individuals or groups are responsible for them or can be constrained to "set things right."

How can we constantly keep in the forefront of our minds dangers which are enormously threatening, yet so remote from individual control? The answer is that most of us cannot. People who worry all day, every day, about the possibility of nuclear war, as was noted earlier, are liable to be thought disturbed. While it would be difficult to deem irrational someone who was constantly and consciously anxious in this way, this outlook would paralyse ordinary day-to-day life. Even a person who raises the topic at a social gathering is prone to be thought hysterical or gauche. In Carolyn See's novel *Golden Days*, which finishes in the aftermath of a nuclear war, the main character relates her fear of a nuclear holocaust to another guest at a dinner party:

> Her eyes were wide. She gazed at me with terrific concentration. "Yes," she said, "I understand what you're saying. I get it. But isn't it true that your fear of nuclear war is a metaphor for all the *other* fears that plague us today?"
>
> My mind has never been exactly fine. But sometimes it has been good. "No," I said. I may have shouted it through the beautiful, sheltered room. "It's my view that the other fears, all those of which we have spoken, are a metaphor of my fear of nuclear war!"
>
> She stared at me incredulously, but was spared the difficulty of a response when we were all called to a very pleasant late supper.[iii]

The incredulity of the dinner party guest has nothing to do with the argument expressed; it registers disbelief that anyone should become emotional about such an issue in such a setting.

The large majority of people do not spend much of their time, on a conscious level at least, worrying about nuclear war or about the other major hazards for which it may or may not be a metaphor. The need to get on with the more local practicalities of day-to-day life is no doubt one reason, but much more is involved psychologically. In a secular environment, low-probability high-consequence risks tend to conjure up anew a sense of *fortuna* closer to the pre-modern outlook than that cultivated by minor superstitions. A sense of "fate," whether positively or negatively tinged—a vague and generalised sense of trust in distant events over which one has no control—relieves the individual of the burden of engagement with an existential situation which might otherwise be chronically disturbing. Fate, a feeling that things will take their own course anyway, thus reappears at the core of a world which is supposedly taking rational control of its own

affairs. Moreover, this surely exacts a price on the level of the unconscious, since it essentially presumes the repression of anxiety. The sense of dread which is the antithesis of basis trust is likely to infuse unconscious sentiments about the uncertainties faced by humanity as a whole.

Low-probability high-consequence risks will not disappear in the modern world, although in an optimal scenario they could be minimised. Thus, were it to be the case that all existing nuclear weapons were done away with, no other weapons of comparable destructive force were invented, and no comparably catastrophic disturbances of socialised nature were to loom, a profile of global danger would still exist. For if it is accepted that the eradication of established technical knowledge could not be achieved, nuclear weaponry could be reconstructed at any point. Moreover, any major technological initiative could thoroughly disturb the overall orientation of global affairs. The juggernaut effect is inherent in modernity, for reasons I shall amplify in the next section of this work.

The heavily counterfactual character of the most consequential risks is closely bound up with the numbness that a listing of them tends to promote. In mediaeval times, the invention of hell and damnation as the fate of the unbeliever in the afterlife was "real." Yet things are different with the most catastrophic dangers which face us today. The greater the danger, measured not in terms of probability of occurrence but in terms of its generalised threat to human life, the more thoroughly counterfactual it is. The risks involved are necessarily "unreal," because we could only have clear demonstration of them if events occurred that are too terrible to contemplate. Relatively small-scale events, such as the dropping of atomic bombs on Hiroshima and Nagasaki or the accidents at Three Mile Island or Chernobyl, give us some sense of what could happen. But these do not in any way bear upon the necessarily counterfactual character of other, more cataclysmic happenings—the main basis of their "unreality" and the narcotising effects produced by the repeated listing of risks. As Susan Sontag remarks, "A permanent modern scenario: apocalypse looms—and it doesn't occur. And still it looms. . . . Apocalypse is now a long-running serial: not 'Apocalypse Now,' but 'Apocalypse from now on.'"[iv] . . .

[iii]Carolyn See, *Golden Days,* London: Arrow, 1989, p. 126.

[iv]Susan Sontag, *AIDS and its Metaphors,* Harmondsworth: Penguin, 1989.

A Phenomenology of Modernity

Two images of what it feels like to live in the world of modernity have dominated the sociological literature, yet both of them seem less than adequate. One is that of Weber, according to which the bonds rationality are drawn tighter and tighter, imprisoning us in a featureless cage of bureaucratic routine. Among the three major founders of modern sociology, Weber saw most clearly the significance of expertise in modern social development and used it to outline a phenomenology of modernity. Everyday experience, according to Weber, retains its colour and spontaneity, but only on the perimeter of the "steel-hard" cage of bureaucratic rationality. The image has a great deal of power and has, of course, featured strongly in fictional literature in the twentieth century as well as in more directly sociological discussions. There are many contexts of modern institutions which are marked by bureaucratic fixity. But they are far from all-pervasive, and even in the core settings of its application, namely, large-scale organisations, Weber's characterisation of bureaucracy is inadequate. Rather than tending inevitably towards rigidity, organisations produce areas of autonomy and spontaneity— which are actually often less easy to achieve in smaller groups. We owe this counterinsight to Durkheim, as well as to subsequent empirical study of organisations. The closed climate of opinion within some small groups and the modes of direct sanction available to its members fix the horizons of action much more narrowly and firmly than in larger organisational settings.

The second is the image of Marx—and of many others, whether they regard themselves as Marxist or not. According to this portrayal, modernity is seen as a monster. More limpidly perhaps than any of his contemporaries, Marx perceived how shattering the impact of modernity would be, and how irreversible at the same time, modernity was for Marx what Habermas has aptly called an "unfinished project." The monster can be tamed, since what human beings have created they can always subject to their own control. Capitalism, simply, is an irrational way to run the modern world, because it substitutes the whims of the market for the controlled fulfillment of human need.

For these images I suggest we should substitute that of the juggernaut[*]—a runaway engine of enormous power which, collectively as human beings, we can drive to some extent but which also threatens to rush out of our control and which could rend itself asunder. The juggernaut crushes those who resist it, and while it sometimes seems to have a steady path, there are times when it veers away erratically in directions we cannot foresee. The ride is by no means wholly unpleasant or unrewarding; it can often be exhilarating and charged with hopeful anticipation. But, so long as the institutions of modernity endure, we shall never be able to control completely either the path or the peace of the journey. In turn, we shall never be able to feel entirely secure, because the terrain across which it runs is fraught with risks of high consequence. Feelings of ontological security and existential anxiety will coexist in ambivalence.

The juggernaut of modernity is not all of one piece, and here the imagery lapses, as does any talk of a single path which it runs. It is not an engine made up of integrated machinery, but one in which there is a tensionful, contradictory, push-and-pull of different influences. Any attempt to capture the experience of modernity must begin from this view, which derives ultimately from the dialectics of space and time, as expressed in the time-space constitution of modern institutions. I shall sketch a phenomenology of modernity in terms of four dialectically related frameworks of experience, each of which connects in an integral way with the preceding discussion in this study:

Displacement and reembedding: the intersection of estrangement and familiarity.

Intimacy and impersonality: the intersection of personal trust and impersonal ties.

Expertise and reappropriation: the intersection of abstract systems and day-to-day knowledgeability.

Privatism and engagement: the intersection of pragmatic acceptance and activism.

---

[*]The term comes from the Hindi *Jagannāth*, "lord of the world," and is a title of Krishna; an idol of this deity was taken each year through the streets on a huge car, which followers are said to have thrown themselves under, to be crushed beneath the wheels.

Modernity "dis-places" in the sense previously analyzed—place becomes phantasmagoric. Yet this is a double-layered, or ambivalent, experience rather than simply a loss of community. We can see this clearly only if we keep in mind the contrasts between the premodern and the modern described earlier. What happens is not simply that localised influences drain away into the more impersonalised relations of abstract systems. Instead, the very tissue of spatial experience alters, conjoining proximity and distance in ways that have few close parallels in prior ages. There is a complex relation here between familiarity and estrangement. Many aspects of life in local contexts continue to have a familiarity and ease to them, grounded in the day-to-day routines individuals follow. But the sense of the familiar is one often mediated by time-space distanciation. It does not derive from the particularities of localised place. And this experience, so far as it seeps into general awareness, is simultaneously disturbing and rewarding. The reassurance of the familiar, so important to a sense of ontological security, is coupled with the realisation that what is comfortable and nearby is actually an expression of distant events and was "placed into" the local environment rather than forming an organic development within it. The local shopping mall is a milieu in which a sense of ease and security is cultivated by the layout of the buildings and the careful planning of public places. Yet everyone who shops there is aware that most of the shops are chain stores, which one might find in any city, and indeed that innumerable shopping malls of similar design exist elsewhere.

A feature of displacement is our insertion into globalised cultural and information settings, which means that familiarity and place are much less consistently connected than hitherto. This is less a phenomenon of estrangement from the local than one of integration within globalised "communities" of shared experience. The boundaries of concealment and disclosure become altered, since many erstwhile quite distinct activities are juxtaposed in unitary public domains. The newspaper and the sequence of television programmes over the day are the most obvious concrete examples of this phenomenon, but it is generic to the time-space organisation of modernity. We are all familiar with events, with actions, and with the visible appearance of physical settings thousands of miles away from where we happen to live. The coming of electronic media has undoubtedly accentuated these aspects of displacement, since they override presence so instantaneously and at such distance. As Joshua Meyrowitz points out, a person on the telephone to another, perhaps on the opposite side of the world, is more closely bound to that distant other than to another individual in the same room (who may be asking, "Who is it? What's she saying?" and so forth).

The counterpart of displacement is reembedding. The disembedding mechanisms lift social relations and the exchange of information out of specific time-space contexts, but at the same time provide new opportunities for their reinsertion. This is another reason why it is a mistake to see the modern world as one in which large, impersonal systems increasingly swallow up most of personal life. The self-same processes that lead to the destruction of older city neighbourhoods and their replacement by towering office-blocks and skyscrapers often permit the gentrification of other areas and a recreation of locality. Although the picture of tall, impersonal clusters of city-centre buildings is often presented as the epitome of the landscape of modernity, this is a mistake. Equally characteristic is the recreation of places of relative smallness and informality. The very means of transportation which help to dissolve the connection between locality and kinship provide the possibility for reembedding, by making it easy to visit "close" relatives who are far away.

Parallel comments can be made about the intersection of intimacy and impersonality in modern contexts of action. It is simply not true that in conditions of modernity we live increasingly in a "world of strangers." We are not required more and more to exchange intimacy for impersonality in the contacts with others we routinely make in the course of our day-to-day lives. Something much more complex and subtle is involved. Day-to-day contacts with others in pre-modern settings were normally based upon a familiarity stemming in part from the nature of place. Yet contacts with familiar others probably rarely facilitated the level of intimacy we associate with personal and sexual relations today. The "transformation of intimacy" of which I have spoken is contingent upon the very distancing which the disembedding mechanisms bring about, combined with the altered environments of trust which they presuppose. There are some very obvious ways in which intimacy and abstract systems interact. Money, for example, can be spent to purchase the expert services of a psychologist who guides the individual in an exploration of the inner universe of the intimate and the personal.

A person walks the streets of a city and encounters perhaps thousands of people in the course of a day, people she or he has never met before—"strangers" in the modern sense of that term. Or perhaps that individual strolls along less crowded thoroughfares, idly scrutinising passers by and the diversity of products for sale in the shops—Baudelaire's *flâneur*. Who could deny that these experiences are an integral element of modernity? Yet the world "out there"— the world that shades off into indefinite time-space from the familiarity of the home and the local neighbourhood—is not at all a purely impersonal one. On the contrary, intimate relationships can be sustained at a distance (regular and sustained contact can be made with other individuals at virtually any point on the earth's surface—as well as some below and above), and personal ties are continually forged with others with whom one was previously unacquainted. We live in a *peopled* world, not merely one of anonymous, blank faces, and the interpolation of abstract systems into our activities is intrinsic to bringing this about.

In relations of intimacy of the modern type, trust is always ambivalent, and the possibility of severance is more or less ever present. Personal ties can be ruptured, and ties of intimacy returned to the sphere of impersonal contacts— in the broken love affair, the intimate suddenly becomes again a stranger. The demand of "opening oneself up" to the other which personal trust relations now presume, the injunction to hide nothing from the other, mix reassurance and deep anxiety. Personal trust demands a level of self-understanding and self-expression which must itself be a source of psychological tension. For mutual self-revelation is combined with the need for reciprocity and support; yet the two are frequently incompatible. Torment and frustration interweave themselves with the need for trust in the other as the provider of care and support.

DESKILLING AND RESKILLING IN EVERYDAY LIFE

Expertise is part of intimacy in conditions of modernity, as is shown not just by the huge variety of forms of psychotherapy and counseling available, but by the plurality of books, articles, and television programmes providing technical information about "relationships." Does this mean that, as Habermas puts it, abstract systems "colonise" a pre-existing "life-world," subordinating personal decisions to technical expertise? It does not. The reasons are twofold. One is that modern institutions do not just implant themselves into a "life-world," the residues of which remain much the same as they always were. Changes in the nature of day-to-day life also affect the disembedding mechanisms in a dialectical interplay. The second reason is that technical expertise is continuously reappropriated by lay agents as part of their routine dealings with abstract systems. No one can become an expert, in the sense of the possession either of full expert knowledge or of the appropriate formal credentials, in more than a few small sectors of the immensely complicated knowledge systems which now exist. Yet no one can interact with abstract systems without mastering some of the rudiments of the principles upon which they are based.

Sociologists often suppose that, in contrast to the pre-modern era, where many things were mysteries, today we live in a world from which mystery has retreated and where the way "the world works" can (in principle) be exhaustively known. But this is not true for either the lay person or the expert, if we consider their experience as individuals. To all of us living in the modern world things are specifically *opaque*, in a way that was not the case previously. In pre-modern environments the "local knowledge," to adapt a phrase from Clifford Geertz, which individuals possessed was rich, varied, and adapted to the requirements of living in the local milieu. But how many of us today when we switch on the light know much about where the electricity supply comes from or even, in a technical sense, what electricity actually is?

Yet, although "local knowledge" cannot be of the same order as it once was, the sieving off of knowledge and skill from everyday life is not a one-way process. Nor are individuals in modern contexts less knowledgeable about their local milieux than their counterparts in pre-modern cultures. Modern social life is a complex affair, and there are many "filter-back" processes whereby technical knowledge, in one shape or another, is reappropriated by lay persons and routinely applied in the course of their day-to-day activities. . . . Economic factors may decide whether a person learns to fix her or his car engine, rewire the electrical system of the house, or fix the roof; but so do the levels of trust that an individual vests in the particular expert systems and known experts involved. Processes of reappropriation relate to all aspects of social life—for example, medical treatment, child-rearing, or sexual pleasure.

For the ordinary individual, all this does not add up to feelings of secure control over day-to-day life circumstances. Modernity expands the arenas of personal fulfillment and of security in respect of large swathes of day-to-day life. But the day person—and *all* of us are lay persons in respect of the vast majority of expert systems—must ride the juggernaut. The lack of control which many of us feel about some of the circumstances of our lives is real. . . .

Balanced against the deep anxieties which such circumstances must produce in virtually everyone is the psychological prop of the feeling that "there's nothing that I as an individual can do," and that at any rate the risk must be very slight. Business-as-usual, as I have pointed out, is a prime element in the establishing of trust and ontological security, and this no doubt applies in respect of high consequence risks just as it does in other areas of trust relations.

Yet obviously even high-consequence risks are not only remote contingencies, which can be ignored in daily life, albeit at some probable psychological cost. Some such risks, and many others which are potentially life-threatening for individuals or otherwise significantly affect them, intrude right into the core of day-to-day activities. This is true, for example, of any pollution damage which affects the health of adults or children, and anything which produces toxic contents in food or affects its nutritional properties. It is also true of a multitude of technological changes that influence life chances, such as reproductive technologies. The mix of risk and opportunity is so complex in many of the circumstances involved that it is extremely difficult for individuals to know how far to vest trust in particular prescriptions or systems, and how far to suspend it. How can one manage to eat "healthily," for example, when all kinds of food are said to have toxic qualities of one sort or another and when what is held to be "good for you" by nutritional experts varies with the sifting state of scientific knowledge?

Trust and risk, opportunity and danger—these polar, paradoxical features of modernity permeate all aspects of day-to-day life, once more reflecting an extraordinary interpolation of the local and the global. Pragmatic acceptance can be sustained towards most of the abstract systems that impinge on individuals' lives, but by its very nature such an attitude cannot be carried on all the while and in respect of all areas of activity. For incoming expert information is often fragmentary or inconsistent,[*] as is the recycled knowledge which colleagues, friends, and intimates pass on to one another. On a personal level, decisions must be taken and policies forged. Privatism, the avoidance of

---

[*]Consider, as one among an indefinite range of examples, the case of cyclamate, an artificial sweetener, and the U.S. authorities. Cyclamate was widely used in the United States until 1970, and the Food and Drug Administration classified it as "generally recognised as safe." The attitude of the FDA changed when scientific research concluded that rats given large doses of the substance were prone to certain types of cancer. Cyclamate was banned from use in foodstuffs. As more and people began to drink low-calorie beverages in the 1970's and early 1980's, however, manufacturers exerted pressure on the FDA to change its stance. In 1984, a committee of the FDA decided that cyclamate was not after all a cancer-producing agent. A year later, the National Academy of Sciences intervened, reaching yet a different conclusion. In its report on the subject, the Academy declared that cyclamate is unsafe when used with sacharin, although probably harmless when used on its own as a sweetener. See James Bellini, *High Tech Holocaust* (London: Tarrant, 1986).

contestatory engagement—which can be supported by attitudes of basic optimism, pessimism, or pragmatic acceptance—can serve the purposes of day-to-day "survival" in many respects. But it is likely to be interspersed with phases of active engagement, even on the part of those most prone to attitudes of indifference or cynicism. For, to repeat, in respect of the balance of security and danger which modernity introduces into our lives, there are no longer "others"—no one can be completely outside. Conditions of modernity, in many circumstances, provoke activism rather than privatism, because of modernity's inherent reflexivity and because there are many opportunities for collective organisation within the polyarchic systems of modern nation-states.

OBJECTIONS TO POST-MODERNITY

. . . I have sought to develop an interpretation of the current era which challenges the usual views of the emergence of post-modernity. As ordinarily understood, conceptions of post-modernity—which mostly have their origin in post-structuralist thought—involve a number of distinct strands. I compare this conception of post-modernity (PM) with my alternative position, which I shall call radicalised modernity (RM), in Table 1.

Table 1 A Comparison of Conceptions of "Post-Modernity" (PM) and "Radicalised Modernity" (RM)

PM	RM
1. Understands current transitions in epistemological terms or as dissolving epistemology altogether.	1. Identifies the institutional developments which create a sense of fragmentation and dispersal.
2. Focuses upon the centrifugal tendencies of current social transformation and their dislocating character.	2. Sees high modernity as a set of circumstances in which dispersal is dialectically connected to profound tendencies towards global integration.
3. Sees the self as dissolved or dismembered by the fragmenting of experience.	3. Sees the self as more than just a site of intersecting forces; active processes of reflexive self-identity are made possible by modernity.
4. Argues for the contextuality of truth claims or sees them as "historical."	4. Argues that the universal features of truth claims force themselves upon us in an irresistible way given the primacy of problems of a global kind. Systematic knowledge about these developments is not precluded by the reflexivity of modernity.
5. Theories powerlessness which individuals feel in the face of globalising tendencies.	5. Analyses a dialectic of powerlessness and empowerment, in terms of both experience and action.
6. Sees the "emptying" of day-to-day life as a result of the intrusion of abstract systems.	6. Sees day-to-day life as an active complex of reactions to abstract systems, involving appropriation as well as loss.
7. Regards coordinated political engagement as precluded by the primacy of contextuality and dispersal.	7. Regards coordinated political engagement as both possible and necessary, on a global level as well as locally.
8. Defines post-modernity as the end of epistemology/the individual/ethics.	8. Defines post-modernity as possible transformations moving "beyond" the institutions of modernity.

Discussion Questions

1. Using Giddens's theory of structuration, how might intergenerational poverty be explained?

2. Bourdieu notes how class relations shape the habitus such that "the dominated perceive the dominant through the categories that the relation of domination has produced and which are thus identical to the interests of the dominant" (Bourdieu 1998:121). In addition to economic classes, how might relations of domination based on gender or race shape the categories of perception that induce the dominated to reproduce their own subordinate position?

3. For Habermas, the strength and vibrancy of democracy lie in the public sphere, that is, spaces where ideas and reasoned arguments can be freely debated. What role do you think the mass media plays in shaping the public sphere? How might the corporate consolidation of media outlets and growing use of the Internet affect public debate?

4. Each of the theorists discussed in this chapter has sought to develop a multidimensional framework that bridges the divide between individualist and collectivist perspectives. Which framework do you think provides the most accurate and balanced account of social life? What are the strengths of this framework relative to the others?

5. Given that each of the theorists discussed in this chapter explores social life through a unique set of concepts, what types of research strategies might be best suited to each approach? In other words, what types of data would you need to collect in order to empirically examine, for instance, the duality of structure, the reproduction of class relations, or the colonization of the lifeworld?

10

THE GLOBAL SOCIETY

Key Concepts

Immanuel Wallerstein

- ❖ World-System
- ❖ World-Empires
- ❖ World-Economies
- ❖ Core
- ❖ Periphery
- ❖ Semiperiphery

Leslie Sklair

- ❖ Globalization
- ❖ Transnational Practices
- ❖ Transnational Corporations
- ❖ Transnational Capitalist Class
- ❖ Transnational Culture-Ideology

Edward Said

- ❖ Orientalism

It was with the emergence of the modern world-economy in sixteenth century Europe that we saw the full development and economic predominance of market trade. This was the system called capitalism. Capitalism and a world-economy . . . are obverse sides of the same coin.

~Wallerstein (1979:6)

S everal years ago I spent some time on an eco-tour in the Amazon rainforest. While the trip was spectacular in every sense, it also provided a first-hand experience of the shrinking of space that increasingly characterizes our (post)modern world. After a full day of travel from New York, which included four different modes of transportation, I had the sense of being far away but, yet, not removed from the world as I know it. For during the four-hour trip down the Napo River in a dugout canoe, we came across an outpost that resembled a small town like those depicted in Western movies. It had a general store, one or two other small, wooden buildings, and what appeared to be a brothel. Just past the outpost was an area of deforestation or clear-cutting where mud roads crisscrossed. The sights and sounds of bulldozers, dump trucks, and the like dominated the landscape. And off the bank of the river a large sign emblazoned with a single word—TEXACO—stood perched some thirty feet off the ground. Here, deep in the Amazonian rain forest, was a transnational corporation, head-quartered in a dominant, global superpower, exploiting the natural resources of an "underdeveloped" country in the name of private profit.

The reach of the modern global society is not simply economic, however. Indeed, international commerce preceded both capitalism and colonization and thus by itself represents nothing new. Rather, it is the scope and speed at which economic capital flows across borders that differentiates the contemporary global society from that of earlier eras. Moreover, it is technological innovations in communications and transportation that are directly responsible for shrinking the size of the globe. For while it took me a day to travel some three thousand miles to the rainforest from New York, it only took me a day. In addition, I was able to make all of the necessary travel plans and plot out my adventure long before I left the comforts of my home.

Yet, my trip highlighted another dimension of the contemporary global society. One day as I ventured from my straw hut to the part of the encampment where the native guides were housed, I happened upon a generator that ran to one of their huts. As I approached the hut I saw the guides huddled around a generator-powered television watching a video of Sylvester Stallone's *Rambo*. So much for my escape from home! And here was a glimpse into how not only Western corporations but also Western culture penetrates even the most remote nooks of our planet. To understand the forces that shape today's global society, then, we must not only be attuned to economic, technological, and political dynamics. We also need to recognize the role played by the spread of Western culture and images. For both individuals and larger collectivities around the globe, the impetus for action is in many ways shaped by encounters with and reactions to the "West" understood not as a place on a map or as a particular form of economy, but as an idea.

In this chapter, we explore three perspectives pertaining to the contemporary global society. We begin with a discussion of Immanuel Wallerstein's world-systems analysis, which focuses on the economic processes that have shaped the modern world. We next turn to the work of Leslie Sklair, who underscores the cultural aspects of globalization. We conclude with a discussion of postcolonial theory and the work of Edward Said, whose analysis of the social and cultural construction of the "Oriental" continues to provoke debate throughout the social sciences and the humanities. These perspectives focus neither on the dynamics of interpersonal interaction nor on the internal forces that give form to a single, self-contained society. Rather, they emphasize how such aspects of social life are themselves embedded in a global context, and how what happens in any given country (or geographical zone) is a function of its interconnections with other geographical regions. Certainly, what happens in Ecuador's rainforest is not solely, or most importantly, a result of internal economic, political, or cultural factors. Rather, Ecuador, like the rest of the world, is but a part of the global society.

DEFINING GLOBALIZATION

Before we turn to the work of these three theorists, we need to clarify further a central concept in this chapter: globalization. In this section we outline some of the major themes that occupy studies of globalization and, in doing so, provide a fuller context for examining the work of the theorists that follows later in the chapter. At the outset, however, it is important to note that despite, or perhaps because of, the vast literature that has been written on the subject, there is no one theory of globalization. Instead, there are "many theoretical discourses . . . that tend to be grounded in broader theoretical traditions and perspectives, such as Marxism, Weberianism, functionalism, postmodernism, critical and feminist theory, and involve a number of distinct approaches to social inquiry, such as cultural studies, international relations, postcolonial studies, literature, and so on" (Robinson, forthcoming).[1]

Globalization can be defined as "the rapidly developing and ever-densening network of interconnections and interdependencies that characterize modern life" (Tomlinson 1999:2). In a very real sense, the modern world is undergoing processes of compression or "shrinking," as geographical distances become less constraining of the flow of information, technology, products, and people across territorial boundaries. Coupled with the increasing interconnectedness is the growing awareness and experience of the world as a "whole" (Robertson 1992:8; Waters 2001:5). While the physical distance separating, say, Japan and England still exists, today the inhabitants of the respective nations experience this distance in ways very different from those living only a century ago. With advances in transportation and communications technology, the six thousand miles between the two nations is routinely traversed through an airplane ride, television show, or click of a mouse (Tomlinson 1992:4). Thus, whether through economic trade, corporate expansion, political alliances, military conquest, the Internet, or TV, the world has become more structurally intertwined, while individuals' everyday lives are increasingly shaped by events taking place outside of their local environment. The world has become, in Marshall McLuhan's words, a "global village."

An endless supply of examples could be used to illustrate this point: through the technology of the Internet, individuals develop virtual relationships with people who live on the other side of the globe; satellites enable us to watch and listen to events— the passing of popes, wars, music concerts, the Olympics—taking place thousands of miles away yet providing us with a sense of connection to distant lands and their people. Or consider the ripple effects of rising gas and oil prices in the United States, triggered in part by China's increasing consumption of petroleum. A rise in gas prices can lead to higher costs for most other goods, as their distribution is dependent on a transportation system fueled by gasoline. Thus, for example, the trucking industry, a key transporter of goods to warehouses and stores across the nation, will have to pass off to consumers the higher fuel costs that otherwise will cut into its profits. If fuel prices remain high, this in turn could produce a significant slowing down of the national economy, as many consumers become less willing and able to spend their wages on anything other than essential items. If prolonged, this slowdown can lead to growing unemployment across the nation as businesses begin to lay off workers in an effort to compensate for declining sales. Moreover, as America is a major trading partner with numerous countries and, for that matter, the leading consumer of countless commodities, a slowdown of its economy could have a devastating impact on virtually

---

[1]This same point also applies to feminist theories and postmodern and poststructural theories (see Chapters 7 and 8).

every nation. What may result is not a local recession or even a national one but, rather, a global recession that affects every region of the world.

When, What, and Where?

While most globalization theorists would agree that increasing connectivity and interdependency—a growing compression of the world—are essential features of the globalization process, disagreements remain over determining some of its fundamental aspects. In particular, theorists have offered competing views concerning *when* the process of globalization began, *what* factors are primarily responsible for shaping its development, and *where* the process ultimately is leading.

Concerning the issue of when the globalization process began, theorists generally ascribe to one of three competing views (Waters 2001:6, 7; Robinson, forthcoming). The first view argues that globalizing forces have been evolving since the beginning of human history; thus, globalization has been occurring for well over five thousand years. A second view, whose adherents include Immanuel Wallerstein, contends that globalization began with the rise of the modern era and the development of capitalism. From this perspective, globalization was born some five hundred years ago as European nations raced to establish colonies and an international network of economic trade relations. The third view argues that globalization is in its infancy, having begun in the second half of the twentieth century. Globalization is here associated with the development of postindustrial economies and the contemporary restructuring of capitalism. Despite the different historical dimensions that scholars assign to globalization, most agree that the pace of the process increased markedly in the last decades of the past century.

Perhaps more thorny is sorting out the factors that are most significant in shaping the process of globalization. While there is a general consensus that globalization involves economic, political, and cultural transformations, theorizing how these domains intersect, overlap, and influence one another remains contentious. A glimpse into the complexity of such transformations is offered in Arjun Appadurai's notion of the "global cultural economy." In his widely cited essay, "Disjuncture and Difference in the Global Cultural Economy," Appadurai (1992) notes that the contemporary global order is marked by "disjunctures" between and within five dimensions or "scapes" of global cultural flows. These scapes, in turn, form the basis of the fluidity of today's world and the multiple perspectives, images, and meanings that inform the worldviews of social actors, whether they be individuals, communities, corporations, or nation-states.[2]

Ethnoscapes are created through the flow of individuals and groups "who constitute the shifting world in which we live" (Appadurai 1992:33). Ethnoscapes are composed of the growing number of exiles, guest workers, tourists, immigrants, and refugees whose movements affect the economic, political, and cultural landscapes of an increasing number of, and increasingly distant, nations. *Technoscapes* refer to the "global configuration . . . of technology and the fact that technology, both high and low, both mechanical and informational, now moves at high speeds across" previously impermeable corporate and national boundaries (ibid.:34). Technologies are now bought and sold and moved across borders at an unprecedented rate. For instance, an automobile plant in the United States may be using parts and technologies imported from Mexico, Japan, and Germany. *Financescapes* represent the rapid flow of massive amounts of currencies and stocks across national boundaries. More than ever, national economies

---

[2]Nation-states are defined as self-governing territories demarcated by recognized spatial boundaries.

are linked globally as the rise and fall of major financial markets, patterns of foreign investment and the purchasing of foreign debt, and the value of national currencies impact the economic stability of not just one country but many countries simultaneously.

Appadurai also notes the growing importance of *mediascapes*, the ability to electronically produce and disseminate information and images on a global scale through television, newspapers, magazines, and films. According to Appadurai, what is most important about mediascapes is that "they provide . . . large and complex repertoires of images, narratives, and ethnoscapes to viewers throughout the world, in which the world of commodities and the world of news and political are profoundly mixed" (1992:35). In turn, the lines between the real and the fictional are blurred, while the audiences for such images often are further and further removed from the direct experience of the mediated narratives that they observe. Thus, from the strips of information presented on the news, viewers form opinions about people and places from around the globe, as they come to "know" about, for instance, civil unrest in France or a community's response to a natural disaster. Meanwhile, the line between news and propaganda, reality and fantasy, is becoming increasingly blurred as television subjects viewers to a steady dose of "infomercials" and "infotainment."

Closely related to mediascapes are *ideoscapes* that likewise entail the dissemination of images. In the case of ideoscapes, however, the images "are often directly political and frequently have to do with the ideologies of states and the counterideologies of movements explicitly oriented to capturing state power or a piece of it" (Appadurai 1992:36). Such politically charged images are tied to an Enlightenment worldview that trumpeted notions of rights, freedom, sovereignty, and democracy. It is these terms and the ideas that they encompass that often form the discourse through which political struggles are cast. For instance, the meaning of elections, military interventions, legal rulings, and protest movements is formed out of the attempts by proponents and opponents to affirm or contest their adherence to the principles of freedom, equality, and democracy. Taken together, these five scapes represent the source of global flows of people, machines, money, and images. While previous periods in history experienced such flows across national boundaries, Appadurai contends that the contemporary era of globalization is witness to an extreme intensification of their speed, scale, and volume such that the disjunctures between them are a major component to the global economic, political, and cultural landscapes. No longer are people, machines, money, and images more or less fixed to an identifiable territory; instead, they traverse the planet with unprecedented ease, creating truly global ideas and practices.

As we noted at the outset of our discussion, the world we live in today is shrinking. National economies are becoming increasingly integrated through expanding trade relationships, the spread of transnational corporations, and organizations such as the International Monetary Fund. Transnational political institutions from world courts, the European Union, the South American Community of Nations, and the United Nations are furthering international, if not global, forms of governance. A "global culture" consisting of common practices, ideas, and images now flows across national boundaries as more people, products, and information move to more places. That nations have become increasingly subject to the push and pull of foreign economic, political, and cultural interests begs what is perhaps the most salient, and controversial, question: where is the world headed?

There are two broad positions into which most scholars fall on this question, depending on whether they view globalization as producing an increasingly homogenous or heterogeneous world. These two broad positions can be further divided into "weak" and "strong" versions. (See Table 10.1 for a summary of these positions.) For those who view globalization as a homogenizing force, technological advances in

Table 10.1   Where Is Globalization Leading?: Four Views on the Consequences of Globalization

	Homogeneity	Heterogeneity
"Weak" Version	Glocalism World democracy Universalism via fusion	Global pluralism Particular colored with the global McArabia
"Strong" Version	Western cultural imperialism McDonaldization Coca-colonization Universalism via conquest	Ethnic and religious conflicts Rising fundamentalism Polarization of cultural identities "Clash of civilizations"

communication and transportation are seen as leading to the creation of a unified, interconnected "world society" where the world's population becomes integrated into a common culture. Yet, to the extent that globalization is tied to the expansion of Western capitalism and culture, this raises the issue of specifying what the West is actually exporting around the globe. For some observers, Westernization primarily implies a sense of universalism in which people around the world come to embrace a common cultural ground rooted in the Western ideals of democracy, human rights, and individual freedom. This could be termed a "weak" form of homogenization in which what is shared is a common appreciation and respect for differences (Tomlinson 1999:69). This openness to difference can in turn lead to a fusion of distinct cultures and practices, giving birth to such things as world music, world cuisine, or world cinema. In essence, a universal trend toward "glocalism" is created, where the local meets the global producing an ever-expanding mixture of cultural practices, meanings, tastes, and personal identities (see Robertson 1992). The crucial point to this notion of homogenization is the sense that globalization is not based on the systematic exploitation or domination of one region of the world by another, but rather on a developing, more humane and tolerant world-as-a-whole.

The "strong" form of the homogenization thesis, however, contends that globalization does indeed involve the destruction of indigenous or national cultures as the West continues its expansion through both economic and cultural imperialism. (Both Wallerstein and Sklair adopt this "strong" position, although they emphasize different dynamics.) This is a homogenization or universalism bred from conquest and the perpetuation of global inequalities as corporate capitalism and the ideology of consumerism continue their invasion of national and local cultures and ways of life. Thus, homogenization doesn't usher in a global democracy, the establishment of universal human rights, or a pastiche of cultural practices but, rather, a "McWorld" or "Coca-colonization" in which Western nations (most notably the U.S.) remodel the world in their image while siphoning off the profits that come with the increasing flows of technology, goods, money, and people across national borders.

One oft-cited description of this viewpoint is George Ritzer's "McDonaldization of Society." Ritzer defines this as "the process by which the principles of the fast-food restaurant are coming to dominate more and more sectors of American society as well as the rest of the world" (2000:1). Drawing from Max Weber's notion of the "iron cage" and his critique of the growing rationalization of the Western world, Ritzer argues that the operating procedures perfected by McDonald's not only have been duplicated in countless sectors of industry (from amusement parks and grocery stores to child care companies, health care organizations, and educational institutions), they have seeped into the routines of everyday life. Specifically, Ritzer notes four dimensions to McDonaldization: (1) Efficiency—optimizing the method for achieving goals, whether it be satisfying one's hunger or mass-producing laptop computers. (2) Calculability—an emphasis on the quantitative aspects of goods and services, for instance, how *much* they cost or how *long* it takes to receive them. As a result the importance of quality becomes secondary. Big Macs and Domino's Pizza may not taste as good as a home-made burger or pizza, but they are relatively inexpensive, and you get them fast. (3) Predictability—the comforting promise that goods and services will be the same whenever or wherever they are produced or consumed. (4) Control through nonhuman technology—the use of machines to replace workers or, at the very least, to routinize their tasks, while controlling the behavior of consumers through techniques such as offering drive-through windows and limited menu options, clearly marking queues for ordering, and providing uncomfortable seats and inhospitable lighting. All are designed to encourage individuals to leave as quickly as possible in order to make room for new paying customers (2000:12–15). In the end, McDonaldization promotes a standardized, homogenized approach to both production and consumption. To the extent that it has been adopted globally, everyday life has become the same the world over.

Moreover, as Mike Featherstone (1995) points out, the homogenizing effects of exporting McDonald's means more than spreading a particular method for producing and consuming goods and services. With restaurants in more than sixty countries, McDonald's serves as an icon of America and an American "way of life." Those who dine at McDonald's in South Africa, Thailand, India, Uruguay, and around the world are eating more than just a burger; they are "consuming" America and images associated with it: power, wealth, beauty, freedom, youth. This is true not only for McDonald's but also for other American products that have penetrated global markets such as Nike, Hollywood movies, Coca-Cola, and pop music. In the process, indigenous types of food, clothing, and music are displaced as a country's population adopts "American style."

We must not be too quick to assume, however, that McDonald's, Hollywood, and American CEOs have carte blanche to remake the world as they see fit. The consumption of goods and images is not a simple, unidirectional process, but instead one that often involves a reconfiguring of products on the part of consumers. There are a number of reasons to doubt that the sights, sounds, and tastes of America—and the West more generally—are sweeping the globe in some monolithic fashion. While American television shows and movies are beamed across the world, audiences do not assign identical meanings to them: *CSI* and *Desperate Housewives* can mean one thing (or many things, for that matter) to white, suburban viewers in America and something entirely different to those watching in Seoul, Korea. This holds true even more so when considering the meaning of ideals such as democracy, justice, and human rights. There is much variation in how particular countries define these terms and in how they are implemented in political institutions. What a Saudi might see as evidence of democracy, a Swede might view as promoting dictatorship. Or consider how Coke, a "simple" soft drink, is consumed throughout the world. As Howes (1996) notes:

> No imported object, Coca-Cola included, is completely immune from creolization. Indeed, one finds that Coke is often attributed with meanings and uses within particular cultures that are different from those imagined by the manufacturer. These include that it can smooth wrinkles (Russia), that it can revive a person from the dead (Haiti), and that it can turn copper into silver (Barbados). . . . Coke is also indigenised through being mixed with other drinks, such as rum in the Caribbean to make *Cuba Libre* or *augadiente* in Bolivia to produce *Ponche*

Negro. Finally it seems that Coke is perceived as a "native product" in many places—that is you will often find people who believe the drink originated in their country not in the United States. (cited in Tomlinson 1999:84)

For some final food for thought, in addition to offering the standard menu items found in their "home" country, fast-food chains often provide options tailored to the local culture. Thus, in Norway, McDonald's features the "McLaks" (a grilled salmon sandwich with dill sauce), in the Philippines one can indulge in "McSpaghetti," in Uruguay the McHuevo (hamburgers with poached egg), in Japan a "Teriyaki McBurger" (sausage patty with teriyaki sauce), in the Middle East diners can enjoy the McArabia (grilled chicken wrapped in flatbread), and in India, where neither beef nor pork products are served, the menu offers the Chicken Maharaja Mac and the Chicken McCurry Pan. The examples above suggest that, at the very least, it is premature to portend of a homogeneous global order in which the economies, political systems, and cultures of countries around the world are becoming exact duplicates of one another.

The second broad position adopted by scholars concerning where globalization is leading gives us even more cause to be cautious about such projections. For some, globalization is linked more to an increasing global pluralism or to the intensification of existing cultural differences. The world society is thus seen as characterized by a growing heterogeneity that highlights the distinctiveness of local cultures and ways of life. For example, proponents of this view would see in McDonald's global expansion not an invasion of the Big Mac, but rather a force that has created novel products that incorporate local ingredients and tastes like the McLak. Thus, while the global mass-marketing of products leads to homogenization in the sense that the same goods can be found in virtually every corner of the globe, this also means that in any one place there exists the possibility for increased choice and, with it, greater heterogeneity at the local level (Waters 2001:196). This view, emphasizing the combining of particular, local practices and ideas with those of foreign origin, represents what we call here a "weak" form of the heterogeneity thesis. In short, the process of globalization is seen as penetrating the regions of the world without, however, producing a uniform global culture. Regional distinctions remain, albeit colored by a constant interweaving with "outside" cultural and economic influences.

Last, we can speak of a "strong" form of heterogeneity. (Edward Said's work is aligned most closely with this perspective.) Those who adopt this position maintain that globalization is leading to an increasingly fragmented world where local communities organize to resist the homogenizing tendencies associated with the spread of global, and more often than not Western, influences. Far from promoting global unity or uniformity, scholars here note that the interconnectedness spawned by globalization sparks religious, ethnic, and cultural conflicts as people fight to preserve their identity and particular way of life. For instance, in response to the increasing encroachment of Western culture and ideals, Asian leaders have sought to articulate a unique model of human rights based on Confucianism to counter Western conceptions of individualism and liberty. Moreover, globalization is seen as providing fertile ground not only for the rise of Islamic fundamentalism in the Middle East but also for an intensifying ethnocentrism witnessed in many countries such as Germany, where Turkish immigrants are subjected to violent attacks; England, where South Asians face similar hostilities; and the United States, where armed "minutemen" take to patrolling the border with Mexico in order to slow the "tide" of illegal immigrants. Rejecting globalization's trend toward universalism, these reactions are symptomatic of a "clash of civilizations" that pits the West against the Rest (Huntington 1993).

Photo 10.1   Democracy, Iranian Style: While they have popular elections for both the office of the president and the national assembly, Iran is a theocracy governed according to Shari'a or Islamic law. The "Supreme Leader" of the country is a cleric who is appointed for life. In this "democracy" there is no separation between church and state, while under Islamic law women can be stoned to death for adultery, have unequal rights to divorce and child custody, can be married off at the age of nine, are able to work or travel only with the permission of their father or husband, and in the court of law, evidence and testimony offered by a female witness is valued at half that offered by a male. Pictured above is Supreme Leader of the Islamic Revolution Ayatollah Seyed Ali Khamenei, confirming Mahmoud Ahmadinejad as the sixth president of the Islamic Republic of Iran in a special ceremony.

SOURCE: © Mohsen Shandiz/CORBIS; used with permission.

Outside of Europe and the United States, this resistance to global homogeneity is in large part a response to the history of Western colonialism (a theme Said addresses later in the chapter). Many nations that were once colonies or "client states" of Western powers have sought to combine the economic modernization that globalization has brought with a rekindling of their traditional cultural identities.[3] This entails embracing the economic advantages and technological advances flowing from the West without embracing Western culture. A similar stance is often adopted by non-Western nations (for instance, China, Japan, and Saudi Arabia) that remained largely free from direct or indirect rule by Western powers. As these nations struggle for and win greater political, economic, and military power, the clash between their religious and cultural orientations and those of the West will likewise increase. No longer mere pawns on the world stage, nations whose religious and political cultures are based on Islamic, Hindu, and Buddhist traditions are gaining greater voice and are using it to nurture a way of life

---

[3]The list of such nations is long. Some that students may be more familiar with are Algeria, Egypt, Hong Kong, India, Iran, Kuwait, Pakistan, and Vietnam.

that contrasts in fundamental ways with the "universal" values and ideals of the West. "For the relevant future, there will be no universal civilization, but instead a world of different civilizations," where the West seeks to maintain its dominance as other nations attempt to assert their own cultural identities and priorities (Huntington 1993:49).

Having provided an overview of some of the central themes that inform studies of the global society, we now turn to our discussion of the work of Immanuel Wallerstein, Leslie Sklair, and Edward Said.

IMMANUEL WALLERSTEIN (1930–): A BIOGRAPHICAL SKETCH

SOURCE: Photo courtesy of Yale University; used with permission.

Immanuel Wallerstein was born in New York City in 1930. He spent his childhood and early adult years in the city, attending the local high school and going on to Columbia University, where he received his bachelor's, master's, and doctorate degrees. While finishing his doctorate, he took a position as an instructor in Columbia's sociology department. He remained there for the next thirteen years, advancing to the position of associate professor, and then, in 1971, he took a position at McGill University in Montreal. In 1976, he returned to New York to become director of the newly established Fernand Braudel Center for the Study of Economics, Historical Systems, and Civilizations at the State University of New York at Binghamton. While he continues to be the director of the Center, Wallerstein now holds a position at Yale University.

Wallerstein grew up in a politically minded family, and early socialization into political discussions played an important role in shaping his intellectual interests. He became involved both politically and as a scholar in the national liberation movements spreading through Africa during the early 1950s. During the next two decades, Wallerstein would become a leading specialist in the study of African political and economic affairs, producing numerous books and articles on the subject. His early experiences in Africa led to his "gut feeling . . . that the most important thing that was happening in the twentieth-century world was the struggle to overcome the control by the Western world of the rest of the world" (Wallerstein: http://www.yale.edu/socdept/faculty/wallerstein.html). His solidarity with those struggling for independence from colonial exploitation also shaped his development of "world-systems analysis" in the 1970s.

One additional aspect of Wallerstein's intellectual position is worth noting here. While objectivity is often proclaimed as a hallmark of scientific inquiry, Wallerstein argues that the intellectual detachment necessary to achieving such a perspective is, in fact, impossible to maintain. Moreover, by attempting to detach one's self from the subject of study, the "disengaged" scholar will produce knowledge that is less capable of fostering positive social change. Wallerstein, however, does not suggest that scholars should produce knowledge to serve the interests of particular political parties or to serve their own political loyalties. Rather, his point is that there is not or could not "be such a thing as value-free historical social science. Every choice of conceptual framework is a political option. Every assertion of 'truth,' even if one qualifies it as transitory truth or heuristic theory, is an assertion of value" (Wallerstein 1979:x). Scholars who are convinced otherwise are merely attempting to hide their value assertions behind the transparent cloak of scientific neutrality and objectivity.

Wallerstein states his position on the relationship between politics and scientific research thusly:

> It seems to me that it is the duty of the scholar to be politically and intellectually subversive of received truths, but that the only way this subversion can be socially useful is if it reflects a serious attempt to engage with and understand the real world as best we can. . . . I have argued that world-systems analysis is not a theory but a protest against neglected issues and deceptive epistemologies. It is a call for intellectual change, indeed for "unthinking" the premises of nineteenth-century social science. It is an intellectual task that is and has to be a political task as well, because—I insist—the search for the true and the search for the good is but a single quest. (Wallerstein: www.yale.edu/socdept/faculty/wallerstein.html)

Not surprisingly, Wallerstein's criticisms of mainstream theories and research practices and his own emphasis on qualitative and historical methods were not enthusiastically received by all social scientists. Nevertheless, he has established himself as a leading intellectual with an international reputation. In addition to serving as president of the International Sociological Association from 1994 to 1998, he has over the years produced an amazing corpus of work comprising more than fifty authored and coauthored books and nearly three hundred articles. However, it is his three-volume study, *The Modern World-System* (1974, 1980, 1989), for which he is most noted. Translated into fourteen languages, the first volume attracted worldwide attention and placed Wallerstein squarely into the pantheon of contemporary intellectual giants.

INTELLECTUAL INFLUENCES AND CORE IDEAS

Wallerstein lists a number of thinkers whose ideas have impacted his intellectual development. Among them are Karl Marx, the economists Joseph Schumpeter (1883–1950) and Karl Polanyi (1886–1964), and Fernand Braudel (1902–1985), the French historian for whom the Center for the Study of Economics, Historical Systems, and Civilizations was named. In what follows we briefly introduce the central ideas associated with these thinkers as they pertain to Wallerstein's own perspective.

Fernand Braudel was a leading figure in the Annales School of history, established in France in the late 1920s. Members of the Annales School revolutionized the study of history by moving from events-based research to the study of *la longue durée*, or the long-term. Up to this point, historians had focused on detailing single accounts of war and diplomacy and the great deeds of great men, but the Annales historians sought to integrate geography, sociology, economics, and, in later generations, a focus on the "mentalities" or psychology of the period into their analyses. This approach produced more sweeping and in-depth social and economic histories such as Braudel's monumental two-thousand-page work *The Mediterranean and the Mediterranean World in the Age of Philip II* (1949). Written largely during his captivity in a German prisoner-of-war camp, this masterpiece of historical reconstruction, produced in the most inhospitable conditions with the barest of resources (including few books), sealed his reputation as one of the world's foremost historians.

In this work and his subsequent publications,[4] Braudel adopted the *longue durée* to complete enormously detailed studies that incorporated analyses of everything from a region's climate, geography, natural catastrophes, and demographics to its social

---

[4]His most notable works include the three-volume *Civilization and Capitalism, 15th–18th Century*; *A History of Civilizations*; and *On History*.

customs, fashions, food, technology, and economic and political institutions. Examining such an extensive array of factors across continents and over centuries, Braudel concluded that historical development is a "messy" project, incapable of being subsumed under one or another general theory. Nevertheless, Braudel maintained that it was the life of the peasant, the craftsman, and the merchant, not the heroics of the prince, the statesman, and the rich, that largely shaped the march of history.

Three aspects of Wallerstein's research demonstrate a particular debt to Braudel. First, like the French historian, Wallerstein's work covers large expanses of time. His three-volume *The Modern World-System* spans some four hundred years while offering detailed accounts of the economic development of several regions of the world. Second, akin to Braudel, Wallerstein sets out to explain the origins of modern capitalism and the causes and consequences of its spread throughout the world. The third Braudelian stamp is evidenced by Wallerstein's rejection of traditional methodological and disciplinary boundaries, particularly those separating history from sociology.[5] While history has typically been devoted to analyses of unique or particular events, sociology (or more accurately, some branches of sociology) has been devoted to the development of abstract or general causal statements. For his part, Wallerstein believed this to be a false dichotomy and instead advocated building upon both the idiographic accounts associated with the humanities and the nomothetic explanations that characterize the sciences. For Wallerstein, both methods are necessary for any attempt to accurately describe and explain the real world.

Wallerstein's history of economic development is also influenced by the work of two renowned economists: Joseph Schumpeter and Karl Polanyi. Schumpeter was an Austrian economist who rose to prominence at the age of twenty-eight with the publication of his *Theory of Economic Development* (1911).[6] His subsequent book, *Capitalism, Socialism and Democracy* (1942), further solidified his reputation in the field while expanding his audience to include, among other scholars, sociologists. In this work, Schumpeter mounted a masterful defense of the virtues of capitalism—a particularly important accomplishment, given the prevailing geopolitical climate. He championed the individual entrepreneur as the source of great innovations that not only advanced capitalism as a system of production and economic organization, but also improved the living standards of the general population. However, like Marx, Schumpeter imagined that the very success of capitalism would ultimately lead to its collapse and to the rise of socialism. Yet, in stark contrast to Marx, who viewed capitalism as inherently exploitative and destined to be overthrown by a proletarian revolution, Schumpeter saw capitalism imploding on itself because of moments of "creative destruction" in which the constant, beneficial innovations sparked by the entrepreneurial spirit would in time lead to the rise of monopolies that are better able to withstand the costs associated with "progress." In short, only monopolies and large corporations that possess the necessary capital and control of the market can bear the rising costs and risks associated with the continual supplanting of "obsolete" technologies, products, and skills by new innovations. With the gradual eclipse of competitive capitalism, the

---

[5]Max Weber, one of the founding figures in sociology, took a similar position on this debate, developing what is now commonly referred to as historical-comparative methods.

[6]Apart from working in academia, Schumpeter also served briefly as Austria's finance minister in 1919, his tenure short-lived in part because of the hyperinflation that was strangling his country's economy. With Hitler's rise to power, however, Schumpeter left Europe and emigrated to the United States in 1932. That same year he accepted a position at Harvard University, where he remained until his retirement in 1949.

individual entrepreneur is himself rendered obsolete as bureaucratic managers take on the administrative task of steering the economy. However, the slow extinction of the entrepreneur produces a workforce increasingly uncertain about its prospects for employment. Coupled with the intellectual class's growing protests against the social inequities stemming from capitalist production, the stage becomes set for the emergence of socialism.

The other economist Wallerstein credits for shaping his approach is Karl Polanyi.[7] Here we note two of Polanyi's most influential works. First is *The Great Transformation* (1944), a now classic study of the emergence of the contemporary market economy in the nineteenth century and its connection to the development of the modern nation-state. In this book, Polanyi details the role that governments played in supporting the economic interests of the rising bourgeoisie. The second work is his coauthored *Trade and Market in the Early Empires* (1957). In his contribution to this volume, Polanyi explored the development of nonmarket forms of economic systems, which he classified as reciprocal, redistributive, and householding. Polanyi's investigations led him to construct a "substantive" approach to the study of economics. Akin to anthropological studies, this approach was based on the premise that economic systems and modes of exchange are not separate from but, rather, are embedded in broader social and cultural relations.

The imprint of these two economists on Wallerstein's world-systems analysis is apparent on several fronts. Like Schumpeter and Polanyi, Wallerstein provides rich, historical accounts of economic developments and connects them to transformations taking place in other domains of society. Similarly, all three view capitalism as an economic system whose reign will eventually come to a close. In Polanyi's perspective, capitalism will collapse not because of the system's successes, as Schumpeter argued, but because of its failures. More specifically, Polanyi asserted that market-based forms of exchange cannot be sustained ecologically over the long term, as the logic of market relations destroys other forms of social relations, such as kinship ties, that are better suited to creating a sense of solidarity or community within populations.

Making the deepest impact on Wallerstein's work, however, is Karl Marx, whose ideas figure prominently also in the work of each of the scholars discussed above. At its most fundamental level, Wallerstein's model is based on the assumption that all social systems, whether a particular nation-state or the more encompassing world-system, are formed, maintained, and destroyed through conflict. To understand the history of social development thus requires an analysis of the struggles that are waged between factions competing over resources. Moreover, in the spirit of Marx's historical materialism, Wallerstein maintained that while the conflicts that form the basis of social systems can be contained through legal or political institutions, they can never be entirely eliminated. For Marx saw that all history is the history of class struggle, a struggle against inequality that is inevitable so long as a society's means of production can be privately owned. (See our overview of Marx's work in Chapter 3 as well as additional remarks in the previous chapter.) Wallerstein expresses a similar view when he remarks that "the history of the world is one of a constant series of revolts against

[7]Polanyi was born in Vienna and raised in Budapest, Hungary. He emigrated to the United States in 1940 and later took a position at Columbia University, where he served on the faculty from 1947 to 1953. However, although he worked in New York City, Polanyi was unable to live there or anywhere else in the United States Because his wife was a one-time communist, she was unable to secure a visa to enter the United States, leaving Karl to commute between New York and Canada, where they took up residence.

inequality—whether that of one people or nation vis-à-vis another or of one class within a geographical area against another" (Wallerstein 1979:49).

To connect the range of intellectual influences outlined to this point, we now turn to an overview of Wallerstein's world-systems analysis. At its root, world-systems analysis is a product of Wallerstein's rejection of the conventional sociological practice of equating states (e.g., France, China) with societies. This intellectual position, according to Wallerstein, leads to erroneous explanations of social history and misguided predictions of future developments. To counter these pitfalls, he insists that the only unit of analysis capable of advancing the knowledge of the social sciences is the "world-system." In essence, social scientists must approach their subject—society—with the understanding that there is only one social system as opposed to viewing the world as made up of a collection of more or less independent societies or nation-states. He defines his central concept, **world-system**, as a

> social system, one that has boundaries, structures, member groups, rules of legitimation, and coherence. Its life is made up of conflicting forces which hold it together by tension, and tear it apart as each group seeks eternally to remold it to its advantage. It has the characteristics of an organism, in that it has a life-span over which its characteristics change in some respects and remain stable in others. (Wallerstein 1979:229)

Such "total" world-systems are distinct from tribal societies or nations in that they contain within their boundaries a diversity of cultures and an expansive division of labor that links together the smaller social units to form a coherent whole.

According to Wallerstein, to this point in history there have been only two types of world-systems in existence: **world-empires** and **world-economies**. Empires, such as those that existed in ancient Rome or Egypt between 8000 B.C. and A.D. 1500, are ruled by, and integrated through, political and military domination. Those regions making up the empire pay taxes in the form of "tributes" to those who control the empire. World-economies, conversely, are not structured according to political rule but, instead, are based on economic exchanges that extend beyond the politically defined boundaries and control of any given state. Thus, it is not politics but economics that is the integrating force within world-economies, an integration that nevertheless remains based on relations of domination. And from roughly the sixteenth century to the present, only one world-system has been in existence: the capitalist world-economy. This economy is the only mode of production in which the maximization of profit is the central reward for participating in economic production. Thus, the capitalist's interest in producing particular goods or services is determined not by their use, but rather by the potential value of their exchange on the market. Moreover, the logic of capitalism demands that those who profit from the market are required to accumulate yet more capital in an effort to further increase their economic reward. This leads in turn to the constant expansion of capitalist enterprises (Wallerstein 1979:85).

Wallerstein (1974) traces the origins of the modern world-capitalist system during the sixteenth century to the convergence of three factors: (1) an expansion of the world's geography due to exploration and colonization, (2) the development of different methods of labor control in different geographical zones, and (3) the development of strong states able to dictate the terms of international economic trade to their relative advantage. As ruling elites in European nations vied to maintain their power, they sought to exploit the natural and human resources of foreign lands. In need of gold, raw materials for production and trade, and the manpower to extract them, factions within the European nobility looked to overseas expansion as a means for securing their positions of dominance. This created a global and hierarchical division of labor and system of economic specialization that to this day serves as the foundation for the world capitalist system, whose essential feature "is production for sale in a market in which the object is to realize the maximum profit" (Wallerstein 1979:15).

In the attempt to consolidate their economic power, emerging capitalist classes appealed to political leaders to intervene in the market on their behalf. Those capitalists who were able to turn to a strong state bureaucracy (which is itself largely a product of large tax revenues) capable of dictating trade policy and possessing the military power to secure its demands were able to reap a greater share of the world's wealth. Indeed, in the world-economy, strong, relatively autonomous states "serve primarily to distort the 'free' workings of the capitalist market" in order to increase one or another group's potential for profit (Wallerstein 1979:223).[8] This dynamic led to the creation of three hierarchically structural positions within the capitalist world-economy: core, periphery, and semiperiphery. As a result, the stability of the modern world-system came to be based on a fundamental inequality in which some regions of the globe accumulate wealth at the expense of the continuing impoverishment of other regions.

The **core** region of the modern world-system first emerged in northwestern Europe and now includes the United States, Canada, Japan, and other similarly industrialized nation-states. Together this "area" controls a vast majority of the world's wealth while producing a highly skilled workforce that is controlled through wage payment. Using its economic and political superiority, the core is able to dominate and control the periphery. The **periphery** is exploited for its raw materials, such as cotton, sugar, rubber, and gold, which are then exported to the core. Often "possessions" or colonies of core states, the periphery is made up of weak nations lacking the economic, political, and military clout necessary for pressing its own agenda. The workforce in the periphery historically has been controlled through coercion and slavery, and today it still breeds the worst of labor conditions. At the outset Eastern Europe and parts of the Western Hemisphere served as the periphery, while today it is comprised of Africa, the Caribbean, Central America, and other "third world" regions. The lack of progress that is often said to characterize peripheral areas is in large measure a result of their economic and political dependence on the core. While the core areas have been enriched through their exploitation of the natural and human resources of the periphery, the periphery has been subject to the "development of underdevelopment" (Frank 1967). In other words, the "backwardness" of the periphery is the result of economic polices strategically intended to maintain its status as an exporter of resources while being prevented from appropriating the profits that they generate. An example of this phenomenon was provided at the beginning of the chapter when we described the multinational corporation Texaco exploiting the rainforests of Ecuador. Unfortunately, the list of examples is exceedingly long: diamonds and coal in Africa, rice and rubber in Cambodia, coffee and sugarcane from Haiti. . . . In each case, core areas institute international economic trade policies and subsidize local governments that perpetuate the underdevelopment of the regions making up the periphery.

The **semiperiphery** occupies a position between the core and the periphery—economically and politically weaker than the former, but stronger than the latter. This

---

[8]Wallerstein defines a "strong state" as one that possesses "strength vis-à-vis other states within the world economy including other core states, and strong vis-à-vis local political units within the boundaries of the state. . . . A strong state then is a partially autonomous entity in the sense that it has a margin of action available to it wherein reflects the compromises of multiple interests, even if the bounds of these margins are set by some groups of primordial strength. To be a partially autonomous entity, there must be a group of people whose direct interests are served by such an entity: state managers and a state bureaucracy" (Wallerstein 1974:232).

area, with a labor force historically controlled through sharecropping, first emerged in the Mediterranean region of Europe, a position that today includes Eastern Europe, Mexico, and parts of South America. Moreover, semiperipheral areas play an essential role in maintaining the political stability of the modern world-system by deflecting some of the protests and political pressures that groups located in the periphery would otherwise direct toward the core states and the economic interests that are aligned with them. These areas prevent a completely polarized world-system from developing such that "the upper stratum is not faced with the *unified* opposition of all the others because the *middle* stratum is both exploited and exploiter" (Wallerstein 1979:23).

In one sense, Wallerstein's notion of the core and periphery resembles Marx's discussion of the struggle between the "two great classes" under capitalism: the bourgeoisie—those who own the means of production—and the proletariat—those who own only their labor power and thus must work for the bourgeoisie. However, a critical distinction separates these two views. While Marx emphasized the conflict between the two classes that occurs within a particular nation, Wallerstein contends that "capitalism involves not only appropriation of the surplus value [profit] by an owner from a laborer, but an appropriation of surplus of the whole world-economy by core areas" (Wallerstein 1979:19). In other words, the reality of the capitalist world-economy is that the surplus value produced by the proletariat is routinely appropriated by a bourgeoisie that is located in a different region of the globe. With the development of the world-economy, no single nation-state or central political system exists that is capable of controlling the flow of capital across national boundaries and its unequal accumulation into "private" hands. Capitalism has no determinate "external" boundaries in the modern world-system, as it has on the basis of its own logic come to expand the globe, absorbing all other social systems (Wallerstein 1987:318). This expansion, however, has served to increase the wealth for some regions while perpetuating the poverty of others.

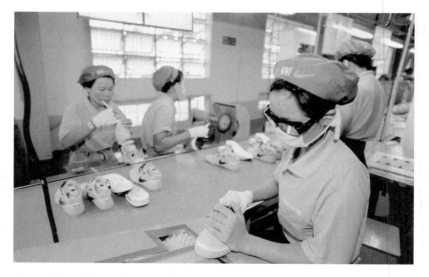

Photo 10.3 Nike in Vietnam. Although a communist country, Vietnam is not isolated from the market forces of the capitalist world-economy. With some fifty thousand employees, Nike is Vietnam's largest private employer, exporting twenty-two million pairs of shoes annually.
SOURCE: © Steve Raymer/CORBIS; used with permission.

There are two other important differences between Marx's analysis and that offered by Wallerstein. First, while Marx envisioned a future utopia brought on by the inevitable revolution of the proletariat and the establishment of communism, Wallerstein's vision of the future is much more cautious. Unlike Marx, Wallerstein does not ascribe a necessary trajectory or path of progress to history. There is no utopian final stage or "end of prehistory" toward which the capitalist world-economy inexorably marches. At best, an entirely new form of world-system—a socialist world-government—may emerge out of the capitalist world-economy as "antisystemic movements" struggle to resist the inequities and injustices resulting from the unchecked expansion of capitalism. Such a world-system may not offer humankind full redemption from the exploitation and destruction wrought by capitalism or the end of class conflict, but it would lead to a more equitable distribution of the world's wealth by maintaining a high level of economic productivity managed more through political planning decisions than market forces. The freedom currently exercised by capitalists and core states to direct profits to their sole advantage would be curtailed, as a single political system whose boundaries encompass (as opposed to being exceeded by) the whole of economic production would be established. This would in turn stabilize economic development by curbing fluctuations in supply and demand. The tighter control exercised over the market would then reduce the level of exploitation and destruction currently tied to the capitalist world-economy.

Second, Wallerstein's studies of the political and economic conditions in Africa, and in the modern world-system more generally, led him to identify not only class but also race as a major locus of conflict within the capitalist world-economy. Indeed, he contends that gender, ethnicity, and nationality are likewise all major sources of divisiveness in the modern world. This emphasis represents a break from more orthodox variants of Marxism that argue that class conflict is the singular site of exploitation and the motor force of all social change. Wallerstein argues that it is not by coincidence that the vast majority of the periphery is peopled by the "darker races," thus directly tying racism to the expansion of the capitalist world-economy. It is not by coincidence that the technologically advanced, wealthy core states compose an area where "whites" constitute a majority of the population. As you will see in the final portion of this chapter when we discuss the work of Edward Said, this point is also taken up in postcolonial theories. Yet, Wallerstein's argument on this point remains ambiguous, for he contends that ethnic and racial struggles and nationalist movements ultimately are generated by the dynamics of the *capitalist* world-economy. (They must be given that the modern world-system is fundamentally organized around the logic of capitalism.) As a result, such struggles are at their root expressions of economic, not racial or nationalist, conflict. Thus, Wallerstein notes that despite the success of some ethno-nationalist movements to win political independence for their countries, they remain dependent and subordinate because of the overwhelming economic power possessed by core

Table 10.2   Comparing the Theories of Marx and Wallerstein on Modern Society

Central Themes	Marx	Wallerstein
Primary social entity	Nation-State	World-System
Basis of society	Capitalist economy	Capitalist economy
Primary social relations	Bourgeoisie and Proletariat	Core, Periphery, Semiperiphery
Basis of social relations	Conflict/Exploitation	Conflict/Exploitation
Future of society	Inevitable communist revolution	Possible socialist world-government

states. Moreover, such movements serve to mute the underlying reality of capitalist exploitation to the extent that calls for ethnic equality and national liberation are the principal battleground for social change (Wallerstein 1979:200).

Consider, for instance, the case of South Africa. First colonized by the Dutch, South Africa became a British colony in the late eighteenth century. After the Anglo-Boer Wars, the Union of South Africa was established in 1910 and with it a political and social environment that promoted the systematic repression of the indigenous nonwhite population. The repression was intensified under the brutally oppressive system of apartheid formally established in 1948. South Africa declared its independence from British rule in 1961, and the Republic of South Africa was created. It would take several decades of domestic protests from the black population and mounting pressure from the international community to end the country's overtly racist policies. Yet, with the dismantling of apartheid in the early 1990s and the granting of political equality for the nonwhite population, South Africa's economic picture remains bleak. With estimates of unemployment ranging from 30 to 40 percent of the population, an annual per capita income of $2,600, and the implementation of socially punishing austerity measures to attract foreign (i.e., core) investment, South Africa remains economically weak in the world capitalist-economy. In the end, the morally motivated battle to end racial injustice may have been won, but the vast majority of South Africans are still not free.

WALLERSTEIN'S THEORETICAL ORIENTATION

The presuppositions underlying Wallerstein's perspective can be gleaned from our preceding discussion. Employing concepts such as core, periphery, and semiperiphery, Wallerstein adopts a decidedly collectivist approach to the issue of order. Indeed, what could be more encompassing than a world-system! From this vantage point, social life is fundamentally patterned according to the economic relationships existing between regions of the globe. As such, individuals and their interactions do not figure prominently in Wallerstein's theoretical framework, creating a fairly "dehumanized" portrait of history.

Figure 10.1   Basic Theoretical Concepts in Wallerstein's World-Systems Analysis

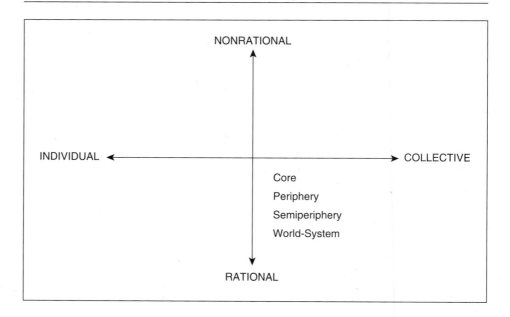

Regarding the issue of action, Wallerstein's emphasis on matters such as capitalist markets, class interests, and the pursuit of profit points to a rationalist orientation. It is important to note, however, that accounting for motivational factors, which is what the question of action addresses, is problematic within world-systems analysis. This is because the central "actors" are not individuals, or even groups of individuals, but rather regions of the globe. At the very least, we must be cautious about projecting motives onto spatial areas. Nevertheless, if we set aside this issue, it is clear that what "motivates" the core is the strategic attempt to maintain its dominant position in the modern world-system. Similarly, the peripheral and semiperipheral regions seek to improve their position through strategic use of the limited resources they possess. Ultimately, the world is shaped by the play of interests, not ideas, as the competing regions struggle to maximize their economic advantage while perpetuating the inequal-ities on which the capitalist world-economy is based.

The collectivistic and rationalistic dimensions of Wallerstein's theoretical orienta-tion are reflected in the following remarks, in which he describes the dynamics of the capitalist world-economy:

> The capitalist world-economy functions, as do most . . . historical systems by means of a pat-tern of cyclical rhythms. . . . One part, however, of the process is that, periodically, the capital-ist world-economy has seen the need to expand the geographic boundaries of the system as a whole, creating thereby new loci of production to participate in its axial division of labor. Over 400 years, these successive expansions have transformed the capitalist world-economy from a system located primarily in Europe to one that covers the entire globe. (Wallerstein 1990:36)

Here Wallerstein posits the existence of an economic system with its own "needs" and that experiences necessary periods of expansion according to its own internal logic, and in classic functionalist—and Marxist—fashion, Wallerstein offers a picture of society in which the primary mover of history is not people but rather an abstract force that carries them along in its own wake.

Reading

Introduction to "The Rise and Future Demise of the World Capitalist System"

In this reading, "The Rise and Future Demise of the World Capitalist System," Wallerstein addresses many of the issues discussed above. He begins by situating his analysis within the debates between the various forms of Marxism. He then describes his notion of the world-system and the nature of the relationship between the core, peripheral, and semiperipheral regions that make up the world-capitalist economy. The last section of the reading finds Wallerstein outlining the historical evolution of the world-capitalist economy, beginning with its initial emergence in the sixteenth century to its current stage of consolidation.

One additional point about this reading bears mentioning: that the world-capitalist economy has evolved over the course of several centuries implies that nations are subject to both advancement and loss of status within the world-system. One need only think of the United States to recognize that a colony located in the periphery can, over time, become a dominant force located in the core region. Similarly, at the present, other nations are vying more or less successfully for improving their status in the world-capitalist economy, for instance, India, Brazil, and Singapore. And as Wallerstein points out, history is filled with nations whose trajectories during certain historical periods have been less fortunate: Russia, Poland, Turkey, Spain, and even Britain, among others. The fate of any one nation or region, however, is tied to the economic dynamics of the overall world-system that experiences cycles of geographical expansion and contraction according to the balance between world supply of raw materials and production of goods, and world demand for them.

The Rise and Future Demise of the World Capitalist System: Concepts for Comparative Analysis (1974)

Immanuel Wallerstein

The growth within the capitalist world-economy of the industrial sector of production, the so-called 'industrial revolution,' was accompanied by a very strong current of thought which defined this change as both a process of organic development and of progress. There were those who considered these economic developments and the concomitant changes in social organization to be some penultimate stage of world development whose final working out was but a matter of time. These included such diverse thinkers as Saint-Simon, Comte, Hegel, Weber, Durkheim. And then there were the critics, most notably Marx, who argued, if you will, that the nineteenth-century present was only an antepenultimate stage of development, that the capitalist world was to know a cataclysmic political revolution which would then lead in the fullness of time to a final societal form, in this case the classless society.

One of the great strengths of Marxism was that, being an oppositional and hence critical doctrine, it called attention not merely to the contradictions of the system but to those of its ideologists, by appealing to the empirical evidence of historical reality which unmasked the irrelevancy of the models proposed for the explanation of the social world. The Marxist critics saw in abstracted models concrete rationalization, and they argued their case fundamentally by pointing to the failure of their opponents to analyze the social whole. As Lukacs put it, 'it is not the primacy of economic motives in historical explanation that constitutes the decisive difference between Marxism and bourgeois thought, but the point of view of totality.'[i]

In the mid twentieth century, the dominant theory of development in the core countries of the capitalist world-economy has added little to the theorizing of the nineteenth-century progenitors of this mode of analysis, except to quantify the models and to abstract them still further, by adding on epicyclical codas to the models in order to account for ever further deviations from empirical expectations. . . .

Shall we then turn to the critical schools, in particular Marxism, to give us a better account of social reality? In principle yes; in practice there are many different, often contradictory, versions extant of 'Marxism.' But what is more fundamental is the fact that in many countries Marxism is now the official state doctrine. Marxism is no

---

[i]George Lukacs, 'The Marxism of Rosa Luxemburg,' in *History and Class Consciousness* (London: Merlin Press, 1968), p. 27.

longer exclusively an oppositional doctrine as it was in the nineteenth century.

The social fate of official doctrines is that they suffer a constant social pressure towards dogmatism and apologia, difficult although by no means impossible to counteract, and that they thereby often fall into the same intellectual dead end of ahistorical model building. Here the critique of Fernand Braudel is most pertinent:

> Marxism is a whole collection of models . . . I shall protest . . . , more or less, not against the model, but rather against the use to which people have thought themselves entitled to put it. The genius of Marx, the secret of his enduring power, lies in his having been the first to construct true social models, starting out from the long term (*la longue durée*). These models have been fixed permanently in their simplicity; they have been given the force of law and they have been treated as ready-made, automatic explanations, applicable in all places to all societies . . . In this way has the creative power of the most powerful social analysis of the last century been shackled. It will be able to regain its strength and vitality only in the long term.[ii]

Nothing illustrates the distortions of ahistorical models of social change better than the dilemmas to which the concept of stages gives rise. If we are to deal with social transformations over long historical time (Braudel's 'the long term'), and if we are to give an explanation of both continuity and transformation, then we must logically divide the long term into segments in order to observe the structural changes from time A to time B. These segments are however not discrete but continuous in reality; *ergo* they are 'stages' in the 'development' of a social structure, a development which we determine however not *a priori* but *a posteriori*. That is, we cannot predict the future concretely, but we can predict the past.

The crucial issue when comparing 'stages' is to determine the units of which the 'stages' are synchronic portraits (or 'ideal types,' if you will). And the fundamental error of ahistorical social science (including ahistorical versions of Marxism) is to reify parts of the totality into

such units and then to compare these reified structures.

For example, we may take modes of disposition of agricultural production, and term them subsistence cropping and cash cropping. We may then see these as entities which are 'stages' of a development. We may talk about decisions of groups of peasants to shift from one to the other. We may describe other partial entities, such as states, as having within them two separate 'economies,' each based on a different mode of disposition of agricultural production. If we take each of these successive steps, all of which are false steps, we will end up with the misleading concept of the 'dual economy' as have many liberal economists dealing with the so-called underdeveloped countries of the world. . . .

Marxist scholars have often fallen into exactly the same trap. If we take modes of payment of agricultural labor and contrast a 'feudal' mode wherein the laborer is permitted to retain for subsistence a part of his agricultural production with a 'capitalist' mode wherein the same laborer turns over the totality of his production to the landowner, receiving part of it back in the form of wages, we may then see these two modes as 'stages' of a development. We may talk of the interests of 'feudal' landowners in preventing the conversion of their mode of payment to a system of wages. We may then explain the fact that in the twentieth century a partial entity, say a state in Latin America, has not yet industrialized as the consequence of its being dominated by such landlords. If we take each of these successive steps, all of which are false steps, we will end up with the misleading concept of a 'state dominated by feudal elements,' as though such a thing could possibly exist in a capitalist world-economy. . . .

Not only does the misidentification of the entities to be compared lead us into false concepts, but it creates a non-problem: can stages be skipped? This question is only logically meaningful if we have 'stages' that 'coexist' within a single empirical framework. If within a capitalist world-economy, we define one state as feudal, a second as capitalist, and a third as socialist, then and only then can we pose the question: can a country 'skip' from the feudal

---

[ii]Fernand Braudel, 'History and the Social Sciences,' in Peter Burke (ed.), *Economy and Society in Early Modern Europe* (London: Routledge and Kegan Paul, 1972), pp. 38–9.

stage to the socialist stage of national development without 'passing through capitalism'?

But if there is no such thing as 'national development' (if by that we mean a natural history), and if the proper entity of comparison is the world system, then the problem of stage skipping is nonsense. If a stage can be skipped, it isn't a stage. And we know this *a posteriori*.

If we are to talk of stages, then—and we should talk of stages—it must be stages of social systems, that is, of totalities. And the only totalities that exist or have historically existed are minisystems and world-systems, and in the nineteenth and twentieth centuries there has been only one world-system in existence, the capitalist world-economy.

We take the defining characteristic of a social system to be the existence within it of a division of labor, such that the various sectors or areas within are dependent upon economic exchange with others for the smooth and continuous provisioning of the needs of the area. Such economic exchange can clearly exist without a common political structure and even more obviously without sharing the same culture.

A minisystem is an entity that has within it a complete division of labor, and a single cultural framework. Such systems are found only in very simple agricultural or hunting and gathering societies. Such minisystems no longer exist in the world. Furthermore, there were fewer in the past than is often asserted, since any such system that became tied to an empire by the payment of tribute as 'protection costs' ceased by that fact to be a 'system,' no longer having a self-contained division of labor. For such an area, the payment of tribute marked a shift, in Polanyi's language, from being a reciprocal economy to participating in a larger redistributive economy.[iii]

Leaving aside the now defunct minisystems, the only kind of social system is a world-system, which we define quite simply as a unit with a single division of labor and multiple cultural systems. It follows logically that there can, however, be two varieties of such world-systems,

one with a common political system and one without. We shall designate these respectively as world-empires and world-economies.

It turns out empirically that world-economies have historically been unstable structures leading either towards disintegration or conquest by one group and hence transformation into a world-empire. Examples of such world-empires emerging from world-economies are all the so-called great civilizations of premodern times, such as China, Egypt, Rome (each at appropriate periods of its history). On the other hand, the so-called nineteenth-century empires, such as Great Britain or France, were not world-empires at all, but nation-states with colonial appendages operating within the framework of a world-economy.

World-empires were basically redistributive in economic form. No doubt they bred clusters of merchants who engaged in economic exchange (primarily long distance trade), but such clusters, however large, were a minor part of the total economy and not fundamentally determinative of its fate. Such long-distance trade tended to be, as Polanyi argues, 'administered trade' and not market trade, utilizing 'ports of trade.'

It was only with the emergence of the modern world-economy in sixteenth-century Europe that we saw the full development and economic predominance of market trade. This was the system called capitalism. Capitalism and a world-economy (that is, a single division of labor but multiple polities and cultures) are obverse sides of the same coin. One does not cause the other. We are merely defining the same indivisible phenomenon by different characteristics. . . .

Let us therefore turn to the capitalist world-economy. We shall seek to deal with two pseudoproblems, created by the trap of not analyzing totalities: the so-called persistence of feudal forms, and the so-called creation of socialist systems. In doing this, we shall offer an alternative model with which to engage in comparative analysis, one rooted in the historically specific totality which is the world capitalist economy. We hope to demonstrate thereby that to be historically specific is not to fail to be

iiiSee Karl Polanyi, 'The Economy as Instituted Process,' in Karl Polanyi, Conrad M. Arsenberg and Harry W. Pearson (eds.), *Trade and Market in the Early Empire* (Glencoe: Free Press, 1957), pp. 243–70.

analytically universal. On the contrary, the only road to nomothetic propositions is through the historically concrete, just as in cosmology the only road to a theory of the laws governing the universe is through the concrete analysis of the historical evolution of this same universe. On the 'feudalism' debate, we take as a starting point Frank's concept of 'the development of underdevelopment,' that is, the view that the economic structures of contemporary underdeveloped countries is not the form which a 'traditional' society takes upon contract with 'developed' societies, not an earlier stage in the 'transition' to industrialization. It is rather the result of being involved in the world-economy as a peripheral, raw material producing area, or as Frank puts it for Chile, 'underdevelopment . . . is the necessary product of four centuries of capitalism itself.'[iv]

This formulation runs counter to a large body of writing concerning the underdeveloped countries that was produced in the period 1950–70, a literature which sought the factors that explained 'development' within non-systems such as 'states' or 'cultures' and, once having presumably discovered these factors, urged their reproduction in underdeveloped areas as the road to salvation.[v]

Frank's theory also runs counter, as we have already noted, to the received orthodox version of Marxism that had long dominated Marxist parties and intellectual circles, for example in Latin America. This older 'Marxist' view of Latin America as a set of feudal societies in a more or less prebourgeois stage of development has fallen before the critiques of Frank and many others as well as before the political reality symbolized by the Cuban revolution and all its many consequences. Recent analysis in Latin America has centered instead around the concept of 'dependence.'

However, recently, Ernesto Laclau has made an attack on Frank which, while accepting the critique of dualist doctrines, refuses to accept the categorization of Latin American states as capitalist. Instead Laclau asserts that 'the world capitalist system . . . includes, *at the level of its definition*, various modes of production.' He accuses Frank of confusing the two concepts of the 'capitalist mode of production' and 'participation in a world capitalist economic system.'. . .[vi]

What is the picture, both analytical and historical, that Laclau constructs? The heart of the problem revolves around the existence of free labor as the defining characteristic of a capitalist mode of production:

> The fundamental economic relationship of capitalism is constituted by the *free* [italics mine] labourer's sale of his labour-power, whose necessary precondition is the loss by the direct producer of ownership of the means of production. . . .
>
> If we now confront Frank's affirmation that the socio-economic complexes of Latin America have been capitalist since the Conquest Period . . . with the currently available empirical evidence, we must conclude that the 'capitalist' thesis is indefensible. In regions with dense indigenous populations—Mexico, Peru, Bolivia, or Guatemala—the direct producers were not despoiled of their ownership of the means of production, while extra-economic coercion to maximize various systems of labour service . . . was progressively intensified. In the plantations of the West Indies, the economy was based on a mode of production constituted by slave labour, while in the mining areas there developed disguised forms of slavery and other types of forced labour which bore not the slightest resemblance to the formation of a capitalist proletariat.[vii]

[iv]Frank, 'The Myth of Feudalism,' p. 3.

[v]Frank's critique, now classic, of these theories is entitled 'Sociology Development and Underdevelopment of Sociology' and is reprinted in *Latin America: Underdevelopment or Revolution* (New York: Monthly Review Press, 1969), pp. 21–94.

[vi]Ernesto Laclau (*h*), 'Feudalism and Capitalism in Latin America,' *New Left Review*, 67 (May–June 1971), 37–8.

[vii]Ernesto Laclau (*h*), 'Feudalism and Capitalism in Latin America,' *New Left Review*, 67 (May–June 1971), 37–8.

There in a nutshell it is. Western Europe, at least England from the late seventeenth century on, had primarily landless, wage-earning laborers. In Latin America, then and to some extent still now, laborers were not proletarians, but slaves or 'serfs.' If proletariat, then capitalism. Of course. To be sure. But is England, or Mexico, or the West Indies a unit of analysis? Does each have a separate 'mode of production'? Or is the unit (for the sixteenth–eighteenth centuries) the European world-economy, including England *and* Mexico, in which case what was the 'mode of production' of this world-economy? . . .

Let us see now if we can reinterpret the issues developed in [this debate] within the framework of a general set of concepts that could be used to analyze the functioning of world-systems, and particularly of the historically specific capitalist world-economy that has existed for about four or five centuries now.

We must start with how one demonstrates the existence of a single division of labor. We can regard a division of labor as a grid which is substantially interdependent. Economic actors operate on some assumption (obviously seldom clear to any individual actor) that the totality of their essential needs—of sustenance, protection, and pleasure—will be met over a reasonable time span by a combination of their own productive activities and exchange in some form. The smallest grid that would substantially meet the expectations of the overwhelming majority of actors within those boundaries constitutes a single division of labor.

The reason why a small farming community whose only significant link to outsiders is the payment of annual tribute does not constitute such a single division of labor is that the assumptions of persons living in it concerning the provisions of protection involve an 'exchange' with other parts of the world-empire.

This concept of a grid of exchange relationships assumes, however, a distinction between *essential* exchanges and what might be called 'luxury' exchanges. This is to be sure a distinction rooted in the social perceptions of the actors and hence in both their social organization and their culture. These perceptions can change. But this distinction is crucial if we are not to fall into the trap of identifying *every* exchange activity

as evidence of the existence of a system. Members of a system (a minisystem or a world-system) can be linked in limited exchanges with elements located outside the system, in the 'external arena' of the system.

The form of such an exchange is very limited. Elements of the two systems can engage in an exchange of preciosities. That is, each can export to the other what is in *its* system socially defined as worth little in return for the import of what in its system is defined as worth much. This is not a mere pedantic definitional exercise, as the exchange of preciosities *between* world-systems can be extremely important in the historical evolution of a given world-system. The reason why this is so important is that in an exchange of preciosities, the importer is 'reaping a windfall' and not obtaining a profit. Both exchange partners can reap windfalls simultaneously but only one can obtain maximum profit, since the exchange of surplus value within a system is a zero-sum game.

We are, as you see, coming to the essential feature of a capitalist world-economy, which is production for sale in a market in which the object is to realize the maximum profit. In such a system production is constantly expanded as long as further production is profitable, and men constantly innovate new ways of producing things that will expand the profit margin. The classical economists tried to argue that such production for the market was somehow the 'natural' state of man. But the combined writings of the anthropologists and the Marxists left few in doubt that such a mode of production (these days called 'capitalism') was only one of several possible modes. . . .

If capitalism is a mode of production, production for profit in a market, then we ought, I should have thought, to look to whether or not such production was or was not occurring [in Europe from the sixteenth to the eighteenth centuries]. It turns out in fact that it was, and in a very substantial form. Most of this production, however, was not industrial production. What was happening in Europe from the sixteenth to the eighteenth centuries is that over a large geographical area going from Poland in the northeast westwards and southwards throughout Europe and including large parts of the Western Hemisphere as well, there grew up a world-economy with a single division of labor within which there was a world market, for which men produced largely agricultural products for sale and profit. I would think the simplest thing to do would be to call this agricultural capitalism.

This then resolves the problems incurred by using the pervasiveness of *wage* labor as a defining characteristic of capitalism. An individual is no less a capitalist exploiting labor because the state assists him to pay his laborers low wages (including wages in kind) and denies these laborers the right to change employment. Slavery and so-called 'second serfdom' are not to be regarded as anomalies in a capitalist system. Rather the so-called serf in Poland or the Indian on a Spanish *encomienda* in New Spain in this sixteenth-century world-economy were working for landlords who 'paid' them (however euphemistic this term) for cash crop production. This is a relationship in which labor power is a commodity (how could it ever be more so than under slavery?), quite different from the relationship of a feudal serf to his lord in eleventh-century Burgundy, where the economy was not oriented to a world market, and where labor power was (therefore?) in no sense bought or sold.

Capitalism thus means labor as a commodity to be sure. But in the era of agricultural capitalism, wage labor is only one of the modes in which labor is recruited and recompensed in the labor market. Slavery, coerced cash-crop production (my name for the so-called 'second feudalism'), sharecropping, and tenancy are all alternative modes. It would be too long to develop here the conditions under which differing regions of the world-economy tend to specialize in different agricultural products. I have done this elsewhere.[viii]

What we must notice now is that this specialization occurs in specific and differing geographic regions of the world-economy. This regional specialization comes about by the attempts of actors in the market to avoid the normal operation of the market whenever it does not maximize their profit. The attempts of these actors to use non-market devices to ensure short-run profits makes them turn to the political entities which have in

fact power to affect the market—the nation-states. (Again, why at this stage they could not have turned to city-states would take us into a long discursus, but it has to do with the state of military and shipping technology, the need of the European landmass to expand overseas in the fifteenth century if it was to maintain the level of income of the various aristocracies, combined with the state of political disintegration to which Europe had fallen in the Middle Ages.)

In any case, the local capitalist classes—cash-crop landowners (often, even usually, nobility) and merchants—turned to the state, not only to liberate them from non-market constraints (as traditionally emphasized by liberal historiography) but to create new constraints on the new market, the market of the European world-economy.

By a series of accidents—historical, ecological, geographic—northwest Europe was better situated in the sixteenth century to diversify its agricultural specialization and add to it certain industries (such as textiles, shipbuilding, and metal wares) than were other parts of Europe. Northwest Europe emerged as the core area of this world-economy, specializing in agricultural production of higher skill levels, which favored (again for reasons too complex to develop) tenancy and wage labor as the modes of labor control. Eastern Europe and the Western Hemisphere became peripheral areas specializing in export of grains, bullion, wood, cotton, sugar—all of which favored the use of slavery and coerced cash-crop labor as the modes of labor control. Mediterranean Europe emerged as the semiperipheral area of this world-economy specializing in high-cost industrial products (for example, silks) and credit and specie transactions, which had as a consequence in the agricultural arena sharecropping as the mode of labor control and little export to other areas.

The three structural positions in a world-economy—core, periphery, and semipheriphery—had become stabilized by about 1640. How certain areas became one and not the other is a long story. The key fact is that given slightly different starting points, the interests of various

viii See my *The Modern World-System*, ch. 2.

local groups converged in northwest Europe, leading to the development of strong state mechanisms, and diverged sharply in the peripheral areas, leading to very weak ones. Once we get a difference in the strength of the state machineries, we get the operation of 'unequal exchange' which is enforced by strong states on weak ones, by core states on peripheral areas. Thus capitalism involves not only appropriation of the surplus value by an owner from a laborer, but an appropriation of surplus of the whole world-economy by core areas. And this was as true in the stage of agricultural capitalism as it is in the stage of industrial capitalism.

In the early Middle Ages, there was to be sure trade. But it was largely either 'local,' in a region that we might call the 'extended' manor, or 'long-distance,' primarily of luxury goods. There was no exchange of 'bulk' goods, of 'staples' across intermediate-size areas, and hence no production for such markets. Later on in the Middle Ages, world-economies may be said to have come into existence, one centering on Venice, a second on the cities of Flanders and the Hanse. For various reasons, these structures were hurt by the retractions (economic, demographic, and ecological) of the period 1300–1450. It is only with the creating of a *European* division of labor after 1450 that capitalism found firm roots.

Capitalism was from the beginning an affair of the world-economy and not of nation-states. It is a misreading of the situation to claim that it is only in the twentieth century that capitalism has become 'world-wide,' although this claim is frequently made in various writings, particularly by Marxists. Typical of this line of argument is Charles Bettelheim's response to Arghiri Emmanuel's discussion of unequal exchange:

> The tendency of the capitalist mode of production to become worldwide is manifested not only through the constitution of a group of national economies forming a complex and hierarchical structure, including an imperialist pole and a dominated one, and not only through the antagonistic relations that develop between the different 'national economies' and the different states, but also through the constant 'transcending' of 'national limits' by big capital (the formation of 'international big capital,' 'world firms,' etc. . . .).[ix]

The whole tone of these remarks ignores the fact that capital has never allowed its aspirations to be determined by national boundaries in a capitalist world-economy, and that the creation of 'national' barriers—generically, mercantilism—has historically been a defensive mechanism of capitalists located in states which are one level below the high point of strength in the system. Such was the case of England *vis-à-vis* the Netherlands in 1660–1715, France *vis-à-vis* England in 1715–1815, Germany *vis-à-vis* Britain in the nineteenth century, the Soviet Union *vis-à-vis* the US in the twentieth. In the process a large number of countries create national economic barriers whose consequences often last beyond their initial objectives. At this later point in the process the very same capitalists who pressed their national governments to impose the restrictions now find these restrictions constraining. This is not an 'internationalization' of 'national' capital. This is simply a new political demand by certain sectors of the capitalist classes who have at all points in time sought to maximize their profits within the real economic market, that of the world-economy.

If this is so, then what meaning does it have to talk of structural positions within this economy and identify states as being in one of these positions? And why talk of three positions, inserting that of 'semiperiphery' in between the widely used concepts of core and periphery? The state machineries of the core states were strengthened to meet the needs of capitalist landowners and their merchant allies. But that does not mean that these state machineries were manipulable puppets. Obviously any organization, once created, has a certain autonomy from those who pressed it into existence for two reasons. It creates a stratum of officials whose own careers and interests are furthered by the

---

[ix]Charles Bettelheim, 'Theoretical Comments,' in Emmanuel, *Unequal Exchange*, p. 295.

continued strengthening of the organization itself, however the interests of its capitalist backers may vary. Kings and bureaucrats wanted to stay in power and increase their personal gain constantly. Secondly, in the process of creating the strong state in the first place, certain 'constitutional' compromises had to be made with other forces within the state boundaries and these institutionalized compromise limit, as they are designed to do, the freedom of maneuver of the managers of the state machinery. The formula of the state as 'executive committee of the ruling class' is only valid, therefore, if one bears in mind that executive committees are never mere reflections of the wills of their constituents, as anyone who has ever participated in any organization knows well.

The strengthening of the state machineries in core areas has as its direct counterpart the decline of the state machineries in peripheral areas. The decline of the Polish monarchy in the sixteenth and seventeenth centuries is a striking example of this phenomenon. There are two reasons for this. In peripheral countries, the interests of the capitalist landowners lie in an opposite direction from those of the local commercial bourgeoisie. Their interests lie in maintaining an open economy to maximize their profit from world-market trade (no restrictions in exports and access to lower-cost industrial products from core countries) and in elimination of the commercial bourgeoisie in favor of outside merchants (who pose no local political threat). Thus, in terms of the state, the coalition which strengthened it in core countries was precisely absent.

The second reason, which has become ever more operative over the history of the modern world-system, is that the strength of the state machinery in core states is a function of the weakness of other state machineries. Hence intervention of outsiders via war, subversion, and diplomacy is the lot of peripheral states.

All this seems very obvious. I repeat it only in order to make clear two points. One cannot reasonably explain the strength of various state machineries at specific moments of the history of the modern world-system primarily in terms of a genetic-cultural line of argumentation, but rather in terms of the structural role a country plays in the world-economy at that moment in time. To be sure, the initial eligibility for a particular role is often decided by an accidental edge a particular country has, and the 'accident' of which one is talking is no doubt located in part in past history, in part in current geography. But once this relatively minor accident is given, it is the operations of the world-market forces which accentuate the differences, institutionalize them, and make them impossible to surmount over the short run.

The second point we wish to make about the structural differences of core and periphery is that they are not comprehensible unless we realize that there is a third structural position: that of the semiperiphery. This is not the result merely of establishing arbitrary cutting-points on a continuum of characteristics. Our logic is not merely inductive, sensing the presence of a third category from a comparison of indicator curves. It is also deductive. The semiperiphery is needed to make a capitalist world-economy run smoothly. Both kinds of world-system, the world-empire with a redistributive economy and the world-economy with a capitalist market economy, involve markedly unequal distribution of rewards. Thus, logically, there is immediately posed the question of how it is possible politically for such a system to persist. Why do not the majority who are exploited simply overwhelm the minority who draw disproportionate benefits? The most rapid glance at the historic record shows that these world-systems have been faced rather rarely by fundamental system-wide insurrection. While internal discontent has been eternal, it has usually taken quite long before the accumulation of the erosion of power has led to the decline of a world-system, and as often as not, an external force has been a major factor in this decline.

There have been three major mechanisms that have enabled world-systems to retain relative political stability (not in terms of the particular groups who will play the leading roles in the system, but in terms of systemic survival itself). One obviously is the concentration of military strength in the hands of the dominant forces. The modalities of this obviously vary with the technology, and there are to be sure political prerequisites for such a concentration, but nonetheless sheer force is no doubt a central consideration.

A second mechanism is the pervasiveness of an ideological commitment to the system as a whole. I do not mean what has often been termed the 'legitimation' of a system, because that term has been used to imply that the lower strata of a system feel some affinity with or loyalty towards the rulers, and I doubt that this has ever been a significant factor in the survival of world-systems. I mean rather the degree to which the staff or cadres of the system (and I leave this term deliberately vague) feel that their own well-being is wrapped up in the survival of the system as such and the competence of its leaders. It is this staff which not only propagates the myths; it is they who believe them.

But neither force nor the ideological commitment of the staff would suffice were it not for the division of the majority into a larger lower stratum and a smaller middle stratum. Both the revolutionary call for polarization as a strategy of change and the liberal encomium to consensus as the basis of the liberal polity reflect this proposition. The import is far wider than its use in the analysis of contemporary political problems suggests. It is the normal condition of either kind of world-system to have a three-layered structure. When and if this ceases to be the case, the world-system disintegrates.

In a world-empire, the middle stratum is in fact accorded the role of maintaining the marginally desirable long-distance luxury trade, while the upper stratum concentrates its resources on controlling the military machinery which can collect the tribute, the crucial mode of redistributing surplus. By providing, however, for an access to a limited portion of the surplus to urbanized elements who alone, in premodern societies, could contribute political cohesiveness to isolated clusters of primary producers, the upper stratum effectively buys off the potential leadership of coordinated revolt. And by denying access to political rights for this commercial-urban middle stratum, it makes them constantly vulnerable to confiscatory measures whenever their economic profits

become sufficiently swollen so that they might begin to create for themselves military strength.

In a world-economy, such 'cultural' stratification is not so simple, because the absence of a single political system means the concentration of economic roles vertically rather than horizontally throughout the system. The solution then is to have three *kinds* of states, with pressures for cultural homogenization within each of them—thus, besides the upper stratum of core states and the lower stratum of peripheral states, there is a middle stratum of semiperipheral ones.

This semiperipheral is then assigned as it were a specific economic role, but the reason is less economic than political. That is to say, one might make a good case that the world-economy as an economy would function every bit as well without a semiperiphery. But it would be far less *politically* stable, for it would mean a polarized world-system. The existence of the third category means precisely that the upper stratum is not faced with the *unified* opposition of all the others because the *middle* stratum is both exploited and exploiter. It follows that the specific economic role is not all that important, and has thus changed through the various historical stages of the modern world-system. We shall discuss these changes shortly.

Where then does class analysis fit in all of this? And what in such a formulation are nations, nationalities, peoples, ethnic groups? First of all, without arguing the point now, I would contend that all these latter terms denote variants of a single phenomenon which I will term 'ethno-nations.'

Both classes and ethnic groups, or status groups, or ethno-nations are phenomena of world-economies and much of the enormous confusion that has surrounded the concrete analysis of their functioning can be attributed quite simply to the fact that they have been analyzed as though they existed within the nation-states of this world-economy, instead of within the world-economy as a whole. This has been a Procrustean bed indeed.

The range of economic activities being far wider in the core than in the periphery, the range of syndical interest groups is far wider there.[x] Thus, it has been widely observed that there does not exist in many parts of the world today a proletariat of the kind which exists in, say, Europe or North America. But this is a confusing way to state the observation. Industrial activity being disproportionately concentrated in certain parts of the world-economy, industrial wage workers are to be found principally in certain geographic regions. Their interests as a syndical group are determined by their collective relationship to the world-economy. Their ability to influence the political functioning of this world-economy is shaped by the fact that they command larger percentages of the population in one sovereign entity than another. The form their organizations take have, in large part, been governed too by these political boundaries. The same might be said about industrial capitalists. Class analysis is perfectly capable of accounting for the political position of, let us say, French skilled workers if we look at their structural position and interests in the world-economy. Similarly with ethno-nations. The meaning of ethnic consciousness in a core area is considerably different from that of ethnic consciousness in a peripheral area precisely because of the different class position such ethnic groups have in the world-economy.

Political struggles of ethno-nations or segments of classes within national boundaries of course are the daily bread and butter of local politics. But their significance or consequences can only be fruitfully analyzed if one spells out the implications of their organizational activity or political demands for the functioning of the world-economy. This also incidentally makes possible more rational assessments of these politics in terms of some set of evaluative criteria such as 'left' and 'right.'

The functioning then of a capitalist world-economy requires that groups pursue their economic interests within a single world market while seeking to distort this market for their benefit by organizing to exert influence on states, some of which are far more powerful than others but none of which controls the world market in its entirety. Of course, we shall find on closer inspection that there are periods where one state is relatively quite powerful and other periods where power is more diffuse and contested, permitting weaker states broader ranges of action. We can talk then of the relative tightness or looseness of the world-system as an important variable and seek to analyze why this dimension tends to be cyclical in nature, as it seems to have been for several hundred years.

We are now in a position to look at the historical evolution of this capitalist world-economy itself and analyze the degree to which it is fruitful to talk of distinct stages in its evolution as a system. The emergence of the European world-economy in the 'long' sixteenth century (1450–1640) was made possible by an historical conjuncture: on those long-term trends which were the culmination of what has been sometimes described as the 'crisis of feudalism' was superimposed a more immediate cyclical crisis plus climatic changes, all of which created a dilemma that could only be resolved by a geographic expansion of the division of labor. Furthermore, the balance of intersystem forces was such as to make this realizable. Thus a geographic expansion did take place in conjunction with a demographic expansion and an upward price rise.

The remarkable thing was not that a European world-economy was thereby created, but that it survived the Hapsburg attempt to transform it into a world-empire, an attempt seriously pursued by Charles V. The Spanish attempt to absorb the whole failed because the rapid economic-demographic-technological burst forward of the preceding century made

[x]'Range' in this sentence means the number of different occupations in which a significant proportion of the population is engaged. Thus peripheral society typically is overwhelmingly agricultural. A core society typically has its occupations well-distributed over all of Colin Clark's three sectors. If one shifted the connotation of range to talk of style of life, consumption patterns, even income distribution quite possibly one might reverse the correlation. In a typical peripheral society, the differences between a subsistence farmer and an urban professional are probably far greater than those which could be found in a typical core state.

the whole enterprise too expensive for the imperial base to sustain, especially given many structural insufficiencies in Castilian economic development. Spain could afford neither the bureaucracy nor the army that was necessary to the enterprise, and in the event went bankrupt, as did the French monarchs making a similar albeit even less plausible attempt.

Once the Hapsburg dream of world-empire was over—and in 1557 it was over forever—the capitalist world-economy was an established system that became almost impossible to unbalance. It quickly reached an equilibrium point in its relations with other world-systems: the Ottoman and Russian world-empires, the Indian Ocean proto-world-economy. Each of the states or potential states within the European world-economy was quickly in the race to bureaucratize, to raise a standing army, to homogenize its culture, to diversity its economic activities. By 1640, those in north-west Europe had succeeded in establishing themselves as the core states; Spain and the northern Italian city-states declined into being semi-peripheral; northeastern Europe and Iberian America had become the periphery. At this point, those in semiperipheral status had reached it by virtue of decline from a former more pre-eminent status.

It was the system-wide recession of 1652–1730 that consolidated the European world-economy and opened stage two of the modern world-economy. For the recession forced retrenchment, and the decline in relative surplus allowed room for only one core state to survive. The mode of struggle was mercantilism, which was a device of partial insulation and withdrawal from the world market of *large* areas themselves hierarchically constructed—that is, empires within the world-economy (which is quite different from world-empires). In this struggle England first ousted the Netherlands from its commercial primacy and then resisted successfully France's attempt to catch up. As England began to speed up the process of industrialization after 1760, there was one last attempt of those capitalist forces located in France to break the imminent British hegemony. This attempt was expressed first in the French Revolution's replacement of the cadres of the regime and then in Napoleon's continental blockade. But it failed.

Stage three of the capitalist world-economy begins then, a stage of industrial rather than of agricultural capitalism. Henceforth, industrial production is no longer a minor aspect of the world market but comprises an ever larger percentage of world gross production—and even more important, of world gross surplus. This involves a whole series of consequences for the world-system.

First of all, it led to the further geographic expansion of the European world-economy to include now the whole of the globe. This was in part the result of its technological feasibility both in terms of improved military firepower and improved shipping facilities which made regular trade sufficiently inexpensive to be viable. But in addition, industrial production *required* access to raw materials of a nature and in a quantity such that the needs could not be supplied within the former boundaries. At first, however, the search for new markets was not a primary consideration in the geographic expansion since the new markets were more readily available within the old boundaries, as we shall see.

The geographic expansion of the European world-economy meant the elimination of other world-systems as well as the absorption of the remaining minisystems. The most important world-system up to then outside of the European world-economy, Russia, entered in semiperipheral status, the consequence of the strength of its state machinery (including its army) and the degree of industrialization already achieved in the eighteenth century. The independences in the Latin American countries did nothing to change their peripheral status. They merely eliminated the last vestiges of Spain's semiperipheral role and ended pockets of noninvolvement in the world-economy in the interior of Latin America. Asia and Africa were absorbed into the periphery in the nineteenth century, although Japan, because of the combination of the strength of its state machinery, the poverty of its resource base (which led to a certain disinterest on the part of world capitalist forces), and its geographic remoteness from the core areas, was able quickly to graduate into semi-pheripheral status.

The absorption of Africa as part of the periphery meant the end of slavery world-wide for two reasons. First of all, the manpower that was used as slaves was now needed for cash-crop production in Africa itself, whereas in the eighteenth century Europeans had sought to *discourage* just such cash-crop production.[xi] In the second place, once Africa was part of the periphery and not the external arena, slavery was no longer economic. To understand this, we must appreciate the economics of slavery. Slaves receiving the lowest conceivable reward for their labor are the least productive form of labor and have the shortest life span, both because of undernourishment and maltreatment and because of lowered psychic resistance to death. Furthermore, if recruited from areas surrounding their workplace the escape rate is too high. Hence, there must be a high transport cost for a product of low productivity. This makes economic sense only if the purchase price is virtually nil. In capitalist market trade, purchase always has a real cost. It is only in long-distance trade, the exchange of preciosities, that the purchase price can be in the social system of the purchaser virtually nil. Such was the slave trade. Slaves were bought at low immediate cost (the production cost of the items actually exchanged) and none of the usual invisible cost. That is to say, the fact that removing a man from West Africa lowered the productive potential of the region was of *zero* cost to the European world-economy since these areas were not part of the division of labor. Of course, had the slave trade totally denuded Africa of all possibilities of furnishing further slaves, then a real cost to Europe

would have commenced. But that point was never historically reached. Once, however, Africa was part of the periphery, then the real cost of a slave in terms of the production of surplus in the world-economy went up to such a point that it became far more economical to use wage labor, even on sugar or cotton plantations, which is precisely what transpired in the nineteenth-century Caribbean and other slave labor regions.

The creation of vast new areas as the periphery of the expanded world-economy made possible a shift in the role of some other areas. Specifically, both the United States and Germany (as it came into being) combined formerly peripheral and semiperipheral regions. The manufacturing sector in each was able to gain political ascendancy, as the peripheral subregions became less economically crucial to the world-economy. Mercantilism now became the major tool of semiperipheral countries seeking to become core countries, thus still performing a function analogous to that of the mercantilist drives of the late seventeenth and eighteenth centuries in England and France. To be sure, the struggle of semiperipheral countries to 'industrialize' varied in the degree to which it succeeded in the period before the First World War: all the way in the United States, only partially in Germany, not at all in Russia.

The internal structure of core states also changed fundamentally under industrial capitalism. For a core area, industrialism involved divesting itself of substantially all agricultural activities (except that in the twentieth century further mechanization was to create a new form of working the land that was so highly mechanized as to warrant the appellation industrial). Thus whereas, in the period 1700–40, England

---

[xi]A. Adu Boahen cites the instructions of the British Board of Trade in 1751 to the Governor of Cape Castle (a small British fort and trading settlement in what is now Ghana) to seek to stop the local people, the Fante, from cultivating cotton. The reason given was the following: 'The introduction of culture and industry among the Negroes is contrary to the known established policy of this country, there is no saying where this might stop, and that it might extend to tobacco, sugar and every other commodity which we now take from our colonies; and thereby the Africans, who now support themselves by wars, would become planters and their slaves be employed in the culture of these articles in Africa, which they are employed in America.' Cited in A. Adu Boahen, *Topics in West Africa History* (London: Longmans, Green and Co., 1966), p. 113.

not only was Europe's leading industrial exporter but was also Europe's leading agricultural exporter—this was at a high point in the economy-wide recession—by 1900, less than 10 percent of England's population were engaged in agricultural pursuits.

At first under industrial capitalism, the core exchanged manufactured products against the periphery's agricultural products—hence, Britain from 1815 to 1873 as the 'workshop of the world.' Even to those semiperipheral countries that had some manufacture (France, Germany, Belgium, the US), Britain in this period supplied about half their needs in manufactured goods. As, however, the mercantilist practices of this latter group both cut Britain off from outlets and even created competition for Britain in sales to peripheral areas, a competition which led to the late nineteenth-century 'scramble for Africa,' the world division of labor was reallocated to ensure a new special role for the core: less the provision of the manufactures, more the provision of the machines to make the manufactures as well as the provision of infrastructure (especially, in this period, railroads).

The rise of manufacturing created for the first time under capitalism a large-scale urban proletariat. And in consequence for the first time there arose what Michels has called the 'anti-capitalist mass spirit,'[xii] which was translated into concrete organizational forms (trade unions, socialist parties). This development intruded a new factor as threatening to the stability of the states and of the capitalist forces now so securely in control of them as the earlier centrifugal thrusts of regional anti-capitalist landed elements had been in the seventeenth century.

At the same time that the bourgeoisies of the core countries were faced by this threat to the internal stability of their state structures, they ware simultaneously faced with the economic crisis of the latter third of the nineteenth century resulting from the more rapid increase of agricultural production (and indeed of light manufactures) than the expansion of a potential market for these goods. Some of the surplus would have to be redistributed to someone to allow these goods to be bought and the economic machinery to return to smooth operation. By expanding the purchasing power of the industrial proletariat of the core countries, the world-economy was unburdened simultaneously of two problems: the bottleneck of demand, and the unsettling 'class conflict' of the core states—hence, the social liberalism or welfare-state ideology that arose just at that point in time.

The First World War was, as men of the time observed, the end of an era; and the Russian Revolution of October 1917 the beginning of a new one—our stage four. This stage was to be sure a stage of revolutionary turmoil but it also was, in a seeming paradox, the stage of the *consolidation* of the industrial capitalist world-economy. The Russian Revolution was essentially that of a semiperipheral country whose internal balance of forces had been such that as of the late nineteenth century it began on a decline towards a peripheral status. This was the result of the marked penetration of foreign capital into the industrial sector which was on its way to eliminating all indigenous capitalist forces, the resistance to the mechanization of the agricultural sector, the decline of relative military power (as evidenced by the defeat by the Japanese in 1905). The Revolution brought to power a group of state managers who reversed each one of these trends by using the classic technique of mercantilist semiwithdrawal from the world-economy. In the process of doing this, the now USSR mobilized considerable popular support, especially in the urban sector. At the end of the Second World War, Russia was reinstated as a very strong member of the semiperiphery and could begin to seek full core status.

Meanwhile, the decline of Britain which dates from 1873 was confirmed and its hegemonic role was assumed by the United States. While the US thus rose, Germany fell further behind as a result of its military defeat. Various German attempts in the 1920s to find new industrial outlets in the Middle East and South America were unsuccessful in the face of the US thrust combined with Britain's continuing relative strength. Germany's thrust of desperation to

---

[xii]Robert Michels, 'The Origins of the Anti-Capitalist Mass Spirit,' in *Man in Contemporary Society* (New York: Columbia University Press, 1955), vol. 1, pp. 740–65.

recoup lost ground took the noxious and unsuccessful form of Nazism.

It was the Second World War that enabled the United States for a brief period (1945–65) to attain the same level of primacy as Britain had in the first part of the nineteenth century. United States growth in this period was spectacular and created a great need for expanded market outlets. The Cold War closure denied not only the USSR but eastern Europe to US exports. And the Chinese Revolution meant that this region, which had been destined for much exploitative activity, was also cut off. Three alternative areas were available and each was pursued with assiduity. First, western Europe had to be rapidly 'reconstructed,' and it was the Marshall Plan which thus allowed this area to play a primary role in the expansion of world productivity. Secondly, Latin America became the reserve of US investment from which now Britain and Germany were completely cut off. Thirdly, southern Asia, the Middle East and Africa had to be decolonized. On the one hand, this was necessary in order to reduce the share of the surplus taken by the western European intermediaries, as Canning covertly supported the Latin American revolutionaries against Spain in the 1820s. But also, these countries had to be decolonized in order to mobilize productive potential in a way that had never been achieved in the colonial era. Colonial rule after all had been an *inferior* mode of relationship of core and periphery, one occasioned by the strenuous late-nineteenth-century conflict among industrial states but one no longer desirable from the point of view of the new hegemonic power.

But a world capitalist economy does not permit true imperium. Charles V could not succeed in his dream of world-empire. The Pax Britannica stimulated its own demise. So too did the Pax Americana. In each case, the cost of *political* imperium was too high economically, and in a capitalist system, over the middle run when profits decline, new *political* formulae are sought. In this case the costs mounted along several fronts. The efforts of the USSR to further its own industrialization, protect a privileged market area (eastern Europe), and force entry into other market areas led to an immense spiralling of military expenditure, which on the Soviet side promised long-run returns whereas for the US it was merely a question of running

very fast to stand still. The economic resurgence of western Europe, made necessary both to provide markets for US sales and investments and to counter the USSR military thrust, meant over time that the west European state structures collectively became as strong as that of the US, which led in the late 1960s to the 'dollar and gold crisis' and the retreat of Nixon from the free-trade stance which is the definitive mark of the self-confident leader in a capitalist market system. When the cumulated Third World pressures, most notably Vietnam, were added on, a restructuring of the world division of labor was inevitable, involving probably in the 1970s a quadripartite division of the larger part of the world surplus by the US, the European Common Market, Japan, and the USSR.

Such a decline in US state hegemony has actually *increased* the freedom of action of capitalist enterprises, the larger of which have now taken the form of multinational corporations which are able to maneuver against state bureaucracies whenever the national politicians become too responsive to internal worker pressures. Whether some effective links can be established between multinational corporations, presently limited to operating in certain areas, and the USSR remains to be seen, but it is by no means impossible. . . .

Are we not seeing the emergence of a political structure for *semiperipheral* nations adapted to stage four of the capitalist world-system? The fact that all enterprises are nationalized in these countries does not make the participation of these enterprises in the world-economy one that does not conform to the mode of operation of a capitalist market system: seeking increased efficiency of production in order to realize a maximum price on sales, thus achieving a more favorable allocation of the surplus of the world-economy. If tomorrow U.S. Steel became a worker's collective in which all employees without exception received an identical share of the profits and all stockholders are expropriated without compensation, would U.S. Steel thereby cease to be a capitalist enterprise operating in a capitalist world-economy?

What then have been the consequences for the world-system of the emergence of many states in which there is no private ownership of the basic means of production? To some extent, this has meant an internal reallocation of consumption. It has certainly undermined the ideological justification in world capitalism, both by showing the political vulnerability of capitalist entrepreneurs and by demonstrating that private ownership is irrelevant to the rapid expansion of industrial productivity. But to the extent that it has raised the ability of the new semiperipheral areas to enjoy a larger share of the world surplus, it has once again depolarized the world, recreating the triad of strata that has been a fundamental element in the survival of the world-system.

Finally, in the peripheral areas of the world-economy, both the continued economic expansion of the core (even though the core is seeing some reallocation of surplus internal to it) and the new strength of the semiperiphery has led to a further weakening of the political and hence economic position of the peripheral areas. The pundits note that 'the gap is getting wider,' but thus for no one has succeeded in doing much about it, and it is not clear that there are very many in whose interests it would be to do so. Far from a strengthening of state authority, in many parts of the world we are witnessing the same kind of deterioration Poland knew in the sixteenth century, a deterioration of which the frequency of military coups is only one of many signposts. And all of this leads us to conclude that stage four has been the stage of the *consolidation* of the capitalist world-economy.

Consolidation, however, does not mean the absence of contradictions and does not mean the likelihood of long-term survival. We thus come to projections about the future, which has always been man's great game, his true *hybris*, the most convincing argument for the dogma of original sin. Having read Dante, I will therefore be brief.

There are two fundamental contradictions, it seems to me, involved in the workings of the capitalist world-system. In the first place, there is the contradiction to which the nineteenth-century Marxian corpus pointed, which I would phrase as follows: whereas in the short run the maximization of profit requires maximizing the withdrawal of surplus from immediate consumption of the majority, in the long run the continued production of surplus requires a mass demand which can only be created by redistributing the surplus withdrawn. Since these two considerations move in opposite directions (a 'contradiction'), the system has constant crises which in the long run both weaken it and make the game for those with privilege less worth playing.

The second fundamental contradiction, to which Mao's concept of socialism as process points, is the following: whenever the tenants of privilege seek to coopt an oppositional movement by including them in a minor share of the privilege, they may no doubt eliminate opponents in the short run; but they also up the ante for the next oppositional movement created in the next crisis of the world-economy. Thus the cost of 'cooption' rises ever higher and the advantages of cooption seem ever less worthwhile.

There are today no socialist systems in the world-economy any more than there are feudal systems because there is only *one* world-system. It is a world-economy and it is by definition capitalist in form. Socialism involves the creation of a new kind of *world*-system, neither a redistributive world-empire nor a capitalist world-economy but a socialist world-government. I don't see this projection as being in the least utopian but I also don't feel its institution is imminent. It will be the outcome of a long struggle in forms that may be familiar and perhaps in very few forms, that will take place in *all* the areas of the world-economy (Mao's continual 'class struggle'). Governments may be in the hands of persons, groups or movements sympathetic to this transformation but *states* as such are neither progressive nor reactionary. It is movements and forces that deserve such evaluative judgments.

Having gone as far as I care to in projecting the future, let me return to the present and to the scholarly enterprise which is never neutral but does have its own logic and to some extent its own priorities. We have adumbrated as our basic unit of observation a concept of world-systems that have structural parts and evolving stages. It is within such a framework, I am arguing, that we can fruitfully make comparative analyses— of the wholes and of parts of the whole. Conceptions precede and govern measurements. I am all for minute and sophisticated quantitative indicators. I am all for minute and diligent archival work that will trace a concrete historical series of events in terms of all its immediate complexities. But the point of either is to enable us to see better what has happened and what is happening. For that we need glasses with which to discern the dimensions of difference, we need models with which to weigh significance, we need summarizing concepts with which to create the knowledge which we then seek to communicate to each other. And all this because we are men with hybris and original sin and therefore seek the good, the true, and the beautiful.

Leslie Sklair (1940–): A Biographical Sketch

Reprinted with permission.

Leslie Sklair was born in Glasgow, Scotland. He received a bachelor's degree in sociology and philosophy from Leeds University in England and his master's degree in sociology from McMaster University in Ontario, Canada. In 1970 he was awarded a doctoral degree in sociology from the prestigious London School of Economics (LSE), where he is now Professor Emeritus. While the LSE is Sklair's academic home, he has also held positions at universities in California, New York, Hong Kong, and Sydney, Australia.

With his work in the area spanning some thirty years, Sklair has become a leading figure in globalization studies. His research and publications concerning global capitalism have explored the links between it and a number of issues, including environmental changes, the rise of social movements contesting the advances of globalization, "iconic" architecture and the development of transnational economic, political, and cultural practices. He has served as a consultant to the United Nations Centre on Transnational Corporations as well as to its International Labor Organization and its Economic Commission on Latin America. He also served as a consultant to the U.S. Congress in its Office of Technology Assessment. In addition, he has served on the editorial boards of major sociological journals and from 2001 to 2005 as vice president of the Global Studies Association.

Sklair's work on globalization has taken him to numerous countries including Ireland, Egypt, China, Mexico, and the United States, and his expertise has made him a much sought-after speaker. He has delivered lectures at universities and conferences across Europe, Asia, and Australia, and the Caribbean, and in countries throughout North, South, and Central America, while his works have been translated into seven languages.

Intellectual Influences and Core Ideas

In contrast to Wallerstein, who traces globalization back to the rise of the modern era and the early development of capitalism, Sklair views globalization as a relatively recent phenomenon, the emergence of which can be traced to the second half of the twentieth century. It was at this time that **transnational practices** (TNPs) became the dominant mechanism for ordering social life across the boundaries of nation-states, effectively supplanting territorial borders and national governments as the basic elements for structuring contemporary life. TNPs are defined as "practices that cross state borders but do not originate with state actors, agencies, or institutions" (Sklair 2002:10). To understand better the modern world, then, one must move beyond studying the actions of, and relations between, particular states and instead examine the "global system." More specifically, this requires recognizing that the most important global force in the world today is the capitalist global system.

Sklair distinguishes between three types of TNPs: economic, political, and culture-ideology. Forming the institutional foundation for transnational economic practices are major **transnational corporations** (TNCs) whose extensive powers have made capitalism the dominant organizing principle of the global system. (General Motors, Monsanto, and Sony are but three examples.) Those who own and oversee TNCs control the manufacturing of goods and the labor necessary to produce and sell them. The **transnational capitalist class** (TCC) is the central shaper of transnational political practices. This class is made up of those who control the major TNCs and media outlets, as well as an elite segment of politicians and state bureaucrats (think Alan Greenspan and his successor, Ben Bernanke), "who see their own interests and/or interests of their social and/or ethnic group . . . as best served by an identification with the interests of the capitalist global system" (Sklair 2002:9). The "state fraction" of this class is charged with stabilizing the political environment in order to ensure the profitable marketing of goods and services across the globe. The primary **transnational culture-ideology** practices are found in consumerism and the meanings attached to the globally marketed goods we purchase. The culture-ideology of consumerism is based on values and attitudes aimed at instilling a "need" for the products produced by the TNCs. As Sklair points out, however, these TNPs represent analytical distinctions that are not neatly separated in the real world. Instead, "TNCs get involved in host country politics, and the culture-ideology of consumerism is largely promulgated through the transnational corporations involved in mass media and advertising. Members of the

Photo 10.5 Transnational Practices: Capitalism Without Borders. Starbucks, a U.S.-based corporation, has stores in more than thirty countries, including one in Shanghai, China. The coffee giant uses beans imported from more than half a dozen countries across four continents. Of course, the company sells more than a drink. Its Web site speaks to the culture-ideology of consumerism as it touts the creation of "The Starbucks Experience" based on a "passion for a quality product, excellent customer service, and people. With more than 1500 coffeehouses in 31 markets outside North America, it is clear that our passion transcends language and culture." We should not overlook the fact, however, that underlying the "passion" and commitment to "bringing the Starbucks Experience to customers worldwide" is a highly successful branding campaign.

SOURCE: © Keren Su/CORBIS; used with permission.

transnational capitalist class often work directly for the TNCs, and their lifestyles are exemplary for the spread of consumerism" (ibid.:85).

Sklair's transnational approach to globalization shares important features with world-systems analysis. Both are rooted in a Marxist-inspired orientation that regards capitalism as the most powerful force shaping the contemporary global order. Likewise, both approaches contend that this global order is organized around relationships based on conflict and institutionalized forms of domination and oppression. However, Sklair's Marxian analysis differs in two respects from that of Wallerstein. First, Sklair emphasizes the role played by nonstate actors and agencies, namely, TNCs and the TCC, that have eclipsed in many ways the power of nation-states to control capitalist development. This shift in power marks a new global phase in the development of capitalism, as recent technological advances in communications, electronics, and transportation have revolutionized the production and distribution of goods as well as the ability to create new needs that are satisfied through consumerism. For Sklair, it is transnational economic and political interests that shape the expansion of capitalism and not interests that stem from the domestic or international arena. Thus, "it is not the state as such that drives globalization, but the transnational capitalist class" (Sklair 2002:10). While this class may include state actors in the form of "globalizing bureaucrats and politicians," it is, nevertheless, those executives at the helm of transnational corporations and media conglomerates that are navigating the course of the global capitalist system (ibid.).

To be sure, the nation-state is far from dead: a country's monopolistic ability to wage war, to implement tax laws for redistributing its wealth, and to enact all manner of international trade agreements (e.g., NAFTA) or sanctions make it clear that (some) nation-states still play a central role in world politics and economics. Yet, the power of the nation-state has been diminished by the increasingly unrestricted flow of economic capital and cultural images across countries. One need only note the power of transnational corporations to shift their resources according to their own profit interests, thus superseding the political and economic interests of at least some sectors of their "home" country.

A second difference is found in Sklair's emphasis on the cultural dimensions of globalization. His notion of culture-ideology derives in part from the work of the Italian Marxist intellectual, journalist, and activist Antonio Gramsci (1891–1937). Gramsci spent the last eleven years of his life as a political prisoner under the fascist regime of Benito Mussolini. During this period, Gramsci wrote some three thousand pages in twenty-nine notebooks that he kept in his various prison cells. The notebooks were smuggled out, and publication of selections began after World War II. In the 1970s, selections were translated into English and compiled under the title *The Prison Notebooks*. In the notebooks, Gramsci reworked a number of ideas central to Marx's theory, most importantly the latter's focus on economic forms of domination and the inevitable triumph of the communist revolution. For Gramsci, class domination and the march of historical change are not tied primarily to the forces and relations of economic production, as Marx attested. Class rule is also exercised through "ideological hegemony" wherein subordinate classes are controlled and manipulated through the spread of ideas, morals, and values that serve the interests of the ruling class. Indoctrinated into mistaking the ideology propagated by the ruling class for a common-sense or natural explanation for how the world works, the dominated classes consent to their own domination. In Gramsci's view, it is ideological control or hegemony that accounted for why the working class had failed to mount a progressive revolution in Italy and elsewhere throughout Western Europe. In short, the working class is unable to recognize the extent and source of its oppression.

The stability of capitalist societies is thus not predicated on overt or threatened uses of force. Neither is it maintained primarily through economic coercion. Instead, long-term stability requires popular support and a belief in the legitimacy of existing social arrangements, arrangements that are rooted in fundamental inequalities. This allegiance to the status quo among the masses is secured ideologically, through the development of a shared culture that leads subordinate groups to identify their own interests with those that reinforce the power of dominant groups. According to Sklair, in the global capitalist society this allegiance is effected through the dominant culture-ideology of consumerism, expressed via the mass media and advertising, that induces individuals to equate personal satisfaction and happiness with the continual purchase of commodities. Although the rewards experienced by individuals are at best fleeting, consumerism generates lasting profits and power for transnational corporations and the transnational capitalist class. Identifying themselves in the products they purchase, individuals lend their monetized consensual support to the very corporations that are responsible for perpetuating both global inequalities and the exploitation of human labor and natural resources.

SKLAIR'S THEORETICAL ORIENTATION

From our foregoing discussion, Sklair's presuppositions regarding the questions of order and action are readily discernible. His emphasis on transnational practices and the centrality of capitalism in the global system attests to his collectivist understanding of the forces that shape the social order. According to his account, globalization is a process steered not by individuals attempting to navigate their everyday lives through a host of interpersonal interactions but, rather, by corporations and the capitalist class. Moreover, the world's population is pictured as increasingly subject to an overarching ideology of consumerism that not only serves the interests of elite groups, it also provides a broad cultural framework for negotiating one's place in the world. While Sklair notes the *types* of individuals who compose the capitalist class and control the major transnational corporations, they are portrayed in typical Marxist fashion as actors whose behaviors and attitudes are determined largely by the structural positions they inhabit. Indeed, recall Sklair's definition of the transnational capitalist class offered earlier in our discussion: "people who see their own interests and/or interests of their social and/or ethnic group . . . as best served by an identification with the interests of the capitalist global

Figure 10.2   Basic Theoretical Concepts in Sklair's Capitalist Global System

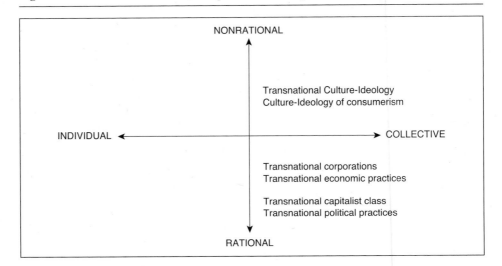

system" (Sklair 2002:9). In suggesting that an abstract economic system has "interests" that mirror the interests of people, Sklair reveals a decidedly collectivist view of what provides the organizing principles for society—for that matter, for the entire globe.

Although Sklair's orientation on the question of order is fairly unidimensional, his understanding of the problem of action is more nuanced. On the one hand, he contends that groups, specifically the TCC, are guided by their "interests." Again, the definition noted above illustrates this point. As such, actors are moved by rational considerations, most notably the strategic pursuit of profit. We should not be surprised by Sklair's position on this issue, however, as he is developing a theory that aims to shed light on the economic motivations of actors. In a capitalist economy, such motivations are framed by a competition for markets and calculated predictions of their rise and fall. Sklair succinctly describes the TCC's motivations thusly: "This class sees its mission [i.e., motivation] as organizing the conditions under which its interests and the interests of the global system . . . can be furthered within the transnational, inter-state, national, and local contexts" (2002:99).

On the other hand, Sklair's notion of the culture-ideology of consumerism represents a nonrational motivating factor. Reminiscent of Marx's notion of the "fetishism of commodities," Sklair notes how the expansion of capitalism is dependent on creating legions of consumers who find in the goods they purchase much more than a practical satisfaction of needs. More important, consumers must see in commodities an avenue for *becoming* something they otherwise cannot be. While the culture-ideology of consumerism exhibits a rationalist component insofar as it leads to increased profits for TNCs and those who control them (and thus serves their interests), at root it points to the nonrational dimension of action, for the ideology of consumerism promotes a hollow, "artificial" worldview. In Sklair's words:

> The culture-ideology project of global capitalism is to persuade people to consume not simply to satisfy their biological and other modest needs but in response to artificially created desires in order to perpetuate the accumulation of capital for private profit. . . . The culture-ideology of consumerism proclaims, literally, that the meaning of life is to be found in the things that we possess. To consume, therefore, is to be alive, and to remain fully alive we must continuously consume, discard, consume. (2002:62)

Reading

Introduction to *Globalization: Capitalism and Its Alternatives*

In this selection taken from *Globalization: Capitalism and Its Alternatives*, Sklair outlines the role of transnational practices in shaping the capitalist global system. In doing so, he explores the relationship between transnational corporations, the transnational capitalist class, and the culture-ideology of consumerism. In addition, Sklair examines how mass media and the advertising industry promote global consumerism and political stability through the messages they spread and the lifestyles they endorse. The selection concludes with a case study in global consumerism: the "cola-wars" waged between Coke and Pepsi. In calling attention to the cultural dimensions of globalization, Sklair's analysis provides an important counterpoint to the economic emphasis found in Wallerstein's work.

❖

Globalization: Capitalism and Its Alternatives (2002)

Leslie Sklair

ECONOMY, POLITY, CULTURE-IDEOLOGY

The bearers of transnational practices within the capitalist global system stand in determinate relationships to all other categories of actors. Groups may be included or excluded from profitable participation in the system. One of the most important historic tasks of capitalist imperialism was to include various previously excluded groups within its realm of influence. This inclusion was, however, partial and differences emerged between the economic, political, and culture-ideology spheres.

In the economic sphere, the capitalist global system offers a more or less circumscribed place to the wage-earning majorities in most countries. The workers, the direct producers of goods and services, have occupational choices that are generally free within the range offered by local economic conditions, but they do change over time and place. For example, as capitalist globalization reduced the numbers of manufacturing jobs in most high-wage countries, workers there have been forced to seek jobs in other, often less well-paid and less secure sectors. Throughout the First World, many older workers displaced from traditional industries (like mining and metal industries) were faced with permanent unemployment. The other side of the coin is that some of the manufacturing jobs lost in relatively high-wage countries have turned up in relatively low-wage countries. This has, undoubtedly, over the last few decades, brought many people from the Third World countryside into urban areas, whether forced off their lands by hunger or predatory landlords, or as willing migrants in search of a better life.

Transnational migration, by no means a novel phenomenon, is also a prominent feature of many communities. In the twentieth century large numbers of people migrated from poor countries to richer countries in search of work and from dangerous regions to safer places in search of personal security. Millions moved from Europe and Asia to the Americas; from black Africa to white-ruled Southern Africa; from Central America and the Caribbean to North America; from the Caribbean and the Indian subcontinent to Britain; and from southern and eastern to north-western Europe. The rapid increase in such migration since the 1950s has prompted one commentator to speak of the creation of new global diasporas (Cohen 1997; see also Portes 2001). In addition, since the 1980s, there has been massive internal migration in search of employment opportunities, notably within China (Cannon 2000). . . .

In those states with substantial migrant minorities as well as in those without, the inclusion of the subordinate classes in the political sphere is very partial. To put it crudely, the capitalist global system has very little need of the subordinate classes in this sphere. In the parliamentary democracies the parties must be able to mobilize the masses to vote every so often, but very few countries make voting compulsory. In many parliamentary democracies voter turn-out tends to be around half to three-quarters of the electorate in general elections and very much less in local elections. While conventional political organization is usually unfettered, the structural obstacles to genuine opposition to the capitalist system are such that there are rarely any serious challenges to it. For example: 'The presidential debates [between Clinton and Dole] were in fact sponsored by an entity called the Commission of Presidential Debates involving executives from an array of big-business firms—Philip Morris, AT&T, Prudential, IBM, Ford, and General Motors,' and they excluded the alternative candidates Ralph Nader and Ross

Perot (Boggs 2000: 64). Boggs concludes that this is a result of a deeply ingrained culture of antipolitics in the USA, and though he considers it exceptional in this respect, many other countries are not far behind.

While the capitalist class is increasingly organized transnationally, the obstacles to transnational class formation among subordinate groups are formidable.

> This is partly because, in the era of globalization, the lines among enemies, friends and allies are blurred, unlike the situation three or four decades ago when the targets of the struggle were much clearer. At the same time, the exclusionary processes of globalization, especially the continuous post-Fordist restructuring, fragment large sections of the subordinate groups, especially the unorganized, peripheral and migrant workers. Thus, resistance to globalization among subordinate groups often remains uncoordinated, diffuse and weak. (Embong 2000: 1000)

Where serious challenges to capitalist globalization do emerge, for example in the case of the election of the socialist Salvador Allende as president of Chile in 1970, the threat is removed by violent overthrow of the constitutional power by the capitalist class through the army and the police, with the support of other key sectors of the establishment. In the Chilean case, as is well known, this was done with the active collaboration of the US government and TNCs. The destabilization of socialist governments in Mozambique and Nicaragua by terrorism sponsored by hostile states (apartheid South Africa and the USA) is also well documented as is terrorism against these states. In one-party states, spontaneous political participation by the masses is usually actively discouraged and realistic threats to the prevailing order tend to be focused on changing the people at the top, *coup d'état*, rather than on changing the conditions under which global capitalism operates.

The culture-ideology sphere is, however, entirely different. Here, the aim of the capitalist global system is total inclusion of all classes, and especially the subordinate classes in so far as the bourgeoisie can be considered already included. The culture-ideology project of global capitalism is to persuade people to consume not simply to satisfy their biological and other

modest needs but in response to artificially created desires in order to perpetuate the accumulation of capital for private profit, in other words, to ensure that the capitalist global system goes on for ever. The culture-ideology of consumerism proclaims, literally, that the meaning of life is to be found in the things that we possess. To consume, therefore, is to be fully alive, and to remain fully alive we must continuously consume, discard, consume. The notions of men and women as economic or political beings are marginalized by global capitalism, quite logically, as the system does not even pretend to satisfy everyone in the economic or the political spheres. Men, women, children, even pets, are consumers. The point of economic activity for ordinary members of the system is simply to provide the resources to be consumers, and the point of political activity is to ensure, usually through political inactivity, that the conditions for consuming are maintained. This system has been evolving for centuries, first for aristocracies and members of the bourgeoisie all over the world, then spreading to the working classes in the First World, and slowly but surely penetrating to all those with disposable income everywhere.

This is why I have persisted in using the label culture-ideology, risking the sin of inelegance for the possibility of clarity. Culture always has an ideological function for consumerism in the capitalist global system, so all transnational cultural practices in this sphere are at the same time ideological practices, thus culture-ideology. This is not an empirical assertion—it is no doubt sometimes false and usually impossible to prove one way or the other. The idea of culture-ideology transnational practices and, in particular, the idea of the culture-ideology of consumerism in the capitalist global system, are conceptual tools in the theory of the global system. Global capitalism does not permit culture-ideology neutrality. Those cultural practices that cannot be incorporated into the culture-ideology of consumerism become oppositional counter-hegemonic forces, to be harnessed or marginalized, and if that fails, destroyed physically. Ordinary so-called counter-cultures are regularly incorporated and commercialized and pose no threat, indeed through the process of differentiation (illusory variety and choice), they are a source of great strength to the capitalist global system. The celebrations of the twentieth anniversary of the student and worker revolts of 1968 became media events and were relentlessly commercially exploited with the willing and presumably lucrative participation of many of those who had then been (and still are) dedicated to the overthrow of the capitalist system. Consumerist appropriations of the bicentennial of the American and French Revolutions are other interesting examples. We shall have to wait for the year 2017 to see what the culture-ideology of consumerism makes of the hundredth anniversary of the Bolshevik revolution!

The culture-ideology of consumerism is, as it were, the fuel that powers the motor of global capitalism. The driver is the transnational capitalist class. But the vehicle itself is the mighty transnational corporation. As those who own and control the TNCs are the main drivers of capitalist globalization, they merit a central place in my analysis. . . .

ECONOMIC TRANSNATIONAL PRACTICES

Economic transnational practices are economic practices that transcend state boundaries. These may seem to be entirely contained within the borders of a single country even though their effects are transnational. For example, within one country there are consumer demands for products that are unavailable, in general or during particular seasons, from domestic sources. Retailers place orders with suppliers who fill the orders from foreign sources. Neither the retailer nor the consumer needs to know or care where the product comes from, though some countries now have country of origin rules making mandatory the display of this information. Many campaigning groups make sure that customers know, for example, that some products come from sweatshops in Asia or the USA (Bonacich and Applebaum 2000, Rosen 2002). There may be a parallel situation in the supplier country. Local producers may simply sell their products to a domestic marketing board or wholesalers and neither know nor care who the final consumer is. Transnational corporations, big or small, enter the scene when sellers, intermediaries, and buyers are parts of the same transnational network (Morgan 2001).

Hundreds of thousands of companies based all over the world export goods and services. In the USA alone in the late 1990s there were more than 200,000 exporting companies according to the website of the US Department of Commerce. Of this large number of exporters only about 15 per cent operated from multiple locations, but these accounted for about 80 per cent of exports from the USA and almost half of manufacturing exports were from the top fifty firms. They, of course, are the major TNCs, comprising the less than 1 per cent of US manufacturers that export to fifty or more countries. Over half of all US export value derives from their transnational economic practices and, significantly, much of their business is comprised of intra-firm transactions. The picture is similar in many other countries with firms that export manufactured goods. The global economy is dominated by a few gigantic transnational corporations marketing their products, many of them global brands, all over the world, some medium-sized companies producing in a few locations and selling in multiple markets, while many more small firms sell from one location to one or a few other locations.

One important consequence of the expansion of the capitalist world economy has been that individual economic actors (like workers and entrepreneurs) and collective economic actors (like trade unions and TNCs) have become much more conscious of the transnationality of their practices and have striven to extend their global influence. As capitalist globalization spread, anti-globalization researchers and activists focused on imports and exports, and vested some products with great political and culture-ideology significance. Increasing numbers of consumers now register where what they are buying comes from, and producers now register where what they are producing will go to, and this knowledge may affect their actions. An important example of this process is the rapid growth of ethical and organic marketing between Third World producers and First World consumers (Barrientos 2000, Raynolds 2000). These transnational practices must be seen within the context of an unprecedented increase in the volume of economic transnational practices since the 1950s, as evidenced by the tremendous growth of cross-border trade. According to the World Bank, global exports rose from $US94 billion in 1965, to $1,365 billion in 1986, $3,500 billion in 1993 and over $5,400 billion in 1999. Foreign investment and other types of capital flows have increased even more rapidly (Streeton, in Bhalla 1998: ch. 1). This means that even some quite poor people in some poor countries now have access to many non-local consumer goods, and through their use of the mass media are becoming more aware of the status-conferring advantages that global branded goods and services have over others. These new economic communities are generally referred to as emerging markets (see Sidaway and Pryke 2000), signifying that their main interest for capitalist globalization is their potential for the profitable sale of goods and services. Transnational corporations are routinely conceived of as the surest route to economic development on a global scale (Hood and Young 2000). This, of course, largely depends on people having the money to buy goods and services, and the primary source of money for most people in the world is their jobs. . . .

THE TRANSNATIONAL CAPITALIST CLASS

The transnational capitalist class is not made up of capitalists in the traditional Marxist sense. Direct ownership or control of the means of production is no longer the exclusive criterion for serving the interests of capital, particularly not the global interests of capital.

The transnational capitalist class (TCC) is transnational in at least five senses. Its members tend to share global as well as local economic interests; they seek to exert economic control in the workplace, political control in domestic and international politics, and culture-ideology control in everyday life; they tend to have global rather than local perspectives on a variety of issues; they tend to be people from many countries, more and more of whom begin to consider themselves citizens of the world as well as of their places of birth; and they tend to share similar lifestyles, particularly patterns of luxury consumption of goods and services. In my formulation, the transnational capitalist class includes the following four fractions:

- TNC executives and their local affiliates (corporate fraction);

- globalizing state and inter-state bureaucrats and politicians (state fraction);
- globalizing professionals (technical fraction); and
- merchants and media (consumerist fraction).

This class sees its mission as organizing the conditions under which its interests and the interests of the global system (which usually but do not always coincide) can be furthered within the transnational, inter-state, national, and local contexts. The concept of the transnational capitalist class implies that there is one central transnational capitalist class that makes system-wide decisions, and that it connects with the TCC in each community, region, and country.

Political transnational practices are not primarily conducted within conventional political organizations. Neither the transnational capitalist class nor any other class operates primarily through transnational political parties. However, loose transnational political groupings do exist and they do have some effects on, and are affected by, the political practices of the TCC in most countries. There are no genuine transnational political parties, though there appears to be a growing interest in international associations of parties, which are sometimes mistaken for transnational parties. The post-Comintern Communist Movement, the Socialist International, international Fascist organizations, and various liberal and neo-liberal multi-state parties have never had much success.

There are, however, various transnational political organizations through which fractions of the TCC operate locally, for example, the Rotary Club and its offshoots and the network of American, European, and Japan-related Chambers of Commerce that straddles the globe. As Errington and Gewertz (1997) show in their study of a Rotary Club in Melanesia as well as my own research on AmCham in Mexico (Sklair 1993: *passim*), these organizations work as crucial transmission belts and lines of communication between global capitalism and local business. . . . At a more elevated level are the Trilateral Commission of the great and good from the United States, Europe, and Japan whose business is 'Elite Planning for World Management' (Sklar 1980); the World Economic Forum which meets at Davos in Switzerland and the annual Global conferences organized by *Fortune* magazine that bring together the corporate and the state fractions of the TCC. Many other similar but less well-known networks for capitalist globalization exist, for example the Bilderberg Group and Caux Round Table of senior business leaders. There are few major cities in any First or Third World (and now New Second World) country that do not have members of or connections with one or more of these organizations. They vary in strength from the major First World political and business capitals, through important Third World cities like Cairo, Singapore, and Mexico City, to nominal presences in some of the poorer countries in Africa, Asia, and Latin America. They are backed up by many powerful official bodies, such as foreign trade and economics departments of the major states. Specialized agencies of the World Bank and the IMF, WTO, US Agency for International Development (USAID), development banks, and the UN work with TNCs, local businesses, and NGOs (willing and not so willing) in projects that promote the agenda of capitalist globalization (Fox and Brown 1998, O'Brien *et al.* 2000). . . .

CULTURE-IDEOLOGY TRANSNATIONAL PRACTICES

There are many theorists who argue that the driving force for globalization lies not in the economic nor in the political sphere, but in the realm of culture and ideology. Those for whom this idea is a novelty may be surprised to learn that it was the writings and political practice of a Marxist, and a communist militant at that, which were largely responsible for the present currency of this view among radical thinkers. Antonio Gramsci, who spent most of his adult life (1926–37) in Mussolini's prisons in Fascist Italy, elaborated on Marx's insight that the ruling ideas of an epoch are the ideas of its ruling class, to create a theory of hegemony and a theory of classes of intellectuals whose function it is in any literate society to propagate or to challenge these leading ideas. Gramsci's *Prison Notebooks* represent not only a stirring monument to the human spirit under adversity but a significant turning point in the history of Marxist ideas and their contemporary relevance.

This is partly because in the sphere of culture and ideology the material conditions have changed to such an extent that what Gramsci was arguing about hegemonic processes in the 1930s has become more, not less, relevant today than it was then. To put the point graphically, while Marx and his nineteenth-century comrades would have no great difficulty in recognizing the economic and the political spheres today, despite the major changes that have undoubtedly taken place in the last 150 years, in the culture-ideology sphere the opportunities for hegemonic control on a global scale have changed out of all recognition. . . .

The 1980s witnessed an unprecedented increase in the scale and scope of the electronic media of communication, as well as genuine innovations in their nature. Technological advances and price reductions in producer and consumer electronics led the TNCs from the USA, Europe, and Japan that for the most part control the electronic media, to become globalizing corporations in ways that would have been technically impossible, and in some cases even unthinkable, a few decades previously (see Schiller 1999). This gave the potential for distribution of messages and images in a scale never before achieved. While of course there are continuities with the past, it is clear that the new forms of communication are of fundamental significance (Sussman and Lent 1991, Tehranian 1999, Thusu 2000). The fact that this is happening within and as a result of capitalist globalization indicates that a qualitatively new relationship between culture and ideology is being forged.

All those who argue that it is the medium not the message that characterizes this revolution are in my view entirely wrong. The fact that a greater variety of messages may be broadcast on a vastly greater scale does not alter the fact that the central messages come from those who own and control the major corporations. McLuhan's famous 'the medium is the message' is true only to the extent that transnational corporations increasingly control the media to propagate their message, as McLuhan himself occasionally acknowledged. A telling indicator of this is the phenomenal increase since the 1980s in commercial sponsorship of what used to be considered purely cultural events, such as operas, museum exhibits, science, and education, and their incorporation into capitalist globalization (Shaw 1993, Sklair 2001: ch. 6) and the commercialization and globalization of sport, notably the Olympic Games and the World Cup, by some of the world's largest TNCs (see Maguire 1999, Sugden and Tomlinson 1998). The television networks in the USA paid over $600m. for the Winter and Summer games of 1988 and Coca-Cola and Visa paid $22m. and $15m. respectively for exclusive use of the five-ring symbol. The four-year cycle is now estimated to create revenues of around $4 billion. The 2008 summer games has a budget of almost $2 billion and the International Olympic Committee announced in July 2001, when the summer Olympics was awarded to Beijing, that over one billion dollars was already under contract. This is driven by a variety of interests around the media and urban boosterism and is a direct consequence of how the culture-ideology of consumerism works to create global mega-events. . . .

The recognition that transnational practices in the culture-ideology sphere were seriously asymmetrical had to be addressed in a way that was not necessary for economic and political TNPs. The reason for this is the peculiar status of culture-ideology in the reproduction of capitalist globalization. Here it is useful to distinguish between private and public media. The main difference between them is that private media are used mainly to transmit commercial data and documents, often under conditions of extreme security, while public (mass) media are used mainly to broadcast entertainment, always under conditions of the greatest visibility to the paying public. Both forms were revolutionized in the 1980s by the development and dissemination of new information and communication technologies, such as cable and satellite television, video, and the Internet. The capacity for total packaging of cultural products was institutionalized in entirely new forms creating new commercial opportunities (Footer and Graber 2000).

Bagdikian (1989) characterized those who control this system as the lords of the global village. They purvey their product (a relatively undifferentiated mass of news, information, ideas, entertainment, and popular culture) to a rapidly expanding public, eventually the whole world. He argued that national boundaries are growing increasingly meaningless as the main actors (five groups at the time he was writing) strive for total control in the production, delivery, and marketing of what we can call the culture-ideology goods of the capitalist global system. Their goal is to create a buying mood for the benefit of the global troika of media, advertising, and consumer goods manufacturers. 'Nothing in human experience has prepared men, women and children for the modern television techniques of fixing human attention and creating the uncritical mood required to sell goods, many of which are marginal at best to human needs' (Bagdikian 1989: 819). Two symbolic facts: by the age of 16, the average North American youth has been exposed to more than 300,000 television commercials; and the former Soviet Union sold advertising slots on cosmonaut suits and space ships! (For many others, see Durning 1992.) In order to connect and explain these facts, we need to generate a new framework, namely the culture-ideology of consumerism.

THE CULTURE-IDEOLOGY OF CONSUMERISM

The transformation of the culture-ideology of consumerism from a sectional preference of the rich to a globalizing phenomenon can be explained in terms of two central factors, factors that are historically unprecedented. First, capitalism entered a qualitatively new globalizing phase in the 1960s. As the electronic revolution got under way, the productivity of capitalist factories, systems of extraction and processing of raw materials, product design, marketing and distribution of goods and services began to be transformed in one sector after another. This golden age of capitalism began in the USA, but spread a little later to Japan and Western Europe and other parts of the First World, to the NICs, and to some cities and enclaves in the Third World. Second, the technical and social relations that structured the mass media all over the world made it very easy for new consumerist lifestyles to become the dominant motif for these media. Therefore, in the second half of the twentieth century, for the first time in human history, the dominant economic system, capitalism, was sufficiently productive to provide a basic package of material possessions and services to almost everyone in the First World and to privileged groups elsewhere. Capitalism, particularly in its neo-liberal phase from the 1980s, promised that eventually the rising tide would raise all boats, that is, everyone else in the world would get rich as long as they did what the transnational capitalist class told to them to do. A rapidly globalizing system of mass media was also geared up to tell everyone what was available and, crucially, to persuade people that this culture-ideology of consumerism was what a happy and satisfying life was all about. In a powerful empirical study of the increasing hours and more intensive nature of work in the United States since the 1950s, Schor (1991) demonstrated how capitalist consumerism led North Americans (and, I would argue, other groups elsewhere) into a sort of Faustian bargain whereby those who can find work trade off their time for more and more consumer goods and services.

Mass media perform many functions for global capitalism. They speed up the circulation of material goods through advertising, which reduces the time between production and consumption. They begin to inculcate the dominant ideology into the minds of viewers, listeners, and readers from an early age, in the words of Esteinou Madrid, 'creating the political/cultural demand for the survival of capitalism' (1986: 119). The systematic blurring of the lines between information, entertainment, and promotion of products lies at the heart of this practice. This has not in itself created consumerism, for consumer cultures have been in place for centuries. What it has created is a reformation of consumerism that transforms all the mass media and their contents into opportunities to sell ideas, values, products, in short, a consumerist world-view . . .

Contemporary consumer culture would not be possible without the shopping mall, both symbolically and substantively. As Crawford (in Sorkin 1992: 3–30) argued, the merging of the architecture of the mall with the culture of the theme park has become the key symbol and the key spatial reference point for consumer capitalism, not only in North America but increasingly all over the world. What Goss (1993) terms the magic of the mall has to be understood on several levels, how the consuming environment is carefully designed and controlled, the seductive nature of

the consuming experience, the transformation of nominal public space into actual private terrain. Although there are certainly anomalies of decaying city districts interspersed with gleaming malls bursting with consumer goods in the First World, it is in the poorer parts of the Third World that these anomalies are at their most stark. This World mall until quite recently catered mainly to the needs and wants of expatriate TNC executives and officials, and local members of the transnational capitalist class. The success of the culture-ideology of consumerism can be observed all over the world in these malls, where now large numbers of workers and their families flock to buy, usually with credit cards, thus locking themselves into the financial system of capitalist globalization. The integration of the medium of the mall and the message of the culture-ideology of consumerism had a formative influence on the trajectory of global capitalism. The medium looks like the message because the message, the culture-ideology of consumerism, has engulfed the medium. The problem, therefore, is not *Understanding Media* (the title of McLuhan's great if somewhat misconceived book) but understanding capitalist globalization, the system that produces and reproduces both the message and the media that incessantly transmit it. . . .

The connections between capitalist globalization and the culture-ideology of consumerism must be laid bare. In an attempt to do this, Featherstone (1987:21) develops a useful composite picture of contemporary consumer culture. He writes:

1. Goods are framed and displayed to entice the customer, and shopping becomes an overtly symbolic event.

2. Images play a central part, constantly created and circulated by the mass media.

3. Acquisition of goods leads to a 'greater aestheticisation of reality.'

The end result of these processes is a new concept of lifestyle, enhanced self-image. This 'glosses over the real distinctions in the capacity to consume and ignores the low paid, the unemployed, the old' (ibid.: 22), though the ubiquity of the culture-ideology of consumerism actually does include everyone (or, at least, all those with the potential to buy) however poor, because no one can escape its images. And, it must be added, very few people would choose to escape its images and what they represent in terms of the good, or better, life. Monga (2000: 193) insightfully analyzes this issue through the stories of women from Africa who eventually found asylum in France and USA (and many more who did not). 'Though the perspectives of these women are in themselves of interest, what is of real import is their fundamental goal: survival in a rapidly changing world where the rhetoric of globalisation poorly conceals the reality of the increasing marginalisation of Africa and its inhabitants [including men].' This is concretely expressed in three strategies for African women and their children mainly through migrating to the USA. The first is through the sale of beauty products for immediate income. The cosmetics industry in the USA, uniquely, has designed a range for black women, so women in Africa are keen to get hold of them, usually through high end informal sector locations. These locations are also socio-economic markers of a system based on credit in which authentic products straight from the USA are at a premium. The second strategy is education of children, a route to intermediate material well-being. The possibility of working through college in the USA makes this an attractive option. While France focuses on rhetoric for African women, the USA focuses on marketable skills, and the myth of America as the land of opportunity contrasts with the racism that black people often find in France. The third, long-term strategy, is the Americanization of children, through giving birth in the USA. This involves the rapid Americanization of names in Africa (usually taken from TV characters) and, Monga argues, illustrates a deeper desire to participate in the global village. She quotes Zhan to the effect that the 'success of American brand-name products abroad is due not to their "Americanism" per se but to their ability to match the demands of a diverse market throughout the world' (cited in Monga 2000: 202, n. 10). Monga is entirely on the mark when she argues: 'whereas women from Africa turn to American culture, some members of the African-American community look to African, or African-inspired culture as a means of expressing their need for self-affirmation and social recognition, often utilizing the same

cultural markers as African women: first names, apparel, and art objects' (Monga 2000:204).

The issue of Americanization is clearly a central dilemma of any critique of consumerism (and also of the politics of the consumer movement). Many scholars (pre-eminently Ewen 1976) point up the distinctive role of the United States in the campaign to make consumer culture universal. Through Hollywood, and the globalization of the movies, via Madison Avenue, from where Ewen's captains of consciousness created the modern advertising industry, to the more geographically diffuse but ideologically monolithic television networking conceptualizers, the consumerist elites of the transnational capitalist class in the United States has assumed leadership of the culture-ideology of consumerism in the interests of global capitalism in the twentieth century.

A good illustration of this is the origin of the soap opera, one of the most highly developed media forms through which mass consumerism is projected. It began in the 1920s when Glen Sample, an American advertising agent, had the idea of adapting a newspaper serial for the radio, a medium already dominated by commercial interests. The programme, *Betty and Bob*, was sponsored by a flour manufacturer, and Sample used the same idea to promote Oxydol washing powder for Procter & Gamble, under siege from Unilever's Rinso in the US market. Oxydol won out, and the so-called soap opera that was used to sell it gave its name to a genre, massively reinforced by its wholesale adoption by television all over the world since the 1950s.

The universal availability of the mass media has been rapidly achieved through relatively cheap transistor radios, cassette recorders, and televisions, which now totally penetrate the First World, almost totally penetrate the urban Second and Third Worlds, and are beginning to penetrate deeply into the countryside even in the poorest places. Thus, the potential of global exposure to global communication, the dream of every merchant in history, has arrived. The socialization process by which people learn what to want, which used to occur mainly in the home and the school, is increasingly taking place through what the theorists of the Frankfurt School had so acutely termed the culture industry (reprinted in Bernstein 1992). . . .

ADVERTISING AND THE
SPREAD OF CONSUMERISM

Transnational advertising agencies (TNAAs) are now big business . . . [as].many have revenues in excess of one billion dollars. They are also increasingly active in the Third World, producing advertisements and marketing strategies often with domestic agencies in joint ventures to promote local and global products and services. Since the 1970s these have taken up more and more Third World radio, TV, and printed media space (Anderson 1984). Studies of the TNAAs, from the USA, Europe, and Japan, provide a good test for the view that we should be looking not at the increase or decrease of Americanization in the Third World but at the inroads that the culture-ideology of consumerism directed by major TNCs is making in Third World societies.

According to Noreene Janus, by 1980 the TNAAs derived more than half of their gross income from overseas, with the Latin American market expanding particularly fast. Brazil, Mexico, and Argentina were among the top twenty advertising markets. Janus's (1986:128) approach is predicated on the claim that: 'lifestyles promoted in advertising include implicit and explicit agendas for social relations, political action, and cultural change.' In most countries advertising is concentrated on a relatively small group of consumer goods, soaps/detergents, tobacco, drugs, perfumes, deodorants, toothpaste, processed foods, alcohol, soft drinks, and cars. Increase in the consumption of these products is less an indicator of level of development than kind of development. All over the world, these products tend to be characterized by high profits, high advertising spent on sales, high barriers to entry, and high levels of penetration by TNCs.

This leads inexorably to the transnationalization of the local mass media. In her own substantive research Janus found that TNCs were responsible for most of the adverts on TV in Mexico and women's magazines in Latin America, and for about one-third of non-government newspaper adverts in Mexico. The next stage in the process, the transnationalization of consumption habits, is not as unproblematic as is sometimes assumed. Janus (1986:133) argued for a 'perpetual confrontation between transnational expansion and local cultural expansion,' and cites as evidence the fact TNCs such as Gerber (baby food) and Nestlé (instant coffee) have acknowledged that customer resistance is their main marketing problem in Latin America. . . . It is for this reason that the TNAAs are not only trying to sell specific products in the Third World but are engineering social, political, and cultural change in order to ensure a level of consumption that is 'the material basis for the promotion of a standardized global culture' (Janus 1986:135). . . .

Global Exposure

The global film, television, and radio broadcasting industries are increasingly organically linked and are still dominated by the commercial interest of US-origin transnationals. Although Hollywood actually produces only a minority of the worldwide total of films and television programmes, its control over marketing and distribution gives it an enormous input onto Third World screens. A report for UNESCO showed that in 1976, 36.5 per cent of Thai TV time was devoted to foreign, mostly US imports; in 1973 almost 90 per cent of the films shown in Argentina were foreign-made, 37 per cent of these from the United States (Guback and Varis 1982: ch.4). . . . The proposition that, in the words of the British media sociologist Jeremy Tunstall, the media are American, became a potent political slogan.

The US-Japanese relationship is of particular significance here. Many in the Third World argue that if the Japanese, so economically powerful, cannot resist American or, more generally, Western consumerism then what chance has anyone else. But the question needs to be reconceptualized in the form: to what extent is the culture ideology of consumerism in Japan an effect of capitalist globalization, or does it have uniquely Japanese (or any other cultural) characteristics? My argument is that the consumerism of capitalist globalization has a universal form but with the permanent potential of national-local cultural contents. A typical, if absurd, example is the new 'fake festival of panty-givers' in Japan. Japanese confectioners take around 10 per cent of their annual sales on St Valentine's Day (whose name was unknown in Japan before the arrival of chocolate). Panty-giving Day 'is an attempt by the lingerie industry to join in the commercial exploitation of fake festivals.' The point is that the culture-ideology of consumerism produces the form, but the content is taken from the film *Working Girl*, whose heroine is given underwear by the boyfriend. Mikiko Taga, the feminist author of a book on *sekihara* (sexual harassment) explains: 'Japanese think this is an American custom and they imitate American actions' (quoted in Sullivan 1990). However, this is driven not by Americanization as such but by the marketing skills of local entrepreneurs. . . .

There are those who would condemn all US culture products, as there are those who would as uncritically endorse them. This is not the point. The point is that Thailand, Argentina, and Nigeria (and most other Third World countries), as well as Japan and Western Europe, are exposed to media messages of US origin extolling the virtues of capitalist consumerism daily and at a high level of intensity. The balance between US/European and local-origin mass media communication globally is skewed towards the former, and Third World-origin mass media messages practically never get exposure in the United States or other First World countries. Under the title 'What's hot on TV Worldwide?' *Advertising Age* (1 Dec. 1986:60) produced a list of the top US and local shows on the television channels of nine Third World and eleven First World countries. Not one of the local shows has ever been networked in the United State. The most popular US shows for the Third World sample were *Knight Rider* (all the way from South Korea to Nicaragua), *The A-Team*, and *Dynasty*. A survey in the *Los Angeles Times* (1992) confirmed the point. In 2001, the shows had changed but the message was similar. All of these programmes, and the many more broadcast in the Third World, present specific messages and convey specific myths about life in the United States and at home (see Barker 1997), as indeed all popular television does in any country. The popularity of such programmes and the annual crop of multi-million-dollar grossing movies that achieve global screening also tell us something about the ways in which the media TNCs have successfully tapped into consumer preferences in the Third World. It must be remembered that these consumers are free to switch on or off, to pay to see films or not. Intellectuals may bemoan the effects of US-influenced public mass media in the Third World, as they bemoan the onward march of the fast food and beverage industries caused by the rise of global franchising, but it cannot be denied that these products of the TNCs are popular and widely sought after all over the world. The inability or unwillingness of local producers, private or state, to compete effectively with the TNCs in these fields does not sufficiently explain the global success that TNC media products enjoy. Further, the Americanization of the mass media is somewhat problematic in light of two facts. First, three of the big five media TNCs (Bertelsman, Vivendi, and NewsCorp) originate in Germany, France, and Australia-UK, and second, many 'American' media companies are actually subsidiaries of these three (Houghton Mifflin publishers, Universal Studios, and Fox, respectively), Sony Corporation from Japan (PlayStation), and others. . . .

Cola Wars

The so-called cola wars provide a telling example of how the TNCs have gone about the creation of a culture-ideology of consumerism in the Third World. Coca-Cola (Coke), the market leader, has been sold outside the United States since the beginning of the twentieth century (Pendergrast 1993). In an article to celebrate the hundredth anniversary of the company and what it stands for, *Beverage World* (May 1986: 48–51) under the revealing title, 'Ambassador to the world,' provided an insight into how the industry sees the product. By 1929 Coke was operating sixty-four bottling plants in twenty-eight different countries. Recalling its diplomatic skills and its very special role as a symbol of the American way of life, the article describes how Coke survived the India-Pakistan War by turning its plants into blood donor stations, how it survived the Arab anti-Zionist boycott, and how it recovered after its major diplomatic setback—losing control of the Russian market to Pepsi. By the mid-1980s Coke was found in 155 countries, over 60 per cent of its sales were outside the United States, and more than 300 million Cokes were drunk every day. By 2000, its worldwide revenues were $35 billion. It is truly globalizing!

Only since the 1980s has the pressure of competition, particularly from its great rival Pepsi, led Coke and its competitors to a more public global strategy and a specific targeting of Third World markets (see Clairmonte and Cavanagh 1988: chs. 7 and 8). In the early 1980s it was reported that the annual consumption of Coke overseas was 49 6.5 oz-units per person, compared with 272 units in the United States. The potential for growth was thus outside the US market rather than in any major expansion of domestic consumption (*Advertising Age*, 29 Oct. 1983: 2, 86). The cola was illustrated in one phase of the continuing campaign orchestrated by the major beverage TNCs to structure new consumption needs, or more accurately induced wants, particularly in the Third World. The cola wars are particularly intense in the struggle for the teenage market. Coca-cola was reported to have been researching the global teenager in a nine-country study and to have discovered that music and associated styles of clothing, sport, and consumer electronics are the three parameters of the global teenage market (Tully 1994). Coca-Cola is constantly connected with all of these in a variety of direct and indirect ways (see Sklair 2001:168–71).

This is true not only for Coca-Cola. Well over half of total world soft drink consumption takes place in the United States. Between the mid-1960s, per capita consumption of soft drinks in the USA more than doubled while that of water appears to have halved (though sales of bottled water, some of it owned by the cola companies, has reversed this to some extent). Soft drink consumption exceeded that of water, coffee, beer, and milk (*Beverage World*, Feb. 1989: 45). While, no doubt, North Americans can always be persuaded to have another one, the greatest challenge for the TNCs is to persuade consumers elsewhere to develop the same habit. As one industry analyst has proclaimed: 'because the international soft drink market is yet in its infancy, the successes of both Coke and Pepsi will serve to grow the entire world market. Their success, in part, hinges on their ability to change the way consumers in foreign markets regard soft drinks. . . . So as a strategy, Coke will target an increasingly younger consumer in an attempt to shape his [*sic*] drinking habits to consume more soft drinks instead of alternative beverages' (Hemphill 1986).

One indication that the beverage industry was gearing itself for an onslaught on the drinking habits of the global consumer came in 1984 when InterBev'84 was staged with 15,000 delegates from nearly thirty countries. Two years later, under the slogan 'Selling the World,' InterBev'86 brought together 25,000 people from eighty countries to ponder the thought expressed by a prominent industry representative: 'You have billions of people around the world that have yet to be exposed to soft drinks.' In the mid-1980s, even Coca-Cola, the market leader, had half its sales in only five countries (*Beverage Industry*, Sept. 1986: 1ff.). The cola wars were well and truly under way!

Announcing that 'Cola wars move to foreign shores,' *Advertising Age* (26 Aug. 1985: 6) described how Pepsi and Coke were locked in global combat in Europe and Asia; in 'Latin soft drink wars' (11 Nov. 1985), how Pepsi's 7UP and Coke's Sprite were engaged in a lemon-lime battle for the allegiance of potential South American consumers: and how Schweppes was challenging in Australia (18 Dec. 1989). 'Pepsi in China' (*Beverage Industry*, Apr. 1986:15, 20) recounted how PepsiCo would invest $100m. over ten years to develop the Chinese soft drinks industry, and secure the company's place as the prime purveyor of non-alcoholic beverages in the communist world. PepsiCO has operated a bottling plant in Canton since the early 1980s, and along with its joint venture Happiness Soft Drinks Corporation in the Shenzhen SEZ, serves the Chinese and South-East Asian markets (Sklair 1985). Coke, however, fought back, and the Chinese authorities have had a certain degree of success in playing the two corporate giants off against each other. By the late 1990s both colas were well established in the Chinese market, and *Fortune* reported that Coca-Cola had signed a distribution deal with neighbourhood committees of the Communist Party in Shanghai (25 May 1998).

India, too, has had its own cola war. The Coca-Cola presence in India dates from 1950 and in alliance with a local bottling company aligned with the politically dominant Gandhi family, it prospered until 1977 when it was forced to withdraw rather than give up its total control (as IBM had also done when threatened with indigenization). A local soft drink, 77 Cola, flopped because of marketing and flavour problems, but a rival Coke clone, Campa-Cola, was more successful (*Advertising Age*, 28 Jan. 1985:63). The cola wars in India were sustained by the bold actions of an Indian entrepreneur, who tried to keep Pepsi out of the country, while sneaking his own brand of fruit juice into the United States (*Forbes*, 22 Sept. 1986: 207; Chakravarty 1989). In July 1994, Hindu fundamentalists in northern India declared a boycott of Coca-Cola and Pepsi-Cola, calling them 'the most visible symbols of the multinational invasion of this country' and threatened a countrywide boycott of foreign consumer goods. The clash of interests between those who want to buy these products, local competitors, and fundamentalists attacking the evils of modern consumerism, is a heady brew. By the late 1990s, Pepsi was said to be winning over the key market of some 200 million middle-class youths (*Fortune*, 27 Apr. 1998). And so it goes on!

In Vietnam, Pepsi-Cola's local partner had its products out on the streets of Ho Chi Minh City hours after President Clinton announced the end of the US trade embargo in 1994 which, Reuters News reported, signalled new cola wars for Vietnam's 70 million consumers. Coca-Cola had previously signed joint-venture agreements with the two local firms to produce the beverage in Vietnam. Cans of these drinks were freely available in Vietnam, smuggled in from neighbouring countries. When democratic elections removed the pressure to boycott the government in South Africa, Pepsi-Cola announced that it was returning to the country in joint ventures with black partners after decades of anti-apartheid protest. Coca-Cola had divested its interests in 1986, but a local firm which had been left with a bottling license had captured most of the market.

While Coca-Cola outsells its main rival by a significant amount worldwide, the next phase of the cola wars is likely to feature other products owned by Coke and Pepsi as much as fizzy drinks. Both are heavily involved in the exceptionally lucrative bottled water business, and Pepsi paid $14 billion for the Quaker Oats food group, outbidding Coca-Cola. In Venezuela, however, the domestic Cisneros Group had ended its relationship with Pepsi in that market and joined up with Coca-Cola, which acquired several popular local brands as part of the deal. Coke was beset with many problems at the turn of the century, being sued by black employees at home and by antitrust authorities in Texas and in

Europe (*Business Week*, 29 May 2000) and in disputes over predatory pricing by US bottlers exporting to Japan, where Coke derived 20 per cent of its profits on just 5 per cent of its production (*New York Times*, 26 Jan. 2000). *Fortune* has speculated that Pepsi might be winning the cola wars (2 Apr. 2001:96–7).

There are very few parts of the world in which the effects of the cola wars have not been felt. In even the most remote places Coke and Pepsi and their ubiquitous marketing slogans and logos are acknowledged as symbols of the American way of life. They are also marketed on the prospect that anyone, however poor, who can afford a bottle or a can, can join in the great project of global consumerism, if only for a few moments. The transnational practices of the capitalist global system fade into the background as the joyous promises of 'Coca Cola is It' or membership of the 'Pepsi Generation' or some new slogan flood the foreground.

Now this may be very welcome news for those who oppose the consumption of alcohol by the young, and it may also be good news for those involved in bottling plants and distribution networks. It is hardly up to the outside observer to decide whether one or other or any fizzy drink is appropriate for anyone's consumption. Nevertheless, it is legitimate to draw attention to the massive marketing budgets and the battery of promotional skills put to work by TNCs like Coca-Cola and PepsiCo in poor communities, and to acknowledge that they really can create new consumption needs for nutritionally worthless products, and dictate the means to satisfy them largely on their own terms.

It is not irrelevant that most of the players in this game are connected with TNCs that originate in the United States with eager associates all over the world, and that what is being marketed is not simply a soft drink but a style of life, specifically a (North) American style of life. An executive of a small cola company put the point plainly when he said: 'our emphasis in Third World countries is to reinforce to the consumer that we are an American soft drink and we do have the quality the consumer has been looking for and not always finding . . . there is a tremendous potential for expanding per capita consumption . . . through impacting lifestyles in the same manner that we have here in the U.S.'

(Jabbonsky 1986: 188). This statement epito- mizes the relationship between Americanization and the culture-ideology of consumerism in the capitalist global system.

Edward Said (1935–2003): A Biographical Sketch

SOURCE: www.frittogvilt.no.

Edward Said was born in Jerusalem in 1935 to a Christian Arab family. At this time Jerusalem was a Palestinian city under British colonial rule. Said spent his formative years living between Jerusalem and Cairo until 1948, when the state of Israel was established and his family became refugees. In 1951, Said emigrated to the United States to attend an elite boarding school in Massachusetts while his family stayed behind in the Middle East. He proved to be an exceptional student in his new country, graduating at the top of his class. The school, however, withheld his deserved title as valedictorian or salutatorian (Said does not recall graduating first or second) on the dubious moral grounds of being unfit for the honor (Said 2000:559). Nevertheless, he would go on to receive his bachelor's degree from Princeton University and his master's and doctorate from Harvard, where he studied Western litera- ture, music, and philosophy.

In 1963, Said joined the faculty of Columbia University, where he would remain for the next four decades as professor of English and compara- tive literature. During this time he also taught courses at Yale, Johns Hopkins, and Harvard Universities and delivered lectures internationally. He received more than half a dozen honorary doctorates from universities in some eight countries. He published more than a dozen books (with translations in thirty-six languages) and wrote countless articles and essays appearing in both scholarly journals and the popular media. Said's writings span from literary criticism and music criticism (he was a Juilliard-trained classical pianist) to the cultural dynamics of colonialism, the Arab-Israeli conflict, media depic- tions of Arabs and Islam, and personal memoirs. Said was a member of the Council on Foreign Relations, the American Academy of Arts and Sciences, and the Royal Society of Literature. He served as president of the Modern Language Association in 1999.

Said is arguably best known for his political views on the "Palestinian question." An ardent supporter of the Palestinians' right of return, he remained an outspoken critic of the Israeli occupation of the West Bank and Gaza Strip and the United States's complicity in the continued degradation of the Palestinian people. He was a regular contributor to news- papers and magazines published in England, France, the United States, and across the Arab world. For more than a decade he served on the Palestinian National Council until a falling out with Yasser Arafat and his leadership of the Palestinian Liberation Organization (PLO) led him to resign his position. Such was Said's vocal opposition to Arafat's leadership that the Palestinian Authority banned the sale of his books. Once an official spokesperson for the Palestinian struggle for independence, Said was now considered a traitor to the cause. His disagreement with the PLO came largely in response to Arafat's signing of the Oslo Peace Accord in 1993. For Said, the Accord was fundamentally flawed, for it did not establish the right of Palestinian refugees to return to their homes in Israel while leaving unchecked the expansion of Israeli settlements in the occupied territories. In his view, a lasting Middle East peace could be secured only through the creation of a single, bi-national state in which Israelis and Palestinians shared political authority. A coexistence between Israeli Jews and Palestinian Arabs based on a mutual equality was for Said the only "road map" capable of ending the continuing oppression of refugees and the violence that occupation breeds. Said summed up his position thusly:

> I've been consistent in my belief that no military option exists for either side, that only a process of peaceful reconciliation, and justice for what the Palestinians have had to endure by way of dispossession and military occupation, would work. (2000:564)

As for his views on the United States and the media's role in the politics of the Middle East, Said noted all too presciently in 1980:

> So far as the United States seems to be concerned, it is only a slight overstatement to say that Moslems and Arabs are essentially seen as either oil suppliers or potential terrorists. Very little of the detail, the human density, the passion of Arab-Moslem life has entered the awareness of even those people whose profession it is to report the Arab world. What we have instead is a series of crude, essentialized caricatures of the Islamic world presented in such a way as to make that world vulnerable to military aggression. ("Islam Through Western Eyes," *The Nation*, April 26, 1980)

Over the decades, Said's position earned him his share of enemies on both the political right and left. His office at Columbia University was set on fire, his family was subjected to countless death threats, and in 1985 he was labeled a Nazi by the Jewish Defense League. His more recent criticisms of the ongoing Iraq War also made him a popular target for those in the media and government who support the invasion and subsequent occupation. Nevertheless, Said remained steadfastly committed to his principles and vision of a humane world until his death at the age of sixty-seven in September 2003.

INTELLECTUAL INFLUENCES AND CORE IDEAS

While both Wallerstein and Sklair emphasize broad, structural aspects of globalization, Said, as a postcolonial theorist, underscores the subjective dimensions of Western expansion into non-Western societies. Developing largely out of English and comparative literature departments, postcolonial studies examines the relationship between the colonizer and the colonized as it is inscribed in language. More specifically, postcolonial theorists analyze how scientists, philosophers, novelists, and political officials from imperialist powers (most notably England, France, and the United States) construct, understand, and subjugate the populations of colonized nations through the written word. In addition, postcolonial theory explores how writers living under colonial rule seek to reconstruct their cultural identity and resist domination through their own appropriation or use of the colonial language (i.e., English or French).

While the term "post"colonial implies a specific relationship between the colonizer and the colonized—after colonial rule has ended—it should not be taken literally. Postcolonial scholars explore writings produced prior to and during colonial rule, as well as after a nation has gained its political independence. Indeed, it is often the case that political independence does not bring with it complete autonomy or freedom from foreign intervention but leads, instead, to neocolonial relations aimed at "modernizing" underdeveloped nations. Under these conditions, Western powers install "puppet regimes" in their former colonies to ensure their continued economic (if not political or military) exploitation of the region. For their part, the leaders of these regimes all too often resort to ruthless repression of their own native populations in order to maintain the favor of Western investors. Unfortunately, the list of such dictators is quite long: Saddam Hussein of Iraq; King Fahd in Saudi Arabia; Reza Muhammed Shah Pahlawi, the former Shah of Iran; Papa Doc and Baby Duc Duvalier of Haiti; Manuel Noriega of Panama; Rafael Trujillo in the Dominican Republic; and Ngo Dinh Diem of South Vietnam, to name but a few.

At its root, postcolonial studies explore relations of power that have defined geopolitics from the age of European colonial expansion to the present-day era of declining Western dominance. Although spearheaded by scholars associated with the field of comparative literature, this emphasis has led to a host of questions that sociologists have recently taken up, a sign of the increasing cross-disciplinary encounters between the humanities and the sciences. Perhaps the most compelling question involves how colonizing powers use language to fix the meaning of the colonized "Other." In other words, how do colonizing powers use texts—the written word—to simplify complex civilizations, to erase the existence of a rich cultural heritage, and to deny the humanity of a population as part of the effort to legitimate the subjugation of those nations they seek to control? Such efforts demand that a population be torn from its history in order to create a new future—a future literally written by the West. For those seeking to fashion an alternative, "postcolonial" means of expression freed from the dehumanizing effects of the colonial language, a central task involves reclaiming the culture, the history, and the language of marginalized populations in order to speak as and for oneself. Examining the promises and pitfalls tied to this struggle for self-representation is a primary concern for Gayatri Chakravorty Spivak, a leading postcolonial theorist whose work we highlight in Significant Others, page 615, and who, as an Indian woman, knows firsthand what it means to be the "Other."

The notion of the "Other" raises several interesting issues, two of which we address here. First, colonization is premised on the notion that the colonized Other is inherently inferior, weak, and evil. This understanding of the native population allows for the implementation of brutal and repressive tactics as a means for "civilizing the savages." Yet, such an understanding must first be constructed, and it is colonial discourse that accomplishes this very objective: "to construe the colonized as a population of degenerate types on the basis of racial origin, in order to justify conquest and to establish systems of administration and instruction. . . . The colonized population is then deemed to be both the cause and effect of the system, imprisoned in the circle of interpretation" (Bhabha 1986:154, 171). Thus, people throughout the Arab world, the Caribbean islands, Africa, and elsewhere have been defined in Western literary texts and in scientific works as simultaneously irrational, bloodthirsty, infantile, and deceitful and in need of "correct training." And who better to provide this correct training than those in the colonizing West, who, by virtue of not being the inferior and degenerate Other, are superior, strong, righteous, and pure? To the colonizers, then, the colonized are an untamed group who, despite their inferiority, are to be feared because of their potential to corrupt civilized Western culture. Hence the need to tame those who are less civilized. Such is the "white man's burden."[9]

---

[9]It is important to note that a similar colonial discourse is often used to subjugate segments of a population within a nation and not only as a means for justifying the oppression of those living in a foreign country. The history of racism within the United States, as well as its contemporary manifestations, provides ample evidence of this. Black Americans in particular have been subjected to a litany of negative depictions, from violent, oversexed, and conniving, to childish, inept, and feeble-minded.

| Significant Others | Gayatri Chakravorty Spivak (1942–): Can the Subaltern Speak? |

Alongside Edward Said, Gayatri Chakravorty Spivak is one of the leading postcolonial scholars. Spivak was born in Calcutta, West Bengal, to an urban middle-class family. After graduating from the University of Calcutta with a degree in English, she moved to the United States to pursue a graduate education in comparative literature at Cornell University. After completing her degree, Spivak achieved notoriety with the publication *Of Grammatology* (1976), an English translation of *De la Grammatologie* (1967) written by the French poststructuralist theorist Jacques Derrida. This work is most notable for Spivak's contribution to "deconstruction," a branch of philosophy that seeks to deconstruct the hierarchical binary oppositions (such as black and white, male and female, good and evil) on which Western thought is based. In doing so, deconstructionists expose how otherwise unquestioned "truths" are produced. However, the practice of deconstruction necessarily involves adopting the existing system of binary codes in order to articulate a critique of that system. Unable to escape from this hierarchical system, the deconstructionist unavoidably reproduces the prevailing patterns of social domination that are understood and legitimated through it.

Spivak's work in large measure addresses this problematic, a problematic that for her takes on a particularly personal dimension. On the one hand, as a woman from a "third world" nation, Spivak inhabits a marginalized social position. Yet, on the other hand, she is a member of the educated elite who enjoys a privileged career as a professor at one of the most prestigious institutions, Columbia University. In what is her most oft-cited piece, "Can the Subaltern Speak?" (1985) Spivak borrows Antonio Gramsci's notion of the "subaltern" to argue that those groups who remain shut out from the dominant social institutions and whose voices do not conform to the assumptions of the dominant discourse are effectively mute. While such groups can indeed speak, they will not be heard by those who occupy positions of privilege. Yet intellectuals committed to dismantling Western imperialism and advocating the independence of colonized nations all too often do a disservice to those oppressed groups on whose behalf they speak. Speaking from a vantage point of privilege, intellectuals cannot help but distort the lived truth of those who, because of their marginalized status, are unable to represent themselves.

In the end, Spivak calls into question the very foundation of postcolonial studies by asking whether or not intellectuals are necessarily complicit in perpetuating the colonizing forces and institutions they are ostensibly seeking to unmask. Aligned with male-dominated educational institutions (many of which have dubious records with regard to foreign investment practices) located in imperialist countries, Spivak asks if it is possible for Western intellectuals to develop a postcolonial discourse that is not, however inadvertently, colonizing. Speaking *for* the subaltern, whether it is "Iraqi women," "Indian women," or East Timorese peasants, intellectuals simultaneously construct the subaltern through a discourse that essentializes what is in reality always a diverse, heterogeneous group. Spivak warns that such a discursive practice is a form of colonization, a way of erasing and remaking the identity and culture of a group that is analogous to the economic exploitation and political domination exercised by colonial powers. For those engaged with postcolonial studies, their best hope is not to "give" the subaltern a voice in hopes of protecting or fighting for "them," for this only reinforces their subaltern status. Rather, they should work toward institutionalizing avenues that allow subalterns to speak for themselves.

This relationship between the Other and the West leads to a central paradox in the development of cultural identity. In a very real sense, the West, despite its alleged superiority and strength, is dependent on the inferior, colonized Other, who alone is capable of producing its sublime identity. In other words, one cannot be "superior" unless there is an "inferior" against which the necessary comparison can be made. As a result, the source of the West's superiority lies not in its own "advanced" civilization but, rather, in constructing non-Western cultures through negative terms that project onto the colonized all those traits that the West cannot possess if it is to legitimate its position as the center of progress and the beacon of humanity. The purity of the West is thus intertwined with the impurity of the non-West. And such oversimplified, homogenized depictions of both Western and non-Western cultures and peoples must be maintained in order to perpetuate existing relations based on domination and subordination.[10] Thus, when a politician remarks that Muslims "hate us for our freedom," this claim is dependent on a purified notion of what Western freedom has promoted around the world, in turn justifying an ennobled aggression against those who are "against freedom."

The second set of issues raised by the notion of the Other turns our attention from the colonizers to the colonized. For colonized groups, or those who have won political independence from colonial rule, the question remains as to how they can shed their identity as an inferior Other. Educated in schools established by the colonizers and adopting the language of their rulers, the colonized are effectively cut off from their history and cultural traditions. What the colonized come to learn about themselves, their identity, and their heritage is shaped by the images and meanings that the colonizers project back onto their subject populations. In this context, reclaiming their past and their precolonized identity becomes a near-impossible task. Yet, doing so is a necessary and fundamental step in the struggle for the freedom to "be." In this regard the colonized share a parallel fate with their oppressors, for they, too, are unable to escape the duality of their identity. Every attempt to shed their "otherness" entails incorporating the very terms that define them as an Other. Even after their independence is won, the colonized are thus condemned to an identity that is at least in part defined through the vision of their colonizers.

The psychological turmoil this situation exacts was described by Frantz Fanon, whose penetrating work represents an important precursor to what would later become postcolonial studies. We outline Fanon's contributions in Significant Others, page 617. (As a black colonial subject, Fanon, like Spivak, draws from his personal experiences as an Other to describe the psyche of the subjugated.)

However, we turn here to an example of the structural consequences of this "othering" by considering the 1994 genocide in Rwanda, in which hundreds of thousands of Tutsis were slaughtered by Hutus with the encouragement and assistance of the Rwandan government. The intense hatred for the Tutsis has its roots in Belgium's colonization of the country. The different ethnicities of these two groups were politicized by the Belgians, who established a caste system in which the Hutu were defined as an inferior, lower-class people and the lighter-skinned Tutsis as an upper-class people worthy of colonial privileges such as an education, good jobs, and access to political positions. While the two groups had coexisted relatively peacefully for centuries prior to the colonization of the region, Hutu resentment and hatred toward the Tutsi mounted under Belgium's colonial rule and the system of discrimination it created. When Rwanda was granted its independence from Belgium in the early 1960s, the stage was set for a massive civil war. The Hutus gained control of the government, and decades of ensuing

---

[10]The use of the term "non-West" itself points to the oversimplified "othering" that we are discussing: the non-West refers to everything that is "not" West. On a parallel note, in discussing the notion of the "other" and the role of identity construction, postcolonial scholars often draw upon psychoanalysis, particularly the work of Sigmund Freud and Jacques Lacan.

Significant Others	Frantz Fanon (1925–1961): The Father of Postcolonial Studies

Frantz Fanon was born in Martinique, a French colony in the Caribbean. After serving in the French army during World War II, he completed his degree in psychiatry at the University of Lyon. In 1953 he was appointed to head the psychiatry department in an Algerian hospital. The following year, however, the war for Algeria's independence from French colonial rule broke out. The horrors and torture associated with the struggle served to amplify Fanon's own personal experiences as a black, colonized subject growing up in a white, colonial world. Fanon formally left his hospital position (a move that signaled a symbolic renunciation of his French upbringing) in 1956 to join the Algerian liberation movement, and in 1960 the Algerian Provisional Government appointed him ambassador to Ghana. In addition to his diplomatic post, Fanon served the revolution through publishing a number of political essays supportive of its cause.

Although a trained psychiatrist, Fanon rose to prominence as a result of his political activism. He was a leading intellectual in the struggle to end colonial rule in Africa and throughout the world. In his now classic works, *Black Skin, White Masks* (1952) and *The Wretched of the Earth* (1961), Fanon emphasized that colonization has both a physical and a psychological dimension. That colonial rule is established on repressive legal and social codes that relegate indigenous populations to an inferior status is plain to anyone who looks. Yet, colonization also exacts a psychological toll on the colonized as the oppressed comes to know himself through the eyes of the oppressor. Thus, the identity of the subjugated is defined through the discourse, ideas, and theories of the subjugator who alone is able to declare what it means to "be" the colonized *other*. As the colonized subject internalizes the "civilization" of the colonizer, he comes to know himself as half-human, inferior, and despicable—ideas sustained by the oppressor to legitimate the act of colonization.

In an attempt to distance himself from this psychologically destructive sense of being, the black subject adopts a "white mask." However, this only serves to further alienate himself from his own identity and consciousness. Moreover, wearing a white mask does not enable the colonized to escape the daily experience of racism, for while he may see himself as "white"—that is, equal—he is forever seen by the colonizer as both "less-than" and dangerous. The only sure path to exterminate this oppressive relationship is "absolute violence," a total revolution that destroys colonial rule and, with it, the categories or identities of black and white. This alone will achieve the necessary "collective catharsis" that will allow subjugated populations to purge themselves of the dehumanizing colonial culture that reduces them to the status of animals. While many find Fanon's insistence on violence to be unnecessary, if not abhorrent, he was nevertheless convinced that militant action was the only means to national and psychological liberation from colonial oppression.

While serving as a diplomat in Ghana, Fanon developed leukemia. He died less than a year later in a Bethesda, Maryland, hospital where he was being treated. He was thirty-six years old. Fanon's insights into the psychology of colonialism would inspire a generation of scholars, including Edward Said. Yet, Fanon's influence extends beyond the boundaries of postcolonial studies. For instance, Immanuel Wallerstein, whose world-systems analysis is discussed earlier, also counts Fanon as an important influence on his intellectual development and his political sympathies with those engaged in anticolonial struggles.

violence culminated in the atrocities committed during the early months of 1994. The ethnic genocide was the tragic consequence of a racially informed caste system installed by a colonial power whose own definitions of the relative worth of the two groups became the reality through which the groups came to define themselves.

That the Hutus would eventually come to govern Rwanda raises an important point. In Rwanda and elsewhere around the world, colonized and enslaved populations have always fought to resist or subvert the domination of their oppressors. Such resistance can take the form of "hybridization," in which the colonized combine or mix their native language and ways of understanding with those imposed by the colonizers, thus creating sites of potential challenge to the authority of their rulers. In expressing their ideas, interests, and desires in words and forms not sanctioned by the colonial powers, the colonized are able to create a sense of identity that, while not identical to their past, is neither wholly owned by the colonizers. Hybridization takes place not only through literary works written by authors subjected to colonial rule, but also through cultural practices such as religion, in which native beliefs and rituals are combined with those imposed by colonialist Christian missionaries.

Having explored some of the broad themes that inform postcolonial studies, we now turn to a discussion of the work of Edward Said. It was Said's 1978 publication, *Orientalism*, that marked the birth of the field. In this book, Said details how Western scientists, philosophers, novelists, poets, and politicians created the reality of the "Orient" through their writings. Of course, to understand Said's position we first need to know what he means by the Orient. At its most inclusive, the Orient refers to the non-West. It is the Other to the West (or Occident) that encompasses the Near East (more commonly called the Middle East) and the Far East (Asia). That these regions are known or understood in relation to Europe is obvious enough from their names, "Near" and "Far," which take for granted that Europe serves as the central point from which the identities of other regions are designated. And it is Said's most basic contention that the Orient, "the place of Europe's greatest and richest and oldest colonies, the source of its civilizations and languages," was in an important sense invented by the West through the process of **Orientalism** (Said 1978:1). Moreover, in inventing the Orient, Orientalism also helped Europe to define itself by creating a contrasting, inferior Other against which its own identity could be formed. In this light, Europe and the Orient (as well as the rest of the world) are less products of nature than they are products of social invention or what Said terms "imaginative geography."

Orientalism has three dimensions to it. First, it refers to all the scientific and academic disciplines whose purpose is to study Oriental cultures and customs. Thus, the Orientalist, whether he or she is a sociologist, an anthropologist, or a historian, is one whose expertise lies in teaching, researching, or writing about the Orient (Said 1978:2). (For example, one might think of a scholar who focuses on the history and culture of Southwest Asia, China, or Egypt.) Such academic interests in the Orient began in earnest during the early nineteenth century as Britain and France entered into a competition for colonial expansion. It was around this time that Orientalism was institutionalized as a field of study within universities across these two countries. In translating Oriental texts, explaining the history of the Orient, and deciphering the culture of the Orient, academics were (are) producing a "manifest" form of Orientalism that, in speaking about the region, interpreted its otherwise obscure, inscrutable meaning. Not coincidentally, many academic experts on the Orient served as advisors to colonial governments, dispensing knowledge on how to best "handle" their subject populations. Today, in the United States, specialists in "area studies" provide government officials with policy advice on international affairs through their association with a number of think tanks and research institutes such as the RAND Corporation, the American Enterprise Institute, the Brookings Institution, and the Heritage Foundation. For its part, the Middle East Institute, a Washington, D.C.–based policy and research center, states that its mission is to "strive to increase knowledge of the Middle East among our own citizens and to promote understanding between the peoples of the Middle East and America." Perhaps recognizing the ill effects that stem from a history of "orientalizing" the region and its people, the Institute's president notes, "Now more than ever, we must replace stereotyped and simplistic notions about the Middle East with detailed, objective understanding."[11]

A second dimension refers to Orientalism in a more general sense as a "style of thought," the "ideological suppositions, images, and fantasies about a region of the world called the Orient" (Said 2000:199). This dimension expresses a "latent" form of Orientalism, an "almost unconscious," and thus taken for granted, understanding of the Orient, its culture, and its people. The unchanging certainty that underlies latent Orientalism is derived from a racial/biological determinism that renders Orientals and their culture as singularly backward, degenerate, uncivilized, and morally corrupt. The Oriental man was thus understood to be inferior, weak, and effeminate, while the women were portrayed as exotic, sensual, and willing to be dominated by European males. This dimension of Orientalism incorporates not only academic scholarship but all accounts of the Orient that are rooted in a fundamental distinction between it and the West. Here we find novels and poems, the letters and diplomacy of colonial administrators, and all manners of philosophical and political theories that in their accounts and explanations of the Orient and its people construct the very subject they describe.

The third dimension speaks of Orientalism as a source of power for "dominating, restructuring, and having authority over the Orient" (Said 1978:3). As a mode of discourse that encompasses a specific vocabulary and set of images, Orientalism spoke the "truth" about the Orient and Orientals. This truth provided the justification for the West's imperialist ambitions. Through the knowledge and descriptions it produced on its subject, Orientalism ruled both a place and its people while simultaneously shaping the identity of the West as a rightly dominant, benevolent ruler. Said sums up the "achievements" of Orientalism as follows:

> [T]he British and the French saw the Orient as a geographical—and cultural, political, demographical, sociological, and historical—entity over whose destiny they believed themselves to have traditional entitlement. The Orient to them was no sudden discovery, no mere historical accident, but an area to the east of Europe whose principal worth was uniformly defined in terms of Europe—European science, scholarship, understanding, and administration—the credit for having made the Orient what it was now. And this had been the achievement . . . of modern Orientalism. (Said 1978:221)

In emphasizing the connection between knowledge and power as it relates to imaginative geography, Said's indebtedness to the work of Antonio Gramsci and Michel Foucault is particularly apparent.[12] As we noted earlier in this chapter, central to Gramsci's perspective is the concept of hegemony. Recall that hegemony refers to a mode of domination in which the rulers secure their dominance not through force but through the "spontaneous consent" of the ruled. This consent is dependent on the

---

[11]http://www.mideasti.org/

[12]The range of Said's intellectual influences is vast. In addition to drawing from Gramsci and Foucault, his work is inspired by the Hungarian Marxist Georg Lukács (1885–1971), the German philosopher Friedrich Nietzsche (1844–1900), the Marxian literary critic Raymond Williams (1921–1988), the French philosopher Maurice Merleau-Ponty (1908–1961), the novelist Joseph Conrad (1857–1924), the Italian historian and philosopher Giambattista Vico (1668–1744), Theodor Adorno (see Chapter 3), and Frantz Fanon (see this chapter).

subordinated classes adopting as their own the values, beliefs, and attitudes that serve the interests of the ruling class. As a result, the ideas propagated by the ruling class take on the appearance of universality and common sense. For Said, Orientalism is an instance of hegemony in which scholars, missionaries, colonial administrators, and literary authors offer a picture of the Orient and its people that prescribes for them an inferior position relative to the West. Europe's superiority over the "backward" Orient becomes a taken-for-granted truth that then justifies the colonial exploitation of the Other.

Said's discussion of Orientalism also draws on Foucault's notion of power/knowledge (see Chapter 9). For Foucault, power/knowledge are two sides of the same coin: power is exercised through knowledge, while knowledge is an exercise of power. Knowledge is constructed and communicated through discourse—words that declare a state of being while simultaneously declaring how things are not. For example, when a person says or writes that Palestinians are terrorists, he is constructing an identity that at the same time excludes other possible identities. Yet, Palestinians are no more any one "thing" than Israelis, Americans, Germans, Mexicans, or Koreans. Nevertheless, such a claim often is offered as "knowledge," and to the extent that it gains credibility, it also becomes infused with the power to produce a reality that does not exist outside of the discourse that constitutes it. In this way, Orientalism is a "world of power and representations, a world that came into being as a series of decisions made by writers,

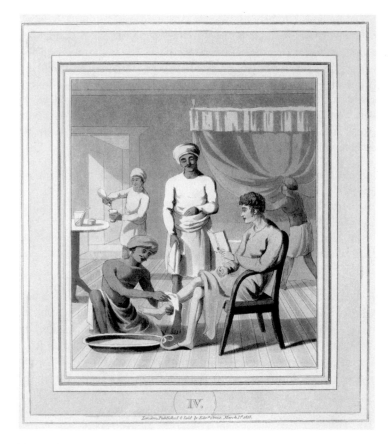

Photo 10.7   Visual Orientalism: The inferiority of Orientals was depicted in pictures as well as in words. Above is an 1813 print entitled "A Gentleman Dressing, Attended by His Head Bearer and Other Servants." Drawn by Charles D'Oyly, it was published in *The European in India*. Such illustrations were commonplace throughout the nineteenth century.

SOURCE: © Stapleton Collection/CORBIS; used with permission.

politicians, philosophers to suggest or adumbrate one reality and at the same time efface others" (Said 2000:563). This approach to knowledge calls attention to the political dimensions of Orientalism as an academic pursuit (and purportedly objective, impartial academic scholarship more generally), for the production of knowledge invariably involves "interests" on the part of the writer that reflect his or her life circumstances. It is impossible to entirely escape one's own beliefs, attitudes, or social position when researching and writing on a given subject. And in the case of Orientalism, this means, at its most basic level, that the scholar "comes up against the Orient as a European or American first, as an individual second. . . [This] means being aware, however dimly, that one belongs to a power with definite interests in the Orient, and more important, that one belongs to a part of the earth with a definite history of involvement in the Orient . . ." (Said 1978:11). In this way the Orient *exists* because of, and for, the West, not because of its own internal reality.

We end this section with a brief discussion of contemporary forms of Orientalism, particularly as they are expressed through American views of Arabs and Islam. The Middle East, home to much of the world's Arab population, has occupied a central position in regard to both government policy and popular culture since the 1950s. Much of the American involvement in, and understanding of, this region has been framed by the conflict between the Arabs and Israelis on which the government, corporate media, and academic establishment have adopted a pro-Israeli position—a position that casts Arabs as "evil, totalitarian, and terroristic." The attention focused on the Middle East and its people has only intensified in the aftermath of the September 11 terrorist attacks. Moreover, this intensity is itself in large measure a product of the immediacy with which information and images are disseminated through the electronic media. Well before the attacks on America, however, the media portrayed Arabs in simplistic, stereotypical terms. In television, films, and cartoons, the Arab was a nomadic camel-jockey; an over-sexed savage; a treacherous, if clever, marauder; or an oil sheik, who despite his obvious inferiority is able to hold the West hostage by controlling the world's energy supply. As for the latter, because Arabs are believed to lack the intelligence and moral qualifications required for possessing such a valuable resource, it is only fitting and right that their oil fields be seized—if necessary, through American military force. Today, this view has taken on renewed significance given the critics of the current Bush administration who claim that the principal motive for invading Iraq was to control that nation's oil supply. Likewise, Said's comments regarding the depiction of Arabs in the news ring as true today as they did twenty-five years ago, when he wrote:

> In newsreels or newsphotos, the Arab is always shown in large numbers. No individuality, no personal characteristics or experiences. Most of the pictures represent mass rage and misery, or irrational (hence hopelessly eccentric) gestures. Lurking behind all of these images is the menace of *jihad*. Consequence: a fear that the Muslims (or Arabs) will take over the world. (Said 1978:287)

SAID'S THEORETICAL ORIENTATION

Said's work is primarily devoted to exploring a single concept, Orientalism; yet, this is by no means a simple theoretical concept. On the contrary, "Orientalism" is a multi-dimensional concept that speaks to each of the quadrants in our action/framework, as shown in Figure 10.3. Because of its theoretical multidimensionality and flexibility, this concept can be used to shed light on a range of real-life issues. Consider first Orientalism's individualist/rational dimension. This comprises the work of specific scholars and colonial administrators who construct the meaning of the Orient in specific

Figure 10.3 Basic Theoretical Dimensions of Said's Concept of Orientalism

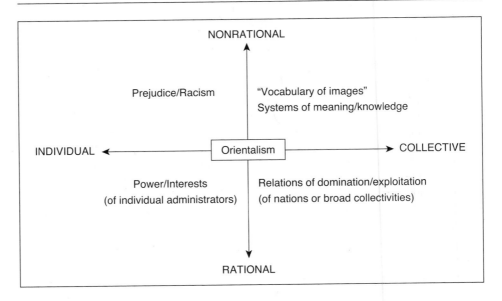

ways that serve their interests. This is the manifest form of Orientalism that calls our attention to the interconnection between knowledge and power and, in this case, how knowledge is used by individuals in their attempt to subjugate populations. For the Western Orientalist, the Orient serves "as a kind of culture and intellectual proletariat useful for [his] grander interpretative activity, necessary for his performance as a superior judge . . ." (Said 1978:208).

The collectivist/rational aspects of Orientalism become apparent when we move from a focus on individuals to one on groups. Thus, we find Said continually speaking of broad collectivities—East and West, or Orient and Occident—as well as nations. On this level, the interactions that occupy Said's analysis are those taking place between, for instance, Britain and India or France and Egypt. The emphasis here is on the relations of domination and exploitation that exist between nations and regions of the globe, relations that are strategically sustained by those in power in order to secure their continued geopolitical and economic advantages.

Orientalism operates on a nonrational level as well. This is suggested by Said's notion of latent Orientalism, discussed above. As a concept that captures the individual/ nonrational dimension, Orientalism refers to an individual's racist attitudes and practices that construct an inferior Other. Thus, individuals use or "mobilize" the dogma of Orientalism in an "almost unconscious" way as they go about the business of describing the world. What an Orientalist (or any person, for that matter) writes and says can betray an underlying racist scheme that positions the Oriental as inherently, and thus undeniably, uncivilized.

Turning to the collectivist/nonrational dimension, Orientalism is that which is mobilized. It is a set of background, taken-for-granted assumptions projected onto the Orient and its people—in short, a hegemonic dogma. Such assumptions are never tested against the reality of the empirical world; they simply exist as an unconscious lens through which the Orient is seen and understood. Orientalism provides a vocabulary of images that "represent or stand for a very large entity, otherwise impossibly diffuse, . . . [that] comes to exert a three-way force, on the Orient, on the Orientalist, and on the Western 'consumer' of Orientalism" (Said 1978:66, 67). In this way, Orientalism possesses structural or collectivist properties that give it a life of its own, separate from those individuals who deploy it.

Reading

Introduction to *Orientalism*

In this chapter, "Knowing the Oriental," excerpted from Said's *Orientalism*, we are introduced to two distinguished English politicians and diplomats, Arthur James Balfour and Evelyn Baring, Lord Cromer. Beginning with a speech Balfour delivered to England's House of Commons in 1910 and then moving to an essay written by Cromer in 1908, Said examines the language employed by these men as they go about the business of justifying colonial rule over Egypt. In doing so, Said reveals how knowledge regarding Egypt, and the Orient more broadly, constructs its inhabitants as an Other whose inferiority requires that they be ruled by a superior, although "benevolent," nation. Thus, Balfour claims that "it is a good thing" for Egypt to be ruled by Britain because the Egyptians "have got under it far better government than in the whole history of the world they ever had before, and which not only is a benefit to them, but is undoubtedly a benefit to the whole of civilised West" (quoted in Said 1978:33). Similarly, with decades of experience serving as a colonial administrator in India and Egypt, Cromer is compelled to note the "fact" that "the Oriental generally acts, speaks, and thinks in a manner exactly opposite to the European" (quoted in Said 1978:39). Chief among their faults, according to Cromer, is that they are "singularly deficient in the logical faculty. They are often incapable of drawing the most obvious conclusions from any simple premises of which they admit the truth" (ibid.:38). Because the Orientals possess "slipshod" reasoning ability, England must decide what "is best for the subject race."

In the concluding portion of this selection, Said turns his attention to the United States to discuss more contemporary instances of Orientalism, particularly as they were expressed by then Secretary of State Henry Kissinger. And although Said's analysis here pertains to the early 1970s, we suggest that, regardless of one's political persuasion, it should provide the reader with reason for pause to consider the parallels between the periods he discusses and the events currently taking place in Iraq, Afghanistan, and throughout the Arab Middle East.

❖

Orientalism (1978)

Edward Said

KNOWING THE ORIENTAL

On June 13, 1910, Arthur James Balfour lectured the House of Commons on "the problems with which we have to deal in Egypt." These, he said, "belong to a wholly different category" than those "affecting the Isle of Wight or the West Riding of Yorkshire." He spoke with the authority of a long-time member of Parliament, former private secretary to Lord Salisbury, former chief secretary for Ireland, former secretary for Scotland, former prime minister, veteran of numerous overseas crises, achievements, and changes. During his involvement in imperial affairs Balfour served a monarch who in 1876 had been declared Empress of India; he had been especially well placed in positions of uncommon influence to follow the Afghan and Zulu wars, the British occupation of Egypt in 1882, the death of General Gordon in the Sudan, the Fashoda Incident, the battle of Omdurman, the Boer War, the Russo-Japanese War. In addition his remarkable social eminence, the breadth of his learning and wit—he could write on such varied subjects as Bergson, Handel, theism, and golf—his education at Eton and Trinity College, Cambridge, and his apparent command over imperial affairs all gave considerable authority to what he told the Commons in June 1910. But there was still more to Balfour's speech, or at least to his need for giving it so didactically and moralistically. Some members were questioning the necessity for "England in Egypt," the subject of Alfred Milner's enthusiastic book of 1892, but here designating a once-profitable occupation that had become a source of trouble now that Egyptian nationalism was on the rise and the continuing British presence in Egypt no longer so easy to defend. Balfour, then, to inform and explain.

Recalling the challenge of J. M. Robertson, the member of Tyneside, Balfour himself put Robertson's question again: "What right have you to take up these airs of superiority with regard to people whom you choose to call Oriental?" The choice of "Oriental" was canonical; it had been employed by Chaucer and Mandeville, by Shakespeare, Dryden, Pope, and Byron. It designated Asia or the East, geographically, morally, culturally. One could speak in Europe of an Oriental personality, an Oriental atmosphere, an Oriental tale, Oriental despotism, or an Oriental mode of production, and be understood. Marx had used the word, and now Balfour was using it; his choice was understandable and called for no comment whatever.

I take up no attitude of superiority. But I ask [Robertson and anyone else] . . . who has even the most superficial knowledge of history, if they will look in the face the facts with which a British statesman has to deal when he is put in a position

of supremacy over great races like the inhabitants of Egypt and countries in the East. We know the civilization of Egypt better than we know the civilization of any other country. We know it further back; we know it more intimately; we know more about it. It goes far beyond the petty span of the history of our race, which is lost in the prehistoric period at a time when the Egyptian civilisation had already passed its prime. Look at all the Oriental countries. Do not talk about superiority or inferiority.

Two great themes dominate his remarks here and in what will follow: knowledge and power, the Baconian themes. As Balfour justifies the necessity for British occupation of Egypt, supremacy in his mind is associated with "our" knowledge of Egypt and not principally with military or economic power. Knowledge to Balfour means surveying a civilization from its origins to its prime to its decline—and of course, it means *being able to do that*. Knowledge means rising above immediacy, beyond self, into the foreign and distant. The object of such knowledge is inherently vulnerable to scrutiny; this object is a "fact" which, if it develops, changes, or otherwise transforms itself in the way that civilizations frequently do, nevertheless is fundamentally, even ontologically stable. To have such knowledge of such a thing is to dominate it, to have authority over it. And authority here means for "us" to deny autonomy to "it"—the Oriental country—since we know it and it exists, in a sense, *as* we know it. British knowledge of Egypt *is* Egypt for Balfour, and the burdens of knowledge make such questions as inferiority and superiority seem petty ones. Balfour nowhere denies British superiority and Egyptian inferiority; he takes them for granted as he describes the consequences of knowledge.

First of all, look at the facts of the case. Western nations as soon as they emerge into history show the beginnings of those capacities for self-government . . . having merits of their own. . . . You may look through the whole history of the Orientals in what is called, broadly speaking, the East, and you never find traces of self-government. All their great centuries—and they have been very great— have been passed under despotisms, under absolute government. All their great contributions to civilisation—and they have been great—have been made under that form of government. Conqueror has succeeded conqueror; one domination has followed another; but never in all the revolutions of fate and fortune have you seen one of those nations of its own motions establish what we, from a Western point of view, call self-government. That is the fact. It is not a question of superiority and inferiority. I suppose a true Eastern sage would say that the working government which we have taken upon ourselves in Egypt and elsewhere is not a work worthy of a philosopher—that it is the dirty work, the inferior work, of carrying on the necessary labour.

Since these facts are facts, Balfour must then go on to the next part of his argument.

Is it a good thing for these great nations—I admit their greatness—that this absolute government should be exercised by us? I think it is a good thing. I think that experience shows that they have got under it far better government than in the whole history of the world they ever had before, and which not only is a benefit to them, but is undoubtedly a benefit to the whole of the civilised West. . . . We are in Egypt not merely for the sake of the Egyptians, though we are there for their sake; we are there also for the sake of Europe at large.

Balfour produces no evidence that Egyptians and "the races with whom we deal" appreciate or even understand the good that is being done them by colonial occupation. It does not occur to Balfour, however, to let the Egyptian speak for himself, since presumably any Egyptian who would speak out is more likely to be "the agitator [who] wishes to raise difficulties" than the good native who overlooks the "difficulties" of foreign domination. And so, having settled the ethical problems, Balfour turns at last to the practical ones. "If it is our business to govern, with or without gratitude, with or without the real and genuine memory of all the loss of which we have relieved the population [Balfour by no means implies as part of that loss, the loss or at least the indefinite postponement of Egyptian independence] and no vivid imagination of all

the benefits which we have given to them; if that is our duty, how is it to be performed?" England exports "our very best to these countries." These selfless administrators do their work "amidst tens of thousands of persons belonging to a different creed, a different race, a different discipline, different conditions of life." What makes their work of governing possible is their sense of being supported at home by a government that endorses what they do. Yet

directly the native populations have that instinctive feeling that those with whom they have got to deal have not behind them the might, the authority, the sympathy, the full and ungrudging support of the country which sent them there, those populations lose all that sense of order which is the very basis of their civilisation, just as our officers lose all that sense of power and authority, which is the very basis of everything they can do for the benefit of those among whom they have been sent.

Balfour's logic here is interesting, not least for being completely consistent with the premises of his entire speech. England knows Egypt; Egypt is what England knows; England knows that Egypt cannot have self-government; England confirms that by occupying Egypt; for the Egyptians, Egypt is what England has occupied and now governs; foreign occupation therefore becomes "the very basis" of contemporary Egyptian civilization; Egypt requires, indeed insists upon, British occupation. But if the special intimacy between governor and governed in Egypt is disturbed by Parliament's doubts at home, then "the authority of what . . . is the dominant race—and as I think ought to remain the dominant race—has been undermined." Not only does English prestige suffer; "it is vain for a handful of British officials—endow them how you like, give them all the qualities of character and genius you can imagine—it is impossible for them to carry out the great task which in Egypt, not we only, but the civilised world have imposed upon them."[i]

As a rhetorical performance Balfour's speech is significant for the way in which he plays the

---

[i]This and the preceding quotations from Arthur James Balfour's speech to the House of Commons are from Great Britain, *Parliamentary Debates* (Commons), 5th ser., 17 (1910): 1140–46.

part of, and represents, a variety of characters. There are of course "the English," for whom the pronoun "we" is used with the full weight of a distinguished, powerful man who feels himself to be representative of all that is best in his nation's history. Balfour can also speak for the civilized world, the West, and the relatively small corps of colonial officials in Egypt. If he does not speak directly for the Orientals, it is because they after all speak another language; yet he knows how they feel since he knows their history, their reliance upon such as he, and their expectations. Still, he does speak for them in the sense that what they might have to say, were they to be asked and might they be able to answer, would somewhat uselessly confirm what is already evident: that they are a subject race, dominated by a race that knows them and what is good for them better than they could possibly know themselves. Their great moments were in the past; they are useful in the modern world only because the powerful and up-to-date empires have effectively brought them out of the wretchedness of their decline and turned them into rehabilitated residents of productive colonies.

Egypt in particular was an excellent case in point, and Balfour was perfectly aware of how much right he had to speak as a member of his country's parliament on behalf of England, the West, Western civilization, about modern Egypt. For Egypt was not just another colony: it was the vindication of Western imperialism; it was, until its annexation by England, an almost academic example of Oriental backwardness; it was to become the triumph of English knowledge and power. Between 1882, the year in which England occupied Egypt and put an end to the nationalist rebellion of Colonel Arabi, and 1907, England's representative in Egypt, Egypt's master, was Evelyn Baring (also known as "Overbaring"), Lord Cromer. On July 30, 1907, it was Balfour in the Commons who had supported the project to give Cromer a retirement prize of fifty thousand pounds as a reward for what he had done in Egypt. Cromer *made* Egypt, said Balfour:

Everything he has touched he has succeeded in. . . . Lord Cromer's services during the past quarter of a century have raised Egypt from the lowest pitch of social and economic degradation until it now stands among Oriental nations, I believe, absolutely alone in its prosperity, financial and moral.[ii]

How Egypt's moral prosperity was measured, Balfour did not venture to say. British exports to Egypt equaled those to the whole of Africa; that certainly indicated a sort of financial prosperity, for Egypt and England (somewhat unevenly) together. But what really mattered was the unbroken, all-embracing Western tutelage of an Oriental country, from the scholars, missionaries, businessmen, soldiers, and teachers who prepared and then implemented the occupation to the high functionaries like Cromer and Balfour who saw themselves as providing for, directing, and sometimes even forcing Egypt's rise from Oriental neglect to its present lonely eminence.

If British success in Egypt was as exceptional as Balfour said, it was by no means an inexplicable or irrational success. Egyptian affairs had been controlled according to a general theory expressed both by Balfour in his notions about Oriental civilization and by Cromer in his management of everyday business in Egypt. The most important thing about the theory during the first decade of the twentieth century was that it worked, and worked staggeringly well. The argument, when reduced to its simplest form, was clear, it was precise, it was easy to grasp. There are Westerners, and there are Orientals. The former dominate; the latter must be dominated, which usually means having their land occupied, their internal affairs rigidly controlled, their blood and treasure put at the disposal of one or another Western power. That Balfour and Cromer, as we shall soon see, could strip humanity down to such ruthless cultural and racial essences was not at all an indication of their particular viciousness. Rather it was an indication of how streamlined a general doctrine had become by the time they put it to use—how streamlined and effective.

[ii]Denis Judd, *Balfour and the British Empire: A Study in Imperial Evolution, 1874–1932* (London: MacMillan & Co., 1968), p. 286.

Unlike Balfour, whose theses on Orientals pretended to objective universality, Cromer spoke about Orientals specifically as what he had ruled or had to deal with, first in India, then for the twenty-five years in Egypt during which he emerged as the paramount consul-general in England's empire. Balfour's "Orientals" are Cromer's "subject races," which he made the topic of a long essay published in the *Edinburgh Review* in January 1908. Once again, knowledge of subject races or Orientals is what makes their management easy and profitable; knowledge gives power, more power requires more knowledge, and so on in an increasingly profitable dialectic of information and control. Cromer's notion is that England's empire will not dissolve if such things as militarism and commercial egotism at home and "free institutions" in the colony (as opposed to British government "according to the Code of Christian morality") are kept in check. For if, according to Cromer, logic is something "the existence of which the Oriental is disposed altogether to ignore," the proper method of ruling is not to impose ultrascientific measures upon him or to force him bodily to accept logic. It is rather to understand his limitations and "endeavor to find, in the contentment of the subject race, a more worthy and, it may be hoped, a stronger bond of union between the rulers and the ruled." Lurking everywhere behind the pacification of the subject race is imperial might, more effective for its refined understanding and infrequent use than for its soldiers, brutal tax gatherers, and incontinent force. In a word, the Empire must be wise; it must temper its cupidity with selflessness, and its impatience with flexible discipline.

To be more explicit, what is meant when it is said that the commercial spirit should be under some control is this—that in dealing with Indians or Egyptians, or Shilluks, or Zulus, the first question is to consider what these people, who are all, nationally speaking, more or less *in statu pupillari*, themselves think is best in their own interests, although this is a point which deserves serious consideration. But it is essential that each special issue should be decided mainly with reference to what, by the light of Western knowledge and experience tempered by local considerations, we conscientiously think is best for the subject race, without reference to any real or supposed advantage which may accrue to England as a nation, or—as is more frequently the case—to the special interests represented by some one or more influential classes of Englishmen. If the British nation as a whole persistently bears this principle in mind, and insists sternly on its application, though we can never create a patriotism akin to that based on affinity of race or community of language, we may perhaps foster some sort of cosmopolitan allegiance grounded on the respect always accorded to superior talents and unselfish conduct, and on the gratitude derived both from favours conferred and from those to come. There may then at all events be some hope that the Egyptian will hesitate before he throws in his lot with any future Arabi. . . . Even the Central African savage may eventually learn to chant a hymn in honour of Astraea Redux, as represented by the British official who denies him gin but gives him justice. More than this, commerce will gain.[iii]

How much "serious consideration" the ruler ought to give proposals from the subject race was illustrated in Cromer's total opposition to Egyptian nationalism. Free native institutions, the absence of foreign occupation, a self-sustaining national sovereignty: these unsurprising demands were consistently rejected by Cromer, who asserted unambiguously that "the real future of Egypt . . . lies not in the direction of a narrow nationalism, which will only embrace native Egyptians . . . but rather in that of an enlarged cosmopolitanism."[iv] Subject races did not have it in them to know what was good for them. Most of them were Orientals, of whose characteristics Cromer was very knowledgeable since he had had experience with them both in India and Egypt. One of the convenient things about Orientals for Cromer was that managing them, although circumstances

[iii]Evelyn Baring, Lord Cromer, *Political and Literary Essays, 1908–1913* (1913; reprint ed., Freeport, N.Y.: Books for Libraries Press, 1969), pp. 40, 53, 12–14.

[iv]Ibid., p. 171.

might differ slightly here and there, was almost everywhere nearly the same.[v] This was, of course, because Orientals were almost everywhere nearly the same.

Now at last we approach the long-developing core of essential knowledge, knowledge both academic and practical, which Cromer and Balfour inherited from a century of modern Western Orientalism: knowledge about and knowledge of Orientals, their race, character, culture, history, traditions, society, and possibilities. This knowledge was effective: Cromer believed he had put it to use in governing Egypt. Moreover, it was tested and unchanging knowledge, since "Orientals" for all practical purposes were a Platonic essence, which any Orientalist (or ruler of Orientals) might examine, understand, and expose. Thus in the thirty-fourth chapter of his two-volume work *Modern Egypt*, the magisterial record of his experience and achievement, Cromer puts down a sort of personal canon of Oriental wisdom:

Sir Alfred Lyall once said to me: "Accuracy is abhorrent to the Oriental mind. Every Anglo-Indian should always remember that maxim." Want of accuracy, which easily degenerates into untruthfulness, is in fact the main characteristic of the Oriental mind.

The European is a close reasoner; his statements of fact are devoid of any ambiguity; he is a natural logician, albeit he may not have studied logic; he is by nature sceptical and requires proof before he can accept the truth of any proposition; his trained intelligence works like a piece of mechanism. The mind of the Oriental, on the other hand, like his picturesque streets, is eminently wanting in symmetry. His reasoning is of the most slipshod description. Although the ancient Arabs acquired in a somewhat higher degree the science of dialectics, their descendants are singularly deficient in the logical faculty. They are often incapable of drawing the most obvious conclusions from any simple premises of which they

may admit the truth. Endeavor to elicit a plain statement of facts from any ordinary Egyptian. His explanation will generally be lengthy, and wanting in lucidity. He will probably contradict himself half-a-dozen times before he has finished his story. He will often break down under the mildest process of cross-examination.

Orientals or Arabs are thereafter shown to be gullible, "devoid of energy and initiative," much given to "fulsome flattery," intrigue, cunning, and unkindness to animals; Orientals cannot walk on either a road or a pavement (their disordered minds fail to understand what the clever European grasps immediately, that roads and pavements are made for walking); Orientals are inveterate liars, they are "lethargic and suspicious," and in everything oppose the clarity, directness, and nobility of the Anglo-Saxon race.[vi]

Cromer makes no effort to conceal that Orientals for him were always and only the human material he governed in British colonies. "As I am only a diplomatist and an administrator, whose proper study is also man, but from the point of view of governing him," Cromer says, ". . . I content myself with noting the fact that somehow or other the Oriental generally acts, speaks, and thinks in a manner exactly opposite to the European."[vii] Cromer's descriptions are of course based partly on direct observation, yet here and there he refers to orthodox Orientalist authorities (in particular Ernest Renan and Constantin de Volney) to support his views. To these authorities he also defers when it comes to explaining why Orientals are the way they are. He has no doubt that *any* knowledge of the Oriental will confirm his views, which, to judge from his description of the Egyptian breaking under cross-examination, find the Oriental to be guilty. The crime was that the Oriental was an Oriental, and it is an accurate sign of how commonly acceptable such a tautology was that it could be written without even an appeal to

[v]Roger Owen, "The Influence of Lord Cromer's Indian Experience on British Policy in Egypt 1883–1907," in *Middle Eastern Affairs, Number Four: St. Antony's Papers Number 17*, ed. Albert Hourani (London: Oxford University Press, 1965), pp. 109–39.

[vi]Evelyn Baring, Lord Cromer, *Modern Egypt* (New York: MacMillan Co., 1908), 2: 146–67.

[vii]Cromer, *Modern Egypt*, 2: 164.

European logic or symmetry of mind. Thus any deviation from what were considered the norms of Oriental behavior was believed to be unnatural; Cromer's last annual report from Egypt consequently proclaimed Egyptian nationalism to be an "entirely novel idea" and "a plant of exotic rather than of indigenous growth."[viii]

We would be wrong, I think, to underestimate the reservoir of accredited knowledge, the codes of Orientalist orthodoxy, to which Cromer and Balfour refer everywhere in their writing and in their public policy. To say simply that Orientalism was rationalization of colonial rule is to ignore the extent to which colonial rule was justified in advance by Orientalism, rather than after the fact. Men have always divided the world up into regions having either real or imagined distinction from each other. The absolute demarcation between East and West, which Balfour and Cromer accept with such complacency, had been years, even centuries, in the making. There were of course innumerable voyages of discovery; there were contacts through trade and war. But more than this, since the middle of the eighteenth century there had been two principal elements in the relation between East and West. One was a growing systematic knowledge in Europe about the Orient, knowledge reinforced by the colonial encounter as well as by the widespread interest in the alien and unusual, exploited by the developing sciences of ethnology, comparative anatomy, philology, and history; furthermore, to this systematic knowledge was added a sizable body of literature produced by novelists, poets, translators, and gifted travelers. The other feature of Oriental-European relations was that Europe was always in a position of strength, not to say domination. There is no way of putting this euphemistically. True, the relationship of strong to weak could be disguised or mitigated, as when Balfour acknowledged the "greatness" of Oriental civilizations. But the essential relationship, on political, cultural, and even religious grounds, was seen—in the West, which is what concerns us here—to be one between a strong and a weak partner.

Many terms were used to express the relation: Balfour and Cromer, typically, used several. The Oriental is irrational, depraved (fallen), childlike, "different"; thus the European is rational, virtuous, mature, "normal." But the way of enlivening the relationship was everywhere to stress the fact that the Oriental lived in a different but thoroughly organized world of his own, a world with its own national, cultural, and epistemological boundaries and principles of internal coherence. Yet what gave the Oriental's world its intelligibility and identity was not the result of his own efforts but rather the whole complex series of knowledgeable manipulations by which the Orient was identified by the West. Thus the two features of cultural relationship I have been discussing come together. Knowledge of the Orient, because generated out of strength, in a sense *creates* the Orient, the Oriental, and his world. In Cromer's and Balfour's language the Oriental is depicted as something one judges (as in a court of law), something one studies and depicts (as in a curriculum), something one disciplines (as in a school or prison), something one illustrates (as in a zoological manual). The point is that in each of these cases the Oriental is *contained* and *represented* by dominating frameworks. Where do these come from?

Cultural strength is not something we can discuss very easily—and one of the purposes of the present work is illustrate, analyze, and reflect upon Orientalism as an exercise of cultural strength. In other words, it is better not to risk generalizations about so vague and yet so important a notion as cultural strength until a good deal of material has been analyzed first. But at the outset one can say that so far as the West was concerned during the nineteenth and twentieth centuries, an assumption had been made that the Orient and everything in it was, if not patently inferior to, then in need of corrective study by the West. The Orient was viewed as if framed by the classroom, the criminal court, the prison, the illustrated manual. Orientalism, then, is knowledge of the Orient that places things Oriental in class, court, prison, or manual for scrutiny, study, judgment, discipline, or governing.

During the early years of the twentieth century, men like Balfour and Cromer could say what they said, in the way they did, because a still earlier tradition of Orientalism than the

---

[viii]Cited in John Marlowe, *Cromer in Egypt* (London: Elek Books, 1970), p. 271.

nineteenth-century one provided them with a vocabulary, imagery, rhetoric, and figures with which to say it. Yet Orientalism reinforced, and was reinforced by, the certain knowledge that Europe or the West literally commanded the vastly greater part of the earth's surface. The period of immense advance in the institutions and content of Orientalism coincides exactly with the period of unparalleled European expansion; from 1815 to 1914 European direct colonial dominion expanded from about 35 percent of the earth's surface to about 85 percent of it.[ix] Every continent was affected, none more so than Africa and Asia. The two greatest empires were the British and the French; allies and partners in some things, in others they were hostile rivals. In the Orient, from the eastern shores of the Mediterranean to Indochina and Malaya, their colonial possessions and imperial spheres of influence were adjacent, frequently overlapped, often were fought over. But it was in the Near Orient, the lands of the Arab Near East, where Islam was supposed to define cultural and racial characteristics, that the British and the French encountered each other and "the Orient" with the greatest intensity, familiarity, and complexity. For much of the nineteenth century, as Lord Salisbury put it in 1881, their common view of the Orient was intricately problematic: "When you have got a . . . faithful ally who is bent on meddling in a country in which you are deeply interested—you have three courses open to you. You may renounce—or monopolize—or share. Renouncing would have been to place the French across our road to India. Monopolizing would have been very near the risk of war. So we resolved to share."[x]

And share they did, in ways that we shall investigate presently. What they shared, however, was not only land or profit or rule; it was the kind of intellectual power I have been calling Orientalism. In a sense Orientalism was a library or archive of information commonly and, in some of its aspects, unanimously held. What

bound the archive together was a family of ideas and a unifying set of values proven in various ways to be effective. These ideas explained the behavior of Orientals; they supplied Orientals with a mentality, a genealogy, an atmosphere; most important, they allowed Europeans to deal with and even to see Orientals as a phenomenon possessing regular characteristics. But like any set of durable ideas, Orientalist notions influenced the people who were called Orientals as well as those called Occidental, European, or Western; in short, Orientalism is better grasped as a set of constraints upon and limitations of thought than it is simply as a positive doctrine. If the essence of Orientalism is the ineradicable distinction between Western superiority and Oriental inferiority, then we must be prepared to note how in its development and subsequent history Orientalism deepened and even hardened the distinction. When it became common practice during the nineteenth century for Britain to retire its administrators from India and elsewhere once they had reached the age of fifty-five, then a further refinement in Orientalism had been achieved; no Oriental was ever allowed to see a Westerner as he aged and degenerated, just as no Westerner needed ever to see himself, mirrored in the eyes of the subject race, as anything but a vigorous, rational, ever-alert young Raj.

Orientalist ideas took a number of different forms during the nineteenth and twentieth centuries. First of all, in Europe there was a vast literature about the Orient inherited from the European past. What is distinctive about the late eighteenth and early nineteenth centuries, which is where this study assumes modern Orientalism to have begun, is that an Oriental renaissance took place, as Edgar Quinet phrased it.[xi] Suddenly it seemed to a wide variety of thinkers, politicians, and artists that a new awareness of the Orient, which extended from China to the Mediterranean, had arisen. This awareness was partly the result of newly discovered and

---

[ix]Harry Magdoff, "Colonialism (1763–c.1970)," *Encyclopedia Britannica,* 15th ed. (1974), pp. 893–4.

[x]Quoted in Afaf Lutfi al-Sayyid, *Egypt and Cromer: A Study in Anglo-Egyptian Relations* (New York: Frederick A. Praeger, 1969), p. 3.

[xi]Edgar Quinet, *Le Génie des religions,* in *Oeuvres complètes* (Paris: Paguerre, 1857), pp. 55–74.

translated Oriental texts in languages like Sanskrit, Zend, and Arabic; it was also the result of a newly perceived relationship between the Orient and the West. For my purposes here, the keynote of the relationship was set for the Near East and Europe by the Napoleonic invasion of Egypt in 1798, an invasion which was in many ways the very model of a truly scientific appropriation of one culture by another, apparently stronger one. For with Napoleon's occupation of Egypt processes were set in motion between East and West that still dominate our contemporary cultural and political perspectives. And the Napoleonic expedition, with its great collective monument of erudition, the *Description de l'Égypte*, provided a scene or setting for Orientalism, since Egypt and subsequently the other Islamic lands were viewed as the live province, the laboratory, the theater of effective Western knowledge about the Orient. I shall return to the Napoleonic adventure a little later.

With such experiences as Napoleon's the Orient as a body of knowledge in the West was modernized, and this is a second form in which nineteenth- and twentieth-century Orientalism existed. From the outset of the period I shall be examining there was everywhere amongst Orientalists the ambition to formulate their discoveries, experiences, and insights suitably in modern terms, to put ideas about the Orient in very close touch with modern realities. Renan's linguistic investigations of Semitic in 1848, for example, were couched in a style that drew heavily for its authority upon contemporary comparative grammar, comparative anatomy, and racial theory; these lent his Orientalism prestige and—the other side of the coin—made Orientalism vulnerable, as it has been ever since, to modish as well as seriously influential currents of thought in the West. Orientalism has been subjected to imperialism, positivism, utopianism, historicism, Darwinism, racism, Freudianism, Marxism, Spenglerism. But Orientalism, like many of the natural and social sciences, has had "paradigms" of research, its own learned societies, its own Establishment. During the nineteenth century the field increased enormously in prestige, as did also the reputation and influence of such institutions as the Société asiatique, the Royal Asiatic Society, the Deutsche Morgenländische Gesellschaft,

and the American Oriental Society. With the growth of these societies went also an increase, all across Europe, in the number of professorships in Oriental studies; consequently there was an expansion in the available means for disseminating Orientalism. Orientalist periodicals, beginning with the *Fundgraben des Orients* (1809), multiplied the quantity of knowledge as well as the number of specialties.

Yet little of this activity and very few of these institutions existed and flourished freely, for in a third form in which it existed, Orientalism imposed limits upon thought about the Orient. Even the most imaginative writers of an age, men like Flaubert, Nerval, or Scott, were constrained in what they could either experience of or say about the Orient. For Orientalism was ultimately a political vision of reality whose structure promoted the difference between the familiar (Europe, the West, "us") and the strange (the Orient, the East, "them"). This vision in a sense created and then served the two worlds thus conceived. Orientals lived in their world, "we" lived in ours. The vision and material reality propped each other up, kept each other going. A certain freedom of intercourse was always the Westerner's privilege; because his was the stronger culture, he could penetrate, he could wrestle with, he could give shape and meaning to the great Asiatic mystery, as Disraeli once called it. Yet what has, I think, been previously overlooked is the constricted vocabulary of such a privilege, and the comparative limitations of such a vision. My argument takes it that the Orientalist reality is both antihuman and persistent. Its scope, as much as its institutions and all-pervasive influence, lasts up to the present.

But how did and does Orientalism work? How can one describe it all together as a historical phenomenon, a way of thought, a contemporary problem, and a material reality? Consider Cromer again, an accomplished technician of empire but also a beneficiary of Orientalism. He can furnish us with a rudimentary answer. In "The Government of Subject Races" he wrestles with the problem of how Britain, a nation of individuals, is to administer a wide-flung empire according to a number of central principles. He contrasts the "local agent," who has both a specialist's knowledge of the native and an Anglo-Saxon individuality, with the central authority at home in London. The former may "treat subjects of local interest in a manner calculated to damage, or even to jeopardize, imperial interests. The central authority is in a position to obviate any danger arising from this cause." Why? Because this authority can "ensure the harmonious working of the different parts of the machine" and "should endeavour, so far as is possible, to realise the circumstances attendant on the government of the dependency."[xii] The language is vague and unattractive, but the point is not hard to grasp. Cromer envisions a seat of power in the West, and radiating out from it towards the East a great embracing machine, sustaining the central authority yet commanded by it. What the machine's branches feed into it in the East— human material, material wealth, knowledge, what have you—is processed by the machine, then converted into more power. The specialist does the immediate translation of mere Oriental matter into useful substance: the Oriental becomes, for example, a subject race, an example of an "Oriental" mentality, all for the enhancement of the "authority" at home. "Local interests" are Orientalist special interests, the "central authority" is the general interest of the imperial society as a whole. What Cromer quite accurately sees is the management of knowledge by society, the fact that knowledge—no matter how special—is regulated first by the local concerns of a specialist, later by the general concerns of a social system of authority. The interplay between local and central interests is intricate, but by no means indiscriminate.

In Cromer's own case as an imperial administrator the "proper study is also man," he says. When Pope proclaimed the proper study of mankind to be man, he meant all men, including "the poor Indian"; whereas Cromer's "also" reminds us that certain men, such as Orientals, can be singled out as the subject for *proper* study. The proper study—in this sense—of Orientals is Orientalism, properly separate from other forms of knowledge, but finally useful (because finite) for the material and social

reality enclosing all knowledge at any time, supporting knowledge, providing it with uses. An order of sovereignty is set up from East to West, a mock chain of being whose clearest form was given once by Kipling.

> Mule, horse, elephant, or bullock, he obeys his driver, and the driver his sergeant, and the sergeant his lieutenant, and the lieutenant his captain, and the captain his major, and the major his colonel, and the colonel his brigadier commanding three regiments, and the brigadier his general, who obeys the Viceroy, who is the servant of the Empress.[xiii]

As deeply forged as is this monstrous chain of command, as strongly managed as is Cromer's "harmonious working," Orientalism can also express the strength of the West and the Orient's weakness—as seen by the West. Such strength and such weakness are as intrinsic to Orientalism as they are to any view that divides the world into large general divisions, entities that coexist in a state of tension produced by what is believed to be radical difference.

For that is the main intellectual issue raised by Orientalism. Can one divide human reality, as indeed human reality seems to be genuinely divided, into clearly different cultures, histories, traditions, societies, even race, and survive the consequences humanly? By surviving the consequences humanly, I mean to ask whether there is any way of avoiding the hostility expressed by the division, say, of men into "us" (Westerners) and "they" (Orientals). For such divisions are generalities whose use historically and actually has been to press the importance of the distinction between some men and some other men, usually towards not specially admirable ends. When one uses categories like Oriental and Western as both the starting and the end points of analysis, research, public policy (as the categories were used by Balfour and Cromer), the result is usually to polarize the distinction—the Oriental becomes more Oriental, the Westerner more Western—and limit the human encounter between different cultures, traditions, and societies. In short, from its earliest modern

---

[xii]Cromer, *Political and Literary Essays*, p. 35.

[xiii]See Jonah Raskin, *The Mythology of Imperialism* (New York: Random House, 1971), p. 40.

history to the present, Orientalism as a form of thought for dealing with the foreign has typically shown the altogether regrettable tendency of any knowledge based on such hard-and-fast distinctions as "East" and "West": to channel thought into a West or an East compartment. Because this tendency is right at the center of Orientalist theory, practice, and values found in the West, the sense of Western power over the Orient is taken for granted as having the status of scientific truth.

A contemporary illustration or two should clarify this observation perfectly. It is natural for men in power to survey from time to time the world with which they must deal. Balfour did it frequently. Our contemporary Henry Kissinger does it also, rarely with more express frankness than in his essay "Domestic Structure and Foreign Policy." The drama he depicts is a real one, in which the United States must manage its behavior in the world under the pressures of domestic forces on the one hand and of foreign realities on the other. Kissinger's discourse must for that reason alone establish a polarity between the United States and the world; in addition, of course, he speaks consciously as an authoritative voice for the major Western power, whose recent history and present reality have placed it before a world that does not easily accept its power and dominance. Kissinger feels that the United States can deal less problematically with the industrial, developed West than it can with the developing world. Again, the contemporary actuality of relations between the United States and the so-called Third World (which includes China, Indochina, the Near East, Africa, and Latin America) is manifestly a thorny set of problems, which even Kissinger cannot hide.

Kissinger's method in the essay proceeds according to what linguists call binary opposition: that is, he shows that there are two styles in foreign policy (the prophetic and the political), two types of technique, two periods, and so forth. When at the end of the historical part of his argument he is brought face to face with the contemporary world, he divides it accordingly into two halves, the developed and the developing countries. The first half, which is the West,

"is deeply committed to the notion that the real world is external to the observer, that knowledge consists of recording and classifying data—the more accurately the better." Kissinger's proof for this is the Newtonian revolution, which has not taken place in the developing world: "Cultures which escaped the early impact of Newtonian thinking have retained the essentially pre-Newtonian view that the real world is almost completely *internal* to the observer." Consequently, he adds, "empirical reality has a much different significance for many of the new countries than for the West because in a certain sense they never went through the process of discovering it."[xiv]

Unlike Cromer, Kissinger does not need to quote Sir Alfred Lyall on the Oriental's inability to be accurate; the point he makes is sufficiently unarguable to require no special validation. We had our Newtonian revolution; they didn't. As thinkers we are better off than they are. Good: the lines are drawn in much the same way, finally, as Balfour and Cromer drew them. Yet sixty or more years have intervened between Kissinger and the British imperialists. Numerous wars and revolutions have proved conclusively that the pre-Newtonian prophetic style, which Kissinger associates both with "inaccurate" developing countries and with Europe before the Congress of Vienna, is not entirely without its successes. Again unlike Balfour and Cromer, Kissinger therefore feels obliged to respect this pre-Newtonian perspective, since "it offers great flexibility with respect to the contemporary revolutionary turmoil." Thus the duty of men in the post-Newtonian (real) world is to "construct an international order *before* a crisis imposes it as a necessity": in other words, *we* must still find a way by which the developing world can be contained. Is this not similar to Cromer's vision of a harmoniously working machine designed ultimately to benefit some central authority, which opposes the developing world?

Kissinger may not have known on what fund of pedigreed knowledge he was drawing when he cut the world up into pre-Newtonian and post-Newtonian conceptions of reality. But his distinction is identical with the orthodox one

[xiv]Henry A. Kissinger, *American Foreign Policy* (New York: W. W. Norton & Co., 1974), pp. 48–9.

made by Orientalists, who separate Orientals from Westerners. And like Orientalism's distinction Kissinger's is not value-free, despite the apparent neutrality of his tone. Thus such words as "prophetic," "accuracy," "internal," "empirical reality," and "order" are scattered throughout his description, and they characterize either attractive, familiar, desirable virtues or menacing, peculiar, disorderly defects. Both the traditional Orientalist, as we shall see, and Kissinger conceive of the difference between cultures, first, as creating a battlefront that separates them, and second, as inviting the West to control, contain, and otherwise govern (through superior knowledge and accommodating power) the Other. With what effect and at what considerable expense such militant divisions have been maintained, no one at present needs to be reminded.

Another illustration dovetails neatly—perhaps too neatly—with Kissinger's analysis. In its February 1972 issue, the *American Journal of Psychiatry* printed an essay by Harold W. Glidden, who is identified as a retired member of the Bureau of Intelligence and Research, United States Department of State; the essay's title ("The Arab World"), its tone, and its content argue a highly characteristic Orientalist bent of mind. Thus for his four-page, double-columned psychological portrait of over 100 million people, considered for a period of 1,300 years, Glidden cites exactly four sources for his views: a recent book on Tripoli, one issue of the Egyptian newspaper *Al-Ahram*, the periodical *Oriente Moderno*, and a book by Majid Khadduri, a well-known Orientalist. The article itself purports to uncover "the inner workings of Arab behavior," which from *our* point of view is "aberrant" but for Arabs is "normal." After this auspicious start, we are told that Arabs stress conformity; that Arabs inhabit a shame culture whose "prestige system" involves the ability to attract followers and clients (as an aside we are told that "Arab society is and always has been based on a system of client-patron relationships"); that Arabs can function only in conflict situations; that prestige is based solely on the ability to dominate others; that a shame culture—and therefore Islam itself—makes a virtue of revenge

(here Glidden triumphantly cites the June 29, 1970 *Ahram* to show that "in 1969 [in Egypt] in 1070 cases of murder where the perpetrators were apprehended, it was found that 20 percent of the murders were based on a desire to wipe out shame, 30 percent on a desire to satisfy real or imaginary wrongs, and 31 percent on a desire for blood revenge"); that if from a Western point of view "the only rational thing for the Arabs to do is to make peace . . . for the Arabs the situation is not governed by this kind of logic, for objectivity is not a value in the Arab system."

Glidden continues, now more enthusiastically: "it is a notable fact that while the Arab value system demands absolute solidarity within the group, it at the same time encourages among its members a kind of rivalry that is destructive of that very solidarity"; in Arab society only "success counts" and "the end justifies the means"; Arabs live "naturally" in a world "characterized by anxiety expressed in generalized suspicion and distrust, which has been labelled free-floating hostility"; "the art of subterfuge is highly developed in Arab life, as well as in Islam itself"; the Arab need for vengeance overrides everything, otherwise the Arab would feel "ego-destroying" shame. Therefore, if "Westerners consider peace to be high on the scale of values" and if "we have a highly developed consciousness of the value of time," this is not true of Arabs. "In fact," we are told, "in Arab tribal society (where Arab values originated), strife, not peace, was the normal state of affairs because raiding was one of the two main supports of the economy." The purpose of this learned disquisition is merely to show how on the Western and Oriental scale of values "the relative position of the elements is quite different."[xv]

This is the apogee of Orientalist confidence. No merely asserted generality is denied the dignity of truth; no theoretical list of Oriental attributes is without application to the behavior of Orientals in the real world. On the one hand there are Westerners, and on the other there are Arab-Orientals; the former are (in no particular order) rational, peaceful, liberal, logical, capable of holding real values, without natural

---

[xv]Harold W. Glidden, "The Arab World," *American Journal of Psychiatry* 128, no. 8 (February 1972): 984–8.

suspicion; the latter are none of these things. Out of what collective and yet particularized view of the Orient do these statements emerge? What specialized skills, what imaginative pressures, what institutions and traditions, what cultural forces produce such similarity in the descriptions of the Orient to be found in Cromer, Balfour, and our contemporary statesmen?

Discussion Questions

1. Wallerstein argues that the capitalist world-economy is based on a division between core, semiperipheral, and peripheral regions. He also notes that any given nation can move from one tier to another. What factors contribute to a nation's advancement or decline? What nations do you think are advancing/declining and why? What, if anything, do you think is happening to the position of the United States?

2. What are some of the positive benefits that globalization has brought about? What are some of the negative consequences? How has the division of the world into core, semiperipheral, and peripheral regions shaped both the positive and negative effects of globalization?

3. Are we moving inevitably, with unstoppable force, into a global society? What are some of the leading factors accounting for this transformation? What factors or conditions are sources of resistance to globalization?

4. Does the fact that the same television shows can be viewed and the same products bought in numerous countries really mean that the world is becoming "one"? What types of data or evidence would you need to conclude that economic and cultural globalization is fundamentally changing the way people see themselves, interact with others, and interpret the world around them?

5. In his discussion of "Orientalism," Said examines how culture and ideas legitimize colonial rule and the subjugation of the colonized. While he focuses on events occurring roughly a century ago, do you think similar processes of Orientalism are taking place today? Do magazines, books, television shows, and movies "orientalize" non-Westerners, or do they typically offer unbiased portrayals? While journalists may claim to be objective in their reporting, does the news orientalize non-Western populations? Provide examples to support your view.

REFERENCES

Adorno, Theodor. 1941. "On Popular Music." *Studies in Philosophy and Social Science, 9,* 17–48.

————. 1967. *Prisms,* translated by Samuel and Sherry Weber. Cambridge, MA: MIT Press.

————. 1991. *The Culture Industry,* edited by J. M. Bernstein. London: Routledge.

Alexander, Jeffrey C. 1987. *Twenty Lectures.* New York: Columbia University Press.

Alsop, Rachel, Annette Fitzsimons, and Kathleen Lennon. 2002. *Theorizing Gender.* Cambridge, England: Polity Press.

Appadurai, Arjun. 1992. *Modernity at Large: Culture Dimensions of Globalization.* Minneapolis: University of Minnesota Press.

Ashe, Fidelma. 1999. "The Subject." pp. 88–110 in *Contemporary Social and Political Theory,* edited by Ashe, Alan Finlayson, Moya Lloyd, Iain MacKenzie, James Martin, and Shane O'Neill. Philadelphia, PA: Open University Press.

Atkinson, J. Maxwell, and John Heritage, eds. 1984. *Structures of Social Action: Studies in Conversation Analysis.* Cambridge: Cambridge University Press.

Benjamin, Walter. 1936/1968. "The Work of Art in the Age of Mechanical Reproduction," pp. 217–252. In *Illuminations,* edited by Hannah Arendt. Translated by Harry Zohn. New York: Harcourt, Brace.

Berger, Peter, and Thomas Luckmann. 1995. *Modernity, Pluralism and the Crisis of Meaning: The Orientation of Modern Man.* Gütersloh: Bertelsmann Foundation Publishers.

Berlant, Lauren. 2000. "Race, Gender, Nation in *The Color Purple*," pp. 3–28. In *Alice Walker's The Color Purple: Critical Interpretations,* edited by Harold Bloom. Philadelphia: Chelsea House.

Bertens, Hans. 1995. *The Idea of Postmodernism.* New York: Routledge.

Best, Steven, and Douglas Kellner. 1991. *Postmodern Theory: Critical Interrogations.* New York: Guilford.

Bhabha, Homi K. 1986. "The Other Question: Difference, Discrimination and the Discourse of Colonialism," pp. 148–172. In *Literature, Politics and Theory,* edited by Francis Barker, Peter Hulme, Margaret Iversen, and Diana Loxley. London: Methuen.

Bierstadt, Robert. 1938. "Is Homo Sapient?" Review of *The Structure of Social Action,* by Talcott Parsons. *The Saturday Review of Literature,* March 12, p. 18.

Blau, Peter. 1964. *Exchange and Social Power.* New York: Wiley.

Blumer, Herbert. 1969. *Symbolic Interaction: Perspective and Method.* Berkeley: University of California Press.

Boden, Diedre. 1990. "The World as It Happens: Ethnomethodology and Conversation Analysis," pp. 185–213. In *Frontiers of Social Theory,* edited by George Ritzer. New York: Columbia University Press.

Bottomore, Tom. 1984. *The Frankfurt School.* Sussex, England: Ellis Horword Limited.

Bourdieu, Pierre. 1964. *Exchange and Power in Social Life.* New York: Wiley.

————. 1984. *Distinction.* Harvard University Press.

Bourdieu, Pierre. 1990a. *In Other Words*. Palo Alto, CA: Stanford University Press.

_____. 1990b. *The Logic of Practice*. Translated by Richard Nice. Palo Alto, CA: Stanford University Press.

_____. 1991. *Language and Symbolic Power*. Edited and introduced by John B. Thompson. Translated by Gino Raymond and Matthew Adamson. Cambridge, MA: Harvard University Press.

_____. 1993. *The Field of Cultural Production*. Edited and introduced by Randal Johnson. New York: Columbia University Press.

_____. 1998. *Practical Reason*. Palo Alto, CA: Stanford University Press.

Branaman, Ann. 1997. "Goffman's Social Theory," pp. xlv–lxxxii. In *The Goffman Reader*, edited by Charles Lemert and Ann Branaman. Oxford: Blackwell.

Bryson, Valerie. 1999. *Feminist Debates*. New York: New York University Press.

Butler, Judith. 1990. *Gender Trouble: Feminism and the Subversion of Identity*. New York: Routledge.

_____. 1993. *Bodies That Matter: On the Discursive Limits of "Sex."* New York: Routledge.

_____. 1999. *Subjects of Desire*. New York: Columbia University Press.

Calhoun, Craig. 1992. "Introduction: Habermas and the Public Sphere," pp. 1–48. In *Habermas and the Public Sphere*, edited by Craig Calhoun. Cambridge, MA: MIT Press.

_____. 1995. *Critical Social Theory*. Oxford, England: Blackwell Cambridge University Press.

_____. 2003. "Robert K. Merton Remembered." *American Sociological Association Footnotes, 31,* 1.

Calhoun, Craig, and Loïc Wacquant. 2002. "Everything Is Social," *American Sociological Association,* Vol. 30, No. 2, pp. 5, 10.

Camic, Charles. 1991. "Introduction." In *Talcott Parsons, The Early Essays*. Chicago: University of Chicago Press.

Campbell, Marie, and Ann Manicom, eds. 1995. *Experience, Knowledge and Ruling Relations: Explorations in the Social Organization of Knowledge*. Toronto, Ontario, Canada: University of Toronto Press.

Carey, P. 1992. "Catching Up with Candid Camera." *Saturday Evening Post*. Indianapolis.

Chodorow, Nancy. 1978. *The Reproduction of Mothering*. Berkeley: University of California Press.

Cicourel, Aaron. 1964. *Method and Measurement in Sociology*. New York: Free Press.

Clayman, Steven. 1993. "Booing: The Anatomy of a Disaffiliative Response." *American Journal of Sociology* 58: 110–130.

Coleman, J. S. 1990. *Foundations of Social Theory*. Cambridge: Belknap/Harvard University Press.

Collins, Patricia Hill. 1990/2000. *Black Feminist Thought: Knowledge, Consciousness, and the Politics of Empowerment*. London: Harper Collins.

_____. 1998. *Fighting Words: Black Women and the Search for Justice*. Minneapolis: University of Minnesota.

_____. 2004. *Black Sexual Politics*. New York: Routledge.

Collins, Randall. 1975. *Conflict Sociology*. New York: Academic Press.

_____. 1979. *The Credential Society*. New York: Academic Press.

_____. 1986. "The Passing of Intellectual Generations: Reflections on the Death of Erving Goffman." *Sociological Theory, 4,* 106–113.

_____. 1994. *Four Sociological Traditions*. New York: Oxford University Press.

_____. 2004. *Interaction Ritual Chains*. Princeton, NJ: Princeton University.

Connell, R. W. 1997. "Why Is Classical Theory Classical," *American Journal of Sociology,* Vol. 102, No. 6, pp. 1511–1557.

Coser, Lewis A. 1977. *Masters of Sociological Thought*. New York: Harcourt, Brace, Jovanovich.

Craib, Ian. 1992. *Anthony Giddens*. London: Routledge.

Crothers, Charles. 1987. *Robert K. Merton*. Sussex, England: Ellis Horwood Limited.

Davis, Kingsley, and Wilbert E. Moore. 1945. "Some Principles of Stratification." *American Sociological Review, 10,* 242–9.

Denning, Steve. 2004. http://www.stevedenning.com/postmodern.html

Donovan, Josephine. 2000/1985. *Feminist Theory: The Intellectual Traditions* (3rd ed.). New York: Continuum.

Dufay, François, and Pierre-Bertand Dufort. 1993. *Les Normaliens.* Paris: Editions Jean-Claude Lattes.

Durkheim, Émile. 1895/1938. *The Rules of Sociological Method.* Translated by Sarah A. Solovay and John H. Mueller. Edited by George E. G. Catlin. New York: Free Press.

———. (1912/1965). *The Elementary Forms of Religious Life.* New York: Free Press.

Duvenage, Pieter. 2003. *Habermas and Aesthetics.* Cambridge, England: Polity.

Edles, L. D., & Appelrouth, S. (2005). *Sociological Theory in the Classical Era: Text and Readings.* Thousand Oaks, CA: Sage.

Ehrenhalt, Alan. 1999. "Because We Like You." Review of *Celebration USA,* by Douglas Frantz and Catherine Collins, and *The Celebration Chronicles* by Andrew Ross. 1999, September 12. *The Los Angeles Times Book Review,* p. 8.

Elliot, Anthony. 2001. "Anthony Giddens," pp. 292–303. In *Profiles in Contemporary Social Theory,* edited by Anthony Elliot and Bryan Turner. Thousand Oaks, CA: Sage.

Erhich, Paul. 2000. *Human Natures.* New York: Penguin Books.

Featherstone, Mike. 1995. *Undoing Culture.* London: Sage.

Frank, Andre Gunder. 1967. *Capitalism and Under-development in Latin America.* New York: Monthly Review Press.

Freud, Sigmund. 1961. *Civilization and Its Discontents.* New York: W. W. Norton.

Funt, Allen. 1952. *Eavesdropping at Large: Adventures in Human Nature with Candid Mike and Candid Camera.* New York: Vanguard Press.

Garfinkel, Harold. 1967. *Studies in Ethnomethodology.* Englewood Cliffs, NJ: Prentice Hall.

Garfinkel, Harold, and Harvey Sacks. 1970. "On formal structures of practical actions," pp. 337–366. In *Theoretical Sociology: Perspectives and Developments,* edited by John C. McKinney and Edward Tiryakian. New York: Appleton-Century-Crofts.

Gerhardt, Uta. 2002. *Talcott Parsons: An Intellectual Biography.* Cambridge: Cambridge University Press.

Gerhenson, Geoffrey, and Michelle Williams. 2001. "Nancy Chodorow," pp. 281–91. In *Profiles in Contemporary Social Theory,* edited by Anthony Elliot and Bryan Turner. Thousand Oaks, CA: Sage.

Giddens, Anthony. 1979. *Central Problems in Social Theory.* Berkeley: University of California Press.

———. 1981. "Agency, Institution, and Time-Space Analysis," pp. 161–74. In *Advances in Social Theory and Methodology,* edited by K. Knorr-Cetina and A. V. Cicourel. London: Routledge and Kegan Paul.

———. 1984. *The Constitution of Society.* Berkeley: University of California Press.

———. 1990. *Consequences of Modernity.* Palo Alto, CA: Stanford University Press.

Goffman, Erving. 1959. *The Presentation of Self in Everyday Life.* New York: Anchor Books.

———. 1961. *Asylums: Essays on the Social Situation of Mental Patients and Other Inmates.* New York: Anchor Books.

———. 1967. *Interaction Ritual.* New York: Anchor Books.

———. 1974. *Frame Analysis: An Essay on the Organization of Experience.* New York: Harper & Row.

———. 1983. "The Interaction Order." *American Sociological Review, 48,* 1–17.

Gramsci, Antonio. 1971. *Prison Notebooks.* Edited and translated by Auintin Hoare and Geoffrey Nowell Smith. New York: International Publishers.

Grenfell, Michael. 2004. *Pierre Bourdieu: Agent Provocateur.* London: Continuum.

Gubrium, Jaber, and James Holstein. 1997. *The New Language of Qualitative Method.* New York: Oxford University Press.

Habermas, Jürgen. 1962. *The Structural Transformation of the Public Sphere: An Inquiry Into a Category of Bourgeois Society.* Cambridge, MA: MIT Press.

_____. 1979. "Toward a Reconceptualization of Historical Materialism," pp. 130–177. In *Communication and the Evolution of Society.* Boston: Beacon Press.

_____. 1984. *The Theory of Communicative Action. Vol. 1, Reason and the Rationalization of Society.* Boston: Beacon Press.

_____. 1987. *The Theory of Communiciative Action. Vol. 2, Lifeworld and System: A Critique of Functionalist Reason.* Boston: Beacon Press.

_____. 1989. *Jürgen Habermas on Society and Politics.* Edited by Steven Seidman. Boston: Beacon Press.

_____. 1996. *Between Facts and Norms.* Cambridge, MA: MIT Press.

Hale, Alison. 1998. *My World Is Not Your World.* Glenville, NY: Archimedes Press.

Halperin, David. 1995. *Saint Foucault: A Gay Hagiography.* New York: Oxford.

Harding, Sandra. 1986. *The Science Question in Feminism.* Ithaca, NY: Cornell University Press.

Harding, Sandra, ed. 2004. *The Feminist Standpoint Reader.* New York: Routledge.

Hartsock, Nancy. 1990. "Foucault on Power: A Theory for Women?" pp. 157–175. In *Feminism/ Postmodernism,* edited by Linda Nicholson. New York: Routledge.

Hassan, Ihab. 1987. *The Postmodern Turn: Essays in Postmodern Theory and Culture.* Columbus: Ohio State University Press.

Heritage, John. 1984. *Garfinkel and Ethnomethodology.* New York: Polity Press.

_____. 1998. "Harold Garfinkel," pp. 175–188. In *Key Sociological Thinkers,* edited by Rob Stones. London: Macmillan.

Heritage, John, and David Greatbatch, 1986. "Generating Applause: A Study of Rhetoric and Response at Party Conferences," *American Journal of Sociology* 92:110–157.

Hochschild, Arlie Russell. 1983. *The Managed Heart.* Berkeley: University of California Press.

_____. 2003. *The Commercialization of Intimate Life.* Berkeley: University of California Press.

Homans, Casper. 1958. "Social Behavior as Exchange." *American Journal of Sociology, 63* (6), 597–606.

_____. 1961. *Social Behavior: Its Elementary Forms.* New York: Harcourt Brace.

_____. 1984. *Coming to My Senses.* New Brunswick, NJ: Transaction Books.

Horkheimer, Max. 1941. "The End of Reason," pp. 366–388. In *Studies in Philosophy and Social Science,* vol. 9.

_____. 1947. *The Eclipse of Reason.* New York: Oxford University Press.

_____. 1972a. "Traditional and Critical Theory," pp. 188–243. In *Critical Theory: Selected Essays,* translated by Matthew J. O'Connell, et al. New York: Herder and Herder.

_____. 1972b. "Postscript," pp. 244–252. In *Critical Theory: Selected Essays,* translated by Matthew J. O'Connell, et al. New York: Herder and Herder.

Horkheimer, Max, and Theodor Adorno. 2002/1944. *Dialectic of Enlightenment.* Palo Alto, CA: Stanford University Press.

Horster, Detlef. 1992. *Habermas: An Introduction.* Philadelphia: Pennbridge.

Huntington, Samuel. 1993. "The Clash of Civilizations?" *Foreign Affairs, 72,* 3. Interview of Judith Butler by Peter Osborne and Lynne Segal, London, 1993.

Jaspers, Karl. 1957/1962. *Socrates, Buddha, Confucius, Jesus.* (The Great Philosophers, vol. 1) New York: Harcourt Brace.

Jefferson, Gail. 1978. "Sequential Aspects of Storytelling in Conversation." In Jim Schenkein, ed., *Studies in the Organization of Conversational Interaction,* pp. 219–248. New York: Academic Press.

Kaspersen, Lars Bo. 2000. *Anthony Giddens.* Oxford, England: Blackwell.

Kellner, Douglas. 2000. "Habermas, the Public Sphere, and Democracy: A Critical Intervention," pp. 259–288. In *Perspectives on Habermas*, edited by Lewis Hahn. Chicago: Open Court Press.

Kirby, Barbara L. 2001/2005. *The OASIS Guide to Asperger Syndrome*. New York: Crown.

———. "What Is Asperger Syndrome?" (http://www.udel.edu/bkirby/asperger/aswhatisit.html)

Klein, Stephen, and William Leiss. 1978. "Advertising, Needs, and Commodity Fetishism." *Canadian Journal of Political and Social Theory*, 2 (1).

Lalonde, Marc. 1999. *Critical Theology and the Challenge of Jürgen Habermas*. NY: Peter Lang.

Lemert, Charles. 1997. "Goffman," pp. ix–xlii. In *The Goffman Reader*, edited by Charles Lemert and Ann Branaman. Oxford, England: Blackwell.

Lévi-Strauss, Claude. 1969. *The Raw and the Cooked*. Chicago: University of Chicago Press.

Lloyd, Stephen. 2003. *The Sociology of Anthony Giddens*. London: Pluto Press.

Lorber, Judith. 1998. *Gender Inequality*. Los Angeles: Roxbury Press.

March, James G., and Herbert A. Simon. 1958. *Organizations*. New York: Wiley.

Marcuse, Herbert. 1941. "Some Implications of Modern Technology." *Studies in Philosophy and Social Science*, 9, 414–439.

———. 1955. *Eros and Civilization: A Philosophical Inquiry into Freud*. Boston: Beacon Press.

———. 1964. *One Dimensional Man*. Boston: Beacon Press.

———. 1970. *Five Lectures: Psychoanalysis, Politics and Utopia*. Boston: Beacon Press.

Martindale, Don. 1981. *The Nature and Types of Sociological Theory*. 2nd ed. Boston, MA: Houghton Mifflin.

Marx, Karl. 1859/1978. "Preface to a Contribution to the Critique of Political Economy," pp. 3–6. In *The Marx/Engels Reader*, edited by Robert C. Tucker. New York: W. W. Norton.

Marx, Karl, and Friedrich Engels. 1846/1978. "The German Ideology," pp. 146–201. In *The Marx/Engels Reader*, edited by Robert C. Tucker. New York: W. W. Norton.

———. 1848/1978. "Communist Manifesto," pp. 469–500. In *The Marx/Engels Reader*, edited by Robert C. Tucker. New York: W. W. Norton.

Matustik, Martin. 2001. *Jürgen Habermas: A Philosophical-Political Profile*. Lanham, MD: Rowman and Littlefield.

McCarthy, Thomas. 1978. *The Critical Theory of Jürgen Habermas*. Cambridge, MA: MIT Press.

McMahon, Darrin. 2001. *Enemies of the Enlightenment*. Oxford, England: Oxford University Press.

Mead, George Herbert. 1934/1962. *Mind, Self and Society*, edited by Charles W. Morris. Chicago: University of Chicago Press.

Merton, Robert. 1949/1957. *Social Theory and Social Structure*. Toronto, Ontario, Canada: Free Press.

———. 1994. *A Life of Learning*. American Council of Learned Societies, Occasional Paper, n. 25.

———. 1996. *On Social Structure and Science*, edited and with an introduction by Piotr Sztompka. Chicago: University of Chicago.

Miller, James. 1959. *Sociological Integration*. New York: Oxford University Press.

———. 1993. *The Passion of Michel Foucault*. New York: Simon & Schuster.

Mills, C. W. 1951. *White Collar*. New York: Oxford University Press.

———. 1959. *The Sociological Imagination*. New York: Oxford University Press.

———. 1958. *Power Elite*. New York: Oxford University Press.

———. 1963. *Power, Politics and People*, edited by Irving Louis Horowitz. New York: Ballantine Books.

Nazir, Sameena. 2004. "Challenging Inequality: Obstacles and Opportunities Toward Women's Rights in the Middle East and Northern Africa."

Nietzsche, Friedrich. 1886/1917. *Beyond Good and Evil*. Translated by Helen Zimmern, introduction by Willard Huntington Wright. New York: Boni & Liveright.

Nietzsche, Friedrich. 1887/1967. *On the Genealogy of Morals*. Translated by Walter Kaufmann, and edited, with commentary by Walter Kaufmann. New York: Vintage.

Parsons, Talcott. 1961. "An Outline of the Social System." In *Theories of Society*, edited by Parsons et al. New York: Free Press.

_____. 1971. *The System of Modern Societies*. Englewood Cliffs, NJ: Prentice Hall.

Parsons, Talcott C., and Edward A. Shils. 2001/1951. *Toward a General Theory of Action*, introduction by Neil Smelser. New Brunswick: Transaction Publishers.

Pollner, Melvin. 1987. *Mundane Reason*. Cambridge: Cambridge University Press.

Poster, Mark. 1989. *Critical Theory and Poststructuralism: In Search of a Context*. Ithaca, NY: Cornell University Press.

Radical Philosophy Ltd. 1994. (http://www.theory.org.uk/but-int1.htm)

Rawls, Anne. 2002. "Editor's Introduction." In *Ethnomethodology's Program: Working Out Durkheim's Aphorism*, edited by H. Garfinkel. Oxford: Rowman & Littlefield.

Ritzer, George. 2000. *The McDonaldization of Society*. Thousands Oaks, CA: Pine Forge Press.

Ritzer, George, and Douglas J. Goodman. 2004. *Modern Sociological Theory, 6th Edition*. New York: McGraw-Hill.

Robbins, Derek. 2000. *Bourdieu and Culture*. London: Sage.

Robertson, Roland. 1992. *Globalization*. London: Sage.

Robinson, William I. (forthcoming). "Theories of Globalization." In *The Blackwell Companion to Globalization*, edited by George Ritzer. London/New York: Blackwell.

Rocher, Guy. 1972/1974. *Talcott Parsons and American Sociology*. London: Nelson.

Rogers, Mary. 1998. *Contemporary Feminist Theory*. Boston: McGraw Hill.

Sacks, Harvey, Emmanual Schegloff, and Gail Jefferson. 1974. "A Simplest Systematics for the Organization of Turn-taking in Conversation." *Language* 50:396–735.

Said, Edward. 1978. *Orientalism*. New York: Vintage Books.

_____. 2000. *Reflections on Exile and Other Essays*. Cambridge, MA: Harvard University Press.

Sartre, Jean-Paul. 1947. *Existentialism*. Translated by Bernard Frechtman. New York: Philosophical Library.

Seidman. Steven. 1989. "Introduction," pp. 1–25. In *Jürgen Habermas on Society and Politics*, edited by Steven Seidman. Boston: Beacon Press.

Simmel, Georg. 1900/1971. "Exchange," pp. 43–69. In *On Individuality and Social Forms*, edited by Donald N. Levine. Chicago: University of Chicago Press.

_____. 1908/1971. "How Is Society Possible," pp. 6–22. In *On Individuality and Social Forms*, edited by Donald N. Levine. Chicago: University of Chicago Press.

Sitton, John. 2003. *Habermas and Contemporary Society*. New York: Palgrave Macmillan.

Sklair, Leslie. 2002. *Globalization: Capitalism and Its Alternatives* (3rd ed.). Oxford, England: Oxford University Press.

Smelser, Neil. 2001. "Introduction." pp. vii–xix in Toward a General Theory of Action, by Talcott Parsons and Edward Shils. New Brunswick, NJ: Transaction Publishers.

Smith, Dorothy. 1977. *Feminism and Marxism*. Vancouver, Canada: New Star Books.

_____. 1987. *The Everyday World as Problematic*. Boston: Northeastern University Press.

_____. 1990a. *The Conceptual Practices of Power: A Feminist Sociology of Knowledge*. Boston: Northeastern University Press.

_____. 1990b. *Texts, Facts, and Femininity: Exploring the Relations of Ruling*. London: Routledge.

_____. 2005. *Institutional Ethnography: A Sociology for People*. Oxford, England: AltaMira.

Stryker, Sheldon. 1980. *Symbolic Interactionism: A Social Structural Version*. Menlo Park, CA: Benjamin/Cummings.

Stryker, Sheldon. 2003. "Whither Symbolic Interaction? Reflections on a Personal Odyssey." *Symbolic Interaction, 26*, 95–109.

Swartz, David. 1997. *Culture and Power: The Sociology of Pierre Bourdieu*. Chicago: University of Chicago Press.

Swartz, David, and Vera Zolberg. 2004. *After Bourdieu*. Dordrecht: Kluwer.

Sztompka, Piotr. 1986. *Robert K. Merton: An Intellectual Profile*. London: MacMillan.

Thomas, William I. 1923. *The Unadjusted Girl*. Boston: Little, Brown.

Thomas, William I. (with Dorothy Swaine Thomas). 1928. *The Child in America*. New York: Alfred A. Knopf.

Tomlinson, John. 1999. *Globalization and Culture*. Chicago: University of Chicago Press.

Tong, Rosemarie. 1998. *Feminist Thought*. Boulder: Westview Press.

Tönnies, Ferdinand. 1963/1935. *Gemeinschaft und Gesellschaft*. Darmstadt: Wissenshaftliche Buchgesellschaft.

Toynbee, Arthur. 1957. *A Study of History*. New York: Oxford University Press.

Tripp, Anna. 2000. *Gender: Readings in Cultural Criticism*. New York: Palgrave.

Turner, Bryan. 2001. "Peter Berger," pp. 107–116. In *Profiles in Contemporary Social Theory*, edited by Anthony Elliot and Bryan S. Turner. Thousand Oaks, CA: Sage.

Venturi, Robert, Denise Scott Brown, and Steven Izenour. 1977. *Learning from Las Vegas: The Forgotten Symbolism of Architectural Form*. Cambridge, MA: MIT Press.

Wagner, Helmut R. 1973. "The Scope of Phenomenological Sociology." In *Phenomenological Sociology*, edited by George Psathas. New York: Wiley.

Wallerstein, Immanuel. 1974. *The Modern World-System: Capitalist Agriculture and the Origins of the European World-Economy in the Sixteenth Century*. New York: Academic Press.

_____. 1979. *The Capitalist World Economy*. Cambridge: Cambridge University Press.

_____. 1987. "World-Systems Analysis," pp. 309–324. In *Social Theory Today*. Palo Alto, CA: Stanford University Press.

_____. 1990. "Culture as the Ideological Battleground of the Modern World-System," pp. 31–56. In *Global Culture*, edited by Mike Featherstone. London: Sage.

Walsh, George. 1967. "Introduction," pp. xv–xxiv. In *The Phenomenology of the Social World*, by Alfred Schutz. Bloomington, Indiana: Northwestern University Press.

Waters, Malcolm. 2001. *Globalization* (2nd ed.). London: Routledge Press.

Weber, Max. 1904/1958. *The Protestant Ethic and the Spirit of Capitalism*. New York: Scribner.

_____. 1925/1978. *Economy and Society*, edited by Guenther Roth and Claus Wittich. Berkeley: University California Press.

Weber, Max. 1947. *The Theory of Social and Economic Organization*. Edited by Talcott Parsons and translated by A. M. Henderson and Talcott Parsons. New York: Oxford University Press.

_____. 1958. "Politics as a Vocation," pp. 77–128. In *From Max Weber*, edited by Hans Gerth and C. Wright Mills. New York: Oxford University Press.

Wiggershaus, Rolf. 1994. *The Frankfort School: Its History, Theories, and Political Significance*, translated by Michael Robertson. Cambridge, MA: MIT Press.

Williams, Christine. 1993. "Psychoanalytic Theory and the Sociology of Gender." In *Theory on Gender, Feminism on Theory*, edited by Paula England. New York: Aldine de Gruyter.

Williams, Jr., Robin. 1980. "Talcott Parsons: The Stereotypes and the Realities." *The American Sociologist, 15*, in Peter Hamilton, ed., *Talcott Parsons: Critical Assessments v. 1*, Routledge.

Wrong, Dennis H. 1994. *The Problem of Order*. Cambridge, MA: Harvard University Press.

Zimbardo, Philip. 1985. "Laugh Where We Must, Be Candid Where We Can." *Psychology Today*.

Zimmerman, Don. 1988. "On Conversation," pp. 406–32. In *Communication Yearbook*, edited by J. Anderson. Beverly Hills: Sage.

Zimmerman, Don, and D. Lawrence Wieder. 1970. "Ethnomethodology and the Problem of Order," pp. 285–298. In *Understanding Everyday Life*, edited by Jack Douglas. Chicago: Aldine.

INDEX